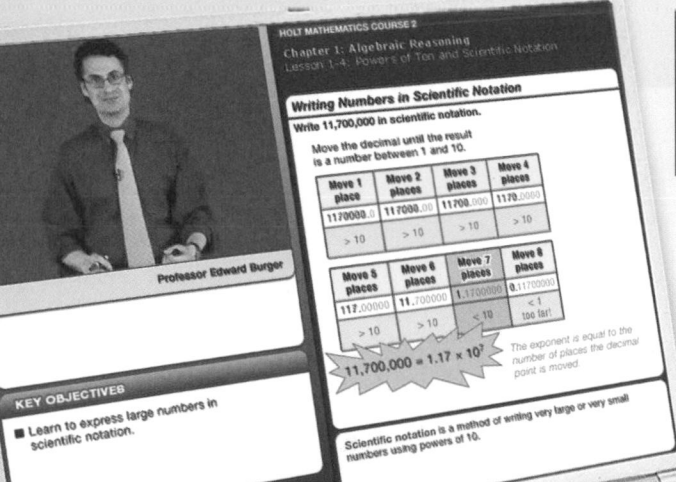

HOLT

NEW YORK

Mathematics
Course 1

Jennie M. Bennett

Edward B. Burger

David J. Chard

Audrey L. Jackson

Paul A. Kennedy

Freddie L. Renfro

Janet K. Scheer

Bert K. Waits

HOLT, RINEHART AND WINSTON

A Harcourt Education Company

Orlando • **Austin** • New York • San Diego • London

Course 1 Contents in Brief

Student Handbook

Printed in the United States of America

ISBN 978-0-03-092875-8

ISBN 0-03-092875-3

7 8 9 10 11 12 073 14 13 12 11 10 09

Cover photo: American Airlines Arena Miami Exterior © Arcaid/Alamy

AUTHORS

Jennie M. Bennett, Ph.D. is a mathematics teacher at Hartman Middle School in Houston, Texas. Jennie is past president of the Benjamin Banneker Association, the Second Vice-President of NCSM, and a former board member of NCTM.

Paul A. Kennedy, Ph.D. is a professor in the Department of Mathematics at Colorado State University. Dr. Kennedy is a leader in mathematics education. His research focuses on developing algebraic thinking by using multiple representations and technology. He is the author of numerous publications.

Edward B. Burger, Ph.D. is Professor of Mathematics and Chair at Williams College and is the author of numerous articles, books, and videos. He has won several of the most prestigious writing and teaching awards offered by the Mathematical Association of America. Dr. Burger has appeared on NBC TV, National Public Radio, and has given innumerable mathematical performances around the world.

Freddie L. Renfro, MA, has 35 years of experience in Texas education as a classroom teacher and director/coordinator of Mathematics PreK-12 for school districts in the Houston area. She has served as TEA TAAS/TAKS reviewer, team trainer for Texas Math Institutes, TEKS Algebra Institute writer, and presenter at math workshops.

David J. Chard, Ph.D., is an Associate Dean of Curriculum and Academic Programs at the University of Oregon. He is the President of the Division for Research at the Council for Exceptional Children, is a member of the International Academy for Research on Learning Disabilities, and is the Principal Investigator on two major research projects for the U.S. Department of Education.

Janet K. Scheer, Ph.D., Executive Director of Create A Vision™, is a motivational speaker and provides customized K-12 math staff development. She has taught internationally and domestically at all grade levels.

Audrey L. Jackson, M. Ed., is on the Board of Directors for NCTM. She is the Program Coordinator for Leadership Development with the St. Louis, public schools and is a former school administrator for the Parkway School District.

Bert K. Waits, Ph.D., is a Professor Emeritus of Mathematics at The Ohio State University and co-founder of T^3 (Teachers Teaching with Technology), a national professional development program.

CONTRIBUTING AUTHORS

Linda Antinone
Fort Worth, TX

Ms. Antinone teaches mathematics at R. L. Paschal High School in Fort Worth, Texas. She has received the Presidential Award for Excellence in Teaching Mathematics and the National Radio Shack Teacher award. She has coauthored several books for Texas Instruments on the use of technology in mathematics.

Carmen Whitman
Pflugerville, TX

Ms. Whitman travels nationally helping districts improve mathematics education. She has been a program coordinator on the mathematics team at the Charles A. Dana Center, and has served as a secondary math specialist for the Austin Independent School District.

NEW YORK ADVISORY PANEL

Carol E. Anderson
High School Special
    Education Consultant
Panama Central School
    District
Panama, New York

Patrick Anderson
Mathematics Teacher
Cassadaga Valley High School
Sinclairville, New York

Suzanne Castren
Mathematics Teacher
Williamsville South
    High School
Williamsville, NY

Kathleen Cole
Math Department Chair
Boynton Middle School
Ithaca, New York

Virginia Cronin, Ed.D.
Math Department Chair
Lincoln High School
Yonkers, New York

Paul Dlug
Math Lead Teacher
Robert Moses Middle School
North Babylon, New York

Arlane Frederick
Math Curriculum & Learning
    Specialist (retired)
Kenmore-Town of
    Tonawanda UFSD
Kenmore, New York

Joseph Furnari
Math Chairman (retired)
Saunders Trades and
    Technical High School
Yonkers, New York

Terri Furnari
Math Teacher
Solomon Schechter
    High School
Hartsdale, New York

Douglas L. Lohnas, Ed.D.
Director of Mathematics
Niskayuna Central School
    District
Niskayuna, New York

Steven Marino
Math Department Chair
Long Beach Middle School
Long Beach, New York

Stephanie Neagle
Math Teacher
Boynton Middle School
Ithaca, New York

Ray Scacalossi Jr.
Math Chairman
Hauppauge UFSD
Hauppauge, New York

Paul Schwiegerling
Mathematics Teacher
Gifted Math Program
SUNY at Buffalo
Buffalo, New York

REVIEWERS

Marilyn Adams
Mathematics Department
    Chair
Eanes ISD
Austin, TX

Thomas J. Altonjy
Assistant Principal
Robert R. Lazar Middle
    School
Montville, NY

Jane Bash, M.A.
Math Education
Eisenhower Middle School
San Antonio, TX

Charlie Bialowas
District Math Coordinator
Anaheim Union High School
    District
Anaheim, CA

Lynn Bodet
Math Teacher
Eisenhower Middle School
San Antonio, TX

Chandra Budd
Mathematics Teacher
Amarillo ISD
Amarillo, TX

Terry Bustillos
Mathematics Teacher
El Paso ISD
El Paso, TX

Preparing for the New York Math Test

Holt Mathematics Course 1 provides many opportunities for you to prepare for the New York State Math Test.

Grade 5 Post-March Diagnostic

Use the Post-March Diagnostic to review content covered at the end of last year.

Practice test items on these pages cover all Post-March Performance Indicators from the previous year.

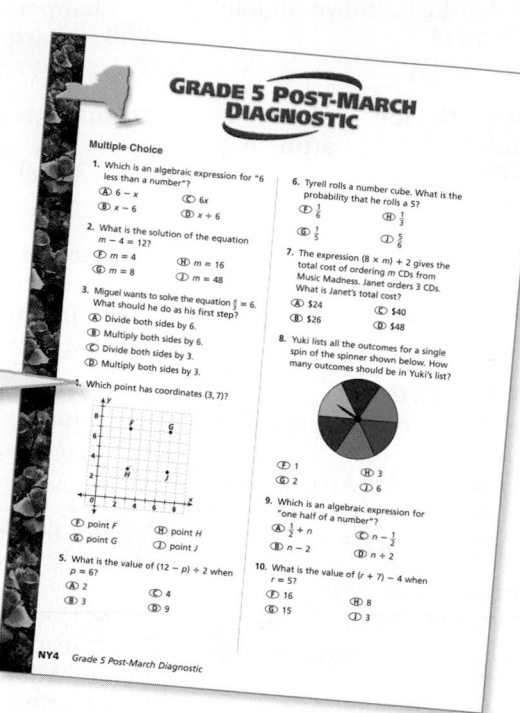

Countdown to Testing

Use the Countdown to Testing to practice for your state test every day.

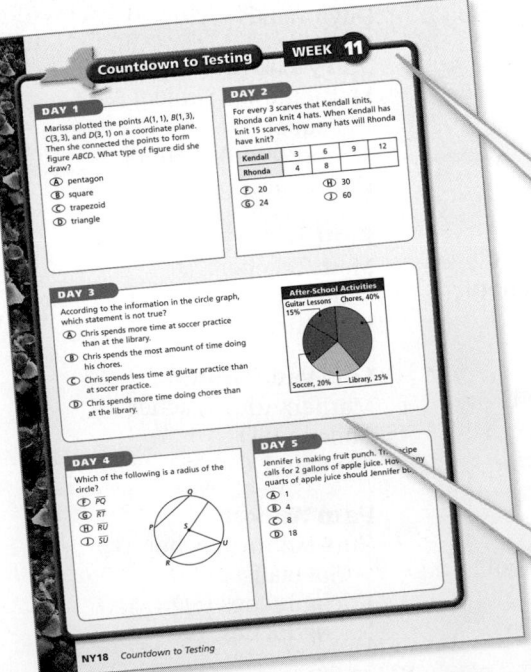

There are 20 pages of practice for your state test. Each page is designed to be used in a week so that all practice will be completed before your state test is given.

Each week's page has five practice test items, one for each day of the week.

New York Math Test Prep

Use the Standardized Test Prep to apply test-taking strategies.

The Hot Tip provides test-taking tips to help you succeed on your tests.

These pages include practice with multiple choice, short response, and extended response test items.

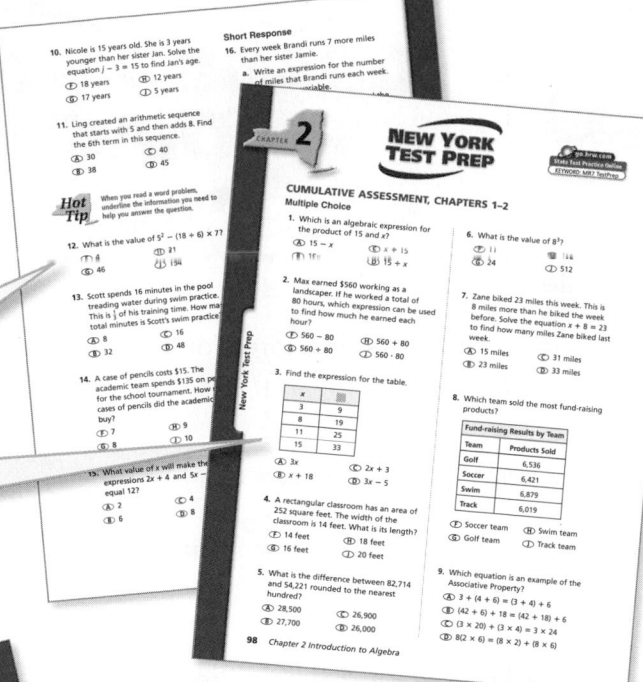

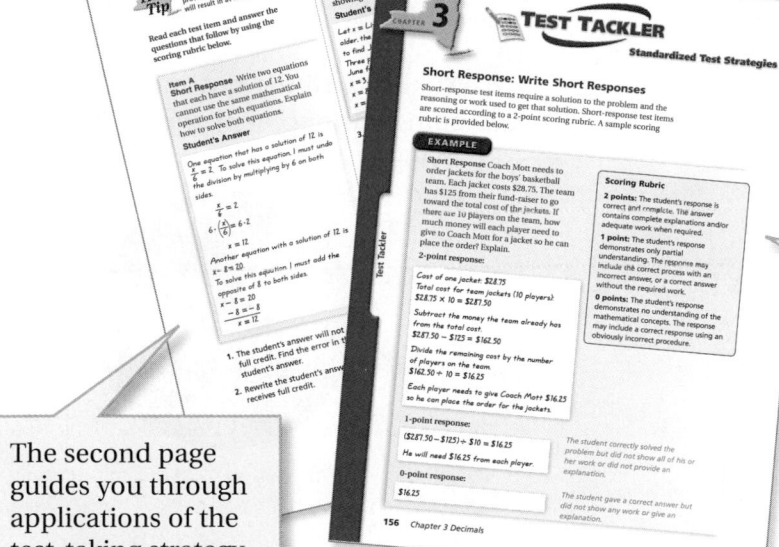

The second page guides you through applications of the test-taking strategy.

Test Tackler

Use the Test Tackler to become familiar with and practice test-taking strategies.

The first page of this feature explains and shows an example of a test-taking strategy.

Test-Taking Tips

☑ Get plenty of sleep the night before the test. A rested mind thinks more clearly and you won't feel like falling asleep while taking the test.

☑ Draw a figure when one is not provided with the problem. If a figure is given, write any details from the problem on the figure.

☑ Read each problem carefully. As you finish each problem, read it again to make sure your answer is reasonable.

☑ Review the formula sheet that will be supplied with the test. Make sure you know when to use each formula.

☑ First answer problems that you know how to solve. If you do not know how to solve a problem, skip it and come back to it when you have finished the others.

☑ Use other test-taking strategies that can be found throughout this book, such as working backward and eliminating answer choices.

GRADE 5 POST-MARCH DIAGNOSTIC

Multiple Choice

1. Which is an algebraic expression for "6 less than a number"?

   Ⓐ 6 − x   Ⓒ 6x

   Ⓑ x − 6   Ⓓ x ÷ 6

2. What is the solution of the equation m − 4 = 12?

   Ⓕ m = 4   Ⓗ m = 16

   Ⓖ m = 8   Ⓙ m = 48

3. Miguel wants to solve the equation $\frac{x}{3} = 6$. What should he do as his first step?

   Ⓐ Divide both sides by 6.

   Ⓑ Multiply both sides by 6.

   Ⓒ Divide both sides by 3.

   Ⓓ Multiply both sides by 3.

4. Which point has coordinates (3, 7)?

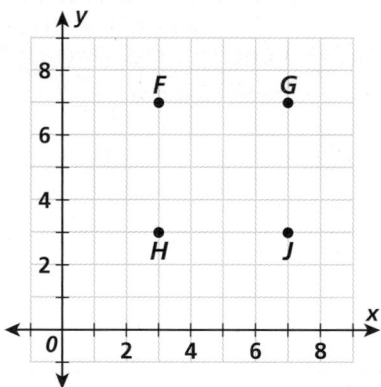

   Ⓕ point F   Ⓗ point H

   Ⓖ point G   Ⓙ point J

5. What is the value of (12 − p) ÷ 2 when p = 6?

   Ⓐ 2   Ⓒ 4

   Ⓑ 3   Ⓓ 9

6. Tyrell rolls a number cube. What is the probability that he rolls a 5?

   Ⓕ $\frac{1}{6}$ Ⓗ $\frac{1}{3}$

   Ⓖ $\frac{1}{5}$ Ⓙ $\frac{5}{6}$

7. The expression (8 × m) + 2 gives the total cost of ordering m CDs from Music Madness. Janet orders 3 CDs. What is Janet's total cost?

   Ⓐ $24   Ⓒ $40

   Ⓑ $26   Ⓓ $48

8. Yuki lists all the outcomes for a single spin of the spinner shown below. How many outcomes should be in Yuki's list?

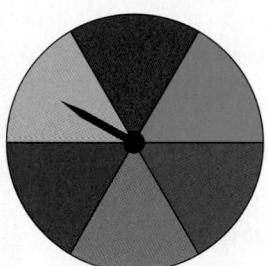

   Ⓕ 1   Ⓗ 3

   Ⓖ 2   Ⓙ 6

9. Which is an algebraic expression for "one half of a number"?

   Ⓐ $\frac{1}{2} + n$ Ⓒ $n - \frac{1}{2}$

   Ⓑ n − 2   Ⓓ n ÷ 2

10. What is the value of (r + 7) − 4 when r = 5?

   Ⓕ 16   Ⓗ 8

   Ⓖ 15   Ⓙ 3

11. David rolled a number cube 24 times. He recorded the results in the table below.

Rolling a Number Cube	
Result	Number of Times Rolled
1	4
2	3
3	3
4	6
5	4
6	4

What fraction of the rolls resulted in a 4?

(A) $\frac{1}{24}$ (C) $\frac{1}{6}$

(B) $\frac{1}{8}$ (D) $\frac{1}{4}$

12. Nicole drew the shape shown below. What is the perimeter, in units, of the shape?

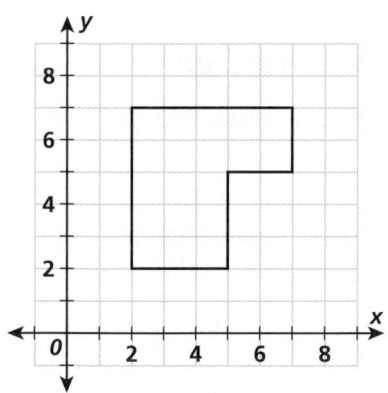

(F) 20   (H) 16

(G) 19   (J) 10

13. Joshua has b baseball cards. Lee has 12 fewer cards than Joshua. Which expression can be used to find the number of cards that Lee has?

(A) $b + 12$ (C) $b - 12$

(B) $12 - b$ (D) $b \div 12$

14. Cheryl's solution for an equation is 4. Which equation could Cheryl have solved?

(F) $x - 1 = 5$ (H) $w - 7 = 3$

(G) $y + 6 = 10$ (J) $z + 8 = 4$

15. Marc wants to draw a pentagon on the grid below by plotting a fifth point and then connecting the points. Which point can be used to complete the pentagon?

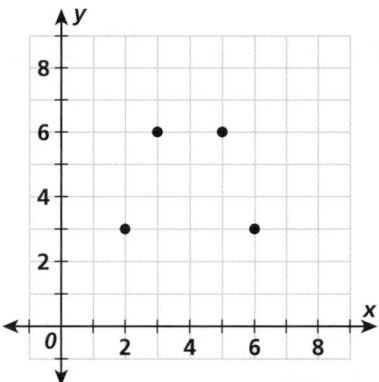

(A) $(4, 6)$ (C) $(3, 3)$

(B) $(5, 3)$ (D) $(4, 2)$

16. Ms. Andrews wrote an equation on the board. She solved it by adding 3 to both sides of the equation. Which equation could she have written?

(F) $m - 6 = 3$ (H) $3 + p = 7$

(G) $n - 3 = 10$ (J) $r + 1 = 3$

17. A bag contains 8 ping pong balls that are numbered 1 through 8. You reach into the bag and choose a ping pong ball without looking. What is the probability that you choose ball number 6?

(A) $\frac{1}{8}$ (C) $\frac{1}{4}$

(B) $\frac{1}{6}$ (D) $\frac{3}{4}$

18. What is the value of the expression $20 - 4 \times n$ when $n = 2$?

(F) 32   (H) 14

(G) 16   (J) 12

19. Graciella plotted the following points on a coordinate plane. Which of the points lies on the x-axis?

(A) $(0, 3)$ (C) $(5, 5)$

(B) $(4, 0)$ (D) $(2, 3)$

20. Jeff tossed a dime ten times and then tossed a nickel ten times. The table shows his results. What fraction of all the tosses resulted in heads?

Coin-Toss Results		
Result	Dime	Nickel
Heads	6	2
Tails	4	8

Ⓕ $\frac{3}{10}$ Ⓗ $\frac{3}{5}$

Ⓖ $\frac{2}{5}$ Ⓙ $\frac{4}{5}$

21. A student plotted the points (2,1), (6,1), (6,3), and (2,3). Then she connected the points. Which shape did she form?

Ⓐ pentagon   Ⓒ square

Ⓑ rectangle   Ⓓ triangle

22. Serena drew the shape shown below. What is the perimeter, in units, of the shape?

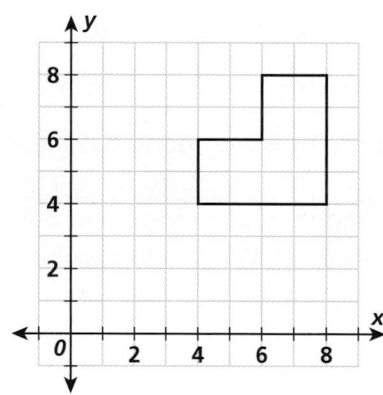

Ⓕ 12   Ⓗ 16

Ⓖ 14   Ⓙ 20

23. What is the value of $(6 + m) \div 3$ when $m = 3$?

Ⓐ 3   Ⓒ 7

Ⓑ 6   Ⓓ 9

24. What is the solution of the equation $\frac{x}{4} = 8$?

Ⓕ $x = 2$ Ⓗ $x = 12$

Ⓖ $x = 4$ Ⓙ $x = 32$

25. Wes is going to solve the equation $n + 26 = 48$. What should he do as his first step?

Ⓐ Add 26 to both sides.

Ⓑ Add 48 to both sides.

Ⓒ Subtract 26 from both sides.

Ⓓ Subtract 48 from both sides.

26. Which of these is the sample space for a single spin of the spinner shown below?

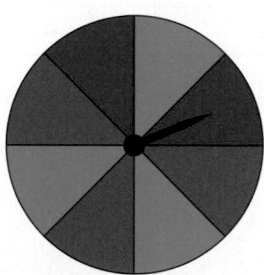

Ⓕ red

Ⓖ red, blue, green

Ⓗ red, red, green, green, blue, blue

Ⓙ red, red, green, green, green, blue, blue, blue

27. Steven is *s* years old. Marcus is 2 years younger than Steven. Which expression can be used to find Marcus's age?

Ⓐ 2s   Ⓒ 2 − s

Ⓑ s + 2   Ⓓ s − 2

28. Mai rolls a number cube. What is the probability that she rolls an even number?

Ⓕ $\frac{1}{6}$ Ⓗ $\frac{1}{2}$

Ⓖ $\frac{1}{3}$ Ⓙ $\frac{2}{3}$

29. A cube has two red faces, two green faces, one blue face, and one yellow face. Allie lists all the possible outcomes for one roll of the cube. How many outcomes are in her list?

Ⓐ 1   Ⓒ 4

Ⓑ 3   Ⓓ 6

30. Dan and Eric have 15 pencils. Dan has 9 pencils. Which equation can be used to find the number of pencils that Eric has?

Ⓕ $p + 9 = 15$ Ⓗ $p - 9 = 15$

Ⓖ $p + 15 = 9$ Ⓙ $p - 15 = 9$

31. What are the coordinates of point *M*?

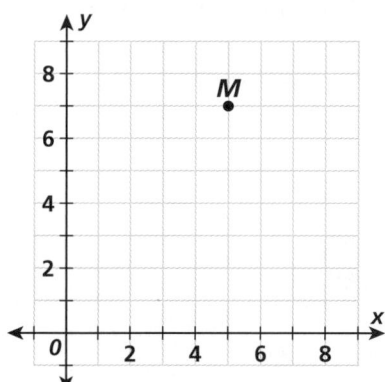

Ⓐ (5,5)   Ⓒ (7,5)

Ⓑ (5,7)   Ⓓ (7,7)

32. Lisa spun a spinner 20 times. The table shows her results.

Spinner Results	
Result	Number of Times
Yellow	5
Red	3
Green	8
Blue	4

Which color did Lisa spin $\frac{1}{5}$ of the time?

Ⓕ yellow   Ⓗ green

Ⓖ red   Ⓙ blue

33. Jamal solved an equation by multiplying both sides of the equation by 4. Which equation could Jamal have solved?

Ⓐ $4x = 20$ Ⓒ $\frac{x}{4} = 20$

Ⓑ $x + 4 = 20$ Ⓓ $x - 4 = 20$

34. Evaluate $(m \div 2) + 4$ when $m = 12$.

Ⓕ 2   Ⓗ 24

Ⓖ 10   Ⓙ 28

35. Singh plotted the points (4,3), (4,5), and (6,5). He wants to plot one more point and then connect the points to form a square. Which point should he plot?

Ⓐ (6,3)   Ⓒ (5,5)

Ⓑ (3,6)   Ⓓ (2,5)

36. Amy spins the spinner shown below. What is the probability that she spins a number greater than 6?

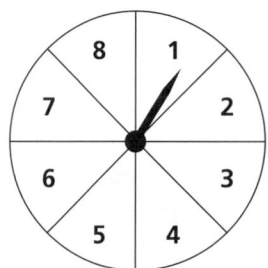

Ⓕ $\frac{1}{8}$ Ⓗ $\frac{3}{8}$

Ⓖ $\frac{1}{4}$ Ⓙ $\frac{3}{4}$

37. Which rectangle has the greatest perimeter?

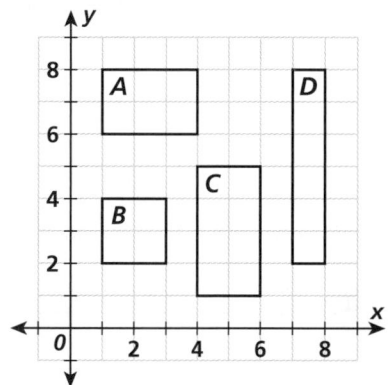

Ⓐ A   Ⓒ C

Ⓑ B   Ⓓ D

38. Danielle's height, in inches, is 6 inches more than Zack's height. Zack's height is *z*. Which expression represents Danielle's height?

Ⓕ $z - 6$ Ⓗ $z + 6$

Ⓖ $6 - z$ Ⓙ $z \div 6$

COUNTDOWN TO TESTING

DAY 1

Chuck is 2 inches shorter than his sister, Jan. If j is Jan's height, which of the following is Chuck's height?

(A) $2 - j$

(B) $j + 2$

(C) $2j$

(D) $j - 2$

DAY 2

In 2000, the population of Brooklyn was two million, four hundred sixty-five thousand, three hundred twenty-six. Which of the following gives the population in standard form?

(F) 240,065,326

(G) 2,465,326

(H) 2,465,300,026

(J) 2,400,650,326

DAY 3

Which point on the number line represents 3.5?

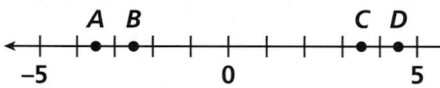

(A) point A   (B) point B   (C) point C   (D) point D

DAY 4

Jerome has a ribbon that is $10\frac{1}{2}$ ft long. He cuts the ribbon into pieces that are each $\frac{3}{4}$ ft long. How many pieces does he have?

(F) 5

(G) 7

(H) 12

(J) 14

DAY 5

The figure gives the formula for the area A of a triangle. Find the area of a triangle with $b = 8$ m and $h = 10$m.

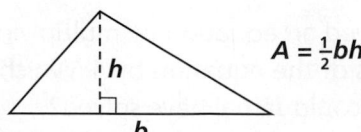

$A = \frac{1}{2}bh$

(A) 9 m²   (C) 40 m²

(B) 14 m²   (D) 80 m²

Countdown to Testing WEEK 2

DAY 1

What is the product of $\frac{3}{8}$ and $\frac{2}{9}$?

(A) $\frac{1}{12}$

(B) $\frac{5}{17}$

(C) $\frac{43}{72}$

(D) $1\frac{11}{16}$

DAY 2

Which of the following is $4 \times 4 \times 4 \times 4 \times 4$ in exponential form?

(F) 4^4

(G) 4^5

(H) 5^4

(J) 5×4

DAY 3

Eric's science class grew plants from bean seeds. The table shows how much each student's plant grew in two weeks. Put the plants in order from least change to greatest change.

Student	Miguel	Eric	Jane	Trisha	Cindy
Plant Heights (in.)	$\frac{1}{2}$	$\frac{5}{12}$	$\frac{3}{16}$	$\frac{1}{8}$	$\frac{4}{5}$

(A) $\frac{1}{2}, \frac{5}{12}, \frac{3}{16}, \frac{1}{8}, \frac{4}{5}$

(B) $\frac{1}{8}, \frac{3}{16}, \frac{5}{12}, \frac{1}{2}, \frac{4}{5}$

(C) $\frac{1}{2}, \frac{4}{5}, \frac{1}{8}, \frac{5}{12}, \frac{3}{16}$

(D) $\frac{1}{2}, \frac{1}{8}, \frac{3}{16}, \frac{4}{5}, \frac{5}{12}$

DAY 4

Evaluate the expression $(10 - m) \times 2$ for $m = 3$.

(F) 4

(G) 7

(H) 9

(J) 14

DAY 5

Admission to Fun Zone costs $5. Each ride costs $3. Yvonne visits Fun Zone and goes on x rides. Which expression gives her total cost?

(A) $3x + 5$

(B) $8x$

(C) $5x + 3$

(D) $5 + 8x$

DAY 1

Peter has $\frac{4}{5}$ yard of fabric. Robert has $\frac{3}{7}$ yard of fabric. How much more fabric does Peter have than Robert?

(A) $\frac{1}{35}$ yard

(B) $\frac{7}{35}$ yard

(C) $\frac{13}{35}$ yard

(D) $\frac{1}{2}$ yard

DAY 2

What is the equivalent decimal form of $\frac{12}{15}$?

(F) 0.008

(G) 0.08

(H) 0.8

(J) 12.15

DAY 3

What percent of the square is shaded?

(A) 40%

(B) 60%

(C) 75%

(D) 80%

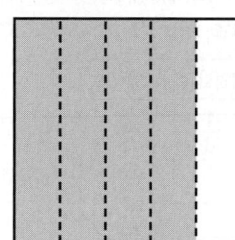

DAY 4

What is the solution of the equation $\frac{m}{4} = 12$?

(F) $m = 3$ (H) $m = 16$

(G) $m = 15$ (J) $m = 48$

DAY 5

Which equation is an example of the Commutative Property of Addition?

(A) $3 + 8 = 8 + 3$

(B) $(4 + 1) + 5 = 4 + (1 + 5)$

(C) $6 + 0 = 6$

(D) $2(4 + 3) = 2 \cdot 4 + 2 \cdot 3$

DAY 1

Omar wrote the equation below in his notebook. Which property does this equation demonstrate?

$6(4 + 3) = 6 \cdot 4 + 6 \cdot 3$

- Ⓐ Associative Property of Multiplication
- Ⓑ Commutative Property of Addition
- Ⓒ Distributive Property of Multiplication Over Addition
- Ⓓ Zero Property of Multiplication

DAY 2

Which of the following is the same as 5^3?

- Ⓕ 5×3
- Ⓖ $5 \times 5 \times 5$
- Ⓗ $5 \times 5 \times 5 \times 5$
- Ⓙ $3 \times 3 \times 3 \times 3 \times 3$

DAY 3

In which month were the savings greatest?

- Ⓐ June
- Ⓑ July
- Ⓒ August
- Ⓓ September

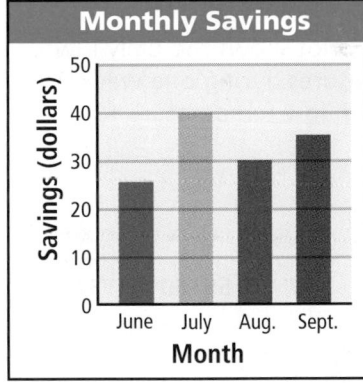

Monthly Savings

DAY 4

Evaluate the expression $2^3 + 3 \times 4 + 1$.

- Ⓕ 19
- Ⓖ 21
- Ⓗ 45
- Ⓙ 55

DAY 5

Miguel has 3 times as many stamps in his collection as Robert. Robert has s stamps in his collection. Which expression represents the number of stamps in Miguel's collection?

- Ⓐ $\frac{s}{3}$
- Ⓑ $s + 3$
- Ⓒ $3s$
- Ⓓ $3 - s$

DAY 1

Evaluate the expression (8 + p) ÷ 2 for p = 4.

Ⓐ 2

Ⓑ 6

Ⓒ 10

Ⓓ 14

DAY 2

Which equation represents the Zero Property of Multiplication?

Ⓕ 3 · 0 = 0

Ⓖ 4 + 0 = 4

Ⓗ 0 · 6 = 6 · 0

Ⓙ 8 + 0 = 0 + 8

DAY 3

The line plot shows the daily low temperatures during one week. What is the mean low temperature for the entire week?

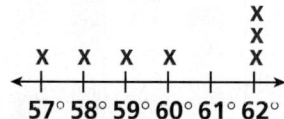

57° 58° 59° 60° 61° 62°

Ⓐ 60°F

Ⓑ 61°F

Ⓒ 62°F

Ⓓ 63°F

DAY 4

What is the equivalent decimal form of $\frac{1}{25}$?

Ⓕ 0.04

Ⓖ 0.25

Ⓗ 0.4

Ⓙ 1.25

DAY 5

How much money does Diego save by buying the shirt on sale?

Ⓐ $2

Ⓑ $2.50

Ⓒ $4

Ⓓ $5

Regular price: $20

SALE! Take 25% off

DAY 1

What is the solution of the equation $5y = 30$?

Ⓐ $y = 5$

Ⓑ $y = 6$

Ⓒ $y = 25$

Ⓓ $y = 150$

DAY 2

Mr. Clarke wrote the equation $5 + 0 = 5$ on the board. Which property does this equation demonstrate?

Ⓕ Associative Property of Addition

Ⓖ Commutative Property of Addition

Ⓗ Identity Property of Addition

Ⓙ Inverse Property of Addition

DAY 3

Triangle *ABC* is similar to triangle *DEF*. What is the length of side $\overline{DE}$?

Ⓐ 6 in. Ⓒ 9 in.

Ⓑ 8 in. Ⓓ 10 in.

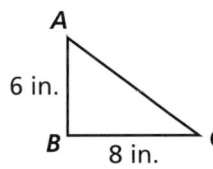
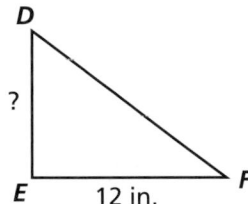

6 in. 8 in. ? 12 in.

DAY 4

Determine which pair of ratios is a proportion.

Ⓕ $\frac{2}{9} \overset{?}{=} \frac{6}{25}$

Ⓖ $\frac{3}{7} \overset{?}{=} \frac{8}{17}$

Ⓗ $\frac{9}{2} \overset{?}{=} \frac{21}{5}$

Ⓙ $\frac{4}{9} \overset{?}{=} \frac{8}{18}$

DAY 5

Simplify the expression $\left(\frac{1}{4}\right)^3$.

Ⓐ $\frac{1}{12}$

Ⓑ $\frac{3}{12}$

Ⓒ $\frac{1}{64}$

Ⓓ $\frac{3}{64}$

DAY 1

There are 149 sixth graders at Whitman Middle School. The principal wants to choose about 10% of the students for a survey. How many students should the principal choose?

Ⓐ 2

Ⓑ 10

Ⓒ 15

Ⓓ 49

DAY 2

John is making birthday cards. He uses 8 stickers to decorate each card. How many stickers will John need for 5 cards?

Ⓕ 5

Ⓖ 13

Ⓗ 35

Ⓙ 40

DAY 3

What is the mean number of candles sold per month?

Ⓐ 25

Ⓑ 35

Ⓒ 40

Ⓓ 45

Candles Sold Per Month

Jan. Feb. Mar. Apr.

🕯 = 5 candles

DAY 4

Luis is going to solve the equation $m + 14 = 35$. Which of the following operations can he use to solve the equation?

Ⓕ Subtract 14 from both sides.

Ⓖ Add 14 to both sides.

Ⓗ Subtract 35 from both sides.

Ⓙ Add 35 to both sides.

DAY 5

Which of the following is the reciprocal of $\frac{3}{5}$?

Ⓐ $\frac{2}{5}$

Ⓑ $\frac{3}{5}$

Ⓒ $-\frac{3}{5}$

Ⓓ $\frac{5}{3}$

Countdown to Testing WEEK 8

DAY 1

Tim's age is 5 years more than twice Beth's age. If b is Beth's age, which expression represents Tim's age?

Ⓐ $2b + 5$

Ⓑ $2b - 5$

Ⓒ $2(b + 5)$

Ⓓ $2(b - 5)$

DAY 2

A factory produces 5,000 car parts per hour. This is an example of which of the following?

Ⓕ percent

Ⓖ proportion

Ⓗ rate

Ⓙ ratio

DAY 3

Kris has four pet turtles. Last week he measured each turtle. What is the order of the turtles from shortest to longest?

Ⓐ Carly, Patty, Bennie, Charley

Ⓑ Patty, Bennie, Charley, Carly

Ⓒ Patty, Carly, Bennie, Charley

Ⓓ Bennie, Patty, Carly, Charley

Turtle	Length (in.)
Bennie	5.67
Charley	5.75
Patty	5.07
Carly	5.5

DAY 4

Ivy's Fresh Eggs transports its eggs in crates. How many crates will 8 trucks carry?

Trucks	2	3	4	5
Crates	80	120	160	200

Ⓕ 220

Ⓖ 280

Ⓗ 320

Ⓙ 360

DAY 5

Mai wants to solve the equation $\frac{n}{4} = 20$. Which operation should she use?

Ⓐ Divide both sides by 20.

Ⓑ Divide both sides by 4.

Ⓒ Multiply both sides by 4.

Ⓓ Subtract $\frac{n}{4}$ from both sides.

DAY 1

The equation (6 + 1) + 2 = 6 + (1 + 2) is an example of which property?

- (A) Associative Property of Addition
- (B) Commutative Property of Addition
- (C) Distributive Property of Multiplication Over Addition
- (D) Identity Property of Addition

DAY 2

Tomas has $8\frac{5}{10}$ feet of fishing line and Mike has $2\frac{8}{16}$ feet of fishing line. How many feet of fishing line do they have together?

- (F) 6
- (G) 10
- (H) $10\frac{1}{2}$
- (J) 11

DAY 3

Which point has coordinates (4, 2)?

- (A) point A
- (B) point B
- (C) point C
- (D) point D

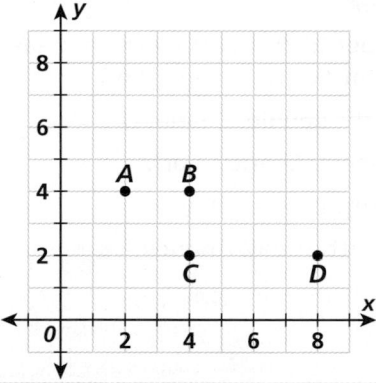

DAY 4

In Mrs. Kendall's class, $\frac{12}{15}$ of the students prefer tennis to basketball. Which decimal shows the part of the class that prefers tennis to basketball?

- (F) 0.08
- (G) 0.8
- (H) 1.25
- (J) 8.0

DAY 5

Which ratio can be used to complete the proportion $\frac{6}{10} = $ ▢ ?

- (A) $\frac{6}{16}$
- (B) $\frac{9}{15}$
- (C) $\frac{12}{18}$
- (D) $\frac{10}{6}$

DAY 1

If 30 buses can carry 1,500 people, how many people can 5 buses carry?

(A) 200

(B) 250

(C) 500

(D) 750

DAY 2

Carlos is buying shirts for the soccer team. Each shirt costs $9.50. Carlos plans to buy 19 shirts. Which of the following is the best estimate of the total cost of the shirts?

(F) $150

(G) $200

(H) $240

(J) $400

DAY 3

What are the coordinates of point *M*?

(A) (3, 5)

(B) (4, 4)

(C) (5, 3)

(D) (6, 3)

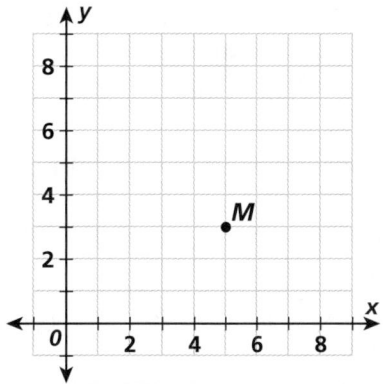

DAY 4

In Amber's science class, quizzes are graded on a scale of 0 to 10. The data set shows Amber's quiz scores. What is the range of the data set?

8, 9, 8, 8, 7, 5, 10, 9

(F) 5

(G) 8

(H) 9

(J) 10

DAY 5

What is the length of the diameter of the circle?

(A) 2 cm

(B) 4 cm

(C) 8 cm

(D) 16 cm

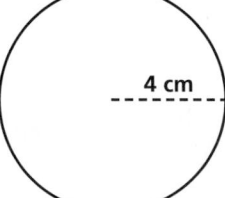

4 cm

DAY 1

Marissa plotted the points $A(1, 1)$, $B(1, 3)$, $C(3, 3)$, and $D(3, 1)$ on a coordinate plane. Then she connected the points to form figure $ABCD$. What type of figure did she draw?

Ⓐ pentagon

Ⓑ square

Ⓒ trapezoid

Ⓓ triangle

DAY 2

For every 3 scarves that Kendall knits, Rhonda can knit 4 hats. When Kendall has knit 15 scarves, how many hats will Rhonda have knit?

Kendall	3	6	9	12
Rhonda	4	8		

Ⓕ 20

Ⓖ 24

Ⓗ 30

Ⓙ 60

DAY 3

According to the information in the circle graph, which statement is not true?

Ⓐ Chris spends more time at soccer practice than at the library.

Ⓑ Chris spends the most amount of time doing his chores.

Ⓒ Chris spends less time at guitar practice than at soccer practice.

Ⓓ Chris spends more time doing chores than at the library.

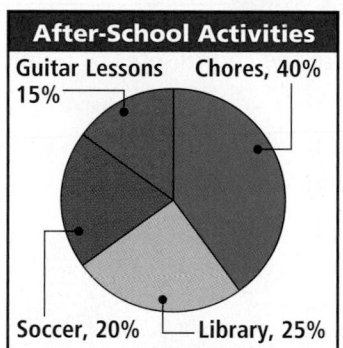

After-School Activities

Guitar Lessons 15% — Chores, 40% — Soccer, 20% — Library, 25%

DAY 4

Which of the following is a radius of the circle?

Ⓕ $\overline{PQ}$

Ⓖ $\overline{RT}$

Ⓗ $\overline{RU}$

Ⓙ $\overline{SU}$

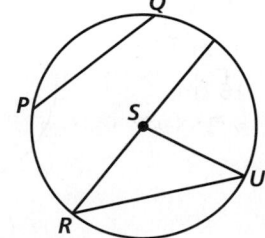

DAY 5

Jennifer is making fruit punch. The recipe calls for 2 gallons of apple juice. How many quarts of apple juice should Jennifer buy?

Ⓐ 1

Ⓑ 4

Ⓒ 8

Ⓓ 18

DAY 1

What is the perimeter of rectangle *ABCD*?

- (A) 10
- (B) 16
- (C) 20
- (D) 24

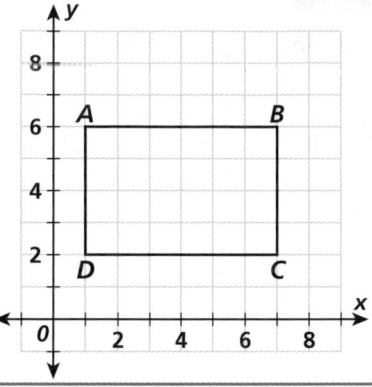

DAY 2

The figure shows a triangular plot in Sam's garden. What is the area of the plot?

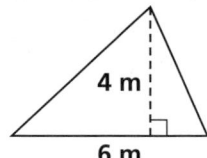

4 m

6 m

- (F) 10 m²
- (G) 12 m²
- (H) 20 m²
- (J) 24 m²

DAY 3

What is the equivalent of $\frac{1}{50}$ in decimal form?

- (A) 0.02
- (B) 0.05
- (C) 0.2
- (D) 5.0

DAY 4

Which unit would be most appropriate for measuring the capacity of a kitchen sink?

- (F) inches
- (G) gallons
- (H) square feet
- (J) yards

DAY 5

Jamal has a pitcher that holds 2 liters of water. How many milliliters of water does the pitcher hold?

- (A) 20 milliliters
- (B) 200 milliliters
- (C) 2,000 milliliters
- (D) 20,000 milliliters

DAY 1

Which equation is shown in the graph?

- (A) $y = x$
- (B) $y = 2x$
- (C) $y = \frac{1}{2}x$
- (D) $y = x + 2$

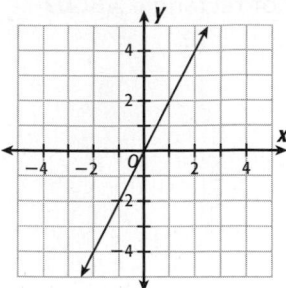

DAY 2

Ted wants to make a small fountain in his garden. The diagram shows the dimensions of the fountain. How much water will Ted need to fill the fountain?

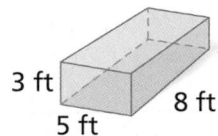

3 ft   5 ft   8 ft

- (F) 18 cubic feet
- (G) 40 cubic feet
- (H) 80 cubic feet
- (J) 120 cubic feet

DAY 3

Wei plotted the points $A(2, 3)$, $B(3, 3)$, $C(4, 2)$, and $D(1, 2)$ on a coordinate plane. Then she connected the points to form figure $ABCD$. What type of figure did she draw?

- (A) parallelogram
- (B) rectangle
- (C) square
- (D) trapezoid

DAY 4

Which of the following is a metric unit of capacity?

- (F) cup
- (G) gallon
- (H) liter
- (J) quart

DAY 5

A rectangular photo is 16 cm long and 10 cm wide. What is the area of the photo?

- (A) 26 cm²
- (B) 52 cm²
- (C) 80 cm²
- (D) 160 cm²

DAY 1

Nancy made this rectangular prism using centimeter cubes. What is the volume of the prism?

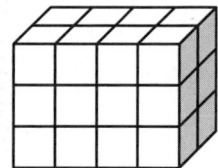

- **A** 12 cm³
- **B** 24 cm³
- **C** 36 cm³
- **D** 48 cm³

DAY 2

Which statement is true for a cylinder, but not for a cone?

- **F** It has two bases.
- **G** It has a curved surface.
- **H** It has a vertex.
- **J** It has a triangular face.

DAY 3

Troy wants to know the number of quarts of water that a goldfish bowl can hold. Which tool would be best for finding the capacity of the bowl?

- **A** measuring cup
- **B** metric ruler
- **C** scale
- **D** yardstick

DAY 4

What is the perimeter of figure *ABCDEF*?

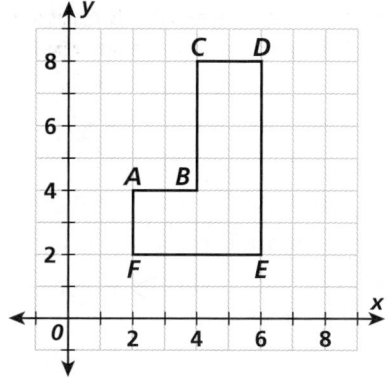

- **F** 10
- **H** 20
- **G** 16
- **J** 24

DAY 5

Estimate the volume of the figure below.

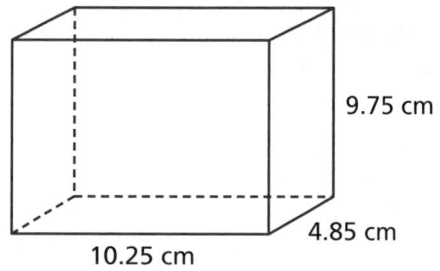

9.75 cm

4.85 cm

10.25 cm

- **A** 300 cubic centimeters
- **B** 450 cubic centimeters
- **C** 500 cubic centimeters
- **D** 650 cubic centimeters

DAY 1

Josh wants to get an idea of what is meant by a pint. Which of the following will give him the best reference for this unit of capacity?

Ⓐ the capacity of a teaspoon

Ⓑ the capacity of a small bottle of ketchup

Ⓒ the capacity of a large milk jug

Ⓓ the capacity of a swimming pool

DAY 2

Devin rolls a number cube. What is the probability that he rolls a 5?

Ⓕ $\frac{1}{6}$

Ⓖ $\frac{1}{3}$

Ⓗ $\frac{1}{2}$

Ⓙ $\frac{5}{6}$

DAY 3

Find the area of the shaded sector of the circle.

Ⓐ 6.3 m²

Ⓑ 12.6 m²

Ⓒ 25.1 m²

Ⓓ 50.3 m²

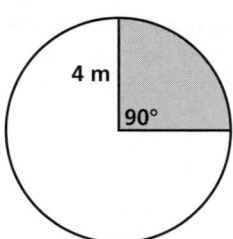

4 m

90°

DAY 4

Evaluate the expression |3 − 7|.

Ⓕ −4

Ⓖ −3

Ⓗ 4

Ⓙ 7

DAY 5

A circle has a diameter of 5.8 m. Mary estimates that the circumference of the circle is about 18 m. Which of the following best describes Mary's estimate?

Ⓐ The estimate is much too low.

Ⓑ The estimate is much too high.

Ⓒ The estimate is reasonable.

Ⓓ The estimate gives the exact value of the circumference.

DAY 1

Which of the following describes the relationship between the circumference *C* of a circle and its diameter *d*?

- **(A)** $C = \pi d$
- **(B)** $d = \pi C$
- **(C)** $C = 2\pi d$
- **(D)** $C = \pi d^2$

DAY 2

Which equation shows the Distributive Property of Multiplication Over Addition?

- **(F)** $7 + (3 + 1) = (7 + 3) + 1$
- **(G)** $2 \times (4 \times 5) = (2 \times 4) \times 5$
- **(H)** $12 + 5 = 5 + 12$
- **(J)** $3 \times (4 + 6) = 3 \times 4 + 3 \times 6$

DAY 3

Jeff wanted to know how many outcomes are possible when tossing a coin and rolling a number cube at the same time. He made this tree diagram.
How many outcomes are possible?

Heads   **Tails**

1 2 3 4 5 6   1 2 3 4 5 6

- **(A)** 2
- **(B)** 6
- **(C)** 12
- **(D)** 14

DAY 4

Donna wants to write the expression $6 \times 6 \times 6 \times 6$ in her notebook using exponential form. Which of the following should she write?

- **(F)** 4^6
- **(G)** 4×6
- **(H)** 6^3
- **(J)** 6^4

DAY 5

Gil wants to fill his fish tank with water. Which is the best estimate of the volume of water he needs?

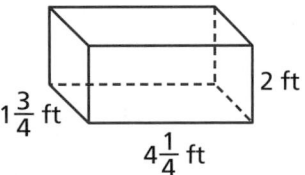

$1\frac{3}{4}$ ft $4\frac{1}{4}$ ft   2 ft

- **(A)** 8 cubic feet
- **(B)** 16 cubic feet
- **(C)** 24 cubic feet
- **(D)** 32 cubic feet

DAY 1

What is the range of the data set shown in the line plot?

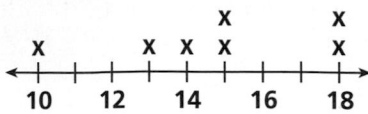

(A) 8

(B) 10

(C) 15

(D) 18

DAY 2

Jorge rolled a number cube 12 times. The frequency table shows his results. What is the experimental probability of rolling a 3?

Number Shown on Cube	Frequency
1	///
2	/
3	///
4	//
5	/
6	//

(F) $\frac{1}{12}$

(H) $\frac{1}{3}$

(G) $\frac{1}{4}$

(J) $\frac{1}{2}$

DAY 3

If △ACE is similar to △BCD, what is the length of AC?

(A) 5.5 centimeters

(B) 13.5 centimeters

(C) 21.5 centimeters

(D) 31.5 centimeters

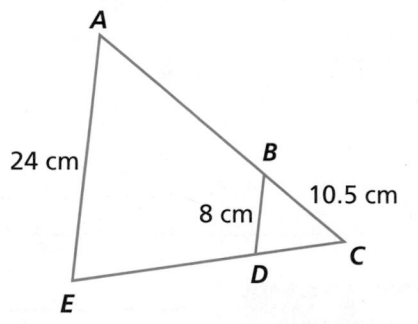

DAY 4

Julia has $\frac{3}{4}$ yard of wrapping paper. She uses $\frac{1}{8}$ yard to wrap a small gift. How much paper does she have left?

(F) $\frac{1}{8}$ yard

(H) $\frac{3}{8}$ yard

(G) $\frac{1}{4}$ yard

(J) $\frac{5}{8}$ yard

DAY 5

At dinner, Mr. and Mrs. Brandt decide to leave a 20% tip for their server. Which is the best estimate of their tip if their meals total $63.20?

(A) $1.20

(B) $12.00

(C) $14.00

(D) $120.00

DAY 1

Roberto wants to pour 8 cups of chicken broth into a pot. How many quarts of chicken broth does he need?

(A) 1

(B) 2

(C) 4

(D) 16

DAY 2

Lisa spins a spinner that is numbered 1 through 4 and tosses a coin at the same time. The tree diagram shows the different outcomes that are possible. How many outcomes are there?

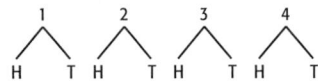

(F) 2

(G) 4

(H) 8

(J) 12

DAY 3

Line *p* is parallel to line *q*. What is $m\angle 1$?

(A) 35°

(B) 55°

(C) 125°

(D) 135°

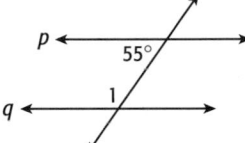

DAY 4

The regular price of a DVD player is $160. Greg buys the DVD player during a 20%-off sale. How much money does Greg save?

(F) $16

(G) $32

(H) $40

(J) $80

DAY 5

Which of the following is greater than 5?

(A) |−3|

(B) |3|

(C) |−6|

(D) |5|

DAY 1

Jeremy spins the spinner shown here. What is the probability that the spinner lands on a vowel?

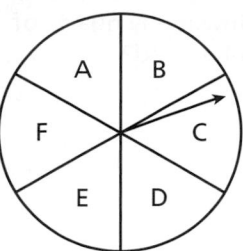

(A) $\frac{1}{6}$

(B) $\frac{1}{3}$

(C) $\frac{1}{2}$

(D) $\frac{2}{3}$

DAY 2

Find the volume of the rectangular prism.

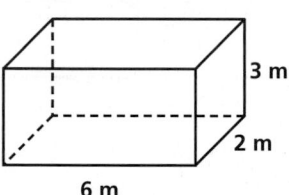

3 m

2 m

6 m

(F) 11 m³

(G) 30 m³

(H) 36 m³

(J) 72 m³

DAY 3

Simplify the expression $(2.5)^2$.

(A) 1.25

(B) 4.5

(C) 5

(D) 6.25

DAY 4

Loretta began writing the following proportion on the board: $\frac{8}{10} = $ ▨. Which ratio could she use to complete the proportion?

(F) $\frac{8}{18}$

(G) $\frac{3}{5}$

(H) $\frac{12}{15}$

(J) $\frac{10}{8}$

DAY 5

Which equation is an example of the Identity Property of Multiplication?

(A) $4 \times 1 = 4$

(B) $5 \times (2 + 1) = 5 \times 2 + 5 \times 1$

(C) $12 \times (8 \times 3) = (12 \times 8) \times 3$

(D) $7 \times 3 = 3 \times 7$

Countdown to Testing WEEK 20

DAY 1

Keisha flipped a coin 12 times. The table shows her results. What is the experimental probability of heads?

Ⓐ $\frac{1}{8}$

Ⓑ $\frac{1}{3}$

Ⓒ $\frac{1}{2}$

Ⓓ $\frac{2}{3}$

Result	Frequency
Heads	~~||||~~ |||
Tails	||||

DAY 2

The figure shows the dimensions of a rectangular garden at Chavez Middle School. What is the area of the garden?

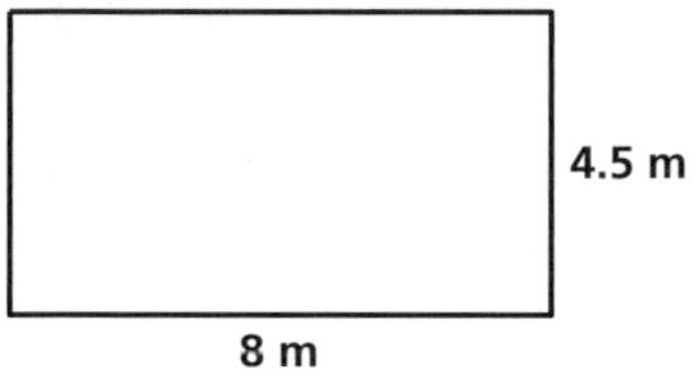

4.5 m
8 m

Ⓕ 18 m^2

Ⓖ 25 m^2

Ⓗ 32 m^2

Ⓙ 36 m^2

DAY 3

Lisa saw this sign outside a restaurant. Which of the following is another way to write the number shown on the sign?

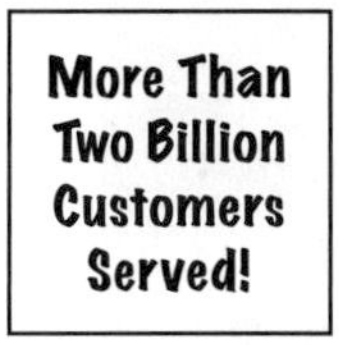

More Than Two Billion Customers Served!

Ⓐ 2,000

Ⓑ 2,000,000

Ⓒ 2,000,000,000

Ⓓ 2,000,000,000,000

DAY 4

Which of the following is NOT a customary unit of capacity?

Ⓕ cup

Ⓖ gallon

Ⓗ pound

Ⓙ quart

DAY 5

What is the reciprocal of $\frac{1}{4}$?

Ⓐ $\frac{1}{4}$

Ⓑ $\frac{1}{2}$

Ⓒ 2

Ⓓ 4

The State Capitol in Albany

Statue of Liberty

Winter in New York

Grade 5 Post-March Performance Indicators

Algebra Strand

Students will represent and analyze algebraically a wide variety of problem solving situations.

Variables and Expressions

5.A.2   Translate simple verbal expressions into algebraic expressions

Students will perform algebraic procedures accurately.

Variables and Expressions

5.A.3   Substitute assigned values into variable expressions and evaluate using order of operations

Equations and Inequalities

5.A.4   Solve simple one-step equations using basic whole-number facts

5.A.5   Solve and explain simple one-step equations using inverse operations involving whole numbers

Students will apply coordinate geometry to analyze problem solving situations.

Coordinate Geometry

5.G.12   Identify and plot points in the first quadrant

5.G.13   Plot points to form basic geometric shapes (identify and classify)

5.G.14   Calculate perimeter of basic geometric shapes drawn on a coordinate plane (rectangles and shapes composed of rectangles having sides with integer lengths and parallel to the axes)

Students will understand and apply concepts of probability.

Probability

5.S.5   List the possible outcomes for a single-event experiment

5.S.6   Record experiment results using fractions/ratios

5.S.7   Create a sample space and determine the probability of a single event, given a simple experiment (e.g., rolling a number cube)

The state bird is the Bluebird

The Rose is the state flower

Grade 6 Performance Indicators

Problem Solving Strand

Students will build new mathematical knowledge through problem solving.

6.PS.1 Know the difference between relevant and irrelevant information when solving problems

6.PS.2 Understand that some ways of representing a problem are more efficient than others

6.PS.3 Interpret information correctly, identify the problem, and generate possible strategies and solutions

Students will solve problems that arise in mathematics and in other contexts.

6.PS.4 Act out or model with manipulatives activities involving mathematical content from literature

6.PS.5 Formulate problems and solutions from everyday situations

6.PS.6 Translate from a picture/diagram to a numeric expression

6.PS.7 Represent problem situations verbally, numerically, algebraically, and/or graphically

6.PS.8 Select an appropriate representation of a problem

6.PS.9 Understand the basic language of logic in mathematical situations (and, or, and not)

Students will apply and adapt a variety of appropriate strategies to solve problems.

6.PS.10 Work in collaboration with others to solve problems

6.PS.11 Translate from a picture/diagram to a number or symbolic expression

6.PS.12 Use trial and error and the process of elimination to solve problems

6.PS.13 Model problems with pictures/ diagrams or physical objects

6.PS.14 Analyze problems by observing patterns

6.PS.15 Make organized lists or charts to solve numerical problems

Students will monitor and reflect on the process of mathematical problem solving.

6.PS.16 Discuss with peers to understand a problem situation

6.PS.17 Determine what information is needed to solve problem

6.PS.18 Determine the efficiency of different representations of a problem

6.PS.19 Differentiate between valid and invalid approaches

6.PS.20 Understand valid counterexamples

6.PS.21 Explain the methods and reasoning behind the problem solving strategies used

6.PS.22 Discuss whether a solution is reasonable in the context of the original problem

6.PS.23 Verify results of a problem

Reasoning and Proof Strand

Students will recognize reasoning and proof as fundamental aspects of mathematics.

6.RP.1 Recognize that mathematical ideas can be supported using a variety of strategies

Continued

6.RP.2 Understand that mathematical statements can be supported, using models, facts, and relationships to explain their thinking

Students will make and investigate mathematical conjectures.

6.RP.3 Investigate conjectures, using arguments and appropriate mathematical terms

6.RP.4 Make and evaluate conjectures, using a variety of strategies

Students will develop and evaluate mathematical arguments and proofs.

6.RP.5 Justify general claims or conjectures, using manipulatives, models, expressions, and mathematical relationships

6.RP.6 Develop and explain an argument verbally, numerically, algebraically, and/or graphically

6.RP.7 Verify claims other students make, using examples and counterexamples when appropriate

Students will select and use various types of reasoning and methods of proof.

6.RP.8 Support an argument through examples/counterexamples and special cases

6.RP.9 Devise ways to verify results

Communication Strand

Students will organize and consolidate their mathematical thinking through communication.

6.CM.1 Provide an organized thought process that is correct, complete, coherent, and clear

6.CM.2 Explain a rationale for strategy selection

6.CM.3 Organize and accurately label work

Students will communicate their mathematical thinking coherently and clearly to peers, teachers, and others.

6.CM.4 Share organized mathematical ideas through the manipulation of objects, numerical tables, drawings, pictures, charts, graphs, tables, diagrams, models, and symbols in written and verbal form

6.CM.5 Answer clarifying questions from others

Students will analyze and evaluate the mathematical thinking and strategies of others.

6.CM.6 Understand mathematical solutions shared by other students

6.CM.7 Raise questions that elicit, extend, or challenge others' thinking

6.CM.8 Consider strategies used and solutions found by others in relation to their own work

Students will use the language of mathematics to express mathematical ideas precisely.

6.CM.9 Increase their use of mathematical vocabulary and language when communicating with others

6.CM.10 Use appropriate vocabulary when describing objects, relationships, mathematical solutions, and rationale

6.CM.11 Decode and comprehend mathematical visuals and symbols to construct meaning

Connections Strand

Students will recognize and use connections among mathematical ideas.

6.CN.1 Understand and make connections and conjectures in their everyday experiences to mathematical ideas

6.CN.2 Explore and explain the relationship between mathematical ideas

6.CN.3 Connect and apply mathematical information to solve problems

Students will understand how mathematical ideas interconnect and build on one another to produce a coherent whole.

6.CN.4 Understand multiple representations and how they are related

6.CN.5 Model situations with objects and representations and be able to draw conclusions

Students will recognize and apply mathematics in contexts outside of mathematics.

6.CN.6 Recognize and provide examples of the presence of mathematics in their daily lives

6.CN.7 Apply mathematics to problem situations that develop outside of mathematics

6.CN.8 Investigate the presence of mathematics in careers and areas of interest

6.CN.9 Recognize and apply mathematics to other disciplines and areas of interest

Representation Strand

Students will create and use representations to organize, record, and communicate mathematical ideas.

6.R.1 Use physical objects, drawings, charts, tables, graphs, symbols, equations, or objects created using technology as representations

6.R.2 Explain, describe, and defend mathematical ideas using representations

6.R.3 Read, interpret, and extend external models

6.R.4 Use standard and nonstandard representations with accuracy and detail

Students will select, apply, and translate among mathematical representations to solve problems.

6.R.5 Use representations to explore problem situations

6.R.6 Investigate relationships between different representations and their impact on a given problem

Buffalo, New York

Students will use representations to model and interpret physical, social, and mathematical phenomena.

6.R.7 Use mathematics to show and understand physical phenomena (e.g., determine the perimeter of a bulletin board)

6.R.8 Use mathematics to show and understand social phenomena (e.g., construct tables to organize data showing book sales)

6.R.9 Use mathematics to show and understand mathematical phenomena (e.g., Find the missing value: $(3 + 4) + 5 = 3 + (4 + \underline{\quad})$)

Number Sense and Operations Strand

Students will understand numbers, multiple ways of representing numbers, relationships among numbers, and number systems.

Number Systems

6.N.1 Read and write whole numbers to trillions

6.N.2 Define and identify the commutative and associative properties of addition and multiplication

6.N.3 Define and identify the distributive property of multiplication over addition

6.N.4 Define and identify the identity and inverse properties of addition and multiplication

6.N.5 Define and identify the zero property of multiplication

6.N.6 Understand the concept of rate

6.N.7 Express equivalent ratios as a proportion

6.N.8 Distinguish the difference between rate and ratio

6.N.9 Solve proportions using equivalent fractions

6.N.10 Verify the proportionality using the product of the means equals the product of the extremes

6.N.11 Read, write, and identify percents of a whole (0% to 100%)

6.N.12 Solve percent problems involving percent, rate, and base

6.N.13 Define absolute value and determine the absolute value of rational numbers (including positive and negative)

6.N.14 Locate rational numbers on a number line (including positive and negative)

6.N.15 Order rational numbers (including positive and negative)

Students will understand meanings of operations and procedures, and how they relate to one another.

Operations

6.N.16 Add and subtract fractions with unlike denominators

6.N.17 Multiply and divide fractions with unlike denominators

6.N.18 Add, subtract, multiply, and divide mixed numbers with unlike denominators

6.N.19 Identify the multiplicative inverse (reciprocal) of a number

6.N.20 Represent fractions as terminating or repeating decimals

6.N.21 Find multiple representations of rational numbers (fractions, decimals, and percents 0 to 100)

6.N.22 Evaluate numerical expressions using order of operations (may include exponents of two and three)

6.N.23 Represent repeated multiplication in exponential form

6.N.24 Represent exponential form as repeated multiplication

6.N.25 Evaluate expressions having exponents where the power is an exponent of one, two, or three

Students will compute accurately and make reasonable estimates.

Estimation

6.N.26 Estimate a percent of quantity (0% to 100%)

6.N.27 Justify the reasonableness of answers using estimation (including rounding)

Algebra Strand

Students will represent and analyze algebraically a wide variety of problem solving situations.

Variables and Expressions

6.A.1 Translate two-step verbal expressions into algebraic expressions

Students will perform algebraic procedures accurately.

Variables and Expressions

6.A.2 Use substitution to evaluate algebraic expressions (may include exponents of one, two and three)

Equations and Inequalities

6.A.3 Translate two-step verbal sentences into algebraic equations

6.A.4 Solve and explain two-step equations involving whole numbers using inverse operations

Continued

NY33

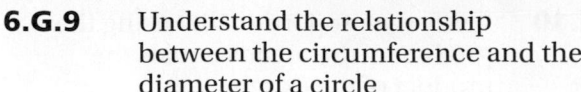
6.A.5   Solve simple proportions within context

6.A.6   Evaluate formulas for given input values (circumference, area, volume, distance, temperature, interest, etc.)

Geometry Strand

Students will use visualization and spatial reasoning to analyze characteristics and properties of geometric shapes.

Shapes

6.G.1   Calculate the length of corresponding sides of similar triangles, using proportional reasoning

6.G.2   Determine the area of triangles and quadrilaterals (squares, rectangles, rhombi, and trapezoids) and develop formulas

6.G.3   Use a variety of strategies to find the area of regular and irregular polygons

6.G.4   Determine the volume of rectangular prisms by counting cubes and develop the formula

6.G.5   Identify radius, diameter, chords and central angles of a circle

6.G.6   Understand the relationship between the diameter and radius of a circle

6.G.7   Determine the area and circumference of a circle, using the appropriate formula

6.G.8   Calculate the area of a sector of a circle, given the measure of a central angle and the radius of the circle

6.G.9   Understand the relationship between the circumference and the diameter of a circle

Students will apply coordinate geometry to analyze problem solving situations.

Coordinate Geometry

6.G.10   Identify and plot points in all four quadrants

6.G.11   Calculate the area of basic polygons drawn on a coordinate plane (rectangles and shapes composed of rectangles having sides with integer lengths)

Measurement Strand

Students will determine what can be measured and how, using appropriate methods and formulas.

Units of Measurement

6.M.1   Measure capacity and calculate volume of a rectangular prism

6.M.2   Identify customary units of capacity (cups, pints, quarts, and gallons)

6.M.3   Identify equivalent customary units of capacity (cups to pints, pints to quarts, and quarts to gallons)

6.M.4   Identify metric units of capacity (liter and milliliter)

6.M.5   Identify equivalent metric units of capacity (milliliter to liter and liter to milliliter)

Tools and Methods

6.M.6   Determine the tool and technique to measure with an appropriate level of precision: capacity

Students will develop strategies for estimating measurements.

Estimation

6.M.7   Estimate volume, area, and circumference (see figures identified in geometry strand)

6.M.8 Justify the reasonableness of estimates

6.M.9 Determine personal references for capacity

Statistics and Probability Strand

Students will collect, organize, display, and analyze data.

Collection of Data

6.S.1 Develop the concept of sampling when collecting data from a population and decide the best method to collect data for a particular question

Organization and Display of Data

6.S.2 Record data in a frequency table

6.S.3 Construct Venn diagrams to sort data

6.S.4 Determine and justify the most appropriate graph to display a given set of data (pictograph, bar graph, line graph, histogram, or circle graph)

Analysis of Data

6.S.5 Determine the mean, mode and median for a given set of data

6.S.6 Determine the range for a given set of data

6.S.7 Read and interpret graphs

Students will make predictions that are based upon data analysis.

Predictions from Data

6.S.8 Justify predictions made from data

Students will understand and apply concepts of probability.

Probability

6.S.9 List possible outcomes for compound events

6.S.10 Determine the probability of dependent events

6.S.11 Determine the number of possible outcomes for a compound event by using the fundamental counting principle and use this to determine the probabilities of events when the outcomes have equal probability

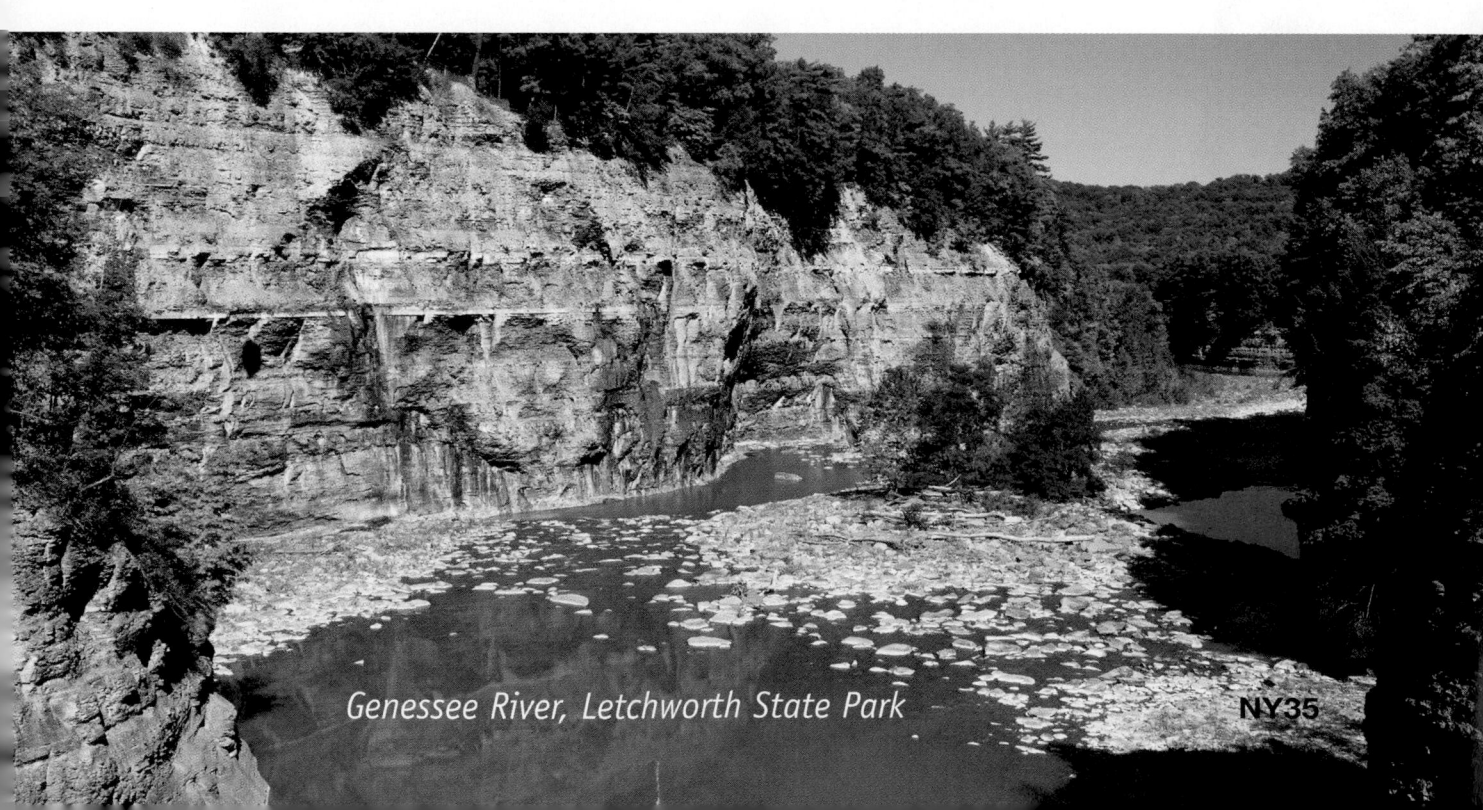

Genessee River, Letchworth State Park

Whole Numbers and Patterns

Career: Veterinary Technician

Tools for Success

Reading Math 5

Writing Math 9, 13, 17, 25, 29, 32, 36

Vocabulary 10, 14, 22, 26, 33

Know-It Notebook Chapter 1

Homework Help Online 8, 12, 16, 24, 28, 31, 35

Student Help 7, 10, 22, 27, 33

Test Prep and Spiral Review 9, 13, 17, 25, 29, 32, 36

Multi-Step Test Prep 39

Test Tackler 46

New York Test Prep 48

Introduction to Algebra

go.hrw.com
Online Resources
Keyword: MR7 TOC

Table of Contents

Career: Traffic Engineer

Tools for Success

Reading Math 70

Writing Math 53, 55, 57, 61, 65, 73, 77, 80, 84, 87

Vocabulary 54, 70, 90

Know-It Notebook Chapter 2

Homework Help Online 56, 60, 64, 72, 76, 79, 83, 86

Student Help 63, 81

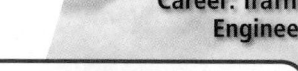

Test Prep and Spiral Review 57, 61, 65, 73, 77, 80, 84, 87

Multi-Step Test Prep 89

 **New York Test Prep** 98

CHAPTER 3

Decimals

go.hrw.com
Online Resources
KEYWORD: MR7 TOC

Career: Sports Historian

Tools for Success

Reading Math 108
Writing Math 105, 111, 115, 121, 127, 133, 136, 140, 143, 147
Vocabulary 112, 124

Know-It Notebook Chapter 3
Homework Help Online 110, 114, 120, 126, 132, 135, 139, 142, 146
Student Help 109, 112, 113, 118, 119, 130, 131, 134, 135, 137, 141, 144, 145

Test Prep and Spiral Review 111, 115, 121, 127, 133, 136, 140, 143, 147
Multi-Step Test Prep 149
Test Tackler 156
New York Test Prep 158

Number Theory and Fractions

go.hrw.com
Online Resources
KEYWORD: MR7 TOC

Career: Plumber

Tools for Success

Reading Math 163, 192
Writing Math 167, 172, 176, 182, 189, 195, 201, 205, 209, 213
Vocabulary 164, 169, 173, 181, 186, 192, 198, 212

Know-It Notebook Chapter 4
Homework Help Online 166, 171, 175, 183, 188, 194, 200, 204, 208
Student Help 169, 170, 174, 181, 187, 198, 199, 202, 203, 207, 213

Test Prep and Spiral Review
167, 172, 176, 184, 189, 195, 201, 205, 209
Multi-Step Test Prep 211
New York Test Prep 220

Fraction Operations

Career: Painter

Tools for Success

Writing Math 231, 237, 241, 247, 251, 257, 263, 267, 273, 277

Vocabulary 228, 234, 270

Know-It Notebook Chapter 5

Study Strategy 227

Homework Help Online 230, 236, 240, 246, 250, 256, 262, 266, 272, 276

Student Help 228, 229, 234, 239, 255, 261, 264, 274

Test Prep and Spiral Review 231, 237, 241, 247, 251, 257, 263, 267, 273, 277

Multi-Step Test Prep 279

Test Tackler 286

New York Test Prep 288

Collecting and Displaying Data

CHAPTER 6

Career: Meteorologist

Tools for Success

Reading Math 293, 309, 314

Writing Math 296, 301, 305, 311, 317, 321, 325, 329, 332, 335

Vocabulary 298, 308, 314, 319, 322, 330

Know-It Notebook Chapter 6

Homework Help Online 295, 300, 304, 310, 316, 320, 324, 328, 331, 334

Student Help 302, 322, 323, 330

Test Prep and Spiral Review 296, 301, 305, 311, 317, 321, 325, 329, 332, 335

Multi-Step Test Prep 337

New York Test Prep 344

Proportional Relationships

go.hrw.com
Online Resources
KEYWORD: MR7 TOC

Career: Fisheries Biologist

Tools for Success

Reading Math 352, 356, 362

Writing Math 351, 355, 359, 365, 369, 372, 377, 384, 388, 393, 397, 401

Vocabulary 362, 366, 370, 374, 381, 394, 400

Know-It Notebook Chapter 7

Homework Help Online 354, 358, 368, 371, 376, 383, 387, 392, 396

Student Help 356, 363, 364, 367, 374, 382, 386, 390, 394

Test Prep and Spiral Review 355, 359, 365, 369, 372, 377, 384, 388, 393, 397

Multi-Step Test Prep 399

Test Tackler 408

New York Test Prep 410

Geometric Relationships

Career: Artist

Tools for Success

Reading and Writing Math

Reading Math 415, 420, 421, 428, 447

Writing Math 419, 423, 427, 431, 440, 445, 449, 453, 458, 462, 467

Vocabulary 416, 420, 424, 428, 437, 442, 446, 459, 464

Study Skills

Know-It Notebook Chapter 8

Homework Help Online 418, 422, 426, 430, 439, 444, 448, 452, 457, 461, 466

Student Help 438, 446, 450

TEST PREP

Test Prep and Spiral Review 419, 423, 427, 431, 440, 445, 449, 453, 458, 462, 467

Multi-Step Test Prep 471

New York Test Prep 478

Measurement and Geometry

Career: Mathematician

Tools for Success

Writing Math 485, 491, 495, 499, 503, 507, 513, 517, 523
Vocabulary 488, 492, 514, 520

Know-It Notebook Chapter 9
Study Strategy 485
Homework Help Online 490, 494, 498, 502, 506, 512, 516, 522
Student Help 496, 497, 500, 501, 505, 510, 511

Test Prep and Spiral Review 491, 495, 499, 503, 507, 513, 517, 523
Multi-Step Test Prep 527
Test Tackler 534
New York Test Prep 536

Measurement: Area and Volume

go.hrw.com
Online Resources
KEYWORD: MR7 TOC

Career: Landscape Architect

Tools for Success

Reading and Writing Math

Reading Math 541

Writing Math 545, 549, 553, 556, 561, 569, 575, 579, 585

Vocabulary 542, 566, 572, 582

Study Skills

Know-It Notebook Chapter 10

Homework Help Online 544, 548, 552, 555, 560, 568, 574, 578, 584

Student Help 546, 552, 567, 572, 577, 583

TEST PREP

Test Prep and Spiral Review
545, 549, 553, 556, 561, 569, 575, 579, 585

Multi-Step Test Prep 587

New York Test Prep 594

Integers, Graphs, and Functions

go.hrw.com
Online Resources
KEYWORD: MR7 TOC

Career:
Geographer

Tools for Success

Reading and Writing Math

Writing Math 601, 605, 609, 613, 617, 620, 624, 627, 631, 643, 649, 653

Vocabulary 602, 610, 640, 646

Study Skills

Know-It Notebook Chapter 11

Homework Help Online 604, 608, 612, 619, 623, 626, 630, 638, 642, 648

Student Help 602, 606, 610, 625, 626, 628, 629, 636, 640, 652

TEST PREP

Test Prep and Spiral Review 605, 609, 613, 620, 624, 627, 631, 639, 643, 649

Multi-Step Test Prep 651

Test Tackler 660

New York Test Prep 662

Probability

go.hrw.com
Online Resources
KEYWORD: MR7 TOC

Career: Financial
Advisor

Tools for Success

Writing Math 671, 673, 675, 681, 685, 691, 697, 701

Vocabulary 668, 672, 678, 682, 688, 694, 700

Know-It Notebook Chapter 12

Study Strategy 667

Homework Help Online 670, 674, 680, 684, 690, 696

Student Help 668, 669, 682, 689

Test Prep and Spiral Review 671, 675, 681, 685, 691, 697

Multi-Step Test Prep 699

New York Test Prep 708

INTERDISCIPLINARY CONNECTIONS

Many fields of study require knowledge of the mathematical skills and concepts taught in *Holt Mathematics Course 1.* Examples and exercises throughout the book highlight the math you will need to understand in order to study other subjects, such as art or finance, or to pursue a career in fields such as medicine or architecture.

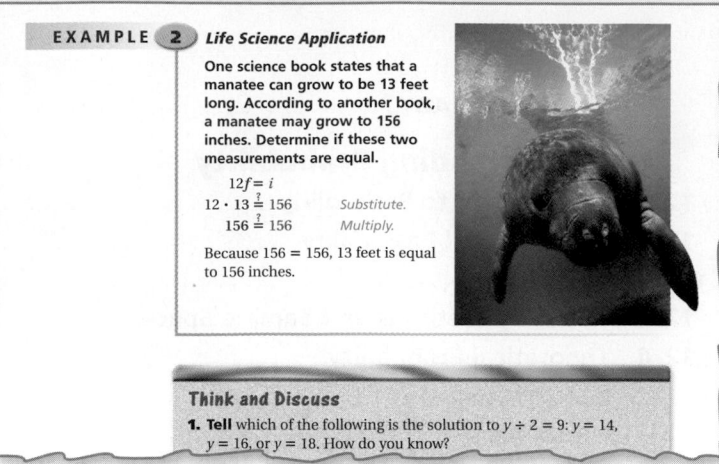

EXAMPLE 2 **Life Science Application**

One science book states that a manatee can grow to be 13 feet long. According to another book, a manatee may grow to 156 inches. Determine if these two measurements are equal.

$12f = i$
$12 \cdot 13 \stackrel{?}{=} 156$ *Substitute.*
$156 \stackrel{?}{=} 156$ *Multiply.*

Because $156 = 156$, 13 feet is equal to 156 inches.

Think and Discuss

1. Tell which of the following is the solution to $y \div 2 = 9$: $y = 14$, $y = 16$, or $y = 18$. How do you know?

Science

Astronomy 30–31, 111, 167, 192, 194, 375, 604
Biology 358, 498
Chemistry 393
Earth Science 28, 65, 87, 109, 127, 140, 355, 382, 561, 605, 609, 618, 620, 624, 627
Life Science 29, 71, 127, 184, 195, 202, 205, 209, 239, 240, 241, 263, 273, 277, 325, 376, 382, 639, 691, 696
Measurement 56, 72, 141, 145, 194, 240, 245, 246, 250, 363, 371, 458, 523, 555, 579
Physical Science 77, 86, 110, 171, 429
Physics 495
Science 130, 579
Technology 126, 391, 393
Weather 290, 294, 675

Language Arts

Language Arts 387, 462

Health and Fitness

Games 685
Health 112, 115
Hobbies 376, 462
Recreation 543
Sports 31, 118, 120, 121, 171, 184, 207, 250, 299, 302, 437, 445, 498, 500, 511, 517, 561, 605, 607, 620, 638

Social Studies

Agriculture 201
Archaeology 25
Architecture 421, 498, 503, 513, 521, 547, 560, 569, 585
Geography 8, 9, 80, 91, 126, 498, 609
History 9, 77, 140, 491, 523
Social Studies 25, 36, 58, 60, 72, 75, 80, 127, 142, 176, 195, 234, 236, 249, 255, 277, 302, 309, 335, 383, 397, 440, 465, 549, 553, 639, 681, 684

Economics

Consumer application 23, 228, 457
Consumer Math 132, 135, 136, 139, 353, 390
Economics 246
Money 57, 72, 115

Fine and Performing Arts

Art 125, 451, 499, 552
Cooking 199, 560
Crafts 250
Entertainment 126, 276, 357, 388
Graphic Art 369
Graphic Design 643
Music 251, 577
Patterns 364, 506
Photography 141

WHY LEARN MATHEMATICS?

Throughout the text, links to interesting application topics, such as entertainment, music, and technology, will help you see how math is used in the real world. Some of these links have additional information and activities at go.hrw.com. For a complete list of all real-world problems in *Holt Mathematics Course 1*, see page 815 in the Index.

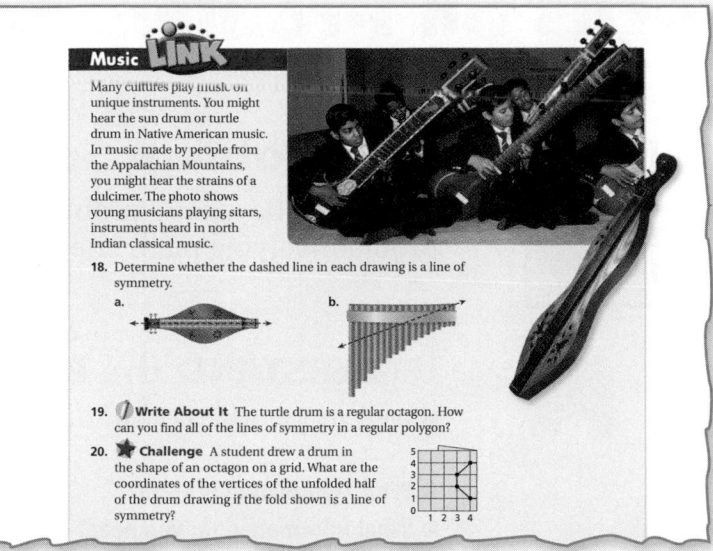

Music LINK

Many cultures play music on unique instruments. You might hear the sun drum or turtle drum in Native American music. In music made by people from the Appalachian Mountains, you might hear the strains of a dulcimer. The photo shows young musicians playing sitars, instruments heard in north Indian classical music.

18. Determine whether the dashed line in each drawing is a line of symmetry.

a.   b.

19. ✏ **Write About It** The turtle drum is a regular octagon. How can you find all of the lines of symmetry in a regular polygon?

20. ⭐ **Challenge** A student drew a drum in the shape of an octagon on a grid. What are the coordinates of the vertices of the unfolded half of the drum drawing if the fold shown is a line of symmetry?

Real-World LINKS

Career LINK

The risk of death in a house fire can be reduced by up to 50% if the home has a working smoke alarm.

Hobbies LINK

In a game of chess, each player has 318,979,564,000 possible ways to make the first four moves.

Weather LINK

The National Weather Service estimated that Mitch's wind speed reached 180 mi/h. This made Mitch a Category 5 hurricane, which is the strongest type.

go.hrw.com
Web Extra!
KEYWORD: MR7 Hurricane

Focus on Problem Solving

The Problem Solving Plan

In order to be a good problem solver, you first need a good problem-solving plan. The plan used in this book is detailed below.

UNDERSTAND the Problem

■ **What are you asked to find?**
Restate the question in your own words.

■ **What information is given?**
Identify the facts in the problem.

■ **What information do you need?**
Determine which facts are needed to answer the question.

■ **Is all the information given?**
Determine whether all the facts are given.

■ **Is there any information given that you will not use?**
Determine which facts, if any, are unnecessary to solve the problem.

Make a PLAN

■ **Have you ever solved a similar problem?**
Think about other problems like this that you successfully solved.

■ **What strategy or strategies can you use?**
Determine a strategy that you can use and how you will use it.

SOLVE

■ **Follow your plan.**
Show the steps in your solution. Write your answer as a complete sentence.

LOOK BACK

■ **Have you answered the question?**
Be sure that you answered the question that is being asked.

■ **Is your answer reasonable?**
Your answer should make sense in the context of the problem.

■ **Is there another strategy you could use?**
Solving the problem using another strategy is a good way to check your work.

■ **Did you learn anything while solving this problem that could help you solve similar problems in the future?**
Try to remember the problems you have solved and the strategies you used to solve them.

Using the Problem Solving Plan

During summer vacation, Nicholas will visit first his cousin and then his grandmother. He will be gone for 5 weeks and 2 days, and he will spend 9 more days with his cousin than with his grandmother. How long will he stay with each family member?

UNDERSTAND the Problem

Identify the important information.

- Nicholas's visits will total 5 weeks and 2 days.
- He will spend 9 more days with his cousin than with his grandmother.

The answer will be how long he will stay with each family member.

Make a PLAN

You can draw a diagram to show how long Nicholas will stay. Use boxes for the length of each stay. The length of each box will represent the length of each stay.

SOLVE

Think: There are 7 days in a week, so 5 weeks and 2 days is 37 days in all. Your diagram might look like this:

Cousin	? days	9 days	= 37 days

Grandmother	? days

Cousin	14 days	9 days	$37 - 9 = 28$

Grandmother	14 days	$28 \div 2 = 14$

So Nicholas will stay with his cousin for 23 days and with his grandmother for 14 days.

LOOK BACK

Twenty-three days is 9 days longer than 14 days. The total of the two stays is $23 + 14$, or 37 days, which is the same as 5 weeks and 2 days. This solution fits the description of Nicholas's trip given in the problem.

USING YOUR BOOK FOR SUCCESS

This book has many features designed to help you learn and study math. Becoming familiar with these features will prepare you for greater success on your exams.

Learn

Preview new **vocabulary** terms listed at the beginning of every lesson.

Look for the **Student Help** for hints and reminders.

Review the New York Performance Indicators the lesson addresses.

Study the **examples** to learn new math ideas and skills. The examples include step-by-step solutions.

Practice

Look back at examples from the lesson to solve the **Guided Practice** exercises.

If you get stuck, use the Internet for **Homework Help Online**.

Review

Study and review **vocabulary** from the entire chapter.

Test yourself with **practice problems** from every lesson in the chapter.

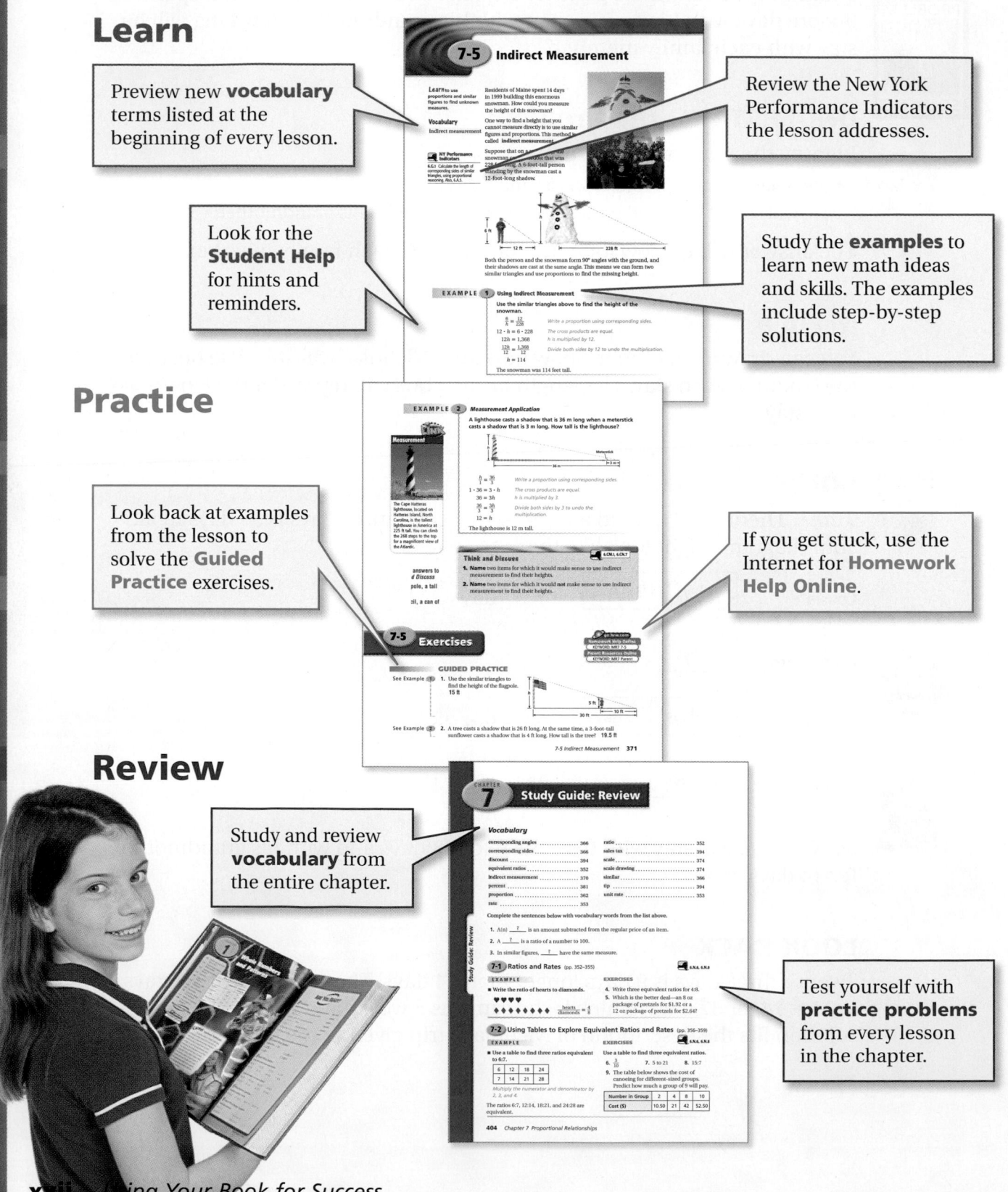

Scavenger Hunt

Holt Mathematics is your resource to help you succeed. Use this scavenger hunt to discover some of the many tools Holt provides to help you be an independent learner. On a separate sheet of paper, fill in the blanks to answer each question below. In each answer, one letter will be in a yellow box. When you have answered every question, use the letters to fill in the blank at the bottom of the page.

1. What is the first key **vocabulary** term in the Study Guide: Preview for Chapter 6?

▢▢▢ ▢▢▢▢▢

2. What are you asked to solve in Chapter 4 **Game Time**?

▢▢▢▢▢▢▢

3. What hobby is explored in **Problem Solving on Location** in Chapter 12?

▢▢▢▢▢▢▢▢▢▢▢ ▢▢▢▢▢▢

4. What is the last key **vocabulary** term in the Study Guide: Review for Chapter 6?

▢▢▢▢ ▢▢▢ ▢▢ ▢▢▢▢ ▢▢▢▢

5. Chapter 5's **Test Tackler** gives strategies for what kind of standardized test item?

▢▢▢▢▢▢▢▢ ▢▢▢▢▢▢▢▢

6. What school subject is connected to math in the **Link** on page 419?

▢▢▢▢▢▢▢▢▢

7. What keyword would you use for Lesson 7-1 **Homework Help Online**?

▢▢▢▢▢▢

8. What **career** is spotlighted on page 412?

▢▢▢▢▢

9. What **study strategy** is described on page 485?

▢▢▢ ▢▢▢▢▢▢▢▢ ▢▢▢▢
▢▢▢▢▢▢▢▢▢▢▢▢▢▢▢

Math Humor

What kind of message do you send a snake?

▢▢▢▢▢▢▢▢▢▢

Whole Numbers and Patterns

go.hrw.com
Chapter Project Online
KEYWORD: MR7 Ch1

African Plant-Eating Animals		
Animal	Weight (lb)	Daily Food Intake (lb)
Buffalo	1,500	45
Elephant	11,000	660
Giraffe	2,500	75
Hippopotamus	5,500	90
Zebra	950	30

Career *Veterinary Technician*

Do you like caring for animals? Veterinary technicians perform many of the same tasks for veterinarians as nurses do for doctors. Veterinary technicians also do research that can help animals. To care for animals, technicians must know what the animals need to eat and how they behave with other types of animals. Large plant-eating animals, many of which live in Africa, need to eat specific kinds of grasses and trees. The table above shows the approximate weight of some animals and the approximate amount of food the animals eat each day.

ARE YOU READY?

✓ Vocabulary

Choose the best term from the list to complete each sentence.

1. The answer in a multiplication problem is called the ___?___ .

2. 5,000 + 400 + 70 + 5 is a number written in ___?___ form.

3. A(n) ___?___ tells about how many.

4. The number 70,562 is written in ___?___ form.

5. Ten thousands is the ___?___ of the 4 in 42,801.

place value

estimate

product

expanded

standard

period

Complete these exercises to review skills you will need for this chapter.

✓ Compare Whole Numbers

Compare. Write < , >, or =.

6. 245 ▓ 219

7. 5,320 ▓ 5,128

8. 64 ▓ 67

9. 784 ▓ 792

✓ Round Whole Numbers

Round each number to the nearest hundred.

10. 567

11. 827

12. 1,642

13. 12,852

14. 1,237

15. 135

16. 15,561

17. 452,801

Round each number to the nearest thousand.

18. 4,709

19. 3,399

20. 9,825

21. 26,419

22. 12,434

23. 4,561

24. 11,784

25. 468,201

✓ Whole Number Operations

Add, subtract, multiply, or divide.

26. 18×22

27. $135 \div 3$

28. $247 + 96$

29. $358 - 29$

✓ Evaluate Whole Number Expressions

Evaluate each expression.

30. $3 \times 4 \times 2$

31. $20 + 100 - 40$

32. $5 \times 20 \div 4$

33. $6 \times 12 \times 5$

Where You've Been

Previously, you

- compared and ordered whole numbers to the hundred thousands.

- used the order of operations without exponents.

- looked for patterns.

In This Chapter

You will study

- comparing and ordering whole numbers to the billions.

- using the order of operations, including exponents.

- how to recognize and extend sequences.

- using properties to compute whole-number operations mentally.

- representing whole numbers by using exponents.

Where You're Going

You can use the skills learned in this chapter

- to express numbers in scientific and standard notation in science classes.

- to recognize and extend geometric sequences.

Key Vocabulary/Vocabulario

Associative Property	propiedad asociativa
base	base (en numeración)
Commutative Property	propiedad conmutativa
Distributive Property	propiedad distributiva
evaluate	evaluar
exponent	exponente
numerical expression	expresión numérica
order of operations	orden de las operaciones
sequence	sucesión
term	término (en una sucesión)

Vocabulary Connections

To become familiar with some of the vocabulary terms in the chapter, consider the following. You may refer to the chapter, the glossary, or a dictionary if you like.

1. The word *evaluate* means "to determine the value of something." What do you think you will **evaluate** in this chapter?

2. An *order* is the way things are arranged one after the other. How do you think an **order of operations** will help you solve math problems?

3. The word *numerical* means "of numbers." The word *expression* can refer to a mathematical symbol or combination of symbols. What do you think a **numerical expression** is?

4. A *sequence* is a list or arrangement that is in a particular order. What kind of **sequence** do you expect to see in this chapter?

Reading Strategy: Use Your Book for Success

Understanding how your textbook is organized will help you locate and use helpful information.

As you read through an example problem, pay attention to the margin notes, such as Reading Math notes, Writing Math notes, Helpful Hints, and Caution notes. These notes will help you understand concepts and avoid common mistakes.

Reading Math
A group of four ta
marks with a line
through it means

Writing Math
To write a repeati
decimal, you can
show three dots

Helpful Hint
Estimating before
you add or subtra
will help you che

Caution!
When you write a
expression for dat
a table, check tha

The Glossary is found in the back of your textbook. Use it as a resource when you need the definition of an unfamiliar word or property.

The Index is located at the end of your textbook. Use it to locate the page where a particular concept is taught.

The Skills Bank is found in the back of your textbook. These pages review concepts from previous math courses, including geometry skills.

Glossary/Glosari

A

ENGLISH

absolute value The distance of a number from zero on a number line; shown by │ │.

valor
está u
numér
absolt

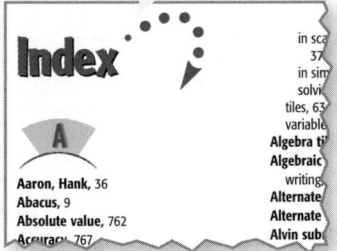

Index

A

Aaron, Hank, 36
Abacus, 9
Absolute value, 762
Accuracy, 767

in sca
37
in sim
solvi
tiles, 63
variable
Algebra ti
Algebraic
writing
Alternate
Alternate
Alvin sub

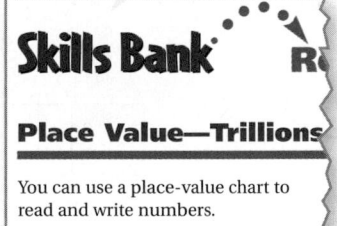

Skills Bank
R

Place Value—Trillions

You can use a place-value chart to read and write numbers.

Try This

Use your textbook.

1. Use the glossary to find the definitions of *bisect* and *factor tree*.

2. Where in the Skills Bank can you review how to round whole numbers and decimals?

3. Use the Problem Solving Handbook to list the four steps of the problem-solving plan and two different problem-solving strategies.

4. Use the index to find the pages where *angles* and *histogram* appear.

Reading and Writing Math

1-1 Comparing and Ordering Whole Numbers

Learn to compare and order whole numbers using place value or a number line.

NY Performance Indicators

6.N.1 Read and write whole numbers.

The midyear world population in 1995 was 5,694,418,460 people. The world population by midyear 2015 is projected to be 7,202,516,136 people.

You can use place value to read and understand large numbers. In the place value chart below, 1 has a value of 1 ten thousand or 1 hundred, depending on its position in the number.

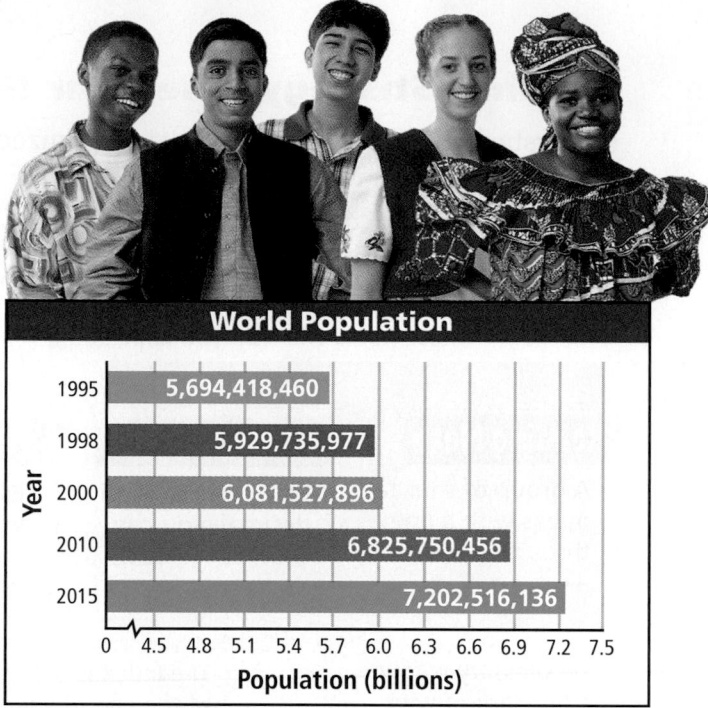

World Population

Year	Population
1995	5,694,418,460
1998	5,929,735,977
2000	6,081,527,896
2010	6,825,750,456
2015	7,202,516,136

Population (billions)

Source: U.S. Bureau of the Census, International Data Base, 2005

Place Value

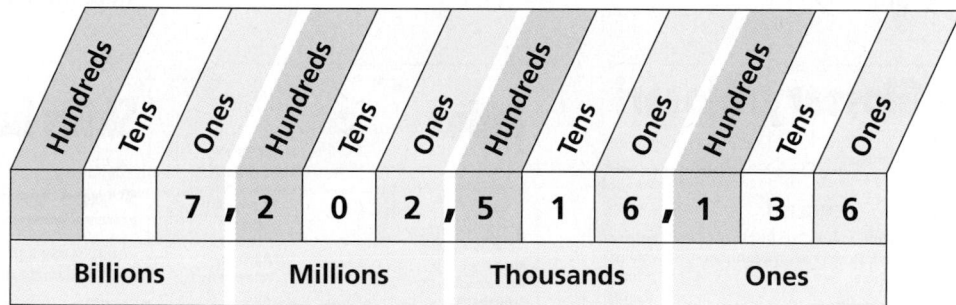

Hundreds	Tens	Ones	Hundreds	Tens	Ones	Hundreds	Tens	Ones	Hundreds	Tens	Ones
		7,	2	0	2,	5	1	6,	1	3	6
Billions			**Millions**			**Thousands**			**Ones**		

Standard form: 7,202,516,136

Expanded form: 7,000,000,000 + 200,000,000 + 2,000,000 + 500,000 + 10,000 + 6,000 + 100 + 30 + 6

Word form: seven billion, two hundred two million, five hundred sixteen thousand, one hundred thirty-six

EXAMPLE 1 Using Place Value to Compare Whole Numbers

Belgium's 2005 population was 10,364,388 people. The Czech Republic's 2005 population was 10,241,138 people. Which country had more people?

Belgium: 1 0, 3 6 4, 3 8 8

Czech Republic: 1 0, 2 4 1, 1 3 8

Start at the left and compare digits in the same place value position. Look for the first place where the values are different.

200 thousand is less than 300 thousand.
10,241,138 is less than 10,364,388.
So, Belgium had more people.

To order numbers, you can compare them using place value and then write them in order from least to greatest. You can also graph the numbers on a number line. As you read the numbers from left to right, they will be ordered from least to greatest.

EXAMPLE 2 Using a Number Line to Order Whole Numbers

Order the numbers from least to greatest.
923; 835; 1,266

Graph the following numbers on a number line:
The number 923 is between 900 and 1,000.
The number 835 is between 800 and 900.
The number 1,266 is between 1,200 and 1,300.

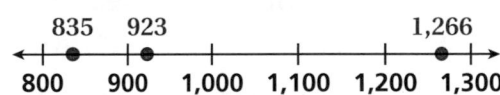

The numbers are ordered when you read the number line from left to right.

The numbers in order from least to greatest are 835, 923, and 1,266.

Remember!

< means
"is less than."
3 < 5   120 < 504
> means
"is greater than."
17 > 9   212 > 83

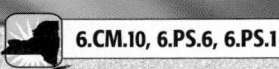

Think and Discuss

1. **Give** the place value of the digit 3 in each of the following numbers: 2,037,912; 2,370,912; 2,703,912.

2. **Read** each of the following numbers: 937,052; 3,012,480; 8,135,712,004.

3. **Look** at the bar graph at the beginning of the lesson. In which years was the population between 5,500,000,000 and 6,500,000,000?

go.hrw.com
Homework Help Online
KEYWORD: MR7 1-1
Parent Resources Online
KEYWORD: MR7 Parent

GUIDED PRACTICE

See Example 1. **Geography** Mount McKinley, in Alaska, is 20,320 feet tall. Mount Aconcagua, in Argentina, is 22,834 feet tall. Which mountain is taller?

2. The area of the Caribbean Sea is 971,400 square miles. The area of the Mediterranean Sea is 969,100 square miles. Which sea is smaller in area?

See Example 2 **Order the numbers from least to greatest.**

3. 726; 349; 642   **4.** 513; 915; 103   **5.** 497; 1,264; 809

6. 672; 1,421; 1,016   **7.** 982; 5,001; 3,255   **8.** 4,079; 9,976; 2,951

INDEPENDENT PRACTICE

See Example 1   **9.** The attendance in 1999 at a theme park was 17,459,000 people. The attendance in 1999 at a water park was 15,200,000 people. Which park had the higher attendance?

10. According to the table, which river is longer, the Missouri or the Mississippi?

11. A New York City driving range reported 413,497 golf balls were hit by customers last year. A Philadelphia range reported customers hit 408,959 golf balls. Which range had more golf balls hit?

River Length (mi)	
Mississippi	2,340
Missouri	2,315
Ohio	618
Red	1,290
Rio Grande	1,900

See Example 2 **Order the numbers from least to greatest.**

12. 367; 597; 279   **13.** 619; 126; 480   **14.** 946; 705; 810

15. 423; 1,046; 805   **16.** 1,523; 2,913; 111   **17.** 1,764; 1,359; 666

18. 742; 777; 711   **19.** 4,228; 1,502; 978   **20.** 6,704; 5,902; 2,792

PRACTICE AND PROBLEM SOLVING

Extra Practice
See page 714.

Compare. Write <, >, or =.

21. 46,495 ▆ 46,594   **22.** 162,648 ▆ 126,498   **23.** 3,654 ▆ 3,654

24. 512,105 ▆ 512,099   **25.** 29,448 ▆ 29,488   **26.** 913,203 ▆ 913,600

27. 23,172,458 ▆ 231,724 **28.** 21,782 ▆ 21,782   **29.** 1,556,982 ▆ 1,556,983

Order the numbers from greatest to least.

30. 591; 924; 341   **31.** 601; 533; 823; 149   **32.** 291; 911; 439; 747

33. 2,649; 3,461; 1,947   **34.** 5,349; 5,389; 5,480   **35.** 7,467; 7,239; 7,498

36. Americans own about 74,000,000 dogs as pets and 90,000,000 cats as pets. Do Americans own more dogs or cats?

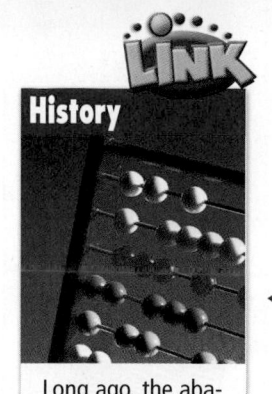
37. Geography The three biggest states in the continental United States are California, 159,869 square miles; Montana, 147,047 square miles; and Texas, 267,277 square miles. Write the states in order from smallest area to largest area.

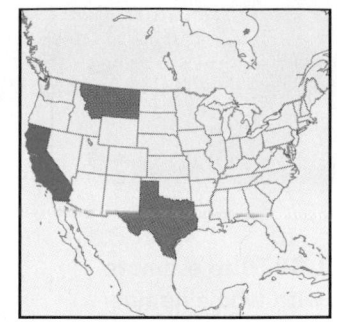

38. History The two drawings show another way to represent numbers. The rod on the far left of each drawing represents the hundred thousands place. The number of beads on a rod tells the value for that place. Which drawing represents the greater number?

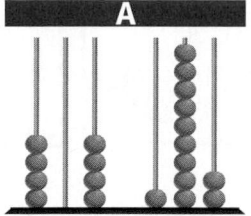
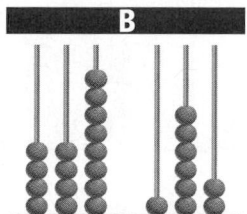

39. What's the Error? A student said 19,465,405 is greater than 19,465,425. Explain the error. Write the statement correctly.

40. Write About It Explain how you would compare 19,465,146 and 19,460,146.

41. Challenge In Roman numerals, letters represent numbers. For example, I = 1, V = 5, X = 10, L = 50, and C = 100. Letters in Roman numerals are written next to each other; this is how the value of the number is shown. To read the numbers below, add the values of all of the letters. What numbers do the following represent?

    a. CLX   **b.** LVI   **c.** CIII

TEST PREP and Spiral Review

42. Multiple Choice Which list shows the numbers in order from least to greatest?

  Ⓐ 101; 10,001; 1,001   Ⓒ 502; 205; 5,002

  Ⓑ 9,428; 9,454; 9,478   Ⓓ 2,123; 2,078; 2,055

43. Multiple Choice The 2000 populations of four major Texas cities were as follows: Amarillo, 17,627; Brownsville, 139,722; Laredo, 176,576; and Lubbock, 199,564. Which of the cities had the greatest population?

  Ⓕ Amarillo   Ⓖ Brownsville   Ⓗ Laredo   Ⓙ Lubbock

Write each number in word form. (Previous course)

44. 1,645   **45.** 24,498   **46.** 306,927   **47.** 4,605,926

Write the value of the red digit in each number. (Previous course)

48. 649,809   **49.** 349,239   **50.** 27,463   **51.** 16,239

1-2 Estimating with Whole Numbers

Learn to estimate with whole numbers.

Vocabulary

compatible number

underestimate

overestimate

NY Performance Indicators

6.CN.7 Apply mathematics to problem situations that develop outside of mathematics.

Sometimes in math you do not need an exact answer. Instead, you can use an estimate. Estimates are close to the exact answer but are usually easier and faster to find.

When estimating, you can round the numbers in the problem to *compatible numbers*. **Compatible numbers** are close to the numbers in the problem, and they can help you do math mentally.

EXAMPLE 1 Estimating a Sum or Difference by Rounding

Estimate each sum or difference by rounding to the place value indicated.

Remember!

When rounding, look at the digit to the right of the place to which you are rounding.

- If that digit is 5 or greater, round up.
- If that digit is less than 5, round down.

A 5,439 + 7,516; thousands

$$
\begin{array}{ll}
5,000 & \textit{Round 5,439 down.} \\
+\,8,000 & \textit{Round 7,516 up.} \\
\hline
13,000 &
\end{array}
$$

The sum is about 13,000.

B 62,167 − 47,511; ten thousands

$$
\begin{array}{ll}
60,000 & \textit{Round 62,167 down.} \\
-\,50,000 & \textit{Round 47,511 up.} \\
\hline
10,000 &
\end{array}
$$

The difference is about 10,000.

An estimate that is less than the exact answer is an **underestimate**.

An estimate that is greater than the exact answer is an **overestimate**.

E X A M P L E **2** **Estimating a Product by Rounding**

Ms. Escobar is planning a graduation celebration for the entire eighth grade. There are 9 eighth-grade homeroom classes of 27 students. Estimate how many cups Ms. Escobar needs to buy for the students if they all attend the celebration.

Find the number of students in the eighth grade.

$9 \times 27 \rightarrow 9 \times 30$ *Overestimate the number of students.*

$9 \times 30 = 270$ *The actual number of students is **less than** 270.*

If Ms. Escobar buys 270 cups, she will have enough for every student.

E X A M P L E **3** **Estimating a Quotient Using Compatible Numbers**

Mrs. Byrd will drive 120 miles to take Becca to the state fair. She can drive 65 mi/h. About how long will the trip take?

To find how long the trip will be, divide the miles Mrs. Byrd has to travel by how many miles per hour she can drive.

miles ÷ miles per hour

$120 \div 65 \rightarrow 120 \div 60$ *120 and 60 are compatible numbers. **Underestimate** the speed.*

$120 \div 60 = 2$ *Because she **underestimated** the speed, the actual time will be **less than** 2 hours.*

It will take Mrs. Byrd about two hours to reach the state fair.

Think and Discuss

 6.CM.1, 6.PS.21, 6.CN.9

1. **Suppose** you are buying items for a party and you have $50. Would it be better to overestimate or underestimate the cost of the items?

2. **Suppose** your car can travel between 20 and 25 miles on a gallon of gas. You want to go on a 100-mile trip. Would it be better to overestimate or underestimate the number of miles per gallon your car can travel?

3. **Describe** situations in which you might want to estimate.

1-2 **Exercises**

go.hrw.com
Homework Help Online
KEYWORD: MR7 1-2
Parent Resources Online
KEYWORD: MR7 Parent

GUIDED PRACTICE

See Example **1**   **Estimate each sum or difference by rounding to the place value indicated.**

1. 4,689 + 2,469; thousands

2. 50,498 − 35,798; ten thousands

See Example **2**   **3.** The graph shows the number of bottles of water used in three bicycle races last year. If the same number of riders enter the races each year, estimate the number of bottles that will be needed for races held in May over the next five years.

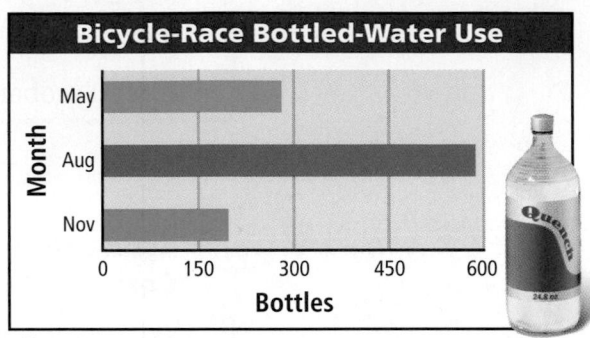

Bicycle-Race Bottled-Water Use

See Example **3**   **4.** If a local business provided half the bottled water needed for the August bicycle race, about how many bottles did the company provide?

5. Carla drives 80 miles on her scooter. If the scooter gets about 42 miles per gallon of gas, about how much gas did she use?

INDEPENDENT PRACTICE

See Example **1**   **Estimate each sum or difference by rounding to the place value indicated.**

6. 6,570 + 3,609; thousands

7. 49,821 − 11,567; ten thousands

8. 3,912 + 1,269; thousands

9. 37,097 − 20,364; ten thousands

See Example **2**   **10.** The recreation center has provided softballs every year to the city league. Use the table to estimate the number of softballs the league will use in 5 years.

See Example **3**   **11.** The recreation center has a girls' golf team with 8 members. About how many golf balls will each girl on the team get?

12. If the recreation center loses about 4 table tennis balls per year, and they are not replaced, about how many years will it take until the center has none left?

Recreation Center Balls Supplied	
Sport	**Number of Balls**
Basketball	21
Golf	324
Softball	28
Table tennis	95

PRACTICE AND PROBLEM SOLVING

Extra Practice
See page 714.

Estimate each sum or difference by rounding to the greatest place value.

13. 152 + 269

14. 797 − 234

15. 242 − 179

16. 6,152 − 3,195

17. 9,179 + 2,206

18. 10,982 + 4,821

19. 82,465 − 38,421

20. 38,347 + 17,039

21. 51,201 + 16,492

22. 639,069 + 283,136

23. 777,060 − 410,364

24. 998,927 − 100,724

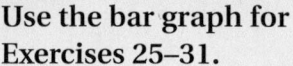

Use the bar graph for Exercises 25–31.

25. On one summer day there were 2,824 sailboats on Lake Erie. Estimate the number of square miles available to each boat.

26. If the areas of all the Great Lakes are rounded to the nearest thousand, which two of the lakes would be the closest in area?

27. About how much larger is Lake Huron than Lake Ontario?

28. The Great Lakes are called "great" because of the huge amount of fresh water they contain. Estimate the total area of all the Great Lakes combined.

29. ❓ **What's the Question?** Lake Erie is about 50,000 square miles smaller. What is the question?

30. ✏️ **Write About It** Explain how you would estimate the areas of Lake Huron and Lake Michigan to compare their sizes.

31. ⭐ **Challenge** Estimate the average area of the Great Lakes.

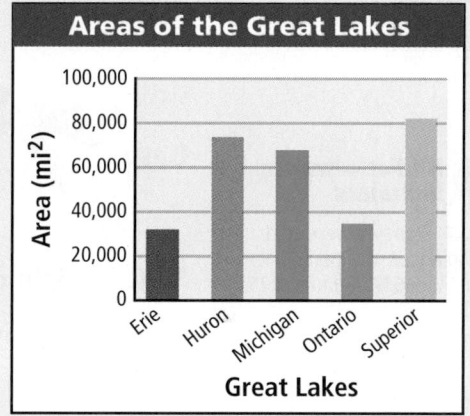

Areas of the Great Lakes

Area (mi²)

Great Lakes: Erie, Huron, Michigan, Ontario, Superior

Area includes the water surface and drainage basin within the United States and Canada.

TEST PREP and Spiral Review

32. Multiple Choice Which number is the best estimate for 817 + 259?

Ⓐ 10,000   Ⓑ 2,000   Ⓒ 1,100   Ⓓ 800

33. Short Response The National Football League requires home teams to have 36 new footballs for outdoor games and 24 new footballs for indoor games. Estimate how many new footballs the Washington Redskins must buy for 8 outdoor games. Explain how you determined your estimate.

Find each product or quotient. (Previous course)

34. $148 \div 4$ **35.** 523×5 **36.** $1,054 \div 31$ **37.** 312×8

Write each number in expanded form. (Lesson 1-1)

38. 269   **39.** 1,354   **40.** 32,498   **41.** 416,703

1-3 Exponents

Learn to represent numbers by using exponents.

Vocabulary

exponent

base

exponential form

The most recent eruption of Mount Vesuvius took place in 1944.

NY Performance Indicators

6.N.23 Represent repeated multiplication in exponential form. Also, 6.N.24 and 6.N.25.

Since 1906, the height of Mount Vesuvius in Italy has increased by 7^3 feet. How many feet is this?

The number 7^3 is written with an exponent. An **exponent** tells how many times a number called the **base** is used as a factor.

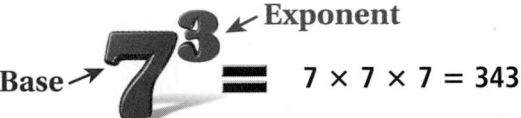

Exponent

Base → 7^3 = 7 × 7 × 7 = 343

So the height of Mount Vesuvius has increased by 343 ft.

A number is in **exponential form** when it is written with a base and an exponent.

Exponential Form	Read	Multiply	Value
10^1	"10 to the 1st power"	10	10
10^2	"10 **squared**," or "10 to the 2nd power"	10 × 10	100
10^3	"10 **cubed**," or "10 to the 3rd power"	10 × 10 × 10	1,000
10^4	"10 to the 4th power"	10 × 10 × 10 × 10	10,000

EXAMPLE 1 Writing Numbers in Exponential Form

Write each expression in exponential form.

A 4 × 4 × 4

4^3 *4 is a factor 3 times.*

B 9 × 9 × 9 × 9 × 9

9^5 *9 is a factor 5 times.*

EXAMPLE 2 Finding the Value of Numbers in Exponential Form

Find each value.

A 2^7

$2^7 = 2 × 2 × 2 × 2 × 2 × 2 × 2$

$= 128$

B 6^4

$6^4 = 6 × 6 × 6 × 6$

$= 1,296$

EXAMPLE 3  **PROBLEM SOLVING APPLICATION**

If Dana's school closes, a phone tree is used to contact each student's family. The secretary calls 3 families. Then each family calls 3 other families, and so on. How many families will be notified during the 6th round of calls?

1 Understand the Problem

The **answer** will be the number of families called in the 6th round.

List the **important information:**
- The secretary calls 3 families.
- Each family calls 3 families.

2 Make a Plan

You can draw a diagram to see how many calls are in each round.

Secretary

1st round—3 calls

2nd round—9 calls

3 Solve

Notice that in each round, the number of calls is a power of 3.
1st round: 3 calls $= 3 = 3^1$
2nd round: 9 calls $= 3 \times 3 = 3^2$

So during the **6**th round there will be 3^6 calls.
$3^6 = 3 \times 3 \times 3 \times 3 \times 3 \times 3 = 729$
During the 6th round of calls, 729 families will be notified.

4 Look Back

Drawing a diagram helps you visualize the pattern, but the numbers become too large for a diagram after the third round of calls. Solving this problem by using exponents can be easier and faster.

Think and Discuss

 6.CM.11, 6.R.9

1. Read each number: $4^8, 12^3, 3^2$.

2. Give the value of each number: $7^1, 13^2, 3^3$.

1-3 **Exercises**

go.hrw.com
Homework Help Online
KEYWORD: MR7 1-3
Parent Resources Online
KEYWORD: MR7 Parent

GUIDED PRACTICE

See Example ① Write each expression in exponential form.

1. $8 \times 8 \times 8$ **2.** 7×7 **3.** $6 \times 6 \times 6 \times 6 \times 6$

4. $4 \times 4 \times 4 \times 4$ **5.** $5 \times 5 \times 5 \times 5 \times 5$ **6.** 1×1

See Example ② Find each value.

7. 4^2 **8.** 3^3 **9.** 5^4 **10.** 8^2 **11.** 7^3

See Example ③ **12.** At Russell's school, one person will contact 4 people and each of those people will contact 4 other people, and so on. How many people will be contacted in the fifth round?

INDEPENDENT PRACTICE

See Example ① Write each expression in exponential form.

13. $2 \times 2 \times 2 \times 2 \times 2 \times 2$ **14.** $9 \times 9 \times 9 \times 9$ **15.** 8×8

16. $1 \times 1 \times 1$ **17.** $6 \times 6 \times 6 \times 6 \times 6$ **18.** $5 \times 5 \times 5$

19. $7 \times 7 \times 7 \times 7 \times 7 \times 7 \times 7$ **20.** $3 \times 3 \times 3 \times 3$ **21.** 4×4

See Example ② Find each value.

22. 2^4 **23.** 3^5 **24.** 6^2 **25.** 9^2 **26.** 7^4

27. 8^3 **28.** 1^4 **29.** 16^2 **30.** 10^8 **31.** 12^2

See Example ③ **32.** To save money for a video game, you put one dollar in an envelope. Each day for 5 days you double the number of dollars in the envelope from the day before. How much will be saved on the fifth day?

PRACTICE AND PROBLEM SOLVING

Extra Practice
See page 714.

Write each expression as repeated multiplication.

33. 16^3 **34.** 22^2 **35.** 31^6 **36.** 46^5 **37.** 50^3

38. 4^1 **39.** 1^9 **40.** 17^6 **41.** 8^5 **42.** 12^4

Find each value.

43. 10^6 **44.** 73^1 **45.** 9^4 **46.** 80^2 **47.** 10^5

48. 19^2 **49.** 2^9 **50.** 57^1 **51.** 5^3 **52.** 11^3

Compare. Write $<$, $>$, or $=$.

53. $6^1 \blacksquare 5^1$ **54.** $9^2 \blacksquare 20^1$ **55.** $10^1 \blacksquare 1{,}000{,}000^1$

56. $7^3 \blacksquare 3^7$ **57.** $5^5 \blacksquare 25^1$ **58.** $100^2 \blacksquare 10^4$

You are able to grow because your body produces new cells. New cells are made when old cells divide. Single-celled bodies, like bacteria, divide by *binary fission*, which means "splitting into two parts." A cycle is the length of time a cell type needs to divide.

59. In science lab, Carol has a dish containing 4^5 cells. How many cells are represented by this number?

60. A certain colony of bacteria triples in length every 15 minutes. Its length is now 1 mm. How long will it be in 1 hour? (*Hint:* There are four cycles of 15 minutes in 1 hour.)

Use the bar graph for Exercises 61–64.

61. Determine how many times cell type A will divide in a 24-hour period. If you begin with one type A cell, how many cells will be produced in 24 hours?

62. Multi-Step If you begin with one type B cell and one type C cell, what is the difference between the number of type B cells and the number of type C cells produced in 24 hours?

63.  **Write About It** Explain how to find the number of type A cells produced in 48 hours.

64. ★ **Challenge** How many hours will it take one C cell to divide into at least 100 C cells?

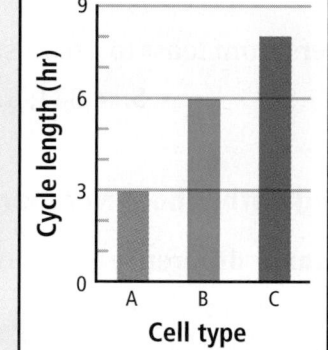

This plant cell shows the anaphase stage of mitosis. Mitosis is the process of nuclear division in complex cells called eukaryotes.

Cell Division Cycles

Cycle length (hr) vs Cell type (A, B, C)

go.hrw.com
Web Extra!
KEYWORD: MR7 Cell

TEST PREP and Spiral Review

65. Multiple Choice Which of the following shows the expression $4 \times 4 \times 4$ in exponential form?

Ⓐ 64   Ⓑ 444   Ⓒ 3^4 Ⓓ 4^3

66. Multiple Choice Which expression has the greatest value?

Ⓕ 2^5 Ⓖ 3^4 Ⓗ 4^3 Ⓙ 5^2

Order the numbers from least to greatest. (Lesson 1-1)

67. 8,452; 8,732; 8,245   **68.** 991; 1,010; 984   **69.** 12,681; 11,901; 12,751

Estimate each sum or difference by rounding to the place value indicated. (Lesson 1-2)

70. $12,876 + 17,986$; thousands   **71.** $72,876 - 15,987$; ten thousands

CHAPTER 1

READY TO GO ON?

SECTION 1A

Quiz for Lessons 1-1 Through 1-3

1-1 Comparing and Ordering Whole Numbers

Compare. Write <, >, or =.

1. 12,563,284 ▢ 12,587,802
2. 783,100,570 ▢ 780,223,104
3. In 2006, a university sold 1,981,299 tickets to its football games. In 2005, the same university sold 1,881,702 tickets. During which year were more tickets sold?

Order the numbers from least to greatest.

4. 1,052; 1,803; 1,231
5. 4,344; 3,344; 3,444
6. 10,463; 14,063; 10,643

1-2 Estimating with Whole Numbers

Estimate each sum or difference by rounding to the place value indicated.

7. 61,582 + 13,281; ten thousands
8. 86,125 − 55,713; ten thousands
9. 7,903 + 2,654; thousands
10. 34,633 − 32,087; thousands
11. 1,896,345 + 3,567,194; hundred thousands
12. 56,129,482 − 37,103,758; ten millions
13. Marcus wants to make a stone walkway in his garden. The rectangular walkway will be 3 feet wide and 18 feet long. Each 2-foot by 3-foot stone covers an area of 6 square feet. How many stones will Marcus need?
14. Jenna's sixth-grade class is taking a bus to the zoo. The zoo is 156 miles from the school. If the bus travels an average of 55 mi/h, about how long will it take the class to get to the zoo?

1-3 Exponents

Write each expression in exponential form.

15. $7 \times 7 \times 7$
16. $5 \times 5 \times 5 \times 5$
17. $3 \times 3 \times 3 \times 3 \times 3 \times 3$
18. $10 \times 10 \times 10 \times 10$
19. $1 \times 1 \times 1 \times 1 \times 1$
20. $4 \times 4 \times 4 \times 4$

Find each value.

21. 3^3
22. 2^4
23. 6^2
24. 8^3
25. To start reading a novel for English class, Sara read 1 page. Each day for 4 days she reads double the number of pages she read the day before. How many pages will she read on the fourth day?

Ready to Go On?

Focus on Problem Solving

Solve

• Choose the operation: addition or subtraction

Read the whole problem before you try to solve it. Determine what action is taking place in the problem. Then decide whether you need to add or subtract in order to solve the problem.

If you need to combine or put numbers together, you need to add. If you need to take away or compare numbers, you need to subtract.

Action	Operation	Picture
Combining Putting together	Add	
Removing Taking away	Subtract	
Comparing Finding the difference	Subtract	

 **Read each problem. Determine the action in each problem. Choose an operation in order to solve the problem. Then solve.**

Most hurricanes that occur over the Atlantic Ocean, the Caribbean Sea, or the Gulf of Mexico occur between June and November. Since 1886, a hurricane has occurred in every month except April.

Number of Out-of-Season Hurricanes Since 1886	
Month	**Number**
Jan	1
Feb	1
Mar	1
May	14
Dec	10

Use the table for problems 1 and 2.

1 How many out-of-season hurricanes have occurred in all?

2 How many more hurricanes have occurred in May than in December?

3 There were 14 named storms during the 2000 hurricane season. Eight of these became hurricanes, and three others became major hurricanes. How many of the named storms were not hurricanes or major hurricanes?

Technology LAB 1-4

Explore the Order of Operations

Use with Lesson 1-4

go.hrw.com
Lab Resources Online
KEYWORD: MR7 Lab1

NY Performance Indicators

6.N.22, 6.PS.19, 6.PS.23

Look at the expression 3 + 2 · 8. To evaluate this expression, decide whether to add first or multiply first. Knowing the correct *order of operations* is important. Without this knowledge, you could get an incorrect result.

Activity 1

Use pencil and paper to evaluate 3 + 2 · 8 two different ways.

Add first, and then multiply by 8.

$3 + 2 = 5$
$5 \cdot 8 = 40$

Multiply first, and then add 3.

$2 \cdot 8 = 16$
$16 + 3 = 19$

Now evaluate 3 + 2 · 8 using a graphing or scientific calculator.

The result, 19, shows that this calculator multiplied first, even though addition came first in the expression.

If there are no parentheses, then multiplication and division are done before addition or subtraction. If the addition is to be done first, parentheses *must* be used.

When you evaluate (3 + 2) · 8 on a calculator, the result is 40. Because of the parentheses, the calculator adds before multiplying.

Graphing and scientific calculators follow a logical system called the algebraic order of operations. The order of operations tells you to multiply and divide before you add or subtract.

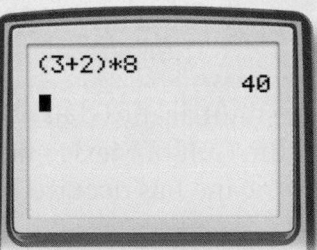

Think and Discuss

1. In 4 + 15 ÷ 5, which operation do you perform first? How do you know?

2. Tell the order in which you would perform the operations in the expression 8 ÷ 2 + 6 · 3 − 4.

Try This

Evaluate each expression with pencil and paper. Check your answer with a calculator.

1. 4 · 12 − 7   2. 15 ÷ 3 + 10   3. 4 + 2 · 6   4. 10 − 4 ÷ 2

Activity 2

What should you do if the same operation appears twice in an expression? Use a calculator to decide which subtraction is done first in the expression $7 - 3 - 2$.

If $7 - 3$ is done first, the value of the expression is $4 - 2 = 2$.

If $3 - 2$ is done first, the value of the expression is $7 - 1 = 6$.

On the calculator, the value of $7 - 3 - 2$ is 2. The subtraction on the left, $7 - 3$, is done first.

Addition and subtraction (or multiplication and division) are done from left to right.

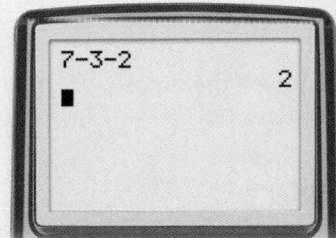

Think and Discuss

1. In $15 + 5 + 4$, does it matter which operation you perform first? Explain.

2. Does it matter which operation you perform first in $15 - 5 + 4$? Explain.

Try This

Evaluate each expression. Check your answer with a calculator.

1. $8 - 6 - 1$ **2.** $20 \div 5 \div 2$ **3.** $3 \cdot 6 \cdot 2$ **4.** $19 + 6 + 5$

Activity 3

Without parentheses, the expression $8 + 2 \cdot 10 - 3$ equals 25. Insert parentheses to make the value of the expression 22.

What happens if you add first?

$(8 + 2) \cdot 10 - 3$
$10 \cdot 10 - 3$
$100 - 3$
97

What happens if you subtract first?

$8 + 2 \cdot (10 - 3)$
$8 + 2 \cdot 7$
$8 + 14$
22

For the expression to equal 22, the subtraction must be done first.

Think and Discuss

1. To evaluate $13 + 5 \cdot 255$ on a calculator, you type $13 + 5$ and then press the ⌗X⌗ key. But before you can type in the 255, the display changes to 18!

  a. Does this calculator follow the correct order of operations? Why?

  b. How could you use this calculator to evaluate $13 + 5 \cdot 255$?

Try This

Insert parentheses to make the value of each expression 12.

1. $56 - 40 + 4$ **2.** $3 - 1 \cdot 10 - 4$ **3.** $18 \div 2 + 1 + 6$ **4.** $100 + 8 \div 2 \cdot 2 + 5$

1-4 Order of Operations

Learn to use the order of operations.

Vocabulary

numerical expression

evaluate

order of operations

**NY Performance Indicators**

6.N.22 Evaluate numerical expressions using order of operations. Also, 6.N.25.

A **numerical expression** is a mathematical phrase that includes only numbers and operation symbols.

Numerical Expressions	4 + 8 ÷ 2 × 6	371 − 203 + 2	5,006 × 19

When you **evaluate** a numerical expression, you find its value.

Erika and Jamie each evaluated 3 + 4 × 6. Their work is shown below. Whose answer is correct?

When an expression has more than one operation, you must know which operation to do first. To make sure that everyone gets the same answer, we use the **order of operations**.

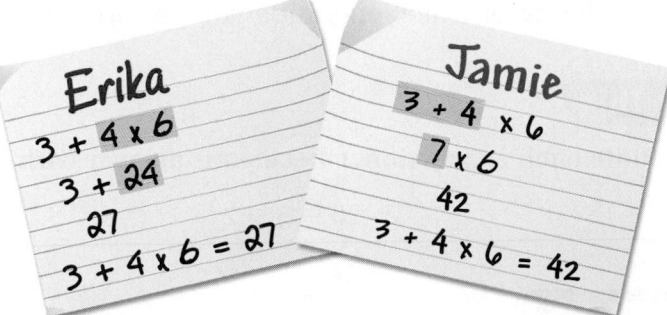

Remember!

The first letters of these words can help you remember the order of operations.

Please	*Parentheses*
Excuse	*Exponents*
My	*Multiply/*
Dear	*Divide*
Aunt	*Add/*
Sally	*Subtract*

ORDER OF OPERATIONS

1. Perform operations in **parentheses**.
2. Find the values of numbers with **exponents**.
3. **Multiply** or **divide** from left to right as ordered in the problem.
4. **Add** or **subtract** from left to right as ordered in the problem.

3 + 4 × 6   *There are no parentheses or exponents. Multiply first.*

3 + 24   *Add.*

27   *Erika has the correct answer.*

E X A M P L E  **Using the Order of Operations**

Evaluate each expression.

A 9 + 12 × 2

9 + 12 × 2   *There are no parentheses or exponents.*

9 +   24   *Multiply.*

33   *Add.*

Evaluate each expression.

B $7 + (12 \times 3) \div 6$

$7 + (12 \times 3) \div 6$

$7 + \quad 36 \quad \div 6$ *Perform operations within parentheses.*

$7 + \qquad\qquad 6$ *Divide.*

$\qquad 13$ *Add.*

EXAMPLE 2   **Using the Order of Operations with Exponents**

Evaluate each expression.

A $3^3 + 8 - 16$

$3^3 + 8 - 16$ *There are no parentheses.*

$27 + 8 - 16$ *Find the values of numbers with exponents.*

$\quad 35 \ - 16$ *Add*

$\qquad 19$ *Subtract.*

B $8 \div (1 + 3) \times 5^2 - 2$

$8 \div (1 + 3) \times 5^2 - 2$

$8 \div \quad 4 \quad \times 5^2 - 2$ *Perform operations within parentheses.*

$8 \div \quad 4 \quad \times 25 - 2$ *Find the values of numbers with exponents.*

$\quad 2 \quad \times 25 - 2$ *Divide.*

$\qquad 50 \ - 2$ *Multiply.*

$\qquad\qquad 48$ *Subtract.*

EXAMPLE 3   *Consumer Application*

Regina bought 5 carved wooden beads for $3 each and 8 glass beads for $2 each. Evaluate $5 \times 3 + 8 \times 2$ to find the amount Regina spent for beads.

$5 \times 3 + 8 \times 2$

$\quad 15 \ + \ 16$

$\qquad 31$

Regina spent $31 for beads.

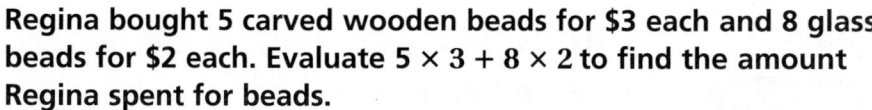

Think and Discuss    **6.RP.2, 6.CN.3**

1. Explain why $6 + 7 \times 10 = 76$ but $(6 + 7) \times 10 = 130$.

2. Tell how you can add parentheses to the numerical expression $2^2 + 5 \times 3$ so that 27 is the correct answer.

1-4 **Exercises**

go.hrw.com
Homework Help Online
KEYWORD: MR7 1-4
Parent Resources Online
KEYWORD: MR7 Parent

GUIDED PRACTICE

See Example **1** Evaluate each expression.

1. $36 - 18 \div 6$ **2.** $7 + 24 \div 6 \times 2$ **3.** $62 - 4 \times (15 \div 5)$

See Example **2**   **4.** $11 + 2^3 \times 5$ **5.** $5 \times (28 \div 7) - 4^2$ **6.** $5 + 3^2 \times 6 - (10 - 9)$

See Example **3**   **7.** Coach Milner fed the team after the game by buying 24 Chicken Deals for $4 each and 7 Burger Deals for $6 each. Evaluate $24 \times 4 + 7 \times 6$ to find the cost of the food.

INDEPENDENT PRACTICE

See Example **1** Evaluate each expression.

8. $9 + 27 \div 3$ **9.** $2 \times 7 - 32 \div 8$ **10.** $45 \div (3 + 6) \times 3$

11. $(6 + 2) \times 4$ **12.** $9 \div 3 + 6 \times 2$ **13.** $5 + 3 \times 2 + 12 \div 4$

See Example **2**   **14.** $4^2 + 48 \div (10 - 4)$ **15.** $100 \div 5^2 + 7 \times 3$ **16.** $6 \times 2^2 + 28 - 5$

17. $6^2 - 12 \div 3 + (15 - 7)$ **18.** $21 \div (3 + 4) \times 9 - 2^3$ **19.** $(3^2 + 6 \div 2) \times (36 \div 6 - 4)$

See Example **3**   **20.** The nature park has a pride of 5 adult lions and 3 cubs. The adults eat 8 lb of meat each day and the cubs eat 4 lb. Evaluate $5 \times 8 + 3 \times 4$ to find the amount of meat consumed each day by the lions.

21. Angie read 4 books that were each 150 pages long and 2 books that were each 325 pages long. Evaluate $4 \times 150 + 2 \times 325$ to find the total number of pages Angie read.

PRACTICE AND PROBLEM SOLVING

Extra Practice
See page 715.

Evaluate each expression.

22. $12 + 3 \times 4$ **23.** $25 - 21 \div 3$ **24.** $1 + 7 \times 2$

25. $60 \div (10 + 2) \times 4^2 - 23$ **26.** $10 \times (28 - 23) + 7^2 - 37$ **27.** $(5 - 3) \div 2$

28. $72 \div 9 - 2 \times 4$ **29.** $12 + (1 + 7^2) \div 5$ **30.** $25 - 5^2$

31. $(15 - 6)^2 - 34 \div 2$ **32.** $(2 \times 4)^2 - 3 \times (5 + 3)$ **33.** $16 + 2 \times 3$

Add parentheses so that each equation is correct.

34. $2^3 + 6 - 5 \times 4 = 12$ **35.** $7 + 2 \times 6 - 4 - 3 = 53$

36. $3^2 + 6 + 3 \times 3 = 36$ **37.** $5^2 - 10 + 5 + 4^2 = 36$

38. $2 \times 8 + 5 - 3 = 23$ **39.** $9^2 - 2 \times 15 + 16 - 8 = 11$

40. $5 + 7 \times 2 - 3 = 21$ **41.** $4^2 \times 3 - 2 \div 4 = 4$

42. **Critical Thinking** Jon says the answer to $1 + 3 \times (6 + 2) - 7$ is 25. Julie says the answer is 18. Who is correct? Explain.

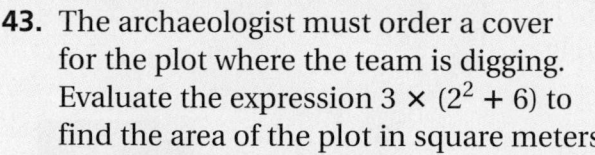
Archaeologists study cultures of the past by uncovering items from ancient cities. An archaeologist has chosen a site in Mexico for her team's next dig. She divides the location into rectangular plots and labels each plot so that uncovered items can be identified by the plot in which they were found.

43. The archaeologist must order a cover for the plot where the team is digging. Evaluate the expression $3 \times (2^2 + 6)$ to find the area of the plot in square meters.

Archaeologists uncovered pieces of pottery at the La Ventilla site in Mexico.

44. In the first week, the archaeology team digs down 2 meters and removes a certain amount of dirt. Evaluate the expression $3 \times (2^2 + 6) \times 2$ to find the volume of the dirt removed from the plot in the first week.

45. Over the next two weeks, the archaeology team digs down an additional 2^3 meters. Evaluate the expression $3 \times (2^2 + 6) \times (2 + 2^3)$ to find the total volume of dirt removed from the plot after 3 weeks.

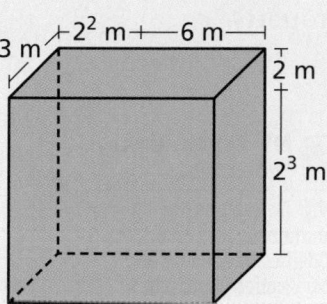

46. **Write About It** Explain why the archaeologist must follow the order of operations to determine the area of each plot.

47. **Challenge** Write an expression for the volume of dirt that would be removed if the archaeologist's team were to dig down an additional 3^2 meters after the first three weeks.

TEST PREP and Spiral Review

48. Multiple Choice Which operation should you perform first when you evaluate $81 - (6 + 30 \div 2) \times 5$?

   Ⓐ Addition   Ⓑ Division   Ⓒ Multiplication   Ⓓ Subtraction

49. Multiple Choice Which expression does NOT have a value of 5?

   Ⓕ $2^2 + (3 - 2)$ Ⓖ $(2^2 + 3) - 2$ Ⓗ $2^2 + 3 - 2$ Ⓙ $2^2 - (3 + 2)$

50. Gridded Response What is the value of the expression $3^2 + (9 \div 3 - 2)$?

Write each number in standard form. (Lesson 1-1)

51. $3,000 + 200 + 70 + 3$ **52.** $10,000 + 500 + 20 + 1$ **53.** $70,000 + 7$

Find each value. (Lesson 1-3)

54. 8^5 **55.** 5^3 **56.** 3^8 **57.** 4^4 **58.** 7^2

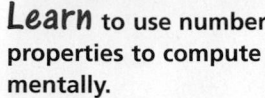 **Mental Math**

Learn to use number properties to compute mentally.

Vocabulary

Commutative Property

Associative Property

Distributive Property

 **NY Performance Indicators**

6.N.2 Define and identify the commutative and associative properties of addition and multiplication. Also, 6.N.3.

Mental math means "doing math in your head." Shakuntala Devi is extremely good at mental math. When she was asked to multiply 7,686,369,774,870 by 2,465,099,745,779, she took only 28 seconds to multiply the numbers mentally and gave the correct answer of 18,947,668,177,995,426,462,773,730!

Most people cannot do calculations like that mentally. But you can learn to solve some problems very quickly in your head.

Many mental math strategies use number properties that you already know.

COMMUTATIVE PROPERTY (Ordering)	
Words	**Numbers**
You can add or multiply numbers in any order.	$18 + 9 = 9 + 18$ $15 \times 2 = 2 \times 15$

ASSOCIATIVE PROPERTY (Grouping)	
Words	**Numbers**
When you are only adding or only multiplying, you can group any of the numbers together.	$(17 + 2) + 9 = 17 + (2 + 9)$ $(12 \times 2) \times 4 = 12 \times (2 \times 4)$

EXAMPLE **Using Properties to Add and Multiply Whole Numbers**

A Evaluate $12 + 4 + 18 + 46$.

$12 + 4 + 18 + 46$	*Look for sums that are multiples of 10.*
$12 + 18 \ + \ 4 + 46$	*Use the Commutative Property.*
$(12 + 18) + (4 + 46)$	*Use the Associative Property to make*
$30 \quad + \quad 50$	*groups of compatible numbers.*
80	*Use mental math to add.*

B Evaluate $5 \times 12 \times 2$.

$5 \times 12 \times 2$	*Look for products that are multiples of 10.*
$12 \times 5 \times 2$	*Use the Commutative Property.*
$12 \times (5 \times 2)$	*Use the Associative Property to group compatible numbers.*
$12 \times \quad 10$	
$\qquad 120$	*Use mental math to multiply.*

DISTRIBUTIVE PROPERTY	
Words	**Numbers**
When you multiply a number times a sum, you can	
• find the sum first and then multiply, or	$6 \times (10 + 4) = 6 \times 14$ $\qquad\qquad\quad = \quad 84$
• multiply by each number in the sum and then add.	$6 \times (10 + 4) = (6 \times 10) + (6 \times 4)$ $\qquad\qquad\quad = \quad 60 \quad + \quad 24$ $\qquad\qquad\quad = \qquad\quad 84$

When you multiply two numbers, you can "break apart" one of the numbers into a sum and then use the Distributive Property.

EXAMPLE 2 Using the Distributive Property to Multiply

Use the Distributive Property to find each product.

A 4×23

$4 \times 23 = 4 \times (20 + 3)$	*"Break apart" 23 into 20 + 3.*
$= (4 \times 20) + (4 \times 3)$	*Use the Distributive Property.*
$= \quad 80 \quad + \quad 12$	*Use mental math to multiply.*
$= \qquad 92$	*Use mental math to add.*

Helpful Hint

Break the greater factor into a sum that contains a multiple of 10 and a one-digit number. You can add and multiply these numbers mentally.

B 8×74

$8 \times 74 = 8 \times (70 + 4)$	*"Break apart" 74 into 70 + 4.*
$= (8 \times 70) + (8 \times 4)$	*Use the Distributive Property.*
$= \quad 560 \quad + \quad 32$	*Use mental math to multiply.*
$= \qquad 592$	*Use mental math to add.*

Think and Discuss  6.CM.4, 6.CN.6

1. Give examples of the Commutative Property and the Associative Property.

2. Name some situations in which you might use mental math.

go.hrw.com
Homework Help Online
KEYWORD: MR7 1-5
Parent Resources Online
KEYWORD: MR7 Parent

GUIDED PRACTICE

See Example **1** Evaluate.

1. $13 + 9 + 7 + 11$ **2.** $19 + 18 + 11 + 32$ **3.** $25 + 7 + 13 + 5$

4. $5 \times 14 \times 4$ **5.** $4 \times 16 \times 5$ **6.** $5 \times 17 \times 2$

See Example **2** Use the Distributive Property to find each product.

7. 5×24 **8.** 8×52 **9.** 4×39 **10.** 6×14

11. 3×33 **12.** 2×78 **13.** 9×12 **14.** 2×87

INDEPENDENT PRACTICE

See Example **1** Evaluate.

15. $15 + 17 + 3 + 5$ **16.** $14 + 7 + 16 + 13$ **17.** $6 + 21 + 14 + 9$

18. $5 \times 25 \times 2$ **19.** $2 \times 32 \times 10$ **20.** $6 \times 12 \times 5$

See Example **2** Use the Distributive Property to find each product.

21. 3×36 **22.** 4×42 **23.** 6×71 **24.** 2×94 **25.** 6×23

26. 5×25 **27.** 6×62 **28.** 7×21 **29.** 8×41 **30.** 2×94

PRACTICE AND PROBLEM SOLVING

Extra Practice
See page 715.

Use mental math to find each sum or product.

31. $8 + 13 + 7 + 12$ **32.** $2 \times 25 \times 4$ **33.** $4 + 22 + 16 + 18$

34. $5 \times 8 \times 12$ **35.** $5 + 98 + 95$ **36.** $6 \times 5 \times 14$

37. $11 + 75 + 25$ **38.** $8 \times 11 \times 5$ **39.** $19 + 1 + 11 + 39$

40. Paul is writing a story for the school newspaper about the landscaping done by his class. The students planted 15 vines, 12 hedges, 8 trees, and 35 flowering plants. How many plants were used in the project?

41. Earth Science The temperature on Sunday was 58°F. The temperature is predicted to rise 4°F on Monday, then rise 2°F more on Tuesday, and then rise another 6°F by Saturday. What is the predicted temperature on Saturday?

42. Multi-Step Janice wants to order disks for her computer. She needs to find the total cost, including shipping and handling. If Janice orders 7 disks, what will her total cost be?

Description	Number	Unit Cost with Tax	Price
Computer Disk	7	$24.00	
		Shipping & Handling	$7.00
		Total	

Poison-dart frogs are members of the family Dendrobatidae, which includes about 170 species. Many are brightly colored.

Multiply using the Distributive Property.

43. 9×17 **44.** 4×27 **45.** 11×18 **46.** 7×51

47. 2×28 **48.** 9×42 **49.** 5×55 **50.** 3×78

51. 4×85 **52.** 6×36 **53.** 8×24 **54.** 11×51

55. Life Science Poison-dart frogs can breed underwater, and the females lay from 4 to 30 eggs. What would be the total number of eggs if four female poison-dart frogs each laid 27 eggs?

Use the table for Exercises 56 and 57.

56. Rickie wants to buy 3 garden hoses at the home center clearance sale. How much will they cost?

57. The boys in Josh's family are saving money to buy 4 ceiling fans at the home center sale. How much will they need to save?

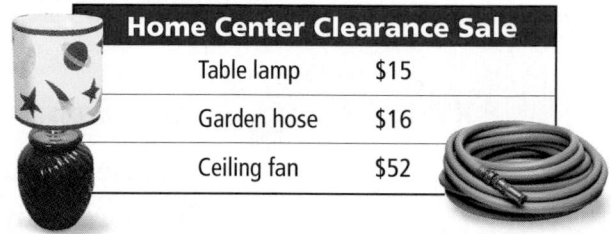

Home Center Clearance Sale	
Table lamp	$15
Garden hose	$16
Ceiling fan	$52

58. Critical Thinking Give a problem that you could simplify using the Commutative and Associative Properties. Then, show the steps to solve the problem and label the Commutative and Associative Properties.

59. What's The Error? A student wrote $5 + 24 + 25 + 6 = 5 + 25 + 24 + 6$ by the Associative Property. What error did the student make?

60. Write About It Why can you simplify $5(50 + 3)$ using the Distributive Property? Why can't you simplify $5(50) + 3$ using the Distributive Property?

61. Challenge Explain how you could find the product of $5^2 \times 112$ using the Distributive Property. Evaluate the expression.

TEST PREP and Spiral Review

62. Multiple Choice Which expression does NOT have the same value as $7 \times (4 + 23)$?

Ⓐ 7×27 Ⓑ $(7 \times 4) + (7 \times 23)$ Ⓒ $7 \times 4 + 23$ Ⓓ $28 + (7 \times 23)$

63. Gridded Response Michelle flew 1,240 miles from Los Angeles to Dallas, and another 718 miles from Dallas to Atlanta. From Atlanta, she flew 760 miles to New York City. How many miles did Michelle fly in all?

Estimate each sum or difference by rounding to the nearest thousands place. (Lesson 1-2)

64. $5,237 - 1,586$ **65.** $915,178 + 451,836$ **66.** $39,187 - 24,999$

Evaluate each expression. (Lesson 1-4)

67. $4 \times 14 + 12 \div 2$ **68.** $16 \div 4^2 + 15 - 2$ **69.** $62 + 14 - (5 \times 4)$

1-6 Choose the Method of Computation

 Problem Solving Skill

Learn to choose an appropriate method of computation and justify your choice.

Earth has one moon. Scientists have determined that other planets in our solar system have as many as 39 moons. Mercury and Venus have no moons at all.

 **NY Performance Indicators**

6.CM.2 Explain a rationale for strategy selection. Also, 6.PS.21.

EXAMPLE 1 **Astronomy Application**

Choose a solution method and solve. Explain your choice.

A How many known moons are in our solar system?

It might be hard to keep track of all of these numbers if you tried to add mentally. But the numbers themselves are small. You can use paper and pencil.

Planet	Moons
Mercury	0
Venus	0
Earth	1
Mars	2
Jupiter	63
Saturn	50
Uranus	27
Neptune	13
Pluto	1

Source: The Planetary Society, 2005

$$
\begin{array}{r}
1 \\
2 \\
63 \\
50 \\
27 \\
13 \\
+\ 1 \\
\hline
157
\end{array}
$$

There are 157 known moons in our solar system.

B The average temperature on Earth is 59°F. The average temperature on Venus is 867°F. How much hotter is Venus's average temperature?

Venus temperature − Earth temperature
    867   −   59

These numbers are small, and 59 is close to a multiple of 10. You can use mental math.

$(867 + 1) − (59 + 1)$ *Think: Add 1 to 59 to make 60. Add 1 to*
      $868 − 60$ *867 to compensate.*
          808

The average temperature on Venus is 808°F hotter than the average temperature on Earth.

Choose a solution method and solve. Explain your choice.

C Every day, about 120 tons of cosmic dust—debris from outer space—enter Earth's atmosphere. How many tons of cosmic dust enter Earth's atmosphere each year?

tons per day × **days per year**   *Think: There are 365 days in a year.*
    120   ×   365

These numbers are not compatible, so mental math is not a good choice.

You could use paper and pencil. But finding a product of 3-digit numbers requires several steps. Using a calculator will probably be faster.

Carefully enter the numbers on a calculator. Record the product.

$120 \times 365 = 43{,}800$

Each year, about 43,800 tons of cosmic dust enter Earth's atmosphere.

Think and Discuss

6.PS.21, 6.CN.6

1. Give an example of a situation in which you would use mental math to solve a problem. When would you use paper and pencil?

2. Tell how you could use mental math in Example 2 if the problem were $867 + 59$.

1-6 Exercises

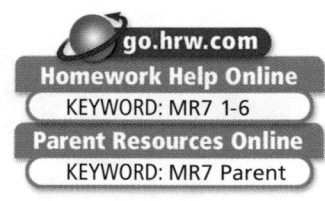

go.hrw.com
Homework Help Online
KEYWORD: MR7 1-6
Parent Resources Online
KEYWORD: MR7 Parent

GUIDED PRACTICE

See Example **1**   Choose a solution method and solve. Explain your choice.

1. Astronomy What is the total number of astronauts who have space flight experience?

U.S.	Germany	France	Canada	Japan	Italy	Russia
244	9	8	7	5	3	88

2. Sports In the 2004 Summer Olympic Games, 929 medals were given. The U.S. team brought home the most medals, 103. How many medals were not won by the U.S. team?

3. A factory produces 126 golf balls per minute. How many golf balls can be produced in 515 minutes?

INDEPENDENT PRACTICE

See Example ① Choose a solution method and solve. Explain your choice.
For 4 and 5, use the diagram at right.

6	9	5
10	20	8
3	7	4

4. The highest score is a total of all the squares on the board. What is that score?

5. What score is higher, the total of the squares in the middle row or middle column?

6. If each store in a chain of 108 furniture stores sells 135 sofas a year, what is the total number of sofas sold?

PRACTICE AND PROBLEM SOLVING

Extra Practice
See page 715.

Evaluate the expression, and state the method of computation you used.

7. $5 + 24 + 7 + 1 + 64 + 2 + 8$ **8.** $16 + 2 + 4 + 13 + 5 + 1 + 14$

9. 828×623 **10.** $742 - 167$ **11.** $41 + 169$ **12.** $499 - 201$ **13.** $338 + 12$

14. A satellite travels 985,200 miles per year. How many miles will it travel if it stays in space for 12 years?

 15. What's the Question? An astronaut has spent the following minutes training in a tank that simulates weightlessness: 2, 15, 5, 40, 10, and 55. The answer is 127. What is the question?

 16. Write About It Explain how you can decide whether to use pencil and paper, mental math, or a calculator to solve a subtraction problem.

 17. Challenge A list of possible astronauts was narrowed down by two committees. The first committee selected 93 people to complete a written form. The second selected 31 of those people to come to an interview. If 837 were not asked to complete a form, how many were on the original list?

TEST PREP and Spiral Review

18. Multiple Choice It takes Mars 687 days to revolve around the Sun. It takes Venus only 225 days to revolve around the Sun. How many more days does it take Mars to revolve around the Sun than it takes Venus?

    Ⓐ 462 days   Ⓑ 500 days   Ⓒ 900 days   Ⓓ 912 days

19. Short Response Hector biked 13 miles on Monday, Wednesday, and Friday of every week for 24 weeks. Find the total number of miles he biked during the 24 weeks. Explain your answer.

Evaluate each expression. (Lesson 1-4)

20. $(2 + 7 - 5) \div 2$ **21.** $10(6 - 3)$ **22.** $5 + 8 \times 7 - 1$ **23.** $5 + (8 + 2) - 3$

Identify the property illustrated by each equation. (Lesson 1-5)

24. $3 + (4 + 5) = (3 + 4) + 5$ **25.** $19(24) = 19(20) + 19(4)$ **26.** $2(13) = 13(2)$

32 *Chapter 1 Whole Numbers and Patterns*

1-7 Patterns and Sequences

Learn to find patterns and to recognize, describe, and extend patterns in sequences.

Vocabulary

sequence

term

arithmetic sequence

NY Performance Indicators

6.PS.14 Analyze problems by observing patterns.

Each month, Eva chooses 3 new DVDs from her DVD club.

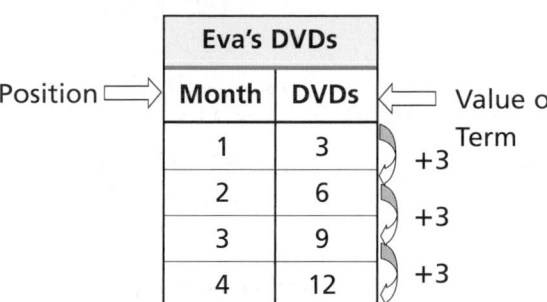

The number of DVDs Eva has after each month shows a pattern: Add 3. This pattern can be written as a sequence. 3, 6, 9, 12, 15, . . .

A **sequence** is an ordered set of numbers. Each number in the sequence is called a **term**. In this sequence, the first term is 3, the second term is 6, and the third term is 9.

When the terms of a sequence change by the same amount each time, the sequence is an **arithmetic sequence**.

EXAMPLE 1 **Extending Arithmetic Sequences**

Helpful Hint

Look for a relationship between the 1st term and the 2nd term. Check if this relationship works between the 2nd term and the 3rd term, and so on.

Identify a pattern in each arithmetic sequence and then find the missing terms.

A 3, 15, 27, 39, ▪, ▪, . . .

Look for a pattern.
A pattern is to add 12 to each term to get the next term.

$3, \ 15, \ 27, \ 39, \ \blacksquare, \ \blacksquare, \ . . .$
$+12 \ +12 \ +12 \ +12 \ +12$

$39 + 12 = 51 \quad 51 + 12 = 63$
So 51 and 63 are the missing terms.

B 12, 21, 30, 39, ▪, ▪, . . .

Use a table to find a pattern.

Position	1	2	3	4	5	6
Value of Term	12	21	30	39	▪	▪

$+9 \quad +9 \quad +9 \quad +9 \quad +9$

A pattern is to add 9 to each term to get the next term.
$39 + 9 = 48 \qquad 48 + 9 = 57$
So 48 and 57 are the missing terms.

Not all sequences are arithmetic sequences.

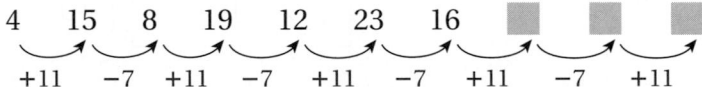

Arithmetic Sequences	Not Arithmetic Sequences

2, 4, 6, 8,...   20, 35, 50, 65,...   1, 3, 6, 10,...   2, 6, 18, 54,...
+2 +2 +2   +15 +15 +15   +2 +3 +4   ×3 ×3 ×3

In nonarithmetic sequences, look for patterns that involve multiplication or division. Some sequences may even be combinations of different operations.

EXAMPLE 2 **Completing Other Sequences**

Identify a pattern in each sequence. Name the missing terms.

A 4, 15, 8, 19, 12, 23, 16, ■, ■, ■,...

4   15   8   19   12   23   16   ■   ■   ■
  +11 −7 +11 −7 +11 −7 +11 −7 +11

A pattern is to add 11 to one term and subtract 7 from the next.

$16 + 11 = 27$ $27 − 7 = 20$ $20 + 11 = 31$

So 27, 20, and 31 are the missing terms.

B

Position	1	2	3	4	5	6	7	8	9
Value of Term	1	6	2	12	■	24	8	■	16

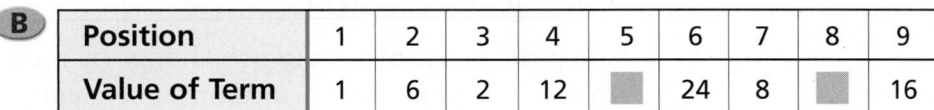

Position	1	2	3	4	5	6	7	8	9
Value of Term	1	6	2	12	■	24	8	■	16

×6 ÷3 ×6 ÷3 ×6 ÷3 ×6 ÷3

A pattern is to multiply one term by 6 and divide the next by 3.

$12 ÷ 3 = 4$ $8 × 6 = 48$

So 4 and 48 are the missing terms.

Think and Discuss

6.PS.21, 6.RP.5, 6.CM.1

1. Tell how you could check whether the next two terms in the arithmetic sequence 5, 7, 9, 11, . . . are 13 and 15.

2. Explain how to find the next term in the sequence 16, 8, 4, 2, ■, ...

3. Explain how to determine whether 256, 128, 64, 32, . . . is an arithmetic or nonarithmetic sequence.

1-7 **Exercises**

go.hrw.com
Homework Help Online
KEYWORD: MR7 1-7
Parent Resources Online
KEYWORD: MR7 Parent

GUIDED PRACTICE

See Example **1** Identify a pattern in each arithmetic sequence and then find the missing terms.

1. 12, 24, 36, 48, ▨, ▨, ▨, . . .   **2.** 105, 90, 75, 60, 45, ▨, ▨, ▨, . . .

3.

Position	1	2	3	4	5	6
Value of Term	7	18	29	40	▨	▨

4.

Position	1	2	3	4	5	6
Value of Term	44	38	32	26	▨	▨

See Example **2** Identify a pattern in each sequence. Name the missing terms.

5. 2, 9, 7, 14, ▨, ▨, . . .   **6.** 80, 8, 40, 4, ▨, 2, 10, ▨, . . .

7.

Position	1	2	3	4	5	6	7	8
Value of Term	1	6	3	18	▨	54	27	▨

INDEPENDENT PRACTICE

See Example **1** Identify a pattern in each arithmetic sequence and then find the missing terms.

8. 9, 19, 29, 39, 49, ▨, ▨, ▨, . . .   **9.** 98, 84, 70, 56, 42, ▨, ▨, ▨, . . .

10.

Position	1	2	3	4	5	6
Value of Term	45	38	31	24	▨	▨

11.

Position	1	2	3	4	5	6
Value of Term	8	11	14	17	▨	▨

See Example **2** Identify a pattern in each sequence. Name the missing terms.

12. 50, 40, 43, 33, ▨, 26, ▨, . . .   **13.** 7, 28, 24, 45, ▨, ▨, ▨, . . .

14.

Position	1	2	3	4	5	6	7
Value of Term	120	60	180	90	▨	▨	405

15.

Position	1	2	3	4	5	6	7
Value of Term	400	100	200	50	▨	▨	50

Extra Practice
See page 715.

Use the pattern to write the first five terms of the sequence.

16. Start with 1; multiply by 3. **17.** Start with 5; add 9. **18.** Start with 100; subtract 7.

19. Social Studies The Chinese lunar calendar is based on a 12-year cycle, with each of the 12 years named after a different animal. The year 2006 is the year of the dog.

   a. When will the next year of the dog occur?

   b. When was the last year of the dog?

   c. Will the year 2030 be a year of the dog? Explain.

Identify whether each given sequences could be arithmetic. If not, identify the pattern of the sequence.

20. 10, 16, 22, 28, 34, . . . **21.** 60, 56, 61, 57, 62, . . . **22.** 111, 121, 131, 141, 151, . . .

23. Choose a Strategy The * shows where a piece is missing from the pattern. What piece is missing?

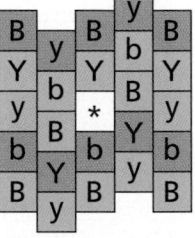

24. Whole numbers raised to the second power are called perfect squares. This is because they can be represented by objects arranged in the shape of a square. Perfect squares can be written as the sequence 1, 4, 9, 16, . . .

   a. Find the next two perfect squares in the sequence.

   b. Explain how can you know whether a number is a perfect square?

 25. Write About It Explain how to determine if a sequence is arithmetic.

 26. Challenge Find the missing terms in the following sequence:

   ■, 2^3, 27, 4^3, 125, ■, 343, . . .

TEST PREP and Spiral Review

27. Multiple Choice Identify the pattern in the sequence 6, 11, 16, 21, 26, . . .

   Ⓐ Add 5.   Ⓑ Add 6.   Ⓒ Multiply by 5.   Ⓓ Multiply by 6.

28. Extended Response Identify the first term and a pattern for the sequence 5, 8, 11, 14, 17, . . . Is the sequence arithmetic? Explain why or why not. Find the next three terms in the sequence.

Use mental math to find each sum or product. (Lesson 1-5)

29. 13 + 6 + 17 + 24   **30.** 4 × 11 × 5   **31.** 45 + 11 + 35 + 29

Choose a solution method and solve. Explain your choice. (Lesson 1-6)

32. As of 2005, Hank Aaron was Major League Baseball's career home run leader with 755 home runs. Sadaharu Oh was the career home run leader of Japanese baseball with 868 home runs. How many more home runs did Oh hit than Aaron?

Technology LAB

Find a Pattern in Sequences

Use with Lesson 1-7

 NY Performance Indicators

6.PS.14

 go.hrw.com
Lab Resources Online
KEYWORD: MR7 Lab1

The numbers 4, 7, 10, 13, 16, 19, … form an arithmetic sequence. To continue the sequence, identify a pattern. Here is a possible pattern:

$$4, \quad 4 + 3 = 7, \quad 7 + 3 = 10, \quad 10 + 3 = 13,…$$

Activity

Use a spreadsheet to generate the first seven terms of the sequence above.

To start with 4, type **4** in cell A1.

To add 3 to the value in cell A1, type **=A1 + 3** in cell B1.

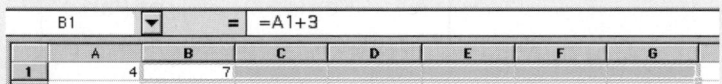

Press ENTER.

To continue the sequence, click the square in the lower right corner of cell B1, hold down the mouse button, and drag the cursor across through cell G1.

When you release the mouse button, A1 through G1 will list the first seven terms of the sequence.

Think and Discuss

1. How do you use a sequence's pattern when you use your spreadsheet to generate the terms?

Try This

Identify a pattern in each sequence. Then use a spreadsheet to generate the first 12 terms.

1. 9, 14, 19, 24, 29, 34, …
2. 7, 13, 19, 25, 31, 37, …
3. 105, 98, 91, 84, 77, 70, …
4. 21, 29, 37, 45, 53, 61, …
5. 150, 174, 198, 222, 246, 270, …
6. 600, 550, 500, 450, 400, 350, …

Quiz for Lessons 1-4 Through 1-7

✓ 1-4 Order of Operations

Evaluate each expression.

1. $3 \times 4 \div (10 - 4)$ **2.** $5^2 + 10 \div 2 - 1$ **3.** $4 + (12 - 8) \times 6$ **4.** $(2^3 + 2) \times 10$

5. Mrs. Webb buys 7 cards for \$2 each, 3 metallic pens for \$1 each, and 1 pad of writing paper for \$4. Evaluate $7 \times 2 + 3 \times 1 + 1 \times 4$ to find the total amount Mrs. Webb spends.

✓ 1-5 Mental Math

Evaluate.

6. $4 + 21 + 9 + 6$ **7.** $5 \times 17 \times 2$ **8.** $45 + 19 + 1 + 55$ **9.** $2 \times 17 \times 10$

Use the Distributive Property to find each product.

10. 5×62 **11.** 9×41 **12.** 4×23 **13.** 7×14 **14.** 5×34

✓ 1-6 Choose the Method of Computation

Choose a solution method and solve.
Explain your choice.

15. How many Texas state parks are shown in the table?

16. How many more parks are there in the Prairies and Lakes region than in the Big Bend region?

Texas State Parks	
Region	Number of Parks
Big Bend	7
Gulf Coast	11
Hill Country	11
Panhandle Plains	12
Pineywoods	13
Prairies and Lakes	22
South Texas Plains	5

✓ 1-7 Patterns and Sequences

Identify a pattern in the arithmetic sequence and then find the missing terms.

17.

Position	1	2	3	4	5	6	7
Value of Term	5	14	23	32	▣	▣	▣

Identify a pattern in each sequence. Name the missing terms.

18. 4, 20, 15, 31, ▣, ▣, 37, …

19. 16, 32, 8, 16, ▣, 8, 2, ▣, 1, …

20. A concert hall has 5 seats in the front row, 9 seats in the second row, 13 seats in the third row, and 17 seats in the fourth row. If this pattern continues, how many seats are in the sixth row?

MULTI-STEP TEST PREP

Go for the Gold The table shows the number of medals won by the United States at four Summer Olympic Games.

1. Find the total number of medals won by the United States at each Olympics. Then order the Olympic sites from the greatest number of medals won to the least.

2. Estimate the total number of gold medals won by the United States at these four Olympics. Explain how you found your estimate.

Olympic Medals Won by U.S. Athletes				
Year	Site	Gold	Silver	Bronze
1992	Barcelona	37	34	37
1996	Atlanta	44	32	25
2000	Sydney	40	24	33
2004	Athens	35	39	29

3. To compare the performances of U.S. athletes at different Olympics, Jocelyn assigns 3 points to each gold medal, 2 points to each silver medal, and 1 point to each bronze medal. To find the total number of U.S. points for the Barcelona Olympics, she writes the expression $3 \times 37 + 2 \times 34 + 1 \times 37$. Explain how to evaluate this expression, and then find the point total.

4. In 1996, Romania won 2^2 gold medals, 7^1 silver medals, and 3^2 bronze medals. How many of each medal did Romania win? Find the difference in the number of medals won by the United States and the number of medals won by Romania in 1996.

5. The total number of medals won by the United States at each Summer Olympics since 1896 is $3^7 + 2$. About how many more medals do U.S. athletes need to win in order to have a total of 2,200?

Game Time

Palindromes

A *palindrome* is a word, phrase, or number that reads the same forward and backward.

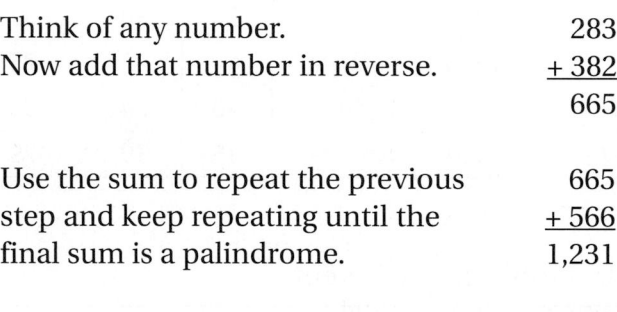

Examples:
race car   Madam, I'm Adam.   3710173

You can turn almost any number into a palindrome with this trick.

Think of any number.	283
Now add that number in reverse.	+ 382
	665

Use the sum to repeat the previous	665
step and keep repeating until the	+ 566
final sum is a palindrome.	1,231

$$1{,}231$$
$$+ 1{,}321$$
$$2{,}552$$

It took only three steps to create a palindrome by starting with the number 283. What happens if you start with the number 196? Do you think you will ever create a palindrome if you start with 196? One man who started with 196 did these steps until he had a number with 70,928 digits and he still had not created a palindrome!

Spin-a-Million

The object of this game is to create the number closest to 1,000,000.

Taking turns, spin the pointer and write the number on your place-value chart. The number cannot be moved once it has been placed.

After six turns, the player whose number is closest to one million wins the round and scores a point. The first player to get five points wins the game.

A complete copy of the rules and game pieces are available online.

go.hrw.com
Game Time Extra
KEYWORD: MR7 Games

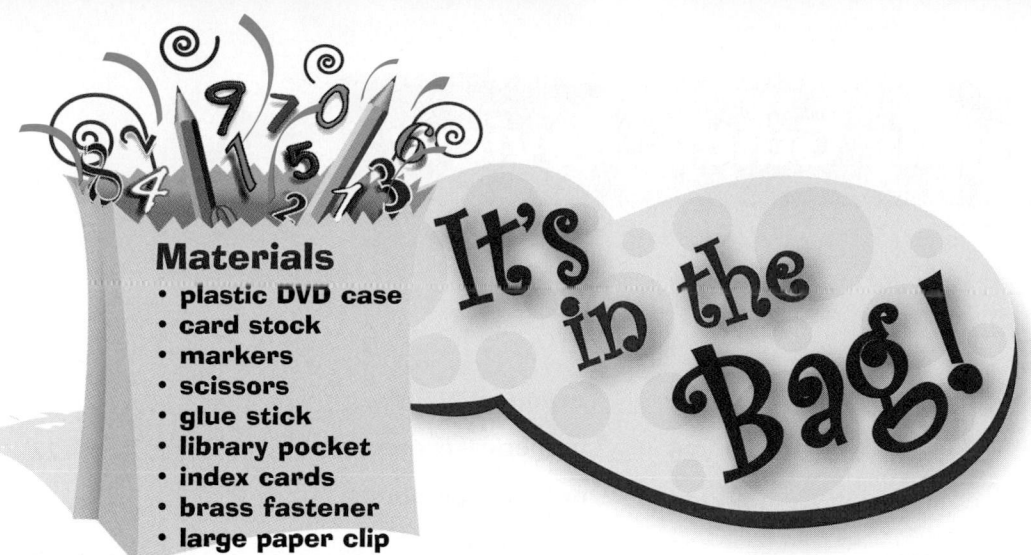

Materials
- plastic **DVD** case
- card stock
- markers
- scissors
- glue stick
- library pocket
- index cards
- brass fastener
- large paper clip

It's in the Bag!

PROJECT **Picture This**

Make a game in an empty DVD case to review concepts from this chapter.

Directions

❶ Cut a piece of card stock that can be folded in half to fit inside the DVD case. Lay the card stock flat and draw a path for a board game. Be sure to have a start and a finish. **Figure A**

❷ Close the game board and decorate the front. Glue a library pocket onto the front to hold the index cards. **Figure B**

❸ On the index cards, write problems that can be solved using math from the chapter. Place the cards in the pocket.

❹ Cut a piece of card stock to fit the other side of the DVD box. Glue directions for your game at the top. At the bottom, make a spinner the size of a DVD. Attach a brass fastener to the middle of the spinner, and then attach a paper clip to the fastener. **Figure C**

Putting the Math into Action

Play your game with a partner. Use buttons or coins as playing pieces. Players should take turns spinning the spinner and then be required to solve a problem correctly in order to move their piece.

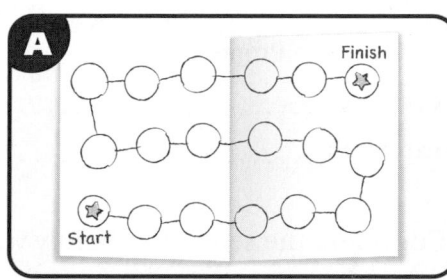

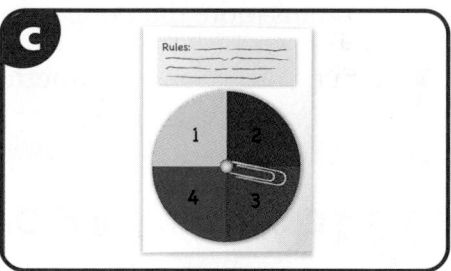

Study Guide: Review

Study Guide: Review

Vocabulary

Complete the sentences below with vocabulary words from the list above.

1. An ordered set of numbers is called a(n) ___?___. Each number in a sequence is called a(n) ___?___.

2. In the expression 8^5, 8 is the ___?___, and 5 is the ___?___.

3. The ___?___ is a set of rules used to evaluate an expression that contains more than one operation.

4. When you ___?___ a numerical expression, you find its value.

1-1 Comparing and Ordering Whole Numbers (pp. 6–9)

 6.N.1

EXAMPLE

■ Order the numbers from least to greatest.

4,913; 4,931; 4,391

4,913
4,931 $4,913 < 4,931$

4,931
4,391 $4,391 < 4,931$

4,913
4,391 $4,391 < 4,913$

$4,391 < 4,913 < 4,931$

```
      4,391          4,913 4,931
   ←+——•——+——————+————••——+→
   4,300  4,500  4,700  4,900  5,100
```

EXERCISES

Order the numbers from least to greatest.

5. 8,731; 8,737; 8,735; 8,740

6. 53,341; 53,337; 53,456; 53,452

7. 87,091; 8,791; 87,901; 81,790

8. 26,551; 25,615; 2,651; 22,561

9. 96,361; 96,631; 93,613; 91,363

10. 10,101; 11,010; 10,110; 11,110

1-2 Estimating with Whole Numbers (pp. 10–13)

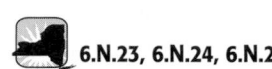

EXAMPLE

■ **Estimate the sum 837 + 710 by rounding to the hundreds place.**
$800 + 700 = 1{,}500$
The sum is about 1,500.

■ **Estimate the quotient of 148 and 31.**
$150 \div 30 = 5$
The quotient is about 5.

EXERCISES

Estimate each sum or difference by rounding to the place value indicated.

11. $4{,}671 - 3{,}954$; thousands

12. $3{,}123 + 2{,}987$; thousands

13. $53{,}465 - 27{,}465$; ten thousands

14. Ralph has 38 photo album sheets with 22 baseball cards in each sheet. About how many baseball cards does he have?

1-3 Exponents (pp. 14–17)

EXAMPLE

■ **Write 6 × 6 in exponential form.**
6^2 *6 is a factor 2 times.*

Find each value.

■ 5^2 ■ 6^3
$5^2 = 5 \times 5$ $6^3 = 6 \times 6 \times 6$
$= 25$ $= 216$

EXERCISES

Write each expression in exponential form.

15. $5 \times 5 \times 5$ **16.** $3 \times 3 \times 3 \times 3$

17. $7 \times 7 \times 7 \times 7 \times 7$ **18.** 8×8

19. $4 \times 4 \times 4 \times 4$ **20.** $1 \times 1 \times 1$

Find each value.

21. 4^4 **22.** 2^4 **23.** 6^3

24. 3^3 **25.** 1^5 **26.** 7^4

27. 5^3 **28.** 10^2 **29.** 9^2

1-4 Order of Operations (pp. 22–25)

6.N.22, 6.N.25

EXAMPLE

■ **Evaluate $8 \div (7 - 5) \times 2^2 - 2 + 9$.**

$8 \div (7 - 5) \times 2^2 - 2 + 9$

$8 \div 2 \times 2^2 - 2 + 9$ *Subtract in parentheses.*

$8 \div 2 \times 4 - 2 + 9$ *Simplify the exponent.*

$4 \times 4 - 2 + 9$ *Divide.*

$16 - 2 + 9$ *Multiply.*

$14 + 9$ *Subtract.*

23 *Add.*

EXERCISES

Evaluate each expression.

30. $9 \times 8 - 13$

31. $21 \div 3 + 4$

32. $6 + 4 \times 5$

33. $19 - 12 \div 6$

34. $30 \div 2 - 5 \times 2$

35. $(7 + 3) \div 2 \times 3^2$

36. $8 \times (7 + 5) \div 4^2 + 9 \div 3$

37. $3^2 \times 5 \div (10 \times 3 \div 2)$

Study Guide: Review

1-5 Mental Math (pp. 26–29)

EXAMPLE

Evaluate.

- 4 + 13 + 6 + 7
  4 + 6 + 13 + 7
  (4 + 6) + (13 + 7)
     10   +   20
         30

- 5 × 9 × 6
  5 × 6 × 9
  (5 × 6) × 9
  30 × 9
    270

- **Use the Distributive Property to find 3 × 16.**

  $3 \times 16 = 3 \times (10 + 6)$
  $= (3 \times 10) + (3 \times 6)$
  $= 30 + 18$
  $= 48$

EXERCISES

Evaluate.

38. 9 + 5 + 1 + 15   **39.** 8 × 13 × 5

40. 31 + 16 + 19 + 14   **41.** 6 × 12 × 15

42. 17 + 12 + 8 + 3   **43.** 16 × 5 × 4

44. 11 + 23 + 27 + 39   **45.** 13 × 5 × 2

Use the Distributive Property to find each product.

46. 7 × 24   **47.** 9 × 15

48. 6 × 34   **49.** 8 × 19

50. 8 × 27   **51.** 5 × 33

1-6 Choose the Method of Computation (pp. 30–32)

EXAMPLE

- **Choose a solution method and solve. Explain your choice.**

  The average annual rainfall in Washington, D.C., is 39 inches. How much rain does Washington, D.C., average in 8 years?

  These numbers are not so big that you must use a calculator. Use pencil and paper to find the answer. 39 × 8 = 312 inches

EXERCISES

Choose a solution method and solve. Explain your choice.

52. The average high temperature for Washington, D.C., in January is 42°F. The record high temperature for Washington, D.C., is 104°F. How much higher is the record temperature than the average high temperature in January?

1-7 Patterns and Sequences (pp. 33–36)

EXAMPLE

Identify a pattern in the sequence. Name the missing terms.

- 1, 3, 5, 7, ▣, ▣, . . .
  +2 +2 +2 +2 +2

  The pattern is to add 2 to each term. The missing terms are 9 and 11.

- 6, 12, 11, 22, ▣, 42, ▣, . . .
  ×2 −1 ×2 −1 ×2 −1

  The pattern is to multiply one term by 2 and subtract the next by 1. The missing terms are 21 and 41.

EXERCISES

Identify the pattern in each arithmetic sequence and then find the missing terms.

53. 4, 9, 14, 19, ▣, ▣, . . .

54. 21, 19, 17, 15, ▣, ▣, . . .

Identify a pattern in each sequence. Name the missing terms.

55. 16, 20, 18, 22, ▣, 24, ▣, . . .

56. 1, 3, 9, 27, ▣, ▣, . . .

57. 65, 70, 68, 73, ▣, 76, ▣, . . .

Compare. Write <, >, or =.

1. 3,241 ▊ 324

2. 16,880,953 ▊ 16,221,773

3. 22,481,093 ▊ 23,662,840

Order the numbers from least to greatest.

4. 801; 798; 921

5. 4,835; 7,505; 4,310

6. 10,101; 101; 1,001

Estimate each sum or difference by rounding to the place value indicated.

7. 8,743 + 3,198; thousands

8. 62,524 − 17,831; ten thousands

Estimate.

9. Kaitlin's family is planning a trip from Washington, D.C., to New York City. New York City is 227 miles from Washington, D.C., and the family can drive an average of 55 mi/h. About how long will the trip take?

Write each expression in exponential form.

10. $4 \times 4 \times 4 \times 4 \times 4$

11. $10 \times 10 \times 10$

12. $6 \times 6 \times 6 \times 6$

Find each value.

13. 2^3

14. 5^2

15. 4^4

16. 11^2

17. 9^3

Evaluate each expression.

18. $12 + 8 \div 2$

19. $3^2 \times 5 + 10 - 7$

20. $12 + (28 - 15) + 4 \times 2$

Evaluate.

21. $15 + 23 + 47 + 5$

22. $5 \times 48 \times 2$

23. $2 \times 5 \times 11$

24. $44 + 18 + 12 + 6$

Use the Distributive Property to find each product.

25. 3×32

26. 52×6

27. 24×5

28. 81×6

29. 6×21

Choose a solution method and solve. Explain your choice.

30. At 5:00 A.M., the temperature was 41°F. By noon, the temperature was 69°F. By how many degrees did the temperature increase?

Identify a pattern in each sequence. Name the missing terms.

31. 8, 22, 36, 50, ▊, ▊, ▊, . . .

32. 2, 10, 7, 15, ▊, 20, ▊, . . .

33. A tile pattern has 1 tile in the first row, 3 tiles in the second row, and 5 tiles in the third row. If this pattern continues, how many tiles are in the fifth row?

Test Tackler

Multiple Choice: Eliminate Answer Choices

You can solve some math problems without doing detailed calculations. You can use mental math, estimation, or logical reasoning to help you eliminate answer choices and save time.

EXAMPLE 1

Which number is the closest estimate for 678 + 189?

(A) 700   (C) 1,000

(B) 900   (D) 5,000

You can use logical reasoning to eliminate choice A because it is too small. The estimated sum has to be greater than 700 because 678 + 189 is greater than 700.

Choice D may also be eliminated because the value is too large. The estimated sum will be less than 5,000.

Round 678 up to 700 and 189 up to 200. Then find the sum of 700 and 200: 700 + 200 = 900. You can eliminate choice C because it is greater than 900.

Choice B is the closest estimate.

EXAMPLE 2

Which of the following numbers is the standard form of four million, six hundred eight thousand, fifteen?

(F) 468,015   (H) 4,068,150

(G) 4,608,015   (J) 4,600,815,000

Logical reasoning can be used to eliminate choices. Numbers that have a place value in the millions must have at least seven but no more than nine digits. Choices F and J can be eliminated because they do not have the correct number of digits.

Both choices G and H have the correct range of digits, so narrow it down further. The number must end in 15. Choice H ends in 50, so it cannot be correct. Eliminate it.

The correct answer choice is G.

Hot Tip Some answer choices, called distracters, may seem correct because they are based on common errors made in calculations.

Read each item and answer the questions that follow.

Item A
Which number is the greatest?

  Ⓐ 599,485   Ⓒ 5,569,003

  Ⓑ 5,571,987   Ⓓ 5,399,879

1. Are there any answer choices you can eliminate immediately? If so, which ones and why?

2. Describe how you can find the correct answer.

City Middle School Populations	
Central Middle School	652
Eastside Middle School	718
Northside Middle School	663
Southside Middle School	731
Westside Middle School	842

Item B
The school district receives $30 a day in state funding for every student enrolled in a public school. Find the approximate number of students that attend all of the city middle schools.

  Ⓕ 2,000   Ⓗ 3,600

  Ⓖ 3,300   Ⓙ 4,000

3. Can F be eliminated? Why or why not?

4. Can H be eliminated? Why or why not?

5. Explain how to use mental math to solve this problem.

Item C
Which expression does NOT have the same value as $8 \times (52 + 12)$?

  Ⓐ 8×64

  Ⓑ $(8 \times 52) + (8 \times 12)$

  Ⓒ $8(60) + 8(4)$

  Ⓓ $8 \times 52 + 12$

6. Which answer choice can be eliminated immediately? Explain.

7. Explain how you can use the Distributive Property to solve this problem.

Item D
Stacey is beginning a new exercise program. She plans to cycle 2 kilometers on her first day. Each day after that, she will double the number of kilometers she cycled from the day before. Which expression shows how many kilometers she will cycle on the sixth day?

  Ⓕ 2×6 Ⓗ 2^6

  Ⓖ $2 + 2 + 2 + 2 + 2 + 2$ Ⓙ 6^2

8. Are there any answer choices you can eliminate immediately? If so, which choices and why?

9. Explain how you can use a table to help you solve this problem.

Item E
James is driving to his aunt's house. If he drives about 55 miles per hour for 5 hours, about how many miles will he have driven?

  Ⓐ 12 miles   Ⓒ 60 miles

  Ⓑ 300 miles   Ⓓ 600 miles

10. Which answer choice(s) can be immediately eliminated and why?

11. Explain how to solve this problem.

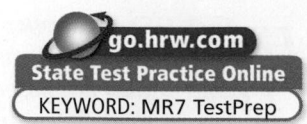
CUMULATIVE ASSESSMENT, CHAPTER 1

Multiple Choice

1. Jonah has 31 boxes of baseball cards. If each box contains 183 cards, about how many baseball cards does Jonah have in his collection?

   Ⓐ 3,000 cards   Ⓒ 9,000 cards

   Ⓑ 6,000 cards   Ⓓ 12,000 cards

2. Which of the following does NOT have a value of 27?

   Ⓕ 3^3 Ⓗ $3 \times 3 + 18$

   Ⓖ $3^2 + 3 \times 7$ Ⓙ $9^2 \div 3$

3. What are the next two terms in the following sequence?

   $$6, 3, 12, 6, 24, \ldots$$

   Ⓐ 3, 12   Ⓒ 12, 48

   Ⓑ 6, 36   Ⓓ 18, 72

4. Which of the following correctly shows the use of the Distributive Property to find the product of 64 and 8?

   Ⓕ $64 \times 8 = (8 \times 60) + (8 \times 4)$

   Ⓖ $64 \times 8 = 8 \times 64$

   Ⓗ $64 \times 8 = 8 + (60 + 4)$

   Ⓙ $64 \times 8 = (8 \times 4) \times 60$

5. What is five billion, two hundred fifty-two million, six hundred thousand, three hundred eleven in standard form?

   Ⓐ 5,252,603,011   Ⓒ 5,252,600,311

   Ⓑ 52,526,311   Ⓓ 5,252,060,311

6. The attendance at a local library is shown in the table below. How many people visited the library last week?

Last Week's Attendance	
Sunday	Closed
Monday	78
Tuesday	125
Wednesday	122
Thursday	96
Friday	104
Saturday	225

   Ⓕ 450   Ⓗ 650

   Ⓖ 550   Ⓙ 750

7. Which number is the greatest?

   Ⓐ 5,432,873   Ⓒ 5,221,754

   Ⓑ 5,201,032   Ⓓ 5,332,621

8. What is $6 \times 6 \times 6 \times 6$ written in exponential form?

   Ⓕ 24^4

   Ⓖ 1,296

   Ⓗ 6^4

   Ⓙ $1000 + 200 + 90 + 6$

9. The expression $6 \times 3 \times 4 = 3 \times 6 \times 4$ is an example of which property?

   Ⓐ Associative   Ⓒ Distributive

   Ⓑ Commutative   Ⓓ Exponential

New York Test Prep

10. Which list of numbers is in order from least to greatest?

- (F) 1,231; 1,543; 1,267; 1,321
- (G) 3,210; 3,357; 3,366; 3,401
- (H) 4,321; 4,312; 4,211; 4,081
- (J) 5,019; 5,187; 5,143; 5,314

11. There are 2,347 seats in the town theater. A ticket to the Friday night concert costs $32. Which method of computation should be used to find how much money the theater will make if the Friday night concert sells out?

- (A) Paper and pencil
- (B) Calculator
- (C) Mental Math
- (D) Estimation

 *Hot Tip* When you read a word problem, underline the information you need to help you answer the question.

12. What is the value of
$3 + 8 \times 6 - (12 \div 4)$?

- (F) 13
- (H) 48
- (G) 27
- (J) 63

13. What is the value of 2^4?

- (A) 4
- (C) 8
- (B) 6
- (D) 16

14. At 2:00 P.M., the water temperature in the pool was 88°F. By 10:00 P.M. the water temperature in the pool was 75°F. By how many degrees did the water temperature drop?

- (F) 8°
- (H) 52°
- (G) 13°
- (J) 104°

15. Estimate the sum of 3,820 and 4,373 by rounding to the nearest thousand.

- (A) 8,000
- (C) 9,000
- (B) 8,100
- (D) 9,200

Short Response

16. Megan deposited $2 into her savings account on the first Friday of the month. Each week she doubles her deposit from the week before.

a. If this pattern continues, how much money will she deposit in week 4?

b. What is the total amount in Megan's account after her fourth deposit? Explain how you found your answer.

17. Create a numerical expression that can be simplified in four steps. Include one set of parentheses and an exponent. The same mathematical operation may be used no more than two times. Show how to evaluate your expression.

Extended Response

18. The student population at Southside Middle School is listed in the table below.

Student Population at Southside Middle School		
	Boys	**Girls**
6th Grade	98	102
7th Grade	89	105
8th Grade	123	117

a. Use the information in the table to find the total number of students who attend Southside Middle School. Show your work.

b. About how many more girls are enrolled in the school than boys? Show your work. Explain how you found your answer.

c. The school board wants the school to have one teacher for every 20 students. If there are 8 sixth-grade teachers, does the school need to hire more sixth-grade teachers? If so, how many more? Explain your answer.

Introduction to Algebra

NEW YORK TEST PREP

go.hrw.com
Chapter Project Online
KEYWORD: MR7 Ch2

Number of Cars Traveling in Each Direction				
	North	South	East	West
6–8 A.M.	114	36	48	57
8–10 A.M.	97	52	57	52
10 A.M.–noon	35	24	65	56
noon–2 P.M.	23	109	61	56
2–4 P.M.	18	138	70	72
4–6 P.M.	11	54	47	40

Career *Traffic Engineer*

Have you ever wondered why traffic moves quickly through one intersection but slowly through another? Traffic engineers program stoplights so that vehicles can move smoothly through intersections. There are many variables at a traffic intersection—the number of vehicles that pass, the time of day, and the direction in which each vehicle travels are examples. Traffic engineers use this information to control the timing of stoplights. The table lists traffic movement through a given intersection during a given weekday.

ARE YOU READY?

✓ Vocabulary

Choose the best term from the list to complete each sentence.

1. Multiplication is the __?__ of division.
2. The __?__ of 12 and 3 is 36.
3. The __?__ of 12 and 3 is 15.
4. Addition, subtraction, multiplication, and division are called __?__.
5. The answer to a division problem is called the __?__.

dividend

factor

inverse

operations

product

quotient

sum

Complete these exercises to review skills you will need for this chapter.

✓ Multiplication Facts

Multiply.

6. 7×4
7. 8×9
8. 9×6
9. 7×7
10. 6×5
11. 3×8
12. 5×5
13. 2×9

✓ Division Facts

Divide.

14. $64 \div 8$
15. $63 \div 9$
16. $56 \div 7$
17. $54 \div 6$
18. $49 \div 7$
19. $30 \div 5$
20. $32 \div 4$
21. $18 \div 3$

✓ Whole Number Operations

Add, subtract, multiply, or divide.

22. $\begin{array}{r} 28 \\ + 15 \end{array}$
23. $\begin{array}{r} 71 \\ + 38 \end{array}$
24. $\begin{array}{r} 1{,}218 \\ + 430 \end{array}$
25. $\begin{array}{r} 2{,}218 \\ + 1{,}135 \end{array}$

26. $\begin{array}{r} 72 \\ - 35 \end{array}$
27. $\begin{array}{r} 98 \\ - 45 \end{array}$
28. $\begin{array}{r} 1{,}642 \\ - 249 \end{array}$
29. $\begin{array}{r} 3{,}408 \\ - 1{,}649 \end{array}$

30. 6×13
31. 8×15
32. 16×22
33. 20×35
34. $9\overline{)72}$
35. $7\overline{)84}$
36. $16\overline{)112}$
37. $23\overline{)1{,}472}$

Where You've Been

Previously, you

- wrote numerical expressions involving whole numbers.

- solved problems using addition, subtraction, multiplication, and division of whole numbers.

In This Chapter

You will study

- writing algebraic expressions involving whole numbers.

- using addition, subtraction, multiplication, and division to solve one-step equations involving whole numbers.

- determining whether a number is a solution to an equation.

Where You're Going

You can use the skills learned in this chapter

- to solve one-step equations involving decimals and fractions.

- to solve one-step inequalities.

Key Vocabulary/Vocabulario

algebraic expression	expresión algebraica
constant	constante
equation	ecuación
solution of an equation	solución de una ecuación
variable	variable

Vocabulary Connections

To become familiar with some of the vocabulary terms in the chapter, consider the following. You may refer to the chapter, the glossary, or a dictionary if you like.

1. *Algebra* is a type of math that uses letters to represent numbers. The word *algebraic* means "relating to algebra." What do you think an **algebraic expression** contains?

2. When something is *constant,* it does not change. If there is a **constant** in an expression, do you think the number changes? Explain.

3. When something is *variable,* it is able to vary, or change. What do you think a **variable** in an expression is able to do?

4. An *equation* shows that two expressions are equal. What mathematical symbol would you expect to see in an **equation**?

 **Reading** and **Writing Math**

Writing Strategy: Use Your Own Words

Sometimes when you are reading about a new math concept for the first time from a textbook, the concept is difficult to understand.

As you go through each lesson, do the following:

- Look for the key ideas.
- Rewrite explanations given as paragraphs as steps or a list.
- Add an example when possible.

What Lupe Reads

To order numbers, you can compare them using place value and then write them in order from least to greatest.

What Lupe Writes

● To Order Numbers:

Step 1: Compare place value.
Step 2: Write numbers in order from least to greatest.

Example: Order from least to greatest: 2,456; 2,265; 2,981.

Compare place value.
2,456   The thousands values are the
2,265   same so, compare the hundreds
2,981   values.

Write in order.
2,265; 2,456; 2,981

Try This

Rewrite the paragraph in your own words.

1. Sometimes in math you do not need an exact answer. Instead, you can use an estimate. Estimates are close to the exact answer but are usually easier and faster to find. When estimating, you can round the numbers in the problem to compatible numbers. Compatible numbers are close to the numbers in the problem, and they can help you do math mentally.

Variables and Expressions

Learn to identify and evaluate expressions.

Vocabulary

variable

constant

algebraic expression

NY Performance Indicators

6.A.2 Use substitution to evaluate algebraic expressions. Also, 5.A.3.

Inflation is the rise in prices that occurs over time. For example, you would have paid about $7 in the year 2000 for something that cost only $1 in 1950.

With this information, you can convert prices in 1950 to their equivalent prices in 2000.

Input

Output

1950	2000
$1	$7
$2	$14
$3	$21
$p	$p × 7

A **variable** is a letter or symbol that represents a quantity that can change. In the table above, p is a variable that stands for any price in 1950. A **constant** is a quantity that does not change. For example, the price of something in 2000 is always 7 times the price in 1950.

An **algebraic expression** contains one or more variables and may contain operation symbols. So $p \times 7$ is an algebraic expression.

Algebraic Expressions	NOT Algebraic Expressions
$150 + y$	$85 \div 5$
$35 \times w + z$	$10 + 3 \times 5$

To evaluate an algebraic expression, substitute a number for the variable and then find the value.

EXAMPLE 1 Evaluating Algebraic Expressions

Evaluate each expression to find the missing values in the tables.

A

w	$w \div 11$
55	5
66	■
77	■

Substitute for w in w ÷ 11.

w = 55; 55 ÷ 11 = 5

w = 66; 66 ÷ 11 = 6

w = 77; 77 ÷ 11 = 7

The missing values are 6 and 7.

Evaluate each expression to find the missing values in the tables.

B

n	$4 \times n + 6^2$
1	40
2	
3	

Substitute for n in $4 \times n + 6^2$.
Use the order of operations.
$n = 1$; $4 \times 1 + 36 = 40$
$n = 2$; $4 \times 2 + 36 = 44$
$n = 3$; $4 \times 3 + 36 = 48$

The missing values are 44 and 48.

You can write multiplication and division expressions without using the symbols $\times$ and $\div$.

Writing Math

When you are multiplying a number times a variable, the number is written first. Write "$3x$" and not "$x3$." Read $3x$ as "three x."

Instead of . . .	You can write . . .
$x \times 3$	$x \cdot 3$ $x(3)$ $3x$
$35 \div y$	$\dfrac{35}{y}$

EXAMPLE ② **Evaluating Expressions with Two Variables**

A rectangle is 2 units wide. How many square units does the rectangle cover if it is 4, 5, 6, or 7 units long?

You can multiply length and width to find the number of square units. Let ℓ be length and w be width.

ℓ	w	$\ell \times w$
4	2	8
5	2	
6	2	
7	2	

Make a table to help you find the number of square units for each length.
$\ell = 4$; $4 \times 2 = 8$ square units
$\ell = 5$; $5 \times 2 = 10$ square units
$\ell = 6$; $6 \times 2 = 12$ square units
$\ell = 7$; $7 \times 2 = 14$ square units

The rectangle will cover 8, 10, 12, or 14 square units.

Check

Draw a rectangle 2 units wide. Then find the total number of units when the rectangle is 4, 5, 6, and 7 units long.

length

width

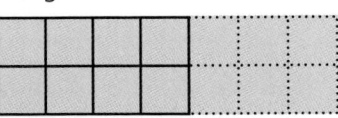

Think and Discuss

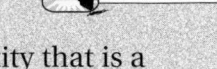

6.RP.2, 6.CM.4

1. **Name** a quantity that is a variable and a quantity that is a constant.

2. **Explain** why $45 + x$ is an algebraic expression.

go.hrw.com
Homework Help Online
KEYWORD: MR7 2-1
Parent Resources Online
KEYWORD: MR7 Parent

GUIDED PRACTICE

See Example ① Evaluate each expression to find the missing values in the tables.

1.

n	$n + 7$
38	45
49	▨
58	▨

2.

x	$12x + 2^3$
8	104
9	▨
10	▨

See Example ② **3.** A rectangle is 4 units wide. How many square units does the rectangle cover if it is 6, 7, 8, or 9 units long?

INDEPENDENT PRACTICE

See Example ① Evaluate each expression to find the missing values in the tables.

4.

x	$4x$
50	200
100	▨
150	▨

5.

n	$2n - 3^2$
10	11
16	▨
17	▨

See Example ② **6.** A builder is designing a rectangular patio that has a length of 12 units. Find the total number of square units the patio will cover if the width is 4, 5, 6, or 7 units.

PRACTICE AND PROBLEM SOLVING

Extra Practice
See page 716.

7. Estimation Bobby drives his truck at a rate of 50 to 60 miles per hour.
  a. Approximately how far can Bobby drive in 2, 3, 4, and 5 hours?
  b. Bobby plans to take an 8-hour trip, which will include a 1-hour stop for lunch. What is a reasonable distance for Bobby to drive?

8. Multi-Step Each table in the cafeteria seats 8 people. Find the total number of people that can be seated at 7, 8, 9, and 10 tables. If the average bill per person is $12, how much money can the cafeteria expect from 7, 8, 9, and 10 tables that have no empty seats?

9. Measurement When traveling in Europe, Jessika converts the temperature given in degrees Celsius to a Fahrenheit temperature by using the expression $9x \div 5 + 32$, where x is the Celsius temperature. Find the temperature in degrees Fahrenheit when it is 0°C, 10°C, and 25°C.

10. Geometry To find the area of a triangle, you can use the expression $b \times h \div 2$, where b is the base of the triangle and h is its height. Find the area of a triangle with a base of 5 and a height of 6.

Money

Why does a Polish coin show Australia and a kangaroo? This coin honors Pawel Edmund Strzelecki, a Pole who explored and mapped much of Australia.

go.hrw.com
Web Extra!
KEYWORD: MR7 Money

Evaluate each expression for the given value of the variable.

11. $3h + 2$ for $h = 10$ **12.** $2x^2$ for $x = 3$ **13.** $t - 7$ for $t = 20$

14. $4p - 3$ for $p = 20$ **15.** $\frac{c}{7}$ for $c = 56$ **16.** $10 + 2r$ for $r = 5$

17 $3x + 17$ for $x = 13$ **18.** $5p$ for $p = 12$ **19.** $s^2 - 15$ for $s = 5$

20. $14 - 2c$ for $c = 2$ **21.** $10x$ for $x = 11$ **22.** $4j + 12$ for $j = 9$

23. **Money** The zloty is the currency in Poland. In 2005, 1 U.S. dollar was worth 3 zlotys. How many zlotys were equivalent to 8 U.S. dollars?

24. Use the graph to complete the table.

Cups of Water	Number of Lemons
8	
12	
16	
w	

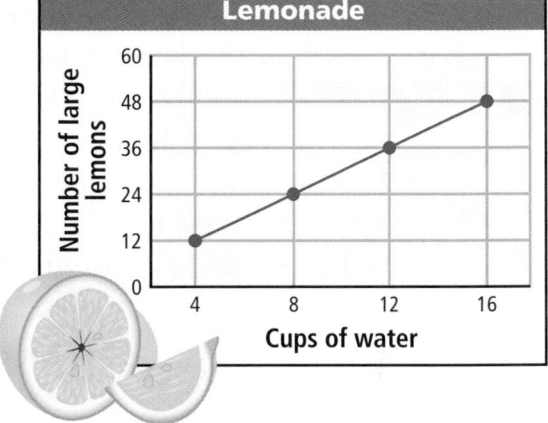

25. **What's the Error?** A student evaluated the expression $x \div 2$ for $x = 14$ and gave an answer of 28. What did the student do wrong?

26. **Write About It** How would you evaluate the expression $2x + 5$ for $x = 1, 2, 3,$ and 4?

27. **Challenge** Using the algebraic expression $3n - 5$, what is the smallest whole-number value for n that will give you a result greater than 100?

TEST PREP and Spiral Review

28. **Multiple Choice** Evaluate $8m - 5$ for $m = 9$.

(A) 67   (B) 83   (C) 84   (D) 94

29. **Gridded Response** Evaluate the expression $4p + 18$ for $p = 5$.

Write each expression in exponential form. (Lesson 1-3)

30. $3 \times 3 \times 3$ **31.** $5 \times 5 \times 5 \times 5 \times 5 \times 5$ **32.** $10 \times 10 \times 10 \times 10$

Choose a solution method and solve. Explain your choice. (Lesson 1-6)

33. Al earns $16 per hour for his work at a factory. He works 32 hours per week and gets paid every 2 weeks. If the factory takes $105 out of each check for taxes, how much money will Al be paid?

Translate Between Words and Math

Problem Solving Skill

Learn to translate between words and math.

NY Performance Indicators

5.A.2 Translate simple verbal expressions into algebraic expressions.

The earth's core is divided into two parts. The inner core is solid and dense, with a radius of 1,228 km. Let c stand for the thickness in kilometers of the liquid outer core. What is the total radius of the earth's core?

In word problems, you may need to identify the action to translate words to math.

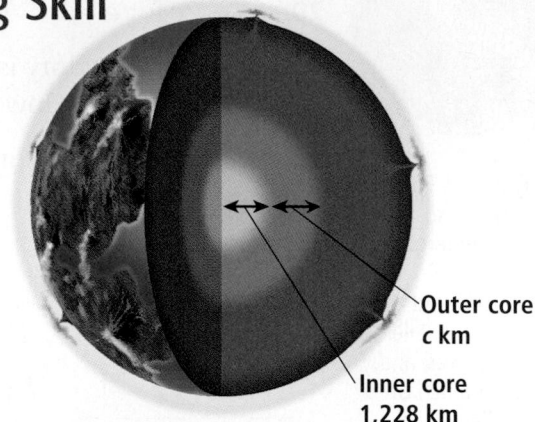

Outer core
c km

Inner core
1,228 km

Action	Put together or combine	Find how much more or less	Put together groups of equal parts	Separate into equal groups
Operation	Add	Subtract	Multiply	Divide

To solve this problem, you need to *put together* the measurements of the inner core and the outer core. To put things together, add.

$$1{,}228 + c$$

The total radius of the earth's core is $1{,}228 + c$ km.

EXAMPLE 1 *Social Studies Applications*

A The Nile River is the world's longest river. Let n stand for the length in miles of the Nile. The Amazon River is 4,000 miles long. Write an expression to show how much longer the Nile is than the Amazon.

To *find how much longer,* subtract the **length of the Amazon** from the **length of the Nile.**

$$n \qquad - \qquad 4{,}000$$

The Nile is $n - 4{,}000$ miles longer than the Amazon.

B Let s represent the number of senators that each of the 50 states has in the U.S. Senate. Write an expression for the total number of senators.

To *put together 50 equal groups of s,* multiply 50 times s.

$$50s$$

There are $50s$ senators in the U.S. Senate.

There are several different ways to write math expressions with words.

Operation	**+**	**–**	**✖**	**÷**
Numerical Expression	37 + 28	90 − 12	8 × 48 or 8 · 48 or (8)(48) or 8(48) or (8)48	327 ÷ 3 or $\frac{327}{3}$
Words	• 28 added to 37 • 37 plus 28 • the sum of 37 and 28 • 28 more than 37	• 12 subtracted from 90 • 90 minus 12 • the difference of 90 and 12 • 12 less than 90 • take away 12 from 90	• 8 times 48 • 48 multiplied by 8 • the product of 8 and 48 • 8 groups of 48	• 327 divided by 3 • the quotient of 327 and 3
Algebraic Expression	$x + 28$	$k - 12$	$8 \cdot w$ or $(8)(w)$ or $8w$	$n \div 3$ or $\frac{n}{3}$
Words	• 28 added to x • x plus 28 • the sum of x and 28 • 28 more than x	• 12 subtracted from k • k minus 12 • the difference of k and 12 • 12 less than k • take away 12 from k	• 8 times w • w multiplied by 8 • the product of 8 and w • 8 groups of w	• n divided by 3 • the quotient of n and 3

EXAMPLE 2 **Translating Words into Math**

Write each phrase as a numerical or algebraic expression.

A 287 plus 932

287 + 932

B b divided by 14

$b \div 14$ or $\frac{b}{14}$

EXAMPLE 3 **Translating Math into Words**

Write two phrases for each expression.

A $a - 45$
• a minus 45
• take away 45 from a

B (34)(7)
• the product of 34 and 7
• 7 multiplied by 34

6.PS.7, 6.CM.10

Think and Discuss

1. Tell how to write each of the following phrases as a numerical or algebraic expression: 75 less than 1,023; the product of 125 and z.

2. Give two examples of "$a \div 17$" expressed with words.

go.hrw.com
Homework Help Online
KEYWORD: MR7 2-2
Parent Resources Online
KEYWORD: MR7 Parent

GUIDED PRACTICE

See Example **1**   **1. Social Studies** The Big Island of Hawaii is the largest Hawaiian island, with an area of 4,028 mi^2. The next biggest island is Maui. Let *m* represent the area of Maui. Write an expression for the difference between the two areas.

See Example **2**   Write each phrase as a numerical or algebraic expression.

    2. 279 minus 125   **3.** the product of 15 and *x*   **4.** 17 plus 4

    5. *p* divided by 5   **6.** the sum of 9 and *q*   **7.** 149 times 2

See Example **3**   Write two phrases for each expression.

    8. $r + 87$ **9.** 345×196 **10.** $476 \div 28$ **11.** $d - 5$

INDEPENDENT PRACTICE

See Example **1**   **12. Social Studies** In 2005, California had 21 more seats in the U.S. Congress than Texas had. If *t* represents the number of seats Texas had, write an expression for the number of seats California had.

    13. Let *x* represent the number of television show episodes that are taped in a season. Write an expression for the number of episodes taped in 5 seasons.

See Example **2**   Write each phrase as a numerical or algebraic expression.

    14. 25 less than *k*   **15.** the quotient of 325 and 25

    16. 34 times *w*   **17.** 675 added to 137

    18. the sum of 135 and *p*   **19.** take away 14 from *j*

See Example **3**   Write two phrases for each expression.

    20. $h + 65$ **21.** $243 - 19$ **22.** $125 \div n$ **23.** $342(75)$

    24. $\dfrac{d}{27}$ **25.** $45 \cdot 23$ **26.** $629 + c$ **27.** $228 - b$

PRACTICE AND PROBLEM SOLVING

Extra Practice
See page 716.

Translate each phrase into a numerical or algebraic expression.

    28. 13 less than *z*   **29.** 15 divided by *d*

    30. 874 times 23   **31.** *m* multiplied by 67

    32. the sum of 35, 74, and 21   **33.** 319 less than 678

    34. Critical Thinking Paula and Manda were asked to write an expression to find the total number of shoes in a closet. Let *s* represent the number of pairs of shoes. Paula wrote *s* and Manda wrote 2*s*. Who is correct? Explain.

     35. Write About It Write a situation that could be modeled by the expression *x* + 5.

The graph shows the number of U.S. space exploration missions from 1961 to 2005.

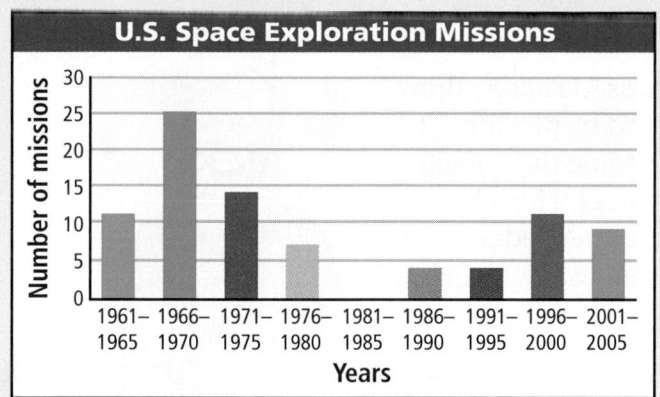

U.S. Space Exploration Missions

36. Between 1966 and 1970, the Soviet Union had *m* fewer space missions than the United States. Write an algebraic expression for this situation.

37. Let *d* represent the number of dollars that the United States spent on space missions from 1986 to 1990. Write an expression for the cost per mission.

38.  **Write a Problem** Use the data in the graph to write a word problem that can be answered with a numerical or algebraic expression.

39. Critical Thinking Let *p* stand for the number of missions between 1996 and 2000 that had people aboard. What operation would you use to write an expression for the number of missions without people? Explain.

40. ⭐ **Challenge** Write an expression for the following: two more than the number of missions from 1971 to 1975, minus the number of missions from 1986 to 1990. Then evaluate the expression.

TEST PREP and Spiral Review

41. Multiple Choice Which expression represents the product of 79 and *x*?

    Ⓐ $79 + x$ Ⓑ $x - 79$ Ⓒ $79x$ Ⓓ $\frac{x}{79}$

42. Extended Response Tim is driving from Ames, Iowa to Canton, Ohio. He is 280 miles from Ames when he stops for gas. Write an expression to represent the number of miles Tim has left to drive. Explain. Translate your expression into two different word phrases.

Use mental math to find each sum or product. (Lesson 1-5)

43. $8 \times 5 \times 9$ **44.** $49 + 26 + 11 + 14$ **45.** $4 \times 15 \times 6$

Evaluate each expression for the given value of the variable. (Lesson 2-1)

46. $2y + 6$ for $y = 4$ **47.** $\frac{z}{5}$ for $z = 40$ **48.** $7r - 3$ for $r = 18$ **49.** $\frac{p}{7} + 12$ for $p = 28$

2-3 Translating Between Tables and Expressions

 **Learn** to write expressions for tables and sequences.

NY Performance Indicators

6.PS.7 Represent problem situations verbally, numerically, algebraically and/or graphically. Also, 6.PS.12.

In 2004, International Chess Master Andrew Martin broke a world record by playing 321 games of chess at the same time. Each game required 32 chess pieces. The table shows the number of pieces needed for different numbers of games.

Games	Pieces
1	32
2	64
3	96
n	$32n$

The number of pieces is always 32 times the number of games. For n games, the expression $32n$ gives the number of pieces that are needed.

EXAMPLE 1 Writing an Expression

Write an expression for the missing value in each table.

A

Reilly's Age	Ashley's Age
9	11
10	12
11	13
12	14
n	▨

Ashley's age is Reilly's age plus 2.

$9 + 2 = 11$
$10 + 2 = 12$
$11 + 2 = 13$
$12 + 2 = 14$
$n + 2$

When Reilly's age is n, Ashley's age is $n + 2$.

B

Eggs	Dozens
12	1
24	2
36	3
48	4
e	▨

The number of dozens is the number of eggs divided by 12.

$12 \div 12 = 1$
$24 \div 12 = 2$
$36 \div 12 = 3$
$48 \div 12 = 4$
$e \div 12$

When there are e eggs, the number of dozens is $e \div 12$, or $\frac{e}{12}$.

You can look for a pattern in a table to help you write an expression.

EXAMPLE 2 **Writing an Expression for a Sequence**

Write an expression for the sequence in the table.

Position	1	2	3	4	5	n
Value of Term	3	5	7	9	11	

Look for a relationship between the positions and the values of the terms in the sequence. Use guess and check.

Guess $2n$.

Check by substituting 3.

$2 \times 3 \neq 7$ ✗

Guess $2n + 1$.

Check by substituting 3.

$2 \times 3 + 1 = 7$ ✔

The expression $2n + 1$ works for the entire sequence.

$2 \times 1 + 1 = 3, 2 \times 2 + 1 = 5, 2 \times 3 + 1 = 7,$

$2 \times 4 + 1 = 9, 2 \times 5 + 1 = 11$

The expression for the sequence is $2n + 1$.

EXAMPLE 3 **Writing an Expression for the Area of a Figure**

A triangle has a base of 8 inches. The table shows the area of the triangle for different heights. Write an expression that can be used to find the area of the triangle when its height is *h* inches.

Base (in.)	Height (in.)	Area (in²)
8	1	4
8	2	8
8	3	12
8	4	16
8	h	

$8 \times 1 = 8, \quad 8 \div 2 = 4$

$8 \times 2 = 16, 16 \div 2 = 8$

$8 \times 3 = 24, 24 \div 2 = 12$

$8 \times 4 = 32, 32 \div 2 = 16$

$8 \times h = 8h, 8h \div 2$

In each row of the table, the area is half the product of the base and the height. The expression is $\frac{8h}{2}$, or $4h$.

Think and Discuss  6.RP.6, 6.CM.1

1. **Describe** how to write an expression for a sequence given in a table.

2. **Explain** why it is important to check your expression for all of the data in a table.

2-3 **Exercises**

go.hrw.com
Homework Help Online
KEYWORD: MR7 2-3
Parent Resources Online
KEYWORD: MR7 Parent

GUIDED PRACTICE

See Example 1   Write an expression for the missing value in each table.

1.

Go-Carts	1	2	3	4	n
Wheels	4	8	12	16	▧

See Example 2   Write an expression for the sequence in the table.

2.

Position	1	2	3	4	5	n
Value of Term	9	10	11	12	13	▧

See Example 3   **3.** A rectangle has a length of 5 inches. The table shows the area of the rectangle for different widths. Write an expression that can be used to find the area of the rectangle when its width is w inches.

Length (in.)	Width (in.)	Area (in²)
5	2	10
5	4	20
5	6	30
5	8	40
5	w	▧

INDEPENDENT PRACTICE

See Example 1   Write an expression for the missing value in each table.

4.

Players	Soccer Teams
22	2
44	4
66	6
88	8
n	▧

5.

Weeks	Days
4	28
8	56
12	84
16	112
n	▧

See Example 2   Write an expression for the sequence in the table.

6.

Position	1	2	3	4	5	n
Value of Term	7	12	17	22	27	▧

See Example 3   **7.** The table shows the area of a square with different side lengths. Write an expression that can be used to find the area of a square when its side length is s feet.

Length (ft)	2	4	6	8	s
Area (ft²)	4	16	36	64	▧

PRACTICE AND PROBLEM SOLVING

Extra Practice
See page 716.

Make a table for each sequence. Then write an expression for the sequence.

8. 2, 4, 6, 8, . . .   **9.** 6, 7, 8, 9, . . .   **10.** 10, 20, 30, 40, . . .

11. Earth Science The planet Mercury takes 88 days to make a complete orbit of the Sun. The table shows the number of orbits and the number of days it takes to make the orbits. Write an expression for the number of days it takes Mercury to make n orbits.

Orbits	Days
1	88
2	176
3	264
n	

12. Multi-Step The entry fee for a county fair is $10. Each ride at the fair costs $2. The table shows the total cost to go on various numbers of rides. Write an expression for the cost of r rides. Then use the expression to find the cost of 12 rides.

Number of Rides	1	3	5	8	10	r
Total Cost ($)	12	16	20	26	30	

13. Critical Thinking Write two different expressions that describe the relationship in the table.

14. Write About It Explain how you can make a table of values for the expression $4n + 3$.

Position (n)	Value of Term
3	10

15. Challenge Can there be more than one expression that describes a set of data in a table? Explain.

TEST PREP and Spiral Review

16. Multiple Choice Which expression describes the sequence in the table?

Position	1	2	3	4	5	n
Value of Term	6	11	16	21	26	

Ⓐ $n + 5$ Ⓑ $5n + 1$ Ⓒ $6n$ Ⓓ $6n - 1$

17. Multiple Choice Find the missing value in the sequence 1, 3, 5, ▓, 9, ...

Ⓕ 6   Ⓖ 7   Ⓗ 8   Ⓙ 9

Evaluate each expression. (Lesson 1-4)

18. $14 + 8 \times 2$ **19.** $6^2 - (4 + 3)$ **20.** $5 \times 8 \div (3 + 1)$ **21.** $45 \div 3^2 + 16$

Use the Distributive Property to find each product. (Lesson 1-5)

22. 3×21 **23.** 7×35 **24.** 6×19 **25.** 2×63

Hands-On LAB 2-3

Explore Area and Perimeter of Rectangles

Use with Lesson 2-3

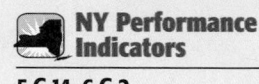
go.hrw.com
Lab Resources Online
KEYWORD: MR7 Lab2

REMEMBER
- Perimeter is the distance around a figure.
- Area is the amount of space a figure covers. It is measured in square units.

NY Performance Indicators
5.G.14, 6.G.2

You can use graph paper to model the area of different rectangles.

Activity 1

Sarita is digging rectangular vegetable gardens. To prevent weeds from growing she will cover each garden with a mesh sheet the exact size of the garden before planting the vegetables. Complete the table to find the size of sheet needed for each garden.

Each sheet will be the same size as the garden it covers. Complete the table at right to show the area of each garden.

 Garden A  Garden B

Areas of Gardens			
Garden	Length (ℓ)	Width (w)	Area (A)
A	4	2	8
B	4	3	▪
C	▪	▪	▪
D	▪	▪	▪

Garden C   Garden D

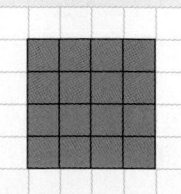 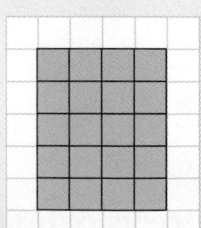

Think and Discuss

1. If you had a garden with a length of 4 and an area of 24, what would the width be? How did you get your answer?

2. The area of each garden is equal to its length times its width. Using the variables ℓ and w, what expression can you use to find the area of a rectangle? A = _____.

Complete a table like the one in Activity 1 to find the area of each rectangle.

1. length = 10, width = 5   **2.** length = 10, width = 6   **3.** length = 10, width = 7

You can use graph paper to model the perimeters of different rectangles.

Activity 2

Jorge's family recently returned from vacation. They took many pictures that they want to frame, and they decide to make their own frames. Complete the table to find the amount of wood needed for each frame.

The amount of wood needed for each frame is the perimeter of the frame. Complete the table at right to show the perimeter of each frame.

Perimeters of Picture Frames			
Frame	Length (ℓ)	Width (w)	Perimeter (P)
A	4	2	12
B	4	3	▨
C	▨	▨	▨
D	▨	▨	▨

Frame A

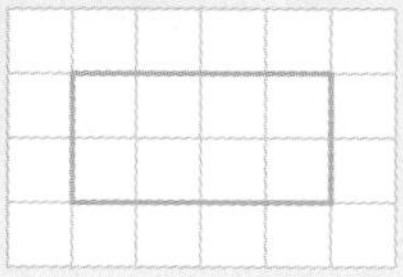

Frame B

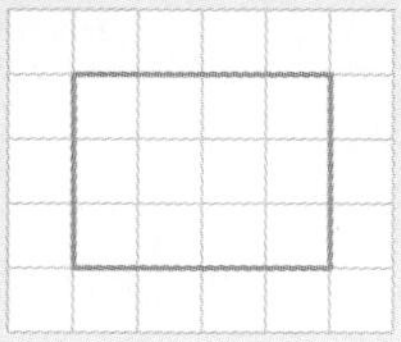

Frame C

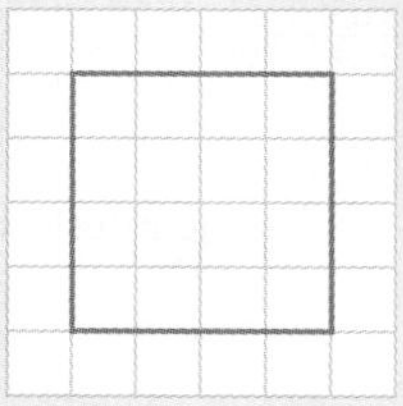

Frame D

Think and Discuss

1. How did you find the perimeter of each frame?

2. A rectangle has one pair of sides with the same measure, called the length, and another pair with the same measure, called the width. We can say two lengths and two widths equal the perimeter. Using the variables ℓ and w, what expression can you use to find the perimeter of a rectangle?
$P = $ _____.

Try This

Complete a table like the one in Activity 2 to find the perimeter of each rectangle.

1. length = 8, width = 3   **2.** length = 20, width = 4   **3.** length = 7, width = 7

Quiz for Lessons 2-1 Through 2-3

✅ **2-1** **Variables and Expressions**

Evaluate each expression to find the missing values in the tables.

1.

y	$23 + y$
17	40
27	▨
37	▨

2.

w	$w \times 3 + 10$
4	22
5	▨
6	▨

3. Stephanie's CD holder holds 6 CDs per page. How many CDs does Stephanie have if she fills 2, 3, 4, or 5 pages?

✅ **2-2** **Translate Between Words and Math**

4. The small and large intestines are part of the digestive system. The small intestine is longer than the large intestine. Let n represent the length in feet of the small intestine. The large intestine is 5 feet long. Write an expression to show how much longer the small intestine is than the large intestine.

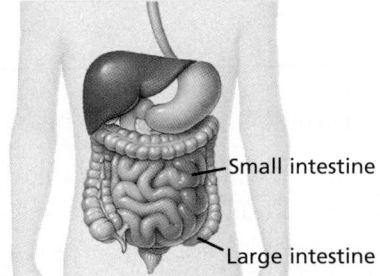

Small intestine

Large intestine

5. Let h represent the number of times your heart beats in 1 minute. Write an expression for the total number of times it beats in 1 hour. (*Hint:* 1 hour = 60 minutes)

Write each phrase as a numerical or algebraic expression.

6. 719 plus 210   **7.** t multiplied by 7   **8.** the sum of n and 51

Write two phrases for each expression.

9. $n + 19$ **10.** $12 \cdot 13$ **11.** $72 - x$ **12.** $\frac{t}{12}$ **13.** $15s$

✅ **2-3** **Translating Between Tables and Expressions**

Write an expression for the sequence in the table.

14.

Position	1	2	3	4	5	n
Value of Term	8	16	24	32	40	▨

Make a table for each sequence. Then write an expression for the sequence.

15. 3, 4, 5, 6, . . .   **16.** 4, 7, 10, 13, . . .

Ready to Go On?

Focus on Problem Solving

Understand the Problem

• **Identify too much or too little information**

Problems often give too much or too little information. You must decide whether you have enough information to work the problem.

Read the problem and identify the facts that are given. Can you use any of these facts to arrive at an answer? Are there facts in the problem that are not necessary to find the answer? These questions can help you determine whether you have too much or too little information.

If you cannot solve the problem with the information given, decide what information you need. Then read the problem again to be sure you haven't missed the information in the problem.

Copy each problem. Circle the important facts. Underline any facts that you do not need to answer the question. If there is not enough information, list the additional information you need.

1 The reticulated python is one of the longest snakes in the world. One was found in Indonesia in 1912 that was 33 feet long. At birth, a reticulated python is 2 feet long. Suppose an adult python is 29 feet long. Let f represent the number of feet the python grew since birth. What is the value of f?

2 The largest flying flag in the world is 7,410 square feet and weighs 180 pounds. There are a total of 13 horizontal stripes on it. Let h represent the height of each stripe. What is the value of h?

3 The elevation of Mt. McKinley is 20,320 ft. People who climb Mt. McKinley are flown to a base camp located at 7,200 ft. From there, they begin a climb that may last 20 days or longer. Let d represent the distance from the base camp to the summit of Mt. McKinley. What is the value of d?

4 Let c represent the cost of a particular computer in 1981. Six years later, in 1987, the price of the computer had increased to $3,600. What is the value of c?

2-4 Equations and Their Solutions

Learn to determine whether a number is a solution of an equation.

Vocabulary

equation

solution

NY Performance Indicators

6.A.2 Use substitution to evaluate algebraic expressions. Also, 5.A.3.

An **equation** is a mathematical statement that two quantities are equal. You can think of a correct equation as a balanced scale.

Equations may contain variables. If a value for a variable makes an equation true, that value is a **solution** of the equation.

You can test a value to see if it is a solution of an equation by substituting the value for the variable.

$$s + 15 = 27$$

$s = 12$ $s = 10$

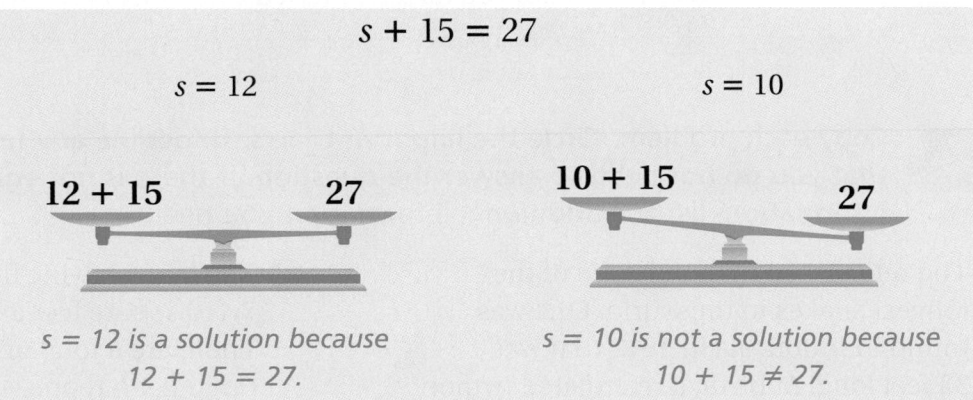

$s = 12$ is a solution because $12 + 15 = 27$.

$s = 10$ is not a solution because $10 + 15 \neq 27$.

Reading Math

The symbol $\neq$ means "is not equal to."

EXAMPLE **1** **Determining Solutions of Equations**

Determine whether the given value of the variable is a solution.

A $a + 23 = 82$ for $a = 61$

$a + 23 = 82$

$61 + 23 \overset{?}{=} 82$ *Substitute 61 for a.*

$84 \overset{?}{=} 82$ *Add.*

84   82

Since $84 \neq 82$, 61 is not a solution to $a + 23 = 82$.

Determine whether the given value of the variable is a solution.

B $60 \div c = 6$ for $c = 10$

$60 \div c = 6$

$60 \div 10 \overset{?}{=} 6$ *Substitute 10 for c.*

$6 \overset{?}{=} 6$ *Divide.*

| 6 | 6 |

Because $6 = 6$, 10 is a solution to $60 \div c = 6$.

You can use equations to check whether measurements given in different units are equal.

For example, there are 12 inches in one foot. If you have a measurement in feet, multiply by 12 to find the measurement in inches: $12 \cdot \text{feet} = \text{inches}$, or $12f = i$.

If you have one measurement in feet and another in inches, check whether the two numbers make the equation $12f = i$ true.

EXAMPLE 2 *Life Science Application*

One science book states that a manatee can grow to be 13 feet long. According to another book, a manatee may grow to 156 inches. Determine if these two measurements are equal.

$12f = i$

$12 \cdot 13 \overset{?}{=} 156$ *Substitute.*

$156 \overset{?}{=} 156$ *Multiply.*

Because $156 = 156$, 13 feet is equal to 156 inches.

Think and Discuss

 6.PS.8, 6.RP.6

1. **Tell** which of the following is the solution to $y \div 2 = 9$: $y = 14$, $y = 16$, or $y = 18$. How do you know?

2. **Give an example** of an equation with a solution of 15.

2-4 **Exercises**

go.hrw.com
Homework Help Online
KEYWORD: MR7 2-4
Parent Resources Online
KEYWORD: MR7 Parent

GUIDED PRACTICE

See Example **1** Determine whether the given value of the variable is a solution.

1. $c + 23 = 48$ for $c = 35$ **2.** $z + 31 = 73$ for $z = 42$

3. $96 = 130 - d$ for $d = 34$ **4.** $85 = 194 - a$ for $a = 105$

5. $75 \div y = 5$ for $y = 15$ **6.** $78 \div n = 13$ for $n = 5$

See Example **2** **7. Social Studies** An almanac states that the Minnehaha Waterfall in Minnesota is 53 feet tall. A tour guide said the Minnehaha Waterfall is 636 inches tall. Determine if these two measurements are equal.

INDEPENDENT PRACTICE

See Example **1** Determine whether the given value of the variable is a solution.

8. $w + 19 = 49$ for $w = 30$ **9.** $d + 27 = 81$ for $d = 44$

10. $g + 34 = 91$ for $g = 67$ **11.** $k + 16 = 55$ for $k = 39$

12. $101 = 150 - h$ for $h = 49$ **13.** $89 = 111 - m$ for $m = 32$

14. $116 = 144 - q$ for $q = 38$ **15.** $92 = 120 - t$ for $t = 28$

16. $80 \div b = 20$ for $b = 4$ **17.** $91 \div x = 7$ for $x = 12$

18. $55 \div j = 5$ for $j = 10$ **19.** $49 \div r = 7$ for $r = 7$

See Example **2** **20. Money** Kent earns $6 per hour at his after-school job. One week, he worked 12 hours and received a paycheck for $66. Determine if Kent was paid the correct amount of money. (*Hint:* $6 · hours = total pay)

21. Measurement The Eiffel Tower in Paris, France, is 300 meters tall. A fact page states that it is 30,000 centimeters tall. Determine if these two measurements are equal. (*Hint:* 1 m = 100 cm)

PRACTICE AND PROBLEM SOLVING

Extra Practice
See page 717.

Determine whether the given value of the variable is a solution.

22. $93 = 48 + u$ for $u = 35$ **23.** $112 = 14 \times f$ for $f = 8$

24. $13 = m \div 8$ for $m = 104$ **25.** $79 = z - 23$ for $z = 112$

26. $64 = l - 34$ for $l = 98$ **27.** $105 = p \times 7$ for $p = 14$

28. $94 \div s = 26$ for $s = 3$ **29.** $v + 79 = 167$ for $v = 88$

30. $m + 36 = 54$ for $m = 18$ **31.** $x - 35 = 96$ for $x = 112$

32. $12y = 84$ for $y = 7$ **33.** $7x = 56$ for $x = 8$

34. Estimation A large pizza has 8 slices. Determine if 6 large pizzas will be enough to feed 24 people, if each person eats 2 to 3 slices of pizza.

35. Multi-Step Rebecca has 17 one-dollar bills. Courtney has 350 nickels. Do the two girls have the same amount of money? (*Hint*: First find how many nickels are in a dollar.)

Replace each ▨ with a number that makes the equation correct.

36. $4 + 1 = \boxed{} + 2$

37. $2 + \boxed{} = 6 + 2$

38. $\boxed{} - 5 = 9 - 2$

39. $5(4) = 10(\boxed{})$

40. $3 + 6 = \boxed{} - 4$

41. $12 \div 4 = 9 \div \boxed{}$

42. Critical Thinking Linda is building a rectangular playhouse. The width is x feet. The length is $x + 3$ feet. The distance around the base of the playhouse is 36 feet. Is 8 the value of x? Explain.

 43. Choose a Strategy What should replace the question mark to keep the scale balanced?

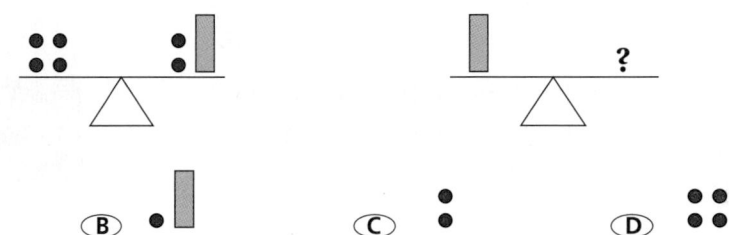

(A) ● **(B)** ●▮ **(C)** ⋮ **(D)** ∷

 44. Write About It Explain how to determine if a value is a solution to an equation.

★ **45. Challenge** Is $n = 4$ a solution for $n^2 + 79 = 88$? Explain.

TEST PREP and Spiral Review

46. Multiple Choice For which equation is $b = 8$ a solution?

(A) $13 - b = 8$ **(B)** $8 + b = 21$ **(C)** $b - 13 = 21$ **(D)** $b + 13 = 21$

47. Multiple Choice When Paul gets 53 more postcards, he will have 82 cards in his collection. Solve the equation $n + 53 = 82$ to find how many postcards Paul has in his collection now.

(F) 135 **(G)** 125 **(H)** 29 **(J)** 27

Write each expression in exponential form. (Lesson 1-3)

48. $3 \times 3 \times 3 \times 3 \times 3$ **49.** $9 \times 9 \times 9 \times 9$ **50.** $13 \times 13 \times 13$ **51.** 8×8

Write an expression for the sequence in the table. (Lesson 2-3)

52.

Position	1	2	3	4	5	n
Value of Term	4	7	10	13	16	▨

2-5 Addition Equations

Learn to solve whole-number addition equations.

NY Performance Indicators

5.A.4 Solve simple one-step equations using basic whole-number facts. Also, 5.A.5.

Some surfers recommend that the length of a beginner's surfboard be 14 inches greater than the surfer's height. If a surfboard is 82 inches, how tall should the surfer be to ride it?

The height of the surfer *combined* with 14 inches equals 82 inches. To combine amounts, you need to add.

Let *h* stand for the surfer's height. You can use the equation $h + 14 = 82$.

The equation $h + 14 = 82$ can be represented as a balanced scale.

To find the value of h, you need h by itself on one side of a balanced scale.

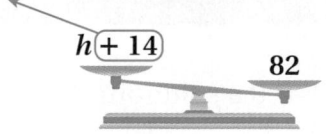

To get h by itself, first take away 14 from the left side of the scale. Now the scale is unbalanced.

To rebalance the scale, take away 14 from the other side.

Taking away 14 from both sides of the scale is the same as subtracting 14 from both sides of the equation.

$$
\begin{array}{rcr}
h + 14 &=& 82 \\
-\ 14 & & -\ 14 \\
\hline
h &=& 68
\end{array}
$$

A surfer using an 82-inch surfboard should be 68 inches tall.

Subtraction is the inverse, or opposite, of addition. If an equation contains addition, solve it by subtracting from both sides to "undo" the addition.

A surfer using an 82-inch surfboard should be 68 inches tall.

Subtraction is the inverse, or opposite, of addition. If an equation contains addition, solve it by subtracting from both sides to "undo" the addition.

EXAMPLE 1 Solving Addition Equations

Solve each equation. Check your answers.

A $x + 62 = 93$

$$
\begin{array}{rl}
x + 62 = & 93 \\
- 62 \quad & - 62 \\
\hline
x \quad = & 31
\end{array}
$$

62 is added to x.
Subtract 62 from both sides to undo the addition.

Check $x + 62 = 93$

$$31 + 62 \overset{?}{=} 93$$
$$93 \overset{?}{=} 93 \checkmark$$

Substitute 31 for x in the equation.
31 is the solution.

B $81 = 17 + y$

$$
\begin{array}{rl}
81 = & 17 + y \\
- 17 \quad & - 17 \\
\hline
64 = & \quad y
\end{array}
$$

17 is added to y.
Subtract 17 from both sides to undo the addition.

Check $81 = 17 + y$

$$81 \overset{?}{=} 17 + 64$$
$$81 \overset{?}{=} 81 \checkmark$$

Substitute 64 for y in the equation.
64 is the solution.

EXAMPLE 2 *Social Studies Application*

Dyersberg, Newton, and St. Thomas are located along Ventura Highway, as shown on the map. Find the distance d between Newton and Dyersberg.

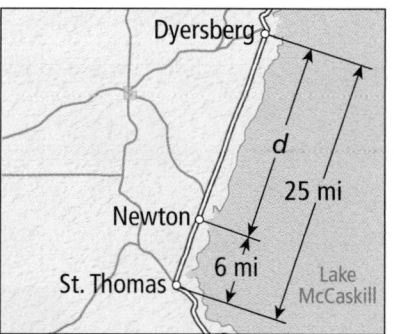

distance between Dyersberg and St. Thomas	=	distance between Newton and St. Thomas	+	distance between Newton and Dyersberg
25	=	6	+	d

$$
\begin{array}{rl}
25 = & 6 + d \\
- 6 \quad & - 6 \\
\hline
19 = & \quad d
\end{array}
$$

6 is added to d.
Subtract 6 from both sides to undo the addition.

The distance between Newton and Dyersberg is 19 miles.

Think and Discuss

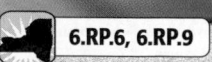

6.RP.6, 6.RP.9

1. **Tell** whether the solution of $c + 4 = 21$ will be less than 21 or greater than 21. Explain.

2. **Describe** how you could check your answer in Example 2.

2-5 **Exercises**

go.hrw.com
Homework Help Online
KEYWORD: MR7 2-5
Parent Resources Online
KEYWORD: MR7 Parent

GUIDED PRACTICE

See Example ① **Solve each equation. Check your answers.**

1. $x + 54 = 90$ **2.** $49 = 12 + y$ **3.** $n + 27 = 46$

4. $22 + t = 91$ **5.** $31 = p + 13$ **6.** $c + 38 = 54$

See Example ② **7.** Lou, Michael, and Georgette live on Mulberry Street, as shown on the map. Lou lives 10 blocks from Georgette. Georgette lives 4 blocks from Michael. How many blocks does Michael live from Lou?

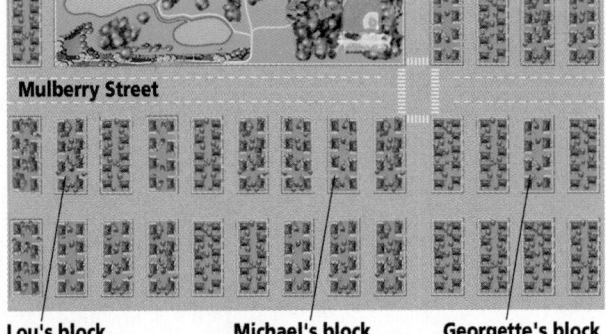

Mulberry Street

Lou's block   Michael's block   Georgette's block

INDEPENDENT PRACTICE

See Example ① **Solve each equation. Check your answers.**

8. $x + 19 = 24$ **9.** $10 = r + 3$ **10.** $s + 11 = 50$

11. $b + 17 = 42$ **12.** $12 + m = 28$ **13.** $z + 68 = 77$

14. $72 = n + 51$ **15.** $g + 28 = 44$ **16.** $27 = 15 + y$

See Example ② **17.** What is the length of a killer whale?

21 m

Fin whale

Gray whale

Killer whale

15 m   ?

PRACTICE AND PROBLEM SOLVING

Extra Practice
See page 717.

Solve each equation.

18. $x + 12 = 16$ **19.** $n + 32 = 39$ **20.** $23 + q = 34$

21. $52 + y = 71$ **22.** $73 = c + 35$ **23.** $93 = h + 15$

24. $125 = n + 85$ **25.** $87 = b + 18$ **26.** $12 + y = 50$

27. $t + 17 = 43$ **28.** $k + 9 = 56$ **29.** $25 + m = 47$

Write an equation for each statement.

30. The number of eggs *e* increased by 3 equals 14.

31. The number of new photos taken *p* added to 20 equals 36.

32. **Physical Science** Temperature can be measured in degrees Fahrenheit, degrees Celsius, or kelvins. To convert from degrees Celsius to kelvins, add 273 to the Celsius temperature. Complete the table.

	Kelvins (K)	°C + 273 = K	Celsius (°C)
Water Freezes	273	°C + 273 = 273	
Body Temperature	310		
Water Boils	373		

Popular items like the ball and the mood rings above are made of heat-sensitive materials. Changes in temperature, cause these materials to change color.

33. **History** In 1520, the explorer Ferdinand Magellan tried to measure the depth of the ocean. He weighted a 370 m rope and lowered it into the ocean. This rope was not long enough to reach the ocean floor. Suppose the depth at this location was 1,250 m. How much longer would Magellan's rope have to have been to reach the ocean floor?

 34. **Write a Problem** Use data from your science book to write a problem that can be solved using an addition equation. Solve your problem.

 35. **Write About It** Why are addition and subtraction called inverse operations?

 36. **Challenge** In the magic square at right, each row, column, and diagonal has the same sum. Find the values of *x*, *y*, and *z*.

7	61	*x*
y	37	1
31	*z*	67

TEST PREP and Spiral Review

37. **Multiple Choice** Pauline hit 6 more home runs than Danielle. Pauline hit 18 home runs. How many home runs did Danielle hit?

Ⓐ 3 Ⓑ 12 Ⓒ 18 Ⓓ 24

38. **Multiple Choice** Which is the solution to the equation $79 + r = 118$?

Ⓕ $r = 39$ Ⓖ $r = 52$ Ⓗ $r = 79$ Ⓙ $r = 197$

Order the numbers from least to greatest. (Lesson 1-1)

39. 798; 648; 923   **40.** 1,298; 876; 972   **41.** 1,498; 2,163; 1,036

Evaluate each expression to find the missing values in the tables. (Lesson 2-1)

42.

x	5	6	7	8
9x	45			

43.

y	121	99	77	55
y ÷ 11	11			

2-6 Subtraction Equations

Learn to solve whole-number subtraction equations.

NY Performance Indicators

5.A.5 Solve and explain simple one-step equations using inverse operations involving whole numbers. Also, 5.A.4.

When John F. Kennedy became president of the United States, he was 43 years old. He was 8 years younger than Abraham Lincoln was when Lincoln became president. How old was Lincoln when he became president?

Let *a* represent Abraham Lincoln's age.

Kennedy was President from 1961 to 1963.

Lincoln was President from 1861 to 1865.

Abraham Lincoln's age	−	8	=	John F. Kennedy's age
a	−	8	=	43

Remember that addition and subtraction are inverse operations. When an equation contains subtraction, use addition to "undo" the subtraction. Remember to add the same amount to both sides of the equation.

$$
\begin{aligned}
a - 8 &= 43 \\
+8 \quad &\quad +8 \\
\hline
a &= 51
\end{aligned}
$$

Abraham Lincoln was 51 years old when he became president.

EXAMPLE **Solving Subtraction Equations**

A Solve $p - 2 = 5$. Check your answer.

$$
\begin{aligned}
p - 2 &= 5 \\
+2 \quad &\quad +2 \\
\hline
p &= 7
\end{aligned}
$$

2 is subtracted from p.

Add 2 to both sides to undo the subtraction.

Check $p - 2 = 5$

$7 - 2 \overset{?}{=} 5$ Substitute 7 for p in the equation.

$5 \overset{?}{=} 5$ ✔   7 is the solution.

B Solve $40 = x - 11$. Check your answer.

$$40 = x - 11$$
$$\underline{+\ 11 \qquad\quad +\ 11}$$
$$51 = x$$

11 is subtracted from x.

Add 11 to both sides to undo the subtraction.

Check $40 = x - 11$

$$40 \overset{?}{=} 51 - 11$$

Substitute 51 for x in the equation.

$$40 \overset{?}{=} 40 \checkmark$$

51 is the solution.

C Solve $x - 56 = 19$. Check your answer.

$$x - 56 = 19$$
$$\underline{+\ 56 \qquad +\ 56}$$
$$x \qquad = \quad 75$$

56 is subtracted from x.

Add 56 to both sides to undo the subtraction.

Check $x - 56 = 19$

$$75 - 56 \overset{?}{=} 19$$

Substitute 75 for x in the equation.

$$19 \overset{?}{=} 19 \checkmark$$

75 is the solution.

Think and Discuss

 6.PS.21, 6.RP.6

1. **Tell** whether the solution of $b - 14 = 9$ will be less than 9 or greater than 9. Explain.

2. **Explain** how you know what number to add to both sides of an equation containing subtraction.

2-6 Exercises

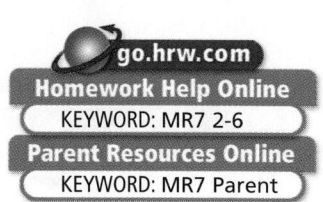

go.hrw.com
Homework Help Online
KEYWORD: MR7 2-6
Parent Resources Online
KEYWORD: MR7 Parent

GUIDED PRACTICE

See Example **1** Solve each equation. Check your answers.

1. $p - 8 = 9$ **2.** $3 = x - 16$ **3.** $a - 13 = 18$

4. $15 = y - 7$ **5.** $n - 24 = 9$ **6.** $39 = d - 2$

INDEPENDENT PRACTICE

See Example **1** Solve each equation. Check your answers.

7. $y - 18 = 7$ **8.** $8 = n - 5$ **9.** $a - 34 = 4$

10. $c - 21 = 45$ **11.** $a - 40 = 57$ **12.** $31 = x - 14$

13. $28 = p - 5$ **14.** $z - 42 = 7$ **15.** $s - 19 = 12$

PRACTICE AND PROBLEM SOLVING

Extra Practice
See page 716.

Solve each equation.

16. $r - 57 = 7$

17. $11 = x - 25$

18. $8 = y - 96$

19. $a - 6 = 15$

20. $q - 14 = 22$

21. $f - 12 = 2$

22. $18 = j - 19$

23. $109 = r - 45$

24. $d - 8 = 29$

25. $g - 71 = 72$

26. $p - 13 = 111$

27. $13 = m - 5$

28. Geography Mt. Rainier, in Washington, has a higher elevation than Mt. Shasta. The difference between their elevations is 248 feet. What is the elevation of Mt. Rainier? Write an equation and solve.

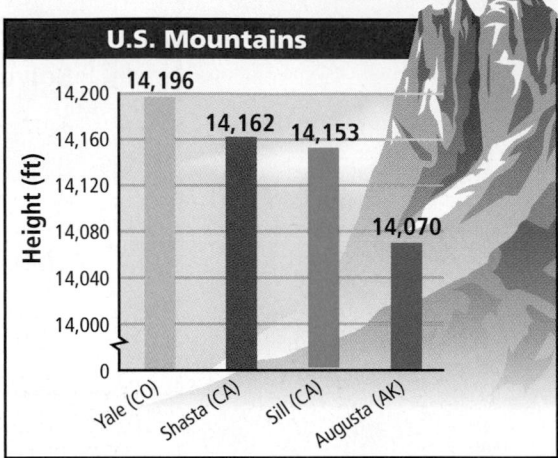

29. Social Studies In 2004, the population of New York City was 5 million less than the population of Shanghai, China. The population of New York City was 8 million. Solve the equation $8 = s - 5$ to find the population of Shanghai.

 30. Write About It Suppose $n - 15$ is a whole number. What do you know about the value of n? Explain.

 31. What's the Error? Look at the student paper at right. What did the student do wrong? What is the correct answer?

 32. Challenge Write "the difference between n and 16 is 5" as an algebraic equation. Then find the solution.

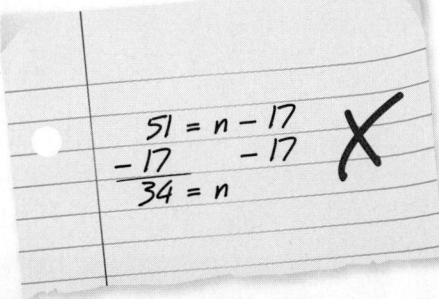

$$51 = n - 17$$
$$-17 \qquad -17$$
$$\overline{34 = n}$$

 ## TEST PREP and Spiral Review

33. Multiple Choice Which is a solution to the equation $j - 39 = 93$?

Ⓐ $j = 54$ 　　　 Ⓑ $j = 66$ 　　　 Ⓒ $j = 93$ 　　　 Ⓓ $j = 132$

34. Short Response When 17 is subtracted from a number, the result is 64. Write an equation that can be used to find the original number. Then find the original number.

Evaluate each expression. (Lesson 1-4)

35. $81 - 4 \times 3 + 18 \div (6 + 3)$ 　　 **36.** $17 \times (5 - 3) + 16 \div 8$ 　　 **37.** $3^2 - (15 - 8) + 4 \times 5$

Solve each equation. (Lesson 2-5)

38. $a + 3 = 18$ 　　 **39.** $y + 7 = 45$ 　　 **40.** $x + 16 = 71$ 　　 **41.** $87 = b + 31$

2-7 Multiplication Equations

Learn to solve whole-number multiplication equations.

NY Performance Indicators

5.A.5 Solve and explain simple one-step equations using inverse operations involving whole numbers. Also, 5.A.4.

Nine-banded armadillos are always born in groups of 4. If you count 32 babies, what is the number of mother armadillos?

To put together equal groups of 4, multiply. Let m represent the number of mother armadillos. There will be m equal groups of 4.

You can use the equation $4m = 32$.

Division is the inverse of multiplication. To solve an equation that contains multiplication, use division to "undo" the multiplication.

Caution!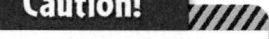

$4m$ means "$4 \times m$."

$$4m = 32$$
$$\frac{4m}{4} = \frac{32}{4}$$
$$m = 8$$

There are 8 mother armadillos.

EXAMPLE 1 **Solving Multiplication Equations**

Solve each equation. Check your answers.

A $3x = 12$

$3x = 12$ *x is multiplied by 3.*

$\frac{3x}{3} = \frac{12}{3}$ *Divide both sides by 3 to undo the multiplication.*

$x = 4$

Check $3x = 12$

$3(4) \stackrel{?}{=} 12$ *Substitute 4 for x in the equation.*

$12 \stackrel{?}{=} 12$ ✔   *4 is the solution.*

B $8 = 4w$

$8 = 4w$ *w is multiplied by 4.*

$\frac{8}{4} = \frac{4w}{4}$ *Divide both sides by 4 to undo the multiplication.*

$2 = w$

Check $8 = 4w$

$8 \stackrel{?}{=} 4(2)$ *Substitute 2 for w in the equation.*

$8 \stackrel{?}{=} 8$ ✔   *2 is the solution.*

EXAMPLE **2**

PROBLEM SOLVING APPLICATION

The area of a rectangle is 36 square inches. Its length is 9 inches. What is its width?

1. Understand the Problem

The **answer** will be the width of the rectangle in inches.

List the **important information:**

- The area of the rectangle is 36 square inches.
- The length of the rectangle is 9 inches.

Draw a diagram to represent this information.

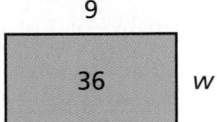

2. Make a Plan

You can write and solve an equation using the formula for area. To find the area of a rectangle, multiply its length by its width.

$$A = \ell w$$
$$36 = 9w$$

3. Solve

$36 = 9w$ *w is multiplied by 9.*

$\dfrac{36}{9} = \dfrac{9w}{9}$ *Divide both sides by 9 to undo the multiplication.*

$4 = w$

So the width of the rectangle is 4 inches.

4. Look Back

Arrange 36 identical squares in a rectangle. The length is 9, so line up the squares in rows of 9. You can make 4 rows of 9, so the width of the rectangle is 4.

Think and Discuss

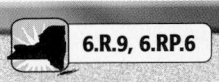

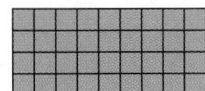 6.R.9, 6.RP.6

1. Tell what number you would use to divide both sides of the equation $15x = 60$.

2. Tell whether the solution of $10c = 90$ will be less than 90 or greater than 90. Explain.

go.hrw.com
Homework Help Online
KEYWORD: MR7 2-7
Parent Resources Online
KEYWORD: MR7 Parent

GUIDED PRACTICE

See Example **1** Solve each equation. Check your answers.

1. $7x = 21$ **2.** $27 = 3w$ **3.** $90 = 10a$

4. $56 = 7b$ **5.** $3c = 33$ **6.** $12 = 2n$

See Example **2** **7.** The area of a rectangular deck is 675 square feet. The deck's width is 15 feet. What is its length?

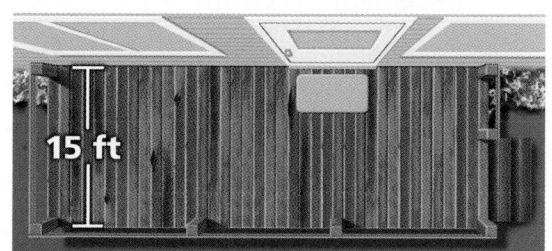

15 ft

INDEPENDENT PRACTICE

See Example **1** Solve each equation. Check your answers.

8. $12p = 36$ **9.** $52 = 13a$ **10.** $64 = 8n$

11. $20 = 5x$ **12.** $6r = 30$ **13.** $77 = 11t$

14. $14s = 98$ **15.** $12m = 132$ **16.** $9z = 135$

See Example **2** **17.** Marcy spreads out a rectangular picnic blanket with an area of 24 square feet. Its width is 4 feet. What is its length?

PRACTICE AND PROBLEM SOLVING

Extra Practice
See page 717.

Solve each equation.

18. $5y = 35$ **19.** $18 = 2y$ **20.** $54 = 9y$ **21.** $15y = 120$

22. $4y = 0$ **23.** $22y = 440$ **24.** $3y = 63$ **25.** $z - 6 = 34$

26. $6y = 114$ **27.** $161 = 7y$ **28.** $135 = 3y$ **29.** $y - 15 = 3$

30. $81 = 9y$ **31.** $4 + y = 12$ **32.** $7y = 21$ **33.** $a + 12 = 26$

34. $10x = 120$ **35.** $36 = 12x$ **36.** $s - 2 = 7$ **37.** $15 + t = 21$

38. Estimation Colorado is almost a perfect rectangle on a map. Its border from east to west is about 387 mi, and its area is about 104,247 mi^2. Estimate the length of Colorado's border from north to south. (Area = length × width)

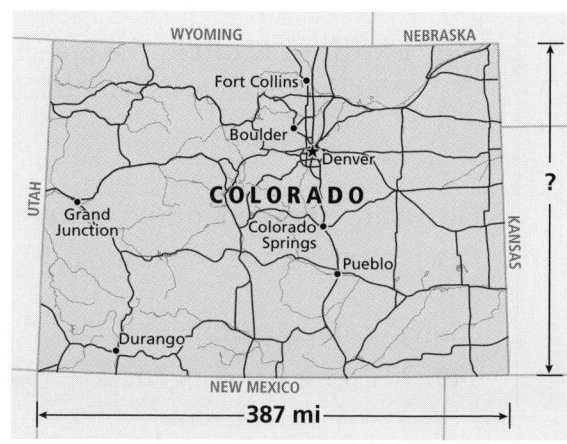

Arthropods make up the largest group of animals on Earth. They include insects, spiders, crabs, and centipedes. Arthropods have segmented bodies. In centipedes and millipedes, all of the segments are identical.

39. Centipedes have 2 legs per segment. They can have from 30 to 354 legs. Find a range for the number of segments a centipede can have.

40. Millipedes have 4 legs per segment. The record number of legs on a millipede is 752. How many segments did this millipede have?

Many arthropods have compound eyes. Compound eyes are made up of tiny bundles of identical light-sensitive cells.

41. A dragonfly has 7 times as many light-sensitive cells as a housefly. How many of these cells does a housefly have?

42. Find how many times more light-sensitive cells a dragonfly has than a butterfly.

43. *Write About It* A trapdoor spider can pull with a force that is 140 times its own weight. What other information would you need to find the spider's weight? Explain.

44. ★ *Challenge* There are about 6 billion humans in the world. Scientists estimate that there are a billion billion arthropods in the world. About how many times larger is the arthropod population than the human population?

A horsefly magnified to twelve times its actual size

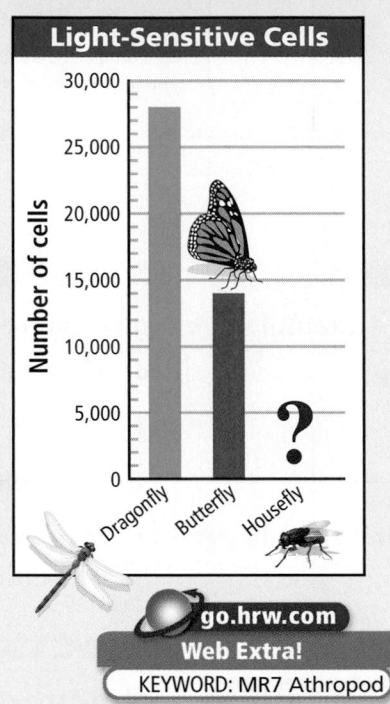

go.hrw.com
Web Extra!
KEYWORD: MR7 Athropod

TEST PREP and Spiral Review

45. Multiple Choice Solve the equation $25x = 175$.

   Ⓐ $x = 5$ Ⓑ $x = 6$ Ⓒ $x = 7$ Ⓓ $x = 8$

46. Multiple Choice The area of a rectangle is 42 square inches. Its width is 6 inches. What is its length?

   Ⓕ 5 inches   Ⓖ 7 inches   Ⓗ 9 inches   Ⓙ 11 inches

Estimate each sum or difference by rounding to the place value indicated. (Lesson 1-2)

47. 4,798 + 2,118; thousands   **48.** 49,169 − 13,919; ten thousands

Solve each equation. (Lessons 2-5 and 2-6)

49. $b + 53 = 95$ **50.** $a - 100 = 340$ **51.** $n - 24 = 188$ **52.** $w + 20 = 95$

Division Equations

Learn to solve whole-number division equations.

NY Performance Indicators

5.A.4 Solve simple one-step equations using basic whole-number facts. Also, 5.A.5.

Japanese pearl divers go as deep as 165 feet underwater in search of pearls. At this depth, the pressure on a diver is much greater than at the water's surface. Water pressure can be described using equations containing division.

Multiplication is the inverse of division. When an equation contains division, use multiplication to "undo" the division.

EXAMPLE **1** **Solving Division Equations**

Solve each equation. Check your answers.

A $\frac{y}{5} = 4$

$\frac{y}{5} = 4$ *y is divided by 5.*

$5 \cdot \frac{y}{5} = 5 \cdot 4$ *Multiply both sides by 5 to undo the division.*

$y = 20$

Check

$\frac{y}{5} = 4$

$\frac{20}{5} \overset{?}{=} 4$ *Substitute 20 for y in the equation.*

$4 \overset{?}{=} 4$ ✔   *20 is the solution.*

B $12 = \frac{z}{4}$

$12 = \frac{z}{4}$ *z is divided by 4.*

$4 \cdot 12 = 4 \cdot \frac{z}{4}$ *Multiply both sides by 4 to undo the division.*

$48 = z$

Check

$12 = \frac{z}{4}$

$12 \overset{?}{=} \frac{48}{4}$ *Substitute 48 for z in the equation.*

$12 \overset{?}{=} 12$ ✔   *48 is the solution.*

EXAMPLE 2 *Physical Science Application*

Pressure is the amount of force exerted on an area. Pressure can be measured in pounds per square inch, or psi.

The pressure at the surface of the water is half the pressure at 30 ft underwater.

$$\text{pressure at surface} = \frac{\text{pressure at 30 ft underwater}}{2}$$

The pressure at the surface is 15 psi. What is the water pressure at 30 ft underwater?

Let p represent the pressure at 30 ft underwater.

$15 = \frac{p}{2}$ *Substitute 15 for pressure at the surface.*
p is divided by 2.

$2 \cdot 15 = 2 \cdot \frac{p}{2}$ *Multiply both sides by 2 to undo the division.*

$30 = p$

The water pressure at 30 ft underwater is 30 psi.

Think and Discuss

6.RP.5, 6.RP.6, 6.RP.9

1. **Tell** whether the solution of $\frac{c}{10} = 70$ will be less than 70 or greater than 70. Explain.

2. **Describe** how you would check your answer to Example 2.

3. **Explain** why $13 \cdot \frac{x}{13} = x$.

2-8 Exercises

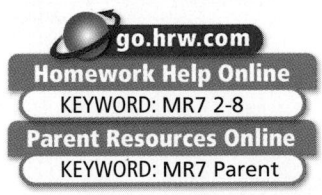
go.hrw.com
Homework Help Online
KEYWORD: MR7 2-8
Parent Resources Online
KEYWORD: MR7 Parent

GUIDED PRACTICE

See Example 1   Solve each equation. Check your answers.

1. $\frac{y}{4} = 3$

2. $14 = \frac{z}{2}$

3. $\frac{r}{9} = 7$

4. $\frac{s}{10} = \frac{4}{40}$

5. $12 = \frac{j}{3}$

6. $9 = \frac{x}{5}$

7. $\frac{f}{12} = 5$

8. $\frac{g}{2} = 1$

See Example 2   9. Irene mowed the lawn and planted flowers. The amount of time she spent mowing the lawn was one-third the amount of time it took her to plant flowers. It took her 30 minutes to mow the lawn. Find the amount of time Irene spent planting flowers.

See Example ① Solve each equation. Check your answers.

10. $\dfrac{d}{3} = 12$ **11.** $\dfrac{c}{2} = 13$ **12.** $7 = \dfrac{m}{7}$ **13.** $\dfrac{g}{7} = 14$

14. $6 = \dfrac{f}{4}$ **15.** $\dfrac{x}{12} = 12$ **16.** $\dfrac{j}{20} = 10$ **17.** $9 = \dfrac{r}{9}$

See Example ② **18.** The area of Danielle's garden is one-twelfth the area of her entire yard. The area of the garden is 10 square feet. Find the area of the yard.

PRACTICE AND PROBLEM SOLVING

Extra Practice
See page 717.

Find the value of c in each equation.

19. $\dfrac{c}{12} = 8$ **20.** $4 = \dfrac{c}{9}$ **21.** $\dfrac{c}{15} = 11$ **22.** $c + 21 = 40$

23. $14 = \dfrac{c}{5}$ **24.** $\dfrac{c}{4} = 12$ **25.** $\dfrac{c}{4} = 15$ **26.** $5c = 120$

27. Multi-Step The Empire State Building is 381 m tall. At the Grand Canyon's widest point, 76 Empire State Buildings would fit end to end. Write and solve an equation to find the width of the Grand Canyon at this point.

28. Earth Science You can estimate the distance of a thunderstorm in kilometers by counting the number of seconds between the lightning flash and the thunder and then dividing this number by 3. If a storm is 5 km away, how many seconds will you count between the lightning flash and the thunder?

 29. Write a Problem Write a problem about money that can be solved with a division equation.

 30. Write About It Use a numerical example to explain how multiplication and division undo each other.

 31. Challenge A number halved and then halved again is equal to 2. What was the original number?

TEST PREP and Spiral Review

32. Multiple Choice Carl has n action figures in his collection. He wants to place them in 6 bins with 12 figures in each bin. Solve the equation $\dfrac{n}{6} = 12$ to determine the number of action figures Carl has.

ⓐ $n = 2$ ⓑ $n = 6$ ⓒ $n = 18$ ⓓ $n = 72$

33. Multiple Choice Which equation does NOT have $k = 28$ as a solution?

Ⓕ $\dfrac{k}{14} = 2$ Ⓖ $\dfrac{k}{7} = 4$ Ⓗ $\dfrac{k}{28} = 1$ Ⓙ $\dfrac{k}{6} = 12$

Identify a pattern in each sequence. Name the next three terms. (Lesson 1-7)

34. 3, 10, 17, 24, . . .   **35.** 5, 10, 15, 20, . . .   **36.** 1, 4, 2, 5, 3, . . .

Solve each equation. (Lesson 2-7)

37. $4r = 52$ **38.** $8k = 128$ **39.** $81 = 9p$ **40.** $119 = 17q$

Quiz for Lessons 2-4 Through 2-8

2-4 Equations and Their Solutions

Determine whether the given value of the variable is a solution.

1. $c - 13 = 54$ for $c = 67$ **2.** $5r = 65$ for $r = 15$ **3.** $48 \div x = 6$ for $x = 8$

4. Brady buys 2 notebooks and should get $3 back in change. The cashier gives him 12 quarters. Determine if Brady was given the correct amount of change.

2-5 Addition Equations

Solve each equation. Check your answers.

5. $p + 51 = 76$ **6.** $107 = 19 + j$ **7.** $45 = s + 27$

8. A large section of the original Great Wall of China is now in ruins. As measured today, the length of the wall is about 6,350 kilometers. When the length of the section now in ruins is included, the length of the wall is about 6,850 kilometers. Write and solve an equation to find the approximate length of the section of the Great Wall that is now in ruins.

2-6 Subtraction Equations

Solve each equation. Check your answers.

9. $k - 5 = 17$ **10.** $150 = p - 30$ **11.** $n - 24 = 72$

12. The Kingda Ka roller coaster at Six Flags® Great Adventure in New Jersey is taller than the Top Thrill Dragster located at Cedar Point™ in Ohio. The difference between their heights is 36 feet. The Top Thrill Dragster is 420 feet high. Write and solve an equation to find the height of Kingda Ka.

2-7 Multiplication Equations

Solve each equation. Check your answers.

13. $6f = 18$ **14.** $105 = 5d$ **15.** $11x = 99$

16. Taryn buys 8 identical glasses. Her total is $48 before tax. Write and solve an equation to find out how much Taryn pays per glass.

2-8 Division Equations

Solve each equation. Check your answers.

17. $10 = \frac{j}{9}$ **18.** $5 = \frac{t}{6}$ **19.** $\frac{r}{15} = 3$

20. Paula is baking peach pies for a bake sale. Each pie requires 2 pounds of peaches. She bakes 6 pies. Write and solve an equation to find how many pounds of peaches Paula had to buy.

MULTI-STEP TEST PREP

Super Squid! For centuries, sailors have told tales of ships being captured by giant squid. Although the stories may be myths, scientists have concluded that giant squid can reach a total length of up to 60 feet.

The figure shows different ways a squid can be measured.

1. A giant squid washed ashore in New Zealand in 1887. It had a total length of 55 feet. In some sources, the squid's length is reported as 660 inches. Determine if these two measurements are equal. Explain.

2. The giant squid's total length of 55 feet was 49 feet more than its mantle length. What equation could you use to find the length of the mantle? Solve your equation.

3. The difference between the standard length and mantle length for this squid was 10 feet. Explain which operation you would use to write an equation to find the standard length of the squid, and then find the standard length.

4. Suppose the giant squid had 240 suction cups on each arm. Let n represent the number of arms. What expression could be used to find the total number of suction cups found on a giant squid? Explain.

5. The squid had a total of 1,920 suction cups. How many arms did the squid have?

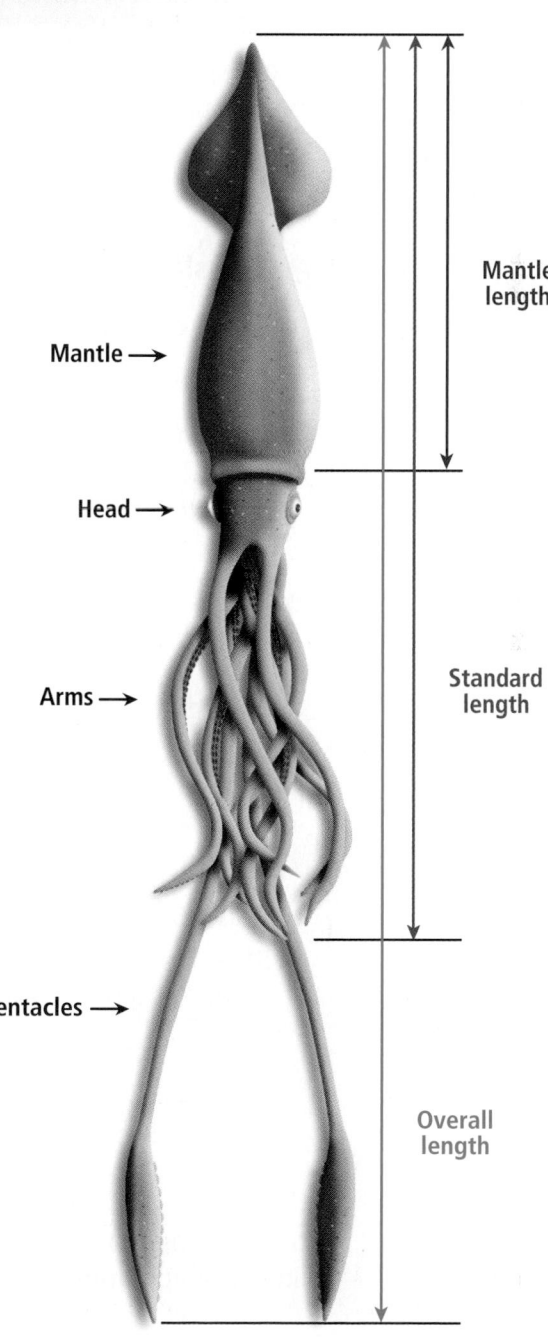

Mantle →

Head →

Arms →

Tentacles →

Mantle length

Standard length

Overall length

Multi-Step Test Prep

Two-Step Algebraic Equations

Learn to translate two-step verbal expressions into algebraic expressions and equations and to solve two-step equations.

NY Performance Indicators

6.A.4 Solve and explain two-step equations involving whole numbers using imverse operations. Also, 6.A.1, 6.A.3.

At a frog jumping contest, Alison's frog jumped 55 inches, which is 3 inches more than 2 times the distance that Justin's frog jumped. How far did Justin's frog jump?

When solving real-world problems, you need to translate words, or verbal expressions, into algebraic expressions.

EXAMPLE 1 Translating Verbal Expressions

Write each phrase as an algebraic expression or equation.

A 8 times a number decreased by 12

8 times a number decreased by 12

$$8 \quad \times \quad\quad\quad\quad n - 12$$

$$8(n - 12)$$

B the quotient of 3 more than a number and 20 is 1

3 more than a number divided by 20 is 1

$$3 \quad + \quad\quad n \quad\quad \div \quad 20 = 1$$

$$\frac{3 + n}{20} = 1$$

EXAMPLE 2 Solving Two-Step Equations

Solve $5x - 7 = 8$.

$$5x - 7 = 8$$

$$\underline{\quad +7 \quad +7} \quad\quad \textit{Add 7 to both sides.}$$

$$5x \quad\quad = 15$$

$$\frac{5x}{5} = \frac{15}{5} \quad\quad\quad \textit{Divide both sides by 5.}$$

$$x = 3$$

When solving real-world problems, you need to determine the action to know which operation to use.

EXAMPLE **3** *Recreation Application*

At a frog jumping contest, Alison's frog jumped 55 inches, which is 3 inches more than 2 times the distance that Justin's frog jumped. How far did Justin's frog jump?

Let x represent the distance Justin's frog jumped in inches.

Alison's frog	is	3 in.	more than	2	times	Justin's frog
55	=	3	+	2	·	x

$$55 = 3 + 2x$$
$$\frac{-3}{52} = \frac{-3}{2x}$$
$$\frac{52}{2} = \frac{2x}{2}$$
$$x = 26$$

Justin's frog jumped 26 inches.

EXTENSION

Exercises

Write each phrase as an algebraic expression.

1. 9 times a number minus 4

2. 8 divided into a number plus 12

3. the product of 3 and a number increased by 2

Write each phrase as an algebraic equation.

4. 3 more than a number divided by 12 equals 40

5. a number minus 15 times 2 is equal to 10

6. a number less 8 divided by 4 is 24

Solve.

7. $3x + 8 = 29$ 8. $-2r + 14 = 10$ 9. $12a - 11 = 49$

10. $-9f - 15 = 93$ 11. $-8 = \frac{g}{7} + 2$ 12. $15 = -7 + \frac{b}{3}$

13. $10 = -8 + \frac{t}{4}$ 14. $\frac{q}{5} - 13 = 4$ 15. $-7 = 7x - 8$

16. During a 5-mile road race for charity, John completed the race in 55 minutes, which is 40 minutes longer than $\frac{1}{3}$ Theresa's race time. What was Theresa's race time?

Game Time

Math Magic

Guess what your friends are thinking with this math magic trick.

Copy the following number charts.

1	10	19
2, 2	11, 11	20, 20
4	13	22
5, 5	14, 14	23, 23
7	16	25
8, 8	17, 17	26, 26

3	12	21
4	13	22
5	14	23
6, 6	15, 15	24, 24
7, 7	16, 16	25, 25
8, 8	17, 17	26, 26

9	15	21, 21
10	16	22, 22
11	17	23, 23
12	18, 18	24, 24
13	19, 19	25, 25
14	20, 20	26, 26

Step 1: Ask a friend to think of a number from 1 to 26.
Example: Your friend thinks of 26.

Step 2: Show your friend the first chart and ask how many times the chosen number appears. Remember the answer.
Your friend says the chosen number appears twice on the first chart.

2

Step 3: Show the second chart and ask the same question. Multiply the answer by 3. Add your result to the answer from step 2. Remember this answer.
Your friend says the chosen number appears twice.
The answer from step 2 is 2.

$3 \cdot 2 = 6$
$6 + 2 = 8$

Step 4: Show the third chart and ask the same question. Multiply the answer by 9. Add your result to the answer from step 3. The answer is your friend's number.
Your friend says the chosen number appears twice.
The answer from step 3 is 8.

$9 \cdot 2 = 18$
$18 + 8 = 26$

↑
Your friend's number

How does it work?

Your friend's number will be the following:

(answer from step 2) + (3 · answer from step 3) + (9 · answer from step 4)

This is an expression with three variables: $a + 3b + 9c$. A number will be on a particular chart 0, 1, or 2 times, so a, b, and c will always be 0, 1, or 2. With these values, you can write expressions for each number from 1 to 26.

a	b	c	$a + 3b + 9c$
1	0	0	$1 + 3(0) + 9(0) = 1$
2	0	0	$2 + 3(0) + 9(0) = 2$
0	1	0	$0 + 3(1) + 9(0) = 3$

Can you complete the table for 4–26?

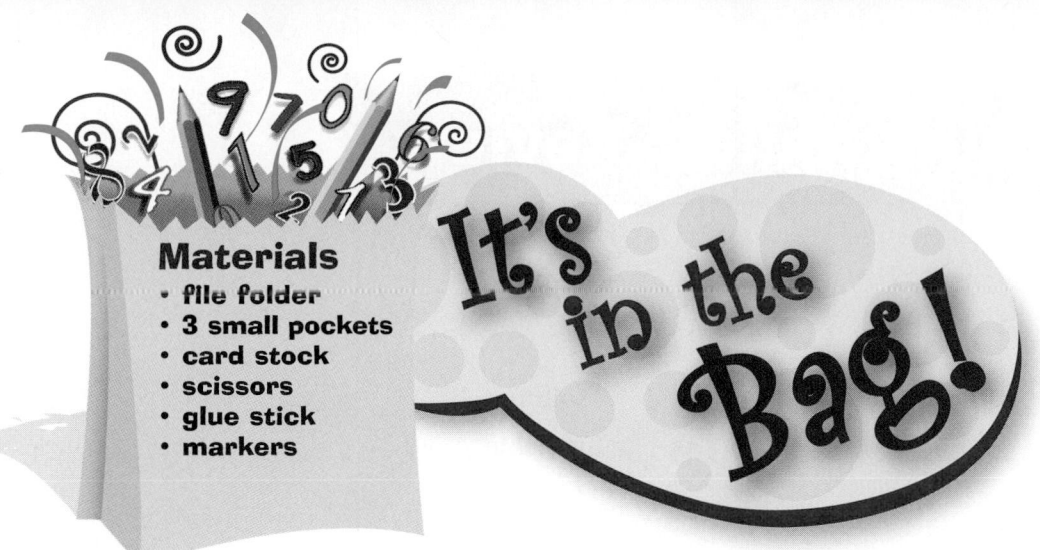

Materials

- file folder
- 3 small pockets
- card stock
- scissors
- glue stick
- markers

PROJECT **Tri-Sided Equations**

Use a colorful file folder to prepare a three-sided review of algebra!

Directions

1 Close the file folder. Fold one side down to the folded edge. Turn the folder over and fold the other side down to the folded edge. **Figure A**

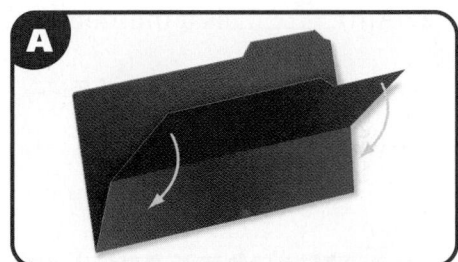

2 Open the folder. It will be divided into four sections. On the top section, cut off $\frac{1}{4}$ inch from each edge. On the bottom section, make a 1 inch diagonal slit in the top left corner and in the top right corner. **Figure B**

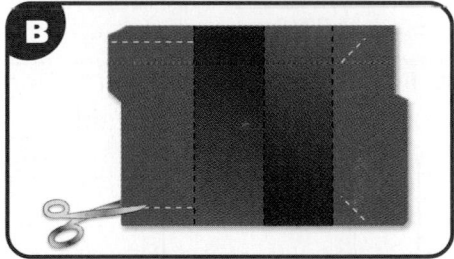

3 Fold the folder so that the corners of the smaller top section fit into the slits. This will create your three-sided holder for notes. **Figure C**

4 Write the definition of an equation on one side of your note holder. Write the order of operations on another side. Write examples of expressions on the third side.

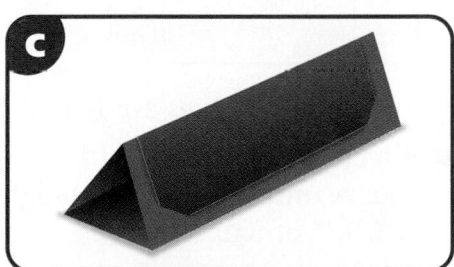

Taking Note of the Math

Glue a small pocket made from construction paper or card stock onto each side of your note holder. On rectangular slips of card stock, write problems that demonstrate your knowledge of equations, order of operations, and expressions. Store the note cards in the appropriate pockets.

Vocabulary

algebraic expression 54

constant 54

equation 70

solution 70

variable 54

Complete the sentences below with vocabulary words from the list above.

1. A(n) __?__ contains one or more variables.

2. A(n) __?__ is a mathematical statement that says two quantities are equal.

3. In the equation $12 + t = 22$, t is a __?__.

4. A(n) __?__ is a quantity that does not change.

2-1 Variables and Expressions (pp. 54–57)

 5.A.3, 6.A.2

EXAMPLE

■ Evaluate the expression to find the missing values in the table.

n	$3n + 4$	
1	7	$n = 1$; $3 \times 1 + 4 = 7$
2	▮	$n = 2$; $3 \times 2 + 4 = 10$
3	▮	$n = 3$; $3 \times 3 + 4 = 13$

The missing values are 10 and 13.

■ A rectangle is 3 units wide. How many square units does the rectangle cover if it is 5, 6, 7, or 8 units long?

ℓ	w	$\ell \times w$	
5	3	15	$5 \times 3 = 15$ square units
6	3	▮	$6 \times 3 = 18$ square units
7	3	▮	$7 \times 3 = 21$ square units
8	3	▮	$8 \times 3 = 24$ square units

The rectangle will cover a total of 15, 18, 21, or 24 square units.

EXERCISES

Evaluate each expression to find the missing values in the tables.

5.

y	$y \div 7$
56	8
49	▮
42	▮

6.

k	$k \times 4 - 6$
2	2
3	▮
4	▮

7. A rectangle is 9 units long. How many square units does the rectangle cover if it is 1, 2, 3, or 4 units wide?

8. Karen buys 3 bouquets of flowers. How many flowers does she buy if each bouquet contains 10, 11, 12, or 13 flowers?

9. Ron buys 5 bags of marbles. How many marbles does he buy if each bag contains 15, 16, 17, or 18 marbles?

2-2 Translate Between Words and Math (pp. 58–61)

 5.A.2

EXAMPLE

Write each phrase as a numerical or algebraic expression.

- 617 minus 191
  617 − 191
- d multiplied by 5
  $5d$ or $5 \cdot d$ or $(5)(d)$

Write two phrases for each expression.

- $a \div 5$
  - a divided by 5
  - the quotient of a and 5
- 67 + 19
  - the sum of 67 and 19
  - 19 more than 67

EXERCISES

Write each phrase as a numerical or algebraic expression.

10. 15 plus b
11. the product of 6 and 5
12. 9 times t
13. the quotient of g and 9

Write two phrases for each expression.

14. $4z$
15. $15 + x$
16. $54 \div 6$
17. $\frac{m}{20}$
18. $3 - y$
19. $5{,}100 + 64$
20. $y - 3$
21. $g - 20$

2-3 Translating Between Tables and Expressions (pp. 62–65)

 6.PS.7

EXAMPLE

- Write an expression for the sequence in the table.

Position	1	2	3	4	n
Value of Term	9	18	27	36	■

To go from the position to the value of the term, multiply the position by 9. The expression is $9n$.

EXERCISES

Write an expression for the sequence in each table.

22.

Position	1	2	3	4	n
Value of Term	4	7	10	13	■

23.

Position	1	2	3	4	n
Value of Term	0	1	2	3	■

2-4 Equations and Their Solutions (pp. 70–73)

 5.A.3, 6.A.2

EXAMPLE

- Determine whether the given value of the variable is a solution.

  $f + 14 = 50$ for $f = 34$
  $34 + 14 \overset{?}{=} 50$ *Substitute 34 for f.*
  $48 \neq 50$ *Add.*
  34 is not a solution.

EXERCISES

Determine whether the given value of each variable is a solution.

24. $28 + n = 39$ for $n = 11$
25. $12t = 74$ for $t = 6$
26. $y - 53 = 27$ for $y = 80$
27. $96 \div w = 32$ for $w = 3$

2-5 Addition Equations (pp. 74–77)

 5.A.4, 5.A.5

EXAMPLE

■ Solve the equation $x + 18 = 31$.

$$\begin{array}{rl} x + 18 = & 31 \\ -18 & -18 \\ \hline x \quad = & 13 \end{array}$$

18 is added to x.
Subtract 18 from both sides to undo the addition.

EXERCISES

Solve each equation.

28. $4 + x = 10$ **29.** $n + 10 = 24$
30. $c + 71 = 100$ **31.** $y + 16 = 22$
32. $44 = p + 17$ **33.** $94 + w = 103$
34. $23 + b = 34$ **35.** $56 = n + 12$
36. $39 = 23 + p$ **37.** $d + 28 = 85$

2-6 Subtraction Equations (pp. 78–80)

 5.A.4, 5.A.5

EXAMPLE

■ Solve the equation $c - 7 = 16$.

$$\begin{array}{rl} c - 7 = & 16 \\ +7 & +7 \\ \hline c \quad = & 23 \end{array}$$

7 is subtracted from c.
Add 7 to each side to undo the subtraction.

EXERCISES

Solve each equation.

38. $28 = k - 17$ **39.** $d - 8 = 1$
40. $p - 55 = 8$ **41.** $n - 31 = 36$
42. $3 = r - 11$ **43.** $97 = w - 47$
44. $12 = h - 48$ **45.** $9 = p - 158$

2-7 Multiplication Equations (pp. 81–84)

 5.A.4, 5.A.5

EXAMPLE

■ Solve the equation $6x = 36$.

$$6x = 36$$
$$\frac{6x}{6} = \frac{36}{6}$$
$$x = 6$$

x is multiplied by 6.
Divide both sides by 6 to undo the multiplication.

EXERCISES

Solve each equation.

46. $5v = 40$ **47.** $27 = 3y$
48. $12c = 84$ **49.** $18n = 36$
50. $72 = 9s$ **51.** $11t = 110$
52. $7a = 56$ **53.** $8y = 64$

2-8 Division Equations (pp. 85–87)

5.A.4, 5.A.5

EXAMPLE

■ Solve the equation $\frac{k}{4} = 8$.

$$\frac{k}{4} = 8$$
$$4 \cdot \frac{k}{4} = 4 \cdot 8$$
$$k = 32$$

k is divided by 4.
Multiply both sides by 4 to undo the division.

EXERCISES

Solve each equation.

54. $\frac{r}{7} = 6$ **55.** $\frac{t}{5} = 3$
56. $6 = \frac{y}{3}$ **57.** $12 = \frac{n}{6}$
58. $\frac{z}{13} = 4$ **59.** $20 = \frac{b}{5}$
60. $\frac{n}{11} = 7$ **61.** $10 = \frac{p}{9}$

Evaluate each expression to find the missing values in the tables.

1.

a	$a + 18$
10	28
12	▨
14	▨

2.

y	$y \div 6$
18	3
30	▨
42	▨

3.

n	$n \div 5 + 7$
10	9
20	▨
30	▨

4. A van can seat 6 people. How many people can ride in 3, 4, 5, and 6 vans?

5. A rectangle is 5 units wide. How many square units does the rectangle cover if it is 10, 11, 12, or 13 units long?

Write an expression for the missing value in each table.

6.

Packages	Rolls
1	8
2	16
3	24
4	32
p	▨

7.

Students	Groups
5	1
10	2
15	3
20	4
s	▨

Write an expression for the sequence in the table.

8.

Position	1	2	3	4	5	n
Value of Term	4	7	10	13	16	▨

9. There are more reptile species than amphibian species. There are 3,100 living species of amphibians. Write an expression to show how many more reptile species there are than amphibian species.

Write each phrase as a numerical or algebraic expression.

10. 26 more than n **11.** g multiplied by 4   **12.** the quotient of 180 and 15

Write two phrases for each expression.

13. $(14)(16)$ **14.** $n \div 8$ **15.** $p + 11$ **16.** $s - 6$

Determine whether the given value of the variable is a solution.

17. $5d = 70$ for $d = 12$ **18.** $29 = 76 - n$ for $n = 46$

19. $108 \div a = 12$ for $a = 9$ **20.** $15 + m = 27$ for $m = 12$

Solve each equation.

21. $a + 7 = 25$ **22.** $121 = 11d$ **23.** $3 = t - 8$ **24.** $6 = \frac{k}{9}$

25. Air typically has about 4,000 bacteria per cubic meter. If your room is 30 cubic meters, about how many bacteria would there be in the air in your room?

Chapter Test

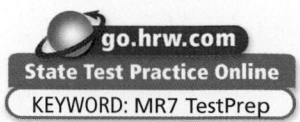
CUMULATIVE ASSESSMENT, CHAPTERS 1–2

Multiple Choice

1. Which is an algebraic expression for the product of 15 and x?

    (A) $15 - x$ (C) $x + 15$

    (B) $15x$ (D) $15 \div x$

2. Max earned $560 working as a landscaper. If he worked a total of 80 hours, which expression can be used to find how much he earned each hour?

    (F) $560 - 80$ (H) $560 + 80$

    (G) $560 \div 80$ (J) $560 \cdot 80$

3. Find the expression for the table.

x	▩
3	9
8	19
11	25
15	33

    (A) $3x$ (C) $2x + 3$

    (B) $x + 18$ (D) $3x - 5$

4. A rectangular classroom has an area of 252 square feet. The width of the classroom is 14 feet. What is its length?

    (F) 14 feet   (H) 18 feet

    (G) 16 feet   (J) 20 feet

5. What is the difference between 82,714 and 54,221 rounded to the nearest hundred?

    (A) 28,500   (C) 26,900

    (B) 27,700   (D) 26,000

6. What is the value of 8^3?

    (F) 11   (H) 192

    (G) 24   (J) 512

7. Zane biked 23 miles this week. This is 8 miles more than he biked the week before. Solve the equation $x + 8 = 23$ to find how many miles Zane biked last week.

    (A) 15 miles   (C) 31 miles

    (B) 23 miles   (D) 33 miles

8. Which team sold the most fund-raising products?

Fund-raising Results by Team	
Team	**Products Sold**
Golf	6,536
Soccer	6,421
Swim	6,879
Track	6,019

    (F) Soccer team   (H) Swim team

    (G) Golf team   (J) Track team

9. Which equation is an example of the Associative Property?

    (A) $3 + (4 + 6) = (3 + 4) + 6$

    (B) $(42 + 6) + 18 = (42 + 18) + 6$

    (C) $(3 \times 20) + (3 \times 4) = 3 \times 24$

    (D) $8(2 \times 6) = (8 \times 2) + (8 \times 6)$

New York Test Prep

10. Nicole is 15 years old. She is 3 years younger than her sister Jan. Solve the equation $j - 3 = 15$ to find Jan's age.

F 18 years   H 12 years

G 17 years   J 5 years

11. Ling created an arithmetic sequence that starts with 5 and then adds 8. Find the 6th term in this sequence.

A 30   C 40

B 38   D 45

 *Hot Tip* When you read a word problem, underline the information you need to help you answer the question.

12. What is the value of $5^2 - (18 \div 6) \times 7$?

F 4   H 31

G 46   J 154

13. Scott spends 16 minutes in the pool treading water during swim practice. This is $\frac{1}{3}$ of his training time. How many total minutes is Scott's swim practice?

A 8   C 16

B 32   D 48

14. A case of pencils costs $15. The academic team spends $135 on pencils for the school tournament. How many cases of pencils did the academic team buy?

F 7   H 9

G 8   J 10

15. What value of x will make the expressions $2x + 4$ and $5x - 8$ equal 12?

A 2   C 4

B 6   D 8

Short Response

16. Every week Brandi runs 7 more miles than her sister Jamie.

  a. Write an expression for the number of miles that Brandi runs each week. Identify the variable.

  b. Evaluate your expression to find the number of miles Brandi runs when Jamie runs 5 miles.

17. A vacation tour costs $450. Additional outings cost $25 each. The table shows the total cost to go on additional outings.

Outings	1	2	3	n
Total Cost ($)	475	500	525	

Write an expression for the cost of n outings. Use the expression to find how much it costs to go on 5 outings.

Extended Response

18. Chrissy and Kathie are sisters. Chrissy was born on Kathie's birthday and is exactly 8 years younger. Chrissy celebrated her 16th birthday on December 8, 2005.

  a. Complete the table to show the ages of the sisters in the years 2005, 2008, and 2011.

Year	Kathie's Age	Chrissy's Age
2005		
2008		
2011		

  b. Write an equation that could be used to find Chrissy's age in 2011. Identify the variable in the equation.

  c. Solve the equation. Show your work. Compare your answer to the value in the table. Are the two solutions the same? Explain your answer.

 **Problem Solving on Location**

PENNSYLVANIA

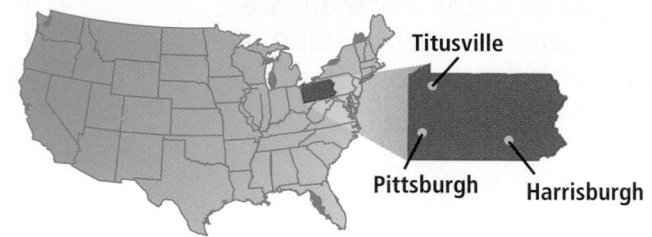

Titusville

Pittsburgh   Harrisburg

⭐ The First Superhighway

The Pennsylvania Turnpike was the first highway designed for modern long-distance travel. Completed in 1940, the turnpike crossed the Allegheny Mountains between Harrisburg and Pittsburgh. It shortened travel time between these cities by 3 hours.

Choose one or more strategies to solve each problem.

1. In its first 4 days, 24,000 vehicles traveled on the turnpike. After 7 days, 42,000 vehicles had used the turnpike. If this trend continued, how many vehicles would have used the turnpike in the first 18 days?

2. It took $5\frac{1}{2}$ hours to drive the old route from Harrisburg to Pittsburgh. A driver wants to make the trip on the turnpike and arrive in Pittsburgh at 4:00 P.M. At what time should she leave Harrisburg if she wants to take a 15-minute break during the trip?

For 3, use the map.

3. Valley Forge is 24 miles from Philadelphia. The distance from Blue Mountain to Valley Forge is 100 miles more than the distance from Valley Forge to Philadelphia. How far is it from Pittsburgh to Philadelphia?

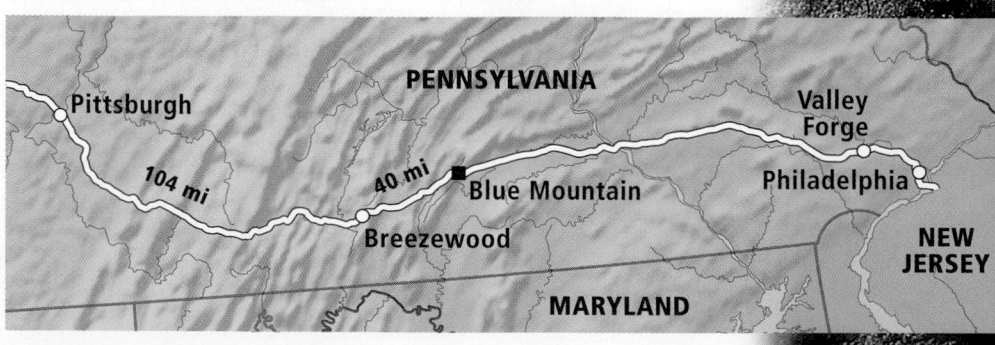

PENNSYLVANIA

Pittsburgh

104 mi   40 mi
Blue Mountain

Valley Forge

Philadelphia

Breezewood

NEW JERSEY

MARYLAND

⭐ The First Oil Well

In 1859, Edwin L. Drake drilled the world's first oil well, beside Oil Creek near Titusville, Pennsylvania.

Before Drake drilled his well, people collected small amounts of oil that seeped from the ground near Oil Creek. Drake's well produced about 210 times as much oil each day as could be collected aboveground.

Problem Solving Strategies
Draw a Diagram
Make a Model
Guess and Test
Work Backward
Find a Pattern
Make a Table
Solve a Simpler Problem
Use Logical Reasoning
Act It Out
Make an Organized List

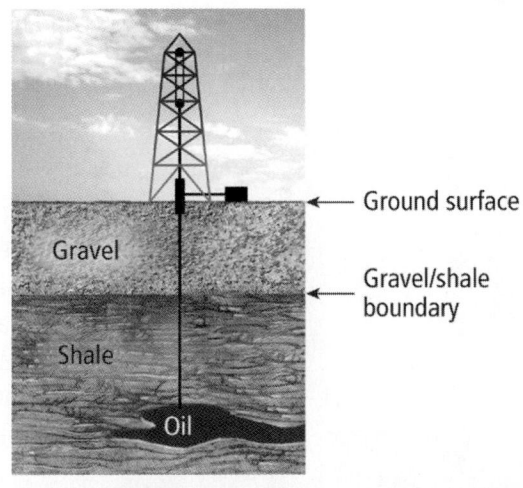

Ground surface

Gravel/shale boundary

Gravel

Shale

Oil

Choose one or more strategies to solve each problem.

1. The success of Drake's well attracted people to the area. In Drake's day, the town of Titusville had about 10,000 people. There were 2,000 more permanent residents than temporary residents. How many temporary residents were there?

2. The surface of the ground at Drake's well is 1,200 ft above sea level. To reach oil, Drake first drilled through gravel to a point 1,168 ft above sea level. He then drilled an additional 38 ft through shale. What was the total depth of the well?

3. About 5 gallons of oil could be collected aboveground each day. Given that there are 42 gallons in one barrel, find the daily production in barrels of Drake's well.

4. In 3 days, Drake's well produced oil worth $1,500. What was the value of the oil produced in one week?

Decimals

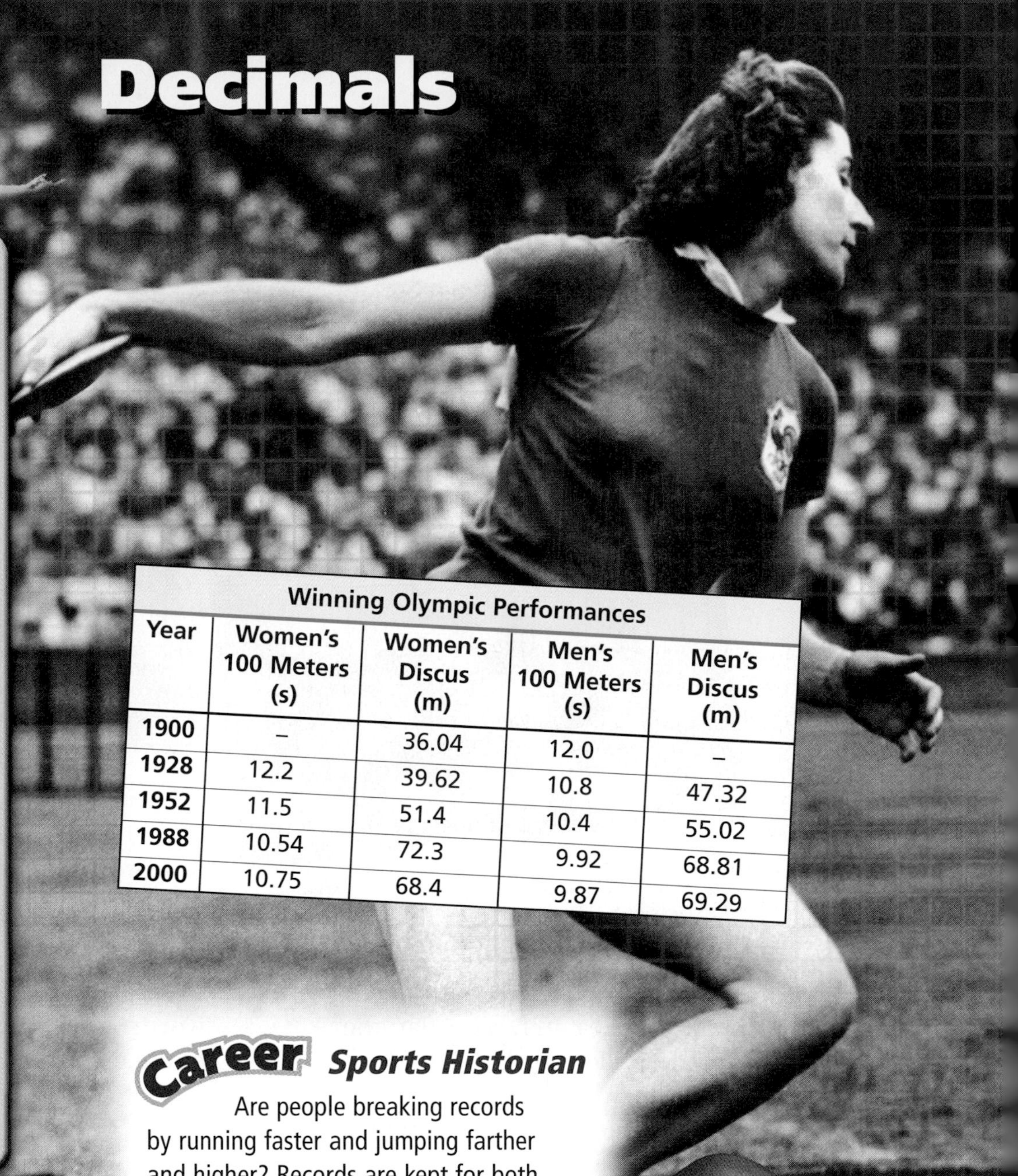

NEW YORK TEST PREP

go.hrw.com
Chapter Project Online
KEYWORD: MR7 Ch3

Winning Olympic Performances				
Year	Women's 100 Meters (s)	Women's Discus (m)	Men's 100 Meters (s)	Men's Discus (m)
1900	–	36.04	12.0	–
1928	12.2	39.62	10.8	47.32
1952	11.5	51.4	10.4	55.02
1988	10.54	72.3	9.92	68.81
2000	10.75	68.4	9.87	69.29

Career Sports Historian

Are people breaking records by running faster and jumping farther and higher? Records are kept for both professional and amateur sports. Many schools keep records of their individual athletes' and teams' performances. Keeping track of sports records is the job of sports historians. One of the most complete records is that of the Olympic games. The table shows the changes in the last century of the winning performances in some men's and women's Olympic sports.

ARE YOU READY?

✓ Vocabulary

Choose the best term from the list to complete each sentence.

1. The first place value to the left of the decimal point is the ___?___ place, and the place value two places to the left of the decimal point is the ___?___ place.

2. In the expression $72 \div 9$, 72 is the ___?___, and 9 is the ___?___.

3. The answer to a subtraction expression is the ___?___.

4. A(n) ___?___ is a mathematical statement that says two quantities are equivalent.

difference

dividend

divisor

equation

ones

quotient

tens

Complete these exercises to review skills you will need for this chapter.

✓ Place Value of Whole Numbers

Identify the place value of each underlined digit.

5. 1<u>5</u>2
6. <u>7</u>,903
7. <u>1</u>45,072

8. 4,8<u>9</u>3,025
9. 13<u>,</u>796,020
10. 1<u>4</u>5,683,032

✓ Add and Subtract Whole Numbers

Find each sum or difference.

11. $425 − $75
12. 532 + 145
13. 160 − 82

✓ Multiply and Divide Whole Numbers

Find each product or quotient.

14. $320 × 5
15. 125 ÷ 5
16. 54 × 3

✓ Exponents

Find each value.

17. 10^3
18. 3^6
19. 10^5

20. 4^5
21. 8^3
22. 2^7

✓ Solve Whole Number Equations

Solve each equation.

23. $y + 382 = 743$
24. $n − 150 = 322$
25. $9x = 108$

Study Guide: Preview

Where You've Been

Previously, you

- compared and ordered whole numbers.

- wrote large whole numbers in standard form.

- rounded numbers to a given place value.

- used addition, subtraction, multiplication, and division of whole numbers to solve problems.

In This Chapter

You will study

- reading, writing, comparing, and ordering decimals.

- writing large whole numbers in scientific notation.

- using rounding to estimate answers to problems that involve decimals.

- solving decimal equations.

Where You're Going

You can use the skills learned in this chapter

- to solve two-step decimal equations in higher-level math classes, such as Algebra 1.

- to solve problems using scientific notation in science classes, such as Astronomy.

Key Vocabulary/Vocabulario

clustering	aproximación
front-end estimation	estimación por partes
scientific notation	notación científica

Vocabulary Connections

To become familiar with some of the vocabulary terms in the chapter, consider the following. You may refer to the chapter, the glossary, or a dictionary if you like.

1. When you estimate, you approximate the value of something. What part of a decimal do you think you are using to approximate a value when you use **front-end estimation**?

2. *Notation* is a way of expressing something. In what other classes do you think you will use **scientific notation**?

3. A *cluster* is a close grouping of similar items. When do you think **clustering** might be a good method of estimation?

Reading and Writing Math

Writing Strategy: Keep a Math Journal

You can help improve your writing and reasoning skills by keeping a math journal. When you express your thoughts on paper, you can make sense of confusing math concepts.

You can also record your thoughts about each lesson and reflect on what you learned in class. Your journal will become a personal math reference book from which to study.

Journal Entry:
Read the entry Jaime wrote in his math journal about translating between math and words.

> **Journal Entry 2**   October
>
> Today's lesson was on translating between words and math. I understand that a math expression like 18 x 2 can be written as "18 multiplied by 2." However, I am confused which symbol to use when translating from words to math. My teacher suggested that I make a list in this journal of common terms and their symbols.
>
> | Words | Symbols |
> |---|---|
> | sum, added, plus | + |
> | difference, less than | − |
> | product, times | x or • |
> | divide, quotient | ÷ |
>
> Now I understand!
> This list will help me when I need to know which symbol goes with which word.

Try This

Begin a math journal. Make an entry every day for one week. Use the following ideas to start your journal entries. Be sure to date each entry.

- What I already know about this lesson is . . .
- The skills I used to complete this lesson were . . .
- What problems did I have? How did I deal with these problems?
- What I liked/did not like about this lesson . . .

Model Decimals

Use with Lesson 3-1

go.hrw.com
Lab Resources Online
KEYWORD: MR7 Lab3

NY Performance Indicators

6.R.1, 6.R.5, 6.R.6

KEY

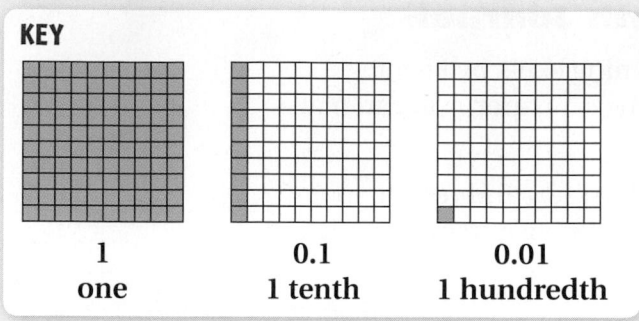

| 1 | 0.1 | 0.01 |
| one | 1 tenth | 1 hundredth |

You can use decimal grids to model decimals. The grid is divided into 100 small squares. One square represents 1 hundredth, or 0.01. Ten squares form a column, which represents 1 tenth, or 0.1. Ten columns make up the grid, which represents one whole, or 1. By shading hundredths, tenths, or whole grids, you can model decimal numbers.

Activity 1

Write the decimal that is represented by each model.

a.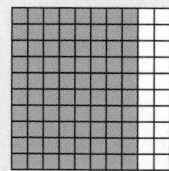

24 hundredths squares are shaded.

So the model represents 0.24.

b.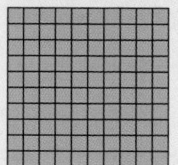

1 whole grid and 8 columns are shaded.

So the model represents 1.8.

c.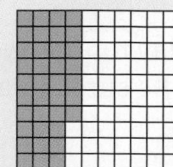

2 whole grids and 37 hundredths are shaded.

So the model represents 2.37.

1. Explain how a decimal grid can show that 0.30 = 0.3.

Try This

Write the decimal that is represented by each model.

1. 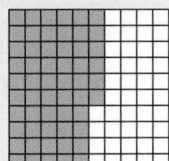   **2.** 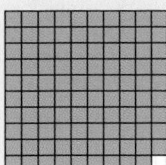   **3.**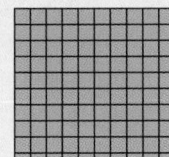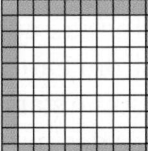

Activity 2

Use a decimal grid to model each decimal.

a. 0.42

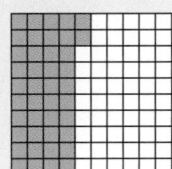   *Shade 42 hundredths squares.*

b. 1.88

 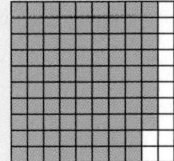   *Shade 1 whole grid, 8 columns, and 8 small squares.*

c. 2.75

  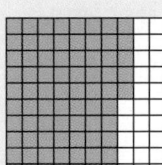   *Shade 2 whole grids, 7 columns, and 5 small squares.*

Think and Discuss

1. Explain how to model 0.46 by shading only 10 sections on the grid.
(Hint: A section is a grid, column, or small square.)

Try This

Use a decimal grid to model each decimal.

1. 1.02   **2.** 0.04   **3.** 0.4   **4.** 2.14   **5.** 0.53

3-1 Representing, Comparing, and Ordering Decimals

The smaller the apparent magnitude of a star, the brighter the star appears when viewed from Earth. The magnitudes of some stars are listed in the table as decimal numbers.

Decimal numbers represent combinations of whole numbers and numbers between whole numbers.

Apparent Magnitudes of Stars	
Star	**Magnitude**
Procyon	0.38
Proxima Centauri	11.0
Wolf 359	13.5
Vega	0.03

Place value can help you understand and write and compare decimal numbers.

Place Value

Hundreds	Tens	Ones	Tenths	Hundredths	Thousandths	Ten-Thousandths	Hundred-Thousandths
2	3 • 0	0	5	0	3		

EXAMPLE 1 Reading and Writing Decimals

Write each decimal in standard form, expanded form, and words.

A 1.05

Expanded form: 1 + 0.05
Word form: one *and* five hundredths

B 0.05 + 0.001 + 0.0007

Standard form: 0.0517
Word form: five hundred seventeen ten-thousandths

C sixteen and nine hundredths

Standard form: 16.09
Expanded form: 10 + 6 + 0.09

You can use place value to compare decimal numbers.

EXAMPLE 2 **Earth Science Application**

Rigel and Betelgeuse are two stars in the constellation Orion. The apparent magnitude of Rigel is 0.12. The apparent magnitude of Betelgeuse is 0.50. Which star has the smaller magnitude? Which star appears brighter?

Betelgeuse
Rigel

0.⬚1⬚2   *Line up the decimal points. Start from the left and compare the digits.*

0.⬚5⬚0   *Look for the first place where the digits are different.*

1 is less than 5.
0.12 < 0.50

Rigel has a smaller apparent magnitude than Betelgeuse.
The star with the smaller magnitude appears brighter. When seen from Earth, Rigel appears brighter than Betelgeuse.

EXAMPLE 3 **Comparing and Ordering Decimals**

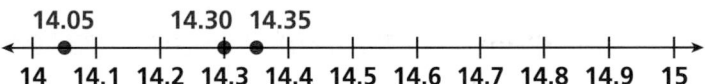

Order the decimals from least to greatest.
14.35, 14.3, 14.05

Helpful Hint

Writing zeros at the end of a decimal does not change the value of the decimal.

0.3 = 0.30 = 0.300

14.35 14.30	14.30 < 14.35	*Compare two of the numbers at a time. Write 14.3 as "14.30."*
14.35 14.05	14.05 < 14.35	*Start at the left and compare the digits.*
14.30 14.05	14.05 < 14.30	*Look for the first place where the digits are different.*

Graph the numbers on a number line.

14.05   14.30 14.35

14 14.1 14.2 14.3 14.4 14.5 14.6 14.7 14.8 14.9 15

The numbers are ordered when you read the number line from left to right. The numbers in order from least to greatest are 14.05, 14.3, and 14.35.

6.RP.6

Think and Discuss

1. Explain why 0.5 is greater than 0.29 even though 29 is greater than 5.

2. Name the decimal with the least value: 0.29, 2.09, 2.009, 0.029

3. Name three numbers between 1.5 and 1.6.

3-1 Representing, Comparing, and Ordering Decimals **109**

go.hrw.com
Homework Help Online
KEYWORD: MR7 3-1
Parent Resources Online
KEYWORD: MR7 Parent

GUIDED PRACTICE

See Example ① **Write each decimal in standard form, expanded form, and words.**

1. 1.98

2. ten and forty-one thousandths

3. 0.07 + 0.006 + 0.0005

4. 0.0472

See Example ② **5. Physical Science** Osmium and iridium are precious metals. The density of osmium is 22.58 g/cm³, and the density of iridium is 22.56 g/cm³. Which metal is denser?

See Example ③ **Order the decimals from least to greatest.**

6. 9.5, 9.35, 9.65

7. 4.18, 4.1, 4.09

8. 12.39, 12.09, 12.92

INDEPENDENT PRACTICE

See Example ① **Write each decimal in standard form, expanded form, and words.**

9. 7.0893

10. 12 + 0.2 + 0.005

11. seven and fifteen hundredths

12. 3 + 0.1 + 0.006

See Example ② **13. Astronomy** Two meteorites landed in Mexico. The one found in Bacuberito weighed 24.3 tons, and the one found in Chupaderos weighed 26.7 tons. Which meteorite weighed more?

See Example ③ **Order the decimals from least to greatest.**

14. 15.25, 15.2, 15.5

15. 1.56, 1.62, 1.5

16. 6.7, 6.07, 6.23

PRACTICE AND PROBLEM SOLVING

Extra Practice
See page 718.

Write each number in words.

17. 9.007

18. 5 + 0.08 + 0.004

19. 10.022

20. 4.28

21. 142.6541

22. 0.001 + 0.0007

23. 0.92755

24. 1.02

Compare. Write <, >, or =.

25. 8.04 ▮ 8.403

26. 0.907 ▮ 0.6801

27. 1.246 ▮ 1.29

28. one and fifty-two ten-thousandths ▮ 1.0052

29. ten and one hundredth ▮ 10.100

Write the value of the red digit in each number.

30. 3.026

31. 17.53703

32. 0.000598

33. 425.1055

Order the numbers from greatest to least.

34. 32.525, 32.5254, 31.6257

35. 0.34, 1.43, 4.034, 1.043, 1.424

36. 1.01, 1.1001, 1.101, 1.0001

37. 652.12, 65.213, 65.135, 61.53

Proxima Centauri, the closest star to Earth other than the Sun, was discovered in 1913. It would take about 115,000 years for a spaceship traveling from Earth at 25,000 mi/h to reach Proxima Centauri.

Use the table for Exercises 38–44.

38. Order the stars Sirius, Luyten 726-8, and Lalande 21185 from closest to farthest from Earth.

39. Which star in the table is farthest from Earth?

40. How far in light-years is Ross 154 from Earth? Write the answer in words and expanded form.

41. List the stars that are less than 5 light-years from Earth.

42. **What's the Error?** A student wrote the distance of Proxima Centauri from Earth as "four hundred and twenty-two hundredths." Explain the error. Write the correct answer.

43. **Write About It** Which star is closer to Earth, Alpha Centauri or Proxima Centauri? Explain how you can compare the distances of these stars. Then answer the question.

Distance of Stars from Earth	
Star	**Distance (light-years)**
Alpha Centauri	4.35
Barnard's Star	5.98
Lalande 21185	8.22
Luyten 726-8	8.43
Proxima Centauri	4.22
Ross 154	9.45
Sirius	8.65

44. **Challenge** Wolf 359 is located 7.75 light-years from Earth. If the stars in the table were listed in order from closest to farthest from Earth, between which two stars would Wolf 359 be located?

Test Prep and Spiral Review

45. Multiple Choice What is the standard form of "five and three hundred twenty-one hundred-thousandths"?

　Ⓐ 5.321　　　　Ⓑ 5.0321　　　　Ⓒ 5.00321　　　　Ⓓ 5.000321

46. Gridded Response Write $30 + 2 + 0.8 + 0.009$ in standard form.

Estimate each sum or difference by rounding to the place value indicated. (Lesson 1-2)

47. $6,832 + 2,078$; thousands　　　　**48.** $52,854 - 25,318$; ten thousands

Solve each equation. (Lesson 2-6)

49. $n - 52 = 71$　　　　**50.** $30 = k - 15$　　　　**51.** $c - 22 = 30$

3-2 Estimating Decimals

Learn to estimate decimal sums, differences, products, and quotients.

Vocabulary

clustering

front-end estimation

NY Performance Indicators

6.CN.7 Apply mathematics to problem situations that develop outside of mathematics.

Beth's health class is learning about fitness and nutrition. The table shows the approximate number of calories burned by someone who weighs 90 pounds.

Activity (45 min)	Calories Burned (App.)
Cycling	198.45
Playing ice hockey	210.6
Rowing	324
Water skiing	194.4

When numbers are about the same value, you can use *clustering* to estimate. **Clustering** means rounding the numbers to the same value.

EXAMPLE **Health Application**

Beth wants to cycle, play ice hockey, and water ski. If Beth weighs 90 pounds and spends 45 minutes doing each activity, *about* how many calories will she burn in all?

198.45 →	200	*The addends cluster around 200.*
210.6 →	200	*To estimate the total number of calories,*
+ 194.4 →	+ 200	*round each addend to 200.*
	600	*Add.*

Beth burns about 600 calories.

EXAMPLE **Rounding Decimals to Estimate Sums and Differences**

Estimate by rounding to the indicated place value.

A 3.92 + 6.48; ones

3.92 + 6.48   *Round to the nearest whole number.*

4 + 6 = 10   *The sum is about 10.*

B 8.6355 − 5.039; hundredths

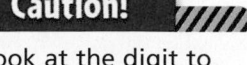
Caution!

Look at the digit to the right of the place to which you are rounding.
- If it is *5 or greater*, round *up*.
- If it is *less than 5*, round *down*.

8.6355	8.64	*Round to the hundredths.*
− 5.039	− 5.04	*Align the decimals.*
	3.60	*Subtract.*

EXAMPLE 3 Using Compatible Numbers to Estimate Products and Quotients

Estimate each product or quotient.

A 26.76×2.93

$25 \times 3 = 75$ *25 and 3 are compatible.*

So 26.76×2.93 is about 75.

B $42.64 \div 16.51$

$45 \div 15 = 3$ *45 and 15 are compatible.*

So $42.64 \div 16.51$ is about 3.

You can also use *front-end estimation* to estimate with decimals. **Front-end estimation** means to use only the whole-number part of the decimal.

EXAMPLE 4 Using Front-End Estimation

Estimate a range for the sum.

$9.99 + 22.89 + 8.3$

Use front-end estimation.

9.99	→	9
22.89	→	22
+ 8.30	→	+ 8
	at least	39

Add the whole numbers only.
The whole-number values of the decimals are less than the actual numbers, so the answer is an underestimate.

The exact answer of $9.99 + 22.89 + 8.3$ is greater than 39.

You can estimate a range for the sum by adjusting the decimal part of the numbers. Round the decimals to 0.5 or 1.

0.99	→	1.00
0.89	→	1.00
+ 0.30	→	+ 0.50
		2.50

$39.00 + 2.50 = 41.50$

Add the adjusted decimal part of the numbers. Add the whole-number estimate and this sum.
The adjusted decimals are greater than the actual decimals, so 41.50 is an overestimate.

The estimated range for the sum is between 39.00 and 41.50.

Think and Discuss  6.RP.5, 6.CN.3

1. **Tell** what number the following decimals cluster around: 34.5, 36.78, and 35.234.

2. **Determine** whether a front-end estimation without adjustment is always an overestimation or an underestimation.

go.hrw.com
Homework Help Online
KEYWORD: MR7 3-2
Parent Resources Online
KEYWORD: MR7 Parent

GUIDED PRACTICE

See Example 1
1. Elba runs every Monday, Wednesday, and Friday. Last week she ran 3.62 miles on Monday, 3.8 miles on Wednesday, and 4.3 miles on Friday. About how many miles did she run last week?

See Example 2 **Estimate by rounding to the indicated place value.**

2. $2.746 - 0.866$; tenths

3. $6.735 + 4.9528$; ones

4. $10.8071 + 5.392$; hundredths

5. $5.9821 - 0.48329$; ten-thousandths

See Example 3 **Estimate each product or quotient.**

6. $38.92 \div 4.06$

7. 14.51×7.89

8. $22.47 \div 3.22$

See Example 4 **Estimate a range for each sum.**

9. $7.8 + 31.39 + 6.95$

10. $14.27 + 5.4 + 21.86$

INDEPENDENT PRACTICE

See Example 1
11. **Multi-Step** Before Mike's trip, the odometer in his car read 146.8 miles. He drove 167.5 miles to a friend's house and 153.9 miles to the beach. About how many miles did the odometer read when he arrived at the beach?

12. The rainfall in July, August, and September was 16.76 cm, 13.97 cm, and 15.24 cm, respectively. About how many total centimeters of rain fell during those three months?

See Example 2 **Estimate by rounding to the indicated place value.**

13. $2.0993 + 1.256$; tenths

14. $7.504 - 2.3792$; hundredths

15. $0.6271 + 4.53027$; thousandths

16. $13.274 - 8.5590$; tenths

See Example 3 **Estimate each product or quotient.**

17. 9.64×1.769

18. $11.509 \div 4.258$

19. $19.03 \div 2.705$

See Example 4 **Estimate a range for each sum.**

20. $17.563 + 4.5 + 2.31$

21. $1.620 + 10.8 + 3.71$

PRACTICE AND PROBLEM SOLVING

Extra Practice
See page 718.

Estimate by rounding to the nearest whole number.

22. $8.456 + 7.903$

23. 12.43×3.72

24. $1,576.2 - 150.50$

25. Estimate the quotient of 67.55 and 3.83.

26. Estimate $84.85 divided by 17.

Use the table for Exercises 27–31.

Long-Distance Costs for Callers in the United States	
Country	Cost per Minute (¢)
Venezuela	22
Russia	9.9
Japan	7.9
United States	3.7

27. **Money** Round each cost in the table to the nearest cent. Write your answer using a dollar sign and decimal point.

28. About how much does it cost to phone someone in Russia and talk for 8 minutes?

29. About how much more does it cost to make a 12-minute call to Japan than to make an 18-minute call within the United States?

30. Will the cost of a 30-minute call to someone within the United States be greater or less than $1.20? Explain.

31. **Multi-Step** Kim is in New York. She calls her grandmother in Venezuela and speaks for 20 minutes, then calls a friend in Japan and talks for 15 minutes, and finally calls her mother in San Francisco and talks for 30 minutes. Estimate the total cost of all her calls.

32. **Health** The recommended daily allowance (RDA) for iron is 15 mg/day for teenage girls. Julie eats a hamburger that contains 3.88 mg of iron. About how many more milligrams of iron does she need to meet the RDA?

 33. **Write a Problem** Write a problem with three decimal numbers that have a total sum between 30 and 32.5.

 34. **Write About It** How do you adjust a front-end estimation? Why is this done?

 35. **Challenge** Place a decimal point in each number so that the sum of the numbers is between 124 and 127: 1059 + 725 + 815 + 1263.

Test Prep and Spiral Review

36. **Multiple Choice** Which is the estimated difference of $34.45 - 24.71$ by rounding to the nearest whole number?

   Ⓐ 11   Ⓑ 10   Ⓒ 9   Ⓓ 8

37. **Short Response** The average rainfall in Oklahoma City is 2.8 inches in April, 5.3 inches in May, and 4.3 inches in June. A weather forecaster predicts that the rainfall one year will double the average in April and May and half the average in June. Estimate the predicted rainfall each month to the nearest inch.

Solve each equation. (Lesson 2-5)

38. $83 + n = 157$ **39.** $x + 23 = 92$ **40.** $25 + c = 145$

Order the decimals from least to greatest. (Lesson 3-1)

41. 8.304, 8.009, 8.05   **42.** 5.62, 15.34, 1.589   **43.** 30.211, 30.709, 30.75

Explore Decimal Addition and Subtraction

Use with Lesson 3-3

go.hrw.com
Lab Resources Online
KEYWORD: MR7 Lab3

NY Performance Indicators
6.R.1, 6.R.5, 6.R.6

KEY

1	0.1	0.01
one	1 tenth	1 hundredth

You can model addition and subtraction of decimals with decimal grids.

Activity 1

Use decimal grids to find each sum.

a. 0.24 + 0.32

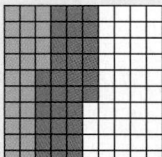

To represent 0.24, shade 24 squares.

To represent 0.32, shade 32 squares in another color.

There are 56 shaded squares representing 0.56.

0.24 + 0.32 = 0.56

b. 1.56 + 0.4

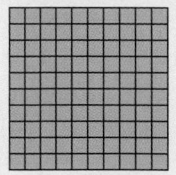 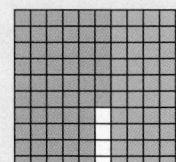

To represent 1.56, shade a whole grid and 56 squares of another.

To represent 0.4, shade 4 columns in another color.

One whole grid and 96 squares are shaded.

1.56 + 0.4 = 1.96

c. 0.75 + 0.68

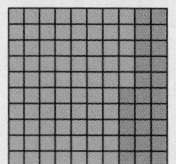 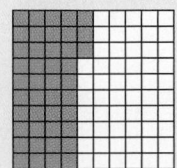

To represent 0.75, shade 75 squares.

To represent 0.68, shade 68 squares in another color. You will need to use another grid.

One whole grid and 43 squares are shaded.

0.75 + 0.68 = 1.43

Think and Discuss

1. How would you shade a decimal grid to represent 0.2 + 0.18?

Try This

Use decimal grids to find each sum.

1. 0.2 + 0.6   **2.** 1.07 + 0.03   **3.** 1.62 + 0.08

4. 0.45 + 0.29   **5.** 0.88 + 0.12   **6.** 1.29 + 0.67

7. 0.07 + 0.41   **8.** 0.51 + 0.51   **9.** 1.01 + 0.23

Activity 2

Use a decimal grid to find each difference.

a. 0.6 − 0.38

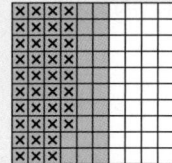

To represent 0.6, shade 6 columns.

Subtract 0.38 by removing 38 squares.

There are 22 remaining squares.

0.6 − 0.38 = 0.22

b. 1.22 − 0.41

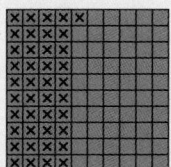 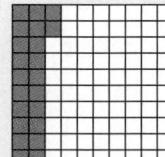

To represent 1.22, shade an entire decimal grid and 22 squares of another.

Subtract 0.41 by removing 41 squares.

There are 81 remaining squares.

1.22 − 0.41 = 0.81

Think and Discuss

1. How would you shade a decimal grid to represent 1.3 − 0.6?

Try This

Use decimal grids to find each difference.

1. 0.9 − 0.3   **2.** 1.2 − 0.98   **3.** 0.6 − 0.41

4. 1.6 − 0.07   **5.** 0.35 − 0.03   **6.** 2.12 − 0.23

7. 2.0 − 0.86   **8.** 0.78 − 0.76   **9.** 1.06 − 0.55

3-3 Adding and Subtracting Decimals

Learn to add and subtract decimals.

NY Performance Indicators

6.A.2 Use substitution to evaluate algebraic expressions. Also, 5.A.3.

At the 2004 U.S. Gymnastics Championships, Carly Patterson and Courtney Kupets tied for the All-Around title.

Carly Patterson's Preliminary Scores	
Event	**Points**
Floor exercise	9.7
Balance beam	9.7
Vault	9.3
Uneven bars	9.45

To find the total number of points, you can add all of the scores.

Carly Patterson also won a gold medal in the Women's Individual All-Around in the 2004 Olympic Games.

EXAMPLE 1 *Sports Application*

A **What was Carly Patterson's preliminary total score in the 2004 U.S. Championships?**

First estimate the sum of 9.7, 9.7, 9.3, and 9.45.

$$9.7 + 9.7 + 9.3 + 9.45$$

↓   ↓   ↓   ↓   *Estimate by rounding to the nearest whole number.*

$$10 + 10 + 9 + 9 = 38$$ *The total is about 38 points.*

Then add.

Helpful Hint

Estimating before you add or subtract will help you check whether your answer is reasonable.

9.70	*Align the decimal points.*
9.70	
9.30	*Use zeros as placeholders.*
+ 9.45	
38.15	*Add. Then place the decimal point.*

Since 38.15 is close to the estimate of 38, the answer is reasonable. Patterson's total preliminary score was 38.15 points.

B **How many more points did Patterson need on the uneven bars to have a perfect score of 10?**

Find the difference between 10 and 9.45.

10.00	*Align the decimal points.*
− 9.45	*Use zeros as placeholders.*
0.55	*Subtract. Then place the decimal point.*

Patterson needed another 0.55 points to have a perfect score.

EXAMPLE **2** **Using Mental Math to Add and Subtract Decimals**

Find each sum or difference.

A 1.6 + 0.4

1.6 + 0.4   *Think: 0.6 + 0.4 = 1*

1.6 + 0.4 = 2

B 3 − 0.8

3 − 0.8   *Think: What number added to*

3 − 0.8 = 2.2   *0.8 is 1? 0.8 + 0.2 = 1*

So 1 − 0.8 = 0.2.

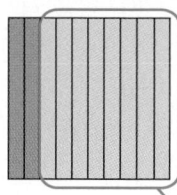

EXAMPLE **3** **Evaluating Decimal Expressions**

Evaluate 7.52 − *s* for each value of *s*.

A *s* = 2.9

$$7.52 - s$$

7.52 − 2.9   *Substitute 2.9 for s.*

7.52   *Align the decimal points.*

− 2.90   *Use a zero as a placeholder.*

4.62   *Subtract.*

Place the decimal point.

Remember!

You can place any number of zeros at the end of a decimal number without changing its value.

B *s* = 4.5367

$$7.52 - s$$

7.52 − 4.5367   *Substitute 4.5367 for s.*

7.5200   *Align the decimal points.*

− 4.5367   *Use zeros as placeholders.*

2.9833   *Subtract.*

Place the decimal point.

Think and Discuss 6.RP.6, 6.CM.4, 6.CN.3

1. Show how you would write 2.678 + 124.5 to find the sum.

2. Tell why it is a good idea to estimate the answer before you add and subtract.

3. Explain how you can use mental math to find how many more points Carly Patterson would have needed to have scored a perfect 10 on the floor exercise.

3-3 **Exercises**

go.hrw.com
Homework Help Online
KEYWORD: MR7 3-3
Parent Resources Online
KEYWORD: MR7 Parent

GUIDED PRACTICE

See Example ① Use the table for Exercises 1–3.

1. How many miles in all is Rea's triathlon training?

2. How many miles did Rea run and swim in all?

3. How much farther did Rea cycle than swim?

Rea's Triathlon Training	
Sport	**Distance (mi)**
Cycling	14.25
Running	4.35
Swimming	1.6

See Example ② Find each sum or difference.

4. $2.7 + 0.3$ **5.** $6 - 0.4$ **6.** $5.2 + 2.8$ **7.** $8.9 - 4$

See Example ③ Evaluate $5.35 - m$ for each value of m.

8. $m = 2.37$ **9.** $m = 1.8$ **10.** $m = 4.7612$ **11.** $m = 0.402$

INDEPENDENT PRACTICE

See Example ① **12. Sports** During a diving competition, Phil performed two reverse dives and two dives from a handstand position. He received the following scores: 8.765, 9.45, 9.875, and 8.025. What was Phil's total score?

13. Brad works after school at a local grocery store. How much did he earn in all for the month of October?

Brad's Earnings for October				
Week	1	2	3	4
Earnings	$123.48	$165.18	$137.80	$140.92

See Example ② Find each sum or difference.

14. $7.2 + 1.8$ **15.** $8.5 - 7$ **16.** $3.3 + 0.7$ **17.** $15.9 + 2.1$

18. $7 - 0.6$ **19.** $7.55 - 3.25$ **20.** $21.4 + 3.6$ **21.** $5 - 2.7$

See Example ③ Evaluate $9.67 - x$ for each value of x.

22. $x = 1.52$ **23.** $x = 3.8$ **24.** $x = 7.21$ **25.** $x = 0.635$

26. $x = 6.9$ **27.** $x = 1.001$ **28.** $x = 8$ **29.** $x = 9.527$

PRACTICE AND PROBLEM SOLVING

Extra Practice
See page 718.

Add or subtract.

30. $5.62 + 4.19$ **31.** $10.508 - 6.73$ **32.** $13.009 + 12.83$

33. Find the sum of 0.0679 and 3.75.   **34.** Subtract 3.0042 from 7.435.

35. Sports Terin Humphrey was ranked third at the 2004 U.S. Gymnastics Championships with a score of 75.45. What was the difference between her score and Courtney Kupet's and Carly Patterson's score of 76.45?

Evaluate each expression.

36. $8.09 - a$ for $a = 4.5$

37. $7.03 + 33.8 + n$ for $n = 12.006$

38. $b + (5.68 - 3.007)$ for $b = 6.134$

39. $(2 \times 14) - a + 1.438$ for $a = 0.062$

40. $5^2 - w$ for $w = 3.5$

41. $100 - p$ for $p = 15.034$

42. **Career** A fire helmet must be sturdy enough to protect the firefighter's head from dangerous objects and extremely hot temperatures while still being as lightweight as possible. One fire helmet weighs 1.616 kg, and another fire helmet weighs 1.403 kg. What is the difference in weights?

43. **Multi-Step** Logan wants to buy a new bike that costs $135.00. He started with $14.83 in his savings account. Last week, he deposited $15.35 into his account. Today, he deposited $32.40. How much more money does he need to buy the bike?

44. **Sports** With a time of 60.35 seconds, Martina Moracova broke Jennifer Thompson's world record time in the women's 100-meter medley. How much faster was Thompson than Moracova when, in the next heat, she reclaimed the record with a time of 59.30 seconds?

45. **Sports** The highest career batting average ever achieved by a professional baseball player is 0.366. Bill Bergen finished with a career 0.170 average. How much lower is Bergen's career average than the highest career average?

46. **What's the Question?** A cup of rice contains 0.8 mg of iron, and a cup of lima beans contains 4.4 mg of iron. If the answer is 6 mg, what is the question?

47. **Write About It** Why is it important to align the decimal points before adding or subtracting decimal numbers?

48. **Challenge** Evaluate $(5.7 + a) \times (9.75 - b)$ for $a = 2.3$ and $b = 7.25$.

Test Prep and Spiral Review

49. **Multiple Choice** What is the sum of 24.91 and 35.8?

Ⓐ 28.49   Ⓑ 59.99   Ⓒ 60.71   Ⓓ 60.99

50. **Multiple Choice** Lead has an atomic weight of 207.19. Mercury has an atomic weight of 200.6. How much greater is the atomic weight of lead than mercury?

Ⓕ 6.59   Ⓖ 7.41   Ⓗ 7.59   Ⓙ 187.13

Solve each equation. (Lesson 2-6)

51. $s - 47 = 23$

52. $73 = a - 78$

53. $823 = t - 641$

Estimate each product or quotient. (Lesson 3-2)

54. 15.72×4.08

55. 14.87×3.78

56. $53.67 \div 9.18$

Quiz for Lessons 3-1 Through 3-3

✓ **3-1** **Representing, Comparing, and Ordering Decimals**

Write each decimal in standard form, expanded form, and words.

1. 4.012

2. ten and fifty-four thousandths

3. On Monday Jamie ran 3.54 miles. On Wednesday he ran 3.6 miles. On which day did he run farther?

Order the decimals from least to greatest.

4. 3.406, 30.08, 3.6

5. 10.10, 10.01, 101.1

6. 16.782, 16.59, 16.79

7. 62.0581, 62.148, 62.0741

8. 123.05745, 132.05628, 123.05749

✓ **3-2** **Estimating Decimals**

9. Matt drove 106.8 miles on Monday, 98.3 miles on Tuesday, and 103.5 miles on Wednesday. About how many miles did he drive in all?

Estimate.

10. $8.345 - 0.6051$; round to the hundredths

11. $16.492 - 2.613$; round to the tenths

12. 18.79×4.68

13. $71.378 \div 8.13$

14. 52.055×7.18

Estimate a range for each sum.

15. $7.42 + 13.87 + 101.2$

16. $1.79 + 3.45 + 7.92$

✓ **3-3** **Adding and Subtracting Decimals**

17. Greg's scores at four gymnastic meets were 9.65, 8.758, 9.884, and 9.500. What was his total score for all four meets?

18. Mrs. Henry buys groceries each week and uses a spreadsheet to keep track of how much she spends. How much did she spend in all for the month of December?

Grocery Spending for December				
Week	1	2	3	4
Amount Spent ($)	52.35	77.97	90.10	42.58

19. Sally walked 1.2 miles on Monday, 1.6 miles on Wednesday, and 2.1 miles on Friday. How many miles did she walk in all?

Find each sum or difference.

20. $0.47 + 0.03$

21. $8 - 0.6$

22. $2.2 + 1.8$

Evaluate $8.67 - s$ for each value of s.

23. $s = 3.4$

24. $s = 2.0871$

25. $s = 7.205$

Focus on Problem Solving

Solve

• **Write an equation**

Read the whole problem before you try to solve it. Sometimes you need to solve the problem in more than one step.

Read the problem. Determine the steps needed to solve the problem.

Brian buys erasers and pens for himself and 4 students in his class. The erasers cost $0.79 each, and the pens cost $2.95 each. What is the total amount that Brian spends on the erasers and pens?

Here is one way to solve the problem.

5 erasers cost	5 pens cost
5 · $0.79	5 · $2.95

$$(5 \cdot \$0.79) \ + \ (5 \cdot \$2.95)$$

Read each problem. Decide whether you need more than one step to solve the problem. List the possible steps. Then choose an equation with which to solve the problem.

1 Joan is making some costumes. She cuts 3 pieces of fabric, each 3.5 m long. She has 5 m of fabric left. Which equation can you use to find f, the amount of fabric she had to start with?

- **A** $(3 \cdot 3.5) + 5 = f$
- **B** $3 + 3.5 + 5 = f$
- **C** $(5 \times 3.5) \div 3 = f$
- **D** $5 - (3 \cdot 3.5) = f$

2 Mario buys 4 chairs and a table. He spends $245.99 in all. If each chair costs $38.95, which equation can you use to find T, the cost of the table?

- **F** $4 + \$245.99 + \$38.95 = T$
- **G** $(4 \cdot \$38.95) + \$245.99 = T$
- **H** $\$245.99 - (4 \cdot \$38.95) = T$
- **J** $\$245.99 \div (4 \cdot \$38.95) = T$

3 Mya skis down Ego Bowl three times and down Fantastic twice. Ego Bowl is 5.85 km long, and Fantastic is 8.35 km long. Which equation can you use to estimate d, the distance Mya skis in all?

- **A** $(6 \cdot 3) + (8 \cdot 2) = d$
- **B** $(6 + 8) + (3 + 2) = d$
- **C** $3(6 + 8) = d$
- **D** $(6 \div 3) + (8 \div 2) = d$

Focus on Problem Solving **123**

3-4 Scientific Notation

Learn to write large numbers in scientific notation.

Vocabulary

scientific notation

NY Performance Indicators

6.CN.4 Understand multiple representations and how they are related.

Artist Georges Seurat used the technique *pointillism* in his 1884 painting *A Sunday on La Grande Jatte.*

In pointillism, an artist places many small dots close together to create a picture. Seurat's painting is made up of about 3,456,000 dots.

The dots in the painting are as small as ¹⁄₁₆ inch. It took Seurat about two years to complete the painting.

You can write large numbers such as 3,456,000 as the product of a number and a power of 10. Look for a pattern in the table below.

Number	×	Power of 10	Product	Number of Places the Decimal Point Moves
3.456	×	10	34.56	1
3.456	×	100	345.6	2
3.456	×	1,000	3,456	3
3.456	×	10,000	34,560	4

EXAMPLE 1 Multiplying by Powers of Ten

Find each product.

A 4,325 × 1,000

4,325.000   *There are 3 zeros in 1,000.*
              To multiply, move the decimal point 3 places right.
= 4,325,000   *Write 3 placeholder zeros.*

B 2.54 × 10,000

2.5400   *There are 4 zeros in 10,000.*
              To multiply, move the decimal point 4 places right.
= 25,400   *Write 2 placeholder zeros.*

Scientific notation is a shorthand method for writing large numbers.

A number written in scientific notation has two numbers that are multiplied.

$$4.123 \times 10^5$$

The first part is a number that is greater than or equal to 1 and less than 10.

The second part is a power of 10.

EXAMPLE 2 **Writing Numbers in Scientific Notation**

Write 8,296,000 in scientific notation.

8,296,000

8,296,000   *Move the decimal point 6 places left.*
            The power of 10 is 6.

$8{,}296{,}000 = 8.296 \times 10^6$

You can write a large number written in scientific notation in standard form. Look at the power of 10 and move the decimal point that number of places to the right.

EXAMPLE 3 **Writing Numbers in Standard Form**

Write 3.2×10^7 in standard form.

3.2×10^7 *The power of 10 is 7.*

3.2000000   *Move the decimal point 7 places right.*
                            Use zeros as placeholders.

$3.2 \times 10^7 = 32{,}000{,}000$

EXAMPLE 4 *Art Application*

Write the number of dots in Seurat's painting *A Sunday on La Grande Jatte*, 3,456,000, in scientific notation.

3,456,000   *Move the decimal point left to form a number that is greater than 1 and less than 10.*

3,456,000   *Multiply that number by a power of ten.*

3.456×10^6 *The power of 10 is 6, because the decimal point is moved 6 places left.*

The number of dots in Seurat's painting is 3.456×10^6.

Think and Discuss 6.CM.1, 6.RP.6, 6.R.6

1. Explain how you can check whether a number is written correctly in scientific notation.

2. Tell why 782.5×10^8 is not correctly written in scientific notation.

3. Tell the advantages of writing a number in scientific notation over writing it in standard form. Explain any disadvantages.

go.hrw.com
Homework Help Online
KEYWORD: MR4 3-4
Parent Resources Online
KEYWORD: MR7 Parent

GUIDED PRACTICE

See Example **1** Find each product.

1. $5{,}937 \times 100$ **2.** $719.25 \times 1{,}000$ **3.** $6.0912 \times 100{,}000$

See Example **2** Write each number in scientific notation.

4. 62,000   **5.** 500,000   **6.** 6,913,000

See Example **3** Write each number in standard form.

7. 6.793×10^6 **8.** 1.4×10^4 **9.** 3.82×10^5

See Example **4** **10.** **Geography** The Atlantic Ocean has a surface area of 31,660,000 square miles. Write the surface area of the Atlantic Ocean in scientific notation.

INDEPENDENT PRACTICE

See Example **1** Find each product.

11. $278 \times 1{,}000$ **12.** 74.1×100 **13.** $381.8 \times 10{,}000$

14. $1.97 \times 10{,}000$ **15.** $4{,}129 \times 100$ **16.** $62.4 \times 1{,}000$

See Example **2** Write each number in scientific notation.

17. 90,000   **18.** 186,000   **19.** 1,607,000

20. 240,000   **21.** 6,000,000   **22.** 16,900,000

See Example **3** Write each number in standard form.

23. 3.211×10^5 **24.** 1.63×10^6 **25.** 7.7×10^3

26. 2.14×10^4 **27.** 4.03×10^6 **28.** 8.1164×10^8

See Example **4** **29.** **Entertainment** *Star Wars: Episode III—Revenge of the Sith* made $6,200,000 from its opening-night midnight screenings. Write this amount in scientific notation.

PRACTICE AND PROBLEM SOLVING

Extra Practice
See page 718.

Write each number in standard form.

30. 7.21×10^3 **31.** 1.234×10^5 **32.** 7.200×10^2

33. 2.08×10^5 **34.** 6.954×10^3 **35.** 5.43×10^1

Write each number in scientific notation.

36. 112,050   **37.** 150,000   **38.** 4,562   **39.** 652

40. 1,000   **41.** 65,342   **42.** 95   **43.** 28,001

44. **Technology** In the year 2005, there were about 1 billion computers in the world. Write this number in standard form and scientific notation.

45. Life Science Genes carry the codes used for making proteins that are necessary for life. No one knows yet how many human genes there are. Estimates range from 2.0×10^4 to 2.5×10^4. Write a number in standard form that is within this range.

46. Earth Science The speed of light is about 300,000 km/s. The speed of sound in air that has a temperature of 20°C is 1,125 ft/s. Write both of these values in scientific notation.

Use the pictograph for Exercises 47 and 48.

47. Write the capacity of Rungnado Stadium in scientific notation.

48. Estimation Estimate the capacity of the largest stadium. Write the estimate in scientific notation.

World's Largest Stadiums

Strahov

Maracana Municipal

Rungnado

= 25,000 seats

49. Social Studies The Library of Congress, in Washington, D.C., is the largest library in the world. It has 24,616,867 books. Round the number of books to the nearest hundred thousand, and write that number in scientific notation.

50. What's the Error? A student said 56,320,000 written in scientific notation is 56.32×10^6. Describe the error. Then write the correct answer.

51. Write About It How does writing numbers in scientific notation make it easier to compare and order the numbers?

52. Challenge What is 5.32 written in scientific notation?

TEST PREP and Spiral Review

53. Multiple Choice What is 23,600,000 in scientific notation?

    (A) 236×10^5 (B) 23.6×10^6 (C) 2.36×10^6 (D) 2.36×10^7

54. Gridded Response Rhode Island has an area of 1.045×10^3 square miles. What is this number in standard form?

Identify the property illustrated by each equation. (Lesson 1-5)

55. $4 + 5 = 5 + 4$ **56.** $3(4 - 1) = 3(4) - 3(1)$ **57.** $(9 \times 80) \times 72 = 9 \times (80 \times 72)$

Evaluate each expression for $a = 4$, $b = 2.8$, and $c = 0.9$. (Lesson 3-3)

58. $a + b$ **59.** $b - c$ **60.** $a + c$ **61.** $a - b$ **62.** $a - c$

Hands-On LAB 3-5

Explore Decimal Multiplication and Division

Use with Lessons 3-5 and 3-6

go.hrw.com
Lab Resources Online
KEYWORD: MR7 Lab3

NY Performance Indicators
6.R.1, 6.R.5, 6.R.6

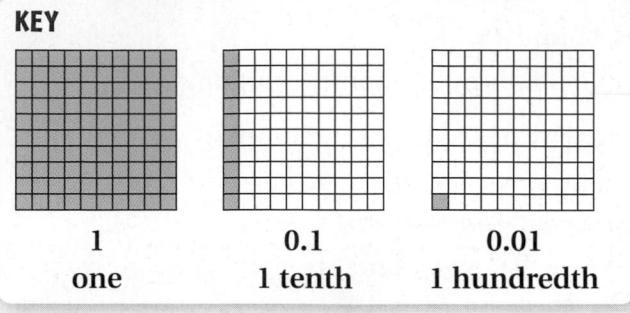

KEY		
1	0.1	0.01
one	1 tenth	1 hundredth

You can use decimal grids to model multiplication and division of decimals.

Activity 1

Use decimal grids to find each product.

a. $3 \cdot 0.32$

To represent $3 \cdot 0.32$, shade 32 small squares three times.

Use a different color to shade a different group of 32 small squares each time.

There are 96 shaded squares.

$$3 \cdot 0.32 = 0.96$$

b. $0.3 \cdot 0.5$

To represent 0.3, shade 3 columns.

To represent 0.5, shade 5 rows in another color.

There are 15 squares in the area where the shading overlaps.

$$0.3 \cdot 0.5 = 0.15$$

Think and Discuss

1. How is multiplying a decimal by a decimal different from multiplying a decimal by a whole number?

2. Why can you shade 5 rows to represent 0.5?

Try This

Use decimal grids to find each product.

1. $3 \cdot 0.14$ **2.** $5 \cdot 0.18$ **3.** $0.7 \cdot 0.5$ **4.** $0.6 \cdot 0.4$

5. $4 \cdot 0.25$ **6.** $0.2 \cdot 0.9$ **7.** $9 \cdot 0.07$ **8.** $8 \cdot 0.15$

Activity 2

Use decimal grids to find each quotient.

a. 3.66 ÷ 3

Shade 3 grids and 66 small squares of a fourth grid to represent 3.66.

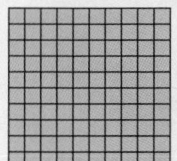 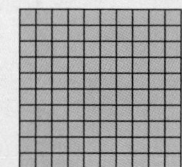 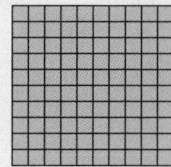 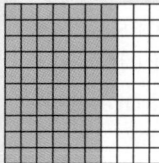

Divide the shaded wholes into 3 equal groups. Use scissors to divide the 66 hundredths into 3 equal groups.

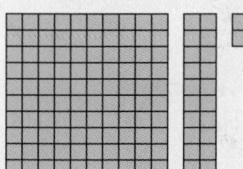 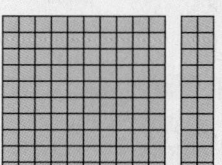 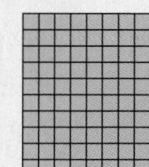

3.66 ÷ 3 = 1.22   *One whole grid and 22 small squares are in each group.*

b. 3.6 ÷ 1.2

Shade 3 grids and 6 columns of a fourth grid to represent 3.6. Cut apart the 6 tenths.

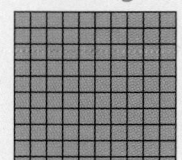   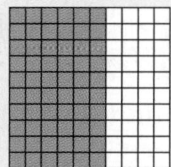

Divide the grids and tenths into equal groups of 1.2.

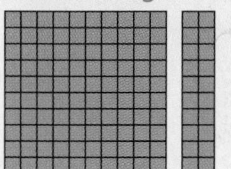 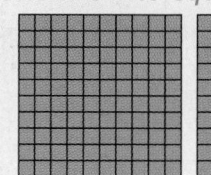 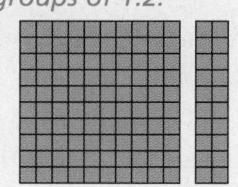

3.6 ÷ 1.2 = 3   *There are 3 equal groups of 1.2.*

Think and Discuss

1. Find 36 ÷ 12. How does this problem and its quotient compare to 3.6 ÷ 1.2?

Try This

Use decimal grids to find each quotient.

1. 4.04 ÷ 4   **2.** 3.25 ÷ 5   **3.** 7.8 ÷ 1.3   **4.** 5.6 ÷ 0.8

5. 6.24 ÷ 2   **6.** 5.1 ÷ 1.7   **7.** 5.7 ÷ 3   **8.** 5.4 ÷ 0.9

Learn to multiply decimals by whole numbers and by decimals.

Gravity on Earth is about six times the gravity on the surface of the Moon.

Because the Moon has less mass than Earth, it has a smaller gravitational effect. An object that weighs 1 pound on Earth weighs only 0.17 pound on the Moon.

You can multiply the weight of an object on Earth by 0.17 to find its weight on the Moon.

You can multiply decimals by first multiplying as you would whole numbers. Then place the decimal point by finding the total of the number of decimal places in the factors. The product will have the same number of decimal places.

NY Performance Indicators

6.A.2 Use substitution to evaluate algebraic expressions. Also, 5.A.3.

E X A M P L E *Science Application*

A flag weighs 3 pounds on Earth. What is the weight of the flag on the Moon?

3 × 0.17 Multiply 3 by 0.17, since 1 pound on Earth is 0.17 pound on the Moon.

$$
\begin{array}{r}
17 \\
\times\ 3 \\
\hline
51
\end{array}
$$

Multiply as you would with whole numbers.

Place the decimal point by adding the number of decimal places in the numbers multiplied.

Check
$$
\begin{array}{r}
0.17 \\
\times\ \ \ 3 \\
\hline
0.51
\end{array}
$$

2 decimal places
+ 0 decimal places
2 decimal places

A 3 lb flag on Earth weighs 0.51 lb on the Moon.

E X A M P L E **Multiplying a Decimal by a Decimal**

Helpful Hint

You can use a decimal grid to model multiplication of decimals.

Find each product.

A 0.2 × 0.6

Multiply. Then place the decimal point.

$$
\begin{array}{r}
0.2 \\
\times\ 0.6 \\
\hline
0.12
\end{array}
$$

1 decimal place
+ 1 decimal place
2 decimal places

Find each product.

B 3.25×4.8

$3 \times 5 = 15$ *Estimate the product. Round each factor to the nearest whole number.*

       3.25   *Multiply. Then place the decimal point.*

$$
\begin{array}{r}
3.25 \\
\times\ 4.8 \\
\hline
2600 \\
13000 \\
\hline
15.600
\end{array}
$$

       2 decimal places
       + 1 decimal place
       3 decimal places

15.600 is close to the estimate of 15. The answer is reasonable.

C 0.05×0.9

$0.05 \times 1 = 0.05$ *Estimate the product. 0.9 is close to 1.*

            Multiply. Then place the decimal point.

$$
\begin{array}{r}
0.05 \\
\times\ \ 0.9 \\
\hline
0.045
\end{array}
$$

       2 decimal places
       + 1 decimal place
       3 decimal places; use a placeholder zero.

0.045 is close to the estimate of 0.05. The answer is reasonable.

EXAMPLE 3   **Evaluating Decimal Expressions**

Evaluate **3x** for each value of **x**.

Remember!

These notations all mean multiply 3 times *x*.

$3 \cdot x$ $3x$ $3(x)$

A $x = 4.047$

$3x = 3(4.047)$ *Substitute 4.047 for x.*

$$
\begin{array}{r}
4.047 \\
\times\ \ \ \ 3 \\
\hline
12.141
\end{array}
$$

       3 decimal places
       + 0 decimal places
       3 decimal places

B $x = 2.95$

$3x = 3(2.95)$ *Substitute 2.95 for x.*

$$
\begin{array}{r}
2.95 \\
\times\ \ \ \ 3 \\
\hline
8.85
\end{array}
$$

       2 decimal places
       + 0 decimal places
       2 decimal places

Think and Discuss

6.CM.4, 6.CN.2

1. Tell how many decimal places are in the product of 235.2 and 0.24.

2. Tell which is greater, 4×0.6 or 4×0.006.

3. Describe how the products of 0.3×0.5 and 3×5 are similar. How are they different?

3-5 Exercises

go.hrw.com
Homework Help Online
KEYWORD: MR7 3-5
Parent Resources Online
KEYWORD: MR7 Parent

GUIDED PRACTICE

See Example 1
1. Each can of cat food costs $0.28. How much will 6 cans of cat food cost?

2. Jorge buys 8 baseballs for $9.29 each. How much does he spend in all?

See Example 2 **Find each product.**

3. 0.6
× 0.4

4. 0.008
× 0.5

5. 3.0
× 0.07

6. 0.12
× 0.6

See Example 3 **Evaluate 5x for each value of x.**

7. $x = 3.304$ **8.** $x = 4.58$ **9.** $x = 7.126$ **10.** $x = 1.9$

INDEPENDENT PRACTICE

See Example 1
11. Gwenyth walks her dog each morning. If she walks 0.37 kilometers each morning, how many kilometers will she have walked in 7 days?

12. Consumer Math Apples are on sale for $0.49 per pound. What is the price for 4 pounds of apples?

See Example 2 **Find each product.**

13. 0.9
× 0.03

14. 4.5
× 0.5

15. 0.31
× 0.7

16. 1.6
× 0.08

17. 0.007×0.06 **18.** 0.04×3.0 **19.** 2.0×0.006 **20.** 0.005×0.003

See Example 3 **Evaluate 7x for each value of x.**

21. $x = 1.903$ **22.** $x = 2.461$ **23.** $x = 3.72$ **24.** $x = 4.05$

25. $x = 0.164$ **26.** $x = 5.89$ **27.** $x = 0.3702$ **28.** $x = 1.82$

PRACTICE AND PROBLEM SOLVING

Extra Practice
See page 719.

Multiply.

29. 0.3×0.03 **30.** 1.4×0.21 **31.** 0.06×1.02 **32.** 8.2×4.1

33. 12.6×2.1 **34.** 3.04×0.6 **35.** 0.66×2.52 **36.** 3.08×0.7

37. $0.2 \times 0.94 \times 1.3$ **38.** $1.54 \times 3.05 \times 2.6$ **39.** $1.98 \times 0.4 \times 5.2$

40. $1.7 \times 2.41 \times 0.5$ **41.** $2.5 \times 1.52 \times 3.7$ **42.** $6.5 \times 0.15 \times 3.8$

Evaluate.

43. $6n$ for $n = 6.23$ **44.** $5t + 0.462$ for $t = 3.04$

45. $8^2 - 2b$ for $b = 0.95$ **46.** $4^3 + 5c$ for $c = 1.9$

47. $3h - 15 + h$ for $h = 5.2$ **48.** $5^2 + 6j + j$ for $j = 0.27$

Saturn is the second-largest planet in the solar system. Saturn is covered by thick clouds. Saturn's density is very low. Suppose you weigh 180 pounds on Earth. If you were able to stand on Saturn, you would weigh only 165 pounds. To find the weight of an object on another planet, multiply its weight on Earth by the gravitational pull listed in the table.

Gravitational Pull of Planets (Compared with Earth)	
Planet	**Gravitational Pull**
Mercury	0.38
Venus	0.91
Mars	0.38
Jupiter	2.54
Saturn	0.93
Neptune	1.2

49. Christopher found a rock that weighs 5 pounds on Earth. How much would the rock weigh on Saturn?

50. On which two planets would the weight of an object be the same?

51. **Multi-Step** An object weighs 9 pounds on Earth. How much more would this object weigh on Neptune than on Mars?

52. **Write a Problem** Use the data in the table to write a word problem that can be answered by evaluating an expression with multiplication. Solve your problem.

53. **What's the Error?** A student said that his new baby brother, who weighs 10 pounds, would weigh 120 pounds on Neptune. What is the error? Write the correct answer.

54. **Challenge** An object weighs between 2.79 lb and 5.58 lb on Saturn. Give a range for the object's weight on Earth.

Galileo Galilei was the first person to look at Saturn through a telescope. He thought there were groups of stars on each side of the planet, but it was later determined that he had seen Saturn's rings.

go.hrw.com
Web Extra!
KEYWORD: MR7 Saturn

TEST PREP and Spiral Review

55. **Multiple Choice** Max uses 1.6 liters of gasoline each hour mowing lawns. How much gas does he use in 5.8 hours?

  (A) 7.4 liters   (B) 9.28 liters   (C) 92.8 liters   (D) 928 liters

56. **Multiple Choice** What is the value of $5x$ when $x = 3.2$?

  (F) 16   (G) 1.6   (H) 0.16   (J) 8.2

Solve each equation. (Lesson 2-8)

57. $\frac{x}{8} = 4$ 58. $\frac{y}{12} = 5$ 59. $3 = \frac{t}{17}$ 60. $2 = \frac{s}{21}$

Write each decimal in expanded form. (Lesson 3-1)

61. 1.23   62. 0.45   63. 26.07   64. 116.2   65. 80.002

3-6 Dividing Decimals by Whole Numbers

Learn to divide decimals by whole numbers.

Ethan and two of his friends are going to share equally the cost of making a sculpture for the art fair.

To find how much each person should pay for the materials, you will need to divide a decimal by a whole number.

EXAMPLE **1** **Dividing a Decimal by a Whole Number**

Find each quotient.

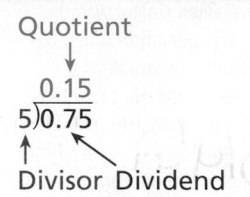

Remember!

$$\underset{\text{Divisor}}{\overset{\text{Quotient}}{\underset{\uparrow}{5}}}\,\underset{\underset{\text{Dividend}}{\uparrow}}{\overline{)0.75}}$$

A 0.75 ÷ 5

$$\begin{array}{r} 0.15 \\ 5\overline{)0.75} \\ -\,5 \\ \hline 25 \\ -\,25 \\ \hline 0 \end{array}$$

Place a decimal point in the quotient directly above the decimal point in the dividend.
Divide as you would with whole numbers.

B 2.52 ÷ 3

$$\begin{array}{r} 0.84 \\ 3\overline{)2.52} \\ -\,24 \\ \hline 12 \\ -\,12 \\ \hline 0 \end{array}$$

Place a decimal point in the quotient directly above the decimal point in the dividend.
Divide as you would with whole numbers.

EXAMPLE **2** **Evaluating Decimal Expressions**

Evaluate 0.435 ÷ x for each given value of x.

NY Performance Indicators

6.A.2 Use substitution to evaluate algebraic expressions. Also, **5.A.3**.

A x = 3

$0.435 \div x$

$0.435 \div 3$ *Substitute 3 for x.*

$$\begin{array}{r} 0.145 \\ 3\overline{)0.435} \\ -\,3 \\ \hline 13 \\ -\,12 \\ \hline 15 \\ -\,15 \\ \hline 0 \end{array}$$

Divide as you would with whole numbers.

B x = 15

$0.435 \div x$

$0.435 \div 15$ *Substitute 15 for x.*

$$\begin{array}{r} 0.029 \\ 15\overline{)0.435} \\ -\,0 \\ \hline 43 \\ -\,30 \\ \hline 135 \\ -135 \\ \hline 0 \end{array}$$

Sometimes you need to use a zero as a placeholder.

15 > 4, so place a zero in the quotient and divide 15 into 43.

EXAMPLE **3** *Consumer Math Application*

Ethan and two of his friends are making a papier-mâché sculpture using balloons, strips of paper, and paint. The materials cost **$11.61. If they share the cost equally, how much should each person pay?**

$11.61 should be divided into three equal groups.
Divide $11.61 by 3.

$$
\begin{array}{r}
3.87 \\
3\overline{)11.61} \\
-9 \\
\hline
2\,6 \\
-2\,4 \\
\hline
21 \\
-21 \\
\hline
0
\end{array}
$$

Place a decimal point in the quotient directly above the decimal point in the dividend.

Divide as you would with whole numbers.

Remember!

Multiplication can "undo" division. To check your answer to a division problem, multiply the divisor by the quotient.

Check

$3.87 \times 3 = 11.61$

Each person should pay $3.87.

Think and Discuss 6.CM.1, 6.CN.2

1. **Tell** how you know where to place the decimal point in the quotient.

2. **Explain** why you can use multiplication to check your answer to a division problem.

Exercises

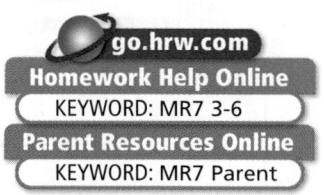
go.hrw.com
Homework Help Online
KEYWORD: MR7 3-6
Parent Resources Online
KEYWORD: MR7 Parent

GUIDED PRACTICE

See Example **1** **Find each quotient.**

1. $1.38 \div 6$ **2.** $0.96 \div 8$ **3.** $1.75 \div 5$ **4.** $0.72 \div 4$

See Example **2** **Evaluate $0.312 \div x$ for each given value of x.**

5. $x = 4$ **6.** $x = 6$ **7.** $x = 3$ **8.** $x = 12$

See Example **3** **9. Consumer Math** Mr. Richards purchased 8 T-shirts for the volleyball team. The total cost of the T-shirts was $70.56. How much did each shirt cost?

INDEPENDENT PRACTICE

See Example ① **Find each quotient.**

10. $0.91 \div 7$ **11.** $1.32 \div 6$ **12.** $4.68 \div 9$ **13.** $0.81 \div 3$

See Example ② **Evaluate $0.684 \div x$ for each given value of x.**

14. $x = 3$ **15.** $x = 4$ **16.** $x = 18$ **17.** $x = 9$

See Example ③ **18. Consumer Math** Charles, Kate, and Kim eat lunch in a restaurant. The bill is $27.12. If they share the bill equally, how much will each person pay?

PRACTICE AND PROBLEM SOLVING

Extra Practice
See page 719.

Find the value of each expression.

19. $(0.49 + 0.045) \div 5$ **20.** $(4.9 - 3.125) \div 5$ **21.** $(13.28 - 7.9) \div 4$

Evaluate the expression $x \div 4$ for each value of x.

22. $x = 0.504$ **23.** $x = 0.944$ **24.** $x = 57.484$ **25.** $x = 1.648$

26. Multi-Step At the grocery store, a 6 lb bag of oranges costs $2.04. Is this more or less expensive than the price shown at the farmers' market?

Oranges
$0.30/lb

27. Critical Thinking How could you use rounding to check your answer to the problem $5.58 \div 6$?

 28. Choose a Strategy Sarah had $1.19 in coins. Jeff asked her for change for a dollar, but she did not have the correct change. What coins did she have?

 29. Write About It When do you use a placeholder zero in the quotient?

 30. Challenge Evaluate the expression $x \div 2$ for the following values of $x = 520$, 52, and 5.2. Try to predict the value of the same expression for $x = 0.52$.

TEST PREP and Spiral Review

31. Multiple Choice What is the value of $0.98 \div x$ when $x = 2$?

Ⓐ 49   Ⓑ 4.9   Ⓒ 0.49   Ⓓ 0.049

32. Gridded Response Danika spent $89.24 on two pairs of shoes. Each pair of shoes cost the same amount. How much, in dollars, did each pair cost?

Identify a pattern in each sequence. Name the missing term. (Lesson 1-7)

33. 85, 80, 75, 70, 65, ▇, . . .   **34.** 2, 6, 5, 9, 8, ▇, . . .   **35.** 10, 17, 12, 19, 14, ▇, . . .

Write each number in standard form. (Lesson 3-4)

36. 6.479×10^3 **37.** 0.208×10^2 **38.** 13.507×10^4 **39.** 7.1×10^5

3-7 Dividing by Decimals

Learn to divide whole numbers and decimals by decimals.

 NY Performance Indicators

6.N.27 Justify the reasonableness of answers using estimation (including rounding).

Julie and her family traveled to the Grand Canyon. They stopped to refill their gas tank with 13.4 gallons of gasoline after they had driven 368.5 miles.

To find the miles that they drove per gallon, you will need to divide a decimal by a decimal.

EXAMPLE 1 **Dividing a Decimal by a Decimal**

Find each quotient.

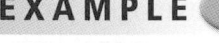 **Helpful Hint**

Multiplying the divisor and the dividend by the same number does not change the quotient.

$$
\begin{array}{c}
42 \div 6 = 7 \\
\times 10 \downarrow \quad \times 10 \downarrow \\
420 \div 60 = 7
\end{array}
$$

$$
\begin{array}{c}
42 \div 6 = 7 \\
\times 100 \downarrow \quad \times 100 \downarrow \\
4{,}200 \div 600 = 7
\end{array}
$$

A 3.6 ÷ 1.2

$$1.2\overline{)3.6}$$

Multiply the divisor and dividend by the same power of ten.

There is one decimal place in the divisor. Multiply by 10¹, or 10.

$$
\begin{array}{r}
3 \\
12\overline{)36} \\
-36 \\
\hline
0
\end{array}
$$

Think: 1.2 × 10 = 12   3.6 × 10 = 36

Divide.

3.6 ÷ 1.2 = 3

B 42.3 ÷ 0.12

$$0.12\overline{)42.3}$$

Make the divisor a whole number by multiplying the divisor and dividend by 10², or 100.
Think: 0.12 × 100 = 12   42.3 × 100 = 4,230

$$
\begin{array}{r}
352.5 \\
12\overline{)4230.0} \\
-36 \\
\hline
63 \\
-60 \\
\hline
30 \\
-24 \\
\hline
60 \\
-60 \\
\hline
0
\end{array}
$$

Place the decimal point in the quotient.
Divide.

When there is a remainder, place a zero after the decimal point in the dividend and continue to divide.

42.3 ÷ 0.12 = 352.5

EXAMPLE 2 **PROBLEM SOLVING APPLICATION**

After driving 368.5 miles, Julie and her family refilled the tank of their car with 13.4 gallons of gasoline. On average, how many miles did they drive per gallon of gas?

1 Understand the Problem

The **answer** will be the average number of miles per gallon.

List the **important information:**

- They drove 368.5 miles.
- They used 13.4 gallons of gas.

2 Make a Plan

Solve a simpler problem by replacing the decimals in the problem with whole numbers.

If they drove 10 miles using 2 gallons of gas, they averaged 5 miles per gallon. You need to divide miles by gallons to solve the problem.

3 Solve

First estimate the answer. You can use compatible numbers.
$368.5 \div 13.4 \longrightarrow 360 \div 12 = 30$

$$13.4\overline{)368.5}$$ *Multiply the divisor and the dividend by 10.*
Think: $13.4 \times 10 = 134$ $368.5 \times 10 = 3,685$

$$
\begin{array}{r}
27.5 \\
134\overline{)3685.0} \\
-268 \\
\hline
1005 \\
-938 \\
\hline
67\,0 \\
-67\,0 \\
\hline
0
\end{array}
$$

Place the decimal point in the quotient.
Divide.

Julie and her family averaged 27.5 miles per gallon.

4 Look Back

The answer is reasonable, since 27.5 is close to the estimate of 30.

Think and Discuss

1. Tell how the quotient of $48 \div 12$ is similar to the quotient of $4.8 \div 1.2$. How is it different?

Exercises

go.hrw.com
Homework Help Online
KEYWORD: MR7 3-7
Parent Resources Online
KEYWORD: MR7 Parent

GUIDED PRACTICE

See Example **1** Find each quotient.

1. $6.5 \div 1.3$ **2.** $20.7 \div 0.6$ **3.** $25.5 \div 1.5$

4. $5.4 \div 0.9$ **5.** $13.2 \div 2.2$ **6.** $63.39 \div 0.24$

See Example **2** **7.** Marcus drove 354.9 miles in 6.5 hours. On average, how many miles per hour did he drive?

8. Consumer Math Anthony spends $87.75 on shrimp. The shrimp cost $9.75 per pound. How many pounds of shrimp does Anthony buy?

INDEPENDENT PRACTICE

See Example **1** Find each quotient.

9. $3.6 \div 0.6$ **10.** $8.2 \div 0.5$ **11.** $18.4 \div 2.3$

12. $4.8 \div 1.2$ **13.** $52.2 \div 0.24$ **14.** $32.5 \div 2.6$

15. $49.5 \div 4.5$ **16.** $96.6 \div 0.42$ **17.** $6.5 \div 1.3$

See Example **2** **18.** Jen spends $5.98 on ribbon. Ribbon costs $0.92 per meter. How many meters of ribbon does Jen buy?

19. Kyle's family drove 329.44 miles. Kyle calculated that the car averaged 28.4 miles per gallon of gas. How many gallons of gas did the car use?

20. Consumer Math Peter is saving $4.95 each week to buy a DVD that costs $24.75, including tax. For how many weeks will he have to save?

PRACTICE AND PROBLEM SOLVING

Extra Practice
See page 719.

Divide.

21. $2.52 \div 0.4$ **22.** $12.586 \div 0.35$ **23.** $0.5733 \div 0.003$

24. $10.875 \div 1.2$ **25.** $92.37 \div 0.5$ **26.** $8.43 \div 0.12$

Evaluate.

27. $0.732 \div n$ for $n = 0.06$ **28.** $73.814 \div c$ for $c = 1.3$

29. $b \div 0.52$ for $b = 6.344$ **30.** $r \div 4.17$ for $r = 10.5918$

Find the value of each expression.

31. $6.35 \times 10^2 \div 0.5$ **32.** $8.1 \times 10^2 \div 0.9$ **33.** $4.5 \times 10^3 \div 4$

34. $20.1 \times 10^3 \div 0.1$ **35.** $2.76 \times 10^2 \div 0.3$ **36.** $6.2 \times 10^3 \div 8$

37. Multi-Step Find the value of $6.45 \times 10^6 \div 0.3$. Write your answer in scientific notation.

 History

The U.S. Mint was established by the Coinage Act in 1792. The first coins were copper and were made in Philadelphia.

38. **Earth Science** A planet's year is the time it takes that planet to revolve around the Sun. A Mars year is 1.88 Earth years. If you are 13 years old in Earth years, about how old would you be in Mars years?

39. **History** The U.S. Treasury first printed paper money in 1862. The paper money we use today is 0.0043 inch thick. Estimate the number of bills you would need to stack to make a pile that is 1 inch thick. If you stacked $20 bills, what would be the total value of the money in the pile?

Use the map for Exercises 40 and 41.

40. **Multi-Step** Bill drove from Washington, D.C., to Charlotte in 6.5 hours. What was his average speed in miles per hour?

41. **Estimation** Betty drove a truck from Richmond to Washington, D.C. It took her about 2.5 hours. Estimate the average speed she was driving.

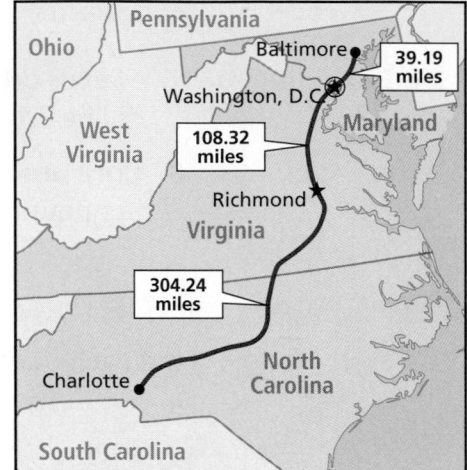

 42. **What's the Error?** A student incorrectly answered the division problem below. Explain the error and write the correct quotient.

$$0.004\overline{)53.824} = 13.456$$

 43. **Write About It** Explain how you know where to place the decimal point in the quotient when you divide by a decimal number.

44. **Challenge** Find the value of a in the division problem.

$$4a3\overline{)0417.13} = 1.01$$

TEST PREP and Spiral Review

45. **Multiple Choice** Nick bought 2.5 pounds of popcorn for $8.35. How much did he pay for each pound of popcorn?

　Ⓐ $20.88　　　　Ⓑ $3.43　　　　Ⓒ $3.34　　　　Ⓓ $33.40

46. **Extended Response** In the 2004–2005 NBA season, Tracy McGrady earned a salary of $14,487,000. He played in 78 games and averaged 40.8 minutes per game. How much money did Tracy McGrady earn each minute he played? Round your answer to the nearest dollar. Explain how you solved the problem.

Compare. Write <, >, or =. (Lesson 1-1)

47. 56,902 ▨ 56,817　　　　48. 14,562 ▨ 14,581　　　　49. 1,240,518 ▨ 1,208,959

Evaluate $4y$ for each value of y. (Lesson 3-5)

50. $y = 2.13$　　51. $y = 4.015$　　52. $y = 3.6$　　53. $y = 0.78$　　54. $y = 1.4$

3-8 Interpret the Quotient

 Problem Solving Skill

Learn to solve problems by interpreting the quotient.

In science lab, Kim learned to make slime from corn starch, water, and food coloring. She has 0.87 kg of corn starch, and the recipe for one bag of slime calls for 0.15 kg. To find the number of bags of slime Kim can make, you need to divide.

EXAMPLE **1**   *Measurement Application*

Remember!

To divide decimals, first write the divisor as a whole number. Multiply the divisor and dividend by the same power of ten.

Kim will use 0.87 kg of corn starch to make gift bags of slime for her friends. If each bag requires 0.15 kg of corn starch, how many bags of slime can she make?

The question asks how many whole bags of slime can be made when the corn starch is divided into groups of 0.15 kg.

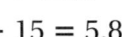
$$0.87 \div 0.15 = ?$$
$$87 \div 15 = 5.8$$

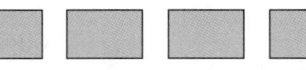  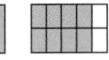

Think: The quotient shows that there is not enough to make 6 bags of slime that are 0.15 kg each. There is only enough for 5 bags. The decimal part of the quotient will not be used in the answer.

Kim can make **5** gift bags of slime.

EXAMPLE **2**   *Photography Application*

NY Performance Indicators

6.PS.7 Represent problem situations verbally, numerically, algebraically, and/or graphically.

There are 246 students in the sixth grade. If Ms. Lee buys rolls of film with 24 exposures each, how many rolls will she need to take every student's picture?

The question asks how many whole rolls are needed to take a picture of every one of the students.

$$246 \div 24 = ?$$
$$246 \div 24 = 10.25$$

Think: Ten rolls of film will not be enough to take every student's picture. Ms. Lee will need to buy another roll of film. The quotient must be rounded up to the next highest whole number.

Ms. Lee will need 11 rolls of film.

EXAMPLE 3

Social Studies Application

Marissa is drawing a time line of the Stone Age. She plans for 6 equal sections, two each for the Paleolithic, Mesolithic, and Neolithic periods. If she has 7.8 meters of paper, how long is each section?

The question asks exactly how long each section will be when the paper is divided into 6 sections.

$7.8 \div 6 = 1.3$ *Think: The question asks for an exact answer, so do not estimate. Use the entire quotient.*

Each section will be **1.3** meters long.

When the question asks	→ You should
How many whole groups can be made when you divide?	→ Drop the decimal part of the quotient.
How many whole groups are needed to put all items from the dividend into a group?	→ Round the quotient up to the next highest whole number.
What is the exact number when you divide?	→ Use the entire quotient as the answer.

Think and Discuss

1. **Tell** how you would interpret the quotient: A group of 27 students will ride in vans that carry 12 students each. How many vans are needed?

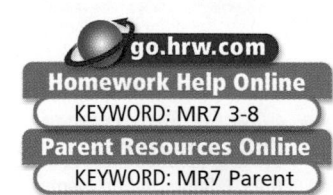

3-8 Exercises

go.hrw.com
Homework Help Online
KEYWORD: MR7 3-8
Parent Resources Online
KEYWORD: MR7 Parent

GUIDED PRACTICE

See Example 1. Kay is making beaded belts for her friends from 6.5 meters of cord. One belt uses 0.625 meter of cord. How many belts can she make?

See Example 2   2. Julius is supplying cups for a party of 136 people. If cups are sold in packs of 24, how many packs of cups will he need?

See Example 3. Miranda is decorating for a party. She has 13 balloons and 29.25 meters of ribbon. She wants to tie the same length of ribbon on each balloon. How long will each ribbon be?

See Example **1** **4.** There are 0.454 kg of corn starch in a container. How many 0.028 kg portions are in one container?

 See Example **2** **5.** Tina needs 36 flowers for her next project. The flowers are sold in bunches of 5. How many bunches will she need?

See Example **3** **6.** Bobby's goal is to run 27 miles a week. If he runs the same distance 6 days a week, how many miles would he have to run each day?

PRACTICE AND PROBLEM SOLVING

Extra Practice
See page 719.

7. Nick wants to write thank-you notes to 15 of his friends. The cards are sold in packs of 6. How many packs does Nick need to buy?

8. Multi-Step The science teacher has 7 packs of seeds and 36 students. If the students should each plant the same number of seeds, how many can each student plant?

9. Critical Thinking How do you know when to round your answer up to the next whole number?

10. Write a Problem Create a problem that is solved by interpreting the quotient.

11. Write About It Explain how a calculator shows the remainder when you divide 145 by 8.

12. Challenge Leonard wants to place a fence on both sides of a 10-meter walkway. If he puts a post at both ends and at every 2.5 meters in between, how many posts does he use?

TEST PREP and Spiral Review

13. Multiple Choice There are 375 students going on a field trip. Each bus holds 65 students. How many buses are needed for the field trip?

    Ⓐ 4   Ⓑ 5   6   Ⓓ 7

14. Multiple Choice Mrs. Neal has 127 stickers. She wants to give each of the 22 students in her class the same number of stickers. Which expression can be used to find how many stickers each student will get?

    Ⓕ $127 - 22$ $127 \div 22$ Ⓗ $127 + 22$ Ⓙ 127×22

Solve for y. (Lessons 2-4, 2-5, 2-6)

15. $y - 23 = 40$ **16.** $14y = 168$ **17.** $36 + y = 53$ **18.** $\frac{y}{5} = 7$

Find each quotient. (Lesson 3-7)

19. $45.5 \div 5$ **20.** $103.7 \div 2$ **21.** $35 \div 2.5$ **22.** $4.25 \div 0.25$

3-9 Solving Decimal Equations

Learn to solve equations involving decimals.

NY Performance Indicators

5.A.4 Solve simple one-step equations using basic whole-number facts.

Felipe has earned $45.20 by mowing lawns for his neighbors. He wants to buy inline skates that cost $69.95. Write and solve an equation to find how much more money Felipe must earn to buy the skates.

Let m be the amount of money Felipe needs. $45.20 + m = $69.95

You can solve equations with decimals using inverse operations just as you solved equations with whole numbers.

$$\begin{array}{r} \$45.20 + m = \$69.95 \\ -\ \$45.20 \qquad -\ \$45.20 \\ \hline m = \$24.75 \end{array}$$

Felipe needs $24.75 more to buy the inline skates.

EXAMPLE 1 Solving One-Step Equations with Decimals

Solve each equation. Check your answer.

Remember!

Use inverse operations to get the variable alone on one side of the equation.

A $g - 3.1 = 4.5$

$$\begin{array}{r} g - 3.1 = \quad 4.5 \\ +\ 3.1 \quad +\ 3.1 \\ \hline g = \quad 7.6 \end{array}$$

3.1 is subtracted from g.

Add 3.1 to both sides to undo the subtraction.

Check

$g - 3.1 = 4.5$

$7.6 - 3.1 \overset{?}{=} 4.5$ Substitute 7.6 for g in the equation.

$4.5 \overset{?}{=} 4.5 ✔$ 7.6 is the solution.

B $3k = 8.1$

$3k = 8.1$ k is multiplied by 3.

$\dfrac{3k}{3} = \dfrac{8.1}{3}$ Divide both sides by 3 to undo the multiplication.

$k = 2.7$

Check

$3k = 8.1$

$3(2.7) \overset{?}{=} 8.1$ Substitute 2.7 for k in the equation.

$8.1 \overset{?}{=} 8.1 ✔$ 2.7 is the solution.

Solve each equation. Check your answer.

C $\dfrac{m}{5} = 1.5$

$\dfrac{m}{5} = 1.5$ *m is divided by 5.*

$\dfrac{m}{5} \cdot 5 = 1.5 \cdot 5$ *Multiply both sides by 5 to undo the division.*

$m = 7.5$

Check

$\dfrac{m}{5} = 1.5$

$\dfrac{7.5}{5} \overset{?}{=} 1.5$ *Substitute 7.5 for m in the equation.*

$1.5 \overset{?}{=} 1.5$ ✔   *7.5 is the solution.*

EXAMPLE 2   *Measurement Application*

Remember!

The area of a rectangle is its length times its width.

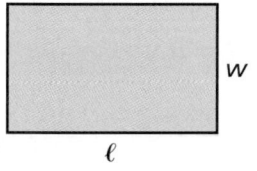

$A = \ell w$

A The area of the floor in Jonah's bedroom is 28 square meters. If its length is 3.5 meters, what is the width of the bedroom?

area	=	length	·	width
28	=	3.5	·	w

Write the equation for the problem.

$28 = 3.5w$ *Let w be the width of the room.*

$\dfrac{28}{3.5} = \dfrac{3.5w}{3.5}$ *w is multiplied by 3.5.*
       Divide both sides by 3.5 to undo the

$8 = w$ *multiplication.*

The width of Jonah's bedroom is 8 meters.

B Jonah is carpeting his bedroom. The carpet costs $22.50 per square meter. What is the total cost to carpet the bedroom?

total cost = area · cost of carpet per square meter

$C = 28 \cdot 22.50$ *Let C be the total cost. Write the equation for the problem.*

$C = 630$ *Multiply.*

The cost of carpeting the bedroom is $630.

Think and Discuss

1. Explain whether the value of m will be less than or greater than 1 when you solve $5m = 4.5$.

2. Tell how you can check the answer in Example 2A.

go.hrw.com
Homework Help Online
KEYWORD: MR7 3-9
Parent Resources Online
KEYWORD: MR7 Parent

GUIDED PRACTICE

See Example **1** Solve each equation. Check your answer.

1. $a - 2.3 = 4.8$ **2.** $6n = 8.4$ **3.** $\dfrac{c}{4} = 3.2$

4. $8.5 = 2.49 + x$ **5.** $\dfrac{d}{3.2} = 1.09$ **6.** $1.6 = m \cdot 4$

See Example **2** **7.** The length of a window is 10.5 meters, and the width is 5.75 meters. Solve the equation $a \div 10.5 = 5.75$ to find the area of the window.

8. Gretchen wants to add a wallpaper border along the top of the walls of her square room. The distance around her room is 20.4 meters.

   a. What is the length of each wall of Gretchen's room?

   b. The price of wallpaper border is $1.25 per meter. What is the total cost to add the border to her room?

INDEPENDENT PRACTICE

See Example **1** Solve each equation. Check your answer.

9. $b - 5.6 = 3.7$ **10.** $1.6 = \dfrac{p}{7}$ **11.** $3r = 62.4$

12. $9.5 = 5x$ **13.** $a - 4.8 = 5.9$ **14.** $\dfrac{n}{8} = 0.8$

15. $8 + f = 14.56$ **16.** $5.2s = 10.4$ **17.** $1.95 = z - 2.05$

See Example **2** **18.** **Geometry** The area of a rectangle is 65.8 square units. The length is 7 units. Solve the equation $7 \cdot w = 65.8$ to find the width of the rectangle.

19. Ken wants to fence his square garden. He will need 6.4 meters of fence to enclose all four sides of the garden.

   a. How long is each side of his garden?

   b. The price of fencing is $2.25 per meter. What is the total cost to fence Ken's garden?

PRACTICE AND PROBLEM SOLVING

Extra Practice
See page 719.

Solve each equation and check your answer.

20. $9.8 = t - 42.1$ **21.** $q \div 2.6 = 9.5$ **22.** $45.36 = 5.6 \cdot m$

23. $1.3b = 5.46$ **24.** $4.93 = 0.563 + m$ **25.** $\dfrac{a}{5} = 2.78$

26. $w - 64.99 = 13.044$ **27.** $6.205z = 80.665$ **28.** $74.2 = 38.06 + c$

29. **Geometry** The shortest side of the triangle is 10 units long.

   a. What are the lengths of the other two sides of the triangle?

   b. What is the perimeter of the triangle?

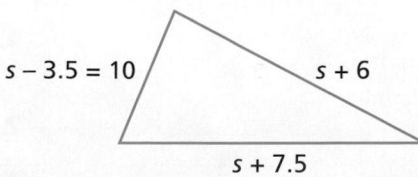

$s - 3.5 = 10$ $s + 6$ $s + 7.5$

The London Eye is the world's largest Ferris wheel. Use the table for Exercises 30–32.

30. Write the height of the wheel in kilometers.

31. Multi-Step There are 1,000 kilograms in a metric ton. What is the weight of the wheel in kilograms written in scientific notation?

32. a. How many seconds does it take for the wheel to make one revolution?
b. The wheel moves at a rate of 0.26 meters per second. Use the equation $d \div 0.26 = 1,800$ to find the distance of one revolution.

33. Each capsule can hold 25 passengers. How many capsules are needed to hold 210 passengers?

Weight of wheel	1,900 metric tons
Time to revolve	30 minutes
Height of wheel	135 meters

34. Fifteen adult tickets for the London Eye cost £187.50 (about $356.25). What is the cost for one ticket? Give the answer in both pounds sterling (£) and U.S. dollars.

35. What's the Error? When solving the equation $b - 12.98 = 5.03$, a student said that $b = 7.95$. Describe the error. What is the correct value for b?

36. Write About It Explain how you solve for the variable in a multiplication equation such as $2.3a = 4.6$.

37. Challenge Solve $1.45n \times 3.2 = 23.942 + 4.13$.

TEST PREP and Spiral Review

38. Multiple Choice Solve the equation $d \div 4 = 6.7$ for d.

Ⓐ $d = 26.8$ Ⓑ $d = 10.7$ Ⓒ $d = 2.7$ Ⓓ $d = 1.675$

39. Multiple Choice Kelly bought 2.8 pounds of beef for $5.04. How much did she pay for each pound of beef?

Ⓕ $18.00   Ⓖ $7.84   Ⓗ $1.80   Ⓙ $0.18

Write each phrase as a numerical or algebraic expression. (Lesson 2-2)

40. 103 less than 739   **41.** the product of 7 and z **42.** the difference of 12 and n

Find each quotient. (Lesson 3-6)

43. $25.5 \div 5$ **44.** $44.7 \div 3$ **45.** $96.48 \div 6$ **46.** $0.0378 \div 9$

READY TO GO ON?

Quiz for Lessons 3-4 Through 3-9

3-4 Scientific Notation

Find each product.

1. $516 \times 10,000$ **2.** 16.82×100 **3.** $5,217 \times 1,000$

Write each number in scientific notation.

4. $102,000$ **5.** $5,480,000$ **6.** $100,000,000$

3-5 Multiplying Decimals

Evaluate $5x$ for each value of x.

7. $x = 1.025$ **8.** $x = 6.2$ **9.** $x = 2.64$

10. Neptune has a gravitational pull 1.2 times that of Earth. If an object weighs 15 pounds on Earth, how much would it weigh on Neptune?

3-6 Dividing Decimals by Whole Numbers

Find each quotient.

11. $17.5 \div 5$ **12.** $11.6 \div 8$ **13.** $23.4 \div 6$ **14.** $35.5 \div 5$

15. Five apples cost $4.90. How much does each apple cost?

3-7 Dividing Decimals

Find each quotient.

16. $2.226 \div 0.42$ **17.** $13.49 \div 7.1$ **18.** $35.34 \div 6.2$ **19.** $178.64 \div 81.2$

20. Peri spent $21.89 on material to make a skirt. The material cost $3.98 per yard. How many yards did Peri buy?

3-8 Interpret the Quotient

21. There are 352 students graduating from high school. The photographer takes one picture of each student as the student receives his or her diploma. If the photographer has 36 exposures on each roll of film, how many rolls will she have to buy to take each student's picture?

3-9 Solving Decimal Equations

Solve each equation.

22. $t - 6.3 = 8.9$ **23.** $4h = 20.4$ **24.** $\frac{p}{7} = 4.6$ **25.** $d + 2.8 = 9.5$

MULTI-STEP TEST PREP

Read All About It! Most Americans read a newspaper at least once a week. In fact, about 55 million newspapers are sold in the United States each day. The table shows the approximate daily circulation of some of the most popular U.S. newspapers.

1. Order the newspapers from the least daily circulation to the greatest.

2. Estimate the total circulation of the eight newspapers. Explain how you made your estimate.

3. The *Wall Street Journal,* the *New York Post,* and the *New York Times* are all published in New York. What is the total circulation for these newspapers?

4. Write the circulation of the *Wall Street Journal* in scientific notation. (*Hint:* 2.09 million is the same as 2,090,000.)

5. The circulation of *USA Today* is about 4.2 times the circulation of the *San Francisco Chronicle.* Find the circulation of *USA Today.*

6. The daily circulation of the *Los Angeles Times* is about 3 times the daily circulation of the *Orange County Register.* Write and solve an equation to find the daily circulation of the *Orange County Register.*

U.S. Newspaper Circulation	
Newspaper	**Daily Circulation (Millions)**
Chicago Tribune	0.681
Dallas Morning News	0.51
Houston Chronicle	0.553
Los Angeles Times	0.915
New York Post	0.652
New York Times	1.12
San Francisco Chronicle	0.513
Wall Street Journal	2.09

Multi-Step Test Prep

Game Time

Jumbles

Do you know what eleven plus two equals?

Use your calculator to evaluate each expression. Keep the letters under the expressions with the answers you get. Then order the answers from least to greatest, and write down the letters in that order. You will spell the answer to the riddle.

$4 - 1.893$	$0.21 \div 0.3$	$0.443 - 0.0042$	$4.509 - 3.526$	$3.14 \cdot 2.44$	$1.56 \cdot 3.678$
E	**L**	**E**	**V**	**E**	**N**

$6.34 \div 2.56$	$1.19 + 1.293$	$8.25 \div 2.5$	$7.4 - 2.356$
P	**L**	**U**	**S**

$0.0003 + 0.003$	$0.3 \cdot 0.04$	$2.17 + 3.42$
T	**W**	**O**

Make A Buck

The object of the game is to win the most points by adding decimal numbers to make a sum close to but not over $1.00.

Most cards have a decimal number on them representing an amount of money. Others are wild cards: The person who receives a wild card decides its value.

The dealer gives each player four cards. Taking turns, players add the numbers in their hand. If the sum is less than $1.00, a player can either draw a card from the top of the deck or pass.

When each player has taken a turn or passed, the player whose sum is closest to but not over $1.00 scores a point. If players tie for the closest sum, each of those players scores a point. All cards are then discarded and four new cards are dealt to each player.

When all of the cards have been dealt, the player with the most points wins.

A complete copy of the rules and game pieces are available online.

go.hrw.com
Game Time Extra
KEYWORD: MR7 Games

Materials
- 2 plastic slide holders
- squares of card stock
- clear tape
- permanent marker

It's in the Bag!

PROJECT | **Project E Z 2 C Decimals**

Practice reading decimals by making this see-through decimal holder.

Directions

1 Cut out about 40 small squares of colored card stock. Remove ten of the squares. On these squares, write "Ones," "Tens," "Hundreds," "Thousands," "Ten-Thousands," "Tenths," "Hundredths," "Thousandths," "Ten-Thousandths," and "Hundred-Thousandths." **Figure A**

2 On each of the remaining squares, write a number from 0 to 9.

3 Tape the two slide holders together. Using a permanent marker, draw decimal points down the middle where the holders are taped together. **Figure B**

4 Put the squares with the names of the place values in the correct slots along the top row.

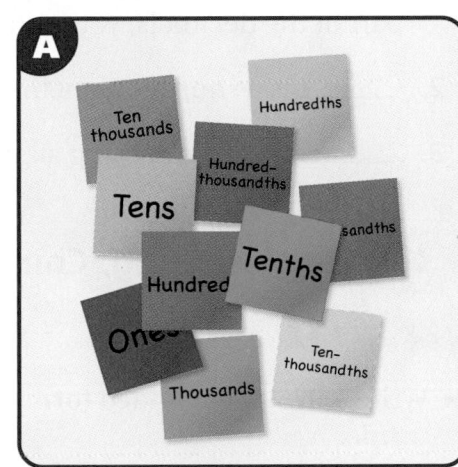

Putting the Math into Action

Put numbered squares in the remaining slots. Work with a partner to practice reading the resulting decimals. Mix up the numbered squares and repeat the process several more times, sometimes using all of the slots in a row and sometimes making shorter decimals.

Study Guide: Review

CHAPTER **3**

Vocabulary

clustering . . . . 112 scientific notation 124

front-end estimation 113

Complete the sentences below with vocabulary words from the list above.

1. When you estimate a sum by using only the whole-number part of the decimals, you are using __?__.

2. __?__ is a shorthand method for writing large numbers.

3. __?__ means rounding all the numbers to the same value.

3-1 Representing, Comparing, and Ordering Decimals (pp. 108–111)

 6.N.14, 6.N.15

EXAMPLE

■ Write 4.025 in expanded form and words.

Expanded form: 4 + 0.02 + 0.005

Word form: four and twenty-five thousandths

■ Order the decimals from least to greatest. 7.8, 7.83, 7.08

7.08 < 7.80 < 7.83   *Compare the numbers.*
7.08, 7.8, 7.83   *Then order the numbers.*

EXERCISES

Write each in expanded form and words.

4. 5.68   5. 1.0076
6. 1.203   7. 23.005
8. 71.038   9. 99.9999

Order the decimals from least to greatest.

10. 1.2, 1.3, 1.12   11. 11.17, 11.7, 11.07
12. 0.3, 0.303, 0.033   13. 5.009, 5.950, 5.5
14. 101.52, 101.25, 101.025

3-2 Estimating Decimals (pp. 112–115)

6.CN.7

EXAMPLE

■ Estimate.

5.35 − 0.7904; round to tenths

  5.4   *Align the decimals.*
− 0.8   *Subtract.*
  4.6

■ Estimate 49.67 × 2.88.

49.67 × 2.88
 50 × 3 = 150

EXERCISES

Estimate.

15. 8.0954 + 3.218; round to the hundredths
16. 6.8356 − 4.507; round to the tenths
17. 9.258 + 4.97; round to the ones

Estimate each product or quotient.

18. 21.19 × 4.23   19. 53.98 ÷ 5.97
20. 102.89 × 19.95

152 *Chapter 3 Decimals*

3-3 Adding and Subtracting Decimals (pp. 118–121)

6.A.2, 5.A.3

EXAMPLE

■ **Find the sum.**

7.62 + 0.563

$$
\begin{array}{r}
7.620 \\
+\ 0.563 \\
\hline
8.183
\end{array}
$$

Align the decimal points.
Use zeros as placeholders.
Add. Place the decimal point.

EXERCISES

Find each sum or difference.

21. $7.08 + 4.5 + 13.27$ **22.** $6 - 0.7$

23. $6.21 + 5.8 + 21.01$ **24.** $7.001 - 2.0785$

25. $5.1 + 7.98 + 19.25$ **26.** $15.704 - 1.08$

Evaluate $6.48 - s$ **for each value of s.**

27. $s = 3.9$ **28.** $s = 3.6082$

29. $s = 5.01$ **30.** $s = 0.057$

31. $s = 4.48$ **32.** $s = 1.65$

3-4 Scientific Notation (pp. 124–127)

6.CN.4

EXAMPLE

■ **Find the product.**

$326 \times 10,000$
$= 326.0000$ *Move the decimal point 4 places right.*
$= 3,260,000$ *Write 4 placeholder zeros.*

■ **Write the number in scientific notation.**

$60,000$ *Move the decimal point 4 places to the left.*

$= 6.0 \times 10^4$

■ **Write each number in standard form.**

7.18×10^5

$= 718,000$ *Move the decimal point 5 places right.*

EXERCISES

Find each product.

33. $12.6 \times 10,000$ **34.** 546×100

35. $67 \times 100,000$ **36.** $180.6 \times 1,000$

37. $4.2 \times 1,000$ **38.** 78.9×100

Write each number in scientific notation.

39. $550,000$ **40.** $7,230$

41. $1,300,000$ **42.** 14.8

43. 902.4 **44.** $891,402,000$

Write each number in standard form.

45. 3.02×10^4 **46.** 4.293×10^5

47. 1.7×10^6 **48.** 5.39×10^3

49. 6.85×10^2 **50.** 1.45×10^7

3-5 Multiplying Decimals (pp. 130–133)

6.A.2, 5.A.3

EXAMPLE

■ **Find the product.**

$$
\begin{array}{r}
0.3 \\
\times\ 0.08 \\
\hline
0.024
\end{array}
$$

1 decimal place
+ 2 decimal places
3 decimal places

EXERCISES

Find each product.

51. 4×2.36 **52.** 0.5×1.73

53. 0.6×0.012 **54.** 8×3.052

55. 1.2×0.45 **56.** 9.7×1.084

57. 9×1.08 **58.** 7.2×5.49

3-6 Dividing Decimals by Whole Numbers (pp. 134–136)

 6.A.2, 5.A.3

EXAMPLE

■ Find the quotient.

0.95 ÷ 5

Place a decimal point directly above the decimal point in the dividend. Then divide.

$$\begin{array}{r} 0.19 \\ 5\overline{)0.95} \end{array}$$

EXERCISES

Find each quotient.

59. $6.18 \div 6$ **60.** $2.16 \div 3$

61. $34.65 \div 9$ **62.** $20.72 \div 8$

63. If four people equally share a bill for $14.56, how much should each person pay?

3-7 Dividing by Decimals (pp. 137–140)

 6.N.27

EXAMPLE

■ Find the quotient.

9.65 ÷ 0.5

Make the divisor a whole number. Place the decimal point in the quotient.

$$\begin{array}{r} 19.3 \\ 5\overline{)96.5} \end{array}$$

EXERCISES

Find each quotient.

64. $4.86 \div 0.6$ **65.** $1.85 \div 0.3$

66. $34.89 \div 9$ **67.** $62.73 \div 1.2$

68. Ana cuts some wood that is 3.75 meters long into 5 pieces of equal length. How long is each piece?

3-8 Interpret the Quotient (pp. 141–143)

 6.PS.7

EXAMPLE

■ Ms. Ald needs 26 stickers for her preschool class. Stickers are sold in packs of 8. How many packs should she buy?

$26 \div 8 = 3.25$

3.25 is between 3 and 4.
3 packs will not be enough.

Ms. Ald should buy 4 packs of stickers.

EXERCISES

69. Billy has 3.6 liters of juice. How many 0.25 L containers can he fill?

70. There are 34 people going on a field trip. If each car holds 4 people, how many cars will they need for the field trip?

3-9 Solving Decimal Equations (pp. 144–147)

5.A.4

EXAMPLE

■ Solve $4x = 20.8$.

$4x = 20.8$ *x is multiplied by 4.*

$\dfrac{4x}{4} = \dfrac{20.8}{4}$ *Divide both sides by 4.*

$x = 5.2$

EXERCISES

Solve each equation.

71. $a - 6.2 = 7.18$ **72.** $3y = 7.86$

73. $n + 4.09 = 6.38$ **74.** $\dfrac{p}{7} = 8.6$

75. Jasmine buys 2.25 kg of apples for $11.25. How much does 1 kg of apples cost?

CHAPTER TEST

1. The New York Philharmonic Orchestra performs at Avery Fisher Hall in New York City. It seats 2,738 people. The Boston Symphony Orchestra performs at Symphony Hall in Boston, Massachusetts. It seats 2,625 people. Which hall seats more people?

Order the decimals from least to greatest.

2. 12.6, 12.07, 12.67

3. 3.5, 3.25, 3.08

4. 0.10301, 0.10318, 0.10325

Estimate by rounding to the indicated place value.

5. 6.178 − 0.2805; hundredths

6. 7.528 + 6.075; ones

Estimate.

7. 21.35×3.18

8. $98.547 \div 4.93$

9. 11.855×8.45

Estimate a range for each sum.

10. 3.89 + 42.71 + 12.32

11. 20.751 + 2.55 + 17.4

12. 4.987 + 28.27 + 0.098

13. Britney wants to exercise in a step aerobics class. The class uses the 4-inch step for 15 minutes and the 6-inch step for 15 minutes. About how many calories will she burn in all?

Step Height (in.)	Calories Burned in 15 minutes
4	67.61
6	82.2
8	96

Evaluate.

14. 0.76 + 2.24

15. 7 − 0.4

16. 0.12×0.006

17. $5.85 \div 3.9$

Find each product.

18. $516 \times 10,000$

19. 16.82×100

20. $521.7 \times 100,000$

21. $423.6 \times 1,000$

Write each number in scientific notation.

22. 16,900

23. 180,500

24. 3,190,000

Write each number in standard form.

25. 3.08×10^5

26. 1.472×10^6

27. 2.973×10^4

Solve each equation.

28. $b - 4.7 = 2.1$

29. $5a = 4.75$

30. $\frac{y}{6} = 7.2$

31. $c + 1.9 = 26.04$

32. The school band is going to a competition. There are 165 students in the band. If each bus holds 25 students, how many buses will be needed?

33. Six girls went shopping. All sweaters were on sale for the same price. Each girl chose a sweater. The total bill was $126.24. How much did each sweater cost?

Short Response: Write Short Responses

Short-response test items require a solution to the problem and the reasoning or work used to get that solution. Short-response test items are scored according to a 2-point scoring rubric. A sample scoring rubric is provided below.

EXAMPLE

Short Response Coach Mott needs to order jackets for the boys' basketball team. Each jacket costs $28.75. The team has $125 from their fund-raiser to go toward the total cost of the jackets. If there are 10 players on the team, how much money will each player need to give to Coach Mott for a jacket so he can place the order? Explain.

2-point response:

> Cost of one jacket: $28.75
> Total cost for team jackets (10 players):
> $28.75 × 10 = $287.50
>
> Subtract the money the team already has from the total cost.
> $287.50 − $125 = $162.50
>
> Divide the remaining cost by the number of players on the team.
> $162.50 ÷ 10 = $16.25
>
> Each player needs to give Coach Mott $16.25 so he can place the order for the jackets.

1-point response:

> ($287.50 − $125) ÷ $10 = $16.25
>
> He will need $16.25 from each player.

The student correctly solved the problem but did not show all of his or her work or did not provide an explanation.

0-point response:

> $16.25

The student gave a correct answer but did not show any work or give an explanation.

Scoring Rubric

2 points: The student's response is correct and complete. The answer contains complete explanations and/or adequate work when required.

1 point: The student's response demonstrates only partial understanding. The response may include the correct process with an incorrect answer, or a correct answer without the required work.

0 points: The student's response demonstrates no understanding of the mathematical concepts. The response may include a correct response using an obviously incorrect procedure.

Hot Tip Never leave a short-response test item blank. Showing your work and providing a reasonable explanation will result in at least some credit.

Read each test item and answer the questions that follow by using the scoring rubric.

Item A
Short Response Write two equations that each have a solution of 12. You cannot use the same mathematical operation for both equations. Explain how to solve both equations.

Student's Answer

One equation that has a solution of 12 is $\frac{x}{6} = 2$. To solve this equation, I must undo the division by multiplying by 6 on both sides.

$$\frac{x}{6} = 2$$

$$6 \cdot \left(\frac{x}{6}\right) = 6 \cdot 2$$

$$x = 12$$

Another equation with a solution of 12 is $x - 8 = 20$.

To solve this equation, I must add the opposite of 8 to both sides.

$$x - 8 = 20$$
$$\underline{-8 = -8}$$
$$x = 12$$

1. The student's answer will not receive full credit. Find the error in the student's answer.

2. Rewrite the student's answer so that it receives full credit.

Item B
Short Response June is 8 years older than her cousin Liv. Write an expression to find June's age. Identify the variable and list three possible solutions showing the ages of June and Liv.

Student's Answer

Let x = Liv's age. Since June is 8 years older, the expression $x + 8$ can be used to find June's age.

Three possible solutions for Liv and June follow:

$x = 3$, $3 + 8 = 11$; Liv: 3, June: 11
$x = 8$, $8 + 8 = 16$; Liv: 8, June: 16
$x = 11$, $11 + 8 = 19$; Liv: 11, June: 19

3. What score should the student's answer receive? Explain your reasoning.

4. What additional information, if any, should the student's answer include in order to receive full credit?

Item C
Short Response Write an equation to represent the following situation. Define the variable. Solve the problem. *Sam has two kittens. The larger kitten weighs 3.2 kg. The other kitten needs to gain 1.9 kg to weigh as much as the larger kitten. How much does the smaller kitten weigh?*

Student's Answer

Let x = the weight of the smaller kitten.
$x + 1.9 = 3.2$
$3.2 + 1.9 = 5.1$

5. How would you score the student's response? Explain.

6. Rewrite the response so that it receives full credit.

CUMULATIVE ASSESSMENT, CHAPTERS 1–3

Multiple Choice

1. Which of the following is the standard form for six and eighty-six thousandths?

   Ⓐ 6.860   Ⓒ 6.0086

   Ⓑ 6.086   Ⓓ 6.00086

2. The weights of three backpacks are 15.8 pounds, 18.1 pounds, and 16.7 pounds. About how many pounds do the backpacks weigh all together?

   Ⓕ 30 pounds   Ⓗ 50 pounds

   Ⓖ 40 pounds   Ⓙ 60 pounds

3. For which equation is $c = 8$ NOT a solution?

   Ⓐ $\frac{c}{4} = 2$ Ⓒ $4c = 28$

   Ⓑ $c + 4 = 12$ Ⓓ $c - 5 = 3$

4. Jerah scored 15 more points in a basketball game than his brother Jim did. Jim scored 7 points. Which expression can be used to find the number of points Jerah scored?

   Ⓕ $15 - 7$ Ⓗ $15 \div 7$

   Ⓖ 15×7 Ⓙ $15 + 7$

5. Find the sum of 1.4 and 0.9.

   Ⓐ 0.1   Ⓒ 1.3

   Ⓑ 0.5   Ⓓ 2.3

6. Which number is the greatest?

   Ⓕ 18.095   Ⓗ 18.907

   Ⓖ 18.9   Ⓙ 18.75

7. The heights of four different plants are listed below. Which statement is supported by the data?

Plant Height (in.)				
Plant	T	S	U	W
Week 1	15.9	23.6	17.1	12.5
Week 2	21.4	27.4	22.9	16.4

   Ⓐ Plant T was the shortest during week 1.

   Ⓑ Plant S grew more than 4 inches between week 1 and week 2.

   Ⓒ Plant U grew the most between week 1 and week 2.

   Ⓓ Plant W is the tallest.

8. What is the value of 3^4?

   Ⓕ 7   Ⓗ 81

   Ⓖ 12   Ⓙ 96

9. There are 58,000 seats in a football stadium. Which of the following is the correct way to write 58,000 in scientific notation?

   Ⓐ 580×10^2 Ⓒ 5.8×10^4

   Ⓑ 58×10^3 Ⓓ 0.58×10^5

10. Tomas needs 42 cups for a party. The cups are sold in packages of 5. How many packages should he buy?

    Ⓕ 10 packages   Ⓗ 8 packages

    Ⓖ 9 packages   Ⓙ 7 packages

11. What is $7.89 \div 3$?

    Ⓐ 263   Ⓒ 0.263

    Ⓑ 26.3   Ⓓ 2.63

12. Which set of numbers is in order from least to greatest?

　(F) 23.7, 23.07, 23.13, 23.89

　(G) 21.4, 21.45, 21.79, 21.8

　(H) 22, 22.09, 21.9, 22.1

　(J) 25.4, 25.09, 25.6, 25.7

13. Megan is beginning an exercise routine. She plans to walk 1 mile on day 1 and increase her distance each day by 0.25 mile. How many miles will she be walking on day 10?

　(A) 2.5 miles　　(C) 4.75 miles

　(B) 3.25 miles　　(D) 6.0 miles

 **Hot Tip** Estimate your answer before solving the question. Use your estimate to check the reasonableness of your answer.

14. What is the value of c in the equation $\frac{c}{6} = 3.4$?

　(F) 0.57　　(H) 9.4

　(G) 4　　(J) 20.4

15. What is the missing term in the following sequence?

5, 12, 26, 47, ▨, 110, . . .

　(A) 68　　(C) 78.5

　(B) 75　　(D) 99

16. Cindy bought 3 bunches of daisies and 4 bunches of carnations. There are 6 daisies and 10 carnations in a bunch. How many flowers does she have in all?

　(F) 58　　(H) 112

　(G) 72　　(J) 720

17. Bart and his 2 friends buy lunch. The total is $13.74. If they share the cost equally, how much, in dollars, should each person pay?

　(A) $4.58　　(C) $6.37

　(B) $5.87　　(D) $6.87

Short Response

18. Kevin buys 5 steaks for $43.75. Let b equal the cost of one steak. Write and solve the equation to find the cost of one steak.

19. Ms. Maier has 8 packs of pencils to give out to students taking a state test. Each pack has 8 pencils. There are 200 students taking the test who need pencils.

　a. How many more packs of pencils does Ms. Maier need to buy? Explain your answer and show your work.

　b. If each pack of pencils costs $0.79, how much money will Ms. Maier need to spend to buy the extra pencils? Show your work.

Extended Response

20. Admission to the Children's Museum is listed below. Use the chart to answer the following questions.

Admission Costs ($)	
Adult	7.50
Child	5.75

　a. Write an expression to find the cost of admission for 2 adults and c children.

　b. Use your expression to find the total cost for Mr. and Mrs. Chu and their 8-year-old triplets. Show your work.

　c. If Mr. Chu pays for admission using a $50 bill, how much change does he get back? Show your work.

　d. On the Chu's next visit, Mrs. Chu plans to use a coupon and will only pay $28.50 for the family. How much will she save using the coupon?

Number Theory and Fractions

NEW YORK TEST PREP

go.hrw.com
Chapter Project Online
KEYWORD: MR7 Ch4

ABS Plastic Drain Pipe	
Component	Cost ($)
Pipe 4 in. × 10 ft	11.99
Pipe 4 in. × 20 ft	22.57
Straight coupling	2.19
$\frac{1}{4}$-bend connection	6.49
$\frac{1}{8}$-bend connection	5.99
$\frac{1}{6}$-bend connection	7.49

Career Plumber

Do you like working with your hands to solve problems? If so, you might want to become a skilled trade worker, such as a master plumber.

To calculate the cost of parts and labor, plumbers use basic mathematical formulas. For example, some plumbers might calculate the cost of a new sewer line with a formula like the following:

$$\text{cost of installed line} = \frac{\text{cost of pipe}}{3} \times 49 + \frac{\text{cost of pipe fittings}}{2}$$

ARE YOU READY?

✓ Vocabulary

Choose the best term from the list to complete each sentence.

1. To find the sum of two numbers, you should __?__.
2. Fractions are written as a __?__ over a __?__.
3. In the equation 4 · 3 = 12, 12 is the __?__.
4. The __?__ of 18 and 10 is 8.
5. The numbers 18, 27, and 72 are __?__ of 9.

add
denominator
difference
multiples
numerator
product
quotient

Complete these exercises to review skills you will need for this chapter.

✓ Write and Read Decimals

Write each decimal in word form.

6. 0.5	**7.** 2.78	**8.** 0.125
9. 12.8	**10.** 125.49	**11.** 8.024

✓ Multiples

List the first four multiples of each number.

12. 6	**13.** 8	**14.** 5	**15.** 12
16. 7	**17.** 20	**18.** 14	**19.** 9

✓ Evaluate Expressions

Evaluate each expression for the given value of the variable.

20. $y + 4.3$ for $y = 3.2$
21. $\frac{x}{5}$ for $x = 6.4$
22. $3c$ for $c = 0.75$
23. $a + 4 \div 8$ for $a = 3.75$
24. $27.8 - d$ for $d = 9.25$
25. $2.5b$ for $b = 8.4$

✓ Factors

Find all the whole-number factors of each number.

26. 8	**27.** 12	**28.** 24	**29.** 30
30. 45	**31.** 52	**32.** 75	**33.** 150

Study Guide: Preview

Where You've Been

Previously, you

- identified a number as prime or composite.
- identified common factors of a set of whole numbers.
- generated equivalent fractions.
- compared two fractions with common denominators.

In This Chapter

You will study

- writing the prime factorization of a number.
- finding the greatest common factor (GCF) of a set of whole numbers.
- generating equivalent forms of numbers, including whole numbers, fractions, and decimals.
- comparing and ordering fractions, decimals, and whole numbers.

Where You're Going

You can use the skills learned in this chapter

- to double or halve recipes when cooking.
- to add together fractions when determining volume in a science class.

Key Vocabulary/Vocabulario

common denominator	común denominador
composite number	número compuesto
equivalent fractions	fracciones equivalentes
factor	factor
greatest common factor (GCF)	máximo común divisor (MCD)
improper fraction	fracción impropia
prime factorization	factorización prima
prime number	número primo
terminating decimal	decimal cerrado

Vocabulary Connections

To become familiar with some of the vocabulary terms in the chapter, consider the following. You may refer to the chapter, the glossary, or a dictionary if you like.

1. The word *equivalent* means "equal in value." What do you think **equivalent fractions** are?

2. To *terminate* something means to bring it to an end. If a decimal is a **terminating decimal**, what do you think happens to it? Explain.

3. When people have something in *common*, they have something that they share. What do you think **common denominators** share?

4. If something is *improper*, it is not right. In fractions, it is *improper* to have the numerator be greater than the denominator. How would you expect an **improper fraction** to look?

Reading and Writing Math

Reading Strategy: Read a Lesson for Understanding

Reading ahead will prepare you for new ideas and concepts presented in class. As you read a lesson, make notes. Write down the main points of the lesson, math terms that you do not understand, examples that need more explanation, and questions you can ask during class.

Learn to solve equations involving decimals.

The objective tells you the main idea of the lesson.

Work through the examples and write down any questions you have.

Solving One-Step Equations with Decimals

Solve each equation. Check your answer.

A $g - 3.1 = 4.5$

$$
\begin{array}{rl}
g - 3.1 = & 4.5 \\
+\,3.1 \quad & +\,3.1 \\
\hline
g = & 7.6
\end{array}
$$

3.1 is subtracted from g.

Add 3.1 to both sides to undo the subtraction.

Check

$g - 3.1 = 4.5$

$7.6 - 3.1 \overset{?}{=} 4.5$ *Substitute 7.6 for g in the equation.*

$4.5 \overset{?}{=} 4.5$ ✔   *7.6 is the solution.*

Questions:
- *How do I know what operation to use?*
- *What should I do if I check my answer and the two sides are not equal?*

Write down questions you have as you read the lesson.

Try This

Read Lesson 4-1 before your next class and answer the following questions.

1. What is the objective of the lesson?

2. Are there new vocabulary terms, formulas, or symbols? If so, what are they?

Reading and Writing Math

4-1 Divisibility

NY Performance Indicators

6.RP.2 Understand that mathematical statements can be supported, using models, facts, and relationships to explain their thinking.

Learn to use divisibility rules.

Vocabulary

divisible

composite number

prime number

This year, 42 girls signed up to play basketball for the Junior Girls League, which has 6 teams. To find whether each team can have the same number of girls, decide if 42 is divisible by 6.

A number is **divisible** by another number if the quotient is a whole number with no remainder.

$$42 \div 6 = 7 \leftarrow \text{Quotient}$$

Since there is no remainder, 42 is divisible by 6. The Junior Girls League can have 6 teams with 7 girls each.

Divisibility Rules		
A number is divisible by...	**Divisible**	**Not Divisible**
2 if the last digit is even (0, 2, 4, 6, or 8).	3,978	4,975
3 if the sum of the digits is divisible by 3.	315	139
4 if the last two digits form a number divisible by 4.	8,512	7,518
5 if the last digit is 0 or 5.	14,975	10,978
6 if the number is divisible by both 2 and 3.	48	20
9 if the sum of the digits is divisible by 9.	711	93
10 if the last digit is 0.	15,990	10,536

EXAMPLE **Checking Divisibility**

A Tell whether 610 is divisible by 2, 3, 4, and 5.

2	*The last digit, 0, is even.*	Divisible
3	*The sum of the digits is 6 + 1 + 0 = 7. 7 is not divisible by 3.*	Not divisible
4	*The last two digits form the number 10. 10 is not divisible by 4.*	Not divisible
5	*The last digit is 0.*	Divisible

So 610 is divisible by 2 and 5.

B Tell whether 387 is divisible by 6, 9, and 10.

6	*The last digit, 7, is odd, so 387 is not divisible by 2.*	Not divisible
9	*The sum of the digits is 3 + 8 + 7 = 18. 18 is divisible by 9.*	Divisible
10	*The last digit is 7, not 0.*	Not divisible

So 387 is divisible by 9.

Any number greater than 1 is divisible by at least two numbers— 1 and the number itself. Numbers that are divisible by more than two numbers are called **composite numbers**.

A **prime number** is divisible by only the numbers 1 and itself. For example, 11 is a prime number because it is divisible by only 1 and 11. The numbers 0 and 1 are neither prime nor composite.

EXAMPLE 2 **Identifying Prime and Composite Numbers**

Tell whether each number is prime or composite.

A 45
divisible by 1, 3, 5, 9, 15, 45
composite

B 13
divisible by 1, 13
prime

C 19
divisible by 1, 19
prime

D 49
divisible by 1, 7, 49
composite

The prime numbers from 1 through 50 are highlighted below.

1	2	3	4	5	6	7	8	9	10
11	12	13	14	15	16	17	18	19	20
21	22	23	24	25	26	27	28	29	30
31	32	33	34	35	36	37	38	39	40
41	42	43	44	45	46	47	48	49	50

6.PS.21, 6.RP.5

Think and Discuss

1. Tell which whole numbers are divisible by 1.

2. Explain how you know that 87 is a composite number.

3. Tell how the divisibility rules help you identify composite numbers.

4-1 Exercises

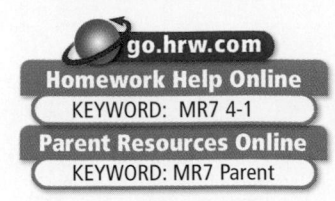
go.hrw.com
Homework Help Online
KEYWORD: MR7 4-1
Parent Resources Online
KEYWORD: MR7 Parent

GUIDED PRACTICE

See Example **1** Tell whether each number is divisible by 2, 3, 4, 5, 6, 9, and 10.

1. 508   **2.** 432   **3.** 247   **4.** 189

See Example **2** Tell whether each number is prime or composite.

5. 75   **6.** 17   **7.** 27   **8.** 63

9. 72   **10.** 83   **11.** 99   **12.** 199

INDEPENDENT PRACTICE

See Example **1** Tell whether each number is divisible by 2, 3, 4, 5, 6, 9, and 10.

13. 741   **14.** 810   **15.** 675   **16.** 480

17. 908   **18.** 146   **19.** 514   **20.** 405

See Example **2** Tell whether each number is prime or composite.

21. 34   **22.** 29   **23.** 61   **24.** 81

25. 51   **26.** 23   **27.** 97   **28.** 93

29. 77   **30.** 41   **31.** 67   **32.** 39

PRACTICE AND PROBLEM SOLVING

Extra Practice
See page 720.

Copy and complete the table. Write *yes* if the number is divisible by the given number. Write *no* if it is not.

		2	3	4	5	6	9	10
33.	677	*no*	▪	▪	*no*	▪	▪	*no*
34.	290	*yes*	▪	▪	▪	▪	▪	▪
35.	1,744	▪	▪	▪	▪	▪	▪	▪
36.	12,180	▪	▪	▪	▪	▪	▪	▪

Tell whether each statement is true or false. Explain your answers.

37. All even numbers are divisible by 2.

38. All odd numbers are divisible by 3.

39. Some even numbers are divisible by 5.

40. All odd numbers are prime.

Replace each box with a digit that will make the number divisible by 3.

41. 74▪   **42.** 8,10▪   **43.** 3,▪41

44. ▪,335   **45.** 67,▪11   **46.** 10,0▪1

47. Make a table that shows the prime numbers from 50 to 100.

48. Astronomy Earth has a diameter of 7,926 miles. Tell whether this number is divisible by 2, 3, 4, 5, 6, 9, and 10.

49. On which of the bridges in the table could a light fixture be placed every 6 meters so that the first light is at the beginning of the bridge and the last light is at the end of the bridge? Explain.

Golden Gate Bridge

Longest Bridges in the U.S.	
Name and State	**Length (m)**
Verrazano Narrows, NY	1,298
Golden Gate, CA	1,280
Mackinac Straits, MI	1,158
George Washington, NY	1,067

50. Critical Thinking A number is between 80 and 100 and is divisible by both 5 and 6. What is the number?

 51. Choose a Strategy Find the greatest four-digit number that is divisible by 1, 2, 3, and 4.

 52. What's the Error? To find whether 3,463 is divisible by 4, a student added the digits. The sum, 16, is divisible by 4, so the student stated that 3,463 is divisible by 4. Explain the error.

 53. Write About It If a number is divisible by both 4 and 9, by what other numbers is it divisible? Explain.

 54. Challenge Find a number that is divisible by 2, 3, 4, 5, 6, and 10, but not 9.

TEST PREP and Spiral Review

55. Multiple Choice _____?_____ numbers are divisible by more than two numbers.

Ⓐ Whole   Ⓑ Prime   Ⓒ Equivalent   Ⓓ Composite

56. Short Response What is the least three-digit number that is divisible by both 5 and 9? Show your work.

Use the pattern to write the first five terms of each sequence. (Lesson 1-7)

57. Start with 7; add 4.   **58.** Start with 78; subtract 9.   **59.** Start with 6; multiply by 5.

Evaluate each expression for the given value of the variable. (Lesson 2-1)

60. $2x + 28$ for $x = 4$ **61.** $x + 18$ for $x = 12$ **62.** $\frac{x}{5}$ for $x = 25$

Hands-On LAB 4-2

Explore Factors

Use with Lesson 4-2

go.hrw.com
Lab Resources Online
KEYWORD: MR7 Lab4

NY Performance Indicators
6.CN.4, 6.R.1, 6.R.5

You can use graph paper or unit cubes to model *factors* of a number and determine whether the number is a prime number or a composite number.

Activity

Use graph paper to show the different ways the number 16 can be modeled.

1 The number 16 can be modeled by drawing a rectangle 2 units wide and 8 units long. The dimensions, 2 and 8, are factors of 16. This means that $2 \times 8 = 16$.

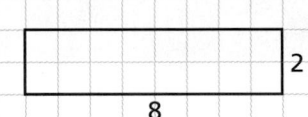

What other ways can 16 be modeled?
A rectangle 1 unit wide and 16 units long and a 4-unit-by-4 unit square can also model 16.

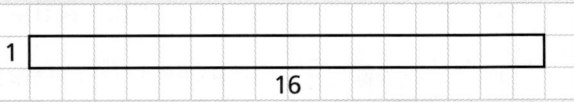

The factors of 16 are 1, 2, 4, 8, and 16. Because you can model 16 in more than one way, 16 is a composite number.

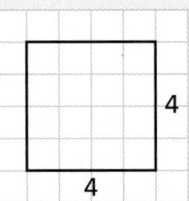

Use graph paper to show the different ways the number 3 can be modeled.

2 The number 3 can be modeled by drawing a rectangle 1 unit wide and 3 units long. The dimensions, 1 and 3, are factors of 3. This means that $1 \times 3 = 3$.
Because 3 cannot be modeled any other way, 3 is a prime number.

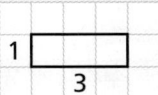

Think and Discuss

1. How can you use the rules of divisibility to determine whether there is more than one way to model a number?

2. Find the factors of 2. Is 2 prime or composite? Explain.

Try This

1. Use graph paper to model two prime numbers and two composite numbers. Find their factors.

4-2 Factors and Prime Factorization

Learn to write prime factorizations of composite numbers.

Vocabulary
factor
prime factorization

Whole numbers that are multiplied to find a product are called **factors** of that product. A number is divisible by its factors.

$$2 \cdot 3 = 6 \qquad 6 \div 3 = 2$$

$$6 \div 2 = 3$$

6 is divisible by 3 and 2.

Factors   Product

EXAMPLE 1   Finding Factors

NY Performance Indicators

6.PS.15 Make organized lists or charts to solve numerical problems. Also, 6.R.6.

Helpful Hint

When the pairs of factors begin to repeat, then you have found all of the factors of the number you are factoring.

List all of the factors of each number.

A 18

Begin listing factors in pairs.

$18 = 1 \cdot 18$	*1 is a factor.*
$18 = 2 \cdot 9$	*2 is a factor.*
$18 = 3 \cdot 6$	*3 is a factor.*
	4 is not a factor.
	5 is not a factor.
$18 = 6 \cdot 3$	*6 and 3 have already been listed, so stop here.*

1   2   3   6   9   18

You can draw a diagram to illustrate the factor pairs.

The factors of 18 are 1, 2, 3, 6, 9, and 18.

B 13

$13 = 1 \cdot 13$

Begin listing factors in pairs. 13 is not divisible by any other whole numbers.

The factors of 13 are 1 and 13.

You can use factors to write a number in different ways.

Factorization of 12			
$1 \cdot 12$	$2 \cdot 6$	$3 \cdot 4$	$3 \cdot 2 \cdot 2$

◄— *Notice that these factors are all prime.*

The **prime factorization** of a number is the number written as the product of its prime factors.

EXAMPLE 2 **Writing Prime Factorizations**

Write the prime factorization of each number.

A 36

Method 1: Use a factor tree.

Choose any two factors of 36 to begin. Keep finding factors until each branch ends at a prime factor.

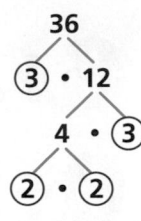

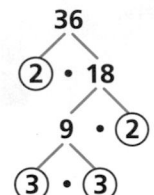

$$36 = 3 \cdot 2 \cdot 2 \cdot 3 \qquad\qquad 36 = 2 \cdot 3 \cdot 3 \cdot 2$$

The prime factorization of 36 is $2 \cdot 2 \cdot 3 \cdot 3$, or $2^2 \cdot 3^2$.

> **Helpful Hint**
>
> You can use exponents to write prime factorizations. Remember that an exponent tells you how many times the base is a factor.

B 54

Method 2: Use a ladder diagram.

Choose a prime factor of 54 to begin. Keep dividing by prime factors until the quotient is 1.

$$
\begin{array}{r|r}
2 & 54 \\
\hline
3 & 27 \\
\hline
3 & 9 \\
\hline
3 & 3 \\
\hline
 & 1
\end{array}
\qquad\qquad
\begin{array}{r|r}
3 & 54 \\
\hline
3 & 18 \\
\hline
2 & 6 \\
\hline
3 & 3 \\
\hline
 & 1
\end{array}
$$

$$54 = 2 \cdot 3 \cdot 3 \cdot 3 \qquad\qquad 54 = 3 \cdot 3 \cdot 2 \cdot 3$$

The prime factorization of 54 is $2 \cdot 3 \cdot 3 \cdot 3$, or $2 \cdot 3^3$.

In Example 2, notice that the prime factors may be written in a different order, but they are still the same factors. Except for changes in the order, there is only one way to write the prime factorization of a number.

Think and Discuss

6.RP.6, 6.CM.10

1. Tell how you know when you have found all of the factors of a number.

2. Tell how you know when you have found the prime factorization of a number.

3. Explain the difference between factors of a number and prime factors of a number.

4-2 **Exercises**

go.hrw.com
Homework Help Online
KEYWORD: MR7 4-2
Parent Resources Online
KEYWORD: MR7 Parent

GUIDED PRACTICE

See Example **1** List all of the factors of each number.

   1. 12   **2.** 21   **3.** 52   **4.** 75

See Example **2** Write the prime factorization of each number.

   5. 48   **6.** 20   **7.** 66   **8.** 34

INDEPENDENT PRACTICE

See Example **1** List all of the factors of each number.

   9. 24   **10.** 37   **11.** 42   **12.** 56

   13. 67   **14.** 72   **15.** 85   **16.** 92

See Example **2** Write the prime factorization of each number.

   17. 49   **18.** 38   **19.** 76   **20.** 60

   21. 81   **22.** 132   **23.** 140   **24.** 87

PRACTICE AND PROBLEM SOLVING

Extra Practice
See page 720.

Write each number as a product in two different ways.

25. 34   **26.** 82   **27.** 88   **28.** 50

29. 15   **30.** 78   **31.** 94   **32.** 35

33. Sports Little League Baseball began in 1939 in Pennsylvania. When it first started, there were 45 boys on 3 teams.

   a. If the teams were equally sized, how many boys were on each team?

   b. Name another way the boys could have been divided into equally sized teams. (Remember that a baseball team must have at least 9 players.)

34. Critical Thinking Use the divisibility rules to list the factors of 171. Explain how you determined the factors.

Find the prime factorization of each number.

35. 99   **36.** 249   **37.** 284   **38.** 620

39. 840   **40.** 150   **41.** 740   **42.** 402

43. The prime factorization of 50 is $2 \cdot 5^2$. Without dividing or using a diagram, find the prime factorization of 100.

44. Geometry The area of a rectangle is the product of its length and width. Suppose the area of a rectangle is 24 in². What are the possible whole number measurements of its length and width?

45. Physical Science The speed of sound at sea level at 20°C is 343 meters per second. Write the prime factorization of 343.

Climate changes, habitat destruction, and overhunting can cause animals and plants to die in large numbers. When the entire population of a species begins to die out, the species is considered endangered.

The graph shows the number of endangered species in each category of animal.

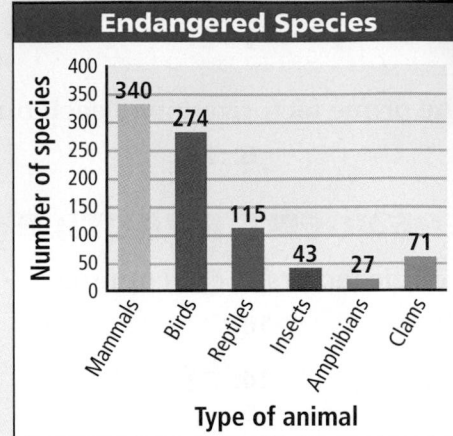

Endangered Species

46. How many species of mammals are endangered? Write this number as the product of prime factors.

47. Which categories of animals have a prime number of endangered species?

48. How many species of reptiles and amphibians combined are endangered? Write the answer as the product of prime factors.

49. **What's the Error?** When asked to write the prime factorization of the number of endangered amphibian species, a student wrote 3 × 9. Explain the error and write the correct answer.

50. **Write About It** A team of five scientists is going to study endangered insect species. The scientists want to divide the species evenly among them. Will they be able to do this? Why or why not?

51. ★ **Challenge** Add the number of endangered mammal species to the number of endangered bird species. Find the prime factorization of this number.

Laysan albatross chicks often die from eating plastic that pollutes the oceans and beaches. Clean-up efforts may prevent the albatross from becoming endangered.

go.hrw.com
Web Extra!
KEYWORD: MR7 Endangered

TEST PREP and Spiral Review

52. **Multiple Choice** Which expression shows the prime factorization of 50?

Ⓐ 2×5^2 Ⓑ 2×5^{10} Ⓒ 10^5 Ⓓ 5×10

53. **Gridded Response** What number has a prime factorization of $2 \times 2 \times 3 \times 5$?

54. Damien's favorite song is 4.2 minutes long. Jan's favorite song is 2.89 minutes long. Estimate the difference in the lengths of the songs by rounding to the nearest whole number. (Lesson 3-2)

Tell whether each number is divisible by 2, 3, 4, 5, 6, 9, and 10. (Lesson 4-1)

55. 105   56. 198   57. 360   58. 235

59. 100   60. 92   61. 540   62. 441

4-3 Greatest Common Factor

Learn to find the greatest common factor (GCF) of a set of numbers.

Vocabulary

greatest common factor (GCF)

Factors shared by two or more whole numbers are called common factors. The largest of the common factors is called the **greatest common factor**, or **GCF**.

Factors of 24: **1, 2, 3, 4, 6, 8, 12, 24**

Factors of 36: **1, 2, 3, 4, 6, 9, 12, 18, 36**

Common factors: 1, 2, 3, 4, 6, ⑫

The greatest common factor (GCF) of 24 and 36 is 12.

Example 1 shows three different methods for finding the GCF.

EXAMPLE 1 Finding the GCF

Find the GCF of each set of numbers.

NY Performance Indicators

6.PS.15 Make organized lists or charts to solve numerical problems. Also, 6.PS.23.

A 16 and 24

Method 1: List the factors.

factors of 16: 1, 2, 4, ⑧, 16   *List all the factors.*

factors of 24: 1, 2, 3, 4, 6, ⑧, 12, 24   *Circle the GCF.*

The GCF of 16 and 24 is 8.

B 12, 24, and 32

Method 2: Use prime factorization.

$12 = 2 \cdot 2 \cdot 3$ *Write the prime factorization of each number.*

$24 = 2 \cdot 2 \cdot 2 \cdot 3$

$32 = 2 \cdot 2 \cdot 2 \cdot 2 \cdot 2$ *Find the common prime factors.*

$2 \cdot 2 = 4$ *Find the product of the common prime factors.*

The GCF of 12, 24, and 32 is 4.

C 12, 18, and 60

Method 3: Use a ladder diagram.

2	12	18	60
3	6	9	30
	2	3	10

Begin with a factor that divides into each number. Keep dividing until the three numbers have no common factors.

$2 \cdot 3 = 6$ *Find the product of the numbers you divided by.*

The GCF is 6.

EXAMPLE 2

PROBLEM SOLVING

PROBLEM SOLVING APPLICATION

There are 12 boys and 18 girls in Mr. Ruiz's science class. The students must form lab groups. Each group must have the same number of boys and the same number of girls. What is the greatest number of groups Mr. Ruiz can make if every student must be in a group?

1. Understand the Problem

The **answer** will be the *greatest* number of groups 12 boys and 18 girls can form so that each group has the same number of boys, and each group has the same number of girls.

2 Make a Plan

You can make an organized list of the possible groups.

3 Solve

There are more girls than boys in the class, so there will be more girls than boys in each group.

Boys	Girls	Groups
1	2	(B GG) (B GG) (B GG) (B GG) (B GG) (B GG) (B GG) (B GG) (B GG) 9 boys, 18 girls: There are 3 boys not in groups. ✗
2	3	(BB GGG) (BB GGG) (BB GGG) (BB GGG) (BB GGG) (BB GGG) 12 boys, 18 girls: Every student is in a group. ✓

The greatest number of groups is 6.

4 Look Back

The number of groups will be a common factor of the number of boys and the number of girls. To form the largest number of groups, find the GCF of 12 and 18.

factors of 12: 1, 2, 3, 4, ⑥, 12   factors of 18: 1, 2, 3, ⑥, 9, 18

The GCF of 12 and 18 is 6.

Helpful Hint

If more students are put in each group, there will be fewer groups. You need the most groups possible, so put the smallest possible number of students in each team. Start with 1 boy in each group.

6.CM.1, 6.CM.9

Think and Discuss

1. Explain what the GCF of two prime numbers is.

2. Tell what the least common factor of a group of numbers would be.

4-3 **Exercises**

go.hrw.com
Homework Help Online
KEYWORD: MR7 4-3
Parent Resources Online
KEYWORD: MR7 Parent

GUIDED PRACTICE

See Example **1**   Find the GCF of each set of numbers.

1. 18 and 27 **2.** 32 and 72 **3.** 21, 42, and 56

4. 15, 30, and 60 **5.** 18, 24, and 36 **6.** 9, 36, and 81

See Example **2**   **7.** Kim is making flower arrangements. She has 16 red roses and 20 pink roses. Each arrangement must have the same number of red roses and the same number of pink roses. What is the greatest number of arrangements Kim can make if every flower is used?

INDEPENDENT PRACTICE

See Example **1**   Find the GCF of each set of numbers.

8. 10 and 35 **9.** 28 and 70 **10.** 36 and 72

11. 26, 48, and 62 **12.** 16, 40, and 88 **13.** 12, 60, and 68

14. 30, 45, and 75 **15.** 24, 48, and 84 **16.** 16, 48, and 72

See Example **2**   **17.** The local recreation center held a scavenger hunt. There were 15 boys and 9 girls at the event. The group was divided into the greatest number of teams possible with the same number of boys on each team and the same number of girls on each team. How many teams were made if each person was on a team?

18. Ms. Kline makes balloon arrangements. She has 32 blue balloons, 24 yellow balloons, and 16 white balloons. Each arrangement must have the same number of each color. What is the greatest number of arrangements that Ms. Kline can make if every balloon is used?

PRACTICE AND PROBLEM SOLVING

Extra Practice
See page 720.

Write the GCF of each set of numbers.

19. 60 and 84 **20.** 14 and 17 **21.** 10, 35, and 110

22. 21 and 306 **23.** 630 and 712 **24.** 16, 24, and 40

25. 75, 225, and 150 **26.** 42, 112, and 105 **27.** 12, 16, 20, and 24

28. Jared has 12 jars of grape jam, 16 jars of strawberry jam, and 24 jars of raspberry jam. He wants to place the jam into the greatest possible number of boxes so that each box has the same number of jars of each kind of jam. How many boxes does he need?

29. Pam is making fruit baskets. She has 30 apples, 24 bananas, and 12 oranges. What is the greatest number of baskets she can make if each type of fruit is distributed equally among the baskets?

30. Critical Thinking Write a set of three different numbers that have a GCF of 9. Explain your method.

Life Science

The biggest flower in the world is the Rafflesia. It grows in the Indonesian rain forest. Blossoms can measure four feet across, weigh about 15 pounds, and contain about 1.5 gallons of water.

Write the GCF of each set of numbers.

31. 16, 24, 30, and 42   **32.** 25, 90, 45, and 100   **33.** 27, 90, 135, and 72

34. $2 \times 2 \times 3$ and 2×2 **35.** $2 \times 3^2 \times 7$ and $2^2 \times 3$ **36.** $3^2 \times 7$ and $2 \times 3 \times 5^2$

37. Mr. Chu is planting 4 types of flowers in his garden. He wants each row to contain the same number of each type of flower. What is the greatest number of rows Mr. Chu can plant if every bulb is used?

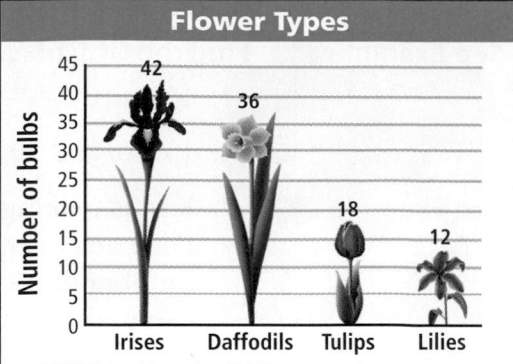

Flower Types

38. In a parade, one school band will march directly behind another school band. All rows must have the same number of students. The first band has 36 students, and the second band has 60 students. What is the greatest number of students who can be in each row?

39. Social Studies Branches of the U.S. Mint in Denver and Philadelphia make all U.S. coins for circulation. A tiny *D* or *P* on the coin tells you where the coin was minted. Suppose you have 32 *D* quarters and 36 *P* quarters. What is the greatest number of groups you can make with the same number of *D* quarters in each group and the same number of *P* quarters in each group so that every quarter is placed in a group?

 40. What's the Error? Mike says if $12 = 2^2 \cdot 3$ and $24 = 2^3 \cdot 3$, then the GCF of 12 and 24 is $2 \cdot 3$, or 6. Explain Mike's error.

 41. Write About It What method do you like best for finding the GCF? Why?

 42. Challenge The GCF of three numbers is 9. The sum of the numbers is 90. Find the three numbers.

TEST PREP and Spiral Review

43. Multiple Choice For which set of numbers is 16 the GCF?

Ⓐ 16, 32, 48   Ⓑ 12, 24, 32   Ⓒ 24, 48, 60   Ⓓ 8, 80, 100

44. Multiple Choice Mrs. Lyndon is making baskets of muffins. She has 48 lemon muffins, 120 blueberry muffins, and 112 banana nut muffins. How many baskets can Mrs. Lyndon make with each type of muffin distributed evenly?

Ⓕ 4   Ⓖ 6   Ⓗ 8   Ⓙ 12

Solve each equation. (Lessons 2-4, 2-5, 2-6, 2-7)

45. $y + 37 = 64$ **46.** $c - 5 = 19$ **47.** $72 \div z = 9$ **48.** $3v = 81$

Write the prime factorization of each number. (Lesson 4-2)

49. 42   **50.** 19   **51.** 51   **52.** 132   **53.** 200

Technology LAB 4-3

Greatest Common Factor

Use with Lesson 4-3

NY Performance Indicators

6.PS.21

go.hrw.com
Lab Resources Online
KEYWORD: MR7 Lab4

You can use a graphing calculator to quickly find the greatest common factor (GCF) of two or more numbers. A calculator is particularly useful when you need to find the GCF of large numbers.

Activity

Find the GCF of 504 and 3,150.

The GCF is also known as the *greatest common divisor,* or GCD. The GCD function is found on the **MATH** menu.

To find the GCD on a graphing calculator, press **MATH**. Press ▶ to highlight **NUM**, and then use ▼ to scroll down and highlight **9:**.

Press **ENTER** 504 **,** 3150 **)** **ENTER**.

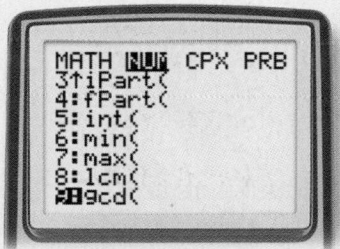

The greatest common factor of 504 and 3,150 is 126.

Think and Discuss

1. Suppose your calculator will not allow you to enter three numbers into the GCD function. How could you still use your calculator to find the GCF of the three following numbers: 4,896; 2,364; and 656? Explain your strategy and why it works.

2. Would you use your calculator to find the GCF of 6 and 18? Why or why not?

Try This

Find the GCF of each set of numbers.

1. 14, 48   **2.** 18, 54   **3.** 99, 121   **4.** 144, 196

5. 200, 136   **6.** 246, 137   **7.** 72, 860   **8.** 55, 141, 91

CHAPTER

4

SECTION 4A

Quiz for Lessons 4-1 Through 4-3

4-1 Divisibility

Tell whether each number is divisible by 2, 3, 4, 5, 6, 9, and 10.

1. 708 **2.** 514 **3.** 470 **4.** 338

5. A highway loop around a city is 45 miles long. If exits are placed every 5 miles, will the exits be evenly spaced around the loop? Explain.

6. Hoover Dam is 1,244 feet across at the top. Tell whether this number is divisible by 2, 3, 4, 5, 6, 9, and 10.

Tell whether each number is prime or composite.

7. 76 **8.** 59 **9.** 69 **10.** 33

4-2 Factors and Prime Factorization

List all of the factors of each number.

11. 26 **12.** 32 **13.** 39 **14.** 84

15. Mr. Collins's bowling league has 48 members. If the league splits into teams of 12 members each, how many equally sized teams will there be?

Write the prime factorization of each number.

16. 96 **17.** 50 **18.** 104 **19.** 63

20. Scientists classify many sunflowers in the genus *Helianthus*. There are approximately 67 species of *Helianthus*. Write the prime factorization of 67.

4-3 Greatest Common Factor

Find the GCF of each set of numbers.

21. 16 and 36 **22.** 22 and 88 **23.** 65 and 91 **24.** 20, 55, and 85

25. There are 36 sixth-graders and 40 seventh-graders. What is the greatest number of teams that the students can form if each team has the same number of sixth-graders and the same number of seventh-graders and every student must be on a team?

26. There are 14 girls and 21 boys in Mrs. Sutter's gym class. To play a certain game, the students must form teams. Each team must have the same number of girls and the same number of boys. What is the greatest number of teams Mrs. Sutter can make if every student is on a team?

27. Mrs. Young, an art teacher, is organizing the art supplies. She has 76 red markers, 52 blue markers, and 80 black markers. She wants to divide the markers into boxes with the same number of red, the same number of blue, and the same number of black markers in each box. What is the greatest number of boxes she can have if every marker is placed in a box?

Ready to Go On?

Focus on Problem Solving

Understand the Problem

• Interpret unfamiliar words

You must understand the words in a problem in order to solve it. If there is a word you do not know, try to use context clues to figure out its meaning. Suppose there is a problem about red, green, blue, and chartreuse fabric. You may not know the word *chartreuse*, but you can guess that it is probably a color. To make the problem easier to understand, you could replace *chartreuse* with the name of a familiar color, like *white*.

In some problems, the name of a person, place, or thing might be difficult to pronounce, such as *Mr. Joubert*. When you see a proper noun that you do not know how to pronounce, you can use another proper noun or a pronoun in its place. You could replace *Mr. Joubert* with *he*. You could replace *Koenisburg Street* with *K Street*.

Copy each problem. Underline any words that you do not understand. Then replace each word with a more familiar word.

1. Grace is making flower bouquets. She has 18 chrysanthemums and 42 roses. She wants to arrange them in groups that each have the same number of chrysanthemums and the same number of roses. What is the fewest number of flowers that Grace can have in each group? How many chrysanthemums and how many roses will be in each group?

2. Most marbles are made from glass. The glass is liquefied in a furnace and poured. It is then cut into cylinders that are rounded off and cooled. Suppose 1,200 cooled marbles are put into packages of 8. How many packages could be made? Would there be any marbles left over?

3. In ancient times, many civilizations used calendars that divided the year into months of 30 days. A year has 365 days. How many whole months were in these ancient calendars? Were there any days left over? If so, how many?

4. Mrs. LeFeubre is tiling her garden walkway. It is a rectangle that is 4 feet wide and 20 feet long. Mrs. LeFeubre wants to use square tiles, and she does not want to have to cut any tiles. What is the size of the largest square tile that Mrs. LeFeubre can use?

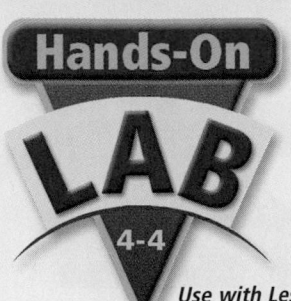

Hands-On LAB 4-4

Explore Decimals and Fractions

Use with Lesson 4-4

go.hrw.com
Lab Resources Online
KEYWORD: MR7 Lab4

NY Performance Indicators
6.R.1, 6.R.2, 6.R.5, 6.R.6

KEY

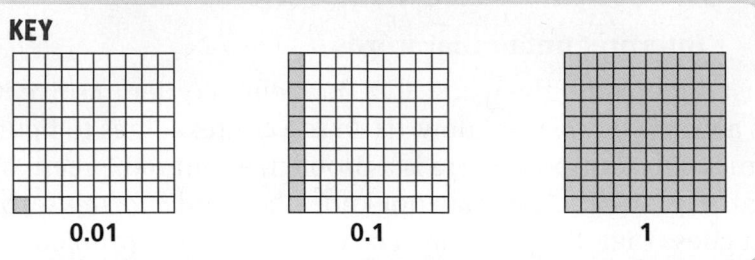

| 0.01 | 0.1 | 1 |

You can use decimal grids to show the relationship between fractions and decimals.

Activity

Write the number represented on each grid as a fraction and as a decimal.

1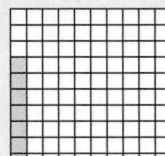

Seven hundredths squares are shaded → 0.07

How many squares are shaded? 7 ← numerator
How many squares are in the whole? $\overline{100}$ ← denominator

$0.07 = \frac{7}{100}$

2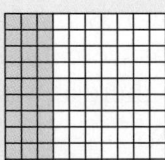

Three tenths columns are shaded →   0.3

How many complete columns are shaded? 3
How many columns are in the whole? $\overline{10}$

$0.3 = \frac{3}{10}$

Think and Discuss

1. Is 0.09 the same as $\frac{9}{10}$? Use decimal grids to support your answer.

Try This

Use decimal grids to represent each number.

1. 0.8   **2.** $\frac{37}{100}$ **3.** 0.53   **4.** $\frac{1}{10}$ **5.** $\frac{67}{100}$

6. For 1–5, write each decimal as a fraction and each fraction as a decimal.

4-4 Decimals and Fractions

Learn to convert between decimals and fractions.

Vocabulary

mixed number

terminating decimal

repeating decimal

NY Performance Indicators

6.N.20 Represent fractions as terminating or repeating decimals. Also, 6.N.14, 6.N.15, 6.N.21.

Decimals and fractions can often be used to represent the same number.

For example, a baseball player's or baseball team's batting average can be represented as a fraction:

$$\frac{\text{number of hits}}{\text{number of times at bat}}$$

The University of Texas baseball team has participated in the College World Series more times than any other school.

In 2005, the University of Texas baseball team won its sixth College World Series title. During that season, the team had 734 hits and 2,432 at bats. The team's batting average was $\frac{734}{2,432}$.

$$734 \div 2,432 = 0.3018092105\ldots$$

The 2005 batting average for the University of Texas baseball team is reported as .302.

Decimals can be written as fractions or mixed numbers. A number that contains both a whole number greater than 0 and a fraction, such as $1\frac{3}{4}$, is called a **mixed number**.

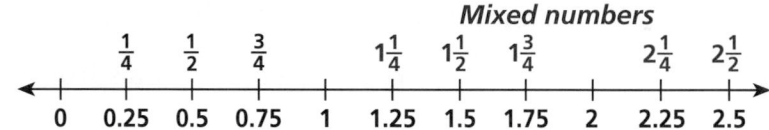

Mixed numbers

$\frac{1}{4}$ $\frac{1}{2}$ $\frac{3}{4}$ $1\frac{1}{4}$ $1\frac{1}{2}$ $1\frac{3}{4}$ $2\frac{1}{4}$ $2\frac{1}{2}$

0   0.25   0.5   0.75   1   1.25   1.5   1.75   2   2.25   2.5

EXAMPLE **1** **Writing Decimals as Fractions or Mixed Numbers**

Write each decimal as a fraction or mixed number.

Remember!

Place Value			
Ones	Tenths	Hundredths	Thousandths

A 0.23

0.23   *Identify the place value of the digit farthest to the right.*

$\frac{23}{100}$ *The 3 is in the **hundred**ths place, so use **100** as the denominator.*

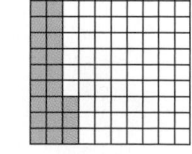

B 1.7

1.7   *Identify the place value of the digit farthest to the right.*

$1\frac{7}{10}$ *Write the whole number, 1. The 7 is in the **ten**ths place, so use **10** as the denominator.*

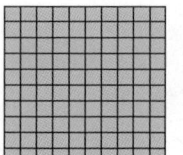 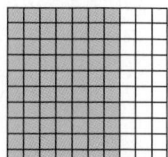

EXAMPLE **2** **Writing Fractions as Decimals**

Write each fraction or mixed number as a decimal.

A $\frac{3}{4}$

$$
\begin{array}{r}
0.75 \\
4\overline{)3.00} \\
-28 \\
\hline
20 \\
-20 \\
\hline
0
\end{array}
$$

Divide 3 by 4.
Add zeros after the decimal point.
The remainder is 0.

$\frac{3}{4} = 0.75$

B $5\frac{2}{3}$

$$
\begin{array}{r}
0.666 \\
3\overline{)2.000} \\
-18 \\
\hline
20 \\
-18 \\
\hline
20 \\
-18 \\
\hline
2
\end{array}
$$

Divide 2 by 3.
Add zeros after the decimal point.
The 6 repeats in the quotient.

$5\frac{2}{3} = 5.666... = 5.\overline{6}$

Writing Math

To write a repeating decimal, you can show three dots or draw a bar over the repeating part:
$0.666... = 0.\overline{6}$

A **terminating decimal**, such as 0.75, has a finite number of decimal places. A **repeating decimal**, such as 0.666..., has a block of one or more digits that repeat continuously.

Common Fractions and Equivalent Decimals								
$\frac{1}{5}$	$\frac{1}{4}$	$\frac{1}{3}$	$\frac{2}{5}$	$\frac{1}{2}$	$\frac{3}{5}$	$\frac{2}{3}$	$\frac{3}{4}$	$\frac{4}{5}$
0.2	0.25	$0.\overline{3}$	0.4	0.5	0.6	$0.\overline{6}$	0.75	0.8

EXAMPLE **3** **Comparing and Ordering Fractions and Decimals**

Order the fractions and decimals from least to greatest.

$0.5, \frac{1}{5}, 0.37$

First rewrite the fraction as a decimal. $\frac{1}{5} = 0.2$
Order the three decimals.

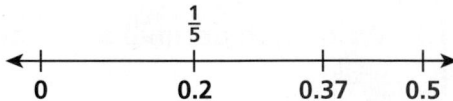

The numbers in order from least to greatest are $\frac{1}{5}$, 0.37, and 0.5.

Think and Discuss

1. **Tell** how reading the decimal 6.9 as "six and nine tenths" helps you to write 6.9 as a mixed number.

2. **Look** at the decimal 0.121122111222.... If the pattern continues, is this a repeating decimal? Why or why not?

go.hrw.com
Homework Help Online
KEYWORD: MR7 4-4
Parent Resources Online
KEYWORD: MR7 Parent

GUIDED PRACTICE

See Example 1 Write each decimal as a fraction or mixed number.

1. 0.15 **2.** 1.25 **3.** 0.43 **4.** 2.6

See Example 2 Write each fraction or mixed number as a decimal.

5. $\frac{2}{5}$ **6.** $2\frac{7}{8}$ **7.** $\frac{1}{8}$ **8.** $4\frac{1}{10}$

See Example 3 Order the fractions and decimals from least to greatest.

9. $\frac{2}{3}$, 0.78, 0.21 **10.** $\frac{5}{16}$, 0.67, $\frac{1}{6}$ **11.** 0.52, $\frac{1}{9}$, 0.3

INDEPENDENT PRACTICE

See Example 1 Write each decimal as a fraction or mixed number.

12. 0.31 **13.** 5.71 **14.** 0.13 **15.** 3.23

16. 0.5 **17.** 2.7 **18.** 0.19 **19.** 6.3

See Example 2 Write each fraction or mixed number as a decimal.

20. $\frac{1}{9}$ **21.** $1\frac{3}{5}$ **22.** $\frac{8}{9}$ **23.** $3\frac{11}{40}$

24. $2\frac{5}{6}$ **25.** $\frac{3}{8}$ **26.** $4\frac{4}{5}$ **27.** $\frac{5}{8}$

See Example 3 Order the fractions and decimals from least to greatest.

28. 0.49, 0.82, $\frac{1}{2}$ **29.** $\frac{3}{8}$, 0.29, $\frac{1}{9}$ **30.** 0.94, $\frac{4}{5}$, 0.6

31. 0.11, $\frac{1}{10}$, 0.13 **32.** $\frac{2}{3}$, 0.42, $\frac{2}{5}$ **33.** $\frac{3}{7}$, 0.76, 0.31

PRACTICE AND PROBLEM SOLVING

Extra Practice
See page 720.

Write each decimal in expanded form and use a whole number or fraction for each place value.

34. 0.81 **35.** 92.3 **36.** 13.29 **37.** 107.17

Write each fraction as a decimal. Tell whether the decimal terminates or repeats.

38. $\frac{7}{9}$ **39.** $\frac{1}{6}$ **40.** $\frac{17}{20}$ **41.** $\frac{5}{12}$ **42.** $\frac{7}{8}$

43. $\frac{4}{5}$ **44.** $\frac{9}{5}$ **45.** $\frac{15}{18}$ **46.** $\frac{7}{3}$ **47.** $\frac{11}{12}$

Compare. Write < , >, or =.

48. 0.75 ▨ $\frac{3}{4}$ **49.** $\frac{5}{8}$ ▨ 0.5 **50.** 0.78 ▨ $\frac{7}{9}$ **51.** $\frac{1}{3}$ ▨ 0.35

52. $\frac{2}{5}$ ▨ 0.4 **53.** 0.75 ▨ $\frac{4}{5}$ **54.** $\frac{3}{8}$ ▨ 0.25 **55.** 0.8 ▨ $\frac{5}{6}$

56. Multi-Step Peter walked $1\frac{3}{5}$ miles on a treadmill. Sally walked 1.5 miles on the treadmill. Who walked farther? Explain.

Order the mixed numbers and decimals from greatest to least.

57. $4.48, 3.92, 4\frac{1}{2}$ **58.** $10\frac{5}{9}, 10.5, 10\frac{1}{5}$ **59.** $125.205, 125.25, 125\frac{1}{5}$

Sports The table shows batting averages for two baseball seasons. Use the table for Exercises 60–62.

Player	Season 1	Season 2
Pedro	0.360	$\frac{3}{10}$
Jill	0.380	$\frac{3}{8}$
Lamar	0.290	$\frac{1}{3}$
Britney	0.190	$\frac{3}{20}$

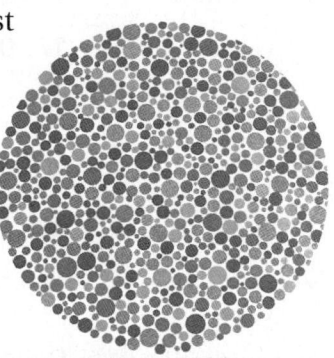

60. Which players had higher batting averages in season 1 than they had in season 2?

61. Who had the highest batting average in either season?

62. Multi-Step Whose batting average changed the most between season 1 and season 2?

63. Life Science Most people with color deficiency (often called color blindness) have trouble distinguishing shades of red and green. About 0.05 of men in the world have color deficiency. What fraction of men have color deficiency?

 64. What's the Error? A student found the decimal equivalent of $\frac{7}{18}$ to be $0.\overline{38}$. Explain the error. What is the correct answer?

People with normal color vision will see "7" in this color-blindness test.

 65. Write About It The decimal for $\frac{1}{25}$ is 0.04, and the decimal for $\frac{2}{25}$ is 0.08. Without dividing, find the decimal for $\frac{6}{25}$. Explain how you found your answer.

66. Challenge Write $\frac{1}{999}$ as a decimal.

TEST PREP and Spiral Review

67. Multiple Choice Which numbers are listed from least to greatest?

   Ⓐ $0.65, 0.81, \frac{4}{5}$ Ⓑ $0.81, 0.65, \frac{4}{5}$ Ⓒ $\frac{4}{5}, 0.81, 0.65$ Ⓓ $0.65, \frac{4}{5}, 0.81$

68. Gridded Response Write $5\frac{1}{8}$ as a decimal.

Find each sum or difference. (Lesson 3-3)

69. $12.56 + 8.91$ **70.** $19.05 - 2.27$ **71.** $5 + 8.25 + 10.2$

Find the GCF of each set of numbers. (Lesson 4-3)

72. 235 and 35   **73.** 28 and 154   **74.** 90 and 56   **75.** 16 and 112

Model Equivalent Fractions

Use with Lesson 4-5

NY Performance Indicators

6.R.1, 6.R.2, 6.R.5, 6.R.6

go.hrw.com
Lab Resources Online
KEYWORD: MR7 Lab4

KEY

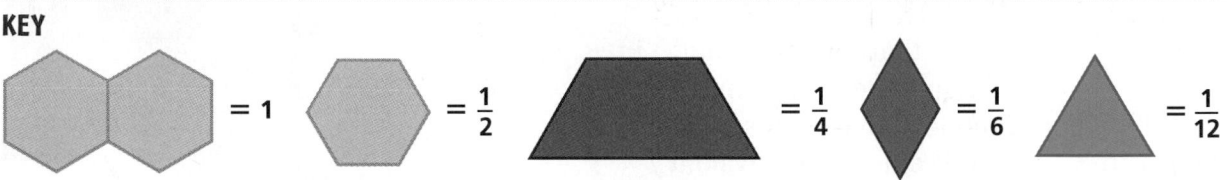

Pattern blocks can be used to model equivalent fractions. To find a fraction that is equivalent to $\frac{1}{2}$, first choose the pattern block that represents $\frac{1}{2}$. Then find all the pieces of one color that will fit evenly on the $\frac{1}{2}$ block. Count these pieces to find the equivalent fraction. You may be able to find more than one equivalent fraction.

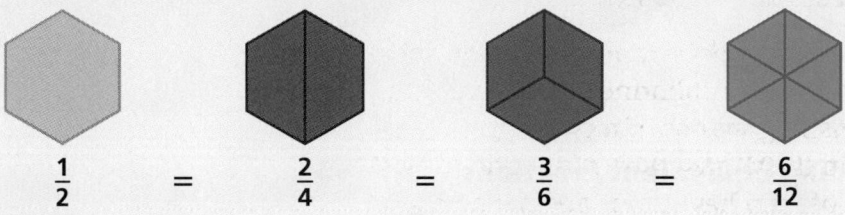

Activity

Use pattern blocks to find an equivalent fraction for $\frac{8}{12}$.

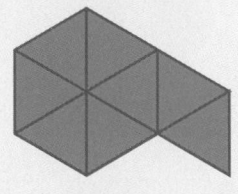

First show $\frac{8}{12}$.

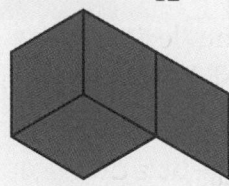

You can cover $\frac{8}{12}$ with four of the $\frac{1}{6}$ pieces.

$$\frac{8}{12} = \frac{4}{6}$$

Think and Discuss

1. Can you find a combination of pattern blocks for $\frac{1}{3}$? Find an equivalent fraction for $\frac{1}{3}$.

2. Are $\frac{9}{12}$ and $\frac{3}{6}$ equivalent? Use pattern blocks to support your answer.

Try This

Write the fraction that is modeled. Then find an equivalent fraction.

1.
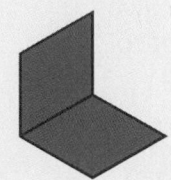

2.
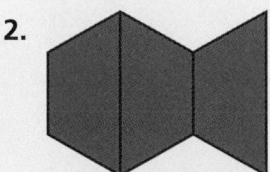

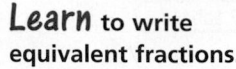

4-5 Equivalent Fractions

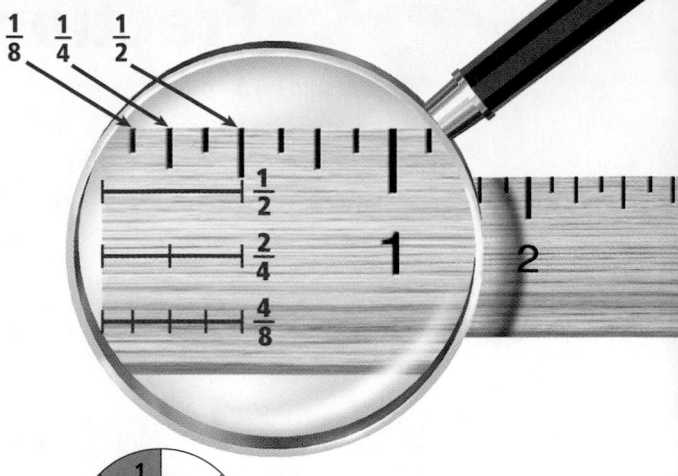

Learn to write equivalent fractions.

Vocabulary

equivalent fractions

simplest form

NY Performance Indicators

6.CN.4 Understand multiple representations and how they are related. Also, 6.R.5.

Rulers often have marks for inches, $\frac{1}{2}$, $\frac{1}{4}$, and $\frac{1}{8}$ inches.

Notice that $\frac{1}{2}$ in., $\frac{2}{4}$ in., and $\frac{4}{8}$ in. all name the same length. Fractions that represent the same value are **equivalent fractions**. So $\frac{1}{2}$, $\frac{2}{4}$, and $\frac{4}{8}$ are equivalent fractions.

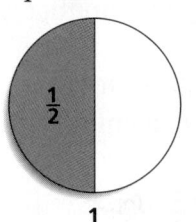 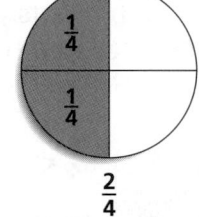 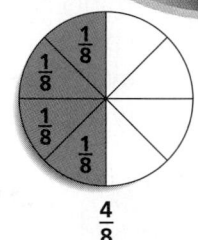

$$\frac{1}{2} \quad = \quad \frac{2}{4} \quad = \quad \frac{4}{8}$$

EXAMPLE 1 **Finding Equivalent Fractions**

Find two equivalent fractions for $\frac{6}{8}$.

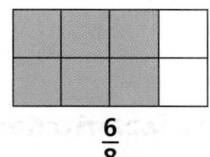 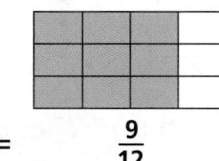 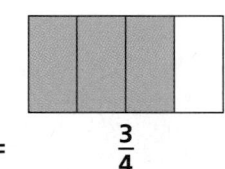

$$\frac{6}{8} \quad = \quad \frac{9}{12} \quad = \quad \frac{3}{4}$$

The same area is shaded when the rectangle is divided into 8 parts, 12 parts, and 4 parts.

So $\frac{6}{8}$, $\frac{9}{12}$, and $\frac{3}{4}$ are all equivalent fractions.

EXAMPLE 2 **Multiplying and Dividing to Find Equivalent Fractions**

Find the missing number that makes the fractions equivalent.

A $\quad \frac{2}{3} = \frac{\blacksquare}{18}$

$\quad \dfrac{2 \cdot 6}{3 \cdot 6} = \dfrac{12}{18}$ *In the denominator, 3 is multiplied by 6 to get 18.*
Multiply the numerator, 2, by the same number, 6.

So $\frac{2}{3}$ is equivalent to $\frac{12}{18}$.

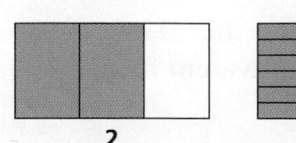

$$\frac{2}{3} \quad = \quad \frac{12}{18}$$

Find the missing number that makes the fractions equivalent.

B $\dfrac{70}{100} = \dfrac{7}{\blacksquare}$

$\dfrac{70 \div 10}{100 \div 10} = \dfrac{7}{10}$ *In the numerator, 70 is divided by 10 to get 7. Divide the denominator by the same number, 10.*

So $\dfrac{70}{100}$ is equivalent to $\dfrac{7}{10}$.

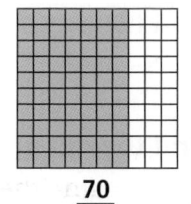 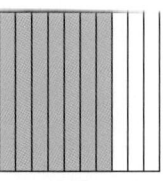

$$\dfrac{70}{100} \quad = \quad \dfrac{7}{10}$$

Every fraction has one equivalent fraction that is called the simplest form of the fraction. A fraction is in **simplest form** when the GCF of the numerator and the denominator is 1.

Example 3 shows two methods for writing a fraction in simplest form.

EXAMPLE 3 **Writing Fractions in Simplest Form**

Write each fraction in simplest form.

 A $\dfrac{18}{24}$

The GCF of 18 and 24 is 6, so $\dfrac{18}{24}$ is not in simplest form.

Method 1: Use the GCF.

$\dfrac{18 \div 6}{24 \div 6} = \dfrac{3}{4}$ *Divide 18 and 24 by their GCF, 6.*

Method 2: Use prime factorization.

$\dfrac{18}{24} = \dfrac{\cancel{2} \cdot \cancel{3} \cdot 3}{\cancel{2} \cdot 2 \cdot 2 \cdot \cancel{3}} = \dfrac{3}{4}$ *Write the prime factors of 18 and 24. Simplify.*

So $\dfrac{18}{24}$ written in simplest form is $\dfrac{3}{4}$.

 B $\dfrac{8}{9}$

The GCF of 8 and 9 is 1, so $\dfrac{8}{9}$ is already in simplest form.

> **Helpful Hint**
>
> Method 2 is useful when you know that the numerator and denominator have common factors, but you are not sure what the GCF is.

Think and Discuss 6.PS.3, 6.CM.1, 6.CM.10

1. **Explain** whether a fraction is equivalent to itself.

2. **Tell** which of the following fractions are in simplest form: $\dfrac{9}{21}$, $\dfrac{20}{25}$, and $\dfrac{5}{13}$. Explain.

3. **Explain** how you know that $\dfrac{7}{16}$ is in simplest form.

4-5 **Exercises**

go.hrw.com
Homework Help Online
KEYWORD: MR4 4-5
Parent Resources Online
KEYWORD: MR7 Parent

GUIDED PRACTICE

See Example 1 Find two equivalent fractions for each fraction.

1. $\frac{4}{6}$ **2.** $\frac{3}{12}$ **3.** $\frac{3}{6}$ **4.** $\frac{6}{16}$

See Example 2 Find the missing numbers that make the fractions equivalent.

5. $\frac{2}{5} = \frac{10}{\blacksquare}$ **6.** $\frac{7}{21} = \frac{1}{\blacksquare}$ **7.** $\frac{3}{4} = \frac{\blacksquare}{28}$ **8.** $\frac{8}{12} = \frac{\blacksquare}{3}$

See Example 3 Write each fraction in simplest form.

9. $\frac{2}{10}$ **10.** $\frac{6}{18}$ **11.** $\frac{4}{16}$ **12.** $\frac{9}{15}$

INDEPENDENT PRACTICE

See Example 1 Find two equivalent fractions for each fraction.

13. $\frac{3}{9}$ **14.** $\frac{2}{10}$ **15.** $\frac{3}{21}$ **16.** $\frac{3}{18}$

17. $\frac{12}{15}$ **18.** $\frac{4}{10}$ **19.** $\frac{10}{12}$ **20.** $\frac{6}{10}$

See Example 2 Find the missing numbers that make the fractions equivalent.

21. $\frac{3}{7} = \frac{\blacksquare}{35}$ **22.** $\frac{6}{48} = \frac{1}{\blacksquare}$ **23.** $\frac{2}{5} = \frac{28}{\blacksquare}$ **24.** $\frac{12}{18} = \frac{\blacksquare}{3}$

25. $\frac{2}{7} = \frac{\blacksquare}{21}$ **26.** $\frac{8}{32} = \frac{\blacksquare}{4}$ **27.** $\frac{2}{7} = \frac{40}{\blacksquare}$ **28.** $\frac{3}{5} = \frac{21}{\blacksquare}$

See Example 3 Write each fraction in simplest form.

29. $\frac{2}{8}$ **30.** $\frac{10}{15}$ **31.** $\frac{6}{30}$ **32.** $\frac{6}{14}$

33. $\frac{12}{16}$ **34.** $\frac{4}{28}$ **35.** $\frac{4}{8}$ **36.** $\frac{10}{35}$

PRACTICE AND PROBLEM SOLVING

Extra Practice
See page 720.

Write the equivalent fractions represented by each picture.

37. 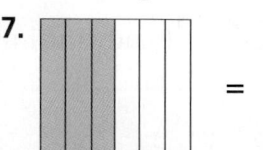 = 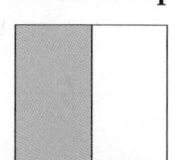   **38.** 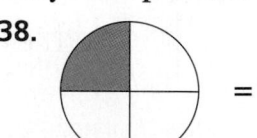 =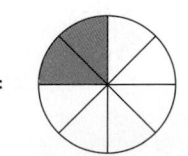

39. 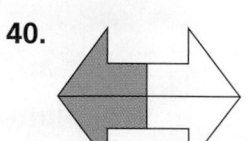   **40.**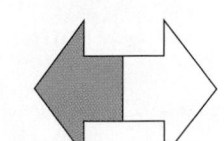

Write each fraction in simplest form. Show two ways to simplify.

41. $\frac{5}{20}$ **42.** $\frac{4}{52}$ **43.** $\frac{14}{35}$ **44.** $\frac{112}{220}$

The Old City Market is a public market in Charleston, South Carolina. Local artists, craftspeople, and vendors display and sell their goods in open-sided booths.

45. You can buy food, such as southern sesame seed cookies, at $\frac{1}{10}$ of the booths. Write two equivalent fractions for $\frac{1}{10}$.

46. Handwoven sweetgrass baskets are a regional specialty. About 8 out of every 10 baskets sold are woven at the market. Write a fraction for "8 out of 10." Then write this fraction in simplest form.

47. Suppose the circle graph shows the number of each kind of craft booth at the Old City Market. For each type of booth, tell what fraction it represents of the total number of craft booths. Write these fractions in simplest form.

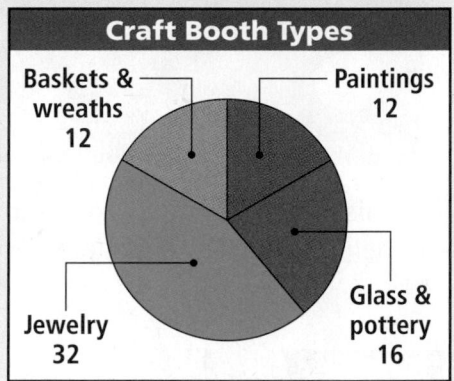

Craft Booth Types

Baskets & wreaths 12

Paintings 12

Jewelry 32

Glass & pottery 16

48. Customers can buy packages of dried rice and black-eyed peas, which can be made into black-eyed pea soup. One recipe for black-eyed pea soup calls for $\frac{1}{2}$ tsp of basil. How could you measure the basil if you had only a $\frac{1}{4}$ tsp measuring spoon? What if you had only a $\frac{1}{8}$ tsp measuring spoon?

49. **Write About It** The recipe for soup also calls for $\frac{1}{4}$ tsp of pepper. How many fractions are equivalent to $\frac{1}{4}$? Explain.

50. ★ **Challenge** Silver jewelry is a popular item at the market. Suppose there are 28 bracelets at one jeweler's booth and that $\frac{3}{7}$ of these bracelets have red stones. How many bracelets have red stones?

TEST PREP and Spiral Review

51. Multiple Choice Which fraction is NOT equivalent to $\frac{1}{6}$?

Ⓐ $\frac{2}{12}$ Ⓑ $\frac{6}{1}$ Ⓒ $\frac{3}{18}$ Ⓓ $\frac{6}{36}$

52. Multiple Choice Which denominator makes the fractions $\frac{7}{28}$ and $\frac{21}{\square}$ equivalent?

Ⓕ 3   Ⓖ 4   Ⓗ 84   Ⓙ 112

Solve each equation. Check your answer. (Lesson 2-7)

53. $\frac{x}{3} = 15$ **54.** $8 = \frac{h}{8}$ **55.** $\frac{w}{2} = 9$ **56.** $\frac{p}{5} = 10$

Write each fraction or mixed number as a decimal. (Lesson 4-4)

57. $\frac{2}{3}$ **58.** $\frac{7}{8}$ **59.** $3\frac{1}{5}$ **60.** $2\frac{9}{16}$

Explore Fraction Measurement

Use with Lesson 4-5

NY Performance Indicators

6.PS.14, 6.CN.2, 6.R.1, 6.R.5

go.hrw.com
Lab Resources Online
KEYWORD: MR7 Lab4

Look at a standard ruler. It probably has marks for inches, half inches, quarter inches, eighth inches, and sixteenth inches.

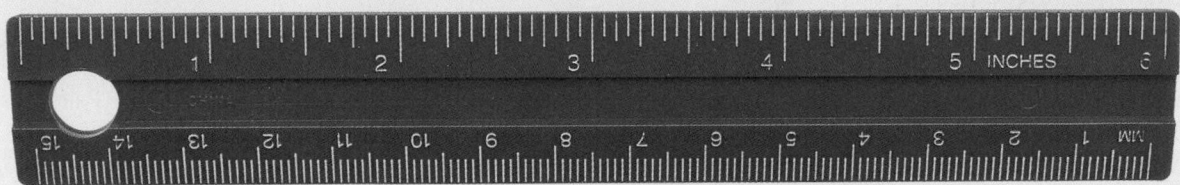

In this activity, you will make some of your own rulers and use them to help you find and understand equivalent fractions.

Activity

1 You will need four strips of paper. On one strip, use your ruler to make a mark for every half inch. Number each mark, beginning with 0. Label this strip "half-inch ruler."

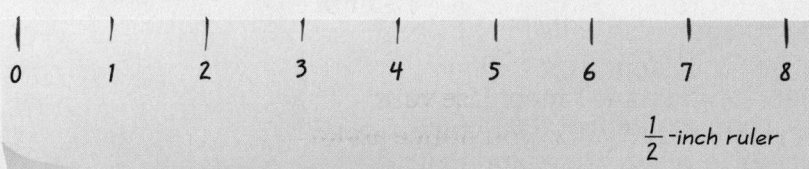

$\frac{1}{2}$-inch ruler

On a second strip, make a mark for every quarter inch. Again, number each mark, beginning with 0. Label this strip "quarter-inch ruler."

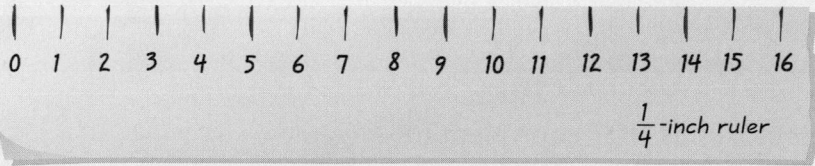

$\frac{1}{4}$-inch ruler

Do the same thing for eighth inches and sixteenth inches.

$\frac{1}{8}$-inch ruler

$\frac{1}{16}$-inch ruler

2 Now use the half-inch ruler you made to measure the green line segment at right. How many half inches long is the segment?

Use your quarter-inch ruler to measure the line segment again. How many quarter inches long is the segment?

How many eighth inches long is the segment?

How many sixteenth inches?

Fill in the blanks: $\frac{1}{2} = \frac{\blacksquare}{4} = \frac{\blacksquare}{8} = \frac{\blacksquare}{16}$.

3 Use your quarter-inch ruler to measure the green line segment below.

How long is the segment?

Now use your eighth-inch ruler to measure the line segment again. How many eighth inches long is the segment?

How many sixteenth inches?

Fill in the blanks: $\frac{3}{4} = \frac{\blacksquare}{8} = \frac{\blacksquare}{16}$.

Think and Discuss

1. How does a ruler show that equivalent fractions have the same value?

2. Look at your lists of equivalent fractions from **2** and **3**. Do you notice any patterns? Describe them.

3. Use your rulers to measure an object longer than 1 inch. Use your measurements to write equivalent fractions. What do you notice about these fractions?

Try This

1. Use your rulers to measure the length of the items below. Use your measurements to write equivalent fractions.

2. Use your rulers to measure several items in your classroom. Use your measurements to write equivalent fractions.

4-6 Mixed Numbers and Improper Fractions

Learn to convert between mixed numbers and improper fractions.

Vocabulary

improper fraction

proper fraction

Reading Math

$\frac{11}{4}$ is read as "eleven-fourths."

Have you ever witnessed a total eclipse of the sun? It occurs when the sun's light is completely blocked out. A total eclipse is rare—only three have been visible in the continental United States since 1963.

The graph shows that the eclipse in 2017 will last $2\frac{3}{4}$ minutes. There are eleven $\frac{1}{4}$-minute sections, so $2\frac{3}{4} = \frac{11}{4}$.

An **improper fraction** is a fraction in which the numerator is greater than or equal to the denominator, such as $\frac{11}{4}$.

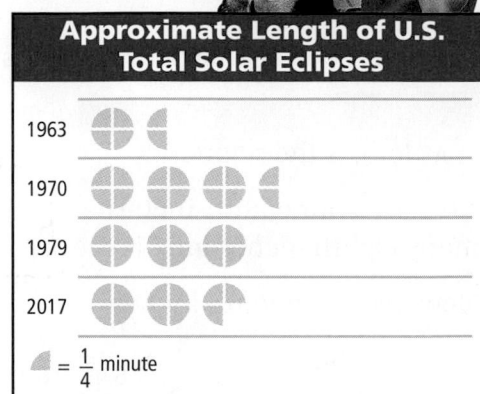

Approximate Length of U.S. Total Solar Eclipses

1963

1970

1979

2017

◢ = $\frac{1}{4}$ minute

Whole numbers can be written as improper fractions. The whole number is the numerator, and the denominator is 1. For example, $7 = \frac{7}{1}$.

When the numerator is less than the denominator, the fraction is called a **proper fraction**.

Improper and Proper Fractions		
Improper Fractions		
• Numerator equals denominator ➤ fraction is equal to 1	$\frac{3}{3} = 1$	$\frac{102}{102} = 1$
• Numerator greater than denominator ➤ fraction is greater than 1	$\frac{9}{5} > 1$	$\frac{13}{1} > 1$
Proper Fractions		
• Numerator less than denominator ➤ fraction is less than 1	$\frac{2}{5} < 1$	$\frac{102}{351} < 1$

You can write an improper fraction as a mixed number.

EXAMPLE 1 · Astronomy Application

NY Performance Indicators

6.PS.13 Model problems with pictures/diagrams or physical objects. Also, 6.R.1.

The longest total solar eclipse in the next 200 years will take place in 2186. It will last about $\frac{15}{2}$ minutes. Write $\frac{15}{2}$ as a mixed number.

Method 1: Use a model.

Draw squares divided into half sections. Shade 15 of the half sections.

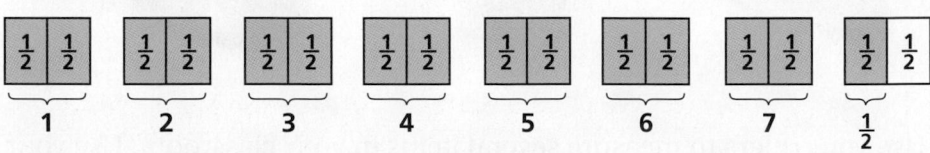

There are 7 whole squares and 1 half square, or $7\frac{1}{2}$ squares, shaded.

Method 2: Use division.

$$7\tfrac{1}{2}$$
$$2\overline{)15}$$
$$\underline{-14}$$
$$1$$

Divide the numerator by the denominator.

To form the fraction part of the quotient, use the remainder as the numerator and the divisor as the denominator.

The 2186 eclipse will last about $7\tfrac{1}{2}$ minutes.

Mixed numbers can be written as improper fractions.

EXAMPLE 2 Writing Mixed Numbers as Improper Fractions

Write $2\tfrac{1}{5}$ as an improper fraction.

Method 1: Use a model.
You can draw a diagram to illustrate the whole and fractional parts.

 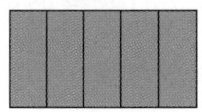 

There are 11 fifths, or $\tfrac{11}{5}$.   *Count the fifths in the diagram.*

Method 2: Use multiplication and addition.
When you are changing a mixed number to an improper fraction, spiral clockwise as shown in the picture. The order of operations will help you remember to multiply before you add.

Then add.

Multiply.

$$2\tfrac{1}{5} = \frac{(5 \cdot 2) + 1}{5}$$

$$= \frac{10 + 1}{5}$$

$$= \frac{11}{5}$$

Multiply the whole number by the denominator and add the numerator. Keep the same denominator.

6.RP.6, 6.CM.10, 6.CN.3

Think and Discuss

1. **Read** each improper fraction: $\tfrac{10}{7}, \tfrac{25}{9}, \tfrac{31}{16}$.

2. **Tell** whether each fraction is less than 1, equal to 1, or greater than 1: $\tfrac{21}{21}, \tfrac{54}{103}, \tfrac{9}{11}, \tfrac{7}{3}$.

3. **Explain** why any mixed number written as a fraction will be improper.

4-6 **Exercises**

go.hrw.com
Homework Help Online
KEYWORD: MR7 4-6
Parent Resources Online
KEYWORD: MR7 Parent

GUIDED PRACTICE

See Example ① 1. The fifth largest meteorite found in the United States is named the Navajo. The Navajo weighs $\frac{12}{5}$ tons. Write $\frac{12}{5}$ as a mixed number.

See Example ② Write each mixed number as an improper fraction.

2. $1\frac{1}{4}$ **3.** $2\frac{2}{3}$ **4.** $1\frac{2}{7}$ **5.** $2\frac{2}{5}$

INDEPENDENT PRACTICE

See Example ① 6. **Astronomy** Saturn is the sixth planet from the Sun. It takes Saturn $\frac{59}{2}$ years to revolve around the Sun. Write $\frac{59}{2}$ as a mixed number.

7. **Astronomy** Pluto has the lowest surface gravity of all the planets in the solar system. A person who weighs 143 pounds on Earth weighs $\frac{43}{5}$ pounds on Pluto. Write $\frac{43}{5}$ as a mixed number.

See Example ② Write each mixed number as an improper fraction.

8. $1\frac{3}{5}$ **9.** $2\frac{2}{9}$ **10.** $3\frac{1}{7}$ **11.** $4\frac{1}{3}$

12. $2\frac{3}{8}$ **13.** $4\frac{1}{6}$ **14.** $1\frac{4}{9}$ **15.** $3\frac{4}{5}$

PRACTICE AND PROBLEM SOLVING

Extra Practice
See page 721.

Write each improper fraction as a mixed number or whole number. Tell whether your answer is a mixed number or whole number.

16. $\frac{21}{4}$ **17.** $\frac{32}{8}$ **18.** $\frac{20}{3}$ **19.** $\frac{43}{5}$

20. $\frac{108}{9}$ **21.** $\frac{87}{10}$ **22.** $\frac{98}{11}$ **23.** $\frac{105}{7}$

Write each mixed number as an improper fraction.

24. $9\frac{1}{4}$ **25.** $4\frac{9}{11}$ **26.** $11\frac{4}{9}$ **27.** $18\frac{3}{5}$

28. **Measurement** The actual dimensions of a piece of lumber called a 2-by-4 are $1\frac{1}{2}$ inches and $3\frac{1}{2}$ inches. Write these numbers as improper fractions.

Replace each shape with a number that will make the equation correct.

29. $\blacksquare\frac{2}{5} = \frac{17}{\bullet}$ **30.** $\blacksquare\frac{6}{11} = \frac{83}{\bullet}$ **31.** $\blacksquare\frac{1}{9} = \frac{118}{\bullet}$

32. $\blacksquare\frac{6}{7} = \frac{55}{\bullet}$ **33.** $\blacksquare\frac{9}{10} = \frac{29}{\bullet}$ **34.** $\blacksquare\frac{1}{3} = \frac{55}{\bullet}$

35. Daniel is a costume designer for movies and music videos. He recently purchased $\frac{256}{9}$ yards of metallic fabric for space-suit costumes. Write a mixed number to represent the number of yards of fabric Daniel purchased.

Write the improper fraction as a decimal. Then use <, >, or = to compare.

36. $\frac{7}{5}$ $\blacksquare$ 1.8   **37.** 6.875 $\blacksquare$ $\frac{55}{8}$ **38.** $\frac{27}{2}$ $\blacksquare$ 13   **39.** $\frac{20}{5}$ $\blacksquare$ 4.25

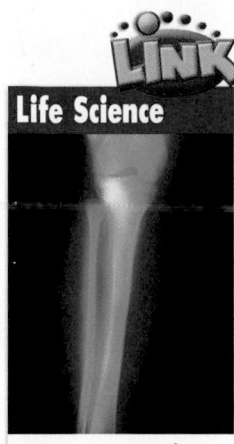

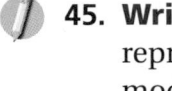
Life Science The table lists the lengths of the longest bones in the human body. Use the table for Exercises 40–42.

40. Write the length of the ulna as an improper fraction. Then do the same for the length of the humerus.

41. Write the length of the fibula as a mixed number. Then do the same for the length of the femur.

42. Use the mixed-number form of each length. Compare the whole-number part of each length to write the bones in order from longest to shortest.

43. **Social Studies** The European country of Monaco, with an area of only $1\frac{4}{5}$ km², is one of the smallest countries in the world. Write $1\frac{4}{5}$ as an improper fraction.

44. **What's the Question?** The lengths of Victor's three favorite movies are $\frac{11}{4}$ hours, $\frac{9}{4}$ hours, and $\frac{7}{4}$ hours. The answer is $2\frac{1}{4}$ hours. What is the question?

 45. **Write About It** Draw models representing $\frac{4}{4}$, $\frac{5}{5}$, and $\frac{9}{9}$. Use your models to explain why a fraction whose numerator is the same as its denominator is equal to 1.

46. **Challenge** Write $\frac{65}{12}$ as a decimal.

Longest Human Bones	
Fibula (outer lower leg)	$\frac{81}{2}$ cm
Ulna (inner lower arm)	$28\frac{1}{5}$ cm
Femur (upper leg)	$\frac{101}{2}$ cm
Humerus (upper arm)	$36\frac{1}{2}$ cm
Tibia (inner lower leg)	43 cm

TEST PREP and Spiral Review

47. **Multiple Choice** What is $3\frac{2}{11}$ written as an improper fraction?

Ⓐ $\frac{35}{11}$ Ⓑ $\frac{35}{3}$ Ⓒ $\frac{33}{22}$ Ⓓ $\frac{70}{11}$

48. **Multiple Choice** It takes $\frac{24}{5}$ new pencils placed end to end to be the same length as one yardstick. What is this improper fraction written as a mixed number?

Ⓔ $3\frac{4}{5}$ Ⓕ $4\frac{1}{4}$ Ⓖ $4\frac{1}{5}$ Ⓗ $4\frac{4}{5}$

Order the numbers from least to greatest. (Lesson 1-1)

49. 1,497; 2,560; 1,038

50. 10,462; 9,198; 11,320

51. 4,706; 11,765; 1,765

Estimate a range for each sum. (Lesson 3-2)

52. 19.85 + 6.7 + 12.4

53. 2.456 + 8.3 + 11.05

54. 15.36 + 10.75 + 6.1

List all the factors of each number. (Lesson 4-2)

55. 57

56. 36

57. 54

Quiz for Lessons 4-4 Through 4-6

4-4 Decimals and Fractions

Write each decimal as a fraction.

1. 0.67   **2.** 0.9   **3.** 0.43

Write each fraction as a decimal.

4. $\frac{2}{5}$ **5.** $\frac{1}{6}$ **6.** $\frac{3}{4}$

Compare. Write $<$, $>$, or $=$.

7. $\frac{7}{10}$ ▨ 0.9   **8.** 0.4 ▨ $\frac{2}{5}$ **9.** $\frac{3}{5}$ ▨ 0.5

10. Jamal got $\frac{4}{5}$ of the questions correct on his quiz. Dominic got 0.75 of the questions correct. Who got more questions correct?

4-5 Equivalent Fractions

Write two equivalent fractions for each fraction.

11. $\frac{9}{12}$ **12.** $\frac{18}{42}$ **13.** $\frac{25}{30}$

Write each fraction in simplest form.

14. $\frac{20}{24}$ **15.** $\frac{14}{49}$ **16.** $\frac{12}{28}$

17. Mandy ate $\frac{1}{6}$ of a pizza. Write two equivalent fractions for $\frac{1}{6}$.

18. Liane is making fruit salad. The recipe calls for $\frac{1}{2}$ cup shredded coconut. Liane has only a $\frac{1}{4}$-cup measure. How can she measure the correct $\frac{1}{2}$-cup amount?

4-6 Mixed Numbers and Improper Fractions

Replace each shape with a number that will make the equation correct.

19. ■$\frac{2}{7}$ = $\frac{9}{●}$ **20.** 6$\frac{■}{8}$ = $\frac{49}{●}$ **21.** ■$\frac{4}{9}$ = $\frac{157}{●}$

Use the table for Exercises 22–24.

22. Write the lengths of *1900* and *Empire* as mixed numbers in simplest form.

23. Write the lengths of *Fanny and Alexander* and *War and Peace* as improper fractions.

24. Write the movies in order from longest to shortest.

25. The proboscis bat, with a length of $\frac{19}{5}$ cm, is one of the smallest bats. Write $\frac{19}{5}$ as a mixed number.

World's Longest Movies	
Title	Length (h)
1900	$\frac{318}{60}$
Empire	$\frac{480}{60}$
Fanny and Alexander	$5\frac{1}{5}$
War and Peace	$8\frac{31}{60}$

Focus on Problem Solving

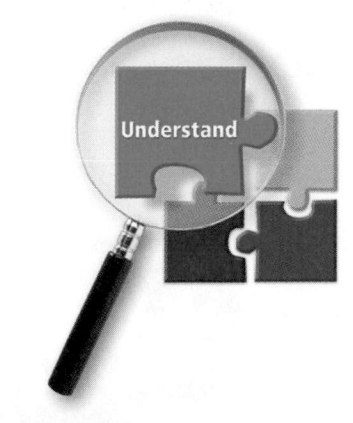

Understand the Problem

• **Write the problem in your own words**

One way to understand a problem better is to write it in your own words. Before you do this, you may need to read it over several times, perhaps aloud so that you can hear yourself say the words.

When you write a problem in your own words, try to make the problem simpler. Use smaller words and shorter sentences. Leave out any extra information, but make sure to include all the information you need to answer the question.

Write each problem in your own words. Check that you have included all the information you need to answer the question.

1 Martin is making muffins for his class bake sale. The recipe calls for $2\frac{1}{3}$ cups of flour, but Martin's only measuring cup holds $\frac{1}{3}$ cup. How many of his measuring cups should he use?

2 Mariko sold an old book to a used bookstore. She had hoped to sell it for $0.80, but the store gave her $\frac{3}{4}$ of a dollar. What is the difference between the two amounts?

3 Koalas of eastern Australia feed mostly on eucalyptus leaves. They select certain trees over others to find the $1\frac{1}{4}$ pounds of food they need each day. Suppose a koala has eaten $1\frac{1}{8}$ pounds of food. Has the koala eaten enough food for the day?

4 The first day of the Tour de France is called the prologue. Each of the days after that is called a stage, and each stage covers a different distance. The total distance covered in the race is about 3,600 km. If a cyclist has completed $\frac{1}{3}$ of the race, how many kilometers has he ridden?

4-7 Comparing and Ordering Fractions

Learn to use pictures and number lines to compare and order fractions.

Vocabulary

like fractions

unlike fractions

common denominator

NY Performance Indicators

6.N.15 Order rational numbers. Also, 6.N.14.

Rachel and Hannah are making a kind of cookie called *hamantaschen*. They have $\frac{1}{2}$ cup of strawberry jam, but the recipe requires $\frac{1}{3}$ cup.

To determine if they have enough for the recipe, they need to compare the fractions $\frac{1}{2}$ and $\frac{1}{3}$.

Hamantaschen

1/2 cup butter
2 egg yolks
1 1/2 cups flour
2 tablespoons sugar
3 tablespoons ice water
1/3 cup strawberry jam

When you are comparing fractions, first check their denominators. When fractions have the same denominator, they are called **like fractions** . For example, $\frac{1}{8}$ and $\frac{5}{8}$ are like fractions. When two fractions have different denominators, they are called **unlike fractions** . For example, $\frac{7}{10}$ and $\frac{1}{2}$ are unlike fractions.

EXAMPLE 1 Comparing Fractions

Compare. Write <, >, or =.

Helpful Hint

When two fractions have the same denominator, the one with the larger numerator is greater.

$\frac{2}{5} < \frac{3}{5}$ $\frac{3}{8} > \frac{1}{8}$

A $\frac{1}{8}$ ☐ $\frac{5}{8}$

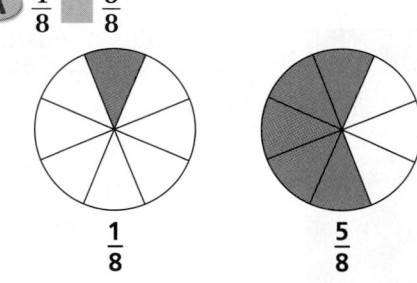

$\frac{1}{8}$ $\frac{5}{8}$

Model $\frac{1}{8}$ and $\frac{5}{8}$.

From the model, $\frac{1}{8} < \frac{5}{8}$.

B $\frac{7}{10}$ ☐ $\frac{1}{2}$

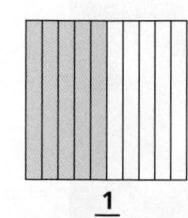

$\frac{7}{10}$ $\frac{1}{2}$

Model $\frac{7}{10}$ and $\frac{1}{2}$.

From the model, $\frac{7}{10} > \frac{1}{2}$.

To compare unlike fractions without models, first rename the fractions so they have the same denominator. This is called finding a **common denominator**. This method can be used to compare mixed numbers as well.

EXAMPLE 2 *Cooking Application*

Rachel and Hannah have $1\frac{2}{3}$ cups of flour. They need $1\frac{1}{2}$ cups to make hamantaschen. Do they have enough flour for the recipe?

Compare $1\frac{2}{3}$ and $1\frac{1}{2}$.

Compare the whole-number parts of the numbers.
$1 = 1$ The whole-number parts are equal.

Compare the fractional parts. Find a common denominator by multiplying the denominators. $2 \cdot 3 = 6$

Find equivalent fractions with 6 as the denominator.

$$\frac{2}{3} = \frac{\boxed{}}{6} \qquad\qquad \frac{1}{2} = \frac{\boxed{}}{6}$$

$$\frac{2 \cdot 2}{3 \cdot 2} = \frac{4}{6} \qquad\qquad \frac{1 \cdot 3}{2 \cdot 3} = \frac{3}{6}$$

$$\frac{2}{3} = \frac{4}{6} \qquad\qquad \frac{1}{2} = \frac{3}{6}$$

Compare the like fractions. $\frac{4}{6} > \frac{3}{6}$, so $\frac{2}{3} > \frac{1}{2}$.

Therefore, $1\frac{2}{3}$ is greater than $1\frac{1}{2}$.

Since $1\frac{2}{3}$ cups is more than $1\frac{1}{2}$ cups, they have enough flour.

EXAMPLE 3 **Ordering Fractions**

Order $\frac{3}{7}$, $\frac{3}{4}$, and $\frac{1}{4}$ from least to greatest.

$$\frac{3 \cdot 4}{7 \cdot 4} = \frac{12}{28} \qquad \frac{3 \cdot 7}{4 \cdot 7} = \frac{21}{28} \qquad \frac{1 \cdot 7}{4 \cdot 7} = \frac{7}{28}$$

Rename with like denominators.

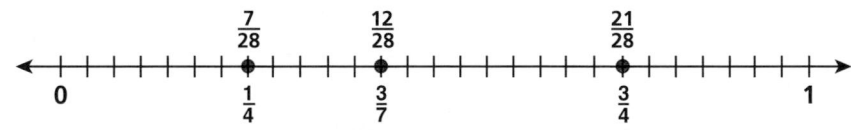

The fractions in order from least to greatest are $\frac{1}{4}$, $\frac{3}{7}$, $\frac{3}{4}$.

Remember!

Numbers increase in value as you move from left to right on a number line.

6.PS.21, 6.CN.4

Think and Discuss

1. **Tell** whether the values of the fractions change when you rename two fractions so that they have common denominators.

2. **Explain** how to compare $\frac{2}{5}$ and $\frac{4}{5}$.

4-7 **Exercises**

go.hrw.com
Homework Help Online
KEYWORD: MR7 4-7
Parent Resources Online
KEYWORD: MR7 Parent

GUIDED PRACTICE

See Example ① **Compare. Write <, >, or =.**

1. $\frac{3}{5} \blacksquare \frac{2}{5}$　　**2.** $\frac{1}{9} \blacksquare \frac{2}{9}$　　**3.** $\frac{6}{8} \blacksquare \frac{3}{4}$　　**4.** $\frac{3}{7} \blacksquare \frac{6}{7}$

See Example ② **5.** Arsenio has $\frac{2}{3}$ cup of brown sugar. The recipe he is using requires $\frac{1}{4}$ cup of brown sugar. Does he have enough brown sugar for the recipe? Explain.

See Example ③ **Order the fractions from least to greatest.**

6. $\frac{3}{8}, \frac{1}{5}, \frac{2}{3}$　　**7.** $\frac{1}{4}, \frac{2}{5}, \frac{1}{3}$　　**8.** $\frac{5}{9}, \frac{1}{8}, \frac{2}{7}$　　**9.** $\frac{1}{2}, \frac{1}{6}, \frac{2}{3}$

INDEPENDENT PRACTICE

See Example ① **Compare. Write <, >, or =.**

10. $\frac{2}{5} \blacksquare \frac{4}{5}$　　**11.** $\frac{1}{10} \blacksquare \frac{3}{10}$　　**12.** $\frac{3}{4} \blacksquare \frac{3}{8}$　　**13.** $\frac{5}{6} \blacksquare \frac{4}{6}$

14. $\frac{4}{5} \blacksquare \frac{5}{5}$　　**15.** $\frac{2}{4} \blacksquare \frac{1}{2}$　　**16.** $\frac{4}{8} \blacksquare \frac{16}{24}$　　**17.** $\frac{11}{16} \blacksquare \frac{9}{16}$

See Example ② **18.** Kelly needs $\frac{2}{3}$ gallon of paint to finish painting her deck. She has $\frac{5}{8}$ gallon of paint. Does she have enough paint to finish her deck? Explain.

See Example ③ **Order the fractions from least to greatest.**

19. $\frac{1}{2}, \frac{3}{5}, \frac{3}{7}$　　**20.** $\frac{1}{6}, \frac{2}{5}, \frac{1}{4}$　　**21.** $\frac{4}{9}, \frac{3}{8}, \frac{1}{3}$　　**22.** $\frac{1}{4}, \frac{5}{6}, \frac{5}{9}$

23. $\frac{3}{4}, \frac{7}{10}, \frac{2}{3}$　　**24.** $\frac{13}{18}, \frac{5}{9}, \frac{5}{6}$　　**25.** $\frac{3}{8}, \frac{1}{4}, \frac{2}{3}$　　**26.** $\frac{3}{10}, \frac{2}{3}, \frac{5}{11}$

PRACTICE AND PROBLEM SOLVING

Extra Practice
See page 721.

Compare. Write <, >, or =.

27. $\frac{4}{15} \blacksquare \frac{3}{10}$　　**28.** $\frac{7}{12} \blacksquare \frac{13}{30}$　　**29.** $\frac{5}{9} \blacksquare \frac{4}{11}$　　**30.** $\frac{8}{14} \blacksquare \frac{8}{9}$

31. $\frac{3}{5} \blacksquare \frac{26}{65}$　　**32.** $\frac{3}{5} \blacksquare \frac{2}{21}$　　**33.** $\frac{24}{41} \blacksquare \frac{2}{7}$　　**34.** $\frac{10}{38} \blacksquare \frac{1}{4}$

Order the fractions from least to greatest.

35. $\frac{2}{5}, \frac{1}{2}, \frac{3}{10}$　　**36.** $\frac{3}{4}, \frac{3}{5}, \frac{7}{10}$　　**37.** $\frac{7}{15}, \frac{2}{3}, \frac{1}{5}$　　**38.** $\frac{3}{4}, \frac{1}{3}, \frac{8}{15}$

39. $\frac{2}{5}, \frac{4}{9}, \frac{11}{15}$　　**40.** $\frac{7}{12}, \frac{5}{8}, \frac{1}{2}$　　**41.** $\frac{5}{8}, \frac{3}{4}, \frac{5}{12}$　　**42.** $\frac{2}{3}, \frac{7}{8}, \frac{7}{15}$

43. Laura and Kim receive the same amount of allowance each week. Laura spends $\frac{3}{5}$ of it on going to the movies. Kim spends $\frac{4}{7}$ of it on a CD. Which girl spent more of her allowance? Explain.

44. Kyle operates a hot dog cart in a large city. He spends $\frac{2}{5}$ of his budget on supplies, $\frac{1}{12}$ on advertising, and $\frac{2}{25}$ on taxes and fees. Does Kyle spend more on advertising or more on taxes and fees?

Order the numbers from least to greatest.

45. $1\frac{2}{5}$, $1\frac{1}{8}$, $3\frac{4}{5}$, 3, $3\frac{2}{5}$

46. $7\frac{1}{2}$, $9\frac{4}{7}$, $9\frac{1}{2}$, 8, $8\frac{3}{4}$

47. $\frac{1}{2}$, $3\frac{1}{5}$, $3\frac{1}{10}$, $\frac{3}{4}$, $3\frac{1}{15}$

48. Agriculture The table shows the fraction of the world's total corn each country produces. List the countries in order from the country that produces the most corn to the country that produces the least corn.

World's Corn Production	
United States	$\frac{41}{100}$
China	$\frac{1}{5}$
Brazil	$\frac{1}{20}$

49. Multi-Step The Dixon Dragons must win at least $\frac{3}{7}$ of their remaining games to qualify for their district playoffs. If they have 15 games left and they win 7 of them, will the Dragons compete in the playoffs? Explain.

50. Write a Problem Write a problem that involves comparing two fractions with different denominators.

 51. Write About It Compare the following fractions.

$\frac{1}{2}$ ▪ $\frac{1}{4}$ $\frac{2}{3}$ ▪ $\frac{2}{5}$ $\frac{3}{4}$ ▪ $\frac{3}{7}$ $\frac{4}{5}$ ▪ $\frac{4}{9}$

What do you notice about two fractions that have the same numerator but different denominators? Which one is greater?

 52. Challenge Name a fraction that would make the inequality true.

$$\frac{1}{4} > \blacksquare > \frac{1}{5}$$

TEST PREP and Spiral Review

53. Multiple Choice Which fraction has the least value?

Ⓐ $\frac{1}{5}$ Ⓑ $\frac{3}{11}$ Ⓒ $\frac{2}{15}$ Ⓓ $\frac{4}{18}$

54. Extended Response Kevin is making potato soup. The recipe shows that he needs $\frac{1}{2}$ gallon of milk and 3.5 pounds of potatoes. He has $\frac{2}{5}$ gallon of milk and $\frac{21}{5}$ pounds of potatoes. Does Kevin have enough milk and potatoes to make the soup? Show your work and explain your answer.

Write each number in scientific notation. (Lesson 3-4)

55. 45   **56.** 405,000   **57.** 1,600,000   **58.** 23,000,000

Write each fraction in simplest form. (Lesson 4-5)

59. $\frac{3}{36}$ **60.** $\frac{4}{42}$ **61.** $\frac{6}{20}$ **62.** $\frac{12}{30}$ **63.** $\frac{5}{55}$

4-8 # Adding and Subtracting with Like Denominators

Learn to add and subtract fractions with like denominators.

You can estimate the age of an oak tree by measuring around the trunk at four feet above the ground.

The distance around a young oak tree's trunk increases at a rate of approximately $\frac{1}{8}$ inch per month.

NY Performance Indicators

6.A.2 Use substitution to evaluate algebraic expressions. Also, 5.A.3.

EXAMPLE **1** *Life Science Application*

Sophie plants a young oak tree in her backyard. The distance around the trunk grows at a rate of $\frac{1}{8}$ inch per month. Use pictures to model how much this distance will increase in two months, then write your answer in simplest form.

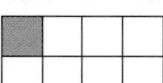

$\frac{1}{8} + \frac{1}{8}$

$\frac{1}{8} + \frac{1}{8} = \frac{2}{8}$ *Add the numerators. Keep the same denominator.*

$\qquad = \frac{1}{4}$ *Write your answer in simplest form.*

The distance around the trunk will increase by $\frac{1}{4}$ inch.

EXAMPLE **2** **Subtracting Like Fractions and Mixed Numbers**

Subtract. Write each answer in simplest form.

A $1 - \frac{2}{3}$

$\downarrow \qquad \downarrow$

$\frac{3}{3} - \frac{2}{3} = \frac{1}{3}$

To get a common denominator, rewrite 1 as a fraction with a denominator of 3.

Subtract the numerators. Keep the same denominator.

Check

 $-$ 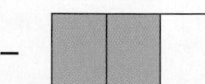 $=$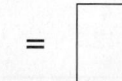

Remember!

When the numerator equals the denominator, the fraction is equal to 1.

$\frac{3}{3} = 1 \qquad \frac{173}{173} = 1$

Subtract. Write each answer in simplest form.

B $3\frac{7}{12} - 1\frac{1}{12}$

$3\frac{7}{12} - 1\frac{1}{12}$ *Subtract the fractions. Then subtract the whole numbers.*

$2\frac{6}{12}$

$2\frac{1}{2}$ *Write your answer in simplest form.*

Check

EXAMPLE 3   **Evaluating Expressions with Fractions**

Evaluate each expression for $x = \frac{3}{8}$. Write each answer in simplest form.

A $\frac{5}{8} - x$

$\frac{5}{8} - x$ *Write the expression.*

$\frac{5}{8} - \frac{3}{8} = \frac{2}{8}$ *Substitute $\frac{3}{8}$ for x and subtract the numerators. Keep the same denominator.*

$= \frac{1}{4}$ *Write your answer in simplest form.*

B $x + 1\frac{1}{8}$

$x + 1\frac{1}{8}$ *Write the expression.*

$\frac{3}{8} + 1\frac{1}{8} = 1\frac{4}{8}$ *Substitute $\frac{3}{8}$ for x. Add the fractions. Then add the whole numbers.*

$= 1\frac{1}{2}$ *Write your answer in simplest form.*

C $x + \frac{7}{8}$

$x + \frac{7}{8}$ *Write the expression.*

$\frac{3}{8} + \frac{7}{8} = \frac{10}{8}$ *Substitute $\frac{3}{8}$ for x and add the numerators. Keep the same denominator.*

$= \frac{5}{4}$ or $1\frac{1}{4}$ *Write your answer in simplest form.*

> **Helpful Hint**
>
> When adding a fraction to a mixed number, you can think of the fraction as having a whole number of 0.
>
> $\frac{3}{8} = 0\frac{3}{8}$

Think and Discuss

1. **Explain** how to add or subtract like fractions.

2. **Tell** why the sum of $\frac{1}{5}$ and $\frac{3}{5}$ is not $\frac{4}{10}$. Give the correct sum.

3. **Describe** how you would add $2\frac{3}{8}$ and $1\frac{1}{8}$. How would you subtract $1\frac{1}{8}$ from $2\frac{3}{8}$?

4-8 **Exercises**

go.hrw.com
Homework Help Online
KEYWORD: MR7 4-8
Parent Resources Online
KEYWORD: MR7 Parent

GUIDED PRACTICE

See Example ① **1.** Marta is filling a bucket with water. The height of the water is increasing $\frac{1}{6}$ foot each minute. Use pictures to model how much the height of the water will change in three minutes, and then write your answer in simplest form.

See Example ② **Subtract. Write each answer in simplest form.**

2. $2 - \frac{3}{5}$ **3.** $8 - \frac{6}{7}$ **4.** $4\frac{2}{3} - 1\frac{1}{3}$ **5.** $8\frac{7}{12} - 3\frac{5}{12}$

See Example ③ **Evaluate each expression for $x = \frac{3}{10}$. Write each answer in simplest form.**

6. $\frac{9}{10} - x$ **7.** $x + \frac{1}{10}$ **8.** $x + \frac{9}{10}$ **9.** $x - \frac{1}{10}$

INDEPENDENT PRACTICE

See Example ① **10.** Wesley drinks $\frac{2}{13}$ gallon of juice each day. Use pictures to model the number of gallons of juice Wesley drinks in 5 days, and then write your answer in simplest form.

See Example ② **Subtract. Write each answer in simplest form.**

11. $1 - \frac{5}{7}$ **12.** $1 - \frac{3}{8}$ **13.** $2\frac{4}{5} - 1\frac{1}{5}$ **14.** $9\frac{9}{14} - 5\frac{3}{14}$

See Example ③ **Evaluate each expression for $x = \frac{11}{20}$. Write each answer in simplest form.**

15. $x + \frac{13}{20}$ **16.** $x - \frac{3}{20}$ **17.** $x - \frac{9}{20}$ **18.** $x + \frac{17}{20}$

PRACTICE AND PROBLEM SOLVING

Extra Practice
See page 721.

Write each sum or difference in simplest form.

19. $\frac{1}{16} + \frac{9}{16}$ **20.** $\frac{15}{26} - \frac{11}{26}$ **21.** $\frac{10}{33} + \frac{4}{33}$

22. $1 - \frac{9}{10}$ **23.** $\frac{26}{75} + \frac{24}{75}$ **24.** $\frac{100}{999} + \frac{899}{999}$

25. $37\frac{13}{18} - 24\frac{7}{18}$ **26.** $\frac{1}{20} + \frac{7}{20} + \frac{3}{20}$ **27.** $\frac{11}{24} + \frac{1}{24} + \frac{5}{24}$

28. Lily took $\frac{5}{6}$ lb of peanuts to a baseball game. She ate $\frac{2}{6}$ lb. How many pounds of peanuts does she have left? Write the answer in simplest form.

Evaluate. Write each answer in simplest form.

29. $a + \frac{7}{18}$ for $a = \frac{1}{18}$ **30.** $\frac{6}{13} - j$ for $j = \frac{4}{13}$

31. $c + c$ for $c = \frac{5}{14}$ **32.** $m - \frac{6}{17}$ for $m = 1$

33. $8\frac{14}{15} - z$ for $z = \frac{4}{15}$ **34.** $13\frac{1}{24} + y$ for $y = 2\frac{5}{24}$

35. Sheila spent x hour studying on Tuesday and $\frac{1}{4}$ hour studying on Thursday. What was the total amount of time in hours Sheila spent studying if $x = \frac{2}{4}$?

36. Carlos had 7 cups of chocolate chips. He used $1\frac{2}{3}$ cups to make a chocolate sauce and $3\frac{1}{3}$ cups to make cookies. How many cups of chocolate chips does Carlos have now?

37. A concert was $2\frac{1}{4}$ hr long. The first musical piece lasted $\frac{1}{4}$ hr. The intermission also lasted $\frac{1}{4}$ hr. How long was the rest of the concert?

38. A flight from Washington, D.C., stops in San Francisco and then continues to Seattle. The trip to San Francisco takes $4\frac{5}{8}$ hr. The trip to Seattle takes $1\frac{1}{8}$ hr. What is the total flight time?

Life Science Use the graph for Exercises 39–41. Sheila performed an experiment to find the most effective plant fertilizer. She used a different fertilizer on each of 5 different plants. The heights of the plants at the end of her experiment are shown in the graph.

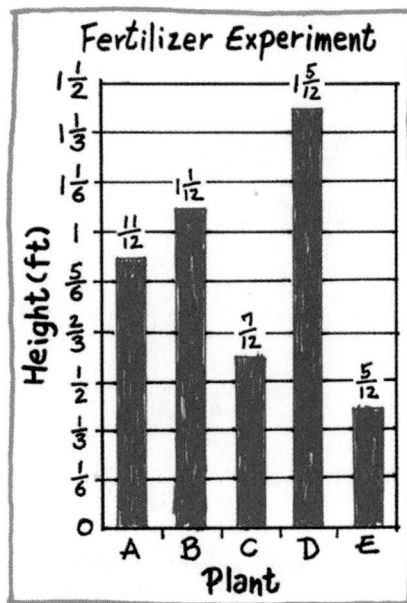

39. What is the combined height of plants C and E?

40. What is the difference in height between the tallest plant and the shortest plant?

41. **What's the Error?** Sheila found the combined heights of plants B and E to be $1\frac{6}{24}$ feet. Explain the error and give the correct answer in simplest form.

 42. **Write About It** When writing 1 as a fraction in a subtraction problem, how do you know what the numerator and denominator should be? Give an example.

 43. **Challenge** Explain how you might estimate the difference between $\frac{3}{4}$ and $\frac{6}{23}$.

TEST PREP and Spiral Review

44. **Multiple Choice** Solve. $x - \frac{6}{11} = \frac{5}{11}$

   Ⓐ $\frac{1}{22}$ Ⓑ $\frac{1}{11}$ Ⓒ 1   Ⓓ 11

45. **Short Response** Your friend was absent from school and asked you for help with the math assignment. Give your friend detailed instructions on how to subtract $4\frac{7}{12}$ from $13\frac{11}{12}$.

Find two equivalent fractions for each fraction. (Lesson 4-5)

46. $\frac{4}{7}$ 47. $\frac{3}{4}$ 48. $\frac{2}{9}$ 49. $\frac{3}{5}$ 50. $\frac{1}{10}$

Order the fractions from least to greatest. (Lesson 4-7)

51. $\frac{3}{7}, \frac{5}{4}, \frac{2}{6}$ 52. $\frac{2}{3}, \frac{4}{11}, \frac{5}{8}$ 53. $\frac{3}{10}, \frac{3}{8}, \frac{1}{3}$

Estimating Fraction Sums and Differences

4-9

Learn to estimate sums and differences of fractions and mixed numbers.

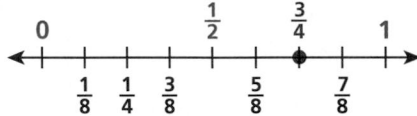
NY Performance Indicators

6.N.14 Locate rational numbers on a number line.

Members of the Nature Club went mountain biking in Canyonlands National Park, Utah. They biked $10\frac{3}{10}$ miles on Monday.

You can estimate fractions by rounding to 0, $\frac{1}{2}$, or 1.

```
        1/2   3/4
0              •      1
|  |  |  |  |  |  |  |
  1/8 1/4 3/8 5/8   7/8
```

The fraction $\frac{3}{4}$ is halfway between $\frac{1}{2}$ and 1, but we usually round up. So the fraction $\frac{3}{4}$ rounds to 1.

Canyonlands National Park, Utah, is a 337,570-acre park that has many canyons, mesas, arches, and spires.

You can round fractions by comparing the numerator and denominator.

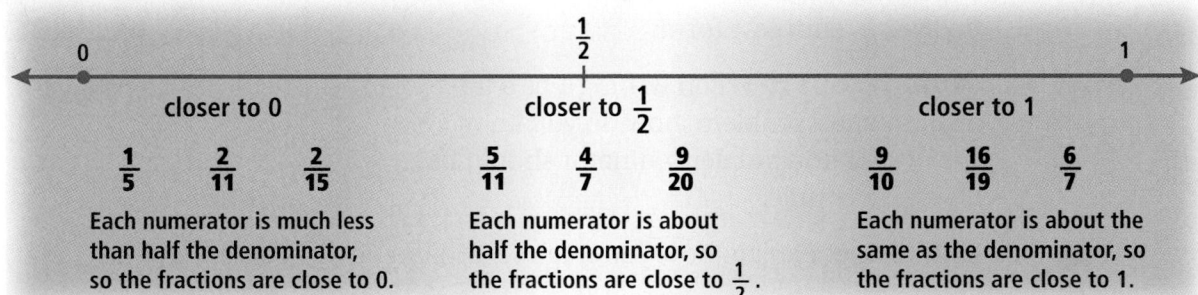

closer to 0	closer to $\frac{1}{2}$	closer to 1
$\frac{1}{5}$ $\frac{2}{11}$ $\frac{2}{15}$	$\frac{5}{11}$ $\frac{4}{7}$ $\frac{9}{20}$	$\frac{9}{10}$ $\frac{16}{19}$ $\frac{6}{7}$
Each numerator is much less than half the denominator, so the fractions are close to 0.	Each numerator is about half the denominator, so the fractions are close to $\frac{1}{2}$.	Each numerator is about the same as the denominator, so the fractions are close to 1.

EXAMPLE **1** **Estimating Fractions**

Estimate each sum or difference by rounding to 0, $\frac{1}{2}$, or 1.

A $\frac{8}{9} + \frac{2}{11}$

$\frac{8}{9} + \frac{2}{11}$ *Think: $\frac{8}{9}$ rounds to 1 and $\frac{2}{11}$ rounds to 0.*

$1 + 0 = 1$

$\frac{8}{9} + \frac{2}{11}$ is about 1.

B $\frac{7}{12} - \frac{8}{15}$

$\frac{7}{12} - \frac{8}{15}$ *Think: $\frac{7}{12}$ rounds to $\frac{1}{2}$ and $\frac{8}{15}$ rounds to $\frac{1}{2}$.*

$\frac{1}{2} - \frac{1}{2} = 0$

$\frac{7}{12} - \frac{8}{15}$ is about 0.

You can also estimate by rounding mixed numbers. Compare the mixed number to the two nearest whole numbers and the nearest $\frac{1}{2}$.

Does $10\frac{3}{10}$ round to 10, $10\frac{1}{2}$, or 11?

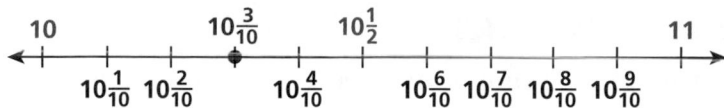

The mixed number $10\frac{3}{10}$ rounds to $10\frac{1}{2}$.

EXAMPLE 2 · Sports Application

A About how far did the Nature Club ride on Monday and Tuesday?

$$10\frac{3}{10} + 9\frac{3}{4}$$
$$\downarrow \qquad \downarrow$$
$$10\frac{1}{2} + 10 = 20\frac{1}{2}$$

They rode about $20\frac{1}{2}$ miles.

Nature Club's Biking Distances	
Day	Distances (mi)
Monday	$10\frac{3}{10}$
Tuesday	$9\frac{3}{4}$
Wednesday	$12\frac{1}{4}$
Thursday	$4\frac{7}{10}$

Helpful Hint

$\frac{1}{4}$ is halfway between 0 and $\frac{1}{2}$. Round $\frac{1}{4}$ up to $\frac{1}{2}$.

B About how much farther did the Nature Club ride on Wednesday than on Thursday?

$$12\frac{1}{4} - 4\frac{7}{10}$$
$$\downarrow \qquad \downarrow$$
$$12\frac{1}{2} - 4\frac{1}{2} = 8$$

They rode about 8 miles farther on Wednesday than on Thursday.

C Estimate the total distance that the Nature Club rode on Monday, Tuesday, and Wednesday.

$$10\frac{3}{10} + \quad 9\frac{3}{4} + 12\frac{1}{4}$$
$$\downarrow \qquad \quad \downarrow \qquad \downarrow$$
$$10\frac{1}{2} + \quad 10 + 12\frac{1}{2} = 33$$

They rode about 33 miles.

Think and Discuss

 6.PS.17, 6.CM.1

1. Tell whether each fraction rounds to 0, $\frac{1}{2}$, or 1: $\frac{5}{6}, \frac{2}{15}, \frac{7}{13}$.

2. Explain how to round mixed numbers to the nearest whole number.

3. Determine whether the Nature Club met their goal to ride at least 35 total miles.

Exercises

go.hrw.com
Homework Help Online
KEYWORD: MR7 4-9
Parent Resources Online
KEYWORD: MR7 Parent

GUIDED PRACTICE

See Example 1 **Estimate each sum or difference by rounding to 0, $\frac{1}{2}$, or 1.**

1. $\frac{8}{9} + \frac{1}{6}$

2. $\frac{11}{12} - \frac{4}{9}$

3. $\frac{3}{7} + \frac{1}{12}$

4. $\frac{6}{13} - \frac{2}{5}$

See Example 2 **Use the table for Exercises 5 and 6.**

5. About how far did Mark run during week 1 and week 2?

6. About how much farther did Mark run during week 2 than during week 3?

Mark's Running Distances	
Week	**Distance (mi)**
1	$8\frac{3}{4}$
2	$7\frac{1}{5}$
3	$5\frac{5}{6}$

INDEPENDENT PRACTICE

See Example 1 **Estimate each sum or difference by rounding to 0, $\frac{1}{2}$, or 1.**

7. $\frac{7}{8} - \frac{3}{8}$

8. $\frac{3}{10} + \frac{3}{4}$

9. $\frac{5}{6} - \frac{7}{8}$

10. $\frac{7}{10} + \frac{1}{6}$

11. $\frac{3}{4} + \frac{7}{10}$

12. $\frac{9}{20} - \frac{1}{6}$

13. $\frac{8}{9} + \frac{4}{5}$

14. $\frac{19}{20} + \frac{9}{10}$

See Example 2 **Use the table for Exercises 15–17.**

15. About how much do the meteorites in Brenham and Goose Lake weigh together?

16. About how much more does the meteorite in Willamette weigh than the meteorite in Norton County?

17. About how much do the two meteorites in Kansas weigh together?

Meteorites in the United States	
Location	**Weight (tons)**
Willamette, AZ	$16\frac{1}{2}$
Brenham, KS	$2\frac{3}{5}$
Goose Lake, CA	$1\frac{3}{10}$
Norton County, KS	$1\frac{1}{10}$

PRACTICE AND PROBLEM SOLVING

Extra Practice
See page 721.

Estimate each sum or difference to compare. Write < or >.

18. $\frac{5}{6} + \frac{7}{9}$ ▢ 3

19. $2\frac{8}{15} - 1\frac{1}{11}$ ▢ 1

20. $1\frac{2}{21} + \frac{3}{7}$ ▢ 2

21. $1\frac{7}{13} - \frac{8}{9}$ ▢ 1

22. $3\frac{2}{10} + 2\frac{2}{5}$ ▢ 6

23. $4\frac{6}{9} - 2\frac{3}{19}$ ▢ 2

24. **Critical Thinking** Describe a situation in which it is better to round a mixed number up to the next whole number even if the fraction in the mixed number is closer to $\frac{1}{2}$ than 1.

Estimate.

25. $\frac{7}{8} + \frac{4}{7} + \frac{7}{13}$

26. $\frac{6}{11} + \frac{9}{17} + \frac{3}{5}$

27. $\frac{8}{9} + \frac{3}{4} + \frac{9}{10}$

28. $1\frac{5}{8} + 2\frac{1}{15} + 2\frac{12}{13}$

29. $4\frac{11}{12} + 3\frac{1}{19} + 5\frac{4}{7}$

30. $10\frac{1}{9} + 8\frac{5}{9} + 11\frac{13}{14}$

Life Science Use an inch ruler for Exercises 31–32. Measure to the nearest $\frac{1}{4}$ inch.

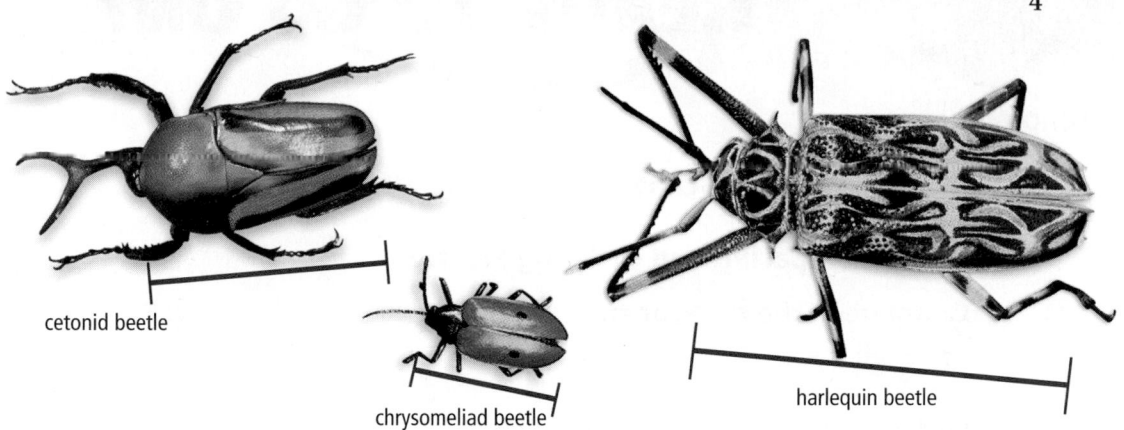

cetonid beetle

chrysomeliad beetle

harlequin beetle

31. About how much longer is the harlequin beetle than the cetonid beetle?

32. About how much longer is the harlequin beetle than the chrysomeliad beetle?

33. Use the table to estimate the total weekly snowfall.

Day	Mon	Tue	Wed	Thu	Fri	Sat	Sun
Snowfall (in.)	$3\frac{4}{7}$	$\frac{7}{8}$	0	$2\frac{1}{6}$	$\frac{2}{11}$	$1\frac{9}{20}$	$1\frac{4}{7}$

34. Write a Problem Write a problem about a trip that can be solved by estimating fractions. Exchange with a classmate and solve.

35. Write About It Explain how to estimate the sum of two mixed numbers. Give an example to explain your answer.

36. Challenge Estimate. $\left[5\frac{7}{8} - 2\frac{3}{20}\right] + 1\frac{4}{7}$

37. Multiple Choice Larry ran $3\frac{1}{3}$ miles on Monday and $5\frac{3}{4}$ miles on Tuesday. About how many miles did Larry run on Monday and Tuesday?

Ⓐ 8   Ⓑ 9   Ⓒ 10   Ⓓ 11

38. Multiple Choice Marie used $2\frac{4}{5}$ cups of flour for a recipe. Linda used $1\frac{1}{4}$ cups of flour for a recipe. About how many more cups of flour did Marie use than Linda?

Ⓕ 1   Ⓖ 2   Ⓗ 3   Ⓙ 4

Evaluate each expression. (Lesson 1-4)

39. $6 \times (21 - 15) \div 12$ **40.** $72 \div 8 + 2^3 \times 5 - 19$ **41.** $5 + (6 - 1) \times 2 \div 2$

Write an expression for the missing value in each table. (Lesson 2-3)

42.

Games Played	2	4	6	8	n
Points Scored	14	28	42	56	▮

43.

Month	1	3	5	7	n
Hours Worked	6	8	10	12	▮

READY TO GO ON?

Quiz for Lessons 4-7 Through 4-9

✓ 4-7 Comparing and Ordering Fractions

Compare. Write <, >, or =.

1. $\frac{3}{4} \blacksquare \frac{2}{3}$
2. $\frac{7}{9} \blacksquare \frac{5}{6}$
3. $\frac{4}{9} \blacksquare \frac{4}{7}$
4. $\frac{5}{11} \blacksquare \frac{3}{5}$

Order the fractions from least to greatest.

5. $\frac{5}{8}, \frac{1}{2}, \frac{3}{4}$
6. $\frac{3}{4}, \frac{3}{5}, \frac{7}{10}$
7. $\frac{1}{3}, \frac{3}{8}, \frac{1}{4}$
8. $\frac{2}{5}, \frac{4}{9}, \frac{11}{15}$

9. Mrs. Wilson split a bag of marbles between her three sons. Ralph got $\frac{1}{10}$, Pete got $\frac{1}{2}$, and Jon got $\frac{8}{20}$. Who got the most marbles?

✓ 4-8 Adding and Subtracting with Like Denominators

10. The average growth rate for human hair is $\frac{1}{2}$ inch per month. On average, how much hair will a person grow in 3 months? Write your answer in simplest form.

11. A recipe for fruit salad calls for $\frac{1}{5}$ cup coconut. Ryan wants to double the recipe. How much coconut should he use? Write your answer in simplest form.

Subtract. Write each answer in simplest form.

12. $1 - \frac{3}{4}$
13. $6\frac{5}{9} - 5\frac{1}{9}$
14. $10\frac{7}{16} - 4\frac{3}{16}$

15. $5\frac{8}{9} - 1\frac{7}{9}$
16. $8\frac{4}{17} - 6\frac{2}{17}$
17. $1 - \frac{7}{8}$

Evaluate each expression for $x = \frac{5}{7}$. Write your answer in simplest form.

18. $x + 2\frac{1}{7}$
19. $x - \frac{3}{7}$
20. $10 + x$

21. $3\frac{2}{7} + x$
22. $6\frac{6}{7} - x$
23. $x + \frac{2}{7}$

✓ 4-9 Estimating Fraction Sums and Differences

Estimate each sum or difference.

24. $\frac{3}{4} - \frac{1}{10}$
25. $\frac{7}{9} + \frac{7}{9}$
26. $\frac{15}{16} - \frac{4}{5}$
27. $3\frac{7}{8} - 1\frac{1}{10}$

Use the table for problems 28–30.

28. About how far did Mrs. Ping walk during week 1 and week 2?

29. About how much farther did Mrs. Ping walk in week 2 than in week 3?

30. About how far did Mrs. Ping walk during the three weeks?

Mrs. Ping's Walking Distances	
Week	Distance (mi)
1	$2\frac{3}{4}$
2	$3\frac{1}{8}$
3	$2\frac{4}{7}$

A Party with Palm Trees

Jamal and Sarah are planning an end-of-year party for the Spanish Club. They want it to have a tropical theme.

Thirst Quencher One Serving

$\frac{2}{3}$ cup	Orange juice
$\frac{1}{3}$ cup	Cranberry juice
$\frac{2}{3}$ cup	Pineapple juice

1. There will be 16 girls and 12 boys at the party. Jamal wants to set up the tables so that every table has the same number of girls and the same number of boys. How many tables will there be? How many girls and boys will be at each table?

2. Sarah finds three recipes for fruit punch. She wants to choose the recipe that calls for the greatest amount of pineapple juice per serving. Which recipe should she choose? Explain.

3. Jamal thinks they should choose the recipe that makes the largest serving of punch. Which recipe should they choose in this case? Explain.

4. Each punch glass holds 2 cups of liquid. If they use the recipe that makes the largest serving, will there be room in each glass for ice? Explain.

Sea Breeze One Serving

$\frac{1}{4}$ cup	Orange juice
$\frac{1}{4}$ cup	Cranberry juice
$\frac{3}{4}$ cup	Pineapple juice

Tropical Mist One Serving

0.75 cup	Orange juice
0.25 cup	Cranberry juice
0.5 cup	Pineapple juice

EXTENSION

Sets of Numbers

**Learn** to make Venn diagrams to describe number sets.

Vocabulary

set   empty set

element

subset

intersection

union

Venn diagram

A group of items is called a **set** . The items in a set are called **elements** . In this chapter, you saw several sets of numbers, such as prime numbers, composite numbers, and factors.

In a **Venn diagram** , circles are used to show relationships between sets. The overlapped region represents elements that are in both set A *and* set B. This set is called the **intersection** of A and B. Elements that are in set A *or* set B make up the **union** of A and B.

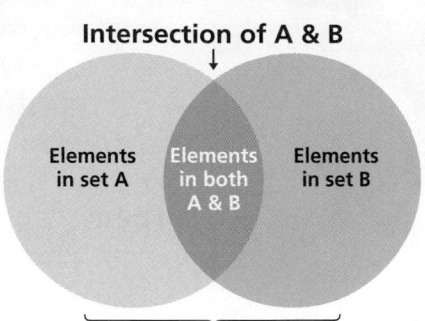

Intersection of A & B

Elements in set A | Elements in both A & B | Elements in set B

Union of A & B

EXAMPLE **1** **Identifying Elements and Drawing Venn Diagrams**

**NY Performance Indicators**

6.S.3 Construct Venn diagrams to sort data. Also, 6.PS.9.

Identify the elements in each set. Then draw a Venn diagram. What is the intersection? What is the union?

A Set A: prime numbers   Set B: composite numbers
Elements of A: 2, 3, 5, 7, …   Elements of B: 4, 6, 8, 9, …

A **2, 3, 5, 7,...**   B **4, 6, 8, 9,...**

The circles do not overlap because no number is both prime and composite.

Intersection: none. When a set has no elements, it is called an **empty set** . The intersection of A and B is empty.

Union: all numbers that are prime *or* composite—all whole numbers except 0 and 1.

B Set A: factors of 36   Set B: factors of 24
Elements of A: 1, 2, 3, 4, 6, 9, 12, 18, 36
Elements of B: 1, 2, 3, 4, 6, 8, 12, 24

A 18 24 B
9 1 2 3 4 6 12
36 8

The circles overlap because some factors of 36 are also factors of 24.

Intersection: 1, 2, 3, 4, 6, 12   *factors of 36 **and** 24*
Union: 1, 2, 3, 4, 6, 8, 9, 12, 18, 24, 36   *factors of 36 **or** 24*

Identify the elements in each set. Then draw a Venn diagram. What is the intersection? What is the union?

C Set A: factors of 36   Set B: factors of 12

Elements of A: 1, 2, 3, 4, 6, 9, 12, 18, 36

Elements of B: 1, 2, 3, 4, 6, 12

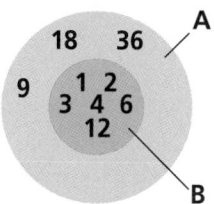

The circle for set B is entirely inside the circle for set A because all factors of 12 are also factors of 36.

Intersection: 1, 2, 3, 4, 6, 12   *factors of 36 **and** 12*

Union: 1, 2, 3, 4, 6, 9, 12, 18, 36   *factors of 36 **or** 12*

Helpful Hint

To decide whether set B is a subset of set A, ask yourself, "Is every element of B also in A?" If the answer is yes, then B is a subset of A.

Look at Example 1C. When one set is entirely contained in another set, we say the first set is a **subset** of the second set.

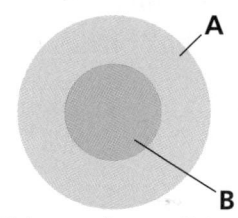

B is a subset of A.

EXTENSION

Exercises

Identify the elements in each set. Then draw a Venn diagram. What is the intersection? What is the union?

1. Set A: even numbers
Set B: odd numbers

2. Set A: factors of 18
Set B: factors of 40

3. Set A: factors of 72
Set B: factors of 36

4. Set A: even numbers
Set B: composite numbers

Tell whether set A is a subset of set B.

5. Set A: whole numbers less than 10
Set B: whole numbers less than 12

6. Set A: whole numbers less than 8
Set B: whole numbers greater than 9

7. Set A: prime numbers
Set B: odd numbers

8. Set A: numbers divisible by 6
Set B: numbers divisible by 3

 9. Write About It How could you use a Venn diagram to help find the greatest common factor of two numbers? Give an example.

 10. Challenge How could you use a Venn diagram to help find the greatest common factor of three numbers? Give an example.

Game Time

Riddle Me This

"When you go from there to here,
you'll find I disappear.
Go from here to there, and then
you'll see me again.
What am I?"

To solve this riddle, copy the square below. If a number is divisible by 3, color that box red. Remember the divisibility rule for 3. If a number is not divisible by 3, color that box blue.

102	981	210	6,015	72
79	1,204	576	10,019	1,771
548	3,416	12,300	904	1,330
217	2,662	1,746	3,506	15,025
34,351	725	2,352	5,675	6,001

On a Roll

The object is to be the first person to fill in all the squares on your game board.

On your turn, roll a number cube and record the number rolled in any blank square on your game board. Once you have placed a number in a square, you cannot move that number. If you cannot place the number in a square, then your turn is over. The winner is the first player to complete their game board correctly.

go.hrw.com
Game Time Extra
KEYWORD: MR7 Games

A complete copy of the rules and game pieces are available online.

Materials
- tan card stock
- scissors
- reinforcements
- hole punch
- wire ring
- markers

It's in the Bag!

PROJECT **Spec-Tag-Ular Number Theory**

Tags will help you keep notes about number theory and fractions on an easy-to-use reference ring.

Directions

❶ Make tags by cutting ten rectangles from card stock, each approximately $2\frac{3}{4}$ inches by $1\frac{1}{2}$ inches.

❷ Use scissors to clip off two corners at the end of each tag. **Figure A**

❸ Punch a hole between the clipped corners of each tag. Put a reinforcement around the hole on both sides of the tag. **Figure B**

❹ Hook all of the tags together on a wire ring. On one of the tags, write the number and name of the chapter. **Figure C**

Taking Note of the Math

On each tag, write a divisibility rule from the chapter. You can also use the tags to record important facts about fractions.

Chapter 4 Number Theory and Fractions

SPEC-TAG-ULAR NUMBER THEORY

Study Guide: Review

Vocabulary

common denominator 199	mixed number 181
composite number 165	prime factorization 169
divisible 164	prime number 165
equivalent fractions 186	proper fraction 192
factor 169	repeating decimal 182
greatest common factor (GCF) 173	simplest form 187
improper fraction 192	terminating decimal 182
like fractions 198	unlike fractions 198

Complete the sentences below with vocabulary words from the list above.

1. The number $\frac{11}{9}$ is an example of a(n) ___?___, and $3\frac{1}{6}$ is an example of a(n) ___?___.

2. A(n) ___?___, such as 0.3333..., has a block of one or more digits that repeat without end. A(n) ___?___, such as 0.25, has a finite number of decimal places.

3. A(n) ___?___ is divisible by only two numbers, 1 and itself. A(n) ___?___ is divisible by more than two numbers.

4-1 Divisibility (pp. 164–167)

6.RP.2

EXAMPLE

■ Tell whether 210 is divisible by 2, 3, 4, and 6.

2	*The last digit, 0, is even.*	Divisible
3	*The sum of the digits is divisible by 3.*	Divisible
4	*The number formed by the last two digits is not divisible by 4.*	Not divisible
6	*210 is divisible by 2 and 3.*	Divisible

■ Tell whether each number is prime or composite.

17 *only divisible by 1 and 17* prime
25 *divisible by 1, 5, and 25* composite

EXERCISES

Tell whether each number is divisible by 2, 3, 4, 5, 6, 9, and 10.

4. 118   5. 90

6. 342   7. 284

8. 170   9. 393

Tell whether each number is prime or composite.

10. 121   11. 77

12. 13   13. 118

14. 67   15. 93

16. 39   17. 97

18. 85   19. 61

4-2 Factors and Prime Factorization (pp. 169–172)

6.PS.15

EXAMPLE

- List all the factors of 10.

  $10 = 1 \cdot 10$ $\qquad$ $10 = 2 \cdot 5$

  The factors of 10 are 1, 2, 5, and 10.

- Write the prime factorization of 30.

  30
  ② · 15
  $\qquad$ ③ · ⑤

  $30 = 2 \cdot 3 \cdot 5$

EXERCISES

List all the factors of each number.

20. 60 $\qquad$ 21. 72
22. 29 $\qquad$ 23. 56
24. 85 $\qquad$ 25. 71

Write the prime factorization of each number.

26. 65 $\qquad$ 27. 94 $\qquad$ 28. 110
29. 81 $\qquad$ 30. 99 $\qquad$ 31. 76
32. 97 $\qquad$ 33. 55 $\qquad$ 34. 46

4-3 Greatest Common Factor (pp. 173–176)

6.PS.15

EXAMPLE

- Find the GCF of 35 and 50.

  factors of 35: 1, ⑤, 7, 35
  factors of 50: 1, 2, ⑤, 10, 25, 50

  The GCF of 35 and 50 is 5.

EXERCISES

Find the GCF of each set of numbers.

35. 36 and 60
36. 50, 75, and 125
37. 45, 81, and 99

4-4 Decimals and Fractions (pp. 181–184)

6.N.14, 6.N.15, 6.N.20, 6.N.21

EXAMPLE

- Write 1.29 as a mixed number.

  $1.29 = 1\frac{29}{100}$

- Write $\frac{3}{5}$ as a decimal.

  $\begin{array}{r} 0.6 \\ 5\overline{)3.0} \end{array}$ $\qquad$ $\frac{3}{5} = 0.6$

EXERCISES

Write as a fraction or mixed number.

38. 0.37 $\qquad$ 39. 1.8 $\qquad$ 40. 0.4

Write as a decimal.

41. $\frac{7}{8}$ $\qquad$ 42. $\frac{2}{5}$ $\qquad$ 43. $\frac{7}{9}$

4-5 Equivalent Fractions (pp. 186–189)

6.CN.4

EXAMPLE

- Find an equivalent fraction for $\frac{4}{5}$.

  $\frac{4}{5} = \frac{\blacksquare}{15}$ $\qquad$ $\frac{4 \cdot 3}{5 \cdot 3} = \frac{12}{15}$

- Write $\frac{8}{12}$ in simplest form.

  $\frac{8 \div 4}{12 \div 4} = \frac{2}{3}$

EXERCISES

Find two equivalent fractions.

44. $\frac{4}{6}$ $\qquad$ 45. $\frac{4}{5}$ $\qquad$ 46. $\frac{3}{12}$

Write each fraction in simplest form.

47. $\frac{14}{16}$ $\qquad$ 48. $\frac{9}{30}$ $\qquad$ 49. $\frac{7}{10}$

4-6 Mixed Numbers and Improper Fractions (pp. 192–195)

 6.PS.13

EXAMPLE

■ Write $3\frac{5}{6}$ as an improper fraction.

$$3\frac{5}{6} = \frac{(3 \cdot 6) + 5}{6} = \frac{18 + 5}{6} = \frac{23}{6}$$

■ Write $\frac{19}{4}$ as a mixed number.

$$\begin{array}{r} 4R3 \\ 4\overline{)19} \end{array} \qquad \frac{19}{4} = 4\frac{3}{4}$$

EXERCISES

Write as an improper fraction.

50. $3\frac{7}{9}$ **51.** $2\frac{5}{12}$ **52.** $5\frac{2}{7}$

Write as a mixed number.

53. $\frac{23}{6}$ **54.** $\frac{17}{5}$ **55.** $\frac{41}{8}$

4-7 Comparing and Ordering Fractions (pp. 198–201)

 6.N.14, 6.N.15

EXAMPLE

■ Order from least to greatest.

$\frac{3}{5}, \frac{2}{3}, \frac{1}{3}$ *Rename with like denominators.*

$$\frac{3 \cdot 3}{5 \cdot 3} = \frac{9}{15} \qquad \frac{2 \cdot 5}{3 \cdot 5} = \frac{10}{15} \qquad \frac{1 \cdot 5}{3 \cdot 5} = \frac{5}{15}$$

$$\frac{1}{3}, \frac{3}{5}, \frac{2}{3}$$

EXERCISES

Compare. Write $<$, $>$, or $=$.

56. $\frac{6}{8}$ ▨ $\frac{3}{8}$ **57.** $\frac{7}{9}$ ▨ $\frac{2}{3}$

Order from least to greatest.

58. $\frac{3}{8}, \frac{2}{3}, \frac{7}{8}$ **59.** $\frac{4}{6}, \frac{3}{12}, \frac{1}{3}$

4-8 Adding and Subtracting with Like Denominators (pp. 202–205)

5.A.3, 6.A.2

EXAMPLE

■ Subtract $4\frac{5}{6} - 2\frac{1}{6}$. Write your answer in simplest form.

$$4\frac{5}{6} - 2\frac{1}{6} = 2\frac{4}{6} = 2\frac{2}{3}$$

EXERCISES

Add or subtract. Write each answer in simplest form.

60. $\frac{1}{5} + \frac{4}{5}$ **61.** $1 - \frac{3}{12}$

62. $\frac{9}{10} - \frac{3}{10}$ **63.** $4\frac{2}{7} + 2\frac{3}{7}$

4-9 Estimating Fraction Sums and Differences (pp. 206–209)

6.N.14

EXAMPLE

■ Estimate the sum or difference by rounding fractions to 0, $\frac{1}{2}$, or 1.

$\frac{7}{8} + \frac{1}{7}$ *Think: $1 + 0$.*

$\frac{7}{8} + \frac{1}{7}$ is about 1.

EXERCISES

Estimate each sum or difference by rounding fractions to 0, $\frac{1}{2}$, or 1.

64. $\frac{3}{5} + \frac{3}{7}$ **65.** $\frac{6}{7} - \frac{5}{9}$

66. $4\frac{9}{10} + 6\frac{1}{5}$ **67.** $7\frac{5}{11} - 4\frac{3}{4}$

CHAPTER TEST

List all the factors of each number. Then tell whether each number is prime or composite.

1. 98

2. 40

3. 45

Write the prime factorization of each number.

4. 64

5. 130

6. 49

Find the GCF of each set of numbers.

7. 24 and 108

8. 45, 18, and 39

9. 49, 77, and 84

10. Ms. Arrington is making supply boxes for her students. She has 63 pencils, 42 pens, and 21 packs of markers. Each type of supply must be evenly distributed. What is the greatest number of supply boxes she can make if every supply is used?

Write each decimal as a fraction or mixed number.

11. 0.37

12. 1.9

13. 0.92

Write each fraction or mixed number as a decimal.

14. $\frac{3}{8}$

15. $9\frac{3}{5}$

16. $\frac{2}{3}$

Write each fraction in simplest form.

17. $\frac{4}{12}$

18. $\frac{6}{9}$

19. $\frac{3}{15}$

Write each mixed number as an improper fraction.

20. $4\frac{7}{8}$

21. $7\frac{5}{12}$

22. $3\frac{5}{7}$

Compare. Write $<$, $>$, or =.

23. $\frac{5}{6}$ ■ $\frac{3}{6}$

24. $\frac{3}{4}$ ■ $\frac{7}{8}$

25. $\frac{4}{5}$ ■ $\frac{7}{10}$

Order the fractions and decimals from least to greatest.

26. $2.17, 2.3, 2\frac{1}{9}$

27. $0.1, \frac{3}{8}, 0.3$

28. $0.9, \frac{2}{8}, 0.35$

29. On Monday, it snowed $2\frac{1}{4}$ inches. On Tuesday, an additional $3\frac{3}{4}$ inches of snow fell. How much snow fell altogether on Monday and Tuesday?

Estimate each sum or difference by rounding to 0, $\frac{1}{2}$, or 1.

30. $\frac{1}{8} + \frac{4}{7}$

31. $\frac{11}{12} - \frac{4}{9}$

32. $\frac{4}{5} + \frac{1}{9}$

33. $2\frac{9}{10} - 2\frac{1}{7}$

CHAPTER 4

NEW YORK
TEST PREP

go.hrw.com
State Test Practice Online
KEYWORD: MR7 TestPrep

CUMULATIVE ASSESSMENT, CHAPTERS 1–4

Multiple Choice

New York Test Prep

1. Which of the following numbers is divisible by 3, 4, and 8?

   (A) 12

   (B) 16

   (C) 20

   (D) 24

2. When June sits down today to read, she notices she is on page 20 of a 200-page book. She decides to read 4 pages of this book every day until she is finished. If this pattern continues, what page of the book will June be on in 10 more days?

   (F) 24

   (G) 44

   (H) 60

   (J) 120

3. Alice is using three different colors of beads to make necklaces. She has 48 blue beads, 56 pink beads, and 32 white beads. She wants to use the same number of pink, same number of blue, and same number of white beads on each necklace. What is the greatest number of necklaces she can make if she uses all of the beads?

   (A) 16

   (B) 12

   (C) 8

   (D) 4

4. A writer spends $144.75 on 5 ink cartridges. Which equation can be used to find the cost c of one ink cartridge?

   (F) $5c = 144.75$

   (G) $\frac{c}{144.75} = 5$

   (H) $5 + c = 144.75$

   (J) $144.75 - c = 5$

5. Which fraction is equal to 0.25?

   (A) $\frac{1}{3}$

   (B) $\frac{1}{4}$

   (C) $\frac{2}{5}$

   (D) $\frac{1}{25}$

6. Which fraction is NOT equivalent to $\frac{4}{6}$?

   (F) $\frac{2}{3}$

   (G) $\frac{10}{15}$

   (H) $\frac{8}{12}$

   (J) $\frac{16}{18}$

7. Which fraction is equivalent to the shaded area of the model?

   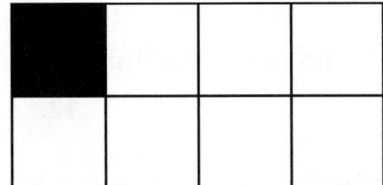

   (A) $\frac{2}{4}$

   (B) $\frac{3}{24}$

   (C) $\frac{6}{32}$

   (D) $\frac{4}{40}$

8. Steve bought a movie ticket for $6.25, a box of popcorn for $2.25, and a large drink for $4.75. How much money did he spend at the movie?

   (F) $12.00

   (G) $12.75

   (H) $13.25

   (J) $13.50

9. Four boys each order their own small pizza. William eats $\frac{2}{3}$ of his pizza. Mike eats $\frac{2}{5}$ of his pizza. Julio eats $\frac{1}{2}$ of his pizza. Lee eats $\frac{3}{8}$ of his pizza. Who ate the least amount of pizza?

   (A) Lee

   (B) Mike

   (C) Julio

   (D) William

10. There are 78 students going on a field trip to the state capitol. The students are in groups of 4. Each group must have an adult leader. How many adult leaders are needed for each student group to have an adult leader?

- (F) 15
- (H) 20
- (G) 19
- (J) 22

11. Which of the following is equivalent to 2.52?

- (A) $2\frac{52}{100}$
- (C) $\frac{52}{200}$
- (B) $2\frac{52}{10}$
- (D) $\frac{2}{52}$

Hot Tip You can answer some problems without doing many calculations. Use mental math, estimation, or logical reasoning to eliminate answer choices and save time.

12. Which of the following numbers is prime?

- (F) 91
- (H) 97
- (G) 93
- (J) 98

13. What is the least common multiple of 4 and 6.

- (A) 2
- (C) 12
- (B) 6
- (D) 24

14. Suppose you are making fruit baskets that contain 4 oranges and 5 apples each. If you have 100 oranges and 100 apples, how many baskets can you make?

- (F) 20
- (H) 100
- (G) 25
- (J) 500

15. What is the prime factorization of 120?

- (A) $2^2 \times 3 \times 5$
- (B) $2^3 \times 3 \times 5$
- (C) $2^3 \times 3^2 \times 5$
- (D) $2 \times 4 \times 3 \times 5$

Short Response

16. Stacie has $16\frac{3}{8}$ yards of material. She uses $7\frac{1}{8}$ yards for a skirt. How much material does she have left? Write your answer as a mixed number in simplest form. Then give three other equivalent answers, including one decimal.

17. Maggie says that 348 is divisible by 2, 4, and 8. Is she correct? Give any other numbers by which 348 is divisible. Explain.

18. Write the numbers 315 and 225 as products of prime factors. Then list all the factors of each number and find the GCF. Are 315 and 225 prime or composite? Explain.

19. Suzanne has 317 flyers to mail. Each flyer requires 1 stamp. If she buys books of stamps that contain 20 stamps each, how many books will she need to mail the flyers?

Extended Response

20. Mr. Peters needs to build a rectangular pig pen $14\frac{4}{5}$ meters long and $5\frac{1}{5}$ meters wide.

- **a.** How much fencing does Mr. Peters need to buy? Show how you found your answer. Write your answer in simplest form.

- **b.** Mr. Peters's pig pen will need 6 meters more fencing than the rectangular pig pen his neighbor is building. Write and solve an equation to find how much fencing his neighbor needs to buy. Show your work.

- **c.** If the neighbor's pig pen is going to be 4 meters wide, how long will it be? Show your work.

 **Problem Solving on Location**

OHIO

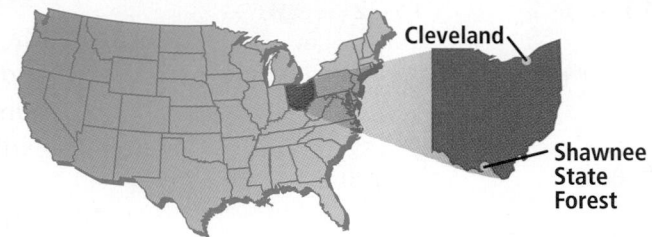

Cleveland

Shawnee State Forest

⭐ Shawnee State Forest

Nestled in the Appalachian foothills of southern Ohio, Shawnee State Forest covers 60,000 acres of wooded hills that are home to colorful wildflowers and various wildlife. Since the state first purchased the land in 1922, the forest has been a popular destination for nature lovers throughout the region.

Choose one or more strategies to solve each problem.

For 1, use the table.

1. The Shawnee State Forest Backpack Trail is a 40-mile loop that begins at the trailhead parking area. The table shows the seven camping areas available along the trail. What is the distance from camp 7 to the trailhead parking area?

2. A hiker on the 40-mile loop stops every 2 miles to take pictures. She also stops every 3 miles to rest. At how many stops along the trail does she both take a picture and rest?

3. Shawnee State Forest began with a land purchase in 1922. The forest is now 12 times its original size. What was the size, in acres, of the original purchase?

4. Two out of every 15 acres of the forest have been set aside and labeled as wilderness. How many acres of wilderness are there?

Backpack Trail Distances	
Portion of Trail	**Distance (mi)**
Trailhead to camp 1	6.2
Camp 1 to camp 2	5.8
Camp 2 to camp 3	5.7
Camp 3 to camp 4	5.2
Camp 4 to camp 5	4.6
Camp 5 to camp 6	3.0
Camp 6 to camp 7	5.0

ENTERING SHAWNEE STATE FOREST AREA CLOSES 11:00 P.M.

NATURAL RESOURCES 14

Problem Solving Strategies

Draw a Diagram
Make a Model
Guess and Test
Work Backward
Find a Pattern
Make a Table
Solve a Simpler Problem
Use Logical Reasoning
Act It Out
Make an Organized List

★ Cleveland Metroparks Zoo

Visitors to the Cleveland Metroparks Zoo can view animals in their natural surroundings. Such surroundings include a rain forest, an African savannah, and the Australian outback. The zoo is home to 84 endangered species and the largest collection of primate species in North America. More than 1.2 million people visit the zoo each year.

Choose one or more strategies to solve each problem.

1. A baby female black rhinoceros was born at the zoo in August 2003. The rhino, named Kibibi, weighed 106 pounds at birth and gained about 28.5 pounds per month. About how much did she weigh in December 2005?

2. Of the 600 animal species at the zoo, 3 out of every 40 are primates. How many primate species are there?

For 3, use the table.

3. The table shows average body and tail lengths for some of the primate species at the zoo. Use the information in the table and the clues below to determine which of these species is found in South America.

   • Four of the species are found only in Africa. One of the species is found only in South America.

   • The species with the longest and shortest body lengths come from the same continent.

   • The two species with tails that are longer than 24.5 inches are found in Africa.

Primate Species at Cleveland Metroparks Zoo		
Species Name	**Body Length (in.)**	**Tail Length (in.)**
Allen's swamp monkey	18	$19\frac{1}{2}$
Colobus monkey	$27\frac{3}{4}$	$24\frac{3}{5}$
Hamadryas baboon	$27\frac{7}{8}$	$24\frac{1}{2}$
Pale-headed saki	$27\frac{1}{2}$	$21\frac{4}{5}$
Collared lemur	$18\frac{1}{2}$	$24\frac{5}{6}$

Fraction Operations

NEW YORK TEST PREP

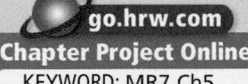

go.hrw.com
Chapter Project Online
KEYWORD: MR7 Ch5

Painting Times

Object	Paint	Time (hr)
Wall (100 ft^2)	Oil-based	$\frac{3}{10}$
Wall (100 ft^2)	Latex	$\frac{2}{5}$
Chair rail (100 ft)	Latex	$\frac{3}{4}$
Chair rail (100 ft)	Stain	$\frac{3}{5}$
Door	Oil-based	$\frac{1}{2}$
Window	Oil-based	$\frac{3}{4}$

Career   *Painter*

Have you ever wondered how painters estimate how much to charge for a job? Professional painters might paint houses, schools, office buildings, sports stadiums, or even music halls. To estimate how much to charge, many painters use a table that lists the average time it should take to prepare and paint certain objects. The table shows some painting jobs and the amount of time they take to complete.

ARE YOU READY?

✓ Vocabulary

Choose the best term from the list to complete each sentence.

1. The first five ___?___ of 6 are 6, 12, 18, 24, and 30. The ___?___ of 6 are 1, 2, 3, and 6.

2. Fractions with the same denominator are called ___?___.

3. A fraction is in ___?___ when the GCF of the numerator and the denominator is 1.

4. The fraction $\frac{13}{9}$ is a(n) ___?___ because the ___?___ is greater than the ___?___.

denominator
factors
improper fraction
like fractions
multiples
numerator
proper fraction
simplest form
unlike fractions

Complete these exercises to review skills you will need for this chapter.

✓ Simplify Fractions

Write each fraction in simplest form.

5. $\frac{6}{10}$

6. $\frac{5}{15}$

7. $\frac{14}{8}$

8. $\frac{8}{12}$

9. $\frac{10}{100}$

10. $\frac{12}{144}$

11. $\frac{33}{121}$

12. $\frac{15}{17}$

✓ Write Mixed Numbers as Fractions

Write each mixed number as an improper fraction.

13. $1\frac{1}{8}$

14. $2\frac{3}{4}$

15. $2\frac{4}{5}$

16. $1\frac{7}{9}$

17. $3\frac{1}{5}$

18. $5\frac{2}{3}$

19. $4\frac{4}{7}$

20. $3\frac{11}{12}$

✓ Add and Subtract Like Fractions

Add or subtract. Write each answer in simplest form.

21. $\frac{5}{8} + \frac{1}{8}$

22. $\frac{3}{7} + \frac{5}{7}$

23. $\frac{9}{10} - \frac{3}{10}$

24. $\frac{5}{9} - \frac{2}{9}$

25. $\frac{1}{2} + \frac{1}{2}$

26. $\frac{7}{12} - \frac{5}{12}$

27. $\frac{3}{5} + \frac{4}{5}$

28. $\frac{4}{15} - \frac{1}{15}$

✓ Multiplication Facts

Multiply.

29. 8×11

30. 7×8

31. 4×12

32. 12×7

33. 10×13

34. 9×7

35. 6×8

36. 11×12

Where You've Been

Previously, you

- modeled addition and subtraction of fractions with like denominators.

- estimated sums and differences of whole numbers.

- wrote equivalent fractions.

In This Chapter

You will study

- modeling addition and subtraction situations involving fractions.

- estimating sums and differences of fractions.

- adding, subtracting, multiplying, and dividing fractions and mixed numbers with unlike denominators.

- solving equations with fractions.

Where You're Going

You can use the skills learned in this chapter

- to solve measurement problems that involve fractions and mixed numbers.

- to estimate sums and differences between distances that involve fractions.

Key Vocabulary/Vocabulario

least common denominator (LCD)	mínimo común denominador (MCD)
least common multiple (LCM)	mínimo común múltiplo (MCM)
reciprocals	recíproco

Vocabulary Connections

To become familiar with some of the vocabulary terms in the chapter, consider the following. You may refer to the chapter, the glossary, or a dictionary if you like.

1. The word *reciprocal* means "inversely related or opposite." What do you think the **reciprocal** of a fraction will look like?

2. When people have something in *common,* they have something that they share. What do you think two numbers with a common multiple share? What do you think the **least common multiple** of two numbers is?

3. Fractions with the same denominator have a common denominator. What do you think the **least common denominator** of two fractions is?

 **Reading** and *Writing* **Math**

Study Strategy: Make Flash Cards

Create flash cards to help you learn a sequence of steps, vocabulary, math symbols, formulas, or mathematical rules. Study your flash cards often.

Use these suggestions to make flash cards.

- Label each card with the lesson number so you can look back at your textbook when studying.

- Write the name of the formula, term, or rule on one side of the card, and the meaning or an example on the other side of the card.

- Write definitions using your own words.

From Lesson 4-8

Life Science Application

Sophie plants a young oak tree in her backyard. The distance around the trunk grows at a rate of $\frac{1}{8}$ inch per month. Use pictures to model how much this distance will increase in two months, then write your answer in simplest form.

$$\frac{1}{8} + \frac{1}{8}$$

$\frac{1}{8} + \frac{1}{8} = \frac{2}{8}$ *Add the numerators. Keep the same denominator.*

$= \frac{1}{4}$ *Write your answer in simplest form.*

The distance around the trunk will increase by $\frac{1}{4}$ inch.

Sample Flash Card

Lesson 4-8
Pages 202–205

Adding and Subtracting
Fractions with
Like Denominators

	$\frac{1}{8} + \frac{1}{8}$
Keep the denominators.	$\frac{1}{8} + \frac{1}{8} = \frac{\ }{8}$
Add the numerators.	$\frac{1}{8} + \frac{1}{8} = \frac{2}{8}$
Write in simplest form.	$\frac{1}{4}$

Front   **Back**

Try This

1. Use Lesson 4-6 to make flash cards for the rules for writing mixed numbers as improper fractions.

5-1 Least Common Multiple

 **Learn** to find the least common multiple (LCM) of a group of numbers.

Vocabulary

least common multiple (LCM)

NY Performance Indicators

6.N.14 Locate rational numbers on a number line. Also, 6.PS.13, 6.PS.15.

After games in Lydia's soccer league, one player's family brings snacks for both teams to share. This week Lydia's family will provide juice boxes and granola bars for 24 players.

You can make a model to help you find the least number of juice and granola packs Lydia's family should buy. Use colored counters, drawings, or pictures to illustrate the problem.

EXAMPLE 1 *Consumer Application*

Remember!

A multiple of a number is the product of the number and any nonzero whole number.

Juice comes in packs of 6, and granola bars in packs of 8. If there are 24 players, what is the least number of packs needed so that each player has a drink and granola bar and there are none left over?

Draw juice boxes in groups of 6. Draw granola bars in groups of 8. Stop when you have drawn the same number of each.

There are 24 juice boxes and 24 granola bars.

Lydia's family should buy 4 packs of juice and 3 packs of granola bars.

The smallest number that is a multiple of two or more numbers is the **least common multiple (LCM)**. In Example 1, the LCM of 6 and 8 is 24.

228 *Chapter 5 Fraction Operations*

EXAMPLE 2 Using Multiples to Find the LCM

Find the least common multiple (LCM).

Method 1: Use a number line.

A 6 and 9

Use a number line to skip count by 6 and 9.

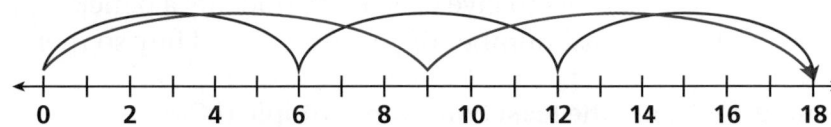

The least common multiple (LCM) of 6 and 9 is 18.

Method 2: Use a list.

B 3, 5, and 6

3: 3, 6, 9, 12, 15, 18, 21, 24, 27, **30**, 33, . . .

5: 5, 10, 15, 20, 25, **30**, 35, . . .

6: 6, 12, 18, 24, **30**, 36, . . .

List multiples of 3, 5, and 6.

Find the smallest number that is in all the lists.

LCM: 30

Method 3: Use prime factorization.

C 8 and 12

$8 = 2 \cdot 2 \cdot 2$

$12 = 2 \cdot 2 \cdot \quad 3$

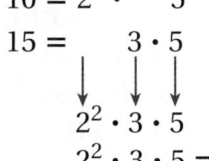

$2 \cdot 2 \cdot 2 \cdot 3$

$2 \cdot 2 \cdot 2 \cdot 3 = 24$

LCM: 24

Write the prime factorization of each number. Line up the common factors. To find the LCM, multiply one number from each column.

> **Remember!**
>
> The prime factorization of a number is the number written as a product of its prime factors.

D 12, 10, and 15

$12 = 2^2 \cdot 3$

$10 = 2 \cdot \quad 5$

$15 = \quad 3 \cdot 5$

$2^2 \cdot 3 \cdot 5$

$2^2 \cdot 3 \cdot 5 = 60$

LCM: 60

Write the prime factorization of each number in exponential form.

To find the LCM, multiply each prime factor once with the greatest exponent used in any of the prime factorizations.

6.RP.5, 6.RP.6

Think and Discuss

1. Explain why you cannot find a greatest common multiple for a group of numbers.

2. Tell whether the LCM of a set of numbers can ever be smaller than any of the numbers in the set.

go.hrw.com
Homework Help Online
KEYWORD: MR7 5-1
Parent Resources Online
KEYWORD: MR7 Parent

GUIDED PRACTICE

See Example ① **1.** Pencils are sold in packs of 12, and erasers in packs of 9. Mr. Joplin wants to give each of 36 students a pencil and an eraser. What is the least number of packs he should buy so there are none left over?

See Example ② **Find the least common multiple (LCM).**

2. 3 and 5	**3.** 4 and 9	**4.** 2, 3, and 6	**5.** 2, 4, and 5
6. 4 and 12	**7.** 6 and 16	**8.** 4, 6, and 8	**9.** 2, 5, and 8
10. 6 and 10	**11.** 21 and 63	**12.** 3, 5, and 9	**13.** 5, 6, and 25

INDEPENDENT PRACTICE

See Example ① **14.** String-cheese sticks are sold in packs of 10, and celery sticks in packs of 15. Ms. Sobrino wants to give each of 30 students one string-cheese stick and one celery stick. What is the least number of packs she should buy so there are none left over?

See Example ② **Find the least common multiple (LCM).**

15. 2 and 8	**16.** 3 and 7	**17.** 4 and 10	**18.** 3 and 9
19. 3, 6, and 9	**20.** 4, 8, and 10	**21.** 4, 6, and 12	**22.** 4, 6, and 7
23. 3, 8, and 12	**24.** 3, 7, and 10	**25.** 2, 6, and 11	**26.** 2, 3, 6, and 9
27. 2, 4, 5, and 6	**28.** 10 and 11	**29.** 4, 5, and 7	**30.** 2, 3, 6, and 8

PRACTICE AND PROBLEM SOLVING

Extra Practice
See page 722.

31. What is the LCM of 6 and 12? **32.** What is the LCM of 5 and 11?

33. The diagram at right is a Venn diagram. The numbers in the red circle are multiples of 4. The numbers in the blue circle are multiples of 6. The numbers in the purple section are multiples of both 4 and 6.

Find the missing numbers in the Venn diagram.

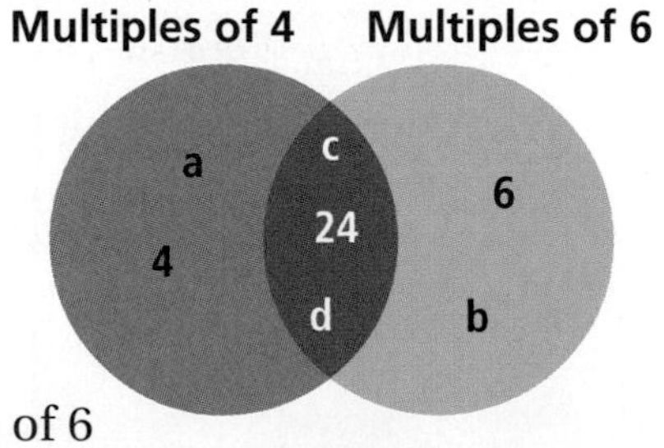

Multiples of 4   Multiples of 6

a. a two-digit multiple of 4 that is not a multiple of 6

b. a two-digit multiple of 6 that is not a multiple of 4

c. the LCM of 4 and 6

d. a three-digit common multiple of 4 and 6

Find a pair of numbers that has the given characteristics.

34. The LCM of the two numbers is 26. One number is even and one is odd.

35. The LCM of the two numbers is 48. The sum of the numbers is 28.

36. The LCM of the two numbers is 60. The difference of the two numbers is 3.

37. During its grand opening weekend, a restaurant gave every eighth customer a free appetizer, every twelfth customer a free beverage, and every fifteenth customer a free dish of frozen yogurt.

    a. Which customer was the first to receive all three free items?

    b. Which customer was the first to receive a free appetizer and frozen yogurt?

    c. If the restaurant served 500 customers that weekend, how many of those customers received all three free items?

 38. Choose a Strategy Sophia gave $\frac{1}{2}$ of her semi-precious-rock collection to her son. She gave $\frac{1}{2}$ of what she had left to her grandson. Then she gave $\frac{1}{2}$ of what she had left to her great-grandson. She kept 10 rocks for herself. How many rocks did she have in the beginning?

    Ⓐ 40   Ⓑ 80   Ⓒ 100   Ⓓ 160

 39. Write About It Explain the steps you can use to find the LCM of two numbers. Choose two numbers to show an example of your method.

 40. Challenge Find the LCM of each pair of numbers.

    a. 4 and 6   **b.** 8 and 9   **c.** 5 and 7   **d.** 8 and 10

When is the LCM of two numbers equal to the product of the two numbers?

TEST PREP and Spiral Review

41. Multiple Choice Cheese cubes are sold in packs of 60. Crackers are sold in packs of 12. To make 60 snacks of 2 cheese cubes and 1 cracker, what is the least number of packs of each type needed?

    Ⓐ 2 cheese, 1 cracker   Ⓒ 2 cheese, 2 cracker

    Ⓑ 2 cheese, 5 cracker   Ⓓ 5 cheese, 2 cracker

42. Multiple Choice What is the least common multiple of 5 and 8?

    Ⓕ 40   Ⓖ 20   Ⓗ 80   Ⓙ 60

Multiply. (Lesson 3-6)

43. 0.3×0.1 **44.** 0.16×0.5 **45.** 1.2×0.2 **46.** 0.7×9

Compare. Write $<$, $>$, **or** $=$. (Lesson 4-7)

47. $\frac{2}{9}$ ▨ $\frac{2}{13}$ **48.** $\frac{10}{11}$ ▨ $\frac{100}{110}$ **49.** $5\frac{2}{7}$ ▨ $3\frac{5}{7}$

Add or subtract. (Lesson 4-8)

50. $\frac{5}{6} + \frac{11}{6}$ **51.** $\frac{3}{7} + 4\frac{2}{7}$ **52.** $6\frac{2}{3} - 3\frac{1}{3}$

Hands-On LAB 5-2

Model Fraction Addition and Subtraction

Use with Lesson 5-2 and 5-3

When fractions have different denominators, you need to find a common denominator before you can add or subtract them. Write equivalent fractions with the same denominator and then perform the operation.

NY Performance Indicators

6.N.16, 6.CN.5, 6.R.1, 6.R.5

Activity 1

1 Find $\frac{1}{8} + \frac{1}{4}$.

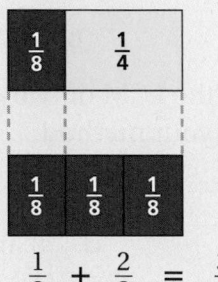

$$\frac{1}{8} + \frac{2}{8} = \frac{3}{8}$$

Use fraction bars to represent both fractions.

Find one size of fraction bars to model both fractions.

$\frac{1}{8} = \frac{1}{8}$ and $\frac{1}{4}$ is equivalent to $\frac{2}{8}$.

Find the total number of $\frac{1}{8}$ fraction bars.

2 Find $\frac{2}{3} + \frac{1}{2}$.

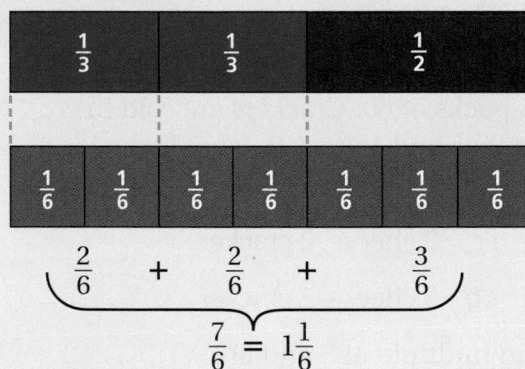

$$\frac{2}{6} + \frac{2}{6} + \frac{3}{6}$$

$$\frac{7}{6} = 1\frac{1}{6}$$

Use fraction bars to represent both fractions.

Find one size of fraction bars to model both fractions.

$\frac{1}{3}$ is equivalent to $\frac{2}{6}$ and $\frac{1}{2}$ is equivalent to $\frac{3}{6}$.

Find the total number of $\frac{1}{6}$ fraction bars.

Think and Discuss

1. Explain what the denominators of $\frac{1}{6}, \frac{1}{4}, \frac{2}{3},$ and $\frac{1}{2}$ have in common?
(Hint: Think of common multiples.)

Try This

Model each addition expression with fraction bars, draw the model, and find the sum.

1. $\frac{1}{4} + \frac{1}{2}$
2. $\frac{3}{8} + \frac{1}{4}$
3. $\frac{1}{2} + \frac{2}{5}$
4. $\frac{3}{4} + \frac{1}{6}$
5. $\frac{1}{3} + \frac{1}{6}$
6. $\frac{7}{8} + \frac{3}{4}$
7. $\frac{2}{3} + \frac{1}{4}$
8. $\frac{5}{8} + \frac{1}{4}$

Activity 2

1 Find $\frac{1}{3} - \frac{1}{6}$.

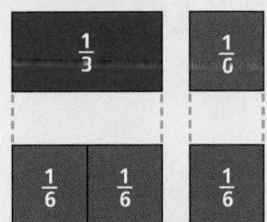

Use fraction bars to represent both fractions.

Find one size of fraction bars to model both fractions.

$\frac{1}{3}$ is equivalent to $\frac{2}{6}$ and $\frac{1}{6} = \frac{1}{6}$.

Take away $\frac{1}{6}$ from $\frac{2}{6}$.

$\frac{2}{6} \quad - \quad \frac{1}{6} \quad = \quad \frac{1}{6}$

2 Find $\frac{1}{2} - \frac{1}{3}$.

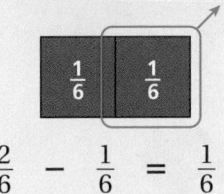

Use fraction bars to represent both fractions.

Find one size of fraction bars to model both fractions.

$\frac{1}{2}$ is equivalent to $\frac{3}{6}$ and $\frac{1}{3}$ is equivalent to $\frac{2}{6}$.

Take away $\frac{2}{6}$ from $\frac{3}{6}$.

$\frac{3}{6} \quad - \quad \frac{2}{6} \quad = \quad \frac{1}{6}$

Think and Discuss

1. What size fraction bar would you use to model $\frac{1}{2} - \frac{1}{4}$? Is there another size fraction bar you could use? Explain.

2. What size fraction bar would you use to model $\frac{4}{5} - \frac{1}{2}$? Explain.

Try This

Model each subtraction expression with fraction bars, draw the model, and find the difference.

1. $\frac{3}{4} - \frac{1}{3}$
2. $\frac{1}{3} - \frac{1}{4}$
3. $\frac{1}{2} - \frac{2}{5}$
4. $\frac{5}{6} - \frac{1}{3}$
5. $\frac{1}{2} - \frac{5}{12}$
6. $\frac{7}{8} - \frac{3}{4}$
7. $\frac{1}{4} - \frac{1}{8}$
8. $\frac{1}{4} - \frac{1}{6}$

5-2 Adding and Subtracting with Unlike Denominators

Learn to add and subtract fractions with unlike denominators.

Vocabulary

least common denominator (LCD)

NY Performance Indicators

6.N.16 Add and subtract fractions with unlike denominators. Also, 6.CN.4, 6.CN.9.

Remember!

Fractions that represent the same value are equivalent.

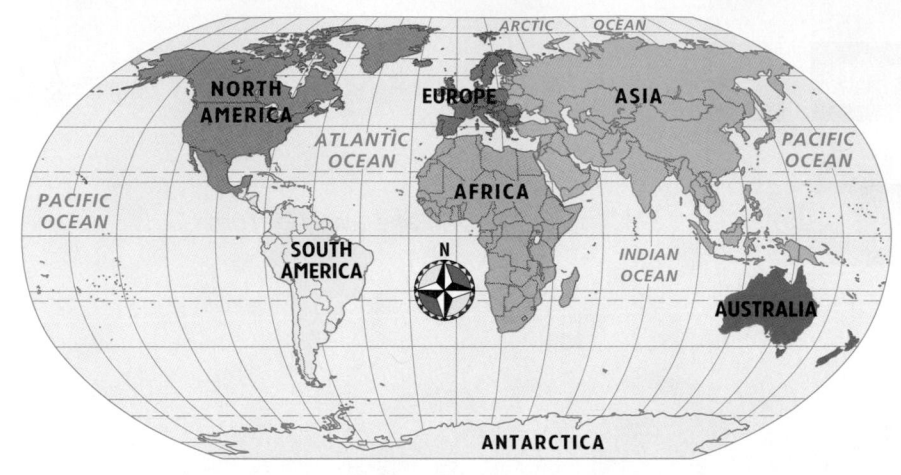

The Pacific Ocean covers $\frac{1}{3}$ of Earth's surface. The Atlantic Ocean covers $\frac{1}{5}$ of Earth's surface. To find the fraction of Earth's surface that is covered by both oceans, you can add $\frac{1}{3}$ and $\frac{1}{5}$, which are unlike fractions.

To add or subtract unlike fractions, first rewrite them as equivalent fractions with a common denominator.

EXAMPLE 1 *Social Studies Application*

What fraction of Earth's surface is covered by the Atlantic and Pacific Oceans? Add $\frac{1}{3}$ and $\frac{1}{5}$.

$$\frac{1}{3}$$
$$+\frac{1}{5}$$

Find a common denominator for 3 and 5.

$$\frac{1}{3} \rightarrow \frac{5}{15}$$
$$+\frac{1}{5} \rightarrow \frac{3}{15}$$

Write equivalent fractions with 15 as the common denominator.

$$\frac{8}{15}$$

Add the numerators. Keep the common denominator.

The Pacific and Atlantic Oceans cover $\frac{8}{15}$ of Earth's surface.

You can use *any* common denominator or the *least common denominator* to add and subtract unlike fractions. The **least common denominator (LCD)** is the least common multiple of the denominators.

EXAMPLE **2** **Adding and Subtracting Unlike Fractions**

Add or subtract. Write each answer in simplest form.

Method 1: Multiply the denominators.

A $\dfrac{9}{10} - \dfrac{7}{8}$

$\dfrac{9}{10} - \dfrac{7}{8}$ *Multiply the denominators. 10 · 8 = 80*

$\dfrac{72}{80} - \dfrac{70}{80}$ *Write equivalent fractions with a common denominator.*

$\dfrac{2}{80}$ *Subtract.*

$\dfrac{1}{40}$ *Write the answer in simplest form.*

Method 2: Use the LCD.

B $\dfrac{9}{10} - \dfrac{7}{8}$ *Multiples of 10: 10, 20, 30, 40, . . .*

$\dfrac{9}{10} - \dfrac{7}{8}$ *Multiples of 8: 8, 16, 24, 32, 40, . . . The LCD is 40.*

$\dfrac{36}{40} - \dfrac{35}{40}$ *Write equivalent fractions with a common denominator.*

$\dfrac{1}{40}$ *Subtract.*

Method 3: Use mental math.

C $\dfrac{5}{12} + \dfrac{1}{6}$

$\dfrac{5}{12} + \dfrac{1}{6}$ *Think: 12 is a multiple of 6, so the LCD is 12.*

$\dfrac{5}{12} + \dfrac{2}{12}$ *Rewrite $\frac{1}{6}$ with a denominator of 12.*

$\dfrac{7}{12}$ *Add.*

D $\dfrac{1}{3} - \dfrac{2}{9}$

$\dfrac{1}{3} - \dfrac{2}{9}$ *Think: 9 is a multiple of 3, so the LCD is 9.*

$\dfrac{3}{9} - \dfrac{2}{9}$ *Rewrite $\frac{1}{3}$ with a denominator of 9.*

$\dfrac{1}{9}$ *Subtract.*

6.PS.2, 6.CM.1

Think and Discuss

1. **Explain** an advantage of using the least common denominator (LCD) when adding unlike fractions.

2. **Tell** when the least common denominator (LCD) of two fractions is the product of their denominators.

3. **Explain** how you can use mental math to subtract $\frac{1}{12}$ from $\frac{3}{4}$.

5-2 **Exercises**

go.hrw.com
Homework Help Online
KEYWORD: MR7 5-2
Parent Resources Online
KEYWORD: MR7 Parent

GUIDED PRACTICE

See Example ① 1. A trailer hauling wood weighs $\frac{2}{3}$ ton. The trailer weighs $\frac{1}{4}$ ton without the wood. What is the weight of the wood?

See Example ② Add or subtract. Write each answer in simplest form.

2. $\frac{1}{3} + \frac{1}{9}$ 3. $\frac{7}{10} - \frac{2}{5}$ 4. $\frac{2}{3} - \frac{2}{5}$ 5. $\frac{1}{2} + \frac{3}{7}$

INDEPENDENT PRACTICE

See Example ① 6. **Social Studies** Approximately $\frac{1}{5}$ of the world's population lives in China. The people of India make up about $\frac{1}{6}$ of the world's population. What fraction of the world's people live in either China or India?

7. Cedric is making an Italian dish using a recipe that calls for $\frac{2}{3}$ cup of grated mozarella cheese. If Cedric has grated $\frac{1}{2}$ cup of mozarella cheese, how much more does he need to grate?

See Example ② Add or subtract. Write each answer in simplest form.

8. $\frac{3}{4} - \frac{1}{2}$ 9. $\frac{1}{6} + \frac{5}{12}$ 10. $\frac{5}{6} - \frac{3}{4}$ 11. $\frac{1}{5} + \frac{1}{4}$

12. $\frac{7}{10} + \frac{1}{8}$ 13. $\frac{1}{3} + \frac{4}{5}$ 14. $\frac{8}{9} - \frac{2}{3}$ 15. $\frac{5}{8} + \frac{1}{2}$

PRACTICE AND PROBLEM SOLVING

Extra Practice
See page 722.

Find each sum or difference. Write your answer in simplest form.

16. $\frac{3}{10} + \frac{1}{2}$ 17. $\frac{4}{5} - \frac{1}{3}$ 18. $\frac{5}{8} - \frac{1}{6}$ 19. $\frac{1}{6} + \frac{2}{9}$

20. $\frac{2}{7} + \frac{2}{5}$ 21. $\frac{7}{12} - \frac{1}{4}$ 22. $\frac{7}{8} - \frac{2}{3}$ 23. $\frac{2}{11} + \frac{2}{3}$

Evaluate each expression for $b = \frac{1}{2}$. Write your answer in simplest form.

24. $b + \frac{1}{3}$ 25. $\frac{8}{9} - b$ 26. $b - \frac{2}{11}$ 27. $\frac{7}{10} - b$

28. $\frac{2}{7} + b$ 29. $b + b$ 30. $b - b$ 31. $b + \frac{5}{8}$

Evaluate. Write each answer in simplest form.

32. $\frac{1}{3} + \frac{1}{9} + \frac{1}{3}$ 33. $\frac{9}{10} - \frac{2}{10} - \frac{1}{5}$ 34. $\frac{1}{2} + \frac{1}{4} - \frac{1}{8}$ 35. $\frac{3}{7} + \frac{1}{14} + \frac{2}{28}$

36. $\frac{5}{6} - \frac{2}{3} + \frac{7}{12}$ 37. $\frac{2}{3} + \frac{1}{4} - \frac{1}{6}$ 38. $\frac{2}{9} + \frac{1}{6} + \frac{1}{3}$ 39. $\frac{1}{2} - \frac{1}{4} + \frac{5}{8}$

40. Bailey spent $\frac{2}{3}$ of his monthly allowance at the movies and $\frac{1}{5}$ of it on baseball cards. What fraction of Bailey's allowance is left?

41. **Multi-Step** Betty is making punch for a party. She needs a total of $\frac{9}{10}$ gallon of water to add to fruit juice. In one container she has $\frac{1}{3}$ gallon water, and in another she has $\frac{2}{5}$ gallon. How much more water does she need?

The red lorikeet, galah cockatoo, and green-cheeked Amazon are three very colorful birds. The African grey parrot is known for its ability to mimic sounds it hears. In fact, one African grey named Prudle had a vocabulary of almost 1,000 words.

42. Which bird weighs more, the green-cheeked Amazon or the red lorikeet?

43. What is the difference in weights between the green-cheeked Amazon and the red lorikeet?

44. Does the red lorikeet weigh more or less than $\frac{1}{2}$ lb? Explain.

45. **What's the Error?** A student found the difference in weight between the African grey parrot and the galah cockatoo to be 1 lb. Explain the error. Then find the correct difference between the weights of these birds.

46. **Write About It** Explain how you find the difference in weight between the galah cockatoo and green-cheeked Amazon.

47. **Challenge** Find the average weight of the birds.

Red lorikeet, $\frac{3}{8}$ lb, $11\frac{2}{5}$ in.

Galah cockatoo, $\frac{3}{4}$ lb, $13\frac{9}{10}$ in.

Green-cheeked Amazon, $\frac{3}{5}$ lb, $13\frac{1}{5}$ in.

African grey parrot, $\frac{7}{8}$ lb, 13 in.

TEST PREP and Spiral Review

48. Multiple Choice One apple weighs $\frac{1}{4}$ lb and another apple weighs $\frac{3}{16}$ lb. Find the difference in their weights.

Ⓐ $\frac{1}{16}$ lb Ⓑ $\frac{1}{6}$ lb Ⓒ $\frac{1}{4}$ lb Ⓓ $\frac{7}{16}$ lb

49. Short Response Wanda walked $\frac{7}{24}$ mile more than Lori. Lori walked $\frac{5}{6}$ mile less than Jack. Wanda walked $\frac{3}{8}$ mile. How many miles did Jack walk? Give your answer in simplest form. Explain how you solved the problem.

Divide. (Lesson 3-7)

50. $1.40 \div 2$ **51.** $3.3 \div 3$ **52.** $0.85 \div 5$ **53.** $0.375 \div 3$

Estimate each sum or difference to compare. Write < or >. (Lesson 4-9)

54. $\frac{4}{5} + \frac{2}{3}$ ▦ 1 **55.** $6\frac{1}{3} - 2\frac{1}{9}$ ▦ 4 **56.** $8\frac{7}{10} - 1\frac{3}{7}$ ▦ 8 **57.** $5\frac{1}{5} + \frac{8}{9}$ ▦ 6

Adding and Subtracting Mixed Numbers

Learn to add and subtract mixed numbers with unlike denominators.

NY Performance Indicators

6.N.18 Add and subtract mixed numbers with unlike denominators. Also, 6.N.16.

Chameleons can change color at any time to camouflage themselves. They live high in trees and are seldom seen on the ground.

A Parsons chameleon, which is the largest kind of chameleon, can extend its tongue $1\frac{1}{2}$ times the length of its body. This allows the chameleon to capture food it otherwise would not be able to reach.

To add or subtract mixed numbers with unlike denominators, you must first find a common denominator for the fractions.

The chameleon is the only animal capable of moving each eye independently of the other. A chameleon can turn its eyes about 360°.

E X A M P L E **1** **Adding and Subtracting Mixed Numbers**

Find each sum or difference. Write the answer in simplest form.

A $2\frac{3}{4} + 1\frac{1}{6}$

$$
\begin{array}{ccc}
2\frac{3}{4} & \longrightarrow & 2\frac{18}{24} \\
+ 1\frac{1}{6} & \longrightarrow & + 1\frac{4}{24} \\
\hline
 & & 3\frac{22}{24} = 3\frac{11}{12}
\end{array}
$$

Multiply the denominators. 4 · 6 = 24
Write equivalent fractions with a common denominator of 24.
Add the fractions and then the whole numbers, and simplify.

B $4\frac{5}{6} - 2\frac{2}{9}$

$$
\begin{array}{ccc}
4\frac{5}{6} & \longrightarrow & 4\frac{15}{18} \\
- 2\frac{2}{9} & \longrightarrow & - 2\frac{4}{18} \\
\hline
 & & 2\frac{11}{18}
\end{array}
$$

The LCD of 6 and 9 is 18.
Write equivalent fractions with a common denominator of 18.
Subtract the fractions and then the whole numbers.

C $2\frac{2}{3} + 1\frac{3}{4}$

$$
\begin{array}{ccc}
2\frac{2}{3} & \longrightarrow & 2\frac{8}{12} \\
+ 1\frac{3}{4} & \longrightarrow & + 1\frac{9}{12} \\
\hline
 & & 3\frac{17}{12} = 4\frac{5}{12}
\end{array}
$$

The LCD of 3 and 4 is 12.
Write equivalent fractions with a common denominator of 12.
Add the fractions and then the whole numbers, and simplify. $3\frac{17}{12} = 3 + 1\frac{5}{12}$

Find each sum or difference. Write the answer in simplest form.

D $8\frac{2}{5} - 6\frac{3}{10}$

$$8\frac{2}{5} \longrightarrow \quad 8\frac{4}{10}$$

$$-\ 6\frac{3}{10} \longrightarrow -\ 6\frac{3}{10}$$

$$\overline{\qquad\qquad 2\frac{1}{10}}$$

Think: 10 is a multiple of 5, so 10 is the LCD.

Write equivalent fractions with a common denominator of 10.

Subtract the fractions and then the whole numbers.

EXAMPLE 2 *Life Science Application*

The length of a Parsons chameleon's body is $23\frac{1}{2}$ inches. The chameleon can extend its tongue $35\frac{1}{4}$ inches. What is the total length of its body and its tongue?

Add $23\frac{1}{2}$ and $35\frac{1}{4}$.

$$23\frac{1}{2} \longrightarrow \quad 23\frac{2}{4}$$

$$+\ 35\frac{1}{4} \longrightarrow +\ 35\frac{1}{4}$$

$$\overline{\qquad\qquad 58\frac{3}{4}}$$

Find a common denominator. Write equivalent fractions with the LCD, 4, as the denominator.

Add the fractions and then the whole numbers.

The total length of the chameleon's body and tongue is $58\frac{3}{4}$ inches.

Helpful Hint

You can use mental math to find an LCD. *Think:* 4 is a multiple of 2 and 4.

Think and Discuss 6.CM.8, 6.PS.19, 6.PS.22

1. **Tell** what mistake was made when subtracting $2\frac{1}{2}$ from $5\frac{3}{5}$ gave the following result: $5\frac{3}{5} - 2\frac{1}{2} = 3\frac{2}{3}$. Then find the correct answer.

2. **Explain** why you first find equivalent fractions when adding $1\frac{1}{5}$ and $1\frac{1}{2}$.

3. **Tell** how you know that $5\frac{1}{2} - 3\frac{1}{4}$ is more than 2.

5-3 **Exercises**

go.hrw.com
Homework Help Online
KEYWORD: MR7 5-3
Parent Resources Online
KEYWORD: MR7 Parent

GUIDED PRACTICE

See Example **1** Find each sum or difference. Write the answer in simplest form.

1. $7\frac{1}{12} + 3\frac{1}{3}$ **2.** $2\frac{1}{6} + 2\frac{3}{8}$ **3.** $8\frac{5}{6} - 2\frac{3}{4}$ **4.** $6\frac{6}{7} - 1\frac{1}{2}$

See Example **2** **5. Life Science** A sea turtle traveled $7\frac{3}{4}$ hours in two days. It traveled $3\frac{1}{2}$ hours on the first day. How many hours did it travel on the second day?

INDEPENDENT PRACTICE

See Example **1** Find each sum or difference. Write the answer in simplest form.

6. $3\frac{9}{10} - 1\frac{2}{5}$ **7.** $2\frac{1}{6} + 4\frac{5}{12}$ **8.** $5\frac{9}{11} + 5\frac{1}{3}$ **9.** $9\frac{3}{4} - 3\frac{1}{2}$

10. $6\frac{3}{10} + 3\frac{2}{5}$ **11.** $10\frac{2}{3} - 2\frac{1}{12}$ **12.** $14\frac{3}{4} - 6\frac{5}{12}$ **13.** $19\frac{1}{10} + 10\frac{1}{2}$

See Example **2** **14. School** The drama club rehearsed $1\frac{3}{4}$ hours Friday and $3\frac{1}{6}$ hours Saturday. How many total hours did the students rehearse?

PRACTICE AND PROBLEM SOLVING

Extra Practice
See page 722.

Add or subtract. Write each answer in simplest form.

15. $15\frac{5}{6} + 18\frac{2}{3}$ **16.** $17\frac{1}{6} + 12\frac{1}{4}$ **17.** $23\frac{9}{10} - 20\frac{3}{9}$ **18.** $32\frac{5}{7} - 13\frac{2}{5}$

19. $28\frac{11}{12} - 8\frac{5}{9}$ **20.** $12\frac{2}{11} + 20\frac{2}{3}$ **21.** $36\frac{5}{8} - 24\frac{5}{12}$ **22.** $48\frac{9}{11} + 2\frac{1}{4}$

23. Measurement Kyle's backpack weighs $14\frac{7}{20}$ lb. Kirsten's backpack weighs $12\frac{1}{4}$ lb.

    a. How much do the backpacks weigh together?

    b. How much more does Kyle's backpack weigh than Kirsten's backpack?

    c. Kyle takes his $3\frac{1}{4}$ lb math book out of his backpack. How much does his backpack weigh now?

Add or subtract. Write each answer as a fraction in simplest form.

24. $0.3 + \frac{2}{5}$ **25.** $\frac{4}{5} + 0.9$ **26.** $5\frac{4}{5} - 3.2$ **27.** $14\frac{1}{4} + 9.5$

28. $6.3 + \frac{4}{5}$ **29.** $23\frac{3}{4} - 10.5$ **30.** $18.9 - 6\frac{1}{2}$ **31.** $21.8 - 3\frac{3}{5}$

32. A wheelbarrow can hold $52\frac{1}{2}$ lb. Five rocks that weigh $9\frac{5}{8}$ lb, $12\frac{1}{6}$ lb, $9\frac{1}{4}$ lb, $11\frac{1}{8}$ lb, and $10\frac{1}{2}$ lb are to be loaded into the wheelbarrow. Can the wheelbarrow hold all five rocks? Explain.

33. The route Jo usually takes to work is $4\frac{2}{5}$ mi. After heavy rains, when that road is flooded, she must take a different route that is $4\frac{9}{10}$ mi. How much longer is Jo's alternate route?

34. Multi-Step Mr. Hansley used $1\frac{2}{3}$ c of flour to make muffins and $4\frac{1}{2}$ c to make bread. If he has $3\frac{5}{6}$ c left, how much flour did Mr. Hansley have before making the muffins and bread?

Life Science

Evaluate each expression for $n = 2\frac{1}{3}$. Write your answer in simplest form.

35. $2\frac{2}{3} + n$

36. $5 - \left(1\frac{2}{3} + n\right)$

37. $n - 1\frac{1}{4}$

38. $5 - n$

39. $n + 5\frac{7}{9}$

40. $6 + \left(3\frac{4}{9} + n\right)$

41. $2\frac{1}{3} - n$

42. $3 + \left(2\frac{3}{4} - n\right)$

43. Life Science Elephants can communicate through low-frequency infrasonic rumbles. Such sounds can travel from $\frac{1}{8}$ km to $9\frac{1}{2}$ km. Find the difference between these two distances.

Use the drawing for Exercises 44–47.

44. Sarah is a landscape architect designing a garden. Based on her drawing, how much longer is the south side of the building than the west side?

45. Sarah needs to determine how many azalea bushes she can plant along both sides of the path. What is the sum of the lengths of the two sides of the path?

46. How wide is the path?

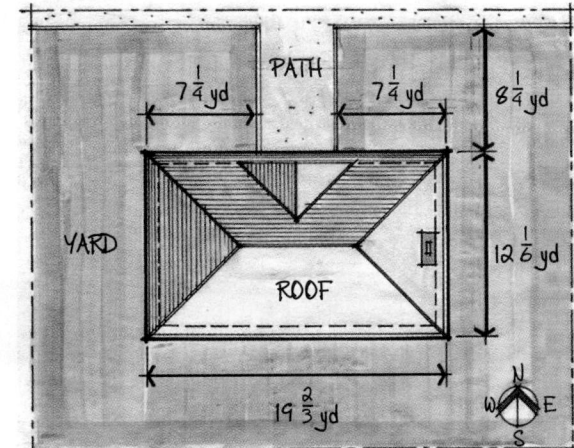

 47. What's the Question? The answer is $63\frac{2}{3}$ yd. What is the question?

 48. Write About It Explain how you would use the sum of $\frac{2}{5}$ and $\frac{1}{3}$ to find the sum of $10\frac{2}{5}$ and $6\frac{1}{3}$.

 49. Challenge Find each missing numerator.

a. $3\frac{x}{9} + 4\frac{2}{9} = 7\frac{7}{9}$

b. $1\frac{3}{10} + 9\frac{x}{2} = 10\frac{4}{5}$

TEST PREP and Spiral Review

50. Multiple Choice Which expression does NOT have a sum of $6\frac{3}{10}$?

Ⓐ $1\frac{1}{20} + 5\frac{1}{4}$

Ⓑ $3\frac{1}{5} + 3\frac{1}{10}$

Ⓒ $3\frac{2}{5} + 3\frac{1}{5}$

Ⓓ $4\frac{3}{20} + 2\frac{3}{20}$

51. Multiple Choice A bumblebee bat is $1\frac{1}{5}$ inches in length. A thread snake is $4\frac{1}{4}$ inches in length. How much longer is a thread snake than a bumblebee bat?

Ⓕ $3\frac{1}{4}$ inches

Ⓖ $3\frac{1}{5}$ inches

Ⓗ $3\frac{1}{10}$ inches

Ⓙ $3\frac{1}{20}$ inches

Write each decimal as a fraction or mixed number. (Lesson 4-4)

52. 0.35

53. 1.5

54. 0.7

55. 1.4

Evaluate each expression for $x = \frac{2}{5}$. Write your answer in simplest form. (Lesson 5-2)

56. $x - \frac{3}{10}$

57. $x + \frac{5}{12}$

58. $\frac{7}{8} - x$

59. $\frac{2}{3} + x$

Model Subtraction with Regrouping

Use with Lesson 5-4

go.hrw.com
Lab Resources Online
KEYWORD: MR7 Lab5

Sometimes you need to regroup a mixed number before you can subtract. To regroup a mixed number, divide one or more of the whole numbers into fractional parts.

NY Performance Indicators
6.N.16, 6.N.18, 6.R.1, 6.R.5

Activity

1 Find $1\frac{1}{3} - \frac{2}{3}$.

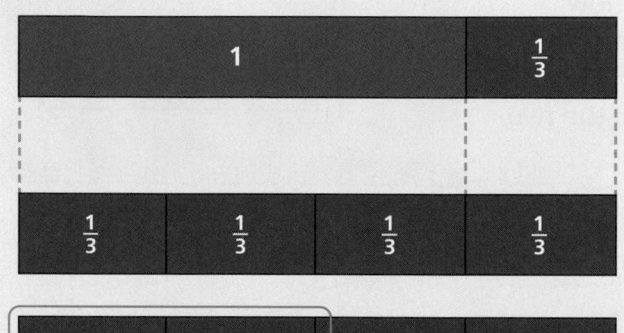

Use fraction bars to model the first mixed number, $1\frac{1}{3}$.

The model does not show $\frac{2}{3}$ that can be removed. You need to regroup $1\frac{1}{3}$.

1 is equivalent to $\frac{3}{3}$.

Now you can subtract $\frac{2}{3}$ from $\frac{4}{3}$.

$$1\frac{1}{3} - \frac{2}{3} \rightarrow \frac{4}{3} - \frac{2}{3} = \frac{2}{3}$$

2 Find $1\frac{1}{6} - \frac{5}{12}$.

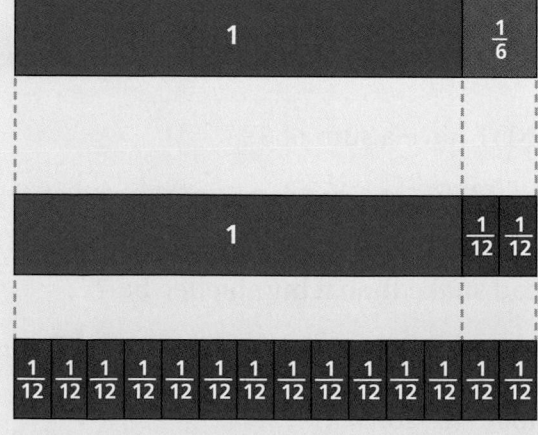

Use fraction bars to model the first mixed number, $1\frac{1}{6}$.

You need to remove $\frac{5}{12}$, so model $1\frac{1}{6}$ using $\frac{1}{12}$ fraction bars.

The model does not show $\frac{5}{12}$ that can be removed. You need to regroup $1\frac{1}{6}$.

1 is equivalent to $\frac{12}{12}$.

Now you can subtract $\frac{5}{12}$ from $\frac{14}{12}$.

$$1\frac{1}{6} - \frac{5}{12} \rightarrow \frac{14}{12} - \frac{5}{12} - \frac{9}{12}, \text{ or } \frac{3}{4}$$

3 Find $1\frac{1}{3} - \frac{1}{2}$.

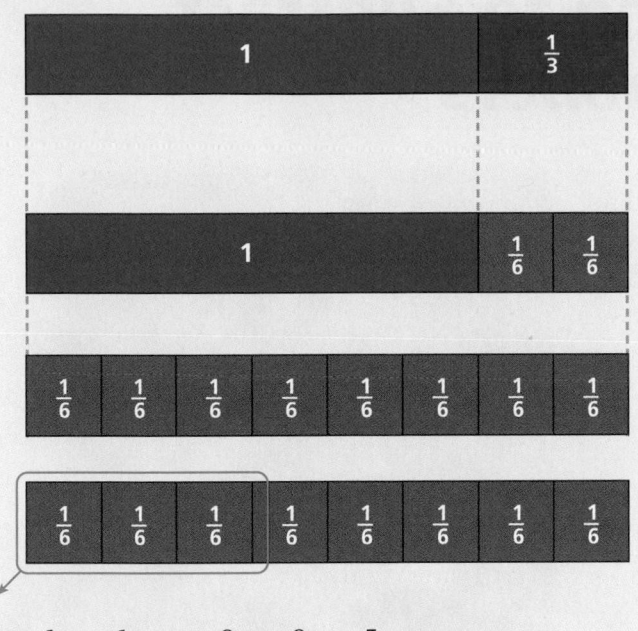

Use fraction bars to model the first mixed number, $1\frac{1}{3}$.

You need to remove $\frac{1}{2}$. Model $1\frac{1}{3}$ using one size fraction bar that can model $1\frac{1}{3}$ and $\frac{1}{2}$.

The model does not show $\frac{1}{2}$ that can be removed. You need to regroup $1\frac{1}{3}$.

1 is equivalent to $\frac{6}{6}$.

Now you can subtract $\frac{1}{2}$ from $\frac{8}{6}$.

$$1\frac{1}{3} - \frac{1}{2} \quad \rightarrow \quad \frac{8}{6} - \frac{3}{6} = \frac{5}{6}$$

Think and Discuss

1. Tell whether you need to regroup before you subtract $3\frac{3}{8} - 1\frac{1}{8}$.

2. Tell whether you need to regroup before you subtract $4\frac{3}{5} - 1\frac{7}{10}$.

Try This

Give the subtraction expression that is modeled.

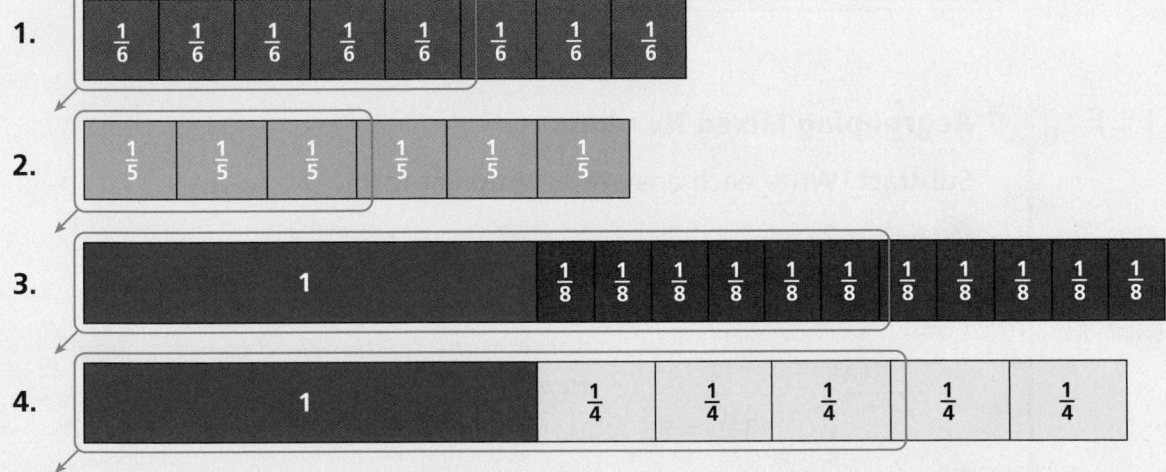

1.

2.

3.

4.

Model each subtraction expression with fraction bars, draw the model, and find the difference.

5. $1\frac{3}{4} - 1\frac{1}{8}$

6. $1\frac{1}{2} - \frac{3}{4}$

7. $1\frac{2}{6} - \frac{5}{6}$

8. $1\frac{1}{6} - \frac{3}{4}$

9. $2\frac{3}{8} - 1\frac{1}{2}$

10. $3\frac{1}{3} - 1\frac{2}{3}$

11. $4\frac{1}{4} - 2\frac{5}{6}$

12. $3\frac{1}{6} - 1\frac{1}{4}$

5-4 Regrouping to Subtract Mixed Numbers

Learn to regroup mixed numbers to subtract.

NY Performance Indicators

6.N.18 Add and subtract mixed numbers with unlike denominators. Also, 6.N.16.

Jimmy and his family planted a tree when it was $1\frac{3}{4}$ ft tall. Now the tree is $2\frac{1}{4}$ ft tall. How much has the tree grown since it was planted?

The difference in the heights can be represented by the expression $2\frac{1}{4} - 1\frac{3}{4}$.

You will need to regroup $2\frac{1}{4}$ because the fraction in $1\frac{3}{4}$ is greater than $\frac{1}{4}$.

Divide *one whole* of $2\frac{1}{4}$ into fourths.

1	1	$\frac{1}{4}$

1	$\frac{1}{4}$	$\frac{1}{4}$	$\frac{1}{4}$	$\frac{1}{4}$	$\frac{1}{4}$

Regroup $2\frac{1}{4}$ as $1\frac{5}{4}$.

1	$\frac{1}{4}$	$\frac{1}{4}$	$\frac{1}{4}$	$\frac{1}{4}$	$\frac{1}{4}$

$$\begin{array}{r} 2\frac{1}{4} \rightarrow \quad 1\frac{5}{4} \\ -\ 1\frac{3}{4} \rightarrow -\ 1\frac{3}{4} \\ \hline \frac{2}{4} = \frac{1}{2} \end{array}$$

The tree has grown $\frac{1}{2}$ ft since it was planted.

EXAMPLE 1 **Regrouping Mixed Numbers**

Subtract. Write each answer in simplest form.

A $6\frac{5}{12} - 2\frac{7}{12}$

$$\begin{array}{r} 6\frac{5}{12} \longrightarrow \quad 5\frac{17}{12} \\ -\ 2\frac{7}{12} \longrightarrow -\ 2\frac{7}{12} \\ \hline 3\frac{10}{12} = 3\frac{5}{6} \end{array}$$

Regroup $6\frac{5}{12}$ as $5 + 1\frac{5}{12} = 5 + \frac{12}{12} + \frac{5}{12}$.

Subtract the fractions and then the whole numbers.

Write the answer in simplest form.

B $7\frac{2}{3} - 2\frac{5}{6}$

$$\begin{array}{r} 7\frac{4}{6} \longrightarrow \quad 6\frac{10}{6} \\ -\ 2\frac{5}{6} \longrightarrow -\ 2\frac{5}{6} \\ \hline 4\frac{5}{6} \end{array}$$

6 is a multiple of 3, so 6 is a common denominator.

Regroup $7\frac{4}{6}$ as $6 + 1\frac{4}{6} = 6 + \frac{6}{6} + \frac{4}{6}$.

Subtract the fractions and then the whole numbers.

Subtract. Write each answer in simplest form.

C $8\frac{1}{4} - 5\frac{2}{3}$

$$8\frac{3}{12} \longrightarrow 7\frac{15}{12}$$
$$-5\frac{8}{12} \longrightarrow -5\frac{8}{12}$$
$$\overline{\phantom{-5\frac{8}{12}}2\frac{7}{12}}$$

The LCM of 4 and 3 is 12.
Regroup $8\frac{3}{12}$ as $7 + 1\frac{3}{12} = 7 + \frac{12}{12} + \frac{3}{12}$.
Subtract the fractions and then the whole numbers.

D $8 - 5\frac{3}{4}$

$$8 \longrightarrow 7\frac{4}{4}$$
$$-5\frac{3}{4} \longrightarrow -5\frac{3}{4}$$
$$\overline{\phantom{-5\frac{3}{4}}2\frac{1}{4}}$$

Write 8 as a mixed number with a denominator of 4. Regroup 8 as $7 + \frac{4}{4}$.
Subtract the fractions and then the whole numbers.

EXAMPLE 2 *Measurement Application*

Dave is re-covering an old couch and cushions. He determines that he needs 17 yards of fabric for the job.

A Dave has $1\frac{2}{3}$ yards of fabric. How many more yards does he need?

$$17 \longrightarrow 16\frac{3}{3}$$
$$-1\frac{2}{3} \longrightarrow -1\frac{2}{3}$$
$$\overline{\phantom{-1\frac{2}{3}}15\frac{1}{3}}$$

Write 17 as a mixed number with a denominator of 3. Regroup 17 as $16 + \frac{3}{3}$.
Subtract the fractions and then the whole numbers.

Dave needs another $15\frac{1}{3}$ yards of material.

B If Dave uses $9\frac{5}{6}$ yards of fabric to cover the couch frame, how much of the 17 yards will he have left?

$$17 \longrightarrow 16\frac{6}{6}$$
$$-9\frac{5}{6} \longrightarrow -9\frac{5}{6}$$
$$\overline{\phantom{-9\frac{5}{6}}7\frac{1}{6}}$$

Write 17 as a mixed number with a denominator of 6. Regroup 17 as $16 + \frac{6}{6}$.

Subtract the fractions and then the whole numbers.

Dave will have $7\frac{1}{6}$ yards of material left.

Think and Discuss

1. **Explain** why you regroup 2 as $1\frac{8}{8}$ instead of $1\frac{3}{3}$ when you find $2 - 1\frac{3}{8}$.

2. **Give an example** of a subtraction expression in which you would need to regroup the first mixed number to subtract.

go.hrw.com
Homework Help Online
KEYWORD: MR7 5-4
Parent Resources Online
KEYWORD: MR7 Parent

GUIDED PRACTICE

See Example 1 Subtract. Write each answer in simplest form.

1. $2\frac{1}{2} - 1\frac{3}{4}$ **2.** $8\frac{2}{9} - 2\frac{7}{9}$ **3.** $3\frac{2}{6} - 1\frac{2}{3}$ **4.** $7\frac{1}{4} - 4\frac{11}{12}$

See Example 2 **5.** Mr. Jones purchased a 4-pound bag of flour. He used $1\frac{2}{5}$ pounds of flour to make bread. How many pounds of flour are left?

INDEPENDENT PRACTICE

See Example 1 Subtract. Write each answer in simplest form.

6. $6\frac{3}{11} - 3\frac{10}{11}$ **7.** $9\frac{2}{5} - 5\frac{3}{5}$ **8.** $4\frac{3}{10} - 3\frac{3}{5}$ **9.** $10\frac{1}{2} - 2\frac{5}{8}$

10. $11\frac{1}{4} - 9\frac{3}{8}$ **11.** $7\frac{5}{9} - 2\frac{5}{6}$ **12.** $6 - 2\frac{2}{3}$ **13.** $5\frac{3}{10} - 3\frac{1}{2}$

See Example 2 **14. Measurement** A standard piece of notebook paper has a length of 11 inches and a width of $8\frac{1}{2}$ inches. What is the difference between these two measures?

15. Chad opened a 10-pound bag of birdseed to refill his feeders. He used $3\frac{1}{3}$ pounds to fill them. How many pounds of birdseed were left?

PRACTICE AND PROBLEM SOLVING

Extra Practice
See page 722.

Find each difference. Write the answer in simplest form.

16. $8 - 6\frac{4}{7}$ **17.** $13\frac{1}{9} - 11\frac{2}{3}$ **18.** $10\frac{3}{4} - 6\frac{1}{2}$ **19.** $13 - 4\frac{2}{11}$

20. $15\frac{2}{5} - 12\frac{3}{4}$ **21.** $17\frac{5}{9} - 6\frac{1}{3}$ **22.** $18\frac{1}{4} - 14\frac{3}{8}$ **23.** $20\frac{1}{6} - 7\frac{4}{9}$

24. Economics A single share of stock in a company cost $23\frac{2}{5}$ on Monday. By Tuesday, the cost of a share in the company had fallen to $19\frac{1}{5}$. By how much did the price of a share fall?

25. Jasmine is $62\frac{1}{2}$ inches tall. Her brother, Antoine, is $69\frac{3}{4}$ inches tall. What is the difference, in inches, in their heights?

Simplify each expression. Write the answer in simplest form.

26. $4\frac{2}{3} + 5\frac{1}{3} - 7\frac{1}{8}$ **27.** $12\frac{5}{9} - 6\frac{2}{3} + 1\frac{4}{9}$ **28.** $7\frac{7}{8} - 4\frac{1}{8} + 1\frac{1}{4}$

29. $7\frac{4}{11} - 2\frac{8}{11} - \frac{10}{11}$ **30.** $8\frac{1}{3} - 5\frac{8}{9} + 8\frac{1}{2}$ **31.** $5\frac{2}{7} - 2\frac{1}{14} + 8\frac{5}{14}$

32. Multi-Step Octavio used a brand new 6-hour tape to record some television shows. He recorded a movie that is $1\frac{1}{2}$ hours long and a cooking show that is $1\frac{1}{4}$ hours long. How much time is left on the tape?

Evaluate each expression for $a = 6\frac{2}{3}$, $b = 8\frac{1}{2}$, and $c = 1\frac{3}{4}$. Write the answer in simplest form.

33. $a - c$ **34.** $b - c$ **35.** $b - a$ **36.** $10 - b$

37. $b - (a + c)$ **38.** $c + (b - a)$ **39.** $(a + b) - c$ **40.** $(10 - c) - a$

Use the table for Exercises 41–44.

41. Gustavo is working at a gift wrap center. He has 2 yd² of wrapping paper to wrap a small box. How much wrapping paper will be left after he wraps the gift?

42. Gustavo must now wrap two extra-large boxes. If he has 6 yd² of wrapping paper, how much more wrapping paper will he need to wrap the two gifts?

43. To wrap a large box, Gustavo used $\frac{3}{4}$ yd² less wrapping paper than the amount listed in the table. How many square yards did he use to wrap the gift?

Gustavo's Gift Wrap Table

Gift Size	Paper Needed (yd²)
Small	$\frac{11}{12}$
Medium	$1\frac{5}{9}$
Large	$2\frac{2}{3}$
X-large	$3\frac{1}{9}$

 44. **What's the Error?** Gustavo calculated the difference between the amount needed to wrap an extra-large box and the amount needed to wrap a medium box to be $2\frac{4}{9}$ yd². Explain his error and find the correct answer.

 45. **Write About It** Explain why you write equivalent fractions before you regroup them. Explain why you do not regroup them first.

 46. **Challenge** Fill in the box with a mixed number that makes the inequality true.

$$12\frac{1}{2} - 8\frac{3}{4} > 10 - \blacksquare$$

TEST PREP and Spiral Review

47. Multiple Choice Find the difference of $5 - \frac{4}{9}$.

  Ⓐ $5\frac{5}{9}$ Ⓑ $5\frac{1}{9}$ Ⓒ $4\frac{5}{9}$ Ⓓ $4\frac{1}{9}$

48. Gridded Response Tami worked 4 hours on Saturday at the city pool. She spent $1\frac{3}{4}$ hours cleaning the pool and the remaining time working as a lifeguard. How many hours did Tami spend working as a lifeguard?

Find the missing numbers that make the fractions equivalent. (Lesson 4-5)

49. $\frac{1}{2} = \frac{8}{a}$ **50.** $\frac{x}{5} = \frac{3}{15}$ **51.** $\frac{3}{z} = \frac{7}{21}$ **52.** $\frac{7}{8} = \frac{d}{56}$

Estimate. (Lesson 4-9)

53. $6\frac{7}{8} + 3\frac{2}{15} + 7\frac{1}{20}$ **54.** $2\frac{3}{4} + 8\frac{9}{10} + 3\frac{1}{9}$ **55.** $12\frac{8}{15} + 2\frac{1}{6} + 7\frac{3}{5}$

5-5 Solving Fraction Equations: Addition and Subtraction

Learn to solve equations by adding and subtracting fractions.

NY Performance Indicators

6.N.18 Add and subtract mixed numbers with unlike denominators. Also, 6.N.16.

Sugarcane is the main source of the sugar we use to sweeten our foods. It grows in tropical areas, such as Costa Rica and Haiti.

In one year, the average person in Costa Rica consumes $24\frac{1}{4}$ lb less sugar than the average person in the United States consumes.

This painting depicts the landscape of Haiti, a tropical area where sugarcane grows.

EXAMPLE 1 Solving Equations by Adding and Subtracting

Solve each equation. Write the solution in simplest form.

A $x + 6\frac{2}{3} = 11$

$$x + 6\frac{2}{3} = 11$$
$$-6\frac{2}{3} \qquad -6\frac{2}{3}$$

Subtract $6\frac{2}{3}$ from both sides to undo the addition.

$$x = 10\frac{3}{3} - 6\frac{2}{3}$$ Regroup 11 as $10\frac{3}{3}$.

$$x = 4\frac{1}{3}$$ Subtract.

B $2\frac{1}{4} = x - 3\frac{1}{2}$

$$2\frac{1}{4} = x - 3\frac{1}{2}$$
$$+3\frac{1}{2} \qquad +3\frac{1}{2}$$

Add $3\frac{1}{2}$ to both sides to undo the subtraction.

$$2\frac{1}{4} + 3\frac{2}{4} = x$$ Find a common denominator. $3\frac{1}{2} = 3\frac{2}{4}$

$$5\frac{3}{4} = x$$ Add.

C $5\frac{3}{5} = m + \frac{7}{10}$

$$5\frac{3}{5} = m + \frac{7}{10}$$
$$-\frac{7}{10} \qquad -\frac{7}{10}$$

Subtract $\frac{7}{10}$ from both sides to undo the addition.

$$5\frac{6}{10} - \frac{7}{10} = m$$ Find a common denominator. $5\frac{3}{5} = 5\frac{6}{10}$

$$4\frac{16}{10} - \frac{7}{10} = m$$ Regroup $5\frac{6}{10}$ as $4\frac{10}{10} + \frac{6}{10}$.

$$4\frac{9}{10} = m$$ Subtract.

Solve each equation. Write the solution in simplest form.

 D $w - \frac{1}{2} = 2\frac{3}{4}$

$$w - \frac{1}{2} = 2\frac{3}{4}$$

$$\underline{+\frac{1}{2} \quad +\frac{1}{2}}$$ *Add $\frac{1}{2}$ to both sides to undo the subtraction.*

$$w = 2\frac{3}{4} + \frac{1}{2}$$

$$w = 2\frac{3}{4} + \frac{2}{4}$$ *Find a common denominator. $\frac{1}{2} = \frac{2}{4}$*

$$w = 2\frac{5}{4}$$ *Add.*

$$w = 3\frac{1}{4}$$ $\quad 2\frac{5}{4} = 2 + 1\frac{1}{4}$

EXAMPLE **2** **Social Studies Application**

On average, a person in Costa Rica consumes $132\frac{1}{4}$ lb of sugar per year. If the average person in Costa Rica consumes $24\frac{1}{4}$ lb less than the average person in the U.S., what is the average sugar consumption per year by a person in the U.S.?

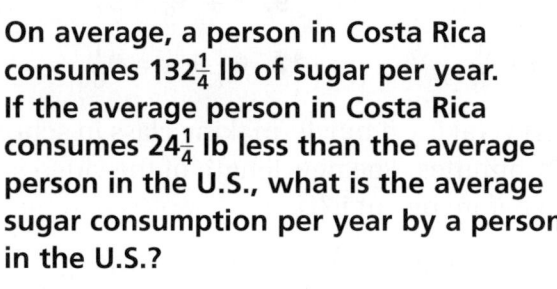

Costa Rica

$$u - 24\frac{1}{4} = 132\frac{1}{4}$$ *Let u represent the average amount of sugar consumed in the U.S.*

$$\underline{+24\frac{1}{4} \quad +24\frac{1}{4}}$$ *Add $24\frac{1}{4}$ to both sides to undo the subtraction.*

$$u = 156\frac{2}{4} = 156\frac{1}{2}$$ *Simplify.*

Check

$$u - 24\frac{1}{4} = 132\frac{1}{4}$$

$$156\frac{1}{2} - 24\frac{1}{4} \stackrel{?}{=} 132\frac{1}{4}$$ *Substitute $156\frac{1}{2}$ for u.*

$$156\frac{2}{4} - 24\frac{1}{4} \stackrel{?}{=} 132\frac{1}{4}$$ *Find a common denominator.*

$$132\frac{1}{4} \stackrel{?}{=} 132\frac{1}{4}\checkmark$$ *$156\frac{1}{2}$ is the solution.*

On average, a person in the U.S. consumes $156\frac{1}{2}$ lb of sugar per year.

6.PS.7, 6.PS.21

Think and Discuss

1. **Explain** how regrouping a mixed number when subtracting is similar to regrouping when subtracting whole numbers.

2. **Give an example** of an addition equation with a solution that is a fraction between 3 and 4.

go.hrw.com
Homework Help Online
KEYWORD: MR7 5-5
Parent Resources Online
KEYWORD: MR7 Parent

GUIDED PRACTICE

See Example ① Solve each equation. Write the solution in simplest form.

1. $x + 2\frac{1}{2} = 7$ **2.** $3\frac{1}{3} = x - 5\frac{1}{9}$ **3.** $9\frac{3}{4} = x + 4\frac{1}{8}$

4. $x + 1\frac{1}{5} = 5\frac{3}{10}$ **5.** $3\frac{2}{5} + x = 7\frac{1}{2}$ **6.** $8\frac{7}{10} = x - 4\frac{1}{4}$

See Example ② **7.** A tailor increased the length of a robe by $2\frac{1}{4}$ inches. The new length of the robe is 60 inches. What was the original length?

INDEPENDENT PRACTICE

See Example ① Solve each equation. Write the solution in simplest form.

8. $x - 4\frac{3}{4} = 1\frac{1}{12}$ **9.** $x + 5\frac{3}{8} = 9$ **10.** $3\frac{1}{2} = 1\frac{3}{10} + x$

11. $4\frac{2}{3} = x - \frac{1}{6}$ **12.** $6\frac{3}{4} + x = 9\frac{1}{8}$ **13.** $x - 3\frac{7}{9} = 5$

See Example ② **14.** Robert is taking a movie-making class in school. He edited his short video and cut $3\frac{2}{5}$ minutes. The new length of the video is $12\frac{1}{10}$ minutes. How long was his video before he cut it?

15. An extension for a table increased its length by $2\frac{1}{2}$ feet. The new length of the table is $8\frac{3}{4}$ feet. What was the original length?

PRACTICE AND PROBLEM SOLVING

Extra Practice
See page 722.

Find the solution to each equation. Check your answers.

16. $y + 8\frac{2}{4} = 10$ **17.** $p - 1\frac{2}{5} = 3\frac{7}{10}$ **18.** $6\frac{2}{3} + n = 7\frac{5}{6}$

19. $5\frac{3}{5} = s - 2\frac{3}{10}$ **20.** $k - 8\frac{1}{4} = 1\frac{1}{3}$ **21.** $\frac{23}{24} = c + \frac{5}{8}$

22. The difference between Cristina's and Erin's heights is $\frac{1}{2}$ foot. Erin's height is $4\frac{1}{4}$ feet, and she is shorter than Cristina. How tall is Cristina?

23. **Measurement** Lori used $2\frac{5}{8}$ ounces of shampoo to wash her dog. When she was finished, the bottle contained $13\frac{3}{8}$ ounces of shampoo. How many ounces of shampoo were in the bottle before Lori washed her dog?

24. **Sports** Jack decreased his best time in the 400-meter race by $1\frac{3}{10}$ seconds. His new best time is $52\frac{3}{5}$ seconds. What was Jack's old time in the 400-meter race?

25. **Crafts** Juan makes bracelets to sell at his mother's gift shop. He alternates between green and blue beads.

What is the length of the green bead?

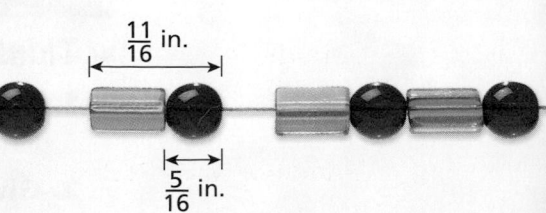

$\frac{11}{16}$ in.

$\frac{5}{16}$ in.

Find the solution to each equation. Check your answers.

26. $m + 4 = 6\frac{3}{8} - 1\frac{1}{4}$ **27.** $3\frac{2}{9} - 1\frac{1}{3} = p - 5\frac{1}{2}$ **28.** $q - 4\frac{1}{4} = 1\frac{1}{6} + 1\frac{1}{2}$

29. $a + 5\frac{1}{4} + 2\frac{1}{2} = 13\frac{1}{6}$ **30.** $11\frac{2}{7} = w + 3\frac{1}{2} - 1\frac{1}{7}$ **31.** $9 - 5\frac{7}{8} = x - 1\frac{1}{8}$

32. Music A string quartet is performing Antonio Vivaldi's *The Four Seasons*. The concert is scheduled to last 45 minutes.

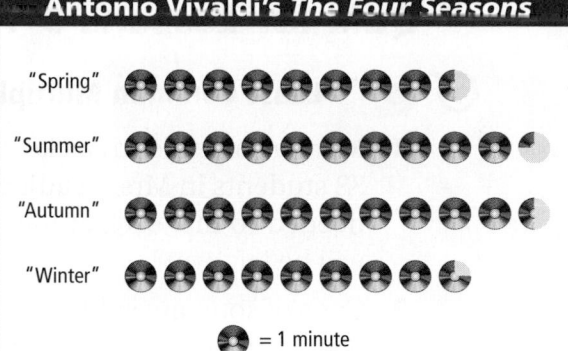

Antonio Vivaldi's *The Four Seasons*

"Spring"

"Summer"

"Autumn"

"Winter"

● = 1 minute

  a. After playing "Spring," "Summer," and "Autumn," how much time will be left in the concert?

  b. Is the concert long enough to play the four movements and another piece that is $6\frac{1}{2}$ minutes long? Explain.

33. Write a Problem Use the pictograph to write a subtraction problem with two mixed numbers.

34. Choose a Strategy How can you draw a line that is 5 inches long using only one sheet of $8\frac{1}{2}$ in. × 11 in. notebook paper?

35. Write About It Explain how you know whether to add a number to or subtract a number from both sides of an equation in order to solve the equation.

36. Challenge Use the numbers 1, 2, 3, 4, 5, and 6 to write a subtraction problem with two mixed numbers that have a difference of $4\frac{13}{20}$.

37. Multiple Choice Solve $4\frac{1}{2} + x = 6\frac{1}{6}$ for x.

  Ⓐ $x = 1\frac{1}{4}$ Ⓑ $x = 1\frac{2}{3}$ Ⓒ $x = 2\frac{1}{4}$ Ⓓ $x = 2\frac{2}{3}$

38. Multiple Choice Ambra's hair was $7\frac{2}{3}$ inches long. After she got her hair cut, the length of her hair was $5\frac{4}{5}$ inches. How many inches of hair were cut?

  Ⓕ $1\frac{13}{15}$ Ⓖ $2\frac{2}{5}$ Ⓗ $2\frac{2}{3}$ Ⓙ $2\frac{13}{15}$

Find the least common multiple (LCM). (Lesson 5-1)

39. 4 and 12   **40.** 7, 14, and 21   **41.** 6, 9, and 24

Evaluate. Write each answer as a fraction in simplest form. (Lesson 5-3)

42. $2.5 + 5\frac{3}{8}$ **43.** $3.1 - 2\frac{3}{4}$ **44.** $15\frac{1}{5} - 8.2$ **45.** $6\frac{1}{6} + 1.4$

READY TO GO ON?

Quiz for Lessons 5-1 Through 5-5

5-1 Least Common Multiple

1. Markers are sold in packs of 8, and crayons are sold in packs of 16. If there are 32 students in Mrs. Reading's art class, what is the least number of packs needed so that each student can have one marker and one crayon and none will be left over?

2. Cans of soup are sold in packs of 24, and packets of crackers are sold in groups of 4. If there are 120 people to be fed and each will get one can of soup and one packet of crackers, what is the least number of packs needed to feed everyone such that no crackers or soup are left over?

Find the least common multiple (LCM).

3. 4 and 6   4. 2 and 15   5. 3, 5, and 9   6. 4, 6, and 10

5-2 Adding and Subtracting with Unlike Denominators

Add or subtract. Write each answer in simplest form.

7. $\frac{5}{7} - \frac{3}{14}$ 8. $\frac{7}{8} + \frac{1}{24}$ 9. $\frac{8}{9} - \frac{1}{10}$ 10. $\frac{1}{6} + \frac{1}{2}$

11. Alexia needs to add $\frac{2}{3}$ cup of sugar for the recipe she is making. She has added $\frac{1}{2}$ cup already. How much more sugar does she need to add?

5-3 Adding and Subtracting Mixed Numbers

Find each sum or difference. Write each answer in simplest form.

12. $2\frac{9}{13} - 1\frac{1}{26}$ 13. $9\frac{5}{10} + 11\frac{4}{5}$ 14. $7\frac{8}{9} - 1\frac{1}{18}$ 15. $2\frac{4}{5} + 1\frac{1}{10}$

5-4 Regrouping to Subtract Mixed Numbers

Subtract. Write each answer in simplest form.

16. $2\frac{1}{13} - 1\frac{1}{26}$ 17. $7\frac{1}{3} - 5\frac{7}{9}$ 18. $3\frac{3}{10} - 1\frac{4}{5}$ 19. $10\frac{1}{2} - 5\frac{2}{3}$

20. Mary Ann buys $4\frac{2}{5}$ pounds of bananas. She uses $1\frac{1}{2}$ pounds making banana bread. How many pounds of bananas does she have left?

5-5 Solving Fraction Equations: Addition and Subtraction

Solve each equation. Write the solution in simplest form.

21. $t + 2\frac{5}{8} = 9$ 22. $5\frac{1}{6} = x - \frac{7}{8}$ 23. $g + \frac{1}{4} = 2\frac{9}{10}$ 24. $a + \frac{3}{5} = 1\frac{7}{10}$

25. Bryn bought $5\frac{1}{8}$ yards of material. She used $3\frac{7}{9}$ yards to make a dress. How much material does she have left?

Focus on Problem Solving

Solve

Choose the operation: multiplication or division

Read the whole problem before you try to solve it. Determine what action is taking place in the problem. Then decide whether you need to multiply or divide in order to solve the problem.

If you are asked to combine equal groups, you need to multiply. If you are asked to share something equally or to separate something into equal groups, you need to divide.

Action	Operation	
Combining equal groups	Multiplication	
Sharing things equally or separating into equal groups	Division	

 Read each problem, and determine the action taking place. Choose an operation to solve the problem. Then solve, and write the answer in simplest form.

1 Jason picked 30 cups of raspberries. He put them in giant freezer bags with 5 cups in each bag. How many bags does he have?

2 When the cranberry flowers start to open in June, cranberry growers usually bring in about $2\frac{1}{2}$ beehives per acre of cranberries to pollinate the flowers. A grower has 36 acres of cranberries. About how many beehives does she need?

3 A recipe that makes 3 cranberry banana loaves calls for 4 cups of cranberries. Linh wants to make only 1 loaf. How many cups of cranberries does she need?

4 Clay wants to double a recipe for blueberry muffins that calls for 1 cup of blueberries. How many blueberries will he need?

5-6 Multiplying Fractions by Whole Numbers

Learn to multiply fractions by whole numbers.

NY Performance Indicators

6.A.2 Use substitution to evaluate algebraic expressions. Also, 6.N.17.

Recall that multiplication by a whole number can be represented as repeated addition. For example, $4 \cdot 5 = 5 + 5 + 5 + 5$. You can multiply a whole number by a fraction using the same method.

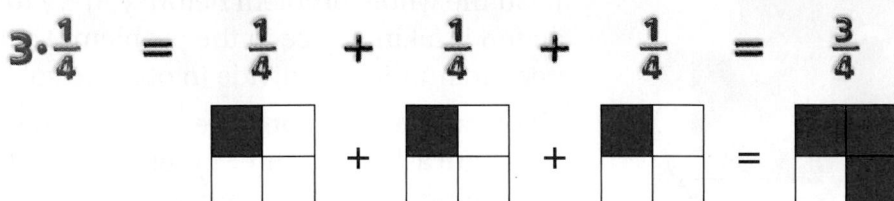

$$3 \cdot \frac{1}{4} = \frac{1}{4} + \frac{1}{4} + \frac{1}{4} = \frac{3}{4}$$

There is another way to multiply with fractions. Remember that a whole number can be written as an improper fraction with 1 in the denominator. So $3 = \frac{3}{1}$.

$$\frac{3}{1} \cdot \frac{1}{4} = \frac{3 \cdot 1}{1 \cdot 4} = \frac{3}{4} \longleftarrow \text{Multiply numerators.}$$
$$\longleftarrow \text{Multiply denominators.}$$

EXAMPLE **Multiplying Fractions and Whole Numbers**

Multiply. Write each answer in simplest form.

Method 1: Use repeated addition.

A $5 \cdot \frac{1}{8}$

$5 \cdot \frac{1}{8} = \frac{1}{8} + \frac{1}{8} + \frac{1}{8} + \frac{1}{8} + \frac{1}{8}$ *Write $5 \cdot \frac{1}{8}$ as addition. Add the numerators.*

$= \frac{5}{8}$

B $3 \cdot \frac{1}{9}$

$3 \cdot \frac{1}{9} = \frac{1}{9} + \frac{1}{9} + \frac{1}{9}$ *Write $3 \cdot \frac{1}{9}$ as addition. Add the numerators.*

$= \frac{3}{9}$

$= \frac{1}{3}$ *Write your answer in simplest form.*

Method 2: Multiply.

C $4 \cdot \frac{7}{8}$

$\frac{4}{1} \cdot \frac{7}{8} = \frac{28}{8}$ *Multiply.*

$= \frac{7}{2} \text{ or } 3\frac{1}{2}$ *Write your answer in simplest form.*

EXAMPLE 2 **Evaluating Fraction Expressions**

Evaluate 6x for each value of x. Write each answer in simplest form.

A $x = \frac{1}{8}$

$6x$	*Write the expression.*
$6 \cdot \frac{1}{8}$	*Substitute $\frac{1}{8}$ for x.*
$\frac{6}{1} \cdot \frac{1}{8} = \frac{6}{8}$	*Multiply.*
$= \frac{3}{4}$	*Write your answer in simplest form.*

B $x = \frac{2}{3}$

$6x$	*Write the expression.*
$6 \cdot \frac{2}{3}$	*Substitute $\frac{2}{3}$ for x.*
$\frac{6}{1} \cdot \frac{2}{3} = \frac{12}{3}$	*Multiply.*
$= \frac{4}{1}$	
$= 4$	

Remember!

$\frac{12}{3}$ means $12 \div 3$.

Sometimes the denominator of an improper fraction will divide into the numerator without a remainder, as in Example 2B. When this happens, the improper fraction is equivalent to a whole number, not a mixed number.

$$\frac{12}{3} = 4$$

EXAMPLE 3 **Social Studies Application**

Any proposed amendment to the U.S. Constitution must be ratified, or approved, by $\frac{3}{4}$ of the states. When the 13th Amendment abolishing slavery was proposed in 1865, there were 36 states. How many states needed to ratify this amendment in order for it to pass?

To find $\frac{3}{4}$ of 36, multiply.

$$\frac{3}{4} \cdot 36 = \frac{3}{4} \cdot \frac{36}{1}$$
$$= \frac{108}{4}$$ *Divide 108 by 4 and write your answer in simplest form.*
$$= 27$$

For the 13th Amendment to pass, 27 states had to ratify it.

Think and Discuss

6.CM.4, 6.PS.19, 6.PS.21

1. Describe a model you could use to show the product of $4 \cdot \frac{1}{5}$.

2. Choose the expression that is correctly multiplied.

$$2 \cdot \frac{3}{7} = \frac{6}{7} \qquad 2 \cdot \frac{3}{7} = \frac{6}{14}$$

3. Explain how you know without actually multiplying that $\frac{5}{8} \cdot 16$ is greater than 8.

5-6 **Exercises**

go.hrw.com
Homework Help Online
KEYWORD: MR7 5-6
Parent Resources Online
KEYWORD: MR7 Parent

GUIDED PRACTICE

See Example 1 **Multiply. Write each answer in simplest form.**

1. $8 \cdot \frac{1}{9}$ **2.** $2 \cdot \frac{1}{5}$ **3.** $12 \cdot \frac{1}{4}$ **4.** $7 \cdot \frac{4}{9}$

5. $3 \cdot \frac{1}{7}$ **6.** $4 \cdot \frac{2}{11}$ **7.** $8 \cdot \frac{3}{4}$ **8.** $18 \cdot \frac{1}{3}$

See Example 2 **Evaluate 12x for each value of x. Write each answer in simplest form.**

9. $x = \frac{2}{3}$ **10.** $x = \frac{1}{2}$ **11.** $x = \frac{3}{4}$ **12.** $x = \frac{5}{6}$

See Example 3 **13.** The school Community Service Club has 45 members. Of these 45 members, $\frac{3}{5}$ are boys. How many boys are members of the Community Service Club?

INDEPENDENT PRACTICE

See Example 1 **Multiply. Write each answer in simplest form.**

14. $4 \cdot \frac{1}{10}$ **15.** $6 \cdot \frac{1}{8}$ **16.** $3 \cdot \frac{1}{12}$ **17.** $2 \cdot \frac{2}{5}$

18. $6 \cdot \frac{10}{11}$ **19.** $2 \cdot \frac{3}{11}$ **20.** $15 \cdot \frac{2}{15}$ **21.** $20 \cdot \frac{1}{2}$

See Example 2 **Evaluate 8x for each value of x. Write each answer in simplest form.**

22. $x = \frac{1}{2}$ **23.** $x = \frac{3}{4}$ **24.** $x = \frac{1}{8}$ **25.** $x = \frac{1}{4}$

26. $x = \frac{2}{5}$ **27.** $x = \frac{5}{7}$ **28.** $x = \frac{7}{8}$ **29.** $x = \frac{4}{9}$

See Example 3 **30. School** Kiesha spent 120 minutes completing her homework last night. Of those minutes, $\frac{1}{6}$ were spent on Spanish. How many minutes did Kiesha spend on her Spanish homework?

PRACTICE AND PROBLEM SOLVING

Extra Practice
See page 722.

Evaluate each expression. Write each answer in simplest form.

31. $12b$ for $b = \frac{7}{12}$ **32.** $20m$ for $m = \frac{1}{20}$ **33.** $33z$ for $z = \frac{5}{11}$

34. $\frac{2}{3}y$ for $y = 18$ **35.** $\frac{1}{4}x$ for $x = 20$ **36.** $\frac{3}{5}a$ for $a = 30$

37. $\frac{4}{5}c$ for $c = 12$ **38.** $14x$ for $x = \frac{3}{8}$ **39.** $\frac{9}{10}n$ for $n = 50$

Compare. Write <, >, or =.

40. $9 \cdot \frac{1}{16}$ ▨ $\frac{1}{2}$ **41.** $15 \cdot \frac{2}{5}$ ▨ 5 **42.** $\frac{8}{13}$ ▨ $4 \cdot \frac{2}{13}$

43. $3 \cdot \frac{2}{9}$ ▨ $\frac{2}{3}$ **44.** $6 \cdot \frac{4}{15}$ ▨ $\frac{11}{24}$ **45.** 5 ▨ $12 \cdot \frac{3}{4}$

46. $3 \cdot \frac{1}{7}$ ▨ $3 \cdot \frac{1}{5}$ **47.** $7 \cdot \frac{3}{4}$ ▨ $6 \cdot \frac{3}{7}$ **48.** $2 \cdot \frac{5}{6}$ ▨ $6 \cdot \frac{2}{5}$

49. Denise spent $55 shopping. Of that $55, she spent $\frac{3}{5}$ on a pair of shoes. How much money did Denise spend on the pair of shoes?

The General Sherman, a giant sequoia tree in California's Sequoia National Park, is one of the largest trees in the world at 275 ft tall.

California also has some of the nation's tallest grand firs, ponderosa pines, and sugar pines. The table shows how the heights of these trees compare with the height of the General Sherman. For example, the grand fir is $\frac{23}{25}$ the height of the General Sherman.

50. Find the heights of the trees in the table. Write your answers in simplest form.

51. The world's tallest bluegum eucalyptus tree is $\frac{3}{5}$ the height of the General Sherman tree. How tall is this bluegum eucalyptus?

52. ❓ **What's the Question?** Joshua trees can grow to be 40 ft tall. The answer is $\frac{8}{55}$. What is the question?

53. ✏️ **Write About It** Find $\frac{1}{5}$ the height of the General Sherman. Then divide the height of the General Sherman by 5. What do you notice? Why does this make sense?

54. ⭐ **Challenge** The world's tallest incense cedar tree is 152 ft tall. What is $\frac{1}{5}$ of $\frac{1}{2}$ of $\frac{1}{4}$ of 152?

GENERAL SHERMAN

Tree Heights Compared with the General Sherman	
Tallest Grand Fir	$\frac{23}{25}$
Tallest Ponderosa Pine	$\frac{41}{50}$
Tallest Sugar Pine	$\frac{21}{25}$

Source: The Top 10 of Everything 2000

TEST PREP and Spiral Review

55. Multiple Choice A recipe uses $\frac{1}{3}$ cup of sugar. Daniela doubled the recipe. How much sugar did she use?

Ⓐ $\frac{1}{4}$ cup Ⓑ $\frac{1}{3}$ cup Ⓒ $\frac{2}{3}$ cup Ⓓ $\frac{3}{4}$ cup

56. Extended Response Mario bought $\frac{1}{5}$ pound of turkey. Rose bought four times as much turkey as Mario. And Celia bought 2 times as much as Rose. How many pounds of turkey did Rose buy? How many pounds did Celia buy? How much more did Celia buy than Mario? Show your work.

Write each phrase as a numerical or algebraic expression. (Lesson 2-2)

57. w less than 75   **58.** the product of n and 16   **59.** the quotient of p and 7

Subtract. Write each answer in simplest form. (Lesson 5-4)

60. $5\frac{2}{3} - 4\frac{5}{6}$ **61.** $12\frac{4}{7} - 3\frac{6}{7}$ **62.** $9\frac{7}{12} - 2\frac{1}{3}$ **63.** $11\frac{5}{8} - 5\frac{1}{4}$

Model Fraction Multiplication

Use with Lessons 5-7 and 5-8

go.hrw.com
Lab Resources Online
KEYWORD: MR7 Lab5

You can use grids to help you understand fraction multiplication.

NY Performance Indicators
6.N.17, 6.PS.11, 6.R.1, 6.R.2

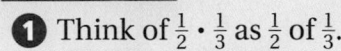
Activity 1

1 Think of $\frac{1}{2} \cdot \frac{1}{3}$ as $\frac{1}{2}$ of $\frac{1}{3}$.

Shade $\frac{1}{3}$ of a square.   Divide the square into halves.

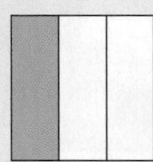   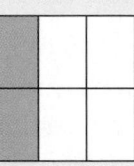

Look at $\frac{1}{2}$ of the part you shaded.

What fraction of the whole is this?   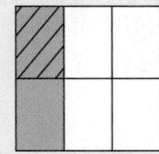 $\frac{1}{2}$ of $\frac{1}{3}$ is $\frac{1}{6}$.

2 Think of $\frac{2}{3} \cdot \frac{1}{2}$ as $\frac{2}{3}$ of $\frac{1}{2}$.

Shade $\frac{1}{2}$ of a square.   Divide the square into thirds. $\frac{2}{3}$ of $\frac{1}{2}$ is $\frac{2}{6}$, or $\frac{1}{3}$.

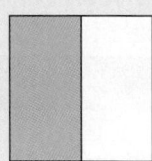   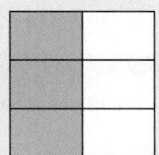   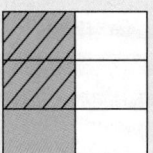

Think and Discuss

1. Tell whether the product is greater than or less than the fractions you started with.

Try This

Write the multiplication expression modeled on each grid.

1.   2.   3.

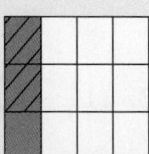   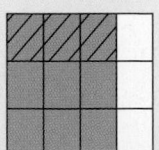   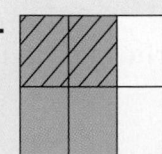

Use a grid to model each multiplication expression.

4. $\frac{1}{3} \cdot \frac{1}{2}$ **5.** $\frac{2}{3} \cdot \frac{1}{3}$ **6.** $\frac{1}{4} \cdot \frac{2}{3}$ **7.** $\frac{1}{3} \cdot \frac{3}{4}$

You can also use grids to model multiplication of mixed numbers.

Activity 2

Think of $\frac{1}{2} \cdot 2\frac{1}{2}$ as $\frac{1}{2}$ of $2\frac{1}{2}$.

Shade $2\frac{1}{2}$ squares.

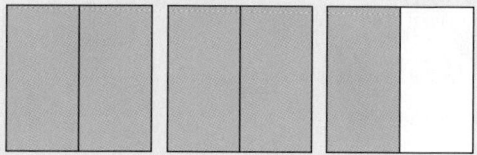

Divide the squares into halves.

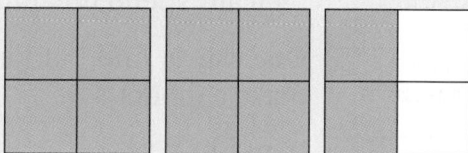

Look at $\frac{1}{2}$ of the part you shaded.

What fraction of the model is this?

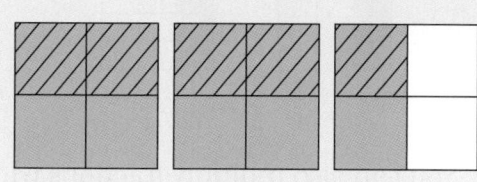

$\frac{1}{2}$ of $2\frac{1}{2}$ is $\frac{5}{4}$, or $1\frac{1}{4}$.

Think and Discuss

1. Describe how modeling multiplication of mixed numbers is like modeling multiplication of fractions.

Try This

Write the multiplication expression modeled on each grid.

1. 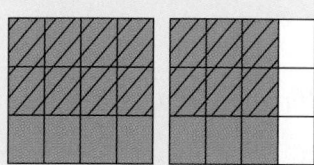   **2.**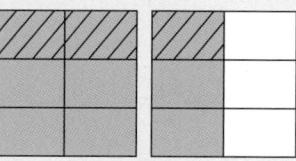

3.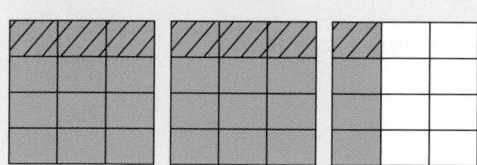

Use a grid to model each multiplication expression.

4. $\frac{1}{3} \cdot 1\frac{1}{2}$ **5.** $\frac{2}{3} \cdot 2\frac{1}{3}$ **6.** $\frac{1}{4} \cdot 2\frac{2}{3}$ **7.** $\frac{1}{3} \cdot 1\frac{3}{4}$

8. $\frac{3}{4} \cdot 1\frac{1}{3}$ **9.** $\frac{1}{2} \cdot 3\frac{1}{3}$ **10.** $\frac{2}{3} \cdot 1\frac{3}{4}$ **11.** $\frac{1}{4} \cdot 2\frac{1}{2}$

5-7 Multiplying Fractions

Learn to multiply fractions.

NY Performance Indicators

6.A.2 Use substitution to evaluate algebraic expressions. Also, **6.N.17.**

On average, people spend $\frac{1}{3}$ of their lives asleep. About $\frac{1}{4}$ of the time they sleep, they dream. What fraction of a lifetime does a person typically spend dreaming?

One way to find $\frac{1}{4}$ of $\frac{1}{3}$ is to make a model.

Find $\frac{1}{4}$ of $\frac{1}{3}$.

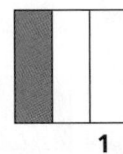 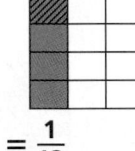

$$\frac{1}{4} \cdot \frac{1}{3} = \frac{1}{12}$$

Your brain keeps working even when you're asleep. It makes sure that you keep breathing and that your heart keeps beating.

You can also multiply fractions without making a model.

$$\frac{1}{4} \cdot \frac{1}{3} = \frac{1 \cdot 1}{4 \cdot 3}$$ ← *Multiply the numerators.*
                      ← *Multiply the denominators.*

$$= \frac{1}{12}$$ *The answer is in simplest form.*

A person typically spends $\frac{1}{12}$ of his or her lifetime dreaming.

EXAMPLE 1 Multiplying Fractions

Multiply. Write each answer in simplest form.

A $\frac{1}{3} \cdot \frac{3}{5}$

$$\frac{1}{3} \cdot \frac{3}{5} = \frac{1 \cdot 3}{3 \cdot 5}$$ *Multiply numerators. Multiply denominators.*

$$= \frac{3}{15}$$ *The GCF of 3 and 15 is 3.*

$$= \frac{1}{5}$$ *The answer is in simplest form.*

B $\frac{6}{7} \cdot \frac{2}{3}$

$$\frac{\overset{2}{\cancel{6}}}{7} \cdot \frac{2}{\underset{1}{\cancel{3}}} = \frac{2}{7} \cdot \frac{2}{1}$$ *Use the GCF to simplify the fractions before multiplying. The GCF of 6 and 3 is 3.*

$$= \frac{2 \cdot 2}{7 \cdot 1}$$ *Multiply numerators. Multiply denominators.*

$$= \frac{4}{7}$$ *The answer is in simplest form.*

Multiply. Write each answer in simplest form.

C $\frac{3}{8} \cdot \frac{2}{9}$

$\frac{3}{8} \cdot \frac{2}{9} = \frac{3 \cdot 2}{8 \cdot 9}$ *Multiply numerators. Multiply denominators.*

$= \frac{6}{72}$ *The GCF of 6 and 72 is 6.*

$= \frac{1}{12}$ *The answer is in simplest form.*

EXAMPLE **2** **Evaluating Fraction Expressions**

Evaluate the expression $a \cdot \frac{1}{3}$ for each value of a. Write the answer in simplest form.

A $a = \frac{5}{8}$ $a \cdot \frac{1}{3}$

$\frac{5}{8} \cdot \frac{1}{3}$ *Substitute $\frac{5}{8}$ for a.*

$\frac{5 \cdot 1}{8 \cdot 3}$ *Multiply.*

$\frac{5}{24}$ *The answer is in simplest form.*

> **Helpful Hint**
>
> You can look for a common factor in a numerator and a denominator to determine whether you can simplify before multiplying.

B $a = \frac{9}{10}$ $a \cdot \frac{1}{3}$

$\frac{9}{10} \cdot \frac{1}{3}$ *Substitute $\frac{9}{10}$ for a.*

$\frac{\overset{3}{\cancel{9}}}{10} \cdot \frac{1}{\underset{1}{\cancel{3}}}$ *Use the GCF to simplify.*

$\frac{3 \cdot 1}{10 \cdot 1}$ *Multiply.*

$\frac{3}{10}$ *The answer is in simplest form.*

C $a = \frac{3}{4}$ $a \cdot \frac{1}{3}$

$\frac{3}{4} \cdot \frac{1}{3}$ *Substitute $\frac{3}{4}$ for a.*

$\frac{3 \cdot 1}{4 \cdot 3}$ *Multiply numerators. Multiply denominators.*

$\frac{3}{12}$ *The GCF of 3 and 12 is 3.*

$\frac{1}{4}$ *The answer is in simplest form.*

Think and Discuss   6.RP.4, 6.R.9, 6.CM.10

1. Determine whether the product of two proper fractions is greater than or less than each factor.

2. Name the missing denominator in the equation $\frac{1}{\blacksquare} \cdot \frac{2}{3} = \frac{2}{21}$.

3. Tell how to find the product of $\frac{4}{21} \cdot \frac{6}{10}$ in two different ways.

5-7 **Exercises**

go.hrw.com
Homework Help Online
KEYWORD: MR7 5-7
Parent Resources Online
KEYWORD: MR7 Parent

GUIDED PRACTICE

See Example **1** Multiply. Write each answer in simplest form.

1. $\frac{1}{2} \cdot \frac{1}{3}$
2. $\frac{2}{5} \cdot \frac{1}{4}$
3. $\frac{4}{7} \cdot \frac{3}{4}$
4. $\frac{5}{6} \cdot \frac{3}{5}$

See Example **2** Evaluate the expression $b \cdot \frac{1}{5}$ for each value of b. Write the answer in simplest form.

5. $b = \frac{2}{3}$
6. $b = \frac{5}{8}$
7. $b = \frac{1}{4}$
8. $b = \frac{3}{5}$

INDEPENDENT PRACTICE

See Example **1** Multiply. Write each answer in simplest form.

9. $\frac{1}{3} \cdot \frac{2}{7}$
10. $\frac{1}{3} \cdot \frac{1}{5}$
11. $\frac{5}{6} \cdot \frac{2}{3}$
12. $\frac{1}{3} \cdot \frac{6}{7}$

13. $\frac{3}{10} \cdot \frac{5}{6}$
14. $\frac{7}{9} \cdot \frac{3}{5}$
15. $\frac{1}{2} \cdot \frac{10}{11}$
16. $\frac{3}{5} \cdot \frac{3}{4}$

See Example **2** Evaluate the expression $x \cdot \frac{1}{6}$ for each value of x. Write the answer in simplest form.

17. $x = \frac{4}{5}$
18. $x = \frac{6}{7}$
19. $x = \frac{3}{4}$
20. $x = \frac{5}{6}$

21. $x = \frac{8}{9}$
22. $x = \frac{9}{10}$
23. $x = \frac{5}{8}$
24. $x = \frac{3}{8}$

PRACTICE AND PROBLEM SOLVING

Extra Practice
See page 723.

Find each product. Simplify the answer.

25. $\frac{3}{5} \cdot \frac{4}{9}$
26. $\frac{5}{12} \cdot \frac{9}{10}$
27. $\frac{2}{5} \cdot \frac{2}{7} \cdot \frac{5}{8}$
28. $\frac{2}{7} \cdot \frac{1}{8}$

29. $\frac{6}{7} \cdot \frac{9}{10}$
30. $\frac{4}{9} \cdot \frac{2}{3}$
31. $\frac{1}{2} \cdot \frac{2}{5} \cdot \frac{9}{11}$
32. $\frac{1}{12} \cdot \frac{3}{7}$

33. A walnut muffin recipe calls for $\frac{3}{4}$ cup walnuts. Mrs. Hooper wants to make $\frac{1}{3}$ of the recipe. What fraction of a cup of walnuts will she need?

34. Jim spent $\frac{5}{6}$ of an hour doing chores. He spent $\frac{2}{5}$ of that time washing dishes. What fraction of an hour did he spend washing dishes?

Compare. Write $<$, $>$, or $=$.

35. $\frac{2}{3} \cdot \frac{1}{4}$ ▨ $\frac{1}{3} \cdot \frac{3}{4}$
36. $\frac{3}{5} \cdot \frac{3}{4}$ ▨ $\frac{1}{2} \cdot \frac{9}{10}$
37. $\frac{5}{6} \cdot \frac{2}{3}$ ▨ $\frac{1}{3} \cdot \frac{2}{3}$

38. $\frac{5}{8} \cdot \frac{1}{4}$ ▨ $\frac{2}{9} \cdot \frac{1}{7}$
39. $\frac{2}{5} \cdot \frac{1}{10}$ ▨ $\frac{3}{5} \cdot \frac{2}{5}$
40. $\frac{1}{2} \cdot \frac{4}{5}$ ▨ $\frac{10}{20} \cdot \frac{16}{20}$

41. A multiplying number machine uses a rule to change one fraction into another fraction. The machine changed $\frac{1}{2}$ into $\frac{1}{8}$, $\frac{1}{5}$ into $\frac{1}{20}$, and $\frac{5}{7}$ into $\frac{5}{28}$.

   a. What is the rule?

   b. Into what fraction will the machine change $\frac{1}{3}$?

42. Alex exercised for $\frac{3}{4}$ hour. He lifted weights for $\frac{1}{5}$ of that time. What fraction of an hour did he spend lifting weights?

43. **Life Science** A bat can eat half its weight in insects in one night. If a bat weighing $\frac{3}{4}$ lb eats half its weight in insects, how much do the insects weigh?

44. **Multi-Step** The number of American bison has steadily declined throughout the years. Once, 20 million bison roamed the United States. Now, there are only $\frac{1}{80}$ of that number of bison. Of those, only $\frac{8}{125}$ roam in the wild. The number of American bison currently roaming in the wild is what fraction of 20 million? How many bison is that?

45. The seating plan shows Oak School's theater. The front section has $\frac{3}{4}$ of the seats, and the rear section has $\frac{1}{4}$ of the seats. The school has reserved $\frac{1}{2}$ of the seats in the front section for students. What fraction of the seating is reserved for students?

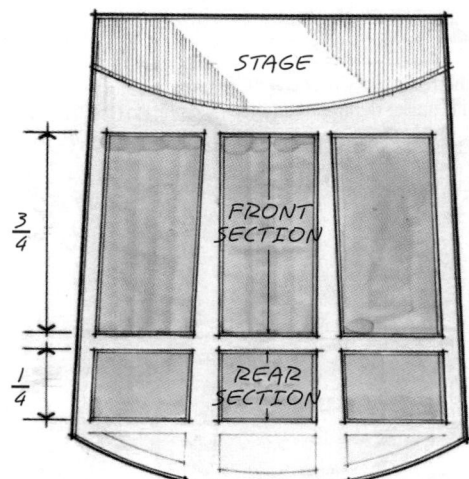

 $\frac{3}{4}$

 $\frac{1}{4}$

46. **Write a Problem** Use the seating plan to write a problem in which you need to multiply two fractions. Then solve the problem.

47. **Write About It** Explain how you can use the GCF before multiplying so that the product of two fractions is in simplest form.

48. **Challenge** Evaluate the expression. Then simplify your answer.

$$\frac{(2+6)}{5} \cdot \frac{1}{4} \cdot 6$$

TEST PREP and Spiral Review

49. **Multiple Choice** Which shows the product of $\frac{4}{5}$ and $\frac{3}{5}$ in simplest form?

Ⓐ $1\frac{2}{5}$ Ⓑ $1\frac{1}{3}$ Ⓒ $\frac{3}{5}$ Ⓓ $\frac{12}{25}$

50. **Multiple Choice** Julie spent $\frac{1}{3}$ of her birthday money on new clothes. She spent $\frac{3}{10}$ of that money on shoes. What fraction of her birthday money did Julie spend on shoes?

Ⓕ $\frac{1}{30}$ Ⓖ $\frac{1}{10}$ Ⓗ $\frac{2}{15}$ Ⓚ $\frac{3}{13}$

Solve each equation. (Lesson 2-7)

51. $15n = 45$ **52.** $7t = 147$ **53.** $6a = 78$ **54.** $12b = 216$

Find each sum or difference. (Lesson 5-2)

55. $\frac{1}{9} + \frac{1}{3}$ **56.** $\frac{11}{12} - \frac{5}{6}$ **57.** $\frac{2}{7} + \frac{6}{21}$ **58.** $\frac{1}{5} + \frac{3}{10} - \frac{1}{15}$

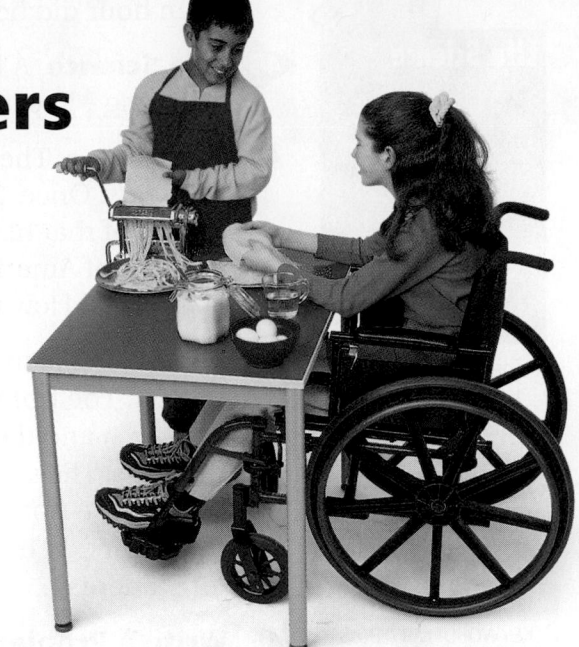

5-8 Multiplying Mixed Numbers

Learn to multiply mixed numbers.

 NY Performance Indicators

6.N.18 Multiply mixed numbers with unlike denominators. Also, 6.N.17.

Janice and Carlos are making homemade pasta from a recipe that calls for $1\frac{1}{2}$ cups of flour. They want to make $\frac{1}{3}$ of the recipe.

You can find $\frac{1}{3}$ of $1\frac{1}{2}$, or multiply $\frac{1}{3}$ by $1\frac{1}{2}$, to find how much flour Janice and Carlos need.

EXAMPLE 1 Multiplying Fractions and Mixed Numbers

Multiply. Write each answer in simplest form.

> **Remember!**
>
> To write a mixed number as an improper fraction, start with the denominator, multiply by the whole number, and add the numerator. Use the same denominator.
>
> $1\frac{1}{5} = \frac{1 \cdot 5 + 1}{5} = \frac{6}{5}$

A $\frac{1}{3} \cdot 1\frac{1}{2}$

$\frac{1}{3} \cdot \frac{3}{2}$ *Write $1\frac{1}{2}$ as an improper fraction. $1\frac{1}{2} = \frac{3}{2}$*

$\frac{1 \cdot 3}{3 \cdot 2}$ *Multiply numerators. Multiply denominators.*

$\frac{3}{6}$

$\frac{1}{2}$ *Write the answer in simplest form.*

B $1\frac{1}{5} \cdot \frac{2}{3}$

$\frac{6}{5} \cdot \frac{2}{3}$ *Write $1\frac{1}{5}$ as an improper fraction. $1\frac{1}{5} = \frac{6}{5}$*

$\frac{6 \cdot 2}{5 \cdot 3}$ *Multiply numerators. Multiply denominators.*

$\frac{12}{15}$

$\frac{4}{5}$ *Write the answer in simplest form.*

C $\frac{3}{4} \cdot 2\frac{1}{3}$

$\frac{3}{4} \cdot \frac{7}{3}$ *Write $2\frac{1}{3}$ as an improper fraction. $2\frac{1}{3} = \frac{7}{3}$*

$\frac{\overset{1}{\cancel{3}}}{4} \cdot \frac{7}{\underset{1}{\cancel{3}}}$ *Use the GCF to simplify before multiplying.*

$\frac{1 \cdot 7}{4 \cdot 1}$

$\frac{7}{4} = 1\frac{3}{4}$ *You can write the answer as a mixed number.*

EXAMPLE **2** **Multiplying Mixed Numbers**

Find each product. Write the answer in simplest form.

A $2\frac{1}{2} \cdot 1\frac{1}{3}$

$\dfrac{5}{2} \cdot \dfrac{4}{3}$ *Write the mixed numbers as improper fractions.* $2\frac{1}{2} = \frac{5}{2}$ $1\frac{1}{3} = \frac{4}{3}$

$\dfrac{5 \cdot 4}{2 \cdot 3}$ *Multiply numerators.*
Multiply denominators.

$\dfrac{20}{6}$

$3\dfrac{2}{6}$ *Write the improper fraction as a mixed number.*

$3\dfrac{1}{3}$ *Simplify.*

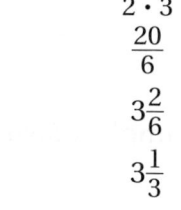

B $1\frac{1}{4} \cdot 1\frac{1}{3}$

$\dfrac{5}{4} \cdot \dfrac{4}{3}$ *Write the mixed numbers as improper fractions.* $1\frac{1}{4} = \frac{5}{4}$ $1\frac{1}{3} = \frac{4}{3}$

$\dfrac{5}{\underset{1}{\cancel{4}}} \cdot \dfrac{\overset{1}{\cancel{4}}}{3}$ *Use the GCF to simplify before multiplying.*

$\dfrac{5 \cdot 1}{1 \cdot 3}$ *Multiply numerators. Multiply denominators.*

$\dfrac{5}{3}$

$1\dfrac{2}{3}$ *Write the answer as a mixed number.*

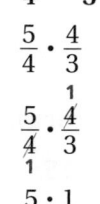

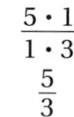

C $5 \cdot 3\frac{2}{11}$

$5 \cdot 3\dfrac{2}{11}$

$5 \cdot \left(3 + \dfrac{2}{11}\right)$

$(5 \cdot 3) + \left(5 \cdot \dfrac{2}{11}\right)$ *Use the Distributive Property.*

$(5 \cdot 3) + \left(\dfrac{5}{1} \cdot \dfrac{2}{11}\right)$

$15 + \dfrac{10}{11}$ *Multiply.*

$15\dfrac{10}{11}$ *Add.*

Think and Discuss

 6.CM.1, 6.CM.10, 6.CN.3

1. Tell how you multiply a mixed number by a mixed number.

2. Explain two ways you would multiply a mixed number by a whole number.

3. Tell how multiplying mixed numbers is similar to multiplying fractions.

5-8
Exercises

go.hrw.com
Homework Help Online
KEYWORD: MR7 5-8
Parent Resources Online
KEYWORD: MR7 Parent

GUIDED PRACTICE

See Example 1 Multiply. Write each answer in simplest form.

1. $1\frac{1}{4} \cdot \frac{2}{3}$

2. $2\frac{2}{3} \cdot \frac{1}{4}$

3. $\frac{3}{7} \cdot 1\frac{5}{6}$

4. $1\frac{1}{3} \cdot \frac{6}{7}$

5. $\frac{2}{3} \cdot 1\frac{3}{10}$

6. $2\frac{6}{11} \cdot \frac{2}{7}$

See Example 2 Find each product. Write the answer in simplest form.

7. $1\frac{5}{6} \cdot 1\frac{1}{8}$

8. $2\frac{2}{5} \cdot 1\frac{1}{12}$

9. $4 \cdot 5\frac{3}{7}$

10. $2\frac{3}{4} \cdot 1\frac{5}{6}$

11. $2\frac{3}{8} \cdot 5\frac{1}{5}$

12. $10\frac{1}{2} \cdot 1\frac{1}{4}$

INDEPENDENT PRACTICE

See Example 1 Multiply. Write each answer in simplest form.

13. $1\frac{1}{4} \cdot \frac{3}{4}$

14. $\frac{4}{7} \cdot 1\frac{1}{4}$

15. $1\frac{1}{6} \cdot \frac{2}{5}$

16. $2\frac{1}{6} \cdot \frac{3}{7}$

17. $\frac{5}{9} \cdot 1\frac{9}{10}$

18. $2\frac{2}{9} \cdot \frac{3}{5}$

19. $1\frac{3}{10} \cdot \frac{5}{7}$

20. $\frac{3}{4} \cdot 1\frac{2}{5}$

See Example 2 Find each product. Write the answer in simplest form.

21. $1\frac{1}{3} \cdot 1\frac{5}{7}$

22. $1\frac{2}{3} \cdot 2\frac{3}{10}$

23. $4 \cdot 3\frac{7}{8}$

24. $6 \cdot 2\frac{1}{3}$

25. $5 \cdot 4\frac{7}{10}$

26. $2\frac{2}{3} \cdot 3\frac{5}{8}$

27. $1\frac{1}{2} \cdot 2\frac{2}{5}$

28. $3\frac{5}{6} \cdot 2\frac{3}{4}$

PRACTICE AND PROBLEM SOLVING

Extra Practice
See page 723.

Write each product in simplest form.

29. $1\frac{2}{3} \cdot \frac{2}{9}$

30. $3\frac{1}{3} \cdot \frac{7}{10}$

31. $2 \cdot \frac{5}{8}$

32. $2\frac{8}{11} \cdot \frac{3}{10}$

33. $\frac{3}{8} \cdot \frac{4}{9}$

34. $2\frac{1}{12} \cdot 1\frac{3}{5}$

35. $3\frac{3}{10} \cdot 4\frac{1}{6}$

36. $2\frac{1}{4} \cdot 1\frac{2}{9}$

37. $2 \cdot \frac{4}{5} \cdot 1\frac{2}{3}$

38. $3\frac{5}{6} \cdot \frac{9}{10} \cdot 4\frac{2}{3}$

39. $1\frac{7}{8} \cdot 2\frac{1}{3} \cdot 4$

40. $1\frac{2}{7} \cdot 3 \cdot 2\frac{5}{8}$

41. Multi-Step Jared used $1\frac{2}{5}$ bags of soil for his garden. He is digging another garden that will need $\frac{1}{5}$ as much soil as the original. How much will he use total?

42. Milo is making $1\frac{1}{2}$ batches of muffins. If one batch calls for $1\frac{3}{4}$ cups flour, how much flour will he need?

43. Critical Thinking Is the product of two mixed numbers always greater than 1? Explain.

Evaluate each expression.

44. $\frac{1}{2} \cdot c$ for $c = 4\frac{2}{5}$

45. $1\frac{5}{7} \cdot x$ for $x = \frac{5}{6}$

46. $1\frac{3}{4} \cdot b$ for $b = 1\frac{1}{7}$

47. $1\frac{5}{9} \cdot n$ for $n = 18$

48. $2\frac{5}{9} \cdot t$ for $t = 4$

49. $3\frac{3}{4} \cdot p$ for $p = \frac{1}{2}$

50. $\frac{4}{5} \cdot m$ for $m = 2\frac{2}{3}$

51. $6y$ for $y = 3\frac{5}{8}$

52. $2\frac{3}{5} \cdot c$ for $c = 1\frac{1}{5}$

In a survey, 240 people were asked how many hours per week they spend using the Internet. The circle graph shows which fractions of the people use the Internet for which amounts of time.

Use the graph for Exercises 54–58.

53. How many people in all were surveyed?

54. Find the number of people who said they use the Internet for 12 hours to 24 hours a week.

55. Toni's grandfather uses the Internet for $1\frac{1}{2}$ hours each day.

    a. How many hours does he use the Internet in one week? (Write the answer as a mixed number.)

    b. If Toni's grandfather were included in the survey, in which time section of the circle graph would his data be?

56. 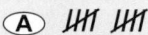 **Choose a Strategy** Which set of tallies could represent the number of people who use the Internet for fewer than 12 hours a week?

    Ⓐ ⅄⅄⅄ ⅄⅄⅄   Ⓑ ⅄⅄⅄ ⅄⅄⅄ ‖   Ⓒ ⅄⅄⅄ ⅄⅄⅄ ⅄⅄⅄ ⅄⅄⅄   Ⓓ ⅄⅄⅄ ⅄⅄⅄ ⅄⅄⅄ ⅄⅄⅄ ‖‖‖‖

57. **Write About It** Explain how you can find the number of people surveyed who use the Internet for more than 36 hours a week.

58. **Challenge** Five-sixths of the people who use the Internet for 25 hours to 36 hours said they use it for 30 hours each week. Find the number of people who use the Internet for 30 hours each week.

Using the Internet

More than 36 hr   12 hr to 24 hr

$\frac{1}{4}$ $\frac{1}{3}$

$\frac{3}{8}$

Less than 12 hr   25 hr to 36 hr
$\frac{1}{24}$

go.hrw.com
Web Extra!
KEYWORD: MR7 Internet

 **TEST PREP and Spiral Review**

59. **Multiple Choice** A chef uses $2\frac{1}{4}$ cups of water for a recipe. The chef doubled the recipe. How much water did the chef use?

    Ⓐ 4 cups   Ⓑ $4\frac{1}{4}$ cups   Ⓒ $4\frac{1}{2}$ cups   Ⓓ $4\frac{3}{4}$ cups

60. **Gridded Response** Keith ate $\frac{1}{3}$ pound of grapes last week. Jamal ate five times as many grapes as Keith last week. How many pounds of grapes did Jamal eat?

Write each number in scientific notation. (Lesson 3-4)

61. 540   62. 1,400   63. 54,000   64. 508,000,000

Multiply. Write each answer in simplest form. (Lesson 5-6)

65. $5 \times \frac{1}{10}$ 66. $21 \times \frac{1}{3}$ 67. $\frac{2}{7} \times 14$ 68. $\frac{5}{12} \times 2$

Model Fraction Division

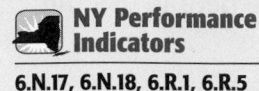
NY Performance Indicators
6.N.17, 6.N.18, 6.R.1, 6.R.5

go.hrw.com
Lab Resources Online
KEYWORD: MR7 Lab5

You can use grids to help you understand division of fractions.

Activity 1

Find $4\frac{1}{2} \div 3$.

Think of $4\frac{1}{2} \div 3$ as dividing $4\frac{1}{2}$ into 3 equal groups.

Shade $4\frac{1}{2}$ squares.

Divide the shaded parts into 3 equal groups.

Look at one of the shaded groups.

What fraction is this?

$$4\frac{1}{2} \div 3 = 1\frac{1}{2}$$

Think and Discuss

1. Explain how you know the number of groups into which you must divide the squares.

Try This

Write the division expression modeled on each grid.

1. 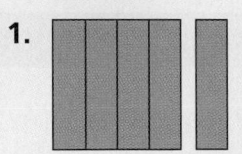 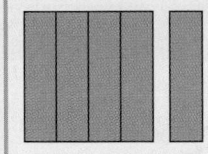  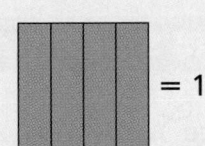 = 1

Draw a model for each division expression. Then find the value of the expression.

2. $9\frac{1}{3} \div 4$ **3.** $3\frac{3}{4} \div 5$ **4.** $4\frac{2}{3} \div 2$ **5.** $4\frac{1}{5} \div 3$

Activity 2

❶ Find $2\frac{2}{3} \div \frac{2}{3}$.

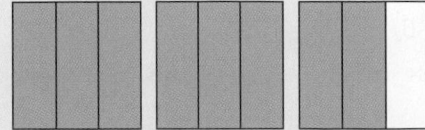

Shade $2\frac{2}{3}$ squares.

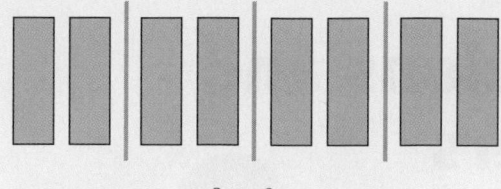

Divide the shaded squares and shaded thirds into equal groups of $\frac{2}{3}$.

There are 4 groups of $\frac{2}{3}$ in $2\frac{2}{3}$.

$$2\frac{2}{3} \div \frac{2}{3} = 4$$

2

To find $3 \div \frac{3}{4}$, think, "How many groups of $\frac{3}{4}$ are in 3?"

Shade 3 squares. Then divide the squares into fourths because the denominator of $\frac{3}{4}$ is 4.

Divide the shaded squares into equal groups of $\frac{3}{4}$.

There are 4 groups of $\frac{3}{4}$ in 3.

$$3 \div \frac{3}{4} = 4$$

Think and Discuss

1. Explain what prediction you can make about the value of $6 \div \frac{3}{4}$ if you know that $3 \div \frac{3}{4}$ is 4.

Try This

Write the division expression modeled by each grid.

1. 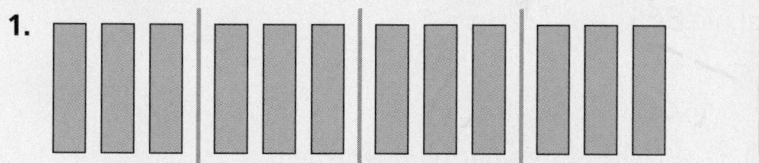 = 1

2. 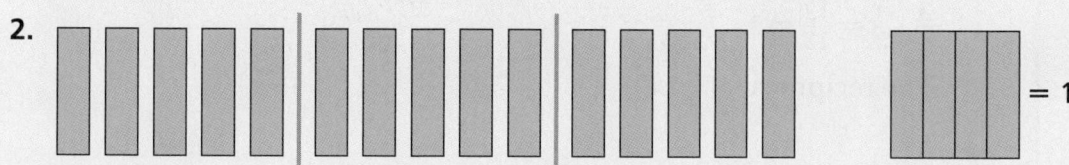 = 1

Draw a model for each division expression. Then find the value of the expression.

3. $4 \div 1\frac{1}{3}$ 4. $3\frac{3}{4} \div \frac{3}{4}$ 5. $5\frac{1}{3} \div \frac{2}{3}$ 6. $6\frac{2}{3} \div 1\frac{2}{3}$

5-9 Dividing Fractions and Mixed Numbers

**Learn** to divide fractions and mixed numbers.

Vocabulary

reciprocal

NY Performance Indicators

6.N.19 Identify the multiplicative inverse (reciprocal) of a number. Also, 6.N.17, 6.N.18.

Curtis is making sushi rolls. First, he will place a sheet of seaweed, called *nori,* on the sushi rolling mat. Then, he will use the mat to roll up rice, cucumber, avocado, and crabmeat. Finally, he will slice the roll into smaller pieces.

Curtis has 2 cups of rice and will use $\frac{1}{3}$ cup for each sushi roll. How many sushi rolls can he make?

Think: How many $\frac{1}{3}$ pieces equal 2 wholes?

There are six $\frac{1}{3}$ pieces in 2 wholes.

Curtis can make 6 sushi rolls.

Reciprocals can help you divide by fractions. Two numbers are **reciprocals** if their product is 1.

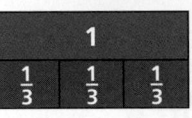

EXAMPLE 1 Finding Reciprocals

Find the reciprocal.

A $\frac{1}{5}$

$\frac{1}{5} \cdot \blacksquare = 1$ *Think: $\frac{1}{5}$ of what number is 1?*

$\frac{1}{5} \cdot 5 = 1$ *$\frac{1}{5}$ of $\frac{5}{1}$ is 1.*

The reciprocal of $\frac{1}{5}$ is 5.

B $\frac{3}{4}$

$\frac{3}{4} \cdot \blacksquare = 1$ *Think: $\frac{3}{4}$ of what number is 1?*

$\frac{3}{4} \cdot \frac{4}{3} = \frac{12}{12} = 1$ *$\frac{3}{4}$ of $\frac{4}{3}$ is 1.*

The reciprocal of $\frac{3}{4}$ is $\frac{4}{3}$.

C $2\frac{1}{3}$

$\frac{7}{3} \cdot \blacksquare = 1$ *Write $2\frac{1}{3}$ as $\frac{7}{3}$.*

$\frac{7}{3} \cdot \frac{3}{7} = \frac{21}{21} = 1$ *$\frac{7}{3}$ of $\frac{3}{7}$ is 1.*

The reciprocal of $\frac{7}{3}$ is $\frac{3}{7}$.

Look at the relationship between the fractions $\frac{3}{4}$ and $\frac{4}{3}$. If you switch the numerator and denominator of a fraction, you will find its reciprocal. Dividing by a number is the same as multiplying by its reciprocal.

$$24 \div 4 = 6 \qquad 24 \cdot \frac{1}{4} = 6$$

EXAMPLE 2 **Using Reciprocals to Divide Fractions and Mixed Numbers**

Divide. Write each answer in simplest form.

A $\frac{4}{5} \div 5$

$\frac{4}{5} \div 5 = \frac{4}{5} \cdot \frac{1}{5}$ *Rewrite as multiplication using the reciprocal of 5, $\frac{1}{5}$.*

$= \frac{4 \cdot 1}{5 \cdot 5}$ *Multiply by the reciprocal.*

$= \frac{4}{25}$ *The answer is in simplest form.*

B $\frac{3}{4} \div \frac{1}{2}$

$\frac{3}{4} \div \frac{1}{2} = \frac{3}{4} \cdot \frac{2}{1}$ *Rewrite as multiplication using the reciprocal of $\frac{1}{2}$, $\frac{2}{1}$.*

$= \frac{3 \cdot \overset{1}{\cancel{2}}}{\underset{2}{\cancel{4}} \cdot 1}$ *Simplify before multiplying.*

$= \frac{3}{2}$ *Multiply.*

$= 1\frac{1}{2}$ *You can write the answer as a mixed number.*

C $2\frac{2}{3} \div 1\frac{1}{6}$

$2\frac{2}{3} \div 1\frac{1}{6} = \frac{8}{3} \div \frac{7}{6}$ *Write the mixed numbers as improper fractions. $2\frac{2}{3} = \frac{8}{3}$ and $1\frac{1}{6} = \frac{7}{6}$*

$= \frac{8}{3} \cdot \frac{6}{7}$ *Rewrite as multiplication.*

$= \frac{8 \cdot \overset{2}{\cancel{6}}}{\underset{1}{\cancel{3}} \cdot 7}$ *Simplify before multiplying.*

$= \frac{16}{7}$ *Multiply.*

$= 2\frac{2}{7}$ *You can write the answer as a mixed number.*

Think and Discuss

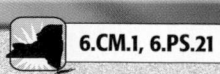
6.CM.1, 6.PS.21

1. Explain how you can use mental math to find the value of n in the equation $\frac{5}{8} \cdot n = 1$.

2. Explain how to find the reciprocal of $3\frac{6}{11}$.

go.hrw.com
Homework Help Online
KEYWORD: MR7 5-9
Parent Resources Online
KEYWORD: MR7 Parent

GUIDED PRACTICE

See Example 1   Find the reciprocal.

1. $\frac{2}{7}$ 2. $\frac{5}{9}$ 3. $\frac{1}{9}$ 4. $\frac{3}{11}$ 5. $2\frac{3}{5}$

See Example 2   Divide. Write each answer in simplest form.

6. $\frac{5}{6} \div 3$ 7. $2\frac{1}{7} \div 1\frac{1}{4}$ 8. $\frac{5}{12} \div 5$ 9. $1\frac{5}{8} \div \frac{3}{4}$

10. $\frac{2}{3} \div \frac{1}{6}$ 11. $\frac{3}{10} \div 1\frac{2}{3}$ 12. $\frac{4}{7} \div 1\frac{1}{7}$ 13. $4 \div \frac{7}{8}$

INDEPENDENT PRACTICE

See Example 1   Find the reciprocal.

14. $\frac{7}{8}$ 15. $\frac{1}{10}$ 16. $\frac{3}{8}$ 17. $\frac{11}{12}$ 18. $2\frac{5}{8}$

19. $\frac{8}{11}$ 20. $\frac{5}{6}$ 21. $\frac{6}{7}$ 22. $\frac{2}{9}$ 23. $5\frac{1}{4}$

See Example 2   Divide. Write each answer in simplest form.

24. $\frac{7}{8} \div 4$ 25. $2\frac{3}{8} \div 1\frac{3}{4}$ 26. $\frac{8}{9} \div 12$ 27. $9 \div \frac{3}{4}$

28. $3\frac{5}{6} \div 1\frac{5}{9}$ 29. $\frac{9}{10} \div 3$ 30. $2\frac{4}{5} \div 1\frac{5}{7}$ 31. $3\frac{1}{5} \div 1\frac{2}{7}$

32. $\frac{5}{8} \div \frac{1}{2}$ 33. $1\frac{1}{2} \div 2\frac{1}{4}$ 34. $\frac{7}{12} \div 2\frac{5}{8}$ 35. $\frac{1}{8} \div 5$

PRACTICE AND PROBLEM SOLVING

Extra Practice
See page 723.

Multiply or divide. Write each answer in simplest form.

36. $2\frac{3}{4} \div 2\frac{1}{5}$ 37. $4\frac{4}{5} \div 2\frac{6}{7}$ 38. $\frac{3}{8} \cdot \frac{5}{12}$

39. $6 \cdot \frac{7}{9}$ 40. $3\frac{1}{7} \div 5$ 41. $\frac{9}{14} \cdot \frac{1}{6}$

42. At Lina's restaurant, one serving of chili is $1\frac{1}{2}$ cups. The chef makes 48 cups of chili each night. How many servings of chili are in 48 cups?

43. Rhula bought 12 lb of raisins. She packed them into freezer bags so that each bag weighs $\frac{3}{4}$ lb. How many freezer bags did she pack?

Decide whether the fractions in each pair are reciprocals. If not, write the reciprocal of each fraction.

44. $\frac{1}{2}, 2$ 45. $\frac{3}{8}, \frac{16}{6}$ 46. $\frac{7}{9}, \frac{21}{27}$ 47. $\frac{5}{6}, \frac{12}{10}$

48. $1\frac{1}{2}, \frac{2}{3}$ 49. $\frac{2}{5}, \frac{4}{25}$ 50. $\frac{3}{7}, 2\frac{1}{3}$ 51. $5, \frac{5}{1}$

52. Lisa had some wood that was $12\frac{1}{2}$ feet long. She cut it into 5 pieces that are equal in length. How long is each piece of wood?

53. **Critical Thinking** How can you recognize the reciprocal of a fraction?

Multiply or divide. Write each answer in simplest form.

54. $\frac{11}{12} \cdot \frac{9}{10} \div 1\frac{1}{4}$

55. $2\frac{3}{4} \cdot 1\frac{2}{3} \div 5$

56. $1\frac{1}{2} \div \frac{3}{4} \cdot \frac{2}{5}$

57. $\frac{3}{4} \cdot \left(\frac{5}{7} \div \frac{1}{2}\right)$

58. $4\frac{2}{3} \div \left(6 \cdot \frac{3}{5}\right)$

59. $5\frac{1}{5} \cdot \left(3\frac{2}{5} \cdot 2\frac{1}{3}\right)$

Life Science The bar graph shows the lengths of some species of snakes found in the United States. Use the bar graph for Exercises 60–62.

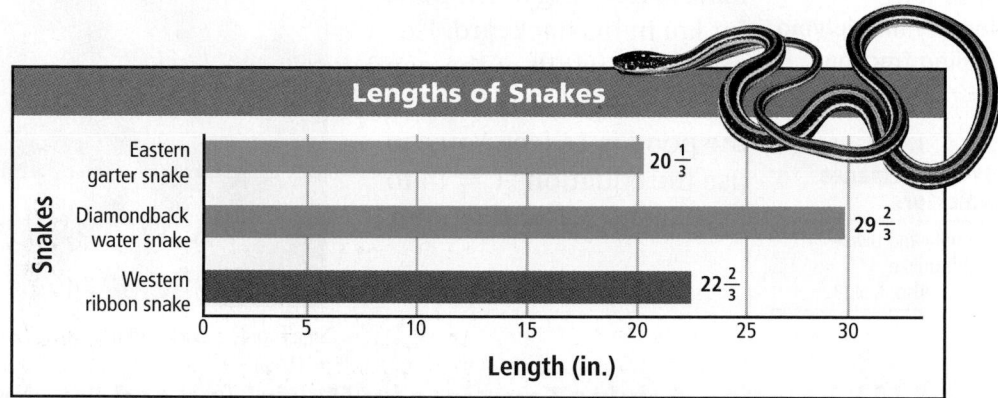

60. Is the length of the eastern garter snake greater than or less than $\frac{1}{2}$ yd? Explain.

61. What is the average length of all the snakes?

62. Jim measured the length of a rough green snake. It was $27\frac{1}{3}$ in. long. What would the average length of the snakes be if Jim's measure of a rough green snake were added?

 63. What's the Error? A student said the reciprocal of $6\frac{2}{3}$ is $6\frac{3}{2}$. Explain the error. Then write the correct reciprocal.

 64. Write About It Explain how to divide fractions to find $\frac{3}{4} \div 2\frac{1}{3}$.

 65. Challenge Evaluate the expression $\frac{(6-3)}{4} \div \frac{1}{8} \cdot 5$.

TEST PREP and Spiral Review

66. Multiple Choice A piece of wood was 12 feet long. Gene cut the wood into pieces $\frac{2}{3}$ foot long. How many pieces did Gene have?

Ⓐ 4   Ⓑ 8   Ⓒ 16   Ⓓ 18

67. Multiple Choice Which product is NOT equal to 1?

Ⓕ $\frac{2}{3} \cdot \frac{3}{2}$ Ⓖ $8 \cdot \frac{1}{8}$ Ⓗ $\frac{1}{9} \cdot \frac{9}{3}$ Ⓙ $\frac{2}{13} \cdot \frac{13}{2}$

Find the number of decimal places in each product. Then multiply. (Lesson 3-5)

68. 2.4×1.8 **69.** 19×0.5 **70.** 7.04×2.3 **71.** 0.4×0.1

Find each product. (Lesson 5-8)

72. $2\frac{2}{3} \cdot \frac{1}{8}$ **73.** $\frac{1}{4} \cdot 3\frac{1}{2}$ **74.** $1\frac{1}{4} \cdot 1\frac{2}{5}$ **75.** $2\frac{1}{5} \cdot 2\frac{2}{3}$

Learn to solve equations by multiplying and dividing fractions.

NY Performance Indicators

6.N.17 Multiply and divide fractions with unlike denominators. Also, 6.N.18.

Josef is building a fish pond for koi in his backyard. He makes the width of the pond $\frac{2}{3}$ of the length. The width of the pond is 14 feet. You can use the equation $\frac{2}{3}\ell = 14$ to find the length of the pond.

Small koi in a backyard pond usually grow 2 to 4 inches per year.

EXAMPLE 1 Solving Equations by Multiplying and Dividing

Solve each equation. Write the answer in simplest form.

A $\frac{2}{3}\ell = 14$

$$\frac{2}{3}\ell = 14$$

$$\frac{2}{3}\ell \div \frac{2}{3} = 14 \div \frac{2}{3} \qquad \textit{Divide both sides of the equation by } \frac{2}{3}.$$

$$\frac{2}{3}\ell \cdot \frac{3}{2} = 14 \cdot \frac{3}{2} \qquad \textit{Multiply by } \frac{3}{2}, \textit{ the reciprocal of } \frac{2}{3}.$$

$$\ell = 14 \cdot \frac{3}{2}$$

$$\ell = \frac{14 \cdot 3}{1 \cdot 2}$$

$$\ell = \frac{42}{2}, \text{ or } 21$$

Remember!

Dividing by a number is the same as multiplying by its reciprocal.

B $2x = \frac{1}{3}$

$$2x = \frac{1}{3}$$

$$\frac{2x}{1} \cdot \frac{1}{2} = \frac{1}{3} \cdot \frac{1}{2} \qquad \textit{Multiply both sides by the reciprocal of 2.}$$

$$x = \frac{1 \cdot 1}{3 \cdot 2}$$

$$x = \frac{1}{6} \qquad \textit{The answer is in simplest form.}$$

C $\frac{5x}{6} = 4$

$$\frac{5x}{6} = 4$$

$$\frac{5x}{6} \div \frac{5}{6} = \frac{4}{1} \div \frac{5}{6} \qquad \textit{Divide both sides by } \frac{5}{6}.$$

$$\frac{5x}{6} \cdot \frac{6}{5} = \frac{4}{1} \cdot \frac{6}{5} \qquad \textit{Multiply by the reciprocal of } \frac{5}{6}.$$

$$x = \frac{24}{5}, \text{ or } 4\frac{4}{5}$$

EXAMPLE 2

PROBLEM SOLVING

Life Science

No more than $\frac{1}{10}$ of a dog's diet should consist of treats and biscuits.

PROBLEM SOLVING APPLICATION

Dexter makes dog biscuits for the animal shelter. He makes $\frac{3}{4}$ of a recipe and uses 15 cups of powdered milk. How many cups of powdered milk are in the recipe?

1 Understand the Problem

The **answer** will be the number of cups of powdered milk in the recipe.

List the **important information:**

- He makes $\frac{3}{4}$ of the recipe.
- He uses 15 cups of powdered milk.

2 Make a Plan

You can write and solve an equation. Let x represent the number of cups in the recipe.

He uses 15 cups, which is three-fourths of the amount in the recipe. $15 = \frac{3}{4}x$

3 Solve

$$15 = \frac{3}{4}x$$

$$15 \cdot \frac{4}{3} = \frac{3}{4}x \cdot \frac{4}{3} \qquad \textit{Multiply both sides by } \frac{4}{3}, \textit{ the reciprocal of } \frac{3}{4}.$$

$$\overset{5}{\underset{1}{\frac{15}{1}}} \cdot \frac{4}{\underset{1}{3}} = x \qquad \textit{Simplify. Then multiply.}$$

$$20 = x$$

There are 20 cups of powdered milk in the recipe.

4 Look Back

Check $15 = \frac{3}{4}x$

$$15 \overset{?}{=} \frac{3}{4}(20) \qquad \textit{Substitute 20 for x.}$$

$$15 \overset{?}{=} \frac{\overset{15}{60}}{\underset{1}{4}} \qquad \textit{Multiply and simplify.}$$

$$15 \overset{?}{=} 15 \checkmark \qquad \textit{20 is the solution.}$$

Think and Discuss

 6.CM.1, 6.CM.10

1. **Explain** whether $\frac{2}{3}x = 4$ is the same as $\frac{2}{3} = 4x$.

2. **Tell** how you know which numbers to divide by in the following equations: $\frac{2}{3}x = 4$ and $\frac{4}{5} = 8x$.

go.hrw.com
Homework Help Online
KEYWORD: MR7 5-10
Parent Resources Online
KEYWORD: MR7 Parent

GUIDED PRACTICE

See Example 1 Solve each equation. Write the answer in simplest form.

1. $\frac{3}{4}z = 12$ **2.** $4n = \frac{3}{5}$ **3.** $\frac{2x}{3} = 5$ **4.** $2c = \frac{9}{10}$

See Example 2 **5. School** In PE class, $\frac{3}{8}$ of the students want to play volleyball. If 9 students want to play volleyball, how many students are in the class?

INDEPENDENT PRACTICE

See Example 1 Solve each equation. Write the answer in simplest form.

6. $3t = \frac{2}{7}$ **7.** $\frac{1}{3}x = 3$ **8.** $\frac{3r}{5} = 9$ **9.** $8t = \frac{4}{5}$

10. $\frac{4}{5}a = 1$ **11.** $\frac{y}{4} = 5$ **12.** $2b = \frac{6}{7}$ **13.** $\frac{7}{9}j = 10$

See Example 2 **14.** Jason uses 2 cans of paint to paint $\frac{1}{2}$ of his room. How many cans of paint will he use to paint the whole room?

15. Cassandra baby-sits for $\frac{4}{5}$ of an hour and earns $8. What is her hourly rate?

PRACTICE AND PROBLEM SOLVING

Extra Practice
See page 723.

Solve each equation. Write the answer in simplest form.

16. $m = \frac{3}{8} \cdot 4$ **17.** $\frac{3y}{5} = 6$ **18.** $4z = \frac{7}{10}$ **19.** $t = \frac{4}{5} \cdot 20$

20. $\frac{3}{5}a = \frac{3}{5}$ **21.** $\frac{1}{6}b = 2\frac{1}{3}$ **22.** $5c = \frac{2}{3} \div \frac{2}{3}$ **23.** $\frac{3}{4}x = 7$

24. $\frac{1}{2} = \frac{w}{4}$ **25.** $8 = \frac{2n}{3}$ **26.** $\frac{1}{4} \cdot \frac{1}{2} = 4d$ **27.** $2y = \frac{4}{5} \div \frac{3}{5}$

Write each equation. Then solve, and check the solution.

28. A number n is divided by 4 and the quotient is $\frac{1}{2}$.

29. A number n is multiplied by $1\frac{1}{2}$ and the product is 9.

30. A recipe for a loaf of bread calls for $\frac{3}{4}$ cup of oatmeal.
   a. How much oatmeal do you need if you make half the recipe?
   b. How much oatmeal do you need if you double the recipe?

31. Entertainment Connie rode the roller coaster at the amusement park. After 3 minutes, the ride was $\frac{3}{4}$ complete. How long did the entire ride take?

32. Zac moved $\frac{1}{5}$ of the things from his old bedroom to his new dorm room in $32\frac{1}{2}$ minutes. How long will it take in minutes for him to move all of his things to his new dorm room?

33. A dress pattern requires $3\frac{1}{8}$ yards of fabric. Jody wants to make matching dresses for the girls in her sewing club so she purchased $34\frac{3}{8}$ yards of fabric. How many dresses can Jody make using this pattern?

34. **Multi-Step** Alder cut 3 pieces of fabric from a roll. Each piece of fabric she cut is $1\frac{1}{2}$ yd long. She has 2 yards of fabric left on the roll. How much fabric was on the roll before she cut it?

35. **Life Science** Sasha's book report is about animals in Madagascar. She writes 10 pages, which represents $\frac{1}{3}$ of her report, about lemurs. How many more pages does Sasha have to write to complete her book report?

36. **Critical Thinking** How can you tell, without solving the equation $\frac{1}{2}x = 4\frac{7}{8}$, that x is greater that $4\frac{7}{8}$?

The northwest corner of Madagascar is home to black lemurs. These primates live in groups of 7–10, and they have an average life span of 20–25 years. Much of their habitat is being destroyed by human agricultural activity.

Use the circle graph for Exercises 37 and 38.

37. The circle graph shows the results of a survey of people who were asked to choose their favorite kind of bagel.

    a. One hundred people chose plain bagels as their favorite kind of bagel. How many people were surveyed in all?

    b. One-fifth of the people who chose sesame bagels also chose plain cream cheese as their favorite spread. How many people chose plain cream cheese? (*Hint*: Use the answer to part **a** to help you solve this problem.)

Favorite Bagels

$\frac{1}{4}$ Sesame $\frac{1}{2}$ Plain

$\frac{1}{8}$ Poppy

$\frac{1}{8}$ Raisin

38. **What's the Question?** If the answer is 25 people, what is the question?

39. **Write About It** Explain how to solve $\frac{3}{5}x = 4$.

40. **Challenge** Solve $2\frac{3}{4}n = \frac{11}{12}$.

TEST PREP and Spiral Review

41. **Multiple Choice** Solve $\frac{3}{10}x = 9$.

    (A) $x = 15$ (B) $x = 30$ (C) $x = 60$ (D) $x = 90$

42. **Multiple Choice** Which of the following is a solution to $4x = \frac{3}{4}$?

    (F) $x = \frac{3}{16}$ (G) $x = \frac{3}{4}$ (H) $x = 3$ (J) $x = 5\frac{1}{3}$

43. **Gridded Response** What value of y is a solution to $\frac{4}{5}y = 28$?

Find the GCF of each set of numbers. (Lesson 4-3)

44. 6 and 15   45. 18 and 56   46. 12, 16, and 32   47. 24, 63, and 81

Divide. Write each answer in simplest form. (Lesson 5-9)

48. $\frac{2}{3} \div \frac{1}{3}$ 49. $\frac{9}{10} \div \frac{3}{4}$ 50. $2\frac{3}{8} \div \frac{1}{4}$ 51. $1\frac{1}{4} \div 2\frac{1}{3}$

READY TO GO ON?

Quiz for Lessons 5-6 Through 5-10

✓ **5-6** **Multiplying Fractions by Whole Numbers**

1. Multiply $4 \cdot \frac{2}{3}$. Write your answer in simplest form.

2. Michelle ordered 5 lb of fruit for a family picnic. Of that fruit, $\frac{1}{3}$ was watermelon. How much of the fruit was watermelon?

3. Philip has 35 comic books. Of those comics, $\frac{2}{10}$ take place in space. How many of Philip's comic books take place in space?

✓ **5-7** **Multiplying Fractions**

Multiply. Write each answer in simplest form.

4. $\frac{2}{7} \cdot \frac{3}{4}$

5. $\frac{3}{5} \cdot \frac{2}{3}$

6. $\frac{7}{12} \cdot \frac{4}{5}$

Evaluate the expression $t \cdot \frac{1}{8}$ for each value of t. Write the answer in simplest form.

7. $t = \frac{4}{9}$

8. $t = \frac{4}{5}$

9. $t = \frac{2}{3}$

✓ **5-8** **Multiplying Mixed Numbers**

Multiply. Write each answer in simplest form.

10. $\frac{1}{4} \cdot 2\frac{1}{3}$

11. $1\frac{1}{6} \cdot \frac{2}{3}$

12. $\frac{7}{8} \cdot 2\frac{2}{3}$

Find each product. Write the answer in simplest form.

13. $2\frac{1}{4} \cdot 1\frac{1}{6}$

14. $1\frac{2}{3} \cdot 2\frac{1}{5}$

15. $3 \cdot 4\frac{2}{7}$

✓ **5-9** **Dividing Fractions and Mixed Numbers**

Find the reciprocal.

16. $\frac{2}{7}$

17. $\frac{5}{12}$

18. $\frac{3}{5}$

Divide. Write each answer in simplest form.

19. $\frac{3}{5} \div 4$

20. $1\frac{3}{10} \div 3\frac{1}{4}$

21. $1\frac{1}{5} \div 2\frac{1}{3}$

✓ **5-10** **Solving Fraction Equations: Multiplication and Division**

Solve each equation.

22. $\frac{2y}{3} = 10$

23. $6p = \frac{3}{4}$

24. $\frac{2x}{3} = 9$

25. Michael has a black cat and a gray kitten. The black cat weighs 12 pounds. The gray kitten weighs $\frac{3}{5}$ the weight of the black cat. How much does the gray kitten weigh?

Something's Fishy! Maria and Victor are setting up a 20-gallon aquarium. They want to choose fish for the aquarium using the rule "1 inch of fish per gallon of water." This means that the total length of the fish in their tank should be no more than 20 inches.

1. Maria considers getting one of each fish shown in the table. Estimate the total length of the fish. Could she add more fish? Explain.

2. Victor would like to have a neon tetra and a guppy in the tank. What is the total length of the two fish?

3. What is the total length of the remaining fish that Victor could add to the tank? Explain.

4. Is there enough room left for Victor to add 4 clown barbs to the tank? Why or why not?

5. Maria and Victor decide to fill the tank with neon tetras only. Write and solve an equation to find out how many neon tetras they can put in the tank.

| Common Aquarium Fish ||
Name	Length (in.)
Zebra danio	$2\frac{1}{2}$
Neon tetra	$1\frac{1}{4}$
Clown barb	$4\frac{7}{16}$
Platy	$1\frac{3}{4}$
Guppy	$2\frac{3}{8}$

Multi-Step Test Prep

Game Time

Fraction Riddles

1 What is the value of one-half of two-thirds of three-fourths of four-fifths of five-sixths of six-sevenths of seven-eighths of eight-ninths of nine-tenths of one thousand?

2 What is the next fraction in the sequence below?

$$\frac{1}{12}, \frac{1}{6}, \frac{1}{4}, \frac{1}{3}, \cdots$$

3 I am a three-digit number. My hundreds digit is one-third of my tens digit. My tens digit is one-third of my ones digit. What number am I?

4 A *splorg* costs three-fourths of a dollar plus three-fourths of a *splorg*. How much does a *splorg* cost?

5 How many cubic inches of dirt are in a hole that measures $\frac{1}{3}$ feet by $\frac{1}{4}$ feet by $\frac{1}{2}$ feet?

Fraction Bingo

The object is to be the first player to cover five squares in a row horizontally, vertically, or diagonally.

One person is the caller. On each of the caller's cards, there is an expression containing fractions. When the caller draws a card, he or she reads the expression aloud for the players.

The players must find the value of the expression. If a square on the player's card has that value or a fraction equivalent to that value, they cover the square.

go.hrw.com
Game Time Extra
KEYWORD: MR7 Games

The first player to cover five squares in a row is the winner. Take turns being the caller. A variation can be played in which the winner is the first person to cover all their squares.

A complete copy of the rules and game pieces are available online.

Materials
- file folder
- scissors
- white paper
- hole punch
- chenille stem
- surveyor's flagging tape
- tape

PROJECT **Flipping over Fractions**

Make a flip-flop book to take notes and work sample problems related to fraction operations.

Directions

❶ Cut the folder in half from the fold to the edge. Then cut out a flip-flop shape, with the "toe" of the flip-flop along the folded edge. **Figure A**

❷ Cut about ten flip-flop shapes out of the white paper. They should be slightly smaller than the flip-flop you cut out of the file folder.

❸ Put the white flip-flops inside the file-folder flip-flop. Punch a hole at the top through all the layers. Also punch holes at the sides of the flip-flip cover. These side holes should go through only the cover. **Figure B**

❹ Insert the chenille stem into the hole at the top, make a loop, and trim. Insert the surveyor's flagging tape through the loop, and insert the ends into the holes at the sides of the flip-flop. Tape the surveyor's flagging tape to the back of the cover to hold it in place. **Figure C**

Taking Note of the Math

Write the chapter number and title on the flip-flop. Then use the inside pages to work problems from the chapter. Choose problems that will help you remember the most important concepts.

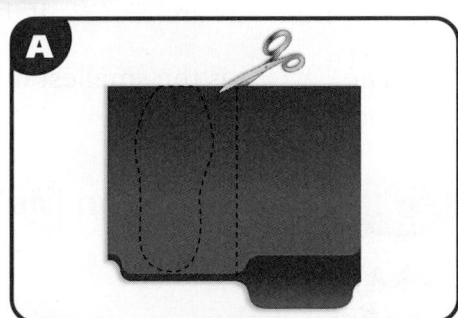

A

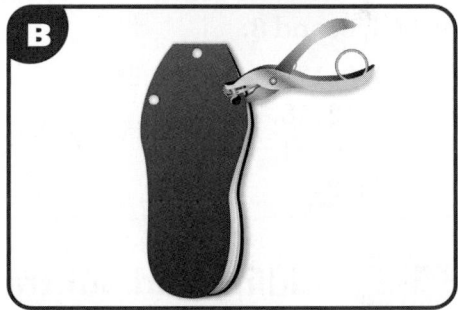

B

C

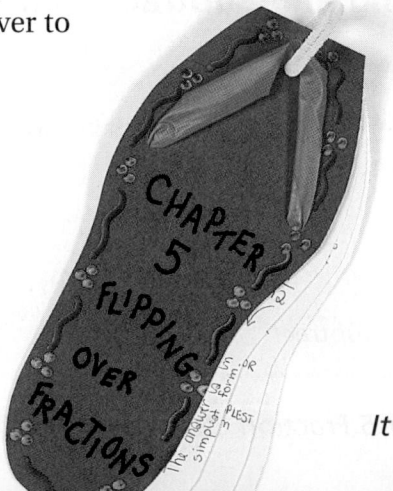

CHAPTER 5 FLIPPING OVER FRACTIONS

Study Guide: Review

Vocabulary

least common denominator (LCD) 234   reciprocals 270

least common multiple (LCM) 228

Complete the sentences below with vocabulary words from the list above.

1. Two numbers are ___?___ if their product is 1.

2. The ___?___ is the smallest number that is a common multiple of two or more denominators.

5-1 Least Common Multiple (pp. 228–231)    6.N.14

EXAMPLE

- Find the least common multiple (LCM) of 4, 6, and 8.

  4: 4, 8, 12, 16, 20, 24, 28, . . .
  6: 6, 12, 18, 24, 30, . . .
  8: 8, 16, 24, 32, . . .
  LCM: 24

EXERCISES

Find the least common multiple (LCM).

3. 3, 5, and 10   4. 6, 8, and 16

5. 3, 9, and 27   6. 4, 12, and 30

7. 25 and 45   8. 12, 22, and 30

5-2 Adding and Subtracting with Unlike Denominators (pp. 234–237)    6.N.16

EXAMPLE

- $\frac{7}{9} + \frac{2}{3}$

  $\frac{7}{9} + \frac{2}{3}$ *Write equivalent fractions. Add.*

  $\frac{7}{9} + \frac{6}{9} = \frac{13}{9} = 1\frac{4}{9}$

EXERCISES

Add or subtract. Write each answer in simplest form.

9. $\frac{1}{5} + \frac{5}{8}$ 10. $\frac{1}{6} + \frac{7}{12}$

11. $\frac{13}{15} - \frac{4}{5}$ 12. $\frac{7}{8} - \frac{2}{3}$

5-3 Adding and Subtracting Mixed Numbers (pp. 238–241)    6.N.16, 6.N.18

EXAMPLE

- Find the difference. Write the answer in simplest form.

  $5\frac{5}{8} - 3\frac{1}{6}$

  $5\frac{15}{24} - 3\frac{4}{24}$ *Write equivalent fractions.*

  $2\frac{11}{24}$ *Subtract.*

EXERCISES

Find each sum or difference. Write the answer in simplest form.

13. $1\frac{3}{10} + 3\frac{2}{5}$ 14. $4\frac{5}{9} - 1\frac{1}{2}$

15. Angela had $\frac{7}{10}$ gallon of paint. She used $\frac{1}{3}$ gallon for a project. How much paint did she have left?

5-4 Regrouping to Subtract Mixed Numbers (pp. 244–247)  6.N.16, 6.N.18

EXAMPLE

■ Subtract.

$4\frac{7}{10} - 2\frac{9}{10}$

$3\frac{17}{10} - 2\frac{9}{10}$ *Regroup $4\frac{7}{10}$. Subtract.*

$1\frac{8}{10}$

$1\frac{4}{5}$

EXERCISES

Subtract. Write each answer in simplest form.

16. $7\frac{2}{9} - 3\frac{5}{9}$ **17.** $3\frac{1}{5} - 1\frac{7}{10}$

18. $8\frac{7}{12} - 2\frac{11}{12}$ **19.** $5\frac{3}{8} - 2\frac{3}{4}$

20. $11\frac{6}{7} - 4\frac{13}{14}$ **21.** $10 - 8\frac{7}{8}$

22. Georgette needs 8 feet of ribbon to decorate gifts. She has $3\frac{1}{4}$ feet of ribbon. How many more feet of ribbon does Georgette need?

5-5 Solving Fraction Equations: Addition and Subtraction (pp. 248–251)

EXAMPLE

 6.N.16, 6.N.18

■ Solve $n + 2\frac{5}{7} = 8$.

$n + 2\frac{5}{7} - 2\frac{5}{7} = 8 - 2\frac{5}{7}$

$n = 8 - 2\frac{5}{7}$

$n = 7\frac{7}{7} - 2\frac{5}{7}$

$n = 5\frac{2}{7}$

EXERCISES

Solve each equation. Write the solution in simplest form.

23. $x - 12\frac{3}{4} = 17\frac{2}{5}$ **24.** $t + 6\frac{11}{12} = 21\frac{5}{6}$

25. $3\frac{2}{3} = m - 1\frac{3}{4}$ **26.** $5\frac{2}{3} = p + 2\frac{2}{9}$

27. $y - 1\frac{2}{3} = 3\frac{4}{5}$ **28.** $4\frac{2}{5} + j = 7\frac{7}{10}$

29. Jon poured $1\frac{1}{2}$ oz of lemon juice onto a salad. He has $5\frac{1}{2}$ oz lemon juice left in the bottle. How many ounces of lemon juice were in the bottle before Jon poured some on the salad?

5-6 Multiplying Fractions by Whole Numbers (pp. 254–257) 6.N.17, 6.A.2

EXAMPLE

■ Multiply $3 \cdot \frac{3}{5}$. Write your answer in simplest form.

$3 \cdot \frac{3}{5} = \frac{3}{5} + \frac{3}{5} + \frac{3}{5} = \frac{9}{5}$ or $1\frac{4}{5}$

EXERCISES

Multiply. Write each answer in simplest form.

30. $5 \cdot \frac{1}{7}$ **31.** $2 \cdot \frac{3}{8}$ **32.** $3 \cdot \frac{6}{7}$

33. $4 \cdot \frac{5}{8}$ **34.** $6 \cdot \frac{1}{2}$ **35.** $2 \cdot \frac{3}{5}$

36. There are 105 members of the high school band. Of these members, $\frac{1}{5}$ play percussion instruments. How many members play percussion?

5-7 Multiplying Fractions (pp. 260–263)

 6.N.17, 6.A.2

EXAMPLE

■ Multiply. Write the answer in simplest form.

$\frac{3}{4} \cdot \frac{1}{3}$ *Multiply. Then simplify.*

$\frac{3 \cdot 1}{4 \cdot 3} = \frac{3}{12} = \frac{1}{4}$

EXERCISES

Multiply. Write each answer in simplest form.

37. $\frac{5}{6} \cdot \frac{2}{5}$ **38.** $\frac{5}{7} \cdot \frac{3}{4}$ **39.** $\frac{4}{5} \cdot \frac{1}{8}$

40. $\frac{7}{10} \cdot \frac{2}{5}$ **41.** $\frac{1}{9} \cdot \frac{5}{9}$ **42.** $\frac{1}{4} \cdot \frac{6}{7}$

43. Andrew's hockey team won $\frac{4}{5}$ of their games. Andrew scored in $\frac{2}{3}$ of the games his team won. In what fraction of his team's games did Andrew score?

5-8 Multiplying Mixed Numbers (pp. 264–267)

 6.N.17, 6.N.18

EXAMPLE

■ Multiply. Write the answer in simplest form.

$\frac{2}{5} \cdot 1\frac{2}{3} = \frac{2}{5} \cdot \frac{5}{3} = \frac{10}{15} = \frac{2}{3}$

EXERCISES

Multiply. Write each answer in simplest form.

44. $\frac{2}{5} \cdot 2\frac{1}{4}$ **45.** $\frac{3}{4} \cdot 1\frac{2}{3}$ **46.** $3\frac{1}{3} \cdot \frac{3}{5}$

5-9 Dividing Fractions and Mixed Numbers (pp. 270–273)

6.N.17, 6.N.18, 6.N.19

EXAMPLE

■ Divide. Write the answer in simplest form.

$\frac{3}{4} \div 6 = \frac{3 \cdot 1}{4 \cdot 6} = \frac{3}{24} = \frac{1}{8}$

EXERCISES

Divide. Write each answer in simplest form.

47. $\frac{4}{7} \div 3$ **48.** $\frac{3}{10} \div 2$ **49.** $1\frac{1}{3} \div 2\frac{2}{5}$

50. Beverly needs to measure $2\frac{2}{3}$ cups of bread crumbs. She has a $\frac{1}{3}$ cup measuring scoop. How many times must she fill the $\frac{1}{3}$ cup measuring scoop to get $2\frac{2}{3}$ cups of bread crumbs?

5-10 Solving Fraction Equations: Multiplication and Division (pp. 274–277)

6.N.17, 6.N.18

EXAMPLE

■ Solve the equation.

$\frac{4}{5}n = 12$

$\frac{4}{5}n \div \frac{4}{5} = 12 \div \frac{4}{5}$ *Divide both sides by $\frac{4}{5}$.*

$\frac{4}{5}n \cdot \frac{5}{4} = 12 \cdot \frac{5}{4}$ *Multiply by the reciprocal.*

$n = \frac{60}{4} = 15$

EXERCISES

Solve each equation.

51. $4a = \frac{1}{2}$ **52.** $\frac{3b}{4} = 1\frac{1}{2}$

53. $\frac{2m}{7} = 5$ **54.** $6g = \frac{4}{5}$

55. $\frac{5}{6}r = 9$ **56.** $\frac{s}{8} = 6\frac{1}{4}$

57. $6p = \frac{2}{3}$ **58.** $\frac{8j}{9} = 1\frac{5}{8}$

Find the least common multiple (LCM).

1. 10 and 15   **2.** 4, 6, and 18   **3.** 9, 10, and 12   **4.** 6, 15, and 20

Add or subtract. Write the answer in simplest form.

5. $4\frac{1}{9} - 2\frac{4}{9}$ **6.** $1\frac{7}{10} + 3\frac{3}{4}$ **7.** $\frac{2}{3} - \frac{3}{8}$ **8.** $2\frac{1}{3} - \frac{5}{6}$

9. $4 + 2\frac{2}{7}$ **10.** $\frac{1}{12} + \frac{5}{6}$ **11.** $\frac{3}{8} + \frac{3}{4}$ **12.** $\frac{5}{6} - \frac{2}{5}$

13. On Saturday, Cecelia ran $3\frac{3}{7}$ miles. On Sunday, she ran $4\frac{5}{6}$ miles. How much farther did Cecelia run on Sunday than on Saturday?

14. Michael studied social studies for $\frac{3}{4}$ of an hour, Spanish for $1\frac{1}{2}$ hours, and math for $1\frac{1}{4}$ hours. How many hours did Michael spend studying all three subjects?

15. Quincy needs $6\frac{1}{3}$ feet of rope to tie down the things he is hauling in his truck. He finds a 9 foot long rope in his garage. How much extra rope does Quincy have?

Find the reciprocal.

16. $\frac{3}{5}$ **17.** $\frac{7}{11}$ **18.** $\frac{5}{9}$ **19.** $\frac{1}{8}$

Multiply or divide. Write the answer in simplest form.

20. $\frac{3}{7} \cdot \frac{4}{9}$ **21.** $1\frac{3}{8} \cdot \frac{6}{11}$ **22.** $2\frac{1}{4} \cdot 2\frac{2}{3}$ **23.** $\frac{7}{8} \div 2$

24. $3\frac{1}{3} \div 1\frac{5}{12}$ **25.** $\frac{4}{5} \cdot 1\frac{1}{3}$ **26.** $3\frac{1}{8} \div 1\frac{1}{4}$ **27.** $\frac{3}{8} \cdot \frac{2}{3}$

Evaluate the expression $n \cdot \frac{1}{4}$ for each value of n. Write the answer in simplest form.

28. $n = \frac{7}{8}$ **29.** $n = \frac{2}{5}$ **30.** $n = \frac{8}{9}$ **31.** $n = \frac{4}{11}$

32. Twenty-four students tried out for the cheerleading squad. Only $\frac{5}{6}$ of the students will be chosen. How many students will be chosen for the squad?

33. A recipe for granola bars require $1\frac{1}{2}$ cups of flour. How much flour is needed to make a triple batch of granola bars?

Solve each equation. Write the solution in simplest form.

34. $3r = \frac{9}{10}$ **35.** $n + 3\frac{1}{6} = 12$ **36.** $5\frac{5}{6} = x - 3\frac{1}{4}$

37. $\frac{2}{5}t = 9$ **38.** $\frac{4}{5}m = 7$ **39.** $y - 15\frac{3}{5} = 2\frac{1}{3}$

40. Jessica purchased a bag of cat food. She feeds her cat 1 cup of cat food each day. After 7 days, she has fed her cat $\frac{2}{3}$ of the food in the bag. How many cups of food were in the bag of cat food when Jessica bought it?

TEST TACKLER

Standardized Test Strategies

Gridded Response: Write Gridded Responses

When responding to a test item that has an answer grid, you must fill out the grid correctly, or the item will be marked as incorrect.

EXAMPLE 1

Gridded Response: Simplify the expression $(8 \times 3) - 5 \times (6 - 3)$.

$(8 \times 3) - 5 \times (6 - 3)$

$24 - 5 \times 3$ *Perform operations within parentheses.*

$24 - 15$ *Multiply.*

9 *Subtract.*

The expression simplifies to 9.

- Use a pencil to write your answer in the answer boxes at the top of the grid.

- The answer can be entered starting in the far left column, or in the far right column, but not in the middle.

- Write only one digit in each box. Do not leave a blank box in the middle of an answer.

- Shade the correct bubble below your written digit.

EXAMPLE 2

Gridded Response: Evaluate $2\frac{1}{4} + 1\frac{1}{4} + 3\frac{3}{4}$.

$2\frac{1}{4} + 1\frac{1}{4} + 3\frac{3}{4}$

$6\frac{5}{4}$ *Add the fractions and then add the whole numbers.*

$6\frac{5}{4} = 6 + 1\frac{1}{4} = 7\frac{1}{4}$ or 7.25 or $\frac{29}{4}$ *Simplify.*

- You cannot fill in mixed numbers. You must fill in the answer as an improper fraction or a decimal.

- Use a pencil to write your answer in the answer boxes at the top of the grid.

- Write only one digit or symbol in each box. On some grids, the fraction bar and the decimal point have a special box. If so, write your fraction or decimal around it correctly. Do not leave a blank box in the middle of an answer.

- Shade the correct bubble below your written digit.

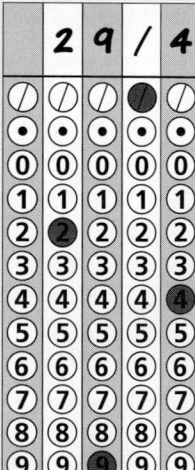

Test Tackler

Hot Tip
When filling out a grid be sure to use a pencil and completely fill in the bubbles directly below each digit or symbol you wrote.

Read each sample and then answer the questions that follow.

Sample A
A student divided two fractions and got $\frac{4}{25}$ as a result. Then the student filled in the grid as shown.

1. What error did the student make when filling in the grid?

2. Explain how to fill in the answer correctly.

Sample B
A student solved the equation $x + 2.1 = 5$, and found that $x = 2.9$. This answer is displayed in the grid below.

3. What error did the student make when filling in the grid?

4. Explain how to fill in the answer correctly.

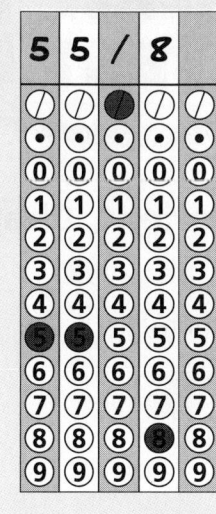

Sample C
A student correctly simplified the expression $6\frac{7}{8} + 1\frac{3}{8} - 2\frac{5}{8}$. Then the student filled in the grid as shown.

5. What answer does the grid show?

6. Explain why you cannot grid a mixed number.

7. Write the answer $5\frac{5}{8}$ in two forms that could be entered in the grid correctly.

Sample D
A student wrote the standard form of the decimal one and twenty-five hundredths and then filled in the grid as shown.

8. What error did the student make when filling in the grid?

9. Explain how to fill in the answer correctly.

Cumulative Assessment, Chapters 1–5

Multiple Choice

1. Which number is less than $\frac{3}{4}$?

   (A) $\frac{2}{3}$ (C) $\frac{5}{6}$

   (B) $\frac{4}{5}$ (D) $\frac{9}{10}$

2. Mr. Ledden's briefcase has a mass of 9.4 kilograms on Earth. How much would his briefcase weigh on Jupiter?

Gravitational Pull of Planets (Compared with Earth)	
Planet	**Gravitational Pull**
Mercury	0.38
Venus	0.91
Mars	0.38
Jupiter	2.54
Saturn	0.93
Neptune	1.2

   (F) 8.554 kg   (H) 11.94 kg

   (G) 11.28 kg   (J) 23.876 kg

3. Brandon's family is planning a trip from Dallas to San Antonio. Dallas is about 272 miles from San Antonio. If Brandon's dad drives an average of 60 miles per hour, about how long will the trip take?

   (A) 3 hours   (C) 6 hours

   (B) 5 hours   (D) 7 hours

4. What is the value of 5^4?

   (F) 9   (H) 625

   (G) 20   (J) 1,000

5. A recipe calls for $\frac{1}{4}$ cup of sugar and $\frac{2}{3}$ cup of flour. How much more flour than sugar is needed for this recipe?

   (A) $\frac{1}{7}$ cup   (C) $\frac{1}{2}$ cup

   (B) $\frac{5}{12}$ cup   (D) $\frac{3}{4}$ cup

6. Maggie needs $15\frac{3}{8}$ yards of blue rope, $24\frac{1}{3}$ yards of white rope, and $8\frac{3}{4}$ yards of red rope. About how many yards of rope does she need in all?

   (F) 38 yards   (H) 48 yards

   (G) 45 yards   (J) 55 yards

7. Let d represent the number of dogs that Max walks in 1 day. Which expression shows the number of dogs Max walks in 7 days?

   (A) $7 + d$ (C) $7d$

   (B) $d - 7$ (D) $\frac{d}{7}$

8. Charlie eats $\frac{5}{8}$ of a pizza. One-fifth of the pizza he eats is covered with mushrooms. How much of Charlie's pizza is covered with mushrooms?

   (F) $\frac{1}{8}$ pizza   (H) $\frac{1}{5}$ pizza

   (G) $\frac{5}{13}$ pizza   (J) $3\frac{1}{8}$ pizza

9. Which of the following sets of decimals is ordered from least to greatest?

   (A) 3.8, 3.89, 3.08, 3.9

   (B) 3.89, 3.8, 3.9, 3.08

   (C) 3.08, 3.89, 3.8, 3.9

   (D) 3.08, 3.8, 3.89, 3.9

10. Samantha gets to choose a number for her soccer jersey. She picks a number that is divisible by 3, 5, and 9, but not by 2, 4, or 6. Which of the following can be Samantha's jersey number?

  (F) 15   (H) 30

  (G) 27   (J) 45

11. A theater has 145 rows of seats. There are 12 seats in each row. The sixth grade class from Brookpark Middle School has 168 students and 15 chaperones that are attending a play next week. How many rows will they need to reserve for the upcoming play?

  (A) 14 rows   (C) 16 rows

  (B) 15 rows   (D) 17 rows

 **Hot Tip**   Underline key words given in the test question so you know for certain what the question is asking.

12. What is the least common denominator for the following fractions: $\frac{4}{5}$, $\frac{3}{4}$, and $\frac{1}{10}$?

  (F) 20   (H) 50

  (G) 40   (J) 100

13. During a walk-a-thon, Brian walks $3\frac{1}{4}$ kilometers, and Stacey walks $2\frac{7}{8}$ kilometers. How many more kilometers does Brian walk than Stacy?

  (A) $\frac{3}{8}$ (C) $1\frac{1}{8}$

  (B) $\frac{7}{8}$ (D) $\frac{7}{4}$

14. What is the reciprocal of $6\frac{1}{7}$?

  (F) $\frac{7}{43}$ (H) $\frac{7}{6}$

  (G) $\frac{6}{7}$ (J) 6

15. Natalie lives $\frac{1}{6}$ mile from school. Peter lives $\frac{3}{10}$ mile from school. How many miles further does Peter live from the school than Natalie?

  (A) $\frac{1}{20}$ (C) $\frac{2}{15}$

  (B) $\frac{1}{30}$ (D) $\frac{6}{60}$

Short Response

16. Jane is building a tank for her pet snake. The tank's minimum length should equal two-thirds of the snake's length, and the tank's width should be equal to half the snake's length. Jane's snake is $2\frac{1}{2}$ feet long. Calculate and explain how to find the dimensions of the tank.

17. Lucy has $\frac{5}{6}$ yard of ribbon to wrap gifts for her friends. The bow on each gift requires $\frac{1}{6}$ yard of ribbon. Write an equation to determine how many b bows Lucy can make. Solve and interpret your answer.

Extended Response

18. Garrett attends a summer day camp for 6 hours each day. The circle graph below shows what fraction of each day he spends doing different activities.

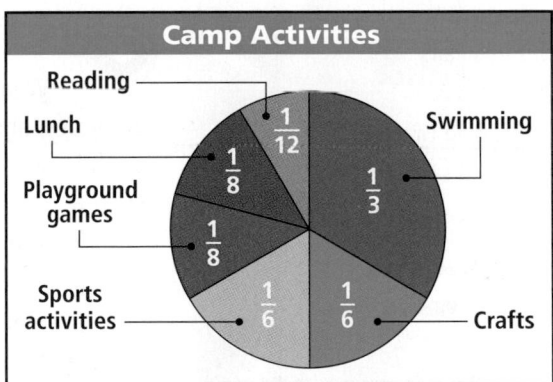

Camp Activities

a. How long does Garrett spend doing each activity? Write the activities in order from longest to shortest.

b. Sports activities and playground games are all held on the camp fields. What fraction of the day does Garrett spend on the fields? Write your answer in simplest form.

c. Lunch and crafts are held in the cafeteria. How many hours does Garrett spend in the cafeteria during a 5-day week at day camp? Write your answer in simplest form, and show the work necessary to determine the correct answer.

Collecting and Displaying Data

NEW YORK TEST PREP

go.hrw.com
Chapter Project Online
KEYWORD: MR7 Ch6

	Average High Temperatures (°C)		
National Park	**Jun**	**Jul**	**Aug**
Badlands, SD	27	33	32
Big Bend, TX	32	31	31
Crater Lake, OR	19	25	24
Everglades, FL	31	32	32

Career *Meteorologist*

Weather affects our daily activities, and weather information is useful and often necessary. Businesses such as farms, ski resorts, and airlines need to know weather conditions.

This information comes from meteorologists, people who study and forecast the weather. They gather data such as temperature, wind speed, and rainfall. They then study this data and make predictions.

The table lists the average daily high temperatures during the summer in some popular national parks.

ARE YOU READY?

✓ Vocabulary

Choose the best term from the list to complete each sentence.

1. The answer to an addition problem is called the ___?___.

2. The ___?___ of the 6 in 5,672 is hundreds.

3. When you move ___?___, you move left or right.
   When you move ___?___, you move up or down.

horizontally

place value

quotients

sum

vertically

Complete these exercises to review skills you will need for this chapter.

✓ Place Value

Write the digit in the tens place of each number.

4. 718   **5.** 989   **6.** 55   **7.** 7,709

✓ Compare and Order Whole Numbers

Order the numbers from least to greatest.

8. 40, 32, 51, 78, 26, 43, 27   **9.** 132, 150, 218, 176, 166

10. 92, 91, 84, 92, 87, 90   **11.** 23, 19, 33, 27, 31, 31, 28, 18

Find the greatest number in each set.

12. 452, 426, 502, 467, 530, 512   **13.** 711, 765, 723, 778, 704, 781

14. 143, 122, 125, 137, 140, 118, 139   **15.** 1,053; 1,106; 1,043; 1,210; 1,039; 1,122

✓ Write Fractions as Decimals

Write each fraction as a decimal.

16. $\frac{1}{4}$ **17.** $\frac{5}{8}$ **18.** $\frac{1}{6}$ **19.** $\frac{2}{5}$

20. $\frac{5}{6}$ **21.** $\frac{1}{2}$ **22.** $\frac{3}{4}$ **23.** $\frac{9}{11}$

✓ Locate Points on a Number Line

Name the point on the number line that corresponds to each given value.

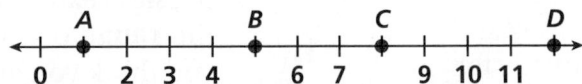

24. 5   **25.** 12   **26.** 8   **27.** 1

Study Guide: Preview

Where You've Been

Previously, you

- described characteristics of data such as the shape of the data and the middle number.
- graphed a given set of data using an appropriate graphical representation.
- used tables of related number pairs to make line graphs.

In This Chapter

You will study

- using mean, median, mode, and range to describe data.
- solving problems by collecting, organizing, and displaying data.
- drawing and comparing different graphical representations of the same data.

Where You're Going

You can use the skills learned in this chapter

- to recognize misuses of graphical information and evaluate conclusions based on data analysis.
- to display data correctly for projects in social studies and science.

Key Vocabulary/Vocabulario

bar graph	gráfica de barras
coordinate grid	cuadrícula de coordenadas
line graph	gráfica lineal
mean	media
median	mediana
mode	moda
ordered pair	par ordenado
outlier	valor extremo
range	rango (en estadística)
stem-and-leaf plot	diagrama de tallo y hojas

Vocabulary Connections

To become familiar with some of the vocabulary terms in the chapter, consider the following. You may refer to the chapter, the glossary, or a dictionary if you like.

1. A *bar* can be a straight stripe or band. What do you think a **bar graph** uses to display data?

2. A *grid* is a network of uniformly spaced horizontal and perpendicular lines. What do you think a **coordinate grid** looks like?

3. *Ordered* means "to be arranged." The word *pair* can mean "two things designed for use together." What do you think an **ordered pair** is made up of?

4. A *range* can mean the distance between possible extremes. If you are looking for the **range** of a set of numbers, what do you think you are looking for?

5. The *stem* is the main trunk of a plant. The *leaves* are the outgrowth from the stem. How do you think a **stem-and-leaf plot** is made?

Reading and *Writing* Math

Reading Strategy: Read and Interpret Graphics

Figures, diagrams, charts, and graphs are used to illustrate data. Knowing how to understand these visual aids will help you learn the important facts and details of a problem.

Chart

Gustavo's Gift Wrap Table

Gift Size	Paper Needed (yd²)
Small	$\frac{11}{12}$
Medium	$1\frac{5}{9}$
Large	$2\frac{2}{3}$
X-large	$3\frac{1}{9}$

Read and understand each column head and each row head.

- **Title:** Gustavo's Gift Wrap Table
- **Gift Size:** Small, Medium, Large, and X-large
- **Paper Needed (yd²):** Tells how much paper is needed to wrap the given gift size.

Graph

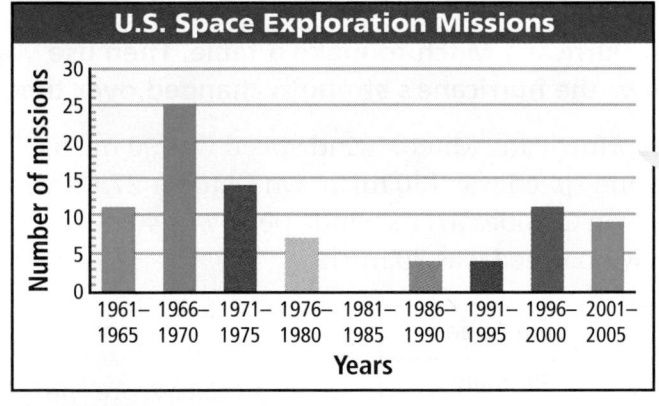

U.S. Space Exploration Missions

The titles of the graph describe what information is being graphed. Read the label on each axis.

- **Title:** U.S. Space Exploration Missions
- **x-axis:** Years (given as 5-year intervals)
- **y-axis:** Number of missions

Try This

Look up each exercise in your textbook and answer the following questions.

1. Lesson 5-5, Exercise 32: What type of graph is shown? How many minutes long is "Winter"? Explain.

2. Lesson 5-10, Exercise 37: What is the title of the circle graph? What types of bagels are listed?

6-1 Make a Table

 Problem Solving Strategy

Learn to use tables to record and organize data.

NY Performance Indicators

6.CM.4 Share organized mathematical ideas through numerical tables. Also, 6.CM.3, 6.CN.5, 6.R.1, 6.R.8.

Weather forecasters collect data about weather. By organizing and interpreting this data, they can often warn people of severe weather before it happens. This advance warning can save lives.

This satellite image shows a hurricane approaching Florida's coastline.

One way to organize data is to make a table. By looking at a table, you may see patterns and relationships.

EXAMPLE 1 *Weather Application*

Weather

The National Weather Service estimated that Mitch's wind speed reached 180 mi/h. This made Mitch a Category 5 hurricane, which is the strongest type.

go.hrw.com
Web Extra!
KEYWORD: MR7 Hurricane

Use the data about Hurricane Mitch to make a table. Then use your table to describe how the hurricane's strength changed over time.

On October 24, 1998, Hurricane Mitch's wind speed was 90 mi/h. On October 26, its wind speed was 130 mi/h. On October 27, its wind speed was 150 mi/h. On October 31, its wind speed was 40 mi/h. On November 1, its wind speed was 30 mi/h.

Date (1998)	Wind Speed
October 24	90 mi/h
October 26	130 mi/h
October 27	150 mi/h
October 31	40 mi/h
November 1	30 mi/h

Make a table. Write the dates in order so that you can see how the hurricane's strength changed over time.

From the table, you can see that Hurricane Mitch became stronger from October 24 to October 27 and then weakened from October 27 to November 1.

EXAMPLE 2 Organizing Data in a Table

Use the temperature data to make a table. Then use your table to find a pattern in the data and draw a conclusion.

At 10 A.M., the temperature was 62°F. At noon, it was 65°F. At 2 P.M., it was 68°F. At 4 P.M., it was 70°F. At 6 P.M., it was 66°F.

Time	Temperature (°F)
10 A.M.	62
Noon	65
2 P.M.	68
4 P.M.	70
6 P.M.	66

The temperature rose until 4 P.M., and then it dropped. One conclusion is that the high temperature on this day was at least 70°F.

Think and Discuss

1. **Tell** how a table helps you organize data.

2. **Explain** why the data in Example 2 was arranged from earliest to latest time instead of from lowest to highest temperature.

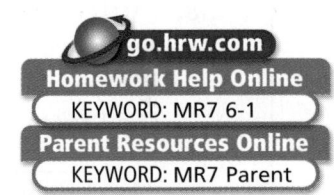

6-1 Exercises

go.hrw.com
Homework Help Online
KEYWORD: MR7 6-1
Parent Resources Online
KEYWORD: MR7 Parent

GUIDED PRACTICE

See Example **1.** On Monday, the high temperature was 72°F. On Tuesday, the high was 75°F. On Wednesday, the high was 68°F. On Thursday, the high was 62°F. On Friday, the high was 55°F. Use this data to make a table.

See Example 2 **2.** Use your table from Exercise 1 to find a pattern in the data and draw a conclusion.

INDEPENDENT PRACTICE

See Example **3.** On his first math test, Joe made a grade of 70. On the second test, Joe made a grade of 75. On the third test, Joe made a grade of 80. On the fourth test, Joe made a grade of 85. On the fifth test, Joe made a grade of 90. Use this data to make a table.

See Example **4.** Use your table from Exercise 3 to find a pattern in the data and draw a conclusion.

5. Multi-Step For ice-skating on a frozen pond to be safe, the ice should be at least 7 inches thick. Use the data below to make a table, and estimate the date on which it first became safe to ice-skate.

On December 3, the ice was 1 in. thick. On December 18, the ice was 2 in. thick. On January 3, the ice was 5 in. thick. On January 18, the ice was 11 in. thick. On February 3, the ice was 17 in. thick.

6. Write About It The tables below were made using identical data that have been organized differently. When might each table be useful?

Time	Temperature (°F)
6 A.M.	55
10 A.M.	68
2 P.M.	75

Time	Temperature (°F)
2 P.M.	75
10 A.M.	68
6 P.M.	62

7. Challenge Arthur, Victoria, and Jeffrey are in the sixth, seventh, and eighth grades, although not necessarily in that order. Victoria is not in eighth grade. The sixth-grader is in choir with Arthur and in band with Victoria. Which student is in which grade? Use a yes/no table like the one at right to help you answer this question.

	Arthur	Victoria	Jeffrey
6th			
7th			
8th		No	

TEST PREP and Spiral Review

8. Multiple Choice In 1999, an earthquake that measured 7.4 on the Richter scale occurred in Turkey. In 2001, an earthquake that measured 7.9 on the Richter scale occurred in India. In 2003, an earthquake that measured 6.5 on the Richter scale occurred in Iran. Which shows the data accurately in a table?

Ⓐ
Country	Turkey	India	Iran
Measure	7.4	6.5	7.9

Ⓒ
Country	Turkey	India	Iran
Measure	6.5	7.4	7.9

Ⓑ
Country	Turkey	India	Iran
Measure	7.9	7.4	6.5

Ⓓ
Country	Turkey	India	Iran
Measure	7.4	7.9	6.5

9. Short Response Make a table to show the following data: Ty builds model cars. He built 2 the first week, 5 the second week, 8 the third week, and 11 the fourth week. Use your table to find a pattern in the data and draw a conclusion.

Find each value. (Lesson 1-3)

10. 5^3 **11.** 3^4 **12.** 2^6 **13.** 6^3

Write two phrases for each expression. (Lesson 2-2)

14. $b + 13$ **15.** $(2)(12)$ **16.** $26 - c$ **17.** $m \div 3$

Collect Data to Explore Mean

Use with Lesson 6-2

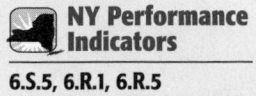

NY Performance Indicators

6.S.5, 6.R.1, 6.R.5

go.hrw.com
Lab Resources Online
KEYWORD: MR7 Lab6

You can use counters to find a single number that describes an entire set of data. Consider the set of data in the table.

2	5	4	3	6

First use counters to make stacks that match the data.

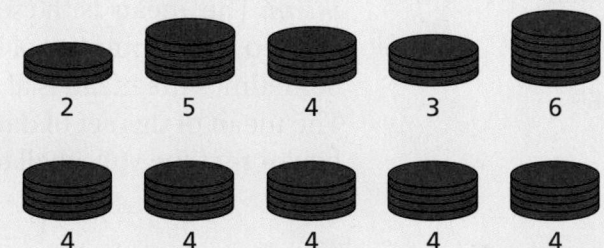

2 5 4 3 6

Now move some of the counters so that all of the stacks are the same height.

4 4 4 4 4

All of the stacks have 4 counters. The set of data can be described by the number 4. It is the *mean* (average) of the set of data.

Activity

1. Ella surveys five people to find out how many brothers and sisters they have.

2. She collects the data and records the results.

3. Use counters to show the data.

4. Move counters so that all of the stacks are the same height. The mean is 2.

Number of Siblings

2	3	1	1	3

2 3 1 1 3

2 2 2 2 2

Think and Discuss

1. Suppose one of the people surveyed had 8 brothers and sisters instead of 3. How would this change the mean?

2. All of the students in a classroom have 3 textbooks. What is the mean of the set of data? How do you know?

Try This

1. Collect data by surveying four friends to find out how many pets they have. Use counters to find the mean of the set of data.

Mean, Median, Mode, and Range

Learn to find the mean, median, mode, and range of a data set.

Players on a volleyball team measured how high they could jump. The results in inches are recorded in the table.

13	23	21	20	21	24	18

One way to describe this data set is to find the *mean*. The **mean** is the sum of all the items divided by the number of items in the set. Sometimes the mean is also called the *average*. The mean of this set of data is the average height that the volleyball team could jump.

Vocabulary

mean

median

mode

range

EXAMPLE 1 Finding the Mean of a Data Set

Find the mean of each data set.

NY Performance Indicators

6.S.5 Determine the mean, mode and median for a given set of data. Also, 6.S.6.

A

Heights of Vertical Jumps (in.)						
13	23	21	20	21	24	18

$13 + 23 + 21 + 20 + 21 + 24 + 18 = 140$ *Add all values.*
$140 \div 7 = 20$ *Divide the sum by the number of items.*

The mean is 20 inches.

B

Numbers of Pets Owned				
2	4	1	1	2

$2 + 4 + 1 + 1 + 2 = 10$ *Add all values.*
$10 \div 5 = 2$ *Divide the sum by the number of items.*

The mean is 2. The average number of pets that these five people own is 2.

Check

Move the chips so that each stack has the same number.

The mean is 2.

Some other descriptions of a set of data are called the *median*, *mode*, and *range*.

- The **median** is the middle value when the data are in numerical order, or the mean of the two middle values if there are an even number of items.

- The **mode** is the value or values that occur most often. There may be more than one mode for a data set. When all values occur an equal number of times, the data set has no mode.

- The **range** is the difference between the least and greatest values in the set.

EXAMPLE 2 **Finding the Mean, Median, Mode, and Range of a Data Set**

Find the mean, median, mode, and range of each data set.

NFL Career Touchdowns			
Marcus Allen	145	Franco Harris	100
Jim Brown	126	Walter Payton	125

mean: $\dfrac{145 + 126 + 100 + 125}{4}$ *Add all values. Divide the sum by the number of items.*

$= 124$

Write the data in numerical order: 100, 125, 126, 145

median: 100, (125, 126) 145 *There are an even number of items, so find the mean of the two middle values.*

$\dfrac{125 + 126}{2} = 125.5$

mode: none *No value occurs most often.*

range: $145 - 100 = 45$ *Subtract least value from greatest value.*

The mean is 124 touchdowns; the median is 125.5 touchdowns; there is no mode; and the range is 45 touchdowns.

6.RP.4, 6.R.9, 6.CN.3

Think and Discuss

1. Describe what you can say about the values in a data set if the set has a small range.

2. Tell how many modes are in the following data set. Explain your answer. 15, 12, 13, 15, 12, 11

3. Describe how adding 20 inches to the data set in Example 1A would affect the mean.

6-2 Exercises

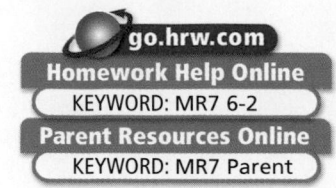

go.hrw.com
Homework Help Online
KEYWORD: MR7 6-2
Parent Resources Online
KEYWORD: MR7 Parent

GUIDED PRACTICE

See Example **1** Find the mean of the data set.

1.
Number of Petals	13	24	35	18	15	27

See Example **2** Find the mean, median, mode, and range of the data set.

2.
Heights of Students (in.)	51	67	63	52	49	48	48

INDEPENDENT PRACTICE

See Example **1** Find the mean of the data set.

3.
Numbers of Books Read	6	4	10	5	6	8

See Example **2** Find the mean, median, mode, and range of each data set.

4.
Ages of Students (yr)	14	16	15	17	16	12

5.

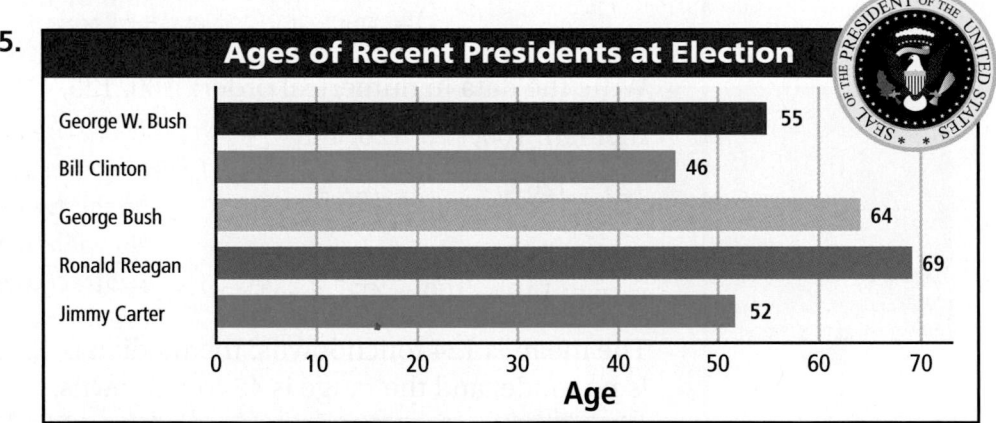

Ages of Recent Presidents at Election

George W. Bush — 55
Bill Clinton — 46
George Bush — 64
Ronald Reagan — 69
Jimmy Carter — 52

Age

PRACTICE AND PROBLEM SOLVING

Extra Practice
See page 724.

6. Frank has 3 nickels, 5 dimes, and 2 quarters. Find the range, mean, median, and mode of the values of Frank's coins.

7. **Education** For the six New England states, the mean scores on the math section of the SAT one year were as follows: Connecticut, 509; Maine, 500; Massachusetts, 513; New Hampshire, 519; Rhode Island, 500; and Vermont, 508. Create a table using this data. Then find the range, mean, median, and mode.

8. **Critical Thinking** Gina spent $4, $5, $7, $7, and $6 over the past 5 days buying lunch. Is the mean, median, mode, or range the most useful way to describe this data set? Explain.

Find each missing value.

9. 3, 5, 7, 9, ; mean: 7

10. 15, 17, , 28, 30; mean: 23

11. 10, 9, , 4, 8, 8, 4, 7; mode: 4

12. 7, 2, ▨, 15, 20, 8, 14, 29; median: 13

13. 50, 100, 75, 60, ▨, 25, 105, 40; median: 65

14. 14, 8, 17, 21, ▨, 11, 3, 13; range: 20

15. Critical Thinking Find the set of 5 items of data that has a range of 9, a mean of 11, a median of 12, and a mode of 15.

16. What's the Error? Joey says that the mean of the set of data is 23.5. Describe Joey's error.

Numbers of Flowers in Bouquets	25	20	21	22	25	25

17. What's the Question? On an exam, three students scored 75, four students scored 82, three students scored 88, four students scored 93, and one student scored 99. If the answer is 88, what is the question?

18. Challenge In the Super Bowls from 1997 to 2002, the winning team won by a mean of $12\frac{1}{6}$ points. By how many points did the Green Bay Packers win in 1997?

Year	Super Bowl Champion	Points Won By
2002	New England Patriots	3
2001	Baltimore Ravens	27
2000	St. Louis Rams	7
1999	Denver Broncos	15
1998	Denver Broncos	7
1997	Green Bay Packers	▨

TEST PREP and Spiral Review

19. Multiple Choice Over 5 days, Pedro jogged 6.5 miles, 5 miles, 2 miles, 2 miles, and 4.5 miles. Find the mean distance that Pedro jogged.

Ⓐ 2 miles   Ⓑ 3.5 miles   Ⓒ 4 miles   Ⓓ 4.75 miles

20. Multiple Choice Which value is NOT always a number in the data set it represents?

Ⓕ Mode   Ⓖ Mean   Ⓗ Least value   Ⓙ Greatest value

21. Gridded Response The mean of 12, 15, 20 and x is 18. Find the value of x.

Tell whether each number is divisible by 2, 3, or 5. (Lesson 4-1)

22. 155   **23.** 14   **24.** 99   **25.** 2,345

26. Make a table to show the number of days in each month of a non-leap year. (Lesson 6-1)

6-3 Additional Data and Outliers

Learn the effect of additional data and outliers.

The mean, median, and mode may change when you add data to a data set.

Vocabulary

outlier

USA's Jim Shea in Men's Skeleton at the 2002 Winter Olympics

E X A M P L E 1 *Sports Application*

A Find the mean, median, and mode of the data in the table.

U.S. Winter Olympic Medals Won								
Year	2002	1998	1994	1992	1988	1984	1980	1976
Medals	34	13	13	11	6	8	12	10

mean = 13.375   mode = 13   median = 11.5

B The United States also won 8 medals in 1972 and 5 medals in 1968. Add this data to the data in the table and find the mean, median, and mode.

mean = 12   *The mean decreased by 1.375.*
modes = 8, 13   *There is an additional mode.*
median = 10.5   *The median decreased by 1.*

NY Performance Indicators

6.CN.7 Apply mathematics to problem situations that develop outside of mathematics.
Also, 6.PS.8, 6.CM.1, 6.CN.4.

An **outlier** is a value in a set that is very different from the other values.

E X A M P L E 2 *Social Studies Application*

In 2001, 64-year-old Sherman Bull became the oldest person to reach the top of Mount Everest. Other climbers to reach the summit that day were 33, 31, 31, 32, 33, and 28 years old. Find the mean, median, and mode without and with Bull's age, and explain the changes.

Data without Bull's age: mean ≈ 31.3   modes = 31, 33   median = 31.5

Data with Bull's age: mean = 36   modes = 31, 33   median = 32

When you add Bull's age, the mean increases by 4.7, the modes stay the same, and the median increases by 0.5. The mean is the most affected by the outlier.

Helpful Hint

Sherman Bull's age is an outlier because he is much older than the others in the group.

Sometimes one or two data values can greatly affect the mean, median, or mode. When one of these values is affected like this, you should choose a different value to best describe the data set.

EXAMPLE 3 Describing a Data Set

The Seawells are shopping for a DVD player. They found ten DVD players with the following prices:

$175, $180, $130, $150, $180, $500, $160, $180, $150, $160

What are the mean, median, and mode of this data set? Which one best describes the data set?

mean = $196.50   mode = $180   median = $167.50

The median price is the best description of the prices. Most of the DVD players cost *about* $167.50.

The mean is higher than most of the prices because of the $500 player, and the mode is higher because of the three players that cost $180 each.

Some data sets do not contain numbers. For example, the circle graph shows the results of a survey to find people's favorite color.

When it does not contain numbers, the only way to describe the data set is with the mode. You cannot find a mean or a median for a set of colors.

The mode for this data set is blue. Most people in this survey chose blue as their favorite color.

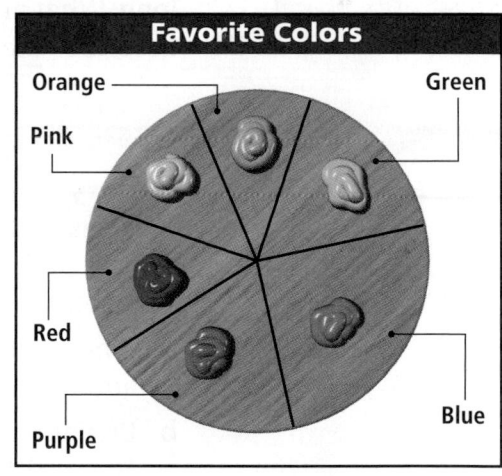

Favorite Colors

Orange
Pink
Red
Purple
Green
Blue

Think and Discuss   6.RP.4, 6.CM.1

1. **Explain** how an outlier with a large value will affect the mean of a data set. What is the effect of a small outlier value?

2. **Explain** why the mean would not be a good description of the following high temperatures that occurred over 7 days: 72°F, 73°F, 70°F, 68°F, 70°F, 71°F, and 39°F.

3. **Give an example** of a data set that could be described only by its mode.

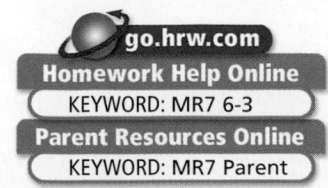

go.hrw.com
Homework Help Online
KEYWORD: MR7 6-3
Parent Resources Online
KEYWORD: MR7 Parent

GUIDED PRACTICE

See Example 1

1. **Sports** The graph shows how many times some countries have won the Davis Cup in tennis from 1900 to 2000.

   a. Find the mean, median, and mode of the data.

   b. The United States won 31 Davis Cups between 1900 and 2000. Add this number to the data in the graph and find the mean, median, and mode.

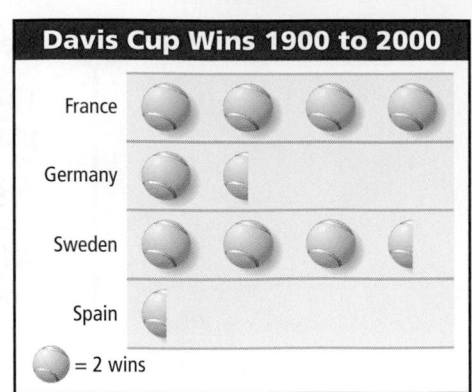

Davis Cup Wins 1900 to 2000

France

Germany

Sweden

Spain

= 2 wins

See Example 2

2. In 1998, 77-year-old John Glenn became the oldest person to travel into space. Other astronauts traveling on that same mission were 43, 37, 38, 46, 35, and 42 years old. Find the mean, median, and mode of all their ages with and without Glenn's age, and explain the changes.

See Example 3

3. Kate read books that were 240, 450, 180, 160, 195, 170, 240, and 165 pages long. What are the mean, median, and mode of this data set? Which one best describes the data set?

INDEPENDENT PRACTICE

See Example 1

4. **History** The table shows the ages of the 10 youngest signers of the Declaration of Independence.

   a. Find the mean, median, and mode of the data.

   b. Benjamin Franklin was 70 years old when he signed the Declaration of Independence. Add his age to the data in the table and find the mean, median, and mode.

Ages of 10 Youngest Signers of Declaration of Independence						
Age	26	29	30	31	33	34
Number Of Signers	//	/	/	/	///	//

See Example 2

5. **Geography** The map shows the population densities of several states along the Atlantic coast. Find the mean, median, and mode of the data with and without Maine's population density, and explain the changes.

See Example 3

6. The passengers in a van are 16, 19, 17, 18, 15, 14, 32, 32, and 41 years old. What are the mean, median, and mode of this data set? Which one best describes the data set?

Extra Practice
See page 724.

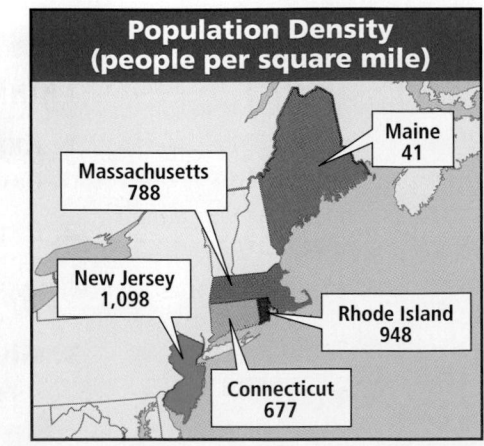

Population Density (people per square mile)

Maine
41

Massachusetts
788

New Jersey
1,098

Rhode Island
948

Connecticut
677

On September 13, 1922, the temperature in El Azizia, Libya, reached 136°F, the record high for the planet. (*Source: The World Almanac and Book of Facts*)

7. What are the mean, median, and mode of the highest recorded temperatures on each continent?

8. a. Which temperature is an outlier?

   b. What are the mean, median, and mode of the temperatures if the outlier is not included?

Continent	Highest Temperature (°F)
Africa	136
Antarctica	59
Asia	129
Australia	128
Europe	122
North America	134
South America	120

This satellite map shows the world's surface temperature. The dark blue areas are coldest, and the deep red areas are hottest.

go.hrw.com
Web Extra!
KEYWORD: MR7 Heat

9. **What's the Error?** A student stated that the median temperature would rise to 120.6°F if a new record high of 75°F were recorded in Antarctica. Explain the error. How would the median temperature actually be affected if a high of 75°F were recorded in Antarctica?

10. **Write About It** Is the data in the table best described by the mean, median, or mode? Explain.

11. **Challenge** Suppose a new high temperature were recorded in Europe, and the new mean temperature became 120°F. What is Europe's new high temperature?

 **TEST PREP and Spiral Review**

12. Multiple Choice Which value will change the most when 16 is added to the data set 0, 1, 4, 0, 3, 4, 2, and 1?

   (A) Mean   (B) Median   (C) Mode   (D) Outlier

13. Gridded Response The table shows the speeds, in miles per hour, of certain animals. Which speed is an outlier?

Animal	House cat	Rabbit	Cheetah	Reindeer	Zebra	Elk	Elephant
Speed (mi/h)	30	35	70	32	40	45	25

Solve each equation. Check your answer. (Lesson 5-5)

14. $\frac{1}{2} + m = 2$ **15.** $n - \frac{4}{5} = \frac{1}{10}$ **16.** $\frac{1}{3} + x = \frac{2}{3}$

17. Find the median, mode, and range of the animal speeds in Exercise 13. (Lesson 6-2)

Quiz for Lessons 6-1 Through 6-3

✓ 6-1 Make a Table

1. The local dance studio holds a spring recital each year. Five years ago, 220 people attended the recital. Four years ago, 235 people attended. Three years ago, 250 people attended. Two years ago, 242 people attended. Last year, 258 people attended. Use the attendance data to make a table. Then use your table to describe how attendance changed over time.

✓ 6-2 Mean, Median, Mode, and Range

Find the mean, median, mode, and range of each data set.

2.
Distance (mi)					
5	6	4	7	3	5

3.
Test Scores				
78	80	85	92	90

4.
Ages of Students (yr)							
11	13	12	12	12	13	9	14

5.
Number of Pages in Each Book						
145	119	156	158	125	128	135

✓ 6-3 Additional Data and Outliers

6. The table shows the number of people who attended each monthly meeting from January to May.

Number of People Attending				
Jan	Feb	Mar	Apr	May
27	26	32	30	30

   a. Find the mean, median, and mode of the attendances.

   b. In June, 39 people attended the meeting, and in July, 26 people attended the meeting. Add this data to the table and find the mean, median, and mode with the new data.

7. The four states with the longest coastlines are Alaska, Florida, California, and Hawaii. Alaska's coastline is 6,640 miles. Florida's coastline is 1,350 miles. California's coastline is 840 miles, and Hawaii's coastline is 750 miles. Find the mean, median, and mode of the lengths with and without Alaska's, and explain the changes.

8. The daily snowfall amounts for the first ten days of December are listed below.

   2 in., 5 in., 0 in., 0 in., 15 in., 1 in., 0 in., 3 in., 1 in., 4 in.

   What are the mean, median, and mode of this data set? Which one best describes the data set?

Ready to Go On?

Focus on Problem Solving

Make a Plan

• **Prioritize and sequence information**

Some problems give you a lot of information. Read the entire problem carefully to be sure you understand all of the facts. You may need to read it over several times, perhaps aloud so that you can hear yourself say the words.

Then decide which information is most important (prioritize). Is there any information that is absolutely necessary to solve the problem? This information is important.

Finally, put the information in order (sequence). Use comparison words like *before, after, longer, shorter,* and so on to help you. Write the sequence down before you try to solve the problem.

 **Read the problems below and answer the questions that follow.**

1 The compact disc (CD) was invented 273 years after the piano. The tape recorder was invented in 1898. Thomas Edison invented the phonograph 21 years before the tape recorder and 95 years before the compact disc. What is the date of each invention?

a. Which invention's date can you use to find the dates of all the others?

b. Can you solve the problem without this date? Explain.

c. List the inventions in order from earliest invention to latest invention.

2 Jon recorded the heights of his family members. There are 4 people in Jon's family, including Jon. Jon's mother is 2 inches taller than Jon's father. Jon is 56 inches tall. Jon's sister is 4 inches taller than Jon and 5 inches shorter than Jon's father. What are the heights of Jon and his family members?

a. Whose height can you use to find the heights of all the others?

b. Can you solve the problem without this height? Explain.

c. List Jon's family members in order from shortest to tallest.

?

1898

?

?

Deciduous Forest

Tundra

Rain Forest

Savannah

6-4 Bar Graphs

Learn to display and analyze data in bar graphs.

Vocabulary

bar graph

double-bar graph

A biome is a large region characterized by a specific climate. There are ten land biomes on Earth. Some are pictured at right. Each gets a different amount of rainfall.

A *bar graph* can be used to display and compare data about rainfall. A **bar graph** displays data with vertical or horizontal bars.

EXAMPLE 1 **Reading a Bar Graph**

NY Performance Indicators

6.S.7 Read and interpret graphs. Also, 6.R.1.

Use the bar graph to answer each question.

A Which biome in the graph has the most rainfall?

Find the highest bar.

The rain forest has the most rainfall.

B Which biomes in the graph have an average yearly rainfall less than 40 inches?

Find the bar or bars whose heights measure less than 40.

The tundra has an average yearly rainfall less than 40 inches.

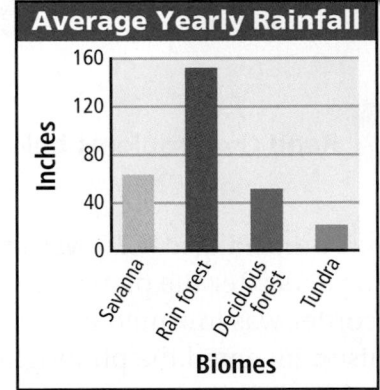

Average Yearly Rainfall

EXAMPLE 2 **Making a Bar Graph**

Use the given data to make a bar graph.

Coal Reserves (billion metric tons)		
Asia	Europe	Africa
695	404	66

Step 1: Find an appropriate scale and interval. The scale must include all of the data values. The interval separates the scale into equal parts.

Step 2: Use the data to determine the lengths of the bars. Draw bars of equal width. The bars cannot touch.

Step 3: Title the graph and label the axes.

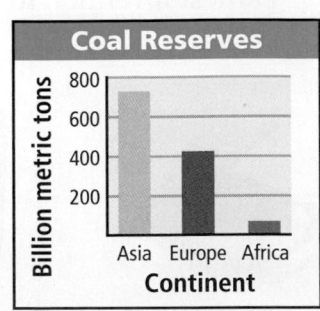

Coal Reserves

A **double-bar graph** shows two sets of related data.

EXAMPLE 3 PROBLEM SOLVING APPLICATION

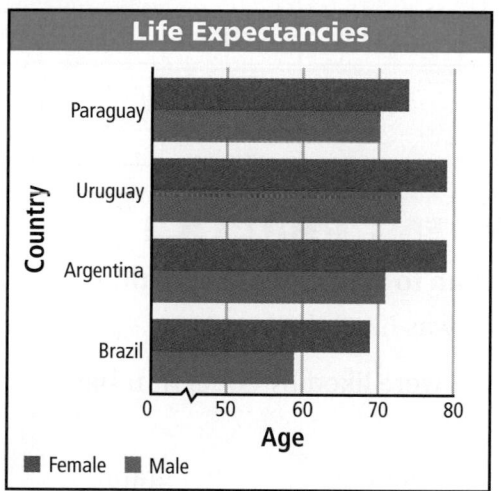

Make a double-bar graph to compare the data in the table.

Life Expectancies in Atlantic South America				
	Brazil	Argentina	Uruguay	Paraguay
Male (yr)	59	71	73	70
Female (yr)	69	79	79	74

1 Understand the Problem

You are asked to use a graph to compare the data given in the table. You will need to use all of the information given.

2 Make a Plan

You can make a double-bar graph to display the two sets of data.

Reading Math

This symbol means there is a break in the scale. Some intervals were left out because they were not needed for the graph.

3 Solve

Determine appropriate scales for both sets of data.

Use the data to determine the lengths of the bars. Draw bars of equal width. Bars should be in pairs. Use a different color for male ages and female ages.

Title the graph and label both axes.

Include a key to show what each bar represents.

4 Look Back

You could make two separate graphs, one of male ages and one of female ages. However, it is easier to compare the two data sets when they are on the same graph.

Think and Discuss

 6.R.5, 6.CM.1, 6.CN.3

1. **Give** comparisons you can make by looking at a bar graph.

2. **Describe** the kind of data you would display in a bar graph.

3. **Tell** why the graph in Example 3 needs a key.

Exercises

go.hrw.com
Homework Help Online
KEYWORD: MR7 6-4
Parent Resources Online
KEYWORD: MR7 Parent

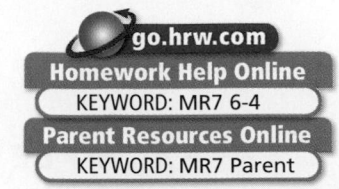

GUIDED PRACTICE

See Example **1** **Use the bar graph to answer each question.**

1. Which color was the least common among the cars in the parking lot?

2. Which colors appeared more than ten times in the parking lot?

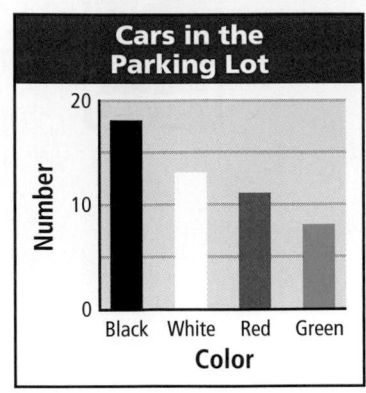

See Example **2** 3. Use the given data to make a bar graph.

Students in Mr. Jones's History Classes			
Period 1	28	Period 6	22
Period 2	27	Period 7	7

See Example **3** 4. Make a bar graph to compare the data in the table.

Movie Preferences of Men and Women Polled at the Mall						
	Comedy	Action	Sci-Fi	Horror	Drama	Other
Men	16	27	16	23	12	6
Women	21	14	8	18	30	9

INDEPENDENT PRACTICE

See Example **1** **Use the bar graph to answer each question.**

5. Which fruit was liked the best?

6. Which fruits were liked by equal numbers of people?

See Example **2** 7. Use the given data to make a bar graph.

Days with Rainfall			
January	14	March	16
February	12	April	23

See Example **3** 8. Make a bar graph to compare the data in the table.

Heart Rates Before and After Exercise (beats per minute)						
	Jason	Jamal	Ray	Tonya	Peter	Brenda
Before	60	62	61	65	64	65
After	131	140	128	140	135	120

PRACTICE AND PROBLEM SOLVING

Extra Practice
See page 724.

Social Studies Use the bar graph for Exercises 9–12.

9. What is the range of the land area of the continents?

10. What is the mode of the land area of the continents?

11. What is the mean of the land area of the continents?

12. What is the median of the land area of the continents?

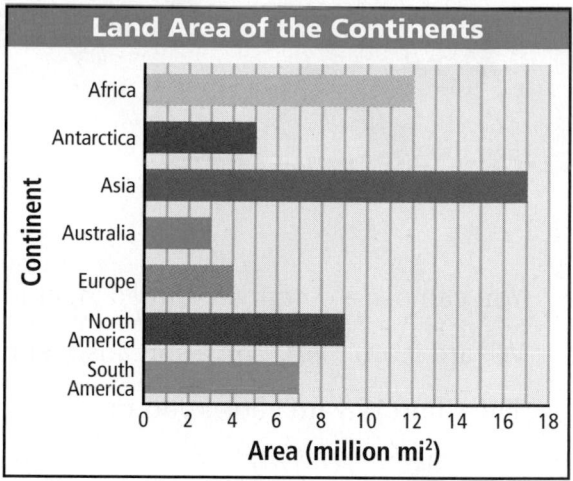

Land Area of the Continents

13. The basketball coach divided the team into two practice squads, the Blue Squad and the Green Squad. The table shows the scores from 6 weeks of practice games.

   a. Draw a double bar graph.

   b. Find the mean score and range for each squad.

   c. Which squad would you pick to play in an upcoming tournament? Explain your reasoning.

 14. **Write About It** Explain how you would make a bar graph of the five most populated cities in the United States.

 15. **Challenge** Create a bar graph displaying the number of A's, B's, C's, D's, and F's in Ms. Walker's class if the grades were the following: 81, 87, 80, 75, 77, 98, 52, 78, 75, 82, 74, 95, 76, 52, 76, 53, 86, 77, 90, 83, 96, 83, 74, 67, 90, 65, 69, 93, 68, and 76.

Scores of Practice Games		
	Blue	**Green**
Week 1	62	40
Week 2	40	44
Week 3	42	44
Week 4	54	48
Week 5	36	52
Week 6	50	56

Grading System	
A	90–100
B	80–89
C	70–79
D	60–69
F	0–59

TEST PREP and Spiral Review

Use the bar graph for Exercises 16 and 17.

16. **Multiple Choice** Which animal has the longest life span?

   Ⓐ Lion   Ⓑ Horse   Ⓒ Squirrel   Ⓓ Cow

17. **Multiple Choice** Which two animals have the same life span?

   Ⓕ Lion and horse   Ⓖ Squirrel and cow   Ⓗ Horse and squirrel   Ⓙ Lion and cow

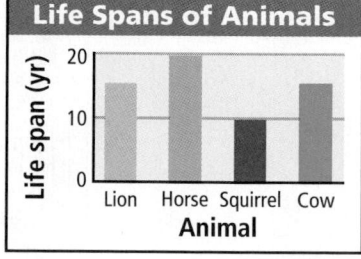

Life Spans of Animals

Find each sum or difference. Write the answer in simplest form. (Lessons 5-2 and 5-3)

18. $\frac{1}{7} + \frac{1}{4}$ 19. $\frac{1}{2} - \frac{3}{10}$ 20. $1\frac{3}{4} + 2\frac{1}{8}$ 21. $8\frac{2}{5} - 6\frac{1}{15}$

Technology LAB 6-4

Create Bar Graphs

Use with Lesson 6-4

go.hrw.com
Lab Resources Online
KEYWORD: MR7 Lab6

NY Performance Indicators
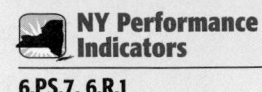
6.PS.7, 6.R.1

You can use a computer spreadsheet to draw bar graphs. The Chart Wizard icon, 📊 , on a spreadsheet menu looks like a bar graph. The Chart Wizard allows you to create different types of graphs.

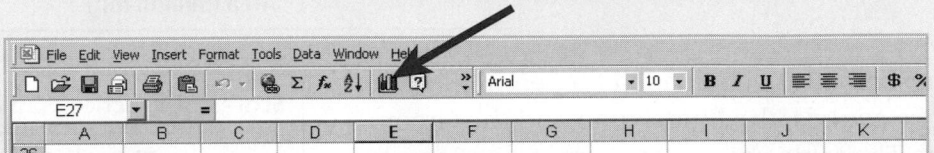

Activity

In a study conducted in December 2001 at Texas A&M University, the population of Texas through 2035 was projected. Make a bar graph of this data.

Texas Population	
Year	**Population**
2000	20,851,820
2005	23,207,929
2010	25,897,018
2015	28,971,283
2020	32,427,282
2025	36,273,829
2030	40,538,290
2035	45,283,746

1 Type the titles *Year* and *Population* into cells A1 and B1. Then type the data into columns A (year) and B (population).

2 Select the cells containing the titles and the data. Do this by placing your pointer in A1, clicking and holding the mouse button, and dragging the pointer down to B9.

3 Click the Chart Wizard icon. Highlight **Column** to make a vertical bar graph. Click **Next**.

4 The next screen shows where the data from the graph comes from. Click **Next**.

5 Title your graph and both axes. Click the **Legend** tab. Click the box next to **Show Legend** to turn off the key. (You would need a key if you were making a double-bar graph.) Click **Next** when you are finished.

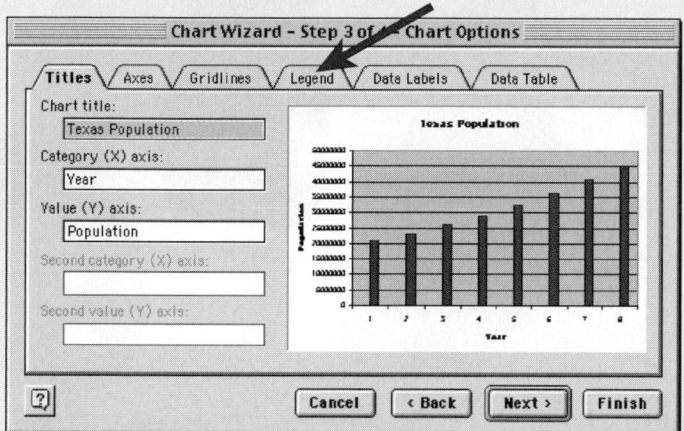

6 The next screen asks you where you want to place your chart. Click **Finish** to place it in your spreadsheet.

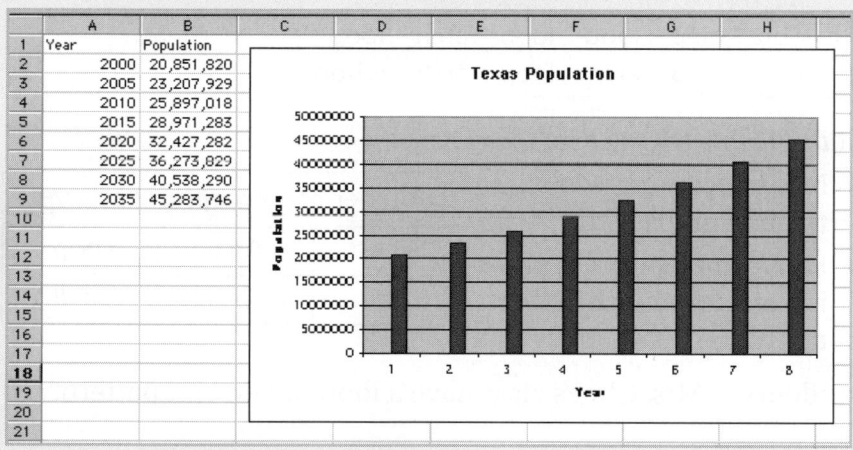

Think and Discuss

1. Do you think the population of Texas will be 32,427,282 in the year 2020 as shown in the graph? Explain.

Try This

1. Redraw the bar graph in the activity to show the population of Texas as 39,000,000 in 2035 and 33,000,000 in 2040.

2. Find the number of Texas counties that begin with the letter *A, B, C,* or *D.* Make a bar graph of the data.

Line Plots, Frequency Tables, and Histograms

Learn to organize data in line plots, frequency tables, and histograms.

Vocabulary

line plot

frequency table

histogram

Your fingerprints are unlike anyone else's. Even identical twins have slightly different fingerprint patterns.

All fingerprints have one of three patterns: whorl, arch, or loop.

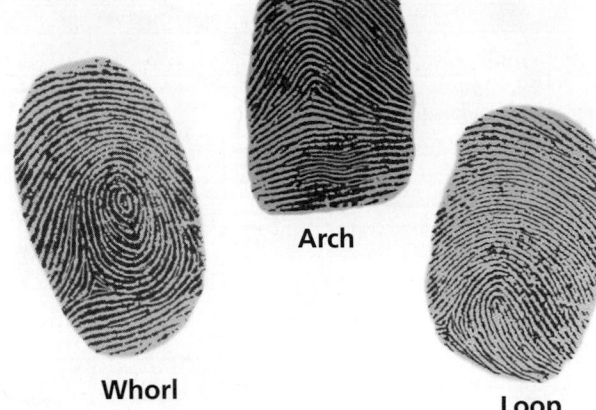

Arch

Whorl

Loop

EXAMPLE **1** **Making a Tally Table**

Each student in Mrs. Choe's class recorded their fingerprint pattern. Which type do most students in Mrs. Choe's class have?

| whorl | loop | loop | loop | loop | arch | loop |
| whorl | arch | loop | arch | loop | arch | whorl |

Make a *tally table* to organize the data.

Step 1: Make a column for each fingerprint pattern.

Step 2: For each fingerprint, make a tally mark in the appropriate column.

Reading Math

A group of four tally marks with a line through it means five.

卌 = 5

卌 卌 = 10

Number of Fingerprint Patterns		
Whorl	**Arch**	**Loop**
///	////	卌 //

Most students in Mrs. Choe's class have a loop fingerprint pattern.

A **line plot** uses a number line and *x*'s or other symbols to show frequencies of values.

EXAMPLE **2** **Making a Line Plot**

NY Performance Indicators

6.S.2 Record data in a frequency table. Also, 6.S.7.

Students in Mr. Lee's class each ran several miles in a week. Make a line plot of the data.

Number of Miles Run
8 3 5 6 7 8 5 5 3 6 10 7 5

Step 1: Draw a number line.

Step 2: For each student, use an *x* on the number line to represent how many miles he or she ran.

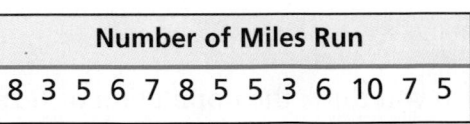

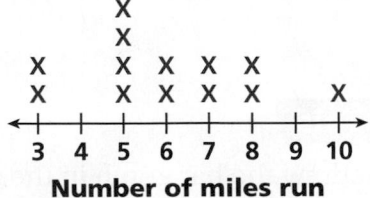

Number of miles run

A **frequency table** tells the number of times an event, category, or group occurs.

EXAMPLE **3** Making a Frequency Table with Intervals

Use the data in the table to make a frequency table with intervals.

Number of Representatives per State in the U.S. House of Representatives												
7	1	6	4	52	6	6	1	1	23	11	2	2
20	10	5	4	6	7	2	8	10	16	8	5	9
1	3	2	2	13	3	31	12	1	19	6	5	21
2	6	1	9	30	3	1	11	9	3	9		

Step 1: Choose equal intervals.

Step 2: Find the number of data values in each interval. Write these numbers in the "Frequency" row.

Number of Representatives per State in the U.S. House of Representatives									
Number	0–5	6–11	12–17	18–23	24–29	30–35	36–41	42–47	48–53
Frequency	22	18	3	4	0	2	0	0	1

This table shows that 22 states have between 0 and 5 representatives, 18 states have between 6 and 11 representatives, and so on.

A **histogram** is a bar graph that shows the number of data items that occur within each interval.

EXAMPLE **4** Making a Histogram

Use the frequency table in Example 3 to make a histogram.

Step 1: Choose an appropriate scale and interval.

Step 2: Draw a bar for the number of states in each interval. The bars should touch but not overlap.

Step 3: Title the graph and label the axes.

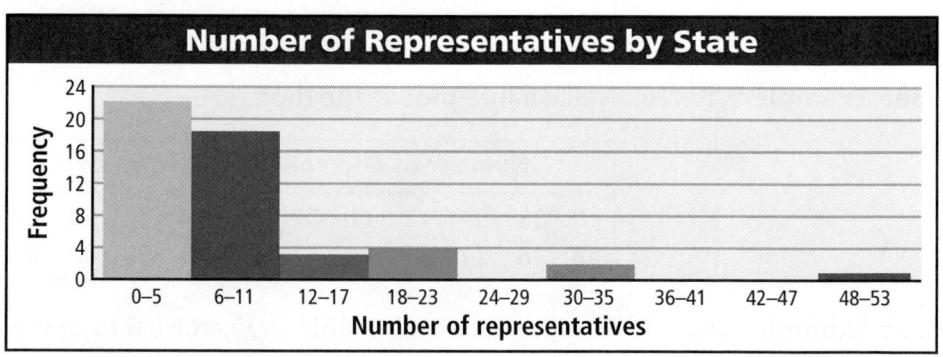

Think and Discuss

1. Describe a data set that can appropriately be displayed using a histogram.

Exercises

go.hrw.com
Homework Help Online
KEYWORD: MR7 6-5
Parent Resources Online
KEYWORD: MR7 Parent

GUIDED PRACTICE

See Example 1

1. Each student in the band recorded the type of instrument he or she plays. The results are shown in the box. Make a tally table to organize the data. Which instrument do the fewest students play?

trumpet	tuba	French horn	drums	trombone
drums	trombone	trombone	trumpet	trumpet
trumpet	French horn	trumpet	French horn	French horn

See Example 2

2. Make a line plot of the data.

Length of Each U.S. Presidency (yr)
8 4 8 8 8 4 8 4 0 4 4 1 3 4 4 4 4 8 4 0 4
4 4 4 4 8 4 8 2 6 4 12 8 8 2 6 5 3 4 8 4 8

See Example 3

3. Use the data in the table in Exercise 2 to make a frequency table with intervals.

See Example 4

4. Use your frequency table from Exercise 3 to make a histogram.

INDEPENDENT PRACTICE

See Example 1

5. Students recorded the type of pet they own. The results are shown in the box. Make a tally table. Which type of pet do most students own?

cat	cat	bird	dog	dog
dog	bird	dog	bird	fish
bird	cat	fish	dog	cat
fish	hamster	cat	hamster	dog

See Example 2

6. Make a line plot of the data.

Number of Olympic Medals Won by 27 Countries
8 88 59 12 11 57 38 17 14 28 28 26 25 23
18 8 29 34 14 17 13 13 58 12 97 10 9

See Example 3

7. Use the data in the table in Exercise 6 to make a frequency table with intervals.

See Example 4

8. Use your frequency table from Exercise 7 to make a histogram.

PRACTICE AND PROBLEM SOLVING

Extra Practice
See page 725.

9. **Critical Thinking** Would a bar graph or a histogram be more appropriate to display the state test scores for an entire sixth grade class? Explain.

10. **Multi-Step** Gather data on the number of pairs of shoes your classmates own. Make two line plots of the data, one for the boys and one for the girls. Compare the data.

11. **Social Studies** The map shows the populations of Australia's states and territories. Use the data to make a frequency table with intervals.

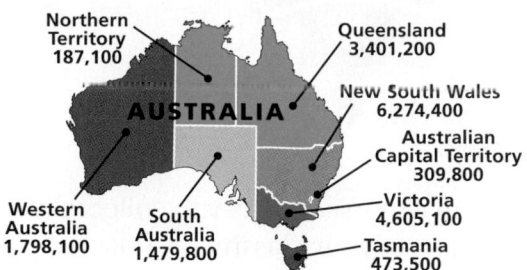

Northern Territory 187,100
Queensland 3,401,200
New South Wales 6,274,400
Australian Capital Territory 309,800
Victoria 4,605,100
Tasmania 473,500
Western Australia 1,798,100
South Australia 1,479,800

12. **Social Studies** Use your frequency table from Exercise 11 to make a histogram.

13. **Critical Thinking** Can a frequency table have intervals of 0–5, 5–10, and 10–15? Why or why not?

14. **What's the Error?** Reading from the line plot, Kathryn says that there are 10 campers who are three years old. What is Kathryn's error?

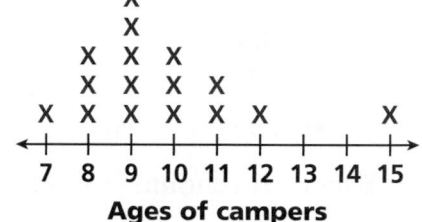

Ages of campers

15. **Write About It** Choose one of the histograms you made for this lesson and redraw it using different intervals. How did the histogram change? Explain.

16. **Challenge** Can you find the mean, median, and mode price using this frequency table? If so, find them. If not, explain why not.

Cost of Video Game Rentals at Different Stores			
Price	$2.00–$2.99	$3.00–$3.99	$4.00–$4.99	$5.00–$5.99
Frequency	5	12	8	5

TEST PREP and Spiral Review

17. **Multiple Choice** Emily is making a histogram for the data 12, 24, 56, 7, 34, 75, 34, 86, 34, 78, and 96. Which is the most appropriate first interval?

　Ⓐ 0–5　　　Ⓑ 0–10　　　Ⓒ 0–50　　　Ⓓ 0–100

18. **Short Response** Use the data in the table to make a frequency table with three-goal intervals. How many times were 6–8 goals scored?

Number of Goals Scored Each Game
3 5 2 5 4 7 1 0 6 4 8 5 3 2 4 5 9

Write each decimal in expanded form and word form. (Lesson 3-1)

19. 1.23　　　　20. 0.45　　　　21. 26.07　　　　22. 80.002

Find the outlier in each data set. (Lesson 6-3)

23. 3, 6, 19, 4, 2, and 5　　　24. 564, 514, 723, and 573　　　25. 34, 37, 41, 9, and 34

Use a Survey to Collect Data

NY Performance
Indicators

6.S.1

go.hrw.com
Lab Resources Online
KEYWORD: MR7 Lab6

You can use a survey to collect data. In this lab, you will split into teams and ask your classmates how long it takes them to get to school.

Work in teams of 2 or 3 students. Each team will survey students as they arrive at school, but the teams will work in different locations:

- Half the teams should survey students outside as they get off the school buses.

- The other teams should survey students as they enter their homerooms.

Each team should follow the steps below for their survey.

Activity

1 Ask students if they have been surveyed by any other team. If not, ask them what time they left their house that morning. Try to get 10 to 15 responses.

2 After you've finished surveying, calculate the time between when each student left the house and the time that first period of school starts. Record your data in a table like the one at right.

3 Calculate the mean travel time for the students you surveyed.

Time Student Left Home	Total Time Spent Getting to First Period (min)
6:57 A.M.	33
7:05 A.M.	25

Think and Discuss

1. Do you think the mean times will be longer for the bus teams or for the homeroom teams? Explain why.

2. As a class, find the mean time of all the students surveyed by the bus teams. Then find the mean time of all the students surveyed by the homeroom teams. Do the results match your prediction from problem **1**?

3. Do you think the bus mean or the homeroom mean is a more accurate estimate of the average time students take to get to school? Why?

Try This

1. Draw a histogram to display your team's data.

2. Think of something you'd like to know about the students in your school and write a survey question to find the answer. Explain how you would conduct the survey to get accurate results.

6-6 Ordered Pairs

Learn to graph ordered pairs on a coordinate grid.

Vocabulary

coordinate grid

ordered pair

NY Performance Indicators

6.G.10 Identify and plot points.

Cities, towns, and neighborhoods are often laid out on a grid. This makes it easier to map and find locations.

A **coordinate grid** is formed by horizontal and vertical lines and is used to locate points.

Each point on a coordinate grid can be located by using an **ordered pair** of numbers, such as (4, 6). The starting point is (0, 0).

San Diego, CA. Image courtesy of spaceimaging.com.

• The first number tells how far to move horizontally from (0, 0).

• The second number tells how far to move vertically.

EXAMPLE **1** **Identifying Ordered Pairs**

Name the ordered pair for each location.

A library

Start at (0, 0). Move right 2 units and then up 3 units.

The library is located at (2, 3).

B school

Start at (0, 0). Move right 6 units and then up 5 units.

The school is located at (6, 5).

C pool

Start at (0, 0). Move right 12 units and up 1 unit.

The pool is located at (12, 1).

EXAMPLE 2 Graphing Ordered Pairs

Graph and label each point on a coordinate grid.

A $Q\left(4\frac{1}{2}, 6\right)$ *Start at (0, 0).*
Move right $4\frac{1}{2}$ units.
Move up 6 units.

B $S(0, 4)$ *Start at (0, 0).*
Move right 0 units.
Move up 4 units.

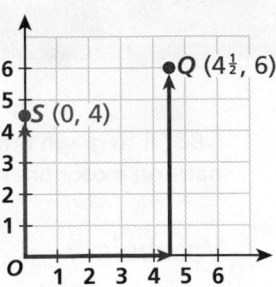

Think and Discuss

6.CM.1

1. **Tell** what point is the starting location when you are graphing on a coordinate grid.

2. **Describe** how to graph $(2\frac{1}{2}, 8)$ on a coordinate grid.

6-6 Exercises

go.hrw.com
Homework Help Online
KEYWORD: MR7 6-6
Parent Resources Online
KEYWORD: MR7 Parent

GUIDED PRACTICE

See Example 1   Name the ordered pair for each location.

1. school
2. store
3. hospital
4. mall
5. office
6. hotel

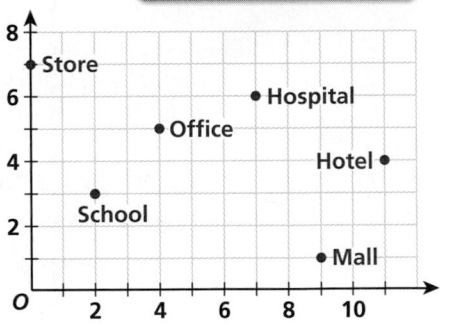

See Example 2   Graph and label each point on a coordinate grid.

7. $T\left(3\frac{1}{2}, 4\right)$
8. $S(2, 8)$
9. $U(5, 5)$
10. $V\left(4\frac{1}{2}, 1\right)$

INDEPENDENT PRACTICE

See Example 1   Name the ordered pair for each location.

11. diner
12. library
13. store
14. bank
15. theater
16. town hall

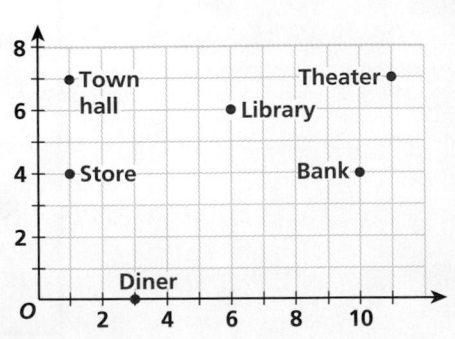

320   *Chapter 6 Collecting and Displaying Data*

Graph and label each point on a coordinate grid.

17. $P\left(5\frac{1}{2}, 1\right)$ **18.** $R(2, 4)$ **19.** $Q\left(3\frac{1}{2}, 2\right)$

20. $V(6, 5)$ **21.** $X\left(1\frac{1}{2}, 3\right)$ **22.** $Y(7, 4)$

PRACTICE AND PROBLEM SOLVING

Extra Practice
See page 725.

Use the coordinate grid for Exercises 23–35.
Name the point found at each location.

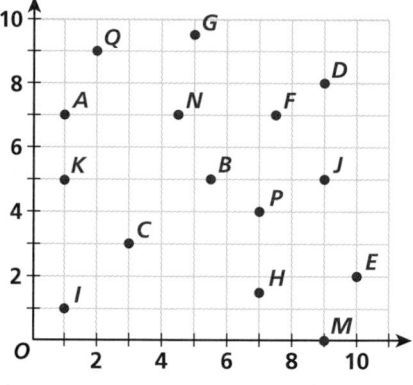

23. $(1, 7)$ **24.** $\left(5, 9\frac{1}{2}\right)$ **25.** $(3, 3)$

26. $\left(4\frac{1}{2}, 7\right)$ **27.** $(7, 4)$ **28.** $\left(7\frac{1}{2}, 7\right)$

Give the ordered pair for each point.

29. D **30.** H **31.** K

32. Q **33.** M **34.** B

35. Multi-Step The coordinates of points B, J, and M in the coordinate grid above form three of the corners of a rectangle. What are the coordinates of the fourth corner? Explain how you found your answer.

 36. Write About It Explain the difference between the points $(3, 2)$ and $(2, 3)$.

 37. What's the Question? If the answer is "Start at $(0, 0)$ and move 3 units to the right," what is the question?

 38. Challenge Locate and graph points that can be connected to form your initials. What are the ordered pairs for these points?

TEST PREP and Spiral Review

Use the coordinate grid for Exercises 39 and 40.

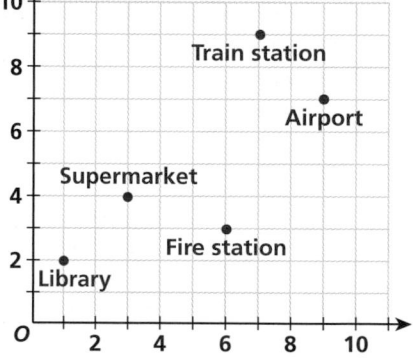

39. Multiple Choice At which ordered pair is the airport located?

  Ⓐ $(7, 9)$ Ⓑ $(3, 4)$ Ⓒ $(6, 3)$ Ⓓ $(9, 7)$

40. Multiple Choice Which location is at $(1, 2)$?

  Ⓕ Airport   Ⓗ Supermarket

  Ⓖ Library   Ⓙ Train station

Write each expression in exponential form. (Lesson 1-3)

41. $3 \times 3 \times 3 \times 5 \times 5$ **42.** $7 \times 7 \times 4 \times 4$ **43.** $2 \times 2 \times 3 \times 3 \times 5$

Find each product. Write each answer in simplest form. (Lesson 5-7)

44. $\frac{2}{3} \cdot \frac{1}{5}$ **45.** $\frac{3}{7} \cdot \frac{1}{4}$ **46.** $\frac{2}{9} \cdot \frac{3}{8}$ **47.** $\frac{1}{4} \cdot \frac{6}{7}$

6-7 Line Graphs

Learn to display and analyze data in line graphs.

Vocabulary

line graph

double-line graph

NY Performance Indicators

6.S.7 Read and interpret graphs.
Also, 6.R.1, 6.R.5.

The first permanent English settlement in the New World was founded in 1607. It contained 104 colonists. Population increased quickly as more and more immigrants left Europe for North America.

The table shows the estimated population of English American colonies from 1650 to 1700.

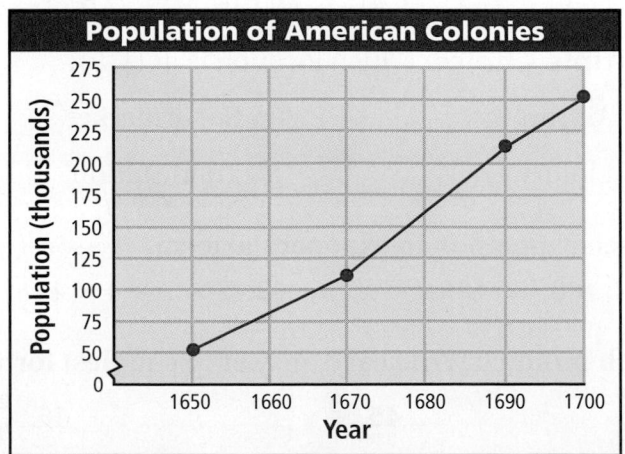
A New England Dame School, 1713

Population of American Colonies				
Year	1650	1670	1690	1700
Population	50,400	111,900	210,400	250,900

Data that shows change over time is best displayed in a *line graph*. A **line graph** displays a set of data using line segments.

EXAMPLE 1 Making a Line Graph

Use the data in the table above to make a line graph.

Step 1: Place *years* on the horizontal axis and *population* on the vertical axis. Label the axes.

Step 2: Determine an appropriate scale and interval for each axis.

Step 3: Mark a point for each data value. Connect the points with straight lines.

Step 4: Title the graph.

Caution!

Because time passes whether or not the population changes, time is *independent* of population. Always put the independent quantity on the horizontal axis.

Population of American Colonies

(Line graph showing Population (thousands) on the vertical axis from 0 to 275, and Year on the horizontal axis from 1650 to 1700. Points plotted: 1650 at about 50, 1670 at about 112, 1690 at about 210, 1700 at about 251.)

EXAMPLE 2

Reading a Line Graph

Use the line graph to answer each question.

A In which year did mountain bikes cost the least? 1997

B About how much did mountain bikes cost in 1999? about $300

C Did mountain bike prices increase or decrease from 1997 through 2001? They increased.

Line graphs that display two sets of data are called **double-line graphs**.

EXAMPLE 3

Making a Double-Line Graph

Use the data in the table to make a double-line graph.

Life Expectancy in the United States							
	1970	**1975**	**1980**	**1985**	**1990**	**1995**	**2000**
Male (yr)	67	69	70	71	72	73	74
Female (yr)	71	77	77	78	79	79	80

Helpful Hint

Use different colors of lines to connect the male and female values so you will easily be able to tell the data apart.

Step 1: Determine an appropriate scale and interval.

Step 2: Mark a point for each male value and connect the points.

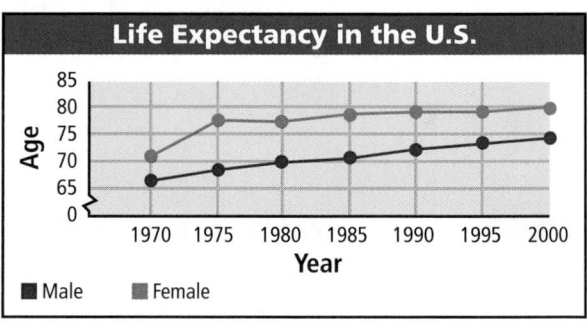

Step 3: Mark a point for each female value and connect the points.

Step 4: Title the graph and label both axes. Include a key.

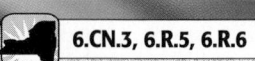

Think and Discuss

1. Explain when it would be helpful to use a line graph instead of a bar graph to display data.

2. Describe how you might use a line graph to make predictions.

3. Tell why the graph in Example 3 needs a key.

6-7 **Exercises**

go.hrw.com
Homework Help Online
KEYWORD: MR7 6–7
Parent Resources Online
KEYWORD: MR7 Parent

GUIDED PRACTICE

See Example **1**

1. Use the data in the table to make a line graph.

School Enrollment				
Year	2000	2001	2002	2003
Students	2,000	2,500	2,750	3,500

See Example **2**

Use the line graph to answer each question.

2. In which year did the most students participate in the science fair?

3. About how many students participated in 2002?

4. Did the number of students increase or decrease from 2000 to 2001?

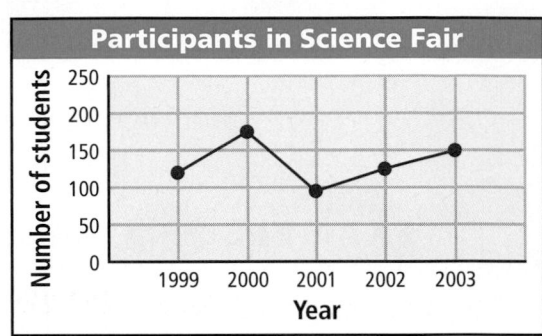

See Example **3**

5. Use the data in the table to make a double-line graph.

	January	February	March	April	May
Stock A	$10	$12	$20	$25	$22
Stock B	$8	$8	$12	$20	$30

INDEPENDENT PRACTICE

See Example **1**

6. Use the data in the table to make a line graph.

Winning Times in the Iditarod Trail Sled Dog Race							
Year	1995	1996	1997	1998	1999	2000	2001
Time (hr)	219	222	225	222	231	217	236

See Example **2**

Use the line graph to answer each question.

7. About how many personal computers were in use in the United States in 1996?

8. When was the number of personal computers in use about 105 million?

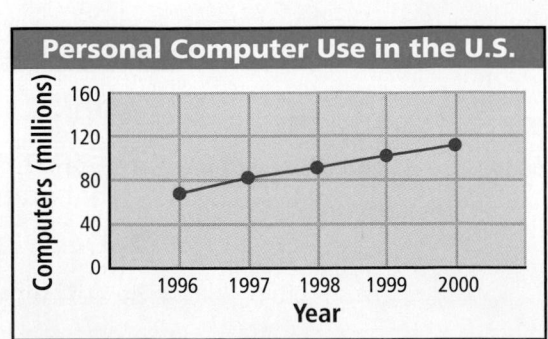

See Example **3** **9.** Use the data in the table to make a double-line graph.

Soccer Team's Total Fund-Raising Sales						
Day	0	1	2	3	4	5
Team A	$0	$100	$225	$300	$370	$450
Team B	$0	$50	$100	$150	$200	$250

PRACTICE AND PROBLEM SOLVING

Life Science

Larger dogs usually have shorter life spans than smaller dogs. Great Danes live an average of 8.4 years, and Jack Russell terriers live an average of 13.6 years.

Use the line graph for Exercises 10 and 11.

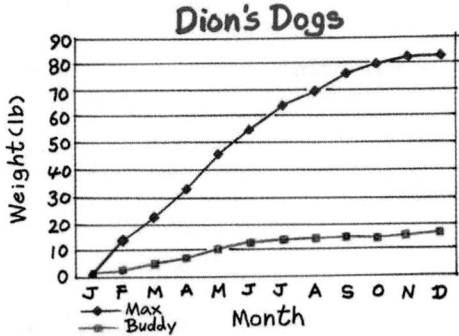

10. Life Science Estimate the difference in the dogs' weights in March.

11. Life Science One of Dion's dogs is a Great Dane, and the other is a Jack Russell Terrier. Which dog is probably the Great Dane? Justify your answer.

12. Life Science The table shows the weights in pounds for Sara Beth's two pets. Use the data to make a line graph that is similar to Dion's.

	Jan	Feb	Mar	Apr	May	Jun	Jul	Aug	Sep	Oct	Nov	Dec
Ginger	3	9	15	21	24	25	26	25	26	27	26	28
Toto	4	8	13	17	24	26	27	29	25	26	28	28

13. Write About It You have a bowl of soup for lunch. Draw a line graph that could represent the changes in the soup's temperature during lunch. Explain.

14. Challenge Describe a situation that this graph could represent.

TEST PREP and Spiral Review

15. Multiple Choice Which type of graph would you use to display two sets of data that change over time?

(A) Bar graph (B) Pictograph (C) Double-line graph (D) Line graph

16. Short Response Use the graph from Exercises 10 and 11. Did Max's weight increase or decrease between September and October? Explain.

Solve each equation. (Lesson 2-7)

17. $5s = 90$ **18.** $4g = 128$ **19.** $8m = 120$ **20.** $17a = 544$

21. A survey of 100 people found that 48 of the people have had 0 speeding tickets, 34 have had 1 ticket, 10 have had 2 tickets, 5 have had 3 tickets, and 2 have had 4 or more tickets. Create a bar graph to display the data. (Lesson 6-4)

6-8 Misleading Graphs

Learn to recognize misleading graphs.

NY Performance Indicators

6.S.7 Read and interpret graphs. Also, 6.R.1.

Data can be displayed in many different ways. Sometimes people who make graphs choose to display data in a misleading way.

This bar graph was created by a group of students who believe their school should increase support of the football team. How could this bar graph be misleading?

At a glance, you might conclude that about three times as many students prefer football to basketball. But if you look at the values of the bars, you can see that only 20 students chose football over basketball.

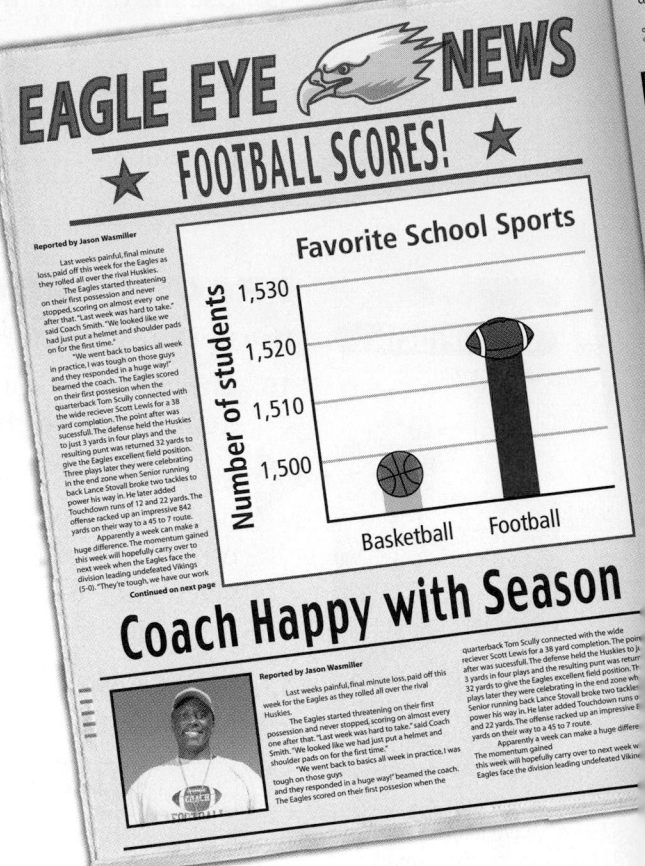

EXAMPLE **1** Misleading Bar Graphs

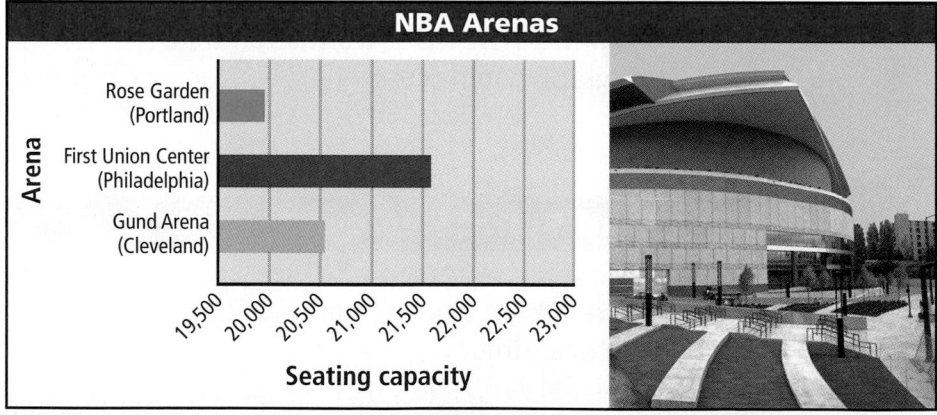

A **Why is this bar graph misleading?**

Because the lower part of the horizontal scale is missing, the differences in seating capacities are exaggerated.

B **What might people believe from the misleading graph?**

People might believe that the First Union Center holds 2–4 times as many people as Gund Arena and the Rose Garden. In reality, the First Union Center holds only one to two thousand more people than the other two arenas.

EXAMPLE **2** Misleading Line Graphs

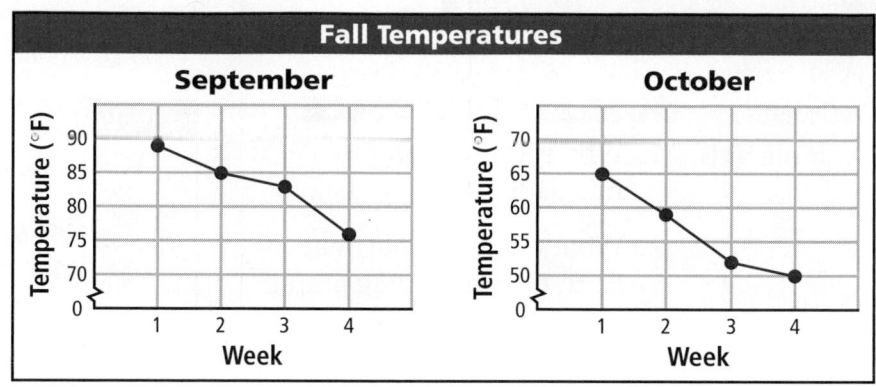

A Why are these line graphs misleading?

If you look at the scale for each graph, you will notice that the September graph goes from 75°F to 90°F and the October graph goes from 50°F to 65°F.

B What might people believe from these misleading graphs?

People might believe that the temperatures in October were about the same as the temperatures in September. In reality, the temperatures in September were 20–30 degrees higher.

C Why is this line graph misleading?

The scale does not have equal intervals. So, for example, an increase from 35 sit-ups to 40 sit-ups looks greater than an increase from 30 sit-ups to 35 sit-ups.

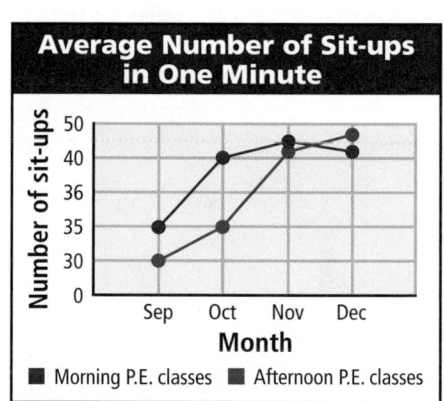

Think and Discuss

1. Give an example of a situation in which you think someone would intentionally try to make a graph misleading.

2. Tell who might have made the misleading graph in Example 2C.

3. Tell how you could change the graph in Example 2C so that it is not misleading.

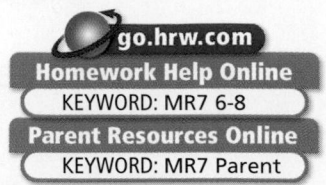

6-8 Exercises

go.hrw.com
Homework Help Online
KEYWORD: MR7 6-8
Parent Resources Online
KEYWORD: MR7 Parent

GUIDED PRACTICE

See Example 1

1. Why is this bar graph misleading?

2. What might people believe from the misleading graph?

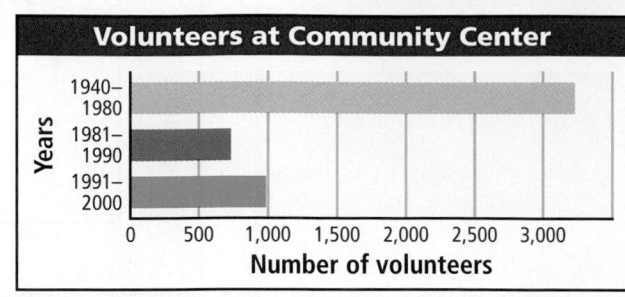

See Example 2

3. Why is this line graph misleading?

4. What might people believe from the misleading graph?

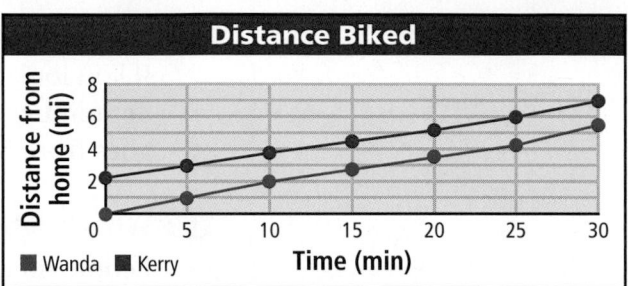

INDEPENDENT PRACTICE

See Example 1

5. Why is this bar graph misleading?

6. What might people believe from the misleading graph?

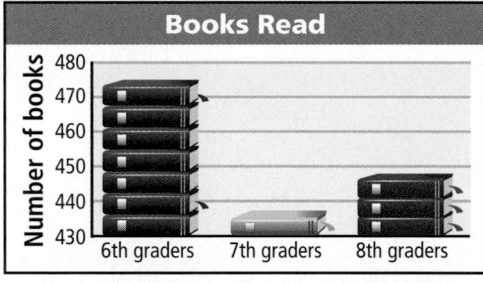

See Example 2

7. Why is this line graph misleading?

8. What might people believe from the misleading graph?

PRACTICE AND PROBLEM SOLVING

Extra Practice
See page 725.

9. Critical Thinking In a survey, people were asked which teeth-whitening product they found worked best. The results stated that 1,007 people chose strips, 995 people chose paste, and 998 chose paint. Make two bar graphs, one to show that the strips are significantly more effective than the paste or paint, and the other to show that the paste is the most effective.

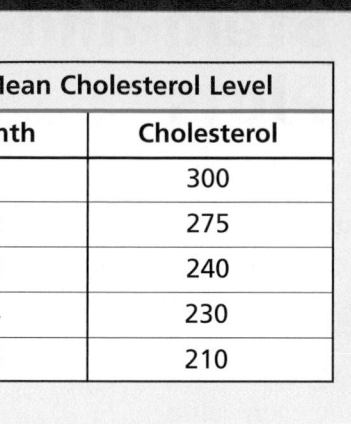
A research company has developed a cholesterol medication. The table shows the mean monthly cholesterol levels for patients who have been taking the medication for 5 months.

Mean Cholesterol Level	
Month	Cholesterol
1	300
2	275
3	240
4	230
5	210

10. What kind of graph would you make to display this data? Why?

11. Make a graph that suggests the medication greatly reduces cholesterol levels. Explain how your graph does this.

12. Make a graph that suggests the medication has little effect on cholesterol levels. Explain how your graph does this.

13. **What's the Question?** Look at the entries in the table. If the answer is 90, what is the question?

14. **Write About It** Suppose you saw your graph from Exercise 12 in an advertisement. What do you think it might be an advertisement for? Explain.

15. **Challenge** What additional information could the research company gather and use to make a double-line graph that shows how its medication affects cholesterol levels?

A heart with coronary artery disease, caused by buildup of fatty deposits

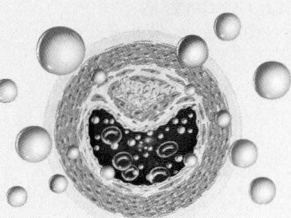

An artery that has been narrowed by high levels of blood cholesterol

TEST PREP and Spiral Review

16. Multiple Choice Which statement is supported by the information in the bar graph?

Ⓐ Damon scored twice as high as Kyle on the test.
Ⓑ Kyle scored the highest on the test.
Ⓒ Brent scored twice as high as Julie on the test.
Ⓓ Deb scored the second-highest on the test.

17. Short Response What might readers believe from the misleading line graph? Explain how to redraw the graph so that it is not as misleading.

Test Scores

Temperatures

Evaluate each expression. (Lesson 1-4)

18. $6 \times 2^3 + 17 - 3 \times 2$ **19.** $85 - (44 + 33) \div 7 + (62 - 12)$

Plot each point on a coordinate grid. (Lesson 6-6)

20. $A(3, 5)$ **21.** $B(6, 2)$ **22.** $C(0, 4)$ **23.** $D(1, 0)$ **24.** $E(5.5, 7)$

Stem-and-Leaf Plots

Learn to make and analyze stem-and-leaf plots.

Vocabulary

stem-and-leaf plot

NY Performance Indicators

6.R.1 Use charts as representations. Also, 6.R.5.

A **stem-and-leaf plot** shows data arranged by place value. You can use a stem-and-leaf plot when you want to display data in an organized way that allows you to see each value.

The Explorer Scouts had a competition to see who could build the highest card tower. The table shows the number of levels reached by each scout.

Bryan Berg and his card model of the Iowa State Capitol

Number of Card-Tower Levels									
12	23	31	50	14	17	25	44	51	20
23	18	35	15	19	15	23	42	21	13

EXAMPLE 1 Creating Stem-and-Leaf Plots

Use the data in the table above to make a stem-and-leaf plot.

Step 1: Group the data by tens digits.

Step 2: Order the data from least to greatest.

Step 3: List the tens digits of the data in order from least to greatest. Write these in the "stems" column.

Step 4: For each tens digit, record the ones digits of each data value in order from least to greatest. Write these in the "leaves" column.

Step 5: Title the graph and add a key.

| 12 13 14 15 15 17 18 19 |
| 20 21 23 23 23 25 |
| 31 35 |
| 42 44 |
| 50 51 |

Helpful Hint

To write 42 in a stem-and-leaf plot, write each digit in a separate column.

4 | 2
↗ ↖
Stem   Leaf

Number of Card Tower Levels

Stems	Leaves
1	2 3 4 5 5 7 8 9
2	0 1 3 3 3 5
3	1 5
4	2 4
5	0 1

Key: 1|5 means 15

EXAMPLE 2 **Reading Stem-and-Leaf Plots**

Stems	Leaves
5	8
6	8 9
7	2 4 8
8	0 4 5 6 8
9	0 0 2 3 6 7 8
10	
11	7

Key: 5|8 means 58

Find the least value, greatest value, mean, median, mode, and range of the data.

The least stem and least leaf give the least value, 58.

The greatest stem and greatest leaf give the greatest value, 117.

Use the data values to find the mean.
$(58 + \ldots + 117) \div 19 = 85$

The median is the middle value in the table, 86.

To find the mode, look for the number that occurs most often in a row of leaves. Then identify its stem. The mode is 90.

The range is the difference between the greatest and least value.
$117 - 58 = 59$

> **Caution!**
>
> If a stem has no leaves, there are no data points with that stem. In the stem-and-leaf plot in Example 2, there are no data values between 100 and 109.

Think and Discuss

6.CM.1

1. **Describe** how to show 25 on a stem-and-leaf plot.

6-9 Exercises

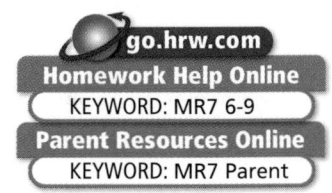

go.hrw.com
Homework Help Online
KEYWORD: MR7 6-9
Parent Resources Online
KEYWORD: MR7 Parent

GUIDED PRACTICE

See Example 1

1. Use the data in the table to make a stem-and-leaf plot.

Daily High Temperatures (°F)	45	56	40	39	37	48	51

See Example 2

Find each value of the data.

2. smallest value   3. largest value

4. mean   5. median

6. mode   7. range

Stems	Leaves
1	0 2
2	
3	2
4	1 4

Key: 1|0 means 10

INDEPENDENT PRACTICE

See Example 1

8. Use the data in the table to make a stem-and-leaf plot.

Heights of Plants (cm)	30	12	27	28	15	47	37	28	40	20

See Example ② **Find each value of the data.**

9. least value   10. greatest value

11. mean   12. median

13. mode   14. range

Stems	Leaves
4	1 2 2
5	1 3
6	7 8

Key: 4|1 means 41

PRACTICE AND PROBLEM SOLVING

Extra Practice

See page 725.

For Exercises 15 and 16, write the letter of the stem-and-leaf plot described.

A.
Stems	Leaves
1	0 3 4
2	0 0 1 1 1 3
3	4 5 9
4	8

Key: 1|0 means 10

B.
Stems	Leaves
1	6
2	2 3
3	0 1 4
4	1 4 8

Key: 1|6 means 16

C.
Stems	Leaves
1	4
2	
3	6
4	3 6 8

Key: 1|4 means 14

15. The data set has a mode of 21.   16. The data set has a median of 31.

Use the table for Exercises 17 and 18.

17. Karla recorded the number of cars with only one passenger that came through a toll booth each day. Use Karla's data to make a stem-and-leaf plot.

Cars with Only One Passenger					
82	103	95	125	88	94
89	92	94	99	87	80
109	101	100	83	124	81

 18. **What's the Error?** Karla's classmate looked at the stem-and-leaf plot and said that the mean number of cars with only one passenger is 4. Explain Karla's classmate's error. What is the correct mean?

 19. **Challenge** Josh is the second youngest of 4 teenage boys, all 2 years apart in age. Josh's mother is 3 times as old as Josh is, and she is 24 years younger than her father. Make a stem-and-leaf plot to show the ages of Josh, his brothers, his mother, and his grandfather.

TEST PREP and Spiral Review

20. **Multiple Choice** What is the value of 1|2 in the stem-and-leaf plot?

Stems	Leaves
1	0 1 2 3
2	7 9 9 9

Key: 1|1 means 1,100

Ⓐ 12   Ⓒ 100,002

Ⓑ 1,200   Ⓓ 100,200

21. **Gridded Response** What is the median of the data in Exercise 20?

Order the numbers from least to greatest. (Lesson 1-1)

22. 3,673,809; 3,708,211; 3,671,935   23. 2,004,801; 225,971; 298,500,004

Find the reciprocal. (Lesson 5-9)

24. 6   25. $\frac{4}{7}$ 26. $\frac{2}{9}$ 27. $\frac{1}{5}$ 28. $\frac{9}{8}$

Choosing an Appropriate Display

Learn to choose an appropriate way to display data.

 NY Performance Indicators

6.S.4 Determine and justify the most appropriate graph to display a given set of data. Also, 6.S.7.

A neighborhood community center offers programs for people of all ages. Its recent brochure includes a bar graph that shows the number of people, by age, enrolled in various programs.

Depending on the data to be displayed, some types of graphs are more useful than others.

Commom Uses of Data Displays			
	You can use a line plot to show how often each number occurs.		You can use a bar graph to display and compare data in separate categories.
	You can use a line graph to show how data change over a period of time.		You can use a stem-and-leaf plot to show how often data values occur and how they are distributed.

EXAMPLE 1 Choosing an Appropriate Data Display

A The table shows the number of miles of coastline for states bordering the Gulf of Mexico. Which graph would be more appropriate to show the data—a bar graph or a line graph? Draw the more appropriate graph.

State	AL	FL	LA	MS	TX
Miles of Coastline	33	770	397	44	367

Think: Is the information in the table describing a change over time? Is the information in the table divided into different categories?

The table shows the number of miles of coastline in different states. The data should be displayed in separate categories. So a bar graph is more appropriate than a line graph.

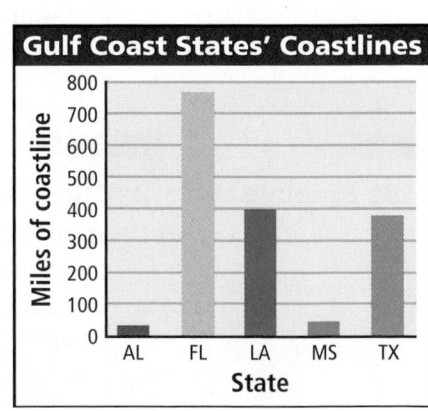

B The table shows the lengths of some animals. Which graph would be more appropriate to show the data— a stem-and-leaf plot or a line graph? Draw the more appropriate graph.

Lengths of Animals (in.)					
70	43	42	50	35	32
32	45	61	35	40	30

Think: The table shows a number of different lengths. It does not show data changing over time.

A stem-and-leaf plot shows how often data values occur. So a stem-and-leaf plot is more appropriate than a line graph.

Lengths of Animals (in.)

Stems	Leaves
3	0 2 2 5 5
4	0 2 3 5
5	0
6	1
7	0

Key: 3|2 means 32

Think and Discuss

 6.CM.1, 6.R.6

1. **Describe** a situation when a line graph would be a more appropriate choice than a bar graph to show data.

2. **Describe** another type of graph that could be used to display the data shown in the table in Example 1B.

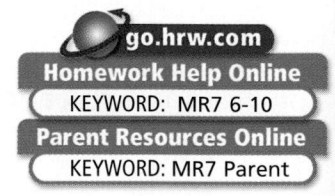

go.hrw.com
Homework Help Online
KEYWORD: MR7 6-10
Parent Resources Online
KEYWORD: MR7 Parent

6-10 Exercises

GUIDED PRACTICE

See Example **1**

1. The table shows the average high temperatures in Atlanta for six months of one year. Which graph would be more appropriate to show the data—a bar graph or a line graph? Draw the more appropriate graph.

Month	Jan	Mar	May	Jul	Sep	Nov
Temp. (°F)	54	63	81	88	83	62

INDEPENDENT PRACTICE

See Example **1**

2. The table shows the percentages of students who bought a hot lunch from the school cafeteria. Which graph would be more appropriate to show the data— a bar graph or a line graph? Draw the more appropriate graph.

September	30%	November	27%	January	45%
October	28%	December	27%	February	42%

Extra Practice
See page 725.

Year	Population
1900	76,094,000
1925	115,829,000
1950	152,271,417
1975	215,973,199
2000	281,421,906

3. **Social Studies** The table shows the U.S. population from 1900 through 2000.

   a. What graph would be most appropriate to show the data? Why?

   b. Make a graph of the data.

4. **Critical Thinking** The total wins that teams in the Western Conference of the National Hockey League had in a recent year are as follows: 48, 39, 38, 25, 20, 43, 40, 42, 36, 30, 43, 22, 29, 41, 28. Which graph would be more appropriate to show the data—a line plot or a bar graph? Draw the more appropriate graph. Then explain how to use the graph to find the median and mode.

5. **Write a Problem** Use the information in the table to write a problem that can be solved by drawing a graph. Tell which type of graph you would use.

Animal	Life Span (yr)
Bear	40
Carp	100
Elephant	70
Tiger	22

6. **Write About It** Explain the similarities and differences between a bar graph and a line graph.

7. **Challenge** The stem-and-leaf plot shows the number of hours 20 students spent studying over a two-week period. Make a line plot to show the data. What does the line plot show more clearly than a stem-and-leaf plot would?

Study Times

Stems	Leaves
1	5 6 6 6 7 7 9 9
2	0 0 1 1 1 1 2 2 3
3	5 7 9

Key: 1|5 means 15

8. **Multiple Choice** Which graph would be most appropriate to show the number of miles each student walked in one week for a charity walk-a-thon?

   Ⓐ Circle graph   Ⓑ Stem-and-leaf plot   Ⓒ Line graph   Ⓓ Bar graph

9. **Extended Response** People leaving a gym were asked how long they exercised. The results in minutes are: 15, 10, 35, 35, 60, 65, 15, 60, 20, 35. Which type of graph would be most appropriate to show the data? Explain. Make a graph of the data. What is the median amount of time spent exercising?

Find the GCF of each set of numbers. (Lesson 4-3)

10. 4 and 16   11. 15 and 50   12. 15, 60, and 75   13. 4, 8, and 80

14. Ashlee spent 50 minutes washing and waxing her car. She spent $\frac{2}{5}$ of that time washing the car. How many minutes did Ashlee spend washing her car? (Lesson 5-6)

READY TO GO ON?

Quiz for Lessons 6-4 Through 6-10

✓ 6-4 Bar Graphs

The students in Ms. Bain's class voted on their favorite fruit juice. Use the bar graph to answer each question.

1. How many more students prefer orange juice than prefer grape juice?

2. How many students in all voted?

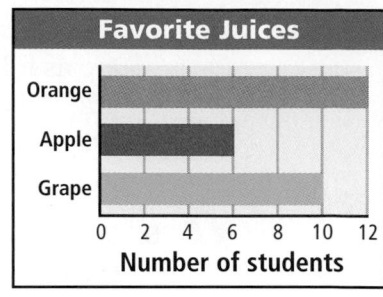

Favorite Juices

Number of students

✓ 6-5 Line Plots, Frequency Tables, and Histograms

Shoppers leaving Midtown Mall were each asked to give their age. Use the line plot to answer each question.

3. What are the range and mode of the data?

4. How many of the shoppers surveyed were older than 20?

Shoppers at Midtown Mall

```
                        X
   X                    X       X
   X                    X  X    X
X  X        X  X  X  X  X       X
<--+--+--+--+--+--+--+--+-->
  15 16 17 18 19 20 21 22
```

Ages of shoppers

✓ 6-6 Ordered Pairs

Graph and label each point on a coordinate grid.

5. $A(4, 5)$

6. $B\left(0, 3\frac{1}{2}\right)$

✓ 6-7 Line Graphs

7. Use the data in the table to make a line graph.

Graphicworks	
Year	Numbers of Employees
2003	852
2004	1,098
2005	1,150
2006	1,150

✓ 6-8 Misleading Graphs

8. Bob drew a line graph of the Graphicworks data. For the vertical scale representing the number of employees, he used these intervals: 0; 800; 1,000; and 1,500. Explain why his graph is misleading.

✓ 6-9 Stem-and-Leaf Plots

9. Use the data in the line plot in problems 3 and 4 to make a stem-and-leaf plot.

✓ 6-10 Choosing an Appropriate Display

10. Would it also be appropriate to use a line graph to represent the data that is shown in the bar graph in problems 1 and 2? Explain.

Ready to Go On?

Deet's Treats Trail mix at Deet's Treats is priced at $2 for 8 ounces. The trail mix is sold in 4-ounce and 8-ounce packages. The manager at the shop decides to put a graph on display to show the cost of trail mix. He asks three employees to each make a graph. Their graphs are shown at right.

1. For each graph, make a table that shows the data in the graph.

2. The manager wants to display the most appropriate graph for his customers to get detailed and accurate information about the trail mix. Explain in what ways, if any, the graphs are misleading.

3. To help clerks sell trail mix, create a table of prices for selling up to 4 pounds of trail mix. Explain your table. (*Hint:* 16 oz = 1 lb)

4. How many different ways can you purchase 4 pounds of trail mix when buying 4-ounce and 8-ounce packages? Explain.

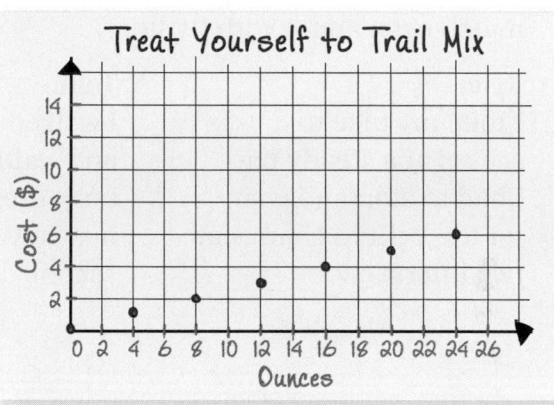

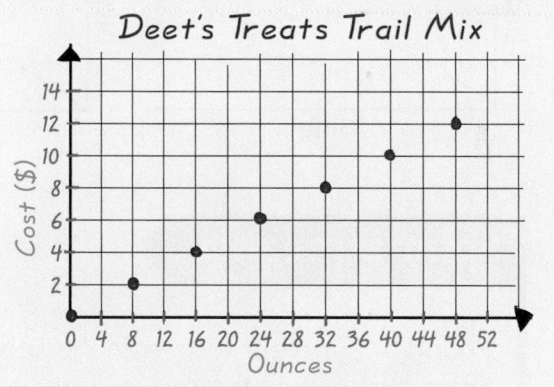

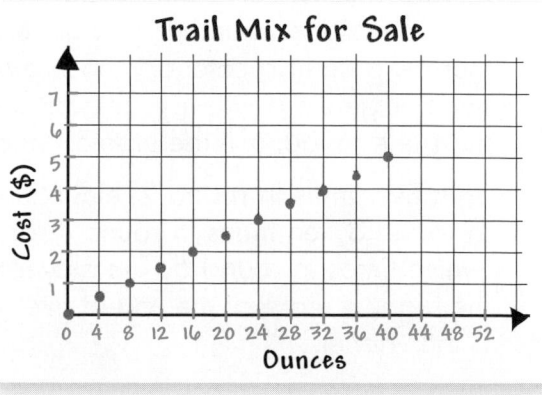

Game Time

A Thousand Words

Did you ever hear the saying "A picture is worth a thousand words"?
A graph can be worth a thousand words too!

Each of the graphs below tells a story about a student's trip to school.
Read each story and think about what each graph is showing. Can you
match each graph with its story?

Kyla:
I rode my bike to
school at a steady pace.
I had to stop and wait
for the light to change at
two intersections.

Tom:
I walked to my bus stop
and waited there for the
bus. After I boarded the
bus, it was driven straight to
school.

Megan:
On my way to school, I
stopped at my friend's
house. She wasn't ready
yet, so I waited for her.
Then we walked to school.

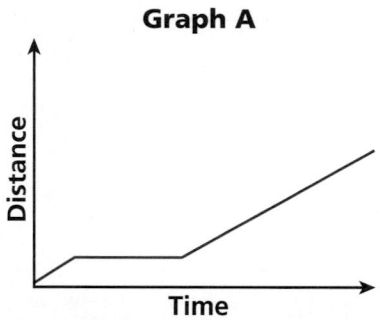

Graph A

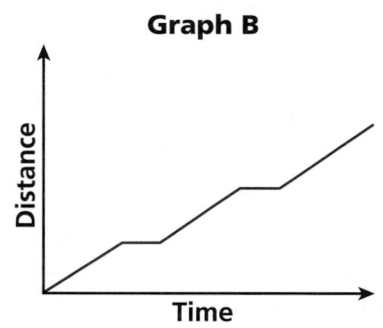

Graph B

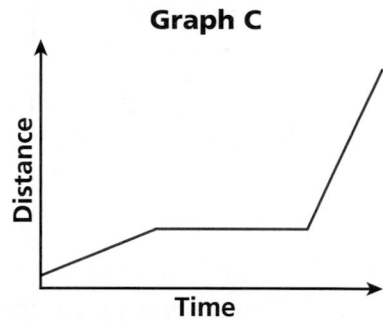

Graph C

Spinnermeania

Round 1: On your turn, spin the spinner four
times and record the results. After everyone has
had a turn, find the mean, median, and mode
of your results. For every category in which you
have the highest number, you get one point. If
there is a tie in a category, each player with that
number gets a point. If your data set has more
than one mode, use the greatest one.

Spin five times in round 2, eight times
in round 3, ten times in round 4, and
twelve times in round 5. The player with
the highest score at the end of five rounds
is the winner.

go.hrw.com
Game Time Extra
KEYWORD: MR7 Games

A complete copy of the rules and
game pieces are available online.

Materials
- 2 pieces of card stock
- 6 sandwich-size zipper bags
- clear packaging tape
- graph paper
- scissors

PROJECT ## Graphing According to Me

Create different types of graphs and make a zippered accordion book to hold them all.

Directions

1 Place one piece of card stock that is $6\frac{1}{2}$ inches by 7 inches next to one of the bags. The opening of the bag should be at the top, and there should be a small space between the card stock and the bag. Tape the card stock and bag together on the front and back sides. **Figure A**

2 Lay another bag down next to the first, keeping a small space between them. Tape them together, front and back. **Figure B**

3 Continue with the rest of the bags. At the end of the chain, tape a second piece of card stock that is $6\frac{1}{2}$ inches by 7 inches to the last bag. **Figure C**

4 Fold the bags accordion-style, back and forth, with the two card stock covers on the front and back.

5 Cut out squares of graph paper so they will fit in the bags.

Taking Note of the Math

Write the number and title of the chapter on the cover. On each piece of graph paper, draw and label an example of one type of graph from the chapter. Store the graphs in the bags.

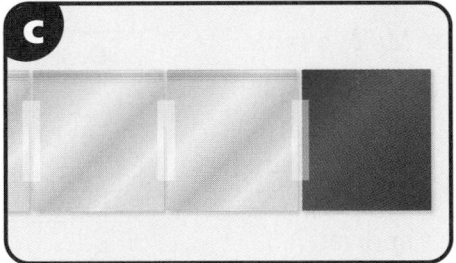

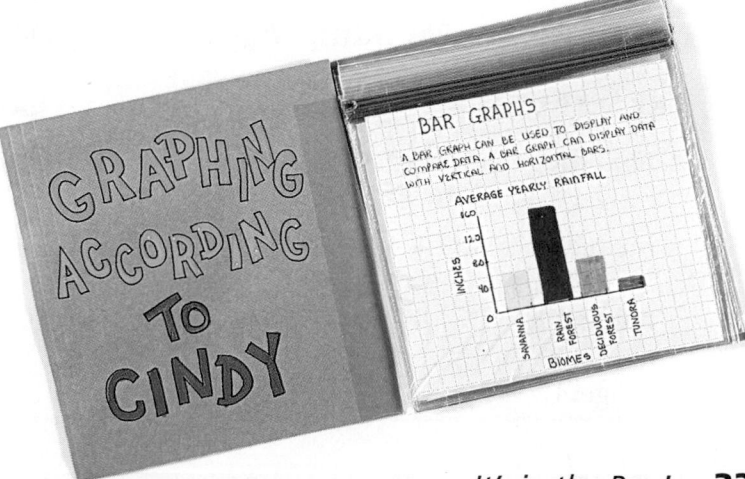

Study Guide: Review

Vocabulary

Complete the sentences below with vocabulary words from the list above.

1. A(n) ___?___ uses vertical or horizontal bars to show the number of items within each interval.

2. A point can be located by using a(n) ___?___ of numbers such as (3, 5).

3. In a data set, the ___?___ is the value or values that occur most often.

6-1 Make a Table (pp. 294–296)

 6.CM.4

EXAMPLE

- **Make a table using the data.**

  Monday it snowed 2 inches. Tuesday it snowed 3.5 inches. Thursday it snowed 4.25 inches.

Day	Snowfall
Mon	2 in.
Tue	3.5 in.
Thu	4.25 in.

EXERCISES

4. Make a table using the data on snake lengths.

   An anaconda can be up to 35 ft long. A diamond python can be up to 21 ft long. A king cobra can be up to 19 ft long. A boa constrictor can be up to 16 ft long.

6-2 Mean, Median, Mode, and Range (pp. 298–301)

 6.S.5, 6.S.6

EXAMPLE

- **Find the mean, median, mode, and range. 7, 8, 12, 10, 8**

  mean: $7 + 8 + 8 + 10 + 12 = 45$

  $45 \div 5 = 9$

  median: 8

  mode: 8

  range: $12 - 7 = 5$

EXERCISES

Find the mean, median, mode, and range.

5.

Hours Worked Each Week						
32	39	39	38	36	39	36

6-3 Additional Data and Outliers (pp. 302–305)

 6.CN.7

EXAMPLE

■ Find the mean, median, and mode with and without the outlier.

10, 4, 7, 8, 34, 7, 7, 12, 5, 8   *The outlier is 34.*
With: **mean** = 10.2, **mode** = 7, **median** = 7.5
Without: **mean** ≈ 7.555, **mode** = 7,
median = 7

EXERCISES

Find the mean, median, and mode of each data set with and without the outlier.

6. 12, 11, 9, 38, 10, 8, 12

7. 34, 12, 32, 45, 32

8. 16, 12, 15, 52, 10, 13

6-4 Bar Graphs (pp. 308–311)

6.S.7

EXAMPLE

■ Which grades have more than 200 students? 6th grade and 8th grade

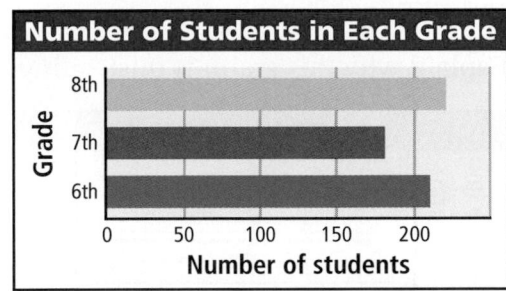

EXERCISES

Use the bar graph at left for Exercise 9.

9. Which grade has the most students?

10. Use the data to make a bar graph.

Test	Math	English	History	Science
Grade	95	85	90	80

6-5 Line Plots, Frequency Tables, and Histograms (pp. 314–317)

6.S.2. 6.S.7

EXAMPLE

■ Make a frequency table with intervals.

Ages of people at Irene's birthday party:
37, 39, 18, 15, 13

Ages of People at Irene's Birthday Party			
Ages	13–19	20–26	27–33	34–40
Frequency	3	0	0	2

EXERCISES

11. Make a frequency table with intervals.

Points Scored					
6	4	5	4	7	10

12. Use the frequency table from Exercise 11 to make a histogram.

6-6 Ordered Pairs (pp. 319–321)

6.G.10

EXAMPLE

■ Name the ordered pair for *A*.

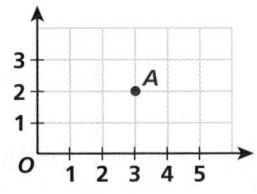

A is at (3, 2).

EXERCISES

Name the ordered pair for each location.

13. Bob's house

14. toy store

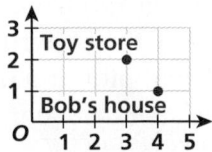

Study Guide: Review

Study Guide: Review   **341**

6-7 Line Graphs (pp. 322–325)

EXAMPLE

- **Use the temperature data to make a line graph.**

  Day 1: 32°F; Day 2: 36°F; Day 3: 38°F; Day 4: 40°F; Day 5: 36°F

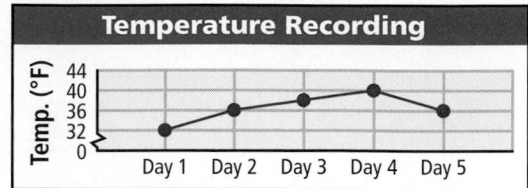

EXERCISES

15. Use the bookstore sales data to make a line graph.

    Jan: $425; Feb: $320; Mar: $450; Apr: $530

Use your line graph from Exercise 15.

16. When were bookstore sales the greatest?

17. Describe the trend in bookstore sales over the four months.

6-8 Misleading Graphs (pp. 326–329)

EXAMPLE

- **Why is this graph misleading?**

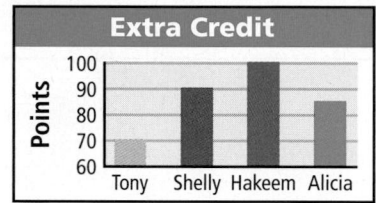

The lower part of the scale is missing.

EXERCISES

18. Explain why this graph is misleading.

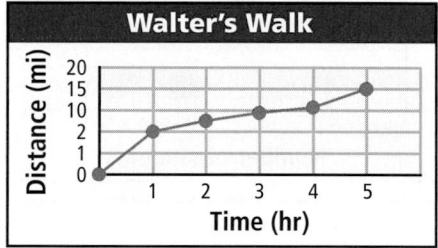

6-9 Stem-and-Leaf Plots (pp. 330–332)

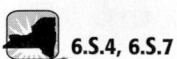

EXAMPLE

- **Make a stem-and-leaf plot of the following test scores.**
  80, 92, 88, 86, 85, 94

Stems	Leaves
8	0 5 6 8
9	2 4

  Key: 8|0 means 80

EXERCISES

19. Make a stem-and-leaf plot of the following basketball scores.

    22, 26, 34, 46, 20, 44, 40, 28

20. List the least value, greatest value, mean, median, mode, and range of the data from Exercise 19.

6-10 Choosing an Appropriate Display (pp. 333–335)

6.S.4, 6.S.7

EXAMPLE

- **Which graph would be more appropriate to show time spent shopping—a stem-and-leaf plot or a line graph?**

  Use a stem-and-leaf plot to see how often data values occur.

EXERCISES

21. Which graph would be more appropriate to show the number of books read over the school year by a class—a bar graph or a line graph?

1. Use the data about sound to make a table.

   The loudness of a sound is measured by the size of its vibrations. The unit of measurement is the decibel (dB). A soft whisper is 30 dB. Conversation is 60 dB. A loud shout is 100 dB. The pain threshold for humans is 130 dB. An airplane takeoff at 100 ft is 140 dB.

Use the bar graph for Exercises 2–4.

2. Find the mean, median, mode, and range of the rainfall amounts.

3. Which month had the lowest average rainfall?

4. Which months had rainfall amounts greater than 2 inches?

5. The table shows the number of strawberries picked by customers at a pick-your-own strawberry patch. Organize the data in a line plot.

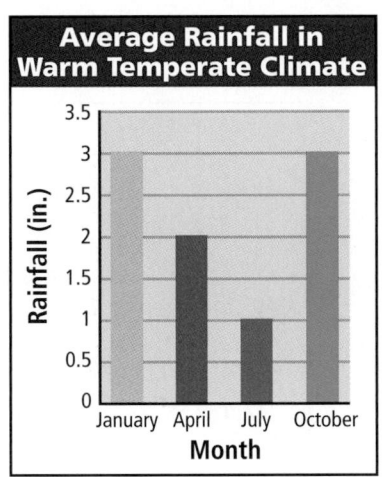

Number of Strawberries Picked							
28	33	35	27	35	28	35	29
30	27	30	35	28	27	31	32

Name the ordered pair for each point on the grid.

6. A
10. E

7. B
11. F

8. C
12. G

9. D
13. H

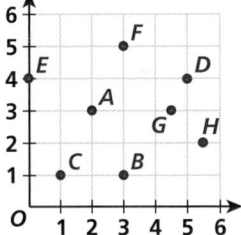

Graph and label each point on a coordinate grid.

14. $T(3, 4)$
15. $M\left(\frac{1}{2}, 6\right)$
16. $P(5, 1)$
17. $S\left(3\frac{1}{2}, 2\right)$
18. $N(0, 5)$

19. Make a stem-and-leaf plot of the push-up data. Use your stem-and-leaf plot to find the mean, median, and mode of the data.

Number of Push-ups Performed						
35	33	25	45	52	21	18
41	27	35	40	53	24	38

20. The table shows the population of a small town over a 5-year period. Which graph would be more appropriate to show the data—a bar graph or a line graph? Draw the more appropriate graph.

Year	2002	2003	2004	2005
Population	852	978	1,125	1,206

Chapter Test

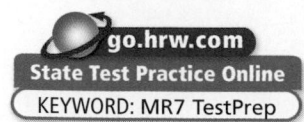
Cumulative Assessment, Chapters 1–6

Multiple Choice

1. The stem-and-leaf plot shows the ages of the volunteers who work at a local food bank. What is the median of this set of data?

Stems	Leaves
1	6
2	2 3
3	0 1 4
4	1 4 8

   Key: 1|6 means 16

   (A) 31   (C) 41

   (B) 32.1   (D) 48

2. In a vacuum, light travels at a speed of 299,792,458 meters per second. Which of the following approximates this rate in scientific notation?

   (F) 2.9×10^7 meters per second

   (G) 2.9×10^8 meters per second

   (H) 2.9×10^9 meters per second

   (J) 2.9×10^{10} meters per second

3. Harrison spends $3\frac{1}{2}$ hours a week working in his yard. He spends $1\frac{1}{3}$ hours pulling weeds. He spends the rest of the time mowing the yard. How much time does he spend mowing the yard?

   (A) $1\frac{1}{6}$ hours   (C) $2\frac{1}{3}$ hours

   (B) $2\frac{1}{6}$ hours   (D) $3\frac{1}{3}$ hours

4. Which value is equivalent to 4^4?

   (F) 8   (H) 64

   (G) 16   (J) 256

5. Jamie is making a fruit salad. She needs $2\frac{1}{4}$ cups of crushed pineapple, $3\frac{3}{4}$ cups of sliced apples, $1\frac{1}{3}$ cups of mandarin oranges, and $2\frac{2}{3}$ cups of red grapes. How many cups total of fruit does she need for the fruit salad?

   (A) 6 cups   (C) 10 cups

   (B) 8 cups   (D) 12 cups

6. The line plot shows the ages of the number of participants in a science fair. Which of the following statements is NOT supported by the line plot?

   Ages of Science Fair Participants

   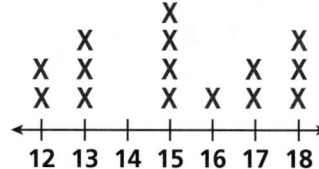

   (F) The range is 6.

   (G) The mean age of the participants in the science fair is 15.1.

   (H) The mode of the ages of the participants in the science fair is 16.

   (J) The median age of the participants in the science fair is 15.

7. What is the mode of the following data? 17, 13, 14, 13, 21, 18, 16, 19

   (A) 13   (C) 16.5

   (B) 16   (D) 16.375

8. Which is a type of graph that uses bars and intervals to display data?

   (F) Stem-and-leaf plot

   (G) Histogram

   (H) Double-line graph

   (J) Line plot

9. Which equation has a solution of 8?

   (A) $2x = 18$ (C) $x + 6 = 24$

   (B) $x - 4 = 12$ (D) $\frac{x}{4} = 2$

 **Hot Tip** Read graphs and diagrams carefully. Look at the labels for important information.

Use the following data set for items 10 and 11.

   4, 13, 7, 26, 6, 7, 3, 4, 2, 8, 10, 9

10. Which number in the data set is an outlier?

    (F) 3   (H) 7

    (G) 6   (J) 26

11. What is the mean of the data set?

    (A) 7.0   (C) 8.75

    (B) 8.25   (D) 9.5

12. Miguel has a piece of lumber that is 48.6 centimeters long. How many centimeters does he need to cut off if he wants the piece of lumber to measure 32.8 centimeters?

    (F) 15.2   (H) 16.8

    (G) 15.8   (J) 17.2

13. What is the least common multiple of 5, 6, and 8?

    (A) 30   (C) 60

    (B) 40   (D) 120

Short Response

14. Look at the bar graph of favorite flavors of frozen fruit bars. Explain why the graph is misleading. Use the same data to make a graph that is not misleading.

15.

Stems	Leaves
2	1 3 6
3	2 2 5 9
4	0 3
5	1 5 5 5

   Key: 2|1 means 21

   a. Find the range, mean, median, and mode of the data in the stem-and-leaf plot.

   b. How does adding 82, 18, and 42 to the data change the range, mean, median, and mode?

Extended Response

16. The high temperature on Monday was 54°F. On Tuesday, it was 62°F. On Wednesday, it was 65°F. On Thursday, it was 60°F. On Friday, it was 62°F.

   a. Organize this data in a table. Find the range, mean, median, and mode of the data.

   b. Which graph would be more appropriate to show the data—a bar graph or a line graph? Explain.

   c. Make a graph of the data.

 # Problem Solving on Location

ARIZONA

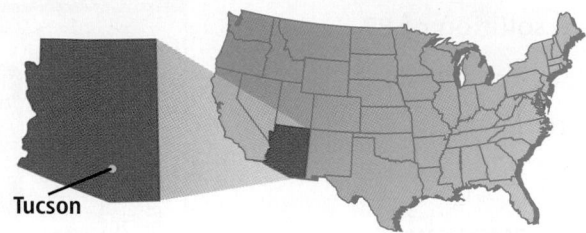

Tucson

⭐ Scenic Roads

Arizona has 22 byways (minor roads) that are officially recognized by the state as scenic roads. These routes take motorists past soaring cliffs, Native American reservations, and ghost towns of the old West.

Choose one or more strategies and use the map to solve each problem.

1. The state wants to put markers along Sky Island Parkway to designate it as a scenic road. The project planners intended to place the markers at the beginning and end of the route and every $\frac{1}{5}$ mile along the way. How many markers are needed?

2. Red Rock Scenic Road is $3\frac{2}{5}$ miles shorter than White River Scenic Road. White River Scenic Road is $42\frac{3}{5}$ miles shorter than Joshua Forest Scenic Road. How long is Red Rock Scenic Road?

3. The Chen family is driving along the Coronado Trail. They have driven the first $50\frac{1}{2}$ miles of the road. A gas station is located $10\frac{1}{5}$ miles from the other end of the road. How much farther do they have to drive to reach the gas station?

4. The Patagonia Scenic Road goes from Nogales to Route 10 and passes through the town of Sonoita along the way. Sonoita is 4 miles farther from Nogales than it is from Route 10. What is the distance from Nogales to Sonoita?

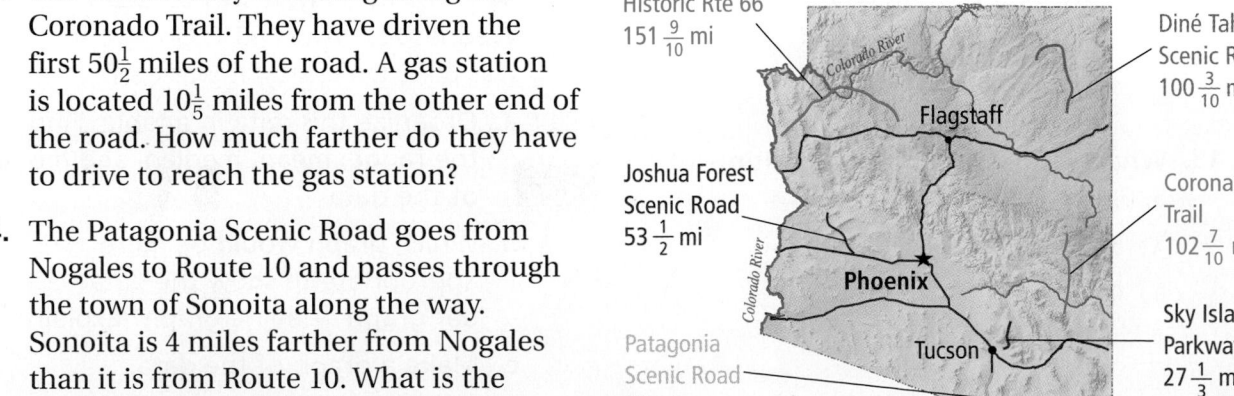

Historic Rte 66
$151\frac{9}{10}$ mi

Diné Tah
Scenic Road
$100\frac{3}{10}$ mi

Colorado River

Flagstaff

Joshua Forest
Scenic Road
$53\frac{1}{2}$ mi

Coronado
Trail
$102\frac{7}{10}$ mi

Colorado River

Phoenix

Patagonia
Scenic Road
52 mi

Tucson

Sky Island
Parkway
$27\frac{1}{3}$ mi

Problem Solving Strategies

Draw a Diagram
Make a Model
Guess and Test
Work Backward
Find a Pattern
Make a Table
Solve a Simpler Problem
Use Logical Reasoning
Act It Out
Make an Organized List

 # The Arizona-Sonora Desert Museum

The Arizona-Sonora Desert Museum (ASDM) is a zoo, botanical garden, and natural history museum all in one. Located on the outskirts of Tucson, ASDM teaches visitors about the plants and animals of the desert in an authentic setting. In fact, 85% of the museum is located outdoors.

Choose one or more strategies to solve each problem.

1. The museum has 4 times as many plant species as animal species. There are 1,500 plant and animal species altogether. How many plant species are there?

2. ASDM offers a daily lecture about poisonous reptiles. Each day, two of the following five reptiles are featured: Mexican bearded lizard, diamond-backed rattlesnake, Mohave rattlesnake, black-tailed rattlesnake, Gila monster. How many different lectures are possible?

For 3–4, use the graph.

3. The museum's soaptree yucca is 16 feet shorter than a typical saguaro cactus. A typical saguaro cactus is 3 times as tall as a senita cactus. What is the height of the soaptree yucca?

4. Only one of the cactus species in the graph produces green flowers.

   • The cactus that produces green flowers is less than 10 feet tall.

   • The shortest cactus produces orange flowers.

   • The Englemann prickly pear produces yellow flowers.

   Which cactus produces green flowers?

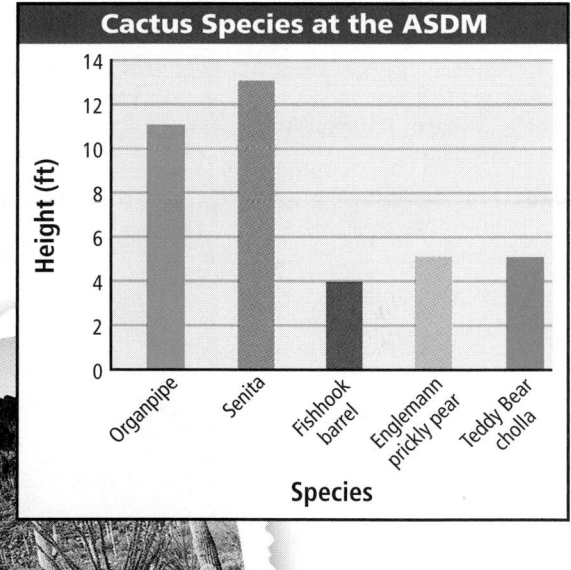

Cactus Species at the ASDM

Height (ft) vs. Species

Species: Organpipe, Senita, Fishhook barrel, Englemann prickly pear, Teddy Bear cholla

Proportional Relationships

NEW YORK TEST PREP

go.hrw.com
Chapter Project Online
KEYWORD: MR7 Ch7

Career *Fisheries Biologist*

A fisheries biologist interacts with nature and with people. Fisheries biologists complete surveys, improve habitats, monitor water conditions, and work with land developers.

Fisheries biologists often must determine the number of fish in a lake or pond. They use the tag, release, and recapture method to estimate this number.

$$\frac{\text{tagged number in recapture}}{\text{total number recaptured}} = \frac{\text{number originally tagged}}{\text{total number in lake}}$$

Lake	Tagged Number in Recapture	Total Number Recaptured	Number Originally Tagged
Duck	23	96	108
Los Dos Perros	32	40	56
Robyn	18	26	75

ARE YOU READY?

✓ Vocabulary

Choose the best term from the list to complete each sentence.

1. A(n) ___?___ is a three-sided polygon, and a(n) ___?___ is a four-sided polygon.

2. A(n) ___?___ is used to name a part of a whole.

3. When two numbers have the same value, they are said to be ___?___.

4. When writing 0.25 as a fraction, 25 is the ___?___ and 100 is the ___?___.

angle

denominator

equivalent

fraction

numerator

pentagon

quadrilateral

triangle

Complete these exercises to review skills you will need for this chapter.

✓ Simplify Fractions

Write each fraction in simplest form.

5. $\frac{6}{10}$ 6. $\frac{9}{12}$ 7. $\frac{8}{6}$

✓ Write Equivalent Fractions

Write three equivalent fractions for each given fraction.

8. $\frac{4}{16}$ 9. $\frac{5}{10}$ 10. $\frac{5}{6}$

✓ Compare Fractions

Compare. Write >, <, or =.

11. $\frac{3}{10} \bigcirc \frac{2}{5}$ 12. $1\frac{3}{4} \bigcirc 1\frac{5}{7}$ 13. $\frac{5}{8} \bigcirc \frac{1}{2}$ 14. $2\frac{11}{12} \bigcirc \frac{35}{12}$

✓ Write Decimals as Fractions

Write each decimal as a fraction in simplest form.

15. 0.5   16. 0.35   17. 0.08   18. 0.12

✓ Multiply Decimals

Multiply.

19. $0.42 \cdot 10$ 20. $0.3 \cdot 52$ 21. $20.5 \cdot 0.25$ 22. $6.75 \cdot 0.40$

23. $9.8 \cdot 0.2$ 24. $0.8 \cdot 7.4$ 25. $0.52 \cdot 0.64$ 26. $0.75 \cdot 8.9$

Study Guide: Preview

Where You've Been

Previously, you

- used fractions to represent situations involving division.
- generated equivalent fractions and decimals.
- used multiplication and division to find equivalent fractions.

In This Chapter

You will study

- using ratios to describe proportional situations.
- representing ratios and percents with concrete models, fractions, and decimals.
- using multiplication and division to solve problems involving equivalent ratios and rates.
- using ratios to make predictions in proportional situations.

Where You're Going

You can use the skills learned in this chapter

- to find discounts and sales tax on retail items at stores.
- to know how much of a tip to leave at restaurants.

Key Vocabulary/Vocabulario

corresponding angles	ángulos correspondientes (en polígonos)
equivalent ratios	razones equivalentes
indirect measurement	medición indirecta
percent	porcentaje
proportion	proporción
rate	tasa
ratio	razón
scale drawing	dibujo a escala
similar	semejantes
unit rate	tasa unitaria

Vocabulary Connections

To become familiar with some of the vocabulary terms in the chapter, consider the following. You may refer to the chapter, the glossary, or a dictionary if you like.

1. *Equivalent* can mean "equal in value." How do you think **equivalent ratios** are related?

2. *Indirect* means "not direct." Do you think you will use a ruler to find an **indirect measurement**?

3. *Percent* comes from *per* and the Latin word *centum,* meaning "hundred." What do you think **percent** means?

4. *Ratio* can mean "the relationship in quantity, amount, or size between two things." How many numbers do you think a **ratio** will have?

5. A *scale* shows the relationship in size between two or more things. If you are making a **scale drawing** of a room, what do you think you would include on the drawing to show the room's actual size?

 **Reading** and **Writing Math**

Writing Strategy: Write a Convincing Explanation

You will see the Write About It icons  throughout the book. These icons show exercises that require you to write a convincing explanation.

A convincing explanation should include

- a restatement of the question or problem.

- a complete solution to the problem.

- any work, definitions, diagrams, or charts needed to answer the problem.

From Lesson 6-8

C Why is this line graph misleading?

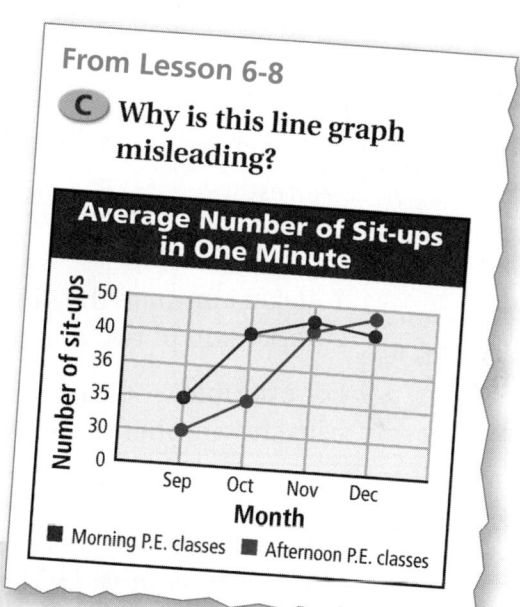

Step 1 **Restate the question.**
The graph is misleading because the scale does not have equal intervals.

Step 2 **Provide a complete solution to the problem with facts and an explanation.**
For example, an increase from 35 sit-ups to 40 sit-ups appears greater than an increase from 30 sit-ups to 35 sit-ups. By reading the scale, you know that this is incorrect. Therefore, the graph is misleading.

Try This

Use your textbook.

1. Write a convincing explanation to explain why there are two modes in the data set 4, 6, 1, 0, 4, 8, 9, 0.

2. Look at one of your previous Write About It exercises. Does your answer follow the method outlined above? If so, label the items that should be included. If not, rewrite the explanation.

Reading and Writing Math

7-1 Ratios and Rates

Learn to write ratios and rates and to find unit rates.

Vocabulary

ratio

equivalent ratios

rate

unit rate

For a time, the Boston Symphony Orchestra was made up of 95 musicians.

Violins	29	Violas	12
Cellos	10	Basses	9
Flutes	5	Trumpets	3
Double reeds	8	Percussion	5
Clarinets	4	Harp	1
Horns	6	Trombones	3

You can compare the different groups by using ratios. A **ratio** is a comparison of two quantities using division.

For example, you can use a ratio to compare the number of violins with the number of violas. This ratio can be written in three ways.

$$Terms \left\langle \begin{array}{c} \\ \\ \end{array} \right. \quad \frac{29}{12} \qquad 29 \text{ to } 12 \qquad 29{:}12$$

Reading Math

Read the ratio $\frac{29}{12}$ as "twenty-nine to twelve."

Notice that the ratio of **violins** to **violas**, $\frac{29}{12}$, is different from the ratio of **violas** to **violins**, $\frac{12}{29}$. The order of the terms is important.

Ratios can be written to compare a part to a part, a part to the whole, or the whole to a part.

EXAMPLE 1 **Writing Ratios**

Use the table above to write each ratio.

NY Performance Indicators

6.N.6 Understand the concept of rate. Also, **6.N.8**.

A flutes to clarinets

$\frac{5}{4}$ *or*   5 to 4   *or*   5:4   *Part to part*

B trumpets to total instruments

$\frac{3}{95}$ *or*   3 to 95   *or*   3:95   *Part to whole*

C total instruments to basses

$\frac{95}{9}$ *or*   95 to 9   *or*   95:9   *Whole to part*

Equivalent ratios are ratios that name the same comparison. You can find an equivalent ratio by multiplying or dividing both terms of a ratio by the same number.

EXAMPLE 2 Writing Equivalent Ratios

Write three equivalent ratios to compare the number of stars with the number of moons in the pattern.

$$\frac{\text{number of stars}}{\text{number of moons}} = \frac{4}{6}$$ *There are 4 stars and 6 moons.*

$$\frac{4}{6} = \frac{4 \div 2}{6 \div 2} = \frac{2}{3}$$ *There are 2 stars for every 3 moons.*

$$\frac{4}{6} = \frac{4 \cdot 2}{6 \cdot 2} = \frac{8}{12}$$ *If you double the pattern, there will be 8 stars and 12 moons.*

So $\frac{4}{6}$, $\frac{2}{3}$, and $\frac{8}{12}$ are equivalent ratios.

A **rate** compares two quantities that have different units of measure.

Suppose a 2-liter bottle of soda costs $1.98.

$$\text{rate} = \frac{\text{price}}{\text{number of liters}} = \frac{\$1.98}{2 \text{ liters}} \qquad \$1.98 \text{ for 2 liters}$$

When the comparison is to one unit, the rate is called a **unit rate**.

Divide both terms by the second term to find the unit rate.

$$\text{unit rate} = \frac{\$1.98}{2} = \frac{\$1.98 \div 2}{2 \div 2} = \frac{\$0.99}{1} \qquad \$0.99 \text{ for 1 liter}$$

When the prices of two or more items are compared, the item with the lowest unit rate is the best deal.

EXAMPLE 3 *Consumer Math Application*

A 2-liter bottle of soda costs $2.02. A 3-liter bottle of the same soda costs $2.79. Which is the better deal?

2-liter bottle		3-liter bottle	
$\dfrac{\$2.02}{2 \text{ liters}}$	*Write the rate.*	$\dfrac{\$2.79}{3 \text{ liters}}$	*Write the rate.*
$\dfrac{\$2.02 \div 2}{2 \text{ liters} \div 2}$	*Divide both terms by 2.*	$\dfrac{\$2.79 \div 3}{3 \text{ liters} \div 3}$	*Divide both terms by 3.*
$\dfrac{\$1.01}{1 \text{ liter}}$	*$1.01 for 1 liter*	$\dfrac{\$0.93}{1 \text{ liter}}$	*$0.93 for 1 liter*

The 3-liter bottle is the better deal.

Think and Discuss

1. Explain the difference between a ratio and a rate.

2. Describe how to determine what number to divide by when finding a unit rate.

go.hrw.com
Homework Help Online
KEYWORD: MR7 7-1
Parent Resources Online
KEYWORD: MR7 Parent

GUIDED PRACTICE

See Example **Use the table to write each ratio.**

1. music programs to art programs

2. arcade games to entire collection

3. entire collection to educational games

Jacqueline's Software Collection	
Educational games	16
Word processing	2
Art programs	10
Arcade games	10
Music programs	3

See Example 2 **4.** Write three equivalent ratios to compare the number of red hearts in the picture with the total number of hearts.

See Example 3 **5. Consumer Math** An 8-ounce bag of sunflower seeds costs $1.68. A 4-ounce bag of sunflower seeds costs $0.88. Which is the better deal?

INDEPENDENT PRACTICE

See Example **Use the table to write each ratio.**

6. Redbirds to Blue Socks

7. right-handed Blue Socks to left-handed Blue Socks

8. left-handed Redbirds to total Redbirds

	Redbirds	Blue Socks
Left-Handed Batters	8	3
Right-Handed Batters	11	19

See Example 2 **9.** Write three equivalent ratios to compare the number of stars in the picture with the number of stripes.

See Example 3 **10.** Gina charges $28 for 3 hours of swimming lessons. Hector charges $18 for 2 hours of swimming lessons. Which instructor offers a better deal?

11. Consumer Math A 12-pound bag of dog food costs $12.36. A 15-pound bag of dog food costs $15.30. Which is the better deal?

PRACTICE AND PROBLEM SOLVING

Extra Practice
See page 726.

Write each ratio three different ways.

12. ten to seven

13. $\frac{24}{11}$

14. 4 to 30

15. $\frac{7}{10}$

16. 16 to 20

17. $\frac{5}{9}$

18. 50 to 79

19. one hundred to one hundred one

20. A florist can create 16 bouquets during an 8-hour work day. How many bouquets can the florist create per hour?

Use the diagram of an oxygen atom and a boron atom for Exercises 21–24. Find each ratio. Then give two equivalent ratios.

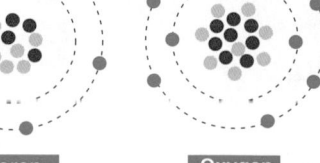

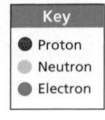

21. oxygen protons to boron protons

22. boron neutrons to boron protons

23. boron electrons to oxygen electrons

24. oxygen electrons to oxygen protons

Boron   Oxygen

25. A lifeguard received 16 hours of first aid training and 8 hours of cardiopulmonary resuscitation (CPR) training. Write the ratio of hours of CPR training to hours of first aid training.

26. Critical Thinking Cassandra has three pictures on her desk. The pictures measure 4 in. long by 6 in. wide, 24 mm long by 36 mm wide, and 6 cm long by 7 cm wide. Which photos have a length-to-width ratio equivalent to 2:3?

27. Multi-Step On which day did Alfonso run faster?

Day	Distance (m)	Time (min)
Monday	1,020	6
Wednesday	1,554	9

28. Earth Science Water rushes over Niagara Falls at the rate of 180 million cubic feet every 30 minutes. How much water goes over the falls in 1 minute?

 29. What's the Question? The ratio of total students in Mr. Avalon's class to students in the class who have a blue backpack is 3 to 1. The answer is 1:2. What is the question?

 30. Write About It How are equivalent ratios like equivalent fractions?

 31. Challenge There are 36 performers in a dance recital. The ratio of men to women is 2:7. How many men are in the dance recital?

TEST PREP and Spiral Review

32. Multiple Choice Which ratio is equivalent to $\frac{1}{20}$?

(A) 9:180   (B) 180 to 9   (C) 4 to 100   (D) 100:4

33. Short Response A 24-ounce box of raisins costs $4.56. A 15-ounce box of raisins costs $3.15. Which is the better deal? Explain.

Find the GCF of each set of numbers. (Lesson 4-3)

34. 12, 36   **35.** 15, 24   **36.** 18, 24, 42   **37.** 5, 14, 17

Solve each equation. Write the solution in simplest form. (Lesson 5-5)

38. $g + \frac{3}{10} = \frac{2}{5}$ **39.** $m - \frac{1}{2} = \frac{1}{9}$ **40.** $\frac{2}{3} = p + \frac{1}{6}$ **41.** $h - \frac{1}{4} = \frac{5}{12}$

Using Tables to Explore Equivalent Ratios and Rates

Learn to use a table to find equivalent ratios and rates.

NY Performance Indicators

6.N.6 Understand the concept of rate. Also, 6.N.8.

Mrs. Kennedy's students are painting a mural in their classroom. They mixed yellow and blue paints for a green background and found that the ratio of the amount of yellow to the amount of blue is 3 to 2.

Now they need to make more green paint, using the same ratio as before.

Use a table to find ratios equivalent to 3 to 2.

Reading Math

Finding equivalent ratios is sometimes referred to as "scaling up" or "scaling down."

Original ratio $3 \cdot 2$ $3 \cdot 3$ $3 \cdot 4$

		↓	↓	↓
Pints of yellow	3	6	9	12
Pints of blue	2	4	6	8

         $2 \cdot 2$ $2 \cdot 3$ $2 \cdot 4$

You can increase amounts but keep them in the same ratio by multiplying both the numerator and denominator of the ratio by the same number.

The ratios 3 to 2, 6 to 4, 9 to 6, and 12 to 8 are equivalent.

You can also decrease amounts in the same ratio by dividing the numerator and denominator by the same number.

EXAMPLE **1**   **Making a Table to Find Equivalent Ratios**

Helpful Hint

Multiplying by 2, 3, and 4 will give you three equivalent ratios, but there are many other equivalent ratios that are correct.

Use a table to find three equivalent ratios.

A $\dfrac{8}{3}$

Original ratio $8 \cdot 2$ $8 \cdot 3$ $8 \cdot 4$

	↓	↓	↓
8	16	24	32
3	6	9	12

     $3 \cdot 2$ $3 \cdot 3$ $3 \cdot 4$

Multiply the numerator and the denominator by 2, 3, and 4.

The ratios $\dfrac{8}{3}$, $\dfrac{16}{6}$, $\dfrac{24}{9}$, and $\dfrac{32}{12}$ are equivalent.

Use a table to find three equivalent ratios.

B 4 to 7

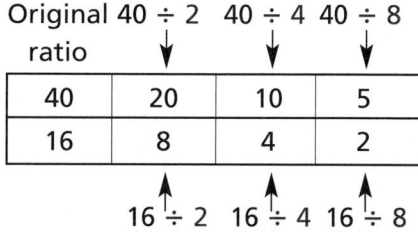

Original 4 · 2   4 · 3   4 · 4
ratio

4	8	12	16
7	14	21	28

7 · 2   7 · 3   7 · 4

Multiply the numerator and the denominator by 2, 3, and 4.

The ratios 4 to 7, 8 to 14, 12 to 21, and 16 to 28 are equivalent.

C 40:16

Original 40 ÷ 2   40 ÷ 4 40 ÷ 8
ratio

40	20	10	5
16	8	4	2

16 ÷ 2   16 ÷ 4   16 ÷ 8

Divide the numerator and the denominator by 2.

The ratios 40:16, 20:8, 10:4, and 5:2 are equivalent.

Ratios in tables can be used to make estimates or predictions.

EXAMPLE 2 *Entertainment Application*

A group of 10 friends is in line to see a movie. The table shows how much different groups will pay in all. Predict how much the group of 10 will pay.

Number in Group	3	5	6	12
Amount Paid ($)	15	25	30	60

$6 < 10 < 12$; therefore, the group will pay between $30 and $60.

Use the amount paid by the group of 5.   *The only factor of 10 in the table is 5.*

$2 \cdot 5 = 10$ *Multiply the numerator and*
$2 \cdot \$25 = \$50$ *denominator by the same factor, 2.*

A group of 10 friends would pay $50.00.

Think and Discuss

6.PS.22, 6.CM.1

1. When you have multiplied or divided a ratio to find equivalent ratios, how can you be sure that all the ratios you have written are correct?

2. If two ratios have colons and you rewrite the ratios as fractions, how can you be sure that you have written the numerator and denominator in the correct order?

7-2 **Exercises**

go.hrw.com
Homework Help Online
KEYWORD: MR7 7-2
Parent Resources Online
KEYWORD: MR7 Parent

GUIDED PRACTICE

See Example ① **Use a table to find three equivalent ratios.**

1. $\frac{2}{7}$ **2.** 7 to 12 **3.** 96:48 **4.** $\frac{3}{5}$

5. 5 to 8 **6.** $\frac{9}{4}$ **7.** 24 to 16 **8.** 25:26

See Example ② **9. Sports** Leo runs laps around a track. The table shows how long it takes him to run different numbers of laps. Predict how long it will take Leo to run 7 laps.

Number of Laps	2	4	6	8	10
Time (min)	10	20	30	40	50

INDEPENDENT PRACTICE

See Example ① **Use a table to find three equivalent ratios.**

10. 6:5 **11.** 8 to 15 **12.** $\frac{12}{4}$ **13.** 6 to 7

14. $\frac{13}{20}$ **15.** 11:25 **16.** 5 to 18 **17.** $\frac{51}{75}$

See Example ② **18.** Lee Middle School orders 15 textbooks for every 12 students. The table shows how many textbooks the school orders for certain numbers of students. Predict the number of textbooks that the school would order for 72 students.

Students	12	24	48	96	192
Textbooks	15	30	60	120	240

PRACTICE AND PROBLEM SOLVING

Extra Practice
See page 726.

19. Biology Brown bats vary in length from 3 to 6 inches and have wing spans from 8 to 16 inches. Write a ratio in simplest form of a bat's wing span to the bat's body length.

20. Buy-A-Lot Market has tomatoes on sale. The table shows some sale prices. Predict how much a restaurant owner will pay for 25 pounds of tomatoes at the rate shown in the table.

Amount (lb)	30	20	15	10	5
Cost ($)	11.70	7.80	5.85	3.90	1.95

Complete each table to find the missing ratios.

21.

6	12	18	■
5	10	■	20

22.

96	48	24	■
48	24	■	6

History

President Lyndon Baines Johnson, often referred to as LBJ, was born in Stillwater, Texas, in 1908. President Johnson had no vice president from November 1963 to January 1965.

Multiply and divide each ratio to find two equivalent ratios.

23. 36:48

24. $\frac{4}{60}$

25. $\frac{128}{48}$

26. 15:100

27. **Multi-Step** Lyndon Johnson was elected president in 1964. The ratio of the number of votes he received to the number of votes that Barry Goldwater received was about 19:12. About how many votes were cast for both candiates?

Candidates	Number of Votes
Lyndon Johnson	43,121,085
Barry Goldwater	▨

28. **What's the Error?** A student said that 3:4 is equivalent to 9:16 and 18:64. What did the student do wrong? Correct the ratios so they are equivalent.

29. **Write About It** If Daniel drives the same distance each day, will he be able to complete a 4,500-mile trip in 2 weeks? Explain how you solved the problem.

Days	Distance (mi)
3	1,020
5	1,700
9	3,060

 **30.** **Challenge** The table shows the regular and sale prices of CDs at Bargain Blast. How much money will you save if you buy 10 CDs on sale?

Number of CDs	Regular Price ($)	Sale Price ($)
2	17.00	14.40
3	25.50	21.60
6	51.00	43.20

TEST PREP and Spiral Review

31. **Multiple Choice** Which ratio is NOT equivalent to 3 to 7?

(A) 9:21 (B) 36:77 (C) 45:105 (D) 54:126

32. **Short Response** The table shows the distances traveled and the numbers of gallons of gas used on four automobile trips. Predict the number of gallons of gas that would be used for a trip of 483 miles.

Distance (mi)	552	414	276	138
Gas Used (gal)	24	18	12	6

33. In 2005, the heights of the world's tallest buildings were 509, 452, 452, 442, 421, and 415 meters. Find the mean, median, mode, and range of the data set. (Lesson 6-2)

34. Javier saved $65, $82, $58, $74, $65, and $72 each month from his part-time job for six months. The next month he worked full-time and saved $285. Find the mean, median, and mode of the amounts saved with and without the full-time savings. (Lesson 6-3)

7-2 Using Tables to Explore Equivalent Ratios and Rates   **359**

Explore Proportions

7-3

Use with Lesson 7-3

NY Performance Indicators

6.N.7, 6.N.9, 6.R.1

go.hrw.com
Lab Resources Online
KEYWORD: MR7 Lab7

You can use counters to model equivalent ratios.

Activity 1

Find three ratios that are equivalent to $\frac{6}{12}$.

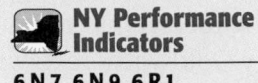

1 Show 6 red counters and 12 yellow counters.

2 Separate the red counters into two equal groups. Then separate the yellow counters into two equal groups.

3 Write the ratio of red counters in each group to yellow counters in each group.

$$\frac{3 \text{ red counters}}{6 \text{ yellow counters}} = \frac{3}{6}$$

4 Now separate the red counters into three equal groups. Then separate the yellow counters into three equal groups.

5 Write the ratio of red counters in each group to yellow counters in each group.

$$\frac{2 \text{ red counters}}{4 \text{ yellow counters}} = \frac{2}{4}$$

6 Now separate the red counters into six equal groups. Then separate the yellow counters into six equal groups.

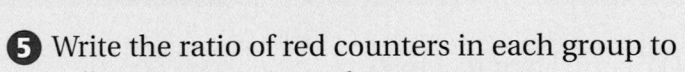

7 Write the ratio of red counters in each group to yellow counters in each group.

$$\frac{1 \text{ red counter}}{2 \text{ yellow counters}} = \frac{1}{2}$$

The three ratios you wrote are equivalent to $\frac{6}{12}$.

$$\frac{6}{12} = \frac{3}{6} = \frac{2}{4} = \frac{1}{2}$$

When you write an equation showing equivalent ratios, that equation is called a *proportion*.

Think and Discuss

1. How do the models show that the ratios are equivalent?

Try This

Use models to determine whether the ratios form a proportion.

1. $\frac{1}{3}$ and $\frac{4}{12}$ **2.** $\frac{3}{4}$ and $\frac{6}{9}$ **3.** $\frac{4}{10}$ and $\frac{2}{5}$

Activity 2

Write a proportion in which one of the ratios is $\frac{1}{3}$.

1 You must find a ratio that is equivalent to $\frac{1}{3}$. First show one red counter and three yellow counters.

2 Show one more group of one red counter and three yellow counters.

3 Write the ratio of red counters to yellow counters for the two groups.

$$\frac{2 \text{ red counters}}{6 \text{ yellow counters}} = \frac{2}{6}$$

4 The two ratios are equivalent. Write the proportion $\frac{1}{3} = \frac{2}{6}$.

You can find more equivalent ratios by adding more groups of one red counter and three yellow counters. Use your models to write proportions.

$$\frac{3 \text{ red counters}}{9 \text{ yellow counters}} = \frac{3}{9} \qquad \frac{4 \text{ red counters}}{12 \text{ yellow counters}} = \frac{4}{12}$$

$$\frac{3}{9} = \frac{1}{3} \qquad\qquad\qquad \frac{4}{12} = \frac{1}{3}$$

Think and Discuss

1. The models above show that $\frac{1}{3}$, $\frac{2}{6}$, $\frac{3}{9}$, and $\frac{4}{12}$ are equivalent ratios. Do you see a pattern in this list of ratios?

2. Use counters to find another ratio that is equivalent to $\frac{1}{3}$.

Try This

Use counters to write a proportion containing each given ratio.

1. $\frac{1}{4}$ **2.** $\frac{1}{5}$ **3.** $\frac{3}{7}$ **4.** $\frac{1}{6}$ **5.** $\frac{4}{9}$

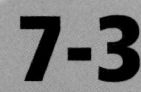 **Proportions**

Learn to write and solve proportions.

Vocabulary
proportion

NY Performance Indicators

6.A.5 Solve simple proportions within context. Also, 6.N.7, 6.N.10.

Reading Math

Read the proportion $\frac{2}{1} = \frac{4}{2}$ as "two is to one as four is to two."

Have you ever heard water called H_2O? H_2O is the scientific formula for water. One molecule of water contains two hydrogen atoms (H_2) and one oxygen atom (O). No matter how many molecules of water you have, hydrogen and oxygen will always be in the ratio 2 to 1.

Water Molecules	1	2	3	4
Hydrogen Oxygen	$\frac{2}{1}$	$\frac{4}{2}$	$\frac{6}{3}$	$\frac{8}{4}$

Notice that $\frac{2}{1}$, $\frac{4}{2}$, $\frac{6}{3}$, and $\frac{8}{4}$ are equivalent ratios.

A **proportion** is an equation that shows two equivalent ratios.

$$\frac{2}{1} = \frac{4}{2} \qquad \frac{4}{2} = \frac{8}{4} \qquad \frac{2}{1} = \frac{6}{3}$$

E X A M P L E **1** **Modeling Proportions**

Write a proportion for the model.

    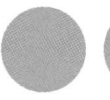

First write the ratio of triangles to circles.

$$\frac{\text{number of triangles}}{\text{number of circles}} = \frac{4}{2}$$

Next separate the triangles and the circles into two equal groups.

Now write the ratio of triangles to circles in each group.

$$\frac{\text{number of triangles in each group}}{\text{number of circles in each group}} = \frac{2}{1}$$

A proportion shown by the model is $\frac{4}{2} = \frac{2}{1}$.

CROSS PRODUCTS

Cross products in proportions are equal.

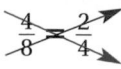	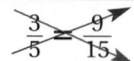	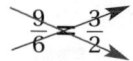	$\frac{14}{7} \times \frac{2}{1}$
$8 \cdot 2 = 4 \cdot 4$	$5 \cdot 9 = 3 \cdot 15$	$6 \cdot 3 = 9 \cdot 2$	$7 \cdot 2 = 14 \cdot 1$
$16 = 16$	$45 = 45$	$18 = 18$	$14 = 14$

EXAMPLE 2 **Using Cross Products to Complete Proportions**

Find the missing value in the proportion $\frac{3}{4} = \frac{n}{16}$.

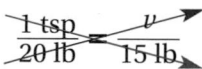   *Find the cross products.*

$4 \cdot n = 3 \cdot 16$ *The cross products are equal.*

$4n = 48$ *n is multiplied by 4.*

$\frac{4n}{4} = \frac{48}{4}$ *Divide both sides by 4 to undo the multiplication.*

$n = 12$

EXAMPLE 3 **Measurement Application**

Caution!

In a proportion, the units must be in the same order in both ratios.

$$\frac{tsp}{lb} = \frac{tsp}{lb}$$

or $\frac{lb}{tsp} = \frac{lb}{tsp}$

The label from a bottle of pet vitamins shows recommended dosages. What dosage would you give an adult dog that weighs 15 lb?

Pet Vitamins

- **Adult dogs:**
  1 tsp per 20 lb body weight
- **Puppies, pregnant dogs, or nursing dogs:**
  1 tsp per 10 lb body weight
- **Cats:**
  1 tsp per 12 lb body weight

$\frac{1 \text{ tsp}}{20 \text{ lb}} = \frac{v}{15 \text{ lb}}$ *Let v be the amount of vitamins for a 15 lb dog.*

$\frac{1 \text{ tsp}}{20 \text{ lb}} \times \frac{v}{15 \text{ lb}}$ *Write a proportion.*

$20 \cdot v = 1 \cdot 15$ *The cross products are equal.*

$20v = 15$ *v is multiplied by 20.*

$\frac{20v}{20} = \frac{15}{20}$ *Divide both sides by 20 to undo the multiplication.*

$v = \frac{3}{4} \text{ tsp}$ *Write your answer in simplest form.*

You should give $\frac{3}{4}$ tsp of vitamins to a 15 lb dog.

Think and Discuss   6.CM.1, 6.CN.2

1. **Tell** whether $\frac{7}{8} = \frac{4}{14}$ is a proportion. How do you know?

2. **Give an example** of a proportion. Tell how you know that it is a proportion.

7-3 **Exercises**

go.hrw.com
Homework Help Online
KEYWORD: MR7 7-3
Parent Resources Online
KEYWORD: MR7 Parent

GUIDED PRACTICE

See Example ① **1.** Write a proportion for the model.

See Example ② **Find the missing value in each proportion.**

2. $\frac{12}{9} = \frac{n}{3}$ **3.** $\frac{t}{5} = \frac{28}{20}$ **4.** $\frac{1}{c} = \frac{6}{12}$ **5.** $\frac{6}{7} = \frac{30}{b}$

See Example ③ **6.** Ursula is entering a bicycle race for charity. Her mother pledges $0.75 for every 0.5 mile she bikes. If Ursula bikes 17.5 miles, how much will her mother donate?

INDEPENDENT PRACTICE

See Example ① **7.** Write a proportion for the model.

See Example ② **Find the missing value in each proportion.**

8. $\frac{3}{2} = \frac{24}{d}$ **9.** $\frac{p}{40} = \frac{3}{8}$ **10.** $\frac{6}{14} = \frac{x}{7}$ **11.** $\frac{5}{p} = \frac{7}{77}$

See Example ③ **12.** According to Ty's study guidelines, how many minutes of science reading should he do if his science class is 90 minutes long?

Ty's Study Guidelines	
Class	**Reading Time**
Literature	35 minutes for every 50 minutes of class time
Science	20 minutes for every 60 minutes of class time
History	30 minutes for every 55 minutes of class time

PRACTICE AND PROBLEM SOLVING

Extra Practice
See page 726.

Find the value of p in each proportion.

13. $\frac{18}{6} = \frac{6}{p}$ **14.** $\frac{4}{p} = \frac{48}{60}$ **15.** $\frac{p}{10} = \frac{15}{50}$ **16.** $\frac{3}{5} = \frac{12}{p}$

17. $\frac{21}{15} = \frac{p}{5}$ **18.** $\frac{3}{6} = \frac{p}{8}$ **19.** $\frac{15}{5} = \frac{9}{p}$ **20.** $\frac{6}{p} = \frac{4}{28}$

21. Patterns Given that the first term in a sequence is $\frac{7}{2}$, the second term is $\frac{14}{4}$, the fourth term is $\frac{28}{8}$, and the fifth term is $\frac{35}{10}$, find the value of the third term.

The value of the U.S. dollar as compared to the values of currencies from other countries changes every day. The graph shows the recent value of various currencies compared to the U.S. dollar. Use the graph for Exercises 22–26.

22. What is the value of 9.72 European euros in U.S. dollars?

23. Multi-Step You have $100 in U.S. dollars. Determine how much money this is in euros, Canadian dollars, renminbi, shekels, and Mexican pesos.

24. ? What's the Error? A student set up the proportion $\frac{1}{8.10} = \frac{x}{30}$ to determine the value of 30 U.S. dollars in China. Why is this proportion incorrect? Write the correct proportion, and find the missing value.

25. ✍ Write About It Which is worth more: five U.S. dollars or five Canadian dollars? Why?

26. ★ Challenge A dime is worth about how many Mexican pesos?

go.hrw.com
Web Extra!
KEYWORD: MR7 Value

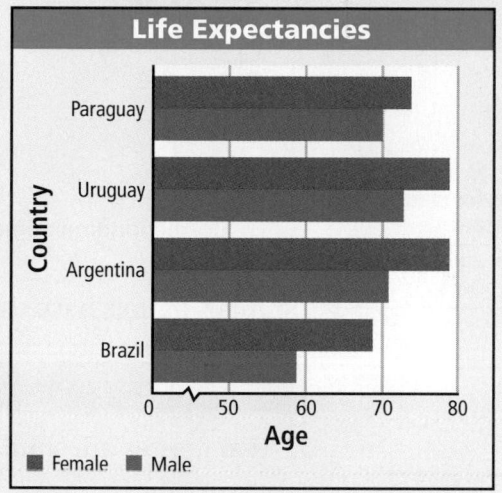

Life Expectancies

Bar graph showing life expectancy (Age, 0–80) for Female and Male in Paraguay, Uruguay, Argentina, and Brazil.

■ Female ■ Male

TEST PREP and Spiral Review

27. Multiple Choice A recipe calls for 4 cups of sugar and 16 cups of water. If the recipe is reduced, how many cups of water should be used with 1 cup of sugar?

Ⓐ 0.25 cups   Ⓑ 1.6 cups   Ⓒ 4 cups   Ⓓ 16 cups

28. Multiple Choice Li mixes 3 units of red paint with 8 units of white paint to get pink. How many units of red paint should she mix with 12 units of white paint to get the same pink shade?

Ⓕ $2\frac{3}{4}$ Ⓖ 3   Ⓗ $3\frac{1}{4}$ Ⓙ $4\frac{1}{2}$

Compare. Write <, >, or =. (Lesson 4-7)

29. $\frac{4}{7}$ ■ $\frac{7}{10}$ **30.** $\frac{3}{5}$ ■ $\frac{14}{15}$ **31.** $\frac{9}{27}$ ■ $\frac{6}{18}$ **32.** $\frac{45}{18}$ ■ $\frac{18}{9}$

Write each ratio two different ways. (Lesson 7-1)

33. 4:9   **34.** eight to eleven   **35.** $\frac{6}{13}$ **36.** 7:5

7-4 Similar Figures

Learn to use proportions to find missing measures in similar figures.

Matching sides of two or more polygons are called **corresponding sides**, and matching angles are called **corresponding angles**.

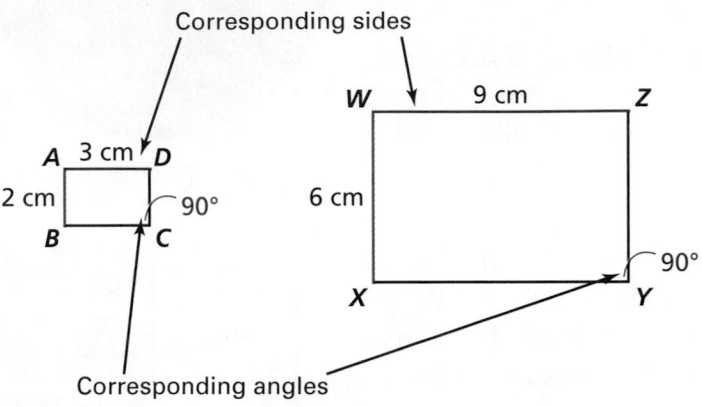

Corresponding sides

Corresponding angles

Vocabulary

corresponding sides

corresponding angles

similar

NY Performance Indicators

6.A.5 Solve simple proportions within context. Also, 6.G.1, 6.N.27.

Similar figures have the same shape but not necessarily the same size.

SIMILAR FIGURES

Two figures are similar if

- the measures of the corresponding angles are equal.

- the ratios of the lengths of the corresponding sides are proportional.

In the rectangles above, one proportion is $\frac{AB}{WX} = \frac{AD}{WZ}$, or $\frac{2}{6} = \frac{3}{9}$.

EXAMPLE 1 **Finding Missing Measures in Similar Figures**

The two triangles are similar. Find the missing length x and the measure of $\angle A$.

$$\frac{8}{12} = \frac{6}{x}$$ *Write a proportion using corresponding side lengths.*

$12 \cdot 6 = 8 \cdot x$ *The cross products are equal.*

$72 = 8x$ *x is multiplied by 8.*

$$\frac{72}{8} = \frac{8x}{8}$$ *Divide both sides by 8 to undo the multiplication.*

$9 \text{ cm} = x$

Angle A corresponds to angle B, and the measure of $\angle B = 65°$. The measure of $\angle A = 65°$.

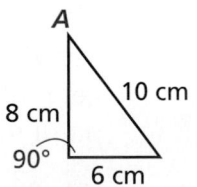

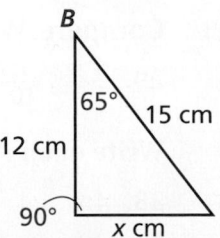

EXAMPLE 2

PROBLEM SOLVING APPLICATION

PROBLEM SOLVING

The Boating Party was painted by American artist Mary Cassatt. This reduction is similar to the actual painting. The height of the actual painting is 90.2 cm. To the nearest centimeter, what is the width of the actual painting?

4.6 cm

|← 6 cm →|

1 **Understand the Problem**

The **answer** will be the width of the actual painting.

List the **important information:**
- The actual painting and the reduction above are similar.
- The reduced painting is 4.6 cm tall and 6 cm wide.
- The actual painting is 90.2 cm tall.

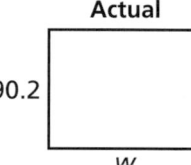

Reduced
4.6
6

2 **Make a Plan**

Draw a diagram to represent the situation.
Use the corresponding sides to write a proportion.

Actual
90.2
w

3 **Solve**

$$\frac{4.6 \text{ cm}}{90.2 \text{ cm}} = \frac{6 \text{ cm}}{w \text{ cm}}$$ *Write a proportion.*

$90.2 \cdot 6 = 4.6 \cdot w$ *The cross products are equal.*

$541.2 = 4.6w$ *w is multiplied by 4.6.*

$$\frac{541.2}{4.6} = \frac{4.6w}{4.6}$$ *Divide both sides by 4.6 to undo the multiplication.*

$118 \approx w$ *Round to the nearest centimeter.*

The width of the actual painting is about 118 cm.

4 **Look Back**

Estimate to check your answer. The ratio of the heights is about 5:90, or 1:18. The ratio of the widths is about 6:120, or 1:20. Since these ratios are close to each other, 118 cm is a reasonable answer.

Remember!

The symbol ≈ means "is approximately equal to."

Think and Discuss

6.CM.1, 6.CN.6

1. Name two items in your classroom that appear to be similar figures.

2. Describe how similar figures are different from congruent figures.

7-4 **Exercises**

go.hrw.com
Homework Help Online
KEYWORD: MR7 7-4
Parent Resources Online
KEYWORD: MR7 Parent

GUIDED PRACTICE

See Example **1** 1. The two triangles are similar. Find the missing length x and the measure of $\angle G$.

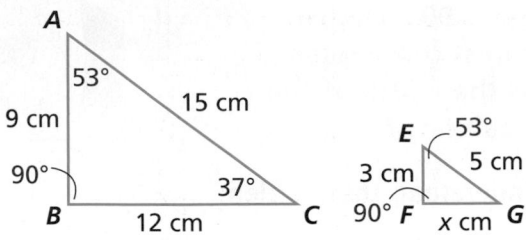

See Example **2** 2. Pat's school photo package includes one large photo and several smaller photos. The large photo is similar to the photo at right. If the height of the large photo is 10 in., what is its width?

2 in.

1.5 in.

INDEPENDENT PRACTICE

See Example **1** 3. The two triangles are similar. Find the missing length n and the measure of $\angle M$.

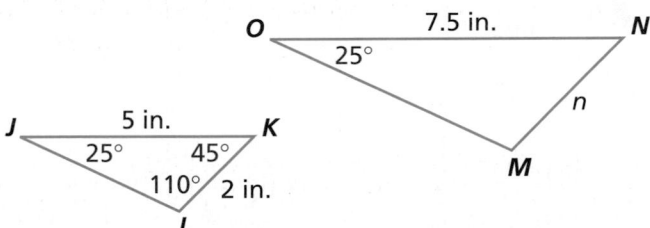

See Example **2** 4. LeJuan swims in a pool that is similar to an Olympic-sized pool. LeJuan's pool is 30 m long by 8 m wide. The length of an Olympic-sized pool is 50 m. To the nearest meter, what is the width of an Olympic-sized pool?

PRACTICE AND PROBLEM SOLVING

Extra Practice
See page 726.

Name the corresponding sides and angles for each pair of similar figures.

5.

6.

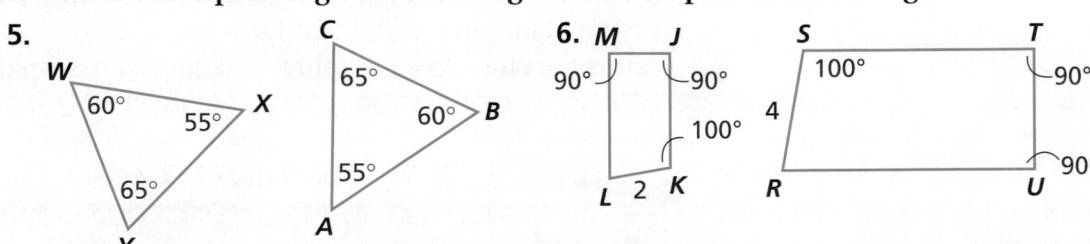

7. **Critical Thinking** The ratio of the lengths of two similar paintings is $\frac{100}{32}$. If the length of one painting is 100 cm, is the length of the other less than or greater than 100 cm? Explain.

The figures in each pair are similar. Find the unknown measures.

8.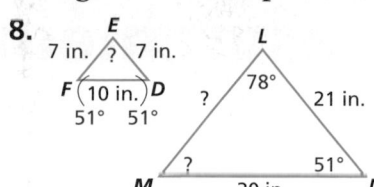

9.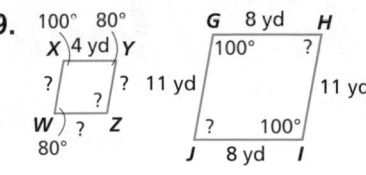

Tell whether the figures in each pair are similar. Explain your answers.

10.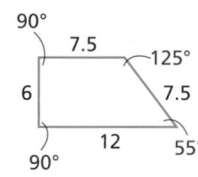

11.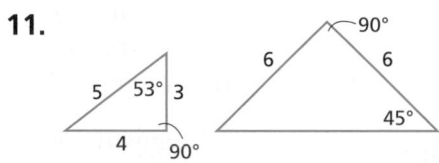

12. Graphic Art Lenny sketches designs for billboards. The sketch and the billboard are similar. If the height of the billboard is 30 ft, what is the width to the nearest foot of the billboard?

1.5 in.

2.5 in.

 13. What's the Error? A student drew two rectangles with dimensions 10 in. by 9 in. and 5 in. by 3 in. The student said that the rectangles are similar. What's the error?

 14. Write About It Are all triangles that have one 90° angle similar? Explain your answer.

 15. Challenge Draw two similar rectangles whose sides are in a ratio of 5:2.

16. Multiple Choice The triangles are similar. Find the missing angle measure.

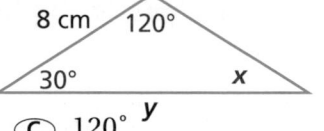   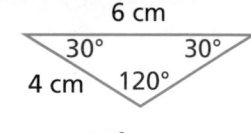

Ⓐ 30° Ⓑ 60° Ⓒ 120° Ⓓ 180°

17. Multiple Choice Use the similar triangles in Exercise 16. Find the missing length *y*.

Ⓕ 4 cm Ⓖ 12 cm Ⓗ 18 cm Ⓙ 24 cm

Identify the property that is illustrated by each equation. (Lesson 1-5)

18. $3 + (4 + 5) = (3 + 4) + 5$ **19.** $19(24) = 19(20) + 19(4)$ **20.** $(2)(13) = (13)(2)$

Find the value of *n* in each proportion. (Lesson 7-3)

21. $\dfrac{n}{7} = \dfrac{30}{42}$

22. $\dfrac{4}{n} = \dfrac{16}{8}$

23. $\dfrac{1}{9} = \dfrac{n}{6.3}$

Learn to use proportions and similar figures to find unknown measures.

Vocabulary

indirect measurement

NY Performance Indicators

6.G.1 Calculate the length of corresponding sides of similar triangles, using proportional reasoning. Also, 6.A.5.

Residents of Maine spent 14 days in 1999 building this enormous snowman. How could you measure the height of this snowman?

One way to find a height that you cannot measure directly is to use similar figures and proportions. This method is called **indirect measurement** .

Suppose that on a sunny day, the snowman cast a shadow that was 228 feet long. A 6-foot-tall person standing by the snowman cast a 12-foot-long shadow.

Both the person and the snowman form 90° angles with the ground, and their shadows are cast at the same angle. This means we can form two similar triangles and use proportions to find the missing height.

EXAMPLE **Using Indirect Measurement**

Use the similar triangles above to find the height of the snowman.

$$\frac{6}{h} = \frac{12}{228}$$ *Write a proportion using corresponding sides.*

$$12 \cdot h = 6 \cdot 228$$ *The cross products are equal.*

$$12h = 1{,}368$$ *h is multiplied by 12.*

$$\frac{12h}{12} = \frac{1{,}368}{12}$$ *Divide both sides by 12 to undo the multiplication.*

$$h = 114$$

The snowman was 114 feet tall.

EXAMPLE 2 **Measurement Application**

A lighthouse casts a shadow that is 36 m long when a meterstick casts a shadow that is 3 m long. How tall is the lighthouse?

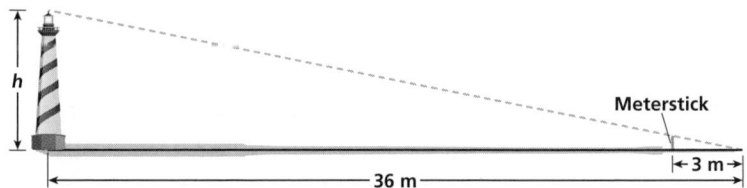

Meterstick

36 m   ← 3 m →

$$\frac{h}{1} = \frac{36}{3}$$ *Write a proportion using corresponding sides.*

$1 \cdot 36 = 3 \cdot h$ *The cross products are equal.*

$36 = 3h$ *h is multiplied by 3.*

$$\frac{36}{3} = \frac{3h}{3}$$ *Divide both sides by 3 to undo the multiplication.*

$12 = h$

The lighthouse is 12 m tall.

6.CM.1, 6.CN.7

Think and Discuss

1. **Name** two items for which it would make sense to use indirect measurement to find their heights.

2. **Name** two items for which it would **not** make sense to use indirect measurement to find their heights.

7-5 Exercises

GUIDED PRACTICE

See Example 1   1. Use the similar triangles to find the height of the flagpole.

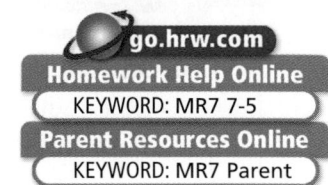

h

5 ft

10 ft

30 ft

See Example 2   2. A tree casts a shadow that is 26 ft long. At the same time, a 3-foot-tall sunflower casts a shadow that is 4 ft long. How tall is the tree?

See Example 3. Use the similar triangles to find the height of the lamppost.

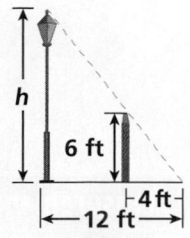

See Example 4. The Eiffel Tower casts a shadow that is 328 feet long. A 6-foot-tall person standing by the tower casts a 2-foot-long shadow. How tall is the Eiffel Tower?

PRACTICE AND PROBLEM SOLVING

Extra Practice
See page 726.

Find the unknown heights.

5.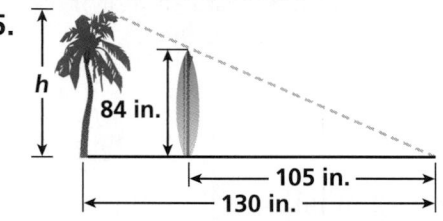

6.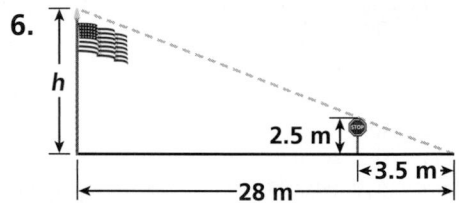

7. A statue casts a shadow that is 360 m long. At the same time, a person who is 2 m tall casts a shadow that is 6 m long. How tall is the statue?

 8. **Write About It** How are indirect measurements useful?

 9. **Challenge** A 5.5-foot-tall girl stands so that her shadow lines up with the shadow of a telephone pole. The tip of her shadow is even with the tip of the pole's shadow. If the length of the pole's shadow is 40 feet and the girl is standing 27.5 feet away from the pole, how tall is the telephone pole?

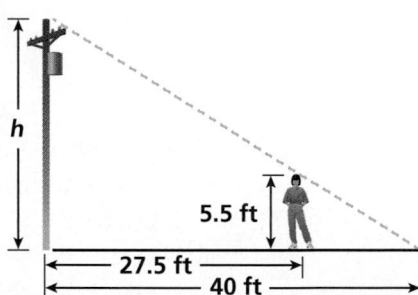

TEST PREP and Spiral Review

10. **Multiple Choice** An 18-foot-tall telephone pole casts a shadow that is 28.8 feet long. At the same time, a woman casts a shadow that is 8.8 feet long. How tall is the woman?

   (A) 4.4 feet   (B) 5.5 feet   (C) 14.08 feet   (D) 158.4 feet

11. **Gridded Response** A 4-foot-tall girl casts a shadow that is 7.2 feet long. A nearby tree casts a shadow that is 25.56 feet long. How tall, in feet, is the tree?

Estimate by rounding to the indicated place value. (Lesson 3-2)

12. $4.325 - 1.895$; tenths   13. $5.121 - 0.1568$; tenths   14. $7.592 + 9.675$; hundredths

Solve each equation. Write the solution in simplest form. (Lesson 5-5)

15. $x - 1\frac{1}{4} = 7$ 16. $4\frac{1}{3} = x + \frac{5}{6}$ 17. $x - 8\frac{1}{2} = \frac{3}{10}$ 18. $6\frac{2}{3} = 4\frac{1}{6} + x$

Sketch Scale Drawings

Use with Lesson 7-6

NY Performance Indicators
6.PS.13, 6.PS.22, 6.CM.3, 6.CN.3

go.hrw.com
Lab Resources Online
KEYWORD: MR7 Lab7

REMEMBER
- Similar figures are exactly the same shape, but they may be different sizes.

You can use a *scale factor* to sketch scale drawings. A *scale drawing* is a drawing of an object that is proportionally smaller or larger than the object. A *scale factor* is the ratio that describes how much a figure is enlarged or reduced.

Activity

Draw triangle A on graph paper with height 1 and base 3 as shown.

To draw a similar triangle using a scale factor of 3, draw another triangle whose sides are 3 times as long as the corresponding sides of the original.

To find the height of the new triangle, multiply the height of triangle A by 3.
height = 1 × 3 = 3; the new height will be 3 units.

To find the base of the new triangle, multiply the base of triangle A by 3.
base = 3 × 3 = 9; the new base will be 9 units.

Label the new figure triangle B.

For every 1 unit of length on the original triangle, the second triangle has 3 units of length.

Think and Discuss

1. How does knowing the scale factor help you find the dimensions of a similar figure?

2. If you use a scale factor of $\frac{3}{2}$, will the new figure be larger or smaller than the original? Explain.

Try This

Use the given scale factor to draw a figure similar to triangle A.

1. 4　　　　　2. $\frac{1}{2}$　　　　　3. 2　　　　　4. $\frac{3}{2}$

Scale Drawings and Maps

Learn to read and use map scales and scale drawings.

Vocabulary

scale drawing

scale

NY Performance Indicators

6.A.5 Solve simple proportions within context.

The map of Yosemite National Park shown above is a *scale drawing*. A **scale drawing** is a drawing of a real object that is proportionally smaller or larger than the real object. In other words, measurements on a scale drawing are in proportion to the measurements of the real object.

A **scale** is a ratio between two sets of measurements. In the map above, the scale is 1 in:2 mi. This ratio means that 1 inch on the map represents 2 miles in Yosemite National Park.

EXAMPLE **1** **Finding Actual Distances**

On the map, the distance between El Capitan and Panorama Cliff is 2 inches. What is the actual distance?

$$\frac{1 \text{ in.}}{2 \text{ mi}} = \frac{2 \text{ in.}}{x \text{ mi}}$$ *Write a proportion using the scale. Let x be the actual number of miles from El Capitan to Panorama Cliff.*

$2 \cdot 2 = 1 \cdot x$ *The cross products are equal.*

$\qquad 4 = x$

The actual distance from El Capitan to Panorama Cliff is 4 miles.

Helpful Hint

In Example 1, think "1 inch is 2 miles, so 2 inches is how many miles?" This approach will help you set up proportions in similar problems.

EXAMPLE **2** *Astronomy Application*

Mercury

Earth

1 in:30 million km

A **What is the actual distance from Mercury to Earth?**

Use your inch ruler to measure the distance from the center of Mercury to the center of Earth on the drawing. Mercury and Earth are about 3 inches apart.

$$\frac{1 \text{ in.}}{30 \text{ million km}} = \frac{3 \text{ in.}}{x \text{ million km}}$$ *Write a proportion. Let x be the actual distance from Mercury to Earth.*

$$30 \cdot 3 = 1 \cdot x$$ *The cross products are equal.*

$$90 = x$$

The actual distance from Mercury to Earth is about 90 million km.

B **The actual distance from Mercury to Venus is 50 million kilometers. How far apart should Mercury and Venus be drawn?**

$$\frac{1 \text{ in.}}{30 \text{ million km}} = \frac{x \text{ in.}}{50 \text{ million km}}$$ *Write a proportion. Let x be the distance from Mercury to Venus on the drawing.*

$$30 \cdot x = 1 \cdot 50$$ *The cross products are equal.*

$$30x = 50$$ *x is multiplied by 30.*

$$\frac{30x}{30} = \frac{50}{30}$$ *Divide both sides by 30 to undo the multiplication.*

$$x = 1\frac{2}{3}$$

Mercury and Venus should be drawn $1\frac{2}{3}$ inches apart.

Think and Discuss

1. Give an example of when you would use a scale drawing.

2. Suppose that you are going to make a scale drawing of your classroom with a scale of 1 inch:3 feet. Select a distance in your classroom and measure it. What will this distance be on your drawing?

go.hrw.com
Homework Help Online
KEYWORD: MR7 7-6
Parent Resources Online
KEYWORD: MR7 Parent

GUIDED PRACTICE

See Example ① **1.** On the map, the distance between the post office and the fountain is 6 cm. What is the actual distance?

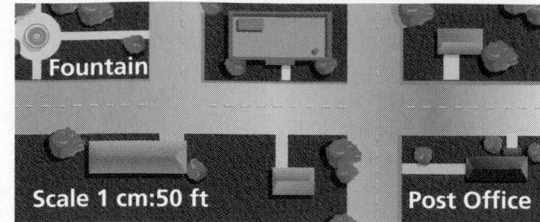

Fountain

Scale 1 cm:50 ft   Post Office

See Example ② **2.** What is the actual length of the car?

3. The actual height of the car is 1.6 meters. Is the car's height in the drawing correct?

Scale: 1 cm:0.8 m

INDEPENDENT PRACTICE

See Example ① **4.** On the map of California, Los Angeles is 1.25 inches from Malibu. Find the actual distance from Los Angeles to Malibu.

See Example ② **5.** Riverside, California, is 50 miles from Los Angeles. On the map, how far should Riverside be from Los Angeles?

Scale: 1 in:20 mi

6. Life Science A paramecium is a one-celled organism. The scale drawing at right is larger than an actual paramecium. Find the actual length of the paramecium.

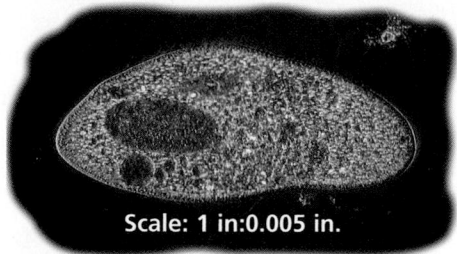

Scale: 1 in:0.005 in.

PRACTICE AND PROBLEM SOLVING

Extra Practice
See page 726.

7. Suppose you are asked to make a scale drawing of a room. The room has four walls. The lengths of the walls are as follows: north wall, 8 ft; west wall, 12 ft; south wall, 20 ft; slanted east wall, 17 ft. The scale for the drawing is 1 in:4 ft.

   a. Use the actual lengths of the walls to find the lengths in the drawing.

   b. Sketch the room and label each wall. What shape does the room resemble?

   c. Mark a 2.5 ft wide window on the west wall, and a 3.5 ft wide door on the south wall. Give the width of each on the scale drawing.

8. Hobbies A popular scale used in model trains is called HO. The scale for HO is 1 ft:87 ft. If a model train is 3 feet long, how long is the actual train?

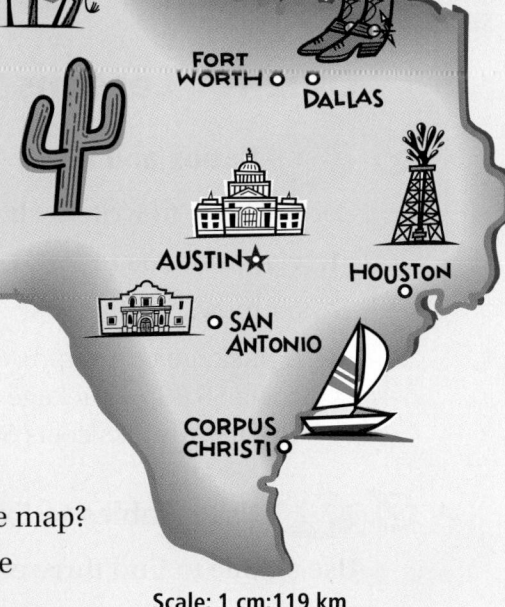

Texas is the second largest state in the country and is the largest state in the lower 48 states. It is more than 1,120 kilometers across. There is even a ranch in Texas that is larger than Rhode Island!

9. What is the distance in kilometers from Houston to Dallas?

10. What is the distance in kilometers from Corpus Christi to San Antonio?

11. Name two cities on the map that are more than 200 kilometers apart.

12. Wichita Falls is about 480 kilometers from San Antonio.

   a. About how far apart should these two cities be on the map?

   b. What else would you need to know to be able to place Wichita Falls on the map?

Scale: 1 cm:119 km

13. ✏️ **Write a Problem** Write a problem using the map and its scale.

14. ✏️ **Write About It** Explain how to find the actual distance between two cities if you know the distance on a map and the scale of the map.

15. ⭐ **Challenge** If you drive at a constant speed of 100 kilometers per hour, about how long will it take you to drive from Amarillo to San Antonio?

TEST PREP and Spiral Review

16. **Multiple Choice** The distance between towns A and C on a map is 13 centimeters. What is the actual distance between towns B and C?

5 cm

Town A   Town B   Town C

Scale: 1 cm:30 km

   Ⓐ 0.27 kilometers   Ⓑ 150 kilometers   Ⓒ 240 kilometers   Ⓓ 390 kilometers

17. **Gridded Response** Tanya has a 1 in:32 in. scale model car. The length of the model car is 2 inches. What is the actual length of the car?

Find each sum or difference. (Lesson 3-3)

18. $8.3 - 6.7$ 19. $25.6 + 12.8$ 20. $14 - 5.9$ 21. $8.62 - 4.75$ 22. $15.75 + 9.38$

Find the missing value in each proportion. (Lesson 7-3)

23. $\frac{9}{15} = \frac{x}{5}$ 24. $\frac{b}{20} = \frac{3}{15}$ 25. $\frac{1}{7} = \frac{6}{k}$ 26. $\frac{8}{3} = \frac{a}{9}$ 27. $\frac{p}{4} = \frac{11}{44}$

READY TO GO ON?

CHAPTER

7

SECTION 7A

Quiz for Lessons 7-1 Through 7-6

☑ **7-1** **Ratios and Rates**

Use the table to write each ratio.

Types of CDs in Mark's Music Collection			
Classical	4	Jazz	3
Country	9	Pop	14
Dance	8	Rock	10

1. classical CDs to rock CDs

2. country to total CDs

3. A package containing 6 pairs of socks costs $6.89. A package containing 4 pairs of socks costs $4.64. Which is the better deal?

☑ **7-2** **Using Tables to Explore Equivalent Ratios and Rates**

Use a table to find three equivalent ratios.

4. $\frac{21}{30}$

5. 15:6

6. 3 to 101

7. The table shows the wait time for different groups at a restaurant. Predict how long a group of 8 will wait.

Number in Group	1	2	5	7	10
Wait Time (min)	3	6	15	21	30

☑ **7-3** **Proportions**

Find the missing value in each proportion.

8. $\frac{1}{4} = \frac{n}{12}$

9. $\frac{3}{n} = \frac{15}{25}$

10. $\frac{n}{4} = \frac{18}{6}$

11. $\frac{10}{4} = \frac{5}{n}$

☑ **7-4** **Similar Figures**

12. The two triangles are similar. Find the missing length n and the measure of $\angle R$.

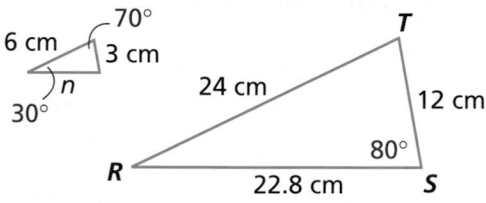

☑ **7-5** **Indirect Measurement**

13. A tree casts a shadow that is 18 feet long. At the same time, a 5-foot-tall person casts a shadow that is 3.6 feet long. How tall is the tree?

☑ **7-6** **Scale Drawings and Maps**

Use the scale drawing and a metric ruler to answer each question.

14. What is the actual length of the kitchen?

15. What are the actual length and width of bedroom 1?

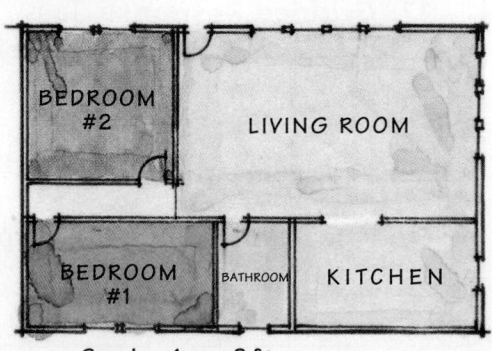

Scale: 1cm:8ft

Focus on Problem Solving

Make a Plan

• **Estimate or find an exact answer**

Sometimes an estimate is all you need to solve a problem, and sometimes you need to find an exact answer.

One way to decide whether you can estimate is to see if you can rewrite the problem using the words *at most, at least,* or *about.* For example, suppose Laura has $30. Then she could spend *at most* $30. She would not have to spend *exactly* $30. Or, if you know it takes 15 minutes to get to school, you must leave your house *at least* (not exactly) 15 minutes before school starts.

Read the problems below. Decide whether you can estimate or whether you must find the exact answer. How do you know?

1 Alex is a radio station disc jockey. He is making a list of songs that should last no longer than 30 minutes total when played in a row. His list of songs and their playing times are given in the table. Does Alex have the right amount of music?

Song Title	Length (min)
Color Me Blue	4.5
Hittin' the Road	7.2
Stand Up, Shout	2.6
Top Dog	3.6
Kelso Blues	4.3
Smile on Me	5.7
A Long Time Ago	6.4

2 For every 10 minutes of music, Alex has to play 1.5 minutes of commercials. If Alex plays the songs on the list, how much time does he need to allow for commercials?

3 If Alex must play the songs on the list and the commercials in 30 minutes, how much music time does he need to cut to allow for commercials?

Model Percents

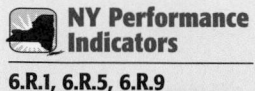

NY Performance Indicators

6.R.1, 6.R.5, 6.R.9

go.hrw.com
Lab Resources Online
KEYWORD: MR7 Lab7

A *percent* shows the ratio of a number to 100. You can model percents by using a 10-by-10 grid on graph paper.

Activity

1 Model 55% on a 10-by-10 grid.

Write 55% as a ratio comparing 55 to 100.

$55\% = \frac{55}{100}$

Since there are 100 squares in a 10 × 10 grid, shade in 55 squares.

$\frac{\text{number of squares shaded}}{\text{total number of squares}} = \frac{55}{100} = 55\%$

The model represents 55%.

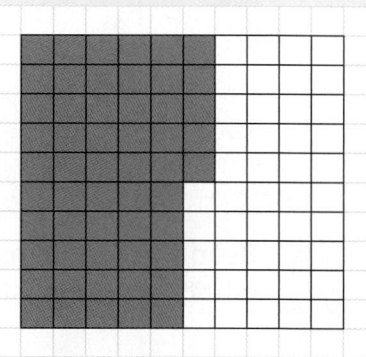

2 What percent of grid A is shaded?

Find the number of squares shaded in grid A. Compare it with the total number of squares.

$\frac{\text{number of squares shaded}}{\text{total number of squares}} = \frac{42}{100}$

Since 42 out of 100 squares are shaded, the grid models 42%.

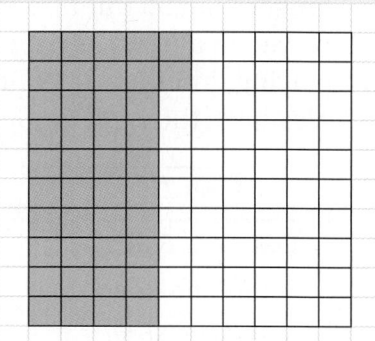

Grid A

Think and Discuss

1. Shade in $\frac{3}{4}$ of a 10-by-10 grid. What percent of the grid is shaded? Explain.

2. How can equivalent ratios help you find your answer to **1**?

3. How would you model 105%? 0.5%? Explain your answer.

Try This

Model each percent on a 10-by-10 grid.

1. 50% **2.** 68% **3.** 4% **4.** 91% **5.** 100%

7-7 Percents

Learn to write percents as decimals and as fractions.

Vocabulary

percent

 NY Performance Indicators

6.N.11 Read, write, and identify percents of a whole (0% to 100%). Also, 6.N.12, 6.N.21.

Most states charge sales tax on items you purchase. Sales tax is a percent of the item's price. A **percent** is a ratio of a number to 100.

You can remember that *percent* means "per hundred." For example, 8% means "8 per hundred," or "8 out of 100."

If a sales tax rate is 8%, the following statements are true:

- For every $1.00 you spend, you pay $0.08 in sales tax.
- For every $10.00 you spend, you pay $0.80 in sales tax.
- For every $100 you spend, you pay $8 in sales tax.

At a sales tax rate of 8%, the tax on this guitar and amplifier would be $36.56.

Because *percent* means "per hundred," 100% means "100 out of 100." This is why 100% is often used to mean "all" or "the whole thing."

EXAMPLE 1 Modeling Percents

Use a 10-by-10-square grid to model 8%.

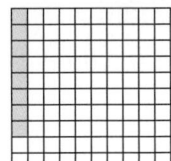

A 10-by-10-square grid has 100 squares.

8% means "8 out of 100," or $\frac{8}{100}$.

Shade 8 squares out of 100 squares.

EXAMPLE 2 Writing Percents as Fractions

Write 40% as a fraction in simplest form.

$40\% = \frac{40}{100}$ *Write the percent as a fraction with a denominator of 100.*

$\frac{40 \div 20}{100 \div 20} = \frac{2}{5}$ *Write the fraction in simplest form.*

Written as a fraction, 40% is $\frac{2}{5}$.

EXAMPLE 3 *Life Science Application*

Up to 55% of the heat lost by your body can be lost through your head. Write 55% as a fraction in simplest form.

$55\% = \frac{55}{100}$ *Write the percent as a fraction with a denominator of 100.*

$\frac{55 \div 5}{100 \div 5} = \frac{11}{20}$ *Write the fraction in simplest form.*

Written as a fraction, 55% is $\frac{11}{20}$.

EXAMPLE 4 **Writing Percents as Decimals**

Write 24% as a decimal.

$24\% = \frac{24}{100}$ *Write the percent as a fraction with a denominator of 100.*

Write the fraction as a decimal.

$$
\begin{array}{r}
0.24 \\
100\overline{)24.00} \\
-200 \\
\hline
400 \\
-400 \\
\hline
0
\end{array}
$$

Written as a decimal, 24% is 0.24.

Remember!

To divide by 100, move the decimal point two places to the left.

$24 \div 100 = 0.24$

EXAMPLE 5 *Earth Science Application*

The water frozen in glaciers makes up almost 75% of the world's fresh water supply. Write 75% as a decimal.

$75\% = \frac{75}{100}$ *Write the percent as a fraction with a denominator of 100.*

$75 \div 100 = 0.75$ *Write the fraction as a decimal.*

Written as a decimal, 75% is 0.75.

Think and Discuss

6.CM.1, 6.CN.4, 6.R.8

1. **Give an example** of a situation in which you have seen percents.

2. **Tell** how much sales tax you would have to pay on $1, $10, and $100 if your state had a 5% sales tax rate.

3. **Explain** how to write a percent as a fraction.

4. **Write** 100% as a decimal and as a fraction.

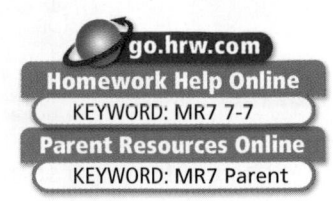
7-7 Exercises

GUIDED PRACTICE

See Example **1** Use a 10-by-10-square grid to model each percent.
   1. 45%   **2.** 3%   **3.** 61%

See Example **2** Write each percent as a fraction in simplest form.
   4. 25%   **5.** 80%   **6.** 54%

See Example **3** **7. Social Studies** Belize is a country in Central America. Of the land in Belize, 92% is made up of forests and woodlands. Write 92% as a fraction in simplest form.

See Example **4** Write each percent as a decimal.
   8. 72%   **9.** 4%   **10.** 90%

See Example **5** **11.** About 64% of the runways at airports in the United States are not paved. Write 64% as a decimal.

INDEPENDENT PRACTICE

See Example **1** Use a 10-by-10-square grid to model each percent.
   12. 14%   **13.** 98%   **14.** 36%   **15.** 28%

See Example **2** Write each percent as a fraction in simplest form.
   16. 20%   **17.** 75%   **18.** 11%   **19.** 72%
   20. 5%   **21.** 64%   **22.** 31%   **23.** 85%

See Example **3** **24.** Nikki must answer 80% of the questions on her final exam correctly to pass her class. Write 80% as a fraction in simplest form.

See Example **4** Write each percent as a decimal.
   25. 44%   **26.** 13%   **27.** 29%   **28.** 51%
   29. 60%   **30.** 92%   **31.** 7%   **32.** 87%

See Example **5** **33.** Brett was absent 2% of the school year. Write 2% as a decimal.

PRACTICE AND PROBLEM SOLVING

Extra Practice
See page 727.

Write each percent as a fraction in simplest form and as a decimal.
   34. 23%   **35.** 1%   **36.** 49%   **37.** 70%   **38.** 10%
   39. 37%   **40.** 85%   **41.** 8%   **42.** 63%   **43.** 75%
   44. 94%   **45.** 100%   **46.** 0%   **47.** 52%   **48.** 12%

49. Model 15%, 52%, 71%, and 100% using different 10-by-10 grids. Then write each percent as a fraction in simplest form.

The circle graph shows the percent of radio stations around the world that play each type of music listed. Use the graph for Exercises 50–57.

50. What fraction of the radio stations play easy listening music? Write this fraction in simplest form.

51. Use a 10-by-10-square grid to model the percent of radio stations that play country music. Then write this percent as a decimal.

52. Which type of music makes up $\frac{1}{20}$ of the graph?

53. Someone reading the graph said, "More than $\frac{1}{10}$ of the radio stations play top 40 music." Do you agree with this statement? Why or why not?

54. Suppose you converted all of the percents in the graph to decimals and added them. Without actually doing this, tell what the sum would be. Explain.

55. ✍ **Write a Problem** Write a question about the circle graph that involves changing a percent to a fraction. Then answer your question.

56. ✍ **Write About It** How does the percent of radio stations that play Spanish music compare with the fraction $\frac{1}{6}$? Explain.

57. ⭐ **Challenge** Name a fraction that is greater than the percent of radio stations that play Spanish music but less than the percent of radio stations that play urban/rap music.

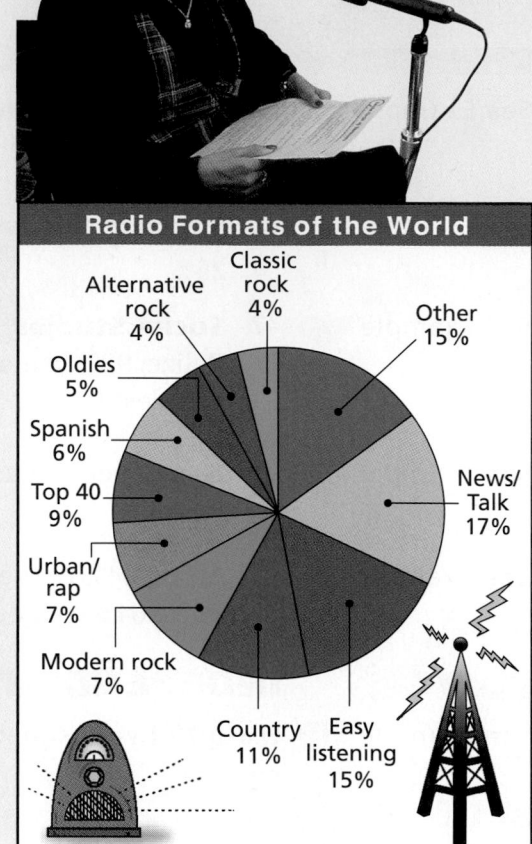

Radio Formats of the World

Alternative rock 4%
Classic rock 4%
Other 15%
Oldies 5%
Spanish 6%
News/Talk 17%
Top 40 9%
Urban/rap 7%
Modern rock 7%
Country 11%
Easy listening 15%

Source: Scholastic Kid's Almanac for the 21st Century

Test Prep and Spiral Review

58. **Multiple Choice** Which decimal is equivalent to 85%?

    Ⓐ 85.0   Ⓑ 8.5   Ⓒ 0.85   Ⓓ 0.085

59. **Multiple Choice** Which term describes a number compared to 100?

    Ⓕ Rate   Ⓖ Ratio   Ⓗ Percent   Ⓙ Proportion

Evaluate each expression. (Lesson 1-4)

60. $45 \div 5 + 2 - 10$ 61. $25 - 4 \times 2$ 62. $18 - 7 \times 2 + 8$ 63. $48 - 9 \times 3 - 11$

64. The Sears Tower in Chicago casts a shadow 580 feet long. At the same time, a 5-foot-tall boy casts a 2-foot shadow. What is the height of the Sears Tower? (Lesson 7-5)

7-8 Percents, Decimals, and Fractions

Learn to write decimals and fractions as percents.

NY Performance Indicators

6.N.21 Find the multiple representations of rational numbers (fractions, decimals, and percents 0 to 100). Also, 6.N.11, 6.N.12.

Percents, decimals, and fractions appear in newspapers, on television, and on the Internet. To fully understand the data you see in your everyday life, you should be able to change from one number form to another.

"Oh yes, a one-half of one percent allowance increase is quite a bit."

EXAMPLE Writing Decimals as Percents

Write each decimal as a percent.

Method 1: Use place value.

A 0.3

$$0.3 = \frac{3}{10}$$ *Write the decimal as a fraction.*

$$\frac{3 \cdot 10}{10 \cdot 10} = \frac{30}{100}$$ *Write an equivalent fraction with 100 as the denominator.*

$$\frac{30}{100} = 30\%$$ *Write the numerator with a percent symbol.*

B 0.43

$$0.43 = \frac{43}{100}$$ *Write the decimal as a fraction.*

$$\frac{43}{100} = 43\%$$ *Write the numerator with a percent symbol.*

Method 2: Multiply by 100.

C 0.7431

$0.7431 \cdot 100$ *Multiply by 100.*

74.31%   *Add the percent symbol.*

D 0.023

$0.023 \cdot 100$ *Multiply by 100.*

2.3%   *Add the percent symbol.*

7-8 Percents, Decimals, and Fractions **385**

EXAMPLE 2 **Writing Fractions as Percents**

Write each fraction as a percent.

Method 1: Write an equivalent fraction with a denominator of 100.

 $\frac{4}{5}$

$$\frac{4 \cdot 20}{5 \cdot 20} = \frac{80}{100}$$ *Write an equivalent fraction with a denominator of 100.*

$$\frac{80}{100} = 80\%$$ *Write the numerator with a percent symbol.*

Method 2: Use division to write the fraction as a decimal.

B $\frac{3}{8}$

$$\begin{array}{r} 0.375 \\ 8\overline{)3.000} \end{array}$$ *Divide the numerator by the denominator.*

$$0.375 = 37.5\%$$ *Multiply by 100 by moving the decimal point right two places. Add the percent symbol.*

EXAMPLE 3 *Earth Science Application*

About $\frac{39}{50}$ of Earth's atmosphere is made up of nitrogen. About what percent of the atmosphere is nitrogen?

$$\frac{39}{50}$$

$$\frac{39 \cdot 2}{50 \cdot 2} = \frac{78}{100}$$ *Write an equivalent fraction with a denominator of 100.*

$$\frac{78}{100} = 78\%$$ *Write the numerator with a percent symbol.*

About 78% of Earth's atmosphere is made up of nitrogen.

Common Equivalent Fractions, Decimals, and Percents									
Fraction	$\frac{1}{5}$	$\frac{1}{4}$	$\frac{1}{3}$	$\frac{2}{5}$	$\frac{1}{2}$	$\frac{3}{5}$	$\frac{2}{3}$	$\frac{3}{4}$	$\frac{4}{5}$
Decimal	0.2	0.25	$0.\overline{3}$	0.4	0.5	0.6	$0.\overline{6}$	0.75	0.8
Percent	20%	25%	$33.\overline{3}\%$	40%	50%	60%	$66.\overline{6}\%$	75%	80%

Think and Discuss   6.CM.2, 6.CN.4, 6.R.9

1. Tell which method you prefer for converting decimals to percents—using equivalent fractions or multiplying by 100. Why?

2. Give two different ways to write three-tenths.

3. Explain how to write fractions as percents using two different methods.

Helpful Hint

When the denominator is a factor of 100, it is often easier to use method 1. When the denominator is not a factor of 100, it is usually easier to use method 2.

7-8 Exercises

go.hrw.com
Homework Help Online
KEYWORD: MR7 7-8

Parent Resources Online
KEYWORD: MR7 Parent

GUIDED PRACTICE

See Example 1 · Write each decimal as a percent.

1. 0.39 **2.** 0.125 **3.** 0.8 **4.** 0.112

See Example 2 · Write each fraction as a percent.

5. $\frac{11}{25}$ **6.** $\frac{7}{8}$ **7.** $\frac{7}{10}$ **8.** $\frac{1}{2}$ **9.** $\frac{9}{15}$

See Example 3 · **10.** Patti spent $\frac{3}{4}$ of her allowance on a new backpack. What percent of her allowance did she spend?

INDEPENDENT PRACTICE

See Example 1 · Write each decimal as a percent.

11. 0.6 **12.** 0.55 **13.** 0.34 **14.** 0.308 **15.** 0.62

See Example 2 · Write each fraction as a percent.

16. $\frac{3}{5}$ **17.** $\frac{3}{10}$ **18.** $\frac{24}{25}$ **19.** $\frac{9}{20}$ **20.** $\frac{17}{20}$

21. $\frac{1}{8}$ **22.** $\frac{11}{16}$ **23.** $\frac{37}{50}$ **24.** $\frac{2}{5}$ **25.** $\frac{18}{45}$

See Example 3 · **26.** About $\frac{1}{125}$ of the people in the United States have the last name *Johnson*. What percent of people in the United States have this last name?

PRACTICE AND PROBLEM SOLVING

Extra Practice
See page 727.

Write each decimal as a percent and a fraction.

27. 0.04 **28.** 0.32 **29.** 0.45 **30.** 0.59 **31.** 0.01

32. 0.81 **33.** 0.6 **34.** 0.39 **35.** 0.14 **36.** 0.62

Write each fraction as a percent and as a decimal. Round to the nearest hundredth, if necessary.

37. $\frac{4}{5}$ **38.** $\frac{1}{3}$ **39.** $\frac{5}{6}$ **40.** $\frac{7}{12}$ **41.** $\frac{17}{50}$

42. $\frac{2}{30}$ **43.** $\frac{1}{25}$ **44.** $\frac{8}{11}$ **45.** $\frac{4}{15}$ **46.** $\frac{22}{35}$

Compare. Write <, >, or =.

47. 70% ▇ $\frac{3}{4}$ **48.** $\frac{5}{8}$ ▇ 6.25% **49.** 0.2 ▇ $\frac{1}{5}$ **50.** 1.25 ▇ $\frac{1}{8}$

51. 0.7 ▇ 7% **52.** $\frac{9}{10}$ ▇ 0.3 **53.** 37% ▇ $\frac{3}{7}$ **54.** $\frac{17}{20}$ ▇ 0.85

55. Language Arts The longest word in all of Shakespeare's plays is *honorificabilitudinitatibus*. About what percent of the letters in this word are vowels? About what percent of the letters are consonants?

Order the numbers from least to greatest.

56. 45%, $\frac{21}{50}$, 0.43

57. $\frac{7}{8}$, 90%, 0.098

58. 0.7, 26%, $\frac{1}{4}$

59. 38%, $\frac{7}{25}$, 0.21

60. $\frac{9}{20}$, 14%, 0.125

61. 0.605, 17%, $\frac{5}{9}$

Entertainment

This photo from 1953 shows one of the first color television cameras.

62. Entertainment About 97 million households in the United States have at least one television. Use the table below to answer the questions that follow.

Television in the United States	
Fraction of households with at least one television	$\frac{49}{50}$
Percent of households with three televisions	38%
Fraction of television owners with basic cable	$\frac{2}{3}$

   a. About what percent of television owners have basic cable?

   b. Write a decimal to express the percent of television owners who have three televisions.

63. Multi-Step A record-company official estimates that 3 out of every 100 albums released become hits. What percent of albums do not become hits?

 64. What's the Question? Out of 25 students, 12 prefer to take their test on Monday, and 5 prefer to take their test on Tuesday. The answer is 32%. What is the question?

 65. Write About It Explain why 0.8 is equal to 80% and not 8%.

 66. Challenge The dimensions of a rectangle are 0.5 yard and 24% of a yard. What is the area of the rectangle? Write your answer as a fraction in simplest form.

TEST PREP and Spiral Review

67. Multiple Choice Which expression is NOT equal to half of *n*?

  Ⓐ 0.5*n*   Ⓑ $\frac{n}{2}$ Ⓒ *n* ÷ 2   Ⓓ 5% of *n*

68. Multiple Choice Approximately $\frac{2}{3}$ of U.S. homeowners own a cell phone. What percent of homeowners do NOT own a cell phone?

  Ⓕ 0.67%   Ⓖ 2.3%   Ⓗ 33.3%   Ⓙ 66.7%

Add or subtract. Write each answer in simplest form. (Lesson 5-2)

69. $\frac{1}{2} + \frac{3}{4}$ **70.** $\frac{2}{3} - \frac{1}{5}$ **71.** $\frac{2}{5} + \frac{1}{2}$ **72.** $\frac{8}{9} - \frac{1}{6}$

The scale for blueprints of a house is 2 in:3 ft. Use the scale to determine the related actual lengths. (Lesson 7-6)

73. porch length: 2 in.   **74.** bedroom wall: 5 in.   **75.** window: 1.5 in.

Technology LAB 7-8

Convert Between Percents, Decimals, and Fractions

Use with Lesson 7-8

NY Performance Indicators

6.N.12, 6.N.21

go.hrw.com
Lab Resources Online
KEYWORD: MR7 Lab7

You can use your calculator to quickly change between percents, decimals, and fractions.

Activity

❶ To write a decimal as a fraction on a graphing calculator, use the **FRAC** command from the **MATH** menu.

Find the fraction equivalent of 0.225 by pressing 0.225
[MATH] 1 [ENTER].

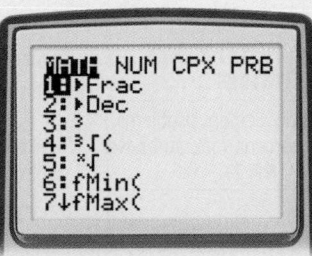

❷ To write a percent as a fraction, first write the percent as a fraction whose denominator is 100. Then use the **FRAC** command to find the simplest form of the fraction.

Find the fraction equivalent of 65% by pressing 65 [÷]
100 [MATH] 1 [ENTER].

❸ To write a fraction as a percent, multiply the fraction by 100.

Find the percent equivalent of $\frac{11}{25}$ by pressing 11 [÷]
25 [×] 100 [ENTER].

$\frac{11}{25} = 44\%$

Think and Discuss

1. Use the **FRAC** command on a graphing calculator to find the fraction equivalent of 0.1428571429 by pressing 0.1428571429
[MATH] 1 [ENTER]. Describe what happens.

Try This

Write each percent as a fraction.

1. 57.5%   **2.** 32.5%   **3.** 3.25%   **4.** 1.65%   **5.** 81.25%

Write each fraction as a percent.

6. $\frac{7}{40}$ **7.** $\frac{3}{8}$ **8.** $\frac{19}{25}$ **9.** $\frac{3}{16}$ **10.** $\frac{17}{20}$

7-9 Percent Problems

Learn to find the missing value in a percent problem.

NY Performance Indicators

6.N.12 Solve percent problems involving percent, rate, and base. Also, 6.N.11, 6.N.27.

The frozen-yogurt stand in the mall sells 420 frozen-yogurt cups per day, on average. Forty-five percent of the frozen-yogurt cups are sold to teenagers. On average, how many frozen-yogurt cups are sold to teenagers each day?

To answer this question, you will need to find 45% of 420.

To find the percent one number is of another, use this proportion:

$$\frac{\%}{100} = \frac{\text{is}}{\text{of}}$$

Because you are looking for **45% of 420**, 45 replaces the **percent sign** and 420 replaces **"of."** The first denominator, 100, always stays the same. The "is" part is what you have been asked to find.

EXAMPLE 1 *Consumer Math Application*

How many frozen-yogurt cups are sold to teenagers each day?

First estimate your answer. Think: $45\% = \frac{45}{100}$, which is close to $\frac{50}{100}$, or $\frac{1}{2}$. So about $\frac{1}{2}$ of the 420 yogurt cups are sold to teenagers.

$\frac{1}{2} \cdot 420 = 210$ ← *This is the estimate.*

Now solve:

Helpful Hint

Think: "45 out of 100 is how many out of 420?"

$\dfrac{45}{100} = \dfrac{y}{420}$	*Let y represent the number of yogurt cups sold to teenagers.*
$100 \cdot y = 45 \cdot 420$	*The cross products are equal.*
$100y = 18{,}900$	*y is multiplied by 100.*
$\dfrac{100y}{100} = \dfrac{18{,}900}{100}$	*Divide both sides of the equation by 100 to undo the multiplication.*
$y = 189$	

Since 189 is close to your estimate of 210, 189 is a reasonable answer. About 189 yogurt cups per day are sold to teenagers.

EXAMPLE 2 **Technology Application**

Heather is downloading a file from the Internet. So far, she has downloaded 75% of the file. If 30 minutes have passed since she started, how long will it take her to download the rest of the file?

$$\frac{\%}{100} = \frac{is}{of}$$

*75% of the file has downloaded, so 30 minutes **is** 75% **of** the total time needed.*

$$\frac{75}{100} = \frac{30}{m}$$

$100 \cdot 30 = 75 \cdot m$ *The cross products are equal.*

$3{,}000 = 75m$ *m is multiplied by 75.*

$$\frac{3{,}000}{75} = \frac{75m}{75}$$

Divide both sides by 75 to undo the multiplication.

$40 = m$

The time needed to download the entire file is 40 min. So far, the file has been downloading for 30 min. Because $40 - 30 = 10$, the remainder of the file will be downloaded in 10 min.

Instead of using proportions, you can also multiply to find a percent of a number.

EXAMPLE 3 **Multiplying to Find a Percent of a Number**

Find 20% of 150.

$20\% = 0.20$ *Write the percent as a decimal.*

$0.20 \cdot 150$ *Multiply using the decimal.*

$\quad 30$

So 30 is 20% of 150.

Check

Use a model to check the answer.

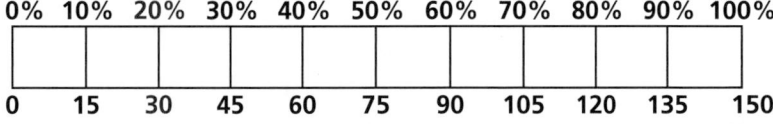

0%	10%	20%	30%	40%	50%	60%	70%	80%	90%	100%
0	15	30	45	60	75	90	105	120	135	150

Think and Discuss

1. Explain why you must subtract 30 from 40 in Example 2.

2. Give an example of a time when you would need to find a percent of a number.

go.hrw.com
Homework Help Online
KEYWORD: MR7 7-9
Parent Resources Online
KEYWORD: MR7 Parent

GUIDED PRACTICE

See Example ① **1.** Members of the drama club sold T-shirts for their upcoming musical. Of the 80 T-shirts sold, 55% were size medium. How many of the T-shirts sold were size medium?

See Example ② **2.** Loni has read 25% of a book. If she has been reading for 5 hours, how many more hours will it take her to complete the book?

See Example ③ **3.** Find 12% of 56. **4.** Find 65% of 240. **5.** Find 2% of 20.

6. Find 85% of 115. **7.** Find 70% of 54. **8.** Find 85% of 355.

INDEPENDENT PRACTICE

See Example ① **9.** Tamara collects porcelain dolls. Of the 24 dolls that she has, 25% have blond hair. How many of her dolls have blond hair?

10. Mr. Green has a garden. Of the 40 seeds he planted, 35% were vegetable seeds. How many vegetable seeds did he plant?

See Example ② **11.** Kevin has mowed 40% of the lawn. If he has been mowing for 20 minutes, how long will it take him to mow the rest of the lawn?

12. Maggie ordered a painting. She paid 30% of the total cost when she ordered it, and she will pay the remaining amount when it is delivered. If she has paid $15, how much more does she owe?

See Example ③ **13.** Find 22% of 130. **14.** Find 78% of 350. **15.** Find 28% of 65.

16. Find 9% of 50. **17.** Find 45% of 210. **18.** Find 54% of 602.

PRACTICE AND PROBLEM SOLVING

Extra Practice
See page 727.

Find the percent of each number.

19. 6% of 38	**20.** 20% of 182	**21.** 13% of 40
22. 32% of 205	**23.** 14% of 88	**24.** 98% of 105
25. 78% of 52	**26.** 31% of 345	**27.** 62% of 50
28. 10% of 50	**29.** 1.5% of 800	**30.** 0.3% of 9

31. Geometry The width of a rectangular room is 75% of the length of the room. The room is 12 feet long.

a. How wide is the room?

b. The area of a rectangle is the product of the length and the width. What is the area of the room?

32. Multi-Step Marissa is shopping and finds a sales rack with items that are 25% off. If Marissa likes a shirt on the rack that originally cost $15, how much will she pay for the shirt before tax?

Technology

Someday you may do all of your schoolwork on a computer, if your school becomes a digital school, like the one pictured above.

33. **Chemistry** Glucose is a type of sugar. A glucose molecule is composed of 24 atoms. Hydrogen atoms make up 50% of the molecule, carbon atoms make up 25% of the molecule, and oxygen atoms make up the other 25%. How many of each atom are in a molecule of glucose?

34. **Technology** Students were asked in a school survey about how they use their computers. The circle graph shows the results.

   a. If there are 850 students in the school, how many spend most of their computer time using e-mail?

   b. Fifty-one students selected "other." What percent of the school population does this represent?

   c. Which choices were selected by more than 200 students?

   d. How many more students chose Internet than chose playing games?

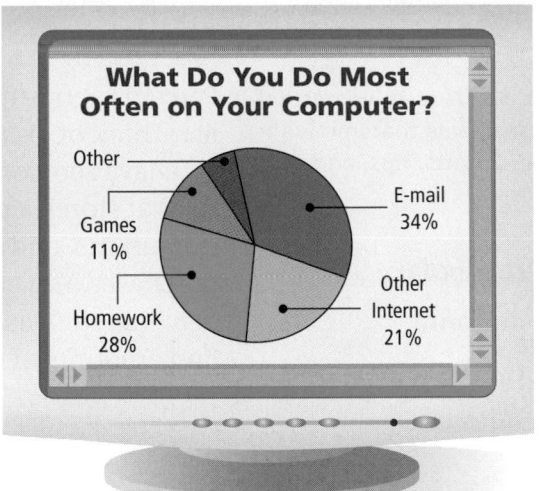

What Do You Do Most Often on Your Computer?

- Other
- Games 11%
- Homework 28%
- E-mail 34%
- Other Internet 21%

 35. **What's the Error?** To find 80% of 130, a student set up the proportion $\frac{80}{100} = \frac{130}{x}$. Explain the error. Write the correct proportion, and find the missing value.

 36. **Write About It** Suppose you were asked to find 48% of 300 and your answer was 6.25. Would your answer be reasonable? How do you know? What is the correct answer?

 37. **Challenge** Mrs. Peterson makes ceramic figurines. She recently made 25 figurines. Of those figurines, 16 are animals. What percent of the figurines are NOT animals?

TEST PREP and Spiral Review

38. **Multiple Choice** Which of the following amounts is greatest?

   Ⓐ 45% of 200   Ⓑ 50% of 150   Ⓒ 60% of 190   Ⓓ 100% of 110

39. **Short Response** If Sara orders 8 sports magazines and 12 health magazines on sale, how much will she save compared to the regular price? Explain.

Magazine Type	Original Price	Sale
Sports	8 for $60	Save 60%
Health	12 for $72	Save 30%

Write each decimal as a fraction or mixed number. (Lesson 4-4)

40. 0.25   41. 0.78   42. 1.4   43. 0.99   44. 5.36

45. About $\frac{7}{8}$ of the flowers in Monica's garden are snapdragons. What percent of the flowers in the garden are snapdragons? (Lesson 7-8)

7-10 Using Percents

Learn to solve percent problems that involve discounts, tips, and sales tax.

Vocabulary

discount

tip

sales tax

![NY] **NY Performance Indicators**

6.N.26 Estimate a percent of quantity (0% to 100%). Also, 6.N.12.

Percents show up often in daily life. Think of examples that you have seen of percents—sales at stores, tips in restaurants, and sales tax on purchases. You can estimate percents such as these to find amounts of money.

Common Uses of Percents	
Discounts	A **discount** is an amount that is subtracted from the regular price of an item. discount = price · discount rate total cost = price − discount
Tips	A **tip** is an amount added to a bill for service. tip = bill · tip rate total cost = bill + tip
Sales tax	**Sales tax** is an amount added to the price of an item. sales tax = price · sales tax rate total cost = price + sales tax

EXAMPLE 1 Finding Discounts

A music store sign reads "10% off the regular price." If Nichole wants to buy a CD whose regular price is $14.99, about how much will she pay for her CD after the discount?

Step 1: First round $14.99 to $15.

Step 2: Find 10% of $15 by multiplying 0.10 · $15. (*Hint:* Moving the decimal point one place left is a shortcut.)

$$10\% \text{ of } 15 = 0.10 \cdot \$15 = \$1.50$$

Remember!

To multiply by 0.10, move the decimal point one place left.

The approximate discount is $1.50. Subtract this amount from $15.00 to estimate the cost of the CD.

$$\$15.00 - \$1.50 = \$13.50$$

Nichole will pay about $13.50 for the CD.

When estimating percents, use percents that you can calculate mentally.

- You can find 10% of a number by moving the decimal point one place to the left.
- You can find 1% of a number by moving the decimal point two places to the left.
- You can find 5% of a number by finding one-half of 10% of the number.

EXAMPLE 2 **Finding Tips**

Leslie's lunch bill is $13.95. She wants to leave a tip that is 15% of the bill. About how much should her tip be?

Step 1: First round $13.95 to $14.

Step 2: Think: 15% = 10% + 5%

10% of $14 = 0.10 · $14 = $1.40

Step 3: 5% = 10% ÷ 2

= $1.40 ÷ 2 = $0.70

Step 4: 15% = 10% + 5%

= $1.40 + $0.70 = $2.10

Leslie should leave about $2.10 as a tip.

EXAMPLE 3 **Finding Sales Tax**

Marc is buying a scooter for $79.65. The sales tax rate is 6%. About how much will the total cost of the scooter be?

Step 1: First round $79.65 to $80.

Step 2: Think: 6% = 6 · 1%

1% of $80 = 0.01 · $80 = $0.80

Step 3: 6% = 6 · 1%

= 6 · $0.80 = $4.80

The approximate sales tax is $4.80. Add this amount to $80 to estimate the total cost of the scooter.

$80 + $4.80 = $84.80

Marc will pay about $84.80 for the scooter.

Think and Discuss

 6.CM.1, 6.CN.9

1. Tell when it would be useful to estimate the percent of a number.

2. Explain how to estimate to find the sales tax of an item.

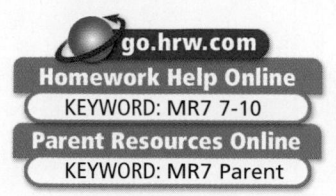

GUIDED PRACTICE

See Example ①   **1.** Norine wants to buy a beaded necklace that is on sale for 10% off the marked price. If the marked price is $8.49, about how much will the necklace cost after the discount?

See Example ②   **2.** Alice and Wagner ordered a pizza to be delivered. The total bill was $12.15. They want to give the delivery person a tip that is 20% of the bill. About how much should the tip be?

See Example ③   **3.** A bicycle sells for $139.75. The sales tax rate is 8%. About how much will the total cost of the bicycle be?

INDEPENDENT PRACTICE

See Example ①   **4.** Peter has a coupon for 15% off the price of any item in a sporting goods store. He wants to buy a pair of sneakers that are priced at $36.99. About how much will the sneakers cost after the discount?

5. All DVDs are discounted 25% off the original price. The DVD that Marissa wants to buy was originally priced at $24.98. About how much will the DVD cost after the discount?

See Example ②   **6.** Michael's breakfast bill came to $7.65. He wants to leave a tip that is 15% of the bill. About how much should he leave for the tip?

7. Betty and her family went out for dinner. Their bill was $73.82. Betty's parents left a tip that was 15% of the bill. About how much was the tip that they left?

See Example ③   **8.** A computer game costs $36.85. The sales tax rate is 6%. About how much will the total cost be for this computer game?

9. Irene is buying party supplies. The cost of her supplies is $52.75. The sales tax rate is 5%. About how much will the total cost of her party supplies be?

PRACTICE AND PROBLEM SOLVING

Extra Practice
See page 727.

10. **Multi-Step** Lenny, Robert, and Katrina went out for lunch. The items they ordered are listed on the receipt. The sales tax rate was 7%, and they left a tip that was 15% of the total bill. How much did the three friends spend in all?

**** Thank you ****	
Chicken Sandwich - 1	$5.95
Hamburger - 1	$4.75
Roast Beef Sandwich - 1	$7.35
Milk - 2	$2.40
Iced Tea - 1	$1.89

11. Jackie has $32.50 to buy a new pair of jeans. The pair she likes costs $38 but is marked "20% off ticketed price." The sales tax rate is 5%. Does Jackie have enough money to buy the jeans? Explain.

12. Evan buys a bike that is on sale for 20% off the original price of $95. His brother Kyle buys the same bike at a different store on sale for 15% off the original price of $90. Who paid more? Explain.

13. **Multi-Step** An electronics store is going out of business. The sign on the door reads "All items on sale for 60% off the ticketed price." A computer has a ticketed price of $649, and a printer has a ticketed price of $199. What is the total cost of both items after the discount?

14. **Social Studies** Use the table.

   a. A shirt costs $18.95. Will the shirt cost more after sales tax in Georgia or in Kentucky? About how much more?

   b. A video game in North Carolina costs $59.75. The same video game in New York costs $60. After sales tax, in which state will the video game cost less? How much less?

State	Sales Tax Rate
Georgia	4%
Kentucky	6%
New York	4%
North Carolina	4.5%

15. **What's the Error?** The original price of an item was $48.65. The item was discounted 40%. A customer calculated the price after the discount to be $19.46. What's the error? Give the correct price after the discount.

16. **Write About It** Discuss the difference between a discount, sales tax, and a tip, in relation to the total cost. How does each affect the total cost? Give examples of situations in which each one is used.

17. **Challenge** Suppose a jacket is discounted 50% off the original price and then discounted an additional 20%. Is this the same as discounting the jacket 70% off the original price? Explain.

TEST PREP and Spiral Review

18. **Multiple Choice** Electric City is offering a 20% discount on all radios. Pedro would like to buy a radio that was originally priced at $36.50. What is the total cost after the discount?

   Ⓐ $7.30   Ⓑ $16.50   Ⓒ $29.20   Ⓓ $36.70

19. **Extended Response** Ann is researching the price of a CD. At Music Place, the CD that Ann wants was originally priced at $15.96 but is discounted 25%. At Awesome Sound, the CD was originally priced at $12.99 but is discounted 10%. What is the sale price of each CD? Which is the better deal? Explain.

Determine whether the given value of the variable is a solution. (Lesson 2-4)

20. $2x + 3 = 10$ for $x = 4$ 21. $5(b - 3) = 25$ for $b = 8$ 22. $18 = 3a - 9$ for $a = 3$

Find 20% of each number. (Lesson 7-9)

23. 15   24. 50   25. 65   26. 200   27. 3,000

 **READY TO GO ON?**

Quiz for Lessons 7-7 Through 7-10

☑ **7-7** **Percents**

Write each percent as a fraction in simplest form.

1. 60%   **2.** 15%   **3.** 75%

Write each percent as a decimal.

4. 34%   **5.** 77%   **6.** 6%

7. About 71% of Earth's surface is covered with water. Write 71% as a decimal.

☑ **7-8** **Percents, Decimals, and Fractions**

Write each fraction as a percent.

8. $\frac{9}{20}$ **9.** $\frac{2}{3}$ **10.** $\frac{21}{50}$

Write each decimal as a percent.

11. 0.28   **12.** 0.9   **13.** 0.02

14. Mike's baseball team won $\frac{17}{20}$ of its games. What percent of the games did Mike's baseball team win?

☑ **7-9** **Percent Problems**

Use the circle graph for problems 15 and 16.

In a survey, 300 students were asked how they contact their friends.

15. How many students said they use text messaging?

16. How many students said they use a cell phone?

17. Find 40% of 80.

18. Find 5% of 30.

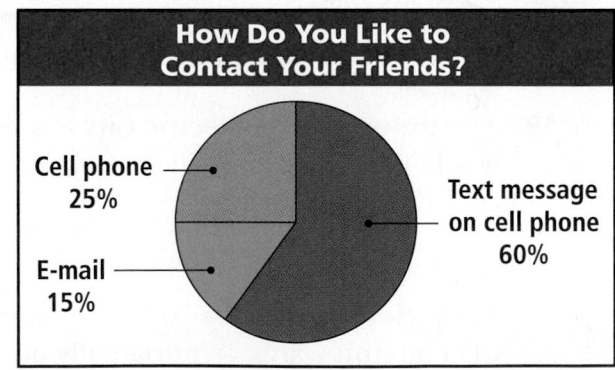

How Do You Like to Contact Your Friends?

Cell phone 25%

E-mail 15%

Text message on cell phone 60%

☑ **7-10** **Using Percents**

19. Max and Dan order a pizza. The total bill is $11.60. If they give the delivery person a tip that is 20% of the bill, how much is the tip?

20. Mia wants to buy a poster that is 10% off the marked price. If the marked price is $15.99, about how much will the poster cost with the discount?

Ready to Go On?

MULTI-STEP TEST PREP

Secret Recipe The ingredients for Sal's famous Old-timer's lemonade are given in the graph below.

Sal's Old-timer's Lemonade

Sweet and Sour Lemonade

Sal's Old-timer's lemonade is so popular that many others have tried to copy the recipe. The graphs at right show some competitors' attempts to copy Sal's recipe. All of the bar graphs are drawn to the same scale.

Yellow Birdie Lemonade

1. In Sal's recipe, what is the ratio of lemon juice to simple syrup? What is the ratio of simple syrup to water?

2. How much simple syrup should you use to make a batch of Sal's recipe that contains 16 ounces of lemon juice?

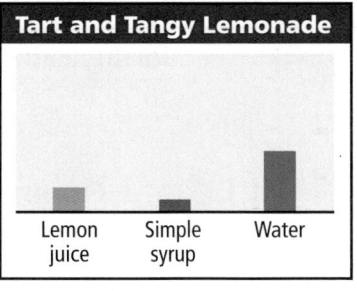

Tart and Tangy Lemonade

3. Which of the competitor's recipes taste identical to Sal's recipe? Explain.

4. Sal poured 1 cup of his Old-timer's lemonade for himself. How much of his glass, in ounces, is lemon juice? simple syrup? water? Explain. (*Hint:* 1 cup = 8 ounces)

5. What fraction of Sal's Old-timer's lemonade is lemon juice? Show how to write this as a percent.

EXTENSION

Simple Interest

Learn to find simple interest.

Vocabulary

interest

principal

simple interest

When you save money in a savings account, you earn money that the bank adds to your account. The added money is called **interest**. The original amount you put into the account is the **principal**. Interest is a percentage of the principal.

One type of interest is called *simple interest*. **Simple interest** is a fixed percentage of the original principal and is often paid over a certain time period. For example, simple interest may be paid once per year or several times per year. In this section, we will assume that simple interest is paid once per year.

NY Performance Indicators

6.N.12 Solve percent problems involving percent, rate, and base. Also, 5.A.4, 6.A.2, 6.A.6.

Simple Interest

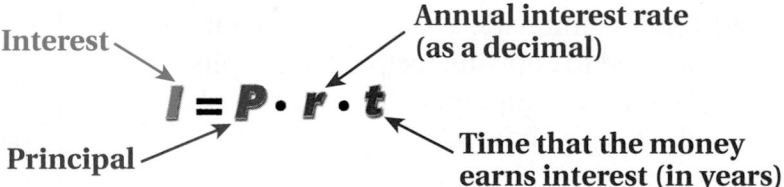

Interest → Annual interest rate (as a decimal)

$$I = P \cdot r \cdot t$$

Principal → Time that the money earns interest (in years)

Note that interest rates are usually given as percents, but you must convert the rates to decimals when you use the simple interest formula above.

EXAMPLE 1 **Finding Simple Interest**

Alyssa put $250 in a savings account at a simple interest rate of 6% per year.

A If she does not add money to or take money from her account, how much interest will she have earned at the end of 3 years?

$I = P \cdot r \cdot t$ *P = $250, r = 0.06, t = 3 years*

$I = 250 \cdot 0.06 \cdot 3$ *Multiply.*

$I = \$45$

Alyssa will earn $45 in interest in 3 years.

B How much money will be in her account after 3 years?

To find the total amount in Alyssa's account after three years, add the interest to the principal.

$$\$250 + \$45 = \$295$$

Alyssa will have $295 in her account after 3 years.

1. Tamara put $425 in a savings account at a simple interest rate of 7% per year. How much interest will she have earned after 5 years?

2. Jerome put $75 in a savings account at a simple interest rate of 3% per year. How much interest will Jerome have earned after 1 year? How much money will he have in his account after 1 year?

Use the equation $I = P \cdot r \cdot t$ to find the missing amount.

3. principal = $320
   interest rate = 5% per year
   time = 2 years
   interest = ▮

4. principal = $150
   interest rate = 2% per year
   time = 7 years
   interest = ▮

5. principal = ▮
   interest rate = 4% per year
   time = 3 years
   interest = $30

6. principal = $456
   interest rate = 6% per year
   time = ▮
   interest = $109.44

7. principal = $100
   interest rate = ▮ per year
   time = 5 years
   interest = $15

8. principal = $750
   interest rate = ▮ per year
   time = 10 years
   interest = $300

9. Mr. Bruckner is saving to go on a vacation. He put $340 in a savings account at a simple interest rate of 4% per year. How much money will he have in the savings account after 2 years?

10. When you borrow money, the amount borrowed is the principal. Instead of receiving interest, you pay interest on the principal. Kendra borrowed $1,500 from the bank to buy a home computer. The bank is charging her a simple interest rate of 7% per year. How much interest will Kendra owe the bank after 1 year?

11. Mr. Pei paid $7,500 in interest over 20 years at 1% per year on a loan. How much money did he borrow?

12. Hunter put $165 in a savings account at a simple interest rate of 6% per year. Nicholas put $145 in a savings account at a simple interest rate of 7% per year. Who will have earned more interest after 3 years? How much more?

 13. **Write About It** Explain the difference between principal and interest.

 14. **Write About It** Would you prefer a high or low interest rate when you are borrowing money? When you are saving money? Explain.

 15. **Challenge** Madison put $200 in a savings account at an interest rate of 5%. Each year the interest is added to the principal, and then the new amount of interest is calculated. If Madison does not add money to or take money out of the account, how much will she have after 3 years?

Game Time

The Golden Rectangle

Which rectangle do you find most visually pleasing?

Did you choose rectangle 3? If so, you agree with artists and architects throughout history. Rectangle 3 is a golden rectangle. Golden rectangles are said to be the most pleasing to the human eye.

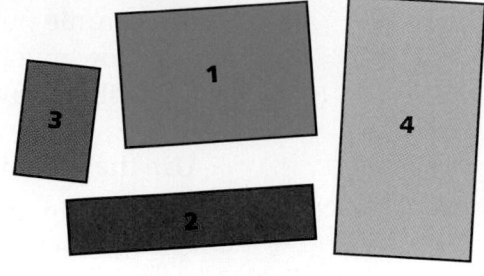

In a golden rectangle, the ratio of the length of the longer side to the length of the shorter side is approximately equal to 1.6. In other words,

$$\frac{\text{length of longer side}}{\text{length of shorter side}} \approx \frac{1.6}{1}$$

Measure the length and width of each rectangle below. Which could be golden rectangles? Are they the most pleasing to your eye?

Triple Play

Number of players: 3–5

Deal five cards to each player. Place the remaining cards in a pile facedown. At any time, you may remove *triples* from your hand. A *triple* is a fraction card, a decimal card, and a percent card that are all equivalent.

On your turn, ask any other player for a specific card. For example, if you have the $\frac{3}{5}$ card, you might ask another player if he or she has the 60% card. If so, he or she must give it to you, and you repeat your turn. If not, take the top card from the deck, and your turn is over.

The first player to get rid of his or her cards is the winner.

go.hrw.com
Game Time Extra
KEYWORD: MR7 Games

A complete copy of the rules and game pieces are available online.

Materials
- construction paper
- $\frac{1}{4}$ in. graph paper
- glue
- scissors
- markers

PROJECT **Double-Door Fractions, Decimals, and Percents**

Open the door to fractions, decimals, and percents by making this handy converter.

Directions

① Cut the construction paper to $6\frac{1}{2}$ inches by $8\frac{1}{2}$ inches. Fold it in half lengthwise and then unfold it. Fold the top and bottom edges to the middle crease to make a double door. **Figure A**

② Cut a strip of graph paper that is 2 inches wide by $8\frac{1}{2}$ inches long. Make a percent number line along the middle of the strip. Include 0%, 5%, 10%, and so on, up to 100%. **Figure B**

③ Cut two 1-by-$8\frac{1}{2}$-inch strips of graph paper. On one strip, make a fraction number line that includes $\frac{0}{20}$, $\frac{1}{20}$, and so on, up to $\frac{20}{20}$. Write the fractions in simplest form. On the other strip, make a decimal number line that includes 0.0, 0.05, 0.1, and so on, up to 1. **Figure C**

④ Glue the percent number line along the center fold of the construction paper. **Figure D**

⑤ Close the double doors. Glue the remaining number lines to the outside of the doors, making sure the number lines match up.

Putting the Math into Action

Team up with a classmate. Use your double-door converters to quiz each other on equivalent fractions, decimals, and percents.

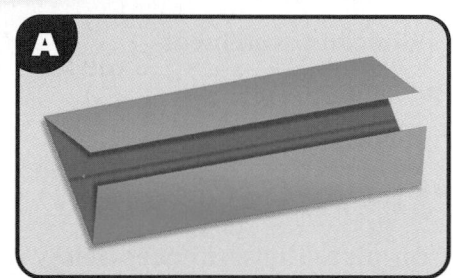

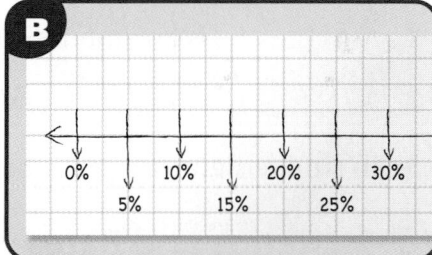

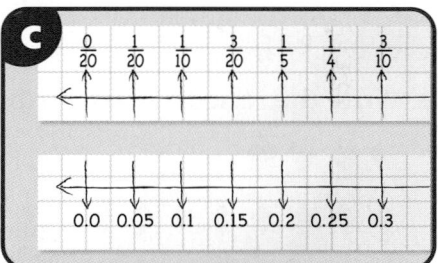

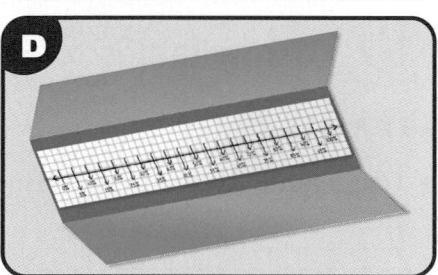

Vocabulary

Complete the sentences below with vocabulary words from the list above.

1. A(n) ___?___ is an amount subtracted from the regular price of an item.

2. A ___?___ is a ratio of a number to 100.

3. In similar figures, ___?___ have the same measure.

7-1 Ratios and Rates (pp. 352–355)

EXAMPLE

■ **Write the ratio of hearts to diamonds.**

$$\frac{\text{hearts}}{\text{diamonds}} = \frac{4}{8}$$

EXERCISES

4. Write three equivalent ratios for 4:8.

5. Which is the better deal—an 8 oz package of pretzels for $1.92 or a 12 oz package of pretzels for $2.64?

7-2 Using Tables to Explore Equivalent Ratios and Rates (pp. 356–359)

EXAMPLE

■ **Use a table to find three ratios equivalent to 6:7.**

6	12	18	24
7	14	21	28

Multiply the numerator and denominator by 2, 3, and 4.

The ratios 6:7, 12:14, 18:21, and 24:28 are equivalent.

EXERCISES

Use a table to find three equivalent ratios.

6. $\frac{3}{10}$ **7.** 5 to 21   **8.** 15:7

9. The table below shows the cost of canoeing for different-sized groups. Predict how much a group of 9 will pay.

Number in Group	2	4	8	10
Cost ($)	10.50	21	42	52.50

7-3 Proportions (pp. 362–365)

 6.N.7, 6.N.10, 6.A.5

EXAMPLE

■ Find the value of n in $\frac{5}{6} = \frac{n}{12}$.

$6 \cdot n = 5 \cdot 12$ *Cross products are equal.*

$\frac{6n}{6} = \frac{60}{6}$ *Divide both sides by 6.*

$n = 10$

EXERCISES

Find the value of n in each proportion.

10. $\frac{3}{5} = \frac{n}{15}$ **11.** $\frac{1}{n} = \frac{3}{9}$

12. $\frac{7}{8} = \frac{n}{16}$ **13.** $\frac{n}{4} = \frac{8}{16}$

7-4 Similar Figures (pp. 366–369)

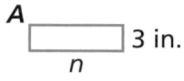 6.N.27, 6.A.5, 6.G.1

EXAMPLE

■ The triangles are similar. Find b.

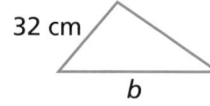

$\frac{1}{32} = \frac{2}{b}$ *Write a proportion.*

$32 \cdot 2 = 1 \cdot b$ *Cross products are equal.*

$64 \text{ cm} = b$

EXERCISES

14. The shapes are similar. Find n and $m\angle A$.

7-5 Indirect Measurement (pp. 370–372)

 6.A.5. 6.G.1

EXAMPLE

■ A tree casts a 12 ft shadow when a 6 ft man casts a 4 ft shadow. How tall is the tree?

$\frac{h}{6} = \frac{12}{4}$ *Write a proportion.*

$6 \cdot 12 = 4 \cdot h$ *The cross products are equal.*

$\frac{72}{4} = \frac{4h}{4}$ *Divide both sides by 4.*

$18 = h$ The tree is 18 ft tall.

EXERCISES

15. Find the height of the building.

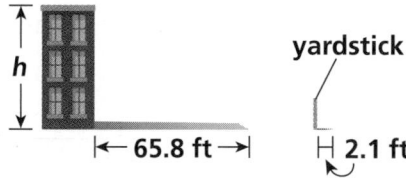

7-6 Scale Drawings and Maps (pp. 374–377)

 6.A.5

EXAMPLE

■ Find the actual distance from A to B.

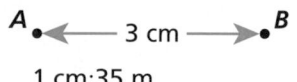

$\frac{1 \text{ cm}}{35 \text{ m}} = \frac{3 \text{ cm}}{x \text{ m}}$ *Write a proportion.*

$35 \cdot 3 = 1 \cdot x$ *Cross products are equal.*

$105 = x$

The actual distance is 105 m.

EXERCISES

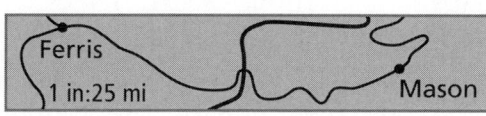

16. Find the actual distance from Ferris to Mason.

17. Renfield is 75 mi from Mason. About how far apart should Renfield and Mason be on the map?

7-7 Percents (pp. 381–384)

6.N.11, 6.N.12, 6.N.21

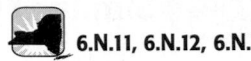

EXAMPLE

■ Write 48% as a fraction in simplest form.

$$48\% = \frac{48}{100} \qquad \frac{48 \div 4}{100 \div 4} = \frac{12}{25}$$

■ Write 16% as a decimal.

$$16\% = \frac{16}{100} \qquad 16 \div 100 = 0.16$$

EXERCISES

Write each as a fraction in simplest form.

18. 75%   **19.** 6%   **20.** 30%

Write each percent as a decimal.

21. 8%   **22.** 65%   **23.** 20%

7-8 Percents, Decimals, and Fractions (pp. 385–388)

6.N.11, 6.N.12, 6.N.21

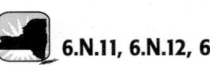

EXAMPLE

■ Write 0.365 as a percent.

$$0.365 = 36.5\% \qquad \textit{Multiply by 100.}$$

■ Write $\frac{3}{5}$ as a percent.

$$\frac{3 \cdot 20}{5 \cdot 20} = \frac{60}{100} = 60\%$$

EXERCISES

Write each decimal or fraction as a percent.

24. 0.896   **25.** 0.70   **26.** 0.057

27. 0.12   **28.** $\frac{7}{10}$ **29.** $\frac{3}{12}$

30. $\frac{7}{8}$ **31.** $\frac{4}{5}$ **32.** $\frac{1}{16}$

7-9 Percent Problems (pp. 390–393)

6.N.11, 6.N.12, 6.N.27

EXAMPLE

■ Find 30% of 85.

$$30\% = 0.30 \qquad \textit{Write 30\% as a decimal.}$$
$$0.30 \cdot 85 = 25.5 \qquad \textit{Multiply.}$$

EXERCISES

33. Find 25% of 48.

34. Find 33% of 18.

35. A total of 325 tickets were sold for the school concert, and 36% of these were sold to students. How many tickets were sold to students?

7-10 Using Percents (pp. 394–397)

6.N.12, 6.N.26

EXAMPLE

■ A DVD costs $24.98. The sales tax is 5%. About how much is the tax?

Step 1: Round $24.98 to $25.

Step 2: 5% = 5 · 1%
    1% of $25 = 0.01 · $25 = $0.25

Step 3: 5% = 5 · 1%
    = 5 · $0.25 = $1.25

The tax is about $1.25.

EXERCISES

36. A sweater is marked 40% off the original price. The original price was $31.75. About how much is the sweater after the discount?

37. Barry and his friends went out for lunch. The bill was $28.68. About how much should they leave for a 15% tip?

38. Ana is purchasing a book for $17.89. The sales tax rate is 6%. About how much will she pay in sales tax?

CHAPTER TEST

Use the table to write each ratio.

1. three equivalent ratios to compare dramas to documentaries

2. documentaries to total videos

3. music videos to exercise videos

4. Which is a better deal—5 videos for $29.50 or 3 videos for $17.25?

Types of Videos in Richard's Collection			
Comedy	5	Cartoon	7
Drama	6	Exercise	3
Music	3	Documentary	2

Find the value of *n* in each proportion.

5. $\dfrac{5}{6} = \dfrac{n}{24}$

6. $\dfrac{8}{n} = \dfrac{12}{3}$

7. $\dfrac{n}{10} = \dfrac{3}{6}$

8. $\dfrac{3}{9} = \dfrac{4}{n}$

9. A cocoa recipe calls for 4 tbsp cocoa mix to make an 8 oz serving. How many tbsp of cocoa mix are needed to make a 15 oz serving?

10. A 3-foot-tall mailbox casts a shadow that is 1.8 feet long. At the same time, a nearby street lamp casts a shadow that is 12 feet long. How tall is the street lamp?

11. The table shows the time it takes Jenny to swim laps. Predict how long it will take her to swim 14 laps.

Number of Laps	4	8	12	16
Time (min)	3	6	9	12

Use the scale drawing for Problems 12 and 13.

12. The length of the court in the drawing is 6 cm. How long is the actual court?

13. The free-throw line is always 15 feet from the backboard. Is the distance between the backboard and the free-throw line correct in the drawing? Explain.

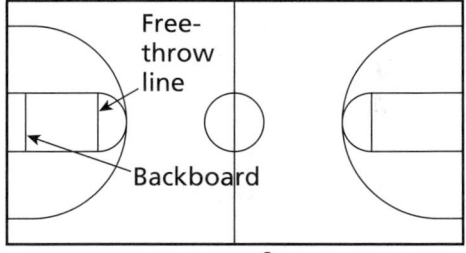

Scale: 1 cm : $15\frac{2}{3}$ ft

Write each percent as a fraction in simplest form and as a decimal.

14. 66%

15. 90%

16. 5%

17. 18%

Write each decimal or fraction as a percent.

18. 0.546

19. 0.092

20. $\dfrac{14}{25}$

21. $\dfrac{1}{8}$

Find each percent.

22. 55% of 218

23. 30% of 310

24. 25% of 78

25. A bookstore sells paperback books at 20% off the listed price. If Brandy wants to buy a paperback book whose listed price is $12.95, about how much will she pay for the book after the discount?

Chapter Test

Extended Response: Write Extended Responses

When you answer an extended-response test item, you need to explain your reasoning clearly. Extended-response items are scored using a 3-point scoring rubric like the one shown below.

Test Tackler

EXAMPLE

Extended Response Amber tracks her math test scores. Her goal is to have a 92% average. Her 10 test scores are 94, 76, 90, 98, 91, 93, 88, 90, 89, and 85. Find the range, mean, median, and mode of the data set. If her lowest score is dropped, will she meet her goal? Explain your answer.

Here is an example of a 3-point response according to the scoring rubric at right.

Scoring Rubric

3 Points: The student's response is correct and complete. The response contains complete explanations and/or adequate work when required.

2 Points: The student's response demonstrates only partial understanding. The response addresses most aspects of the task, and/or may include complete procedures and reasoning but an incorrect answer.

1 Point: The student's response addresses some elements of the task correctly but contains multiple flaws. The response may include a correct answer without the required work.

0 Points: The student's response demonstrates no understanding of the mathematical concepts. The response may include a correct response using an obviously incorrect procedure.

3-point response:

Range: $98 - 76 = 22$
The range is 22.
Mean:
$$\frac{94 + 76 + 90 + 98 + 91 + 93 + 88 + 90 + 89 + 85}{10} = \frac{894}{10} = 89.4$$

The mean is 89.4.

Median: There are an even number of values in this set. The two middle numbers are 90 and 90. The median is 90.

Mode: The value that occurs most often is 90. The mode is 90.

When the lowest score, 76, is dropped, the average is
$\frac{894 - 76}{9} = \frac{818}{9} = 90.9$. This value is less than 92. Even if the lowest score is dropped, Amber will not meet her goal.

The student correctly calculates and shows how to find the range, mean, median, and mode of this data set.

The student correctly answers the questions and shows how the answer is calculated.

Hot Tip Once you have answered an extended-response test item, double-check to make sure that you answered all of the different parts.

Read each test item and use the scoring rubric to answer the questions that follow.

Item A
Extended Response Use the table below to identify a pattern and find the next three terms. Is this sequence arithmetic? Explain.

Position	Value of Term
1	4
2	7
3	10
4	13
5	16
n	▩

1. What needs to be included in a response that would receive 3 points?

2. Write a response that would receive full credit.

Item B
Extended Response Draw a polygon that has three congruent sides. What is true about the measures of the angles of this polygon? Find the measurement of each angle. Classify the type of polygon you drew. Explain your answer.

Kim wrote this response:

Each angle measures 60°.
This is an equilateral triangle.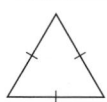

3. Score Kim's response. Explain your scoring decision.

4. Rewrite Kim's response so that it receives full credit.

Item C
Extended Response Look at the graph. Why is this graph misleading? Explain your answer. What might someone believe from this graph? What changes would you make to the graph so it is not misleading?

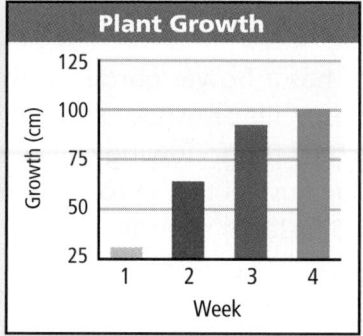

5. What needs to be included in a response that would receive 3 points?

6. Write a response that would receive full credit.

Item D
Extended Response The ages of the employees at a discount store are shown below. Find the mean, median, and mode of the data set. Which one bests describes the data set? Explain your answer.

68	32	16	23	21
17	28	20	39	38
21	22	17	23	37

7. Should the response shown receive a score of 3 points? Why or why not?

The mean is 28.
The modes are 17 and 23.
The median is 22.
The best descriptor is the mode because there is more than one.

8. Correct or add any information, if necessary, for the response to receive full credit.

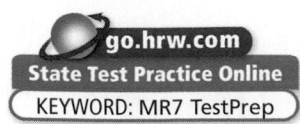
Cumulative Assessment, Chapters 1–7
Multiple Choice

New York Test Prep

1. Janet has a flower garden with 6 rose bushes, 7 lilac bushes, and 5 azaleas. Which of the following shows the ratio of lilac bushes to the total number of plants in Janet's garden?

   Ⓐ 7:11   Ⓒ 11:18

   Ⓑ 7:18   Ⓓ 18:5

2. Jenny lives in Paris, Kentucky. She wants to visit Paris, France, this summer. The distance between the two cities is 6.715×10^3 kilometers. What is this distance in standard form?

   Ⓕ 67.15 kilometers

   Ⓖ 671.5 kilometers

   Ⓗ 6,715 kilometers

   Ⓙ 67,150 kilometers

3. Carina rode her exercise bike 30 minutes on Monday, 45 minutes on Tuesday, 30 minutes on Wednesday, 60 minutes on Thursday, and 50 minutes on Friday. Find the mean amount of time that Carina rode her bike in these 5 days.

   Ⓐ 30 minutes   Ⓒ 45 minutes

   Ⓑ 43 minutes   Ⓓ 215 minutes

4. The sixth grade chorus is going to a competition. There are 116 students in the sixth grade chorus. If each bus holds 35 students, how many buses will be needed to take the students to the competition?

   Ⓕ 5 buses   Ⓗ 3 buses

   Ⓖ 4 buses   Ⓙ 2 buses

5. Which of the following is NOT an example of a proportion?

   Ⓐ $\frac{3}{4} = \frac{9}{12}$ Ⓒ $\frac{1}{3} = \frac{15}{42}$

   Ⓑ $\frac{5}{9} = \frac{45}{81}$ Ⓓ $\frac{7}{8} = \frac{35}{40}$

6. On the map the distance between point R and point T is 1.125 inches. Find the actual distance between point R and point T.

   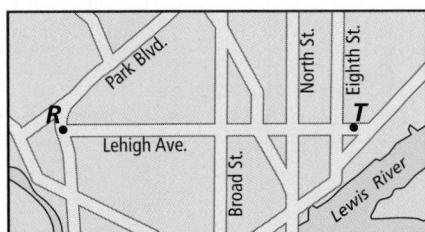

   Scale: 1 in:10 mi

   Ⓕ 10 miles   Ⓗ 12.5 miles

   Ⓖ 11.25 miles   Ⓙ 15 miles

7. Esperanza has a puppy that weighs $3\frac{1}{4}$ pounds. In 3 months, the puppy should weigh 3 times as much as it weighs now. How much weight should the puppy gain in the next 3 months?

   Ⓐ $6\frac{1}{2}$ pounds

   Ⓑ $6\frac{3}{4}$ pounds

   Ⓒ $8\frac{1}{4}$ pounds

   Ⓓ $9\frac{3}{4}$ pounds

8. Which value is greatest?

   Ⓕ $\frac{5}{6}$ Ⓗ 80%

   Ⓖ 0.7   Ⓙ $\frac{6}{7}$

9. Max earns $7.25 per hour working for a florist. His weekly paycheck is $108.75 before taxes. If *h* equals the number of hours worked, which expression can be used to find the number of hours Max works each week?

Ⓐ $7.25 + h = 108.75$

Ⓑ $\frac{7.25}{h} = 108.75$

Ⓒ $108.75 - h = 7.25$

Ⓓ $7.25h = 108.75$

Hot Tip

Estimate your answer before solving the problem. You can often use your estimate to eliminate some of the answer choices.

10. A school is making music kits with 72 recorders, 96 kazoos, and 60 whistles. Each kit has the same number of each instrument. What is the greatest number of kits that can be made?

Ⓕ 6   Ⓗ 15

Ⓖ 12   Ⓙ 30

11. Find the value of $40 \div (3 + 5) \times 2$.

Ⓐ 2.5   Ⓒ 10

Ⓑ 5   Ⓓ 40

12. Write $2\frac{3}{4} + \frac{1}{3}$ as an improper fraction.

Ⓕ $\frac{12}{7}$ Ⓗ $3\frac{1}{12}$

Ⓖ $\frac{16}{7}$ Ⓙ $\frac{37}{12}$

13. Ms. Chavez is ordering art supplies. She orders enough pencils for every student and then adds 20% more for extras. If she has 210 students, how many pencils does she need to order?

Ⓐ 42   Ⓒ 420

Ⓑ 252   Ⓓ 630

Short Response

14. One of the oldest living oak trees is 105 feet tall. One sunny day it casts a shadow that is 75 feet long. At the same time, a younger oak tree casts a shadow that is 15 feet long.

   a. Draw a picture to explain how to find the height of the younger tree.

   b. Use your picture to write a proportion to find the height of the younger tree. Solve the proportion. Show your work.

15. Chrissy is shopping for T-shirts for the pep club. Package A is 10 shirts for $15.50. Package B is 15 shirts for $20.50. Package C is 20 shirts for $25.50. Find the unit price for each package. Which T-shirt package is the best deal? Explain your reasoning and show your work.

16. A computer is marked 30% off the original price. The computer originally cost $685. Find the amount of the discount and the sale price of the computer.

Extended Response

17. A small purple rectangle is 8 millimeters wide and 18 millimeters tall. A larger purple rectangle is 18 millimeters wide and 25 millimeters tall.

   a. Are the two purple rectangles similar? Explain your answer.

   b. A third rectangle is similar to the smaller purple rectangle. The width of the third rectangle is 14 millimeters. Let *x* represent the height of the third rectangle. Write an equation that could be used to find *x*.

   c. Find the height of the third rectangle. Show your work.

Geometric Relationships

NEW YORK TEST PREP

go.hrw.com
Chapter Project Online
KEYWORD: MR7 Ch8

Name of Figure	Number of Sides
Pentagon	5
Hexagon	6
Heptagon	7
Octagon	8
Nonagon	9
Decagon	10
Undecagon	11
Dodecagon	12

Career   *Artist*

Artists help us to see our world in new ways. They use their creativity in many different kinds of careers. Artists might design graphics for Web sites, draw cartoons, design textiles and furniture, paint murals, or even illustrate courtroom scenes. Artists work with many materials, such as different kinds of paints, paper, stone, metal, stained glass, and tile. The table shows some geometric figures that an artist might use in a design.

ARE YOU READY?

✓ Vocabulary

Choose the best term from the list to complete each sentence.

clockwise

counterclockwise

horizontal

protractor

quadrilateral

ruler

triangle

vertical

1. A closed figure with three sides is a ___?___, and a closed figure with four sides is a ___?___.

2. A ___?___ is used to measure and draw angles.

3.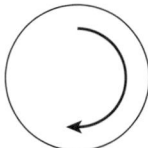

4.

The arrow inside the circle is moving ___?___.

A line that extends left to right is ___?___.

Complete these exercises to review skills you will need for this chapter.

✓ Graph Ordered Pairs

Use the coordinate plane for problems 5–8. Write the ordered pair for each point.

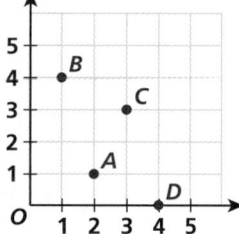

5. A

6. B

7. C

8. D

✓ Identify Polygons

Tell how many sides and angles each figure has.

9.

10.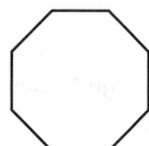

11.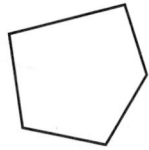

✓ Identify Congruent Figures

Which two figures are exactly the same size and shape but in different positions?

12.

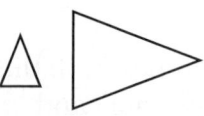

A

B

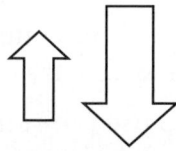

C

D

Where You've Been

Previously, you

- defined geometric shapes.
- identified congruent and similar figures.
- located points on a coordinate plane.

In This Chapter

You will study

- measuring angles.
- using angle measurements to classify angles as acute, obtuse, or right.
- identifying relationships involving angles in triangles and quadrilaterals.
- using congruence and similarity to solve problems.
- transforming figures on the coordinate plane and describing the transformation.

Where You're Going

You can use the skills learned in this chapter

- to solve problems and create geometric proofs by using angle and line relationships in geometry.
- to use transformations to create patterns in art class.

Key Vocabulary/Vocabulario

angle	ángulo
congruent	congruentes
line symmetry	simetría axial
parallel lines	líneas paralelas
perpendicular lines	rectas perpendiculares
polygon	polígono
quadrilateral	cuadrilátero
rotation	rotación
transformation	transformación
vertex	vértice

Vocabulary Connections

To become familiar with some of the vocabulary terms in the chapter, consider the following. You may refer to the chapter, the glossary, or a dictionary if you like.

1. *Congruent* comes from the Latin word *congruere* meaning "to agree, correspond." If two figures are **congruent**, do you think they look the same or different?

2. *Parallel* comes from the Greek words *para* meaning "alongside" and *allenon* meaning "one another." If two lines are **parallel** where do you think they are located in relation to each other?

3. *Polygon* comes from the Greek words *polus* meaning "many" and *gonia* meaning "angle." According to this information, what do you think a shape called a **polygon** includes?

4. *Quadrilateral* comes from the Latin words *quadri* meaning "four" and *latus* meaning "sides." How many sides do you think a **quadrilateral** has?

Reading Strategy: Read Problems for Understanding

It is important to read word problems carefully to make sure you understand the problem and identify all the parts of the problem that need to be answered.

Following these steps can help you understand and answer problems:

1. Read through the problem once.

2. Identify what you are supposed to answer and what skills are needed.

3. Read the problem again carefully and identify key information.

4. Make a plan to solve and answer ALL parts of the problem.

5. Solve.

Lesson 7-9 Percent Problems

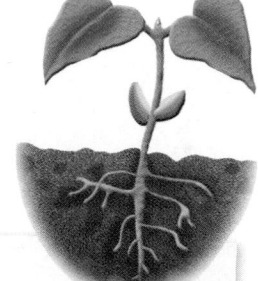

Step 1. Read the problem.

10. Mr. Green has a garden. Of the 40 seeds he planted, 35% were vegetable seeds. How many vegetable seeds did he plant?

Step 2.	What are you supposed to answer, and what skills are needed?	• Find how many vegetable seeds were planted in the garden. • Find the percent of a number.
Step 3.	Identify the key information.	• There were a total of 40 seeds planted. • The vegetable seeds make up 35% of the total number of seeds.
Step 4.	Make a plan to solve and answer all parts of the problem.	• Write 35% as a fraction. • Set up a proportion and solve for the unknown value. • Check your answer by making sure the cross products are equal.
Step 5.	Solve.	

Try This

Read the problem for understanding. Use the steps above to answer the following question.

1. A garden has the shape of a square. The distance around the garden is 200 meters. What is the length of one side of the garden?

Building Blocks of Geometry

Learn to describe figures by using the terms of geometry.

Vocabulary

point

line

plane

line segment

ray

NY Performance Indicators

6.CM.10 Use appropriate vocabulary when describing objects, relationships, mathematical solutions, and rationale.

The building blocks of geometry are *points*, *lines*, and *planes*.

| A **point** is an exact location. | • *P* | point *P*, *P* |

A point is named by a capital letter.

| A **line** is a straight path that extends without end in opposite directions. | 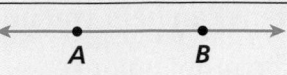 | line *AB*, $\overleftrightarrow{AB}$, line *BA*, $\overleftrightarrow{BA}$ |

A line is named by two points on the line.

| A **plane** is a flat surface that extends without end in all directions. | 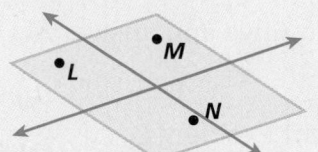 | plane *LMN*, plane *MLN*, plane *NLM* |

A plane is named by three points on the plane that are not on the same line.

E X A M P L E **1** **Identifying Points, Lines, and Planes**

Use the diagram to name each geometric figure.

A three points

A, *C*, and *D*

Five points are labeled: points A, B, C, D, and E.

B two lines

$\overleftrightarrow{AB}$ and $\overleftrightarrow{BE}$

You can also write $\overleftrightarrow{BA}$ and $\overleftrightarrow{EB}$.

C a point shared by two lines

point *B*

Point B is a point on $\overleftrightarrow{AB}$ and $\overleftrightarrow{BE}$.

D a plane

plane *ADC*

Use any three points in the plane that are not on the same line. Write the three points in any order.

Line segments and *rays* are parts of lines. Use points on a line to name line segments and rays.

A **line segment** is made of two endpoints and all the points between the endpoints.		line segment *XY*, $\overline{XY}$, line segment *YX*, $\overline{YX}$
	A line segment is named by its endpoints.	
A **ray** has one endpoint. From the endpoint, the ray extends without end in one direction only.	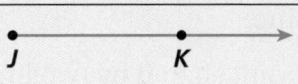	ray *JK*, $\overrightarrow{JK}$
	A ray is named by its endpoint first followed by another point on the ray.	

EXAMPLE 2 **Identifying Line Segments and Rays**

Use the diagram to give a possible name to each figure.

A three different line segments
$\overline{TU}$, $\overline{UV}$, and $\overline{TV}$
You can also write $\overline{UT}$, $\overline{VU}$, and $\overline{VT}$.

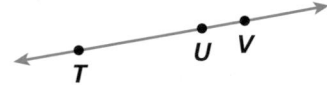

B three ways to name the line
$\overleftrightarrow{UT}$, $\overleftrightarrow{VU}$, and $\overleftrightarrow{VT}$
You can also write $\overleftrightarrow{TU}$, $\overleftrightarrow{UV}$, and $\overleftrightarrow{TV}$.

C six rays
$\overrightarrow{TU}$, $\overrightarrow{TV}$, $\overrightarrow{VT}$, $\overrightarrow{VU}$, $\overrightarrow{UV}$, and $\overrightarrow{UT}$

D another name for ray *TU*
$\overrightarrow{TV}$

T is still the endpoint. V is another point on the ray.

Think and Discuss

6.CN.1, 6.CM.10

1. Name the geometric figure suggested by each of the following: a page of a book; a dot (also called a *pixel*) on a computer screen; the path of a jet across the sky.

2. Explain how $\overrightarrow{XY}$ is different from $\overleftrightarrow{XY}$.

3. Explain how $\overline{AB}$ is different from $\overrightarrow{AB}$.

go.hrw.com
Homework Help Online
KEYWORD: MR7 8-1
Parent Resources Online
KEYWORD: MR7 Parent

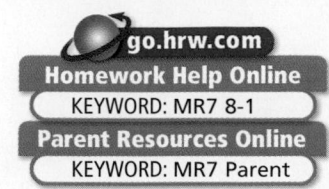

GUIDED PRACTICE

See Example 1 **Use the diagram to name each geometric figure.**

1. two points

2. a line

3. a point shared by two lines

4. a plane

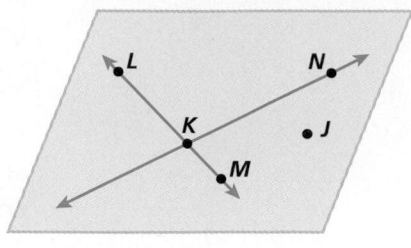

See Example 2 **Use the diagram to give a possible name to each figure.**

5. two different ways to name the line

6. four rays

7. another name for $\overrightarrow{AC}$

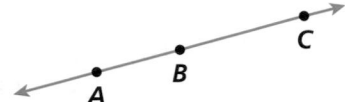

INDEPENDENT PRACTICE

See Example 1 **Use the diagram to name each geometric figure.**

8. three points

9. one line

10. a point shared by a line and a ray

11. a plane

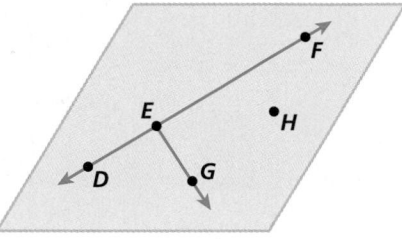

See Example 2 **Use the diagram to give a possible name to each figure.**

12. two different line segments

13. six rays

14. another name for $\overrightarrow{YX}$

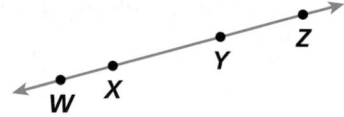

PRACTICE AND PROBLEM SOLVING

Extra Practice
See page 728.

Use the diagram to find a name for each geometric figure described.

15. a point shared by three lines

16. two points on the same line

17. two rays

18. another name for $\overrightarrow{AD}$

19. two different names for the same line

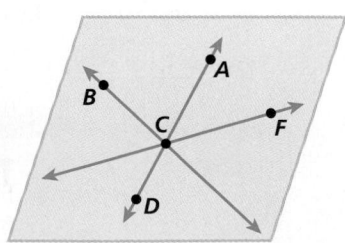

Draw each geometric figure.

20. $\overrightarrow{RS}$

21. $\overline{LM}$

22. $\overleftrightarrow{AB}$

23. $\overline{XY}$ on $\overleftrightarrow{YX}$

24. $\overrightarrow{JK}$ and $\overrightarrow{JH}$ on the same line

Mapmakers often include a *legend* on the maps they create. The legend explains what each symbol or location on the map represents.

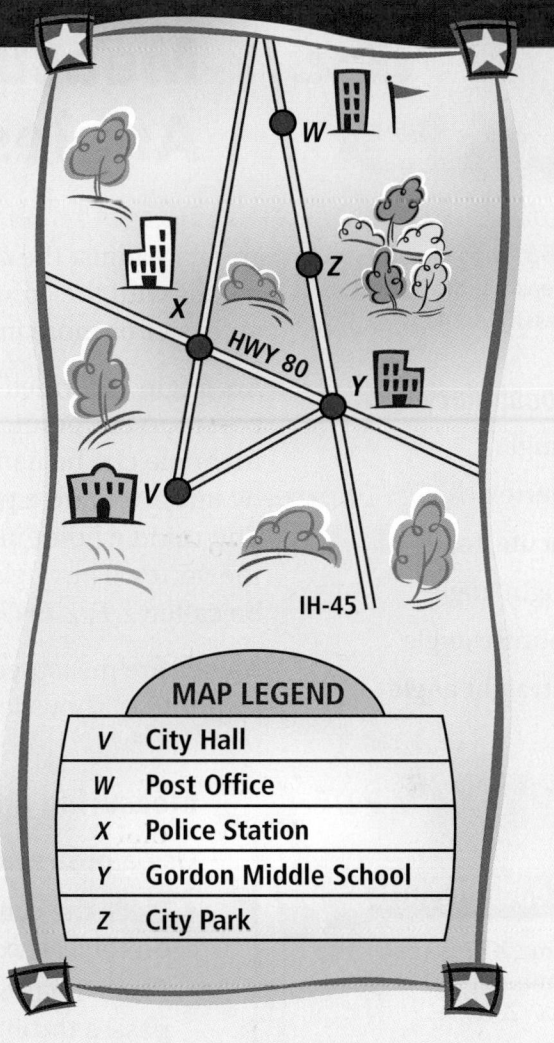

HWY 80

IH-45

MAP LEGEND

V	City Hall
W	Post Office
X	Police Station
Y	Gordon Middle School
Z	City Park

25. Name the geometric figure suggested by each part of the map.

   a. City Hall and Gordon Middle School

   b. Highway 80

   c. the section of the road from the park to the post office

   d. the road from City Hall past the police station

26. A student rides her bike from Gordon Middle School to City Hall. She then rides to the city park, first passing through the intersection near the police station and then passing by the school. List the segments on the map that represent her route.

27. **Critical Thinking** Name a line segment, a ray, and a line that include the same two locations on the map, but do not include the city park.

28. 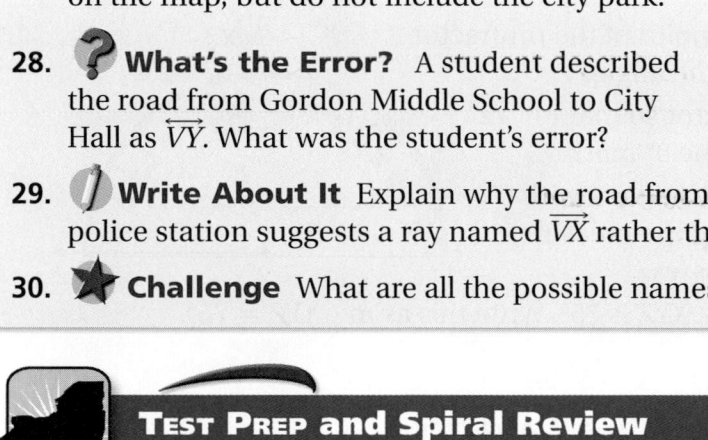 **What's the Error?** A student described the road from Gordon Middle School to City Hall as $\overrightarrow{VY}$. What was the student's error?

29. **Write About It** Explain why the road from City Hall that goes past the police station suggests a ray named $\overrightarrow{VX}$ rather than a ray named $\overrightarrow{XV}$.

30. **Challenge** What are all the possible names for the line suggested by IH-45?

TEST PREP and Spiral Review

31. **Multiple Choice** Which figure is NOT found in the diagram?

   Ⓐ Line   Ⓒ Line segment

   Ⓑ Point   Ⓓ Ray

F   R   M   T

32. **Gridded Response** How many endpoints does a ray have?

Find the value of k in each equation. (Lesson 2-8)

33. $\frac{k}{3} = 7$ 34. $\frac{k}{11} = 4$ 35. $20 = \frac{k}{5}$ 36. $21 = \frac{k}{7}$

Write each improper fraction as a mixed number. (Lesson 4-6)

37. $\frac{13}{4}$ 38. $\frac{70}{9}$ 39. $\frac{41}{3}$ 40. $\frac{75}{6}$ 41. $\frac{81}{7}$

8-2 Measuring and Classifying Angles

Learn to name, measure, draw, and classify angles.

Vocabulary

angle

vertex

acute angle

right angle

obtuse angle

straight angle

You can adjust the *angle* that a treadmill makes with the ground in order to have an easier or more intense workout.

An **angle** is formed by two rays with a common endpoint, called the **vertex**. An angle can be named by its vertex or by its vertex and a point from each ray. The middle point in the name must be the vertex. The angle of the treadmill can be called ∠F, ∠EFG, or ∠GFE.

Angles are measured in degrees. Use the symbol ° to show degrees.

EXAMPLE 1 Measuring an Angle with a Protractor

Reading Math

m∠XYZ is read "the measure of angle XYZ."

Use a protractor to measure the angle.

- Place the center point of the protractor on the vertex of the angle.
- Place the protractor so that ray YZ passes through the 0° mark.
- Using the scale that starts with 0° along ray YZ, read the measure where ray YX crosses.
- The measure of ∠XYZ is 75°. Write this as m∠XYZ = 75°.

EXAMPLE 2 Drawing an Angle with a Protractor

NY Performance Indicators

6.CN.8 Investigate the presence of mathematics in careers and areas of interest.

Use a protractor to draw an angle that measures 150°.

- Draw a ray on a sheet of paper.
- Place the center point of the protractor on the endpoint of the ray.
- Place the protractor so that the ray passes through the 0° mark.
- Make a mark at 150° above the scale on the protractor.
- Draw a ray from the endpoint of the first ray through the mark at 150°.

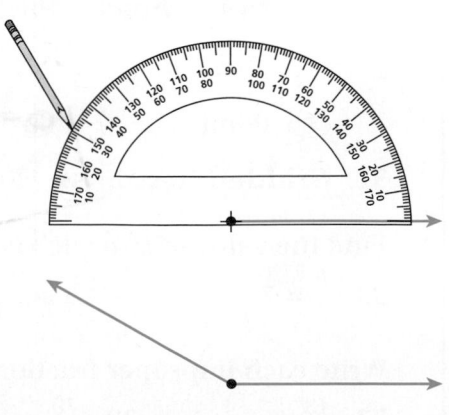

You can classify an angle by its measure.

An **acute angle** measures less than 90°.	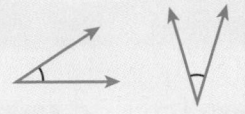
A **right angle** measures exactly 90°.	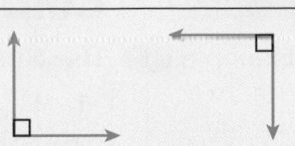
An **obtuse angle** measures more than 90° and less than 180°.	
A **straight angle** measures exactly 180°.	

EXAMPLE 3 **Classifying Angles**

Classify each angle as acute, right, obtuse, or straight.

A

B

The angle measures more than 90° and less than 180°, so it is an obtuse angle.

The angle measures less than 90°, so it is an acute angle.

EXAMPLE 4 *Architectural Application*

An architect designed this floor plan for a five-sided room of a house. Classify ∠A, ∠B, and ∠D in the floor plan.

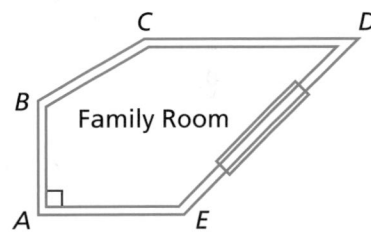

Family Room

∠A   right angle   *The angle is marked as a right angle.*

∠B   obtuse angle   *The angle measures more than 90° and less than 180°.*

∠D   acute angle   *The angle measures less than 90°.*

6.CM.1, 6.CN.6

Think and Discuss

1. **Explain** how you know which point is the vertex of ∠XYZ.

2. **Give an example** of a right angle in your classroom.

3. **Tell** what type of angle is suggested by each of the following.
   a. an open book lying flat   b. the corner of a sheet of paper
   c. the point of a pencil   d. the hands of a clock at 12:25

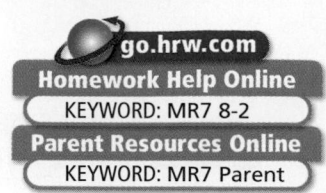

go.hrw.com
Homework Help Online
KEYWORD: MR7 8-2
Parent Resources Online
KEYWORD: MR7 Parent

GUIDED PRACTICE

See Example ① Use a protractor to measure each angle.

1. **2.** 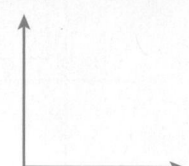 **3.**

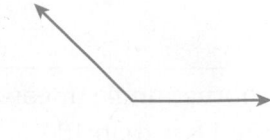

See Example ② Use a protractor to draw an angle with each given measure.

4. 55°   **5.** 135°   **6.** 20°   **7.** 190°

See Example ③ Classify each angle as acute, right, obtuse, or straight.

8. 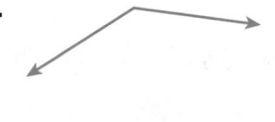   **9.** 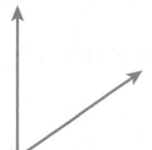   **10.**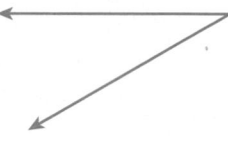

See Example ④ **11.** Kendra is planning a flower bed for her garden, which is shown in the figure. Classify each angle of the flower bed.

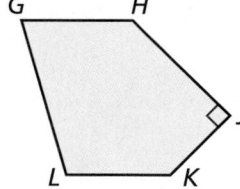

INDEPENDENT PRACTICE

See Example ① Use a protractor to measure each angle.

12.    **13.** 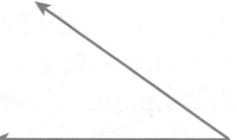   **14.**

See Example ② Use a protractor to draw an angle with each given measure.

15. 150°   **16.** 38°   **17.** 90°   **18.** 72°   **19.** 45°

See Example ③ Classify each angle as acute, right, obtuse, or straight.

20.    **21.**    **22.**

See Example ④ **23.** The figure shows the shape of a ceramic tile. Classify each of the tile's angles.

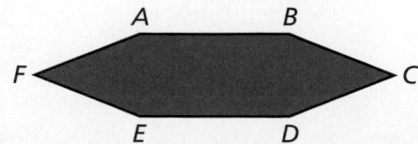

PRACTICE AND PROBLEM SOLVING

Extra Practice

See page 728.

Use a protractor to draw each angle.

24. an acute angle whose measure is less than 45°

25. an obtuse angle whose measure is between 100° and 160°

26. a right angle

Classify the smallest angle formed by the hands on each clock.

27. 　　　　**28.** 　　　　**29.**

30. Critical Thinking Can two acute angles that share a vertex form a right angle? Justify your answer with a diagram.

 31. What's the Error? A student wrote that the measure of this angle is 156°. Explain the error the student may have made, and give the correct measure of the angle. How can the student avoid making the same mistake again?

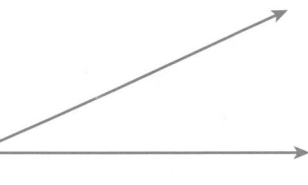

 32. Write About It Describe how an acute angle and an obtuse angle are different.

 33. Challenge How many times during the day do the hands of a clock form a straight angle?

TEST PREP and Spiral Review

34. Multiple Choice The figure shows a plan for a skateboard ramp. What type of angle is ∠B?

   Ⓐ Acute   Ⓑ Right   Ⓒ Obtuse   Ⓓ Straight

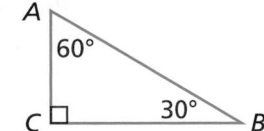

35. Multiple Choice Which of the following is another name for ∠PQR?

   Ⓕ ∠P   Ⓖ ∠RQP   Ⓗ ∠PRQ   Ⓙ ∠QPR

Write each decimal as a percent and a fraction. (Lesson 7-8)

36. 0.09   **37.** 0.4   **38.** 0.65   **39.** 0.9   **40.** 0.76

Find the percent of each number. (Lesson 7-9)

41. 12% of 30   **42.** 30% of 60   **43.** 65% of 110   **44.** 82% of 360

Learn to understand relationships of angles.

Vocabulary

congruent

vertical angles

adjacent angles

complementary angles

supplementary angles

NY Performance Indicators

5.A.5 Solve and explain simple one-step equations using inverse operations involving whole numbers. Also, 5.A.2.

Angle relationships play an important role in many sports and games. Miniature-golf players must understand angles to know where to aim the ball. In the miniature-golf hole shown, m∠1 = m∠2, m∠3 = m∠4, and m∠5 = m∠6.

When angles have the same measure, they are said to be **congruent** .

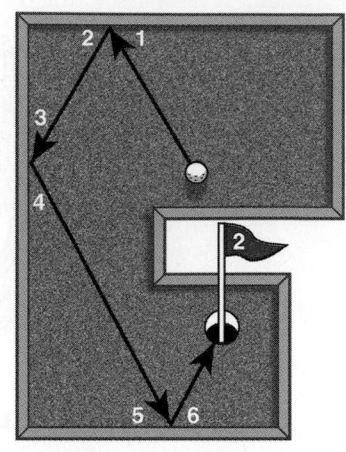

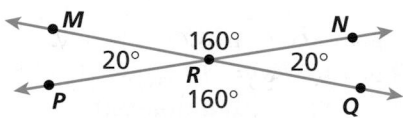

Vertical angles are formed opposite each other when two lines intersect. Vertical angles have the same measure, so they are always congruent.

∠MRP and ∠NRQ are vertical angles.
∠MRN and ∠PRQ are vertical angles.

Adjacent angles are side by side and have a common vertex and ray. Adjacent angles may or may not be congruent.

∠MRN and ∠NRQ are adjacent angles. They share vertex *R* and $\overrightarrow{RN}$.
∠NRQ and ∠QRP are adjacent angles. They share vertex *R* and $\overrightarrow{RQ}$.

E X A M P L E **1** **Identifying Types of Angle Pairs**

Identify the type of each angle pair shown.

A

∠1 and ∠2 are opposite each other and are formed by two intersecting lines.

They are vertical angles.

B

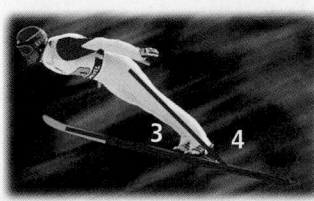

∠3 and ∠4 are side by side and have a common vertex and ray.

They are adjacent angles.

Complementary angles are two angles whose measures have a sum of 90°.

65° + 25° = 90°
∠LMN and ∠NMP are complementary.

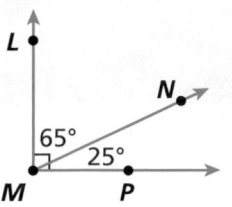

Supplementary angles are two angles whose measures have a sum of 180°.

65° + 115° = 180°
∠GHK and ∠KHJ are supplementary.

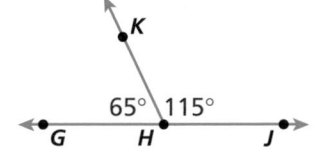

EXAMPLE **2** **Identifying an Unknown Angle Measure**

Find each unknown angle measure.

A The angles are complementary.

$$55° + a = 90°$$
$$\underline{-55° \qquad -55°}$$
$$a = 35°$$

The sum of the measures is 90°.

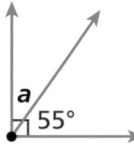

B The angles are supplementary.

$$75° + b = 180°$$
$$\underline{-75° \qquad -75°}$$
$$b = 105°$$

The sum of the measures is 180°.

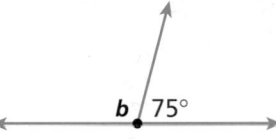

C The angles are vertical angles.

$$c = 51°$$

Vertical angles are congruent.

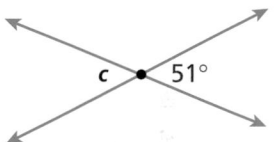

D Angles *JGF* and *KGH* are congruent.

$$d + e + 136° = 180°$$
$$\underline{-136° \quad -136°}$$
$$d + e = 44°$$
$$d = 22° \text{ and } e = 22°$$

The sum of the measures is 180°.
Each angle measures half of 44°.

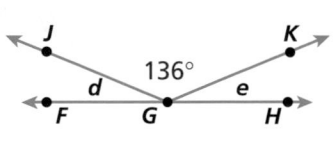

6.CM.10, 6.CN.3

Think and Discuss

1. Give the measure of ∠2 if ∠1 and ∠2 are vertical angles and m∠1 = 40°.

2. Give the measure of ∠3 if ∠3 and ∠4 are supplementary and m∠4 = 150°.

3. Tell whether the angles in Example 1B are supplementary or complementary.

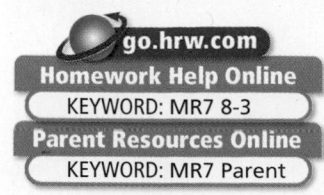

GUIDED PRACTICE

See Example ① **Identify the type of each angle pair shown.**

1.

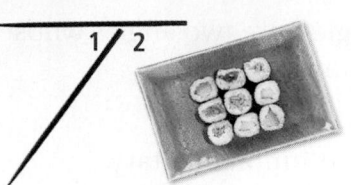

2.

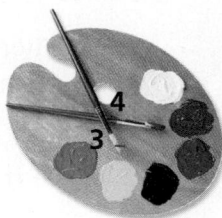

See Example ② **Find each unknown angle measure.**

3. The angles are complementary.

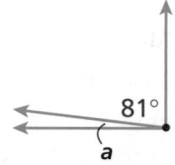

81°

a

4. The angles are supplementary.

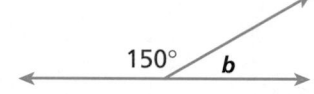

150° *b*

INDEPENDENT PRACTICE

See Example ① **Identify the type of each angle pair shown.**

5.

6.

See Example ② **Find each unknown angle measure.**

7. The angles are vertical angles.

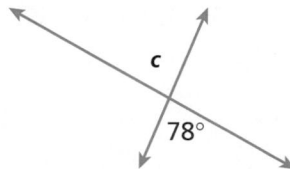

c

78°

8. The angles are supplementary.

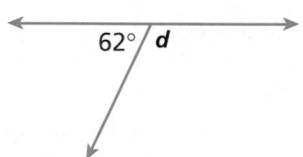

62° *d*

PRACTICE AND PROBLEM SOLVING

Extra Practice
See page 728.

Use the figure for Exercises 9–12.

9. Which angles are not adjacent to ∠3?

10. Name all the pairs of vertical angles that include ∠8.

11. If the m∠6 is 72°, what are the measures of ∠5, ∠7, and ∠8?

12. What is the sum of the measures of ∠1, ∠2, ∠3, and ∠4?

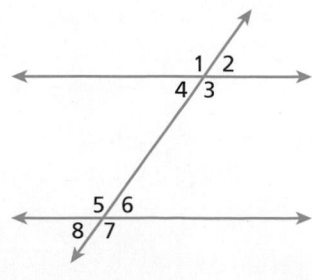

Use the figure for Exercises 13–15.

13. Find the measure of ∠VYW.

14. Find the measure of ∠XYZ.

15. Multi-Step Use the measures of ∠VYW and ∠XYZ to find the measure of ∠WYX.

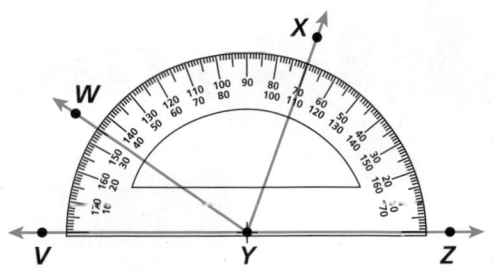

Find the measure of the angle that is complementary to each given angle. Use a protractor to draw both angles.

16. 47°   **17.** 62°   **18.** 55°   **19.** 31°

Find the measure of the angle that is supplementary to each given angle. Use a protractor to draw both angles.

20. 75°   **21.** 102°   **22.** 136°   **23.** 81°

24. Angles A and B are complementary. If the measure of angle A equals the measure of angle B, what is the measure of each angle?

25. Angles C and D are each complementary to angle F. How are angle C and angle D related?

 26. Write a Problem Draw a pair of adjacent supplementary angles. Write a problem in which the measure of one of the angles must be found.

 27. Write About It Two angles are supplementary to the same angle. Explain the relationship between the measures of these angles.

 28. Challenge The measure of angle A is 38°. Angle B is complementary to angle A. Angle C is supplementary to angle B. What is the measure of angle C?

TEST PREP and Spiral Review

29. Multiple Choice Which type of angles are always congruent?

ⓐ Adjacent   ⓑ Complementary   ⓒ Supplementary   ⓓ Vertical

30. Multiple Choice Angle J and angle K are supplementary. What is the measure of ∠K if the measure of ∠J is 75°?

Ⓕ 15°   Ⓖ 25°   Ⓗ 105°   Ⓙ 150°

Find the missing value in each proportion. (Lesson 7-3)

31. $\frac{n}{6} = \frac{5}{15}$ **32.** $\frac{2}{m} = \frac{0.8}{3.6}$ **33.** $\frac{1}{8} = \frac{p}{2}$ **34.** $\frac{30}{8} = \frac{15}{s}$

Classify each angle as acute, right, obtuse, or straight. (Lesson 8-2)

35.    **36.**   **37.**   **38.**

Learn to classify the different types of lines.

Vocabulary

parallel lines

perpendicular lines

skew lines

NY Performance Indicators

6.CN.6 Recognize and provide examples of the presence of mathematics in their daily lives.

The photograph of the houses and the table below show some of the ways that lines can relate to each other. The yellow lines are intersecting. The purple lines are *parallel*. The green lines are *perpendicular*. The white lines are *skew*.

Reading Math

The red arrows on the lines show that the lines are parallel.

Intersecting lines are lines that cross at one common point.	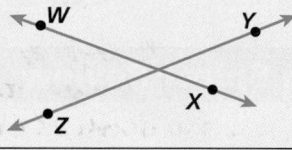	Line *YZ* intersects line *WX*. $\overleftrightarrow{YZ}$ intersects $\overleftrightarrow{WX}$.
Parallel lines are lines in the same plane that never intersect.	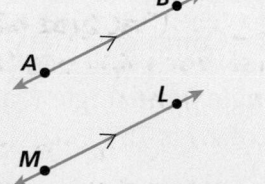	Line *AB* is parallel to line *ML*. $\overleftrightarrow{AB} \parallel \overleftrightarrow{ML}$
Perpendicular lines intersect to form 90° angles, or right angles.	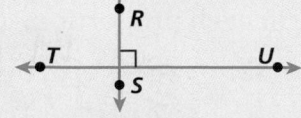	Line *RS* is perpendicular to line *TU*. $\overleftrightarrow{RS} \perp \overleftrightarrow{TU}$
Skew lines are lines that lie in different planes. They are neither parallel nor intersecting.	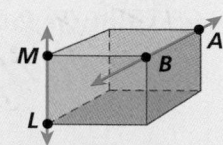	Line *AB* and line *ML* are skew. $\overleftrightarrow{AB}$ and $\overleftrightarrow{ML}$ are skew.

EXAMPLE **1** **Classifying Pairs of Lines**

Classify each pair of lines.

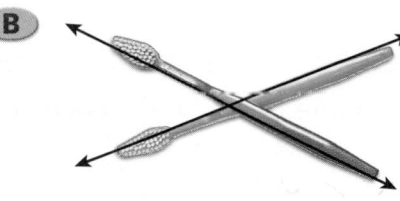

The lines are in the same plane. They do not appear to intersect.
They are parallel.

The lines cross at one common point.
They are intersecting.

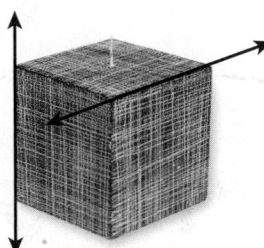

The lines intersect to form right angles.
They are perpendicular.

The lines are in different planes and are not parallel or intersecting.
They are skew.

EXAMPLE **2** *Physical Science Application*

The particles in a transverse wave move up and down as the wave travels to the right. What type of line relationship does this represent?

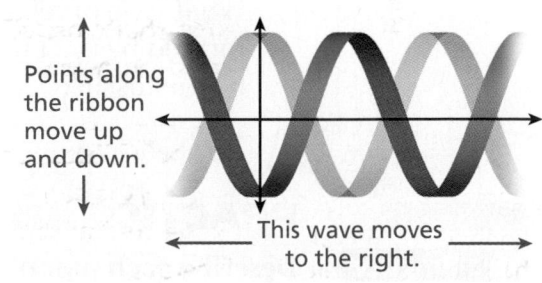

The direction that the particles move forms a right angle with the direction that the wave is traveling. The lines are perpendicular.

Think and Discuss

1. Give an example of intersecting, parallel, perpendicular, and skew lines or line segments in your classroom.

2. Determine whether two lines must be parallel if they do not intersect. Explain.

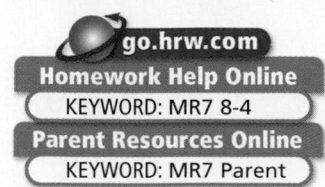

go.hrw.com
Homework Help Online
KEYWORD: MR7 8-4
Parent Resources Online
KEYWORD: MR7 Parent

GUIDED PRACTICE

See Example **1** Classify each pair of lines.

1.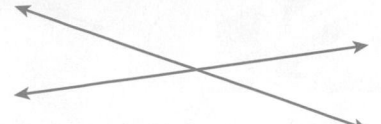

2.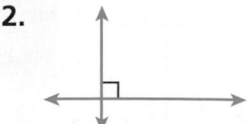

See Example **2** **3.** Jamal dropped a fishing line from a pier, as shown in the drawing. What type of relationship is formed by the lines?

INDEPENDENT PRACTICE

See Example **1** Classify each pair of lines.

4.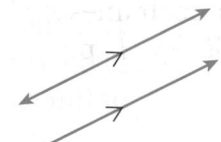

5.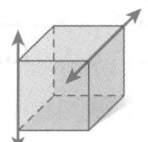

6.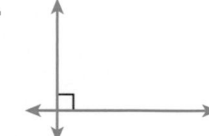

See Example **2** **7.** The drawing shows where an archaeologist found two fossils. What type of relationship is formed by the lines suggested by the fossils?

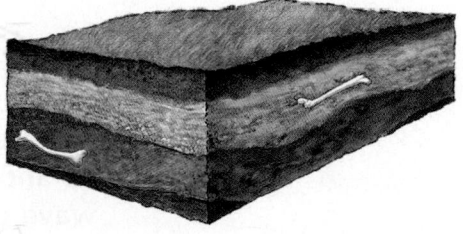

PRACTICE AND PROBLEM SOLVING

Extra Practice
See page 728.

Describe each pair of lines as parallel, skew, intersecting, or perpendicular.

8.

9.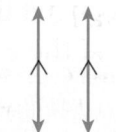

10.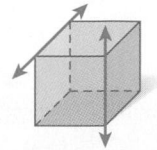

11. Capitol Street intersects 1st, 2nd, and 3rd Avenues, which are parallel to each other. West Street and East Street are perpendicular to 2nd Avenue.

    a. Draw a map showing the six streets.

    b. Suppose East and West Streets were perpendicular to Capitol Street rather than 2nd Avenue. Draw a map showing the streets.

The lines in the figure intersect to form a rectangular box.

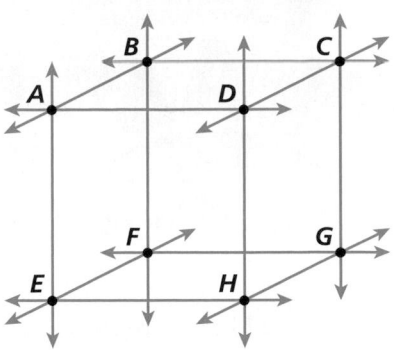

12. Name all the lines that are parallel to $\overleftrightarrow{AD}$.

13. Name all the lines that are perpendicular to $\overleftrightarrow{FG}$.

14. Name a pair of lines that are skew.

15. Name all the lines that are not parallel to and do not intersect $\overleftrightarrow{DH}$.

Tell whether each statement is *always*, *sometimes*, or *never* true.

16. Intersecting lines are parallel.

17. Intersecting lines are perpendicular.

18. Perpendicular lines are intersecting.

19. Parallel lines are skew.

20. Critical Thinking Use *parallel, perpendicular, skew,* or a combination of these terms to describe the lines on a sheet of graph paper. Explain your answer.

21. What's the Error? A student drew two lines and claimed that the lines were both parallel and intersecting. Explain the error.

22. Write About It Explain the similarities and differences between perpendicular and intersecting lines.

23. Challenge Lines *x*, *y*, and *z* are in a plane. If lines *x* and *y* are parallel and line *z* intersects line *x*, does line *z* intersect line *y*? Explain.

TEST PREP and Spiral Review

24. Multiple Choice Which types of lines never intersect when they are in the same plane?

   Ⓐ Intersecting   Ⓑ Parallel   Ⓒ Perpendicular   Ⓓ Skew

25. Multiple Choice Main Street and Elm Street meet at a 90° angle. Which term best describes the streets?

   Ⓕ Intersecting   Ⓖ Parallel   Ⓗ Perpendicular   Ⓙ Skew

26. Extended Response A student draws two lines on the same plane. He claims the lines are skew lines. Is he correct? Explain. What are the possible line types that the student drew?

Graph and label each point on a coordinate grid. (Lesson 6-6)

27. $A(3, 4)$ **28.** $B(1, 5)$ **29.** $C(7, 1)$ **30.** $D\left(8\frac{1}{2}, 5\right)$ **31.** $E\left(2, 3\frac{1}{2}\right)$

Find the measure of the angle that is complementary to each given angle. (Lesson 8-3)

32. 14°   **33.** 57°   **34.** 80°   **35.** 63°   **36.** 21°

Parallel Line Relationships

Use with Lesson 8-4

Parallel lines are in the same plane and never intersect. You can use a straightedge and protractor to draw parallel lines.

NY Performance Indicators

6.R.1, 6.R.5, 6.CM.10

Activity

1 Draw a line on your paper. Label two points *A* and *B*.

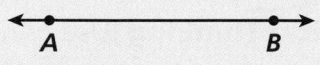

Use your protractor to measure and mark a 90° angle at each point.

Draw rays with endpoints *A* and *B* through the marks you made with the protractor.

Place the point of your compass on point *A*, and draw an arc through the ray.

Use the same compass opening to draw an arc through the ray at point *B*.

Label the points of intersection *X* and *Y*.

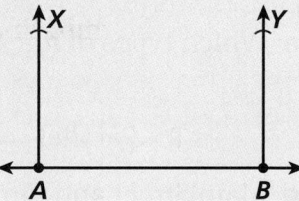

Now use your straightedge to draw a line through *X* and *Y*.

Use the symbol for parallel lines to indicate that $\overleftrightarrow{AB}$ is parallel to $\overleftrightarrow{XY}$.

$\overleftrightarrow{AB} \parallel \overleftrightarrow{XY}$

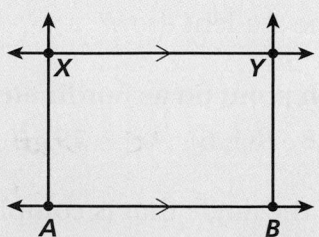

When a pair of parallel lines is intersected by a third line, the angles formed have special relationships.

2 Draw a pair of parallel lines and a third line that intersects them. Label the angles 1 through 8, as shown.

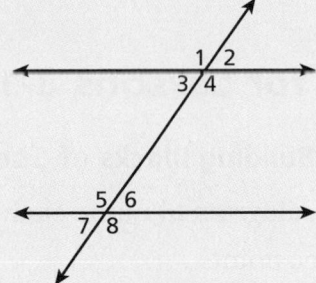

Angles inside the parallel lines are called *interior angles*. The interior angles here are angles 3, 4, 5, and 6.

Angles outside the parallel lines are called *exterior angles*. The exterior angles here are angles 1, 2, 7, and 8.

Measure each angle, and write its measurement inside the angle.

Shade angles with the same measure with the same color.

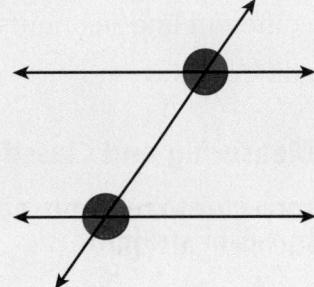

The interior angles with the same measure are called *alternate interior angles*. They are angles 3 and 6 and angles 4 and 5.

The exterior angles with the same measure are called *alternate exterior angles*. They are angles 1 and 8 and angles 2 and 7.

Angles in the same position when the third line intersects the parallel lines are called *corresponding angles*.

Think and Discuss

1. Name three pairs of corresponding angles.

2. Tell the relationship between the measure of interior angles and the measure of exterior angles.

Try This

Follow the steps to construct and label the diagram.

1. Draw a pair of parallel lines, and draw a third line intersecting them where one angle measures 75°.

2. Label each angle on the diagram using the measure you know.

Quiz for Lessons 8-1 Through 8-4

8-1 Building Blocks of Geometry

Use the diagram to name each geometric figure.

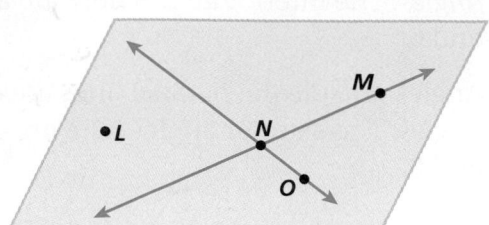

1. three points
2. two lines
3. a point shared by two lines
4. a plane
5. two different line segments
6. two different rays

8-2 Measuring and Classifying Angles

Use a protractor to measure each angle. Then classify each angle as acute, right, obtuse, or straight.

7.   8.   9.   10.

11. The quarterback of a football team throws a long pass, and the angle the path of the ball makes with the ground is 30°. Draw an angle with this measurement.

8-3 Angle Relationships

12. If two angles are supplementary and one angle measures 97°, what is the measure of the other angle?

Find each unknown angle measure.

13. 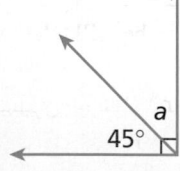   14. 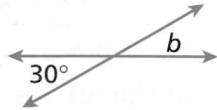   15. 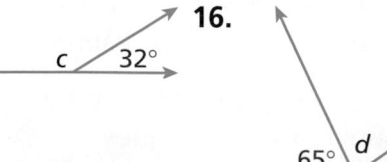   16.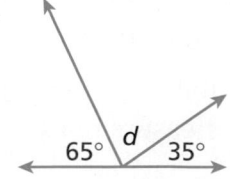

8-4 Classifying Lines

Classify each pair of lines.

17.    18. 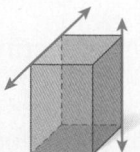   19.    20.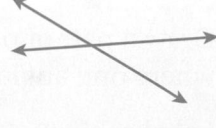

Ready to Go On?

Focus on Problem Solving

Solve

- **Eliminate answer choices**

Sometimes, when a problem has multiple answer choices, you can eliminate some of the choices to help you solve the problem.

For example, a problem reads, "The missing shape is not a red triangle." If one of the answer choices is a red triangle, you can eliminate that answer choice.

 **Read each problem, and look at the answer choices. Determine whether you can eliminate any of the answer choices before solving the problem. Then solve.**

Smileys are letters and symbols that look like faces if you turn them around. When you write an e-mail to someone, you can use smileys to show how you are feeling.

Smileys	
Symbol	**Meaning**
:-(	Frown
:-D	Laugh
:-)	Smile
:-o	Shout
;-)	Wink

For 1–3, use the table.

1 Dora made a pattern with smileys. Which smiley will she probably use next?

:-D :-) :-D :-) :-D :-) :-D :-) :-D

- **Ⓐ** :-D
- **Ⓑ** :-)
- **Ⓒ** :-)
- **Ⓓ** :-D

2 Troy made a pattern with smileys. Identify a pattern. Which smiley is missing?

:-(;-) :-o :-(;-) :-o :-(▢ :-o

- **Ⓕ** :-(
- **Ⓖ** :-o
- **Ⓗ** ;-)
- **Ⓙ** ;-)

3 To end an e-mail, Mya typed four smileys in a row. The shout is first. The wink is between the frown and the smile. The smile is not last. In which order did Mya type the smileys?

- **Ⓐ** :-o :-(;-) :-)
- **Ⓑ** :-o :-) ;-) :-(
- **Ⓒ** :-) ;-) :-o :-(
- **Ⓓ** :-o ;-) :-(:-)

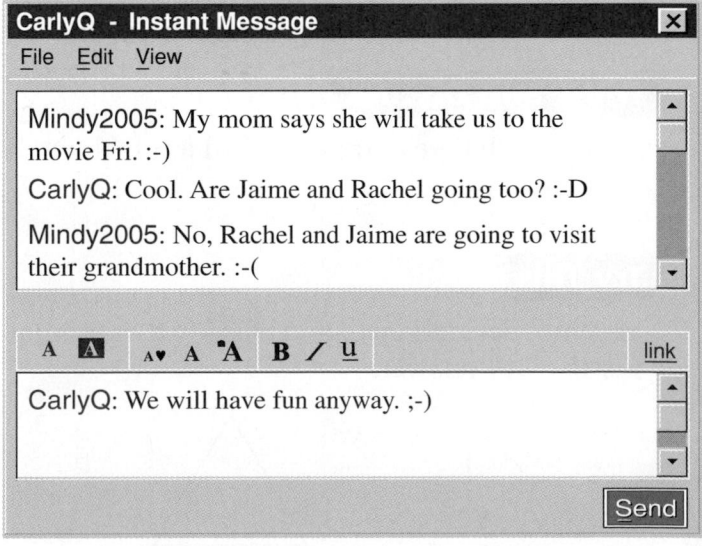

CarlyQ - Instant Message

File Edit View

Mindy2005: My mom says she will take us to the movie Fri. :-)

CarlyQ: Cool. Are Jaime and Rachel going too? :-D

Mindy2005: No, Rachel and Jaime are going to visit their grandmother. :-(

A A   A♥ A ˙A **B** *I* u̲   link

CarlyQ: We will have fun anyway. ;-)

Send

Classify Triangles

NY Performance Indicators

6.RP.8, 6.R.5, 6.CM.10

go.hrw.com
Lab Resources Online
KEYWORD: MR7 Lab8

REMEMBER
• A triangle is a polygon with three sides and three angles.

A triangle can be classified by its sides as either *equilateral, isosceles,* or *scalene.*

Activity

Use a centimeter ruler to measure the sides of each triangle. Sketch each triangle and label the length of each side.

Type of Triangle	Examples	Nonexamples
Equilateral		
Isosceles		
Scalene		

Think and Discuss

1. For each type of triangle, find a rule that relates the side lengths to the type of triangle.

Try This

Measure each triangle and classify it as equilateral, isosceles, or scalene. Justify your answer.

1. 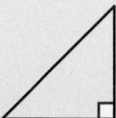　**2.** 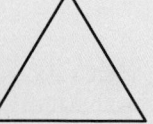　**3.** 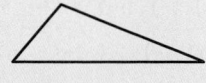　**4.**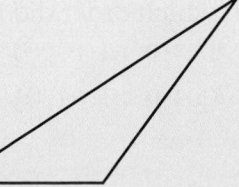

8-5 Triangles

Learn to classify triangles and solve problems involving angle and side measures of triangles.

A triangle is a closed figure with three line segments and three angles. Triangles can be classified by the measures of their angles. An **acute triangle** has only acute angles. An **obtuse triangle** has one obtuse angle. A **right triangle** has one right angle.

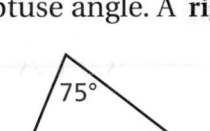

Acute triangle

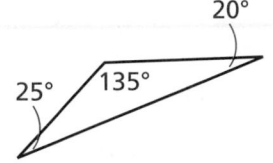

Obtuse triangle

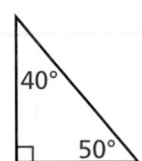

Right triangle

Vocabulary

acute triangle

obtuse triangle

right triangle

scalene triangle

isosceles triangle

equilateral triangle

To decide whether a triangle is acute, obtuse, or right, you need to know the measures of its angles.

The sum of the measures of the angles in any triangle is 180°. You can see this if you tear the corners from a triangle and arrange them around a point on a line.

By knowing the sum of the measures of the angles in a triangle, you can find unknown angle measures.

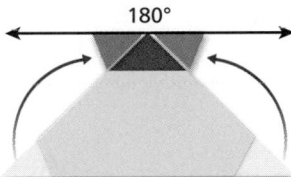

NY Performance Indicators

5.A.5 Solve and explain simple one-step equations using inverse operations involving whole numbers. Also, 5.A.2.

EXAMPLE 1 **Sports Application**

Boat sails are often shaped like triangles. The measure of ∠A is 70°, and the measure of ∠B is 45°. Classify the triangle.

To classify the triangle, find the measure of ∠C on the sail.

$m\angle C = 180° - (70° + 45°)$
$m\angle C = 180° - 115°$ *Subtract the sum of the known*
$m\angle C = 65°$ *angle measures from 180°.*

So the measure of ∠C is 65°. Because △ABC has only acute angles, the boat sail is an acute triangle.

You can use what you know about vertical, adjacent, complementary, and supplementary angles to find the missing measures of angles.

EXAMPLE 2 Using Properties of Angles to Label Triangles

Use the diagram to find the measure of each indicated angle.

A ∠*BDE*

∠*BDE* and ∠*ADC* are vertical angles, so m∠*BDE* = m∠*ADC*.

Remember!

Vertical angles are congruent. The sum of the measures of complementary angles is 90°. The sum of the measures of supplementary angles is 180°.

m∠*ADC* = 180° − (30° + 35°)

= 180° − 65°

= 115°

m∠*BDE* = 115°

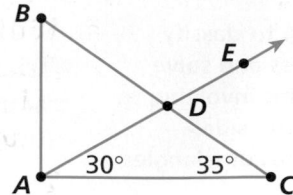

B ∠*ADB*

The sum of m∠*BDE* and m∠*ADB* is 180°.

m∠*ADB* = **180°** − 115°

= 65°

m∠*ADB* = 65°

Triangles can be classified by the lengths of their sides. A **scalene triangle** has no congruent sides. An **isosceles triangle** has at least two congruent sides. An **equilateral triangle** has three congruent sides. You can use tick marks to show congruent sides.

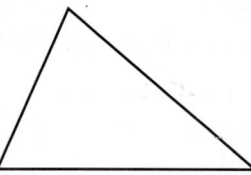

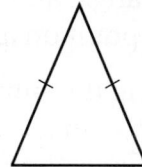

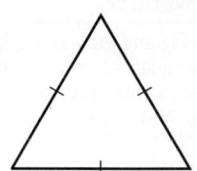

Scalene triangle   Isosceles triangle   Equilateral triangle

EXAMPLE 3 Classifying Triangles by Lengths of Sides

Classify the triangle. The perimeter of the triangle is 7.8 cm.

a + (3.8 + 2) = 7.8

a + 5.8 = 7.8

a + 5.8 − 5.8 = 7.8 − 5.8

a = 2

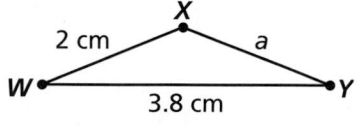

Side *a* is 2 centimeters long. Because △*WXY* has at least two sides, but not three, that are the same length, it is an isosceles triangle.

Think and Discuss

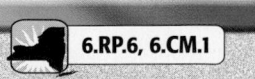

1. **Explain** why a triangle cannot have two obtuse angles.

2. **Tell** whether a right triangle can also be an acute triangle. Explain.

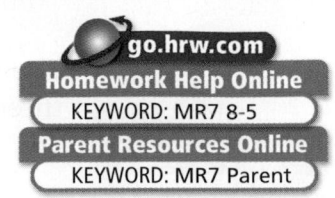

go.hrw.com
Homework Help Online
KEYWORD: MR7 8-5
Parent Resources Online
KEYWORD: MR7 Parent

GUIDED PRACTICE

See Example **1**　**1.** Three stars form a triangular constellation. Two of the angles measure 20° and 50°. Classify the triangle.

See Example **2**　Use the diagram to find the measure of each indicated angle.

2. ∠XZV

3. ∠VZW

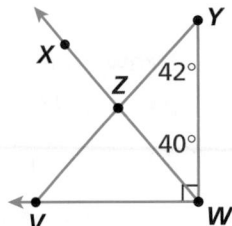

See Example **3**　Classify each triangle using the given information.

4. The perimeter of the triangle is 24 cm.

8 cm　　8 cm

5. The perimeter of the triangle is 30 ft.

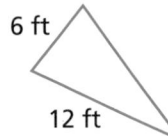

6 ft

12 ft

INDEPENDENT PRACTICE

See Example **1**　**6.** Interstate highways connecting towns R, S, and T form a triangle. Two of the angles measure 40° and 42°. Classify the triangle.

See Example **2**　Use the diagram to find the measure of each indicated angle.

7. ∠KNJ　　　　**8.** ∠LKM

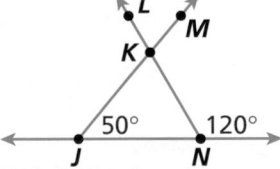

See Example **3**　Classify each triangle using the given information.

9. The perimeter of the triangle is 10.5 in.

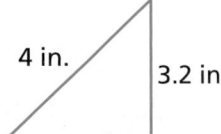

4 in.　3.2 in.

10. The perimeter of the triangle is 231 km.

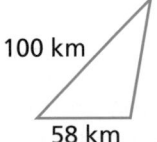

100 km

58 km

PRACTICE AND PROBLEM SOLVING

Extra Practice
See page 729.

If the angles can form a triangle, classify it as acute, obtuse, or right.

11. 45°, 90°, 45°　　　　**12.** 51°, 88°, 41°　　　　**13.** 71°, 40°, 59°

14. 55°, 102°, 33°　　　　**15.** 37°, 40°, 103°　　　　**16.** 90°, 30°, 50°

17. Find a triangle in your classroom or at home. Describe the triangle and classify it. Explain your classification.

The lengths of two sides are given for △*ABC*. Use the sum of the lengths of the three sides to calculate the length of the third side and classify each triangle.

18. *AB* = 7 cm; *BC* = 7 cm;
sum = 15.9 cm

19. *AB* = $1\frac{1}{6}$ ft; *BC* = $1\frac{1}{6}$ ft;
sum = $3\frac{1}{2}$ ft

20. **Social Studies** Some triangular stamps are made by dividing a rectangle into two parts. Classify the triangle that is made by cutting on a line that connects one corner of a rectangle to the opposite corner.

Draw an example of each triangle described.

21. a scalene acute triangle

22. an isosceles right triangle

23. an isosceles obtuse triangle

24. a scalene right triangle

25. **Critical Thinking** Use a centimeter ruler to measure each side of triangle A. Add the lengths of any two sides and compare the sum to the length of the third side. Add a different pair of lengths and compare the sum to the third side. Do the same for triangles B and C. How does the sum of the lengths of any two sides of a triangle compare to the length of the third side?

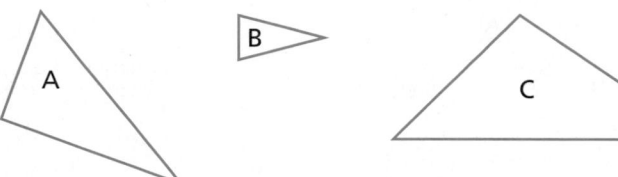

 26. **Choose a Strategy** How many triangles are in the figure at right?

 27. **Write About It** Explain why a triangle cannot have two right angles.

 28. **Challenge** Find the sum of the angles of a square. (*Hint:* Divide the square into two triangles.)

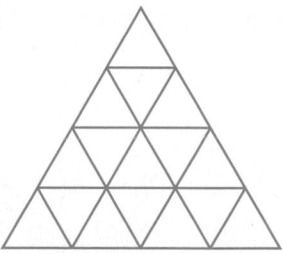

TEST PREP and Spiral Review

29. **Multiple Choice** A triangle has one right angle. What could the measures of the other two angles be?

Ⓐ 20° and 70° Ⓑ 30° and 15° Ⓒ 60° and 120° Ⓓ 90° and 100°

30. **Multiple Choice** The lengths of two sides of a triangle are 54 meters and 45 meters. The sum of the three sides is 126 meters. Find the missing third side.

Ⓕ 27 m Ⓖ 72 m Ⓗ 81 m Ⓙ 99 m

Write each percent as a decimal. (Lesson 7-7)

31. 12% **32.** 55% **33.** 3% **34.** 47% **35.** 76%

Draw each geometric figure. (Lesson 8-1)

36. $\overleftrightarrow{CD}$ **37.** $\overrightarrow{GM}$ **38.** $\overline{XY}$ **39.** point *A*

Technology LAB 8-5

Angles in Triangles

NY Performance Indicators

6.R.1, 6.R.2, 6.R.5

go.hrw.com
Lab Resources Online
KEYWORD: MR7 Lab8

The sum of the angle measures is the same for any triangle. You can use geometry software to find this sum and to check that the sum is the same for many different triangles.

Activity

1 Use the geometry software to make triangle *ABC*. Then use the angle measure tool to measure ∠*B*.

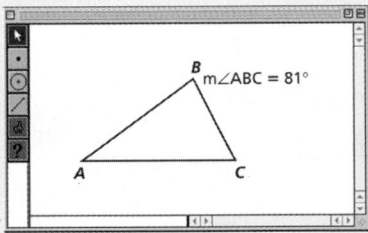

2 Use the angle measure tool to measure ∠*C* and ∠*A*. Then use the calculator tool to add the measures of the three angles. Notice that the sum is 180°.

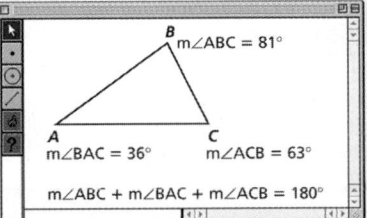

3 Select vertex *A* and drag it around to change the shape of triangle *ABC*. Watch the angle sum. Change the shape of the triangle again and then again. Be sure to make acute and obtuse triangles.

Notice that the sum of the angle measures is always 180°, regardless of the triangle's shape.

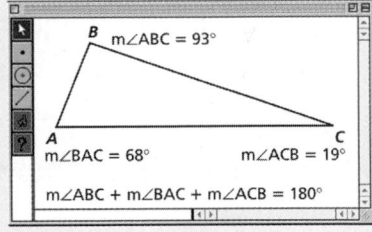

Think and Discuss

1. Can you use geometry software to draw a triangle with two obtuse angles? Explain.

Try This

Solve. Then use geometry software to check each answer.

1. In triangle *ABC*, m∠*B* = 49.15° and m∠*A* = 113.75°. Find m∠*C*.

2. Use geometry software to construct an acute triangle *XYZ*. Give the measures of its angles, and check that their sum is 180°.

Quadrilaterals

Learn to identify, classify, and compare quadrilaterals.

Vocabulary

quadrilateral

parallelogram

rectangle

rhombus

square

trapezoid

 NY Performance Indicators

6.RP.2 Understand that mathematical statements can be supported, using models, facts, and relationships to explain their thinking.

A **quadrilateral** is a plane figure with four sides and four angles.

Five special types of quadrilaterals and their properties are shown in the table below. The tick marks on two or more sides of a figure indicate that the sides are congruent.

Theo van Doesburg painted *Compostion 17*. Many of his abstract paintings consist of different-sized rectangles.

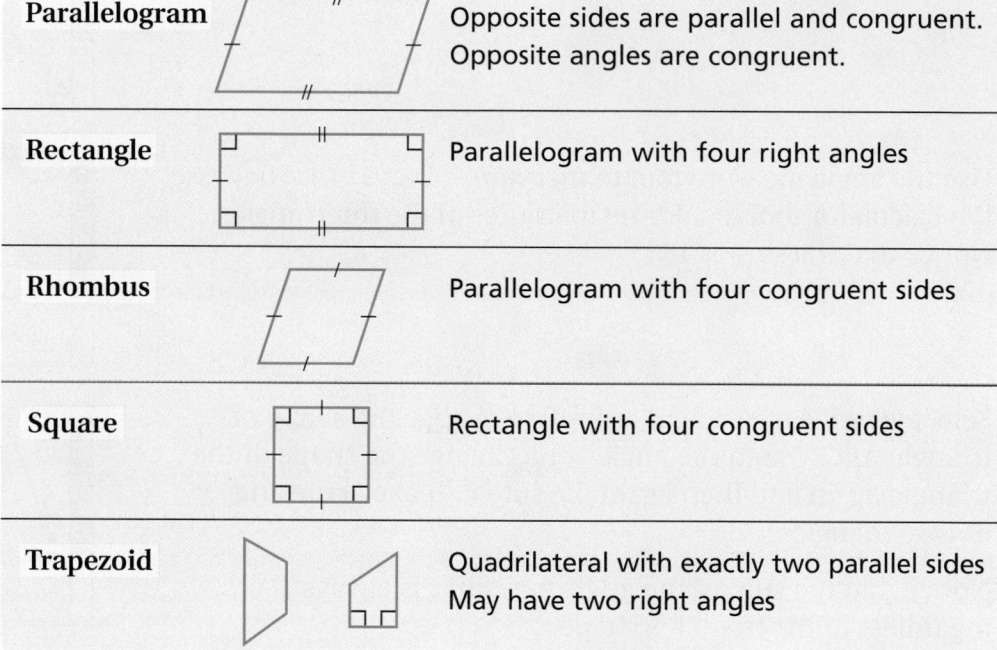

Parallelogram		Opposite sides are parallel and congruent. Opposite angles are congruent.
Rectangle		Parallelogram with four right angles
Rhombus		Parallelogram with four congruent sides
Square		Rectangle with four congruent sides
Trapezoid		Quadrilateral with exactly two parallel sides May have two right angles

EXAMPLE 1 Naming Quadrilaterals

Give the most descriptive name for each figure.

A 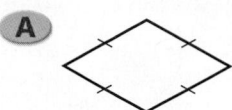 *The figure is a quadrilateral, a parallelogram, and a rhombus.*

Rhombus is the most descriptive name.

B 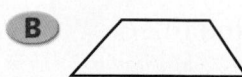 *The figure is a quadrilateral and a trapezoid.*

Trapezoid is the most descriptive name.

Give the most descriptive name for each figure.

C 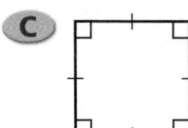   *The figure is a quadrilateral, parallelogram, rectangle, rhombus, and square.*

Square is the most descriptive name.

D 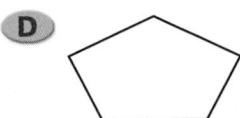   *This figure is a plane figure, but it has more than 4 sides.*

The figure is not a quadrilateral.

You can draw a diagram to classify quadrilaterals based on their properties.

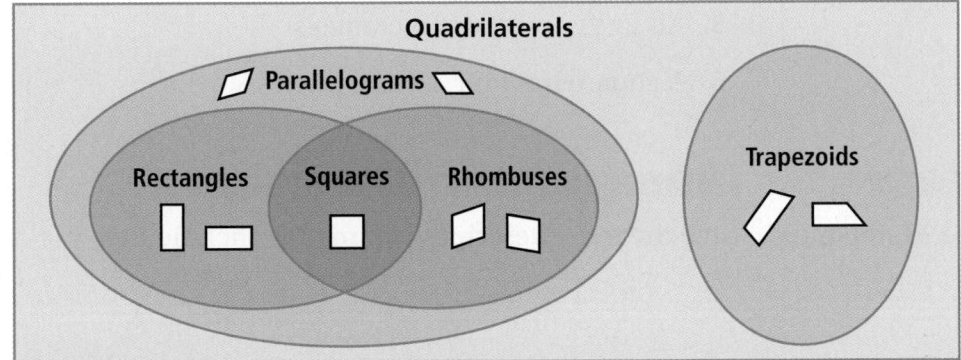

EXAMPLE 2 Classifying Quadrilaterals

Complete each statement.

A A rhombus that is a rectangle is also a ___?___.

A rhombus has four congruent sides, and the opposite sides are parallel. If it is a rectangle, it has four right angles, which makes it a **square**.

B A square can also be called a ___?___, ___?___, and ___?___.

A square has opposite sides that are parallel; it can be called a **parallelogram**.

A square has four congruent sides; it can be called a **rhombus**.

A square has four right angles; it can be called a **rectangle**.

Think and Discuss

1. Tell whether all squares are rhombuses and whether all rhombuses are squares.

2. Compare a trapezoid with a rectangle.

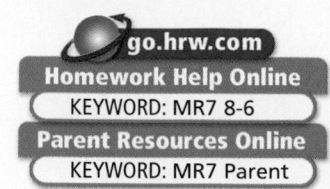
GUIDED PRACTICE

See Example **1** Give the most descriptive name for each figure.

1. 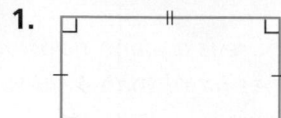 **2.** 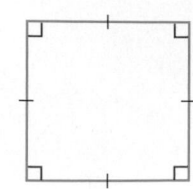 **3.**

See Example **2** Complete each statement.

4. A trapezoid is also a ___?___.

5. All ___?___ are also rectangles.

6. A square has four ___?___ angles.

INDEPENDENT PRACTICE

See Example **1** Give the most descriptive name for each figure.

7. **8.** **9.**

See Example **2** Complete each statement.

10. A rhombus with four right angles is a ___?___.

11. A parallelogram cannot be a ___?___.

12. A quadrilateral with four congruent sides and no right angles can be called a
___?___ and a ___?___.

PRACTICE AND PROBLEM SOLVING

Extra Practice
See page 729.

Give all of the possible names for each figure. Circle the most exact name.

13. 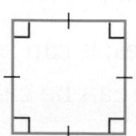 **14.** 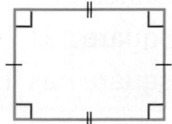 **15.**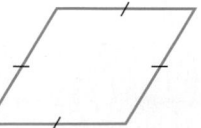

Determine if the given statements are *sometimes*, *always*, or *never* true.

16. A square is a rectangle. **17.** A trapezoid is a parallelogram.

18. A rhombus is a square. **19.** A parallelogram is a quadrilateral.

20. A rectangle is a rhombus. **21.** Four-sided figures are parallelograms.

22. A rectangle is a square. **23.** A trapezoid has one right angle.

Draw each quadrilateral as described. If it is not possible to draw, explain why.

24. a rectangle that is also a square

25. a rhombus that is also a trapezoid

26. a parallelogram that is not a rectangle

27. a square that is not a rhombus

28. **Sports** A baseball diamond is in the shape of a square. The distance from home plate to first base is 90 ft. What is the distance around the baseball diamond?

29. A rectangular picture frame is 3 in. wider than it is tall. The total length of the four sides of the frame is 38 in.

   a. The dimensions of the frame could be 10 in. by 13 in. because one dimension is 3 in. longer than the other. Explain how you know the frame is not 10 in. by 13 in.

   b. **Critical Thinking** How can you use your answer from part **a** to find the dimensions of the frame?

   c. Using parts **a** and **b,** what are the dimensions of the frame?

30. Anika drew a quadrilateral. Then she drew a line segment connecting one pair of opposite corners. She saw that she had divided the original quadrilateral into two right isosceles triangles. Classify the quadrilateral she began with.

31. **What's the Error?** A student said that any quadrilateral with two right angles and a pair of parallel sides is a rectangle. What is the error in the statement?

32. **Write About It** Explain why a square is also a rectangle and a rhombus.

33. **Challenge** Part of a quadrilateral is hidden. What are the possible types of quadrilaterals that the figure could be?

TEST PREP and Spiral Review

34. **Multiple Choice** Which quadrilateral is NOT a parallelogram?

   (A) Rectangle   (B) Rhombus   (C) Square   (D) Trapezoid

35. **Short Response** List all of the names for the figure. Which is the most descriptive?

Use the pattern to write the first five terms of the sequence. (Lesson 1-7)

36. Start with 6; add 5.   37. Start with 2; multiply by 3.

Tell whether each statement is *always, sometimes,* or *never* true. (Lesson 8-4)

38. Perpendicular lines are intersecting lines.   39. Skew lines are on the same plane.

Polygons

Learn to identify regular and not regular polygons and to find the angle measures of regular polygons.

Vocabulary

polygon

regular polygon

Triangles and quadrilaterals are examples of polygons. A **polygon** is a closed plane figure formed by three or more line segments. A **regular polygon** is a polygon in which all sides are congruent and all angles are congruent.

Polygons are named by the number of their sides and angles.

Remember!

An equilateral triangle has three congruent sides.

	Triangle	Quadrilateral	Pentagon	Hexagon	Octagon
Sides and Angles	3	4	5	6	8
Regular	△	□	⬠	⬡	⯃
Not Regular					

EXAMPLE 1   Identifying Polygons

Tell whether each shape is a polygon. If so, give its name and tell whether it appears to be regular or not regular.

NY Performance Indicators

6.PS.15 Make organized lists or charts to solve numerical problems.

A

There are 4 sides and 4 angles.

quadrilateral

The sides and angles appear to be congruent.

regular

B

There are 4 sides and 4 angles.

quadrilateral

All 4 sides do not appear to be congruent.

not regular

The sum of the interior angle measures in a triangle is 180°, so the sum of the interior angle measures in a quadrilateral is 360°.

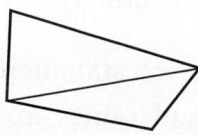 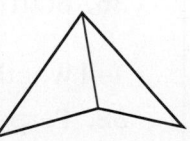

EXAMPLE 2

PROBLEM SOLVING

PROBLEM SOLVING APPLICATION

A stop sign is in the shape of a regular octagon. What is the measure of each angle of the stop sign?

1 **Understand the Problem**

The **answer** will be the measure of each angle in a regular octagon. List the **important information:**

• A regular octagon has 8 congruent sides and 8 congruent angles.

2 **Make a Plan**

Make a table to look for a pattern using regular polygons.

3 **Solve**

Draw some regular polygons and divide each into triangles.

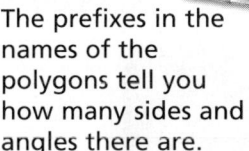

Reading Math

The prefixes in the names of the polygons tell you how many sides and angles there are.

tri- = three
quad- = four
penta- = five
hexa- = six
octa- = eight

Polygon	Sides	Triangles	Sum of Angle Measures
Triangle	3	1	1 × 180° = 180°
Quadrilateral	4	2	2 × 180° = 360°
Pentagon	5	3	3 × 180° = 540°
Hexagon	6	4	4 × 180° = 720°

The number of triangles is always 2 fewer than the number of sides. An octagon can be divided into 8 − 2 = 6 triangles.

The sum of the interior angle measures in an octagon is 6 × 180° = 1,080°.

So the measure of each angle is 1,080° ÷ 8 = 135°.

4 **Look Back**

Each angle in a regular octagon is obtuse. 135° is a reasonable answer, because an obtuse angle is between 90° and 180°.

6.CN.3, 6.CN.6

Think and Discuss

1. **Classify** the angles in each figure: a regular triangle, a regular hexagon, and a rectangle.

2. **Name** an object that is in the shape of a pentagon and an object that is in the shape of an octagon.

go.hrw.com
Homework Help Online
KEYWORD: MR7 8-7
Parent Resources Online
KEYWORD: MR7 Parent

GUIDED PRACTICE

See Example 1 Tell whether each shape is a polygon. If so, give its name and tell whether it appears to be regular or not regular.

1.

2.

3.

See Example 2 **4.** A carpenter is building a deck around a hot tub in the shape of a regular hexagon. What is the measure of each angle of the hexagon?

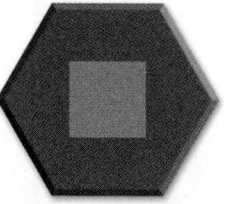

INDEPENDENT PRACTICE

See Example 1 Tell whether each shape is a polygon. If so, give its name and tell whether it appears to be regular or not regular.

5.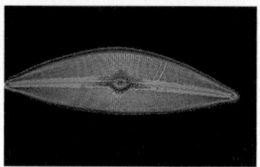

6.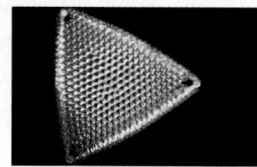

7.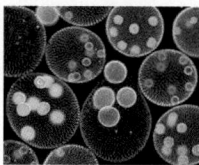

See Example 2 **8.** Janet made a sign for her room in the shape of a regular pentagon. What is the measure of each angle of the pentagon?

PRACTICE AND PROBLEM SOLVING

Extra Practice
See page 729.

Explain why each shape is NOT a polygon.

9.

10.

11.

Name each polygon.

12.

13.

14.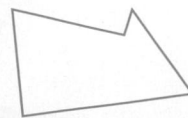

15. Lucy drew a regular decagon (ten-sided figure). What is the sum of the interior angle measures? What is the measure of each angle?

Classify each of the following polygons as either *always* regular, *sometimes* regular, or *never* regular.

		Always	Sometimes	Never
16.	Equilateral triangle	?	?	?
17.	Trapezoid	?	?	?
18.	Right triangle	?	?	?
19.	Parallelogram	?	?	?

Critical Thinking A *diagonal* is a line segment that connects two nonadjacent vertices of a polygon. One diagonal is shown in each figure.

20. a. How many diagonals does a rectangle have?

b. How many diagonals does a pentagon have?

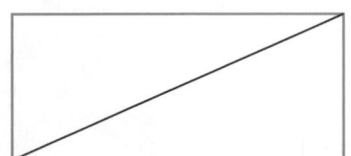   

21. What's the Error? A student said a rectangle is never a regular polygon because the lengths of all the sides are not congruent. What error did the student make? Explain why a rectangle is sometimes a regular polygon.

22. Write About It What polygon is formed when two equilateral triangles are placed side by side, with one upside down? Draw examples, and explain whether the polygon formed by the two triangles is regular.

23. Challenge A figure is formed by placing 6 equilateral triangle tiles around a regular hexagon tile. The distance around the regular hexagon is 60 cm. A snail moves along the sides of the figure. How far will the snail travel until it gets back to its starting point?

 **TEST PREP and Spiral Review**

24. Multiple Choice Which quadrilateral is regular?

Ⓐ Triangle Ⓑ Trapezoid Ⓒ Square Ⓓ Rhombus

25. Gridded Response What is the measure, in degrees, of each angle of a regular pentagon?

Solve each equation. (Lesson 3-9)

26. $5.5 = 5c$ **27.** $d + 4.96 = 9$ **28.** $j - 12.5 = 39.04$ **29.** $\frac{x}{2.4} = 3.5$

30. Can the angles with measurements 34°, 53°, and 93° form a triangle? If so, classify the triangle as acute, obtuse, or right. (Lesson 8-5)

Geometric Patterns

Learn to recognize, describe, and extend geometric patterns.

NY Performance Indicators

6.PS.14 Analyze problems by observing patterns.

Native American art often involves geometric patterns. The patterns are based on the shape, color, size, position, or number of geometric figures.

This blanket has a geometric pattern. The first row with a complete figure has a parallelogram with a horse in its center. The next row has two parallelograms with cows in the centers. This pattern continues. If the weaver wanted to make a longer blanket, the next row would be two parallelograms with pictures of cows.

This Navajo blanket was made in the late seventeenth century.

EXAMPLE **1** **Extending Geometric Patterns**

Identify a possible pattern. Use the pattern to draw the next figure.

Ⓐ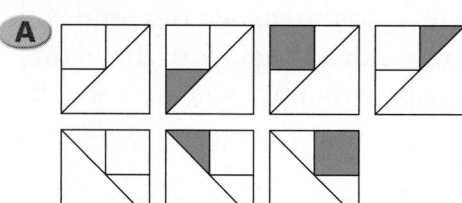

The small shapes within the figure are shaded one at a time from bottom to top. Then the figure is rotated and the top triangle is shaded.

So the next figure might look like this:

Ⓑ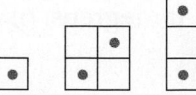

The figures from left to right are a 1 × 1 square, a 2 × 2 square, a 3 × 3 square, and a 4 × 4 square.

So the next figure might look like this: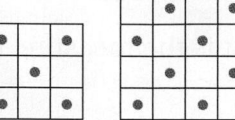

Remember!

Perfect squares, such as 2^2, 3^2, and 4^2, are also called "square numbers" because they can be modeled as a square array.

EXAMPLE 2

EXAMPLE **2** **Completing Geometric Patterns**

Identify a possible pattern. Use the pattern to draw the missing figure.

A   ?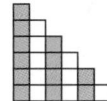

The first figure from the bottom row to the top has 4 squares and then 3, 2, and 1 square. The next figure has 5 squares in the bottom row and then 4, 3, 2, and 1.

So the missing figure might look like this:

B ?

Each figure is an equilateral triangle. The first figure has 3 red triangles along the base. The third figure has 5 red triangles, and the last figure has 6.

So the missing figure might look like this:

EXAMPLE **3** **Art Application**

Dan is painting a clay pot. Identify a pattern in Dan's design and tell what the finished pot might look like.

The pattern from bottom to top is narrow stripe, wide stripe, narrow stripe, wide stripe. The color pattern from bottom to top is blue, green, yellow, blue, green.

If this pattern is followed, the finished pot might look like the pot at left.

Think and Discuss

1. **Explain** how you can use a pattern to find the number of squares in the next, or fifth, figure in Example 2A.

2. **Tell** how you can use a pattern to find the number of small red triangles in the sixth figure in Example 2B.

go.hrw.com
Homework Help Online
KEYWORD: MR7 8-8
Parent Resources Online
KEYWORD: MR7 Parent

GUIDED PRACTICE

See Example **1**   Identify a possible pattern. Use the pattern to draw the next figure.

1.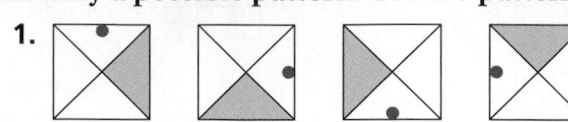

See Example **2**   Identify a possible pattern. Use the pattern to draw the missing figure.

2.

See Example **3**   **3.** Oscar is making a beaded necklace. Identify a pattern in Oscar's design. Then tell which five beads Oscar will probably use next.

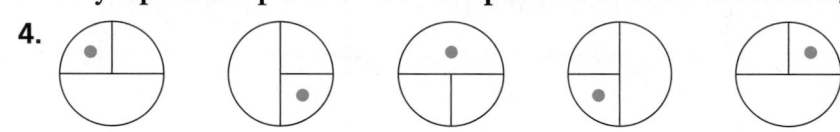

INDEPENDENT PRACTICE

See Example **1**   Identify a possible pattern. Use the pattern to draw the next figure.

4.

See Example **2**   Identify a possible pattern. Use the pattern to draw the missing figure.

5.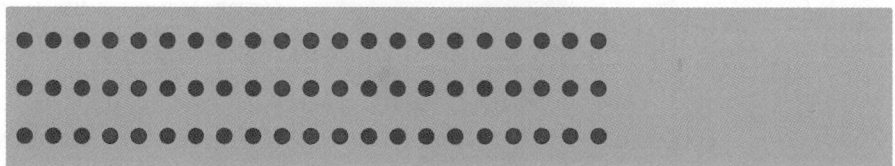

See Example **3**   **6.** Tamara is planting flowers in her garden. She makes groups of purple flowers and groups of pink flowers.

If she continues this pattern, how many flowers might Tamara plant in the next group of purple flowers? How many flowers might she plant in the next group of pink flowers?

PRACTICE AND PROBLEM SOLVING

Extra Practice
See page 729.

Draw the next figure in the pattern.

7. ☐   ☐△   ☐△◯   ☐△◯▢   ☐△◯▢△

8. ◌ ◎ ◉

9. ⌐ ⌐ ⌐ ⌐ ⌐

In South Africa, Ndebele people paint their houses with brightly colored patterns made up of geometric shapes.

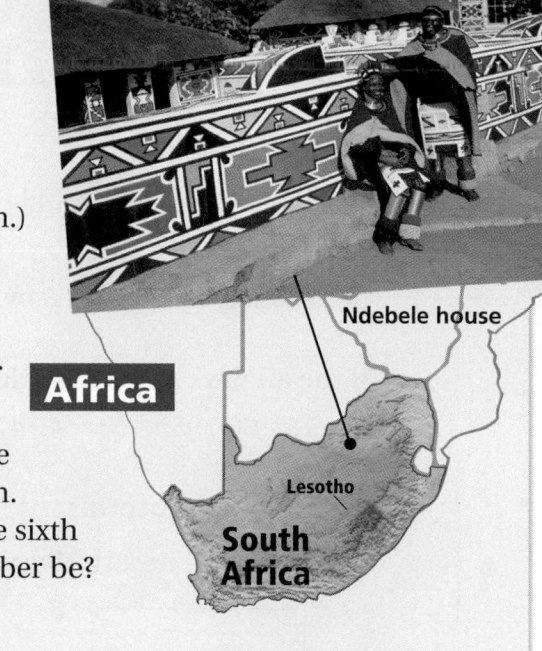

Ndebele house

10. Look at the shapes found on the wall surrounding the Ndebele house. Identify a possible pattern that was used to paint the top band of the wall. Use the pattern to draw the shapes hidden by the Ndebele people. (You do not need to include color in the pattern.)

11. ✏ **Write About It** Look closely at the Ndebele house. Draw four geometric figures you see painted on the house. Then use those figures to make a pattern. Describe your pattern.

Africa

12. ⭐ **Challenge** Look at the designs below, which were made using an African motif. Identify a possible pattern. If the pattern continues, how many motifs will be in the sixth design? If there are 45 motifs, what will the design number be?

Lesotho

South Africa

1   2   3

go.hrw.com
Web Extra!
KEYWORD: MR7 Patterns

TEST PREP and Spiral Review

13. Multiple Choice Identify a possible pattern in the image. Use the pattern to determine the missing figure.

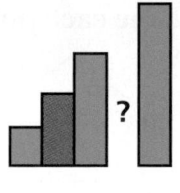
?

Ⓐ    Ⓑ 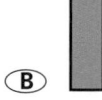   Ⓒ    Ⓓ

14. Short Response Determine the next figure in the pattern. Draw the figure. Explain your answer.

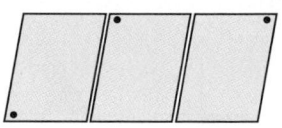

Find each value. (Lesson 1-3)

15. 9^2 **16.** 2^6 **17.** 3^3 **18.** 1^{12} **19.** 4^5

Write the prime factorization of each number. (Lesson 4-2)

20. 38   **21.** 50   **22.** 120   **23.** 214   **24.** 75

READY TO GO ON?

Quiz for Lessons 8-5 Through 8-8

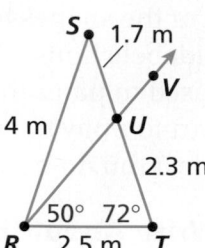

8-5 Triangles

Use the diagram for problems 1 and 2.

1. Find m∠SUV.

2. Classify triangle *STR* by its angles and by its sides.

If the angles can form a triangle, classify it as acute, obtuse, or right.

3. 15°, 60°, 95°   4. 47°, 51°, 82°   5. 94°, 76°, 10°   6. 78°, 102°, 20°

8-6 Quadrilaterals

Give the most descriptive name for each figure.

7. 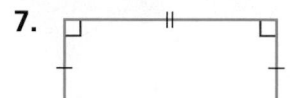   8.    9.    10.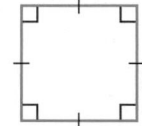

8-7 Polygons

11. Nina cuts a regular hexagon out of poster board. What is the measure of each angle of the hexagon?

12. The perimeter of an equilateral triangle is 186 centimeters. What is the length of one side of the triangle?

Name each polygon, and tell whether it appears to be regular or not regular.

13. 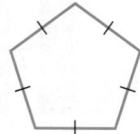   14. 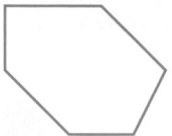   15.    16.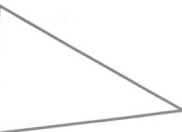

8-8 Geometric Patterns

Identify a possible pattern. Use the pattern to draw the missing figure.

17. 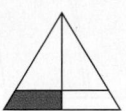 ?   18. 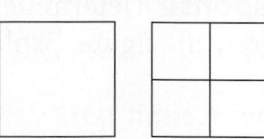 ?

19. 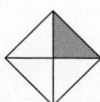 ?   20. 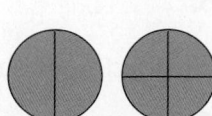 ?

Focus on Problem Solving

Make a Plan

- **Draw a diagram**

Sometimes a problem seems difficult because it is described in words only. You can draw a diagram to help you picture the problem. Try to label all the information you are given on your diagram. Then use the diagram to solve the problem.

Read each problem. Draw a diagram to help you solve the problem. Then solve.

1. Bob used a ruler to draw a quadrilateral. First he drew a line 3 in. long and labeled it $\overline{AB}$. From B, he drew a line 2 in. long and labeled the endpoint C. From A, he drew a line $2\frac{1}{2}$ in. long and labeled the endpoint D. What is the length of $\overline{CD}$ if the perimeter of Bob's quadrilateral is $12\frac{1}{2}$ in?

2. Karen has a vegetable garden that is 12 feet long and 10 feet wide. She plans to plant tomatoes in one-half of the garden. She will divide the other half of the garden equally into three beds, where she'll grow cabbage, pumpkin, and radishes.
   a. What are the possible whole number dimensions of the tomato bed?
   b. What fraction of the garden will Karen use to grow cabbage?

3. Pam draws three parallel lines that are an equal distance apart. The two outside lines are 8 cm apart. How far apart is the middle line from the outside lines?

4. Jan connected the following points on a coordinate grid: (2, 4), (4, 6), (6, 6), (6, 2), (3, 2), and (2, 4).
   a. What figure did Jan draw?
   b. How many right angles does the figure have?

5. Triangle ABC is isoceles. The measure of angle B is equal to the measure of angle C. The measure of angle B equals 50°. What is the measure of angle A?

8-9 Congruence

**Learn** to identify congruent figures and to use congruence to solve problems.

You know that angles that have the same measure are congruent. Figures that have the same shape and same size are also congruent.

You can use stencils to decorate pages of a scrapbook. The stencil helps you draw congruent figures.

NY Performance Indicators

6.RP.6 Develop and explain an argument verbally, numerically, algebraically, and/or graphically.

EXAMPLE 1 Identifying Congruent Figures

Decide whether the figures in each pair are congruent. If not, explain.

A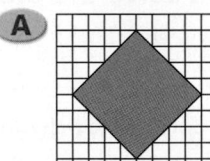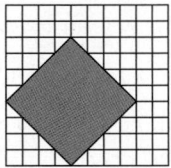

The figures are congruent.

These figures have the same shape and size.

B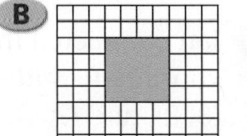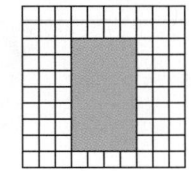

The figures are not congruent.

These figures are both quadrilaterals. But they are neither the same size nor the same shape.

C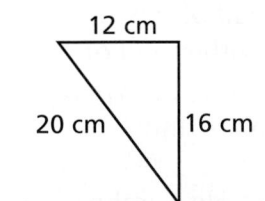

The triangles are congruent.

Each triangle has a 12 cm side, a 16 cm side, and a 20 cm side.

D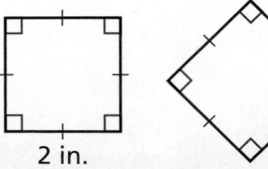

The figures are congruent.

Each figure is a square. Each side of each square measures 2 inches.

EXAMPLE 2 **Consumer Application**

Landra needs a ground cloth that is congruent to the tent floor. Which ground cloth should she buy?

Tent floor

Ground cloth A

Ground cloth B

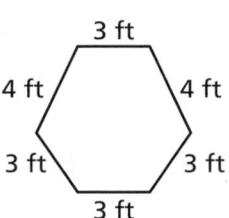
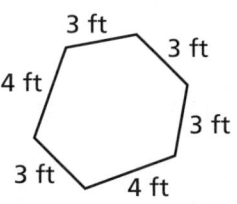
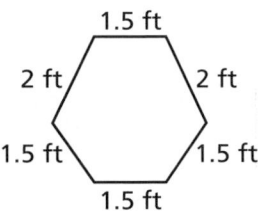

Which ground cloth is the same size and shape as the tent floor?
Both cloths are hexagons. Only Cloth A is the same size as the floor.

Cloth A is congruent to the tent floor.

Think and Discuss

6.PS.17, 6.PS.19

1. **Explain** whether you can determine that figures are congruent just by looking at them.

2. **Tell** what information you would need to know about two rectangles to determine whether they are congruent.

8-9 Exercises

go.hrw.com
Homework Help Online
KEYWORD: MR7 8-9
Parent Resources Online
KEYWORD: MR7 Parent

GUIDED PRACTICE

See Example **1** Decide whether the figures in each pair are congruent. If not, explain.

1.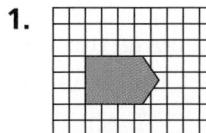

2.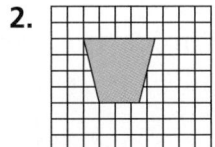

See Example **2** 3. Which quadrilateral is congruent to the bottom of the box?

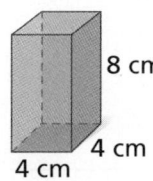
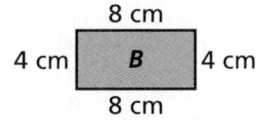
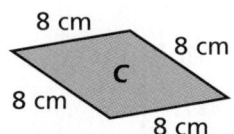

INDEPENDENT PRACTICE

See Example ① Decide whether the figures in each pair are congruent. If not, explain.

4.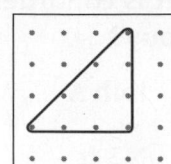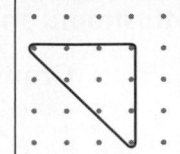

5.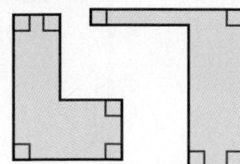

See Example ② **6.** Which puzzle piece will fit into the empty space?

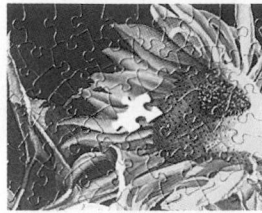

a.  **b.**  **c.**

PRACTICE AND PROBLEM SOLVING

Extra Practice
See page 730.

7. Copy the dot grid. Then draw three figures congruent to the given figure. The figures can have common sides but should not overlap.

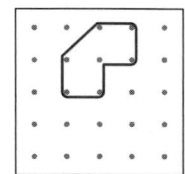

8. Measurement Use an inch ruler to draw two congruent rectangles with side lengths that are longer than 2 in. and shorter than 6 in. Label each side length.

9. Write About It Explain how to tell whether two polygons are congruent.

10. Challenge Two quadrilaterals have side lengths 2 cm, 2 cm, 5 cm, and 5 cm. Are the two quadrilaterals congruent? Explain.

TEST PREP and Spiral Review

11. Multiple Choice Squares *ABCD* and *WXYZ* are congruent. The length of $\overline{AB}$ is 5 in. What is the length of $\overline{WX}$?

Ⓐ 5 in.   Ⓑ 9 in.   Ⓒ 20 in.   Ⓓ 25 in.

12. Multiple Choice Hexagons *FGHJKL* and *RSTWXY* are congruent and regular. The length of $\overline{FG}$ is 7 km. Find the perimeter of hexagon *RSTWXY*.

Ⓕ 7 km   Ⓖ 35 km   Ⓗ 42 km   Ⓙ 49 km

Solve each equation. Check your answers. (Lesson 2-7)

13. $9y = 81$ **14.** $70 = 10x$ **15.** $64 = 8n$ **16.** $60 = 12m$

Multiply. Write each answer in simplest form. (Lesson 5-7)

17. $\frac{2}{3} \cdot \frac{4}{7}$ **18.** $\frac{1}{5} \cdot \frac{3}{8}$ **19.** $\frac{3}{4} \cdot \frac{1}{2}$ **20.** $\frac{4}{5} \cdot \frac{1}{3}$

Transformations

Learn to use translations, reflections, and rotations to transform geometric shapes.

Vocabulary

transformation

translation

rotation

reflection

line of reflection

NY Performance Indicators

6.CM.10 Use appropriate vocabulary when describing objects, relationships, mathematical solutions, and rationale.

A rigid **transformation** moves a figure without changing its size or shape. So the original figure and the transformed figure are always congruent.

The illustrations of the alien show three transformations: a *translation*, a *rotation*, and a *reflection*. Notice the transformed alien does not change in size or shape.

A **translation** is the movement of a figure along a straight line.

Only the location of the figure changes with a translation.

A **rotation** is the movement of a figure around a point. A point of rotation can be on or outside a figure.

The location and position of a figure can change with a rotation.

When a figure flips over a line, creating a mirror image, it is called a **reflection**. The line the figure is flipped over is called the **line of reflection**.

The location and position of a figure change with a reflection.

E X A M P L E **1** **Identifying Transformations**

Tell whether each is a translation, rotation, or reflection.

A

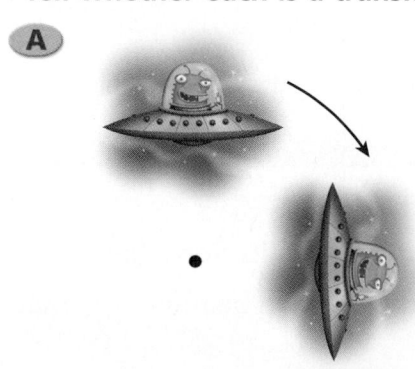

The figure moves around a point.

It is a rotation.

Tell whether each is a translation, rotation, or reflection.

B

The figure is flipped over a line.

It is a reflection.

C

The figure is moved along a line.

It is a translation.

A full turn is a 360° rotation. So a $\frac{1}{4}$ turn is 90°, and a $\frac{1}{2}$ turn is 180°.

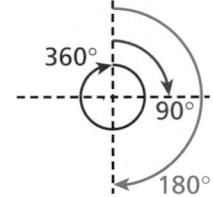

EXAMPLE 2 **Drawing Transformations**

Draw each transformation.

A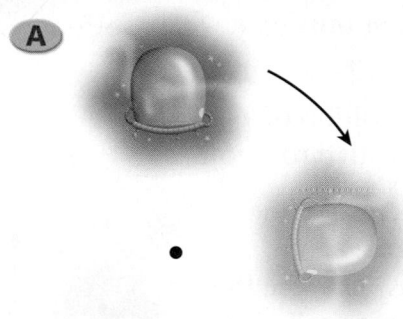

Draw a 90° clockwise rotation about the point shown.

Trace the figure and the point of rotation.

Place your pencil on the point of rotation.

Rotate the figure clockwise 90°.

Trace the figure in its new location.

B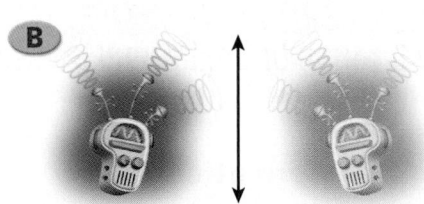

Draw a horizontal reflection.

Trace the figure and the line of reflection.

Fold along the line of reflection.

Trace the figure in its new location.

Think and Discuss

 6.CN.7, 6.CM.1

1. Give examples of reflections that occur in the real world.

2. Name a figure that can be rotated so that it will land on top of itself.

8-10

Exercises

go.hrw.com
Homework Help Online
KEYWORD: MR7 8-10
Parent Resources Online
KEYWORD: MR7 Parent

GUIDED PRACTICE

See Example ① **Tell whether each is a translation, rotation, or reflection.**

1.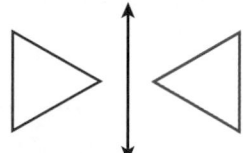

2.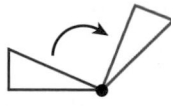

3.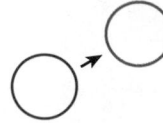

See Example ② **Draw each transformation.**

4. Draw a 180° clockwise rotation about the point shown.

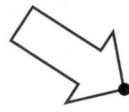

5. Draw a horizontal reflection across the line.

INDEPENDENT PRACTICE

See Example ① **Tell whether each is a translation, rotation, or reflection.**

6.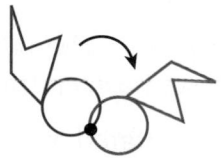

7.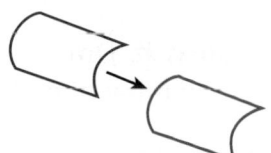

8.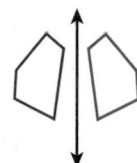

See Example ② **Draw each transformation.**

9. Draw a vertical reflection across the line.

10. Draw a 90° counterclockwise rotation about the point.

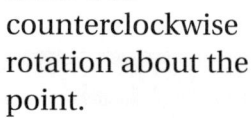

11. Draw a translation.

12. Draw a translation.

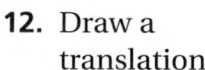

13. Draw a 90° clockwise rotation about the point.

14. Draw a horizontal reflection across the line.

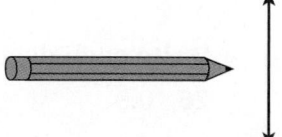

PRACTICE AND PROBLEM SOLVING

Extra Practice
See page 730.

15. Which is a horizontal reflection of this red arrow?

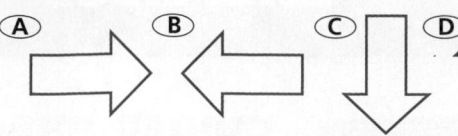

16. Language Arts Which letters in the alphabet can be horizontally reflected and still look the same? Which letters can be vertically reflected and still look the same?

Use the chessboard for Exercises 17–20.

Hobbies Chess is a game of skill that is played on a board divided into 64 squares. Each chess piece is moved differently.

17. Copy the lower left corner of the chessboard. Then show the indicated knight moving in a translation of two forward and one right.

Knight   King   Pawn

Hobbies

In a game of chess, each player has 318,979,564,000 possible ways to make the first four moves.

18. Choose a Strategy If the knight, king, and pawn are placed in a straight line, how many ways can they be arranged?

    (A) 3   (B) 4   (C) 6   (D) 12

19. Write About It Draw one of the chess pieces. Then draw a translation, rotation, and reflection of that piece. Describe each transformation.

20. Challenge Draw one of the chess pieces rotated 90° clockwise around the vertex of a square and then horizontally reflected.

TEST PREP and Spiral Review

21. Multiple Choice What is the movement of a figure about a point?

    (A) Translation   (B) Tessellation   (C) Reflection   (D) Rotation

22. Short Response Tell whether the picture shows a rotation, translation, or reflection. Explain.

Write each phrase as a numerical or algebraic expression.
(Lesson 2-2)

23. 19 times 3   **24.** the quotient of *g* divided by 6   **25.** the sum of 5 and 9

Write each decimal as a fraction or mixed number. *(Lesson 4-4)*

26. 0.9   **27.** 6.71   **28.** 0.20   **29.** 2.88   **30.** 0.55

Transformations in the Coordinate Plane

Use with Lesson 8-10

NY Performance Indicators

5.G.12, 6.R.1, 6.R.5

go.hrw.com
Lab Resources Online
KEYWORD: MR7 Lab8

Activity

1 Draw the first quadrant of a coordinate plane on graph paper.

Place a red pattern block on the coordinate plane so the endpoints are on (1, 1), (1, 6), (3, 5), and (3, 2). Trace around the figure and label it Figure A.

Move the figure so that its endpoints are on (5, 1), (5, 6), (7, 5), and (7, 2). Trace around the figure and label it Figure B.

Describe the shape, size, and position of Figure B compared with those of Figure A.

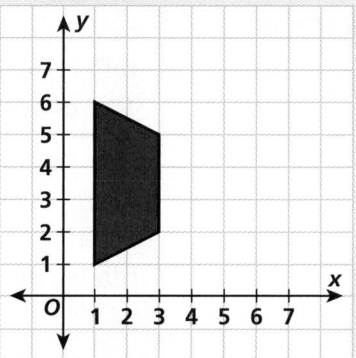

One kind of transformation when only the location of a figure changes is called a *translation*.

2 Draw the first quadrant of a coordinate plane on graph paper.

Place an orange pattern block on the coordinate plane so the endpoints are on (3, 3), (3, 5), (5, 5), and (5, 3). Trace around the figure and label it Figure C.

Draw Figure D so that its endpoints are on (3, 1), (3, 5), (7, 5), and (7, 1).

Describe the shape, size, and position of Figure C compared with those of Figure D.

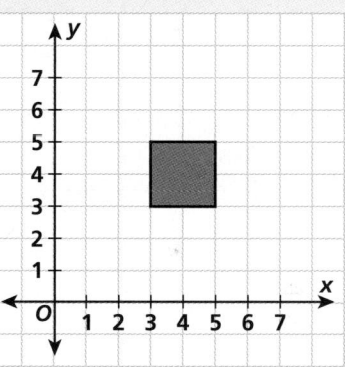

When a figure changes size but keeps the same shape, the transformation is called a *dilation*.

Think and Discuss

1. Which transformation results in a figure that is congruent? similar?

Try This

Draw each transformation.

1. a translation 2 units down

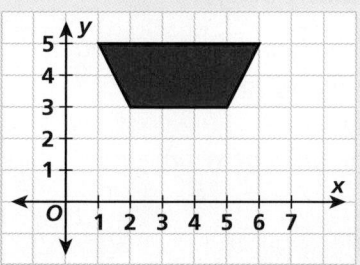

2. a dilation 2 times as big

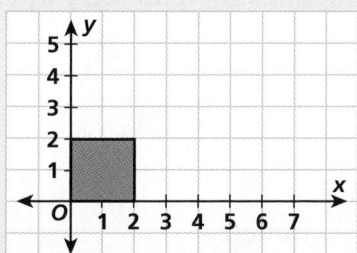

3. a translation 6 units left

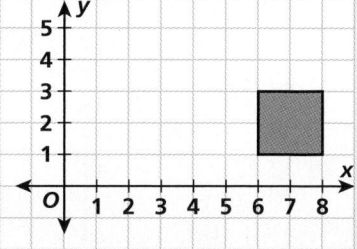

8-11 Line Symmetry

Learn to identify line symmetry.

Vocabulary
line symmetry
line of symmetry

A figure has **line symmetry** if it can be folded or reflected so that the two parts of the figure match, or are congruent. The line of reflection is called the **line of symmetry**.

You can draw a line of symmetry on this windmill. The shape of the building and the position of the blades are symmetrical.

EXAMPLE 1 **Identifying Lines of Symmetry**

Determine whether each dashed line appears to be a line of symmetry.

NY Performance Indicators

6.R.5 Use representations to explore problem situations.

A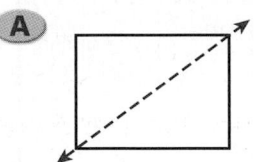

The two parts of the figure are congruent, but they do not match exactly when folded or reflected across the line.

The line does not appear to be a line of symmetry.

B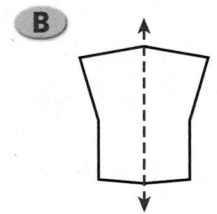

The two parts of the figure appear to match exactly when folded or reflected across the line.

The line appears to be a line of symmetry.

Some figures have more than one line of symmetry.

EXAMPLE 2 **Finding Multiple Lines of Symmetry**

Find all of the lines of symmetry in each regular polygon.

A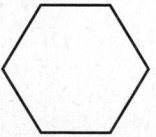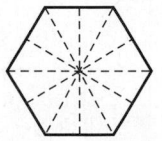

Trace each figure and cut it out. Fold the figure in half in different ways. Count the lines of symmetry.

6 lines of symmetry

Find all of the lines of symmetry in each regular polygon.

 B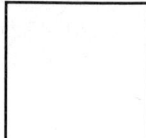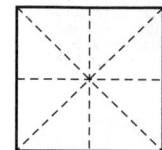

4 lines of symmetry

 C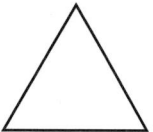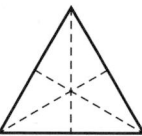

Count the lines of symmetry.

3 lines of symmetry

EXAMPLE **3** *Social Studies Application*

Find all of the lines of symmetry in each flag design.

A Antigua and Barbuda   **B** Macedonia

1 line of symmetry   2 lines of symmetry

C Norway   **D** Lesotho

1 line of symmetry   There are no lines of symmetry.

Think and Discuss

 6.CN.2, 6.CN.6, 6.RP.6

1. Explain how you can use your knowledge of reflection to create a figure that has a line of symmetry.

2. Determine whether all hexagons have six lines of symmetry.

3. Name objects with line symmetry in your classroom. Tell how many lines of symmetry each of these objects has.

go.hrw.com
Homework Help Online
KEYWORD: MR7 8-11
Parent Resources Online
KEYWORD: MR7 Parent

GUIDED PRACTICE

See Example 1   Determine whether each dashed line appears to be a line of symmetry.

1.

2.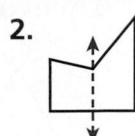

3.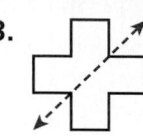

See Example 2   Find all of the lines of symmetry in each regular polygon.

4.

5.

6.

See Example 3   Find all of the lines of symmetry in each design.

7.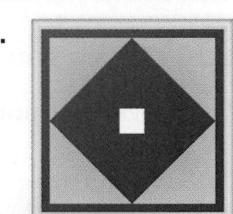

8.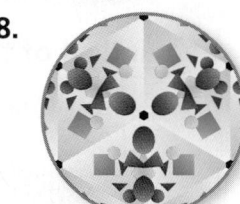

INDEPENDENT PRACTICE

See Example 1   Determine whether each dashed line appears to be a line of symmetry.

9.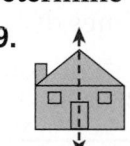

10.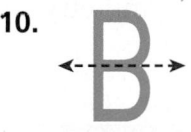

11.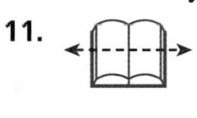

See Example 2   Find all of the lines of symmetry in each regular polygon.

12.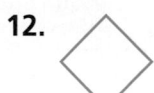

13.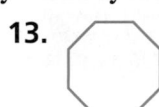

14.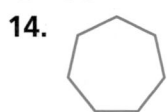

See Example 3   Find all of the lines of symmetry in each object.

15.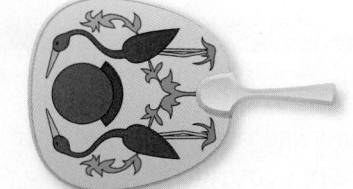

16.

PRACTICE AND PROBLEM SOLVING

Extra Practice
See page 730.

17. How many lines of symmetry does an equilateral triangle have? an isosceles triangle? a scalene triangle? Draw diagrams to support your answer.

Many cultures play music on unique instruments. You might hear the sun drum or turtle drum in Native American music. In music made by people from the Appalachian Mountains, you might hear the strains of a dulcimer. The photo shows young musicians playing sitars, instruments heard in north Indian classical music.

18. Determine whether the dashed line in each drawing is a line of symmetry.

   a.
   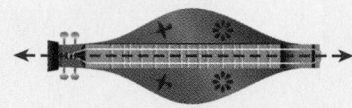

   b.
   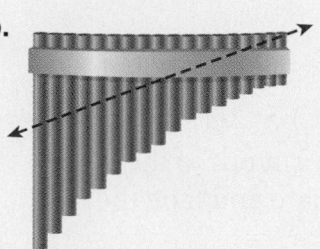

19. ✍ **Write About It** The turtle drum is a regular octagon. How can you find all of the lines of symmetry in a regular polygon?

20. ⭐ **Challenge** A student drew a drum in the shape of an octagon on a grid. What are the coordinates of the vertices of the unfolded half of the drum drawing if the fold shown is a line of symmetry?

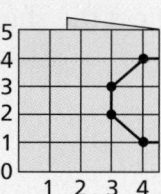

TEST PREP and Spiral Review

21. **Multiple Choice** How many lines of symmetry are in a rectangle that is NOT a square?

   Ⓐ 1   Ⓑ 2   Ⓒ 4   Ⓓ 6

22. **Short Response** Draw the lines of symmetry in the figure.

Compare. Write <, >, or =. (Lesson 1-1)

23. 4,897,204 ☐ 4,895,190

24. 133,099,588 ☐ 133,099,600

Find each sum or difference. (Lesson 3-3)

25. 30 − 5.32

26. 80.37 + 15.125

27. 100 − 25.65

28. 200.6 + 62.78

Create Tessellations

Use with Lesson 8-11

go.hrw.com
Lab Resources Online
KEYWORD: MR7 Lab8

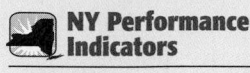
NY Performance Indicators
6.RP.5, 6.R.1, 6.R.5

A repeating arrangement of one or more shapes that completely covers a plane, with no gaps or overlaps, is called a *tessellation*. You can make your own tessellations using paper, scissors, and tape.

Activity

1 Start with a square.

Use scissors to cut out a shape from one side of the square.

Translate the shape you cut out to the opposite side of the square and tape the two pieces together.

Trace this new shape to form at least two rows of a tessellation. You will need to translate, rotate, or reflect the shape.

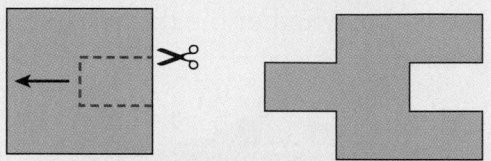

2 Start again with a square.

Use scissors to cut out shapes and move them to the opposite sides of the square.

Trace this new shape to form at least two rows of a tessellation. You will need to translate, rotate, or reflect the shape.

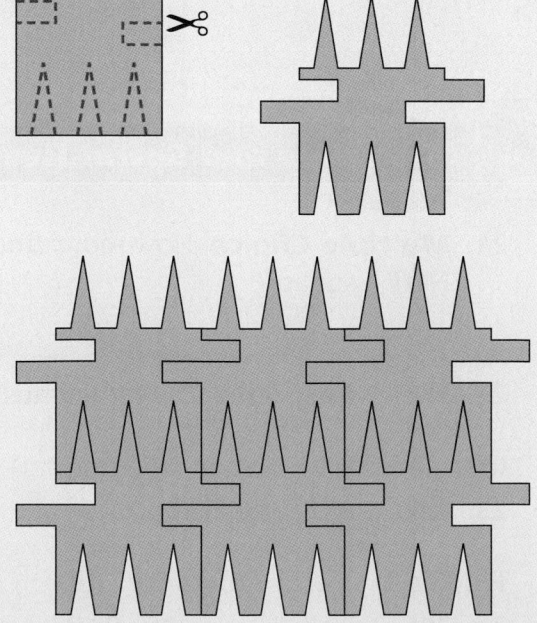

3 You can base a tessellating shape on other polygons.

Try starting with a hexagon.

Use scissors to cut out a shape from one side of the hexagon. Translate the shape to the opposite side of the hexagon.

Try repeating these steps on other sides of the hexagon.

Trace the new shape to form a tessellation. You will need to translate, rotate, or reflect the shape.

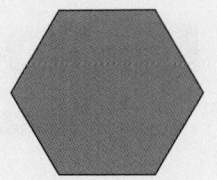 

Think and Discuss

1. Tell whether you can make a tessellation out of circles.

2. Tell whether any polygon can make a tessellation.

Try This

Make each tessellation shape described. Then form two rows of a tessellation.

1.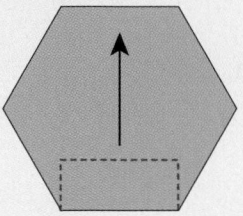

2.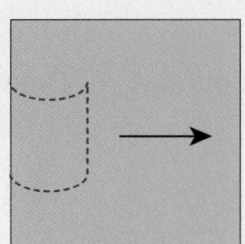

3.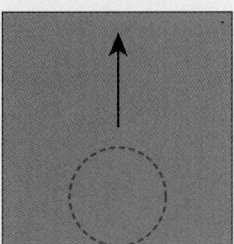

Tell whether each shape can be used to form a tessellation.

4.

5.

6.

7. Cut out a polygon, and then change it by cutting out a part of one side. Translate the cut-out part to the opposite side. Can your shape form a tessellation? Make a drawing to show your answer.

READY TO GO ON?

Quiz for Lessons 8-9 Through 8-11

✓ **8-9** **Congruence**

Decide whether the figures in each pair are congruent. If not, explain.

1.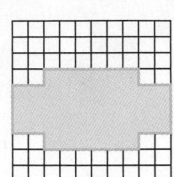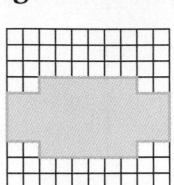

2.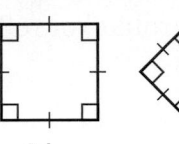

3. Marcus needs a lid for his box. Which lid should he buy?

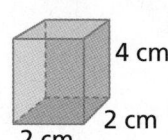 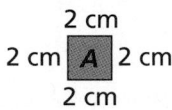 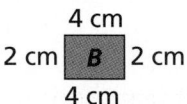 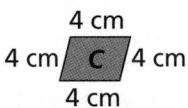

✓ **8-10** **Transformations**

Tell whether each is a translation, rotation, or reflection.

4.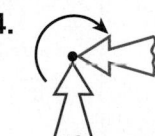

5.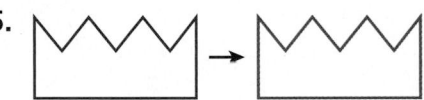

Draw each transformation.

6. Draw a 180° clockwise rotation about the point.

7. Draw a translation.

✓ **8-11** **Line Symmetry**

Determine whether each dashed line appears to be a line of symmetry.

8.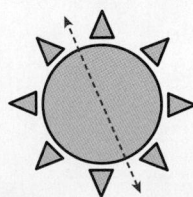

9.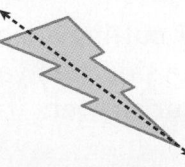

10.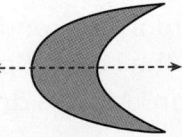

Tonya's Tiles Tonya makes and sells ceramic tiles in the shapes shown at right. She is creating a database that includes information about the tiles.

1. The database includes a description of each tile. Describe each tile by classifying its shape as specifically as possible.

2. The database also includes information about symmetry. Give the number of lines of symmetry for each tile.

3. Tonya wants to provide information about the angles in some of the tiles. In tile G, the two acute angles have the same measure. What is the measure of each acute angle? Explain.

4. Tile C is a regular polygon. What is the measure of each of its angles? Explain how you know the answer.

5. A customer wants to use tiles A and B to create a long strip with the following pattern.

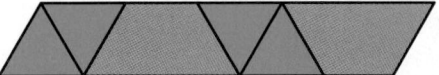

Draw the next five tiles in the pattern.

6. The customer wants the top and bottom edges of the strip to each be 25 inches long. How many of each type of tile will the customer need?

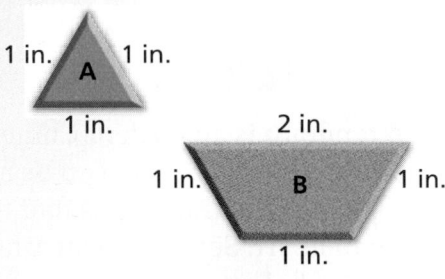

1 in.   1 in.
A
1 in.

2 in.
1 in.   **B**   1 in.
1 in.

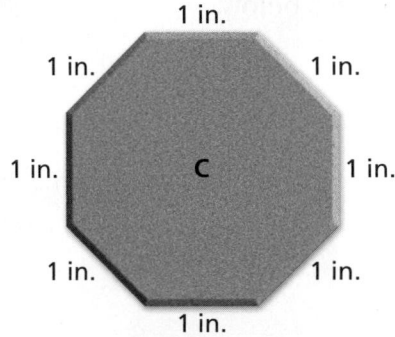

1 in.
1 in.   1 in.
1 in.   **C**   1 in.
1 in.   1 in.
1 in.

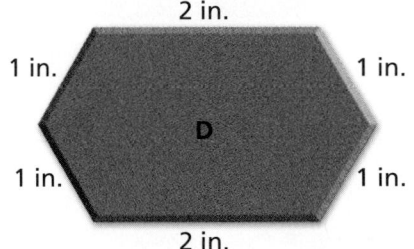

2 in.
1 in.   1 in.
D
1 in.   1 in.
2 in.

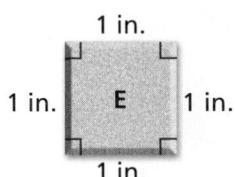

1 in.
1 in.   **E**   1 in.
1 in.

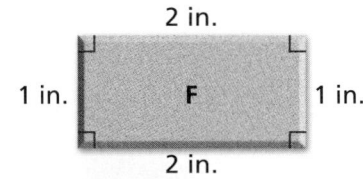

2 in.
1 in.   **F**   1 in.
2 in.

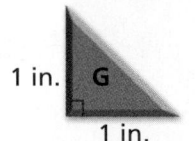

1 in.   **G**
1 in.

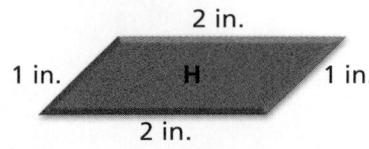

2 in.
1 in.   **H**   1 in.
2 in.

Game Time

Tangrams

A tangram is an ancient Chinese puzzle. The seven shapes that make this square can be arranged to make many other figures. Copy the shapes that make this square, and then cut them apart. See if you can arrange the pieces to make the figures below.

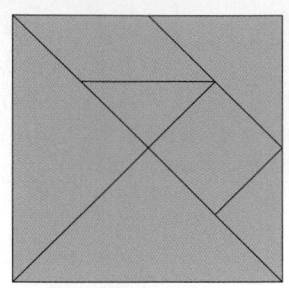

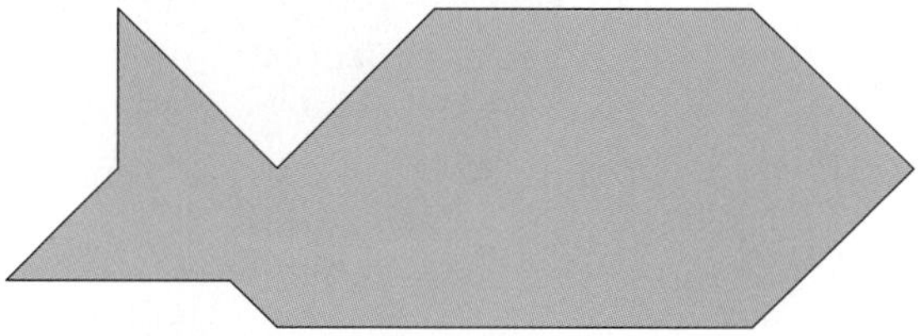

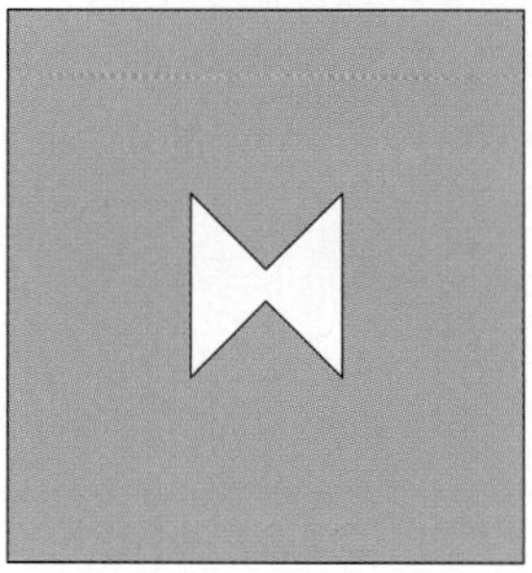

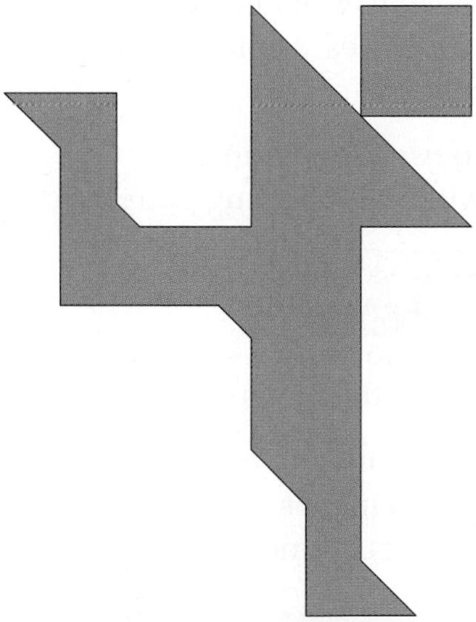

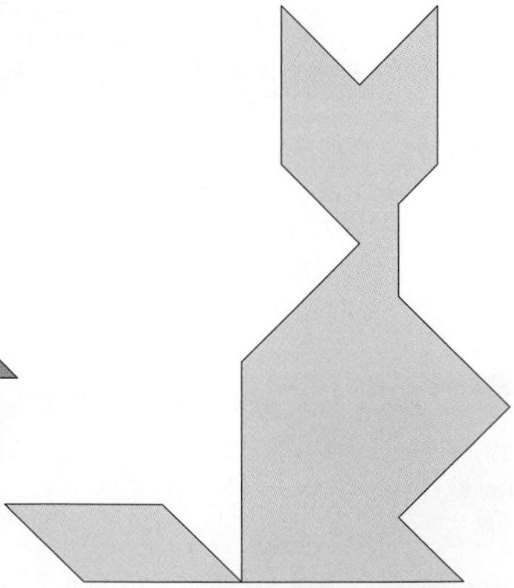

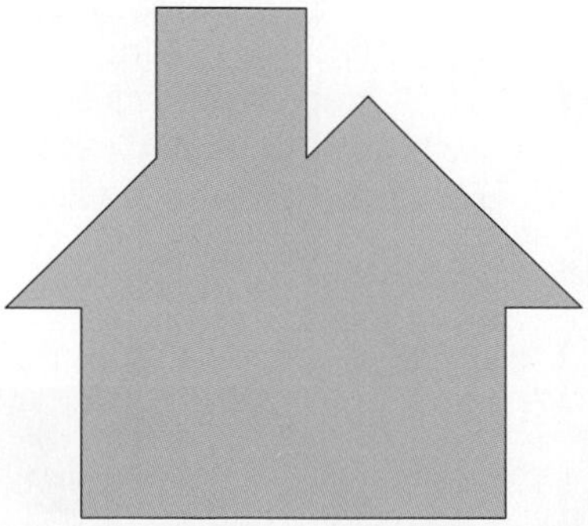

A complete copy of Tangram puzzle pieces is available online.

go.hrw.com
Game Time Extra
KEYWORD: MR7 Games

Materials
- gift bag
- scissors
- tape
- white paper
- card stock
- glue
- markers

PROJECT **Geometry Grab Bag**

Use a recycled gift bag to make a journal for your geometry notes.

Directions

1 Cut away the sides and bottom of the bag. This will leave two rectangles with handles attached. **Figure A**

2 Place the two halves of the bag face down and tape them together as shown, leaving a small space between them. This will form the covers of your journal. **Figure B**

3 Cut several sheets of white paper and the card stock so that they are all the same size and slightly smaller than the covers of the journal. Staple them together, with a piece of card stock on the top and bottom of the stack. **Figure C**

4 Glue the top piece of card stock to the inside front cover. Glue the bottom piece of card stock to the inside back cover.

Taking Note of the Math

Write the number and title of the chapter on the front of the journal. Then use the pages of the journal to take notes on angles, polygons, and transformations.

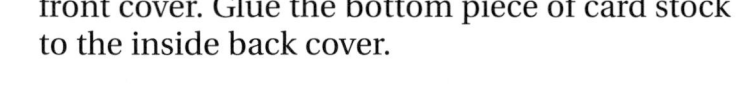

Vocabulary

acute angle 421	obtuse triangle 437	right triangle 437
acute triangle 437	parallel lines 428	rotation 459
adjacent angles 424	parallelogram 442	scalene triangle 438
angle 420	perpendicular lines 428	skew lines 428
complementary angles ..425	plane 416	square 442
congruent 424	point 416	straight angle 421
equilateral triangle 438	polygon 446	supplementary angles ..425
isosceles triangle 438	quadrilateral 442	transformation 459
line 436	ray 417	translation 459
line of reflection 459	rectangle 442	trapezoid 442
line of symmetry 464	reflection 459	vertex 420
line segment 417	regular polygon 446	vertical angles 424
line symmetry 464	rhombus 442	
obtuse angle 421	right angle 421	

Complete the sentences below with vocabulary words from the list above.

1. A quadrilateral with exactly two parallel sides is called a(n) ___?___.

2. A(n) ___?___ is a closed plane figure formed by three or more line segments.

8-1 Building Blocks of Geometry (pp. 416–419)

6.CM.10

E X A M P L E

■ Use the diagram.

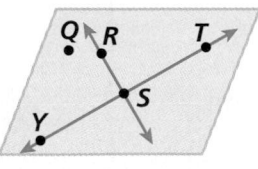

Name a line. $\overleftrightarrow{RS}$
Name a line segment. $\overline{ST}$

EXERCISES

Use the diagram.

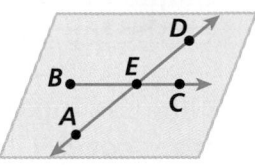

3. Name two lines.

8-2 Measuring and Classifying Angles (pp. 420–423)

6.CN.8

E X A M P L E

■ Classify each angle as acute, right, obtuse, or straight.

$m\angle A = 80°$
$80° < 90°$, so $\angle A$ is acute.

EXERCISES

Classify each angle as acute, right, obtuse, or straight.

4. $m\angle x = 60°$ **5.** $m\angle x = 100°$
6. $m\angle x = 45°$ **7.** $m\angle x = 180°$

8-3 Angle Relationships (pp. 424–427)

5.A.2, 5.A.5

EXAMPLE

■ Find the unknown angle measure.

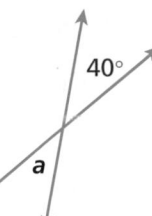

$m\angle a = 40°$ *Vertical angles are congruent.*

EXERCISES

Find each unknown angle measure.

8.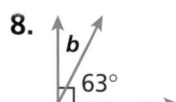

9.

8-4 Classifying Lines (pp. 428–431)

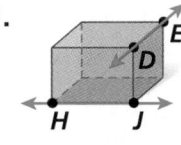
6.CN.6

EXAMPLE

■ Classify each pair of lines.

The red lines are parallel.
The blue lines are perpendicular.

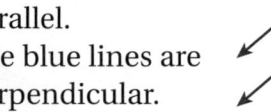

EXERCISES

Classify each pair of lines.

10.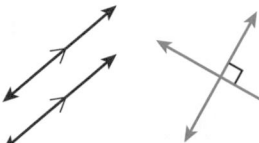

11.

8-5 Triangles (pp. 437–440)

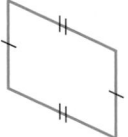
5.A.2, 5.A.5

EXAMPLE

■ Classify the triangle using the given information.

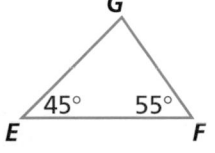

$m\angle G + 45° + 55° = 180°$
$m\angle G = 80°$, so $\triangle EFG$ is an acute triangle.

EXERCISES

Classify the triangle using the given information.

12.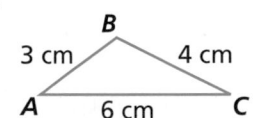

8-6 Quadrilaterals (pp. 442–445)

6.RP.2

EXAMPLE

■ Give the most exact name for the figure.

The most exact name is rectangle.

EXERCISES

Give the most exact name for the figure.

13.

8-7 Polygons (pp. 446–449)

6.PS.15

EXAMPLE

■ Name the polygon and tell whether it appears to be regular or not regular.

It is a regular octagon.

EXERCISES

Name each polygon and tell whether it appears to be regular or not regular.

14.

15.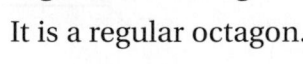

Study Guide: Review

8-8 Geometric Patterns (pp. 450–453)

6.PS.14

EXAMPLE

■ Identify a possible pattern. Use the pattern to draw the missing figure.

 ?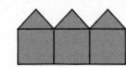

The missing figure might be .

EXERCISES

Identify a possible pattern. Use the pattern to draw the missing figure.

16. 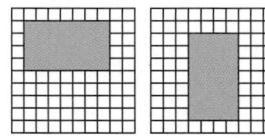 ?

8-9 Congruence (pp. 456–458)

6.RP.6

EXAMPLE

■ Decide whether the figures are congruent. If not, explain.

These figures are congruent.

EXERCISES

Decide whether the figures in each pair are congruent. If not, explain.

17.   18.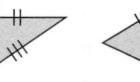

8-10 Transformations (pp. 459–462)

6.CM.10

EXAMPLE

■ Tell whether the transformation is a translation, rotation, or reflection.

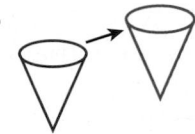

The transformation is a reflection.

■ Draw the transformation.

Draw a horizontal reflection.

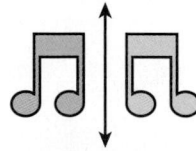

EXERCISES

Tell whether the transformation is a translation, rotation, or reflection.

19.

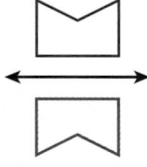

Draw each transformation.

20. Draw a translation.

21. Draw a 90° clockwise rotation about the point.

8-11 Line Symmetry (pp. 464–467)

6.R.5

EXAMPLE

■ Determine whether the dashed line appears to be a line of symmetry.

The line appears to be a line of symmetry.

EXERCISES

Determine whether the dashed line appears to be a line of symmetry.

22.

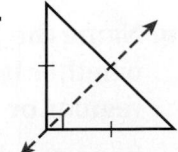

CHAPTER TEST

Classify each pair of angles or lines.

1.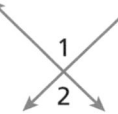

2.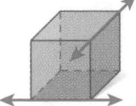

3.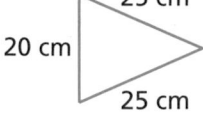

Classify the triangles by angle and side measures.

4.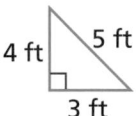

5.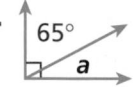

6.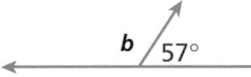

Find the unknown angle measure.

7.

8.

9.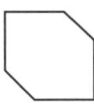

10. Triangle *ABC* has sides of equal length. The measure of $\angle A$ is 60°, and the measure of $\angle B$ is 60°. What is the measure of $\angle C$? Classify the triangle based on the measures of the angles and lengths of the sides.

Draw each transformation.

11. Reflect across the line.

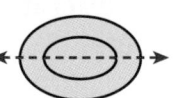

12. Rotate 270° clockwise about the point.

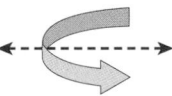

13. Translate $\frac{3}{4}$ in. right.

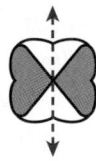

Determine whether each dashed line appears to be a line of symmetry.

14.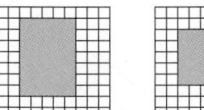

15.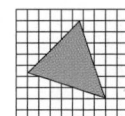

16.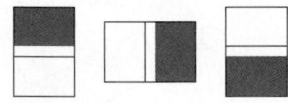

Decide whether the figures in each pair are congruent. If not, explain.

17.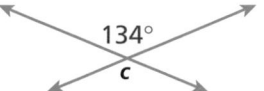

18.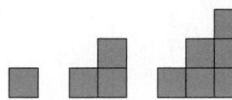

Identify a possible pattern. Use your pattern to draw the next figure.

19.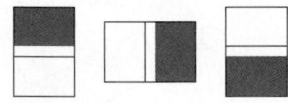

20.

Chapter Test

NEW YORK TEST PREP

Cumulative Assessment, Chapters 1–8

Multiple Choice

1. Which of the following is an example of an obtuse angle?

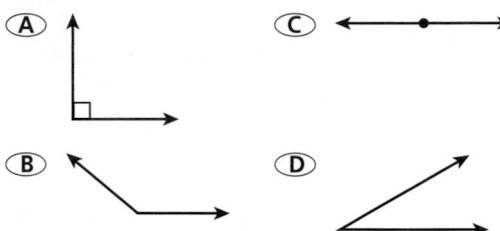

2. Hillary buys 6 flower bouquets for table decorations. Each bouquet costs $16. The sales tax is 6.5%. What is the total cost of her purchase?

   (F) $17.03   (H) $101.70

   (G) $95.94   (J) $102.24

3. Two angles are complementary. If the measure of one angle is 36°, what is the measure of the second angle?

   (A) 36°   (C) 64°

   (B) 54°   (D) 144°

4. Steve, Ashley, and Jeremy work at the same restaurant. Steve works every 4 days. Ashley works every 6 days. Jeremy works every 3 days. If on May 1 they are all working at the restaurant, what is the next date that the three of them will work together?

   (F) May 6   (H) May 18

   (G) May 12   (J) May 24

5. Terri is $60\frac{1}{2}$ inches tall. Steve is $65\frac{1}{4}$ inches tall. What is the difference, in inches, in their heights?

   (A) $4\frac{1}{4}$ (C) $4\frac{3}{4}$

   (B) $4\frac{1}{2}$ (D) $5\frac{1}{4}$

6. In the figure below, which of the following angle pairs are NOT adjacent?

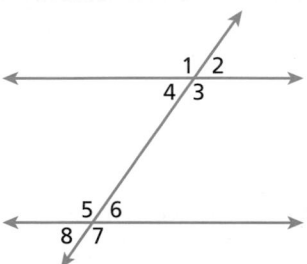

   (F) ∠1 and ∠2   (H) ∠1 and ∠3

   (G) ∠5 and ∠8   (J) ∠6 and ∠7

7. Reggie is a long-distance runner. His daily $2\frac{1}{2}$-hour practice is divided evenly into three areas: warm-up, running, and cool-down. How many minutes total does Reggie spend warming up and cooling down each day at practice?

   (A) 100 min   (C) 60 min

   (B) 75 min   (D) 50 min

8. The arrow is being reflected over the black line. Which of the following correctly shows the arrow after it is reflected over the black line?

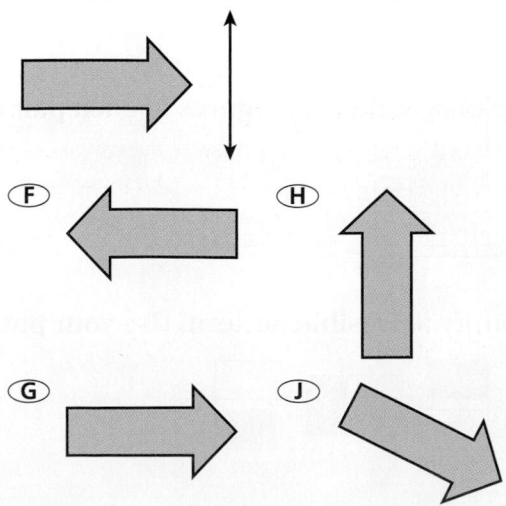

9. Shown below is a map of specific areas at Boone Park. Which of the following is located at the point (7, 6) on the map?

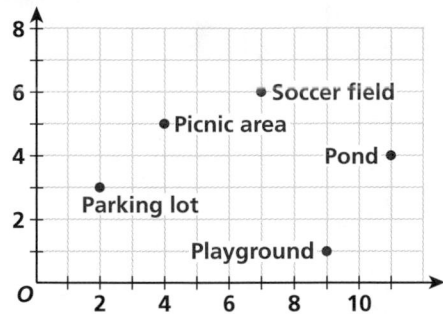

Ⓐ Playground Ⓒ Pond

Ⓑ Parking lot Ⓓ Soccer field

10. What is the most descriptive name for the figure below?

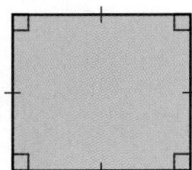

Ⓕ Rhombus Ⓗ Square

Ⓖ Rectangle Ⓙ Parallelogram

After you answer a question, reread it. This will help ensure that you have answered all parts of the question.

11. The distance around a square flower box is 128.4 inches. How many inches long is one side of the flower box?

Ⓐ 32.1 Ⓒ 64.2

Ⓑ 42.8 Ⓓ 256.8

12. There are 120 students trying out for the school play. Only 5% of those trying out will have a speaking part. Write this percent as a fraction in lowest terms.

Ⓕ $\frac{6}{120}$ Ⓗ $\frac{120}{6}$

Ⓖ $\frac{1}{20}$ Ⓙ 20

Short Response

13. Identify the figure shown.

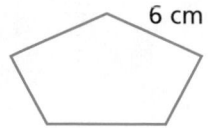

Draw a figure that is congruent to this figure. Explain why your figure is congruent to the given figure.

14. The table shows ten distances hit by a baseball player.

Distances (ft)				
334	360	350	343	330
320	265	327	335	270

Is the mean distance of this player's hits more than or less than the median distance? Explain how you found your answer.

15. Triangle JKL is a right triangle.

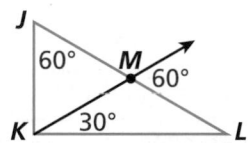

a. What are the angle measurements of ∠JKM, ∠KLM, ∠KML, and ∠KMJ?

b. Name two other triangles. Classify these triangles by their angles. Explain your classifications.

Extended Response

16. A student draws a trapezoid on a coordinate grid. The coordinates are A (3, 1), B (2, 2), C (2, 3), and D (3, 4).

a. Plot these points on a grid and connect the points.

b. Draw a line that passes through points A and D. Reflect the trapezoid over that line, label the points on the new trapezoid, and give the new coordinates.

c. What new plane figure is created? Does this new figure have line symmetry? Explain your answer.

Problem Solving on Location

NEW YORK

Ellis Island

From 1892 to 1954, Ellis Island, located in New York Harbor, was the first stop for many immigrants to the United States. More than 40 percent of all U.S. citizens alive today have an ancestor who came through Ellis Island as an immigrant.

More than 10,700,000 immigrants passed through Ellis Island in its first 40 years of operation. The table shows the number of immigrants from the two countries that had the greatest number of people come through Ellis Island.

Number of Italian and Russian Immigrants Through Ellis Island in its First 40 Years	
Country	**Number of Immigrants**
Italy	2,500,000
Russia	1,900,000

For 1–4, use the table.

1. About what percent of the total number of immigrants came from Italy?

2. About what percent of the total number of immigrants came from Russia?

3. During this period, about 500,000 immigrants came to Ellis Island from Ireland. Estimate the ratio of the immigrants that came from Ireland to the total number of immigrants that came during this period.

4. Estimate the ratio of the immigrants that came from a country other than Italy or Russia during the 40-year period to the total number of immigrants that came during the same time.

The Statue of Liberty

As immigrants sailed toward New York Harbor, their first sight in the distance was the Statue of Liberty. A gift from France in 1886, the statue stands directly across from Ellis Island in New York Harbor.

1. If you visit the Statue of Liberty, you can climb 22 stories to the crown. In all, you would walk up 354 steps. Find the number of steps per story. Round your answer to the nearest whole number.

2. To get to the Statue of Liberty, you take a 2-mile ferry ride from Battery Park in New York City. If the ferry ride takes 15 minutes, what is your speed in miles per hour?

Models of the Statue of Liberty are popular souvenirs in New York. Suppose the scale of a particular model is 1 in:8 ft. The actual dimensions of the statue are given in the table.

For 3–6, use the table.

3. Explain what the scale 1 in:8 ft means.

4. What is the length of the model statue's index finger?

5. What is the length of the model's hand?

6. What is the distance from the bottom of the model's base to the tip of its torch?

Statue of Liberty	
Height of Base	154 ft
Height of Statue	151 ft
Length of Hand	16.5 ft
Length of Index Finger	8 ft

Measurement and Geometry

NEW YORK TEST PREP

go.hrw.com
Chapter Project Online
KEYWORD: MR7 Ch9

Career *Mathematician*

Some mathematicians apply their knowledge in areas such as airplane scheduling, medical safety, and automobile and industrial research. Other mathematicians prefer to study the concepts behind mathematics.

For hundreds of years, mathematicians have studied the relationship between the circumference and the diameter of a circle. This ratio is called *pi* and is represented by the Greek letter π.

ARE YOU READY?

✓ Vocabulary

Choose the best term from the list to complete each sentence.

1. If you find how heavy an object is, you are finding the __?__.

2. A __?__ is used to measure an angle.

3. If you find the amount a container can hold when filled, you are finding the __?__ of the container.

4. A __?__ is an equation that shows two equivalent ratios.

5. A parallelogram with four right angles is a __?__.

capacity
length
proportion
protractor
rectangle
temperature
weight

Complete these exercises to review skills you will need for this chapter.

✓ Write and Read Decimals

Write each decimal in standard form.

6. 12 and 4 tenths   7. 150 and 18 hundredths   8. 1 thousand, 60 and 5 tenths

✓ Simplify Fractions

Write each fraction in simplest form.

9. $\dfrac{8}{12}$ 10. $\dfrac{4}{20}$ 11. $\dfrac{6}{8}$ 12. $\dfrac{8}{16}$

✓ Write Ratios

Write each ratio three different ways.

13. Hearts to rectangles

14. Rectangles to circles

15. Triangles to squares

16. Hexagons to triangles

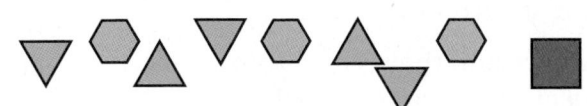

✓ Solve Proportions

Solve for n.

17. $\dfrac{2}{n} = \dfrac{4}{10}$ 18. $\dfrac{3}{8} = \dfrac{6}{n}$ 19. $\dfrac{n}{7} = \dfrac{8}{14}$ 20. $\dfrac{5}{9} = \dfrac{n}{18}$

Study Guide: Preview

Where You've Been

Previously, you

- performed simple conversions within the metric system.

- used angle measurements to classify angles.

- classified polygons according to their sides.

In This Chapter

You will study

- converting measures within the same measurement system.

- identifying relationships involving angles in triangles and quadrilaterals.

- solving problems involving perimeter.

- describing the relationship between the radius, diameter, and circumference of a circle.

Where You're Going

You can use the skills learned in this chapter

- to understand the relationship between the perimeter and the area of a polygon.

- to determine how much fencing to buy to enclose an animal pen or garden.

Key Vocabulary/Vocabulario

center of a circle	centro (de un círculo)
circle	círculo
circumference	circunferencia
customary system	sistema usual de medidas
diameter	diámetro
metric system	sistema métrico
perimeter	perímetro
pi	*pi*
radius	radio

Vocabulary Connections

To become familiar with some of the vocabulary terms in the chapter, consider the following. You may refer to the chapter, the glossary, or a dictionary if you like.

1. The word *perimeter* has the prefix *peri-*, which means "all around or surrounding," and the root *meter*, which is the basic unit of length in the metric system. What do you think the **perimeter** of an object is?

2. The word *circumference* has the prefix *circum-*, which means "around a circle." What do you think you will measure if you find the **circumference** of a circle?

3. The word *radius* is related to the word *radiate*, which means to move outward in all directions from the center. What do you think the **radius** of a circle is?

4. The word *diameter* has the prefix *dia-*, which means "across." What do you think you will measure if you find the **diameter** of a circle?

Study Strategy: Use Multiple Representations

Math concepts can be explained using multiple representations. As you study, pay attention to any tables, lists, graphs, diagrams, symbols, and words used to describe a concept.

From Lesson 8-4

In this example, the concept of classifying lines is explained using words, diagrams, symbols, and examples.

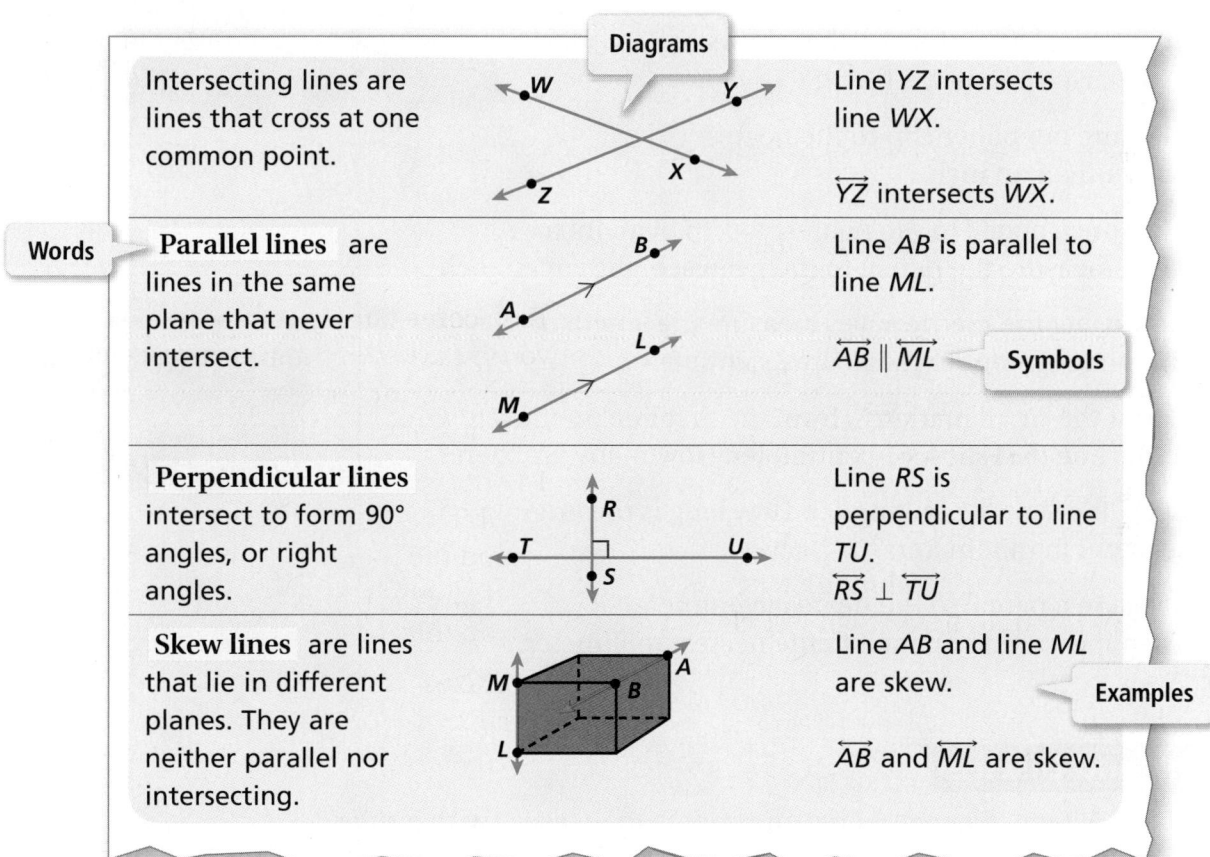

Try This

1. Classify one of the types of triangles in Lesson 8-5 using the four different representations shown above.

2. Review your notes from the previous chapter. Which different representations did you use to explain how to classify lines? Which representation do you prefer? Why?

Select and Use Appropriate Measuring Tools

Use with Lessons 9-1 and 9-2

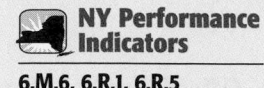
NY Performance Indicators
6.M.6, 6.R.1, 6.R.5

go.hrw.com
Lab Resources Online
KEYWORD: MR7 Lab9

Activity 1

1 Measure the length of a paper clip to the nearest inch. Select an inch or millimeter ruler to measure the length of the paper clip.

2 Count the small markings from the first line on the left to the line that shows 1 inch. How many are there?

Measure the paper clip to the nearest sixteenth of an inch.

3 Measure a pencil to the nearest fourth of an inch. Then measure the pencil to the nearest eighth of an inch.

4 Now using the metric ruler, measure the length of this line segment to the nearest centimeter.

5 Count the small markings from the first line on the left to the line that shows 1 centimeter. How many are there?

6 Each line shows 1 millimeter. How long is the line segment in millimeters?

7 Measure a pencil to the nearest centimeter. Then measure the pencil to the nearest millimeter.

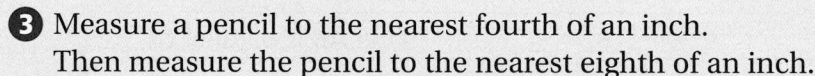

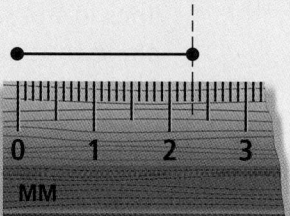

Think and Discuss

1. Name 5 items that would be appropriate to measure with a ruler.

2. *Precision* is the level of detail an instrument can measure. The smaller the unit of measure on the instrument, the more precise the measurement will be. Is the measurement in **1** or **2** more precise? Explain.

Try This

Use a ruler to measure each object to the nearest sixteenth of an inch and to the nearest millimeter.

1. your pinky
2. your desktop
3. your shoe

Activity 2

1 Find the weight of a bunch of grapes.
Use a customary or metric scale to weigh the grapes.

What is the weight of the grapes in pounds?

What is the weight of the grapes in kilograms?

Pounds

Kilograms

2 What is the weight of your math book in pounds and in kilograms?

Think and Discuss

1. Which is heavier, 1 pound of grapes or 1 kilogram of grapes?

Try This

Use a scale to measure each object in pounds and kilograms.

1. your shoe   **2.** 5 pencils   **3.** a tissue box

Activity 3

1 Use a measuring cup that shows fluid ounces and milliliters. Fill the cup with water up to the 8 fluid ounces mark. About how many milliliters is this?

2 Fill a measuring cup with 150 milliliters of water. About how many fluid ounces is this?

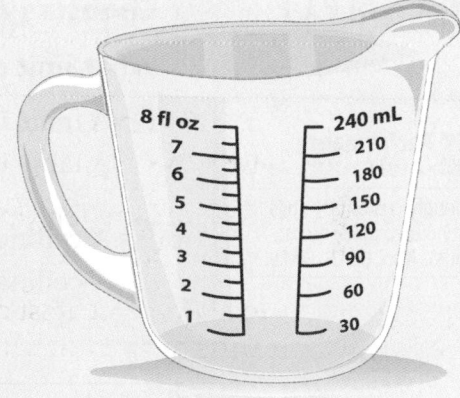

Think and Discuss

1. Explain how you can use a measuring cup and a metric scale to find the mass of 2 cups of water.

2. About how many milliliters are in 2 cups?

Try This

1. Place 25 tablespoons of water in a measuring cup. How many fluid ounces is this? how many milliliters?

2. Find the mass of 2 cups of water.

9-1 Understanding Customary Units of Measure

Learn to understand and select appropriate customary units of measure.

Vocabulary

customary system

If you do not have an instrument, such as a ruler, scale, or measuring cup, you can estimate the length, weight, and capacity of an object by using a benchmark.

The **customary system** is the measurement system often used in the United States. It includes units of measurement for length, weight, and capacity.

Customary Units of Length		
Unit	Abbreviation	Benchmark
Inch	in.	Width of your thumb
Foot	ft	Distance from your elbow to your wrist
Yard	yd	Width of a classroom door
Mile	mi	Total length of 18 football fields

EXAMPLE 1 Choosing Appropriate Units of Length

What unit of measure provides the best estimate? Explain.

A A table is about 4 ___?___ long.
A table is about 4 ft long.

Think: The length of a table is about 4 times the distance from your elbow to your wrist.

NY Performance Indicators

6.M.2 Identify customary units of capacity (cups, pints, quarts, and gallons). Also, 6.M.6, 6.M.9.

B A ceiling is about 3 ___?___ high.
A ceiling is about 3 yd high.

Think: The height of a ceiling is about 3 times the width of a classroom door.

Customary Units of Weight		
Unit	Abbreviation	Benchmark
Ounce	oz	A slice of bread
Pound	lb	A loaf of bread
Ton	T	A small car

EXAMPLE 2 Choosing Appropriate Units of Weight

What unit of measure provides the best estimate? Explain.

A A female elephant can weigh up to 4 ___?___.

Think: An elephant has a weight of about 4 small cars.

A female elephant can weigh up to 4 T.

What unit of measure provides the best estimate? Explain.

B A remote control
weighs about 5 ___?___ .

Think: A remote control has a weight of about 5 slices of bread.

A remote control weighs about 5 oz.

Capacity deals with volume, or the amount a container can hold.

Customary Units of Capacity		
Unit	**Abbreviation**	**Benchmark**
Fluid Ounce	fl oz	A spoonful
Cup	c	A glass of juice
Pint	pt	A small bottle of salad dressing
Quart	qt	A small container of paint
Gallon	gal	A large container of milk

EXAMPLE 3 **Choosing Appropriate Units of Capacity**

What unit of measure provides the best estimate? Explain.

A bathtub holds about
50 ___?___ of water.

Think: A bathtub holds about 50 large containers of milk.

A bathtub holds about 50 gal of water.

Inch rulers are usually separated into sixteenths of an inch.

EXAMPLE 4 **Finding Measurements**

Measure the length of the golf tee to the nearest half, fourth, or eighth inch.

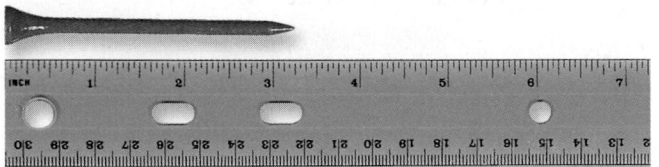

The golf tee is between $3\frac{1}{4}$ in. and $3\frac{3}{8}$ in. It is closer to $3\frac{1}{4}$ in.

The length of the golf tee is about $3\frac{1}{4}$ in.

Think and Discuss

1. **Give an example** of when you might need to estimate the weight of an object.

2. **Give an example** of when you might need to estimate the capacity of a container.

9-1 **Exercises**

go.hrw.com
Homework Help Online
KEYWORD: MR7 9-1
Parent Resources Online
KEYWORD: MR7 Parent

GUIDED PRACTICE

See Example **1** **What unit of measure provides the best estimate? Explain.**

1. A pencil is about 7 ___?___ long.

See Example **2** **2.** A tube of toothpaste weighs about 8 ___?___.

See Example **3** **3.** A swimming pool holds about 20,000 ___?___ of water.

See Example **4** **4.** Measure the length of the key to the nearest half, fourth, or eighth inch.

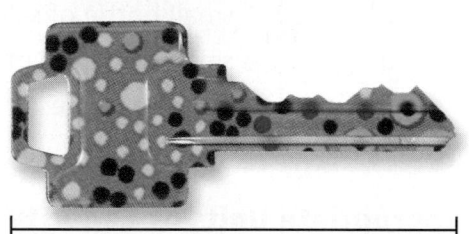

INDEPENDENT PRACTICE

See Example **1** **What unit of measure provides the best estimate? Explain.**

5. The distance from New York City to Boston is about 200 ___?___.

See Example **2** **6.** A small dog weighs about 12 ___?___.

See Example **3** **7.** A pot for cooking soup holds about 10 ___?___ of water.

See Example **4** **8.** Measure the length of the green bean to the nearest half, fourth, or eighth inch.

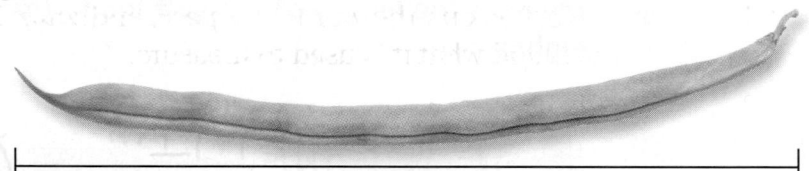

PRACTICE AND PROBLEM SOLVING

Extra Practice
See page 731.

Which unit of measure would you use for each? Justify your answer.

9. the height of a flagpole

10. the width of a CD case

11. the capacity of a car's gas tank

12. the capacity of a baby's bottle

13. the weight of an egg

14. the weight of a chair

Use benchmarks to estimate each measure.

15. the width of your math textbook

16. the width of an armchair

17. the capacity of a flower pot

18. the weight of an alarm clock

19. Critical Thinking When would you choose to measure to the nearest eighth inch rather than the nearest fourth inch?

Find the weight of the object to the nearest half, fourth, or eighth of a pound.

20.

21.

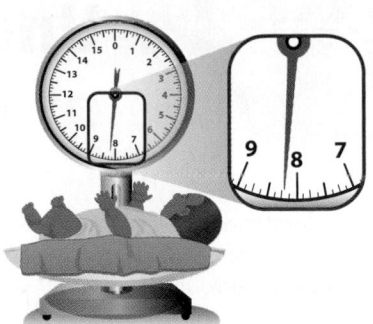

22. History The early Saxon kings of England wore a sash around their waist that they used as a benchmark for measuring length. The name of the sash eventually became the name of one of the customary units of length. What unit of length did the sash represent: the inch, foot, yard, or mile? Explain.

Find how much liquid is in each container to the nearest half, fourth, or eighth of a cup or quart.

23.

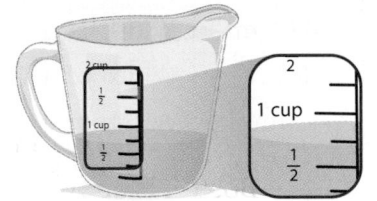

24.

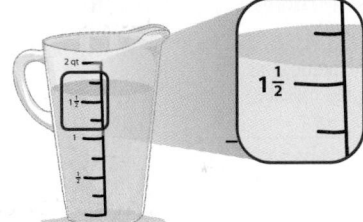

 25. Write a Problem Write a problem that can be answered using a pen as a benchmark.

 26. Write About It Make up your own personal benchmarks for an inch, a cup, and a pound.

 27. Challenge Look up the words *rod, peck,* and *dram* in a dictionary. Tell what each one is and what it is used to measure.

TEST PREP and Spiral Review

28. Multiple Choice Which is the best estimate for the width of a classroom?

   Ⓐ 30 in.   Ⓑ 30 ft   Ⓒ 30 yd   Ⓓ 30 mi

29. Multiple Choice Madison needs to buy a turkey to feed 12 people. What weight turkey should she buy?

   Ⓕ 16 lb   Ⓖ 16 oz   Ⓗ 16 c   Ⓘ 16 T

List all the factors of each number. (Lesson 4-2)

30. 24   **31.** 45   **32.** 56   **33.** 80

Two angles of a triangle are given. Classify the triangle. (Lesson 8-5)

34. 55°, 35°   **35.** 18°, 82°   **36.** 47°, 26°   **37.** 95°, 45°

9-2 Understanding Metric Units of Measure

Learn to understand and select appropriate metric units of measure.

Vocabulary

metric system

NY Performance Indicators

6.M.4 Identify metric units of capacity (liter and milliliter). Also, 6.M.6, 6.M.9.

The **metric system** of measurement is used almost everywhere in the world. Its advantage over the customary system is that all metric units are related by the decimal system.

The shortest Olympic track race is 100 meters. Use the length of your classroom as a benchmark. A classroom is about 10 meters long, so a 100-meter race is about the length of 10 classrooms.

Metric Units of Length

Unit	Abbreviation	Relation to a Meter	Benchmark
Millimeter	mm	0.001 m	Thickness of a dime
Centimeter	cm	0.01 m	Width of a fingernail
Decimeter	dm	0.1 m	Width of a CD case
Meter	m	1 m	Width of a single bed
Kilometer	km	1,000 m	Distance around a city block

EXAMPLE 1 Choosing Appropriate Units of Length

What unit of measure provides the best estimate? Explain.

A A TV remote control is about 19 ___?___ long.

Think: A TV remote control is about 19 times the width of a fingernail.

A TV remote control is about 19 cm long.

B A school auditorium is about 40 ___?___ long.

Think: An auditorium is about 40 times the width of a single bed.

A school auditorium is about 40 m long.

Metric Units of Mass

Unit	Abbreviation	Relation to a Gram	Benchmark
Milligram	mg	0.001 g	Very small insect
Gram	g	1 g	Large paper clip
Kilogram	kg	1,000 g	Textbook

EXAMPLE 2 Choosing Appropriate Units of Mass

What unit of measure provides the best estimate? Explain.

A sandwich has a mass of about 400 ___?___.

Think: A sandwich has a mass of about 400 paperclips.

A sandwich has a mass of about 400 g.

Metric Units of Capacity			
Unit	Abbreviation	Relation to a Liter	Benchmark
Milliliter	mL	0.001 L	Drop of water
Liter	L	1 L	Blender container

EXAMPLE 3 Choosing Appropriate Units of Capacity

What unit of measure provides the best estimate? Explain.

A bucket has a capacity of about 10 ___?___.

Think: A bucket has a capacity of about 10 blender containers.

A bucket has a capacity of about 10 L.

EXAMPLE 4 Finding Measurements

Measure the length of the toothbrush to the nearest centimeter.

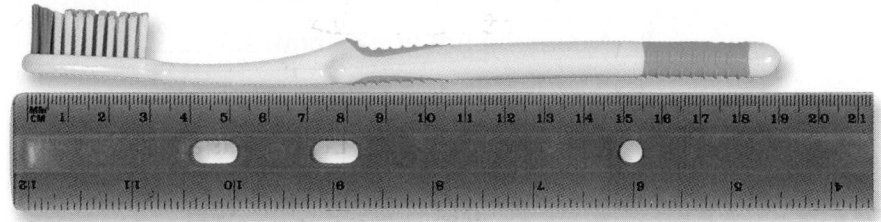

The toothbrush is between 18 and 19 cm. It is closer to 19 cm than 18 cm.

The length of the toothbrush is about 19 cm.

Think and Discuss

1. **Explain** how you would estimate the length of the board in your classroom using the toothbrush in Example 4 as a benchmark.

9-2 Exercises

go.hrw.com
Homework Help Online
KEYWORD: MR7 9-2
Parent Resources Online
KEYWORD: MR7 Parent

GUIDED PRACTICE

See Example **1**   **What unit of measure provides the best estimate? Explain.**

   1. The height of a doorknob from the floor is about 1 ___?___ .

See Example **2**   **2.** A greeting card has a mass of about 28 ___?___ .

See Example **3**   **3.** A kitchen sink holds about 20 ___?___ of water.

   4. A bowl holds about 350 ___?___ of soup.

See Example **4**   **Estimate the length of the party favor to the nearest centimeter.**

5.

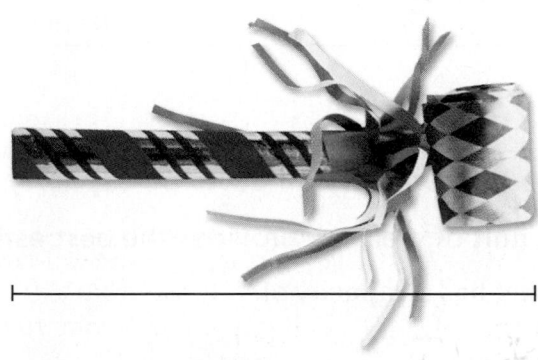

INDEPENDENT PRACTICE

See Example **1**   **What unit of measure provides the best estimate? Explain.**

   6. The width of a desk is about 10 ___?___ .

See Example **2**   **7.** The mass of a packet of sugar is about 3 ___?___ .

See Example **3**   **8.** A bathtub holds about 50 ___?___ of water.

   9. A cooking pot holds about 1.5 ___?___ .

See Example **4**   **Estimate the length of the feather to the nearest centimeter.**

10.

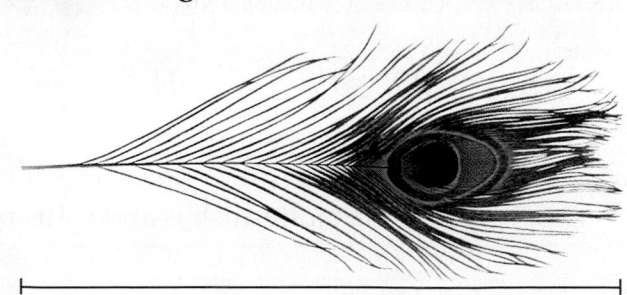

PRACTICE AND PROBLEM SOLVING

Extra Practice
See page 731.

11. Estimation Felipe is estimating the length of his baseball bat using a benchmark. He gets an estimate of about 10 ___?___ . Which benchmark was Felipe most likely using: the width of his fist, the length of his foot, the distance from his elbow to his fingertip, or the length of his baseball cap?

Which unit of measure would you use for each? Justify your answer.

12. the length of a movie screen

13. the length of a walk around a campus

14. the mass of a single flower

15. the mass of a CD case

16. the capacity of a jug

17. the capacity of a thimble

18. Multi-Step A shipment of DVD players contains 8 cartons. Each carton has 6 players in it. A single player weighs 1,500 g. All the players can be unpacked and placed on a shelf in the stockroom. A sign above the shelf reads "Maximum weight 80 ___?___." What is the missing unit of measure on the sign above the shelf?

19. Physics An empty balloon weighs 4.5 g. A filled balloon weighs 5.3 g. Find the mass of the air in the balloon. Does air have mass? Explain.

20. What's the Error? Ellis made a travel brochure for his social studies project. He wrote that the common highway speed in Canada is 8,000 km per hour. What error did Ellis make?

 **21. Write About It** Measure the dimensions of a shoebox and estimate the mass of the box when it contains a pair of shoes. Describe which metric units of measure you used.

22. Challenge Jermaine is trying to limit the amount of fat in his diet to 50 g per day. At breakfast, Jermaine has one serving of milk, two servings of peanut butter, and a serving of apple, which has almost no fat. If his lunch and dinner contain the same amount of fat as his breakfast, is Jermaine likely to meet his goal for the day? Explain.

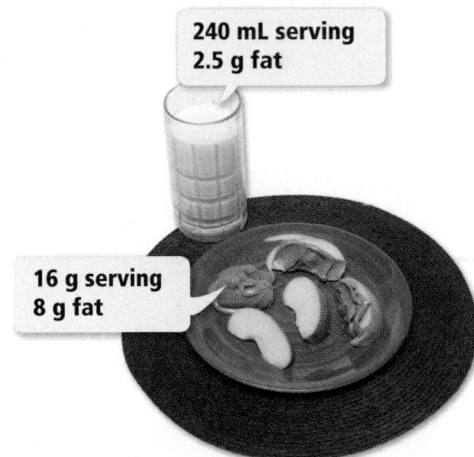

240 mL serving
2.5 g fat

16 g serving
8 g fat

TEST PREP and Spiral Review

23. Multiple Choice Which unit could NOT reasonably be used to measure something involving a home aquarium?

   Ⓐ A liter   Ⓑ A meter   Ⓒ A kilometer   Ⓓ A kilogram

24. Short Response What metric unit of measure provides the best estimate of the width of a bedroom window? Explain your answer.

Find the greatest common factor (GCF) of each set of numbers. (Lesson 4-3)

25. 16 and 24   **26.** 84 and 28   **27.** 48 and 112   **28.** 5, 10, and 105

Find the least common multiple (LCM). (Lesson 5-1)

29. 4 and 9   **30.** 6 and 11   **31.** 15 and 20   **32.** 2, 8, and 10

9-3 Converting Customary Units

Learn to convert customary units of measure.

NY Performance Indicators

6.M.3 Identify equivalent customary units of capacity (cups to pints, pints to quarts, and quarts to gallons). Also, **6.N.27.**

Jacques Freitag is the first athlete to win gold medals at the International Association of Athletic Federations (IAAF) Youth, Junior, and Senior Championships. His personal best in the high jump is over 93 inches. How many feet is this?

You can use the information in the table below to convert one customary unit to another.

Common Customary Measurements		
Length	**Weight**	**Capacity**
1 foot = 12 inch	1 pound = 16 ounces	1 cup = 8 fluid ounces
1 yard = 36 inches	1 ton = 2,000 pounds	1 pint = 2 cups
1 yard = 3 feet		1 quart = 2 pints
1 mile = 5,280 feet		1 quart = 4 cups
1 mile = 1,760 yards		1 gallon = 4 quarts
		1 gallon = 16 cups
		1 gallon = 128 fluid ounces

When you convert one unit of measure to another, you can multiply by a conversion factor.

EXAMPLE **Using a Conversion Factor**

A **Convert 93 inches to feet.**

Set up a conversion factor.

$$93 \text{ in.} \times \frac{1 \text{ ft}}{12 \text{ in.}}$$

$$93 \text{ in.} = 7.75 \text{ ft}$$

Think: inches to feet—1 ft = 12 in., so use $\frac{1 \text{ ft}}{12 \text{ in.}}$.
Multiply 93 in. by the conversion factor.
Cancel the common unit, in.

Caution!

Write the unit you are converting *to* in the numerator and the unit you are converting *from* in the denominator.

B **Convert 2 pounds to ounces.**

Set up a conversion factor.

$$2 \text{ lb} \times \frac{16 \text{ oz}}{1 \text{ lb}} = 32 \text{ oz}$$

$$2 \text{ lb} = 32 \text{ oz}$$

Think: ounces to pounds—16 oz = 1 lb, so use $\frac{16 \text{ oz}}{1 \text{ lb}}$. Multiply 2 lb by the conversion factor. Cancel the common unit, lb.

Another way to convert units is to use proportions.

EXAMPLE 2 Converting Units of Measure by Using Proportions

Convert 48 quarts to gallons.

48 qt = ▧ gal

$$\frac{4 \text{ qt}}{1 \text{ gal}} = \frac{48 \text{ qt}}{x \text{ gal}}$$ *1 gallon is 4 quarts. Write a proportion. Use a variable for the value you are trying to find.*

$4 \cdot x = 1 \cdot 48$ *The cross products are equal.*

$4x = 48$ *Divide both sides by 4 to undo the multiplication.*

$x = 12$

48 qt = 12 gal

EXAMPLE 3 PROBLEM SOLVING APPLICATION

The Washington Monument is about 185 yards tall. This height is almost equal to the length of two football fields. About how many feet is this?

1. Understand the Problem

The **answer** will be the height of the Washington Monument in feet.

List the **important information:**

• The height of the Washington Monument is about 185 yards.

2. Make a Plan

Make a table from the information to show the number of feet in 1, 2, and 3 yards. Then find the number of feet in *n* yards.

3. Solve

Yards	Feet
1	3
2	6
3	9
n	3*n*

Look for a pattern.

1 · 3 = 3

2 · 3 = 6

3 · 3 = 9

n · 3 = 3n

$185 \cdot 3 = 555$ so, the Washington Monument is about 555 ft tall.

4. Look Back

Round 185 to 200. Then multiply by 3.

$200 \cdot 3 = 600$

The answer is reasonable because 555 is close to 600.

Think and Discuss

1. Explain how to set up a proportion to convert miles to yards.

9-3 Exercises

go.hrw.com
Homework Help Online
KEYWORD: MR7 9-3
Parent Resources Online
KEYWORD: MR7 Parent

GUIDED PRACTICE

See Example **1**   Convert.

1. 9 ft = ☐ in.

2. 10 pt = ☐ qt

3. 14,000 lb = ☐ T

4. 5 yd = ☐ ft

5. 24 fl oz = ☐ c

6. 4 lb = ☐ oz

See Example **2**   **7.** 32 qt = ☐ gal

8. 9 lb = ☐ oz

9. 36 in. = ☐ ft

10. 2 yd = ☐ in.

11. 11 qt = ☐ pt

12. 6 T = ☐ lb

See Example **3**   **13. Biology** An adult male of average size normally has about 6 quarts of blood in his body. Approximately how many cups of blood does the average adult male have in his body?

INDEPENDENT PRACTICE

See Example **1**   Convert.

14. 96 oz = ☐ lb

15. 6 c = ☐ fl oz

16. 3 mi = ☐ ft

17. 4,000 lb = ☐ T

18. 6 lb = ☐ oz

19. 3,520 yd = ☐ mi

See Example **2**   **20.** 27 ft = ☐ yd

21. 3 T = ☐ lb

22. 16 qt = ☐ gal

23. 48 oz = ☐ lb

24. 3 yd = ☐ in.

25. 10 pt = ☐ c

See Example **3**   **26. Architecture** The steel used to make the Statue of Liberty weighs about 125 tons. About how many pounds of steel were used to make the Statue of Liberty?

PRACTICE AND PROBLEM SOLVING

Extra Practice
See page 731.

Compare. Use <, >, or =.

27. 18 ft ☐ 220 in.

28. 24 lb ☐ 388 oz

29. $\frac{1}{2}$ pt ☐ 1 c

30. 2 mi ☐ 10,000 ft

31. 12 pt ☐ 3 gal

32. 72 ft ☐ 24 yd

33. 9 c ☐ 72 fl oz

34. 30 yd ☐ 93 ft

35. 145 in. ☐ 4 yd

36. Linda cut off $1\frac{1}{2}$ feet of her hair to donate to an organization that makes wigs for children with cancer. How many inches of hair did Linda cut off?

37. Geography Lake Superior is about 1,302 feet deep at its deepest point. What is this depth in yards?

38. Multi-Step A company produces 3 tons of cereal each week. How many 12-ounce cereal boxes can be filled each week?

39. Sports The width of a singles tennis court is 27 feet.

a. How many yards wide is a singles tennis court?

b. How many inches wide is a singles tennis court?

Art

Long-Term Parking is 65 feet tall and stands in front of a parking lot in Paris.

Convert.

40. 108 in. = ft = yd

41. 10,560 ft = yd = mi

42. 12 qt = c = fl oz

43. 2 gal = qt = pt

44. **Art** In Paris, the sculpture *Long-Term Parking,* created by Armand Fernandez, contains 60 cars embedded in 3.5 million pounds of concrete. How many tons of concrete is this?

45. **Multi-Step** If a half-gallon of milk sells for $1.60, what is the cost of a fluid ounce of milk? (Round your answer to the nearest cent.)

46. **Critical Thinking** Make a table to convert ounces to pounds. Write an expression for the number of pounds in n ounces. Then write an expression for the number of ounces in n pounds.

47. **Multi-Step** If you drink 14 quarts of water per week, on average, how many pints do you drink per day?

48. **What's the Error?** Sari said that she walked a total of 8,800 feet in a 5-mile walk-a-thon. Explain Sari's error.

49. **Write About It** Explain how to compare a length given in inches to a length given in feet.

50. **Challenge** In 1942, there were 15,000 troops on the ship *Queen Mary.* Each soldier was given 2 quarts of fresh water for the entire journey.

   a. How many gallons of fresh water did the soldiers have in all?

   b. **Estimation** If the journey took 5 days, about how many fluid ounces of fresh water should a soldier have rationed himself each day?

TEST PREP and Spiral Review

51. Multiple Choice Which of the following amounts is NOT equivalent to 1 gal?

   Ⓐ 64 fl oz   Ⓑ 16 c   Ⓒ 8 pt   Ⓓ 4 qt

52. Multiple Choice The world's largest ice cream sundae weighed about 55,000 pounds. How many tons did it weigh?

   Ⓕ 2.7 T   Ⓖ 27.5 T   Ⓗ 275 T   Ⓙ 2,750 T

Solve each equation. (Lessons 2-5, 2-6)

53. $6 + x = 15$ **54.** $y - 17 = 29$ **55.** $43 = 26 + d$ **56.** $32 = w - 8$

Give the most descriptive name for each figure. (Lesson 8-6)

57.    **58.** 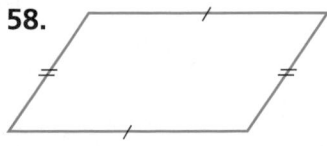   **59.**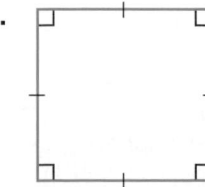

Converting Metric Units

Learn to convert metric units of measure.

NY Performance Indicators

6.M.5 Identify equivalent metric units of capacity (milliliter to liter and liter to milliliter).

The first Tour de France was in 1903 and was 2,428 km long. It had only 6 stages. Compare that to the 2005 Tour de France, which had 21 stages and covered 3,607 km.

During the 2005 Tour de France, Lance Armstrong was the stage winner from Tours to Blois, which has a distance of 67.5 km. How many meters is this distance?

In the metric system, the value of each place is 10 times greater than the value of the place to its right. When you convert one unit of measure to another, you can multiply or divide by a power of 10.

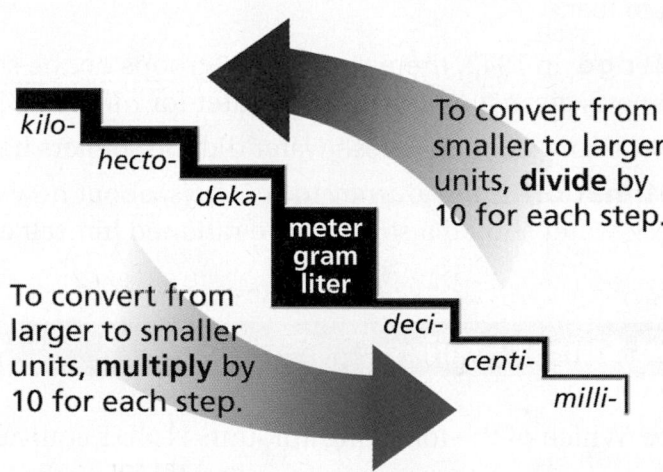

To convert from smaller to larger units, **divide** by 10 for each step.

To convert from larger to smaller units, **multiply** by 10 for each step.

kilo- hecto- deka- meter gram liter deci- centi- milli-

EXAMPLE 1   *Sports Application*

Helpful Hint

To decide whether to multiply or divide, think of a simpler model, such as your fingers and your hand.

fingers → hand
smaller unit → larger
unit ÷ 5

hand → fingers
larger unit → smaller
unit × 5

During the 2005 Tour de France, Lance Armstrong was the stage winner from Tours to Blois, which has a distance of 67.5 km. How many meters is this distance?

67.5 km = ▓ m

Think: Kilometer to meter is going from a bigger unit to a smaller unit. A meter is 3 places to the right of a kilometer in the chart, so $10 \cdot 10 \cdot 10$ or $10^3 = 1,000$.

67.5 km = (67.5 · 1,000) m

1 km = 1,000 m. You are converting a bigger unit to a smaller unit, so multiply by 1,000.

67.5 km = 67,500 m

Move the decimal point 3 places to the right.

EXAMPLE **2**

Using Powers of Ten to Convert Metric Units of Measure

Caution! ///////

Make sure you are multiplying or dividing by the correct power of ten.

Convert.

A The width of a book is about 22 cm. 22 cm = ▮ mm

22 cm = (22 · 10) mm   *1 cm = 10 mm, bigger unit to smaller unit, so multiply by 10.*

22 cm = 220 mm   *Move the decimal point 1 place right.*

B A backpack has a mass of about 6 kg. 6 kg = ▮ g

6 kg = (6 · 1,000) g   *1 kg = 1,000 g, bigger unit to smaller unit, so multiply by 1,000.*

6 kg = 6,000 g   *Move the decimal point 3 places right.*

C A water bottle holds about 400 mL. 400 mL = ▮ L

400 mL = (400 ÷ 1,000) L   *1,000 mL = 1 L, smaller unit to bigger unit, so divide by 1,000.*

400 mL = 0.4 L   *Move the decimal point 3 places left.*

Metric Measurements		
Distance	**Mass**	**Capacity**
1 km = 1,000 m	1 kg = 1,000 g	1 L = 1,000 mL
1 m = 100 cm	1 g = 1,000 mg	
1 cm = 10 mm		

Convert metric measures by using a conversion factor or using proportions.

EXAMPLE 3 **Converting Metric Units of Measure**

Convert.

A Method 1: Use a conversion factor.

11 m = ▮ cm   *Think: 100 cm = 1 m so use $\frac{100\ cm}{1\ m}$.*

$11\ \cancel{m} \cdot \dfrac{100\ cm}{1\ \cancel{m}} = 1,100$ cm   *Multiply 11 m by the conversion factor. Cancel the common unit, m.*

B Method 2: Use proportions.

190 mL = ▮ L

$\dfrac{190\ mL}{x\ L} = \dfrac{1,000\ mL}{1\ L}$ *Write a proportion.*

$1,000x = 190$ *The cross products are equal. Divide both sides by 1,000 to undo the multiplication.*

$x = 0.19$ L

Think and Discuss

6.CM.1

1. Describe how to convert 825 cm to mm.

9-4 Exercises

go.hrw.com
Homework Help Online
KEYWORD: MR7 9-4
Parent Resources Online
KEYWORD: MR7 Parent

GUIDED PRACTICE

See Example ① **1.** The length of a school hallway is 115 meters. How many kilometers long is the hallway?

See Example ② **Convert.**

2. The diameter of a ceiling fan is about 95 cm. 95 cm = ▪ m

3. A rock has a mass of about 852 g. 852 g = ▪ kg

4. A vase holds about 1.25 L of water. 1.25 L = ▪ mL

5. A sheet of paper has a mass of about 3.5 g. 3.5 g = ▪ mg

See Example ③ **6.** 3 kg = ▪ g   **7.** 4.4 L = ▪ mL   **8.** 1 kg = ▪ mg

9. 50 mm = ▪ m   **10.** 21 km = ▪ cm   **11.** 6 ml = ▪ L

INDEPENDENT PRACTICE

See Example ① **12.** A juice container holds 300 milliliters. How many liters of juice are in the container?

See Example ② **Convert.**

13. A teacup holds about 110 mL. 110 mL = ▪ L

14. The distance around a school is about 825 m. 825 m = ▪ km

15. A chair has a mass of about 22.5 kg. 22.5 kg = ▪ g

16. A gas tank holds about 85 L. 85 L = ▪ mL

See Example ③ **17.** 2,460 m = ▪ km   **18.** 842 mm = ▪ cm   **19.** 9,680 mg = ▪ g

20. 25 cm = ▪ mm   **21.** 782 g = ▪ kg   **22.** 1.2 km = ▪ m

PRACTICE AND PROBLEM SOLVING

Extra Practice
See page 731.

23. Multi-Step There are 28 L of soup in a pot. Marshall serves 400 mL in each bowl. If he fills 16 bowls, how much soup is left in the pot? Write your answer two ways: as a number of liters and as a number of milliliters.

24. Multi-Step Joanie wants to frame a rectangular picture that is 1.7 m by 0.9 m. Joanie has 500 cm of wood to use for a frame. Does Joanie have enough wood to frame the picture? Explain.

Convert.

25. $\dfrac{23{,}850 \text{ cm}}{x \text{ km}} = \dfrac{100{,}000 \text{ cm}}{1 \text{ km}}$ **26.** $\dfrac{350 \text{ L}}{x \text{ mL}} = \dfrac{1 \text{ L}}{1{,}000 \text{ mL}}$

27. $7 \text{ km} \cdot \dfrac{1{,}000 \text{ m}}{\text{km}} = $ ▪ m   **28.** $9.5 \text{ L} \cdot \dfrac{1{,}000 \text{ mL}}{\text{L}} = $ ▪ mL

Compare. Use <, >, or =.

29. 1,000 mm ▮ 1 m   **30.** 5.2 kg ▮ 60 g   **31.** 3 L ▮ 6,000 mL

32. 2 g ▮ 20,000 mg   **33.** 0.0065 m ▮ 6.5 mm   **34.** 0.1 km ▮ 10 mm

35. Multi-Step The St. Louis Gateway Arch in Missouri is about 19,200 centimeters tall. The San Jacinto Monument, outside of Houston, Texas, is about 174 m tall. Which structure is taller? by how much? Give your answer in meters.

St. Louis Gateway Arch   San Jacinto Monument

36. Critical Thinking A *millimicron* is equal to one-billionth of a meter. How many millimicrons are there in 2.5 meters?

 37. What's the Error? Edgar wanted to know the mass of a package of cereal in kilograms. The label on the box says 672 g. Edgar said that the mass is 672,000 kg. Explain Edgar's error and give the correct answer.

 38. Write About It Amy ran a 1,000-meter race. Explain how to find the number of centimeters in 1,000 meters.

 39. Challenge The lemonade cooler at the class picnic holds 12.5 L. Each plastic cup holds 225 mL. How many cups can be filled from the cooler? If none of the lemonade is spilled, how many milliliters will be left in the cooler when all possible cups have been filled?

TEST PREP and Spiral Review

40. Multiple Choice Complete the statement with the most reasonable metric unit. A snail might crawl at a rate of about 0.01 ___?___ per hour.

Ⓐ mm   Ⓑ m   Ⓒ mL   Ⓓ km

41. Extended Response Liza, Toni, and Kim used a metric scale to weigh some shells they collected at the beach. The masses of the shells were 29 g, 52 g, 18 g, 103 g, 154 g, and 96 g. What was the combined mass of the shells in kilograms? in milligrams? What is the difference in kilograms between the heaviest and lightest shells?

If the angles can form a triangle, classify it as acute, obtuse, or right. (Lesson 8-5)

42. 49°, 41°, 90°   **43.** 92°, 41°, 47°   **44.** 57°, 63°, 60°

Determine if the given statements are *sometimes, always,* or *never* true. (Lesson 8-6)

45. A rhombus is a square.   **46.** A square is a rhombus.

47. A circle is a polygon.   **48.** A polygon has fewer than 3 sides.

9-5 Time and Temperature

Learn to find measures of time and temperature.

Jamie took a tour of London on a double-decker bus. The tour started at 11:45 A.M. and ended at 3:15 P.M. Jamie was on the bus for 3 hours 30 minutes.

NY Performance Indicators

6.A.6 Evaluate formulas for given input values (circumference, area, volume, distance, temperature, interest, etc.).

You can use the information in the table below to convert one unit of time to another.

Time	
1 year (yr) = 365 days	1 day = 24 hours (hr)
1 year = 12 months (mo)	1 hour = 60 minutes (min)
1 year = 52 weeks	1 minute = 60 seconds (s)
1 week = 7 days	

EXAMPLE 1 Converting Time

Convert.

A 1 min 45 s = ▧ s

1 minute 45 seconds

60 seconds + 45 seconds   *Think: 1 minute = 60 seconds.*

105 seconds

1 min 45 s = 105 s

B 450 min = ▧ hr

$$450 \, \cancel{min} \cdot \frac{1 \, hr}{60 \, \cancel{min}} = \frac{450}{60} \, hr$$ *Think: 1 hour = 60 minutes.*

$$450 \, min = 7\frac{1}{2} \, hr$$ *Write as a mixed number.*

C 6 weeks = ▧ hr

$$6 \, \cancel{wk} \cdot \frac{7 \, \cancel{days}}{1 \, \cancel{wk}} \cdot \frac{24 \, hr}{1 \, \cancel{day}} = 1{,}008 \, hr$$ *Think: 1 week = 7 days and 1 day = 24 hours.*

6 weeks = 1,008 hr

The time between the start of an activity and the end of an activity is called the *elapsed time*.

Chapter 9 Measurement and Geometry

EXAMPLE **2** **Finding Elapsed Time**

A Jamie's flight to London was scheduled to arrive at 9:10 A.M. It was 4 hours 25 minutes late. When did it arrive?

Scheduled time: 9:10 A.M.

Arrival time: 1:35 P.M.

Think: 4 hours after 9:10 A.M. is 1:10 P.M. 25 minutes after 1:10 P.M. is 1:35 P.M.

The flight arrived at 1:35 P.M.

B Jamie's friend Tina joined her in London. Tina's flight arrived at 2:30 P.M. The flight was 3 hours 15 minutes long. At what time did Tina's plane depart?

Arrival time: 2:30 P.M.

Departure: 11:15 A.M.

Think: 3 hours before 2:30 P.M. is 11:30 A.M. 15 minutes before 11:30 A.M. is 11:15 A.M.

The plane departed at 11:15 A.M.

Celsius and Fahrenheit are the scales used to measure temperature. You can use these formulas to convert temperature.

Temperature Conversions	
To convert Celsius to Fahrenheit use $F = \frac{9}{5}C + 32$.	To convert Fahrenheit to Celsius use $C = \frac{5}{9}(F - 32)$.

EXAMPLE **3** **Estimating Temperature**

Estimate the temperature.

Remember!

Dividing by 2 is the same as multiplying by $\frac{1}{2}$.

A 20°C is about ▒°F.

$F = \frac{9}{5} \cdot C + 32$ *Use the formula.*

Round $\frac{9}{5}$ to 2, and 32 to 30.

$F \approx 2 \cdot 20 + 30$ *Use the order of operations.*

$F \approx 40 + 30$

$F \approx 70$

20°C is about 70°F.

B 50°F is about ▒°C.

$C = \frac{5}{9}(F - 32)$ *Use the formula.*

Round $\frac{5}{9}$ to $\frac{1}{2}$, and 32 to 30.

$C \approx \frac{1}{2}(50 - 30)$ *Use the order of operations.*

$C \approx \frac{1}{2}(20)$

$C \approx 10$

50°F is about 10°C.

6.PS.21, 6.CM.1

Think and Discuss

1. **Explain** how to find the number of minutes in a week.

2. **Explain** how to find the elapsed time between 7:45 A.M. and 10:30 P.M. if you know the elapsed time between 7:45 A.M. and 10:30 A.M.

go.hrw.com
Homework Help Online
KEYWORD: MR7 9-5
Parent Resources Online
KEYWORD: MR7 Parent

GUIDED PRACTICE

See Example 1 **Convert.**

1. 20 min = ▪ s   **2.** 98 days = ▪ weeks   **3.** 30 mo = ▪ yr

4. 3 min 25 s = ▪ s   **5.** 8 hr = ▪ min   **6.** 4,320 min = ▪ days

See Example 2 **7.** A movie starts at 11:50 A.M. and runs for 2 hours 25 minutes. At what time does the movie end?

8. Nick drove to visit some friends. If he arrived at 1:30 P.M. and took 4 hours 10 minutes to get there, at what time did Nick start out?

See Example 3 **Estimate the temperature.**

9. 12°C is about ▪ °F   **10.** 78°F is about ▪ °C   **11.** 15°C is about ▪ °F

INDEPENDENT PRACTICE

See Example 1 **Convert.**

12. 2 hr 25 min = ▪ min   **13.** 96 hr = ▪ days   **14.** 1 yr 6 mo = ▪ mo

15. 7,200 s = ▪ hr   **16.** 5 weeks 1 day = ▪ days   **17.** 4,368 hr = ▪ weeks

See Example 2 **18.** A bus arrived at its destination at 2:15 P.M. If the trip took 3 hours 50 minutes, at what time did the bus depart?

19. **Multi-Step** The school play lasts 1 hour 25 minutes, and there is a 15-minute intermission. The play started at 10:30 A.M. When will it end?

See Example 3 **Estimate the temperature.**

20. 56°F is about ▪ °C   **21.** 84°C is about ▪ °F   **22.** 75°F is about ▪ °C

PRACTICE AND PROBLEM SOLVING

Extra Practice
See page 731.

Compare. Use <, >, or =.

23. 21 hr ▪ $\frac{5}{6}$ day   **24.** 2 yr ▪ 104 weeks   **25.** 80,000 s ▪ 1 day

26. **Patterns** The sequence below shows the times that a radio station gives a traffic report. When will the radio station give the next traffic report?
11:18 A.M., 11:30 A.M., 11:42 A.M., 11:54 A.M., …

For Exercises 27 and 28, use the table.

27. Which bus from Miami to Orlando would you take to spend the least amount of time on the bus? the greatest amount of time on the bus?

28. Bus 490 was delayed in traffic for 1 hour 15 minutes. At what time did the bus finally arrive?

Miami to Orlando Schedule		
Bus	Depart	Arrive
460	8:00 A.M.	2:45 P.M.
470	10:50 A.M.	5:45 P.M.
480	1:00 P.M.	7:40 P.M.
490	4:30 P.M.	11:20 P.M.

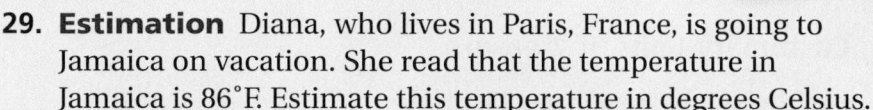

The United States and Jamaica are the only two countries in the world that use the Fahrenheit scale for daily temperature readings. All the other countries in the world use the Celsius scale.

29. Estimation Diana, who lives in Paris, France, is going to Jamaica on vacation. She read that the temperature in Jamaica is 86°F. Estimate this temperature in degrees Celsius.

30. Multi-Step The table shows the average monthly temperatures from April to July in degrees Fahrenheit for New York City and in degrees Celsius for London. In which months is the average monthly temperature in New York City higher than it is in London?

Average Monthly Temperatures		
Month	New York City (°F)	London (°C)
April	50	10
May	61	13
June	70	16
July	76	19

31. Bobby's trip from Paris, Texas, to Paris, France, should have taken $10\frac{1}{2}$ hours, but it was 3 hours and 20 minutes longer. About how long was his trip?

32. ❓ **What's the Error?** David is going to Dublin, Ireland, in July. He read in a travel book that the average temperature in Dublin in July is 15°C. He estimated the temperature in degrees Fahrenheit by adding 30 to the Celsius temperature and then multiplying by 2. What did David do wrong?

33. ✐ **Write About It** How can it be Friday in one part of the United States and Saturday in another?

34. ⭐ **Challenge** Below is a list of the daily high temperatures in Glasgow, Scotland, for one week. What was the mean high temperature in degrees Fahrenheit? 7°C, 12°C, 9°C, 10°C, 14°C, 10°C, 8°C

TEST PREP and Spiral Review

35. Multiple Choice Which measure is NOT equivalent to the others?

Ⓐ 8 hr   Ⓑ 480 min   Ⓒ 28,000 s   Ⓓ $\frac{1}{3}$ day

36. Multiple Choice A flight departs at 11:35 A.M. The flight is 2 hours 45 minutes long, but it is delayed 30 minutes. What is the new arrival time?

Ⓕ 2:20 P.M.   Ⓖ 2:50 P.M.   Ⓗ 3:05 P.M.   Ⓙ 3:15 P.M.

Compare. Write <, >, or =. (Lesson 3-1)

37. 9.17 ▇ 9.107   **38.** 3.456 ▇ 3.65   **39.** 0.051 ▇ 0.052   **40.** 12.5 ▇ 12.50

Evaluate $10.35 - w$ for each value of w. (Lesson 3-3)

41. $w = 4.8$ **42.** $w = 8.62$ **43.** $w = 0.903$ **44.** $w = 5.075$

READY TO GO ON?

Quiz for Lessons 9-1 Through 9-5

9-1 **Understanding Customary Units of Measure**

What unit of measure provides the best estimate? Explain.

1. A fishbowl can hold about 2 ___?___ of water.

2. A Columbian mammoth, which was about the same size as an elephant, lived in Mexico about 1.5 million years ago. A mammoth weighed about 10 ___?___.

9-2 **Understanding Metric Units of Measure**

What unit of measure provides the best estimate? Explain.

3. A cat has a mass of about 3 ___?___.

4. The length of an airport runway is about 3 ___?___.

Measure the length of each line to the nearest centimeter.

5. •————————•   6. •————————————————•

9-3 **Converting Customary Units**

Use the table for Exercises 7 and 8.

7. Convert Ty's length to feet and inches.

8. How many ounces does Ty weigh?

Baby Ty Rodriguez	
Birth Date	July 8, 2005, 11:50 P.M.
Weight	9 lb 8 oz
Length	$21\frac{1}{2}$ in.

9-4 **Converting Metric Units**

Convert.

9. 8 m = ▮ cm   10. 12 kg = ▮ g   11. 2,000 mL = ▮ L

9-5 **Time and Temperature**

Convert.

12. 5 min 32 s = ▮ s   13. 3 days = ▮ min   14. 24 mo = ▮ yr   15. 330 s = ▮ h

Estimate the temperature.

16. 30°C is about ▮°F   17. 80°F is about ▮°C   18. 54°F is about ▮°C

19. What is the elapsed time between 8:45 P.M. and 12:15 A.M.?

20. A train scheduled to arrive at 10:35 A.M. was delayed 3 hours 20 minutes. What time did it arrive?

Focus on Problem Solving

Look Back

• **Check that the question is answered.**

Sometimes a problem requires you to go through a series of steps to find the answer. When you read a question, ask yourself what information you need to find in order to answer it. After you have solved the problem, reread the question to make sure you have answered it completely.

 Read each problem and determine whether the given solution answers the question in the problem. If not, provide the correct answer.

❶ The giant house spider has a leg span of 70 millimeters. The western black widow has a leg span of 4 centimeters. How many centimeters longer is the leg span of the giant house spider?
Solution: 3 centimeters

❷ A recipe for fruit punch calls for 8 fluid ounces of pineapple juice. Daryl pours the required amount of pineapple juice into a bowl that holds 1 gallon. How many additional fluid ounces of liquid can the bowl hold?
Solution: 120 fluid ounces

❸ The distance from Belleville to Cedar Falls is twice the distance from Appleton to Belleville. The distance from Cedar Falls to Donner is twice the distance from Belleville to Cedar Falls. What is the distance from Belleville to Donner?

```
    2 km
 •——————•———————•——————————————•
Appleton Belleville  Cedar Falls        Donner
```

Solution: 8 kilometers

❹ The 1939 film *Gone with the Wind* had a running time of 3 hours 50 minutes. The film was usually shown with one 15-minute intermission. An afternoon showing of the film started at 2:30 P.M. At what time did the film end?
Solution: 4 hr 5 min

❺ A typical chicken egg weighs 2 ounces. A typical ostrich egg weighs 3 pounds. How many times greater is the weight of the ostrich egg than the chicken egg?
Solution: 48 ounces

Finding Angle Measures in Polygons

Learn to find angle measures in polygons.

NY Performance Indicators

6.N.27 Justify the reasonableness of answers using estimation (including rounding). Also, 6.R.1.

All softball and baseball diamonds have a home plate. Home plate is in the shape of a pentagon.

You can use a protractor and your knowledge of angles in polygons to find the measures of the angles in home plate.

EXAMPLE 1 **Subtracting to Find Angle Measures**

Caution! ///////

Ray *BA* can also be read as crossing at 140°, and ray *BC* can be read as crossing at 60°. The angle measure is still 80°. Make sure that you read the measures on the same scale.

Use a protractor to find the measure of ∠ABC. Then classify the angle.

- Place the center point of the protractor on the vertex of the angle.

- Read the measures where ray *BA* and ray *BC* cross.

- Ray *BA* crosses at 40°, and ray *BC* crosses at 120°.

- The measure of ∠ABC is 120° − 40°, or 80°. Write this as m ∠ABC = 80°.

- Since 80° < 90°, the angle is acute.

Check

Use the other scale on the protractor to find the measure of ∠ABC.
140° − 60° = 80°

To estimate the measure of an angle, compare it with an angle whose measure you already know. A right angle has half the measure of a straight angle. A 45° angle has half the measure of a right angle.

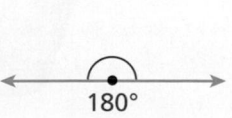
180°

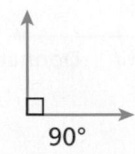
90°

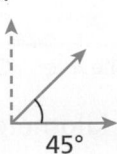
45°

EXAMPLE 2

Estimating Angle Measures

Estimate the measure of ∠J in the parallelogram JKLM. Then use a protractor to check the reasonableness of your answer.

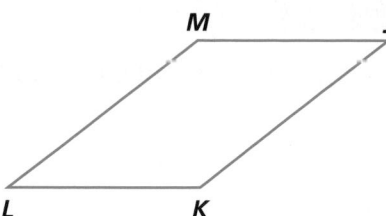

Think: The measure of the angle is close to 45°, but it is a little less. A good estimate would be about 35°.

Caution!

Use the scale on the protractor that starts with 0°.

Remember that in a parallelogram, opposite angles are congruent.

So use the angle opposite ∠J to find its measure.

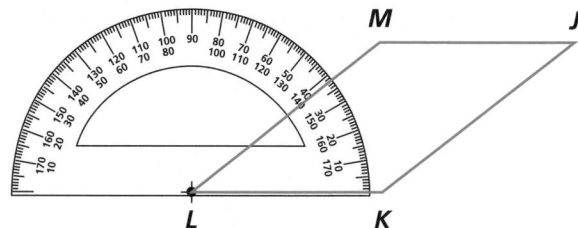

Use the protractor. The measure of the angle is 38°.

m∠J = 38°, so the estimate of 35° is reasonable.

EXAMPLE 3

Sports Application

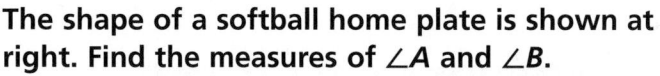

The shape of a softball home plate is shown at right. Find the measures of ∠A and ∠B.

Use a protractor to measure ∠A. $\overrightarrow{AB}$ crosses at 60°, and $\overrightarrow{AE}$ crosses at 150°.

Subtract. 135° − 45° = 90°.

∠A = 90°

Estimate the m∠B.

It is greater than 90°, so it is obtuse. It looks as if the angle measure is 90° + 45°. So, m∠B is about 135°.

Use a protractor to measure ∠B.

∠B = 135°

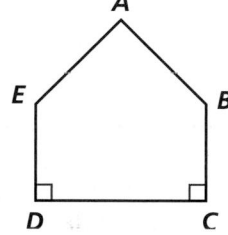

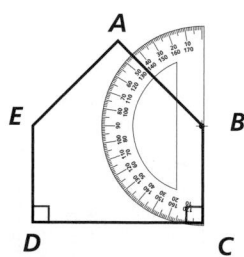

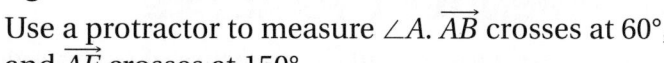

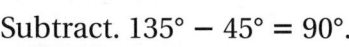

Think and Discuss

6.PS.21

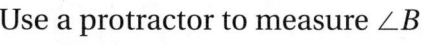

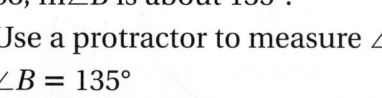

1. Explain how to find the measures of ∠K and ∠M in Example 2 without using a protractor once you know the measure of ∠J.

9-6 Exercises

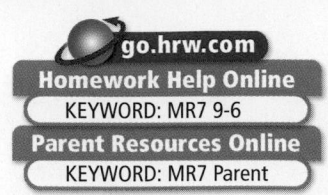
go.hrw.com
Homework Help Online
KEYWORD: MR7 9-6
Parent Resources Online
KEYWORD: MR7 Parent

GUIDED PRACTICE

See Example **1** Use a protractor to find the measure of each angle. Then classify the angle.

1.

2.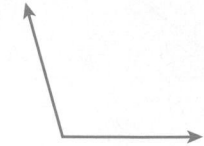

3.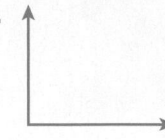

See Example **2** Estimate the measure of ∠A in each figure. Then use a protractor to check the reasonableness of your answer.

4.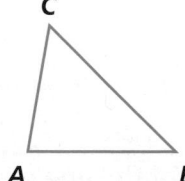

5.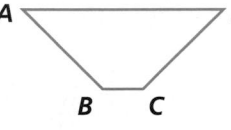

6.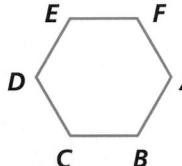

See Example **3** **7.** The shape of a pond is shown at right. Find the measures of ∠A and ∠B.

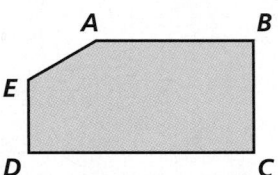

INDEPENDENT PRACTICE

See Example **1** Use a protractor to find the measure of each angle. Then classify the angle.

8.

9.

10.

See Example **2** Estimate the measure of ∠A in each figure. Then use a protractor to check the reasonableness of your answer.

11.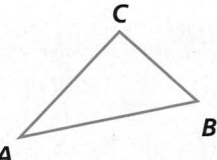

12.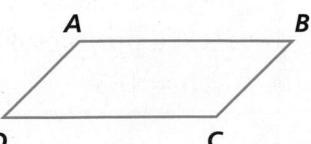

13.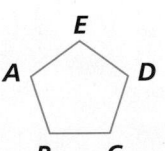

See Example **3** **14.** The shape of a park is shown at right. Find the measures of ∠A and ∠B.

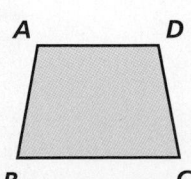

Find the measure of the given angle and the measure of the angle that makes up its supplement.

15.

16.

17. Architecture Most buildings are built at a 90° angle from the ground. The Leaning Tower of Pisa, in Pisa, Italy, is at an angle of approximately 84.5° from the ground. How many degrees is it leaning?

84.5°

18. Critical Thinking Three angles form a 180° angle. If m∠3 = 80° and ∠1 and ∠2 are congruent, what is the measure of ∠1?

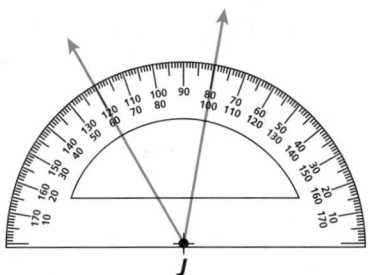

19. What's the Error? Loni said that the measurement of ∠J was 20°. What is her error?

20. Write About It Describe how to measure an angle two different ways.

21. Challenge Another way to measure angles is in radians. 2π radians is equal to 360°. How many radians equal 90°?

22. Multiple Choice Find the measure of ∠C to the nearest degree.

Ⓐ 30°   Ⓑ 60°   Ⓒ 75°   Ⓓ 115°

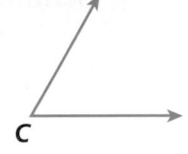
C

23. Short Response Use a protractor to find the measure of ∠A. Classify the angle. Explain.

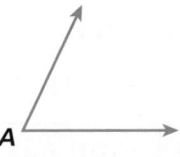
A

Convert. (Lesson 9-3)

24. 6 ft = ▮ in.   **25.** 8 qt = ▮ gal   **26.** 7 lb = ▮ oz   **27.** 4 qt = ▮ pt

28. Pete got into the pool to swim laps at 2:10 P.M. He got out of the pool at 3:25 P.M. How long was he in the pool? (Lesson 9-5)

9-7 Perimeter

Learn to find the perimeter and missing side lengths of a polygon.

Vocabulary

perimeter

One of the biggest finger paintings ever painted is *Ten Fingers, Ten Toes*. It is 8.53 meters wide and 10.66 meters long.

The **perimeter** of a figure is the distance around it. To find the perimeter of the painting, you can add the lengths of the sides.

$8.53 + 10.66 + 8.53 + 10.66 = 38.38$

The perimeter of the painting, is 38.38 meters.

E X A M P L E 1 Finding the Perimeter of a Polygon

NY Performance Indicators

6.A.2 Use substitution to evaluate algebraic expressions (may include exponents of one, two and three). Also, 6.R.1.

Find the perimeter of the figure.

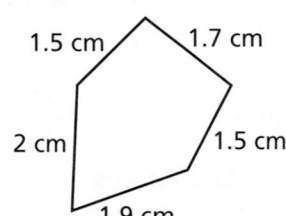

1.5 cm   1.7 cm

2 cm   1.5 cm

1.9 cm

$1.5 + 1.7 + 1.5 + 1.9 + 2 = 8.6$

Add all the side lengths.

The perimeter is 8.6 cm.

PERIMETER OF A RECTANGLE

The opposite sides of a rectangle are equal in length. Find the perimeter of a rectangle by using the formula, in which ℓ is the length and w is the width.

$P = 2\ell + 2w$

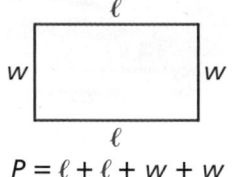

ℓ

w w

ℓ

$P = \ell + \ell + w + w$

E X A M P L E 2 Using a Formula to Find Perimeter

Find the perimeter P of the rectangle.

2 ft

|← 3 ft →|

$P = 2\ell + 2w$

$P = (2 \cdot 3) + (2 \cdot 2)$ *Substitute 3 for ℓ and 2 for w.*

$P = 6 + 4$ *Multiply.*

$P = 10$ *Add.*

The perimeter is 10 feet.

EXAMPLE 3   **Finding Unknown Side Lengths and the Perimeter of a Polygon**

Find each unknown measure.

A What is the length of side a if the perimeter equals 105 m?

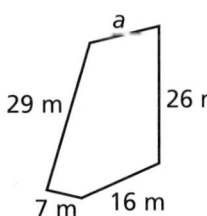

$P =$ sum of side lengths

$105 = a + 26 + 16 + 7 + 29$ *Use the values you know.*

$105 = a + 78$ *Add the known lengths.*

$105 - 78 = a + 78 - 78$ *Subtract 78 from both*
$ 27 = a$ *sides.*

Side a is 27 m long.

B What is the perimeter of the polygon?

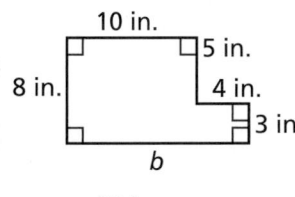

First find the unknown side length.
Find the sides opposite side b.
The length of side b = 10 + 4.
Side b is 14 in. long.
Find the perimeter.
$P = 14 + 8 + 10 + 5 + 4 + 3$
$P = 44$

The perimeter of the polygon is 44 in.

C The width of a rectangle is 12 cm. What is the perimeter of the rectangle if the length is 3 times the width?

$\ell = 3w$ *Find the length.*

$\ell = (3 \cdot 12)$ *Substitute 12 for w.*

$\ell = 36$ *Multiply.*

$P = 2\ell + 2w$ *Use the formula for the*
   perimeter of a rectangle.

$P = 2(36) + 2(12)$ *Substitute 36 and 12.*

$P = 72 + 24$ *Multiply.*

$P = 96$ *Add.*

The perimeter of the rectangle is 96 cm.

Think and Discuss   

1. **Explain** how to find the perimeter of a regular pentagon if you know the length of one side.

2. **Tell** what formula you can use to find the perimeter of a square.

go.hrw.com
Homework Help Online
KEYWORD: MR7 9-7
Parent Resources Online
KEYWORD: MR7 Parent

GUIDED PRACTICE

See Example **1** **Find the perimeter of each figure.**

1.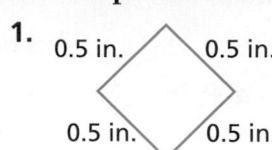
0.5 in. 0.5 in.
0.5 in. 0.5 in.

2.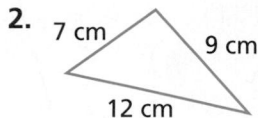
7 cm   9 cm
12 cm

See Example **2** **Find the perimeter P of each rectangle.**

3.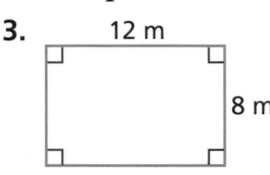
12 m
8 m

4.
7.3 in.
4 in.

See Example **3** **Find the unknown measure.**

5. What is the length of side b
if the perimeter equals 21 yd?

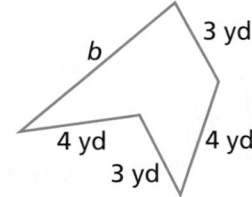
b 3 yd
4 yd   4 yd
3 yd

INDEPENDENT PRACTICE

See Example **1** **Find the perimeter of each figure.**

6.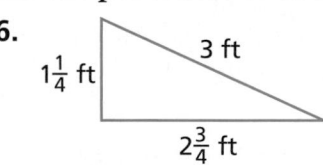
3 ft
$1\frac{1}{4}$ ft
$2\frac{3}{4}$ ft

7. regular octagon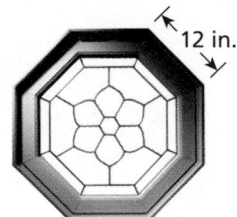
12 in.

See Example **2** **Find the perimeter P of each rectangle.**

8.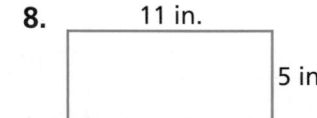
11 in.
5 in.

9.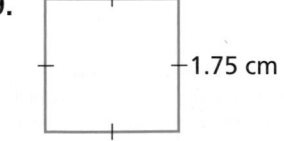
1.75 cm

10.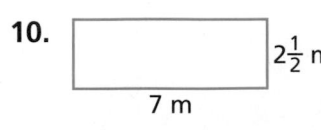
$2\frac{1}{2}$ m
7 m

See Example **3** **Find each unknown measure.**

11. What is the perimeter of the polygon?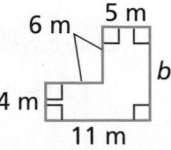
6 m   5 m
b
4 m
11 m

12. The width of a rectangle is 15 ft. What is the perimeter of the rectangle if the length is 5 ft longer than the width?

PRACTICE AND PROBLEM SOLVING

Extra Practice
See page 732.

Use the figure *ACDEFG* for Exercises 13–15.

13. What is the length of side *FE*?

14. If the perimeter of rectangle *BCDE* is 34 in., what is the length of side *BC*?

15. Use your answer from Exercise 14 to find the perimeter of figure *ACDEFG*.

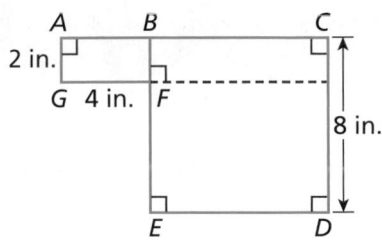

Find the perimeter of each figure.

16. a triangle with side lengths 6 in., 8 in., and 10 in.

17. a regular pentagon with side length $\frac{2}{5}$ km

18. a regular dodecagon (12-sided figure) with side length 3m.

19. **Sports** The diagram shows one-half of a badminton court.

    a. What are the dimensions of the whole court?

    b. What is the perimeter of the whole court?

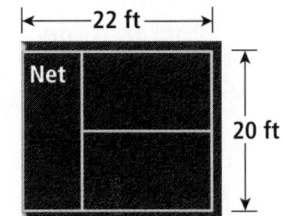

20. **What's the Error?** A student found the perimeter of a 10-inch-by-13-inch rectangle to be 23 inches. Explain the student's error. Then find the correct perimeter.

21. **Write About It** Explain how to find the unknown length of a side of a triangle that has a perimeter of 24 yd and two sides that measure 6 yd and 8 yd.

22. **Challenge** The perimeter of a regular octagon is 20 m. What is the length of one side of the octagon?

TEST PREP and Spiral Review

23. **Multiple Choice** Find the perimeter of the figure.

    (A) 17 cm   (C) 21 cm

    (B) 19 cm   (D) 25 cm

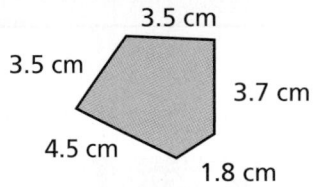

24. **Multiple Choice** The width of a rectangle is 16 m. What is the perimeter of the rectangle if the length is 2 times the width?

    (F) 16 m   (G) 32 m   (H) 64 m   (J) 96 m

Find each sum or difference. (Lesson 3-3)

25. $30 - 5.32$

26. $80.31 + 15.125$

27. $100 - 25.65$

28. $200.6 + 1$

Find the missing value in each proportion. (Lesson 7-3)

29. $\frac{9}{15} = \frac{x}{5}$

30. $\frac{a}{20} = \frac{3}{15}$

31. $\frac{1}{7} = \frac{6}{k}$

32. $\frac{4}{5} = \frac{x}{5}$

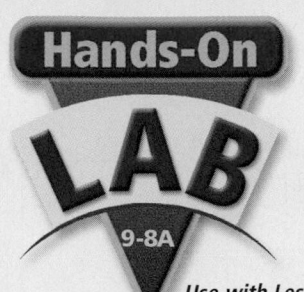

Hands-On LAB
9-8A

Use with Lesson 9-8

Explore Circumference

go.hrw.com
Lab Resources Online
KEYWORD: MR7 Lab9

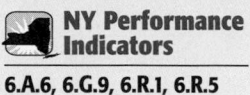
NY Performance Indicators
6.A.6, 6.G.9, 6.R.1, 6.R.5

In this lab, you will measure objects to investigate the distance around a circle. The distance around a circle is called the *circumference*.

Activity 1

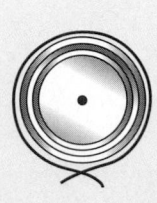

1. Choose a cylindrical object, such as a can or a mug. Tightly wrap a piece of string around the object, and mark the string where it meets itself. Measure this length on the string, and record it in a table like the one below as the circumference.

2. Using a ruler, measure the distance across the object through its center. Record this as the *diameter*.

3. Use a calculator to find the ratio of the circumference C to the diameter d. Round this value to the nearest hundredth, and record it in the table.

4. Repeat the process with three more cylindrical objects.

	Object 1	Object 2	Object 3	Object 4
Circumference C				
Diameter d				
$\frac{C}{d}$				

Think and Discuss

1. Describe what you notice about the ratio $\frac{C}{d}$ in your table.

Try This

Find the ratio $\frac{C}{d}$ for each circle.

1. 4 in. $C = 12.57$ in.

2. 3 cm $C = 9.42$ cm

3. 5 ft $C = 15.71$ ft

The ratio of the circumference of a circle to its diameter is called *pi*, which is represented by the Greek letter π. As you saw in Activity 1, the value of π is close to 3. You can approximate π as 3.14 or $\frac{22}{7}$.

For any circle, $\frac{C}{d} = \pi$. You can solve this equation for C to give an equation for the circumference of a circle in terms of the diameter. The equation is $C = \pi d$.

Activity 2

1 Open your compass to a width of 4 cm. Use the compass to draw a circle with a radius of 4 cm. What is the diameter of the circle?

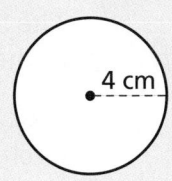

2 Use the equation $C = \pi d$ and the approximation $\pi \approx 3.14$ to predict the circumference of the circle.

3 Carefully lay a piece of string on top of the circle. Make sure the string matches the circle as closely as possible.

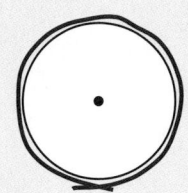

4 Mark the string where it meets itself, and measure this length.

5 Repeat the process, this time starting with a circle whose radius is 3.5 cm. Use the equation $C = \pi d$ to predict the circle's circumference, and then check the prediction by using a string to measure the circumference.

Think and Discuss

1. In each case, how did the length of the string compare with the circumference that you predicted?

2. If you know the diameter of a circle, what should you do to find the circle's circumference?

3. If you know the circumference of a circle, what should you do to find the circle's diameter?

Try This

Find the circumference of each circle. Use 3.14 for π.

1.

9 in.

2.

5 ft

3.

10 cm

Circles and Circumference

Learn to identify the parts of a circle and to find the circumference of a circle.

Vocabulary

circle

center

radius (radii)

diameter

circumference

pi

NY Performance Indicators

6.G.9 Understand the relationship between the circumference and the diameter of a circle. Also, 6.A.2, 6.A.6, 6.G.5, 6.G.6, 6.G.7.

The shape of a drum is a *circle*. A **circle** is the set of all points in a plane that are the same distance from a given point, called the **center**.

The length of the diameter is twice the length of the radius.

Like a polygon, a circle is a plane figure. But a circle is not a polygon because it is not made of line segments.

Center

Circumference

Diameter A line segment that passes through the center of the circle and has both endpoints on the circle.

Radius (plural radii) A line segment with one endpoint at the center of the circle and the other endpoint on the circle.

EXAMPLE **1** **Naming Parts of a Circle**

Name the circle, a diameter, and three radii.

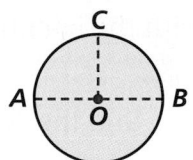

A circle is named by its center, so this is circle O.
$\overline{AB}$ is a diameter.
$\overline{OA}$, $\overline{OB}$, and $\overline{OC}$ are radii.

The distance around a circle is called the **circumference**.

The ratio of the circumference to the diameter, $\frac{C}{d}$, is the same for any circle. This ratio is represented by the Greek letter π, which is read "*pi*."

$$\frac{C}{d} = \pi$$

The decimal representation of *pi* starts with 3.14159265 . . . and goes on forever without repeating. Most people approximate π using either 3.14 or $\frac{22}{7}$. To make multiplying by *pi* easier, you can round π to 3.

The formula for the circumference of a circle is $C = \pi d$, or $C = 2\pi r$.

Circumference of a Circle	
Words	**Formula**
The circumference of any circle is equal to π times the diameter, or 2π times the radius.	$C = \pi d$ or $C = 2\pi r$

EXAMPLE 2 **Architecture Application**

Theater

An architect is making a plan for a new circular theater. Find the circumference of the theater by rounding π to 3.

$C = \pi d$ *Use the formula.*

$C \approx 3 \cdot 32$ *Replace π with 3 and d with 32.*

$C \approx 96$ meters

The circumference of the circle is about 96 meters.

EXAMPLE 3 **Using the Formula for the Circumference of a Circle**

Find each missing value to the nearest hundredth. Use 3.14 for π.

A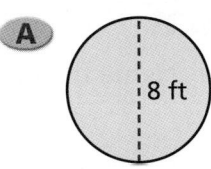

$d = 8$ ft; $C = ?$

$C = \pi d$ *Write the formula.*

$C \approx 3.14 \cdot 8$ *Replace π with 3.14 and d with 8.*

$C \approx 25.12$ ft

B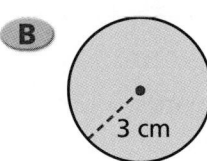

$r = 3$ cm; $C = ?$

$C = 2\pi r$ *Write the formula.*

$C \approx 2 \cdot 3.14 \cdot 3$ *Replace π with 3.14 and r with 3.*

$C \approx 18.84$ cm

C $C = 37.68$ in.; $d = ?$

$C = \pi d$ *Write the formula.*

$37.68 \approx 3.14d$ *Replace C with 37.68, and π with 3.14.*

$\dfrac{37.68}{3.14} \approx \dfrac{3.14d}{3.14}$ *Divide both sides by 3.14.*

12.00 in. $\approx d$

6.PS.17, 6.CM.1, 6.CM.10

Think and Discuss

1. Explain how to find the radius in Example 3C.

2. Tell whether rounding *pi* to 3 will result in an overestimation or an underestimation.

3. Explain why a circle is not a polygon.

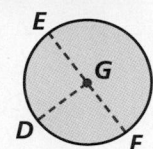

go.hrw.com
Homework Help Online
KEYWORD: MR7 9-8
Parent Resources Online
KEYWORD: MR7 Parent

GUIDED PRACTICE

See Example ① **1.** Point *G* is the center of the circle. Name the circle, a diameter, and three radii.

See Example ② **A builder is putting in a circular window.**
Find the circumference by rounding π to 3.

2. What is the circumference if the diameter is 8 feet?

3. What is the circumference if the radius is 2 feet?

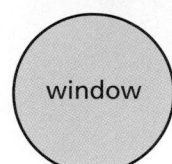
window

See Example ③ **Find each missing value to the nearest hundredth. Use 3.14 for π.**

4. *C* = ?

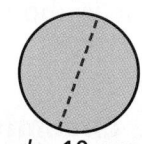
d = 10 mm

5. *C* = ?

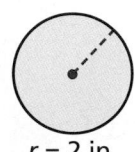
r = 2 in.

INDEPENDENT PRACTICE

See Example ① **6.** Point *P* is the center of the circle. Name the circle, a diameter, and three radii.

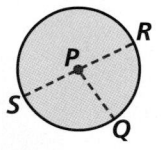

See Example ② **A gardener is digging a circular pond and planting a circular herb garden around it.**
Find the circumference by rounding π to 3.

7. If the diameter of the pond is 5 yards, what is its circumference?

8. If the radius of the garden is 7 yards, what is its circumference?

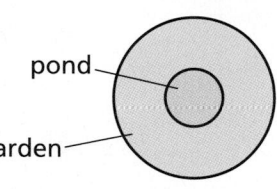
pond

garden

See Example ③ **Find each missing value to the nearest hundredth. Use 3.14 for π.**

9. *C* = ?

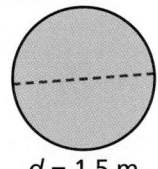
d = 1.5 m

10. *C* = ?

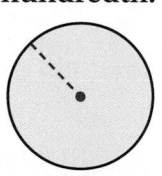
r = 0.8 cm

11. *d* = ?

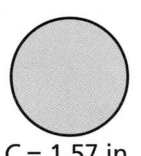
C = 1.57 in.

PRACTICE AND PROBLEM SOLVING

Extra Practice
See page 732.

Fill in the blanks. Use 3.14 for π and round to the nearest hundredth.

12. If *r* = 7 m, then *d* = ___?___, and *C* = ___?___.

13. If *d* = 11.5 ft, then *r* = ___?___, and *C* = ___?___.

14. If *C* = 7.065 cm, then *d* = ___?___, and *r* = ___?___.

15. If *C* = 16.956 in., then *d* = ___?___, and *r* = ___?___.

16. **Measurement** Draw a circle. Name the center P and make the radius 2 in. long.

 a. Draw the diameter $\overline{AB}$ and give its length.

 b. Find the circumference. Use 3.14 for π. Round your answer to the nearest hundredth.

17. **History** The first Hula Hoop® was introduced in 1958. What is the circumference of a Hula Hoop with a 3 ft diameter? Use 3.14 for π.

Use the cylinders for Exercises 18 and 19.

18. **Estimation** About how many times greater is the circumference of the top of the purple cylinder than the top of the blue cylinder?

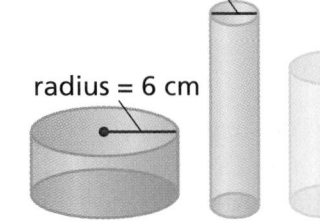

diameter = 4 cm

radius = 6 cm

19. **Choose a Strategy** If the circumference of the top of the yellow cylinder is 22.5 centimeters, which method can you use to find the radius?

 Ⓐ Divide 22.5 by π.

 Ⓑ Multiply 22.5 by π.

 Ⓒ Divide 22.5 by π and then divide the quotient by 2.

 Ⓓ Multiply 22.5 by π and then multiply the product by 2.

20. **Write About It** The circumference of a circle is 3.14 m. Explain how you can find the diameter and radius of the circle.

21. **Challenge** An Olympic outdoor archery target is made up of 10 equally spaced concentric circles. *Concentric* means that the center of each of the circles is the same. If the diameter of the biggest ring on the target is 122 cm and the diameter of the bullseye is 12.2 centimeters, what is the diameter of the fourth ring from the inside?

TEST PREP and Spiral Review

22. **Multiple Choice** A mini-DVD has a radius of 4 centimeters. Which expression can you use to find the circumference of the mini-DVD?

 Ⓐ 4π Ⓑ 8π Ⓒ 16π Ⓓ $2 \cdot 2 \cdot \pi \cdot 8$

23. **Short Response** The wheels on Ryan's bike are each about 2 feet in diameter. If Ryan rides his bike for 1 mile, about how many times will each wheel rotate? Use 3 for π.

Order the fractions from greatest to least. (Lesson 4-7)

24. $\frac{1}{2}, \frac{3}{8}, \frac{5}{8}$ 25. $\frac{3}{4}, \frac{10}{12}, \frac{1}{12}$ 26. $\frac{3}{10}, \frac{3}{5}, \frac{7}{10}$ 27. $\frac{7}{16}, \frac{3}{4}, \frac{5}{8}$

Write each percent as a decimal. (Lesson 7-7)

28. 50%   29. 5%   30. 85%   31. 100%   32. 15%

Construct Circle Graphs

Use with Lesson 9-8

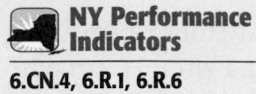

NY Performance Indicators

6.CN.4, 6.R.1, 6.R.6

go.hrw.com
Lab Resources Online
KEYWORD: MR7 Lab9

REMEMBER

The sum of the measures of the angles in any circle is 360°.

A circle graph shows parts of a whole. If you think of a complete circle as 100%, you can express sections of a circle graph as percents.

Money Raised at School Fair

Bake sale — $200
Drinks $50
Crafts $100
Games — $50

- Ms. Shipley's class earned $400 at the school fair. What fraction of the $400 did the class earn at the bake sale?

- What percent of the $400 did the class earn at the bake sale?

Activity

At Mazel Middle School, students were surveyed about their favorite types of TV programs. Make a circle graph to represent the results.

Students' Favorite Programs	
Type of Program	Number of Students
Science	25
Cooking	15
Sports	50
Sitcoms	150
Movies	60
Cartoons	200

1 Find the total number of students surveyed.

$25 + 15 + 50 + 150 + 60 + 200 = 500$

2 Find the percent of the total represented by students who like science programs.

$$\frac{25}{500} = 5\%$$

3 Since there are 360° in a circle, multiply 5% by 360°. This will give you an angle measure in degrees.

$$0.05 \cdot 360° = 18°$$

4 Use a compass to draw a circle. Mark the center and use a straightedge to draw a line from the center to the edge of the circle.

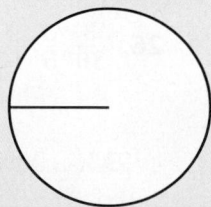

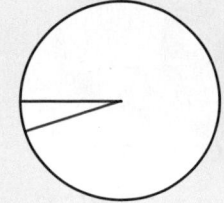

5 Use your protractor to draw an angle measuring 18°. The vertex of the angle will be the center of the circle, and one side will be the line that you drew. The section formed represents the percent of students who prefer science programs.

6 Repeat **2** through **5** for each type of program. Label each section, and give the graph a title.

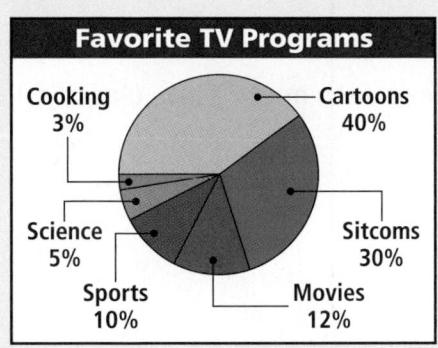

Favorite TV Programs

Cooking 3%
Cartoons 40%
Science 5%
Sitcoms 30%
Sports 10%
Movies 12%

Think and Discuss

1. Looking at your circle graph, discuss five pieces of information you have learned about the TV habits of students at Mazel Middle School.

2. What does the whole circle represent?

3. Why do you need to know that there are 360° in a circle?

4. How does the size of each section of your circle graph relate to the percent that it represents?

Try This

1. People at a mall were surveyed about their favorite pets. Make a circle graph to display the results of the survey. Round to the nearest tenth.

Favorite Pets	
Type of Pet	**Number of People**
Dog	225
Fish	150
Bird	112
Cat	198
Other	65

2. Collect data from your classmates about their favorite colors. Use the data to make a circle graph with no more than five sections.

3. The circle graph shows the results of a survey about what people in the United States like to eat for breakfast. If this survey included 1,500 people, how many people said they like to eat cereal for breakfast?

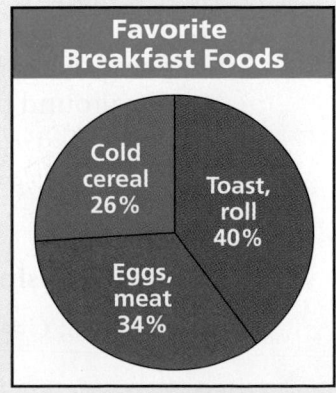

Favorite Breakfast Foods

Cold cereal 26%
Toast, roll 40%
Eggs, meat 34%

READY TO GO ON?

Quiz for Lessons 9-6 Through 9-8

✓ **9-6** **Finding Angle Measures in Polygons**

Use a protractor to find the measure of each angle. Then classify the angle.

1.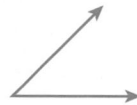

2.

3.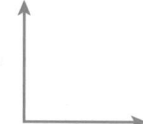

4. A garden plot is shown at right. Find the measures of $\angle A$ and $\angle B$.

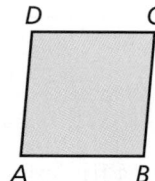

✓ **9-7** **Perimeter**

Find the perimeter of each figure.

5.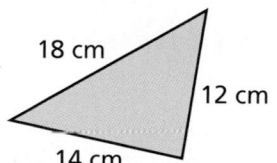

18 cm, 12 cm, 14 cm

6.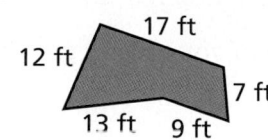

17 ft, 12 ft, 7 ft, 13 ft, 9 ft

7.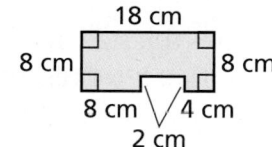

18 cm, 8 cm, 8 cm, 8 cm, 4 cm, 2 cm

✓ **9-8** **Circles and Circumference**

Name the circle and two radii, and then find the circumference for each circle. Use 3.14 for π and round to the nearest hundredth.

8.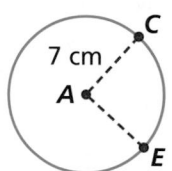

7 cm, A, C, E

9.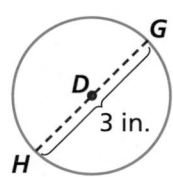

G, D, 3 in., H

10.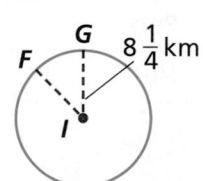

G, F, $8\frac{1}{4}$ km, I

11.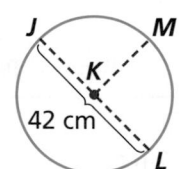

J, M, K, 42 cm, L

12. An architect is making a plan for a new circular playground. Find the circumference of the playground by rounding π to 3.

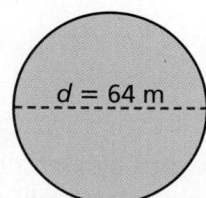

$d = 64$ m

Find each missing value to the nearest hundredth. Use 3.14 for π.

13. $r = 9$ in.; $C = $ ___?___   14. $d = 20$ m; $C = $ ___?___   15. $C = 37.68$ ft; $d = $ ___?___

Ready to Go On?

MULTI-STEP TEST PREP

Fenced In The Midland Botanical Gardens has a rectangular bed of dahlias and a circular bed of tulips. The garden's landscaper has decided to install new fences around both of the flower beds.

1. The length of the dahlia bed is 3 feet longer than its width. What is the perimeter of the dahlia bed?

2. The new fence for the dahlia bed is available in sections that are each 18 inches long. How many sections should the landscaper order? Explain.

3. What is the circumference of the tulip bed to the nearest meter? Round *pi* to 3.

4. The new fence for the tulip bed is available in sections that are each 44 cm long. How many sections should the landscaper order? Explain.

5. The landscaper can install one section of a fence in 6 minutes. How long will it take to install the fences for both beds? Will the landscaper be able to complete the job in less than 5 hours? Why or why not?

Dahlias

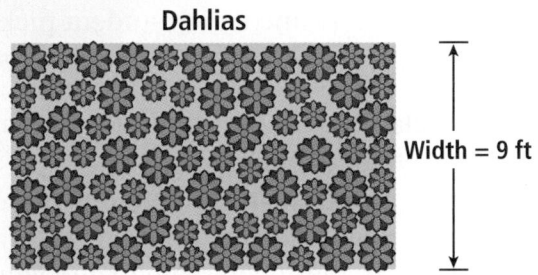

Width = 9 ft

Tulips

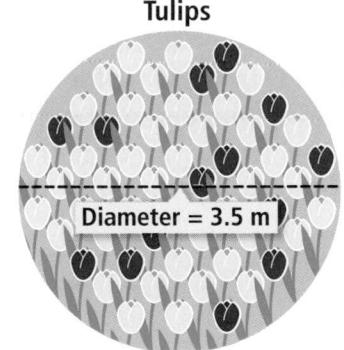

Diameter = 3.5 m

Multi-Step Test Prep

Game Time

Logic Puzzle

Each day from Monday through Friday, Mayuri, Naomi, Brett, Thomas, and Angela took turns picking a restaurant for lunch. They ate at restaurants that serve either Chinese food, hamburgers, pizza, seafood, or tacos. Use the clues below to determine which student picked the restaurant on each day and which restaurant the student picked.

1. Angela skipped Friday's lunch to play in a basketball game.
2. Brett picked the restaurant on Wednesday.
3. The students ate tacos on Friday.
4. Naomi is allergic to seafood and volunteered to pick the first restaurant.
5. Thomas picked a hamburger restaurant on the day before another student chose a pizza restaurant.

You can use a chart like the one below to help you solve this puzzle. Place an *O* in a square for something that is true and an *X* in a square for something that cannot be true. Remember that when you place an *O* in a square, you can put *X*'s in the rest of the squares in that row and column. The information from the first two clues has been entered for you.

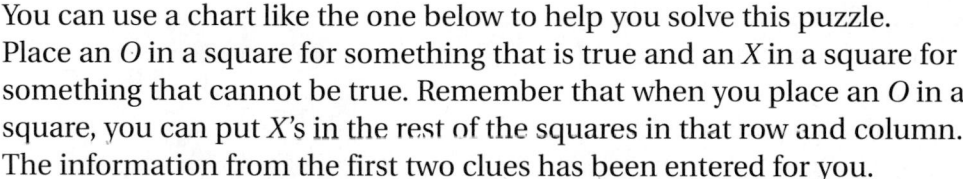

		Student					Restaurant				
		Mayuri	Naomi	Brett	Thomas	Angela	Seafood	Pizza	Hamburger	Chinese	Tacos
Day	Monday			X							
	Tuesday			X							
	Wednesday	X	X	O	X	X					
	Thursday			X							
	Friday			X		X					
Restaurant	Seafood										
	Pizza										
	Hamburgers										
	Chinese										
	Tacos										

A copy of a blank logic puzzle chart is available online.

go.hrw.com
Game Time Extra
KEYWORD: MR7 Games

Materials

- Magnetic strip
- construction paper
- glue
- scissors
- 6 paint chips
- small metal box

It's in the Bag!

PROJECT ▸ **Perfectly Packaged Perimeters**

This metal box stores magnetic vocabulary tiles and small squares that you can use to create a variety of shapes.

Directions

❶ Glue construction paper onto the magnetic strip.

❷ Write vocabulary words from this chapter on the magnetic strip. Then cut the words apart to form magnetic vocabulary tiles. **Figure A**

❸ Cut the paint chips into smaller squares, each approximately $1\frac{1}{4}$ inches by $1\frac{1}{4}$ inches.

❹ Glue a small piece of construction paper onto the lid of the metal box. Label it with the number and title of the chapter. **Figure B**

❺ Store the vocabulary tiles and the small squares in the metal box.

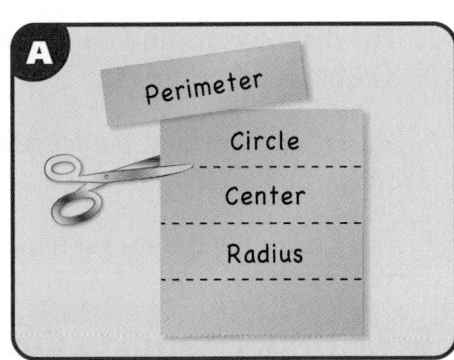

Putting the Math into Action

Place the vocabulary tiles on the outside of the box or on another metal surface to review key terms from the chapter. Arrange the small squares to form shapes with various perimeters. What is the greatest perimeter you can make?

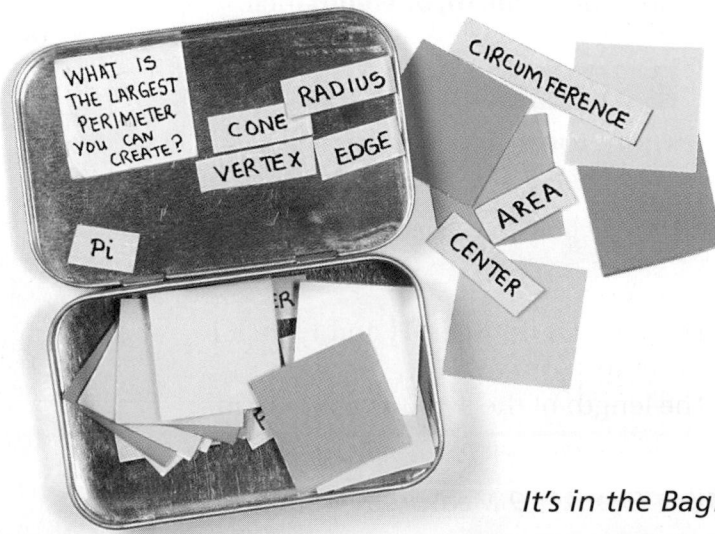

Vocabulary

center 520

circle 520

circumference 520

customary system 488

diameter 520

metric system 492

perimeter 514

pi 520

radius (radii) 520

Complete the sentences below with vocabulary words from the list above.

1. The distance around a polygon is called the ___?___ , and the distance around a circle is called the ___?___ .

2. A line segment that passes through the center of a circle and has both endpoints on the circle is a ___?___ .

3. The ___?___ is the measurement system often used in the United States.

9-1 Understanding Customary Units of Measure (pp. 488–491)

EXAMPLE

■ **What unit of measure provides the best estimate? Explain.**

A desk is about 3 ___?___ long.

Think: The length of a desk is about 3 times the distance from your shoulder to your elbow.

A desk is about 3 ft long.

Measure the length of the arrow to the nearest half, fourth, or eighth inch.

The arrow is between $1\frac{1}{4}$ and $1\frac{3}{8}$ in. It is closer to $1\frac{3}{8}$.
The length of the arrow is about $1\frac{3}{8}$ in.

EXERCISES **6.M.2, 6.M.6, 6.M.9**

What unit of measure provides the best estimate? Explain.

4. A crayon is about 5 ___?___ long.

5. The distance from Denver, CO, to Dallas, TX, is about 800 ___?___ .

6. A bunch of bananas weighs about 2 ___?___ .

7. An eyedropper holds about 1 ___?___ of liquid.

8. Measure the length of the arrow to the nearest half, fourth, or eighth inch.

9-2 Understanding Metric Units of Measure (pp. 492–495)

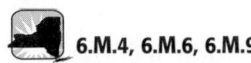

EXAMPLE

■ **What unit of measure provides the best estimate? Explain.**

A sofa is about 3 ___?___ long.

Think: The length of a sofa is about 3 times the width of a single bed.

A sofa is about 3 m long.

Measure the length of the arrow to the nearest centimeter.

The arrow is between 2 and 3 cm. It is closer to 2 cm.

The length of the arrow is about 2 cm.

EXERCISES

What unit of measure provides the best estimate? Explain.

9. A paper clip is about 32 ___?___ long.

10. A grain of rice has a mass of about 5 ___?___.

11. A laptop computer has a mass of about 2 ___?___.

12. A large pitcher has a capacity of about 2 ___?___.

13. Measure the length of the arrow to the nearest centimeter.

9-3 Converting Customary Units (pp. 496–499)

EXAMPLE

■ **Convert 5 yards to feet.**

Set up a conversion factor.

$5 \, \cancel{\text{yd}} \times \dfrac{3 \text{ ft}}{1 \, \cancel{\text{yd}}}$ *Think: yards to feet— 3 ft = 1 yd, so use $\frac{3 \text{ ft}}{yd}$.*

5 yd = 15 ft *Multiply 5 yd by the conversion factor. Cancel the common unit, yd.*

EXERCISES

Convert.

14. 3 mi to feet

15. 18 ft to yards

16. 3 qt to cups

17. 48 c to gal

18. 128 oz to pounds

19. 8,000 lb to tons

20. $\dfrac{64 \text{ oz}}{x \text{ lb}} = \dfrac{16 \text{ oz}}{1 \text{ lb}}$

21. $\dfrac{12 \text{ ft}}{x \text{ in.}} = \dfrac{1 \text{ ft}}{12 \text{ in.}}$

22. $\dfrac{8 \text{ pt}}{x \text{ qt}} = \dfrac{2 \text{ pt}}{1 \text{ qt}}$

23. $\dfrac{3 \text{ ft}}{1 \text{ yd}} = \dfrac{x \text{ ft}}{33 \text{ yd}}$

24. The Golden Gate Bridge, in San Francisco, has a tower height of 750 ft. How many yards tall is this?

9-4 Converting Metric Units (pp. 500–503)

EXAMPLE

■ **Convert.**

29 cm = ▦ m

$29 \, \cancel{\text{cm}} \cdot \dfrac{1 \text{ m}}{100 \, \cancel{\text{cm}}} = 0.29 \text{ m}$ *Cancel the common unit, cm.*

EXERCISES

Convert.

25. 3.2 L = ▦ mL

26. 7 mL = ▦ L

27. 342 m = ▦ km

28. 42 g = ▦ kg

29. 51 mm = ▦ m

30. 71 km = ▦ m

9-5 Time and Temperature (pp. 504–507)

 6.A.6

EXAMPLE

■ Convert.

14 hours = ▨ minutes

$14 \cancel{h} \cdot \dfrac{60 \text{ min}}{1 \cancel{h}} = 840 \text{ min}$ *1 hour =
60 minutes*

EXERCISES

Convert.

31. 3,600 seconds = ▨ hours

32. 990 minutes = ▨ seconds

33. 15 weeks = ▨ days

9-6 Finding Angle Measures in Polygons (pp. 510–513)

6.N.27

EXAMPLE

■ Use a protractor to find the measure of ∠ABC. Then classify the angle.

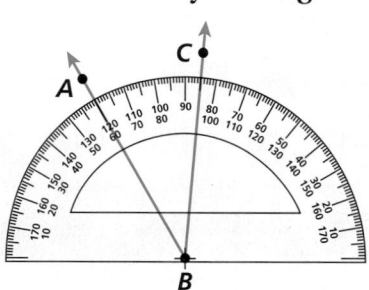

∠ABC = 95° − 60° = 35°
Since 35° < 90°, the angle is acute.

EXERCISES

34. Use a protractor to find the measure of ∠ABC. Then classify the angle.

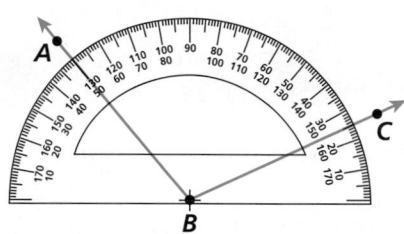

9-7 Perimeter (pp. 514–517)

6.A.2

EXAMPLE

■ Find the perimeter of the figure.

Add all the side lengths.

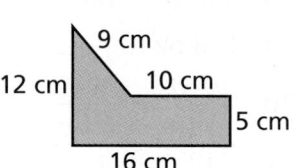

P = 9 + 10 + 5 + 16 + 12 = 52
The perimeter is 52 cm.

EXERCISES

35. Find the perimeter of the figure.

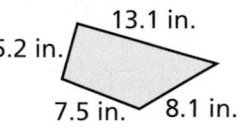

36. What is the length of *n* if the perimeter is 20 ft?

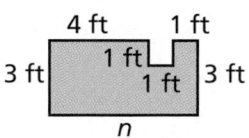

9-8 Circles and Circumference (pp. 520–523)

6.A.2, 6.A.6, 6.G.5, 6.G.6, 6.G.7, 6.G.9

EXAMPLE

■ Find the circumference of the circle. Use 3.14 for π.
C = πd
C ≈ 3.14 · 6
C ≈ 18.84 cm

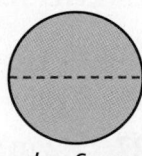

d = 6 cm

EXERCISES

Find each missing value to the nearest hundredth. Use 3.14 for π.

37. d = 10 ft; C = ?   **38.** C = 28.26 m; d = ?

39. r = 8 cm; C = ?   **40.** C = 69.08 ft; r = ?

What metric unit of measure provides the best estimate? Explain.

1. A flower pot can hold about 1 ___?___ of water.

2. A baby bird has a mass of about 15 ___?___.

3. The length of a cricket is about 3 ___?___ long.

Use the table for Problems 4–6.

4. If Darian was moved to the nursery at 2:25 P.M., how long was he in the hospital room?

5. Convert Darian's weight to ounces.

6. How long was Darian in inches?

Baby Darian Cole	
Birth Date	May 1, 2005, 11:45 A.M.
Weight	7 lb
Length	1 ft 8 in.

Estimate the temperature.

7. 48°C is about ▪▪°F.

8. 70°F is about ▪▪°C.

Use a protractor to find the measure of each angle. Then classify the angle.

9.

10.

Find the perimeter of each figure.

11.
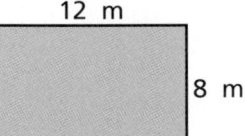
12 m
8 m

12.
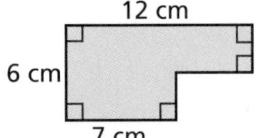
12 cm
6 cm
7 cm

13.
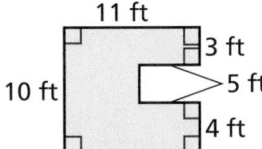
11 ft
3 ft
10 ft
5 ft
4 ft

Name the circle and two radii, and then find the circumference for each circle. Use 3.14 for π and round to the nearest hundredth.

14.
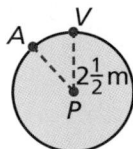
A V
$2\frac{1}{2}$ m
P

15.
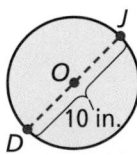
J
O
10 in.
D

16.
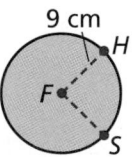
9 cm
H
F
S

Find each missing value to the nearest hundredth. Use 3.14 for π.

17. $r = 4$ cm; $C = $ ___?___

18. $d = 10$ ft; $C = $ ___?___

19. $C = 37.68$ ft; $d = $ ___?___

20. A gardener is digging a rose garden. Find the circumference of the rose garden by rounding π to 3.

$d = 21$ m

TEST TACKLER

Any Question Type: Use a Diagram

Diagrams are a helpful tool. If a diagram is included in a test item, study it closely as it may contain useful information. Sometimes it is helpful to draw your own diagram.

EXAMPLE **1**

Multiple Choice A small circle is inside a large circle. The diameter of the small circle is 10 feet. If the circumference of the large circle is 4 times greater than the circumference of the small circle, what is the radius of the large circle? (Round *pi* to 3.)

(A) 20 ft   (B) 30 ft   (C) 40 ft   (D) 120 ft

Draw a diagram to help you visualize the problem.
Draw two circles and label them with all the information given in the problem.

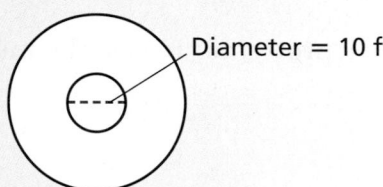

Diameter = 10 ft

The circumference of the small circle is about 30 feet. The circumference of the large circle is about 120 feet. Divide by 2π. $120 \div (3 \cdot 2) = 20$, so the radius is about 20 feet.

Choice A is correct.

EXAMPLE **2**

Short Response $\triangle ABC$ is similar to $\triangle FDE$. Find the missing length.

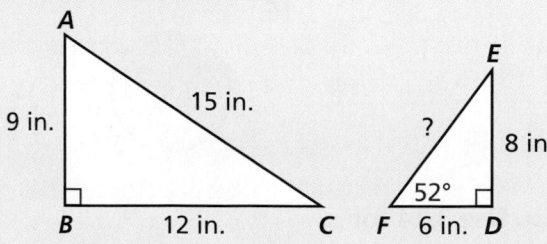

These triangles do not look similar and are not drawn to scale, but the information in the problem says that they are.

Set up a proportion to find the missing length and solve for *x*. $\dfrac{x}{6} = \dfrac{15}{9}$

The unknown side length is 10 in.

If you have trouble understanding what a test item is asking, draw a diagram to help you visualize the question.

Read each test item and answer the questions that follow.

Item A
Multiple Choice The temperature at the ski lodge was 21°F at 9:00 P.M. At sunrise, the temperature was 34°F. How many degrees did the temperature rise overnight?

   Ⓐ 54°F   Ⓒ 13°F

   Ⓑ 25°F   Ⓓ 4°F

1. What information will help you solve the problem?

2. Sketch a diagram to help you solve this problem. Be sure to label the diagram with all of the information you know.

Item B
Short Answer Prove that the two rectangles below are similar. Explain your reasoning.

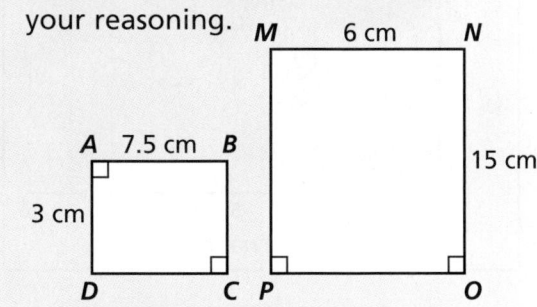

3. What information can you get from the diagram to help you prove that the figures are similar?

4. Do you think the drawings accurately illustrate the given information? If not, why?

5. What is the length of $\overline{DC}$?

Item C
Gridded Response The longest side of a triangle is 14.4 centimeters. Its shortest side is 5.9 centimeters shorter than the longest side. If the perimeter of the triangle is 35.2 centimeters, what is the length of the third side?

6. How do you determine the perimeter of a triangle?

7. Sketch a diagram of the triangle. Explain how sketching the diagram can help you answer the problem.

8. Tell how you would fill in your response to this test item on a grid.

Item D
Multiple Choice Which angle pairs are vertical angles?

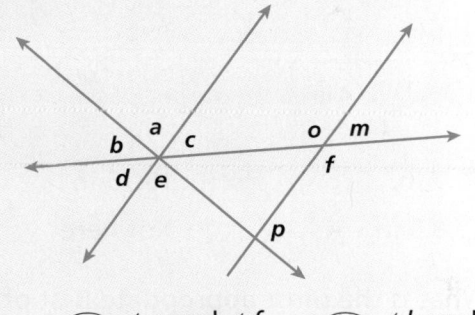

   Ⓕ ∠a and ∠f   Ⓗ ∠b and ∠e

   Ⓖ ∠b and ∠c   Ⓙ ∠c and ∠d

9. Which answer choice can you immediately eliminate? Why?

10. How can you use the diagram to help you eliminate the other choices?

11. Explain which answer choice is correct.

Cumulative Assessment, Chapters 1–9

Multiple Choice

New York Test Prep

1. The world's largest ball of twine is located in Cawker City, Kansas. It weighs 17,571 pounds. About how many tons does this ball of twine weigh?

   (A) 9 tons   (C) 11 tons

   (B) 10 tons   (D) 12 tons

2. The two triangles shown below are similar. What is the length of the unknown side *n*?

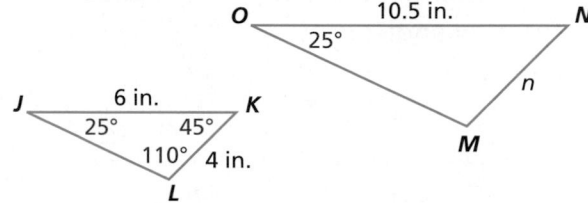

   (F) 7 in.   (H) 15.75 in.

   (G) 8.5 in.   (J) Not here

3. What is the most appropriate unit of measure for the length of a tractor?

   (A) Inches   (C) Millimeters

   (B) Feet   (D) Pounds

4. In 2002, the U.S. Census reported that 37.4 million Latinos were living in the United States. Approximately 3.2 million of these Latinos were from Puerto Rico. What percent of the Latino population in 2002 came from Puerto Rico?

   (F) 0.086%   (H) 8.6%

   (G) 0.86%   (J) 86%

5. Josh's violin lessons start at 8:55 A.M. and last 95 minutes. What time will Josh's lesson end?

   (A) 9:45 A.M.   (C) 10:30 A.M.

   (B) 10:15 A.M.   (D) 10:45 A.M.

6. An online survey by Kids' Money asked children to share how much money they receive for an allowance. The results from 6- to 12-year-olds are shown below. According to this survey, what is the average allowance for children between the ages of 8 and 12?

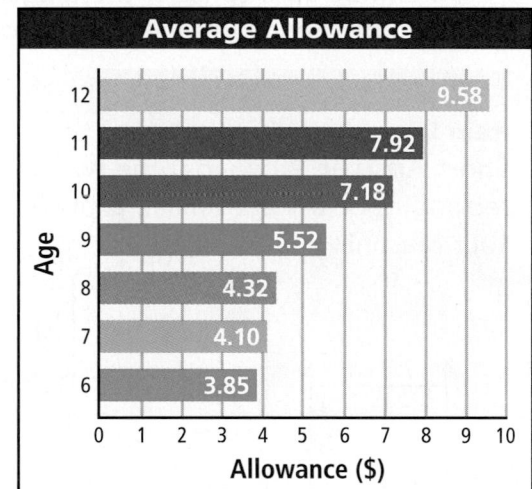

   (F) $6.06   (H) $7.18

   (G) $6.90   (J) $8.49

7. Shelly has a bookshelf that is $48\frac{3}{4}$ inches long. If Shelly's textbooks are each $3\frac{1}{2}$ inches wide, how many books can Shelly fit on a shelf?

   (A) 15 books   (C) 13 books

   (B) 14 books   (D) 12 books

8. Which metric unit should be used to show how much liquid a jar can hold?

   (F) Kilograms (H) Millimeters

   (G) Milligrams (J) Milliliters

9. Which of the following statements about plane figures is NOT true?

   (A) A square is always a rhombus.

   (B) A rectangle is always a square.

   (C) A trapezoid is always a quadrilateral.

   (D) A rhombus is always a parallelogram.

When converting between metric units, multiply by a power of 10 when changing from larger units to smaller units. Divide by a power of 10 when changing from smaller units to larger units.

10. Jordan's locker number is greater than 225 but less than 250. It is divisible by 3 and 9, but not by 2, 4, or 5. What is Jordan's locker number?

    (F) 231 (H) 243

    (G) 237 (J) 249

11. In 1912, a reticulated python was found to be 10.7 meters long. How many centimeters long was this snake?

    (A) 1.07 (C) 107

    (B) 10.7 (D) 1,070

12. What is the 5th term in a sequence that begins on 6 and is divided each time by $\frac{1}{3}$?

    (F) $\frac{2}{9}$ (H) 162

    (G) $\frac{2}{27}$ (J) 486

13. Jessie is $1\frac{1}{2}$ times taller than her sister. If her sister is 4 feet tall, how many inches taller is Jessie than her sister?

    (A) 6 (C) 48

    (B) 24 (D) 72

Short Response

14. Gene and Janice's gas tanks are empty. It cost Gene $48.52 to fill up his 25.7-gallon gas tank. At another gas station, Janice filled up her 13.8 gallon tank and paid $25.80. Who paid the most for a gallon of gas? Explain. **Gene**

15. Larry is making a model of an Olympic-size swimming pool. The scale is 2 cm = 5 m.

    a. An Olympic-size pool is 50 m long by 25 m wide. What are the dimensions of the model? Show your work.
    20 cm × 10 cm

    b. There are 8 lanes in the actual pool. Each lane is 2.5 m wide. How many centimeters wide are the lanes in the model? Show your work. **1 cm**

16. A regulation football field is 160 feet wide and 420 feet long. These dimensions include the end zones.

    a. What is the perimeter of a regulation football field in yards? Show your work. **$386\frac{2}{3}$ yd**

    b. A football field has two end zones at the end of each side of the playing field. If the playing field is 100 yards long, how many inches long is one end zone? Show your work. **720 in.**

Extended Response

17. Teresa is planning to build a stone border around a large walnut tree. The stones are 6 inches long.

    a. How many stones will Teresa need if she creates a square border that is 8 feet long? Show your work.

    b. How many stones will Teresa need if she creates a circular border that has an 8-foot diameter? Use $\frac{22}{7}$ for π. Show your work.

    c. If the stones cost $2.69 each, how much money will Teresa save if she builds a circular border instead of a square border? Explain.

Measurement: Area and Volume

NEW YORK TEST PREP

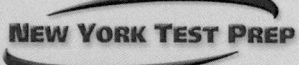

KEYWORD.hmr.com

Chapter Project Online

Coverage Chart (1 yd³ of wood chips)	
Depth of Chips (in.)	Area Covered (ft²)
$\frac{1}{2}$	640
1	320
2	160
3	$106\frac{2}{3}$
4	80

Career *Landscape Architect*

Almost every shopping center has walkways, lawns, and trees. A landscape architect designs these so that they are appealing and well suited to the environment. Landscape architects also plan the layouts of residential areas, office parks, and school campuses.

To calculate costs, landscape architects must estimate how much material is needed to cover planted areas. For example, the table shows the number of square feet that can be covered by 1 cubic yard of wood chips.

ARE YOU READY?

✓ Vocabulary

Choose the best term from the list to complete each sentence.

1. A(n) ___?___ is a quadrilateral with opposite sides that are parallel and congruent.

2. Some customary units of length are ___?___ and ___?___. Some metric units of length are ___?___ and ___?___.

3. A(n) ___?___ is a quadrilateral with side lengths that are all congruent and four right angles.

4. A(n) ___?___ is a polygon with six sides.

centimeters
cube
feet
hexagon
inches
liters
meters
parallelogram
square
trapezoid

Complete these exercises to review skills you will need for this chapter.

✓ Add and Multiply Whole Numbers, Fractions, and Decimals

Find each sum or product.

5. $1.5 + 2.4 + 3.6 + 2.5$ 6. $2 \cdot 3.5 \cdot 4$ 7. $\frac{22}{7} \cdot 21$

8. $\frac{1}{2} \cdot 5 \cdot 4$ 9. $3.2 \cdot 5.6$ 10. $\frac{1}{2} \cdot 10 \cdot 3$

11. $(2 \cdot 5) + (6 \cdot 8)$ 12. $2(3.5) + 2(1.5)$ 13. $9(20 + 7)$

✓ Estimate Metric Lengths

Use a centimeter ruler to measure each line to the nearest centimeter.

14. ───────────────────────

15. ──────────────

✓ Identify Polygons

Name each polygon. Determine whether it appears to be regular or not regular.

16.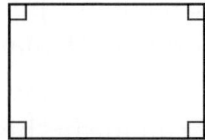

17.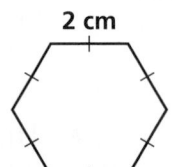

18.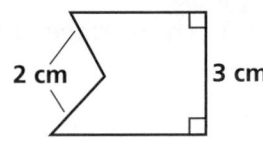

Where You've Been

Previously, you

- selected appropriate units to measure perimeter, area, and volume.
- classified polygons.
- identified three-dimensional figures.

In This Chapter

You will study

- solving problems involving area.
- identifying, drawing, and building three-dimensional figures.
- finding the surface area of prisms, pyramids, and cylinders.
- finding the volume of prisms and cylinders.

Where You're Going

You can use the skills learned in this chapter

- to find the volume of pyramids, cones, and spheres.
- to find the surface area of spheres.

Key Vocabulary/Vocabulario

area	área
base	base (de un polígono o figura tridimensional)
cylinder	cilindro
edge	arista
face	cara
polyhedron	poliedro
pyramid	pirámide
surface area	área total
vertex	vértice
volume	volumen

Vocabulary Connections

To become familiar with some of the vocabulary terms in the chapter, consider the following. You may refer to the chapter, the glossary, or a dictionary if you like.

1. The word *cylinder* comes from the Greek *kylindein,* meaning "to roll." What do you think the three-dimensional shape of a **cylinder** can do? What shape base do you expect it to have?

2. The word *polyhedron* comes from the Greek *polys,* meaning "many" and *hedra,* meaning "base." What do you think **polyhedrons** are made up of?

3. The Egyptian pyramids are huge stone structures whose outside walls, in the form of four triangles, meet in a point at the top. What shapes do you think make up a **pyramid** ?

4. The word *vertex* can mean "highest point." Where do you think you can find one **vertex** of a three-dimensional figure?

Reading Strategy: Learn Math Vocabulary

Many new math terms fill the pages of your textbook. By learning these new terms and their meanings when they are introduced, you will be able to apply this knowledge to different concepts throughout your math classes.

Some ways that may help you learn vocabulary include the following:

- Try to find the meaning of the new term by its context.
- Use the prefix or suffix to figure out the meaning of the term.
- Relate the new term to familiar everyday words or situations.

Vocabulary Word	Definition	Study Tip
Origin	The point (0, 0) where the *x*-axis and *y*-axis intersect on the coordinate plane	The word begins with an "O" which can remind you that the coordinates of the origin are (0, 0).
Quadrants	The *x*- and *y*- axis divide the coordinate plane into four regions. Each region is called a quadrant.	The prefix *quad* means "four." A *quadrilateral* is a four-sided figure, for example.
Coordinate	One of the numbers of an ordered pair that locate a point on a coordinate graph	*Think: x* coordinates with *y*.

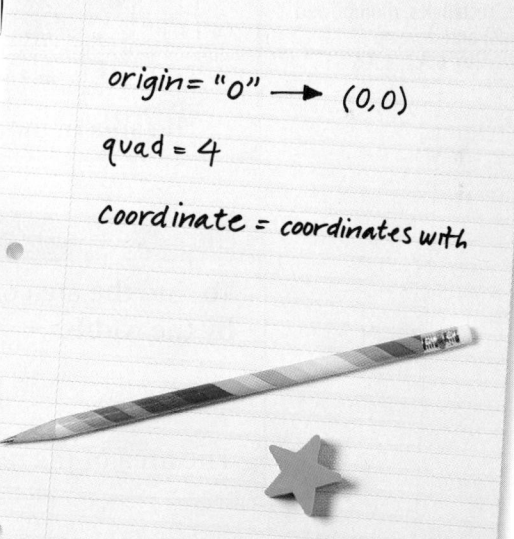

origin = "o" → (0,0)

quad = 4

coordinate = coordinates with

Try This

Complete the table as you work through the chapter to help you learn the vocabulary words.

	Vocabulary Word	Definition	Study Tip
1.	Area	▪	▪
2.	▪	▪	▪
3.	▪	▪	▪

10-1 Estimating and Finding Area

Learn to estimate the area of irregular figures and to find the area of rectangles and parallelograms.

Vocabulary

area

When colonists settled the land that would become the United States, ownership boundaries were sometimes natural landmarks such as rivers, trees, and hills. Landowners who wanted to know the size of their property needed to estimate the area of their land.

The **area** of a figure is the amount of surface it covers. We measure area in square units.

EXAMPLE 1 Estimating the Area of an Irregular Figure

NY Performance Indicators

6.G.2 Determine the area of triangles and quadrilaterals (squares, rectangles, rhombi, and trapezoids) and develop formulas. Also, 6.A.2, 6.A.6.

Estimate the area of the figure.

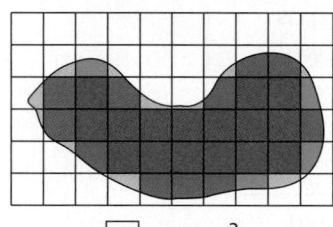

□ = 1 mi²

Count full squares: 16 red squares.

Count almost-full squares: 11 blue squares.

Count squares that are about half-full:
4 green squares ≈ 2 full squares.

Do not count almost empty yellow squares.

Add. 16 + 11 + 2 = 29

The area of the figure is about 29 mi².

AREA OF A RECTANGLE

To find the area of a rectangle, multiply the length by the width.

$$A = \ell w$$
$$A = 4 \cdot 3 = 12$$

The area of the rectangle is 12 square units.

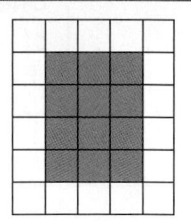

EXAMPLE 2 Finding the Area of a Rectangle

Find the area of the rectangle.

13 m

8 m

$A = \ell w$	*Write the formula.*
$A = 13 \cdot 8$	*Substitute 13 for ℓ and 8 for w.*
$A = 104$	*Multiply.*

The area is 104 m².

You can use the formula for the area of a rectangle to write a formula for the area of a parallelogram. Imagine cutting off the triangle drawn in the parallelogram and sliding it to the right to form a rectangle.

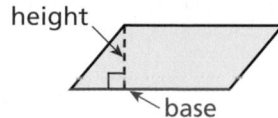

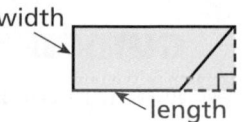

The area of a parallelogram = *bh*.   The area of a rectangle = ℓ*w*.

The **base** of the parallelogram is the **length** of the rectangle.
The **height** of the parallelogram is the **width** of the rectangle.

EXAMPLE **3** **Finding the Area of a Parallelogram**

Find the area of the parallelogram.

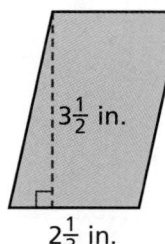

$3\frac{1}{2}$ in.

$2\frac{1}{3}$ in.

$A = bh$	*Write the formula.*
$A = 2\frac{1}{3} \cdot 3\frac{1}{2}$	*Substitute $2\frac{1}{3}$ for b and $3\frac{1}{2}$ for h.*
$A = \frac{7}{3} \cdot \frac{7}{2}$	*Multiply.*
$A = \frac{49}{6}$, or $8\frac{1}{6}$	The area is $8\frac{1}{6}$ in^2.

EXAMPLE **4** *Recreation Application*

A rectangular park is made up of a rectangular spring-fed pool and a limestone picnic ground that surrounds it. The rectangular park is 30 yd by 25 yd, and the pool is 10 yd by 4 yd. What is the area of the limestone picnic ground?

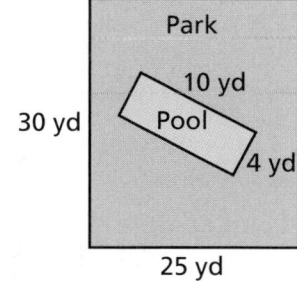

Park

30 yd

10 yd

Pool

4 yd

25 yd

To find the area of the picnic ground, subtract the area of the pool from the area of the park.

park area	–	pool area	=	picnic ground area	
(30 · 25)	–	(10 · 4)	=	*n*	*Substitute for ℓ and w in A = ℓw.*
750	–	40	=	710	*Use the order of operations.*

The area of the limestone picnic ground is 710 yd^2.

6.CN.2, 6.CM.4

Think and Discuss

1. Explain how the area of a triangle and the area of a rectangle that have the same base and the same height are related.

2. Give a formula for the area of a square.

go.hrw.com
Homework Help Online
KEYWORD: MR7 10-1
Parent Resources Online
KEYWORD: MR7 Parent

GUIDED PRACTICE

See Example 1 Estimate the area of each figure.

1.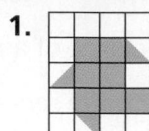

2.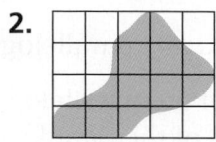

3.

See Example 2 Find the area of each rectangle.

4.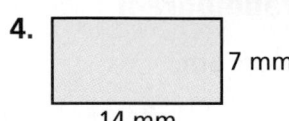
7 mm
14 mm

5.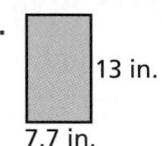
13 in.
7.7 in.

6.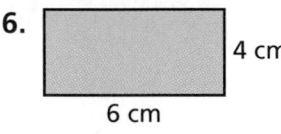
4 cm
6 cm

See Example 3 Find the area of each parallelogram.

7.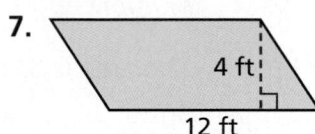
4 ft
12 ft

8.
$2\frac{1}{3}$ cm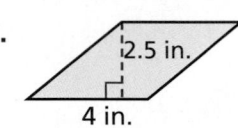
9 cm

9.
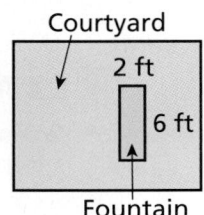
2.5 in.
4 in.

See Example 4 **10.** Mindy is designing a rectangular fountain in a courtyard. The rest of the courtyard will be covered with stone. The rectangular courtyard is 12 ft by 15 ft. What is the area of the courtyard that will be covered with stone?

Courtyard
2 ft
6 ft
Fountain

INDEPENDENT PRACTICE

See Example 1 Estimate the area of each figure.

11.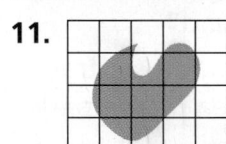

12.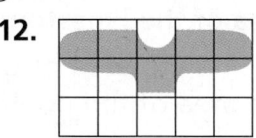

13.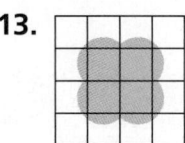

See Example 2 Find the area of each rectangle.

14.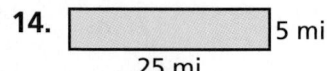
5 mi
25 mi

15.
8.5 m
1.5 m

16.
2 cm
12 cm

See Example 3 Find the area of each parallelogram.

17.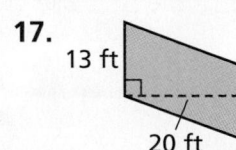
13 ft
20 ft

18.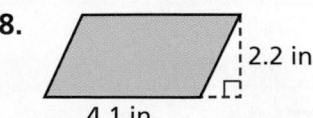
2.2 in.
4.1 in.

19.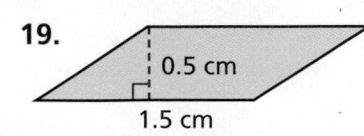
0.5 cm
1.5 cm

See Example 4
Extra Practice
See page 733.

20. Bob is planting in a rectangular container. In the center of the container, he places a smaller rectangular tub with mint. The tub is 8 in. by 3 in. He plants flowers around the tub. What is the area of the container planted with flowers?

38 in.
Flowers
25 in.
Mint
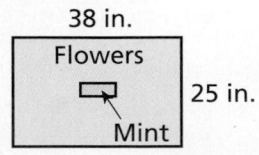

Social Studies LINK

Iceland has many active volcanoes and frequent earthquakes. There are more hot springs in Iceland than in any other country in the world.

Sightseers watch the eruption of Geyser Namafjall in the Myvatn Region of North Iceland.

Use the map for Exercises 21 and 22.

21. **Choose a Strategy** One square on the map represents 1,700 km². Which is a reasonable estimate for the area of Iceland?

Ⓐ Less than 65,000 km²

Ⓑ Between 90,000 and 105,000 km²

Ⓒ Between 120,000 and 135,000 km²

Ⓓ Greater than 150,000 km²

22. **Estimation** About 10% of the area of Iceland is covered with glaciers. Estimate the area covered by glaciers.

23. ✏️ **Write About It** The House is Iceland's oldest building. When it was built in 1765, the builders measured length in *ells*. The base of the House is 14 ells wide and 20 ells long. Explain how to find the area in ells of the House.

24. ⭐ **Challenge** The length of one ell varied from country to country. In England, one ell was equal to $1\frac{1}{4}$ yd. Suppose the House were measured in English ells. Find the area in yards of the House.

go.hrw.com
Web Extra!
KEYWORD: MR7 Iceland

 **TEST PREP and Spiral Review**

25. **Multiple Choice** A small square is inside a larger square. The larger square is 14 feet long. The smaller square is 2 feet long. What is the area of the shaded region?

14 ft

□ 2 ft

Ⓐ 52 ft²   Ⓑ 192 ft²   Ⓒ 196 ft²   Ⓓ 200 ft²

26. **Multiple Choice** Find the area of a rectangle with length 3 in. and width 12 in.

Ⓕ 9 in²   Ⓖ 18 in²   Ⓗ 36 in²   Ⓙ 144 in²

List all the factors of each number. (Lesson 4-2)

27. 20   **28.** 85   **29.** 59   **30.** 40

31. A tree casts a shadow that is 14 feet long. At the same time, a 5.5-foot-tall boy casts a shadow that is 11 feet long. How tall is the tree? (Lesson 7-5)

10-2 Area of Triangles and Trapezoids

Learn to find the area of triangles and trapezoids.

NY Performance Indicators

6.G.2 Determine the area of triangles and quadrilaterals (squares, rectangles, rhombi, and trapezoids) and develop formulas. Also, 6.A.2, 6.A.6.

The Flatiron Building in New York City was built in 1902. Many people consider it to be New York's first skyscraper. The foundation of the building is shaped like a triangle. You can find the area of the triangle to find how much land the building occupies.

You can divide any parallelogram into two congruent triangles. The area of each triangle is half the area of the parallelogram.

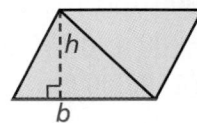 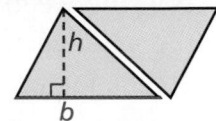

AREA OF A TRIANGLE

The area A of a triangle is half the product of its base b and its height h.

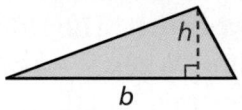

$A = \frac{1}{2} bh$

EXAMPLE 1 Finding the Area of a Triangle

Find the area of each triangle.

A

8 cm

12 cm

$A = \frac{1}{2}bh$ *Write the formula.*

$A = \frac{1}{2}(12 \cdot 8)$ *Substitute 12 for b.*
  Substitute 8 for h.

$A = \frac{1}{2}(96)$ *Multiply.*

$A = 48$

The area is 48 cm^2.

B

$4\frac{1}{2}$ yd

6 yd

$A = \frac{1}{2}bh$ *Write the formula.*

$A = \frac{1}{2}\left(6 \cdot 4\frac{1}{2}\right)$ *Substitute 6 for b.*
  Substitute $4\frac{1}{2}$ for h.

$A = \frac{1}{2}(27)$ *Multiply.*

$A = 13\frac{1}{2}$

The area is $13\frac{1}{2}$ yd^2.

Caution!

The legs of a triangle must meet at a 90° angle in order to use their lengths as the base and height of the triangle.

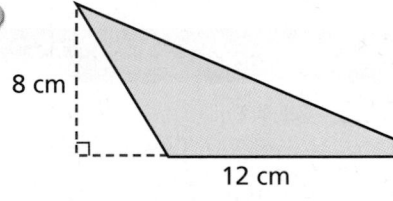

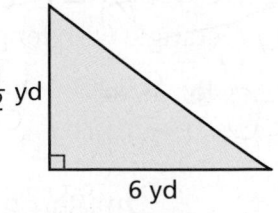

EXAMPLE 2 *Architecture Application*

The diagram shows the outline of the foundation of the Flatiron Building. What is the area of the foundation?

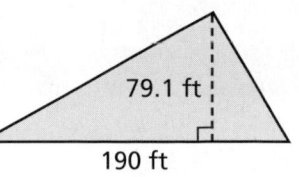

$A = \frac{1}{2}bh$ *Write the formula.*

$A = \frac{1}{2}(190 \cdot 79.1)$ *Substitute 190 for b. Substitute 79.1 for h.*

$A = \frac{1}{2}(15,029) = 7,514.5$ *Multiply.*

The area of the foundation is 7,514.5 ft².

A trapezoid can be divided into a rectangle and two triangles. The area of the trapezoid is the sum of the areas of the rectangle and the triangles.

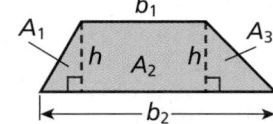

AREA OF A TRAPEZOID

The area A of a trapezoid is the product of half its height h and the sum of its bases b_1 and b_2.

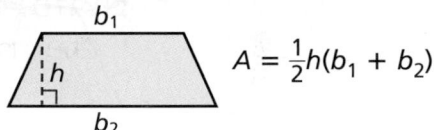

$A = \frac{1}{2}h(b_1 + b_2)$

EXAMPLE 3 **Finding the Area of a Trapezoid**

Find the area of the trapezoid.

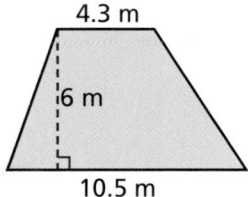

$A = \frac{1}{2}h(b_1 + b_2)$ *Write the formula.*

$A = \frac{1}{2}(6)(4.3 + 10.5)$ *Substitute 6 for h, 4.3 for b_1, and 10.5 for b_2.*

$A = \frac{1}{2}(6)(14.8) = 44.4$ *Multiply.*

The area is 44.4 m².

6.CN.2, 6.CM.8

Think and Discuss

1. **Explain** how the areas of a triangle and a parallelogram with the same base and height are related.

2. **Explain** whether Max's work is correct: To find the area of a trapezoid, Max multiplied the height by the top base and the height by the bottom base. He added the two numbers together and then divided the sum by 2.

10-2 Exercises

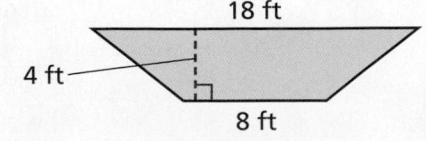

go.hrw.com
Homework Help Online
KEYWORD: MR7 10-2
Parent Resources Online
KEYWORD: MR7 Parent

GUIDED PRACTICE

See Example **1** Find the area of each triangle.

1.

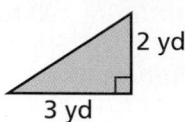

2.

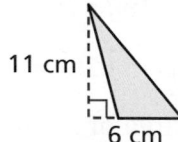

3.

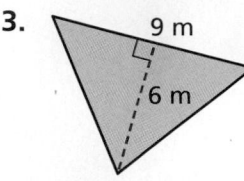

See Example **2** **4.** Harry plans to paint the triangular portion of the side of his house. How many square feet does he need to paint?

See Example **3** Find the area of each trapezoid.

5.

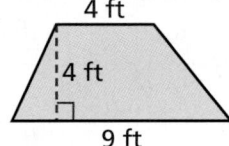

6.

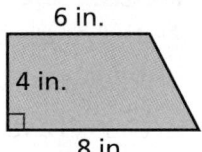

7.

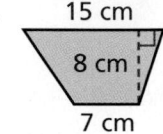

INDEPENDENT PRACTICE

See Example **1** Find the area of each triangle.

8.

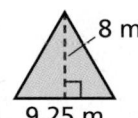

9.

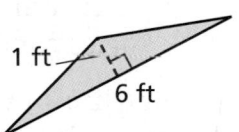

10.

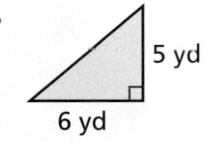

See Example **2** **11.** Sean is making pennants for the school football team. How many square inches of felt does he use for one pennant?

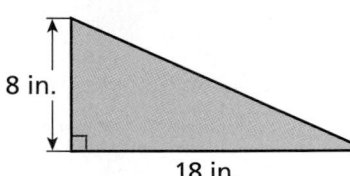

12. Erin has a triangular garden plot that is 5 meters long and 3 meters tall. What is the area of the plot?

See Example **3** Find the area of each trapezoid.

13.

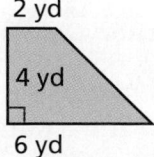

14.

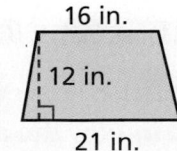

15.

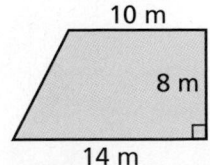

PRACTICE AND PROBLEM SOLVING

Extra Practice
See page 733.

16. The water in a drainage canal is 4 feet deep. What is the area of a cross section of the water in the ditch, which is shaped like a trapezoid?

Social Studies

Nevada has many ghost towns scattered around the state. Many were once boom-towns built during the gold and silver mining rush.

For Exercises 17–21, find the area of each figure.

17.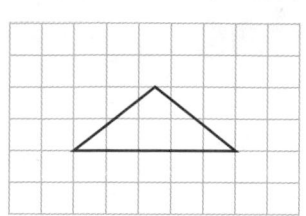

18.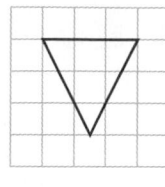

19.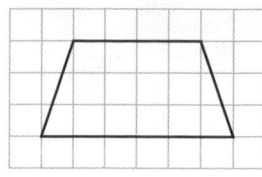

20. triangle: $b = 2\frac{1}{2}$ in.; $h = 1\frac{3}{4}$ in. 21. trapezoid: $b_1 = 18$ m; $b_2 = 27$ m; $h = 15.4$ m

22. **Social Studies** The shape of the state of Nevada is similar to a trapezoid with the measurements shown. Estimate the area of the state in square miles.

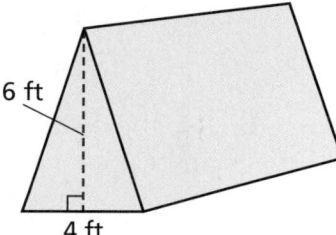

23. Marina is making a tent flap out of netting. The tent opening is 4 feet wide and 6 feet tall. How many square feet of netting will Marina need for the tent flap?

24. **Critical Thinking** The areas and heights of a triangle and a rectangle are the same. How do the lengths of their bases compare?

 25. **Write a Problem** Write a problem about a trapezoid with bases 12 feet and 18 feet and height 10 feet.

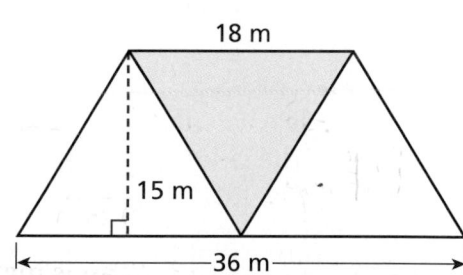

 26. **Write About It** Two triangles have the same base. The height of one triangle is half the height of the other. How do the areas of the triangles compare?

27. **Challenge** Find the area of the unshaded portion of the trapezoid.

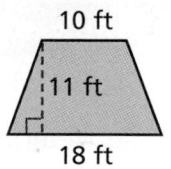

28. **Multiple Choice** A building sign in the shape of a trapezoid has the measurements shown. Which expression can be used to find the area of the sign?

   Ⓐ $\frac{1}{2}(11)(10 + 18)$ Ⓑ $\frac{1}{2}(18)(10)$ Ⓒ $\frac{1}{2}(11)(10)(18)$ Ⓓ $(11)(10 + 18)$

29. **Short Response** Find the area of a right triangle with legs measuring 14 cm and 25 cm.

Multiply. Write each answer in simplest form. (Lesson 5-6)

30. $3 \cdot \frac{2}{7}$ 31. $4 \cdot \frac{3}{5}$ 32. $12 \cdot \frac{9}{10}$ 33. $15 \cdot \frac{1}{2}$

34. Zeb earned $24,000 last year. This year, his salary increased by 5%. How much will he earn? (Lesson 7-9)

Technology LAB 10-2

Area Formulas

Use with Lesson 10-2

NY Performance Indicators

6.RP.2, 6.CN.5, 6.R.5

go.hrw.com
Lab Resources Online
KEYWORD: MR7 Lab10

Geometry software can be used to explore geometric formulas.

Activity

1 Use your geometry software to explore the formula for the area of a rectangle, $A = \ell \cdot w$.

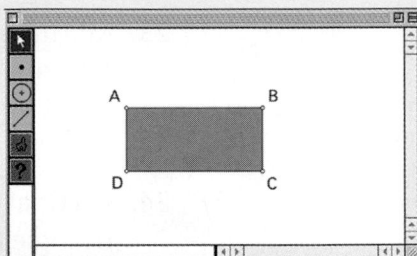

a. Construct a rectangle *ABCD*. Choose four points and connect them with line segments, making sure the opposite sides are parallel.

b. Use the distance tool to measure the length of sides $\overline{AB}$ and $\overline{CB}$.

Select the interior of the rectangle, and then use the area tool to measure the area.

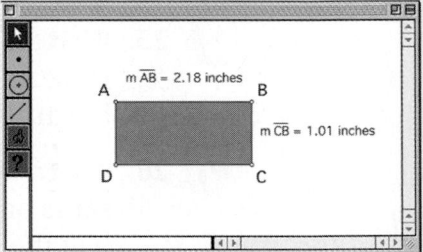

c. Use a calculator or paper and pencil to find the product of the side lengths. Round to the hundredths place.
$2.18 \cdot 1.01 \approx 2.20$

Notice that the geometry software rounds the product to 2.21, which is close to 2.20.
So $Area = AB \cdot CB = \ell \cdot w$.

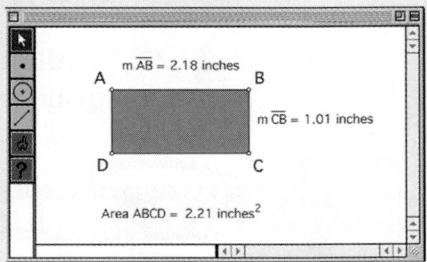

Think and Discuss

1. Tell whether the perimeter *P* of rectangle *ABCD* is equal to $2 \cdot (AB + CB)$.

2. Determine whether the area of rectangle ABCD divided by 2 is equal to the perimeter.

Try This

1. Use geometry software to construct a triangle *ABC* where $m\angle B = 90°$.

a. Measure the area of the triangle and the lengths of sides $\overline{AB}$ and $\overline{CB}$. Find $\frac{1}{2} \cdot AB \cdot CB$.

b. Drag angle *A*, making sure $m\angle B = 90°$. Do this three more times to construct triangles with different areas and side lengths. For each triangle, find $\frac{1}{2} \cdot AB \cdot CB$. What do you conclude?

10-3 Area of Composite Figures

Learn to break a polygon into simpler parts to find its area.

You can find the areas of irregular polygons by breaking them apart into rectangles, parallelograms, and triangles.

NY Performance Indicators

6.G.3 Use a variety of strategies to find the area of regular and irregular polygons.
Also, 6.A.2, 6.A.6.

EXAMPLE 1 Finding Areas of Composite Figures

Find the area of each polygon.

A

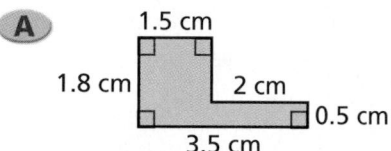

Think: Break the polygon apart into rectangles.

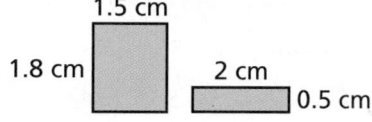

Find the area of each rectangle.

$A = \ell w$ $A = \ell w$

Write the formula for the area of a rectangle.

$A = 1.8 \cdot 1.5$ $A = 2 \cdot 0.5$

$A = 2.7$ $A = 1$

$2.7 + 1 = 3.7$

Add to find the total area.

The area of the polygon is 3.7 cm².

B

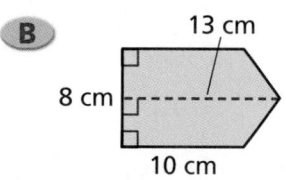

Think: Break the figure apart into a triangle and a rectangle.

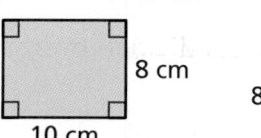 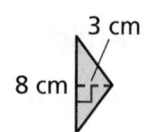

$A = \ell w$ $A = \frac{1}{2}bh$

Find the area of each polygon.

$A = 8 \cdot 10$ $A = \frac{1}{2} \cdot 8 \cdot 3$

$A = 80$ $A = 12$

$80 + 12 = 92$

Add to find the total area of the figure.

The area of the figure is 92 cm².

EXAMPLE 2 **Art Application**

Helpful Hint

You can also count the squares and multiply by the area of one square.
1 square = 4 square units
$17 \cdot 4 = 68$ square units

Stan made a wall hanging. Use the coordinate grid to find its area.

Think: Divide the wall hanging into rectangles.

Find the area of each rectangle.

Rectangle 1
$\ell = 8, w = 4; A = 8 \cdot 4 = 32$

Rectangle 2
$\ell = 6, w = 2; A = 6 \cdot 2 = 12$

Rectangle 3
$\ell = 4, w = 6; A = 4 \cdot 6 = 24$

Add the areas of the three rectangles to find the total area of the wall hanging.

$32 + 12 + 24 = 68$ square units

The area of the wall hanging is 68 square units.

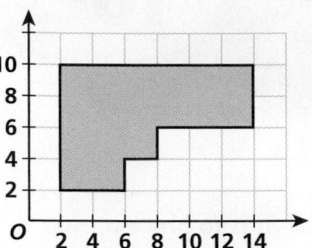

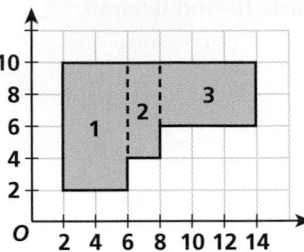

Think and Discuss

6.PS.21, 6.CM.1

1. **Explain** how you can find the area of a regular octagon by breaking it apart into congruent triangles, if you know the area of one triangle.

2. **Explain** another way that you can divide the wall hanging in Example 2.

10-3 Exercises

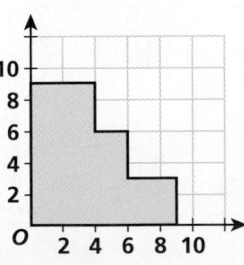
go.hrw.com
Homework Help Online
KEYWORD: MR7 10-3
Parent Resources Online
KEYWORD: MR7 Parent

GUIDED PRACTICE

See Example 1 **Find the area of each polygon.**

1.
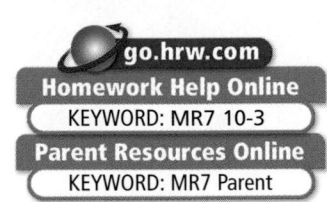

2.
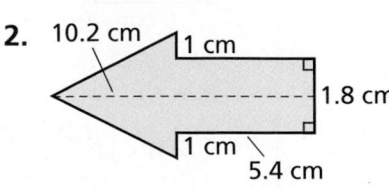

See Example 2 3. Gina used tiles to create a design. Use the coordinate grid to find the area of Gina's design.

INDEPENDENT PRACTICE

See Example ① **Find the area of each polygon.**

4.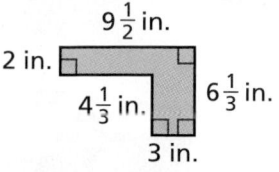

$9\frac{1}{2}$ in.

2 in.

$4\frac{1}{3}$ in. $6\frac{1}{3}$ in.

3 in.

5.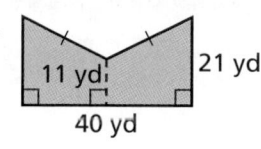

11 yd 21 yd

40 yd

See Example ② **6.** Edgar plants daffodils around a rectangular pond. The yellow part of the diagram shows where the daffodils are planted. Use the coordinate grid to find the area of the yellow part of the diagram.

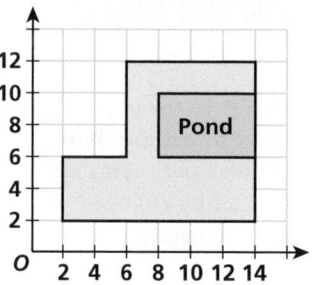

PRACTICE AND PROBLEM SOLVING

Extra Practice
See page 733.

7. Social Studies The map shows the approximate dimensions of the state of South Australia, outlined in red.

a. Estimate the area of the state of South Australia.

b. The total area of Australia is about 7.7 million km². About what fraction of the total area of Australia is the area of the state of South Australia?

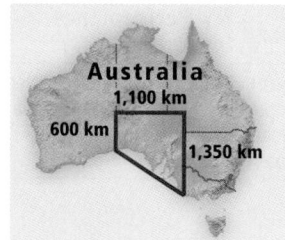

8. Write About It Draw a figure that can be broken up into two rectangles. Label the lengths of each side. Explain how you can find the area of the figure. Then find the area.

9. Challenge The perimeter of the figure is 42.5 cm. Find the area of this figure.

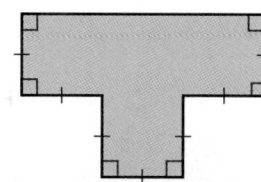

TEST PREP and Spiral Review

10. Multiple Choice What is the area of the polygon?

Ⓕ 40 cm²   Ⓖ 65 cm²   Ⓗ 45 cm²   Ⓙ 90 cm²

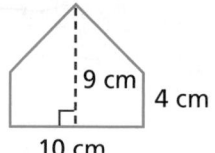

9 cm

4 cm

10 cm

11. Gridded Response Use the coordinate grid to find the area, in square units, of the polygon.

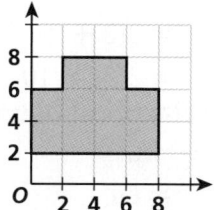

Find each sum or difference. Write the answer in simplest form. (Lesson 5-3)

12. $4\frac{1}{3} + 7\frac{5}{12}$ **13.** $8\frac{1}{2} - 3\frac{1}{3}$ **14.** $6\frac{2}{3} + 3\frac{1}{6}$ **15.** $8\frac{7}{10} - 2\frac{2}{5}$

Find the area of each polygon. (Lesson 10-1)

16. rectangle: $\ell = 14$ m; $w = 11$ m   **17.** parallelogram: $b = 18$ cm; $h = 8$ cm

Comparing Perimeter and Area

Learn to make a model to explore how area and perimeter are affected by changes in the dimensions of a figure.

Ms. Cohn wants to enlarge a photo by doubling its length and width.

Recall that similar figures have exactly the same shape but not necessarily the same size. Doubling the dimensions of the photo will create a larger photo similar to the original.

NY Performance Indicators

6.A.6 Evaluate formulas for given input values (circumference, area, volume, distance, temperature, interest, etc.).

You can draw a model on graph paper to see how the area and the perimeter of a figure change when its dimensions change.

EXAMPLE **1** **Changing Dimensions**

Find how the perimeter and the area of the figure change when its dimensions change.

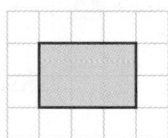

Draw a model of the two figures on graph paper. Label the dimensions.

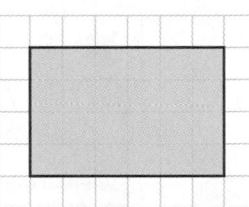

 = 1 in²

The original photo is a 3 in. × 2 in. rectangle.

$P = 2(\ell + w)$

    $= 2(3 + 2)$

    $= 2(5) = 10$

The perimeter is 10 in.

$A = \ell w$

    $= 3 \times 2$

    $= 6$

The area is 6 in².

Use the formula for perimeter of a rectangle.

Substitue for ℓ and w.

Simplify.

Use the formula for area of a rectangle.

Substitute for ℓ and w.

Simplify.

The enlarged photo is a 6 in. × 4 in. rectangle.

$P = 2(\ell + w)$

    $= 2(6 + 4)$

    $= 2(10) = 20$

The perimeter is 20 in.

$A = \ell w$

    $= 6 \times 4$

    $= 24$

The area is 24 in².

When the dimensions of the rectangle are doubled, the perimeter is also doubled, and the area becomes four times as great.

EXAMPLE **2** *Measurement Application*

Use a centimeter ruler to measure the photo. Draw a rectangle whose sides are 3 times as long to enlarge the photo. How do the perimeter and the area change?

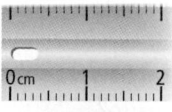

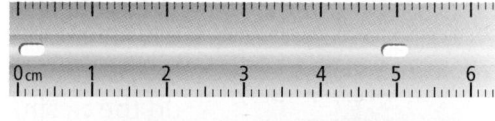

$P = 6$ cm
$A = 2$ cm^2

Multiply each $P = 18$ cm
dimension by 3. $A = 18$ cm^2

When the dimensions of the rectangle are multiplied by 3, the **perimeter** is multiplied by **3**, and the **area** is multiplied by **9**, or 3^2.

Think and Discuss

6.PS.14, 6.CM.1

1. Explain how the perimeter of a triangle changes when all the side lengths are doubled.

2. Tell how the area of a rectangle changes when all the side lengths are divided in half.

10-4 Exercises

go.hrw.com
Homework Help Online
KEYWORD: MR7 10-4
Parent Resources Online
KEYWORD: MR7 Parent

GUIDED PRACTICE

See Example **1**   **1.** Find how the perimeter and the area of the figure change when its dimensions change.

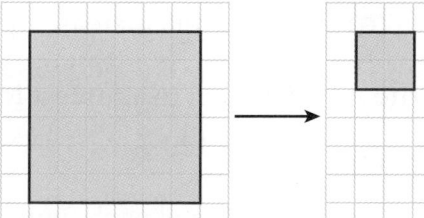

See Example **2**   **2.** Use a centimeter ruler to measure the rectangle. Draw a rectangle whose sides are 2 times as long to enlarge the rectangle. How do the perimeter and the area change?

See Example **3.** Find how the perimeter and the area of the figure change when its dimensions change.

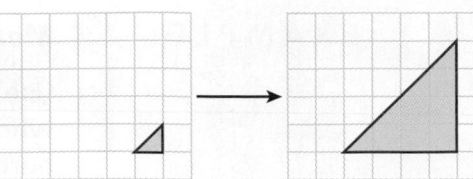

See Example **4.** Use a centimeter ruler to measure the triangle. Draw a triangle whose sides are half as long to reduce the triangle. How do the perimeter and the area change?

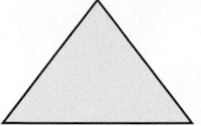

PRACTICE AND PROBLEM SOLVING

Extra Practice
See page 733.

5. The schoolyard is a rectangle with a length of 120 ft and a width of 80 ft. The PE teacher plans to make a field in the schoolyard.

    a. What will the area of the field be if she divides only one of the dimensions of the schoolyard in half?

    b. What will the perimeter of the field be if she divides only the length in half? the width in half?

6. Critical Thinking If George enlarges a 3 in. × 4 in. photo so that it is 12 in. × 16 in., how will its area change?

 **7. Write About It** What happens to the area and the perimeter of a rectangle when the length and width are multiplied by 4?

8. Challenge A rectangle has a perimeter of 24 meters. If its length and width are whole numbers, what is its greatest possible area?

TEST PREP and Spiral Review

9. Multiple Choice A photo is 4 in. × 6 in. long. To enlarge the photo, Lee doubles both the length and width. Find the perimeter of the enlarged photo.

  Ⓐ 8 in.   Ⓑ 12 in.   Ⓒ 20 in.   Ⓓ 40 in.

10. Multiple Choice If Jinny enlarges a 3 in. × 4 in. photo so that it is 12 in. × 16 in., how will its area change?

  Ⓕ The area will increase by 2 times.   Ⓗ The area will increase by 3^2.

  Ⓖ The area will increase by 2^2 times.   Ⓙ The area will increase by 4^2 times.

Write each fraction in simplest form. (Lesson 4-5)

11. $\frac{9}{12}$ **12.** $\frac{4}{16}$ **13.** $\frac{5}{10}$ **14.** $\frac{25}{100}$ **15.** $\frac{65}{100}$

Find the perimeter of each figure. (Lesson 9-7)

16. 125 ft — 30 ft

17. 18 cm, 8 cm, 8 cm, 8 cm, 4 cm, 2 cm

Hands-On LAB
10-5

Use with Lesson 10-5

Explore Area of Circles

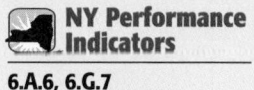

You can use what you know about circles and *pi* to learn about the area of circles.

Activity

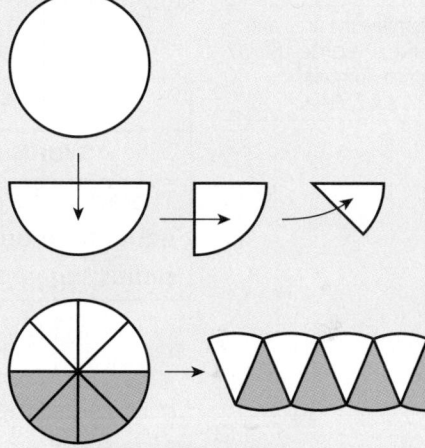

1 The *radius* of a circle is half of its diameter. Use a compass to draw a circle with a 2-inch radius. Cut your circle out and fold it three times as shown.

2 Unfold the circle, trace the folds, and shade one-half of the circle.

3 Cut along the folds, and fit the pieces together to make a figure that looks approximately like a parallelogram.

Think of this figure as a parallelogram. The base and height of the parallelogram relate to the parts of the circle.

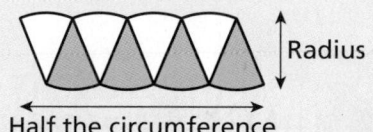

Radius

Half the circumference

base $b = \frac{1}{2}$ the circumference of the circle, or πr

height $h =$ the radius of the circle, or r

To find the area of a parallelogram, use the equation $A = bh$.

To find the area of a circle, use the equation $A = \pi r(r) = \pi r^2$.

Think and Discuss

1. Compare the lengths of all the diameters of a circle.

2. Compare the lengths of all the radii of a circle.

Try This

Find the area of each circle with the given measure. Use 3.14 for π. Round to the nearest tenth.

1. $r = 4$ yd

2.
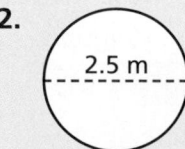
2.5 m

3. $d = 10$ m

4.
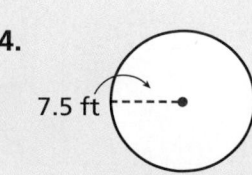
7.5 ft

Learn to find the area of a circle.

In medieval times, circular shields were usually made from wood that was covered with leather or steel. The amount of leather or steel needed to cover a shield depended upon the shield's area.

NY Performance Indicators

6.G.7 Determine the area and circumference of a circle, using the appropriate formula. Also, 6.N.27, 6.A.2, 6.A.6.

Area of a Circle	
Words	**Formula**
The area of a circle is equal to *pi* times the radius squared.	$A = \pi r^2$

You can estimate the area of a circle by using 3 to approximate the value of *pi*.

EXAMPLE 1 **Estimating the Area of a Circle**

Estimate the area of each circle. Use 3 to approximate *pi*.

A 6 in.

$A = \pi r^2$ *Write the formula for the area.*
$A \approx 3 \cdot 6^2$ *Replace π with 3 and r with 6.*
$A \approx 3 \cdot 36$ *Use the order of operations.*
$A \approx 108 \text{ in}^2$ *Multiply.*

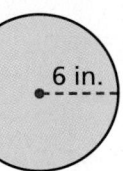
B 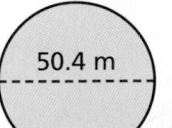 50.4 m

$A = \pi r^2$ *Write the formula for the area.*
$r = d \div 2$ *The length of the radius is half the length of the diameter.*

$r = 50.4 \div 2$
$r = 25.2$ *Divide.*
$r \approx 25$ *Round 25.2 to 25.*
$A \approx 3 \cdot 25^2$ *Replace π with 3 and r with 25.*
$A \approx 3 \cdot 625$ *Use the order of operations.*
$A \approx 1{,}875 \text{ m}^2$ *Multiply.*

EXAMPLE 2 Using the Formula for the Area of a Circle

Find the area of each circle. Use $\frac{22}{7}$ for *pi*.

A

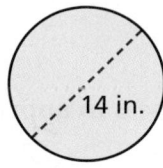

14 in.

$A = \pi r^2$ Write the formula for the area.

$r = d \div 2$ The length of the radius is half the length of the diameter.

$r = 14 \div 2 = 7$ Divide.

$A \approx \frac{22}{7} \cdot 7^2$ Replace π with $\frac{22}{7}$ and r with 7.

$A \approx \frac{22}{\cancel{7}_1} \cdot \overset{7}{\cancel{49}}$ Use the GCF to simplify.

$A \approx 154 \text{ in}^2$ Multiply.

B

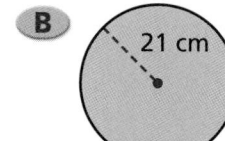

21 cm

$A = \pi r^2$ Write the formula for the area.

$A \approx \frac{22}{7} \cdot 21^2$ Replace π with $\frac{22}{7}$ and r with 21.

$A \approx \frac{22}{7} \cdot 441$ Use the order of operations.

$A \approx \frac{9702}{7}$ Multiply

$A \approx 1386 \text{ cm}^2$ Divide.

EXAMPLE 3 *History Application*

A circular shield has a diameter of 20 inches. Find the area of the steel needed to cover one side of the shield. Use 3.14 for *pi*.

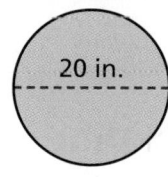

20 in.

$A = \pi r^2$ Write the formula for the area.

$r = d \div 2$ The length of the radius is half the length of the diameter.

$r = 20 \div 2$

$r = 10$ Divide.

$A \approx 3.14 \cdot 10^2$ Replace π with 3.14 and r with 10.

$A \approx 3.14 \cdot 100$ Use the order of operations.

$A \approx 314 \text{ in}^2$ Multiply.

Check Use 3 as an estimate for π. The area, πr^2, is approximately $3 \cdot 10^2 = 3 \cdot 100 = 300$, so the answer is reasonable.

Think and Discuss

6.PS.3, 6.RP.5, 6.RP.9

1. **Describe** how you could estimate the area of a circle whose radius is 1 cm.

2. **Explain** why the area of a circle with a radius of 5 ft must be greater than 75 ft^2.

3. **Tell** how you can check that your answer is reasonable after you have calculated the area of a circle.

10-5 Exercises

go.hrw.com
Homework Help Online
KEYWORD: MR7 10-5

Parent Resources Online
KEYWORD: MR7 Parent

GUIDED PRACTICE

See Example **1** Estimate the area of each circle. Use 3 to approximate *pi.*

1.
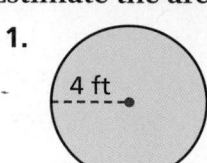
4 ft

2.
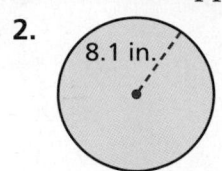
8.1 in.

3.
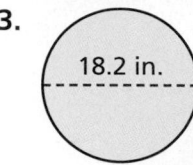
18.2 in.

See Example **2** Find the area of each circle. Use $\frac{22}{7}$ for *pi.*

4.
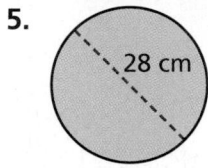
7 ft

5.
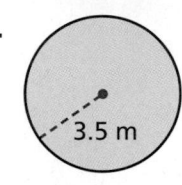
28 cm

6.
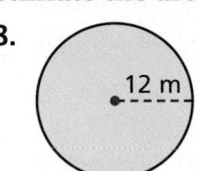
3.5 m

See Example **3** **7. Architecture** A circular window has a diameter of 4 ft. Find the area of the glass needed to fill the window. Use 3.14 for *pi.*

INDEPENDENT PRACTICE

See Example **1** Estimate the area of each circle. Use 3 to approximate *pi.*

8.
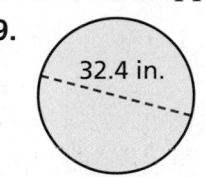
12 m

9.
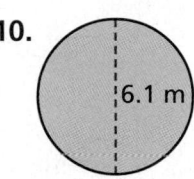
32.4 in.

10.
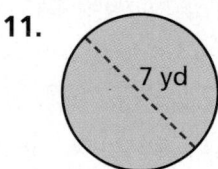
6.1 m

See Example **2** Find the area of each circle. Use $\frac{22}{7}$ for *pi.*

11.
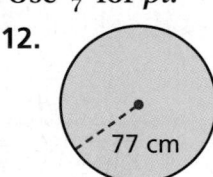
7 yd

12.
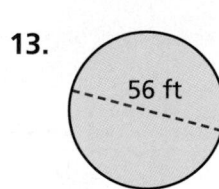
77 cm

13.
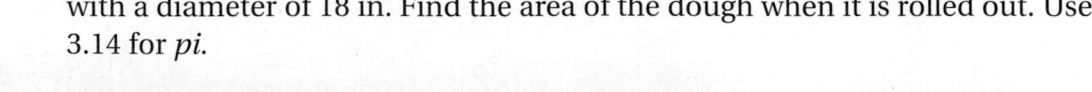
56 ft

See Example **3** **14. Cooking** A pizza recipe calls for the dough to be rolled out to form a circle with a diameter of 18 in. Find the area of the dough when it is rolled out. Use 3.14 for *pi.*

PRACTICE AND PROBLEM SOLVING

Extra Practice
See page 733.

Find the area and circumference of each circle. Use 3.14 for *pi* and round to the nearest hundredth.

15.
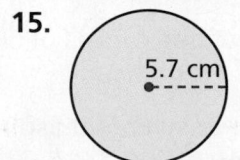
5.7 cm

16.
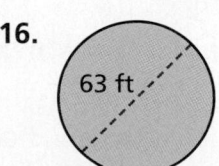
63 ft

17.
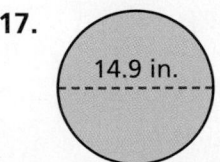
14.9 in.

18. Sports The diameter of the circle that a shot-putter stands in is 7 ft. What is the area of the circle? Use $\frac{22}{7}$ for *pi*.

19. Earth Science Meteor Crater in central Arizona was formed when an asteroid struck Earth between 20,000 and 50,000 years ago. The circular crater has a diameter of 1.2 km. Find the area of the crater to the nearest hundredth. Use 3.14 for *pi*.

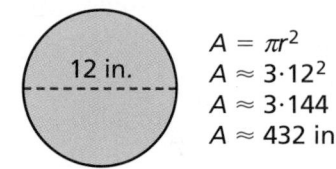

20. Multi-Step A restaurant makes pizzas with 6 in. diameters and 12 in. diameters.

 a. Estimate the difference between the areas of the two sizes of pizzas. (Use 3.14 for *pi*. Round to the nearest whole number.)

 b. Is the area of the 12 in. pizza about twice the area of the 6 in. pizza? Explain.

21. Critical Thinking The area of a circular garden plot is 30 ft². Explain why the diameter of the plot must be greater than 6 ft.

 22. What's the Error? A student estimated the area of this circle as shown. Explain the student's error.

 23. Write About It Describe a step-by-step process you can use to estimate the area of a circle.

 24. Challenge What is the area of the shaded part of the figure? Use 3.14 for *pi*. Round the answer to the nearest hundredth.

12 in.

$A = \pi r^2$
$A \approx 3 \cdot 12^2$
$A \approx 3 \cdot 144$
$A \approx 432 \text{ in}^2$

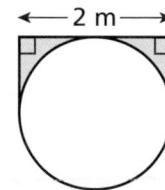

←— 2 m —→

TEST PREP and Spiral Review

25. Multiple Choice Jerome knows the radius of a baking pan. He needs to estimate the pan's area. Which method can Jerome use to estimate the area?

 Ⓐ Multiply the radius by 3.

 Ⓑ Divide the radius by 2 and square the result.

 Ⓒ Square the radius and multiply the result by 3.

 Ⓓ Multiply the radius by 3 and square the result.

26. Gridded Response Find the area, in square inches, of a circle with a diameter of 10 in. Use 3.14 for *pi*.

Multiply. Write each answer in simplest form. (Lesson 5-7)

27. $\frac{3}{8} \cdot \frac{4}{9}$ **28.** $\frac{7}{10} \cdot \frac{3}{14}$ **29.** $\frac{8}{9} \cdot \frac{5}{16}$ **30.** $\frac{6}{15} \cdot \frac{10}{21}$

Divide. Write each answer in simplest form. (Lesson 5-9)

31. $\frac{3}{5} \div 5$ **32.** $\frac{4}{9} \div 12$ **33.** $\frac{5}{6} \div \frac{2}{3}$ **34.** $2\frac{4}{5} \div 1\frac{1}{2}$

READY TO GO ON?

Quiz for Lessons 10-1 Through 10-5

☑ **10-1** Estimating and Finding Area

Find the area of each figure.

1.

41 cm

62 cm

2.

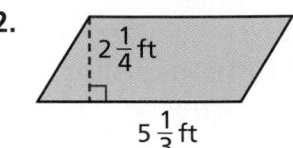

$2\frac{1}{4}$ ft

$5\frac{1}{3}$ ft

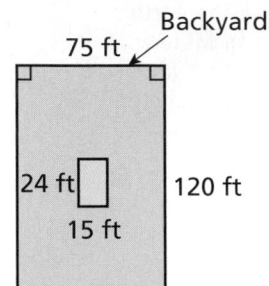

Backyard

75 ft

24 ft   120 ft

15 ft

3. Mark is making a rectangular vegetable garden in his backyard. The rest of the backyard is covered with gravel. What is the area of the backyard that is covered with gravel?

☑ **10-2** Area of Triangles and Trapezoids

Find the area of each figure.

4.

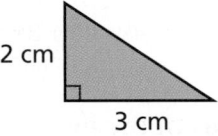

2 cm

3 cm

5.

4.5 ft

3 ft

7.5 ft

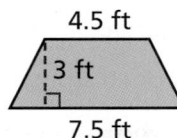

6.

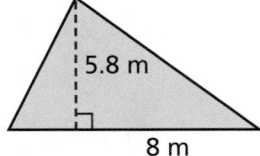

5.8 m

8 m

☑ **10-3** Area of Composite Figures

7. Find the area of the polygon.

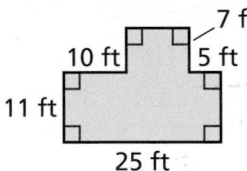

7 ft

10 ft   5 ft

11 ft

25 ft

8. Using the approximate dimensions, estimate the area of the state of Oklahoma.

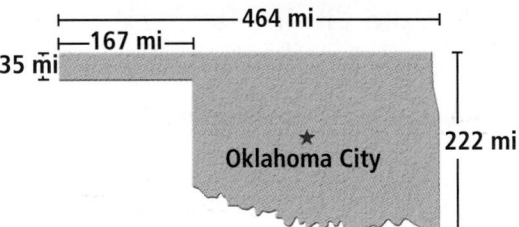

464 mi

167 mi

35 mi

★
Oklahoma City

222 mi

☑ **10-4** Comparing Perimeter and Area

9. The length and width of a rectangle are each multiplied by 4. Find how the perimeter and the area of the rectangle change.

☑ **10-5** Area of Circles

Find the area of each circle. Use 3.14 for *pi*. Round to the nearest hundredth.

10.

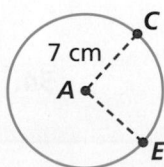

7 cm

C

A

E

11.

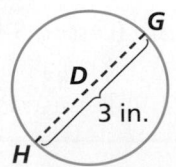

G

D

3 in.

H

12.

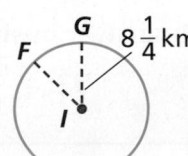

G $8\frac{1}{4}$ km

F

I

13.

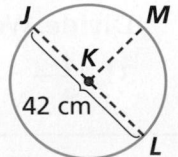

J   M

K

42 cm

L

Focus on Problem Solving

 **Solve**

• **Choose the operation**

Read the whole problem before you try to solve it. Determine what action is taking place in the problem. Then decide whether you need to add, subtract, multiply, or divide in order to solve the problem.

Action	Operation
Combining or putting together	Add
Removing or taking away Comparing or finding the difference	Subtract
Combining equal groups	Multiply
Sharing equally or separating into equal groups	Divide

 **Read each problem and determine the action taking place. Choose an operation, and then solve the problem.**

1 There are 3 lily ponds in the botanical gardens. They are identical in size and shape. The total area of the ponds is 165 ft². What is the area of each lily pond?

2 The greenhouse is made up of 6 rectangular rooms with an area of 4,800 ft² each. What is the total area of the greenhouse?

3 A shady area with 17 different varieties of magnolia trees, which bloom from March to June, surrounds the plaza in Magnolia Park. In the center of the plaza, there is a circular bed of shrubs as shown in the chart. If the total area of the park is 625 ft², what is the area of the plaza?

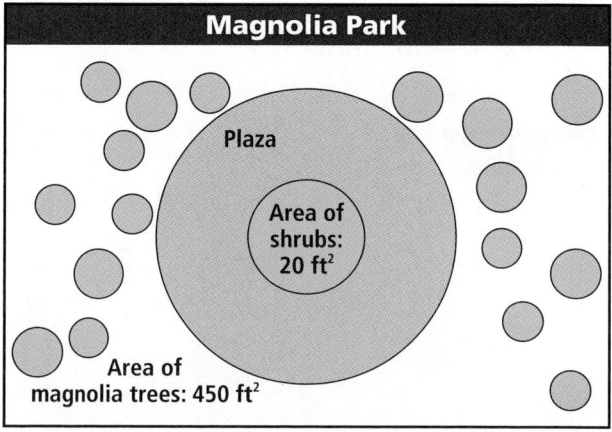

Magnolia Park

Plaza

Area of shrubs: 20 ft²

Area of magnolia trees: 450 ft²

Hands-On LAB 10-6

Draw Views of Three-Dimensional Figures

Use with Lesson 10-6

NY Performance Indicators
6.R.1, 6.R.4, 6.R.6

go.hrw.com
Lab Resources Online
KEYWORD: MR7 Lab10

Activity 1

1 Draw a rectangular prism. Imagine that you are looking at the top of the prism, and draw what you would see. Draw the front and side views of the prism.

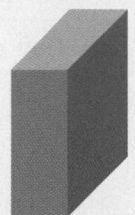 **Top**  **Front**  **Side**

All the faces of a rectangular prism are rectangles.

2 Stack centimeter cubes to make the three-dimensional figure shown. Draw the top, front, and side views.

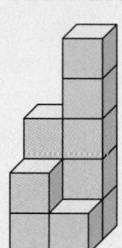 **Top** 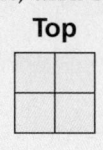 **Front** 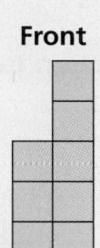 **Side**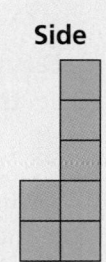

Each view shows a different configuration of squares representing the number of cubes you see.

Think and Discuss

1. Explain why a side view of a three-dimensional figure might change if you look at a different side.

Try This

Draw the top, front, and side views of each three-dimensional figure.

1.
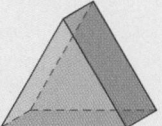

2.

3.

Activity 2

You can use different views of a solid to construct the figure.

Using centimeter cubes, construct a three-dimensional figure that has the given views.

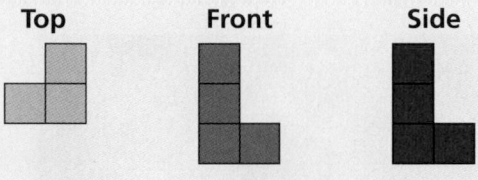

Top **Front** **Side**

 *Step 1: Start with the top view of the solid and place the cubes.*

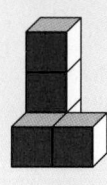 *Step 2: Use the front view to stack two more cubes on the left side.*

Step 3: Check that the side view is correct.
Since the side view is correct, there are no more cubes to add.

This is the three-dimensional figure that has the given views.

Think and Discuss

1. Explain why it is a good idea to start with the top view.

Try This

Using centimeter cubes, construct the three-dimensional figure that has the given views.

1. **Top** **Front** **Side**

2. **Top** **Front** **Side**

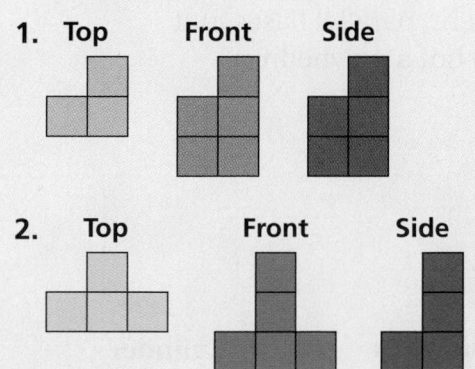

Three-Dimensional Figures

Learn to name three-dimensional figures.

Vocabulary

polyhedron
face
edge
vertex
prism
base
pyramid
cylinder
cone

A **polyhedron** is a three-dimensional object with flat surfaces, called **faces**, that are polygons.

When two faces of a three-dimensional figure share a side, they form an **edge**. A point at which three or more edges meet is a **vertex** (plural: *vertices*).

A cube is formed by 6 square faces. It has 8 vertices and 12 edges. The sculpture in front of this building is based on a cube. The artist's work is not a polyhedron because of the hole cut through the middle.

This sculpture, *Red Cube,* in front of the Marine Midland Bank in New York City was created by Isamu Noguchi.

EXAMPLE **1** **Identifying Faces, Edges, and Vertices**

Identify the number of faces, edges, and vertices on each three-dimensional figure.

 **NY Performance Indicators**

6.CM.10 Use appropriate vocabulary when describing objects, relationships, mathematical solutions, and rationale.

A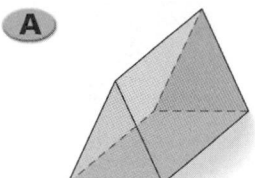

5 faces
9 edges
6 vertices

B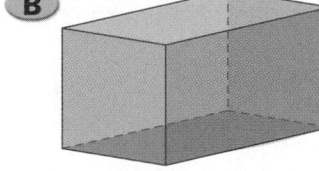

6 faces
12 edges
8 vertices

A **prism** is a polyhedron with two congruent, parallel **bases**, and other faces that are all parallelograms. A prism is named for the shape of its bases. A **cylinder** also has two congruent, parallel bases, but bases of a cylinder are circular. A cylinder is not a polyhedron because not every surface is a polygon.

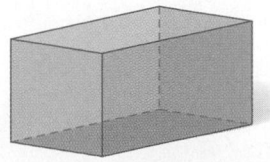

Rectangular prism

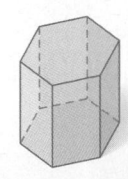

Hexagonal prism

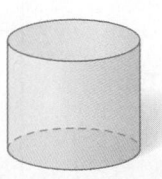

Cylinder

A **pyramid** has one polygon-shaped base and three or more triangular faces that share a vertex. A pyramid is named for the shape of its base. A **cone** has a circular base and a curved surface that comes to a point. A cone is not a polyhedron because not every face is a polygon.

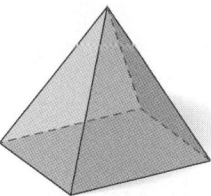

Square pyramid

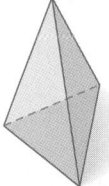

Triangular pyramid

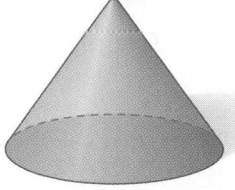

Cone

EXAMPLE 2 Naming Three-Dimensional Figures

Name each three-dimensional figure represented by each object.

 A

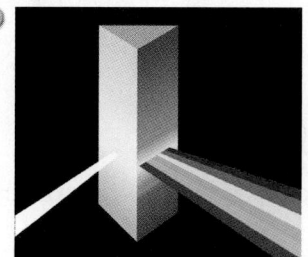

All the faces are flat and are polygons.

The figure is a polyhedron.

There are two congruent, parallel bases, so the figure is a prism.

The bases are triangles.

The figure is a triangular prism.

 B

There is a curved surface.

The figure is not a polyhedron.

There is a flat, circular base.

The lateral surface comes to a point.

The figure represents a cone.

C

All the faces are flat and are polygons.

The figure is a polyhedron.

It has one base and the other faces are triangles that meet at a point, so the figure is a pyramid.

The base is a square.

The figure is a square pyramid.

Think and Discuss

 6.CM.1, 6.CN.2

1. **Explain** how a pyramid and a prism are alike and how they are different.

2. **Explain** how a cone and a pyramid are alike and how they are different.

go.hrw.com
Homework Help Online
KEYWORD: MR7 10-6
Parent Resources Online
KEYWORD: MR7 Parent

GUIDED PRACTICE

See Example **1** Identify the number of faces, edges, and vertices on each three-dimensional figure.

1.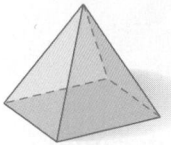

2.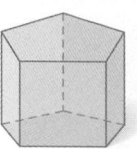

3.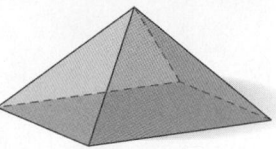

See Example **2** Name each three-dimensional figure represented by each object.

4.

5.

6.

INDEPENDENT PRACTICE

See Example **1** Identify the number of faces, edges, and vertices on each three-dimensional figure.

7.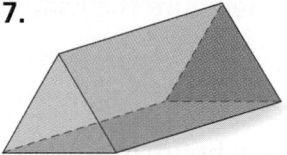

8.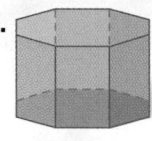

9.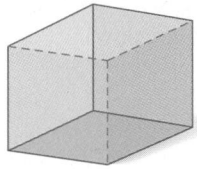

See Example **2** Name each three-dimensional figure represented by each object.

10.

11.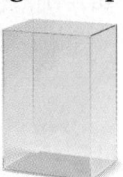

12.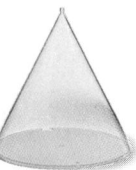

PRACTICE AND PROBLEM SOLVING

Extra Practice
See page 734.

Name each figure and tell whether it is a polyhedron.

13.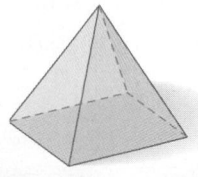

14.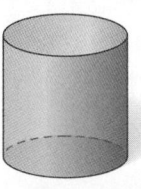

15.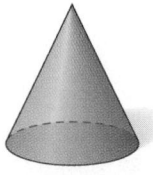

Write the letter of all the figures that match each description.

16. prism

17. has triangular faces

18. has 6 faces

19. has 5 vertices

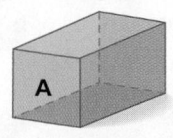
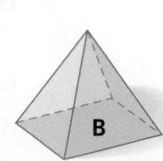
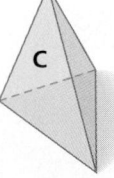
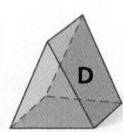

Write *true* or *false* for each statement.

20. A cone does not have a flat surface.

21. The bases of a cylinder are congruent.

22. All pyramids have five or more vertices.

23. All of the edges of a cube are congruent.

24. Architecture Name the three-dimensional figure represented by each building.

a.

b.

c.

25. Critical Thinking Li makes candles with her mother. She made a candle in the shape of a pyramid that had 9 faces. How many sides did the base of the candle have? Name the polyhedron formed by the candle.

 **26. What's the Error?** A student says that any polyhedron can be named if the number of faces it has is known. What is the student's error?

27. Write About It How are a cone and cylinder alike? How are they different?

28. Challenge A square pyramid is cut in half, and the cut is made parallel to the base of the pyramid. What are the shapes of the faces of the bottom half of the pyramid?

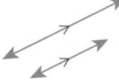

Test Prep and Spiral Review

29. Multiple Choice Which figure has the greatest number of faces?

Ⓐ Cone   Ⓑ Cube   Ⓒ Octagonal prism   Ⓓ Triangular prism

30. Multiple Choice Which figure has a circular base?

Ⓕ Cube   Ⓖ Cylinder   Ⓗ Square pyramid   Ⓙ Triangular prism

Compare. Write <, >, or =. (Lesson 3-1)

31. 9.04 ▨ 9.404   **32.** 12.7 ▨ 12.70   **33.** 0.03 ▨ 0.003   **34.** 5.12 ▨ 5.125

Classify each pair of lines. (Lesson 8-4)

35.
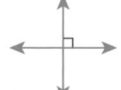

36.
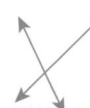

37.

Hands-On LAB 10-7

Explore Volumes of Prisms and Cylinders

Use with Lesson 10-7

go.hrw.com
Lab Resources Online
KEYWORD: MR7 Lab10

NY Performance Indicators

6.G.4, 6.M.6, 6.R.2

REMEMBER
• Volume is the number of cubic units needed to fill a space.

You can use centimeter cubes to help you find the volume of a *prism*.

Activity

Use the steps and diagrams below to fill in the table.

	Length (ℓ)	Width (w)	Height (h)	Total Number of Cubes (V)
Figure A	▨	▨	▨	▨
Figure B	▨	▨	▨	▨
Figure C	▨	▨	▨	▨

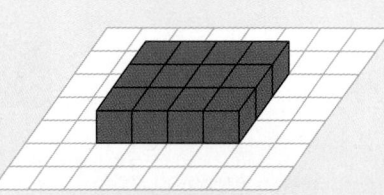

Figure A

1. Draw a 4 × 3 rectangle on centimeter graph paper. Place centimeter cubes on the rectangle. *(Figure A)* How many cubes did you use? What is the height of this prism?

2. Make a prism that is 2 units tall. *(Figure B)* How many cubes did you use?

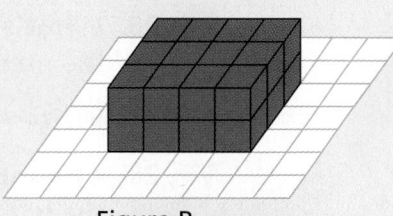

Figure B

3. Make a prism that is 5 units tall. *(Figure C)* How many cubes did you use?

Think and Discuss

1. How can you use the length, width, and height of a prism to find the total number of cubes without counting them?

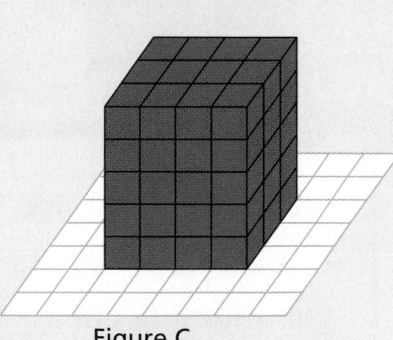

Figure C

2. Use your answer from Problem **1** to write a formula for the volume of a prism.

3. When the height of the prism is doubled, what happens to the volume?

Try This

Build each rectangular prism and find its volume.

1. $\ell = 4$; $w = 2$; $h = 3$ 2. $\ell = 1$; $w = 4$; $h = 5$ 3. $\ell = 3$; $w = 3$; $h = 3$ 4. $\ell = 5$; $w = 10$; $h = 2$

5. Estimate the volume of a shoe box. Fill it with centimeter cubes. How close was your estimate?

You can use graph paper and centimeter cubes to estimate the volume of a *cylinder*.

Use the steps below to fill in the table to estimate the volume of a can.

	Estimated Area of Base (A)	Height (h)	Volume (V)
Can	▪	▪	▪

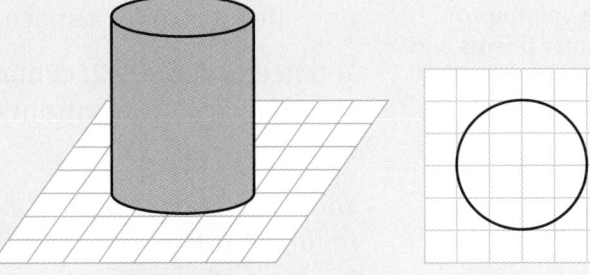

1. Trace around the bottom of a can on graph paper. Count the squares inside the circle to estimate the area *A* of the bottom of the can.

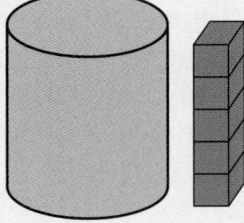

2. Use centimeter cubes to find the height of the can.

3. Use centimeter cubes to build a prism that covers the area of the circle and is the height of the can. Find the volume of the can by counting the cubes used to build the prism or by using $V = A \times h$.

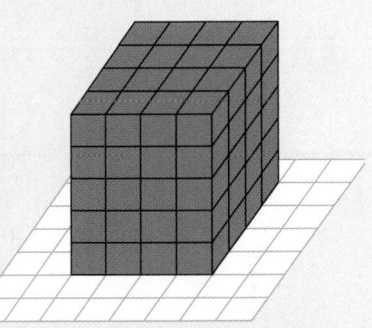

Think and Discuss

1. If you measure the radius of the base, what expression can you use to find the exact area of the circle?

2. Use the expression you found in Problem **1** to write a formula for the volume of a cylinder?

3. When the height of the cylinder is doubled, how does the volume change?

Try This

Estimate the volume of different-sized cans.

		Estimated Area of Base (A)	Height (h)	Volume (V)
1.	Tuna Can	▪	▪	▪
2.		▪	▪	▪
3.		▪	▪	▪

10-7 Volume of Prisms

Learn to estimate and find the volumes of rectangular prisms and triangular prisms.

Vocabulary

volume

NY Performance Indicators

6.M.1 Measure capacity and calculate volume of a rectangular prism. Also, 6.A.2, 6.A.6, 6.M.6.

Volume is the number of cubic units needed to fill a space.

You need 10, or 5 · 2, centimeter cubes to cover the bottom of this rectangular prism.

You need 3 layers of 10 cubes each to fill the prism. It takes 30, or 5 · 2 · 3, cubes.

Volume is expressed in cubic units, so the volume of the prism is 5 cm · 2 cm · 3 cm = 30 cubic centimeters, or 30 cm³.

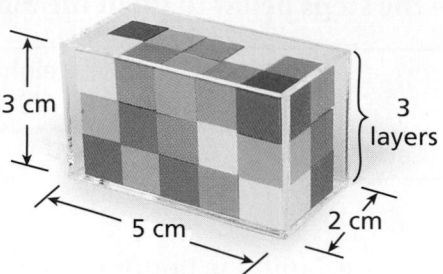

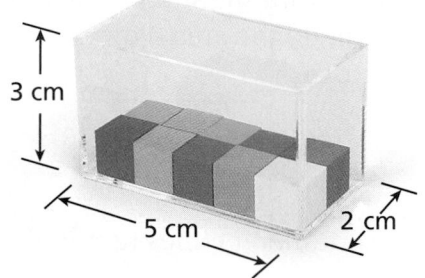

EXAMPLE 1 **Finding the Volume of a Rectangular Prism**

Find the volume of the rectangular prism.

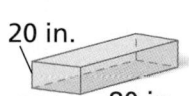

20 in.
36 in.   80 in.

$V = \ell wh$ *Write the formula.*

$V = 80 \cdot 36 \cdot 20$ $\ell = 80; w = 36; h = 20$

$V = 57{,}600 \text{ in}^3$ *Multiply.*

To find the volume of any prism, you can use the formula $V = Bh$, where B is the area of the base, and h is the prism's height.

EXAMPLE 2 **Finding the Volume of a Triangular Prism**

Find the volume of each triangular prism.

A

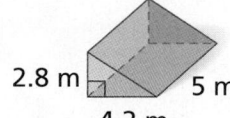

2.8 m   5 m
4.2 m

$V = Bh$ *Write the formula.*

$V = \left(\frac{1}{2} \cdot 2.8 \cdot 4.2 \right) \cdot 5$ $B = \frac{1}{2} \cdot 2.8 \cdot 4.2; h = 5$

$V = 29.4 \text{ m}^3$ *Multiply.*

Caution!

The bases of a prism are always two congruent, parallel polygons.

B

4.3 ft
9 ft   8.2 ft

$V = Bh$ *Write the formula.*

$V = \left(\frac{1}{2} \cdot 8.2 \cdot 4.3 \right) \cdot 9$ $B = \frac{1}{2} \cdot 8.2 \cdot 4.3; h = 9$

$V = 158.67 \text{ ft}^3$ *Multiply.*

EXAMPLE 3

PROBLEM SOLVING

PROBLEM SOLVING APPLICATION

A craft supplier ships 12 cubic trinket boxes in a case. What are the possible dimensions for a case of the trinket boxes?

1 Understand the Problem

The **answer** will be all possible dimensions for a case of 12 cubic boxes.

List the **important information:**

- There are 12 trinket boxes in a case.
- The boxes are cubic, or square prisms.

2 Make a Plan

You can make models using cubes to find the possible dimensions for a case of 12 trinket boxes.

3 Solve

Make different arrangements of 12 cubes.

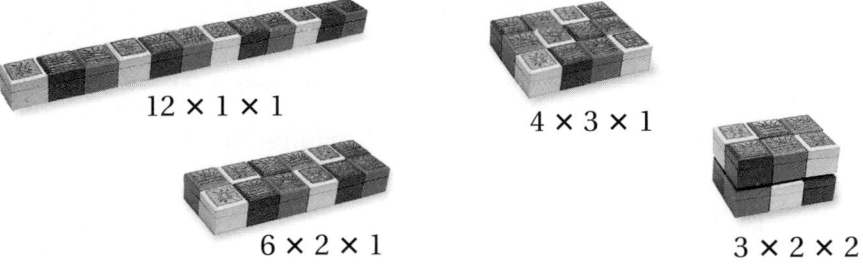

$12 \times 1 \times 1$

$4 \times 3 \times 1$

$6 \times 2 \times 1$

$3 \times 2 \times 2$

The possible dimensions for a case of 12 cubic trinket boxes are the following: $12 \times 1 \times 1$, $4 \times 3 \times 1$, $6 \times 2 \times 1$, and $3 \times 2 \times 2$.

4 Look Back

Notice that each dimension is a factor of 12. Also, the product of the dimensions (length · width · height) is 12, showing that the volume of each case is 12 cubes.

6.PS.21, 6.CM.10

Think and Discuss

1. **Explain** how to find the height of a rectangular prism if you know its length, width, and volume.

2. **Describe** the difference between the units used to measure perimeter, area, and volume.

10-7 Exercises

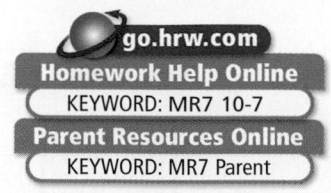
go.hrw.com
Homework Help Online
KEYWORD: MR7 10-7
Parent Resources Online
KEYWORD: MR7 Parent

GUIDED PRACTICE

See Example **1** Find the volume of each rectangular prism.

1.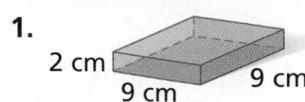
2 cm
9 cm
9 cm

2.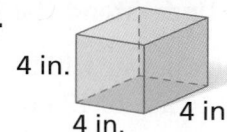
4 in.
4 in.
4 in.

3.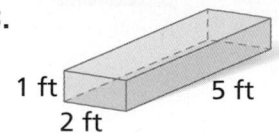
1 ft
2 ft
5 ft

See Example **2** Find the volume of each triangular prism.

4.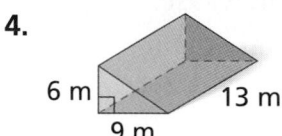
6 m
13 m
9 m

5.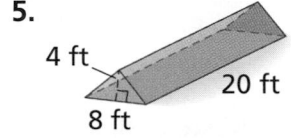
4 ft
20 ft
8 ft

6.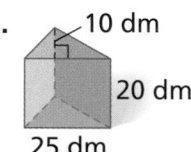
10 dm
20 dm
25 dm

See Example **3** **7.** A toy company packs 10 cubic boxes of toys in a case. What are the possible dimensions for a case of toys?

INDEPENDENT PRACTICE

See Example **1** Find the volume of each rectangular prism.

8.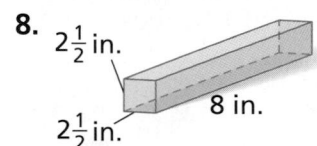
$2\frac{1}{2}$ in.
8 in.
$2\frac{1}{2}$ in.

9.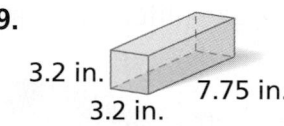
3.2 in.
3.2 in.
7.75 in.

10.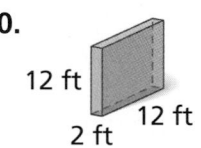
12 ft
12 ft
2 ft

See Example **2** Find the volume of each triangular prism.

11.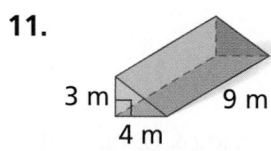
3 m
9 m
4 m

12.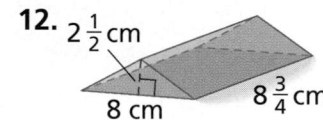
$2\frac{1}{2}$ cm
8 cm
$8\frac{3}{4}$ cm

13.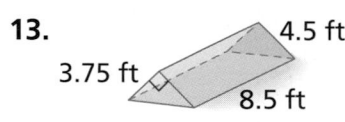
4.5 ft
3.75 ft
8.5 ft

See Example **3** **14.** A printing company packs 18 cubic boxes of business cards in a larger shipping box. What are the possible dimensions for the shipping box?

PRACTICE AND PROBLEM SOLVING

Extra Practice
See page 734.

Find the volume of each figure.

15.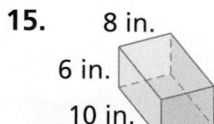
8 in.
6 in.
10 in.

16.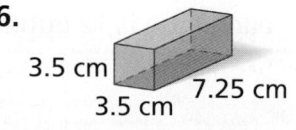
3.5 cm
3.5 cm
7.25 cm

17.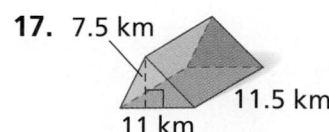
7.5 km
11.5 km
11 km

Find the missing measurement for each prism.

18. $\ell = \underline{\quad?\quad}$; $w = 25$ m; $h = 4$ m; $V = 300$ m³

19. $\ell = 9$ ft; $w = \underline{\quad?\quad}$; $h = 5$ ft; $V = 900$ ft³

20. $B = 9.28$ in.; $h = \underline{\quad?\quad}$; $V = 55.68$ in³

The density of a substance is a measure of its mass per unit of volume. The density of a particular substance is always the same. The formula for density D is the mass m of a substance divided by its volume V, or $D = \frac{m}{V}$.

21. Find the volume of each substance in the table.

22. Calculate the density of each substance.

23. Water has a density of 1 g/cm^3. A substance whose density is less than that of water will float. Which of the substances in the table will float in water?

24. A fresh egg has a density of approximately 1.2 g/cm^3. A spoiled egg has a density of about 0.9 g/cm^3. How can you tell whether an egg is fresh without cracking it open?

25. **Multi-Step** Alicia has a solid rectangular prism of a substance she believes is gold. The dimensions of the prism are 2 cm by 1 cm by 2 cm, and the mass is 20.08 g. Is the substance that Alicia has gold? Explain.

26.  **Write About It** In a science lab, you are given a prism of copper. You determine that its dimensions are 4 cm, 2 cm, and 6 cm. Without weighing the prism, how can you determine its mass? Explain your answer.

27. ★ **Challenge** A solid rectangular prism of silver has a mass of 84 g. What are some possible dimensions of the prism?

Iron filings are attracted by a magnet.

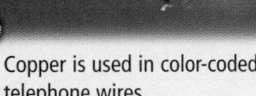
Copper is used in color-coded telephone wires.

Rectangular Prisms				
Substance	Length (cm)	Width (cm)	Height (cm)	Mass (g)
Copper	2	1	5	89.6
Gold	$\frac{2}{3}$	$\frac{3}{4}$	2	19.32
Iron pyrite	0.25	2	7	17.57
Pine	10	10	3	120
Silver	2.5	4	2	210

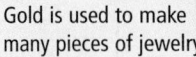
Gold is used to make many pieces of jewelry.

TEST PREP and Spiral Review

28. **Multiple Choice** A rectangular prism has a volume of 1,080 ft^3. The height of the prism is 8 ft, and the width is 9 ft. What is the length of the prism?

   Ⓐ 15 ft   Ⓑ 120 ft   Ⓒ 135 ft   Ⓓ 77,760 ft

29. **Gridded Response** The dimensions of a rectangular prism are 4.3 inches, 12 inches, and 1.5 inches. What is the volume, in cubic inches, of the prism?

Find the GCF of each set of numbers. (Lesson 4-3)

30. 12, 18, 24   31. 15, 18, 30   32. 16, 24, 42   33. 18, 54, 63

Volume of Cylinders

**Learn** to find volumes of cylinders.

NY Performance Indicators

6.A.6 Evaluate formulas for given input values (circumference, area, volume, distance, temperature, interest, etc.). Also, **6.A.2, 6.M.6.**

Thomas Edison invented the first phonograph in 1877. The main part of this phonograph was a cylinder with a 4-inch diameter and a height of $3\frac{3}{8}$ inches.

To find the volume of a cylinder, you can use the same method as you did for prisms: Multiply the area of the base by the height.

volume of a cylinder = area of base × height

The area of the circular base is πr^2, so the formula is $V = Bh = \pi r^2 h$.

EXAMPLE 1 **Finding the Volume of a Cylinder**

Find the volume V of each cylinder to the nearest cubic unit.

A

4 in.
15 in.

$V = \pi r^2 h$ — *Write the formula.*
$V \approx 3.14 \times 4^2 \times 15$ — *Replace π with 3.14, r with 4, and h with 15.*
$V \approx 753.6$ — *Multiply.*

The volume is about 754 in³.

B

6 ft
18 ft

$6 \text{ ft} \div 2 = 3 \text{ ft}$ — *Find the radius.*
$V = \pi r^2 h$ — *Write the formula.*
$V \approx 3.14 \times 3^2 \times 18$ — *Replace π with 3.14, r with 3, and h with 18.*
$V \approx 508.68$ — *Multiply.*

The volume is about 509 ft³.

C

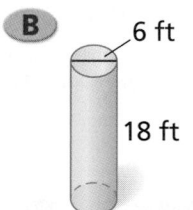
$r = \frac{h}{6} + 1$
$h = 24$ cm

$r = \frac{h}{6} + 1$ — *Find the radius.*
$r = \frac{24}{6} + 1 = 5$ — *Substitute 24 for h.*
$V = \pi r^2 h$ — *Write the formula.*
$V \approx 3.14 \times 5^2 \times 24$ — *Replace π with 3.14, r with 5, and h with 24.*
$V \approx 1,884$ — *Multiply.*

The volume is about 1,884 cm³.

EXAMPLE 2 *Music Application*

The cylinder in Edison's first phonograph had a 4 in. diameter and a height of about 3 in. The standard phonograph manufactured 21 years later had a 2 in. diameter and a height of 4 in. Estimate the volume of each cylinder to the nearest cubic inch.

Remember!

The value of *pi* can be approximated as 3.14 or $\frac{22}{7}$.

A Edison's first phonograph

4 in. ÷ 2 = 2 in.	*Find the radius.*
$V = \pi r^2 h$	*Write the formula.*
$V \approx 3.14 \times 2^2 \times 3$	*Replace π with 3.14, r with 2, and h with 3.*
$V \approx 37.68$	*Multiply.*

The volume of Edison's first phonograph was about 38 in^3.

B Edison's standard phonograph

2 in. ÷ 2 = 1 in.	*Find the radius.*
$V = \pi r^2 h$	*Write the formula.*
$V \approx \frac{22}{7} \times 1^2 \times 4$	*Replace π with $\frac{22}{7}$, r with 1, and h with 4.*
$V \approx \frac{88}{7} = 12\frac{4}{7}$	*Multiply.*

The volume of the standard phonograph was about 13 in^3.

EXAMPLE 3 Comparing Volumes of Cylinders

Find which cylinder has the greater volume.

Cylinder 1: $V = \pi r^2 h$
$\qquad V \approx 3.14 \times 6^2 \times 12$
$\qquad V \approx 1{,}356.48 \text{ cm}^3$

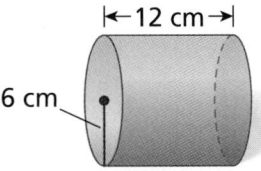

Cylinder 2: $V = \pi r^2 h$
$\qquad V \approx 3.14 \times 4^2 \times 16$
$\qquad V \approx 803.84 \text{ cm}^3$

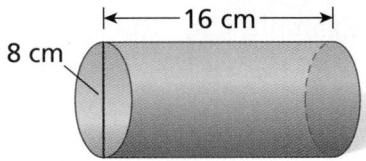

Cylinder 1 has the greater volume because 1,356.48 cm^3 > 803.84 cm^3.

Think and Discuss

1. **Explain** how the formula for the volume of a cylinder is similar to the formula for the volume of a rectangular prism.

2. **Explain** which parts of a cylinder are represented by πr^2 and h in the formula $V = \pi r^2 h$.

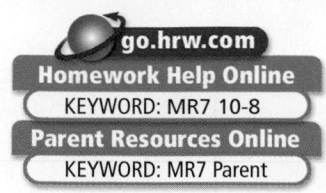

go.hrw.com
Homework Help Online
KEYWORD: MR7 10-8
Parent Resources Online
KEYWORD: MR7 Parent

GUIDED PRACTICE

See Example **1** Find the volume *V* of each cylinder to the nearest cubic unit.

1. 4 m
15 m

2.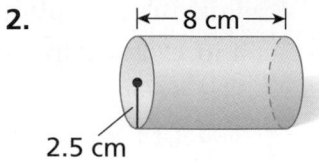
|← 8 cm →|
2.5 cm

3. 10 in.
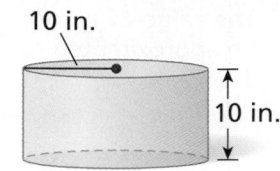
10 in.

See Example **2** **4.** A cylindrical bucket with a diameter of 4 inches is filled with rainwater to a height of 2.5 inches. Estimate the volume of the rainwater to the nearest cubic inch.

See Example **3** **5.** Find which cylinder, A or B, has the greater volume.

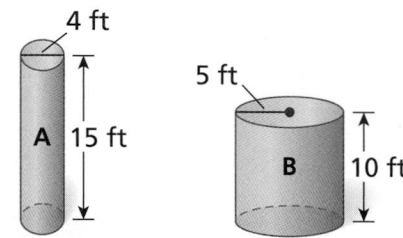
4 ft
A 15 ft
5 ft
B 10 ft

INDEPENDENT PRACTICE

See Example **1** Find the volume *V* of each cylinder to the nearest cubic unit.

6. |← 28 cm →|
14 cm

7.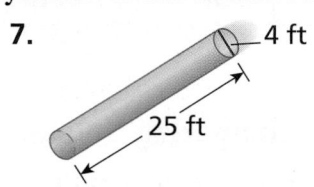
4 ft
25 ft

8. 5 cm
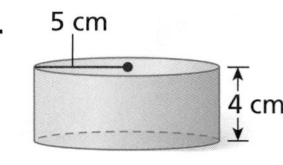
4 cm

See Example **2** **9.** Wooden dowels are solid cylinders of wood. One dowel has a radius of 1 cm, and another dowel has a radius of 3 cm. Both dowels have a height of 10 cm. Estimate the volume of each dowel to the nearest cubic cm.

See Example **3** **10.** Find which cylinder, X or Y, has the greater volume.

6 in.
X 3 in.
3 in.
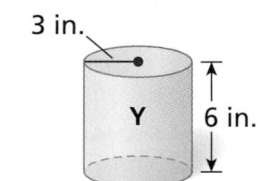
Y 6 in.

PRACTICE AND PROBLEM SOLVING

Extra Practice
See page 734.

Find the volume of each cylinder to the nearest cubic unit.

11. 2.8 in.
5.6 in.

12. |← $5\frac{2}{3}$ cm →|
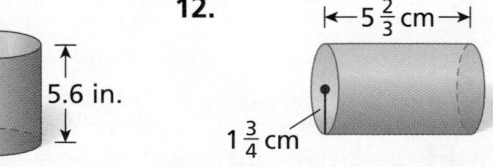
$1\frac{3}{4}$ cm

13.
|← 4.5 m →|
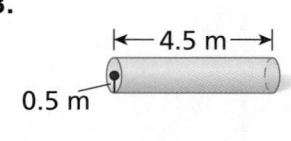
0.5 m

Find the volume of each cylinder using the information given.

14. $r = 6$ cm; $h = 6$ cm   **15.** $d = 4$ in.; $h = 8$ in.   **16.** $r = 2$ m; $h = 5$ m

17. $r = 7.5$ ft; $h = 11.25$ ft **18.** $d = 12\frac{1}{4}$ yd; $h = 5\frac{3}{5}$ yd **19.** $d = 20$ mm; $h = 40$ mm

Multi-Step Find the volume of each shaded cylinder to the nearest cubic unit.

20.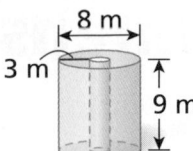
8 m
3 m
9 m

21.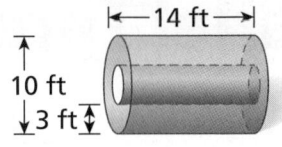
←14 ft→
10 ft
3 ft

22.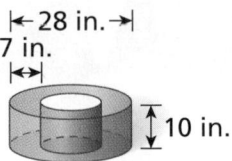
←28 in.→
7 in.
10 in.

23. Measurement Could this blue can hold 200 cm³ of juice? How do you know?

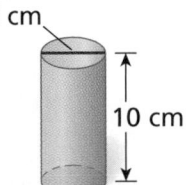
5 cm
10 cm

24. Science A scientist filled a cylindrical beaker with 942 mm³ of a chemical solution. The area of the base of the cylinder is 78.5 mm². What is the height of the solution?

25. Choose a Strategy Fran, Gene, Helen, and Ira have cylinders with different volumes. Gene's cylinder holds more than Fran's. Ira's cylinder holds more than Helen's, but less than Fran's. Whose cylinder has the largest volume? What color cylinder does each person have?

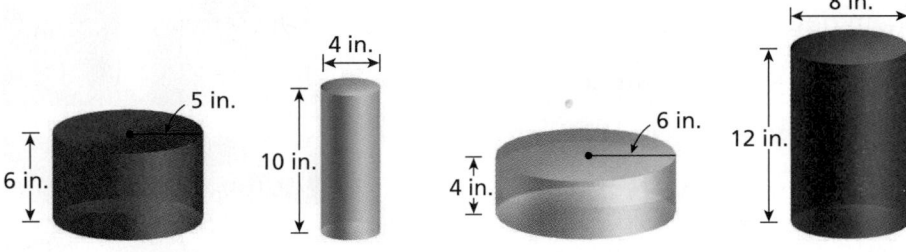
5 in.
6 in.
4 in.
10 in.
6 in.
4 in.
8 in.
12 in.

26. Write About It Explain why volume is expressed in cubic units of measurement.

27. Challenge Find the volume of the shaded area.

1½ cm
4 cm
4 cm
4 cm

TEST PREP and Spiral Review

28. Multiple Choice Find the volume of a cylinder with a height of $2\frac{1}{3}$ feet and a radius of $1\frac{1}{2}$ feet.

 Ⓕ 19.75 ft³   Ⓖ 16.5 ft³   Ⓗ 11 ft³   Ⓙ 5.5 ft³

29. Short Response Chicken noodle soup is sold in a can that is 11 cm tall and has a radius of 2.5 cm. Tomato soup is sold in a can that is 7.5 cm tall and has a radius of 4 cm. Find the volume of both cans. Which can holds more soup?

Identify a pattern in each sequence. Name the missing terms. (Lesson 1-7)

30. 10, 13, 16, 19, ▪, ▪, . . .   **31.** 5, 8, 7, 10, ▪, ▪, . . .   **32.** 4, 16, 64, 256, ▪, ▪, . . .

33. The diagram shows a school yard. What is the measure of ∠W? (Lesson 9-6)

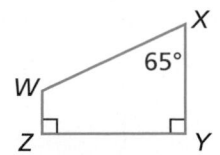
X
65°
W
Z
Y

Model Three-Dimensional Figures

Use with Lesson 10-9

NY Performance Indicators

6.R.1, 6.R.4, 6.R.5

go.hrw.com
Lab Resources Online
KEYWORD: MR7 Lab10

You can build a solid figure by cutting its faces from paper, taping them together, and then folding them to form the solid. A pattern of shapes that can be folded to form a solid figure is called a *net*.

Activity

1 To make a pattern for a rectangular prism follow the steps below.

a. Draw the following rectangles and cut them out:

Two 2 in. × 3 in. rectangles

Two 1 in. × 3 in. rectangles

Two 1 in. × 2 in. rectangles

b. Tape the pieces together to form the prism.

c. Remove the tape from some of the edges so that the pattern lies flat.

2 Create a net for a cylinder.

Think: What shapes can make a cylinder?

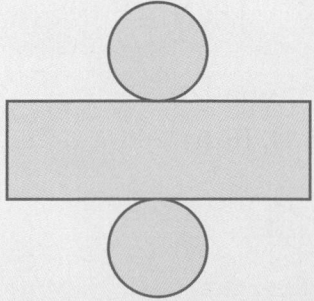

If a cylinder is "unfolded," the bases of the cylinder are circles, and the curved surface is a rectangle.

The net is made up of two circles and a rectangle.

❸ Create a net for a square pyramid.

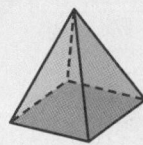

Think: What shapes can make a square pyramid?

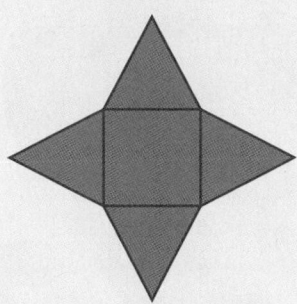

If the square pyramid is "unfolded," the base is a square, and the sides are triangles.

The net is made up of a square and four triangles.

Think and Discuss

1. Compare the nets for a rectangular prism and a cube.

2. Tell what shapes will always appear in a net for a triangular pyramid.

3. Tell what shapes will always appear in a net for a hexagonal prism.

Try This

Tell whether each net can be folded to form a cube. If not, explain.

1.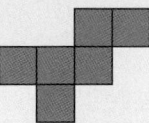

2.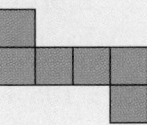

3.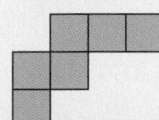

4.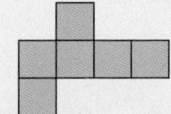

Name the three-dimensional figure that can be formed from each net.

5.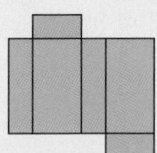

6.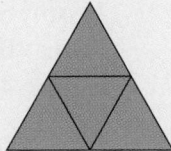

7. Create a net for a cone.

Surface Area

Learn to find the surface areas of prisms, pyramids, and cylinders.

Vocabulary

surface area

net

Katie made a toy for her cat to scratch by attaching carpet to the faces of a wooden box. The amount of carpet needed to cover the box is equal to the surface area of the box.

The **surface area** of a three-dimensional figure is the sum of the areas of its surfaces. To help you see all the surfaces of a three-dimensional figure, you can use a *net*. A **net** is the pattern made when the surface of a three-dimensional figure is layed out flat showing each face of the figure.

EXAMPLE **1** **Finding the Surface Area of a Prism**

Find the surface area *S* of each prism.

NY Performance Indicators

6.A.6 Evaluate formulas for given input values (circumference, area, volume, distance, temperature, interest, etc.). Also, **6.A.2**.

A Method 1: Use a net.

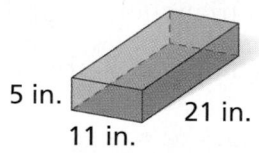

Draw a net to help you see each face of the prism.

Use the formula $A = \ell w$ to find the area of each face.

A: $A = 11 \times 5 = 55$
B: $A = 21 \times 11 = 231$
C: $A = 21 \times 5 = 105$
D: $A = 21 \times 11 = 231$
E: $A = 21 \times 5 = 105$
F: $A = 11 \times 5 = 55$

$S = 55 + 231 + 105 + 231 + 105 + 55 = 782$ *Add the areas of each face.*

The surface area is 782 in^2.

B Method 2: Use a three-dimensional drawing.

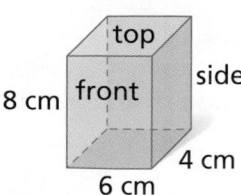

Find the area of the front, top, and side, and multiply each by 2 to include the opposite faces.

Front: $6 \times 8 = 48 \longrightarrow 48 \times 2 = 96$
Top: $6 \times 4 = 24 \longrightarrow 24 \times 2 = 48$
Side: $4 \times 8 = 32 \longrightarrow 32 \times 2 = 64$

$S = 96 + 48 + 64 = 208$ *Add the areas of the faces.*

The surface area is 208 cm^2.

The surface area of a pyramid equals the sum of the area of the base and the areas of the triangular faces. To find the surface area of a pyramid, think of its net.

EXAMPLE ② **Finding the Surface Area of a Pyramid**

Find the surface area S of the pyramid.

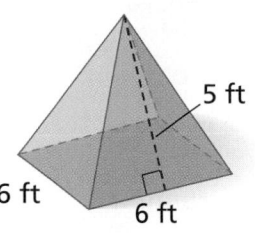
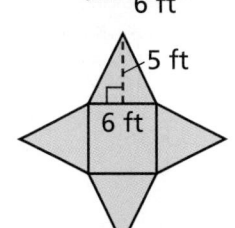

$S = $ area of square $+ 4 \times$ (area of triangular face)

$S = s^2 + 4 \times \left(\frac{1}{2}bh\right)$

$S = 6^2 + 4 \times \left(\frac{1}{2} \times 6 \times 5\right)$ *Substitute.*

$S = 36 + 4 \times 15$

$S = 36 + 60$

$S = 96$

The surface area is 96 ft².

The surface area of a cylinder equals the sum of the area of its bases and the area of its curved surface.

EXAMPLE ③ **Finding the Surface Area of a Cylinder**

Find the surface area S of the cylinder. Use 3.14 for π, and round to the nearest hundredth.

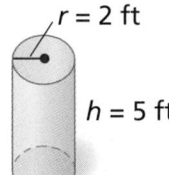
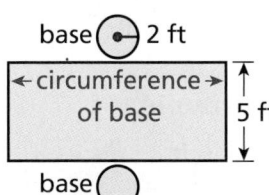

$S = $ area of lateral surface $+ 2 \times$ (area of each base)

$S = h \times (2\pi r) + 2 \times (\pi r^2)$

$S = 5 \times (2 \times \pi \times 2) + 2 \times (\pi \times 2^2)$ *Substitute.*

$S = 5 \times 4\pi + 2 \times 4\pi$

$S \approx 5 \times 4(3.14) + 2 \times 4(3.14)$ *Use 3.14 for π.*

$S \approx 5 \times 12.56 + 2 \times 12.56$

$S \approx 62.8 + 25.12$

$S \approx 87.92$

The surface area is about 87.92 ft².

6.PS.21, 6.CM.1

Think and Discuss

1. Describe how to find the surface area of a pentagonal prism.

2. Tell how to find the surface area of a cube if you know the area of one face.

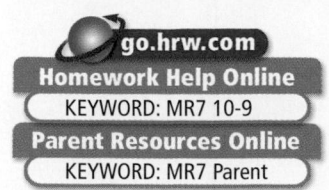
go.hrw.com
Homework Help Online
KEYWORD: MR7 10-9
Parent Resources Online
KEYWORD: MR7 Parent

GUIDED PRACTICE

See Example **1** Find the surface area S of each prism.

1.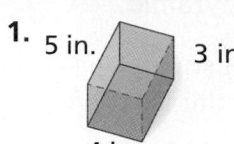
5 in. 3 in. 4 in.

2.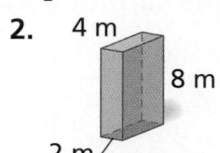
4 m 8 m 2 m

3.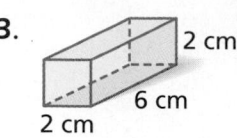
2 cm 6 cm 2 cm

See Example **2** Find the surface area S of each pyramid.

4.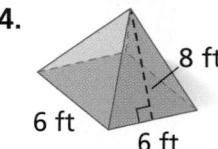
8 ft 6 ft 6 ft

5.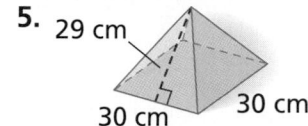
29 cm 30 cm 30 cm

6.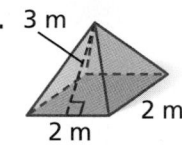
3 m 2 m 2 m

See Example **3** Find the surface area S of each cylinder. Use 3.14 for π, and round to the nearest hundredth.

7.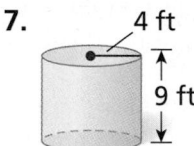
4 ft 9 ft

8.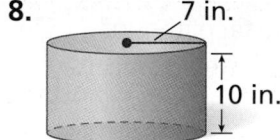
7 in. 10 in.

9.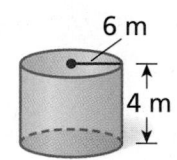
6 m 4 m

INDEPENDENT PRACTICE

See Example **1** Find the surface area S of each prism.

10.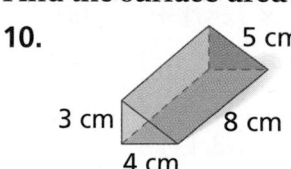
5 cm 3 cm 8 cm 4 cm

11.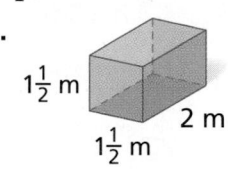
$1\frac{1}{2}$ m 2 m $1\frac{1}{2}$ m

12.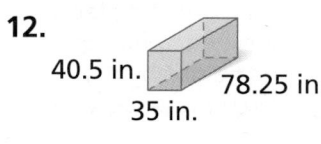
40.5 in. 78.25 in. 35 in.

See Example **2** Find the surface area S of each pyramid.

13.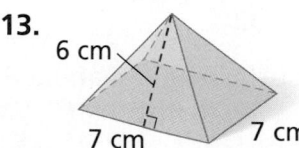
6 cm 7 cm 7 cm

14.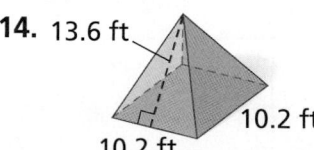
13.6 ft 10.2 ft 10.2 ft

15.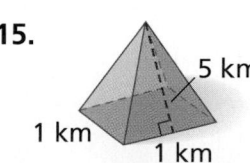
5 km 1 km 1 km

See Example **3** Find the surface area S of each cylinder. Use 3.14 for π, and round to the nearest hundredth.

16.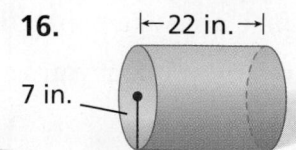
|← 22 in. →| 7 in.

17.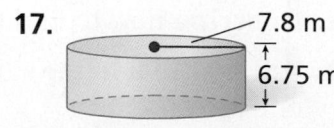
7.8 m 6.75 m

18.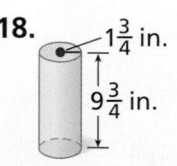
$1\frac{3}{4}$ in. $9\frac{3}{4}$ in.

PRACTICE AND PROBLEM SOLVING

Extra Practice
See page 734.

Architecture

19. You are designing a container for oatmeal. Your first design is a rectangular prism with a height of 12 in., a width of 8 in., and a depth of 3 in.

　　a. What is the surface area of the package?

　　b. You redesign the package as a cylinder with the same surface area as the prism from part **a.** If the radius of the cylinder is 2 in., what is the height of the cylinder? Round to the nearest tenth of an inch.

20. Architecture The entrance to the Louvre Museum is a glass-paned square pyramid. The width of the base is 34.2 m, and the height of the triangular sides is 27 m. What is the surface area of the glass?

Estimation Estimate the surface area of each figure.

21.
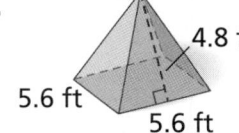
4.8 ft
5.6 ft
5.6 ft

22. 3 m
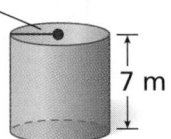
7 m

23.
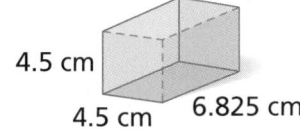
4.5 cm
4.5 cm　6.825 cm

I. M. Pei is the architect of the pyramid-shaped addition to the Louvre in Paris, France.

go.hrw.com
Web Extra!
KEYWORD: MR7 Pei

24. Critical Thinking If each of the dimensions of a rectangular prism is halved, how does this affect the surface area?

 25. What's the Question? The surface area of a cube is 150 cm². The answer is 5 cm. What is the question?

26. Write About It How is finding the surface area of a rectangular pyramid different from finding the surface area of a triangular prism?

27. Challenge This cube is made of 27 smaller cubes whose sides measure 1 in.

　　a. What is the surface area of the large cube?

　　b. Remove one small cube from each of the eight corners of the larger cube. What is the surface area of the solid formed?

TEST PREP and Spiral Review

28. Multiple Choice Find the surface area of a cube with a side length of 9.4 yd.

　Ⓐ 56.4 yd²　　　Ⓑ 88.36 yd²　　　Ⓒ 338.4 yd²　　　Ⓓ 530.16 yd²

29. Gridded Response Find the surface area, in square meters, of a cylinder with a radius of 7 m and a height of 6 m. Use 3.14 for π and round to the nearest hundredth.

Solve each equation. (Lesson 2-5)

30. $12 + y = 23$　　　　**31.** $38 + y = 80$　　　　**32.** $y + 76 = 230$

Find each sum or difference. Write the answer in simplest form. (Lesson 5-3)

33. $5\frac{2}{3} - 1\frac{1}{9}$　　　**34.** $1\frac{1}{4} + 2\frac{3}{8}$　　　**35.** $2\frac{5}{6} - 2\frac{3}{4}$　　　**36.** $4\frac{2}{5} + 3\frac{3}{10}$

Quiz for Lessons 10-6 Through 10-9

✓ 10-6 Three-Dimensional Figures

Identify the number of faces, edges, and vertices on each figure. Then name the figure and tell whether it is a polyhedron.

1.

2.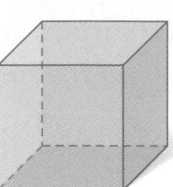

3.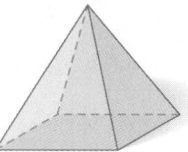

✓ 10-7 Volume of Prisms

Find the volume of each prism.

4.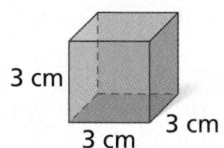
3 cm
3 cm   3 cm

5.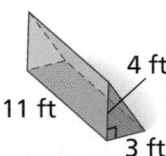
4 ft
11 ft
3 ft

6.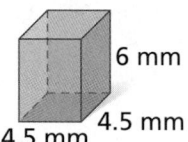
6 mm
4.5 mm   4.5 mm

7. There are 16 cubic boxes of erasers in a case. What are all the possible dimensions for a case of erasers?

✓ 10-8 Volume of Cylinders

Find the volume *v* of each cylinder to the nearest cubic unit. Use 3.14 for *pi*.

8.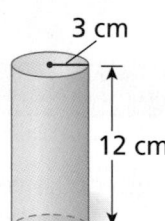
3 cm
12 cm

9.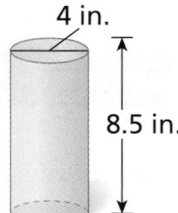
4 in.
8.5 in.

10.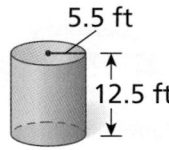
5.5 ft
12.5 ft

11. Which cylinder has the greater volume?

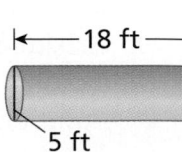
|←9 ft→|
10 ft

|←——18 ft——→|
5 ft

✓ 10-9 Surface Area

Find the surface area *s* of each figure. Use 3.14 for *pi,* and round to the nearest hundredth.

12.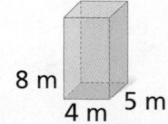
8 m
4 m   5 m

13.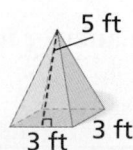
5 ft
3 ft   3 ft

14.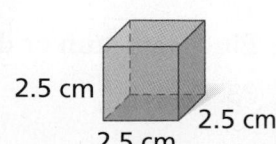
2.5 cm
2.5 cm
2.5 cm

MULTI-STEP TEST PREP

At Home in Space   The International Space Station is a state-of-the-art laboratory in space. It is where we can learn to live and work "off planet." The space station is large enough to accommodate more than 30 experiments and provide living space for 6 astronauts. It is in the shape of a rectangular prism.

1. The table below shows the volumes of rectangular prisms that each have an 18-square-foot area for their bases but have different heights. Describe any patterns or proportional relationships in the table.

2. Write a rule to show how the heights in the table are related to the volumes.

3. According to NASA, the average floor space in U.S. houses is about 1,800 ft². Ceilings are 8 ft high on average. How many cubic feet are in a house with these average measurements?

4. The space station has 43,000 ft³ of pressurized volume. About how many houses with the measurements from Problem 3 would fit in the space station? Explain.

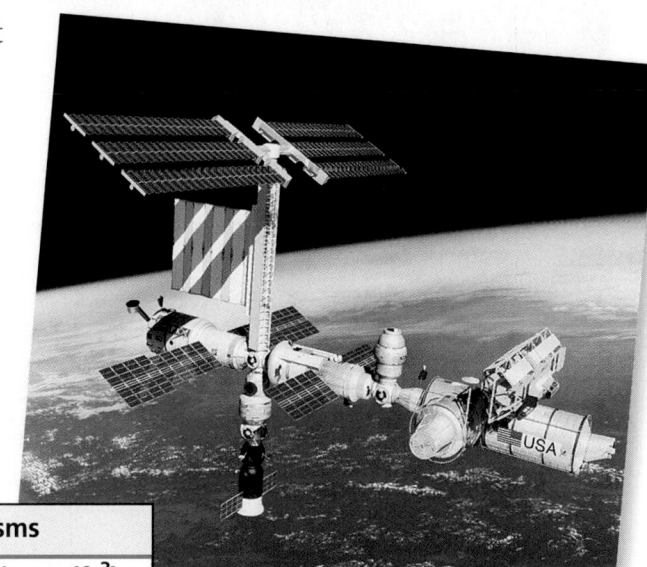

Volume of Rectangular Prisms		
Area (ft²)	Height (ft)	Volume (ft³)
18	1	18
18	2	36
18	3	54
18	4	72
18	5	90
18	6	108
18	7	126
18	8	144

Multi-Step Test Prep

Game Time

Polygon Hide-and-Seek

Use the figure to name each polygon described.

1 an obtuse scalene triangle
2 a right isosceles triangle
3 a parallelogram with no right angles
4 a trapezoid with two congruent sides
5 a pentagon with three congruent sides

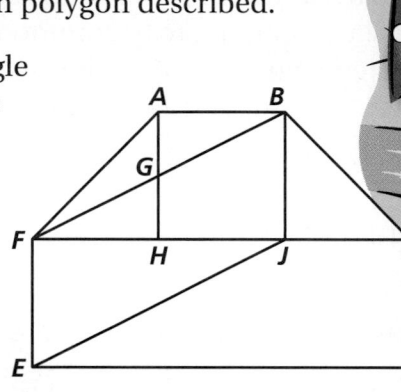

Poly-Cross Puzzle

You will use the names of the figures below to complete a crossword puzzle.

A copy of the crossword puzzle is available online.

go.hrw.com
Game Time Extra
KEYWORD: MR7 Games

ACROSS

1.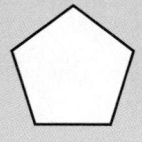

2.

3.

4.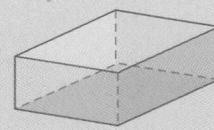

5.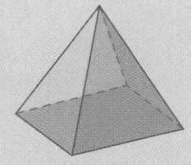

6.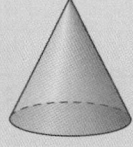

DOWN

1.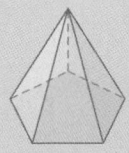

7.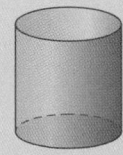

8.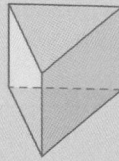

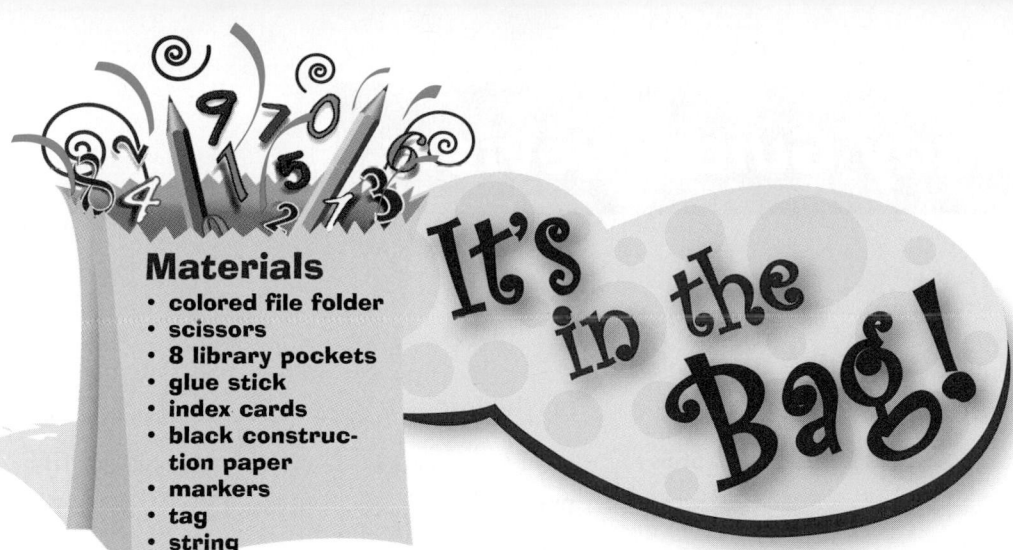

Materials
- colored file folder
- scissors
- 8 library pockets
- glue stick
- index cards
- black construction paper
- markers
- tag
- string

It's in the Bag!

PROJECT **Area and Volume Suitcase**

Carry your notes with you as you travel through Chapter 10.

Directions

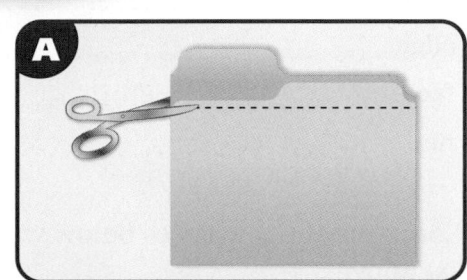

1 Cut the tabs off a colored file folder to form a rectangular folder with straight sides.
Figure A

2 Open the folder. Glue library pockets inside the folder so that there are four on each side. Place an index card in each pocket.
Figure B

3 Cut out "handles" from the construction paper. Glue these to the folder as shown.
Figure C

4 Use a piece of string to attach a tag to one of the handles. Write your name and the name of your class on the tag. Write the name and number of the chapter on the front of the folder.

Taking Note of the Math

Write the names of the chapter's lessons on the library pockets. Then take notes on each lesson on the appropriate index card.

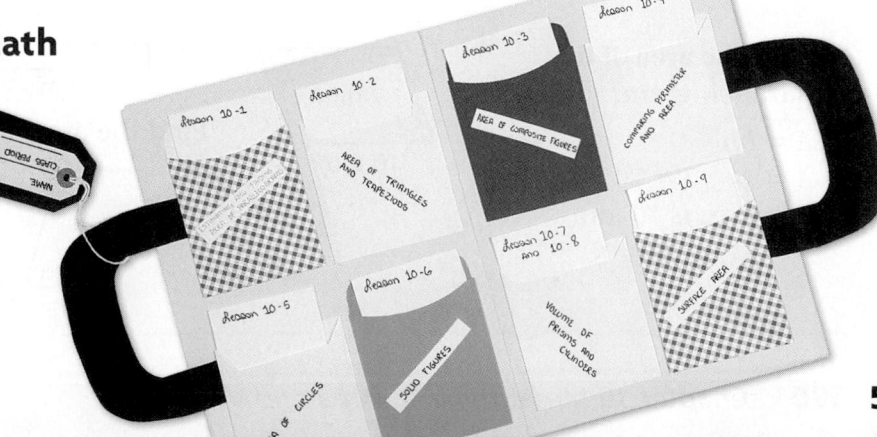

Vocabulary

Complete the sentences below with vocabulary words from the list above.

1. A ___?___ is a three-dimensional object with flat faces that are polygons.

2. The number of cubic units needed to fill a space is called ___?___.

3. The point at which three or more edges meet on a three-dimensional figure is called a ___?___.

10-1 Estimating and Finding Area (pp. 542–545)

6.A.2, 6.A.6, 6.G.2

EXAMPLE

■ **Find the area of the rectangle.**

4 ft [rectangle] 15 ft

$A = \ell w$
$A = 15 \cdot 4 = 60$
The area is 60 ft².

■ **Find the area of the parallelogram.**

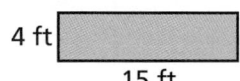
7 mm
10 mm

$A = bh$
$A = 10 \cdot 7 = 70$
The area is 70 mm².

EXERCISES

Find the area of each rectangle.

4.

3 ft
6 ft

5.  1 m
7 m

Find the area of each parallelogram.

6.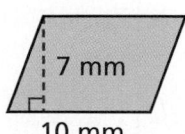
4 in.
3 in.

7.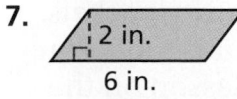
2 in.
6 in.

Study Guide: Review

10-2 Area of Triangles and Trapezoids (pp. 546–549)

6.A.2, 6.A.6, 6.G.2

EXAMPLE

■ Find the area of the trapezoid.

4 m
2 m
10 m

Use $A = \frac{1}{2}h(b_1 + h_2)$.
Substitute 10 for b_1, 4 for b_2, and 2 for h.

$A = \frac{1}{2}(2)(10 + 4)$

$= \frac{1}{2}(2)(14)$

$= \frac{1}{2}(28)$

$= 14 \text{ m}^2$

EXERCISES

Find the area of the triangle.

8.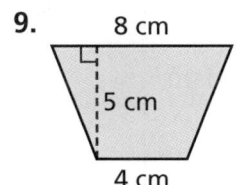
11 in.
28 in.

Find the area of the trapezoid.

9.
8 cm
5 cm
4 cm

10-3 Area of Composite Figures (pp. 551–553)

6.A.2, 6.A.6, 6.G.3

EXAMPLE

■ Find the area of the polygon.

$A = 8 \cdot 12 = 96$

$A = \frac{1}{2} \cdot 12 \cdot 7 = 42$

The area of the figure is
$42 \text{ ft}^2 + 96 \text{ ft}^2 = 138 \text{ ft}^2$.

15 ft
8 ft
12 ft

EXERCISES

Find the area of each polygon.

10.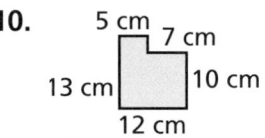
5 cm
7 cm
13 cm
10 cm
12 cm

11.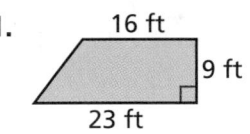
16 ft
9 ft
23 ft

10-4 Comparing Perimeter and Area (pp. 554–556)

6.A.6

EXAMPLE

■ Find how the perimeter and area of a rectangle change when its dimensions change.

When the dimensions of the rectangle are multiplied by x, the perimeter is multiplied by x, and the area is multiplied by x^2.

EXERCISES

Find how the perimeter and area change when its dimensions change.

12.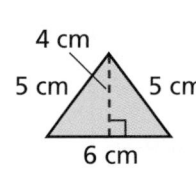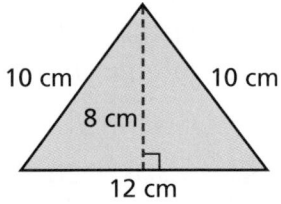
4 cm
5 cm   5 cm
6 cm

10 cm   10 cm
8 cm
12 cm

10-5 Area of Circles (pp. 558–561)

6.N.27, 6.A.2, 6.A.6, 6.G.7

EXAMPLE

■ Find the area of the circle. Use 3.14 for *pi.*

$A = \pi r^2$

$A \approx 3.14 \cdot 3^2$

$A \approx 3.14 \cdot 9 \approx 28.26 \text{ cm}^2$

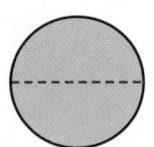
$d = 6$ cm

EXERCISES

Find the area of each circle. Use $\frac{22}{7}$ for *pi.*

13. $d = 10$ ft   **14.** $r = 8$ cm   **15.** $d = 4$ m

16. A circular window has a diameter of 14 ft. Find the area of the glass needed to fill the window. Use 3.14 for *pi.*

10-6 Three-Dimensional Figures (pp. 566–569)

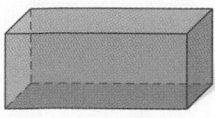 6.CM.10

EXAMPLE

- Identify the number of faces, edges, and vertices on the solid figure. Then name the solid.

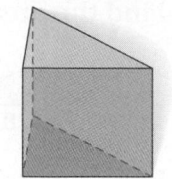

  5 faces; 9 edges; 6 vertices
  There are two congruent parallel bases, so the figure is a prism. The bases are triangles.
  The solid is a triangular prism.

EXERCISES

Identify the number of faces, edges, and vertices on each solid figure. Then name the solid.

17.

18.

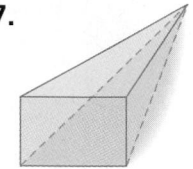

10-7 Volume of Prisms (pp. 572–575)

6.A.2, 6.A.6, 6.M.1, 6.M.6

EXAMPLE

- Find the volume of the rectangular prism.

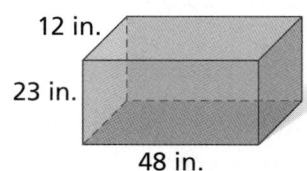

  12 in.
  23 in.
  48 in.

  $V = \ell wh$
  $V = 48 \cdot 12 \cdot 23$
  $V = 13{,}248 \text{ in}^3$

EXERCISES

Find the volume of each prism.

19.

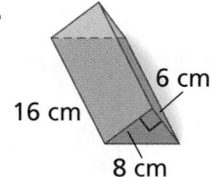

  16 cm
  6 cm
  8 cm

20.

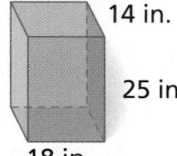

  14 in.
  25 in.
  18 in.

10-8 Volume of Cylinders (pp. 576–579)

6.A.2, 6.A.6, 6.M.6

EXAMPLE

- Find the volume V of the cylinder to the nearest cubic unit.

  $r = 4$ cm
  $h = 16$ cm

  $V \approx 3.14 \cdot 4^2 \cdot 16$
  $V \approx 803.84 \text{ cm}^3$
  The volume is about 804 cm^3.

EXERCISES

Find the volume V of each cylinder to the nearest cubic unit.

21. $h = 12.5$ m

  $r = 3$ m

22. $r = 7$ ft

  $h = 15$ ft

10-9 Surface Area (pp. 582–585)

6.A.2, 6.A.6

EXAMPLE

- Find the surface area S of the cylinder.

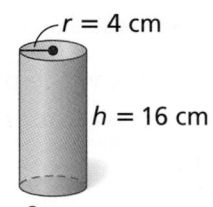

  2 in.
  6 in.

  $S = h \cdot (2\pi r) + 2 \cdot (\pi r^2)$
  $S \approx 6 \cdot (2 \cdot 3.14 \cdot 2) + 2 \cdot (3.14 \cdot 2^2)$
  $S \approx 100.48 \text{ in}^2$

EXERCISES

Find the surface area S of each solid.

23.

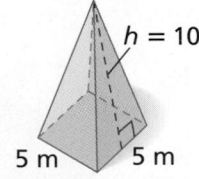

  $h = 10$ m
  5 m   5 m

24.

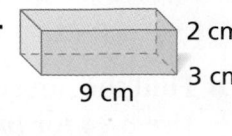

  2 cm
  3 cm
  9 cm

CHAPTER TEST

CHAPTER
10

Find the area of each figure.

1.

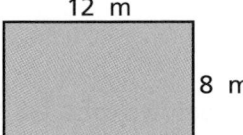

12 m

8 m

2.

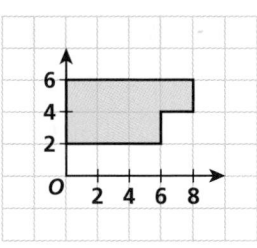

3.

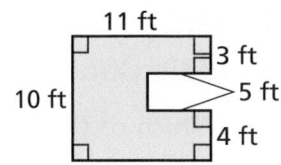

11 ft

3 ft

10 ft

5 ft

4 ft

4. Find how the perimeter and the area of a rectangle change when the length and width are doubled.

5. A patio is in the shape of a trapezoid. What is the area of the patio?

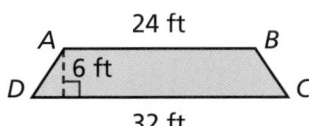

24 ft

A   B

6 ft

D   C

32 ft

Find the area of each circle. Use 3.14 for *pi*. Round to the nearest hundredth.

6.

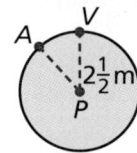

A   V

$2\frac{1}{2}$ m

P

7.

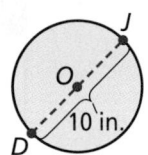

J

O

10 in.

D

8.

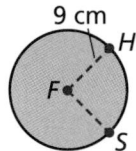

9 cm

H

F

S

Identify the number of faces, edges, and vertices on each three-dimensional figure. Then name the figure and tell whether it is a polyhedron.

9.

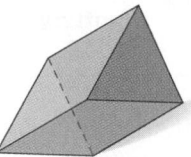

10.

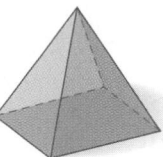

11.

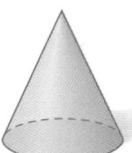

Find the volume of each three-dimensional figure.

12.

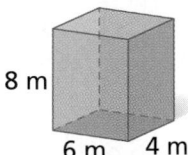

8 m

6 m   4 m

13.

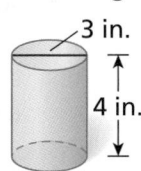

3 in.

4 in.

14.

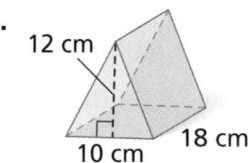

12 cm

10 cm   18 cm

15. Patricia has two cylinder-shaped jars. Jar A has a radius of 6 cm and a height of 9 cm. Jar B has a diameter of 8 cm and a height of 17 cm. Which jar has the greater volume? How much greater?

Find the surface area *S* of each three-dimensional figure.

16.

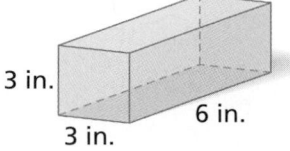

3 in.

3 in.   6 in.

17.

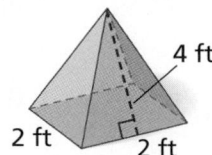

4 ft

2 ft   2 ft

18.

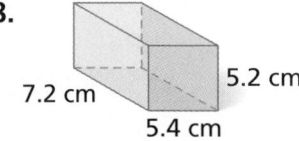

5.2 cm

7.2 cm

5.4 cm

Chapter 10 Test **593**

Cumulative Assessment, Chapters 1–10

Multiple Choice

1. Which of the following solid figures is NOT a polyhedron?

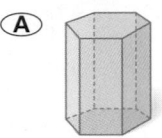

Ⓐ

Ⓒ

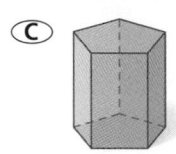

Ⓑ

Ⓓ

2. On May 1, 2005, in Galveston, Texas, the sun rose at 6:37 A.M. The sun set at 7:56 P.M. How much time elapsed from sunrise to sunset?

  Ⓕ 1 hour and 39 minutes

  Ⓖ 12 hours and 29 minutes

  Ⓗ 13 hours and 9 minutes

  Ⓙ 13 hours and 19 minutes

3. A gallon of paint will cover 250 square feet. About how many gallons of paint are needed to paint a rectangular billboard that is 120 feet long and 85 feet tall?

  Ⓐ 2 gallons   Ⓒ 22 gallons

  Ⓑ 10 gallons   Ⓓ 41 gallons

4. Justin has 3 cups of sugar in a canister. He uses $\frac{1}{3}$ cup of sugar in a cookie recipe. He uses $\frac{3}{4}$ of what is remaining in the canister to make a pitcher of lemonade. How much sugar is left?

  Ⓕ $\frac{2}{3}$ cup   Ⓗ $1\frac{11}{12}$ cups

  Ⓖ 1 cup   Ⓙ 2 cups

5. What is the prime factorization of 324?

  Ⓐ $2^2 \times 3^4$ Ⓒ $2^2 \times 3^2 \times 27$

  Ⓑ $2^2 \times 9^2$ Ⓓ $2^2 \times 81$

6. Maysville Middle School is hosting a craft fair. The circle graph shows how many different types of booths will be at the craft fair. To the nearest whole number, what percent of the booths will be selling jewelry?

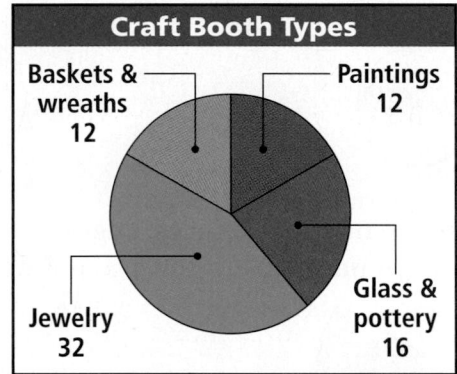

Craft Booth Types

Baskets & wreaths 12

Paintings 12

Jewelry 32

Glass & pottery 16

  Ⓕ 80%   Ⓗ 44%

  Ⓖ 55%   Ⓙ 33%

7. An antique round tabletop has a diameter of 3 feet. What is the area of the tabletop? Use 3.14 for *pi*. Round to the nearest tenth.

  Ⓐ 7.1 ft²   Ⓒ 18.8 ft²

  Ⓑ 9.4 ft²   Ⓓ 28.3 ft²

8. The scale on a map is 1 in:50 mi. If Cincinnati, Ohio, is about 300 miles from Chicago, Illinois, about how far apart are the two cities on the map?

  Ⓕ 5 in.   Ⓗ 7 in.

  Ⓖ 6 in.   Ⓙ 8 in.

9. In March of 2005, Steve Fossett became the first man to complete the first solo, nonstop flight around the world. He did not even stop to refuel. The 36,818-kilometer voyage took 67 hours and 2 minutes. How many kilometers did he travel per minute? Round to the nearest kilometer.

(A) 5 km/min   (C) 23 km/min

(B) 9 km/min   (D) 26 km/min

Hot Tip Pay attention to the units used in problems. If the units used in a problem do not match the units used in the answer choices, you will need to convert from one unit to another.

Use the table for item 10.

Superbowl Attendance					
Year	1967	1968	1969	1970	1971
Number of People	61,946	75,546	75,389	80,562	79,204

10. What was the mean attendance? Round to the nearest thousandth.

(F) 74,000   (H) 74,600

(G) 74,529   (J) 75,000

11. The area of a triangle is 57.12 cm². If the height of the triangle is 8.4 cm, how many centimeters long is the base?

(A) 6.8   (C) 16.8

(B) 13.6   (D) 239.9

12. Solve the equation $\frac{2}{7}k = \frac{1}{6}$ for k.

(F) $\frac{1}{21}$ (H) $\frac{7}{12}$

(G) $\frac{2}{42}$ (J) $\frac{12}{7}$

13. Marcia is weighing her produce. A watermelon weighs 2.89 kg. How many grams are in 2.89 kg?

(A) 2,890   (C) 28.9

(B) 289   (D) 2.89

Short Response

14. Triangle *WXY* is isosceles. The two short sides have a length of 18 mm. The other side has as length of 30 mm.
   a. Draw a triangle that is similar to triangle *WXY*.
   b. Write a proportion to prove that the two triangles are similar.

15. A company's rectangular parking lot is 35 m long and 60 m wide. The company is planning on expanding the area. If the dimensions are doubled, how many times greater will the area of the new parking lot be compared to the area of the original parking lot? Explain how you found your answer.

16. Carole has a piece of fabric that is 2 yards long. She wants to cut the fabric into 2.4-inch strips. Let *s* equal one of the fabric strips. Write and solve an equation to find how many 2.4-inch strips Carole can cut from the piece of fabric.

Extended Response

17. There are 3 pools in Marcie's neighborhood where she can go swimming. The dimensions are listed below. Pool 2 is a circular pool. The width is its radius.

Pool	Length (ft)	Depth (ft)	Width (ft)
1	25	5	8
2	–	6	9
3	15	4	9

   a. Find the volume of each pool. Which pool has the greatest volume? Show your work. Use 3.14 for *pi*.
   b. What is the circumference of pool 2?
   c. Samantha's pool has the same volume as pool 1. However, her pool is in the shape of a cube. What are the dimensions of Samantha's pool?

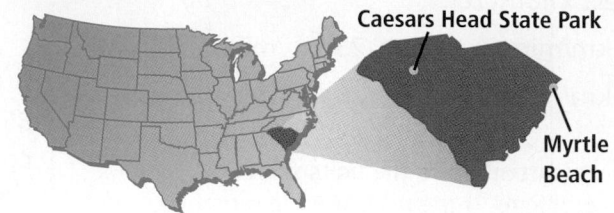

Caesars Head State Park

Myrtle Beach

 ## Raven Cliff Falls

South Carolina has dozens of waterfalls but Raven Cliff Falls may be the most impressive. The 420-foot cascade is one of the highest waterfalls in the eastern United States. Hikers can view Raven Cliff Falls from an observation deck or from a swinging footbridge across the top of the falls.

Choose one or more strategies to solve each problem.

1. An observer spots a bird flying 80 yards above the base of Raven Cliff Falls. How far is the bird from the top of the falls?

For 2 and 3, use the map.

2. Sonia is hiking from the parking lot to the observation deck. After hiking 4,000 feet, she comes across a fallen tree. There is another fallen tree 3,000 feet from the end of the trail. What is the distance between the two trees?

3. Daryl wants to hike from the parking lot to the footbridge and arrive at the footbridge at noon. He plans to take five 15-minute breaks along the way. At what time should he begin his hike?

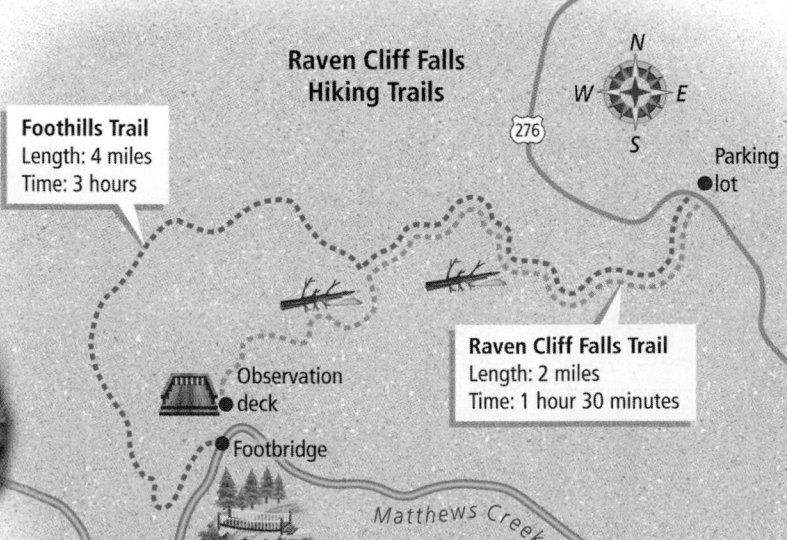

Raven Cliff Falls Hiking Trails

N
W · E
S

276

Parking lot

Foothills Trail
Length: 4 miles
Time: 3 hours

Raven Cliff Falls Trail
Length: 2 miles
Time: 1 hour 30 minutes

Observation deck

Footbridge

Matthews Creek

Problem Solving Strategies

Draw a Diagram
Make a Model
Guess and Test
Work Backward
Find a Pattern
Make a Table
Solve a Simpler Problem
Use Logical Reasoning
Act It Out
Make an Organized List

★ Miniature Golf Tournaments

Many people consider Myrtle Beach, South Carolina, to be the miniature golf capital of the United States. The seaside resort has more than 40 miniature golf courses with a wide variety of themes. Myrtle Beach also hosts two miniature golf tournaments each year—the U.S. Open and the Masters National Championship.

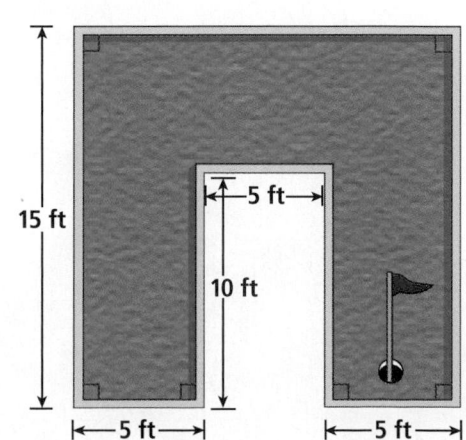

Choose one or more strategies to solve each problem.

1. Hawaiian Rumble is one of the best-known miniature golf courses in Myrtle Beach. It features an artificial volcano that erupts every 20 minutes. Suppose the first eruption occurs at 9:15 A.M. How many eruptions happen between 9 A.M. and 9 P.M.?

2. A miniature golf course includes a rectangular putting green. The area of the green is 240 square feet. The length of the green is 22 feet greater than the width. What is the length of the green?

3. A circular putting green has a diameter of 7 meters. There are lights around the circumference of the green. The lights are evenly spaced, and there are about 2 meters between each light. How many lights are there?

For 4, use the diagram.

4. The surface of the putting green in the diagram needs to be replaced. Artificial grass is available in squares with sides 1 foot long. Each square costs $1.80. How much will it cost to replace the surface of the green?

Problem Solving on Location **597**

CHAPTER 11

Integers, Graphs, and Functions

NEW YORK TEST PREP

go.hrw.com
Chapter Project Online
KEYWORD: MR7 Ch11

Continent	Highest Point (m)	Lowest Point (m)
Africa	Mt. Kilimanjaro: 5,895	Lake Assal: −156
Antarctica	Vinson Massif: 4,897	Bentley Subglacial Trench: −2,538
Asia	Mt. Everest: 8,850	Dead Sea: −411
Australia	Mt. Kosciusko: 2,228	Lake Eyre: −12
Europe	Mt. Elbrus: 5,642	Caspian Sea: −28
North America	Mt. McKinley: 6,194	Death Valley: −86
South America	Mt. Aconcagua: 6,960	Valdes Peninsula: −40

Career ***Geographer***

Geographers are interested in characteristics of our natural world, such as landforms, natural resources, and climate. Some geographers spend time in the field collecting information. Others create maps, charts, and graphs. Geographers use integers to express information such as high and low temperatures and elevations above and below sea level. The table lists the highest and lowest points on each continent.

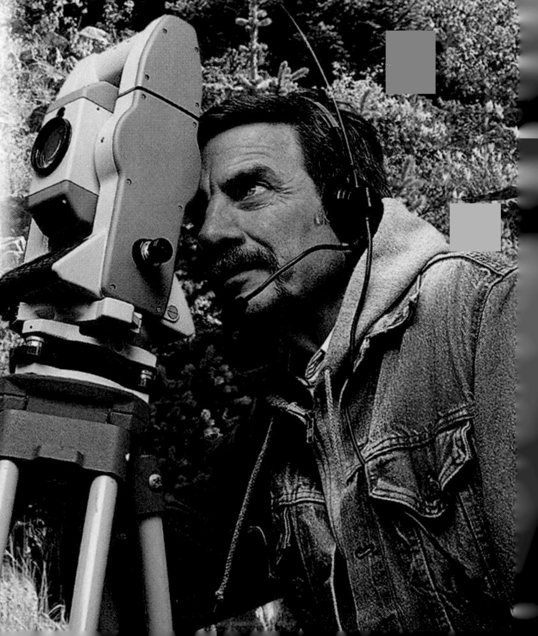

ARE YOU READY?

✓ Vocabulary

Choose the best term from the list to complete each sentence.

1. When you ___?___ a numerical expression, you find its value.

2. ___?___ are the set of numbers 0, 1, 2, 3, 4, ...

3. A(n) ___?___ is an exact location in space.

4. A(n) ___?___ is a mathematical statement that two quantities are equal.

equation

evaluate

exponents

less than

point

whole numbers

Complete these exercises to review skills you will need for this chapter.

✓ Compare Whole Numbers

Write <, >, or = to compare the numbers.

5. 9 ■ 2 **6.** 4 ■ 5 **7.** 8 ■ 1 **8.** 3 ■ 3

9. 412 ■ 214 **10.** 1,076 ■ 1,074 **11.** 502 ■ 520 **12.** 9,123 ■ 9,001

✓ Whole-Number Operations

Add, subtract, multiply, or divide.

13. $7 + 6$ **14.** $15 - 8$ **15.** $6 \cdot 7$ **16.** $25 \div 5$

17. $129 + 30$ **18.** $32 - 25$ **19.** $119 \cdot 5$ **20.** $156 \div 6$

✓ Solve One-Step Equations

Solve each equation.

21. $4t = 32$ **22.** $b - 4 = 12$ **23.** $24 = 6r$

24. $3x = 72$ **25.** $8 = 4a$ **26.** $m + 3 = 63$

✓ Graph Ordered Pairs

Graph each ordered pair.

27. $(1, 3)$ **28.** $(0, 5)$ **29.** $(3, 2)$ **30.** $(4, 0)$

31. $(6, 4)$ **32.** $(2, 5)$ **33.** $(0, 1)$ **34.** $(1, 0)$

Where You've Been

Previously, you

- graphed and located ordered pairs of whole numbers on a coordinate grid.

- graphed a given set of data.

- used equations to represent real-life situations.

In This Chapter

You will study

- using integers to represent real-life situations.

- using tables and symbols to represent sequences.

- using data tables to generate formulas representing relationships like perimeter.

- graphing and locating ordered pairs on four quadrants of a coordinate plane.

Where You're Going

You can use the skills learned in this chapter

- to interpret graphs of functions that represent real-world situations.

- to solve multi-step equations with integers and positive and negative fractions and decimals.

Key Vocabulary/Vocabulario

coordinates	coordenadas
function	función
input	valor de entrada
integer	entero
linear equation	ecuación lineal
opposites	opuestos
origin	origen
output	valor de salida
quadrants	cuadrante

Vocabulary Connections

To become familiar with some of the vocabulary terms in the chapter, consider the following. You may refer to the chapter, the glossary, or a dictionary if you like.

1. The word *input* can mean "an amount put in." What type of **input** do you think you will use to find the output of a function?

2. The word *linear* means "relating to a straight line." What do you think the graph of a **linear equation** will look like?

3. The word *opposite* can mean "across from." Where do you think **opposites** will lie on a number line?

4. The word *origin* can mean "the point at which something begins." At what coordinates do you think the **origin** is?

5. The word *quadrant* comes from the Latin *quattuor*, meaning "four." How many **quadrants** do you think a coordinate plane has?

Reading and Writing Math

Writing Strategy:
Write a Convincing Argument

Being able to write a convincing argument about a math concept proves that you have a solid understanding of the concept.

A good argument should include

- an answer.
- support to prove the statement (including examples if necessary).
- a summary statement.

From Lesson 10-4

6. **Critical Thinking** If George enlarges a 3 in. × 4 in. photo so that it is 12 in. × 16 in., how will its area change?

Step 1 Answer statement:
The area of the new photo will be 16 times as great as that of the original photo.

Step 2 Support:
The dimensions of the 3 in. × 4 in. photo are multiplied by 4 to be enlarged to 12 in. × 16 in.

The area of the new photo is 16 times as great as that of the original photo.

area of original = 3 × 4 = 12 in^2

area of enlarged = 12 × 16 = 192 in^2

area of original: area of enlarged

12:192

1:16

16 in.

4 in.

| Original photo | 3 in.

12 in.

Enlarged photo

Step 3 Summary Statement:
Therefore, to find the area of the enlarged photo, multiply the original area by 4^2, or 16.

Try This

Write a convincing argument to show whether or not a rectangle with whole-number dimensions can have an area of 15 m^2 and a perimeter of 15 m.

Reading and Writing Math

Integers in Real-World Situations

Learn to identify and graph integers, and find opposites.

Vocabulary

positive number

negative number

opposites

integer

The highest temperature recorded in the United States is 134°F, in Death Valley, California. The lowest recorded temperature is 80° below 0°F, in Prospect Creek, Alaska.

Positive numbers are greater than 0. They may be written with a positive sign (+), but they are usually written without it. So, the highest temperature can be written as +134°F or 134°F.

Negative numbers are less than 0. They are always written with a negative sign (−). So, the lowest temperature is written as −80°F.

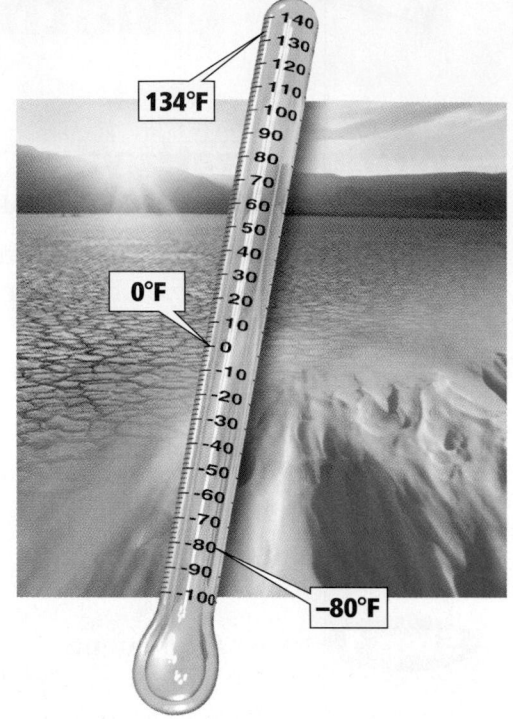

134°F

0°F

−80°F

EXAMPLE 1 **Identifying Positive and Negative Numbers in the Real World**

Name a positive or negative number to represent each situation.

NY Performance Indicators

6.N.14 Locate rational numbers on a number line (including positive and negative). Also, 6.R.5.

A a gain of 20 yards in football

Positive numbers can represent *gains* or *increases*.

+20

B spending $75

Negative numbers can represent *losses* or *decreases*.

−75

C 10 feet below sea level

Negative numbers can represent values *below* or *less than* a certain value.

−10

You can graph positive and negative numbers on a number line.

Remember!

The set of whole numbers includes zero and the counting numbers. {0, 1, 2, 3, 4, ...}

On a number line, **opposites** are the same distance from 0 but on different sides of 0. Zero is its own opposite.

Integers are the set of all whole numbers and their opposites.

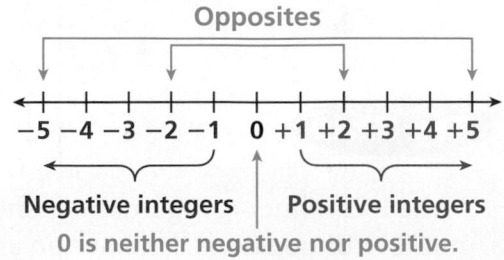

Opposites

−5 −4 −3 −2 −1 0 +1 +2 +3 +4 +5

Negative integers | Positive integers

0 is neither negative nor positive.

EXAMPLE 2 Graphing Integers

Graph each integer and its opposite on a number line.

A −4

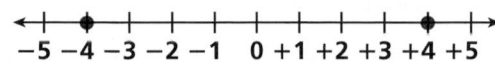

+4 is the same distance from 0 as −4.

B 3

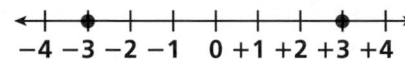

−3 is the same distance from 0 as 3.

C 0

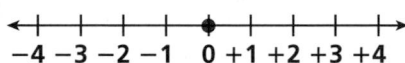

Zero is its own opposite.

EXAMPLE 3 Writing Integer Expressions to Represent Situations

Steffe works on the ground floor of a museum restoring ancient vases. Using the elevator, she goes down 2 floors to get a broken vase, then goes up 6 floors to talk to an ancient civilization expert, and then goes down 3 floors to meet a museum guide. Use integers to model this situation.

You can use a number line to model Steffe's movements on the elevator.

0	*Steffe starts on the ground floor, 0.*
−2	*Steffe goes down two floors.*
+6	*Steffe goes up six floors.*
−3	*Steffe goes back down three floors.*

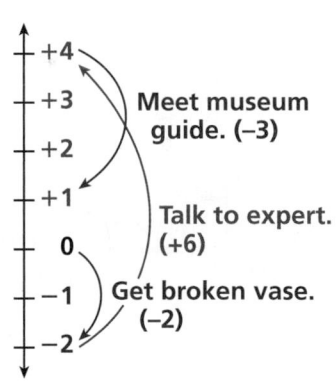

Meet museum guide. (−3)

Talk to expert. (+6)

Get broken vase. (−2)

Think and Discuss

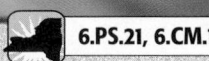
6.PS.21, 6.CM.10

1. Tell whether −3.2 is an integer. Why or why not?

2. Give the opposite of 14. What is the opposite of −11?

3. Explain how you could use the integers in Example 3 to write an expression to represent the situation. Write the expression.

11-1 **Exercises**

go.hrw.com
Homework Help Online
KEYWORD: MR7 11-1
Parent Resources Online
KEYWORD: MR7 Parent

GUIDED PRACTICE

See Example ① **Name a positive or negative number to represent each situation.**

1. an increase of 5 points   **2.** a loss of 15 yards

See Example ② **Graph each integer and its opposite on a number line.**

3. −2   **4.** 1   **5.** −6   **6.** 9

See Example ③ **7.** Arnold has $8 in his piggy bank. He takes out $4 to buy a magazine. Later his mother gives him $5, which he puts in his piggy bank. Use integers to model this situation.

INDEPENDENT PRACTICE

See Example ① **Name a positive or negative number to represent each situation.**

8. earning $50   **9.** 20° below zero

10. 7 feet above sea level   **11.** a decrease of 39 points

See Example ② **Graph each integer and its opposite on a number line.**

12. −5   **13.** 6   **14.** 2   **15.** −3   **16.** 9

See Example ③ **17.** Carla volunteers at the Help for Seniors program. She starts at the volunteers' center on Elm Street and rides her bike to senior citizens' homes. She rides due south 3 blocks to the first senior's home, then she rides 4 blocks due north to the next home, then 2 more blocks due north to the third home, and finally 3 blocks due south back to the center. Use integers to model this situation.

PRACTICE AND PROBLEM SOLVING

Extra Practice
See page 735.

Write a situation that each integer could represent.

18. +49   **19.** −83   **20.** −7   **21.** +15   **22.** −2

Write the opposite of each integer.

23. −92   **24.** +75   **25.** −25   **26.** +1,001   **27.** 0

28. **Astronomy** Use the table to graph the average surface temperatures of the given planets on a number line.

Planet	Earth	Mars	Jupiter
Average Surface Temperature (°C)	15	−65	−110

29. A certain stock dropped 3 points in the stock market. Another stock gained 5 points. Write an integer to represent each stock's gain or loss.

Decimals and fractions can also be positive or negative. Write the opposite of each decimal or fraction.

30. $+\frac{1}{2}$ **31.** −2.7   **32.** $-\frac{3}{8}$ **33.** +6.2   **34.** +0.1

35. Sports When the Mountain Lions football team returned the kickoff, they gained 45 yards. Write an integer to represent this situation.

36. Earth Science The Mariana Trench is the deepest part of the Pacific Ocean, reaching a depth of 10,924 meters. Write the depth in meters of the Mariana Trench as an integer.

37. Earth Science From June 21 to December 21, most of the United States loses 1 to 2 minutes of daylight each day. But on December 21, most of the country begins to gain 1 to 2 minutes of daylight each day. What integer could you write for a gain of 2 minutes? a loss of 2 minutes?

38. Match each temperature with the correct point on the thermometer.

    a. $-10°$F   **b.** $5°$F   **c.** $10°$F

    d. $-2°$F   **e.** $-9°$F   **f.** $7°$F

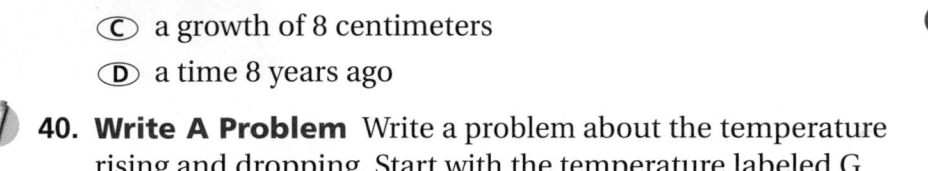

39. Which situation is least likely to be represented by -8?

    Ⓐ a temperature drop of 8°F

    Ⓑ a depth of 8 meters

    Ⓒ a growth of 8 centimeters

    Ⓓ a time 8 years ago

 40. Write A Problem Write a problem about the temperature rising and dropping. Start with the temperature labeled G on the thermometer. Then write an expression to represent the situation.

41. Write About It Is -0.5 an integer? Explain.

42. Challenge What are the opposites of the integers 3 units away from -8? Explain.

TEST PREP and Spiral Review

43. Multiple Choice Which situation could the integer -50 represent?

    Ⓐ An increase of $50 in a bank account

    Ⓑ The temperature on a warm spring day

    Ⓒ The distance driven on the way to the beach

    Ⓓ A decrease of 50 employees

44. Multiple Choice Which integer can represent *200 years ago*?

    Ⓕ -200 Ⓖ $200x$ Ⓗ 200 Ⓙ $x - 200$

Estimate by rounding to the indicated place value. (Lesson 3-2)

45. $1.892 - 0.243$; tenths   **46.** $13.4132 + 0.513$; tenths   **47.** $11.4307 - 5.2164$; thousandths

48. Hugo is filling a tub with water. The height of the water is increasing $\frac{1}{5}$ foot each minute. Use pictures to model how much the height of the water will change in 4 minutes, and then write your answer in simplest form. (Lesson 4-8)

Comparing and Ordering Integers

Learn to compare and order integers.

NY Performance Indicators

6.N.15 Order rational numbers (including positive and negative). Also, 6.N.14, 6.R.5.

The table shows three golfers' scores from a golf tournament.

Player	Score
David Berganio	+6
Sergio Garcia	−16
Tiger Woods	−4

In golf, the player with the lowest score wins the game. You can compare integers to find the winner of the tournament.

Sergio Garcia

EXAMPLE 1 Comparing Integers

Use the number line to compare each pair of integers. Write < or >.

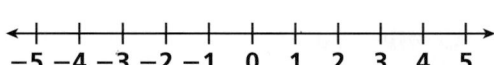

$$-5\ -4\ -3\ -2\ -1\ \ 0\ \ 1\ \ 2\ \ 3\ \ 4\ \ 5$$

Remember!

Numbers on a number line increase in value as you move from left to right.

A −4 ☐ 2

−4 < 2   *−4 is to the left of 2 on the number line.*

B −3 ☐ −5

−3 > −5   *−3 is to the right of −5 on the number line.*

C 0 ☐ −4

0 > −4   *0 is to the right of −4 on the number line.*

EXAMPLE 2 Ordering Integers

Order the integers in each set from least to greatest.

A 4, −2, 1

Graph the integers on the same number line.

$$-5\ -4\ -3\ -2\ -1\ \ 0\ \ 1\ \ 2\ \ 3\ \ 4\ \ 5$$

Then read the numbers from left to right: −2, 1, 4.

Order the integers in each set from least to greatest.

B $-2, 0, 2, -5$

Graph the integers on the same number line.

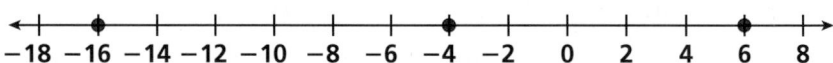

$$-5 \;-4 \;-3 \;-2 \;-1 \quad 0 \quad 1 \quad 2 \quad 3 \quad 4 \quad 5$$

Then read the numbers from left to right: $-5, -2, 0, 2.$

EXAMPLE 3 *Problem Solving Application*

At a golf tournament, David Berganio scored $+6$, Sergio Garcia scored -16, and Tiger Woods scored -4. One of these three players was the winner of the tournament. Who won the tournament?

1 Understand the Problem

The **answer** will be the player with the *lowest* score.
List the **important information:**

- David Berganio scored $+6$.
- Sergio Garcia scored -16.
- Tiger Woods scored -4.

2 Make a Plan

You can draw a diagram to order the scores from least to greatest.

3 Solve

Draw a number line and graph each player's score on it.

$$-18 \;-16 \;-14 \;-12 \;-10 \;-8 \;-6 \;-4 \;-2 \quad 0 \quad 2 \quad 4 \quad 6 \quad 8$$

Sergio Garcia's score, -16, is farthest to the left, so it is the lowest score. Sergio Garcia won this tournament.

4 Look Back

Negative integers are always less than positive integers, so David Berganio cannot be the winner. Since Sergio Garcia's score of -16 is less than Tiger Woods's score of -4, Sergio Garcia won.

Think and Discuss 6.PS.21, 6.CM.1

1. Tell which is greater, a negative or a positive integer. Explain.

2. Tell which is greater, 0 or a negative integer. Explain.

3. Explain how to tell which of two negative integers is greater.

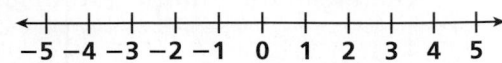
go.hrw.com
Homework Help Online
KEYWORD: MR7 11-2
Parent Resources Online
KEYWORD: MR7 Parent

GUIDED PRACTICE

See Example **1** Use the number line to compare each pair of integers. Write < or >.

−5 −4 −3 −2 −1 0 1 2 3 4 5

1. −4 ▮ −5   **2.** −2 ▮ 0   **3.** −1 ▮ 3

See Example **2** Order the integers in each set from least to greatest.

4. 9, 0, −2   **5.** 7, −4, 3, −5   **6.** 8, −6, −1, 10

See Example **3** **7.** Use the table.

   a. At what time was the temperature the lowest?

   b. What was the highest temperature?

Time	Temperature (°F)
10:00 P.M.	1
Midnight	−4
3:30 A.M.	−6
6:00 A.M.	1

INDEPENDENT PRACTICE

See Example **1** Use the number line to compare each pair of integers. Write < or >.

−5 −4 −3 −2 −1 0 1 2 3 4 5

8. 0 ▮ 2   **9.** 4 ▮ −4   **10.** −3 ▮ −1   **11.** −5 ▮ 2

See Example **2** Order the integers in each set from least to greatest.

12. 11, −6, −3   **13.** 15, −8, 7   **14.** 5, −12, 0, 1

15. −9, 13, −1, −16   **16.** 24, −6, 7, −10, 4   **17.** 22, 0, −19, 8, −3

See Example **3** **18. Earth Science** Use the table, which shows the depths of the world's three largest oceans.

   a. Which ocean is the deepest?

   b. Which oceans are less than 35,000 feet deep?

Ocean	Depth (ft)
Pacific	−36,200
Atlantic	−30,246
Indian	−24,442

PRACTICE AND PROBLEM SOLVING

Extra Practice
See page 735.

Compare. Write < or >.

19. −30 ▮ 25   **20.** 0 ▮ −49   **21.** −16 ▮ −51   **22.** −17 ▮ 17

23. −64 ▮ −15   **24.** 77 ▮ 300   **25.** −28 ▮ 1   **26.** 25 ▮ −30

Order the integers in each set from least to greatest.

27. −39, 14, 21   **28.** −18, −9, −31   **29.** 0, −26, 43, −12

30. 15, −25, −4, 31   **31.** −67, 82, −73, −10, 20   **32.** 42, −27, 69, −50, 38

33. Which set of integers is written in order from greatest to least?

(A) 0, −4, −3, −1   (C) 9, −9, −10, −15

(B) 2, −4, 8, −16   (D) −8, −7, −6, −5

34. Earth Science The normal high temperature in January for Barrow, Alaska, is −7°F. The normal high temperature in January for Los Angeles is 68°F. Compare the two temperatures using < or >.

35. Geography The table shows elevations for several natural features. Write the features in order from the least elevation to the greatest elevation.

Elevations of Natural Features	
Mt. Everest	29,022 ft
Mt. Rainier	14,410 ft
Kilimanjaro	19,000 ft
San Augustin Cave	−2,189 ft
Dead Sea	−1,296 ft

 36. What's the Error? Your classmate says that 0 < −91. Explain why this is incorrect.

 37. Write About It Explain how you would order from least to greatest three numbers that include a positive number, a negative number, and zero.

 38. Challenge There is a missing integer from the list below. The missing integer is both the median and the mode. What is the integer? (*Hint:* There could be more than one correct answer.) 2, −10, 7, −7, 5, −5

39. Multiple Choice Which set of integers is written in order from greatest to least?

(A) −3, −9, −6   (B) −3, 2, 5   (C) 2, −1, −3   (D) 4, 10, 12

40. Short Response The table shows the elevations relative to sea level of several cities. Order the cities from the least elevation to the greatest elevation.

City	Boston	Cincinnati	Death Valley	Salt Lake City	San Antonio
Elevation (ft)	16	483	−282	4,226	807

If the angles can form a triangle, classify it as acute, obtuse, or right. (Lesson 8-5)

41. 45°, 76°, 59°   **42.** 12°, 90°, 78°   **43.** 88°, 22°, 90°   **44.** 10°, 5°, 165°

Graph each integer and its opposite on a number line. (Lesson 11-1)

45. −9   **46.** 7   **47.** −2   **48.** 8   **49.** −5

11-3 The Coordinate Plane

Learn to locate and graph points on the coordinate plane.

Vocabulary

coordinate plane

axes

x-axis

y-axis

quadrants

origin

coordinates

x-coordinate

y-coordinate

A **coordinate plane** is formed by two number lines in a plane that intersect at right angles. The point of intersection is the zero on each number line.

- The two number lines are called the **axes** .

- The horizontal axis is called the **x-axis** .

- The vertical axis is called the **y-axis** .

- The two axes divide the coordinate plane into four **quadrants** .

- The point where the axes intersect is called the **origin** .

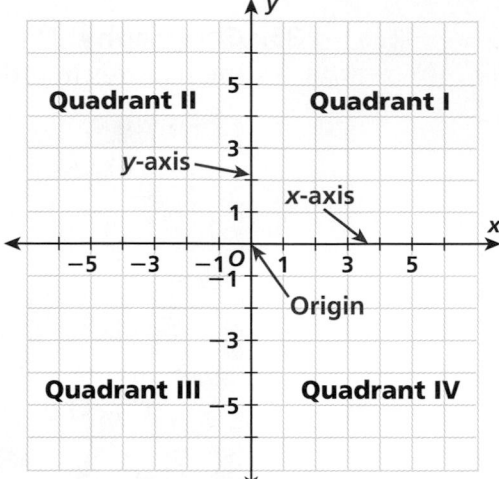

EXAMPLE **1** **Identifying Quadrants**

Name the quadrant where each point is located.

A *M*

Quadrant I

B *J*

Quadrant IV

C *R*

x-axis

no quadrant

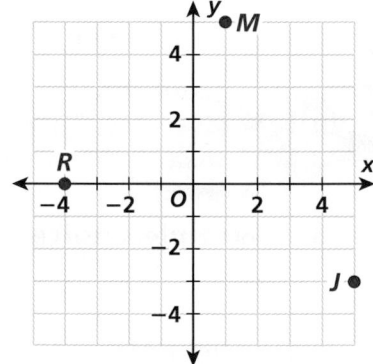

Helpful Hint

Points on the axes are not in any quadrant.

NY Performance Indicators

6.G.10 Identify and plot points in all four quadrants. Also, 5.G.12.

An ordered pair gives the location of a point on a coordinate plane. The first number tells how far to move right (positive) or left (negative) from the origin. The second number tells how far to move up (positive) or down (negative).

The numbers in an ordered pair are called **coordinates** . The first number is called the **x-coordinate** . The second number is called the **y-coordinate** .

The ordered pair for the origin is (0, 0).

EXAMPLE 2 Locating Points on a Coordinate Plane

Give the coordinates of each point.

A *K*

From the origin, K is 1 unit right and 4 units up.

(1, 4)

B *T*

From the origin, T is 2 units left on the x-axis.

(−2, 0)

C *W*

From the origin, W is 3 units left and 4 units down.

(−3, −4)

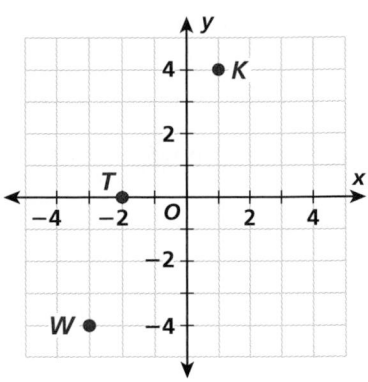

EXAMPLE 3 Graphing Points on a Coordinate Plane

Graph each point on a coordinate plane.

A *P*(−3, −2)

From the origin, move 3 units left and 2 units down.

B *R*(0, 4)

From the origin, move 4 units up.

C *M*(3, −4)

From the origin, move 3 units right and 4 units down.

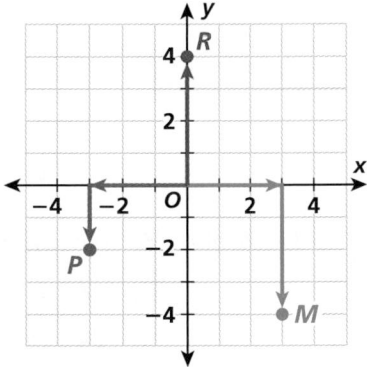

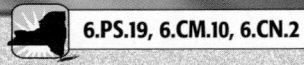
6.PS.19, 6.CM.10, 6.CN.2

Think and Discuss

1. **Tell** which number in an ordered pair indicates how far to move left or right from the origin and which number indicates how far to move up or down.

2. **Describe** how graphing the point (5, 4) is similar to graphing the point (5, −4). How is it different?

3. **Tell** why it is important to start at the origin when you are graphing points.

go.hrw.com
Homework Help Online
KEYWORD: MR7 11-3
Parent Resources Online
KEYWORD: MR7 Parent

GUIDED PRACTICE

Use the coordinate plane for Exercises 1–6.

See Example **1** Name the quadrant where each point is located.

1. T **2.** U **3.** B

See Example **2** Give the coordinates of each point.

4. A **5.** B **6.** U

See Example **3** Graph each point on a coordinate plane.

7. $E(4, 2)$ **8.** $F(-1, -4)$ **9.** $G(0, 2)$

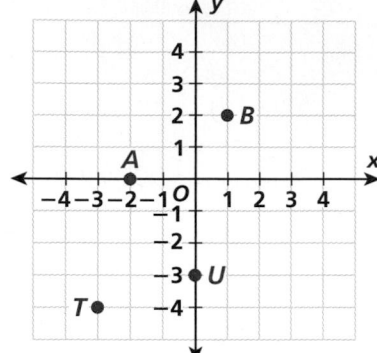

INDEPENDENT PRACTICE

Use the coordinate plane for Exercises 10–21.

See Example **1** Name the quadrant where each point is located.

10. Q **11.** X **12.** H

13. Y **14.** Z **15.** P

See Example **2** Give the coordinates of each point.

16. P **17.** R **18.** Y

19. T **20.** H **21.** Q

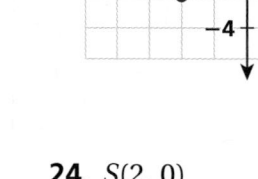

See Example **3** Graph each point on a coordinate plane.

22. $L(0, 3)$ **23.** $M(3, -3)$ **24.** $S(2, 0)$

25. $V(-4, 3)$ **26.** $N(-2, -1)$ **27.** $B(4, 3)$

PRACTICE AND PROBLEM SOLVING

Extra Practice
See page 735.

Name the quadrant where each ordered pair is located.

28. $(3, -1)$ **29.** $(2, 1)$ **30.** $(-2, 3)$ **31.** $(-4, -3)$

32. $\left(4\frac{1}{2}, -3\right)$ **33.** $\left(10, -7\frac{1}{2}\right)$ **34.** $\left(-6, 2\frac{1}{3}\right)$ **35.** $\left(-8\frac{1}{3}, -\frac{1}{2}\right)$

Graph each ordered pair.

36. $(0, -5)$ **37.** $(-4, -4)$ **38.** $(5, 0)$ **39.** $(3, 2)$

40. $(-2, 2)$ **41.** $(0, -3)$ **42.** $(1, -4)$ **43.** $(0, 0)$

44. $\left(-2\frac{1}{2}, 3\right)$ **45.** $\left(5, 3\frac{1}{2}\right)$ **46.** $\left(-4\frac{1}{3}, 0\right)$ **47.** $\left(0, -\frac{1}{2}\right)$

48. Graph points $A(-1, -1)$, $B(2, 1)$, $C(2, -2)$, and $D(-1, -2)$. Connect the points. What type of quadrilateral do the points form?

We use a coordinate system on Earth to find exact locations. The *equator* is like the *x*-axis, and the *prime meridian* is like the *y*-axis.

The lines that run east-west are *lines of latitude*. They are measured in degrees north and south of the equator.

The lines that run north-south are *lines of longitude*. They are measured in degrees east and west of the prime meridian.

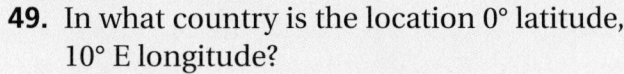
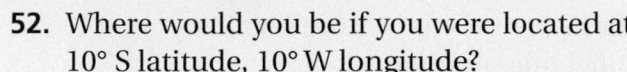
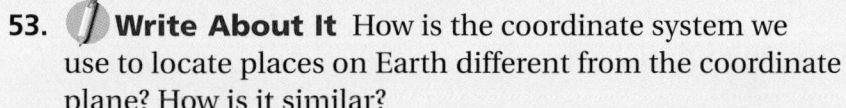

49. In what country is the location 0° latitude, 10° E longitude?

50. Give the coordinates of a location in Algeria.

51. Name two countries that lie along the 30° N line of latitude.

52. Where would you be if you were located at 10° S latitude, 10° W longitude?

53. ✎ **Write About It** How is the coordinate system we use to locate places on Earth different from the coordinate plane? How is it similar?

go.hrw.com
Web Extra!
KEYWORD: MR7 Africa

54. ⭐ **Challenge** Begin at 10° S latitude, 20° E longitude. Travel 40° north and 20° west. What country would you be in now?

TEST PREP and Spiral Review

55. Multiple Choice In which quadrant is the point (−1, 2) located?

   Ⓐ Quadrant I   Ⓑ Quadrant II   Ⓒ Quadrant III   Ⓓ Quadrant IV

56. Multiple Choice Which of the following coordinates is the farthest to the right of the origin on a coordinate plane?

   Ⓕ (−19, 7)   Ⓖ (0, 12)   Ⓗ (4, 15)   Ⓙ (7, 0)

Write each fraction or mixed number as a decimal. (Lesson 4-4)

57. $4\frac{2}{5}$ **58.** $\frac{9}{10}$ **59.** $5\frac{3}{4}$ **60.** $\frac{9}{20}$ **61.** $\frac{1}{5}$

Compare. Write < or >. (Lesson 11-2)

62. 0 ▮ −4   **63.** −345 ▮ 78   **64.** −12 ▮ −6   **65.** 14 ▮ 18

READY TO GO ON?

Quiz for Lessons 11-1 Through 11-3

✓ 11-1 Integers in Real-World Situations

Name a positive or negative number to represent each situation.

1. a gain of 10 yards

2. 45 feet below sea level

3. 5 degrees below zero

4. earning $50

Write the opposite of each integer.

5. 9

6. −17

7. 1

8. −20

9. The average depth of the Atlantic Ocean is 3,926 meters. Write the depth in meters of the Atlantic Ocean as an integer.

10. A company's food service is based on the ground floor of the building. Using the elevator, the chef delivers a fruit tray to the 8th floor. He then goes down 3 floors to deliver drinks. His last stop is up 5 more floors to deliver sandwiches. Use integers to model this situation.

✓ 11-2 Comparing and Ordering Integers

Compare. Write < or >.

11. 9 ▨ −22

12. −7 ▨ 4

13. −10 ▨ −19

Order the integers in each set from least to greatest.

14. 2, −7, 14

15. 25, −9, 4, −21

16. 10, 0, −23, −17, 8

17. During an archaeological dig, the farther down an object is found, the older it is. If pieces of jewelry are found at −7 ft, −17 ft, −4 ft, and −9 ft, which piece is oldest?

✓ 11-3 The Coordinate Plane

Use the coordinate plane for problems 18–25.

Name the quadrant where each point is located.

18. A

19. Y

20. J

21. C

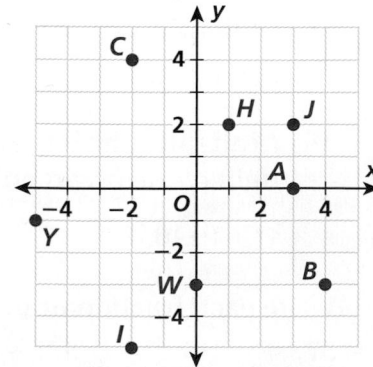

Give the coordinates of each point.

22. H

23. I

24. W

25. B

Graph each point on a coordinate plane.

26. $N(−5, −2)$

27. $S(0, 4)$

28. $R(−2, 6)$

29. $M(2, 2)$

30. $Q(4, −1)$

31. $P(−3, 0)$

32. $T\left(1\frac{1}{2}, 5\right)$

33. $H\left(−3, 1\frac{1}{2}\right)$

Focus on Problem Solving

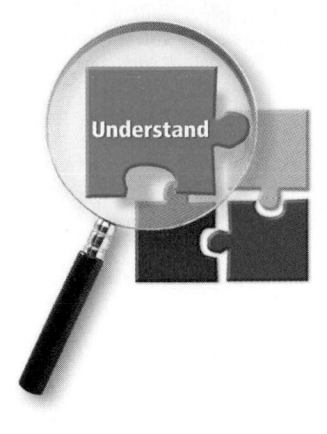

Understand the Problem

• Restate the question

After reading a real-world problem (perhaps several times), look at the question in the problem. Rewrite the question as a statement in your own words. For example, if the question is "How much money did the museum earn?" you could write, "Find the amount of money the museum earned."

Now you have a simple sentence telling you what you must do. This can help you understand and remember what the problem is about. This can also help you find the necessary information in the problem.

 Read the problems below. Rewrite each question as a statement in your own words.

1. Israel is one of the hottest countries in Asia. A temperature of 129°F was once recorded there. This is the opposite of the coldest recorded temperature in Antarctica. How cold has it been in Antarctica?

2. The average recorded temperature in Fairbanks, Alaska, in January is about −10°F. In February, the average temperature is about −4°F. Is the average temperature lower in January or in February?

3. The south pole on Mars is made of frozen carbon dioxide, which has a temperature of −193°F. The coldest day recorded on Earth was −129°F, in Antarctica. Which temperature is lower?

4. The pirate Blackbeard's ship, the *Queen Anne's Revenge,* sank at Beauford Inlet, North Carolina, in 1718. In 1996, divers discovered a shipwreck believed to be the *Queen Anne's Revenge.* The ship's cannons were found 21 feet below the water's surface, and the ship's bell was found 20 feet below the surface. Were the cannons or the bell closer to the surface?

In this photo of Mars, different colors represent different temperature ranges. When the photo was taken, it was summer in the northern hemisphere and winter in the southern hemisphere.

−65°C   −120°C

Hands-On LAB 11-4

Model Integer Addition

Use with Lesson 11-4

go.hrw.com
Lab Resources Online
KEYWORD: MR7 Lab11

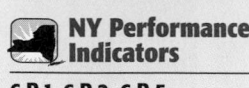
NY Performance Indicators
6.R.1, 6.R.2, 6.R.5

KEY

● = 1   ● = −1

REMEMBER
Subtracting zero from a number does not change the number's value.

Two-color counters can be used to represent integers. Yellow counters represent positive numbers and red counters represent negative numbers.

Activity

Model with two-color counters.

1 3 + 4   ● ● ●   3 + 4 = 7
                     ● ● ● ●

2 −5 + (−3)   ● ● ● ● ●   −5 + (−3) = −8
                  ● ● ●

One red and one yellow counter together equal zero, and are called a zero pair. Whenever you have a zero pair, you can remove it without changing the value of the model.

3 3 + (−4)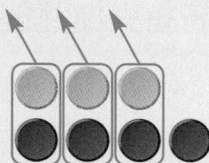

                  3 + (−4) = −1

Think and Discuss

1. When adding integers, would changing the order in which you add them affect the answer? Explain.

2. When can you remove counters from an addition model?

Try This

Model with two-color counters.

1. −8 + (−4)   2. −8 + 4   3. 8 + (−4)   4. 8 + 4

11-4 Adding Integers

Learn to add integers.

NY Performance Indicators

6.A.2 Use substitution to evaluate algebraic expressions (may include exponents of one, two and three). Also, 6.N.14, 6.R.5.

One of the world's most active volcanoes is Kilauea, in Hawaii. Kilauea's base is 9 km below sea level. The top of Kilauea is 10 km above the base of the mountain.

You can add the integers −9 and 10 to find the height of Kilauea above sea level.

Adding Integers on a Number Line
Move **right** on a number line to add a **positive** integer.
Move **left** on a number line to add a **negative** integer.

EXAMPLE **1** **Writing Integer Addition**

Write the addition modeled on each number line.

A

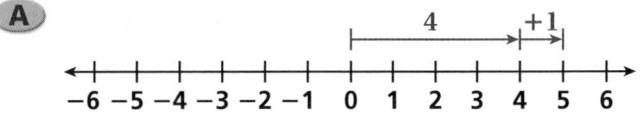

The addition modeled is 4 + 1 = 5.

Writing Math

Parentheses are used to separate addition, subtraction, multiplication, and division signs from negative integers.
−2 + (−5) = −7

B

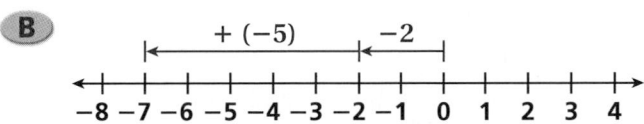

The addition modeled is −2 + (−5) = −7.

C

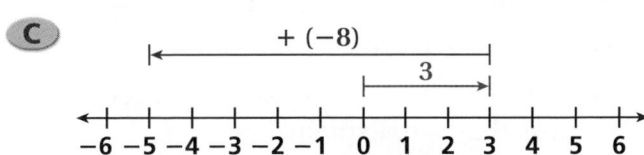

The addition modeled is 3 + (−8) = −5.

EXAMPLE 2 Adding Integers

Find each sum.

A $6 + (-5)$

Think:

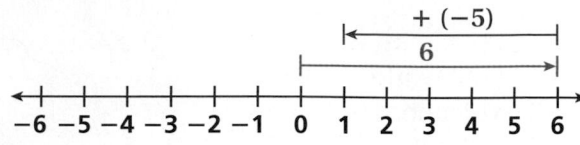
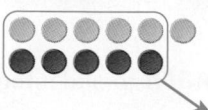

$6 + (-5) = 1$

B $-7 + 4$

Think:

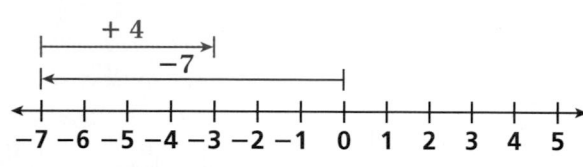
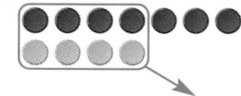

$-7 + 4 = -3$

EXAMPLE 3 Evaluating Integer Expressions

Evaluate $x + 3$ for $x = -9$.

$x + 3$	*Write the expression.*
$-9 + 3$	*Substitute -9 for x.*
-6	*Add.*

Think:

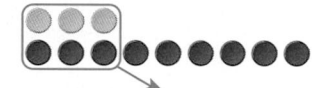

EXAMPLE 4 *Earth Science Application*

The base of Kilauea is 9 km below sea level. The top is 10 km above the base. How high above sea level is Kilauea?

The base is **9 km below sea level** and the top is **10 km above the base.**

$-9 + 10$

1

Kilauea is 1 km above sea level.

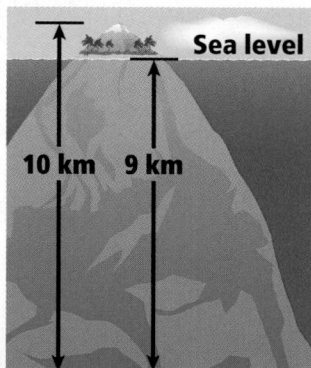

Think and Discuss

6.PS.21

1. Tell if the sum of a positive integer and -8 is greater than -8 or less than -8. Explain.

2. Give the sum of a number and its opposite.

11-4
Exercises

go.hrw.com
Homework Help Online
KEYWORD: MR7 11-4
Parent Resources Online
KEYWORD: MR7 Parent

GUIDED PRACTICE

See Example ① Write the addition modeled on the number line.

1.

See Example ② Find each sum.

2. $-5 + 9$

3. $-3 + (-2)$

4. $8 + (-7)$

5. $10 + (-3)$

6. $-4 + (-8)$

7. $-1 + 5$

See Example ③ Evaluate $n + (-2)$ for each value of n.

8. $n = -10$

9. $n = 2$

10. $n = -2$

11. $n = -15$

12. $n = 12$

13. $n = -20$

See Example ④ **14.** A submarine at the water's surface dropped down 100 ft. After thirty minutes at that depth, it dove an additional 500 ft. What was its depth after the second dive?

INDEPENDENT PRACTICE

See Example ① Write the addition modeled on each number line.

15.
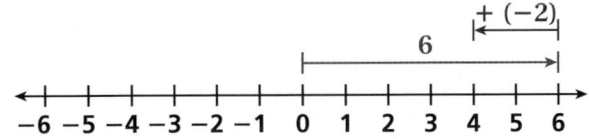

16.
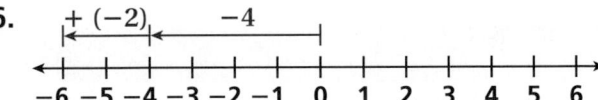

See Example ② Find each sum.

17. $4 + 7$

18. $2 + (-12)$

19. $9 + (-9)$

20. $10 + (-21)$

21. $-8 + 2$

22. $-2 + 8$

23. $-1 + (-6)$

24. $-25 + (14)$

See Example ③ Evaluate $-6 + a$ for each value of a.

25. $a = -10$

26. $a = 7$

27. $a = -2$

28. $a = -6$

29. $a = 4$

30. $a = -9$

31. $a = 8$

32. $a = -20$

See Example ④ **33.** Jon works on a cruise ship and sleeps in a cabin that is 6 feet below sea level. The main deck is 35 feet above Jon's cabin. How far above sea level is the main deck?

34. Recreation Preston dives to a depth of 15 feet. He stops briefly and then dives an additional 17 feet. What is Preston's depth after his second dive?

PRACTICE AND PROBLEM SOLVING

Extra Practice
See page 735.

Model each addition problem on a number line.

35. $3 + (-1)$ **36.** $-2 + (-4)$ **37.** $-6 + 5$ **38.** $1 + (-2)$

39. $-1 + 6$ **40.** $5 + (-3)$ **41.** $-3 + (-1)$ **42.** $0 + (-5)$

History

Find each sum.

43. $-18 + 25$ **44.** $8 + (-2)$ **45.** $-5 + (-6)$ **46.** $-12 + (-7)$

47. $-6 + (-3)$ **48.** $4 + (-1)$ **49.** $20 + (-3)$ **50.** $30 + (-25)$

Evaluate each expression for the given value of the variable.

51. $x + (-3);\ x = 7$ **52.** $-9 + n;\ n = 7$ **53.** $a + 5;\ a = -6$

54. $m + (-2);\ m = -4$ **55.** $-10 + x;\ x = -7$ **56.** $n + 19;\ n = -5$

57. Earth Science The temperature at midnight was –2°F. During the next 4 hours, a decrease of 4°F was recorded. What was the temperature at 4 A.M.?

58. Sports In the 2001 U.S. Women's Open, Cristie Kerr had the following scores for the four rounds of golf: -1, $+3$, $+1$, and 0. What was her total score?

Augustus, originally named Octavian, ruled the Roman Empire for more than 40 years.

59. Choose a Strategy The first Roman emperor, Augustus, was born in 63 B.C.E. and died in 14 C.E. How many years did he live? (*Hint*: Years B.C.E. are like negative numbers. Years C.E. are like positive numbers. There was no year 0.)

60. Critical Thinking Will the expression $-7 + 10$ have the same sum as $10 + (-7)$? Explain your answer.

61. Write About It When adding two integers, what will the sign of the answer be when one integer is positive and the other is negative? Explain.

62. Challenge Evaluate $-3 + (-2) + (-1) + 0 + 1 + 2 + 3 + 4$. Then use this pattern to find the sum of the integers from -10 to 11 and from -100 to 101.

TEST PREP and Spiral Review

63. Multiple Choice Julie earned $1,350 at her part-time job. Her paycheck showed deductions of $148.50. What was the total amount of her paycheck?

   Ⓐ $1,165.50   Ⓑ $1,201.50   Ⓒ $1,498.50   Ⓓ $1,534.50

64. Multiple Choice Which sum is NOT negative?

   Ⓕ $-38 + (-24)$ Ⓖ $-61 + 43$ Ⓗ $-54 + 68$ Ⓙ $-29 + 11$

65. Short Response Evaluate $b + 7$ for $b = -2$, -4, and -8.

Find each value. (Lesson 1-3)

66. 5^3 **67.** 4^1 **68.** 9^2 **69.** 12^3 **70.** 7^4

Graph each point on a coordinate plane. (Lesson 11-3)

71. $J(5, 7)$ **72.** $M(-2, 4)$ **73.** $L(4, -3)$ **74.** $A(-1, -6)$ **75.** $W(0, 5)$

Model Integer Subtraction

11-5

Use with Lesson 11-5

go.hrw.com
Lab Resources Online
KEYWORD: MR7 Lab11

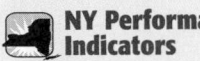
NY Performance Indicators
6.R.1, 6.R.2, 6.R.5

KEY

⬤ = 1   ⬤ = −1

REMEMBER
Adding zero to a number does not change the number's value.

⬤ + ⬤ = 0

Activity

Model with two-color counters.

1 3 − 2

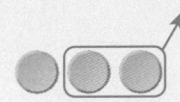

$3 - 2 = 1$

2 −3 − (−2)

$-3 - (-2) = -1$

3 3 − (−2)

You do not have any red counters, so you cannot subtract −2. Add zero pairs until you have enough red counters to subtract.

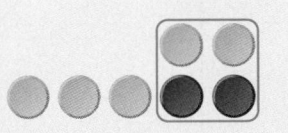 →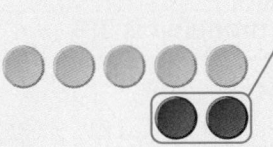

Add 2 zero pairs.   *Now you can subtract −2.*

$3 - (-2) = 5$

Think and Discuss

1. How do you show subtraction with counters?

2. Why can you add zero pairs to a subtraction model?

Try This

Model with two-color counters.

1. 5 − 4   **2.** 4 − (−5)   **3.** −4 − 5   **4.** −4 − (−5)

5. 8 − 5   **6.** 5 − (−8)   **7.** −5 − 8   **8.** −8 − (−8)

11-5 Hands-On Lab **621**

11-5 Subtracting Integers

Learn to subtract integers.

On a number line, integer subtraction is the opposite of integer addition. Integer subtraction "undoes" integer addition.

Subtracting Integers on a Number Line
Move **left** on a number line to subtract a **positive** integer.
Move **right** on a number line to subtract a **negative** integer.

EXAMPLE 1 Writing Integer Subtraction

Write the subtraction modeled on each number line.

A

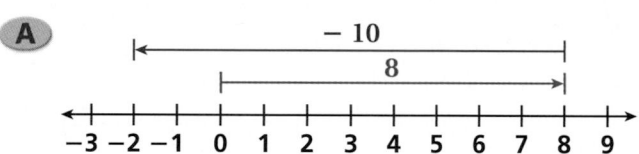

The subtraction modeled is $8 - 10 = -2$.

B

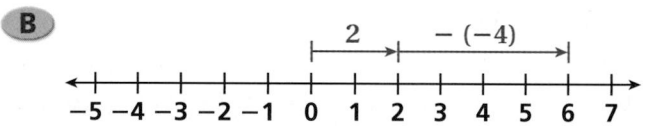

The subtraction modeled is $2 - (-4) = 6$.

NY Performance Indicators

6.A.2 Use substitution to evaluate algebraic expressions. Also, 6.N.14, 6.R.5.

EXAMPLE 2 Subtracting Integers

Find each difference.

A $7 - 4$

Think:

$7 - 4 = 3$

B $-8 - (-2)$

Think:

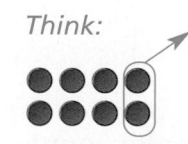

$-8 - (-2) = -6$

622 *Chapter 11 Integers, Graphs, and Functions*

EXAMPLE **3** **Evaluating Integer Expressions**

Evaluate $x - (-4)$ for $x = -5$.

$x - (-4)$	*Write the expression.*
$-5 - (-4)$	*Substitute -5 for x.* *Think:* 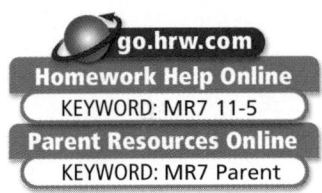
-1	*Subtract.*

Think and Discuss

6.CM.1, 6.CN.2

1. **Describe** the direction you would move to add a positive integer. to subtract a positive integer.

2. **Explain** how the answers to Example 1 help show that addition and subtraction are inverses.

11-5 Exercises

go.hrw.com
Homework Help Online
KEYWORD: MR7 11-5
Parent Resources Online
KEYWORD: MR7 Parent

GUIDED PRACTICE

See Example **1**

1. Write the subtraction modeled on the number line.

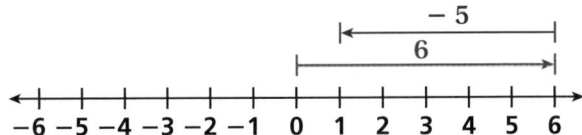

See Example **2**   Find each difference.

2. $6 - 3$ **3.** $3 - 6$ **4.** $10 - (-4)$ **5.** $-12 - (-4)$

See Example **3**   Evaluate $n - (-6)$ for each value of n.

6. $n = -4$ **7.** $n = 2$ **8.** $n = -15$ **9.** $n = 7$

INDEPENDENT PRACTICE

See Example **1**   **10.** Write the subtraction modeled on the number line.

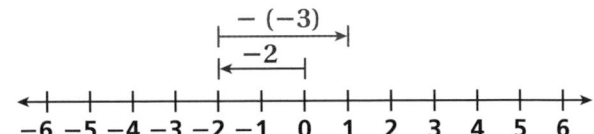

See Example **2**   Find each difference.

11. $3 - 7$ **12.** $-4 - 9$ **13.** $2 - (-9)$ **14.** $-22 - (-2)$

See Example **3**   Evaluate $m - (-3)$ for each value of m.

15. $m = -1$ **16.** $m = 7$ **17.** $m = -8$ **18.** $m = -5$

19. $m = 4$ **20.** $m = -9$ **21.** $m = -15$ **22.** $m = 13$

PRACTICE AND PROBLEM SOLVING

Extra Practice

See page 735.

Find each difference.

23. $-12 - (-6)$ **24.** $7 - (-3)$ **25.** $-4 - (-3)$ **26.** $8 - (-2)$

27. $19 - (-2)$ **28.** $-5 - 10$ **29.** $50 - 20$ **30.** $-2 - 7$

Evaluate each expression for the given value of the variable.

31. $n - (-10), n = 2$ **32.** $-6 - m, m = -9$ **33.** $x - 2, x = 6$

34. $4 - y, y = 9$ **35.** $j - 21, j = -17$ **36.** $101 - h, h = -75$

37. Earth Science The surface of an underground water supply was 10 m below sea level. After one year, the depth of the water supply has decreased by 9 m. How far below sea level is the water's surface now?

38. Construction A 200-foot column holds an oil rig platform above the ocean's surface. The column rests on the ocean floor 175 feet below sea level. How high is the platform above sea level?

39. Earth Science During summer 1997, NASA landed the *Pathfinder* on Mars. On July 9, *Pathfinder* reported a temperature of $-1°F$ on the planet's surface. On July 10, it reported a temperature of $8°F$. Find the difference between the temperature on July 10 and the temperature on July 9.

 40. What's the Error? Ty says that $0 - (-4) = -4$. Explain why this is incorrect.

 41. Write About It Will the difference between two negative numbers ever be positive? Use examples to support your answer.

 42. Challenge This pyramid was built by subtracting integers. Two integers are subtracted from left to right, and their difference is centered above them. Find the missing numbers.

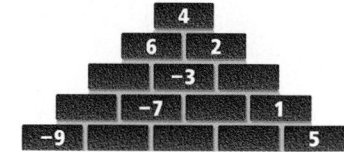

TEST PREP and Spiral Review

43. Multiple Choice Evaluate $h - (-8)$ for $h = 3$.

   Ⓐ -11 Ⓑ -5 Ⓒ 5 Ⓓ 11

44. Multiple Choice Trina's score on a game show was -250 points. Gwen's score was -320 points. By how many points was Trina ahead of Gwen?

   Ⓕ 570 points   Ⓖ 70 points   Ⓗ -70 points   Ⓙ -570 points

Write each decimal as a percent. (Lesson 7-8)

45. 0.02 **46.** 0.53 **47.** 0.26 **48.** 0.44 **49.** 3.1

Name the quadrant where each ordered pair is located. (Lesson 11-3)

50. $(4, -6)$ **51.** $(-1, 5)$ **52.** $(2, 3)$ **53.** $(-2, -4)$ **54.** $(-10, 5)$

11-6 Multiplying Integers

Learn to multiply integers.

 NY Performance Indicators

6.A.2 Use substitution to evaluate algebraic expressions.

You have seen that you can multiply whole numbers to count items in equally sized groups.

There are three sets of twins in the sixth grade. How many sixth graders are twins?

A set of twins is 2 people.

$3 \cdot 2 = 6$ *3 sets of 2 is 6.*

So 6 students in the sixth grade are twins.

Multiplying with integers is similar.

Numbers	$3 \cdot 2$	$-3 \cdot 2$	$3 \cdot (-2)$	$-3 \cdot (-2)$
Words	3 groups of 2	the opposite of 3 groups of 2	3 groups of –2	the opposite of 3 groups of –2
Addition	$2 + 2 + 2$	$-(2 + 2 + 2)$	$(-2) + (-2) + (-2)$	$-[(-2) + (-2) + (-2)]$
Product	6	-6	-6	6

EXAMPLE Multiplying Integers

Find each product.

A $4 \cdot 3$

$4 \cdot 3 = 12$ *Think: 4 groups of 3*

B $2 \cdot (-4)$

$2 \cdot (-4) = -8$ *Think: 2 groups of −4*

C $-5 \cdot 2$

$-5 \cdot 2 = -10$ *Think: **the opposite of** 5 groups of 2*

D $-3 \cdot (-4)$

$-3 \cdot (-4) = 12$ *Think: **the opposite of** 3 groups of −4*

Remember!

To find the opposite of a number, change the sign. The opposite of 6 is −6. The opposite of −4 is 4.

MULTIPLYING INTEGERS

If the signs are the same, the product is positive.

$$4 \cdot 3 = 12 \qquad\qquad -6 \cdot (-3) = 18$$

If the signs are different, the product is negative.

$$-2 \cdot 5 = -10 \qquad\qquad 7 \cdot (-8) = -56$$

The product of any number and 0 is 0.

$$0 \cdot 9 = 0 \qquad\qquad (-12) \cdot 0 = 0$$

EXAMPLE 2 **Evaluating Integer Expressions**

Evaluate 5x for each value of x.

Remember!

$5x$ means $5 \cdot x$.

A $x = -4$

$5x$	*Write the expression.*
$5 \cdot (-4)$	*Substitute −4 for x.*
-20	*The signs are different, so the answer is negative.*

B $x = 0$

$5x$	*Write the expression.*
$5 \cdot 0$	*Substitute 0 for x.*
0	*Any number times 0 is 0.*

Think and Discuss

1. **Explain** how multiplying integers is similar to multiplying whole numbers. How is it different?

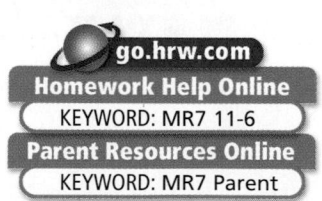

11-6 Exercises

go.hrw.com
Homework Help Online
KEYWORD: MR7 11-6
Parent Resources Online
KEYWORD: MR7 Parent

GUIDED PRACTICE

See Example **1** **Find each product.**

1. $6 \cdot 4$ **2.** $5 \cdot (-2)$ **3.** $-3 \cdot 7$ **4.** $-2 \cdot 3$

5. $-9 \cdot (-1)$ **6.** $13 \cdot 0$ **7.** $-8 \cdot (-2)$ **8.** $-6 \cdot (-6)$

See Example **2** **Evaluate 3n for each value of n.**

9. $n = 3$ **10.** $n = -2$ **11.** $n = 11$ **12.** $n = -5$

13. $n = -8$ **14.** $n = -12$ **15.** $n = 6$ **16.** $n = 10$

See Example ① **Find each product.**

17. $5 \cdot 9$ **18.** $-7 \cdot 6$ **19.** $8 \cdot (-4)$ **20.** $-6 \cdot (-9)$

21. $-13 \cdot (-3)$ **22.** $4 \cdot 12$ **23.** $6 \cdot (-12)$ **24.** $-7 \cdot (-11)$

See Example ② **Evaluate $-4a$ for each value of a.**

25. $a = 6$ **26.** $a = 12$ **27.** $a = 3$ **28.** $a = -7$

29. $a = -10$ **30.** $a = 7$ **31.** $a = -15$ **32.** $a = -22$

PRACTICE AND PROBLEM SOLVING

Extra Practice
See page 736.

Evaluate each expression for the given value of the variable.

33. $n \cdot (-7); n = -2$ **34.** $-6 \cdot m; m = 4$ **35.** $9x; x = 6$

36. $-5m; m = 5$ **37.** $x \cdot 10; x = -9$ **38.** $-8 \cdot n; n = -1$

39. Earth Science When the moon, the sun, and Earth are in a straight line, spring tides occur on Earth. Spring tides may cause high and low tides to be two times as great as normal. If high tides at a certain location are usually 2 ft and low tides are usually -2 ft, what might the spring tides be?

40. Critical Thinking What number property is true for integer multiplication?

 41. What's the Error? Ava says the value of $-6b$ when $b = -6$ is -36. What is her error? What is the correct answer?

 42. Write About It What is the sign of the product when you multiply three negative integers? four negative integers? Use examples to explain.

 43. Challenge Name 2 integers whose product is -36 and whose sum is 0.

TEST PREP and Spiral Review

44. Multiple Choice During a game, Frieda scored -10 points for each question she missed. She missed 5 questions. What was the total number of points she scored on missed questions?

    Ⓐ -50 Ⓑ -2 Ⓒ 2 Ⓓ 50

45. Extended Response What is the sign of the product when 4 negative integers are multiplied? when 5 negative integers are multiplied? Describe a rule that can be used to determine the sign of the product when the number of negative integers is even and when the number of negative integers is odd.

46. Kim cut $6\frac{1}{3}$ yards of ribbon into $\frac{1}{3}$-yard pieces. How many pieces of ribbon did Kim cut? (Lesson 5-9)

Find each sum. (Lesson 11-4)

47. $3 + 6$ **48.** $-5 + 1$ **49.** $-4 + (-9)$ **50.** $7 + (-7)$ **51.** $2 + (-5)$

11-7 Dividing Integers

Learn to divide
integers.

**NY Performance
Indicators**

6.A.2 Use substitution to
evaluate algebraic expressions.

Mona is a biologist studying an
endangered species of wombat.
Each year she records the
change in the wombat
population.

Year	Change in Population
1	−2
2	−5
3	−1
4	−4

Baby Australian wombat

One way to describe the change in the wombat population over time
is to find the mean of the data in the table.

$$\frac{-2 + (-5) + (-1) + (-4)}{4} = \frac{-12}{4} = -12 \div 4 = \blacksquare$$

Remember!

To find the mean of
a list of numbers:
1. Add all the
   numbers together.
2. Divide by how
   many numbers are
   in the list.

Multiplication and division are inverse operations. To solve a division
problem, think of the related multiplication.

To solve −12 ÷ 4, think: What number times 4 equals −12?

$$-3 \cdot 4 = -12, \text{ so } -12 \div 4 = -3$$

The mean change in the wombat population is −3. So on average, the
population **decreased by 3 wombats** per year.

EXAMPLE **Dividing Integers**

Find each quotient.

A $12 \div (-3)$

Think: What number times −3 equals 12?

$-4 \cdot (-3) = 12$, so $12 \div (-3) = -4$.

B $-15 \div (-3)$

Think: What number times −3 equals −15?

$5 \cdot (-3) = -15$, so $-15 \div (-3) = 5$.

Because division is the inverse of multiplication, the rules for dividing integers are the same as the rules for multiplying integers.

DIVIDING INTEGERS

If the signs are the same, the quotient is positive.
$$24 \div 3 = 8 \qquad -6 \div (-3) = 2$$

If the signs are different, the quotient is negative.
$$-20 \div 5 = -4 \qquad 72 \div (-8) = -9$$

Zero divided by any integer equals 0.
$$\frac{0}{14} = 0 \qquad \frac{0}{-11} = 0$$

You cannot divide any integer by 0.

EXAMPLE 2   **Evaluating Integer Expressions**

Evaluate $\frac{x}{3}$ for each value of x.

Remember!

$\frac{x}{3}$ means $x \div 3$.

A $x = 6$

$\dfrac{x}{3}$ *Write the expression.*

$\dfrac{6}{3} = 6 \div 3$ *Substitute 6 for x.*

$\quad\ = 2$ *The signs are the same, so the answer is positive.*

B $x = -18$

$\dfrac{x}{3}$ *Write the expression.*

$\dfrac{-18}{3} = -18 \div 3$ *Substitute −18 for x.*

$\quad\ = -6$ *The signs are different, so the answer is negative.*

C $x = -12$

$\dfrac{x}{3}$ *Write the expression.*

$\dfrac{-12}{3} = -12 \div 3$ *Substitute −12 for x.*

$\quad\ = -4$ *The signs are different, so the answer is negative.*

Think and Discuss

1. Describe the sign of the quotient of two integers with like signs.

2. Describe the sign of the quotient of two integers with unlike signs.

11-7 **Exercises**

go.hrw.com
Homework Help Online
KEYWORD: MR7 11-7
Parent Resources Online
KEYWORD: MR7 Parent

GUIDED PRACTICE

See Example 1 Find each quotient.

1. $64 \div 8$ **2.** $10 \div (-2)$ **3.** $-21 \div (-7)$ **4.** $-64 \div 2$

See Example 2 Evaluate $\frac{m}{2}$ for each value of m.

5. $m = -4$ **6.** $m = 20$ **7.** $m = -30$ **8.** $m = 50$

INDEPENDENT PRACTICE

See Example 1 Find each quotient.

9. $45 \div 9$ **10.** $-42 \div 6$ **11.** $32 \div (-4)$ **12.** $54 \div (-6)$

13. $-60 \div (-10)$ **14.** $-75 \div 15$ **15.** $22 \div 11$ **16.** $-48 \div (-4)$

See Example 2 Evaluate $\frac{n}{4}$ for each value of n.

17. $n = 4$ **18.** $n = -32$ **19.** $n = 12$ **20.** $n = -24$

21. $n = 64$ **22.** $n = -92$ **23.** $n = 56$ **24.** $n = -28$

PRACTICE AND PROBLEM SOLVING

Extra Practice
See page 736.

Divide.

25. $-12 \div 2$ **26.** $\frac{16}{-4}$ **27.** $-6 \div (-6)$ **28.** $-56 \div (-7)$

29. $\frac{-30}{-3}$ **30.** $-45 \div 9$ **31.** $\frac{-35}{5}$ **32.** $\frac{-63}{9}$

Evaluate each expression for the given value of the variable.

33. $n \div (-7); n = -21$ **34.** $\frac{m}{3}; m = -15$ **35.** $\frac{x}{4}; x = 32$

36. $y \div (-3); y = -6$ **37.** $\frac{a}{3}; a = -9$ **38.** $w \div (-2); w = -18$

39. $-48 \div n; n = -8$ **40.** $\frac{p}{-2}; p = -20$ **41.** $j \div 9; j = -99$

42. The graph shows the low temperatures for 5 days in Fairbanks, Alaska.

   a. Find the mean low temperature for Monday, Tuesday, and Wednesday.

   b. Find the mean low temperature for all 5 days.

   c. **Critical Thinking** Which mean low temperature was higher? Explain.

   d. Find the range of the data.

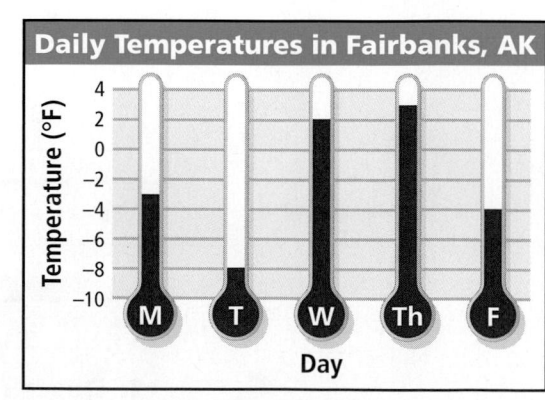

Daily Temperatures in Fairbanks, AK

The Mediterranean monk seal is one of the world's rarest mammals. Monk seals have become endangered largely because divers hunt them for their skin and disturb their habitat.

Annette found this table in a science article about monk seals.

Changes in Population of Monk Seals							
Years	1971–1975	1976–1980	1981–1985	1986–1990	1991–1995	1996–2000	2001–2005
Change	550	−300	−150	−50	100	200	−100

43. a. According to the table, what was the change in the monk seal population from 1976 to 1980?
b. What does this number mean?

44. Find the mean change per year from 1971 to 1975. (*Hint: This is a range of 5 years, so divide by 5.*) What does your answer mean?

45. Find the mean change per year from 1981 to 1990. What does your answer mean?

46. **Write About It** Why is it important to use both positive and negative numbers when tracking the changes in a population?

47. **Challenge** Suppose that there were 250 monk seals in 1971. How many were there in 2005?

TEST PREP and Spiral Review

48. Multiple Choice Which quotient is greatest?

(A) $-8 \div (-2)$ (B) $-10 \div 5$ (C) $-10 \div (-5)$ (D) $15 \div (-5)$

49. Multiple Choice The change in population for a species is recorded in the table. What is the mean of the data?

Year	1	2	3	4
Change in Population	−2	+5	−7	−4

(F) −4   (H) 1
(G) −2   (J) 3

Find the missing measurement for each prism. (Lesson 10-7)

50. $\ell = 9$ cm; $w = 24$ cm; $h = \underline{?}$; $V = 1{,}296$ cm^3 **51.** $\ell = 8$ m; $w = \underline{?}$; $h = 13$ m; $V = 728$ cm^3

Evaluate $k - (-4)$ **for each value of** k. (Lesson 11-5)

52. $k = -5$ **53.** $k = 7$ **54.** $k = -13$ **55.** $k = -4$ **56.** $k = 16$

READY TO GO ON?

Quiz for Lessons 11-4 Through 11-7

✓ **11-4** Adding Integers

Write the addition modeled on each number line.

1.

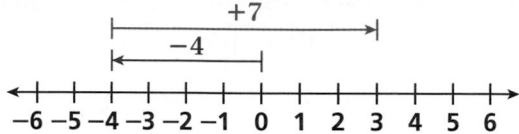

2.

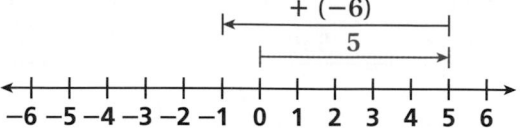

Find each sum.

3. $7 + (-3)$ **4.** $-10 + 6$ **5.** $-7 + (-3)$

Evaluate $-5 + x$ for each value of x.

6. $x = 7$ **7.** $x = -4$ **8.** $x = 2$

9. An archaeological team digs 6 feet below the surface on the first day. The team digs an additional 3 feet on the second day. At what depth is the archaeological team at the end of the second day?

✓ **11-5** Subtracting Integers

Write the subtraction modeled on each number line.

10.

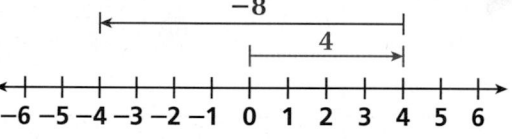

11.

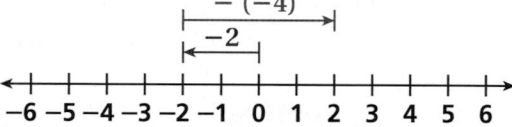

12. Evaluate $x - (-7)$ for $x = -2$.

13. The temperature on January 5 was $-7°F$. On January 6, it was $2°F$. Find the difference between the temperature on January 5 and January 6.

✓ **11-6** Multiplying Integers

Evaluate $6x$ for each value of x.

14. $x = -2$ **15.** $x = 1$ **16.** $x = -7$

Find each product.

17. $3 \cdot (-7)$ **18.** $-10 \cdot 8$ **19.** $-12 \cdot (-5)$

✓ **11-7** Dividing Integers

Evaluate $\frac{x}{4}$ for each value of x.

20. $x = -24$ **21.** $x = 44$ **22.** $x = -124$

Find each quotient.

23. $72 \div (-9)$ **24.** $-15 \div (-3)$ **25.** $-40 \div 10$

Focus on Problem Solving

Make a Plan

• **Choose a problem-solving strategy**

The following strategies can help you solve problems.

- Act It Out
- Draw a Diagram
- Make a Model
- Guess and Test
- Work Backward

- Find a Pattern
- Make a Table
- Solve a Simpler Problem
- Use Logical Reasoning
- Make an Organized List

Tell which strategy from the list above you would use to solve each problem. Explain your choice. Then solve the problem.

1 The temperature on a winter day is −6°F at 8:00 A.M., −4°F at 9:00 A.M., and −2°F at 10:00 A.M. The temperature continues to change by the same amount each hour. What is the temperature at 2:00 P.M.?

2 Caleb lives in one of the states listed in the table. His home is at an elevation of 600 feet. There is a park in his state at an elevation of 150 feet. Which state does Caleb live in?

State	Lowest Elevation (ft)	Highest Elevation (ft)
California	−282	14,494
Louisiana	−8	535
West Virginia	240	4,861

3 On a map of Nadia's town, the library is located at (2, 3), the museum is located at (1, −2), city hall is located at (−2, −3), and the aquarium is located at (−4, 2). She wants to organize a field trip to the two buildings that are closest to each other. Which two buildings should she choose?

4 In the past month, Ethan's savings account had withdrawals and deposits in the amounts of −$25, +$45, +$15, −$40, and +$60. He wants to check the receipts for one of the withdrawals and one of the deposits. How many different combinations of one withdrawal and one deposit are there?

Model Integer Equations

Use with Lesson 11-8

go.hrw.com
Lab Resources Online
KEYWORD: MR7 Lab11

NY Performance Indicators
5.A.5, 6.R.1, 6.R.2, 6.R.5

KEY
■ = 1
■ = −1
▭ = x

REMEMBER
You can add or subtract the same number on both sides of an equation.
Adding or subtracting zero does not change a number's value.

You can use algebra tiles to model equations. An equation mat represents the two sides of an equation. To find the value of the variable, get the *x*-tile by itself on one side of the mat. You may remove the same number of yellow tiles or the same number of red tiles from both sides.

Activity

Use algebra tiles to model and solve each equation.

1 $x + 2 = 6$

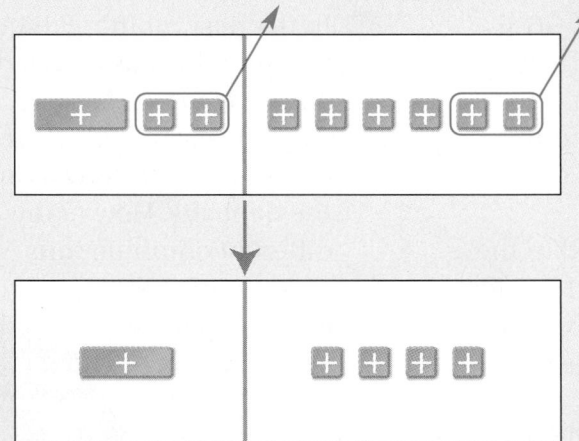

Remove 2 yellow tiles from both sides of the mat.

$x = 4$

2 $x - 3 = -5$

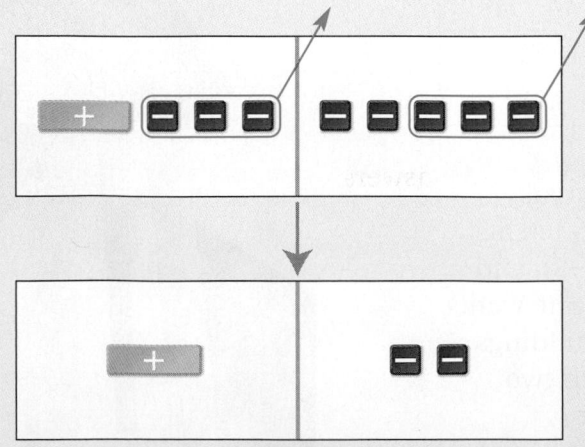

Use red tiles to model subtraction. Remove 3 red tiles from both sides of the mat.

$x = -2$

3 $x + 6 = 2$

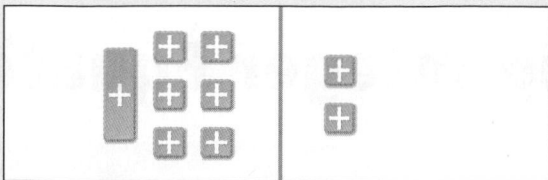

Adding red tiles to both sides will allow you to remove zero pairs. If you add 6 red tiles to the left side, you must add 6 red tiles to the right side to keep the equation balanced.

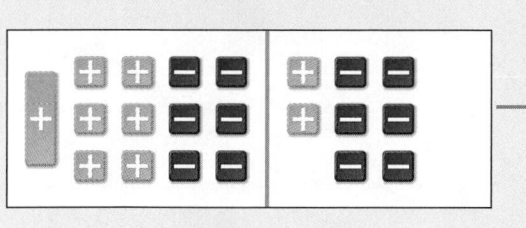

$x = -4$

Add 6 red tiles to both sides.

Now you can remove zero pairs from both sides of the mat.

4 $3x = -9$

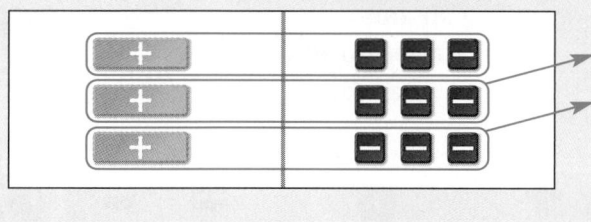

Divide each side into 3 equal groups. Remove all but one of the groups.

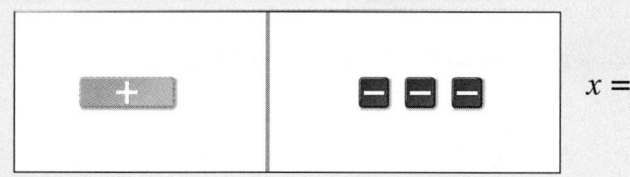

$x = -3$

Think and Discuss

1. In **4**, why did you divide both sides into 3 groups?

2. Why can you add zero pairs to an equation mat? Why is it not necessary to add them to both sides?

3. When you add zero to an equation, how do you know the number of red and yellow tiles to add?

4. How can you use algebra tiles to check your answers?

Try This

Use algebra tiles to model and solve each equation.

1. $x + 6 = 3$ **2.** $x - 1 = -8$ **3.** $2x = 14$ **4.** $4x = -8$

Learn to solve equations containing integers.

NY Performance Indicators

5.A.5 Solve and explain simple one-step equations using inverse operations involving whole numbers. Also, 5.A.4.

The entrance to the Great Pyramid of Khufu is 55 ft above ground. The underground chamber is 102 ft below ground. From the entrance, what is the distance to the underground chamber?

To solve this problem, you can use an equation containing integers.

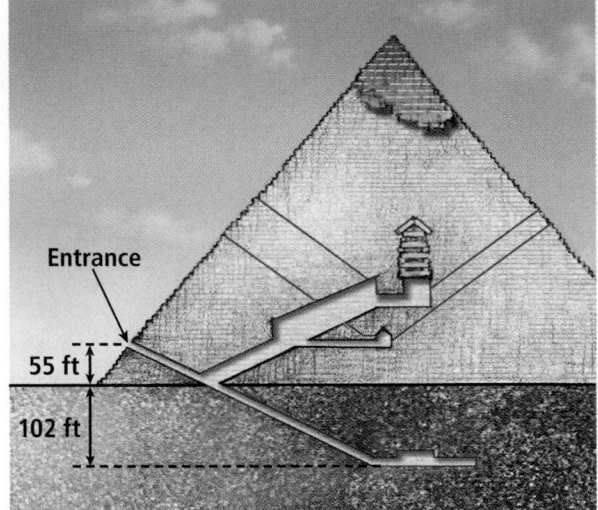

Entrance
55 ft
102 ft

height of entrance	+	distance to underground chamber	=	height of underground chamber

$$55 \quad + \quad d \quad = \quad \text{-}102$$

$$
\begin{array}{ll}
55 + d = -102 & \textit{Write the equation.} \\
\underline{-\,55 \qquad\quad -\,55} & \textit{Subtract 55 from both sides.} \\
\quad\quad d = -157 &
\end{array}
$$

It is -157 ft from the entrance to the underground chamber. The sign is negative, which means you **go down 157 ft.**

EXAMPLE **Adding and Subtracting to Solve Equations**

A Solve $4 + x = -2$. Check your answer.

$$
\begin{array}{ll}
4 + x = -2 & \textit{4 is added to x.} \\
\underline{-4 \qquad\; -4} & \textit{Subtract 4 from both} \\
\qquad x = -6 & \textit{sides to undo the} \\
& \textit{addition.}
\end{array}
$$

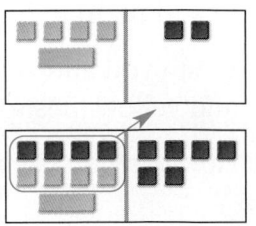

Check

$$
\begin{array}{ll}
4 + x = -2 & \textit{Write the equation.} \\
4 + (-6) \overset{?}{=} -2 & \textit{Substitute −6 for x.} \\
-2 \overset{?}{=} -2 \; ✔ & \textit{−6 is a solution.}
\end{array}
$$

Helpful Hint

Subtracting a number is the same as adding its opposite. To solve this equation using algebra tiles, you can add four red tiles to both sides and then remove zero pairs.

B Solve $y - 6 = -5$. Check your answer.

$$y - 6 = -5 \qquad \text{\textit{6 is subtracted from y.}}$$
$$\underline{+6 \quad +6} \qquad \text{\textit{Add 6 to both sides to}}$$
$$y \qquad = \quad 1 \qquad \text{\textit{undo the subtraction.}}$$

Check

$$y - 6 = -5 \qquad \text{\textit{Write the equation.}}$$
$$1 - 6 \overset{?}{=} -5 \qquad \text{\textit{Substitute 1 for y.}}$$
$$-5 \overset{?}{=} -5 \checkmark \qquad \text{\textit{1 is a solution.}}$$

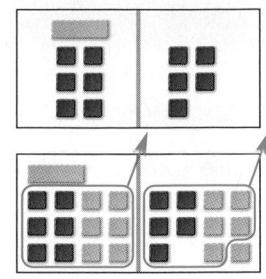

EXAMPLE 2 Multiplying and Dividing to Solve Equations

Solve each equation. Check your answers.

A $-3a = 15$

$$\frac{-3a}{-3} = \frac{15}{-3} \qquad \text{\textit{a is multiplied by −3. Divide both sides}}$$
$$\qquad\qquad\qquad \text{\textit{by −3 to undo the multiplication.}}$$

$$a = -5$$

Check

$$-3a = 15 \qquad \text{\textit{Write the equation.}}$$
$$-3(-5) \overset{?}{=} 15 \qquad \text{\textit{Substitute −5 for a.}}$$
$$15 \overset{?}{=} 15 \checkmark \qquad \text{\textit{−5 is a solution.}}$$

B $\dfrac{b}{-4} = -2$

$$-4 \cdot \frac{b}{-4} = -4 \cdot (-2) \qquad \text{\textit{b is divided by −4. Multiply both sides}}$$
$$\qquad\qquad\qquad\qquad \text{\textit{by −4 to undo the division.}}$$

$$b = 8$$

Check

$$\frac{b}{-4} = -2 \qquad \text{\textit{Write the equation.}}$$
$$8 \div (-4) \overset{?}{=} -2 \qquad \text{\textit{Substitute 8 for b.}}$$
$$-2 \overset{?}{=} -2 \checkmark \qquad \text{\textit{8 is a solution.}}$$

Think and Discuss

1. Tell what operation you would use to solve $x + 12 = -32$.

2. Tell whether the solution to $-9t = -27$ will be positive or negative without actually solving the equation.

3. Explain how to check your answer to an integer equation.

go.hrw.com

Homework Help Online
KEYWORD: MR7 11-8

Parent Resources Online
KEYWORD: MR7 Parent

GUIDED PRACTICE

See Example **1** Solve each equation. Check your answers.

1. $m - 3 = 9$ **2.** $a - 8 = -13$ **3.** $z - 12 = -3$ **4.** $j - 2 = 7$

5. $p + 2 = -7$ **6.** $k - 9 = 21$ **7.** $g - 10 = -2$ **8.** $h + 15 = 25$

See Example **2** **9.** $-4b = 32$ **10.** $\frac{w}{3} = 18$ **11.** $5c = -35$ **12.** $\frac{p}{-5} = 10$

13. $6f = -36$ **14.** $-2c = 72$ **15.** $\frac{r}{10} = -90$ **16.** $\frac{d}{-12} = 144$

INDEPENDENT PRACTICE

See Example **1** Solve each equation. Check your answers.

17. $g - 9 = -5$ **18.** $v - 7 = 19$ **19.** $t - 13 = -27$ **20.** $s - 4 = -21$

21. $x + 2 = -12$ **22.** $y + 9 = -10$ **23.** $20 + w = 10$ **24.** $z + 15 = 50$

See Example **2** **25.** $6j = 48$ **26.** $7s = -49$ **27.** $\frac{a}{-2} = 26$ **28.** $-2r = 10$

29. $\frac{m}{-12} = 4$ **30.** $\frac{k}{5} = -4$ **31.** $u \div 6 = -10$ **32.** $6t = -36$

PRACTICE AND PROBLEM SOLVING

Extra Practice
See page 736.

Solve each equation. Check your answers.

33. $x - 12 = 5$ **34.** $w - 3 = -2$ **35.** $-7k = 28$ **36.** $g \div 7 = -2$

37. $\frac{m}{-3} = 5$ **38.** $a - 10 = 9$ **39.** $n - 19 = -22$ **40.** $2h = 42$

41. $13g = -39$ **42.** $s \div 6 = -3$ **43.** $24 + f = 16$ **44.** $q - 15 = -4$

45. $d - 26 = 7$ **46.** $-6c = 54$ **47.** $h \div (-4) = 21$ **48.** $7k = 70$

49. $b - 17 = 15$ **50.** $u - 82 = -7$ **51.** $-8a = -64$ **52.** $v + 1 = -9$

53. $\frac{t}{11} = -5$ **54.** $31 + j = -14$ **55.** $c + 23 = 10$ **56.** $\frac{r}{-2} = -8$

57. $15n = -60$ **58.** $z \div (-5) = -9$ **59.** $j - 20 = -23$ **60.** $f + 20 = -60$

61. A submarine captain sets the following diving course: dive 200 ft, stop, and then dive another 200 ft. If this pattern is continued, how many dives will be necessary to reach a location 14,000 ft below sea level?

62. While exploring a cave, Lin noticed that the temperature dropped 4°F for every 30 ft that she descended. What is Lin's depth if the temperature is 8° lower than the temperature at the surface?

63. Sports After two rounds in the 2001 LPGA Champions Classic, Wendy Doolan had a score of –12. Her score in the second round was –8. What was her score in the first round?

64. Critical Thinking If the product of a variable and a number is positive and the number is negative, what is the sign of the value of the variable?

Bolivia has two capitals. La Paz is Bolivia's chief industrial city, and the congress meets there. However, the supreme court meets in Sucre.

Use the graph for Exercises 65 and 66.

65. Life Science Scientists have found live bacteria at elevations of 135,000 ft. This is 153,500 ft above one of the animals in the graph. Which one? (*Hint:* Solve $x + 153,500 = 135,000$.)

66. Social Studies The world's highest capital city is La Paz, Bolivia, with an elevation of 11,808 ft. The highest altitude that a yak has been found at is how much higher than La Paz? (*Hint:* Solve $11,808 + x = 20,000$.)

67. Carla is a diver. On Friday, she dove 5 times as deep as she dove on Monday. If she dove to -120 ft on Friday, how deep did she dive on Monday?

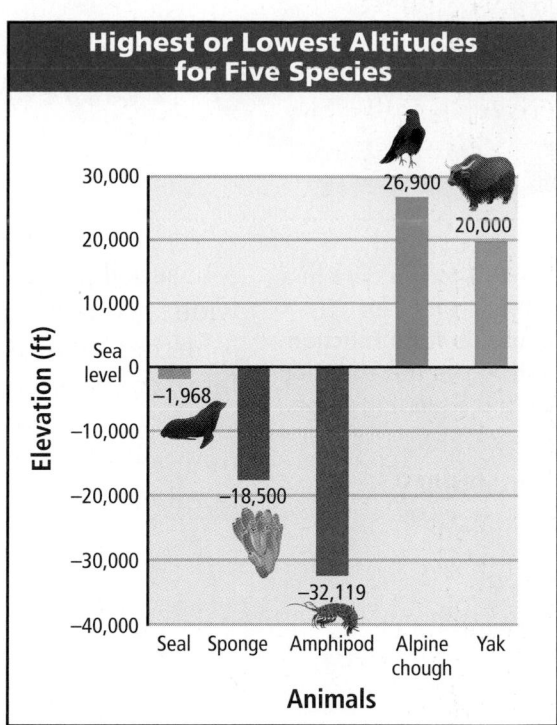

Highest or Lowest Altitudes for Five Species

68. Write A Problem Write a word problem that could be solved using the equation $x - 3 = -15$.

69. Write About It Is the solution to $3n = -12$ positive or negative? How could you tell without solving the equation?

70. Challenge Find each answer.

　a. $12 \div (-3 \cdot 2) \div 2$　　　　**b.** $12 \div (-3 \cdot 2 \div 2)$

Why are the answers different even though the numbers are the same?

TEST PREP and Spiral Review

71. Multiple Choice Kathie and her three friends each owe $24 for dinner. Solve the equation $\frac{t}{4} = 24$ to determine the total amount t of the dinner.

　Ⓐ $96　　　Ⓑ $28　　　Ⓒ $20　　　Ⓓ $6

72. Short Response David is 12 years younger than his sister Candace. David is 9 years old. Write an equation for the situation. Let c be Candace's age. Then solve the equation to find her age.

Determine if the given statements are *sometimes, always,* or *never* true. (Lesson 8-6)

73. A square is a rhombus　　　　　　　**74.** A parallelogram is a square.

Find each product. (Lesson 11-6)

75. $5 \cdot (-7)$　　**76.** $-9 \cdot 9$　　**77.** $2 \cdot 6$　　**78.** $10 \cdot 0$　　**79.** $-8 \cdot (-4)$

Learn to use data in a table to write an equation for a function and to use the equation to find a missing value.

Vocabulary

function

input

output

NY Performance Indicators

6.PS.14 Analyze problems by observing patterns. Also, 6.PS.23.

A baseball pitch thrown too high, low, or wide is considered outside the strike zone. A pitcher threw a ball 4 inches too low. How far in centimeters was the ball outside the strike zone? Make a table to show how the number of centimeters increases as the number of inches increases.

Inches	Centimeters
1	2.54
2	5.08
3	7.62
4	10.16

+1 ... +2.54 (between each row)

"Come on, ump, that pitch was at least four centimeters outside!"

The number of centimeters is 2.54 times the number of inches. Let x represent the number of inches and y represent the number of centimeters. Then the equation $y = 2.54x$ relates centimeters to inches.

A **function** is a rule that relates two quantities so that each **input** value corresponds exactly to one **output** value.

Input 2 → Rule $y = 2.54x$ → Output 5.08

Input 4 → Rule $y = 2.54x$ → Output 10.16

When the input is 4 in., the output is 10.16 cm. So the ball was 10.16 centimeters outside the strike zone.

You can use a function table to show some of the values for a function.

EXAMPLE 1 Writing Equations from Function Tables

Write an equation for a function that gives the values in the table. Use the equation to find the value of y for the indicated value of x.

x	3	4	5	6	7	10
y	7	9	11	13	15	■

Helpful Hint

When all the y-values are greater than the corresponding x-values, use addition and/or multiplication in your equation.

y is 2 times x + 1.　　　*Compare x and y to find a pattern.*

$y = 2x + 1$　　　*Use the pattern to write an equation.*

$y = 2(10) + 1$　　　*Substitute 10 for x.*

$y = 20 + 1 = 21$　　　*Use your function rule to find y when x = 10.*

You can write equations for functions that are described in words.

EXAMPLE 2 **Translating Words into Math**

Write an equation for the function. Tell what each variable you use represents.

The length of a rectangle is 5 times its width.

ℓ = length of rectangle   *Choose variables for the equation.*

w = width of rectangle

$\ell = 5w$ *Write an equation.*

EXAMPLE 3 **PROBLEM SOLVING APPLICATION**

Car washers tracked the number of cars they washed and the total amount of money they earned. They charged the same price for each car they washed. They earned $60 for 20 cars, $66 for 22 cars, and $81 for 27 cars. Write an equation for the function.

1. Understand the Problem

The **answer** will be an equation that describes the relationship between the number of cars washed and the money earned.

2. Make a Plan

You can make a table to display the data.

3. Solve

Let c be the number of cars. Let m be the amount of money earned.

c	20	22	27
m	60	66	81

m is equal to 3 times c.   *Compare c and m.*

$m = 3c$ *Write an equation.*

4. Look Back

Substitute the c and m values in the table to check that they are solutions of the equation $m = 3c$.

$m = 3c$ (20, 60) $m = 3c$ (22, 66) $m = 3c$ (27, 81)

$60 \overset{?}{=} 3 \cdot 20$ $66 \overset{?}{=} 3 \cdot 22$ $81 \overset{?}{=} 3 \cdot 27$

$60 \overset{?}{=} 60$ ✔ $66 \overset{?}{=} 66$ ✔ $81 \overset{?}{=} 81$ ✔

6.PS.21

Think and Discuss

1. Explain how you find the y-value when the x-value is 20 for the function $y = 5x$.

go.hrw.com
Homework Help Online
KEYWORD: MR7 11-9
Parent Resources Online
KEYWORD: MR7 Parent

GUIDED PRACTICE

See Example ① Write an equation for a function that gives the values in each table. Use the equation to find the value of y for the indicated value of x.

1.

x	1	2	3	6	9
y	7	8	9	12	■

2.

x	3	4	5	6	10
y	16	21	26	31	■

See Example ② Write an equation for the function. Tell what each variable you use represents.

3. Jen is 6 years younger than her brother.

See Example ③ **4.** Brenda sells balloon bouquets. She charges the same price for each balloon in a bouquet. The cost of a bouquet with 6 balloons is $3, with 9 balloons is $4.50, and with 12 balloons is $6. Write an equation for the function.

INDEPENDENT PRACTICE

See Example ① Write an equation for a function that gives the values in each table. Use the equation to find the value of y for the indicated value of x.

5.

x	0	1	2	5	7
y	0	4	8	20	■

6.

x	4	5	6	7	12
y	0	2	4	6	■

See Example ② Write an equation for the function. Tell what each variable you use represents.

7. The cost of a case of bottled juices is $2 less than the cost of twelve individual bottles.

8. The population of New York is twice as large as the population of Michigan.

See Example ③ **9.** Oliver is playing a video game. He earns the same number of points for each prize he captures. He earned 1,050 points for 7 prizes, 1,500 points for 10 prizes, and 2,850 points for 19 prizes. Write an equation for the function.

PRACTICE AND PROBLEM SOLVING

Extra Practice
See page 736.

Write an equation for a function that gives the values in each table, and then find the missing terms.

10.

x	−1	0	1	2	5	7
y	■	3.4	4.4	5.4	■	10.4

11.

x	2	3	5	9	11	14
y	−6	−10	−18	−34	−42	■

12.

x	20	24	28	32	36	40
y	−5	−6	−7	■	−9	−10

13.

x	−5	−3	−1	0	1	3
y	−11	−7	■	−1	1	■

14. Multi-Step The height of a triangle is 5 centimeters more than twice the length of its base. Write an equation relating the height of the triangle to the length of its base. Find the height when the base is 20 centimeters long.

Write an equation for each function. Define the variables that you use.

15.

16.

17. **Multi-Step** Georgia earns $6.50 per hour at a part-time job. She wants to buy a sweater that costs $58.50. Write an equation relating the number of hours she works to the amount of money she earns. Find how many hours Georgia needs to work to buy the sweater.

Use the table for Exercises 18–20.

18. **Graphic Design** Margo is designing a Web page displaying similar rectangles. Use the table to write an equation relating the width of a rectangle to the length of a rectangle. Find the length of a rectangle that has a width of 250 pixels.

Width (pixels)	Length (pixels)
30	95
40	125
50	155
60	185

 19. **What's the Error?** Margo predicted that the length of a rectangle with a width of 100 pixels would be 310 pixels. Explain the error she made. Then find the correct length.

 20. **Write About It** Explain how to write an equation for the data in the table.

 21. **Challenge** Write an equation that would give the same y-values as $y = 2x + 1$ for $x = 0, 1, 2, 3$.

22. **Multiple Choice** Sunny Lawn Care charges $25 per visit plus $2 per cubic foot. Which equation models this situation?

Ⓐ $y = x + 2$ Ⓑ $y = x + 25$ Ⓒ $y = 25x + 2$ Ⓓ $y = 2x + 25$

23. **Multiple Choice** Which is an equation for the function that gives the values in the table?

x	3	4	5	6	7
y	8	11	14	17	20

Ⓕ $y = 2x + 2$ Ⓗ $y = 2x + 6$

Ⓖ $y = 3x - 1$ Ⓙ $y = 3x + 1$

Solve each equation. Check your answers. (Lesson 3-9)

24. $4.2 + n = 6.7$ 25. $x - 2.3 = 1.6$ 26. $1.5w = 3.6$ 27. $\frac{p}{4} = 1.3$

Find the volume of each cylinder using the information given. (Lesson 10-8)

28. $r = 6$ cm; $h = 6.4$ cm   29. $r = 5$ ft; $h = 9$ ft   30. $d = 7$ m; $h = 11$ m

Explore Linear and Nonlinear Relationships

Use with Lesson 11-10

You can learn about linear and nonlinear relationships by looking at patterns.

NY Performance Indicators

6.PS.14, 6.R.1, 6.R.5

Activity

1 This model shows stage 1 to stage 3 of a pattern.

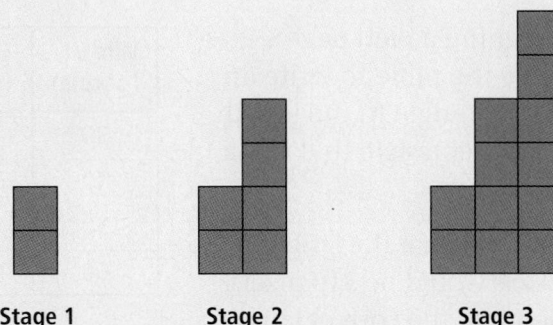

Stage 1   Stage 2   Stage 3

a. Use square tiles or graph paper to model stages 4, 5, and 6.

b. Record each stage and the perimeter of each figure in a table.

c. Graph the ordered pairs (x, y) from the table on a coordinate plane.

Stage (x)	Perimeter (y)
1	6
2	12
3	18
4	24
5	30
6	36

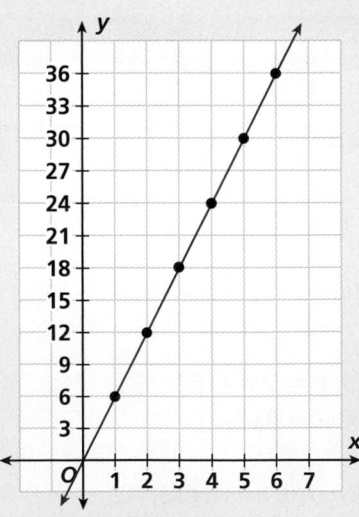

If you connected the points you graphed, you would draw a straight line. This shows that the relationship between the stage and the perimeter of the figure is linear. The equation for this line is $y = 6x$.

2 This table shows the ordered pairs for stages 1, 4, and 9 of a pattern.

Stage (x)	Square Root (y)
1	1
4	2
9	3
16	4
25	5
36	6

$1 = 1 \cdot 1$ or $1 = 1^2$
$4 = 2 \cdot 2$ or $4 = 2^2$
$9 = 3 \cdot 3$ or $9 = 3^2$

The square root of 4 is 2, which is written like this: $\sqrt{4} = 2$.

a. You can model this by arranging squares in 1-by-1, 2-by-2, and 3-by-3 blocks.

b. Record each stage number and the number's square root in a table. Graph the ordered pairs (x, y) from the table on a coordinate plane.

 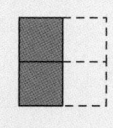 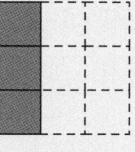

Stage 1   Stage 4   Stage 9

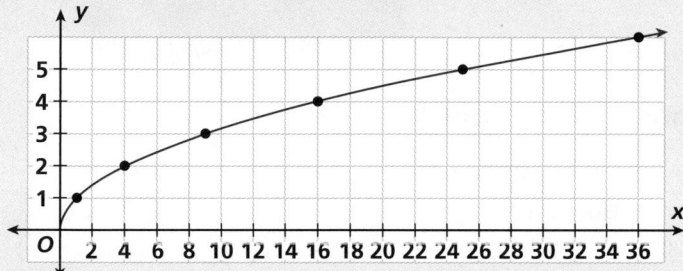

If you connect the graphed points, you draw a curved line. This shows that the relationship between the stage number and that number's square root is nonlinear. The equation for this curve is $y = \sqrt{x}$.

Think and Discuss

1. Explain what pattern you see in the y-values of the ordered pairs from the graph above.

Try This

Use the x-values 1, 2, 3, and 4 to find ordered pairs for each equation. Then graph the equation. Tell whether the relationship between x and y is linear or nonlinear.

1. $y = 2 + x$ **2.** $y = 4x$ **3.** $y = x^3$

4. $y = x + 4$ **5.** $y = x(2 + x)$ **6.** $y = x + x$

7. $y = 2x$ **8.** $y = x^2$ **9.** $y = 3 + 2x$

Learn to represent linear functions using ordered pairs and graphs.

Learn to represent linear functions using ordered pairs and graphs.

Vocabulary

linear equation

Christa is ordering CDs online. Each CD costs $16, and the shipping and handling charge is $6 for the whole order.

The total cost y depends on the number of CDs x. This function is described by the equation $y = 16x + 6$.

To find solutions of an equation with two variables, first choose a replacement value for one variable and then find the value of the other variable.

EXAMPLE **1** **Finding Solutions of Equations with Two Variables**

Use the given x-values to write solutions of the equation $y = 16x + 6$ as ordered pairs.

NY Performance Indicators

6.G.10 Identify and plot points in all four quadrants. Also, 5.G.12, 6.R.1.

Make a function table by using the given values for x to find values for y.

Write these solutions as ordered pairs.

x	$16x + 6$	y	(x, y)
1	$16(1) + 6$	22	$(1, 22)$
2	$16(2) + 6$	38	$(2, 38)$
3	$16(3) + 6$	54	$(3, 54)$
4	$16(4) + 6$	70	$(4, 70)$

Check if an ordered pair is a solution of an equation by putting the x and y values into the equation to see if they make it a true statement.

EXAMPLE **2** **Checking Solutions of Equations with Two Variables**

Determine whether the ordered pair is a solution to the given equation.

$(8, 16)$; $y = 2x$

$y = 2x$ *Write the equation.*

$16 \stackrel{?}{=} 2(8)$ *Substitute 8 for x and 16 for y.*

$16 \stackrel{?}{=} 16$ ✔

So $(8, 16)$ is a solution of $y = 2x$.

You can also graph the solutions of an equation on a coordinate plane. When you graph the ordered pairs of some functions, they form a straight line. The equations that express these functions are called **linear equations**.

EXAMPLE 3 Reading Solutions on Graphs

Use the graph of the linear function to find the value of _y_ for the given value of _x_.

$x = 1$

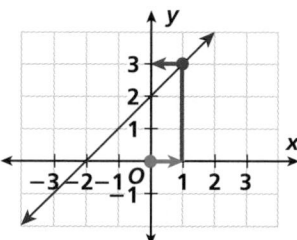

Start at the origin and move 1 unit right.

Move up until you reach the graph. Move left to find the y-value on the y-axis.

When $x = 1$, $y = 3$. The ordered pair is (1, 3).

EXAMPLE 4 Graphing Linear Functions

Graph the function described by the equation.

$y = 2x + 1$

Make a function table. Substitute different values for x.

Write the solutions as ordered pairs.

x	2x + 1	y
−1	2(−1) + 1	−1
0	2(0) + 1	1
1	2(1) + 1	3

(x, y)

(−1, −1)

(0, 1)

(1, 3)

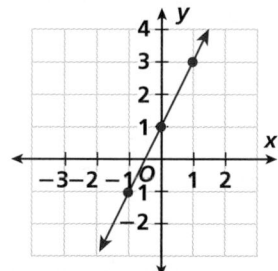

Graph the ordered pairs on a coordinate plane. Draw a line through the points to represent all the values of x you could have chosen and the corresponding values of y.

6.PS.17, 6.RP.6

Think and Discuss

1. **Explain** why the points in Example 4 are not the only points on the graph. Name two points that you did not plot.

2. **Tell** whether the equation $y = 10x - 5$ describes a linear function.

11-10 Exercises

go.hrw.com
Homework Help Online
KEYWORD: MR7 11-10
Parent Resources Online
KEYWORD: MR7 Parent

GUIDED PRACTICE

See Example **1**   Use the given x-values to write solutions of each equation as ordered pairs.

1. $y = 6x + 2$ for $x = 1, 2, 3, 4$ **2.** $y = -2x$ for $x = 1, 2, 3, 4$

See Example **2**   Determine whether each ordered pair is a solution to the given equation.

3. $(2, 12); y = 4x$ **4.** $(5, 9); y = 2x - 1$

See Example **3**   Use the graph of the linear function to find the value of y for each given value of x.

5. $x = 1$ **6.** $x = 0$ **7.** $x = -1$

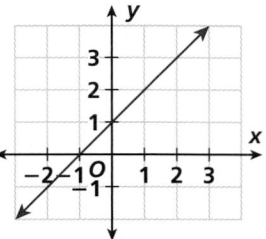

See Example **4**   Graph the function described by each equation.

8. $y = x + 3$ **9.** $y = 3x - 1$ **10.** $y = -2x + 3$

INDEPENDENT PRACTICE

See Example **1**   Use the given x-values to write solutions of each equation as ordered pairs.

11. $y = -4x + 1$ for $x = 1, 2, 3, 4$ **12.** $y = 5x - 5$ for $x = 1, 2, 3, 4$

See Example **2**   Determine whether each ordered pair is a solution to the given equation.

13. $(3, -10); y = -6x + 8$ **14.** $(-8, 1); y = 7x - 15$

See Example **3**   Use the graph of the linear function to find the value of y for each given value of x.

15. $x = -2$ **16.** $x = 1$ **17.** $x = -3$

18. $x = 0$ **19.** $x = -1$ **20.** $x = 2$

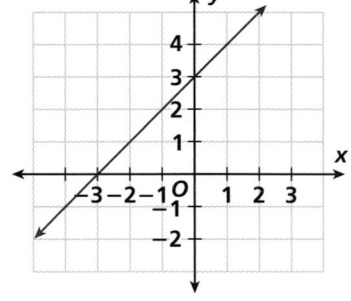

See Example **4**   Graph the function described by each equation.

21. $y = 4x + 1$ **22.** $y = -x - 2$ **23.** $y = x - 2$

24. $y = -2x - 4$ **25.** $y = 3x - 2$ **26.** $y = -x$

PRACTICE AND PROBLEM SOLVING

Extra Practice
See page 736.

Complete each table, and then use the table to graph the function.

27. $y = x - 2$

x	-1	0	1	2
y				

28. $y = 2x - 4$

x	-1	0	1	2
y				

29. Which of the ordered pairs below is not a solution of $y = 4x + 9$?
$(1, 14), (0, 9), (-1, 5), (-2, 1), (2, 17)$

Temperature can be expressed according to different scales. The Kelvin scale is divided into units called kelvins, and the Celsius scale is divided into degrees Celsius.

The table shows several temperatures recorded in degrees Celsius and their equivalent measures in kelvins.

30. Write an equation for a function that gives the values in the table. Define the variables that you use.

31. Graph the function described by your equation.

32. Use your graph to find the value of y when x is 0.

Equivalent Temperatures	
Celsius (°C)	Kelvin (K)
−100	173
−50	223
0	273
50	323
100	373

A technician preserves brain cells in this tank of liquid nitrogen, which is at −196°C, for later research.

33. Use your equation to find the equivalent Kelvin temperature for −54°C.

34. Use your equation to find the equivalent Celsius temperature for 77 kelvins.

go.hrw.com
Web Extra!
KEYWORD: MR7 Temp

35. **? What's the Question?** The answer is −273°C. What is the question?

36. **✏ Write About It** Explain how to use your equation to determine whether 75°C is equivalent to 345 kelvins. Then determine whether the temperatures are equivalent.

37. **★ Challenge** How many ordered-pair solutions exist for the equation you wrote in Exercise 30?

TEST PREP and Spiral Review

38. Multiple Choice Which of the ordered pairs is NOT a solution of $y = -5x + 10$?

Ⓐ $(-20, 6)$ 　　　Ⓑ $(5, -15)$ 　　　Ⓒ $(4, -10)$ 　　　Ⓓ $(2, 0)$

39. Multiple Choice The equation $y = 12x$ shows the number of inches y in x feet. Which ordered pair is on the graph of the equation?

Ⓕ $(-2, 24)$ 　　　Ⓖ $(1, 13)$ 　　　Ⓗ $(4, 48)$ 　　　Ⓙ $(12, 1)$

Find the mean of each data set. (Lesson 6-2)

40. 0, 5, 2, 3, 7, 1 　　　**41.** 6, 6, 6, 6, 6, 6, 6, 6, 6, 6 　　　**42.** 2, 3, 4, 5, 6, 7, 8, 1, 9

Solve each equation. Check your answers. (Lesson 11-8)

43. $\left(\dfrac{y}{-10}\right) = 12$ 　　　**44.** $p + 25 = -4$ 　　　**45.** $j - 3 = -15$ 　　　**46.** $5m = -20$

READY TO GO ON?

Quiz for Lessons 11-8 Through 11-10

☑ **11-8 Solving Integer Equations**

Solve each equation. Check your answers.

1. $5 + x = -20$ **2.** $3a = -27$ **3.** $p \div 2 = -16$ **4.** $c - 2 = -7$

5. The temperature was twice as cold on Monday as it was on Sunday. If it was $-4°F$ on Monday, how cold was it on Sunday?

☑ **11-9 Tables and Functions**

Write an equation for a function that gives the values in each table. Use the equation to find the value of *y* for each indicated value of *x*.

6.

x	2	3	4	5	8
y	7	9	11	13	▉

7.

x	1	4	5	6	8
y	▉	18	23	28	38

For Problems 8–10, write an equation for the function. Tell what each variable you use represents.

8. The number of plates is 5 less than 3 times the number of cups.

9. The time Rodney spends running is 10 minutes more than twice the time he spends stretching.

10. The height of a triangle is twice the length of its base.

11. A store manager tracked T-shirt sales. The store charges the same price for each T-shirt. On Monday, 5 shirts were sold for a total of $60. On Tuesday, 8 shirts were sold for a total of $96. On Wednesday, 11 shirts were sold for a total of $132. Write an equation for the function.

☑ **11-10 Graphing Functions**

Use the given *x*-values to write solutions of each equation as ordered pairs.

12. $y = 4x + 6$ for $x = 1, 2, 3, 4$ **13.** $y = 10x - 7$ for $x = 2, 3, 4, 5$

Use the graph of the linear function at right to find the value of *y* for each given value of *x*.

14. $x = 3$ **15.** $x = 0$

16. $x = -1$ **17.** $x = -2$

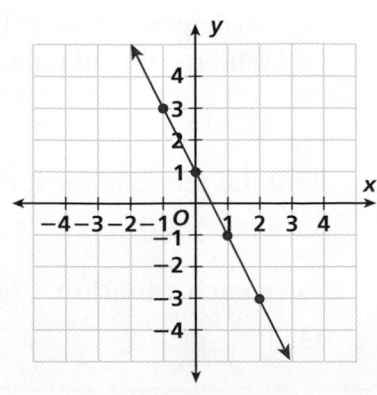

Graph the function described by each equation.

18. $y = x + 5$ **19.** $y = 3x + 2$ **20.** $y = -2x$

MULTI-STEP TEST PREP

It's All Mine Underground mines make it possible to reach coal deposits deep beneath the earth. The headframe is the only part of the mine that is visible above the ground. It contains the machinery that lowers miners into the shaft and carries the coal back to the surface. The diagram shows a typical mining operation.

1. What is the total distance the coal travels as it goes from level C to the top of the headframe?

2. How far do miners travel in the elevator as they descend from level A to level B? from level B to level C?

3. What is the mean depth of the three levels?

4. A new level is added to the mine. It is three times as deep as level A. What is the depth of the new level? Where is it located in relation to the other levels?

5. In 3 hours, each miner produces 18 tons of coal. In 5 hours, each miner produces 30 tons of coal. In 8 hours, each miner produces 48 tons of coal. Make a table and write an equation for the function.

6. Use your equation to find the number of tons of coal that each miner produces in a 40-hour work week.

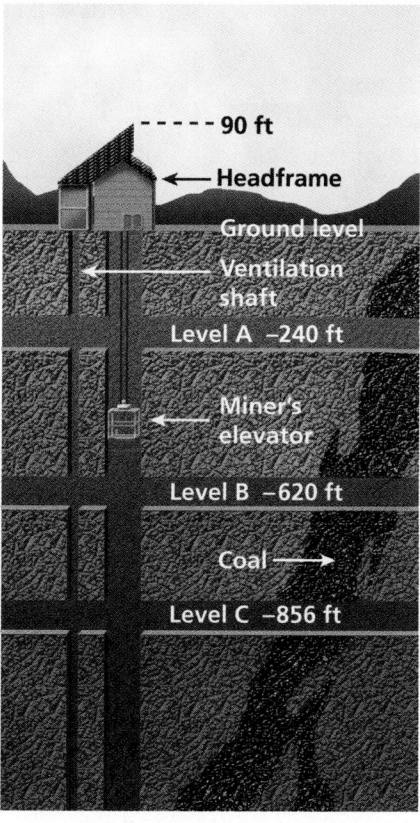

- - - - - **90 ft**

← **Headframe**

Ground level

Ventilation shaft

Level A −240 ft

Miner's elevator

Level B −620 ft

Coal →

Level C −856 ft

Multi-Step Test Prep

Integer Exponents

Learn to recognize negative exponents by examining patterns.

You have already learned about positive exponents. Exponents can be negative, too. To determine the values of negative powers, write some positive powers and look for a pattern.

EXAMPLE 1   Finding Patterns in Exponents

Find a pattern in the table.

Remember!

Exponent

$10^3 = 10 \cdot 10 \cdot 10$

Base

Power	10^3	10^2	10^1	10^0	10^{-1}	10^{-2}
Value	1,000	100	10	1	$\frac{1}{10}$	$\frac{1}{100}$

$\div 10$ $\div 10$ $\div 10$ $\div 10$ $\div 10$

One possible pattern is "divide by 10."

EXAMPLE 2   Using Patterns in Exponents

Find each value: 2^0, 2^{-1}, 2^{-2}, 2^{-3}.

Make a table like the one in Example 1. Write some powers of 2 that you know, and look for a pattern.

NY Performance Indicators

6.PS.14 Analyze problems by observing patterns. Also, 6.CN.2.

Power	2^3	2^2	2^1	2^0	2^{-1}	2^{-2}	2^{-3}
Value	8	4	2	▣	▣	▣	▣

$\div 2$ $\div 2$ $\div 2$ $\div 2$ $\div 2$ $\div 2$

One possible pattern is "divide by 2."

$$2^0 = 2 \div 2 = 1 \quad 2^{-1} = 1 \div 2 = \frac{1}{2} \quad 2^{-2} = \frac{1}{2} \div 2 = \frac{1}{4} \quad 2^{-3} = \frac{1}{4} \div 2 = \frac{1}{8}$$

Look at the table in Example 2. There is another pattern.

$$2^{-1} = \frac{1}{2^1} = \frac{1}{2} \quad\quad 2^{-2} = \frac{1}{2^2} = \frac{1}{4} \quad\quad 2^{-3} = \frac{1}{2^3} = \frac{1}{8}$$

This pattern works for all negative exponents. A number raised to a negative exponent equals 1 divided by that number raised to the opposite (positive) exponent.

Complete each table by extending the pattern.

1.

Power	3^3	3^2	3^1	3^0	3^{-1}	3^{-2}
Value	27	9	3	▨	▨	▨

2.

Power	5^{-2}	5^{-1}	5^0	5^1	5^2	5^3
Value	▨	▨	▨	5	25	125

3.

Power	6^3	6^2	6^1	6^0	6^{-1}	6^{-2}
Value	216	36	6	▨	▨	▨

Find the missing exponent.

4. $81 = 9^{\blacksquare}$

5. $\frac{1}{7} = 7^{\blacksquare}$

6. $64 = 4^{\blacksquare}$

7. $\frac{1}{64} = 8^{\blacksquare}$

8. $49 = 7^{\blacksquare}$

9. $\frac{1}{3} = 3^{\blacksquare}$

10. $25 = 5^{\blacksquare}$

11. $\frac{1}{49} = 7^{\blacksquare}$

12. $64 = 2^{\blacksquare}$

13. $\frac{1}{16} = 4^{\blacksquare}$

14. $\frac{1}{64} = 4^{\blacksquare}$

15. $\frac{1}{81} = 3^{\blacksquare}$

Find each value.

16. 8^3

17. 3^{-3}

18. 6^3

19. 9^{-3}

20. 7^{-3}

21. 4^4

22. 1^{-8}

23. 8^{-2}

24. 1^2

25. 5^{-3}

26. 4^2

27. 1^{-3}

28. For each row of the table, find the number that is not equal to the other three.

a.	10	10^{-1}	$\frac{1}{10}$	0.1
b.	27	3^3	$\frac{1}{3}$	$3 \cdot 3 \cdot 3$
c.	$\frac{1}{25}$	5^{-2}	0.04	-25

29. Critical Thinking What do you think is the value of any number raised to the 0 power?

30. Critical Thinking One million can be written as 10^6. How do you think you can write one millionth using a negative exponent? Explain your answer.

31. Write About It What is the value of 1 raised to a negative exponent? Use examples to support your answer.

32. Write About It You cannot raise 0 to a negative exponent. Why?

Game Time

A Math Riddle

What coin doubles in value when half is subtracted?

To find the answer, graph each set of points. Connect each pair of points with a straight line.

1. $(-8, 3)$ $(-6, 3)$

2. $(-9, 1)$ $(-7, 5)$

3. $(-7, 5)$ $(-5, 1)$

4. $(-3, 1)$ $(-3, 5)$

5. $(-1, 1)$ $(-1, 5)$

6. $(-3, 3)$ $(-1, 3)$

7. $(1, 1)$ $(3, 5)$

8. $(3, 5)$ $(5, 1)$

9. $(2, 3)$ $(4, 3)$

10. $(6, 1)$ $(6, 5)$

11. $(6, 1)$ $(8, 1)$

12. $(9, 1)$ $(9, 5)$

13. $(9, 5)$ $(11, 5)$

14. $(9, 3)$ $(11, 3)$

15. $(-9, -5)$ $(-9, -1)$

16. $(-9, -1)$ $(-7, -3)$

17. $(-7, -3)$ $(-9, -5)$

18. $(-6, -1)$ $(-6, -5)$

19. $(-6, -5)$ $(-4, -5)$

20. $(-4, -5)$ $(-4, -1)$

21. $(-4, -1)$ $(-6, -1)$

22. $(-3, -1)$ $(-3, -5)$

23. $(-3, -5)$ $(-1, -5)$

24. $(1, -1)$ $(1, -5)$

25. $(1, -5)$ $(3, -5)$

26. $(4, -5)$ $(6, -1)$

27. $(6, -1)$ $(8, -5)$

28. $(5, -3)$ $(7, -3)$

29. $(9, -5)$ $(9, -1)$

30. $(9, -1)$ $(11, -3)$

31. $(11, -3)$ $(9, -3)$

32. $(9, -3)$ $(11, -5)$

Zero Sum

Each card contains either a positive number, a negative number, or 0. The dealer deals three cards to each player. On your turn, you may exchange one or two of your cards for new ones, or you may keep your three original cards. After everyone has had a turn, the player whose sum is closest to 0 wins the round and receives everyone's cards. The dealer deals a new round and the game continues until the dealer runs out of cards. The winner is the player with the most cards at the end of the game.

go.hrw.com
Game Time Extra
KEYWORD: MR7 Games

A complete copy of the rules and game pieces are available online.

Materials
- business-size envelope
- ruler
- scissors
- tape
- hole punch
- chenille stem
- adding-machine tape

It's in the Bag!

PROJECT **Positive-Negative Pull-Out**

Pull questions and answers out of the bag to check your knowledge of integers and functions.

Directions

1 Seal the envelope. Then cut it in half.

2 Hold the envelope with the opening at the top. Lightly draw lines $\frac{3}{4}$ inch from the bottom and from each side. Fold the envelope back and forth along these lines until the envelope is flexible and easy to work with. **Figure A**

3 Put your hand into the envelope and push out the sides and bottom to form a bag. There will be two triangular points at the bottom of the bag. Tape these to the bottom so that the bag sits flat. **Figure B**

4 Make a 2-inch slit on the front of the bag about an inch from the bottom. Punch two holes at the top of each side of the bag and insert half of a chenille stem to make handles. **Figure C**

Taking Note of the Math

Starting at the end of the adding-machine tape, write a question about integers and functions, and then write the answer. After you have written several questions and answers, roll up the tape, place it in the bag, and pull the end through the slit.

Vocabulary

Complete the sentences below with vocabulary words from the list above.

1. For the equation $y = 3x$, the ___?___ is 12 when the ___?___ is 4.

2. The axes separate the ___?___ into four ___?___ .

11-1 Integers in Real-World Situations (pp. 602–605)

 **6.N.14**

EXAMPLE

■ **Name a positive or negative number to represent each situation.**

15 feet below sea level −15
a bank deposit of $10 +10

■ **Graph +4 on a number line.**

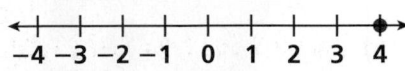
−4 −3 −2 −1 0 1 2 3 4

EXERCISES

Name a positive or negative number to represent each situation.

3. a raise of $10   **4.** a loss of $50

Graph each integer and its opposite on a number line.

5. −3   **6.** 1   **7.** −9   **8.** 0

11-2 Comparing and Ordering Integers (pp. 606–609)

 **6.N.14, 6.N.15**

EXAMPLE

■ **Compare −2 and 3. Write < or >.**

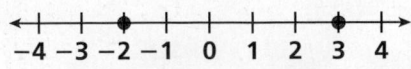
−4 −3 −2 −1 0 1 2 3 4

−2 < 3   −2 is left of 3 on the number line.

EXERCISES

Compare. Write < or >.

9. 3 ▯ 4   **10.** −2 ▯ 5   **11.** 0 ▯ 6

Order the integers in each set from least to greatest.

12. 2, −1, 4   **13.** −3, 0, 4   **14.** −6, −8, 0

11-3 The Coordinate Plane (pp. 610–613)

5.G.12, 6.G.10

EXAMPLE

- **Give the coordinates of A and name the quadrant where it is located.**

  A is in the fourth quadrant. Its coordinates are (2, –3).

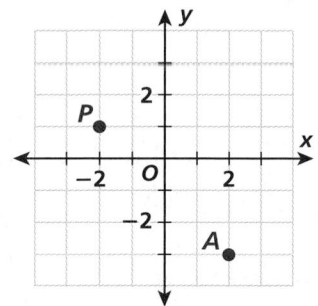

EXERCISES

Give the coordinates of each point.

15. *A*   **16.** *C*

Name the quadrant where each point is located.

17. *A*   **18.** *B*

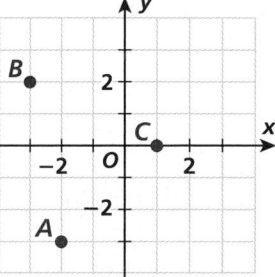

11-4 Adding Integers (pp. 617–620)

6.N.14, 6.A.2

EXAMPLE

- **Find the sum:** $3 + (-2)$.

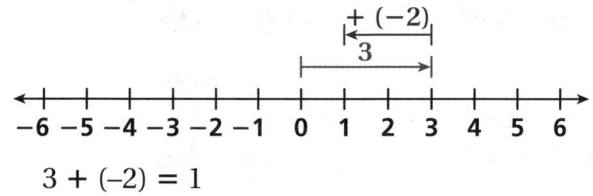

$3 + (–2) = 1$

EXERCISES

Find each sum.

19. $-4 + 2$ **20.** $4 + (-4)$

21. $3 + (-2)$ **22.** $-3 + (-2)$

Evaluate $x + 3$ for each value of x.

23. $x = -20$ **24.** $x = 5$

11-5 Subtracting Integers (pp. 622–624)

6.N.14, 6.A.2

EXAMPLE

- **Evaluate** $n - 4$ **for** $n = -1$.

  $(-1) - 4 = -5$

EXERCISES

Find each difference.

25. $-6 - 2$ **26.** $5 - (-4)$

Evaluate $x - (-1)$ for each value of x.

27. $x = 12$ **28.** $x = -7$

11-6 Multiplying Integers (pp. 625–627)

6.A.2

EXAMPLE

- **Find the product:** $3 \cdot (-2)$.

  Think: 3 groups of –2

  $3 \cdot (-2) = -6$

- **Evaluate** $-2x$ **for** $x = -4$.

  $-2(-4) = 8$

EXERCISES

Find each product.

29. $5 \cdot (-2)$ **30.** $3 \cdot 2$

31. $-3 \cdot (-2)$ **32.** $-4 \cdot 2$

Evaluate $-9y$ for each value of y.

33. $y = 2$ **34.** $y = -5$

11-7 Dividing Integers (pp. 628–631)

6.A.2

EXAMPLE

- $-24 \div 4$

  Think: $-6 \cdot 4 = -24$

  $-24 \div 4 = -6$

EXERCISES

Find each quotient.

35. $6 \div (-2)$ **36.** $9 \div 3$

37. $-14 \div (-7)$ **38.** $-4 \div 2$

11-8 Solving Integer Equations (pp. 636–639)

5.A.4, 5.A.5

EXAMPLE

- Solve $x + 4 = 18$.

  $x + 4 = 18$

  $\underline{-4 \quad -4}$ *Subtract 4 from both sides.*

  $x \quad\quad = 14$

EXERCISES

Solve each equation. Check your answers.

39. $w - 5 = -1$ **40.** $\frac{a}{-4} = 3$

41. $2q = -14$ **42.** $x + 3 = -2$

11-9 Tables and Functions (pp. 640–643)

6.PS.14

EXAMPLE

- Write an equation for a function that gives the values in the table. Use the equation to find the value of y for the indicated value of x.

x	2	3	4	5	6	12
y	5	8	11	14	17	

  y is 3 times x minus 1. *Find a pattern.*

  $y = 3x - 1$ *Write an equation.*

  $y = 3(12) - 1$ *Substitute 12 for x.*

  $y = 36 - 1 = 35$

EXERCISES

Write an equation for a function that gives the values in each table. Use the equation to find the value of y for each indicated value of x.

43.

x	2	3	4	5	6	8
y	6	8	10	12	14	

Write an equation to describe the function. Tell what each variable you use represents.

44. The length of a rectangle is 4 times its width.

11-10 Graphing Functions (pp. 646–649)

5.G.12, 6.G.10

EXAMPLE

- Graph the function described by the equation $y = 3x + 4$.

  Make a table.   *Write as ordered pairs.*

x	3x + 4	y		(x, y)
-2	3(-2) + 4	-2		(-2, -2)
-1	3(-1) + 4	1		(-1, 1)
0	3(0) + 4	4		(0, 4)

  Graph the ordered pairs on a coordinate plane.

EXERCISES

Use the given x-values to write solutions of each equation as ordered pairs.

45. $y = 2x - 5$ for $x = 1, 2, 3, 4$

46. $y = x + 7$ for $x = 1, 2, 3, 4$

Determine whether each ordered pair is a solution to the given equation.

47. $(3, 12)$; $y = 5x - 3$ **48.** $(6, 14)$; $y = x + 7$

Study Guide: Review

Name a positive or negative number to represent each situation.

1. 30° below zero
2. a bank deposit of $75
3. a loss of 5 yards

4. On the first down of a football game, the quarterback threw for a 6-yard gain. On the second down, he was sacked for a 4-yard loss. On the third down, he ran for a 2-yard gain. Use integers to model this situation.

Compare. Write $<$ or $>$.

5. -4 ▨ 4
6. 2 ▨ -9
7. -10 ▨ 8
8. -2 ▨ -12

Order each set of integers from least to greatest.

9. $21, -19, 34$
10. $-16, -2, 13, 46$
11. $-10, 0, 25, -7, 18$

Graph each point on a coordinate plane.

12. $A(2, 3)$
13. $B(3, -2)$
14. $C(-1, 3)$
15. $D\left(-1, 2\frac{1}{2}\right)$
16. $E(0, 1)$

Add, subtract, multiply, or divide.

17. $-4 + 4$
18. $-2 - 9$
19. $-3 \cdot 8$
20. $12 \div (-3)$
21. $-48 \div (-4)$
22. $13 + (-9)$
23. $8 - (-11)$
24. $-7 \cdot (-6)$

Evaluate each expression for the given value of the variable.

25. $n + 3, n = -10$
26. $9 - x, x = -9$
27. $4m, m = -6$
28. $\frac{15}{a}, a = -3$
29. $(-11) + z, z = 28$
30. $w - (-8), w = 13$

Solve each equation.

31. $\frac{b}{7} = -3$
32. $-9 \cdot f = -81$
33. $r - 14 = -32$
34. $y + 17 = 22$

Write an equation for a function that gives the values in each table. Use the equation to find the value of y for each indicated value of x.

35.

x	2	3	4	5	6	7
y	▨	8	11	14	17	20

36.

x	1	2	3	4	5	9
y	8	10	12	14	16	▨

Write an equation for the function. Tell what each variable you use represents.

37. The number of buttons on the jacket is 4 more than the number of zippers.

38. The length of a parallelogram is 2 in. more than twice the height.

Use the given x-values to write solutions of each equation as ordered pairs. Then graph the function described by each equation.

39. $y = 5x - 3$ for $x = 1, 2, 3, 4$
40. $y = 2x - 3$ for $x = 0, 1, 2, 3$

Multiple Choice: Identifying Keywords and Context Clues

When reading a test item, pay attention to key words and context clues given in the problem statement. These clues will guide you in providing a correct response.

EXAMPLE 1

Which angle is obtuse?

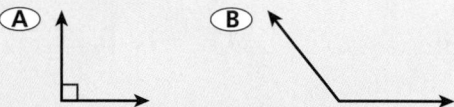 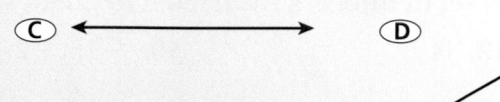 

- Look for context clues. Identify what they mean.
- In this test item, **obtuse** is the context clue. It means an angle whose measure is **greater than** 90°.

Find the choice that shows an **obtuse** angle.

A: This angle's measure is 90° because it has a right angle symbol.

B: This angle's measure is greater than 90°. It is an obtuse angle.

C: This angle's measure is 180° because it is a straight angle.

D: This angle's measure is less than 90°. It is an acute angle.

The correct answer is B.

EXAMPLE 2

Kenneth makes flower deliveries along Oak Street. He starts at the flower shop on Oak Street. His first delivery is 8 blocks directly west of the shop. His second delivery takes him 4 blocks directly east of his first delivery. His third delivery takes him 5 blocks east of his second delivery. Write an expression using integers to model this situation.

    F $-4 - 5 + 8$ **G** $8 + 4 - 5$ **H** $-8 - 4 - 5$ **J** $-8 + 4 + 5$

- Look for key words.
- In this test item, the key words are **expression** and **integers.**

Find the choice that shows the correct **integer expression** to model the situation.

F: The first delivery is 8 blocks west. This expression does not begin with –8.

G: The first delivery is 8 blocks west. This expression does not begin with –8.

H: The expression begins with −8, but 4 blocks east would be + 4.

J: This expression's integers correctly correspond to the deliveries.

The correct answer is J.

Test Tackler

Read each test item and answer the questions that follow.

Item A
Multiple Choice Jenny is trimming the edges of a card with ribbon. The rectangular card measures 8 inches by 12 inches. How much ribbon does Jenny need to trim the card?

- Ⓐ 36 inches
- Ⓑ 40 inches
- Ⓒ 64 inches
- Ⓓ 72 inches

1. What are the dimensions of the card?

2. Which words in the problem statement are clues that you need to find the perimeter of the card?

3. When you calculate the perimeter, why are the units not given in square units?

Item B
Multiple Choice Sam has two cylinders. One cylinder has a height of 25 cm and a diameter of 8 cm. The other cylinder has a height of 15 cm and a diameter of 20 cm. What is the difference between the volumes of the two cylinders?

- Ⓕ $400\pi\,cm^3$
- Ⓖ $1,100\pi\,cm^3$
- Ⓗ $1,500\pi\,cm^3$
- Ⓙ $4,400\pi\,cm^3$

4. Make a list of the key words given in the problem statement and link each word to its mathematical meaning.

5. Which choice, if any, can be eliminated? Why?

Item C
Multiple Choice Madeline has 28 daisies and 42 violets. Find the GCF to find the greatest number of wrist corsages that can be made if each corsage has the same number of daisies and the same number of violets.

- Ⓐ 4
- Ⓑ 7
- Ⓒ 14
- Ⓓ 21

6. What is the math term that describes what is being tested?

7. Identify the keywords in this problem statement.

Item D
Multiple Choice An office supply store states that 4 out of 5 customers would recommend the store to another person. Given this information, what percent of customers would NOT recommend the office supply store to someone else?

- Ⓕ 10%
- Ⓖ 20%
- Ⓗ 40%
- Ⓙ 80%

8. What information is needed to solve this problem?

9. Which choice can be eliminated immediately? Why?

10. Write a proportion to find the percent of customers who would recommend the office store to someone else.

11. Describe two different ways to solve this problem.

Test Tackler

Cumulative Assessment, Chapters 1–11

Multiple Choice

1. Marla bought a shirt on sale for $22, which was $\frac{1}{8}$ off the original price. What decimal represents the discount received?

- (A) 0.125
- (C) 0.725
- (B) 0.225
- (D) 0.825

2. William is bringing small bottles of fruit juice for the company picnic. There are 154 people coming to the company picnic. If the drinks come in packages of 6, how many packages will William need to buy so that each guest can have 3 drinks?

- (F) 20 boxes
- (H) 75 boxes
- (G) 26 boxes
- (J) 77 boxes

3. Ashlee has 36 basketballs, 48 bean bags, and 60 flying disks. She is making playground sets for the teachers. She wants to put the same number of basketballs, bean bags, and flying disks in each set. What is the greatest number of sets she can make if she uses all of the items?

- (A) 3
- (C) 12
- (B) 6
- (D) 18

4. At 5:30 P.M., 75% of the people at company A had gone home. What fraction of people had NOT yet gone home?

- (F) $\frac{3}{4}$
- (H) $\frac{1}{4}$
- (G) $\frac{1}{2}$
- (J) $\frac{1}{25}$

5. What is the ratio of the number of students who play the drums to the number of students who play the trumpet? Give the ratio in simplest form.

School Band	
Instrument	**Number of Students**
Drums	10
Trombone	14
Trumpet	8
Tuba	3

- (A) 10 to 3
- (C) 5 to 7
- (B) 5 to 4
- (D) 10 to 27

6. If $\angle KHG$ and $\angle JHM$ are congruent, what is the measure of $\angle GHJ$?

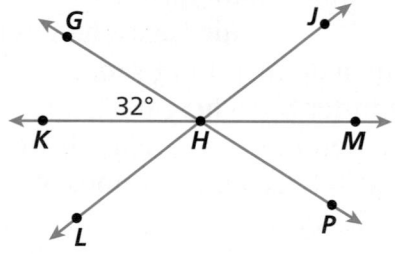

- (F) 148°
- (H) 108°
- (G) 116°
- (J) 96°

7. What is the reciprocal of $1\frac{3}{5}$?

- (A) $-1\frac{3}{5}$
- (C) $\frac{8}{5}$
- (B) $\frac{5}{8}$
- (D) 8

8. Find the prime factorization of 80.

- (F) $2 \cdot 5^2$
- (H) $2^3 \cdot 10$
- (G) $2^2 \cdot 5$
- (J) $2^4 \cdot 5$

9. Louie buys a baseball bat for $125, a catcher's mitt for $55, and a baseball for $3. The tax rate is 5%. If Louie gives the cashier $200, how much change will he get back?

    (A) $6.15   (C) $9.25

    (B) $7.85   (D) $10.75

10. There are 4 shows a day at the local performing arts theater. The first show starts at 10:15 A.M. Each show lasts 30 minutes, and there is a 1 hour and 30 minute break between shows. What time does the third show end?

    (F) 12:15 P.M.   (H) 2:45 P.M.

    (G) 12:45 P.M.   (J) 3:15 P.M.

 **Hot Tip** When adding integers, move right on a number line to add a positive number and move left on a number line to add a negative number.

11. Wyatt has received the following scores on his chapter spelling tests: 92, 98, 90, 97, and 92. What is the mean score of Wyatt's spelling tests?

    (A) 92   (C) 94.5

    (B) 93.8   (D) 97

12. Joshua runs 35% of the way from his house to the gym. If the gym is 5 miles from Joshua's house, how many miles does Joshua run on his way to the gym?

    (F) 1.75   (H) 3.5

    (G) 2.25   (J) 4

13. What is 65 cm expressed in meters?

    (A) 0.065   (C) 6.5

    (B) 0.65   (D) 650

Short Response

14. On Monday, the balance in Graham's checking account was $32. On Tuesday, he wrote three $18 checks. After a deposit on Wednesday, his balance was $15.

    a. Find Graham's balance on Tuesday.

    b. Write and solve an equation that can be used to find the amount of Graham's deposit. Let $d =$ the amount of Graham's deposit. Show your work.

15. Find the coordinates of the vertices of the yellow square. Then explain how to find the new coordinates of the square after it is translated 5 units down and 3 units left.

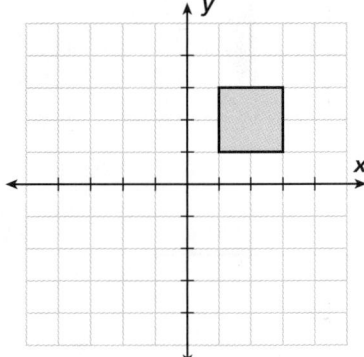

Extended Response

16. A store sold 44 art masks in September for $528. In October, the store sold 41 art masks for $492. In November, the store sold 38 art masks for $456. All the masks cost the same.

    a. Make a table to display the data, and then graph the data. Is the function linear? Explain your answer.

    b. Write an equation to represent the function. Tell what each variable represents.

    c. In December, the store sold 67 masks. What were the total mask sales in December?

Probability

NEW YORK TEST PREP

go.hrw.com
Chapter Project Online
KEYWORD: MR7 Ch12

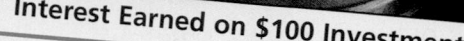

Interest Earned on $100 Investment				
Years Invested	Interest (compounded annually)			
	7%	8%	9%	10%
1	$7	$8	$9	$10
2	$14	$17	$19	$21
5	$40	$47	$54	$61
10	$97	$116	$137	$159

Career *Financial Advisor*

We all must decide how much money to spend and how much to invest and save for the future. Financial advisors help people make these decisions.

Financial advisors must understand the relationship between risk and earnings. An investment with a high probability of returning a profit is less risky than an investment with a lower probability of returning a profit. However, riskier investments may return larger profits. The table lists returns for different investments with different interest rates. Which investment is the most risky? Which do you think is the safest?

ARE YOU READY?

✓ Vocabulary

Choose the best term from the list to complete each sentence.

1. The denominator of a fraction represents the _____?_____, and the numerator represents the _____?_____.

2. Fractions that represent the same value are _____?_____ fractions.

3. A _____?_____ is a comparison of two quantities by division.

4. Tally marks in a table show the _____?_____, or total, for each result.

5. A ratio of a number to 100 is called a _____?_____.

equivalent

frequency

part

percent

ratio

simplest form

table

whole

Complete these exercises to review skills you will need for this chapter.

✓ Model Fractions

Write the fraction in simplest form that represents the shaded portion.

6. 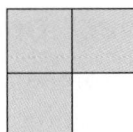 7. 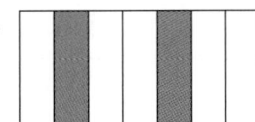 8.

✓ Write Fractions as Decimals

Write each fraction as a decimal.

9. $\frac{9}{10}$ 10. $\frac{1}{2}$ 11. $\frac{12}{25}$ 12. $\frac{11}{20}$

✓ Compare Fractions, Decimals, and Percents

Compare. Write <, >, or =.

13. 0.35 ▧ 0.4 14. 0.25 ▧ 25% 15. $\frac{3}{5}$ ▧ 0.7 16. 0.5 ▧ $\frac{23}{50}$

✓ Write Ratios

Write each ratio.

17. blue circles to total circles

18. squares to triangles

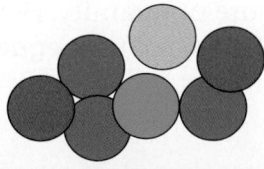 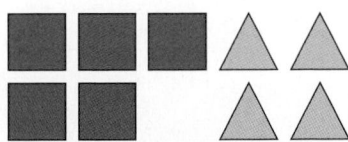

Study Guide: Preview

Where You've Been

Previously, you

- listed all possible outcomes of a probability experiment.
- used fractions to describe the results of an experiment.
- generated equivalent forms of rational numbers.

In This Chapter

You will study

- finding sample spaces using lists and tree diagrams.
- finding the probabilities of simple events and their complements.
- expressing probabilities as fractions, decimals, and percents.
- finding probabilities of compound events.

Where You're Going

You can use the skills learned in this chapter

- to find probabilities involving permutations and combinations.
- to find odds for and against specified outcomes.

Key Vocabulary/Vocabulario

complement	complemento
compound event	suceso compuesto
equally likely	igualmente probables
experiment	experimento (probabilidad)
experimental probability	probabilidad experimental
outcome	resultado (probabilidad)
prediction	predicción
probability	probabilidad
theoretical probability	probabilidad teórica

Vocabulary Connections

To become familiar with some of the vocabulary terms in the chapter, consider the following. You may refer to the chapter, the glossary, or a dictionary if you like.

1. The word *experiment* can mean "the process of testing." What do you think **experimental probability** is based on?

2. The word *compound* can mean "composed of separate elements." Do you think a **compound event** is made up of one event? Why or why not?

3. To *predict* something means to "foretell on the basis of observation, experience, or scientific reason." What do you think a **prediction** is?

4. When things are *equal,* they are of the same measure or quantity. How do you think the chances of two **equally likely** events compare?

 **Reading** and *Writing* **Math**

Study Strategy: Prepare for Your Final Exam

In your math class, you use skills that you have learned throughout the year, so most final exams cover material from the beginning of the course.

A timeline and checklist like the one shown can help you study for the final exam in an organized way.

2 weeks before the final exam I will:

- Gather my notes.
- Review lessons.
- Make a list of all formulas I will probably need to know.
- Create a practice exam using problems from the book that have answers.
- Go over any missed problems from previous tests and quizzes.
- Ask about any concepts that are difficult.

1 week before the final exam I will:

- Take the practice exam and check my answers.
- For each problem I miss, find 2 or 3 other similar problems and work them.
- Look over the *Study Guide: Review* at the end of each chapter.
- Work with a friend from class to quiz each other on formulas from my list and other major concepts.

1 day before the final exam I will:

Make sure I have:
- Sharpened pencils with erasers.
- Calculator (if allowed) with fresh batteries.
- Any other math tools I may need.
- Make sure I get a good night's sleep.

FINAL

Try This

1. Create a timeline and checklist of your own to help you prepare for your final exam.

Reading and Writing Math

12-1 Introduction to Probability

Learn to estimate the likelihood of an event and to write and compare probabilities.

Vocabulary

probability

NY Performance Indicators

6.CM.10 Use appropriate vocabulary when describing objects, relationships, mathematical solutions, and rationale.

The weather report gives a 5% chance of rain today. Will you wear your raincoat? What if the report gives a 95% chance of rain?

In this situation, you are using probability to help make a decision. **Probability** is the measure of how likely an event is to occur. In this case, both 5% and 95% are probabilities of rain.

Probabilities are written as fractions or decimals from 0 to 1 or as percents from 0% to 100%. The higher an event's probability, the more likely that event is to happen.

- Events with a probability of 0, or 0%, never happen.
- Events with a probability of 1, or 100%, always happen.
- Events with a probability of 0.5, or 50%, have the same chance of happening as of not happening.

| Impossible | Unlikely | As likely as not | Likely | Certain |

0   0.5   1
0% $\frac{1}{2}$ 100%
                       50%

A 95% chance of rain means rain is highly likely. A 5% chance of rain means rain is highly unlikely.

EXAMPLE 1 **Estimating the Likelihood of an Event**

Write *impossible, unlikely, as likely as not, likely,* or *certain* to describe each event.

Helpful Hint

A standard number cube is numbered from 1 to 6.

A The month of June has 30 days.

certain

B A coin toss comes up heads.

as likely as not

C You roll a 9 on a standard number cube.

impossible

D This spinner lands on red.

likely

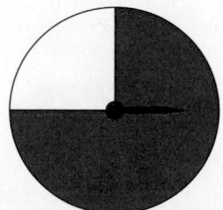

EXAMPLE 2 Writing Probabilities

A The weather report gives a 35% chance of rain for tomorrow. Write this probability as a decimal and as a fraction.

$35\% = 0.35$ *Write as a decimal.*

$35\% = \frac{35}{100} = \frac{7}{20}$ *Write as a fraction in simplest form.*

B The chance that Ethan is chosen to represent his class in the student council is 0.6. Write this probability as a fraction and as a percent.

$0.6 = \frac{6}{10} = \frac{3}{5}$ *Write as a fraction in simplest form.*

$0.6 = 60\%$ *Write as a percent.*

C There is a $\frac{9}{25}$ chance of getting a green gumball out of a certain machine. Write this probability as a decimal and as a percent.

$\frac{9}{25} = 9 \div 25 = 0.36$ *Write as a decimal.*

$\frac{9}{25} = \frac{9 \cdot 4}{25 \cdot 4} = \frac{36}{100} = 36\%$ *Write as a percent.*

> **Helpful Hint**
>
> In Example 2C, after you find the decimal form of $\frac{9}{25}$, you can use it to find the percent.
>
> $0.36 = 36\%$

EXAMPLE 3 Comparing Probabilities

A On a flowering plant called the four o'clock, there is a 50% chance the flowers will be pink, a 25% chance the flowers will be white, and a 25% chance the flowers will be red. Is it more likely that the flowers will be pink or white?

Compare: $50\% > 25\%$

The flowers are more likely to be pink than white.

B When you spin this spinner, there is a 25% chance that it will land on red, a 50% chance that it will land on yellow, and a 25% chance that it will land on blue. Is it more likely to land on red or on blue?

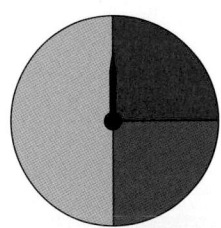

Compare: $25\% = 25\%$

It is as likely to land on red as on blue.

Think and Discuss

1. Give an example of a situation that involves probability.

2. Name events that can be described by each of the following terms: *impossible, likely, as likely as not, unlikely,* and *certain.*

12-1 **Exercises**

go.hrw.com
Homework Help Online
KEYWORD: MR7 12-1
Parent Resources Online
KEYWORD: MR7 Parent

GUIDED PRACTICE

See Example **1** Write *impossible*, *unlikely*, *as likely as not*, *likely*, or *certain* to describe each event.

1. This year has 12 months.   **2.** You win the lottery.

See Example **2** **3.** Suppose that the chance of reaching into a bag of coins and selecting a quarter is 40%. Write this probability as a decimal and as a fraction.

See Example **3** **4.** If there are two children in a family, there is a 25% chance that both children are boys, a 25% chance that both children are girls, and a 50% chance that one child is a boy and the other is a girl. Which is more likely, that both children are boys or that one child is a boy and the other is a girl?

INDEPENDENT PRACTICE

See Example **1** Write *impossible*, *unlikely*, *as likely as not*, *likely*, or *certain* to describe each event.

5. The spinner at right lands on green.

6. The spinner at right lands on blue.

7. You guess one winning number between 1 and 500.

8. You correctly guess one of eight winning numbers between 1 and 10.

See Example **2** **9.** **Sports** The chance of Jill's missing a free throw is $\frac{3}{10}$. Write this probability as a decimal and as a percent.

See Example **3** **10.** The probability of Daniel randomly selecting a long-sleeved shirt from his closet is 0.20. Write this probability as a fraction and a percent.

11. If you choose from a bag of mixed nuts, there is a 45% chance of choosing a peanut, a 20% chance of choosing a pecan, a 15% chance of choosing a cashew, and a 20% chance of choosing a walnut. Is it less likely that you will choose a pecan or a cashew from the bag?

PRACTICE AND PROBLEM SOLVING

Extra Practice
See page 737.

Describe the events as *impossible*, *unlikely*, *as likely as not*, *likely*, or *certain*.

12. The probability of winning a game is $\frac{2}{3}$.

13. The probability of being chosen for a team is 0.09.

14. There is a 50% chance of snow today.

15. Your chances of being struck by lightning are $\frac{1}{2,000,000}$.

16. **Critical Thinking** Why is the event *It will be Saturday in one of the next 7 days* certain?

Each year, millions of people donate blood.

There are eight different human blood types, which are shown in the chart, along with the percent of people who have each type. It is very important that people receive the right type of blood. If they do not, their bodies will not recognize the foreign blood cells and will attack the cells.

17. How would you describe the probability of a person having AB positive blood: impossible, unlikely, as likely as not, likely, or certain? Explain.

18. If a person is randomly chosen, which blood type is he or she most likely to have?

19. If a person is randomly chosen, which blood type is he or she least likely to have?

20. Write the probability that a randomly chosen person will have A negative blood as a decimal and as a fraction in simplest form.

21.  **Write About It** Blood banks especially encourage people with certain types of blood to donate. Which blood types do you think these are? Explain.

22. ★ **Challenge** A person with AB positive blood can safely receive O, A, B, or AB blood. What is the probability that a randomly chosen person could donate blood to a person with AB positive blood?

The donated blood in these bags is Type O.

Blood Types in the United States

O negative, 7%

B positive, 9%

O positive, 38%

A positive, 34%

A negative, 6%

AB positive, 3% B negative, 2% AB negative, 1%

go.hrw.com
Web Extra!
KEYWORD: MR7 Blood

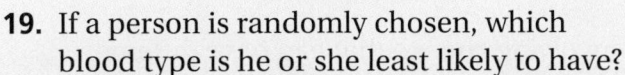

TEST PREP and Spiral Review

23. **Multiple Choice** Eddie has a $\frac{9}{20}$ chance of winning the election. What is the probability of Eddie winning the election written as a percent?

　Ⓐ 0.45　　　　Ⓑ 0.55　　　　Ⓒ 45%　　　　Ⓓ 55%

24. **Gridded Response** There is a $\frac{7}{10}$ chance of rain today. What is this probability written as a decimal?

Write the prime factorization of each number. (Lesson 4-2)

25. 76　　　　26. 12　　　　27. 16　　　　28. 18　　　　29. 128

Find each missing value to the nearest hundredth. Use 3.14 for π. (Lesson 9-8)

30. $d = 2$ in.; $C = ?$　　　31. $r = 5$ cm; $C = ?$　　　32. $C = 28.26$ m; $d = ?$

Experimental Probability

Learn to find the experimental probability of an event.

Vocabulary

experiment

outcome

experimental probability

Four Possibilities

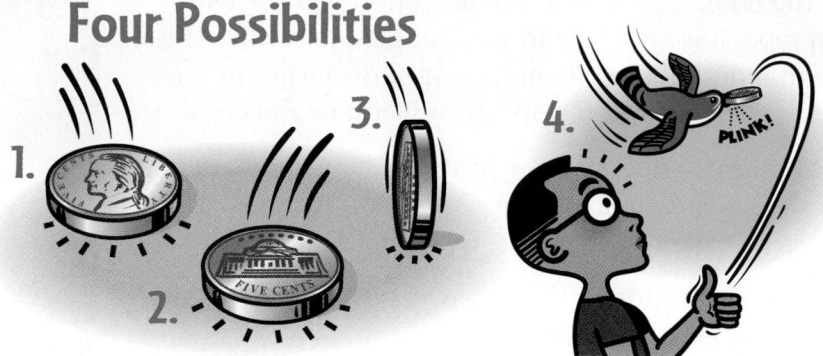

1.

2.

3.

4.

An **experiment** is an activity involving chance that can have different results. Flipping a coin and spinning a spinner are examples of experiments.

The different results that can occur are called **outcomes** of the experiment. If you are flipping a coin, heads is one possible outcome.

E X A M P L E **Identifying Outcomes**

For each experiment, identify the outcome shown.

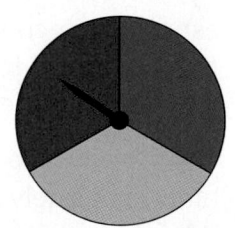

A spinning a spinner

outcome shown: red

B tossing two coins

outcome shown: heads, tails (H, T)

C rolling two number cubes

outcome shown: (3, 5)

 NY Performance Indicators

5.S.5 List the possible outcomes for a single-event experiment. Also, 5.S.6.

Performing an experiment is one way to estimate the probability of an event. If an experiment is repeated many times, the **experimental probability** of an event is the ratio of the number of times the event occurs to the total number of times the experiment is performed.

EXPERIMENTAL PROBABILITY

$$\text{probability} \approx \frac{\text{number of times the event occurs}}{\text{total number of trials}}$$

EXAMPLE 2 **Finding Experimental Probability**

For one month, Tosha recorded the time at which her school bus arrived. She organized her results in a frequency table.

Time	7:00–7:04	7:05–7:09	7:10–7:14
Frequency	8	9	3

Writing Math

The probability of an event can be written as *P*(event). *P*(blue) means "the probability that blue will be the outcome."

A Find the experimental probability that the bus will arrive between 7:00 and 7:04.

$$P(\text{between 7:00 and 7:04}) \approx \frac{\text{number of times the event occurs}}{\text{total number of trials}}$$

$$= \frac{8}{20} = \frac{2}{5}$$

B Find the experimental probability that the bus will arrive before 7:10.

$$P(\text{before 7:10}) \approx \frac{\text{number of times the event occurs}}{\text{total number of trials}}$$

$$= \frac{8+9}{20} \qquad \textit{Before 7:10 includes 7:00–7:04 and 7:05–7:09.}$$

$$= \frac{17}{20}$$

EXAMPLE 3 **Comparing Experimental Probabilities**

Ian tossed a cone 30 times and recorded whether it landed on its base or on its side. Based on Ian's experiment, which way is the cone more likely to land?

On its side   On its base

Outcome	On its base	On its side
Frequency	JHT II	JHT JHT JHT JHT III

$$P(\text{base}) \approx \frac{\text{number of times the event occurs}}{\text{total number of trials}} = \frac{7}{30}$$

$$P(\text{side}) \approx \frac{\text{number of times the event occurs}}{\text{total number of trials}} = \frac{23}{30}$$

Find the experimental probability of each outcome.

$$\frac{7}{30} < \frac{23}{30} \qquad \textit{Compare the probabilities.}$$

It is more likely that the cone will land on its side.

Think and Discuss

1. **Explain** whether you and a friend will get the same experimental probability for an event if you perform the same experiment.

2. **Tell** why it is important to repeat an experiment many times.

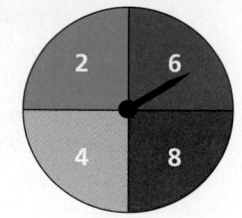
go.hrw.com
Homework Help Online
KEYWORD: MR7 12-2
Parent Resources Online
KEYWORD: MR7 Parent

GUIDED PRACTICE

See Example ① **1.** Identify the outcome shown on the spinner.

Sports Josh recorded the number of hits his favorite baseball player made in each of 15 games. He organized his results in a frequency table.

Number of Hits	0	1	2	3
Frequency	4	8	2	1

See Example ② **2.** Find the experimental probability that this player will get one hit in a game.

See Example ③ **3.** Based on Josh's results, is this player more likely to get two hits in a game or no hits in a game? How many hits will this player most likely get in a game?

INDEPENDENT PRACTICE

See Example ① **For each experiment, identify the outcome shown.**

4.

5.

Jennifer has a bag of marbles. She removed one marble, recorded the color, and placed it back in the bag. She repeated this process several times and recorded her results in the table.

See Example ② **6.** Find the experimental probability that a marble selected from the bag will be red.

7. Find the experimental probability that a marble selected from the bag will not be black.

See Example ③ **8.** Based on Jennifer's experiment, which color marble is she most likely to select from the bag?

Color	Frequency
White	
Red	///
Yellow	
Black	JHT JHT //

PRACTICE AND PROBLEM SOLVING

Extra Practice
See page 737.

Identify the outcome for each situation.

9.

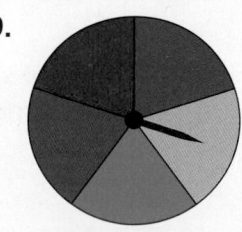

10.

11. Weather Janet recorded the high temperature every day in January. She recorded her results in a frequency table.

Temperature (°F)	26–35	36–45	46–55	56–65
Number of Days	10	9	11	1

According to Janet's results, what is the probability that a day in January will be warmer than 55°F? Describe this probability as certain, likely, as likely as not, unlikely, or impossible.

12. Mariana recorded the results of spinning a spinner with 3 sections.

Outcome	Red	Blue	Green
Spins	25	19	56

a. Use the results in the table to find the experimental probability of the spinner landing on each color.

b. Which section of the spinner do you think might be the greatest? Explain.

 13. Write About It Conduct an experiment in which you toss a coin 100 times. Keep a tally of the number of times the coin shows heads. According to your results, what is the experimental probability that it will show heads? Compare your results with a classmate. Did you both get the same experimental probability? Why or why not?

 14. Challenge Suppose you roll two number cubes and add the two numbers that come up. What do you think the most likely sum would be? (*Hint:* Perform an experiment.)

TEST PREP and Spiral Review

15. Multiple Choice Identify the outcome shown on the spinner.

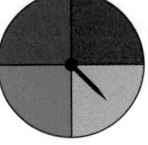

Ⓐ blue   Ⓒ red

Ⓑ green   Ⓓ yellow

16. Multiple Choice Sam plays baseball. Five of his games started at 5:00 P.M. Four started at 5:15 P.M. One started at 5:45 P.M. What is the experimental probability that his next game will start at 5:00 P.M.?

Ⓕ $\frac{1}{10}$ Ⓖ $\frac{2}{5}$ Ⓗ $\frac{1}{2}$ Ⓙ $\frac{9}{10}$

Evaluate each expression for $x = 5$. (Lesson 2-1)

17. $x + 7$ **18.** $4x$ **19.** $3x + 6$ **20.** $x + 5$ **21.** $2x - 7$

22. Arthur has a 91% chance of making a free throw. His brother Lance has a 93% chance of making a free throw. Is it more likely that Arthur or Lance will make the free throw? (Lesson 12-1)

Hands-On LAB 12-2

Simulations

Use with Lesson 12-2

go.hrw.com
Lab Resources Online
KEYWORD: MR7 Lab12

NY Performance Indicators
6.S.2, 6.PS.10, 6.PS.15

A **simulation** is a model of an experiment that would be difficult or inconvenient to actually perform. In this lab, you will conduct simulations.

Activity

A cereal company is having a contest. To win a prize, you must collect six different cards that spell *YOU WIN*. One of the six letters is put into each cereal box. The letters are divided equally among the boxes. How many boxes do you think you will have to buy to collect all six cards?

1 Since there are six different cards that are evenly distributed, you can use a number cube to simulate collecting the letters. Each of the numbers from 1 to 6 will represent a letter. A roll of the number cube will simulate buying one box of cereal, and the number rolled will represent the letter inside that box.

1	2	3	4	5	6
Y	O	U	W	I	N
/	~~IIII~~ I	IIII	II	II	I

2 Roll the number cube, and keep track of the numbers you roll. Continue to roll the number cube until you have rolled every number at least once.

Think and Discuss

1. Look at the results in the table above. What was the last number rolled? How do you know?

2. How many rolls did it take to get all six numbers in your simulation?

3. How many boxes of cereal do you think you would have to buy to get all six letters? If you bought this many boxes, would you be sure to win? Explain.

Try This

1. Repeat the simulation three more times. Record your results.

2. Combine your data with the data of 5 of your classmates. Find the mean number of rolls from all 6 sets of data.

3. How many boxes of cereal do you think you would have to buy to get all six letters? Is this number different from what you thought after the first simulation? Explain.

Activity 2

Amy is a basketball player who usually makes $\frac{1}{2}$ of the baskets that she attempts. Suppose she attempts 20 shots in each game. If she plays ten games, in how many games do you think she will make at least four baskets in a row?

① There are two possible outcomes every time Amy shoots the ball—either she will make the basket or she will miss. Since Amy makes $\frac{1}{2}$ of her shots, you can toss a coin to simulate one shot. Let heads represent making the basket, and let tails represent missing.

② Toss the coin 20 times to simulate one game. Keep track of your results.

③ Repeat **②** nine more times to simulate ten games.

Trial	Results
1	THTHHTTHTTHTHTTHHHTT
2	HHTTTHTHTHHHHHTTHTHT
3	HTTTHTTTHTHTTTHTTHTT
4	HTHTHTHTHTTHTHTTTTTT
5	THTTTTHHTHTHHTHTTHTT
6	HTTHTHHHHHTHHHHHHHHH
7	TTHHTTHHHHTHTHHTTHTTT
8	HTTHTTHTTTHHTTHTTHTT
9	HHHTTTTTHHHHHHTHHTHHT
10	HTTHHTTHHHHTHHTHTHHHH

Think and Discuss

1. Why does tossing a coin 20 times represent only one trial?

2. Do any of your sequences contain four or more heads in a row? How many?

3. In how many games do you think Amy will make at least four baskets in a row? Out of *every* ten games, will Amy always make at least four baskets in a row this number of times?

4. You can use your simulation to find the experimental probability that Amy will make at least four or more baskets in a row. Divide the number of trials in which the coin came up heads at least four times in a row by the total number of trials. What is the experimental probability that Amy will make at least four baskets in a row?

5. Suppose Amy made only $\frac{1}{3}$ of her shots. Would you still be able to use a coin as a simulation? Why or why not?

Try This

1. In a group of ten families that each have four children, how many families do you think will have two girls and two boys? Make a prediction, and then design and carry out a simulation to answer this question. (Assume that having a boy and having a girl are equally likely events.) Was your prediction close?

2. Use your results from the previous problem to give the experimental probability that a family with four children will have two girls and two boys.

3. Think of an experiment, and design your own simulation to model it.

12-3 Counting Methods and Sample Spaces

Learn to use counting methods to find all possible outcomes.

Vocabulary

sample space

Sample spaces are used in finding probability. The **sample space** for an experiment is all the possible outcomes. You can use { } to show sample spaces.

When you need to find many possible outcomes, you can make a tree diagram. A tree diagram is one way to organize information.

EXAMPLE  1 PROBLEM SOLVING APPLICATION

NY Performance Indicators

6.S.11 Determine the number of possible outcomes for a compound event by using the fundamental counting principle. Also, 6.PS.15.

At a circus, the clowns have two choices of clown suits—polka dots or stripes. They have three choices of wigs—pigtails, rainbow hair, or blue hair. What are the different costumes the clowns can wear?

1 Understand the Problem

List the **important information:**

- There are two types of clown suits.
- There are three types of wigs.

2 Make a Plan

You can draw a tree diagram to find all the possible costumes.

3 Solve

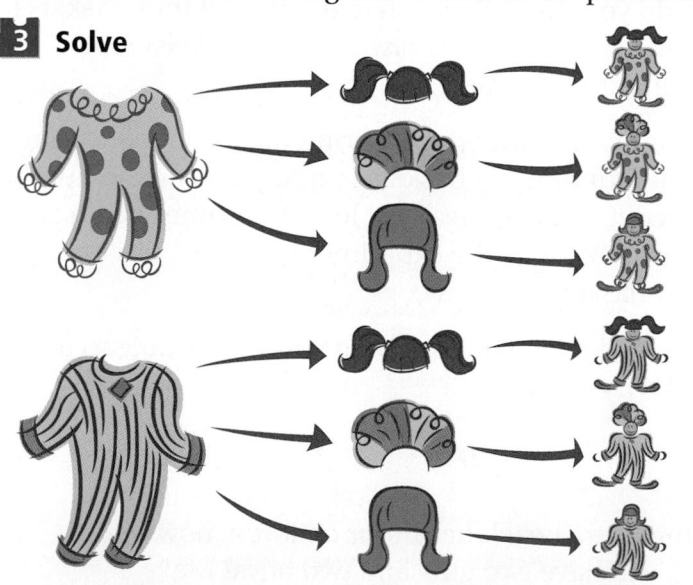

Pair the first pair of pants with each shirt.

Pair the second pair of pants with each shirt.

Follow each branch on the tree diagram to find all of the possible outcomes: {polka dots and pigtails, polka dots and rainbow hair, polka dots and blue hair, stripes and pigtails, stripes and rainbow hair, stripes and blue hair}.

4 Look Back

There are 6 branches at the end of the tree diagram. There are 6 possible costumes listed.

Another way to keep track of possible outcomes is to make an organized list.

EXAMPLE 2 Making an Organized List

Marissa is shopping for a portable MP3 player. The player comes in black, silver, and red. She can choose between models that store 120 songs or 240 songs. What are all the possible MP3 players Marissa can choose from?

black, 120 songs   *List all the players that are black.*
black, 240 songs

silver, 120 songs   *List all the players that are silver.*
silver, 240 songs

red, 120 songs   *List all the players that are red.*
red, 240 songs

The Fundamental Counting Principle is a way to find the number of outcomes in a sample space without making a list. To use the Fundamental Counting Principle, multiply the number of choices in each category.

In the example above, there are 3 colors and 2 models of MP3 players. The total number of MP3 players to choose from is $3 \cdot 2 = 6$.

EXAMPLE 3 Using the Fundamental Counting Principle

Students at Jefferson Middle School must take one fine arts class and one athletics class. The fine arts class choices are band, orchestra, choir, and art. The athletics class choices are P.E., soccer, basketball, volleyball, football, and tennis. How many possible combinations are there?

There are 4 choices for fine arts classes and 6 choices for athletics classes.

$4 \cdot 6 = 24$ *Multiply the number of choices in each category.*

There are 24 possible combinations.

Think and Discuss 6.PS.18, 6.PS.21

1. Explain the advantages of an organized list over a random list.

2. Describe how you can check whether your list is accurate.

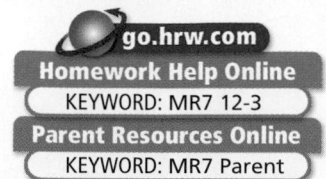

go.hrw.com
Homework Help Online
KEYWORD: MR7 12-3
Parent Resources Online
KEYWORD: MR7 Parent

GUIDED PRACTICE

See Example 1   1. Use the ZCool Foods menu. If Carl chooses a main dish and a side dish, what are all the possible outcomes?

See Example 2   2. **School** Patrice, Jason, and Kenya are auditioning for the school play. The director has two roles available, a doctor and a teacher. Each can be played by either a boy or a girl. What are all the possible ways the two roles can be assigned?

See Example 3   3. **School** Mr. Li is offering a make-up science test. He can give the test on Monday, Tuesday, or Thursday, before school, during lunch, or after school. How many different times can Mr. Li give his make-up test?

INDEPENDENT PRACTICE

See Example 1   4. **Recreation** Use the Outdoor Club flyer. The Outdoor Club is planning its annual Spring Festival. The members must vote to choose the day of the event and the main activity. What are all the possible outcomes?

Day of Event
Saturday or Sunday
Main Activity
Foot race   Hike
Bicycle race
Swimming race
Scavenger hunt

See Example 2   5. Greta's apartment building is protected by a security system that requires a pass code to let in residents. The code is made up of numbers from 1 to 3. The code is three digits long, and a digit cannot repeat. What are all the possible pass codes?

See Example 3   6. **Sports** A middle school is purchasing new basketball jerseys. Each jersey will have a letter and a number on it. The possible letters are A–Z, and the possible numbers are 0–9. How many possible combinations are there?

PRACTICE AND PROBLEM SOLVING

Extra Practice
See page 737.

7. Keisha will choose a shirt and a skirt or a pair of pants from her closet to wear to school. Find the number of different outfits she can make if she has

   a. 3 shirts, 3 pants, and 3 skirts.

   b. 7 shirts, 5 pants, and 3 skirts.

8. Omar is redecorating his bedroom. He can choose one paint color, one border, and one type of brush.

    a. How many different combinations of paint, border, and brush are possible?

    b. If Omar found another brush that he could use, how many different combinations would be possible?

9. **Social Studies** Japanese children play a game called *Jan-Ken-Pon.* You may know it as Rock, Paper, Scissors. Two players shout at the same time, "*jan-ken-pon!*" On "*pon!*" each player shows one of three hand positions—closed fist (*gu*), open hand palm down (*pa*), or index and middle finger extended to form a V (*choki*). How many different outcomes are possible in this game?

10. **Choose a Strategy** At a meeting, each person shook hands with every other person exactly one time. There were a total of 28 handshakes. How many people were at the meeting?

11. **Write About It** Suppose you are going to choose one boy and one girl from your class for a group project. How can you find the number of possible combinations? Explain.

12. **Challenge** A sailor has five flags: blue, green, red, orange, and yellow. Suppose she wants to fly three flags, but their order is not important; red, orange, yellow is the same as yellow, orange, red. List the different combinations of flags that are possible. How many combinations are there?

TEST PREP and Spiral Review

13. **Multiple Choice** A cafeteria sells 3 types of cereal and 2 types of juice for breakfast. Bo can choose 1 cereal and 1 juice. How large is the sample space?

    Ⓐ 2   Ⓑ 3   Ⓒ 6   Ⓓ 18

14. **Gridded Response** Bikes R Us sells customized bicycles. There are 5 different color frames, 2 types of tires, and 4 types of seats. How many different combinations are available for 1 frame, 1 type of tire, and 1 type of seat?

Add or subtract. Write each answer in simplest form. (Lesson 5-2)

15. $\frac{1}{3} + \frac{3}{4}$ **16.** $\frac{3}{8} + \frac{2}{5}$ **17.** $\frac{7}{8} - \frac{1}{4}$ **18.** $\frac{5}{6} - \frac{1}{2}$

19. Use the data in the table to make a stem-and-leaf plot. (Lesson 6-9)

Height of Sunflowers (in.)	18	22	15	17	18	21	16	20

12-4 Theoretical Probability

Learn to find the theoretical probability and complement of an event.

Vocabulary

theoretical probability

equally likely

fair

complement

NY Performance Indicators

5.S.7 Create a sample space and determine the probability of a single event, given a simple experiment (e.g. rolling a number cube).

Another way to describe the probability of an event is to use **theoretical probability**. One situation in which you can use theoretical probability is when all outcomes have the same chance of occurring. In other words, the outcomes are **equally likely**.

Equally likely outcomes

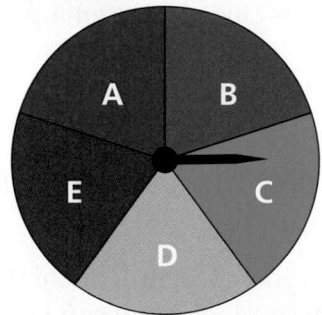

There is the same chance that the spinner will land on any of these letters.

Not equally likely outcomes

There is a greater chance that the spinner will land on 1 than on any other number.

An experiment with equally likely outcomes is said to be **fair**. You can usually assume that experiments involving items such as coins and number cubes are fair.

THEORETICAL PROBABILITY

$$\text{probability} = \frac{\text{number of ways the event can occur}}{\text{total number of equally likely outcomes}}$$

EXAMPLE 1 Finding Theoretical Probability

Remember!

The sample space is heads, tails (H, T).

A **What is the probability that a fair coin will land heads up?**

There are two possible outcomes when flipping a coin, heads or tails. Both are equally likely because the coin is fair.

$$P(\text{heads}) = \frac{\blacksquare}{2 \text{ possible outcomes}}$$

There is only one way for the coin to land heads up.

$$P(\text{heads}) = \frac{1 \text{ way event can occur}}{2 \text{ possible outcomes}}$$

$$P(\text{heads}) = \frac{1 \text{ way event can occur}}{2 \text{ possible outcomes}} = \frac{1}{2}$$

B What is the probability of rolling a number less than 5 on a fair number cube?

There are six possible outcomes when a fair number cube is rolled: 1, 2, 3, 4, 5, or 6.

$$P(\text{less than 5}) = \frac{\blacksquare}{6 \text{ possible outcomes}}$$

There are 4 ways to roll a number less than 5: 1, 2, 3, or 4.

$$P(\text{less than 5}) = \frac{4 \text{ ways event can occur}}{6 \text{ possible outcomes}}$$

$$P(\text{less than 5}) = \frac{4 \text{ ways event can occur}}{6 \text{ possible outcomes}} = \frac{4}{6} = \frac{2}{3}$$

When you toss a coin, there are two possible outcomes: heads or tails. What is $P(\text{heads}) + P(\text{tails})$?

$$P(\text{heads}) + P(\text{tails}) = \frac{1}{2} + \frac{1}{2} = \frac{2}{2} = 1$$

The probabilities of all the outcomes in the sample space add up to 1 (or 100%, if the probabilities are given as percents).

When you combine all the ways that an event can NOT happen, you have the **complement** of the event.

Event	Complement of the Event
A coin landing heads up on a toss	A coin landing tails up on a toss
Rolling 5 on a number cube	Rolling 1, 2, 3, 4, or 6 on a number cube

E X A M P L E ② **Finding the Complement of an Event**

Suppose there is a 10% chance of rain today. What is the probability that it will NOT rain?

In this situation, there are two possible outcomes, either it will rain or it will not rain.

$$P(\textbf{rain}) + P(\text{not rain}) = 100\%$$
$$P(\text{not rain}) = 100\% - 10\% \qquad \textit{Subtract.}$$
$$P(\text{not rain}) = 90\%$$

6.CN.6, 6.CM.1

Think and Discuss

1. **Give an example** of a fair experiment. Give an example of an unfair experiment.

2. **Describe** the complement of the following situation. There is a 60% chance of snow,

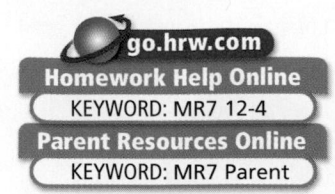

GUIDED PRACTICE

See Example ① **1.** What is the probability that a fair coin will land tails up?

2. What is the probability of randomly choosing a vowel from the letters *A*, *B*, *C*, *D*, and *E*?

See Example ② **3.** The probability that a spinner will land on blue is 26%. What is the probability that it will NOT land on blue?

4. Suppose you have an unfair number cube and the probability of rolling a 2 is 0.7. What is the probability that you will NOT roll a 2?

INDEPENDENT PRACTICE

See Example ① **5.** What is the probability of rolling the number 3 on a fair number cube?

6. What is the probability of rolling a number that is a multiple of 3 on a fair number cube?

7. Find the probability that a yellow marble will be chosen from a bag that contains 3 green marbles, 2 red marbles, and 4 yellow marbles.

See Example ② **8.** **Weather** Suppose there is an 81% chance of snow today. What is the probability that it will NOT snow?

9. On a game show, the chance that the spinner will land on the winning color is 0.04. Find the probability that it will NOT land on the winning color.

PRACTICE AND PROBLEM SOLVING

Extra Practice
See page 738.

A fair number cube is rolled. Find each probability.

10. $P(4)$

11. $P(\text{not } 3)$

12. $P(1, 2, \text{ or } 3)$

13. $P(\text{number greater than } 0)$

14. $P(\text{odd number})$

15. $P(\text{number divisible by } 5)$

16. $P(\text{prime number})$

17. $P(\text{negative number})$

18. **Critical Thinking** This net can be folded to make a solid figure. The solid figure can then be rolled like a number cube. Give the probability of rolling each number with the solid figure.

19. A board game has a die (singular of dice) with 12 faces. Give the probability of rolling a number that is a factor of 12.

20. **Social Studies** In a recent presidential election, the probability that an eligible person voted was about 45%. Is it more likely that an eligible person voted or did not vote?

For Exercises 21–26, *A* represents an event. The probability that *A* will happen is given. Find the probability that *A* will NOT happen.

21. $P(A) = 47\%$
22. $P(A) = 0.9$
23. $P(A) = \frac{7}{12}$

24. $P(A) = \frac{5}{8}$
25. $P(A) = 0.23$
26. $P(A) = 100\%$

27. **Games** Mah Jong is a traditional Chinese game played with 144 decorated tiles—36 Bamboo tiles, 36 Circle tiles, 36 Character tiles, 16 Wind tiles, 12 Dragon tiles, and 8 bonus tiles. The tiles are the same shape and size, and are all blank on the back. Suppose the tiles are all placed face down and you choose one. What is the probability that you will choose a Wind tile? Write your answer as a fraction in simplest form.

Nine pieces of paper with the numbers 1, 2, 2, 3, 4, 4, 5, 6, and 6 printed on them are placed in a bag. A student chooses one without looking. Compare the probabilities. Write <, >, or =.

28. $P(1)$ ▨ $P(5)$
29. $P(3)$ ▨ $P(2)$
30. $P(4)$ ▨ $P(6)$

31. $P(4)$ ▨ $P(5) + P(6)$
32. $P(3) + P(5)$ ▨ $P(6)$
33. $P(\text{less than } 3)$ ▨ $P(6)$

34. **What's the Error?** If you toss a cylinder, it can land on its top, on its bottom, or on its side. Your friend says that $P(\text{top}) = \frac{1}{3}$. What mistake did your friend make?

35. **Write About It** Toss a coin 20 times and record your results. According to your experiment, what is the probability that the coin shows tails? What is the theoretical probability that it shows tails? How do the two probabilities compare? Repeat the experiment, but this time toss the coin 50 times. Now how do the probabilities compare?

36. **Challenge** Suppose you perform an experiment in which you toss a fair coin and roll a fair number cube. Find the theoretical probability that heads *and* 3 will be the outcomes.

TEST PREP and Spiral Review

37. **Multiple Choice** There is a 25% chance of snow on Friday. What is the probability that it will NOT snow on Friday?

　Ⓐ 0%　　　　Ⓑ 25%　　　　Ⓒ 75%　　　　Ⓓ 100%

38. **Extended Response** A drawer contains 6 blue socks, 4 brown socks, and 10 white socks. Arnold chooses one sock without looking. What is the probability of choosing each color sock? Compare the possibilities. Write <, >, or =.

Find each quotient. (Lesson 11-7)

39. $84 \div 4$
40. $-25 \div 5$
41. $-60 \div (-20)$
42. $-55 \div 5$

43. Paulina will use 15 feet of ribbon to decorate baskets for her friends. If each basket requires 1.2 feet of ribbon, how many baskets can she decorate? (Lesson 3-8)

READY TO GO ON?

Quiz for Lessons 12-1 Through 12-4

✓ **12-1** **Introduction to Probability**

For Problems 1 and 2, write *impossible, unlikely, as likely as not, likely,* or *certain* to describe the event.

1. This spinner lands on blue.

2. You roll an even number on a standard number cube.

3. The chance that Mitch will win concert tickets is 0.15. Write this probability as a fraction and as a percent.

4. The chance of rain is 33% on Tuesday, 45% on Wednesday, and 35% on Thursday. On which day is it most likely to rain?

✓ **12-2** **Experimental Probability**

For each experiment, identify the outcome shown.

5.

6.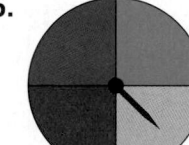

7. Jeremy recorded the number of times a spinner landed on each number. Based on Jeremy's experiment, on which number is the spinner most likely to land?

Outcome	1	2	3
Frequency	卌 II	卌 卌 II	卌 I

✓ **12-3** **Counting Methods and Sample Spaces**

8. Mindy's Deli serves 3 kinds of pasta with 2 kinds of sauce. The different pastas are spaghetti, fettuccine, and bow tie. The different sauces are tomato and pesto. What are all the possible outcomes that include 1 pasta and 1 sauce?

9. Cynthia is choosing an outfit for the first day of class. Her choices are black or blue pants and a white, yellow, or pink shirt. How many possible combinations can she choose from?

✓ **12-4** **Theoretical Probability**

10. What is the probability that this spinner will land on 2?

11. What is the probability of rolling a number less than 3 on a number cube?

12. Kirk has a 33% chance of scoring in the basketball game. What is the probability that Kirk will NOT score in the game?

Focus on Problem Solving

Look Back

• **Estimate to check that your answer is reasonable**

When you have finished solving a problem, take a minute to reread the problem. See if your answer makes sense. Make sure that your answer is reasonable given the situation in the problem.

One way to do this is to estimate the answer before you begin solving the problem. Then when you get your final answer, compare it with your original estimate. If your answer is not close to your estimate, check your work again.

Each problem below has an answer given, but it is not right. How do you know that the answer is not reasonable? Give your own estimate of the correct answer.

1 A rental car agency has 55 blue cars, 32 red cars, and 70 white cars. A customer is given a car at random. How many color outcomes are possible?

Answer: 2,100

2 A box has 120 marbles. If the probability of drawing a blue marble is $\frac{3}{8}$ and the probability of drawing a red marble is $\frac{5}{8}$, how many of each color are in the box?

Answer: 100 blue marbles and 20 red marbles

3 A store manager decides to survey one out of every ten shoppers. How many would be surveyed out of 350 shoppers?

Answer: 3 shoppers

4 Sue has just started to collect old dimes. She has six dimes from 1941, five dimes from 1932, and one dime from 1930. If she chooses one dime at random, what is the probability that it is from before 1932?

Answer: 50%

12-5 Compound Events

Learn to list all the outcomes and find the theoretical probability of a compound event.

Vocabulary
compound event

If a family is going to have four children, there are 16 possibilities for the birth order of the children based on gender (boy, B, or girl, G).

BBBB, BBBG, BBGB, BBGG,
BGBB, BGBG, BGGB, BGGG,
GBBB, GBBG, GBGB, GBGG,
GGBB, GGBG, GGGB, GGGG

A **compound event** consists of two or more single events. For example, the birth of one child is a single event. The births of four children make up a compound event.

EXAMPLE **1** **Finding Probabilities of Compound Events**

Theresa rolls a fair number cube and then flips a fair coin.

 **NY Performance Indicators**

6.S.11 Determine the number of possible outcomes for a compound event by using the fundamental counting principle and use this to determine the probabilities of events when the outcomes have equal probability. Also, 5.S.7, 6.S.9, 6.PS.15.

A Find the probability that the number cube will show an odd number and that the coin will show tails.

First find all of the possible outcomes.

Number Cube

Coin		1	2	3	4	5	6
	H	1, H	2, H	3, H	4, H	5, H	6, H
	T	1, T	2, T	3, T	4, T	5, T	6, T

There are 12 possible outcomes, and all are equally likely.

Three of the outcomes have an odd number and tails:

$$1, T; 3, T; \text{ and } 5, T.$$

$$P(\text{odd, tails}) = \frac{3 \text{ ways event can occur}}{12 \text{ possible outcomes}}$$

$$= \frac{3}{12}$$

$$= \frac{1}{4} \qquad \textit{Write your answer in simplest form.}$$

B Find the probability that the number cube will show a 2 and that the coin will show heads.

Only one outcome is 2, H.

$$P(2, H) = \frac{1 \text{ way event can occur}}{12 \text{ possible outcomes}}$$

$$= \frac{1}{12}$$

C The following experiment is going to be performed.

Step 1: Toss a fair coin.

Step 2: Spin the spinner.

Step 3: Choose a marble.

 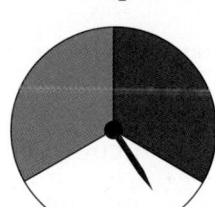 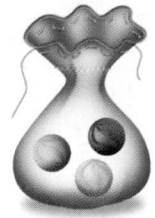

What is the probability that the coin will show heads, the spinner will land on orange, and a red marble will be chosen?

Coin	Spinner	Marble	Outcome
		red →	heads, purple, red
	purple	yellow →	heads, purple, yellow
		green →	heads, purple, green
		red →	heads, orange, red
Heads	orange	yellow →	heads, orange, yellow
		green →	heads, orange, green
		red →	heads, white, red
	white	yellow →	heads, white, yellow
		green →	heads, white, green
		red →	tails, purple, red
	purple	yellow →	tails, purple, yellow
		green →	tails, purple, green
		red →	tails, orange, red
Tails	orange	yellow →	tails, orange, yellow
		green →	tails, orange, green
		red →	tails, white, red
	white	yellow →	tails, white, yellow
		green →	tails, white, green

There are 18 equally likely outcomes.

$$P(\text{heads, orange, red}) = \frac{1 \text{ way event can occur}}{18 \text{ possible outcomes}}$$

$$= \frac{1}{18}$$

Remember!

You could also use the Fundamental Counting Principle to find the total possble outcomes.

coin · spinner · marble

2 · 3 · 3

= 18 total outcomes

Think and Discuss

6.PS.14, 6.CN.6

1. Give an example of a compound event.

2. Explain any pattern you noticed while finding the number of possible outcomes in a compound event.

12-5 **Exercises**

go.hrw.com
Homework Help Online
KEYWORD: MR7 12-5
Parent Resources Online
KEYWORD: MR7 Parent

GUIDED PRACTICE

See Example

1. Patrick rolled a fair number cube twice. Find the probability that the number cube will show an even number both times.

2. A boy and a girl each flip a coin. What is the probability that the boy's coin will show heads and the girl's coin will show tails?

INDEPENDENT PRACTICE

See Example **1**

3. If you spin the spinner twice, what is the probability that it will land on green on the first spin and on purple on the second spin?

4. What is the probability that the spinner will land on either green or purple on the first spin and yellow on the second spin?

5. What is the probability that the spinner will land on the same color twice in a row?

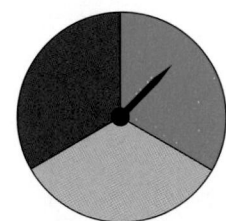

PRACTICE AND PROBLEM SOLVING

Extra Practice
See page 738.

An experiment involves spinning each spinner once. Find each probability.

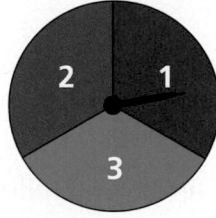 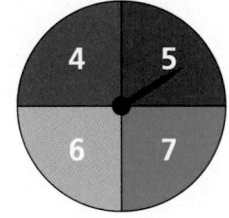

6. *P*(2 on spinner 1 and 5 on spinner 2)

7. *P*(not 1 on spinner 1 and not 7 on spinner 2)

8. *P*(even number on both spinners)

9. *P*(odd number on spinner 1 and even number on spinner 2)

10. *P*(number on spinner 2 is greater than number on spinner 1)

11. *P*(same number on both spinners)

12. *P*(a multiple of 3 on both spinners)

13. *P*(different number on each spinner)

14. A jar contains tiles that are numbered 1, 2, 3, 4, and 5. Danny removes a tile from the jar, replaces the tile, and draws a second tile. What is the probability that Danny will draw the same number both times?

A fair number cube is rolled, and a fair coin is tossed. Compare the probabilities. Write <, >, or =.

15. $P(3 \text{ and tails})$ ▨ $P(5 \text{ and heads})$

16. $P(\text{even number and tails})$ ▨ $P(\text{odd number and heads})$

17. $P(\text{number less than 3 and tails})$ ▨ $P(\text{odd number and tails})$

18. $P(\text{number greater than 5 and heads})$ ▨ $P(\text{prime number and tails})$

19. **Life Science** If a cat has 5 kittens, what is the probability that they are all female? What is the probability that they are all male? (Assume that having a male and having a female are equally likely events.)

20. **Multi-Step** The students in Jared's class have ID numbers made up of two digits from 1 through 6. The same digit can be used twice. In fact, the same digit is used twice in Jared's ID number. If Jared rolls 2 number cubes, what is the probability that he does NOT roll his ID number?

 21. **What's the Error?** One of your classmates said, "If you flip a coin and roll a number cube, the probability of getting heads and a 3 is $\frac{1}{2} + \frac{1}{6} = \frac{2}{3}$." What mistake did your classmate make? Explain how to find the correct answer.

 22. **Write About It** Describe a situation that involves a compound event.

 23. **Challenge** You roll a number cube six times. What is the probability of rolling the numbers 1 through 6 in order?

24. **Multiple Choice** A fair number cube is rolled twice. What is the probability that the first roll will be even and the second roll will be odd?

    Ⓐ $\frac{1}{6}$ Ⓑ $\frac{1}{4}$ Ⓒ $\frac{1}{2}$ Ⓓ $\frac{5}{6}$

25. **Multiple Choice** A fair number cube is rolled once, and a coin is flipped once. What is the probability of a 5 on the number cube and heads on the coin toss?

    Ⓕ $\frac{1}{2}$ Ⓖ $\frac{1}{4}$ Ⓗ $\frac{1}{6}$ Ⓙ $\frac{1}{12}$

Order each set of numbers from least to greatest. (Lesson 3-1)

26. 1.2, 0.445, 1.06, 0.9   27. 2.45, 2.678, 2.007, 2.02   28. 7.99, 7.999, 7.9, 7.09

29. Suppose there is a 15% chance that Cy will finish all his work before he leaves class. What is the probability that he will NOT finish? (Lesson 12-3)

Hands-On LAB 12-5

Explore Permutations and Combinations

Use with Lesson 12-5

go.hrw.com
Lab Resources Online
KEYWORD: MR7 Lab12

NY Performance Indicators

6.PS.15, 6.CM.10

For a compound event, you often must count the arrangements of individual outcomes. To do this, you must know whether the order of the outcomes in these arrangements matters. With three outcomes *A*, *B*, and *C*, when is *A-B-C* different from *C-B-A*, and when is it considered to be the same?

Activity 1

In how many different arrangements can Ellen, Susan, and Jeffrey sit in a row?

① Write each name on 6 index cards. You will have a total of 18 cards. Show all the different ways the cards can be arranged in a row.

Arrangement	1	2	3	4	5	6
First Seat	Ellen	Ellen	Susan	Susan	Jeffrey	Jeffrey
Second Seat	Susan	Jeffrey	Jeffrey	Ellen	Susan	Ellen
Third Seat	Jeffrey	Susan	Ellen	Jeffrey	Ellen	Susan

There are 6 different ways that these three people can sit in a row.

Notice that the order of the students in the different arrangements is important. "Ellen, Susan, Jeffrey" is different from "Ellen, Jeffrey, Susan." An arrangement in which order is important is called a **permutation.**

Think and Discuss

1. Think of another situation in which the order in an arrangement is important. Can you think of a situation in which the order would NOT be important? Explain.

Try This

1. Cindy, Laurie, Marty, and Joel are running for president of their class. The person who gets the second greatest amount of votes will be the vice president. How many different ways can the election turn out?

Activity 2

1 Abe, Babe, Cora, and Dora are going to work on a project in groups of 2. How many different ways can they pair off?

Write each name on 3 index cards. You will have a total of 12 cards. Show all pairings.

Abe	Babe		Babe	Cora		Cora	Dora

Abe	Cora		Babe	Dora

Abe	Dora

There are 6 different possible pairs.

Notice that in this situation, the order in the pairs is not important. "Abe, Cora" is the same as "Cora, Abe." When order is not important, the arrangements are called **combinations.**

Think and Discuss

Tell whether each of the following is a permutation or a combination. Explain.

1. There are 20 horses in a race. Ribbons are given for first, second, and third place. How many possible ways can the ribbons be awarded?

2. There are 20 violin players trying out for the school band and 6 players will be chosen. How many different ways could students be selected for the band?

3. Connie has 10 different barrettes. She wears 2 each day. How many ways can she choose 2 barrettes each morning?

4. Yoko belongs to a book club, and she has just received 25 new books. How many possible ways are there for them to be placed on the shelf?

Try This

1. The video club is sponsoring a double feature. How many ways can club members choose 2 movies from a list of 6 possibilities?

2. Ms. Baker must pick a team of 3 students to send to the state mathematics competition. She has decided to choose 3 students from the 5 with the highest grades in her class. Ms. Baker can either send 3 equal representatives, or she can send a captain, an assistant captain, and a secretary. Which choice results in more possible teams? Explain. Find the number of teams possible for each choice.

12-6 Making Predictions

Learn to use probability to predict events.

Vocabulary

prediction

population

sample

A **prediction** is a guess about something in the future. One way to make a prediction is to collect information by conducting a survey. The **population** is the whole group being surveyed. To save time and money, researchers often make predictions based on a **sample**, which is part of the group being surveyed. Another way to make a prediction is to use probability.

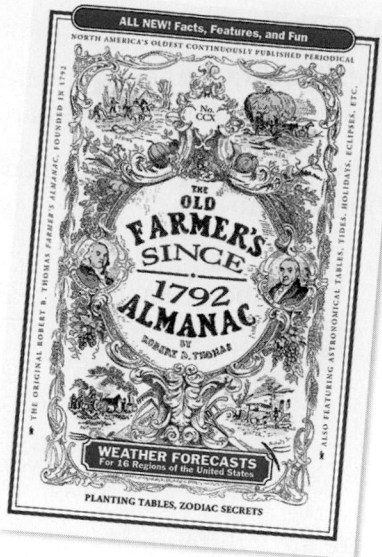

The Old Farmer's Almanac predicts weather, sunrise and sunset times, and tides.

NY Performance Indicators

6.A.5 Solve simple proportions within context. Also, 6.N.27, 6.S.1, 6.S.8.

EXAMPLE 1 Using Sample Surveys to Make Predictions

Based on a sample survey, an airline claims that its flights have a 92% probability of being on time. Out of 1,000 flights, how many would you predict will be on time?

You can write a proportion. Remember that *percent* means "per hundred."

$$\frac{92}{100} = \frac{x}{1,000}$$

Think: 92 out of 100 is how many out of 1,000?

$$100 \cdot x = 92 \cdot 1,000$$

The cross products are equal.

$$100x = 92,000$$

x is multiplied by 100.

$$\frac{100x}{100} = \frac{92,000}{100}$$

Divide both sides by 100 to undo the multiplication.

$$x = 920$$

You can predict that about 920 of 1,000 flights will be on time.

EXAMPLE 2 Using Theoretical Probability to Make Predictions

If you roll a number cube 24 times, how many times do you expect to roll a 5?

$$P(\text{rolling a 5}) = \frac{1}{6}$$

$$\frac{1}{6} = \frac{x}{24}$$

Think: 1 out of 6 is how many out of 24?

$$6 \cdot x = 1 \cdot 24$$

The cross products are equal.

$$6x = 24$$

x is multiplied by 6.

$$\frac{6x}{6} = \frac{24}{6}$$

Divide both sides by 6 to undo the multiplication.

$$x = 4$$

You can expect to roll a 5 about 4 times.

EXAMPLE 3 **PROBLEM SOLVING APPLICATION**

A stadium sells yearly parking passes. If you have a parking pass, you can park at the stadium for any event during that year.

Based on a sample group of fans, the managers of the stadium estimate that the probability that a person with a pass will attend any one event is 80%. The parking lot has 300 spaces. If the managers want the lot to be full at every event, how many passes should they sell?

1. Understand the Problem

The **answer** will be the number of parking passes they should sell.

List the **important information:**

- P(person with pass attends event) = 80%
- There are 300 parking spaces.

2. Make a Plan

The managers want to fill all 300 spaces. But, on average, only 80% of parking pass holders will attend. So 80% of pass holders must equal 300. You can write an equation to find this number.

3. Solve

$$\frac{80}{100} = \frac{300}{x}$$ *Think: 80 out of 100 is 300 out of how many?*

$100 \cdot 300 = 80 \cdot x$ *The cross products are equal.*

$30{,}000 = 80x$ *x is multiplied by 80.*

$$\frac{30{,}000}{80} = \frac{80x}{80}$$ *Divide both sides by 80 to undo the multiplication.*

$375 = x$

The managers should sell 375 parking passes.

4. Look Back

If the managers sold only 300 passes, the parking lot would not usually be full because only about 80% of the people with passes will attend any one event. The managers should sell more than 300 passes, so 375 is a reasonable answer.

6.RP.6

Think and Discuss

1. Tell whether you expect to be exactly right if you make a prediction based on a sample. Explain your answer.

12-6 Exercises

go.hrw.com
Homework Help Online
KEYWORD: MR7 12-6
Parent Resources Online
KEYWORD: MR7 Parent

GUIDED PRACTICE

See Example ① 1. Based on a sample survey, a local newspaper states that 12% of the city's residents have volunteered at an animal shelter. Out of 5,000 residents, how many would you predict have volunteered at the animal shelter?

See Example ② 2. If you roll a fair number cube 30 times, how many times would you expect to roll a number that is a multiple of 3?

See Example ③ 3. **Recreation** Airlines routinely overbook flights, which means that they sell more tickets than there are seats on the planes. Suppose an airline estimates that 93% of customers will show up for a particular flight. If the plane seats 186 people, how many tickets should the airline sell?

INDEPENDENT PRACTICE

See Example ① 4. Based on a sample survey, a local newspaper claims that 64% of the town's households receive their paper. Out of 15,000 households, how many would you predict receive the paper?

See Example ② 5. If you flip a coin 64 times, how many times do you expect the coin to show tails?

6. A bag contains 2 black chips, 5 red chips, and 4 white chips. You pick a chip from the bag, record its color, and put the chip back in the bag. If you repeat this process 99 times, how many times do you expect to remove a red chip from the bag?

See Example ③ 7. **Life Science** The director of a blood bank is eager to increase his supply of O negative blood, because O negative blood can be given to people with any blood type. The probability that a person has O negative blood is 7%. The director would like to have 9 O negative donors each day. How many total donors does the director need to find each day to reach his goal of O negative donors?

PRACTICE AND PROBLEM SOLVING

Extra Practice
See page 738.

8. A sample survey of 50 people in Harrisburg indicates that 10 of them know the name of the mayor of their neighboring city.

   a. Out of 5,500 Harrisburg residents, how many would you expect to know the name of the mayor of the neighboring city?

   b. **Multi-Step** Out of 600 Harrisburg residents, how many would you predict do not know the name of the mayor of the neighboring city?

9. **Critical Thinking** A survey is being conducted as people exit a frozen yogurt store. They are being asked if they prefer frozen yogurt or ice cream. Should predictions be made about the population of the town based on the survey? Explain.

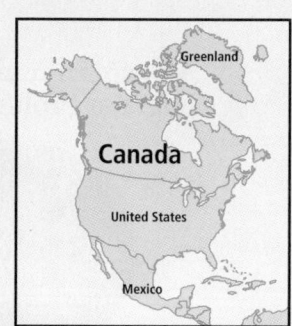

The Native Canadians lived in Canada before the Europeans arrived. The French were the first Europeans to settle successfully in Canada.

The graph shows the results of a survey of 400 Canadian citizens.

10. Out of 75 Canadians, how many would you predict are of French origin?

11. A random group of Canadians includes 18 Native Canadians. How many total Canadians would you predict are in the group?

12. **? What's the Error?** A student said that in any group of Canadians, 20 of them will be Native Canadians. What mistake did this student make?

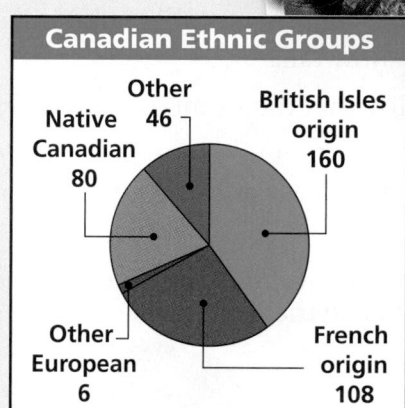

Canadian Ethnic Groups

Other
Native 46
Canadian
80

British Isles
origin
160

Other
European
6

French
origin
108

Canada

13. **/ Write About It** How could you predict the number of people of French *or* Native Canadian origin in a group of 150 Canadians?

14. **★ Challenge** In a group of Canadians, 15 are in the Other European origin category. Predict how many Canadians in the same group are NOT in that category.

TEST PREP and Spiral Review

15. Multiple Choice Jay played a game and won 24 out of 100 times. Which is the best estimate of the experimental probability of Jay winning his next game?

   Ⓐ 5%   Ⓑ 25%   Ⓒ 50%   Ⓓ 75%

16. Multiple Choice You roll a fair number cube 36 times. How many times do you expect to roll a 4?

   Ⓕ 36   Ⓖ 9   Ⓗ 6   Ⓙ $\frac{1}{6}$

Solve each question. Check your answers. (Lesson 11-8)

17. $x + 10 = -2$ **18.** $x - 20 = -5$ **19.** $-9x = 45$ **20.** $x \div (-2) = -5$

A fair number cube is rolled. Find each probability. (Lesson 12-4)

21. $P(5)$ **22.** $P(\text{not } 2)$ **23.** $P(3) + P(4)$ **24.** $P(\text{number divisible by } 3)$

Quiz for Lessons 12-5 Through 12-6

☑ **12-5** **Compound Events**

Billie rolls a fair number cube and then flips a fair coin.

1. Find the probability that the number cube will show an even number and the coin will show tails.

2. Find the probability that the number cube will show a 6 and the coin will show tails.

3. Compare P(4 and heads) and P(odd number and heads). Write $<$, $>$, or $=$.

An experiment involves spinning a spinner and choosing a marble from a bag. For Problems 4–6, use the diagrams.

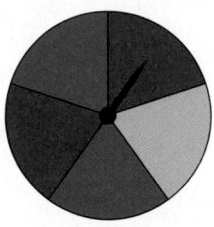

M604SE_EPR011005_A

4. What is the probability of spinning red on the spinner and choosing a red marble from the bag?

5. What is the probability of spinning yellow and choosing a marble that is NOT yellow?

6. What is the probability of spinning a color that is NOT blue and choosing a marble that is NOT blue?

☑ **12-6** **Making Predictions**

7. Based on a sample survey, 26% of the local people have a pet dog. Out of 600 people, how many people do you predict will have a pet dog?

8. If you roll a number cube 54 times, how many times do you expect to roll a number less than 3?

9. Based on previous attendance, the managers for a summer concert series estimate the probability that a person will attend any one event to be 90%. The chairs set up around the stage seat 450 people. If the mangers want to be at full capacity every concert, how many tickets should they sell?

10. Based on a sample survey, a newspaper states that only 45% of the local population gets the recommended amount of sleep each night. If there are 45,000 people in town, how many people are not getting enough sleep?

MULTI-STEP TEST PREP

Spin to Win Jasper Middle School is having a spring carnival for students and their families. Every guest may spin either the Big Wheel or the Lucky Circle. Guests win a door prize if the Big Wheel's spinner lands on *A* or if the Lucky Circle's spinner lands on an even number.

1. Is a guest more likely to win a door prize by spinning the Big Wheel or by spinning the Lucky Circle? Explain.

2. Miguel chooses to spin the Big Wheel. His sister, Anna, chooses to spin the Lucky Circle. How many different outcomes of their spins are possible?

3. What is the probability that Miguel and Anna both win a door prize?

4. Find the probability that two guests in a row win a prize spinning the Big Wheel.

5. During the carnival, 160 guests spin the Big Wheel and 125 guests spin the Lucky Circle. Which spinner do you predict will have the greater number of winners? Explain.

Multi-Step Test Prep

Independent and Dependent Events

Learn to find the probability of independent and dependent events.

Vocabulary

independent events

dependent events

For **independent events**, the occurrence of one event has no effect on the probability that the second event will occur.

To find the probability that two independent events will occur, multiply the probabilities of the two events as follows:

Probability of Two Independent Events

$$P(A \text{ and } B) = P(A) \cdot P(B)$$

Probability of   Probability of   Probability of
both events   first event   second event

EXAMPLE **Finding the Probability of Independent Events**

NY Performance Indicators

6.S.10 Determine the probability of dependent events.

Find the probability of rolling a 3 on a number cube and the spinner shown landing on A.

The outcome of rolling the number cube does not affect the outcome of spinning the spinner, so the events are independent.

$P(3 \text{ and } A) = P(3) \cdot P(A)$ *Use the formula.*

$\qquad = \dfrac{1}{6} \cdot \dfrac{1}{5}$ *The probability of rolling a 3 is $\frac{1}{6}$. The probability of the spinner landing on A is $\frac{1}{5}$.*

$\qquad = \dfrac{1}{30}$ *Multiply.*

The probability of rolling a 3 and the spinner landing on A is $\frac{1}{30}$.

Suppose you have a bag containing 3 red marbles and 2 blue marbles. You draw two marbles, one after the other. The first marble you draw affects the marbles that remain in the bag, so the two draws are *dependent events*. For **dependent events**, the occurrence of one event has an effect on the probability that the second event will occur.

To find the probability that two dependent events will occur, multiply the probabilities of the two events as follows:

Probability of Two Dependent Events

$$P(A \text{ and } B) = P(A) \cdot P(B \text{ after } A)$$

Probability of   Probability of   Probability of second event
both events   first event   *after* the first event has occurred

EXAMPLE 2 **Finding the Probability of Dependent Events**

A bag contains 3 red marbles and 2 blue marbles. Find the probability of drawing a red marble and then a blue marble.

$P(\text{red and blue}) = P(\text{red}) \cdot P(\text{blue after red})$

$P(\text{red}) = \dfrac{3}{5}$ *There are 3 red marbles out of the 5 marbles.*

$P(\text{blue after red}) = \dfrac{2}{4} = \dfrac{1}{2}$ *There are 4 marbles left, and 2 are blue.*

$P(\text{red after blue}) = P(\text{red}) \cdot P(\text{blue after red})$

$= \dfrac{3}{5} \cdot \dfrac{1}{2} = \dfrac{3}{10}$ *Multiply.*

The probability of drawing a red marble and then a blue marble is $\dfrac{3}{10}$.

EXTENSION

Exercises

Determine whether the events are independent or dependent.

1. Adrian chooses a baseball card from a stack. Then Jemma chooses a card from those remaining in the stack.

2. Mike draws a 7 from ten cards numbered 1 through 10. He replaces the card. Then Alison draws a 5.

Find the probability of each event for the spinners shown.

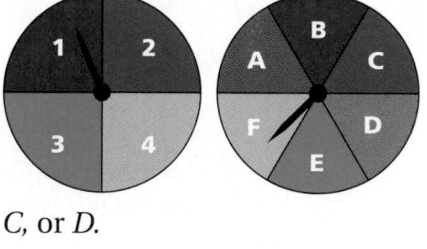

3. The spinners land on 1 and *F*.

4. The spinners land on an even number and *A*.

5. The spinners land on an odd number and *A, B, C,* or *D*.

A bag contains 4 green marbles and 6 yellow marbles. You draw a marble and put it aside. Then you draw a second marble. Find the probability of each event.

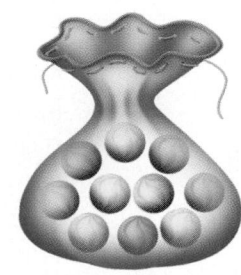

6. You draw a yellow marble and then a green marble.

7. You draw 2 green marbles.

8. **Write About It** Explain the difference between independent and dependent events.

9. **Challenge** Nicole has 10 coins in her purse: 3 pennies, 3 nickels, 2 dimes, and 2 quarters. She removes a coin from the purse and then chooses a second coin without replacing the first. What is the probability that the two coins will add up to exactly 50 cents?

Game Time

Probability Brain Teasers

Can you solve these riddles that involve probability? Watch out—some of them are tricky!

1 In Wade City, 5% of the residents have unlisted phone numbers. If you selected 100 people at random from the town's phone directory, how many of them would you predict have unlisted numbers?

2 Amanda has a drawer that contains 24 black socks and 18 white socks. If she reaches into the drawer without looking, how many socks does she have to pull out in order to be *certain* that she will have two socks of the same color?

3 Dale, Melvin, Carter, and Ken went out to eat. Each person ordered something different. When the food came, the waiter could not remember who had ordered what, so he set the plates down at random in front of the four friends. What is the probability that exactly three of the boys got what they ordered?

Round and Round and Round

This is a game for two players.

The object of this game is to determine which of the three spinners is the winning spinner (lands on the greater number most often).

Both players choose a spinner and spin at the same time. Record which spinner lands on the greater number. Repeat this 19 times, keeping track of which spinner wins each time. Repeat this process until you have played spinner A against spinner B, spinner B against spinner C, and spinner A against spinner C. Spin each pair of spinners 20 times and record the results.

go.hrw.com
Game Time Extra
KEYWORD: MR7 Games

Which spinner wins more often, A or B? Which spinner wins more often, B or C? Which spinner wins more often, A or C? Is there anything surprising about your results?

A complete copy of the rules and game pieces are available online.

Materials
- CD with case
- white paper
- scissors
- markers
- glue
- brass fastener
- large paper clip
- stapler

It's in the Bag!

PROJECT **CD Spinner**

Use a CD to make a spinner. Then take notes on probability in a booklet that you store in the CD case.

Directions

❶ Trace around the CD to make a circle on white paper. Divide the circle into thirds, color each third a different color, and cut out the circle. Glue the circle onto the CD. **Figure A**

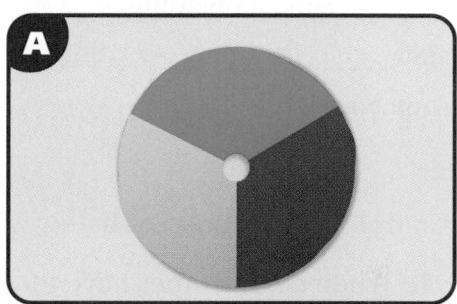

❷ Carefully remove the plastic CD holder from the back of the CD case. Place the CD in the holder and insert a brass fastener into the center of the CD. Bend the ends of the fastener so it stays in place, and put the holder back into the CD case. **Figure B**

❸ Attach a large paper clip to the brass fastener to make a spinner. **Figure C**

❹ Cut several sheets of white paper so they are $4\frac{3}{4}$ inches by $4\frac{3}{4}$ inches. Staple them together to form a booklet that fits in the cover of the CD case.

Taking Note of the Math

Use the booklet to record notes on probability. Be sure to include probabilities related to the spinner that you made.

CHAPTER
12
PROBABILITY

Study Guide: Review

Vocabulary

Complete the sentences below with vocabulary words from the list above.

1. When all outcomes have the same probability of occurring, the outcomes are ___?___.

2. A(n) ___?___ is an activity involving chance that can have different results. Each possible result is called a(n) ___?___.

3. The measure of how likely an event is to occur is the event's ___?___.

4. ___?___ is the ratio of the number of ways an event can occur to the total number of possible outcomes.

5. The set of all possible outcomes for an experiment is the ___?___.

12-1 Introduction to Probability (pp. 668–671)

 6.CM.10

EXAMPLE

■ Is it *impossible, unlikely, as likely as not, likely,* or *certain* that the spinner will land on yellow?

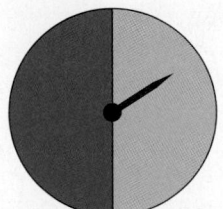

Half of the spinner is yellow, so it is as likely to land on yellow as not.

EXERCISES

6. Is it *impossible, unlikely, as likely as not, likely,* or *certain* that next week will have 7 days?

7. There is a 75% chance that George will win a race. Write this probability as a decimal and as a fraction.

8. Barry has a 30% chance of picking a black sock and a 50% chance of picking a white sock from his drawer. Which color sock is he more likely to pick?

12-2 Experimental Probability (pp. 672–675)

 5.S.5, 5.S.6

EXAMPLE

■ Margie recorded the number of times a spinner landed on each color. Based on Margie's experiment, on which color is the spinner most likely to land?

Outcomes	Red	Blue	Green
Frequency	JHT JHT IIII	IIII	JHT II

$P(\text{red}) \approx \frac{14}{25}$ $P(\text{blue}) \approx \frac{4}{25}$ $P(\text{green}) \approx \frac{7}{25}$

The spinner will most likely land on red.

EXERCISES

9. One day, the cafeteria supervisor recorded the number of students who chose each type of beverage. She organized her results in a table. Find the experimental probability that a student will choose juice.

Beverage	Juice	Milk	Water
Frequency	20	37	18

12-3 Counting Methods and Sample Spaces (pp. 678–681)

 6.S.11

EXAMPLE

■ Liz is wrapping a gift. She can use gold or silver paper and either a red or white ribbon. From how many different combinations can Liz choose?

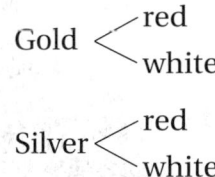

Gold — red
     — white

Silver — red
      — white

Follow each branch to find all outcomes.
There are 4 different combinations.

EXERCISES

10. The local restaurant has a lunch special in which you can pick an appetizer, a sandwich, and a drink. How many different lunch-special combinations are there if you have the following choices?

appetizers: soup or salad
sandwiches: turkey, roast beef, or ham
drinks: juice, milk, or iced tea

12-4 Theoretical Probability (pp. 682–685)

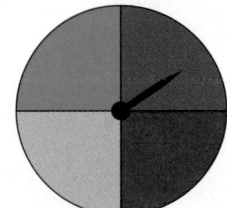 5.S.7

EXAMPLE

■ What is the probability of rolling a 4 on a fair number cube?

There are six possible outcomes when a number cube is rolled: 1, 2, 3, 4, 5, or 6. All are equally likely because the number cube is fair.

$$P = \frac{\text{number of ways event can occur}}{\text{total number of possible outcomes}}$$

$$P(4) = \frac{1 \text{ way event can occur}}{6 \text{ possible outcomes}} = \frac{1}{6}$$

EXERCISES

11. What is the probability that the spinner will land on yellow?

12. What is the probability of rolling a number greater than 3 on a fair number cube?

13. There is a 25% chance of choosing a purple marble from a bag. Find the probability of choosing a marble that is NOT purple.

Study Guide: Review

12-5 Compound Events (pp. 688–691)

5.S.7, 6.S.9, 6.S.11

EXAMPLE

■ What is the probability of spinning red or blue and having the coin land heads up?

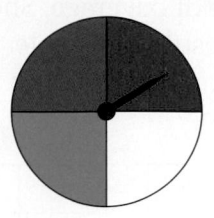 

	Red	Blue	Green	White
Heads	red, H	blue, H	green, H	white, H
Tails	red, T	blue, T	green, T	white, T

There are 8 possible outcomes, and all are equally likely.

$P(\text{red or blue, H}) = \dfrac{2 \text{ ways event can occur}}{8 \text{ possible outcomes}}$

$= \dfrac{2}{8} = \dfrac{1}{4}$

EXERCISES

14. Find the probability that a blue marble will be chosen, the first coin will show heads, and the second coin will show tails.

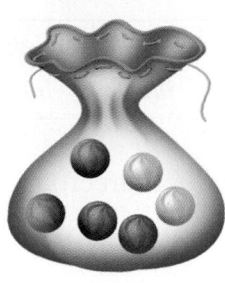  

15. Jacob rolled a fair number cube, flipped a fair penny, and then flipped a fair quarter. Find the probability that the number cube will show an even number and both coins will show heads.

12-6 Making Predictions (pp. 694–697)

6.N.27, 6.A.5, 6.S.1, 6.S.8

EXAMPLE

■ If you spin the spinner 30 times, how many times do you expect it to land on red?

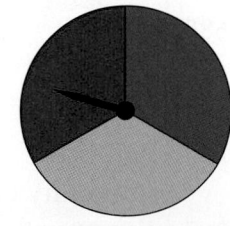

$P(\text{red}) = \dfrac{1}{3}$

$\dfrac{1}{3} = \dfrac{x}{30}$

$3 \cdot x = 1 \cdot 30$ *The cross products are equal.*

$3x = 30$ *x is multiplied by 3.*

$\dfrac{3x}{3} = \dfrac{30}{3}$ *Divide both sides by 3 to undo the multiplication.*

$x = 10$

You can expect it to land on red about 10 times.

EXERCISES

16. Based on a sample survey, about 2% of the items produced by a company are defective. Out of 5,000 items, how many can you predict will be defective?

17. If you roll a fair number cube 50 times, how many times can you expect to roll an even number?

18. In a sample survey, 500 teenagers indicated that 175 of them use their computers regularly. Out of 4,500 teenagers, predict how many use their computers regularly.

19. In a sample survey, 100 sixth-grade students indicated that 20 of them take music lessons. Out of 500 sixth-grade students, predict how many take music lessons.

CHAPTER TEST

For Items 1 and 2, write *impossible, unlikely, as likely as not, likely,* **or** *certain* **to describe each event.**

1. You roll a 3 on a standard number cube.

2. You pick a blue marble from a bag of 5 white marbles and 20 blue marbles.

3. There is a 12% chance of rain tomorrow. Write this probability as a decimal and as a fraction.

4. The probability that Mark will be selected for a scholarship is 0.8. Write this probability as a percent and as a fraction.

5. Iris asked 60 students what time they go to bed. Her results are in the table. Find the experimental probability that a student chosen at random goes to bed at 8:30 P.M.

Time (P.M.)	8:00	8:30	9:00	9:30
Frequency	12	24	18	6

6. Find the experimental probability that a student chosen at random goes to bed before 8:30 P.M.

7. Josh threw darts at a dartboard 10 times. Assume that he threw the darts randomly and did not aim. Based on his results, what is the probability that a dart will land in the center circle?

8. What is the probability of rolling an even number greater than 2 on a fair number cube?

9. The baseball game has a 64% chance of being rained out. What is the probability that it will NOT be rained out?

10. Peter has four photos to arrange in a frame. How many different ways can he arrange the photos?

11. Marsha can wear jeans or black pants with a red, blue, or white shirt. How many different outfits can she choose from?

12. If you roll a number cube 36 times, how many times do you expect to roll an even number?

13. Find the probability that you will pick a blue marble from both bags and that the spinner will land on blue.

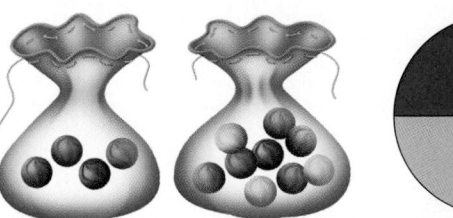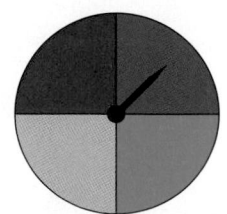

NEW YORK TEST PREP

go.hrw.com
State Test Practice Online
KEYWORD: MR7 TestPrep

Cumulative Assessment, Chapters 1–12

Multiple Choice

1. A humpback whale swimming on the water's surface dives 500 feet. It then dives another 175 feet. Which expression represents this situation?

   Ⓐ $-175 + 500$ Ⓒ $-500 - 175$

   Ⓑ $675 - 175$ Ⓓ $500 + 175$

2. The weather report states that there is a 60% chance of a thunderstorm. What is this probability written as a fraction in simplest form?

   Ⓕ $\frac{3}{5}$ Ⓗ $\frac{30}{60}$

   Ⓖ $\frac{6}{10}$ Ⓙ $\frac{60}{100}$

3. There were 18 teachers and 45 students registered to participate in a 5K walk-a-thon. Which ratio accurately compares the number of students to the number of teachers?

   Ⓐ 1:5   Ⓒ 3:15

   Ⓑ 5:2   Ⓓ 18:45

4. Which three-dimensional figure is a square pyramid?

   Ⓕ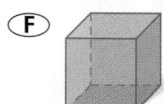

   Ⓖ

   Ⓗ

   Ⓙ

5. Jason delivers newspapers. He earns $0.22 for every newspaper he delivers. He wants to buy a new printer for his computer that costs $264. If n equals the number of newspapers he delivers, which equation can be used to find the number of newspapers Jason needs to deliver in order to have enough money to buy the printer?

   Ⓐ $n - 0.22 = 264$ Ⓒ $\frac{n}{0.22} = 264$

   Ⓑ $0.22 + n = 264$ Ⓓ $0.22n = 264$

6. The two figures are similar. Which proportion can be used to find the missing side length?

   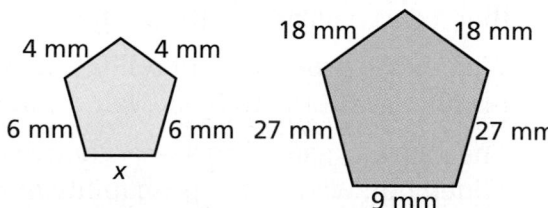

   Ⓕ $\frac{4}{x} = \frac{18}{27}$ Ⓗ $\frac{6}{x} = \frac{9}{18}$

   Ⓖ $\frac{6}{x} = \frac{27}{4}$ Ⓙ $\frac{4}{x} = \frac{18}{9}$

7. Victor owns 638 model trains. He can put 24 trains in a protective case. If each case costs $5.65, how much money will Victor have to spend to put all of his model trains in cases?

   Ⓐ $135.60   Ⓒ $152.55

   Ⓑ $146.90   Ⓓ $158.25

8. What is 70% of 30?

   Ⓕ 0.21   Ⓗ 21

   Ⓖ 2.1   Ⓙ 210

New York Test Prep

9. The weights of four puppies are listed below. Which puppy is the heaviest?

Puppy	Weight (lb)
Toby	$5\frac{1}{4}$
Rusty	$5\frac{2}{5}$
Alex	$5\frac{5}{8}$
Jax	$5\frac{2}{3}$

(A) Toby

(B) Rusty

(C) Alex

(D) Jax

10. A fair number cube is rolled. What is the probability that the cube will NOT land on 4?

(F) $\frac{1}{6}$

(G) $\frac{1}{3}$

(H) $\frac{2}{3}$

(J) $\frac{5}{6}$

Hot Tip

A probability can be written as a decimal, fraction, or percent. Probabilities are always between 0 and 1 (or 0% and 100%). The greater the probability, the more likely the event is to occur.

11. The movie *Gone with the Wind* is 3 hours and 42 minutes long. How many minutes long is the movie?

(A) 180

(B) 202

(C) 222

(D) 284

12. Nancy is stenciling 5-inch-wide stars, end-to-end, around her rectangular bedroom. Her bedroom is $12\frac{3}{4}$ feet wide and $15\frac{1}{4}$ feet long. How many whole stars will Nancy stencil?

(F) 62

(G) 64

(H) 96

(J) 134

13. Carl drives at an average rate of 60 miles per hour. How many hours will it take him to drive 240 miles?

(A) 4

(B) 12

(C) 24

(D) 48

Short Response

14. John asked a group of teenagers how many hours of television they watch per day during the summer. He put his results in a table.

Hours	2	3	4	5
Teenagers	//	JH//	JH/	JH1

a. Based on this survey, what is the probability that a teenager will spend 4 hours a day watching television in the summer?

b. John plans to ask 500 teenagers the same survey question. How many of those teenagers can he predict watch 2 hours of television per day during the summer? Explain.

15. A restaurant offers a choice of roast beef, chicken, or fish; broccoli, carrots, or corn; and soup or salad. If you can choose one main dish, one vegetable, and one side, what are all the possible outcomes?

Extended Response

16. There are 5 blue tiles, 7 red tiles, and 8 yellow tiles in a jar.

a. If you pick a tile without looking, what is the probability of picking a blue tile? Express this probability as a percent, a fraction, and a decimal.

b. If you pick a tile without looking, what is the probability of NOT picking a yellow tile? Write your answer in simplest form.

c. You conduct an experiment in which you pick a tile out of the jar 50 different times. Each time you record the color of tile and then replace the tile before you pick another. How many times would you expect to pick a blue tile? Explain.

 **Problem Solving on Location**

NEW JERSEY

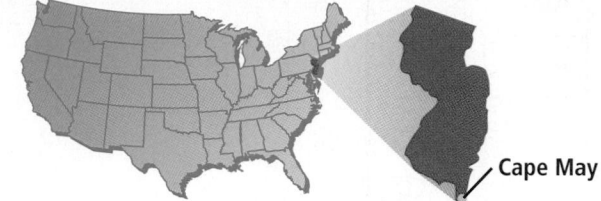

Cape May

 ## Shipwreck Diving

The ocean floor along the New Jersey coast is dotted with shipwrecks. According to some estimates, there may be as many as 7,000 shipwrecks off the New Jersey shore. This makes the area a favorite spot among scuba divers who enjoy exploring the mysterious remains of sunken ships.

Choose one or more strategies to solve each problem.

For 1–3, use the graph.

1. The wreck of the U-869 is 3 times as deep as that of the S.S. *Mohawk*. While descending to the U-869, a scuba diver stops to check her equipment every 20 feet. How many times will she check her equipment *before* reaching the U-869?

2. Carlos is diving to the *Tolten*. He dives $\frac{1}{5}$ of the distance and stops to watch a school of fish. Then he descends another 30 feet and stops to rest. How many more feet must he descend in order to reach the *Tolten*?

3. The depth of the *Eagle* is $\frac{1}{2}$ that of the *Eureka*. The *Eureka* is 15 feet closer to the surface of the water than the *Resor*. What is the depth of the *Eagle*?

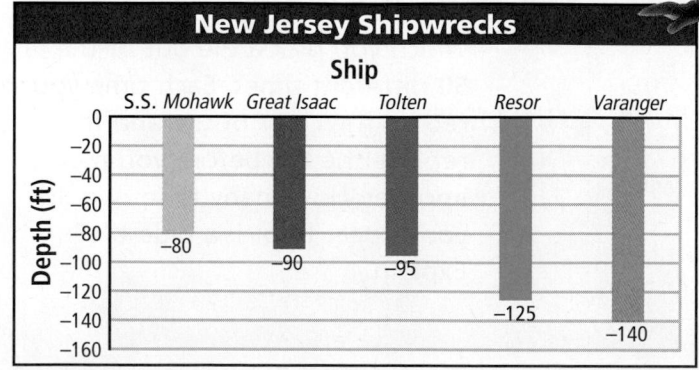

New Jersey Shipwrecks

Ship: S.S. *Mohawk* (−80), Great Isaac (−90), *Tolten* (−95), Resor (−125), Varanger (−140)
Depth (ft): 0, −20, −40, −60, −80, −100, −120, −140, −160

Problem Solving Strategies

Draw a Diagram
Make a Model
Guess and Test
Work Backward
Find a Pattern
Make a Table
Solve a Simpler Problem
Use Logical Reasoning
Act It Out
Make an Organized List

★ Historic Cold Spring Village

Visiting historic Cold Spring Village in Cape May, New Jersey, is like traveling back in time. The village offers a detailed re-creation of life in the nineteenth century. In addition to its 25 historic buildings, the town features costumed "residents" who play the roles of blacksmiths, weavers, and other townspeople.

Choose one or more strategies to solve each problem.

1. The village's welcome center has a 7-minute orientation video. The video plays continually, with 30 seconds between each showing. How many times does the video play in an 8-hour period?

2. A photographer is taking a picture for a brochure about the village. The picture will include a schoolmaster, a farmer, a potter, and an innkeeper. How many different ways can these residents line up for the photo?

For 3 and 4, use the diagram.

3. A school group is putting together their own tour of the village. They plan to start at one of the private homes, then visit one of the barns, and then visit one of the meeting halls. How many different tours are possible?

4. A historian is preparing a talk about five of the village's shops. In how many different ways can she choose a set of five shops for her talk?

Buildings at Historic Cold Spring Village	
Type of Building	**Number of Buildings**
Railroad station	2
Barn	2
Shop	6
Private home	5
Meeting hall	2

 # Student Handbook

Extra Practice • Chapter 1

LESSON 1-1

1. The area of Canada is 3,851,788 square miles. The area of the United States is 3,717,792 square miles. Which country has the greater area?

2. In 2001, it was estimated that 14,902,000 students attended high school and 14,889,000 attended college. Were more students in high school or in college?

Order the numbers from least to greatest.

3. 783; 772; 1,702

4. 10,318; 1,308; 10,301

5. 34,903; 32,788; 32,679

6. 24,615; 24,829; 24,560

7. 1,345; 1,780; 1,356

8. 29,992; 22,929; 22,922

LESSON 1-2

Estimate each sum or difference by rounding to the place value indicated.

9. 7,685 + 8,230; thousands

10. 23,218 + 37,518; ten thousands

11. 52,087 − 35,210; ten thousands

12. 292,801 − 156,127; hundred thousands

13. 14,325 + 25,629; hundreds

14. 9,210 − 396; hundreds

15. Mr. Peterson needs topsoil for his garden. His rectangular garden is 78 in. long and 48 in. wide. A bag of topsoil covers an area of 500 square inches. How many bags should Mr. Peterson buy?

16. Natalie's family is having a picnic at an amusement park. The park is 153 miles from Natalie's house. If the family drives 55 mi/h, about how long will it take them to get to the park?

LESSON 1-3

Write each expression in exponential form.

17. $5 \times 5 \times 5 \times 5 \times 5 \times 5$

18. $3 \times 3 \times 3 \times 3$

19. $10 \times 10 \times 10 \times 10 \times 10$

20. $2 \times 2 \times 2 \times 2$

21. $7 \times 7 \times 7$

22. 9×9

Find each value.

23. 5^2

24. 5^5

25. 6^3

26. 10^5

27. 9^1

28. 3^6

29. 4^3

30. 2^5

31. Patricia e-mailed a joke to 4 of her friends. Each of those friends e-mailed the joke to 4 other friends. If this pattern continues, how many people will receive the e-mail on the fifth round of e-mails?

Extra Practice ▪ Chapter 1

LESSON 1-4

Evaluate each expression.

32. $15 + 7 \times 3$

33. $3 \times 3^2 + 13 - 5$

34. $10 \div (3 + 2) \times 2^3 - 8$

35. $4^2 - 12 \div 3 + (7 - 5)$

36. $10 \times (25 - 11) \div 7 + 6$

37. $(3 + 6) \times 18 \div 2 + 7$

38. The sixth-grade band students sell cases of fruit for a fund-raiser. Emily sold 18 cases of oranges for $12 each, 11 cases of apples for $10 each, and 5 cases of grapefruit for $14 each. Evaluate $18 \times 12 + 11 \times 10 + 5 \times 14$ to find how much money she should collect in all.

LESSON 1-5

Evaluate.

39. $15 + 7 + 23 + 5$

40. $4 \times 13 \times 5$

41. $34 + 16 + 22 + 18$

Use the Distributive Property to find each product.

42. 5×54

43. 3×32

44. 7×26

45. 9×73

LESSON 1-6

For Exercises 46–48, choose a solution method and solve. Explain your choice.

46. The table shows the number of days it rained each month. How many days total did it rain in the year?

47. The coldest temperature in a city was 11°F. The warmest temperature that same year was 89°F. What is the difference between the highest and lowest temperatures?

Month	Days of Rain	Month	Days of Rain
January	6	July	15
February	5	August	9
March	7	September	17
April	14	October	14
May	12	November	8
June	10	December	5

48. Heather is a member of a dance company. She practices 14 hours a week. How many hours does she practice each year? (*Hint*: There are 52 weeks in a year.)

LESSON 1-7

Identify a pattern in each arithmetic sequence and then find the missing terms.

49. 8, 16, 24, ▨, ▨, ▨

50. 6, 11, 16, ▨, ▨, ▨

51. 100, 85, 70, ▨, ▨, ▨

52.

Position	1	2	3	4	5	6	7	8
Value of Term	1	12	23	34	45	▨	▨	▨

Identify a pattern in each sequence. Name the missing terms.

53. 496, 248, 260, ▨, 142, 71, ▨

54. 1, 8, 4, 32, 16, ▨, 64, 512, ▨

Extra Practice ∙ Chapter 2

LESSON 2-1

Evaluate each expression to find the missing values in the tables.

1.
y	23 + y
17	40
27	■
37	■

2.
w	w × 3 + 10
4	22
5	■
6	■

3.
x	x ÷ 8
40	5
48	■
56	■

LESSON 2-2

4. Earth has a diameter of 7,926 miles. Let d represent the diameter of the Moon, which is smaller than the diameter of Earth. Write an expression to show how much larger the diameter of Earth is than the diameter of the Moon.

Write each phrase as a numerical or algebraic expression.

5. the sum of 322 and 18

6. the product of 7 and 12

7. the quotient of n and 8

8. 14 more than x

Write two phrases for each expression.

9. $(23)(6)$

10. $52 - p$

11. $y \div 4$

12. $8 + 4$

13. $13 \cdot m$

LESSON 2-3

Write an expression for the missing value in each table.

14.
Albert's Age	Ashley's Age
10	1
14	5
18	9
n	■

15.
Hooves	Horses
16	4
12	3
8	2
n	■

16. A parallelogram has a base of 4 inches. The table shows the area of the parallelogram for different heights. Write an expression that can be used to find the area of the parallelogram when its height is h inches.

Base (in.)	Height (in.)	Area (in²)
4	4	16
4	5	20
4	6	24
4	h	■

LESSON 2-4

Determine whether the given value of each variable is a solution.

17. $a + 15 = 34$, when $a = 17$

18. $t - 9 = 14$, when $t = 23$

19. Rachel says she is 5 feet tall. Her friend measured her height as 60 inches. Determine if these two measurements are equal.

LESSON 2-5

Solve each equation. Check your answers.

20. $r + 13 = 36$

21. $52 = 24 + n$

22. $6 + s = 10$

23. Towns A, B, and C are located along Main Road, as shown on the map. Town A is 34 miles from town C. Town B is 12 miles from town C. Find the distance d between town A and town B.

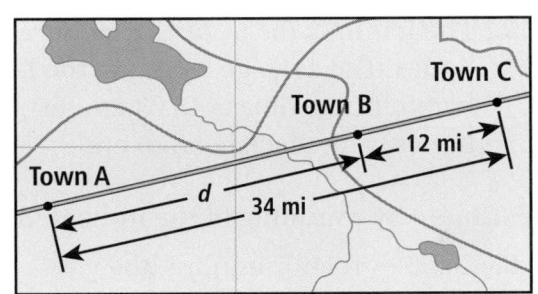

LESSON 2-6

Solve each equation. Check your answers.

24. $z - 9 = 5$

25. $v - 17 = 14$

26. $24 = w - 6$

27. Reggie withdrew $175 from his bank account to go shopping. After his withdrawal, there was $234 left in Reggie's account. How much money did Reggie have in his account before his withdrawal?

LESSON 2-7

Solve each equation. Check your answers.

28. $4y = 20$

29. $21 = 3t$

30. $72 = 9g$

31. The area of a rectangle is 54 in^2. Its width is 6 in. What is its length?

32. A squirrel can run 36 miles in 3 hours. Solve the equation $3m = 36$ to find the number of miles a squirrel can run in 1 hour.

LESSON 2-8

Solve each equation. Check your answers.

33. $\frac{n}{4} = 6$

34. $7 = \frac{t}{5}$

35. $\frac{a}{8} = 12$

36. Sydney likes to run and ride a bike for exercise. Each day, she runs for one-third the time that she rides her bike. Yesterday, Sydney ran for 15 minutes. How many minutes did she ride her bike?

Extra Practice ▪ Chapter 3

LESSON 3-1

Write each decimal in standard form, expanded form, and words.

1. 1.32

2. 0.6 + 0.003 + 0.0008

3. five and three thousandths

4. Joshua ran 1.45 miles, and Jasmine ran 1.5 miles. Who ran farther?

Order the decimals from least to greatest.

5. 3.89, 3.08, 3.8

6. 20.65, 20.09, 20.7

7. 0.053, 0.43, 0.340

LESSON 3-2

8. The femur is the upper leg bone, and the tibia is one of the lower leg bones. The average length of the femur is 50.5 cm, and the average length of the tibia is 43.03 cm. Estimate the total length of the leg if the bones were placed end to end.

Estimate by rounding to the indicated place value.

9. 5.856 − 1.3497; hundredths

10. 4.7609 + 7.2471; tenths

Estimate each product or quotient.

11. 20.84 ÷ 3.201

12. 31.02 × 4.91

13. 39.76 ÷ 7.94

Estimate a range for the sum.

14. 8.38 + 24.92 + 4.8

15. 38.27 + 2.99 + 15.32

LESSON 3-3

Find each sum or difference.

16. 1.65 + 4.53 + 3.2

17. 2.2 + 6.8

18. 7 − 0.6

Evaluate 6.35 − s for each value of s.

19. $s = 3.2$

20. $s = 2.108$

21. $s = 5.0421$

22. Brianna is shopping for school clothes and wants to purchase the following items: a shirt for $19.50, shoes for $35.00, a skirt for $12.39, socks for $6.99, and a pair of jeans for $19.95. Not including tax, how much money will Brianna need to purchase these items?

LESSON 3-4

Write each number in scientific notation.

23. 60,000

24. 423,800

25. 8,500,000

Write each number in standard form.

26. 5.632×10^5

27. 2.1×10^8

28. 1.425×10^4

LESSON 3-5

Find each product.

29. 0.5×0.7

30. 0.3×0.06

31. 6.12×5.9

Evaluate $4x$ for each value of x.

32. $x = 2.071$

33. $x = 5.42$

34. $x = 7.85$

35. Each car tire costs $69.99. How much will 4 tires cost?

LESSON 3-6

Find each quotient.

36. $0.84 \div 6$

37. $11.07 \div 9$

38. $27.6 \div 12$

Evaluate $0.564 \div x$ for each given value of x.

39. $x = 4$

40. $x = 12$

41. $x = 2$

42. Marci pays $8.97 at the grocery store for 3 pounds of cherries. How much does each pound cost?

LESSON 3-7

Find each quotient.

43. $4.5 \div 0.9$

44. $59.7 \div 0.4$

45. $8.32 \div 8$

46. Lisa paid $13.41 for 4.5 pounds of ground chicken. How much did each pound cost?

LESSON 3-8

47. Jocelyn has 3.5 yards of ribbon. She needs 0.6 yards of ribbon to make one bow. How many bows can Jocelyn make?

48. Louie has a piece of wood that is 46.8 cm long. If he cuts the piece into 4 equal sections, how long will each section be?

LESSON 3-9

Solve each equation. Check your answer.

49. $b - 5.2 = 2.6$

50. $5t = 24.5$

51. $\frac{p}{3} = 1.8$

52. The area of a rectangle is 41 cm^2. Its length is 8.2 cm. What is its width?

53. The area of Henry's kitchen is 168 ft^2. The cost of tile is $4.62 per square foot. What is the total cost to tile the kitchen?

Extra Practice ▪ Chapter 4

LESSON 4-1

Tell whether each number is divisible by 2, 3, 4, 5, 6, 9, and 10.

1. 12,680   **2.** 174   **3.** 1,638   **4.** 735

Tell whether each number is prime or composite.

5. 97   **6.** 9   **7.** 111   **8.** 256

LESSON 4-2

List all of the factors of each number.

9. 28   **10.** 51   **11.** 70   **12.** 24

Write the prime factorization of each number.

13. 48   **14.** 72   **15.** 81   **16.** 150

LESSON 4-3

Find the GCF of each set of numbers.

17. 15 and 35   **18.** 16 and 40   **19.** 22 and 68

20. 6, 36, and 60   **21.** 27, 36, and 54   **22.** 14, 28, and 63

23. Alice has 42 red beads and 24 white beads. What is the greatest number of bracelets Alice can make if each bracelet has the same number of red beads and the same number of white beads and if every bead is used?

LESSON 4-4

Write each decimal as a fraction or mixed number.

24. 0.31   **25.** 1.9   **26.** 2.53   **27.** 0.07

Write each fraction or mixed number as a decimal.

28. $1\frac{7}{8}$ **29.** $\frac{5}{9}$ **30.** $6\frac{3}{5}$ **31.** $\frac{5}{6}$

Order the fractions and decimals from least to greatest.

32. $0.3, \frac{3}{5}, 0.53$ **33.** $0.8, 0.67, \frac{7}{8}$ **34.** $0.68, \frac{2}{3}, \frac{3}{4}$

LESSON 4-5

Find the missing numbers that make the fractions equivalent.

35. $\frac{4}{5} = \frac{\blacksquare}{20}$ **36.** $\frac{8}{12} = \frac{2}{\blacksquare}$ **37.** $\frac{6}{7} = \frac{\blacksquare}{28}$ **38.** $\frac{24}{3} = \frac{\blacksquare}{1}$

Write each fraction in simplest form.

39. $\frac{6}{10}$ **40.** $\frac{7}{9}$ **41.** $\frac{4}{16}$ **42.** $\frac{2}{6}$

LESSON 4-6

Write each mixed number as an improper fraction.

43. $3\frac{1}{4}$

44. $6\frac{5}{7}$

45. $1\frac{2}{9}$

46. $2\frac{7}{10}$

47. Brett's favorite soup recipe calls for $\frac{14}{4}$ cups of chicken broth. Write $\frac{14}{4}$ as a mixed number.

LESSON 4-7

Compare. Write $<$, $>$, or $=$.

48. $\frac{2}{5}$ ▨ $\frac{4}{5}$

49. $\frac{5}{6}$ ▨ $\frac{7}{8}$

50. $\frac{1}{3}$ ▨ $\frac{9}{27}$

51. $\frac{9}{15}$ ▨ $\frac{2}{5}$

52. Natalie lives $\frac{1}{6}$ mile from school. Peter lives $\frac{3}{10}$ mile from school. Who lives closer to the school?

Order the fractions from least to greatest.

53. $\frac{3}{5}, \frac{5}{9}, \frac{4}{5}$

54. $\frac{1}{6}, \frac{3}{7}, \frac{1}{3}$

55. $\frac{1}{2}, \frac{5}{8}, \frac{7}{12}$

LESSON 4-8

56. Rose is filling a tub with water. The height of the water is increasing $\frac{1}{8}$ foot each minute. Use pictures to model how much the height of the water will change in 5 minutes, and then write your answer in simplest form.

Subtract. Write each answer in simplest form.

57. $1 - \frac{7}{9}$

58. $2\frac{5}{6} - 1\frac{1}{6}$

59. $5\frac{7}{10} - 3\frac{3}{10}$

60. $2 - \frac{3}{4}$

Evaluate each expression for $x = \frac{7}{12}$. Write each answer in simplest form.

61. $\frac{11}{12} - x$

62. $x + 1\frac{1}{12}$

63. $x - \frac{5}{12}$

LESSON 4-9

Estimate each sum or difference by rounding to 0, $\frac{1}{2}$, or 1.

64. $\frac{7}{8} + \frac{7}{15}$

65. $\frac{5}{6} + \frac{1}{11}$

66. $\frac{7}{12} - \frac{4}{9}$

Use the table for Exercises 67 and 68.

67. The table shows the number of hours each day that Michael worked. About how many hours did Michael work on Monday and Tuesday?

68. About how many more hours did he work on Thursday than on Friday?

Michael's Work Schedule	
Day	**Hours Worked**
Monday	$4\frac{5}{6}$
Tuesday	$5\frac{1}{4}$
Thursday	$6\frac{1}{10}$
Friday	$4\frac{5}{12}$

Extra Practice ▪ Chapter 5

LESSON 5-1

1. There are 18 girls on the dance team. Barrettes are sold in packs of 6. Ponytail holders are sold in packs of 2. What is the least number of packs they could buy so that each girl has a barrette and a ponytail holder and none are left over?

Find the least common multiple (LCM).

2. 9 and 15
3. 12 and 16
4. 10 and 12
5. 3, 4, and 5

LESSON 5-2

Add or subtract. Write each answer in simplest form.

6. $\frac{3}{5} + \frac{2}{3}$
7. $\frac{7}{8} - \frac{1}{6}$
8. $\frac{1}{3} + \frac{1}{2}$

9. About $\frac{1}{3}$ of the animals at the zoo are birds. The mammals make up $\frac{2}{5}$ of the zoo's population. What fraction of the zoo's animals are mammals or birds?

LESSON 5-3

Find each sum or difference. Write the answer in simplest form.

10. $18\frac{1}{3} + 16\frac{1}{6}$
11. $5\frac{3}{4} + 3\frac{5}{12}$
12. $12\frac{1}{2} - 8\frac{2}{5}$

13. Joan has a rottweiler and a Chihuahua. The rottweiler weighs $99\frac{1}{2}$ lb, and the Chihuahua weighs $3\frac{1}{4}$ lb. How much more does Joan's rottweiler weigh than her Chihuahua?

LESSON 5-4

Subtract. Write each answer in simplest form.

14. $4\frac{2}{5} - 2\frac{9}{10}$
15. $9\frac{1}{6} - 5\frac{5}{6}$
16. $6 - 1\frac{7}{12}$

17. Adam purchased a 10 lb bag of dog food. His dog ate $7\frac{1}{3}$ lb. of dog food in one week. How many pounds of dog food were left after one week?

LESSON 5-5

Solve each equation. Write the solution in simplest form.

18. $a + 5\frac{3}{10} = 9$
19. $1\frac{3}{8} = x - 2\frac{1}{4}$
20. $6\frac{5}{6} = t + 1\frac{2}{3}$

21. Taylor needs to change a lightbulb that is $12\frac{1}{3}$ feet above the floor. Without a ladder, Taylor can reach $6\frac{1}{2}$ feet. How tall must her ladder be in order for her to reach the lightbulb?

LESSON 5-6

Multiply. Write each answer in simplest form.

22. $2 \cdot \frac{1}{5}$
23. $3 \cdot \frac{1}{6}$
24. $2 \cdot \frac{2}{11}$

25. There are 16 players on the baseball team. Of these players, $\frac{1}{4}$ are girls. How many girls play on the baseball team?

LESSON 5-7

Multiply. Write each answer in simplest form.

26. $\frac{1}{10} \cdot \frac{5}{6}$ **27.** $\frac{8}{9} \cdot \frac{3}{4}$ **28.** $\frac{5}{7} \cdot \frac{3}{10}$

Evaluate the expression $a \cdot \frac{1}{10}$ for each value of a. Write the answer in simplest form.

29. $a = \frac{4}{5}$ **30.** $a = \frac{2}{3}$ **31.** $a = \frac{5}{9}$

32. Camille spent $\frac{2}{5}$ of her weekly allowance on meals in restaurants. She spent $\frac{1}{2}$ of that money on pizza. What fraction of her weekly allowance did Camille spend on pizza?

LESSON 5-8

Multiply. Write each answer in simplest form.

33. $\frac{1}{4} \cdot 1\frac{2}{3}$ **34.** $2\frac{3}{5} \cdot \frac{1}{3}$ **35.** $\frac{7}{8} \cdot 1\frac{1}{3}$

Find each product. Write the answer in simplest form.

36. $1\frac{1}{3} \cdot 1\frac{3}{5}$ **37.** $4 \cdot 2\frac{6}{7}$ **38.** $\frac{2}{5}$ of $4\frac{1}{2}$

39. An art class has 18 students, and $\frac{1}{3}$ of the students are painting. How many of the students in the class are painting?

LESSON 5-9

Find the reciprocal.

40. $\frac{7}{9}$ **41.** $\frac{2}{13}$ **42.** $\frac{1}{12}$ **43.** $\frac{8}{5}$

Divide. Write each answer in simplest form.

44. $\frac{1}{6} \div 3$ **45.** $\frac{4}{7} \div 2$ **46.** $2\frac{1}{2} \div 1\frac{3}{4}$

47. Debbie bought $8\frac{1}{2}$ lb of ground turkey. She packed the turkey in $\frac{1}{2}$ lb containers and put them in the freezer. How many containers of ground turkey did she pack?

LESSON 5-10

Solve each equation. Write the answer in simplest form.

48. $\frac{3}{5}a = 12$ **49.** $6b = \frac{3}{7}$ **50.** $\frac{3}{8}x = 5$

51. $3s = \frac{7}{9}$ **52.** $\frac{5}{12}m = 3$ **53.** $\frac{9}{10}t = 6$

54. Joanie used $\frac{2}{3}$ of a box of invitations to invite friends to her birthday party. If she sent out 12 invitations, how many total invitations were in the box?

Extra Practice ▪ Chapter 6

LESSON 6-1

1. Each year a community holds a 5 km race. In 1998, 1,345 people participated in the race. In 1999, 1,415 people participated. In 2000, 1,532 people participated. In 2001, 1,607 people participated, and in 2002, 1,781 people participated. Use the data to make a table. Then use your table to describe how participation changed over time.

2. Make a table using the basketball data below. Then use your table to tell which player had the most points, rebounds, and assists.

   In 1,560 games, Kareem Abdul-Jabbar scored 38,387 points, grabbed 17,440 rebounds, and made 5,660 assists. In 897 games, Larry Bird scored 21,791 points, grabbed 8,974 rebounds, and made 5,695 assists. In 963 games, Bill Russell scored 14,522 points, grabbed 21,620 rebounds, and made 4,100 assists.

LESSON 6-2

Find the mean, median, mode, and range of each data set.

3.

Points Scored				
16	18	23	13	15

4.

Hours Worked							
37	42	43	38	39	40	45	40

LESSON 6-3

5. **a.** The table shows a student's test scores. Find the mean, median, and mode of the test scores.

   b. On the next test the student scored a 92. Find the mean, median, and mode with the new test score.

Test Scores			
78	82	87	95

6. The daily temperatures for the first eight days of April were 52°F, 63°F, 61°F, 54°F, 52°F, 55°F, 68°F, and 75°. What are the mean, median, and mode of this data set? Which one best describes the data set?

LESSON 6-4

Use the bar graph to answer each question.

7. Which type of vacation received the most votes?

8. Which types of vacations received more than 20 votes?

9. Use the data given below to make a bar graph.

Number of Days with Temperatures over 100°F			
June	3	August	14
July	5	September	7

Favorite Vacations

Extra Practice ■ Chapter 6

LESSON 6-5

10. Use the data of students' heights to make a frequency table with intervals. Then use your frequency table to make a histogram.

Heights of Students (in.)							
63	58	48	60	60	65	56	57
56	62	61	58	59	55	64	50

11. Make a line plot of the data.

Number of Miles Biked																								
14	45	33	34	32	37	44	19	35	36	17	33	35	40	41	38	47	31	44	23	27	20	33	45	27

LESSON 6-6

Name the ordered pair for each location on the grid.

12. L   **13.** M   **14.** R

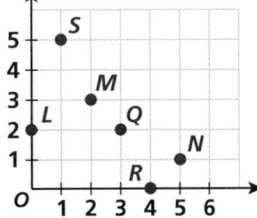

Graph and label each point on a coordinate grid.

15. $A(0, 3)$ **16.** $B(5\frac{1}{2}, 3)$ **17.** $C(2, 1\frac{1}{2})$

LESSON 6-7

18. Use the data in the table to make a double-line graph. Did toy sales increase or decrease for store A?

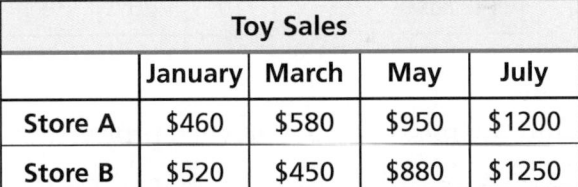

Toy Sales				
	January	March	May	July
Store A	$460	$580	$950	$1200
Store B	$520	$450	$880	$1250

LESSON 6-8

19. Explain why this bar graph is misleading.

20. What might people believe from the misleading graph?

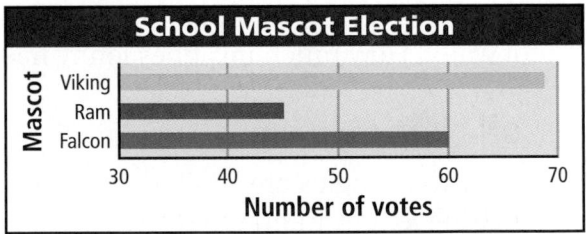

LESSON 6-9

21. Use the data in the table to make a stem-and-leaf plot. Then use your stem-and-leaf plot to find the mean, median, and mode of the data.

Time Spent Doing Homework (min)				
15	35	60	65	15
10	35	60	20	35

LESSON 6-10

22. The table shows the shoe sizes of the female students in Mrs. Woodward's gym class. Which graph would be more appropriate to show the data—a stem-and-leaf plot or a line plot? Draw the more appropriate graph.

Shoe Sizes of Female Students																	
7	8	$7\frac{1}{2}$	8	9	5	$9\frac{1}{2}$	7	$7\frac{1}{2}$	$7\frac{1}{2}$	$8\frac{1}{2}$	8	7	$6\frac{1}{2}$	7	8	10	9

Extra Practice • Chapter 7

LESSON 7-1

Use the table to write each ratio.

1. cooking books to poetry books

2. biography books to total books

3. A pack of 12 pens costs $5.52. A pack of 8 pens costs $3.92. Which is the better deal?

Types of Books in Doug's Collection			
Reference	10	Comic	7
Mystery	8	Poetry	5
Biography	3	Cooking	4

LESSON 7-2

Use a table to find three equivalent ratios.

4. $\frac{2}{5}$

5. 5 to 12

6. 1:2

7. $\frac{6}{7}$

8. The table shows how many pizzas Travis Middle School orders for certain numbers of students. Predict the number of pizzas the school orders for 175 students.

Students	50	100	150	200	250
Pizzas	10	20	30	40	50

LESSON 7-3

Find the missing value in each proportion.

9. $\frac{5}{4} = \frac{n}{12}$

10. $\frac{2}{9} = \frac{4}{n}$

11. $\frac{6}{10} = \frac{n}{5}$

12. $\frac{7}{8} = \frac{21}{n}$

13. To make 2 quarts of punch, Jenny adds 16 grams of juice mix to 2 quarts of water. How much mix does Jenny need to make 3 quarts of punch?

LESSON 7-4

14. The two triangles are similar. Find the missing length y and the measure of $\angle B$.

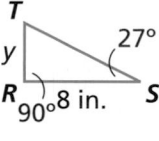
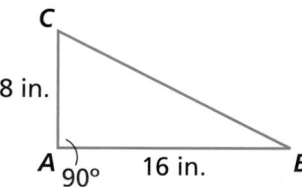

LESSON 7-5

15. A telephone pole casts a shadow that is 32 yd long. At the same time, a yardstick casts a shadow that is 4 yd long. How tall is the telephone pole?

LESSON 7-6

Use the map to answer each question.

16. On the map, the distance from State College to Belmont is 2 cm. What is the actual distance between the two locations?

17. Henderson City is 83 miles from State College. How many centimeters apart should the two locations be placed on the map?

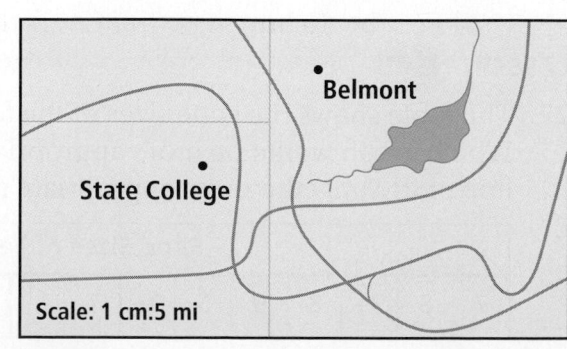

Scale: 1 cm:5 mi

LESSON 7-7

Write each percent as a fraction in simplest form.

18. 50%   **19.** 34%   **20.** 8%   **21.** 12%

22. Michael's baseball team won 85% of its games. Write 85% as a fraction in simplest form.

Write each percent as a decimal.

23. 13%   **24.** 76%   **25.** 5%   **26.** 70%

27. At the toy store, sales increased by 26%. Write 26% as a decimal.

LESSON 7-8

Write each decimal as a percent.

28. 0.56   **29.** 0.092   **30.** 0.4   **31.** 0.735

Write each fraction as a percent.

32. $\frac{4}{5}$ **33.** $\frac{4}{25}$ **34.** $\frac{7}{16}$ **35.** $\frac{5}{8}$

36. In Mrs. Piper's class, $\frac{17}{20}$ of the students have a pet. What percent of the students in the class have pets?

LESSON 7-9

37. A theater sold a total of 570 tickets for a new movie. Of those tickets, 30% were children's tickets. How many children's tickets were sold?

38. Kathy has listened to 80% of the music on a CD. If 26 minutes have passed, how many more minutes of music are left on the CD?

39. Find 30% of 98.   **40.** Find 15% of 220.   **41.** Find 5% of 72.

LESSON 7-10

42. Ashley wants to buy a sweater regularly priced at $19.95. It is on sale for 25% off the regular price. About how much will she pay for the sweater after the discount?

43. Margo and her three friends went to dinner. The bill was $34.62. They left a tip that was 15% of the bill. About how much was the tip?

44. Patricia is buying new roller skates that cost $59.99. The sales tax rate is 7%. About how much will the total cost of the roller skates be?

Extra Practice ▪ Chapter 8

LESSON 8-1

Use the diagram to name each geometric figure.

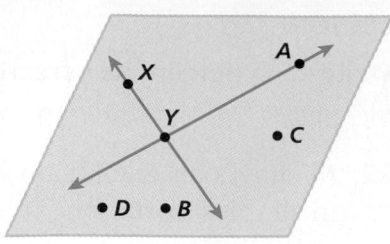

1. three points

2. two lines

3. a point shared by two lines

4. a plane

Use the diagram to give a possible name to each figure.

5. three line segments

6. three ways to name the line

7. six rays

8. another name for ray *XY*

LESSON 8-2

Use a protractor to measure each angle. Classify each angle as acute, right, obtuse, or straight.

9. 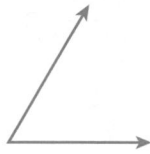　　10. 　　11. 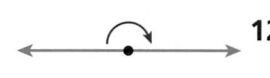　　12.

LESSON 8-3

Find each unknown angle measure.

13. 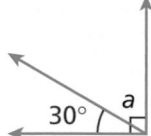　　14. 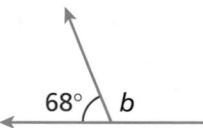　　15. 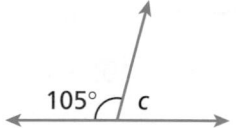　　16.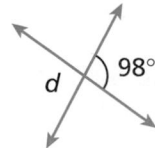

LESSON 8-4

Classify each pair of lines.

17. 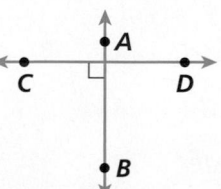　　18. 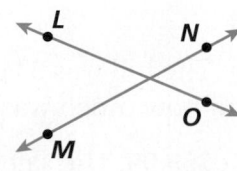　　19. 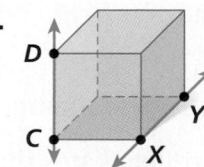　　20.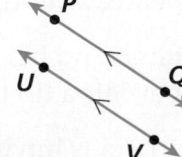

Extra Practice ■ Chapter 8

LESSON 8-5

Use the diagram to find the measure of each indicated angle.

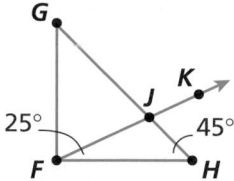

21. ∠FJH

22. ∠FJG

Classify each triangle using the given information.

23. The perimeter of the triangle is 14 in.

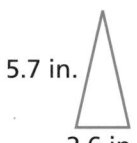

5.7 in.

2.6 in.

24. The perimeter of the triangle is 45 ft.

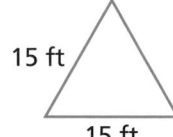

15 ft

15 ft

25. The perimeter of the triangle is 20 ft.

5 ft   6 ft

LESSON 8-6

Give the most descriptive name for each figure.

26.

27.

28.

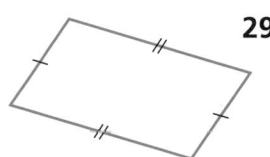

29.

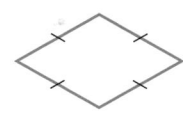

Complete each statement.

30. A parallelogram with four right angles can be a _____?_____ or a _____?_____ .

31. A quadrilateral with two parallel sides is a _____?_____ .

LESSON 8-7

Tell whether each shape is a polygon. If so, give it's name and tell whether it appears to be regular or not regular.

32.

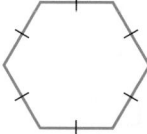

33.

34.

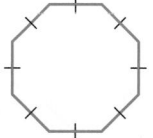

35.

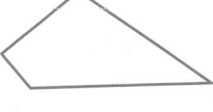

LESSON 8-8

Identify a possible pattern. Use the pattern to draw the missing figure.

36.

   ?

37.

    ?

LESSON 8-9

Decide whether the figures in each pair are congruent. If not, explain.

38.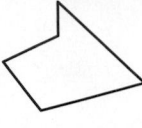

39.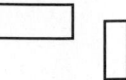

LESSON 8-10

Tell whether each is a translation, rotation, or reflection.

40.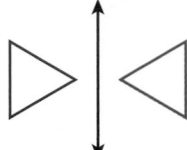

41.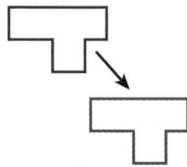

42.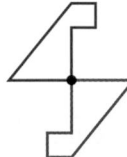

Draw each transformation.

43. Draw a translation 2 cm to the right.

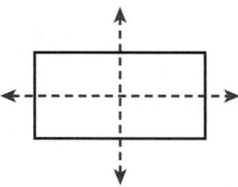

44. Draw a 90° clockwise rotation about the point.

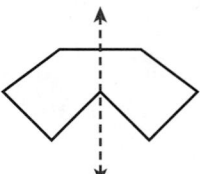

45. Draw a vertical reflection across the line.

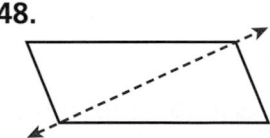

LESSON 8-11

Determine whether each dashed line appears to be a line of symmetry.

46.

47.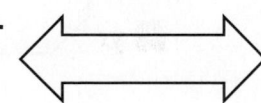

48.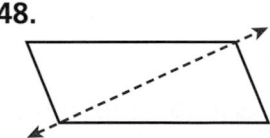

49.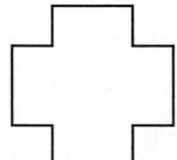

Find all of the lines of symmetry in each design.

50.

51.

52.

LESSON 9-1

What unit of measure provides the best estimate? Explain.

1. A book is about 12 _____?_____ long.

2. A newborn baby weights about 8 _____?_____.

3. A small aquarium holds about 10 _____?_____ of water.

LESSON 9-2

What unit of measure provides the best estimate? Explain.

4. An earthworm is about 10 _____?_____ long.

5. A leaf has a mass of about 250 _____?_____.

6. The mass of a fork is about 40 _____?_____.

LESSON 9-3

Convert.

7. 156 in = ▪ ft

8. 6 T = ▪ lb

9. 24 qt = ▪ gal

10. 13,200 ft = ▪ mi

11. 8 pt = ▪ qt

12. 33 yd = ▪ ft

13. A marathon is about 26.2 miles. How many feet long is a marathon?

LESSON 9-4

14. The height of a telephone pole is 15 meters. How many centimeters is this?

Convert.

15. A hat has a mass of about 86 g. 86 g = ▪ kg

16. A rain gauge holds about 0.5 L of water. 0.5 L = ▪ mL

17. 550 g = ▪ kg

18. 88 cm = ▪ mm

19. 1,585 m = ▪ km

20. 5,500 mg = ▪ g

21. 200 mL = ▪ L

22. 2.2 mL = ▪ L

LESSON 9-5

23. 1,095 days = ▪ yr

24. 4 min 23 s = ▪ s

25. 3 weeks = ▪ hr

26. 96 h = ▪ days

27. 78 weeks = ▪ yr

28. 1h 35 min = ▪ min

29. Rochelle's birthday party starts at 7:30 P.M. and lasts for 3 hours 45 minutes. What time does her party end?

Estimate the temperature.

30. 18º C is about ▪ º F

31. 35º F is about ▪ º C

32. 44º C is about ▪ º F

LESSON 9-6

Estimate the measure of ∠A in each figure. Then use a protractor to check the reasonableness of your answer..

33.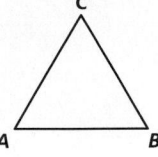

34.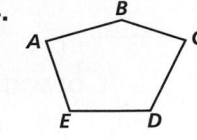

35.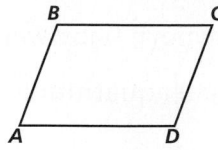

36. The shape of a swimming pool is shown. Find the measures of ∠A and ∠C.

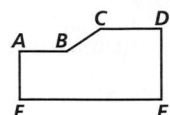

LESSON 9-7

Find the perimeter of each figure.

37.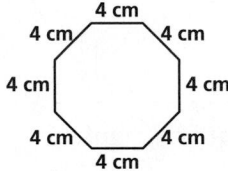

38.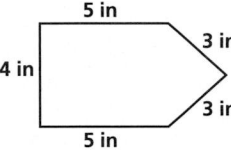

Find the perimeter *P* of each rectangle.

39.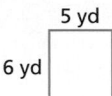

40.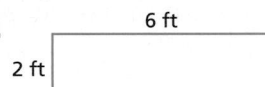

41. 1 in.
4 in.

Find each unknown measure.

42. What is the value of *b* if the perimeter equals 82 cm?

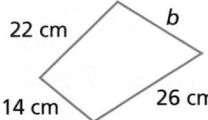

43. What is the value of *x* if the perimeter equals 36?

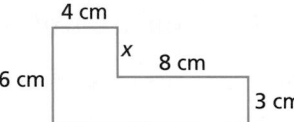

LESSON 9-8

A carpenter is building a circular tabletop. Find the circumference by rounding π to 3.

tabletop

44. What is the circumference if the diameter is 4 feet?

45. If the radius of the tabletop is 3 feet, what is its circumference?

Find each missing value to the nearest hundredth. Use 3.14 for π.

46. $C = ?$

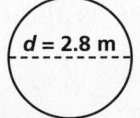

$d = 2.8$ m

47. $r = ?$

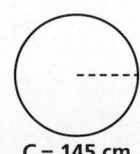

$C = 145$ cm

Extra Practice ▪ Chapter 10

LESSON 10-1

Find the area of each figure.

1.

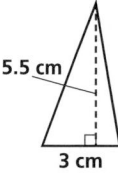

7 m

4 m

2.

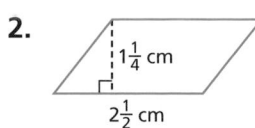

$1\frac{1}{4}$ cm

$2\frac{1}{2}$ cm

3.

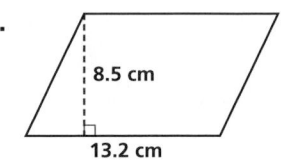

8.5 cm

13.2 cm

LESSON 10-2

Find the area of each triangle or trapezoid.

4.

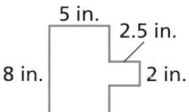

5.5 cm

3 cm

5.

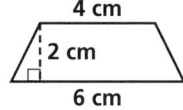

4 cm

2 cm

6 cm

6.

3 cm

4 cm

7. A sailboat's sail is shaped like a triangle with a base of 6 feet and a height of 17 feet. What is the area of the sail?

LESSON 10-3

Find the area of each polygon.

8.

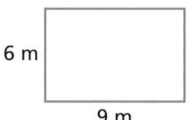

5 in.

2.5 in.

8 in.

2 in.

9.

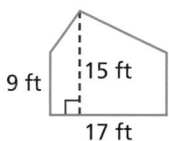

9 ft

15 ft

17 ft

LESSON 10-4

Find how the perimeter and area of each figure change when the dimensions change.

10.

6 m

9 m

→ 2 cm

3 cm

LESSON 10-5

Estimate the area of each circle. Use 3 to approximate *pi*.

11.

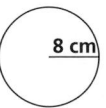

8 cm

12.

2.2 in.

13.

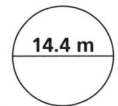

14.4 m

Find the area of each circle. Use $\frac{22}{7}$ for *pi*.

14.

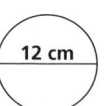

12 cm

15.

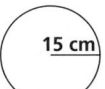

15 cm

16.

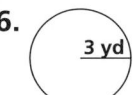

3 yd

17. A pie recipe calls for the crust to be rolled out to form a circle with a diameter of 9 in. Find the area of the dough when it is rolled out. Use 3.14 for *pi*.

Extra Practice ▪ Chapter 10

LESSON 10-6

Identify the number of faces, edges, and vertices on each three-dimensional figure.

18. 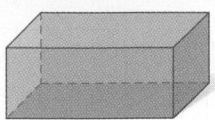   **19.** 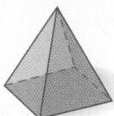   **20.**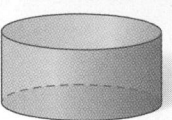

LESSON 10-7

Find the volume of each prism.

21.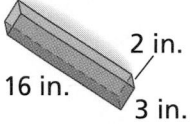
2 in.
16 in.
3 in.

22.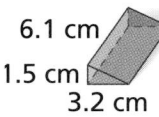
6.1 cm
1.5 cm
3.2 cm

23.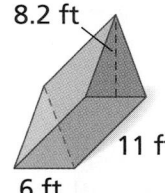
8.2 ft
11 ft
6 ft

LESSON 10-8

Find the volume *V* of each cylinder to the nearest cubic unit. Use 3.14 for π.

24.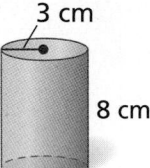
3 cm
8 cm

25.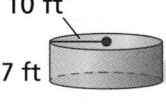
10 ft
7 ft

26.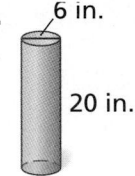
6 in.
20 in.

27. A cylindrical rain gauge with a diameter of 2 inches is filled with rainwater to a height of 8.4 inches. Estimate the volume of the rainwater to the nearest cubic inch.

28. Find which cylinder has the greater volume.

Cylinder A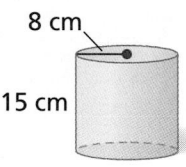
8 cm
15 cm

Cylinder B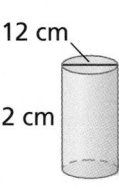
12 cm
22 cm

LESSON 10-9

Find the surface area *S* of each three-dimensional figure. Use 3.14 for π.

29.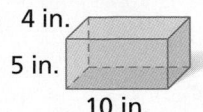
4 in.
5 in.
10 in.

30.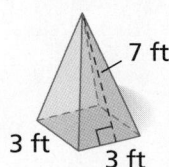
7 ft
3 ft
3 ft

31.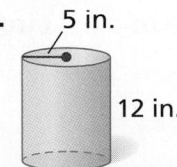
5 in.
12 in.

Extra Practice ▪ Chapter 11

LESSON 11-1

Name a positive or negative number to represent each situation.

1. 120 feet below sea level   2. saving $22   3. a decrease of 5°

Graph each integer and its opposite on a number line.

4. +1   5. −5   6. −3   7. +2

8. Death Valley, California, has an elevation of −282 feet. Long Beach, California, has an elevation of 170 feet. Which location is farther from sea level?

LESSON 11-2

Compare each pair of integers. Write < or >.

9. 15 ▨ −19   10. −7 ▨ −10   11. −3 ▨ 7   12. −8 ▨ 2

Order the integers in each set from least to greatest.

13. −6, 5, −2   14. 12, −25, 10   15. −1, −3, 4, 0

16. On Monday, the temperature was 3°C. On Tuesday, the temperature was −4°C. On Wednesday, the temperature was −1°C. On which day was the temperature the coldest?

LESSON 11-3

Name the quadrant where each point is located.

17. A   18. R   19. C   20. T

Give the coordinates of each point.

21. B   22. S   23. D   24. U

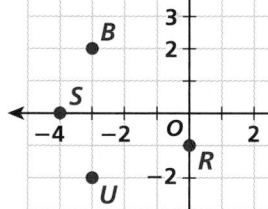

Graph each point on a coordinate plane.

25. M(2, −1)   26. W(−4, −2)   27. A(2, 3)

LESSON 11-4

Evaluate $y + 2$ for each value of y.

28. $y = −5$ 29. $y = −1$ 30. $y = 3$ 31. $y = −8$

32. In the morning, the temperature was −3°C. By the afternoon, the temperature had risen 7°C. What was the temperature in the afternoon?

LESSON 11-5

Evaluate $a − (−5)$ for each value of a.

33. $a = −6$ 34. $a = 2$ 35. $a = 1$ 36. $a = −5$

Extra Practice ■ Chapter 11

LESSON 11-6

Find each product.

37. $5 \cdot (-2)$ **38.** $-3 \cdot (-7)$ **39.** $-4 \cdot 4$ **40.** $8 \cdot (-9)$

Evaluate $3x$ for each value of x.

41. $x = -5$ **42.** $x = 8$ **43.** $x = -9$ **44.** $x = 0$

LESSON 11-7

Find each quotient.

45. $20 \div (-4)$ **46.** $-48 \div (-6)$ **47.** $-24 \div 8$ **48.** $-18 \div (-2)$

Evaluate $\frac{n}{4}$ for each value of n.

49. $n = -36$ **50.** $n = 44$ **51.** $n = -12$ **52.** $n = -60$

LESSON 11-8

Solve each equation. Check your answers.

53. $5 + y = 1$ **54.** $b - 8 = -6$ **55.** $-6 + m = -2$

56. $-6g = 30$ **57.** $-3c = -9$ **58.** $7r = -42$

LESSON 11-9

Write an equation for a function that gives the values in each table. Use the equation to find the value of y for the indicated value of x.

59.

x	1	2	3	4	5	10
y	7	9	11	13	15	■

60.

x	3	5	7	9	11	13
y	5	11	17	23	29	■

Write an equation for the function. Tell what each variable you use represents.

61. The length of a rectangle is 4 cm less than 3 times its width.

62. Darren's age is 5 more than 2 times Nicole's age.

LESSON 11-10

Use the given x-values to write solutions of each equation as ordered pairs.

63. $y = 6x + 2$ for $x = 1, 2, 3, 4$ **64.** $y = 5x - 9$ for $x = 2, 3, 4, 5$

Determine whether the ordered pair is a solution to the given equation.

65. $(2, 3)$; $y = x + 1$ **66.** $(9, 7)$; $y = 3x - 12$

Graph the function described by each equation.

67. $y = 4x - 3$ **68.** $y = x + 1$

Extra Practice ■ Chapter 12

LESSON 12-1

Write *impossible*, *unlikely*, *as likely as not*, *likely*, or *certain* to describe each event.

1. picking a green marble from this bag of marbles

2. picking a red marble from this bag of marbles

3. The chance of winning a sweepstakes is 3%. Write this probability as a decimal and as a fraction.

4. A particular brand of cereal is offering a prize in each box. There is a 34% chance the toy will be a rubber ball, a 50% chance it will be a small figurine, and a 16% chance it will be a game. Is it more likely that the prize will be a rubber ball or a game?

LESSON 12-2

For each experiment, identify the outcome shown.

5.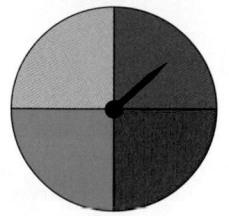

6.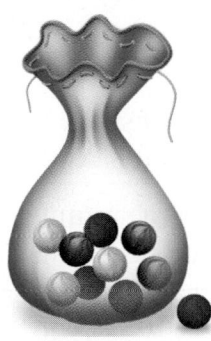

For one month, Maggie recorded the weather. She organized her results in a frequency table.

7. Find the experimental probability of cloudy weather.

8. Based on Maggie's findings, is it more likely that the weather will be cloudy or rainy?

Weather	Sunny	Cloudy	Rainy
Frequency	17	6	7

LESSON 12-3

9. Miguel is buying a new car. He has three choices for the exterior color: black, silver, or blue. He has two choices for the interior color: black or brown. What are the different color combinations Miguel can choose from?

10. For breakfast, Brianna can have oatmeal, cold cereal, or eggs and then a banana, an apple, or an orange. How many different breakfast combinations can Brianna choose from?

11. At summer camp, the campers can participate in 3 different activities each morning: hiking, swimming, and arts and crafts and 2 different activities each afternoon: tennis and biking. How many possible combinations of activities are there?

LESSON 12-4

12. What is the probability of rolling an even number on a fair number cube?

13. What is the probability of randomly choosing the letter *T* from the letters *M, A, T, H, E, M, A, T, I, C, S*?

14. The weather report stated that there is a 42% chance of snow today. What is the probability that it will NOT snow?

15. During its grand opening, a store is giving away prizes. The chance of winning a prize is 0.16. Find the probability of NOT winning a prize.

LESSON 12-5

16. Find the probability of spinning red on the spinner and choosing a red marble from the bag.

17. Find the probability of spinning yellow and choosing a marble that is NOT yellow.

18. Find the probability of spinning a color that is NOT blue and choosing a marble that is NOT blue.

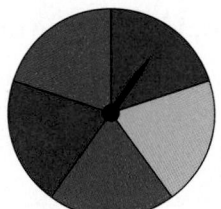
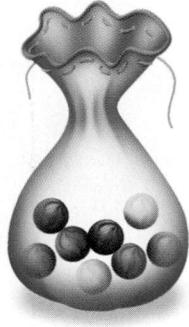

19. You toss two fair coins and roll a fair number cube. What is the probability that both coins will land heads up and the cube will show a number greater than 4?

LESSON 12-6

20. Based on a sample survey, a local newspaper stated that 26% of the population has a pet dog. Out of 600 people, how many people can you predict will have a pet dog?

21. If you roll a number cube 54 times, how many times do you expect to roll a number less than 3?

22. A promotion team is selling tickets for unreserved seats to a concert. The promotion team estimates that 75% of the people who purchase a ticket will attend the concert. If the stadium seats 15,000 people and the promotion team wants to have all of the seats full at the concert, how many concert tickets should they sell?

Draw a Diagram

When problems involve objects, distances, or places, you can **draw a diagram** to make the problem easier to understand. You will often be able to use your diagram to solve the problem.

Problem Solving Strategies

Draw a Diagram	Make a Table
Make a Model	Solve a Simpler Problem
Guess and Test	Use Logical Reasoning
Work Backward	Act It Out
Find a Pattern	Make an Organized List

All city blocks in Sunnydale are the same size. Tina starts her paper route at the corner of two streets. She travels 8 blocks south, 13 blocks west, 8 blocks north, and 6 blocks east. How far is she from her starting point when she finishes her route?

Understand the Problem

Identify the important information.

- Each block is the same size.
- You are given Tina's route.

The answer will be the distance from her starting point.

Make a Plan

Use the information in the problem to **draw a diagram** showing Tina's route. Label her starting and ending points.

Solve

The diagram shows that at the end of Tina's route she is 13 − 6 blocks from her starting point.

$$13 - 6 = 7$$

When Tina finishes, she is 7 blocks from her starting point.

Look Back

Be sure that you have drawn your diagram correctly. Does it match the information given in the problem?

PRACTICE

1. Laurence drives a carpool to school every Monday. He starts at his house and travels 4 miles south to pick up two children. Then he drives 9 miles west to pick up two more children, and then he drives 4 miles north to pick up one more child. Finally, he drives 5 miles east to get to the school. How far does he have to travel to get back home?

2. The roots of a tree reach 12 feet into the ground. A kitten is stuck 5 feet from the top of the tree. From the treetop to the root bottom, the tree measures 32 feet. How far above the ground is the kitten?

Make a Model

If a problem involves objects, you can sometimes **make a model** using those objects or similar objects to act out the problem. This can help you understand the problem and find the solution.

Problem Solving Strategies

Draw a Diagram	Make a Table
Make a Model	Solve a Simpler Problem
Guess and Test	Use Logical Reasoning
Work Backward	Act It Out
Find a Pattern	Make an Organized List

Alice has three pieces of ribbon. Their lengths are 7 inches, 10 inches, and 12 inches. Alice does not have a ruler or scissors. How can she use these ribbons to measure a length of 15 inches?

Understand the Problem

Identify the important information.

- The ribbons are 7 inches, 10 inches, and 12 inches long.

The answer will show how to use the ribbons to measure 15 inches.

Make a Plan

Measure and cut three ribbons or strips of paper to **make a model.** One ribbon should be 7 inches long, one should be 10 inches long, and one should be 12 inches long. Try different combinations of the ribbons to form new lengths.

Solve

When you put any two ribbons together end to end, you can form lengths of 17, 19, and 22 inches. All of these are too long.

Try placing the 10-inch ribbon and the 12-inch ribbon end to end to make 22 inches. Now place the 7-inch ribbon above them. The remaining length that is **not** underneath the 7-inch ribbon will measure 15 inches.

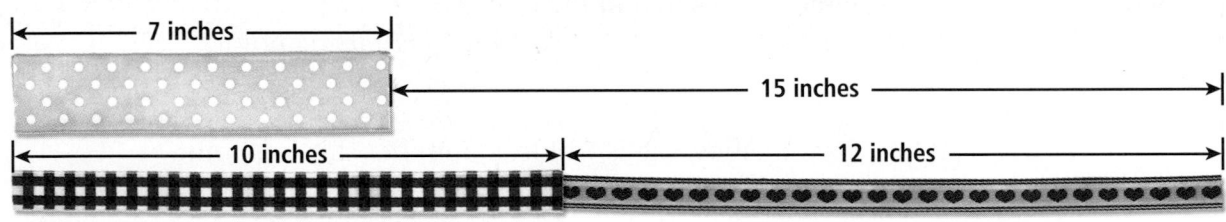

Look Back

Use another strategy. Without using ribbon, you could have **guessed** different ways to add or subtract 7, 10, and 12. Then you could have **tested** to see if any of these gave an answer of 15:

$10 + 12 - 7 = 15$

PRACTICE

1. Find other lengths that you can measure with the three pieces of ribbon.

2. Andy stacks four cubes, one on top of the other, and paints the outside of the stack (not the bottom). How many faces of the cubes are painted?

Guess and Test

If you do not know how to solve a problem, you can always make a **guess**. Then **test** your guess using the information in the problem. Use the result to make a better guess. Repeat until you find the correct answer.

Problem Solving Strategies

Draw a Diagram
Make a Model
Guess and Test
Work Backward
Find a Pattern

Make a Table
Solve a Simpler Problem
Use Logical Reasoning
Act It Out
Make an Organized List

There were 25 problems on a test. For each correct answer, 4 points were given. For each incorrect answer, 1 point was subtracted. Tania answered all 25 problems. Her score was 85. How many correct and incorrect answers did she have?

 **Understand the Problem**

Identify the important information.

- There were 25 problems on the test.
- A correct answer received 4 points, and an incorrect answer lost 1 point.
- Tania answered all of the problems and her score was 85.

The answer will be the number of problems that Tania got correct and incorrect.

 **Make a Plan**

Start with a **guess** for the number of correct answers. Then **test** to see whether the total score is 85.

 **Solve**

Make a first guess of 20 correct answers.

Correct	Incorrect	Score	Result
20	5	$(20 \times 4) - (5 \times 1) = 80 - 5 = 75$	Too low—guess higher
23	2	$(23 \times 4) - (2 \times 1) = 92 - 2 = 90$	Too high—guess lower
22	3	$(22 \times 4) - (3 \times 1) = 88 - 3 = 85$	Correct ✓

Tania had 22 correct answers and 3 incorrect answers.

 **Look Back**

Notice that the guesses made while solving this problem were not just "wild" guesses. Guessing and testing in an organized way will often lead you to the correct answer.

PRACTICE

1. The sum of Joe's age and his younger brother's age is 38. The difference between their ages is 8. How old are Joe and his brother?

2. Amy bought some used books for $4.95. She paid $0.50 each for some books and $0.35 each for the others. She bought fewer than 8 books at each price. How many books did Amy buy? How many cost $0.50?

Work Backward

Some problems give you a sequence of information and ask you to find something that happened at the beginning. To solve a problem like this, you may want to start at the end of the problem and **work backward.**

Problem Solving Strategies

Draw a Diagram	Make a Table
Make a Model	Solve a Simpler Problem
Guess and Test	Use Logical Reasoning
Work Backward	Act It Out
Find a Pattern	Make an Organized List

Jaclyn and her twin sister, Bailey, received money for their birthday. They used half of their money to buy a video game. Then they spent half of the money they had left on a pizza. Finally, they spent half of the remaining money to rent a movie. At the end of the day, they had $4.50. How much money did they have to start out with?

Understand the Problem

Identify the important information.

- The girls ended with $4.50.
- They spent half of their money at each of three stops.

The answer will be the amount of money they started with.

Make a Plan

Start with the amount you know the girls have left, $4.50, and **work backward** through the information given in the problem.

Solve

Jaclyn and Bailey had $4.50 at the end of the day.

They had twice that amount before renting a movie. $2 \times \$4.50 = \$9$

They had twice that amount before buying a pizza. $2 \times \$9 = \$18$

They had twice that amount before buying a video game. $2 \times \$18 = \$36$

The girls started with $36.

Look Back

Using the starting amount of $36, work from the beginning of the problem. Find the amount they spent at each location and see whether they are left with $4.50.

Start: $36
Video game: $36 \div 2 = \$18$
Pizza: $18 \div 2 = \$9$
Movie rental: $9 \div 2 = \$4.50$ ✓

PRACTICE

1. The Lauber family has 4 children. Chris is 5 years younger than his brother Mark. Justin is half as old as his brother Chris. Mary, who is 10, is 3 years younger than Justin. How old is Mark?

2. If you divide a mystery number by 4, add 8, and multiply by 3, you get 42. What is the mystery number?

Find a Pattern

In some problems, there is a relationship between different pieces of information. Examine this relationship and try to **find a pattern.** You can then use this pattern to find more information and the solution to the problem.

Problem Solving Strategies

Draw a Diagram	Make a Table
Make a Model	Solve a Simpler Problem
Guess and Test	Use Logical Reasoning
Work Backward	Act It Out
Find a Pattern	Make an Organized List

Students are using the pattern at right to build stairways for a model house. How many blocks are needed to build a stairway with seven steps?

 **Understand the Problem**

The answer will be the total number of blocks in a stairway with seven steps.

 **Make a Plan**

Try to **find a pattern** between the number of steps and the number of blocks needed.

Notice that the first step is made of one block. The second step is made of two blocks, the third step is made of three blocks, and the fourth step is made of four blocks.

Step	Number of Blocks in Step	Total Number of Blocks in Stairway
2	2	$1 + 2 = 3$
3	3	$1 + 2 + 3 = 6$
4	4	$1 + 2 + 3 + 4 = 10$

To find the total number of blocks, add the number of blocks in the first step, the second step, the third step, and so on.

Solve

The seventh step will be made of seven blocks. The total number of blocks will be $1 + 2 + 3 + 4 + 5 + 6 + 7 = 28$.

Look Back

Use another strategy. You can **draw a diagram** of a stairway with 7 steps. Count the number of blocks in your diagram. There are 28 blocks.

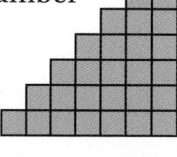

PRACTICE

1. A cereal company adds baseball cards to the 3rd box, the 6th box, the 11th box, the 18th box, and so on of each case of cereal. In a case of 40 boxes, how many boxes will have baseball cards?

2. Describe the pattern and find the missing numbers.

1; 4; 16; 64; 256; ▪; ▪; 16,384

Make a Table

When you are given a lot of information in a problem, it may be helpful to organize that information. One way to organize information is to **make a table.**

Problem Solving Strategies

Draw a Diagram	**Make a Table**
Make a Model	Solve a Simpler Problem
Guess and Test	Use Logical Reasoning
Work Backward	Act It Out
Find a Pattern	Make an Organized List

Mrs. Melo's students scored the following on their math test: 90, 80, 77, 78, 91, 92, 73, 62, 83, 79, 72, 85, 93, 84, 75, 68, 82, 94, 98, and 82. An A is given for 90 to 100 points, a B for 80 to 89 points, a C for 70 to 79 points, a D for 60 to 69 points, and an F for less than 60 points. Find the number of students who scored each letter grade.

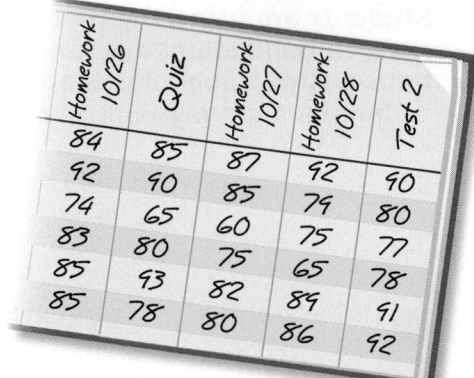

Homework 10/26	Quiz	Homework 10/27	Homework 10/28	Test 2
84	85	87	92	90
92	90	85	79	80
74	65	60	75	77
83	80	75	65	78
85	93	82	89	91
85	78	80	86	92

Understand the Problem

Identify the important information.

- You have been given the list of scores and the letter grades that go with each score.

The answer will be the number of each letter grade.

Make a Plan

Make a table to organize the scores. Use the information in the problem to set up your table. Make one row for each letter grade.

Solve

Read through the list of scores. As you read each score, make a tally in the appropriate place in your table. There are 20 test scores, so be sure you have 20 tallies in all.

Mrs. Melo gave out six A's, six B's, six C's, two D's, and no F's.

Letter Grade	Number
A (90–100)	JHT I
B (80–89)	JHT I
C (70–79)	JHT I
D (60–69)	II
F (below 60)	

Look Back

Use another strategy. Another way you could solve this problem is to **make an organized list.** Order the scores from least to greatest, and count how many scores are in each range.

62, 68, 72, 73, 75, 77, 78, 79, 80, 82, 82, 83, 84, 85, 90, 91, 92, 93, 94, 98
 D   C   B   A

PRACTICE

1. The debate club has 6 members. Each member will debate each of the other members exactly once. How many total debates will there be?

2. At the library, there are three story-telling sessions. Each one lasts 45 minutes, with 30 minutes between sessions. If the first session begins at 10:00 A.M., what time does the last session end?

Solve a Simpler Problem

Problem Solving Strategies

Sometimes a problem contains large numbers or requires many steps. Try to **solve a simpler problem** that is similar. Solve the simpler problem first, and then try the same steps to solve the original problem.

Draw a Diagram	Make a Table
Make a Model	**Solve a Simpler Problem**
Guess and Test	Use Logical Reasoning
Work Backward	Act It Out
Find a Pattern	Make an Organized List

At the end of a soccer game, each player shakes hands with every player on the opposing team. How many handshakes are there at the end of a game between two teams that each have 20 players?

 **Understand the Problem**

Identify the important information.

- There are 20 players on each team.
- Each player will shake hands with every player on the opposing team.

The answer will be the total number of handshakes exchanged.

 **Make a Plan**

Solve a simpler problem. For example, suppose each team had just one player. Then there would only be one handshake between the two players. Expand the number of players to two and then three.

 **Solve**

When there is 1 player, there is $1 \times 1 = 1$ handshake. For 2 players, there are $2 \times 2 = 4$ handshakes. And for 3 players, there are $3 \times 3 = 9$ handshakes.

If each team has 20 players, there will be $20 \times 20 = 400$ handshakes.

Players Per Team	Diagram	Handshakes
1	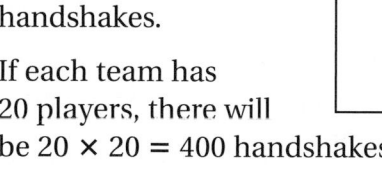	1
2		4
3		9

 **Look Back**

If the pattern is correct, for 4 players there will be 16 handshakes and for 5 players there will be 25 handshakes. Complete the next two rows of the table to check these answers.

PRACTICE

1. Martha has 5 pairs of pants and 4 blouses that she can wear to school. How many different outfits can she make?

2. What is the smallest 5-digit number that can be divided by 50 with a remainder of 17?

Use Logical Reasoning

Sometimes a problem may provide clues and facts that you must use to answer a question. You can **use logical reasoning** to solve this kind of problem.

Problem Solving Strategies

Draw a Diagram	Make a Table
Make a Model	Solve a Simpler Problem
Guess and Test	**Use Logical Reasoning**
Work Backward	Act It Out
Find a Pattern	Make an Organized List

Kevin, Ellie, and Jillian play three different sports. One person plays soccer, one likes to run track, and the other swims. Ellie is the sister of the swimmer. Kevin once went shopping with the swimmer and the track runner. Match each student with his or her sport.

Understand the Problem

Identify the important information.

- There are three people, and each person plays a different sport.
- Ellie is the sister of the swimmer.
- Kevin once went shopping with the swimmer and the track runner.

The answer will tell which student plays each sport.

Make a Plan

Start with clues given in the problem, and **use logical reasoning** to find the answer.

Solve

Make a table with a column for each sport and a row for each person. Work with the clues one at a time. Write "yes" in a box if the clue applies to that person. Write "no" if the clue does not apply.

	Soccer	Track	Swim
Kevin		no	no
Ellie			no
Jillian			

- Ellie is the sister of the swimmer, so she is not the swimmer.
- Kevin went shopping with the swimmer and the track runner. He is not the swimmer or the track runner.

So Kevin must be the soccer player, and Jillian must be the swimmer. This leaves Ellie as the track runner.

Look Back

Compare your answer to the clues in the problem. Make sure none of your conclusions conflict with the clues.

PRACTICE

1. Karin, Brent, and Lola each ordered a different slice of pizza: pepperoni, plain cheese, and ham-pineapple. Karin is allergic to pepperoni. Lola likes more than one topping. Which kind of pizza did each person order?

2. Leo, Jamal, and Kara are in fourth, fifth, and sixth grades. Kara is not in fourth grade. The sixth-grader is in chorus with Kara and has the same lunch time as Leo. Match the students with their grades.

Act It Out

Some problems involve actions or processes. To solve these problems, you can **act it out.** Actively modeling the problem can help you find the solution.

 Problem Solving Strategies

Draw a Diagram	Make a Table
Make a Model	Solve a Simpler Problem
Guess and Test	Use Logical Reasoning
Work Backward	**Act It Out**
Find a Pattern	Make an Organized List

Wei rolls a number cube and flips a coin at the same time. What fraction of all the possible results involve the number cube showing an even number and the coin landing heads up?

Understand the Problem

List the important information.

- Wei is rolling a number cube and flipping a coin at the same time.

The answer will be the fraction of all the possible results in which the number cube shows an even number and the coin lands heads up.

Make a Plan

Act it out to find out how many different results are possible. Then find the fraction of the results that involve an even number and heads.

Solve

Use a number cube and a coin. Turn them over one at a time to list all the possible results. Then circle the results in which the number cube shows an even number and the coin lands heads up.

Count the total number of possible results. There are 12 possible results. Count the number of circled results. There are 3 circled results. The fraction of the results with the number cube showing an even number and the coin landing heads up is $\frac{3}{12}$ or $\frac{1}{4}$.

Look Back

Check the list of all the possible results to make sure you haven't missed any. Also check that you have circled all the results in which the number cube shows an even number and the coin lands heads up.

PRACTICE

1. Jeremy flips a quarter and a nickel at the same time. What fraction of all the possible results involve both coins landing heads up?

2. Alyson rolls a red number cube and a blue number cube at the same time. What fraction of all the possible results involve both number cubes showing a 6?

Make an Organized List

Problem Solving Strategies

Draw a Diagram	Make a Table
Make a Model	Solve a Simpler Problem
Guess and Test	Use Logical Reasoning
Work Backward	Act It Out
Find a Pattern	**Make an Organized List**

In some problems, you will need to find how many different ways something can happen. It is often helpful to **make an organized list.** This will help you count the outcomes and be sure that you have included all of them.

In a game at an amusement park, players throw 3 darts at a target to score points and win prizes. If each dart lands within the target area, how many different total scores are possible?

 **Understand the Problem**

Identify the important information.

• A player throws three darts at the target.

The answer will be the number of different scores a player could earn.

Make a Plan

Make an organized list to determine all possible outcomes and score totals. List the value of each dart and the point total for all three darts.

 **Solve**

You can organize your list by the number of darts that land in the center. All three darts could hit the center circle. Or, two darts could hit the center circle and the third could hit a different circle. One dart could hit the center circle, or no darts could hit the center circle.

3 Darts Hit Center	2 Darts Hit Center	1 Dart Hits Center	0 Darts Hit Center
10 + 10 + 10 = 30	10 + 10 + 5 = 25	10 + 5 + 5 = 20	5 + 5 + 5 = 15
	10 + 10 + 2 = 22	10 + 5 + 2 = 17	5 + 5 + 2 = 12
		10 + 2 + 2 = 14	5 + 2 + 2 = 9
			2 + 2 + 2 = 6

Count the different outcomes. There are 10 possible scores.

Look Back

You could have listed outcomes in random order, but because your list is organized, you can be sure that you have not missed any possibilities. Check to be sure that every score is different.

PRACTICE

1. A restaurant has three different kinds of pancakes: cinnamon, blueberry, and apple. If you order one of each kind, how many different ways can the three pancakes be stacked?

2. How many ways can you make change for a quarter using dimes, nickels, and pennies?

Skills Bank · Review Skills

Place Value—Trillions Through Thousandths

 6.N.1

You can use a place-value chart to read and write numbers.

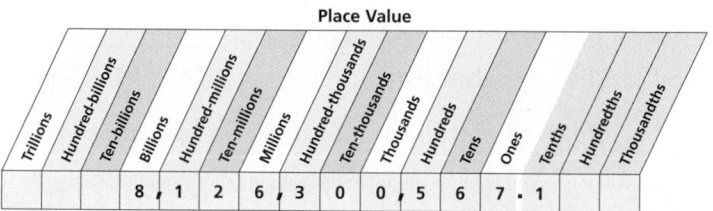

Place Value

EXAMPLE

What is the place value of the digit 3 in 8,126,300,567.1?

The digit 3 is in the hundred-thousands place.

PRACTICE

Write the place value of the underlined digit.

1. 1<u>4</u>,536,992.1
2. 3<u>4</u>.071
3. 6,<u>1</u>90.05
4. <u>5</u>,027,549,757,202
5. 1<u>0</u>3.526
6. 3.7<u>2</u>1
7. <u>6</u>5,331,040,421
8. 75,983.00<u>9</u>

Compare and Order Whole Numbers

 6.N.15

As you read a number line from left to right, the numbers are ordered from least to greatest.

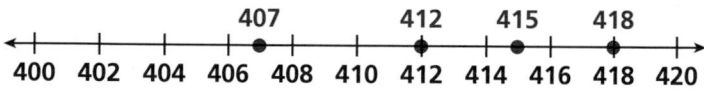

You can use a number line and place value to compare whole numbers. Use the symbols > (is greater than) and < (is less than).

EXAMPLE

Compare. Write <, >, or =.

A 412 ▮ 418
418 is to the right of 412 on a number line.
412 < 418

B 415 ▮ 407
1 ten is greater than 0 tens.
415 > 407

PRACTICE

Compare. Write <, >, or =.

1. 419 ▮ 410
2. 9,161 ▮ 8,957
3. 5,036 ▮ 5,402
4. 617 ▮ 681
5. 700 ▮ 698
6. 1,611 ▮ 1,489

Round Whole Numbers

You can use a number line or rounding rules to round whole numbers to the nearest 10, 100, 1,000, or 10,000.

EXAMPLE 1

Round 547 to the nearest 10.

Look at the number line.

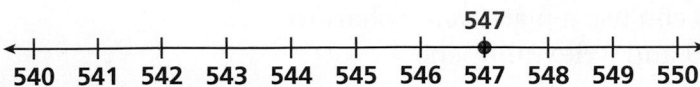

547 is closer to 550 than to 540. So 547 rounded to the nearest 10 is 550.

> **ROUNDING RULES**
>
> If the digit to the right is 5 or greater, increase the digit in the rounding place by 1.
>
> If the digit to the right is less than 5, keep the digit in the rounding place the same.

EXAMPLE 2

Round 12,573 to the nearest 1,000.

12,573   *Find the digit in the thousands place.*

↑ *Digit is 5 or greater. Add 1.*   *Look at the digit to its right.*

12,573 rounded to the nearest 1,000 is 13,000.

PRACTICE

Round each number to the given place value.

1. 15,638; nearest 100
2. 37,519; nearest 1,000
3. 9,298; nearest 10
4. 69,504; nearest 10,000
5. 852; nearest 1,000
6. 33,449; nearest 100

Round Decimals

You can use rounding rules to round decimals to the nearest whole number, tenth, hundredth, thousandth, or ten-thousandth.

EXAMPLE

Round each decimal to the given place value.

A 5.16; whole number

   1 < 5   So 5.16 rounds to 5.

B 13.45605; ten-thousandth

   5 ≥ 5   So 13.45605 rounds to 13.4561.

PRACTICE

Round each decimal to the given place value.

1. 3.982; tenth
2. 6.3174; hundredth
3. 1.471; whole number
4. 48.1526; hundredth
5. 5.03654; ten-thousandth
6. 0.083; tenth

Place Value Patterns

You can use basic facts and place value to solve math problems mentally.

EXAMPLE

Solve mentally.

A $300 + 200$

Basic fact: $3 + 2 = 5$ *Think: 3 hundreds + 2 hundreds*

$300 + 200 = 500$

B 200×600

Basic fact: $2 \times 6 = 12$ *Think: There are four zeros in the factors,*

$200 \times 600 = 120,000$ *so place four zeros in the product.*

PRACTICE

Solve mentally.

1. $500 + 400$ 2. $80 - 50$ 3. 700×30 4. $2,500 \div 50$

5. $1,200 + 600$ 6. $20 \times 9,000$ 7. $650 - 300$ 8. $320 \div 8$

Roman Numerals

Instead of using place value, as with the decimal system, combinations of letters are used to represent numbers in the Roman numeral system.

I = 1	V = 5	X = 10
L = 50	C = 100	D = 500
M = 1,000		

No letter can be written more than three times in a row. If a letter is written before a letter that represents a larger value, then subtract the first letter's value from the second letter's value.

EXAMPLE

Write each decimal number as a Roman numeral and each Roman numeral as a decimal number.

A 3

$3 = I + I + I = III$

B 9

$9 = X - I = IX$

C CLV

$CLV = 100 + 50 + 5 = 155$

D XC

$XC = 100 - 10 = 90$

PRACTICE

Write each decimal number as a Roman numeral and each Roman numeral as a decimal number.

1. 12   2. 25   3. 209   4. 54

5. VIII   6. LXXII   7. XIX   8. MMIV

Addition

Addition is used to find the total of two or more quantities. The answer to an addition problem is called the *sum*.

EXAMPLE

$4,617 + 5,682$

Step 1: Add the ones.	Step 2: Add the tens.	Step 3: Add the hundreds. Regroup.	Step 4: Add the thousands.
$\begin{array}{r} 4,617 \\ + 5,682 \\ \hline 9 \end{array}$	$\begin{array}{r} 4,617 \\ + 5,682 \\ \hline 99 \end{array}$	$\begin{array}{r} {\scriptstyle 1} \\ 4,617 \\ + 5,682 \\ \hline 299 \end{array}$	$\begin{array}{r} {\scriptstyle 1} \\ 4,617 \\ + 5,682 \\ \hline 10,299 \end{array}$

The sum is 10,299.

PRACTICE

Find the sum.

1. $711 + 591$ **2.** $2,580 + 2,345$ **3.** $21,470 + 13,329$

4. $\$165 + \$304$ **5.** $6,905 + 872$ **6.** $47,231 + 3,254$

Subtraction

Subtraction is used to take away one quantity from another quantity or to compare two quantities. The answer to a subtraction problem is called the *difference*. The difference tells how much greater or smaller one number is than the other.

EXAMPLE

$780 - 468$

Step 1: Regroup. Subtract the ones.	Step 2: Subtract the tens.	Step 3: Subtract the hundreds.
$\begin{array}{r} {\scriptstyle 7\ 10} \\ 7\,8\,0 \\ - 4\,6\,8 \\ \hline 2 \end{array}$	$\begin{array}{r} {\scriptstyle 7\ 10} \\ 7\,8\,0 \\ - 4\,6\,8 \\ \hline 1\,2 \end{array}$	$\begin{array}{r} {\scriptstyle 7\ 10} \\ 7\,8\,0 \\ - 4\,6\,8 \\ \hline 3\,1\,2 \end{array}$

The difference is 312.

PRACTICE

Find the difference.

1. $6,785 - 2,426$ **2.** $3,000 - 1,930$ **3.** $932 - 868$

4. $41,003 - 22,500$ **5.** $\$1,075 - \$918$ **6.** $12,035 - 640$

Multiply Whole Numbers

Multiplication is used to combine groups of equal amounts. The answer to a multiplication problem is called the *product*.

EXAMPLE

105 × 214

Step 1: Think of 214 as 2 hundreds, 1 ten, and 4 ones. Multiply by 4 ones.	**Step 2:** Multiply by 1 ten, or 10.	**Step 3:** Multiply by 2 hundreds, or 200.	**Step 4:** Add the partial products.
$\begin{array}{r} 2 \\ 105 \\ \times 214 \\ \hline 420 \end{array}$ ← 4 × 105	$\begin{array}{r} 105 \\ \times 214 \\ \hline 420 \\ 1050 \end{array}$ ← 10 × 105	$\begin{array}{r} 1 \\ 105 \\ \times 214 \\ \hline 420 \\ 1050 \\ 21000 \end{array}$ ← 200 × 105	$\begin{array}{r} 105 \\ \times 214 \\ \hline 420 \\ 1050 \\ +21000 \\ \hline 22,470 \end{array}$

The product is 22,470.

PRACTICE

Find the product.

1. 350 × 112

2. 3,218 × 231

3. 187 × 136

4. 5,028 × 225

5. 642 × 428

6. 2,039 × 570

Multiply by Powers of Ten

You can use mental math to multiply by powers of ten.

EXAMPLE

4,000 × 100

Step 1: Look for a basic fact using the nonzero part of the factors.	**Step 2:** Add the number of zeros in the factors. Place that number of zeros in the product.
4 × 1 = 4	4,000 × 100 = 400,000

The product is 400,000.

PRACTICE

Multiply.

1. 600 × 100

2. 90 × 1,000

3. 2,000 × 10

4. 400 × 10

5. 10,000 × 1,000

6. 7,100 × 1,000

Divide Whole Numbers

Division is used to separate a quantity into equal groups. The answer to a division problem is known as the *quotient*.

EXAMPLE

$672 \div 16$

Step 1: Write the first number inside the long division symbol and the second number to the left. Place the first digit of the quotient.	**Step 2:** Multiply 4 by 16, and place the product under 67.	**Step 3:** Bring down the next digit of the dividend.
  16)672 *16 cannot go into 6, so try 67.*	4 16)672 *Subtract 64 from 67.* − 64 3	42 16)672 *Divide 32 by 16.* − 64↓ 32 −32 0

The quotient is 42.

PRACTICE

Find the quotient.

1. $578 \div 34$ 2. $736 \div 8$ 3. $826 \div 118$

4. $945 \div 45$ 5. $6{,}312 \div 263$ 6. $5{,}989 \div 53$

Divide with Zeros in the Quotient

Sometimes when dividing, you need to use zeros in the quotient as placeholders.

EXAMPLE

$3{,}648 \div 12$

Step 1: Divide 36 by 12 because $12 > 3$.	**Step 2:** Place a zero in the quotient because $12 > 4$.	**Step 3:** Bring down the 8.
3 12)3,648	30 12)3,648 −36↓ 04	304 12)3,648 −36 ↓ 048 −48 0

The quotient is 304.

PRACTICE

Find the quotient.

1. $424 \div 4$ 2. $5{,}796 \div 28$ 3. $540 \div 18$

4. $7{,}380 \div 123$ 5. $12{,}045 \div 3$ 6. $10{,}626 \div 21$

Compatible Numbers

Compatible numbers are numbers that are easy to compute mentally. They are often based on groups of 10 or on basic facts.

EXAMPLE 1

A $7 + 6 + 3 + 4$

$(7 + 3) + (6 + 4)$ *Make groups of 10.*

$10 \quad + \quad 10$

20

B $2 \times 32 \times 5$

$(2 \times 5) \times 32$ *Make a group of 10.*

$10 \quad \times 32$

320

EXAMPLE 2

Estimate $358 \div 9$.

Basic fact: $36 \div 9 = 4$ *360 is compatible with 9. $360 \div 9 = 40$*

$358 \div 9 \approx 40$

PRACTICE

Use compatible numbers to solve.

1. $15 + 42 + 38 + 25$
2. $4 \times 3 \times 25$
3. $17 + 51 + 23 + 19$
4. $6 \times 15 \times 4$
5. $11 + 123 + 57 + 9$
6. $2 \times 7 \times 20 \times 5$

Estimate by rounding to find compatible numbers.

7. $473 \div 80$
8. $118 \div 4$
9. $57 \div 11$

Mental Math

You can use the Distributive Property to find products mentally.

EXAMPLE

6×32

Step 1: Write 32 as the sum of a multiple of 10 and a one-digit number. 6×32 $6 \times (30 + 2)$	**Step 2:** Use the Distributive Property. $6 \times (30 + 2)$ $(6 \times 30) + (6 \times 2)$	**Step 3:** Use mental math to multiply and then to add. $(6 \times 30) + (6 \times 2)$ $180 + 12 = 192$

PRACTICE

Use the Distributive Property to find each product.

1. 5×66
2. 3×42
3. 8×21
4. 7×84
5. 5×93
6. 4×75

Multiples

Multiples of a number can be found by multiplying the number by 1, 2, 3, and so on. *Common multiples* of a set of numbers are multiples of all numbers in the set.

EXAMPLE

Find the first five multiples of 3.

$3 \cdot 1 = 3$ *Multiply 3 times 1.* $3 \cdot 4 = 12$ *Multiply 3 times 4.*
$3 \cdot 2 = 6$ *Multiply 3 times 2.* $3 \cdot 5 = 15$ *Multiply 3 times 5.*
$3 \cdot 3 = 9$ *Multiply 3 times 3.*

The first five multiples of 3 are 3, 6, 9, 12, and 15.

PRACTICE

Find the first five multiples of each number.

1. 9   **2.** 10   **3.** 20   **4.** 15   **5.** 7   **6.** 18

7. Find the first five common multiples of 3, 4, and 6.

8. Find the first five common multiples of 2, 5, and 8.

9. Find the first five common multiples of 3, 5, and 10.

Evaluate Formulas

 6.A.2, 6.A.6

When you **evaluate a formula**, you substitute numerical values for the variables in the formula and then simplify.

EXAMPLE

The formula $d = rt$ is used to find distance. Evaluate the formula for $r = 50$ mi/h and $t = 6$ h.

$d = rt$
$d = 50 \cdot 6$ *Substitute 50 for r and 6 for t.*
$d = 300$ *Multiply.*

The distance d is 300 miles.

PRACTICE

1. Evaluate the formula $d = rt$ for $r = 25$ ft/s and $t = 10$ s.

2. The formula $C = 2\pi r$ is used to find the circumference of a circle. Evaluate the formula for $r = 14$ in. Use $\frac{22}{7}$ for π.

3. The formula $A = \frac{1}{2}bh$ is used to find the area of a triangle. Evaluate the formula for $b = 10$ cm and $h = 8$ cm.

4. The formula $V = \ell wh$ is used to find volume of a rectangular prism. Evaluate the formula for $\ell = 4$ ft, $w = 6$ ft, and $h = 2$ ft.

Properties

Addition and multiplication follow some properties, or laws. Knowing the addition and multiplication properties can help you evaluate expressions.

Addition Properties		
Commutative	You can add numbers in any order.	$5 + 1 = 1 + 5$
Associative	When you are only adding, you can group any of the numbers together.	$(9 + 3) + 2 = 9 + (3 + 2)$
Identity Property of Zero	The sum of any number and zero is equal to the number.	$9 + 0 = 9$
Inverse Property	The sum of any number and its opposite is 0.	$4 + (-4) = 0$

Multiplication Properties		
Commutative	You can multiply numbers in any order.	$5 \times 8 = 8 \times 5$
Associative	When you are only multiplying, you can group any of the numbers together.	$(4 \times 9) \times 7 = 4 \times (9 \times 7)$
Identity Property of One	The product of any number and one is equal to the number.	$6 \times 1 = 6$
Inverse Property	For any number except 0, the product of the number and its reciprocal is 1.	$3 \times \frac{1}{3} = 1$
Property of Zero	The product of any number and zero is zero.	$5 \times 0 = 0$
Distributive	When you multiply a number times a sum, you can find the sum first and then multiply, or multiply each number in the sum and then add.	$6 \times (4 + 5) =$ $6 \times 4 + 6 \times 5$

EXAMPLE

Tell which property is shown in the equation $(3 + 4) + 7 = 3 + (4 + 7)$.

The Associative Property of Addition is shown.

PRACTICE

Tell which property is shown.

1. $6 \times (3 \times 2) = (6 \times 3) \times 2$ **2.** $12 \times 9 = 9 \times 12$ **3.** $0 + d = d$

4. $k \times 1 = k$ **5.** $8 + 5 = 5 + 8$ **6.** $2 \times (3 + 10) = (2 \times 3) + (2 \times 10)$

7. $9 + (-9) = 0$ **8.** $99 \times 0 = 0$ **9.** $y(3 + 10) = 3y + 10y$

Skills Bank

Graph Polygons on a Coordinate Plane

5.G.13, 5.G.14

You can correct ordered pairs graphed on a coordinate plane to form polygons. The perimeter of a polygon is the distance around the figure. You can find the perimeter of a polygon by finding the sum of its side lengths.

EXAMPLE

Plot and label the points at right on a coordinate plane. Determine what figure is formed when the points are connected.

(0, 2), (6, 2), (0, 5), (6, 5)

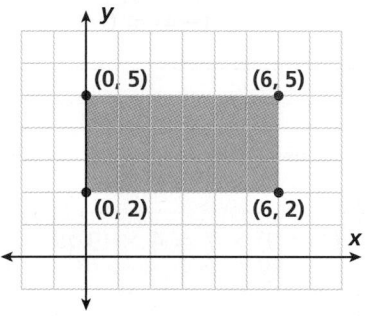

The points form a rectangle.

EXAMPLE

Plot and label the points at right on a coordinate plane. Determine what figure is formed when the points are connected. Then find the perimeter of the figure.

(0, 0), (7, 0), (0, 3), (5, 3), (5, 6), (7, 6)

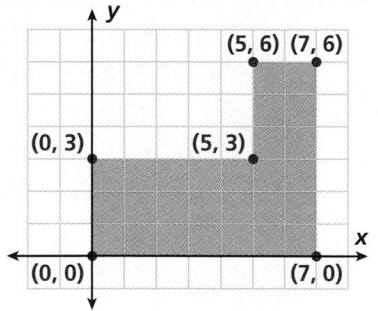

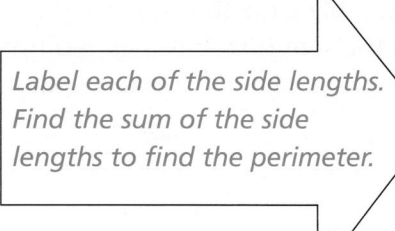
Label each of the side lengths. Find the sum of the side lengths to find the perimeter.

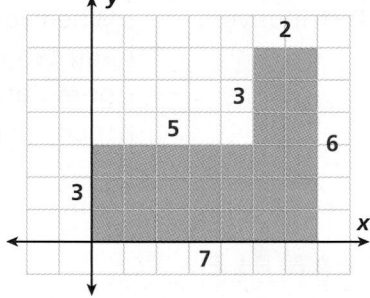

The figure is a hexagon.

$P = 3 + 5 + 3 + 2 + 6 + 7$
$= 26$
The perimeter is 26 units.

PRACTICE

Graph and find the perimeter of each figure with the given vertices.

1. (0, 0), (0, 3), (4, 4), (4, 3)

2. (1, 3), (3, 3), (1, 5), (4, 5)

3. (2, 0), (5, 0), (2, 7), (5, 7)

4. (1, 1), (1, 6), (6, 1), (6, 6)

5. (0, 0), (1, 0), (1, 3), (5, 3), (5, 6), (0, 6)

6. (4, 3), (4, 1), (6, 1), (6, 5), (2, 5), (2, 3)

7. (3, 5), (4, 5), (4, 6), (5, 6), (5, 0), (2, 0), (2, 6), (3, 6)

8. (7, 5), (1, 5), (1, 3), (3, 3), (3, 1), (5, 1), (5, 0), (7, 0)

Pictographs

Pictographs are graphs that use pictures to display data. Pictographs include a key to tell what each picture represents.

EXAMPLE

How many students chose red as their favorite color?

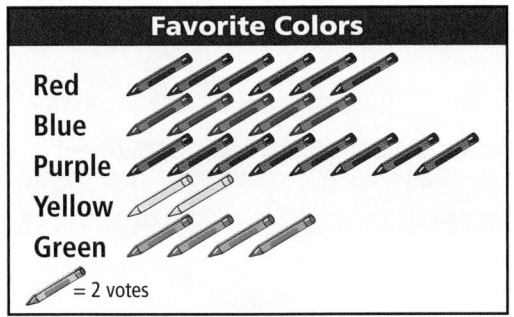

Each ✏ stands for 2 students.

There are 6 ✏ in the row for red.

$6 \times 2 = 12$

So 12 students chose red as their favorite color.

PRACTICE

Use the pictograph for Exercises 1–4.

1. How many tickets did theater A sell?

2. Which theater sold the most tickets?

3. How many more tickets did theater C sell than theater D?

4. Theater E sold 180 tickets. How would this be shown on the pictograph?

Tickets Sold
Theater A 🎟🎟🎟🎟🎟🎟
Theater B 🎟🎟🎟🎟🎟🎟🎟🎟🎟🎟
Theater C 🎟🎟🎟🎟🎟🎟🎟
Theater D 🎟🎟🎟🎟🎟🎟
🎟 = 20 tickets

Use the pictograph for Exercises 5–7.

Mr. Carr took a survey of sixth-graders in his school. He asked them which type of pet they have. He recorded the data in a table.

5. How many students have pet birds?

6. How many more students have pet cats than pet fish?

7. How many students were surveyed?

8. Elizabeth took a survey of her neighbors. She recorded the number of children in each family in a table. Use the data to make a pictograph.

Types of Pets
Dog 🐾🐾🐾🐾🐾🐾
Cat 🐾🐾🐾🐾🐾🐾🐾🐾🐾🐾🐾
Bird 🐾🐾🐾
Fish 🐾🐾🐾🐾🐾🐾🐾
Other 🐾🐾🐾🐾🐾
🐾 = 2 students

Children	Families
0	1
1	6
2	4
3 or more	2

Measure Length to the Nearest $\frac{1}{16}$ Inch

Each inch on this ruler is separated into 16 equal parts. Each mark is $\frac{1}{16}$ inch.

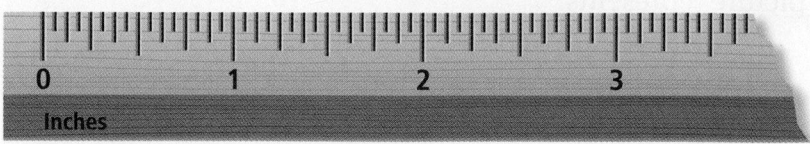

EXAMPLE

What is the length of the pencil?

Count the number of $\frac{1}{16}$ marks after the 5-inch mark. There are 3 marks. The pencil is $5\frac{3}{16}$ inches long.

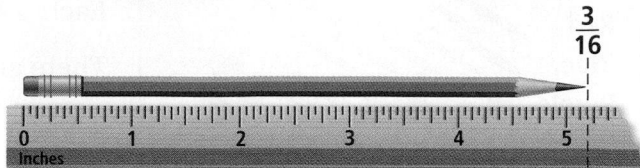

PRACTICE

Use a ruler to find the length of each object to the nearest $\frac{1}{16}$ inch.

1.

2.   3.

Read Scales

 6.M.6

A *scale* is similar to a number line with numbers or marks placed at fixed intervals. You can find scales on graphs and on measuring instruments, such as rulers and thermometers.

EXAMPLE

What temperature is shown on the thermometer?

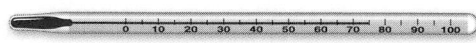

The scale goes from 0°F to 100°F in intervals of 5°F. The temperature shown is 75°F.

PRACTICE

Use the given scale to find each measurement.

1.   3.

2.

Time

Seconds, minutes, hours, days, weeks, months, and years are units you can use to measure time.

EXAMPLE

Which instrument would you use to measure how long it takes to read a page in a book?

A digital clock shows hours and minutes.

An analog clock shows hours, minutes, and seconds.

A calendar shows days, weeks, months, and years.

Since it would take less than a day to read a page in a book, you could use a digital clock or an analog clock.

PRACTICE

Name the appropriate instrument and unit to measure time for each event.

1. completing 6th grade

2. running a mile

3. eating lunch

4. Earth revolving around the Sun

Right Triangle Trigonometry

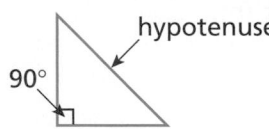

A right triangle has one right angle.
The side opposite the right angle is called the *hypotenuse*.
The hypotenuse is the longest side of a right triangle.
The other sides of a right triangle are called *legs*.

EXAMPLE

Determine if the triangle is a right triangle. If so, identify the hypotenuse.

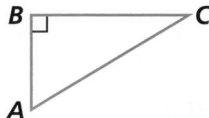

$\triangle ABC$ has a 90° angle.
$\triangle ABC$ is a right triangle.
Line segment CA is the hypotenuse.

PRACTICE

Determine if each triangle is a right triangle. If so, identify the hypotenuse.

1.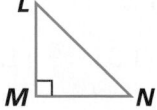

2.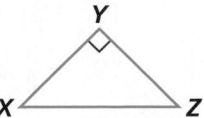

3.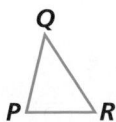

Absolute Value

6.N.13

The **absolute value** of a number is its distance from zero on the number line. The symbol for absolute value is $|\,|$. Since absolute value is a distance, the absolute value of a number can never be less than zero.

Any number and its opposite have the same absolute value. The numbers 5 and -5 are both five units from zero on a number line, so they both have an absolute value of 5. "The absolute value of negative five" is written as $|-5|$.

5 units   **5 units**

$-5\ -4\ -3\ -2\ -1\ \ 0\ \ 1\ \ 2\ \ 3\ \ 4\ \ 5$

$|-5| = 5$ *−5 is five units from 0.*

$|5| = 5$ *5 is five units from 0.*

EXAMPLE

Simplify each expression.

A $|2|$

$|2| = 2$

2 units

$-4\ -3\ -2\ -1\ \ 0\ \ 1\ \ 2\ \ 3\ \ 4$

2 is 2 units from 0.

B $|-3.5|$

$|-3.5| = 3.5$

3.5 units

$-4\ -3\ -2\ -1\ \ 0\ \ 1\ \ 2\ \ 3\ \ 4$

−3.5 is 3.5 units from 0.

C $\left|-1\frac{2}{3}\right|$

$\left|-1\frac{2}{3}\right| = 1\frac{2}{3}$

$1\frac{2}{3}$ units

$-4\ -3\ -2\ -1\ \ 0\ \ 1\ \ 2\ \ 3\ \ 4$

$-1\frac{2}{3}$ is $1\frac{2}{3}$ units from 0.

PRACTICE

Simplify each expression.

1. $|-7|$ 2. $|12|$ 3. $\left|\frac{1}{2}\right|$ 4. $\left|-2\frac{1}{2}\right|$

5. $|-4.8|$ 6. $|0|$ 7. $|483|$ 8. $|-0.66|$

9. $\left|-\frac{5}{2}\right|$ 10. $|4.\overline{3}|$ 11. $|19.1|$ 12. $\left|\frac{1}{100}\right|$

Use <, =, or > to compare each pair of values.

13. $|6|$ ▨ $|7|$ 14. $|-2|$ ▨ $|-9|$ 15. $\left|\frac{3}{7}\right|$ ▨ $\left|-\frac{2}{7}\right|$ 16. 4.5 ▨ $|-4.5|$

17. $\left|3\frac{1}{4}\right|$ ▨ -6.5 18. 0.01 ▨ $|-57|$ 19. $-\frac{3}{2}$ ▨ $|1.5|$ 20. $|-1.\overline{3}|$ ▨ $|1.3|$

Rational Numbers

A **rational number** is any number that can be written as a fraction $\frac{a}{b}$, where a and b are integers and $b \neq 0$. Integers, such as 5 and -7, are rational numbers because they can be written as $\frac{5}{1}$ and $\frac{-7}{1}$. Terminating decimals are also rational numbers. For example, 0.57 may be written as $\frac{57}{100}$.

When a rational number is written in the form $\frac{a}{b}$, it can mean:

- a parts, each of size $\frac{1}{b}$.
- a divided by b.
- the ratio of a to b.

Use a number line to help you order and compare rational numbers.

EXAMPLE 1

Locate each pair of rational numbers on a number line. Then compare the numbers using $<$ or $>$.

A $-\frac{3}{4}$ and $-\frac{1}{2}$

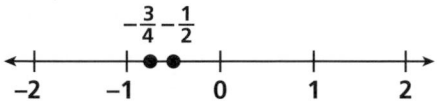

B $\frac{3}{2}$ and 0.75

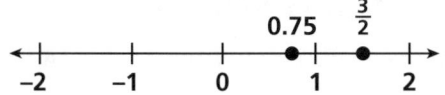

Graph both numbers on a number line. $-\frac{3}{4}$ is to the left of $-\frac{1}{2}$, so $-\frac{3}{4} < -\frac{1}{2}$.

Graph both numbers on a number line. $\frac{3}{2}$ is to the right of 0.75, so $\frac{3}{2} > 0.75$.

Use the order of operations to help you simplify expressions with rational numbers.

EXAMPLE 2

Simplify $1 + (2 \div \frac{1}{3})$.

$1 + (2 \div \frac{1}{3})$	*Simplify using the order of operations.*
$1 + (2 \times \frac{3}{1})$	*Rewrite as multiplication using the reciprocal of $\frac{1}{3}$, $\frac{3}{1}$.*
$1 + (2 \times 3)$	*Remember: $\frac{3}{1} = 3$*
$1 + 6$	*Multiply.*
7	*Add.*

Notice in Example 2 that $2 \div \frac{1}{3} = 6$. In this case, the quotient is greater than the dividend because the divisor is less than 1.

PRACTICE

Locate each pair of rational numbers on a number line. Then compare the numbers using $<$ or $>$.

1. $\frac{1}{3}$ and $-\frac{1}{3}$ **2.** $-\frac{1}{2}$ and $-\frac{3}{2}$ **3.** 0.5 and $\frac{3}{4}$ **4.** $-1\frac{1}{2}$ and -2

Simplify each expression.

5. $(4 \div \frac{1}{4}) + 2$ **6.** $12 - (2 \div \frac{1}{4})$ **7.** $(1 \div \frac{1}{2}) - 0.5$ **8.** $(\frac{2}{3} \times 6) + 3.5$

Sectors of Circles

Two radii form a central angle of a circle. A **sector** of a circle is the part of the circle enclosed by two radii and an arc connecting them. Given a circle of radius r and a central angle that measures $m°$, the area of the sector is $\frac{m}{360}\pi r^2$.

EXAMPLE

Find the area of the sector. Use 3.14 for _pi_.

$A = \frac{m}{360}\pi r^2$

$\quad = \frac{90}{360} \cdot 3.14 \cdot 6^2$ *Substitute 90 for m and 6 for r.*

$\quad = \frac{1}{4} \cdot 3.14 \cdot 36 = 28.26$ *Simplify.*

The area of the sector is 28.26 in^2

PRACTICE

Find the area of each sector. Use 3.14 for _pi_.

1.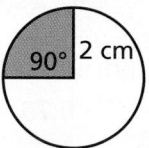

2.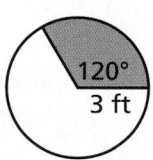

3.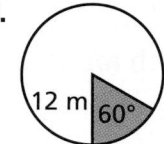

Properties of Ellipses and Spheres

An **ellipse** looks like a stretched out circle. The sum of the distances from any point on the ellipse to its *foci* is constant.

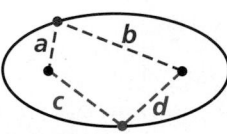

$a + b = c + d$

A **sphere** is a three-dimensional figure whose surface is made up of all the points that are the same distance from a given point called the center.

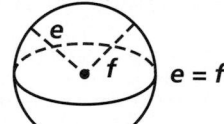

$e = f$

EXAMPLE

Find the value of _x_.

A

$x + 3 = 4 + 4$

$x + 3 = 8$ *Add.*

$x = 5$ *Subtract 3.*

B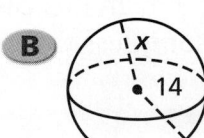

$x = 14$

All points on the surface of the sphere are the same distance from the center.

PRACTICE

Find the value of _x_.

1.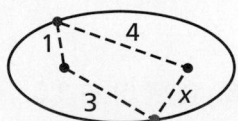

2.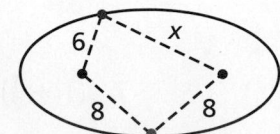

3.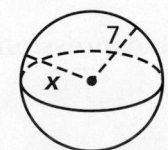

Graph Cumulative Frequency

You have seen how to make a cumulative frequency table for a data set. You can also graph the cumulative frequencies for a data set.

EXAMPLE

The midterm test scores for Mr. Andrews's math class are given in the table at right. Make a cumulative frequency table. Then make a histogram of the cumulative frequencies.

Midterm Test Scores					
70	86	70	74	77	95
82	62	69	79	73	80
87	68	72	72	91	87
98	73	64	81	77	73
99	76	68	95	85	80

Divide the data into equally sized intervals.

Midterm Test Scores	Frequency	Cumulative Frequency
60–64	2	2
65–69	3	5
70–74	8	13
75–79	4	17
80–84	4	21
85–89	4	25
90–94	1	26
95–99	4	30

The cumulative frequency column shows a running total of all frequencies.

The frequency tells the number of times an event, category, or group occurs.

To make a histogram of the cumulative frequencies, draw a bar for the cumulative frequency for each interval.

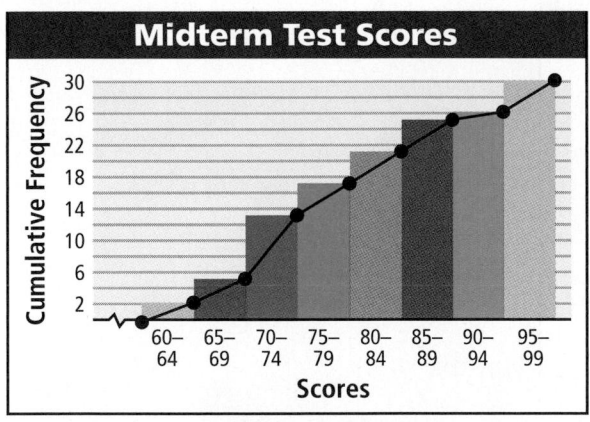

To make a line graph of the cumulative frequencies, place points in the lower left corner of the first bar and upper right corner of every bar. Then connect those points with line segments, as shown.

PRACTICE

1. Make a cumulative frequency histogram and line graph for the data set.

Students' Heights (cm)					
160	130	142	153	164	160
161	162	132	155	140	130
150	145	140	138	166	155
154	155	160	160	155	158

Relative Frequency and Relative Frequency Distributions

In a data set, the relative frequency of a data value is that value's frequency divided by the total number of data values.

$$\text{relative frequency} = \frac{\text{frequency}}{\text{total number of data values}}$$

Relative frequencies can be shown in tables or displayed in histograms.

EXAMPLE

The average class size in 20 schools is given in the table. Make a relative frequency table and a relative frequency histogram of the data.

Average Class Size				
22	25	20	28	31
37	24	19	29	32
38	35	19	32	34
38	25	38	26	33

Divide the data into equally sized intervals.

Class Size	Frequency	Relative Frequency
19–23	4	$\frac{4}{20} = \frac{1}{5}$
24–28	5	$\frac{5}{20} = \frac{1}{4}$
29–33	5	$\frac{5}{20} = \frac{1}{4}$
34–38	6	$\frac{6}{20} = \frac{3}{10}$

There are 20 data points. Divide each frequency by 20 to find the relative frequency.

To make a histogram, draw a bar for each relative frequency.

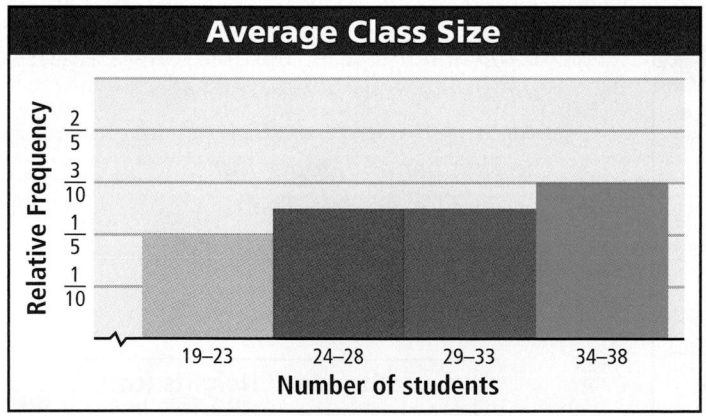

PRACTICE

1. Survey the students in your class and record the number of books read by each student in the past year. Make a relative frequency histogram to display the data.

Angles

Angles are often measured in degrees. Angles may also be measured in radians. A circle of radius 1 has a circumference of 2π. So a full circle measures 2π radians. To find the measure R of an angle in radians, use the formula $R = \frac{m\pi}{180}$, where m is the measure of the angle in degrees.

EXAMPLE

Find the measure of the angle in radians.

$R = \frac{m\pi}{180}$

$R = \frac{90\pi}{180}$ *Substitute 90 for m.*

$R = \frac{\pi}{2}$ *Simplify.*

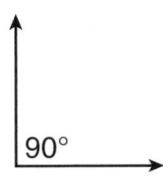

The angle measures $\frac{\pi}{2}$ radians.

PRACTICE

Find the measure of each angle in radians.

1. 45°

2. 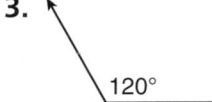 180°

3. 120°

Accuracy

Accuracy is the closeness of a measurement or value to the actual measurement or value. It is usually impossible to measure an object completely accurately. The **degree of accuracy** tells you how close the measurement is to the actual measurement.

EXAMPLE

Measure the line to the nearest $\frac{1}{2}$ inch.

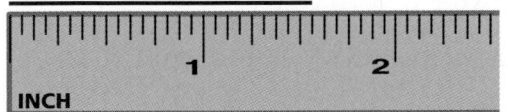

Place a customary ruler next to the line. Read the closest $\frac{1}{2}$-inch mark.

The line is $1\frac{1}{2}$ inches long, plus or minus $\frac{1}{2}$ inch.

PRACTICE

Measure each line to the given degree of accuracy.

1. within $\frac{1}{4}$ inch

2. within $\frac{1}{8}$ inch

3. within 1 inch

Skills Bank

Compute Measurements of Combined Units

Sometimes a measurement is given in a combination of units. For example, a piece of wood may measure 3 feet 4 inches. You can add or subtract measurements that are a combination of units.

EXAMPLE 1

4 ft 8 in. + 5 ft 6 in.

Step 1: Line up the units.	Step 2: Add the inches.	Step 3: Add the feet.	Step 4: Rewrite the answer in simplest form.
4 ft 8 in. + 5 ft 6 in.	4 ft 8 in. + 5 ft 6 in. 14 in.	4 ft 8 in. + 5 ft 6 in. 9 ft 14 in.	*Think: 12 in. = 1 ft* 9 ft 14 in. = 10 ft 2 in.

The sum is 10 ft 2 in.

EXAMPLE 2

3 hr 20 min − 1 hr 50 min

Step 1: Line up the units.	Step 2: Regroup if needed.	Step 3: Subtract the minutes.	Step 4: Subtract the hours.
3 hr 20 min − 1 hr 50 min	2 hr 80 min − 1 hr 50 min	2 hr 80 min − 1 hr 50 min 30 min	2 hr 80 min − 1 hr 50 min 1 hr 30 min

The difference is 1 hr 30 min.

PRACTICE

Add.

1. 7 ft 2 in. + 6 ft 8 in.

2. 8 lb 6 oz + 4 lb 12 oz

3. 2 gal 1 qt + 4 gal 1 qt

4. 12 ft 11 in. + 3 ft 4 in.

5. 4 hr 12 min + 3 hr 42 min

6. 152 yd 2 ft + 75 yd 6 in.

7. 5 yd 2 ft 3 in. + 8 yd 1 ft 8 in.

8. 2 hr 36 min 45 s + 5 hr 42 min 20 s

Subtract.

9. 20 ft 8 in. − 7 ft 6 in.

10. 10 yd 1 ft − 5 yd 2 ft

11. 6 lb 5 oz − 2 lb 8 oz

12. 12 h 13 min − 6 h 25 min

13. 5 min 15 s − 4 min 55 s

14. 3 mi 550 yd − 1 mi 760 yd

15. 4 gal 1 c − 3 qt 1 pt

16. 1 day − 8 hr 36 min

Compare Units

When converting area from one unit to another, you must remember that area is measured in square units.

1 square foot = 1 foot × 1 foot
= 12 inches × 12 inches
= 144 square inches

1 ft (square diagram) 1 ft

Customary Units for Area	
1 square foot (ft^2) = 144 square inches (in^2)	1 acre (a) = 4,840 square yards (yd^2)
1 square yard (yd^2) = 9 square feet (ft^2)	1 acre (a) = 43,560 square feet (ft^2)
1 square yard (yd^2) = 1,296 square inches (in^2)	1 square mile (mi^2) = 640 acres (a)

Multiply to convert from larger units to smaller units.

Divide to convert from smaller units to larger units.

EXAMPLE 1

Find the area of the rectangle in square feet and in square inches.

3 ft × 5 ft = 15 ft^2 *Think: 1 ft^2 = 144 in^2*

15 ft^2 = 15 × 144 in^2 = 2,160 in^2

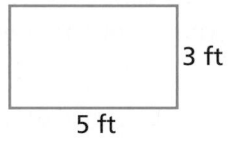
3 ft

5 ft

EXAMPLE 2

Which is the greater area, 3 yd^2 or 25 ft^2?

3 yd^2 = 3 × 9 ft^2 = 27 ft^2 *Think: 1 yd^2 = 9 ft^2*

27 ft^2 > 25 ft^2

3 yd^2 > 25 ft^2

PRACTICE

1. Find the area of the rectangle in square yards and square feet.

2. A plot of land is 1.5 miles long and 1 mile wide. What is the area of the land in square miles and in acres?

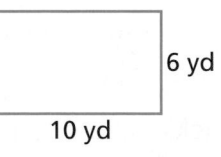
6 yd

10 yd

Compare. Write <, >, or =.

3. 12,500 yd^2 ▓ 3 acres

4. 6 yd^2 ▓ 42 ft^2

5. 4 ft^2 ▓ 576 in^2

6. 5 yd^2 ▓ 6,500 in^2

7. 2.3 mi^2 ▓ 1,430 acres

8. 0.5 acre ▓ 21,700 ft^2

Estimate Measurements

You can use rounding to estimate measurements like perimeter, area, and volume.

EXAMPLE ESTIMATING AREA

A circle has a radius of 6.87 cm. Estimate the area of the circle.

Round π and the radius of the circle to the nearest integers before substituting them into the formula.

$A = \pi r^2$

$\quad \approx 3(7)^2$ *Use 3 for π and 7 for r.*

$\quad = 147$ *Simplify.*

The area of the circle is approximately 147 cm^2.

EXAMPLE ESTIMATING VOLUME

You are buying an angelfish for a pet. The clerk at the pet store tells you that an angelfish needs 10 gallons, or 2,310 in^3, of water to live in. Will the tank at right be large enough? Estimate the volume of the tank and explain your process.

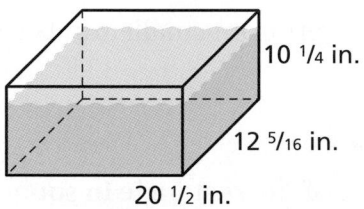

10 ¼ in.

12 ⁵/₁₆ in.

20 ½ in.

If you overestimate the size of the tank, the fish may not have enough water. You should underestimate the size of the tank by rounding the dimensions down before multiplying.

$V = \ell \times w \times h$

$\quad \approx 20 \times 12 \times 10$ *Round the dimensions down to the nearest inch.*

$\quad = 2,400$ *Simplify.*

The volume of the tank is approximately 2,400 in^3. The tank is large enough.

PRACTICE

1. A triangle has a height of 107 mm and a base of 43 mm. Estimate the area of the triangle and explain your process.

2. A cylinder has a radius of $3\frac{11}{16}$ in. and a height of $7\frac{3}{8}$ in. Estimate the volume of the cylinder and explain your process.

3. Jonas is going to use bricks to make a border around a circular garden. How much brick does he need to surround the garden? Estimate the circumference of the garden and explain your process.

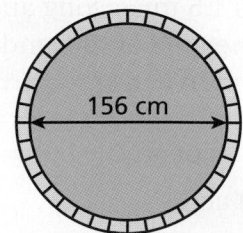

156 cm

Surface Area to Volume Ratio

Surface area is the sum of the areas of all the faces or surfaces of a solid figure. *Volume* is the amount of space within the solid figure. Area is a measurement of two dimensions, length and width. Volume is a measure of three dimensions, length, width, and height. A surface area to volume ratio compares the surface area and volume of a solid.

EXAMPLE 1

Find the surface area and volume of the rectangular prism.

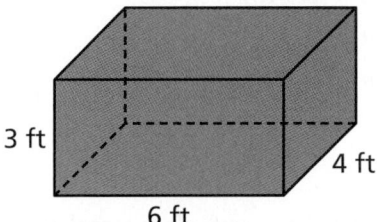

$S = 2wh + 2\ell w + 2\ell h$

$\quad = (2 \times 4 \times 3) + (2 \times 6 \times 4) + (2 \times 6 \times 3)$

$\quad = 24 + 48 + 36$

$\quad = 108 \text{ ft}^2$

$V = \ell \times w \times h$

$\quad = 6 \times 4 \times 3$

$\quad = 72 \text{ ft}^3$

EXAMPLE 2

What is the surface area to volume ratio for the cube?

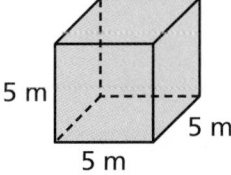

$S = 6s^2 \qquad\qquad V = \ell \times w \times h$

$\quad = 6 \times 5 \times 5 \qquad\quad = 5 \times 5 \times 5$

$\quad = 150 \text{ m}^2 \qquad\qquad = 125 \text{ m}^3$

The ratio of surface area to volume for the cube is $150 \text{ m}^2 : 125 \text{ m}^3$ or $6 \text{ m}^2 : 5 \text{ m}^3$.

PRACTICE

Find the surface area and volume of each rectangular prism.

1.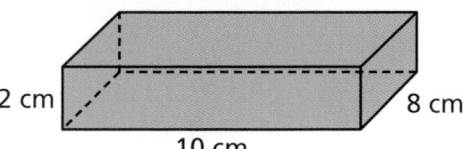

2.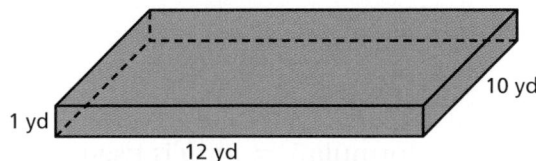

3. a rectangular prism with $\ell = 13$ km, $w = 10$ km, and $h = 3$ km

4. a cube with sides of length 2.5 ft

Write the surface area to volume ratio for each solid.

5.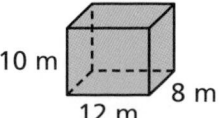

6.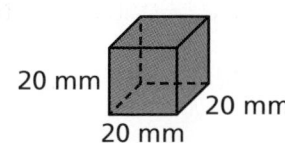

7. a rectangular prism with $\ell = 5$ ft, $w = 4$ ft, and $h = 11$ ft

8. a rectangular prism with $\ell = 8$ dm, $w = 8$ dm, and $h = 4$ dm

Solve Literal Formulas

Formulas are equations that show a relationship between two or more quantities. Formulas can be used to find missing information or to calculate a quantity. For example, the formula $A = \ell w$ is used to find the area of a rectangle. We can solve the formula $A = \ell w$ for w using the same rules used to solve equations.

EXAMPLE

A Solve $A = \ell w$ for w.

$$A = \ell w$$

$$\frac{A}{\ell} = \frac{\ell w}{\ell} \qquad \text{\textit{Divide both sides by } } \ell.$$

$$\frac{A}{\ell} = w$$

B The formula $V = \ell w h$ is used to find the volume of a rectangular prism. Solve $V = \ell w h$ for h.

$$V = \ell w h$$

$$\frac{V}{\ell} = \frac{\ell w h}{\ell} \qquad \text{\textit{Divide both sides by } } \ell.$$

$$\frac{V}{\ell} = wh$$

$$\frac{V}{\ell w} = \frac{wh}{w} \qquad \text{\textit{Divide both sides by } } w.$$

$$\frac{V}{\ell w} = h$$

PRACTICE

Solve.

1. The formula $d = rt$ is used to find distance.

   Solve $d = rt$ for r.

2. The formula $P = 2\ell + 2w$ is used to find the perimeter of a rectangle.

   Solve $P = 2\ell + 2w$ for ℓ.

3. The formula $V = \pi r^2 h$ is used to find the volume of a cylinder.

   Solve $V = \pi r^2 h$ for h.

4. The formula $C = \frac{5}{9}(F - 32)$ is used to convert from degrees Fahrenheit to degrees Celsius.

   Solve $C = \frac{5}{9}(F - 32)$ for F.

5. The formula $A = \frac{1}{2}bh$ is used to find the area of a triangle.

   Solve $A = \frac{1}{2}bh$ for b.

6. The formula $I = Prt$ is used to find simple interest.

   Solve $I = Prt$ for P.

Exponential Function Behavior

Data that changes exponentially increases or decreases by a common factor.

The Richter scale is used to express the magnitude of earthquakes. Each counting number represents a magnitude that is 10 times stronger than the one before it.

Magnitude	Relative Strength
0	1
1	10^1
2	10^2
3	10^3
4	10^4
5	10^5
6	10^6
7	10^7
8	10^8

EXAMPLE

How much stronger is an earthquake of magnitude 4 than one of magnitude 2?

An earthquake of magnitude 4 has a relative strength of 10^4. An earthquake of magnitude 2 has a relative strength of 10^2.

An earthquake of magnitude 4 is 10^2, or 100, times stronger than an earthquake of magnitude 2.

PRACTICE

1. In 1976, an earthquake in China registered 8 on the Richter scale. In 1999, an earthquake in Colombia registered 6 on the Richter scale. Which earthquake was weaker and by what factor?

2. Earthquake A registered 3 on the Richter scale. Earthquake B was 10,000 times stronger than earthquake A. What was the magnitude of earthquake B?

You can see exponential population growth by observing bacteria in an environment with unlimited resources. Use the graph of bacteria growth for Exercises 3–5.

3. By what factor does the graph show the bacteria population increasing each hour?

4. If the bacteria continue to grow at this rate, how many bacteria will there be in 8 hours? Write the answer in both exponential and standard form.

5. How many more bacteria will there be in 10 hours than in 8 hours?

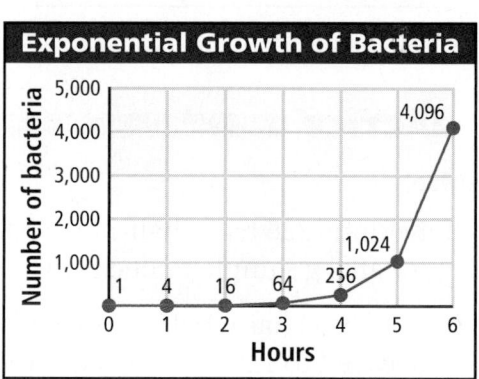

Exponential Growth of Bacteria

Half-life

Half-life is the time that it takes for half of a certain amount of radioactive material to decay. You can use information about the half-life of an element to determine how much of a sample will remain after a given time or to find the age of a sample.

EXAMPLE 1

The half-life of sodium-24 is 15 hours. If you have a 6 g sample of sodium-24, how much will remain after 45 hours?

Every 15 hours, one-half of the sample decays.

Time	0 hours	15 hours	30 hours	45 hours
Amount of Sample	6 g	3 g	1.5 g	0.75 g

After 45 hours, 0.75 g of sodium-24 will remain.

EXAMPLE 2

The half-life of bismuth-212 is 60.5 minutes. If you have a 4 g sample of bismuth-212 from a sample that was originally 16 g, how old is the sample?

Every 60.5 minutes, one-half of the sample decays.

Time	0 min	60.5 min	121 min
Amount of Sample	16 g	8 g	4 g

The sample is 121 minutes old.

PRACTICE

Solve.

1. Radium-226 has a half-life of 1,600 years. How many years will it take for an 8 g sample to decay to 0.5 g?

2. Cobalt-60 has a half-life of 5.26 years. A 10 g sample of cobalt-60 has decayed to 1.25 g. How old is the sample?

3. Iodine-131 has a half-life of 8.07 days. How much of a 4.4 g sample will there be after 40.35 days?

4. A sample of phosphorus-24 decayed from 12 g to 1.5 g in 42.9 days. What is the half-life of phosphorus-24?

5. You have a 0.6 g sample of sodium-24. The half-life of sodium-24 is 15 hours. The original sample size was 9.6 g. How old is the sample?

Notes

Selected Answers

Chapter 1

1-1 Exercises

1. Mount Aconcagua is taller.
3. 349; 642; 726 **5.** 497; 809; 1,264
7. 982; 3,255; 5,001 **9.** the theme
park with 17,459,000 in attendance
11. New York City **13.** 126; 480;
619 **15.** 423; 805; 1,046 **17.** 666;
1,359; 1,764 **19.** 978; 1,502; 4,228
21. < **23.** = **25.** < **27.** > **29.** <
31. 823; 601; 533; 149 **33.** 3,461;
2,649; 1,947 **35.** 7,498; 7,467; 7,239
37. Montana, California, Texas
43. J **45.** twenty-four thousand,
four hundred ninety-eight
47. four million, six hundred five
thousand, nine hundred twenty-
six **49.** 300,000 **51.** 6,000

1-2 Exercises

1. 7,000 **3.** 1,500 bottles of water
5. about 2 gallons **7.** 40,000
9. 20,000 **11.** 40 golf balls **13.** 500
15. 0 **17.** 11,000 **19.** 40,000
21. 70,000 **23.** 400,000 **25.** 10
square miles **27.** 40,000 square
miles **33.** 400; 36 rounds to 40,
and 8 rounds to 10 **35.** 2,615
37. 2,496 **39.** 1,000 + 300 + 50 + 4
41. 400,000 + 10,000 + 6,000 + 700
+ 3

1-3 Exercises

1. 8^3 **3.** 6^5 **5.** 5^5 **7.** 16 **9.** 625
11. 343 **13.** 2^6 **15.** 8^2 **17.** 6^5
19. 7^7 **21.** 4^2 **23.** 243 **25.** 81
27. 512 **29.** 256 **31.** 144 **33.** 16
× 16 × 16 **35.** 31 × 31 × 31 × 31
× 31 × 31 **37.** 50 × 50 × 50 **39.** 1
× 1 × 1 × 1 × 1 × 1 × 1 × 1 × 1
41. 8 × 8 × 8 × 8 × 8
43. 1,000,000 **45.** 6,651
47. 100,000 **49.** 512 **51.** 125
53. > **55.** < **57.** > **59.** 1,024

cells **61.** 8; 2^8, or 256 **65.** D
67. 8,245; 8,452; 8,732 **69.** 11,901;
12,681; 12,751 **71.** 50,000

1-4 Exercises

1. 33 **3.** 50 **5.** 4 **7.** $138 **9.** 10
11. 32 **13.** 14 **15.** 25 **17.** 40
19. 24 **21.** 1,250 pages **23.** 18
25. 57 **27.** 1 **29.** 22 **31.** 64 **33.** 22
35. $(7 + 2) \times 6 - (4 - 3) = 53$
37. $5^2 - 10 + (5 + 4^2) = 36$
39. $9^2 - 2 \times (15 + 16) - 8 = 11$
41. $4^2 \times (3 - 2) \div 4 = 4$ **43.** 30 m^2
45. 300 m^3 **49.** J **51.** 3,273
53. 70,007 **55.** 125 **57.** 256

1-5 Exercises

1. 40 **3.** 50 **5.** 320 **7.** 120 **9.** 156
11. 99 **13.** 108 **15.** 40 **17.** 50
19. 640 **21.** 108 **23.** 426 **25.** 138
27. 372 **29.** 328 **31.** 40 **33.** 60
35. 198 **37.** 111 **39.** 70 **41.** 70°F
43. 153 **45.** 198 **47.** 56 **49.** 275
51. 340 **53.** 192 **55.** 108 eggs
57. $208 **63.** 2,718 mi
65. 1,367,000 **67.** 62 **69.** 56

1-6 Exercises

1. paper and pencil; 364
3. calculator; 64,890 **5.** mental
math; middle row **7.** 111
9. 515,844 **11.** 210 **13.** 350
19. 936; 13 · 3 = 39; 39 · 24 = 936
21. 30 **23.** 12 **25.** Distributive
Property **26.** Commutative
Property

1-7 Exercises

1. add 12; 60; 72; 84 **3.** add 11; 51;
62 **5.** add 7 and subtract 2; 12; 19
7. multiply by 6 and divide by 2; 9;
162 **9.** subtract 14; 28; 14; 0
11. add 3; 20; 23 **13.** add 21 and
subtract 4; 41; 62; 58 **15.** divide by
4 and multiply by 2; 100; 25
17. 5, 14, 23, 32, 41 **19a.** 2018

b. 1994 **c.** yes; 2006 + 2(12) =
2030 **21.** subtract 4 and add 5
27. A **29.** 60 **31.** 120

Chapter 1 Study Guide: Review

1. sequence, term **2.** base,
exponent **3.** order of operations
4. evaluate **5.** 8,731; 8,735; 8,737;
8,740 **6.** 53,337; 53,341; 53,452;
53,456 **7.** 8,791; 81,790; 87,091;
87,901 **8.** 2,651; 22,561; 25,615;
26,551 **9.** 91,363; 93,613; 96,361;
96,631 **10.** 10,101; 10,110; 11,010;
11,110 **11.** 1,000 **12.** 6,000
13. 20,000 **14.** 800 **15.** 5^3 **16.** 3^4
17. 7^5 **18.** 8^2 **19.** 4^4 **20.** 1^3
21. 256 **22.** 16 **23.** 216 **24.** 27
25. 1 **26.** 2,401 **27.** 125 **28.** 100
29. 81 **30.** 59 **31.** 11 **32.** 26
33. 17 **34.** 5 **35.** 45 **36.** 9 **37.** 3
38. 30 **39.** 520 **40.** 80 **41.** 1,080
42. 40 **43.** 320 **44.** 100 **45.** 130
46. 168 **47.** 135 **48.** 204 **49.** 152
50. 216 **51.** 165 **52.** 62° **53.** Add
5; 24, 29. **54.** Subtract 2; 13, 11.
55. Add 4 and subtract 2; 20, 22.
56. Multiply by 3; 81, 243.
57. Add 5 and subtract 2; 71, 74.

Chapter 2

2-1 Exercises

1. 56; 65 **3.** 24; 38; 32; 36 **5.** 23;
25 **7a.** 2 hr: 100 − 120 miles; 3 hr:
150 − 180 miles; 4 hr: 200 − 240
miles; 5 hr: 250 − 300 miles
b. between 350 and 420 miles
9. 32°F; 50°F; 77°F **11.** 32 **13.** 13
15. 8 **17.** 56 **19.** 10 **21.** 110
23. 24 zlotys **29.** 38 **31.** 5^6
33. $919

2-2 Exercises

1. 4,028 − m **3.** 15x **5.** $\frac{p}{5}$

7. (149)(2)   **9.** the product of 345 and 196; 345 times 196   **11.** the difference of d and 5; 5 less than d **13.** $5x$ **15.** $325 \div 25$ **17.** $137 + 675$ **19.** $j - 14$ **21.** take away 19 from 243; 243 minus 19   **23.** 342 multiplied by 75; the product of 342 and 75   **25.** the product of 45 and 23; 45 times 23   **27.** the difference of 228 and b; b less than 228   **29.** $15 \div d$ **31.** $67m$ **33.** $678 - 319$ **37.** $d \div 4$ **41.** C   **43.** 360   **45.** 360   **47.** 8   **49.** 16

2-3 Exercises

1. $4n$ **3.** $5w$ **5.** $7n$ **7.** s^2 **9.** $n + 5$ **11.** $88n$ **13.** $n + 7$; $3n + 1$ **17.** G   **19.** 29   **21.** 21   **23.** 245   **25.** 126

2-4 Exercises

1. no   **3.** yes   **5.** yes   **7.** 53 feet is equal to 636 inches.   **9.** no   **11.** yes   **13.** no   **15.** yes   **17.** no   **19.** yes   **21.** 300 m is equal to 30,000 cm.   **23.** yes   **25.** no   **27.** no   **29.** yes   **31.** no   **33.** yes   **35.** $17 \neq 350 \div 20$; no, they do not have the same amount of money.   **37.** 6   **39.** 2   **41.** 3   **47.** H   **49.** 9^4 **51.** 8^2

2-5 Exercises

1. $x = 36$ **3.** $n = 19$ **5.** $p = 18$ **7.** 6 blocks   **9.** $r = 7$ **11.** $b = 25$ **13.** $z = 9$ **15.** $g = 16$ **17.** 6 meters   **19.** $n = 7$ **21.** $y = 19$ **23.** $h = 78$ **25.** $b = 69$ **27.** $t = 26$ **29.** $m = 22$ **31.** $p + 20 = 36$ **33.** 880 m   **37.** B   **39.** 648; 798; 923   **41.** 1,036; 1,498; 2,163   **43.** 9, 7, 5

2-6 Exercises

1. $p = 17$ **3.** $a = 31$ **5.** $n = 33$ **7.** $y = 25$ **9.** $a = 38$ **11.** $a = 97$ **13.** $p = 33$ **15.** $s = 31$ **17.** $x = 36$ **19.** $a = 21$ **21.** $f = 14$ **23.** $r = 154$ **25.** $g = 143$ **27.** $m = 18$ **29.** 13 million   **33.** D   **35.** 71   **37.** 22   **39.** $y = 38$ **41.** $b = 56$

2-7 Exercises

1. $x = 3$ **3.** $a = 9$ **5.** $c = 11$ **7.** 45 feet   **9.** $a = 4$ **11.** $x = 4$ **13.** $t = 7$ **15.** $m = 11$ **17.** 6 feet   **19.** $y = 9$ **21.** $y = 8$ **23.** $y = 20$ **25.** $z = 40$ **27.** $y = 23$ **29.** $y = 18$ **31.** $y = 8$ **33.** $a = 14$ **35.** $x = 3$ **37.** $t = 6$ **39.** 15 to 177 segments   **41.** 4,000 light-sensitive cells   **45.** C   **47.** 7,000   **49.** $b = 42$ **51.** $n = 212$

2-8 Exercises

1. $y = 12$ **3.** $r = 63$ **5.** $j = 36$ **7.** $f = 60$ **9.** 90 min   **11.** $c = 26$ **13.** $g = 98$ **15.** $x = 144$ **17.** $r = 81$ **19.** $c = 96$ **21.** $c = 165$ **23.** $c = 70$ **25.** $c = 60$ **27.** $\frac{w}{381} = 76$; $w = 28{,}956$ m   **33.** J   **35.** Add 5; 25, 30, 35   **37.** $r = 13$ **39.** $p = 9$

Chapter 2 Extension

1.

3.

5.

7.

9.

11.

13. $t \leq 9$ **15.** $x < 4$ **17.** $c > 1$ **19.** $d \geq 6$ **21.** $p > 6$ **23.** $r \leq 3$ **25.** $f > 27$ **27.** $q \geq 3$ **29.** $p > 11$ **31.** $s + 2 \geq 5$ **33.** $a < 20{,}320$

Chapter 2 Study Guide: Review

1. algebraic expression   **2.** equation   **3.** variable   **4.** constant   **5.** 7, 6   **6.** 6, 10   **7.** 9, 18, 27, 36   **8.** 30, 33, 36, 39   **9.** 75, 80, 85, 90   **10.** $15 + b$ **11.** 6×5 **12.** $9t$ **13.** $g \div 9$ **14.** the product of 4 and z; 4 times z **15.** 15 plus x; the sum of 15 and x **16.** 54 divided by 6; the quotient of 54 and 6   **17.** m divided by 20;

the quotient of m and 20   **18.** 3 minus y; the difference of y and 3   **19.** the sum of 5,100 and 64; 64 added to 5,100   **20.** y minus 3; the difference of y and 3   **21.** g minus 20; the difference of g and 20   **22.** $3n + 1$ **23.** $n - 1$ **24.** yes   **25.** no   **26.** yes   **27.** yes   **28.** $x = 6$ **29.** $n = 14$ **30.** $c = 29$ **31.** $y = 6$ **32.** $p = 27$ **33.** $w = 9$ **34.** $b = 11$ **35.** $n = 44$ **36.** $p = 16$ **37.** $d = 57$ **38.** $k = 45$ **39.** $d = 9$ **40.** $p = 63$ **41.** $n = 67$ **42.** $r = 14$ **43.** $w = 144$ **44.** $h = 60$ **45.** $p = 167$ **46.** $v = 8$ **47.** $y = 9$ **48.** $c = 7$ **49.** $n = 2$ **50.** $s = 8$ **51.** $t = 10$ **52.** $a = 8$ **53.** $y = 8$ **54.** $r = 42$ **55.** $t = 15$ **56.** $y = 18$ **57.** $n = 72$ **58.** $z = 52$ **59.** $b = 100$ **60.** $n = 77$ **61.** $p = 90$

Chapter 3

3-1 Exercises

1. $1 + 0.9 + 0.08$; one and ninety-eight hundredths   **3.** 0.0765; seven hundred sixty-five ten-thousandths   **5.** Osmium   **7.** 4.09, 4.1, 4.18   **9.** $7 + 0.08 + 0.009 + 0.0003$; seven and eight hundred ninety-three ten-thousandths   **11.** 7.15; $7 + 0.1 + 0.05$ **13.** the Chupaderos meteorite   **15.** 1.5, 1.56, 1.62   **17.** nine and seven thousandths   **19.** ten and twenty-two thousandths   **21.** one hundred forty-two and six thousand five hundred forty-one ten-thousandths   **23.** ninety-two thousand, seven hundred fifty-five hundred thousandths   **25.** $<$ **27.** $<$ **29.** $<$ **31.** three hundredths   **33.** one tenth   **35.** 4.034, 1.43, 1.424, 1.043, 0.34   **37.** 652.12, 65.213, 65.135, 61.53   **39.** Ross 154   **41.** Alpha Centauri, Proxima Centauri   **45.** C   **47.** 9,000   **49.** $n = 123$ **51.** $c = 52$

3-2 Exercises

1. about 12 miles **3.** 12 **5.** 5.4988
7. 120 **9.** from 44 to 46.5
11. about 450 miles **13.** 3.4
15. 5.157 **17.** 20 **19.** 6 **21.** from
14 to 17 **23.** 48 **25.** 17 **27.** $0.22,
$0.10, $0.08, $0.04 **29.** $(12 \times 8) -$
$(18 \times 4) = 24$, or about 24 cents
37. 6 inches in April, 10 inches in
May, 2 inches in June **39.** $x = 69$
41. 8.009, 8.05, 8.304 **43.** 30.211,
30.709, 30.75

3-3 Exercises

1. 20.2 miles **3.** 12.65 miles
5. 5.6 **7.** 4.9 **9.** 3.55 **11.** 4.948
13. $567.38 **15.** 1.5 **17.** 18 **19.** 4.3
21. 2.3 **23.** 5.87 **25.** 9.035
27. 8.669 **29.** 0.143 **31.** 3.778
33. 3.8179 **35.** 1 **37.** 52.836
39. 29.376 **41.** 84.966 **43.** $72.42
45. 0.196 **49.** C **51.** $s = 70$
53. $t = 1,464$ **55.** 60

3-4 Exercises

1. 593,700 **3.** 609,120 **5.** 5.0×10^5
7. 6,793,000 **9.** 382,000
11. 278,000 **13.** 3,818,000
15. 412,900 **17.** 9.0×10^4
19. 1.607×10^6 **21.** 6.0×10^6
23. 321,100 **25.** 7,700
27. 4,030,000 **29.** 6.2×10^6
31. 123,400 **33.** 208,000 **35.** 54.3
37. 1.5×10^5 **39.** 6.52×10^2
41. 6.5342×10^4 **43.** 2.8001×10^4
45. Range: 38,000 to 120,000;
possible answer: 100,000
47. $150,000 = 1.5 \times 10^5$
49. $24,600,000$; 2.46×10^7 **53.** D
55. Commutative Property
57. Associative Property **59.** 1.9
61. 1.2

3-5 Exercises

1. $1.68 **3.** 0.24 **5.** 0.21 **7.** 16.52
9. 35.63 **11.** 2.59 km **13.** 0.027
15. 0.217 **17.** 0.00042 **19.** 0.012
21. 13.321 **23.** 26.04 **25.** 1.148
27. 2.5914 **29.** 0.009 **31.** 0.0612

33. 26.46 **35.** 1.6632 **37.** 0.2444
39. 4.1184 **41.** 14.06 **43.** 37.38
45. 62.1 **47.** 5.8 **49.** 4.65 pounds
51. 7.38 lb **55.** B **57.** $x = 32$
59. $t = 51$ **61.** $1 + 0.2 + 0.03$
63. $20 + 6 + 0.07$ **65.** $80 + 0.002$

3-6 Exercises

1. 0.23 **3.** 0.35 **5.** 0.078 **7.** 0.104
9. $8.82 **11.** 0.22 **13.** 0.27
15. 0.171 **17.** 0.076 **19.** 0.107
21. 1.345 **23.** 0.236 **29.** when the
divisor is greater than the portion
of the dividend being divided into
31. C **33.** Subtract 5; 60.
35. Alternate adding 7 and
subtracting 4; 21. **37.** 20.8
39. 710,000

3-7 Exercises

1. 5 **3.** 17 **5.** 6 **7.** 54.6 mi/h **9.** 6
11. 8 **13.** 217.5 **15.** 11 **17.** 5
19. 11.6 gallons of gas **21.** 6.3
23. 191.1 **25.** 184.74 **27.** 12.2
29. 12.2 **31.** 1,270 **33.** 1,125
35. 920 **37.** 2.15×10^7 **39.** about
232 gills; about $4,640 **45.** C
47. > **49.** > **51.** 16.06 **53.** 3.12

3-8 Exercises

1. 10 belts **3.** 2.25 meters
5. 8 bunches **7.** 3 packs
13. C **15.** $y = 63$ **17.** $y = 17$
19. 9.1 **21.** 14

3-9 Exercises

1. $a = 7.1$ **3.** $c = 12.8$ **5.** $d = 3.488$
7. 60.375 m^2 **9.** $b = 9.3$ **11.** $r =$
20.8 **13.** $a = 10.7$ **15.** $f = 6.56$
17. $z = 4$ **19a.** 1.6 meters
b. $14.40 **21.** $q = 24.7$ **23.** $b = 4.2$
25. $a = 13.9$ **27.** $z = 13$ **29a.** 19.5
units, 21 units **b.** 50.5 units
31. 1.9×10^6 **33.** 9 capsules
39. H **41.** $7z$ **43.** 5.1 **45.** 16.08

Chapter 3 Study Guide: Review

1. front-end estimation
2. scientific notation **3.** clustering

4. $5 + 0.6 + 0.08$; five and sixty-
eight hundredths **5.** $1 + 0.007 +$
0.0006; one and seventy-six ten-
thousandths **6.** $1 + 0.2 + 0.003$;
one and two hundred three
thousandths **7.** $20 + 3 + 0.005$;
twenty-three and five thousandths
8. $70 + 1 + 0.03 + 0.008$; seventy-
one and thirty-eight thousandths
9. $90 + 9 + 0.9 + 0.09 + 0.009 +$
0.0009; ninety-nine and nine
thousand, nine hundred ninety-
nine ten thousandths **10.** 1.12,
1.2, 1.3 **11.** 11.07, 11.17, 11.7
12. 0.033, 0.3, 0.303 **13.** 5.009, 5.5,
5.950 **14.** 101.025, 101.25, 101.52
15. 11.32 **16.** 2.3 **17.** 14 **18.** 80
19. 9 **20.** 5 **21.** 24.85 **22.** 5.3
23. 33.02 **24.** 4.9225 **25.** 32.33
26. 14.624 **27.** 2.58 **28.** 2.8718
29. 1.47 **30.** 6.423 **31.** 2 **32.** 4.83
33. 126,000 **34.** 54,600
35. 6,700,000 **36.** 180,600
37. 4,200 **38.** 7,890 **39.** 5.5×10^5
40. 7.23×10^3 **41.** 1.3×10^6
42. 1.48×10^1 **43.** 9.042×10^2
44. 8.91402×10^8 **45.** 30,200
46. 429,300 **47.** 1,700,000
48. 5,390 **49.** 685 **50.** 14,500,000
51. 9.44 **52.** 0.865 **53.** 0.0072
54. 24.416 **55.** 0.54 **56.** 10.5148
57. 9.72 **58.** 39.528 **59.** 1.03
60. 0.72 **61.** 3.85 **62.** 2.59
63. $3.64 **64.** 8.1 **65.** $6.1\overline{6}$
66. $3.87\overline{6}$ **67.** 52.275 **68.** 0.75
meter **69.** 14 containers
70. 9 cars **71.** $a = 13.38$
72. $y = 2.62$ **73.** $n = 2.29$
74. $p = 6.02$ **75.** $5.00

Chapter 4

4-1 Exercises

1. 2, 4 **3.** none **5.** composite
7. composite **9.** composite
11. composite **13.** 3 **15.** 3, 5, 9
17. 2, 4 **19.** 2 **21.** composite
23. prime **25.** composite
27. prime **29.** composite

31. prime   33. no, no, no, no
35. yes, no, yes, no, no, no, no
37. True   39. True   41. 1, 4, or 7
43. 1, 4, or 7   45. 0, 3, 6, or 9
47. Prime numbers from 50 to 100 are 53, 59, 61, 67, 71, 73, 79, 83, 89, and 97.   49. Mackinac Straits
55. D   57. 7, 11, 15, 19, 23
59. 6, 30, 150, 750, 3,750   61. 30

4-2 Exercises

1. 1, 2, 3, 4, 6, 12   3. 1, 2, 4, 13, 26, 52   5. $2^4 \cdot 3$ 7. $2 \cdot 3 \cdot 11$ 9. 1, 2, 3, 4, 6, 8, 12, 24   11. 1, 2, 3, 6, 7, 14, 21, 42   13. 1, 67   15. 1, 5, 17, 85   17. 7^2
19. $2^2 \cdot 19$ 21. 3^4 23. $2^2 \cdot 5 \cdot 7$
33a. 15 boys per team   b. 5 teams of 9 players   35. $3^2 \cdot 11$ 37. $2^2 \cdot 71$
39. $2^3 \cdot 3 \cdot 5 \cdot 7$ 41. $2^2 \cdot 5 \cdot 37$
43. $2^2 \cdot 5^2$ 45. 7^3 47. Insects; Clams   53. 60   55. 3, 5   57. 2, 3, 4, 5, 6, 9, 10   59. 2, 4, 5, 10   61. 2, 3, 4, 5, 6, 9, 10

4-3 Exercises

1. 9   3. 7   5. 6   7. 4 arrangements
9. 14   11. 2   13. 4   15. 12   17. 3 teams   19. 12   21. 5   23. 2   25. 75
27. 4   29. 6 baskets   31. 2   33. 9
35. 6   37. 6 rows   39. 4 groups
43. A   45. $y = 27$ 47. $z = 8$
49. $2 \times 3 \times 7$ 51. 3×17
53. $5^2 \times 2^3$

4-4 Exercises

1. $\frac{3}{20}$ 3. $\frac{43}{10}$ 5. 0.4   7. 0.125
9. 0.21, $\frac{2}{3}$, 0.78   11. $\frac{1}{9}$, 0.3, 0.52
13. $5\frac{71}{100}$ 15. $3\frac{23}{100}$ 17. $2\frac{7}{10}$
19. $6\frac{3}{10}$ 21. 1.6   23. 3.275
25. 0.375   27. 0.625   29. $\frac{1}{9}$, 0.29, $\frac{3}{8}$
31. $\frac{1}{10}$, 0.11, 0.13   33. 0.31, $\frac{3}{7}$, 0.76
35. $90 + 2 + \frac{3}{10}$ 37. $100 + 7 + \frac{1}{10} + \frac{7}{100}$ 39. $0.1\overline{6}$; repeats   41. $0.41\overline{6}$; repeats   43. 0.8; terminates
45. $0.8\overline{3}$; repeats   47. $0.91\overline{6}$; repeats
49. >   51. <   53. <   55. <
57. $4\frac{1}{2}$, 4.48, 3.92   59. 125.25, 125.205, $125\frac{1}{5}$ 61. Jill   63. $\frac{1}{20}$

67. D   69. 21.47   71. 23.45   73. 14
75. 16

4-5 Exercises

1. $\frac{2}{3}$, $\frac{8}{12}$ 3. $\frac{1}{2}$, $\frac{5}{10}$ 5. 25   7. 21   9. $\frac{1}{5}$
11. $\frac{1}{4}$ 21. 15   23. 70   25. 6   27. 140
29. $\frac{1}{4}$ 31. $\frac{1}{5}$ 33. $\frac{3}{4}$ 35. $\frac{1}{2}$
37. $\frac{3}{6} = \frac{1}{2}$ 39. $\frac{2}{3} = \frac{8}{12}$ 41. $\frac{1}{4}$ 43. $\frac{2}{5}$
47. Baskets and wreaths are $\frac{12}{72} = \frac{1}{6}$; jewelry is $\frac{32}{72} = \frac{4}{9}$; glass and pottery are $\frac{16}{72} = \frac{2}{9}$; paintings are $\frac{12}{72} = \frac{1}{6}$.   51. B   53. $x = 45$
55. $w = 18$ 57. $0.\overline{6}$ 59. 3.2

4-6 Exercises

1. $2\frac{2}{5}$ 3. $\frac{8}{3}$ 5. $\frac{12}{5}$ 7. $8\frac{3}{5}$ 9. $\frac{20}{9}$
11. $\frac{13}{3}$ 13. $\frac{25}{6}$ 15. $\frac{19}{5}$ 17. 4; whole number   19. $8\frac{3}{5}$; mixed number   21. $8\frac{7}{10}$; mixed number
23. 15; whole number   25. $\frac{53}{11}$
27. $\frac{93}{5}$ 29. 3; 5   31. 13; 9   33. 2; 10
35. $28\frac{4}{9}$ yards   37. =   39. <
41. $40\frac{1}{2}$; $50\frac{1}{2}$ 43. $\frac{9}{5}$ 47. A
49. 1,038; 1,497; 2,560   51. 1,765; 4,706; 11,765   53. 21 to 22   55. 1, 3, 19, 57   57. 1, 2, 3, 6, 9, 18, 27, 54

4-7 Exercises

1. >   3. =   5. yes   7. $\frac{1}{4}$, $\frac{1}{3}$, $\frac{2}{5}$
9. $\frac{1}{6}$, $\frac{1}{2}$, $\frac{2}{3}$ 11. <   13. >   15. =
17. >   19. $\frac{3}{7}$, $\frac{1}{2}$, $\frac{3}{5}$ 21. $\frac{1}{3}$, $\frac{3}{8}$, $\frac{4}{9}$
23. $\frac{2}{3}$, $\frac{7}{10}$, $\frac{3}{4}$ 25. $\frac{1}{4}$, $\frac{3}{8}$, $\frac{2}{3}$ 27. <
29. >   31. >   33. >   35. $\frac{3}{10}$, $\frac{2}{5}$, $\frac{1}{2}$
37. $\frac{1}{5}$, $\frac{7}{15}$, $\frac{2}{3}$ 39. $\frac{2}{5}$, $\frac{4}{9}$, $\frac{11}{15}$
41. $\frac{5}{12}$, $\frac{5}{8}$, $\frac{3}{4}$ 43. Laura; $\frac{3}{5} > \frac{4}{7}$
45. $1\frac{1}{8}$, $1\frac{2}{5}$, 3, $3\frac{2}{5}$, $3\frac{4}{5}$
47. $\frac{1}{2}$, $\frac{3}{4}$, $3\frac{1}{15}$, $3\frac{1}{10}$, $3\frac{1}{5}$ 49. yes
53. C   55. 4.5×10^1 57. 1.6×10^6
59. $\frac{1}{12}$ 61. $\frac{3}{10}$ 63. $\frac{1}{11}$

4-8 Exercises

1. $\frac{1}{2}$ foot   3. $7\frac{1}{7}$ 5. $5\frac{1}{6}$ 7. $\frac{2}{5}$ 9. $\frac{1}{5}$
11. $\frac{2}{7}$ 13. $1\frac{3}{5}$ 15. $\frac{6}{5}$ or $1\frac{1}{5}$ 17. $\frac{1}{10}$
19. $\frac{5}{8}$ 21. $\frac{14}{33}$ 23. $\frac{2}{3}$ 25. $13\frac{1}{3}$
27. $\frac{17}{24}$ 29. $\frac{4}{9}$ 31. $\frac{5}{7}$ 33. $8\frac{2}{3}$

35. $\frac{3}{4}$ hour   37. $1\frac{3}{4}$ hr   39. 1 foot
51. $\frac{2}{6}$, $\frac{3}{7}$, $\frac{5}{4}$ 53. $\frac{3}{10}$, $\frac{1}{3}$, $\frac{3}{8}$

4-9 Exercises

1. about 1   3. about $\frac{1}{2}$ 5. 16 miles
7. about $\frac{1}{2}$ 9. about 0   11. about $1\frac{1}{2}$ 13. about 2   15. 4 tons
17. $3\frac{1}{2}$ tons   19. >   21. <   23. >
25. about 2   27. about 3
29. about $13\frac{1}{2}$ 31. $\frac{1}{2}$ in.   33. about $9\frac{1}{2}$ in.   37. B   39. 3   41. 10
43. $n + 5$

Chapter 4 Extension

1. intersection: empty; union: all whole numbers   3. intersection: 1, 2, 3, 4, 6, 9, 12, 18, 36; union: 1, 2, 3, 4, 6, 8, 9, 12, 18, 24, 36, 72
5. yes   7. no

Chapter 4 Study Guide: Review

1. improper fraction; mixed number   2. repeating decimal; terminating decimal   3. prime number; composite number   4. 2
5. 2, 3, 5, 6, 9, 10   6. 2, 3, 6, 9   7. 2, 4
8. 2, 5, 10   9. 3   10. composite
11. composite   12. prime
13. composite   14. prime
15. composite   16. composite
17. prime   18. composite
19. prime   20. 1, 2, 3, 4, 5, 6, 10, 12, 15, 20, 30, 60   21. 1, 2, 3, 4, 6, 8, 9, 12, 18, 24, 36, 72   22. 1, 29   23. 1, 2, 4, 7, 8, 14, 28, 56   24. 1, 5, 17, 85
25. 1, 71   26. $5 \cdot 13$ 27. $2 \cdot 47$
28. $2 \cdot 5 \cdot 11$ 29. 3^4 30. $3^2 \cdot 11$
31. $2^2 \cdot 19$ 32. 97   33. $5 \cdot 11$
34. $2 \cdot 23$ 35. 12   36. 25   37. 9
38. $\frac{37}{100}$ 39. $1\frac{4}{5}$ 40. $\frac{2}{5}$ 41. 0.875
42. 0.4   43. $0.\overline{7}$ 44. Possible answer: $\frac{2}{3}$; $\frac{8}{12}$ 45. Possible answer: $\frac{8}{10}$; $\frac{16}{20}$ 46. Possible answer: $\frac{1}{4}$; $\frac{2}{8}$
47. $\frac{7}{8}$ 48. $\frac{3}{10}$ 49. $\frac{7}{10}$ 50. $\frac{34}{9}$
51. $\frac{29}{12}$ 52. $\frac{37}{7}$ 53. $3\frac{5}{6}$ 54. $3\frac{2}{5}$
55. $5\frac{1}{8}$ 56. >   57. >   58. $\frac{3}{8}$, $\frac{2}{3}$, $\frac{7}{8}$

59. $\frac{3}{12}, \frac{1}{3}, \frac{4}{6}$ **60.** 1 **61.** $\frac{3}{4}$ **62.** $\frac{3}{5}$
63. $6\frac{5}{7}$ **64.** 1 **65.** $\frac{1}{2}$ **66.** 11 **67.** $2\frac{1}{2}$

Chapter 5

5-1 Exercises

1. 3 packs of pencils and 4 packs of erasers **3.** 36 **5.** 20 **7.** 48
9. 40 **11.** 63 **13.** 150 **15.** 8
17. 20 **19.** 18 **21.** 12 **23.** 24
25. 66 **27.** 60 **29.** 140 **31.** 12
33c. 12 **d.** Possible answer: 120, 144, 132 **35.** 12 and 16 **37a.** 120
37b. 120 **37c.** 4 **41.** B **43.** 0.03
45. 0.24 **47.** > **49.** > **51.** $4\frac{5}{7}$

5-2 Exercises

1. $\frac{5}{12}$ ton **3.** $\frac{3}{10}$ **5.** $\frac{13}{14}$ **7.** $\frac{1}{6}$ cup
9. $\frac{7}{12}$ **11.** $\frac{9}{20}$ **13.** $1\frac{2}{15}$ **15.** $1\frac{1}{8}$
17. $\frac{7}{15}$ **19.** $\frac{7}{18}$ **21.** $\frac{1}{3}$ **23.** $\frac{28}{33}$
25. $\frac{7}{18}$ **27.** $\frac{1}{5}$ **29.** $\frac{2}{2}$ or 1 **31.** $1\frac{1}{8}$
33. $\frac{1}{2}$ **35.** $\frac{4}{7}$ **37.** $\frac{3}{4}$ **39.** $\frac{7}{8}$
41. $\frac{1}{6}$ gallon **43.** $\frac{9}{40}$ lb **49.** $\frac{11}{12}$ mi
51. 1.1 **53.** 0.125 **55.** > **57.** >

5-3 Exercises

1. $10\frac{5}{12}$ **3.** $6\frac{1}{12}$ **5.** $4\frac{1}{4}$ **7.** $6\frac{7}{12}$
9. $6\frac{1}{4}$ **11.** $8\frac{7}{12}$ **13.** $29\frac{3}{5}$ **15.** $34\frac{1}{2}$
17. $3\frac{51}{90}$ **19.** $20\frac{13}{36}$ **21.** $12\frac{5}{24}$
23a. $26\frac{3}{5}$ lb **b.** $2\frac{1}{10}$ lb **c.** $11\frac{1}{10}$ lb
25. $1\frac{7}{10}$ **27.** $23\frac{3}{4}$ **29.** $13\frac{1}{4}$ **31.** $18\frac{1}{5}$
33. $\frac{1}{2}$ mi **35.** 5 **37.** $1\frac{1}{12}$ **39.** $8\frac{1}{9}$
41. 0 **43.** $9\frac{3}{8}$ km **45.** $16\frac{1}{2}$ yards
51. J **53.** $1\frac{1}{2}$ **55.** $1\frac{2}{5}$ **57.** $\frac{49}{60}$
59. $1\frac{1}{15}$

5-4 Exercises

1. $\frac{3}{4}$ **3.** $1\frac{2}{3}$ **5.** $2\frac{3}{5}$ **7.** $3\frac{4}{5}$ **9.** $7\frac{7}{8}$
11. $4\frac{13}{18}$ **13.** $1\frac{4}{5}$ **15.** $6\frac{2}{3}$ **17.** $1\frac{4}{9}$
19. $8\frac{9}{11}$ **21.** $11\frac{2}{9}$ **23.** $12\frac{13}{18}$
25. $7\frac{1}{4}$ in. **27.** $7\frac{1}{3}$ **29.** $3\frac{8}{11}$
31. $11\frac{4}{7}$ **33.** $4\frac{11}{12}$ **35.** $1\frac{5}{6}$ **37.** $\frac{1}{12}$
39. $13\frac{5}{12}$ **41.** $1\frac{1}{12}$ yards² **43.** $1\frac{11}{12}$
yards² **47.** C **49.** $a = 16$
51. $z = 9$ **53.** 17 **55.** 22

5-5 Exercises

1. $4\frac{1}{2}$ **3.** $5\frac{5}{8}$ **5.** $4\frac{1}{10}$ **7.** $57\frac{3}{4}$ in.
9. $3\frac{5}{8}$ **11.** $4\frac{5}{6}$ **13.** $8\frac{7}{9}$ **15.** $6\frac{1}{4}$ feet
17. $5\frac{1}{10}$ **19.** $7\frac{9}{10}$ **21.** $\frac{1}{3}$
23. 16 ounces **25.** $\frac{3}{8}$ in. **27.** $7\frac{7}{18}$
29. $5\frac{5}{12}$ **31.** $4\frac{1}{4}$ **37.** B **39.** 12
41. 72 **43.** $\frac{7}{20}$ **45.** $7\frac{17}{30}$

5-6 Exercises

1. $\frac{8}{9}$ **3.** 3 **5.** $\frac{3}{7}$ **7.** 6 **9.** 8 **11.** 9
13. 27 boys **15.** $\frac{3}{4}$ **17.** $\frac{4}{5}$ **19.** $\frac{6}{11}$
21. 10 **23.** 6 **25.** 2 **27.** $5\frac{5}{7}$ **29.** $3\frac{5}{9}$
31. 7 **33.** 15 **35.** 5 **37.** $\frac{48}{5}$ or $9\frac{3}{5}$
39. 45 **41.** > **43.** = **45.** < **47.** >
49. $33 **51.** 165 feet tall **55.** C
57. $75 - w$ **59.** $p \div 7$ **61.** $8\frac{5}{7}$
63. $6\frac{3}{8}$

5-7 Exercises

1. $\frac{1}{6}$ **3.** $\frac{3}{7}$ **5.** $\frac{2}{15}$ **7.** $\frac{1}{20}$ **9.** $\frac{2}{21}$
11. $\frac{5}{9}$ **13.** $\frac{1}{4}$ **15.** $\frac{5}{11}$ **17.** $\frac{2}{15}$ **19.** $\frac{1}{8}$
21. $\frac{4}{27}$ **23.** $\frac{5}{48}$ **25.** $\frac{4}{15}$ **27.** $\frac{1}{14}$
29. $\frac{27}{35}$ **31.** $\frac{9}{55}$ **33.** $\frac{1}{4}$ cup **35.** <
37. > **39.** < **41a.** Multiply by $\frac{1}{4}$.
b. $\frac{1}{12}$ **43.** $\frac{3}{8}$ lb **45.** $\frac{3}{8}$ **49.** D
51. $n = 3$ **53.** $a = 13$ **55.** $\frac{4}{9}$ **57.** $\frac{4}{7}$

5-8 Exercises

1. $\frac{5}{6}$ **3.** $\frac{11}{14}$ **5.** $\frac{13}{15}$ **7.** $2\frac{1}{16}$ **9.** $21\frac{5}{7}$
11. $12\frac{7}{20}$ **13.** $\frac{15}{16}$ **15.** $\frac{7}{15}$ **17.** $1\frac{1}{18}$
19. $\frac{13}{14}$ **21.** $2\frac{2}{7}$ **23.** $15\frac{1}{2}$ **25.** $23\frac{1}{2}$
27. $3\frac{3}{5}$ **29.** $\frac{10}{27}$ **31.** $1\frac{1}{4}$ **33.** $\frac{1}{6}$
35. $13\frac{3}{4}$ **37.** $2\frac{2}{3}$ **39.** $17\frac{1}{2}$
41. $1\frac{17}{25}$ bags **43.** yes **45.** $1\frac{3}{7}$
47. 28 **49.** $1\frac{7}{8}$ **51.** $21\frac{3}{4}$ **53.** 240
55a. $1\frac{1}{2} \cdot 7 = 10\frac{1}{2}$ h **b.** less than
12 h **59.** C **61.** 5.4×10^2
63. 5.4×10^4 **65.** $\frac{1}{2}$ **67.** 4

5-9 Exercises

1. $\frac{7}{2}$ **3.** 9 **5.** $\frac{5}{13}$ **7.** $1\frac{5}{7}$ **9.** $2\frac{1}{6}$
11. $\frac{9}{50}$ **13.** $4\frac{4}{7}$ **15.** 10 **17.** $\frac{12}{11}$
19. $\frac{11}{8}$ **21.** $\frac{7}{6}$ **23.** $\frac{4}{21}$ **25.** $1\frac{5}{14}$
27. 12 **29.** $\frac{3}{10}$ **31.** $2\frac{22}{45}$ **33.** $\frac{2}{3}$
35. $\frac{1}{40}$ **37.** $1\frac{17}{25}$ **39.** $4\frac{2}{3}$ **41.** $\frac{3}{28}$

43. 16 bags **45.** yes **47.** yes
49. $\frac{5}{2}, \frac{25}{4}$ **51.** $\frac{1}{5}, \frac{1}{5}$ **53.** The reciprocal of a fraction has the fraction's numerator as its denominator and has the fraction's denominator as its numerator. The product of a fraction and its reciprocal is 1.
55. $\frac{11}{12}$ **57.** $1\frac{1}{14}$ **59.** $41\frac{19}{75}$
61. $24\frac{2}{9}$ in. **67.** H **68.** 2; 4.32
69. 1; 9.5 **70.** 3; 16.192 **71.** 2; 0.04
73. $\frac{7}{8}$ **75.** $5\frac{13}{15}$

5-10 Exercises

1. $z = 16$ **3.** $x = 7\frac{1}{2}$ **5.** 24 **7.** $x = 9$
9. $t = \frac{1}{10}$ **11.** $y = 20$ **13.** $j = 12\frac{6}{7}$
15. $10 **17.** $y = 10$ **19.** $t = 16$
21. $b = 14$ **23.** $x = 9\frac{1}{3}$ **25.** $n = 12$
27. $y = \frac{2}{3}$ **29.** $\frac{3}{2}n = 9; n = 6$
31. 4 minutes **33.** 11 dresses
35. 20 more pages **41.** B **43.** 35
45. 2 **47.** 3 **49.** $1\frac{1}{5}$ **51.** $\frac{15}{28}$

Chapter 5 Study Guide: Review

1. reciprocals **2.** least common denominator **3.** 30 **4.** 48 **5.** 27
6. 60 **7.** 225 **8.** 660 **9.** $\frac{33}{40}$ **10.** $\frac{3}{4}$
11. $\frac{1}{15}$ **12.** $\frac{5}{24}$ **13.** $4\frac{7}{10}$ **14.** $3\frac{1}{18}$
15. $\frac{11}{30}$ **16.** $3\frac{2}{3}$ **17.** $1\frac{1}{2}$ **18.** $5\frac{2}{3}$
19. $2\frac{5}{8}$ **20.** $6\frac{13}{14}$ **21.** $1\frac{1}{8}$
22. $4\frac{3}{4}$ feet **23.** $30\frac{3}{20}$ **24.** $14\frac{11}{12}$
25. $5\frac{5}{12}$ **26.** $3\frac{4}{9}$ **27.** $5\frac{7}{15}$ **28.** $3\frac{3}{10}$
29. 7 oz **30.** $\frac{5}{7}$ **31.** $\frac{3}{4}$ **32.** $2\frac{4}{7}$
33. $2\frac{1}{2}$ **34.** 3 **35.** $1\frac{1}{5}$
36. 21 members **37.** $\frac{1}{3}$
38. $\frac{15}{28}$ **39.** $\frac{1}{10}$ **40.** $\frac{7}{25}$ **41.** $\frac{5}{81}$
42. $\frac{3}{14}$ **43.** $\frac{8}{15}$ **44.** $\frac{9}{10}$ **45.** $1\frac{1}{4}$
46. 2 **47.** $\frac{4}{21}$ **48.** $\frac{3}{20}$ **49.** $\frac{5}{9}$
50. 8 times **51.** $a = \frac{1}{8}$ **52.** $b = 2$
53. $m = 17\frac{1}{2}$ **54.** $g = \frac{2}{15}$
55. $r = 10\frac{4}{5}$ **56.** $s = 50$ **57.** $p = \frac{1}{9}$
58. $j = 1\frac{53}{64}$

Chapter 6

6-1 Exercises

1.

Day	High Temperature (°F)
Mon	72
Tue	75
Wed	68
Thu	62
Fri	55

3.

Test	Grade
1st	70
2nd	75
3rd	80
4th	85
5th	90

5.

Date	Thickness (in.)
December 3	1
December 18	2
January 3	5
January 18	11
February 3	17

7. Jeffery is in sixth grade. Victoria is in seventh, and Arthur is in eighth. **11.** 81 **13.** 216 **15.** Possible answer: 2 times 12; 2 multiplied by 12 **17.** Possible answer: m divided by 3, the quotient of m and 3

6-2 Exercises

1. mean = 22 **3.** mean = 6.5 **5.** mean = 57, median = 54, no mode, range = 23 **7.** range = 19, mean = 508.2, median = 508.5, mode = 500 **9.** 11 **11.** 4 **13.** 70 **15.** 6, 7, 12, 15, 15 **19.** C **21.** 25 **23.** 2 **25.** 5

6-3 Exercises

1a. mean = 4.75, median = 5, no mode **b.** mean = 10, median = 7, no mode **3.** mean = 225, median = 187.5, mode = 240; median **5.** with: mean = 710.4, median = 788, no mode without: mean = 877.75, median = 868, no mode **7.** mean ≈ 118.29, median = 128, no mode **13.** 70 **15.** $n = \frac{9}{10}$ **17.** median: 35; no mode; range = 45

6-4 Exercises

1. green

3.

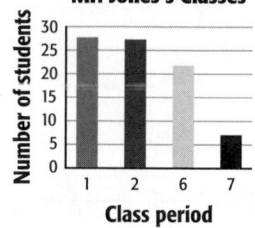

Number of Students in Mr. Jones's Classes

5. orange

7.

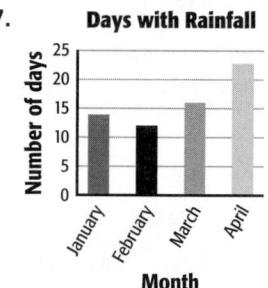

Days with Rainfall

9. 14 million mi² **11.** ≈ 8.14 million mi²

13a.

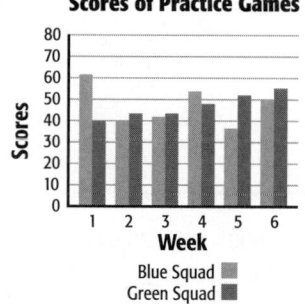

Scores of Practice Games

b. Blue: mean ≈ 47.3, range = 26; Green: mean = 47.3, range = 16 **c.** Possible answer: The green squad; their performance is more consistent, and their scores have steadily increased over time. **17.** J **19.** $\frac{1}{5}$ **21.** $2\frac{1}{3}$

6-5 Exercises

1.

Type of Instrument	
Trumpet	‖‖‖
Drums	‖
Tuba	I
Trombone	‖‖
French horn	‖‖‖

3.

Number of Years of Each Presidential Term		
Number (Intervals)	0–4	5–8	9–12
Frequency	26	15	1

5.

Pets	
Dog	‖‖‖ I
Cat	‖‖‖
Bird	‖‖‖
Fish	‖‖
Hamster	‖

7.

Final Medal Standing at the Summer Olympic Games for the Top 25 Countries					
Number (intervals)	0–20	21–40	41–60	61–80	81–100
Frequency	14	8	3	0	2

9. histogram

11.

Populations of Australia's States and Territories	
Census	Frequency
0–999,999	3
1,000,000–1,999,999	2
2,000,000–2,999,999	0
3,000,000–3,999,999	1
4,000,000–4,999,999	1
5,000,000–5,999,999	0
6,000,000–6,999,999	1

13. no **17.** B **19.** 1 + 0.2 + 0.03; one and twenty-three hundredths **21.** 20 + 6 + 0.07; twenty-six and seven-hundredths **23.** 19 **25.** 9

6-6 Exercises

1. (2, 3) **3.** (7, 6) **5.** (4, 5)

7–9.

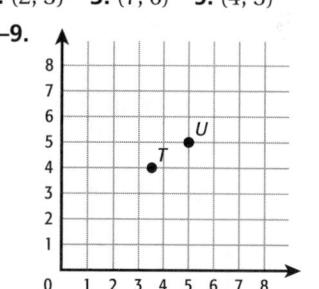

11. (3, 0) **13.** (1, 4) **15.** (11, 7)

17–21.

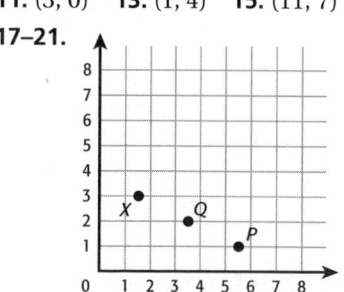

23. A **25.** C **27.** P **29.** (9, 8) **31.** (1, 5) **33.** (9, 0) **35.** $\left(5\frac{1}{2}, 0\right)$

39. D **41.** $3^3 \times 5^2$ **43.** $2^2 \times 3^2 \times 5$
45. $\frac{3}{28}$ **47.** $\frac{3}{14}$

6-7 Exercises

1.
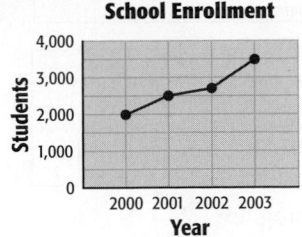
School Enrollment

3. 125

5.
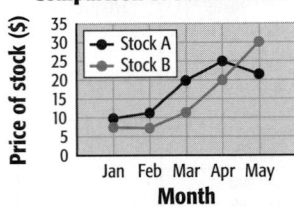
Comparison of Stock Prices

7. 70 million

9.
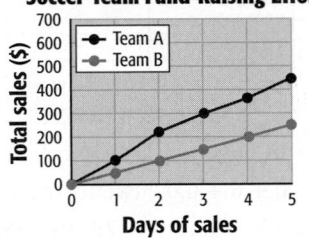
Soccer Team Fund-Raising Efforts

11. Max **15.** C **17.** $s = 18$
19. $m = 15$

6-8 Exercises

5. The vertical axis begins at 430 rather than zero. **7.** the yearly increments changed

9.
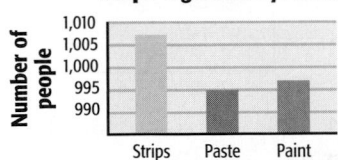
Strips' Significantly Better

Paste is Most Effective

17. Possible answer: The temperature was twice as high at 11:00 A.M. **19.** 124

21–23.
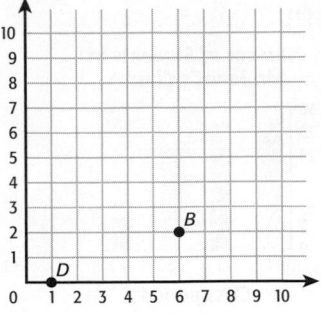

6-9 Exercises

1.

Stems	Leaves
3	7 9
4	0 5 8
5	1 6

Daily High Temperatures (°F)

Key: 3|7 means 37

3. 44 **5.** 32 **7.** 34 **9.** 41 **11.** 52
13. 42 **15.** A

17.

Number of Cars with One Passenger

Stems	Leaves
8	0 1 2 3 7 8 9
9	2 4 4 5 9
10	0 1 3 9
11	
12	4 5

Key: 8|0 means 80

21. 2,000 **23.** 225,971; 2,004,801; 298,500,004 **25.** $\frac{7}{4}$ **27.** 5

6-10 Exercises

1. line graph **3a.** Possible answer: Line graph; it shows change over time.

b.
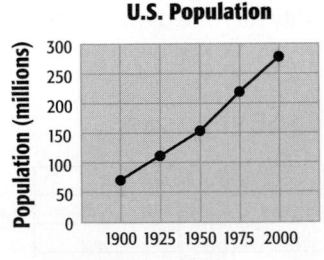
U.S. Population

9. line plot **11.** 5 **13.** 4

Chapter 6 Study Guide: Review

1. histogram **2.** ordered pair
3. mode

4.

Snake Lengths (ft)	
Anaconda	35 ft
Diamond python	21 ft
King cobra	19 ft
Boa constrictor	16 ft

5. mean: 37; median: 38; mode: 39; range: 7 **6.** with outlier: mean ≈ 14.29; median = 11; mode = 12; without outlier: mean ≈ 10.33; median = 10.5; mode = 12
7. with outlier: mean = 31; median = 32; mode = 32; without outlier: mean = 35.75; median = 33; mode = 32 **8.** with outlier: mean ≈ 19.67; median = 14; mode = none; without outlier: mean = 13.2; median = 13; mode = none
9. 8th grade

10.
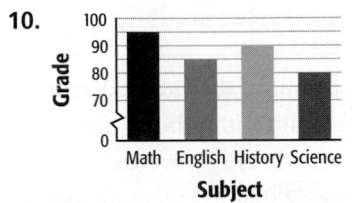

11.

Points Scored			
Points (Intervals)	1–4	5–8	9–12
Frequency	2	3	1

12.
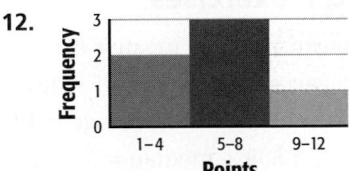

13. (4, 1) **14.** (3, 2)

15.
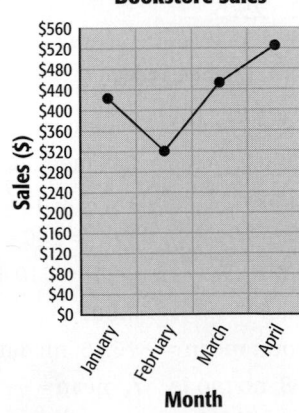
Bookstore Sales

16. April **17.** Sales decreased from January to February and then increased from February to April. **18.** The scale starts out in increments of one mile and then it changes to 5 miles.

19.

Basketball Scores

Stems	Leaves
2	0 2 6 8
3	4
4	0 4 6

Key: 2|0 means 20

20. smallest value: 20, largest value: 46, mean: 32.5, median: 31, no mode, range: 26 **21.** line graph

Chapter 7

7-1 Exercises

1. 3:10 **3.** 41:16 **5.** the 8-ounce bag **7.** 19:3 **11.** the 15 lb bag **13.** 24 to 11, 24:11, twenty-four to eleven **15.** 7 to 10, 7:10, seven to ten **17.** 5 to 9, 5:9, five to nine **19.** $\frac{100}{101}$, 100:101, 100 to 101 **21.** 8:5 **23.** 5:8 **25.** 8:16 **27.** Wednesday **33.** The 24-ounce box is the better deal. **35.** 3 **37.** 1 **39.** $m = \frac{11}{18}$ **41.** $h = \frac{2}{3}$

7-2 Exercises

1.

2	7
4	14
6	21
16	56

3.

96	48
48	24
24	12
12	6

5.

5	10	15	20
8	16	24	32

7.

24	12	6	3
16	8	4	2

9. 35 min

11.

8	15
16	30
24	45
32	60

13.

6	12	18	48	96
7	14	21	56	112

15.

11	22	33	44
25	50	75	100

17.

51	102	153	204
75	150	225	300

19. $\frac{8}{3}$ **21.** 24; 15 **27.** about 70,000,000 **31.** B **33.** 448.5; 447; 452; 94

7-3 Exercises

3. 7 **5.** 35 **9.** 15 **11.** 55 **13.** 2 **15.** 3 **17.** 7 **19.** 3 **21.** $\frac{21}{6}$ **23.** 124 euros, 121 Canadian dollars, 810 renminbi, 448 shekels, and 1,058 Mexican pesos. **27.** C **29.** < **31.** = **33.** 4 to 9, $\frac{4}{9}$ **35.** 6:13, 6 to 13

7-4 Exercises

1. The length of the missing side is 4 cm. m∠G = 37° **3.** The length of the missing side, n, is 3 inches. m∠M = 110° **5.** sides; $\overline{AC}$ and $\overline{XY}$; $\overline{XW}$ and $\overline{AB}$; $\overline{BC}$ and $\overline{WY}$; angles: X and A; W and B; Y and C **9.** m∠H = 80°, m∠J = 80°, m∠Z = 100°; the length of $\overline{WX}$ is 5.5 yd, the length of $\overline{ZY}$ is 5.5 yd, and the length of $\overline{WZ}$ is 4 yd. **11.** No; the corresponding sides are not in proportion. **17.** G **19.** Distributive Property **21.** 5 **23.** 0.7

7-5 Exercises

1. 15 ft **3.** 18 ft **5.** 104 in. **7.** 120 m **11.** 14.2 **13.** 4.9 **15.** $8\frac{1}{4}$ **17.** $8\frac{4}{5}$

7-6 Exercises

1. 300 ft **3.** No **5.** 2.5 inches **7a.** north wall: 2 in.; west wall: 3 in.; south wall: 5 in.; east wall: 4.25 in. **9.** 357 km **17.** 64 in. **19.** 38.4 **21.** 3.87 **23.** $x = 3$ **25.** $k = 42$ **27.** $p = 1$

7-7 Exercises

1.

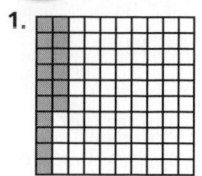

3.

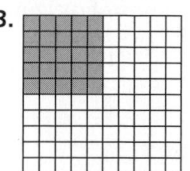

5. $\frac{4}{5}$ **7.** $\frac{23}{25}$ **9.** 0.04 **11.** 0.64

13.

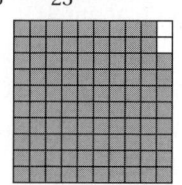

15.

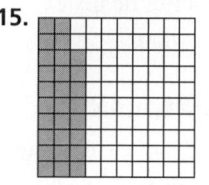

17. $\frac{3}{4}$ **19.** $\frac{18}{25}$ **21.** $\frac{16}{25}$ **23.** $\frac{17}{20}$ **25.** 0.44 **27.** 0.29 **29.** 0.6 **31.** 0.07 **33.** 0.02 **35.** 0.01 **37.** 0.7 **39.** 0.37 **41.** 0.08 **43.** 0.75 **45.** 1 **47.** 0.52 **49.** $\frac{3}{20}$, $\frac{13}{25}$, $\frac{71}{100}$, 1 **51.** 11% = 0.11 **53.** No **59.** H **61.** 17 **63.** 10

7-8 Exercises

1. 39% **3.** 80% **5.** 44% **7.** 70% **9.** 60% **11.** 60% **13.** 34% **15.** 62% **17.** 30% **19.** 45% **21.** 12.5% **23.** 74% **25.** 40% **27.** 4%, $\frac{1}{25}$ **29.** 45%, $\frac{9}{20}$ **31.** 1%, $\frac{1}{100}$ **33.** 60%, $\frac{3}{5}$ **35.** 14%, $\frac{7}{50}$ **37.** 80%, 0.8 **39.** 83.33%, 0.83 **41.** 34%, 0.34 **43.** 4%, 0.04 **45.** 26.67%, 0.27 **47.** < **49.** = **51.** > **53.** < **55.** about 48%; about 52% **57.** 0.098, $\frac{7}{8}$, 90% **59.** 0.21, $\frac{7}{25}$, 38% **61.** 17%, $\frac{5}{9}$, 0.605 **63.** 97% **67.** D **69.** $1\frac{1}{4}$ **71.** $\frac{9}{10}$ **73.** 3 ft **75.** 2.25 ft

7-9 Exercises

1. 44 T-shirts **3.** 6.72 **5.** 0.4

7. 37.8 **9.** 6 dolls **11.** 30 minutes
13. 28.6 **15.** 18.2 **17.** 94.5
19. 2.28 **21.** 5.2 **23.** 12.32
25. 40.56 **27.** 31 **29.** 12
31a. 9 feet **b.** 108 square feet
33. 12 atoms of hydrogen, 6 atoms
of carbon, and 6 atoms of oxygen
39. $57.60 **41.** $\frac{39}{50}$ **43.** $\frac{99}{100}$
45. 87.5%

7-10 Exercises

1. about $7.65 **3.** about $151.20
5. about $18.75 **7.** about $11.10
9. about $55.65 **11.** Yes
13. $339.20 **19.** Music Palace CDs
sell for $11.97. Awesome Sound
CDs sell for $11.69. Awesome
Sound has the better deal. **21.** yes
23. 3 **25.** 13 **27.** 600

Chapter 7 Extension

1. $148.75 **3.** $32 **5.** $250 **7.** 3%
9. $367.20 **11.** $37,500

Chapter 7 Study Guide: Review

1. discount **2.** percent
3. corresponding angles
4. Possible answers: 2:4; 3:6; 6:12
5. 12 oz for $2.64
6. Possible answers:

3	6	9	12
10	20	30	40

7. Possible answers:

5	10	15	20
21	42	63	84

8. Possible answers:

15	30	45	60
7	14	21	28

9. $47.25 **10.** $n = 9$ **11.** $n = 3$
12. $n = 14$ **13.** $n = 2$ **14.** $n =$
11 inches; $m\angle A = 90°$ **15.** 94 ft
16. 43.75 miles **17.** 3 inches
18. $\frac{3}{4}$ **19.** $\frac{3}{50}$ **20.** $\frac{3}{10}$ **21.** 0.08
22. 0.65 **23.** 0.2 **24.** 89.6%
25. 70% **26.** 5.7% **27.** 12%
28. 70% **29.** 25% **30.** 87.5%
31. 80% **32.** 6.25% **33.** 12

34. 5.94 **35.** 117 tickets
36. about $19.20 **37.** about $4.35
38. about $1.08

Chapter 8

8-1 Exercises

3. K **7.** $\overrightarrow{AB}$ **15.** C
21.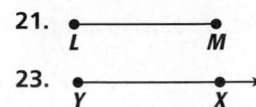
23.

25a. points **b.** line **c.** line
segment **d.** ray **27.** $\overline{XY}$, $\overleftrightarrow{XY}$, $\overrightarrow{XY}$
31. A **33.** $k = 21$ **35.** $k = 100$
37. $3\frac{1}{4}$ **39.** $13\frac{2}{3}$ **41.** $11\frac{4}{7}$

8-2 Exercises

1. 90° **3.** 60°
5.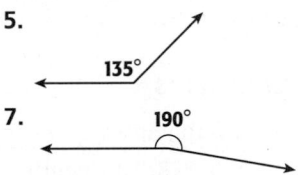

7.

9. acute **11.** $\angle G$ acute;
$\angle H$ obtuse; $\angle J$ right; $\angle K$ obtuse;
$\angle L$ obtuse **13.** 35°
15.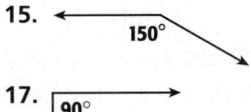

17.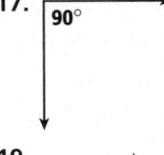

19.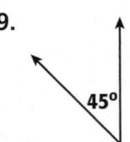

21. acute **23.** $\angle A$ obtuse;
$\angle B$ obtuse; $\angle C$ acute; $\angle D$ obtuse;
$\angle E$ obtuse; $\angle F$ acute
25.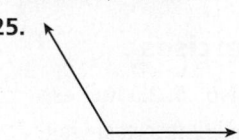

27. straight **29.** acute **35.** G
37. 40%; $\frac{2}{5}$ **39.** 90%; $\frac{9}{10}$ **41.** 3.6
43. 71.5

8-3 Exercises

1. adjacent **3.** $m\angle a = 9°$
5. adjacent **7.** $m\angle c = 78°$
9. angles 1, 5, 6, 7 and 8 **11.** 108°,
108°, 72° **13.** 35° **15.** 75° **17.** 28°
19. 59° **21.** 78° **23.** 99°
25. angles C and D are congruent
angles **29.** D **31.** $n = 2$
33. $p = 0.25$ **35.** straight **37.** acute

8-4 Exercises

1. intersecting **3.** perpendicular
5. skew **7.** skew **9.** parallel
13. $\overrightarrow{BF}$, $\overrightarrow{GH}$, $\overrightarrow{EF}$, $\overrightarrow{CG}$ **15.** $\overrightarrow{AB}$, $\overrightarrow{EF}$,
$\overrightarrow{FG}$, $\overrightarrow{BC}$ **17.** sometimes **19.** never
25. H
27–31.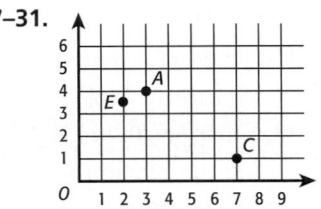

33. 33° **35.** 27°

8-5 Exercises

1. obtuse triangle **3.** 82°
5. isosceles **7.** 60° **9.** scalene
11. yes, right **13.** no **15.** yes,
obtuse **19.** $1\frac{1}{6}$ ft, equilateral
21.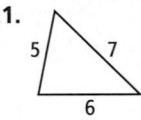

23.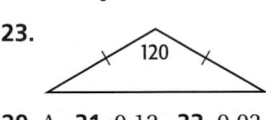

29. A **31.** 0.12 **33.** 0.03 **35.** 0.76
37.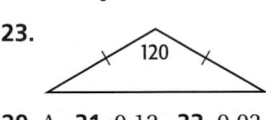

39. •A

8-6 Exercises

1. rectangle **3.** square **5.** squares
7. quadrilateral **9.** parallelogram
11. trapezoid **13.** quadrilateral,
parallelogram, rectangle,
rhombus, square
15. quadrilateral, parallelogram,
rhombus **17.** never **19.** always
21. sometimes **23.** sometimes

25. not possible **27.** not possible
29a. If the frame is 10 in. by 13 in., the total length of the sides is 46 in., not 38 in. **c.** 8 in. by 11 in.
35. Quadrilateral, parallelogram, rhombus; *rhombus* is the most descriptive **37.** 2, 6, 18, 54, 162
39. never

8-7 Exercises

1. polygon, hexagon, regular
3. polygon, triangle, regular
5. not a polygon **7.** not a polygon
9. not formed by line segments
11. not formed by line segments
13. hexagon **15.** 1,440°, 144°
17. never **19.** sometimes **25.** 108
27. $d = 4.04$ **29.** $x = 8.4$

8-8 Exercises

1.

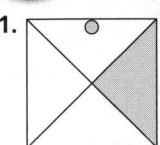

3. Possible answer: purple, purple, red, yellow, green, yellow; red, yellow, green, yellow, purple

5.

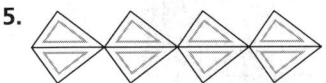

7.

9.

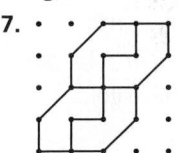

The lines should be green.

13. C **15.** 81 **17.** 27 **19.** 1,024
21. $2 \cdot 5^2$ **23.** $2 \cdot 107$

8-9 Exercises

1. not congruent; different sizes
3. Figure A **5.** The figures are irregular hexagons that are not congruent.

7.

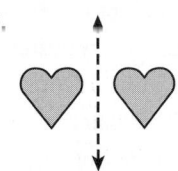

11. A **13.** $y = 9$ **15.** $n = 8$ **17.** $\frac{8}{21}$
19. $\frac{3}{8}$

8-10 Exercises

1. reflection **3.** translation

5.

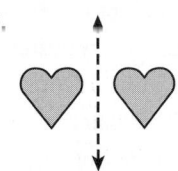

7. translation

9.

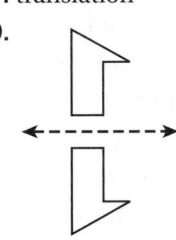

13.

15. A **17.**

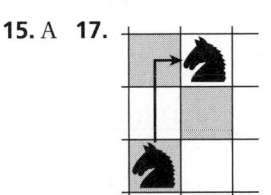

21. D **23.** 19 × 3 **25.** 5 + 9
27. $6\frac{71}{100}$ **29.** $2\frac{22}{55}$

8-11 Exercises

1. The line is a line of symmetry.
3. The line is a line of symmetry.
5. 3 lines of symmetry **7.** 4 lines of symmetry **9.** The line is not a line of symmetry. **11.** The line is not a line of symmetry. **13.** 8 lines of symmetry **15.** 1 line of symmetry **17.** 3; 1; none **21.** B
23. > **25.** 24.68 **27.** 74.35

Chapter 8 Study Guide: Review

1. trapezoid **2.** polygon
3. Possible answer: $\overleftrightarrow{ED}$, $\overrightarrow{AD}$
4. acute **5.** obtuse **6.** acute
7. straight **8.** $b = 27°$ **9.** $d = 98°$

10. perpendicular **11.** skew
12. obtuse scalene
13. parallelogram **14.** triangle; not regular **15.** rectangle; not regular **16.** Add 1 shaded and 1 white triangle each time. **17.** not congruent; different sizes
18. congruent **19.** translation
20.

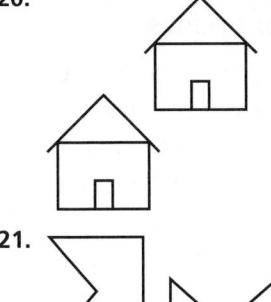

21.

22. The line is a line of symmetry.

Chapter 9

9-1 Exercises

1. in. **3.** gal **5.** mi **7.** qt **9.** ft
11. gal **13.** oz **17.** about 1 qt
21. $8\frac{1}{4}$ lb **27.** Possible answers: *rod*: a unit of length equal to $5\frac{1}{2}$ yards; *peck*: a dry measure of capacity equal to 8 quarts; *dram*: a very small unit of weight equal to 0.0625 ounce **29.** F **31.** 1, 3, 5, 9, 15, 45 **33.** 1, 2, 4, 5, 8, 10, 16, 20, 40, 80 **35.** acute

9-2 Exercises

1. m **3.** L **5.** about 7 cm **7.** g
9. L **11.** the width of his fist
13. km **15.** g **17.** mL **19.** Yes; possible answer: The balloon weighs 0.8 g more with the air.
23. C **25.** 8 **27.** 16 **29.** 36 **31.** 60

9-3 Exercises

1. 108 **3.** 7 **5.** 3 **7.** 8 **9.** 3 **11.** 22
13. about 24 cups **15.** 48 **17.** 2
19. 2 **21.** 6,000 **23.** 3 **25.** 20
27. < **29.** = **31.** < **33.** = **35.** >

37. about 434 yards **39a.** 9 yd
b. 324 in. **41.** 3,520; 2 **43.** 8; 16
47. 4 pints **49.** Possible answer:
First, convert either the inches to
feet or the feet to inches so that
both lengths have the same unit.
Then compare. **51.** A **53.** $x = 9$
55. $d = 17$

9-4 Exercises

1. 0.115 km **3.** 0.852 **5.** 3,500
7. 4,400 **9.** 0.05 **11.** 0.006
13. 0.110 **15.** 22,500 **17.** 2.460
19. 9.68 **21.** 0.782 **23.** 21.6 L;
21,600 mL **25.** $x = 0.23850$
27. 7,000 **29.** = **31.** < **33.** =
35. St. Louis Gateway Arch; 18 m
39. 55 cups; 125 mL **41.** 0.452 kg;
452,000 mg; 0.136 kg **43.** obtuse
45. sometimes **47.** never

9-5 Exercises

1. 1,200 **3.** $2\frac{1}{2}$ **5.** 480 **7.** 2:15 P.M.
9. 54 **11.** 60 **13.** 4 **15.** 2 **17.** 26
19. 12:10 P.M. **21.** 198
23. > **25.** < **27.** 480; 470
29. about 28°C **35.** C **37.** >
39. < **41.** 5.55 **43.** 9.447

9-6 Exercises

1. 52°; acute **3.** 90°; right **5.** 45°
7. $\angle A = 150°$; $\angle B = 90°$ **9.** 180°;
straight **11.** 35° **13.** 108° **17.** 5.5°
23. 65°; acute; 65 < 90 **25.** 2
27. 8

9-7 Exercises

1. 2 in. **3.** 40 m **5.** 7 yd **7.** 96 in.
9. 7 cm **11.** 42 m **13.** 6 in.
15. 42 in. **17.** 2 km **19a.** 44 ft ×
20 ft **b.** 128 ft **25.** 24.68
27. 74.35 **29.** $x = 3$ **31.** $k = 42$

9-8 Exercises

1. circle G, diameter $\overline{EF}$, and radii
$\overline{GF}$, $\overline{GE}$, and $\overline{GD}$ **3.** 12 ft
5. 12.56 in. **7.** 15 yd **9.** 4.71 m
11. 0.5 in. **13.** 5.75 ft, 36.11 ft
15. 5 **17.** 9.42 ft **21.** 48.8 cm

23. 880 revolutions **25.** $\frac{10}{12}, \frac{3}{4}, \frac{1}{12}$
27. $\frac{3}{4}, \frac{5}{8}, \frac{7}{16}$ **29.** 0.05 **31.** 1

Chapter 9 Study Guide: Review

1. perimeter; circumference
2. diameter **3.** customary system
4. in.; about five widths of your
thumbs **5.** mi; about 800 times 18
football fields **6.** lb; about 2
loaves of bread **7.** fl oz; about a
spoonful **8.** $\frac{1}{8}$ in. **9.** mm; about
32 times the thickness of a dime
10. mg; about 5 times the mass of
a very small insect **11.** kg; about
two textbooks **12.** L; about two
blender containers **13.** 2 cm
14. 15, 840 ft **15.** 6 yd **16.** 12 c
17. 3 gal **18.** 8 lb **19.** 4 T **20.** 4 lb
21. 144 in. **22.** 4 qt **23.** 99 ft
24. 250 yd **25.** 3,200 mL
26. 0.007 L **27.** 0.342 km
28. 0.042 kg **29.** 0.051 m
30. 71,000 m **31.** 1 hr **32.** 59,400 s
33. 105 days **34.** 105° **35.** 33.9 in.
36. 6 ft **37.** 31.4 ft **38.** 9 m
39. 50.24 cm **40.** 11 ft

Chapter 10

10-1 Exercises

1. about 8.5 square units **3.** about
6 square units **5.** 100.1 in^2
7. 48 ft^2 **9.** 10 in^2 **11.** about
6 square units **13.** about 4 square
units **15.** 12.75 m^2 **17.** 260 ft^2
19. 0.75 cm^2 **25.** B **27.** 1, 2, 4, 5,
10, 20 **29.** 1, 59 **31.** 7 ft

10-2 Exercises

1. 3 yd^2 **3.** 27 m^2 **5.** 26 ft^2
7. 88 cm^2 **9.** 3 ft^2 **11.** 72 in^2
13. 16 yd^2 **15.** 96 m^2 **17.** 5
square units **19.** 15 square units
21. 346.5 m^2 **23.** 12 ft^2
29. 175 cm^2 **31.** $\frac{12}{5}$ **33.** $\frac{15}{2}$

10-3 Exercises

1. 2,800 m^2 **3.** 57 square units
5. 640 yd^2 **11.** 40 square units
13. $5\frac{1}{6}$ **15.** $6\frac{3}{10}$ **17.** 144 cm^2

10-4 Exercises

1. When the dimensions of the
square are divided by 3, the
perimeter is divided by 3, and the
area is divided by 9 or 3^2.
3. When the dimensions of the
triangle are multiplied by 4, the
perimeter is multiplied by 4, and
the area is multiplied by 16 or 4^2.
5a. 4,800 ft **5b.** 280 ft, 320 ft **9.** D
11. $\frac{3}{4}$ **13.** $\frac{1}{2}$ **15.** $\frac{13}{20}$ **17.** 56 cm

10-5 Exercises

1. 48 ft^2 **3.** 243 in^2 **5.** 616 cm^2
7. 12.56 ft^2 **9.** 768 in^2 **11.** 38.5 yd^2
13. 2,464 ft^2 **15.** A = 102.02 cm^2,
C = 35.8 cm **17.** A = 174.28 in^2,
C = 46.79 in. **19.** 1.13 km^2 **25.** C
27. $\frac{1}{6}$ **29.** $\frac{5}{18}$ **31.** $\frac{3}{25}$ **33.** $1\frac{1}{4}$

10-6 Exercises

1. 5 faces, 8 edges, 5 vertices
3. 5 faces, 8 edges, 5 vertices
5. square pyramid **7.** 5 faces,
9 edges, 6 vertices **9.** 6 faces,
12 edges, 8 vertices
11. rectangular prism **13.** square
pyramid, yes **15.** cone, no
17. B, C and D **19.** B **21.** true
23. true **25.** 8; octagonal pyramid
29. C **31.** < **33.** > **35.** parallel
37. intersecting

10-7 Exercises

1. 162 cm^3 **3.** 10 ft^3 **5.** 320 ft^3
7. 1 × 1 × 10 and 2 × 5 × 1
9. 79.36 in^3 **11.** 54 m^3 **13.** 71.72 ft^3
15. 480 in^3 **17.** 474.375 km^3
19. 20 ft **21.** 10 cm^3, 1 cm^3,
3.5 cm^3, 300 cm^3, 20 cm^3 **23.** pine
25. Alicia does not have gold.
29. 77.4 **31.** 3 **33.** 9

10-8 Exercises

1. 754 m³ **3.** 3,140 in³
5. Cylinder B **7.** 314 ft³ **9.** 31 cm³
and 283 cm³ **11.** 138 in³ **13.** 4 m³
15. 100.48 in³ **17.** 1,987.03 ft³
19. 12,560 mm³ **21.** 923 ft³
23. It cannot hold 200 cm³ of juice
because it only has a volume of
196.25 cm³. **29.** the tomato soup
can holds more soup **31.** 9, 12
33. 115°

10-9 Exercises

1. 94 in² **3.** 56 cm² **5.** 2,640 cm²
7. 326.56 ft² **9.** 376.8 m²
11. $16\frac{1}{2}$ m² **13.** 133 cm²
15. 11 km² **17.** 712.72 m²
21. about 96 ft² **23.** about 190 cm²
27a. 54 in² **b.** 54 in²
29. 571.48 **31.** $y = 42$ **33.** $4\frac{5}{9}$
35. $\frac{1}{12}$

Chapter 10 Study Guide: Review

1. polyhedron **2.** volume
3. vertex **4.** 18 ft² **5.** 7 m²
6. 12 in² **7.** 12 in² **8.** 154 in²
9. 30 cm² **10.** 135 cm²
11. 175.5 ft² **12.** The perimeter is
multiplied by 2, and the area is
multiplied by 4 or 2². **13.** $78\frac{4}{7}$ ft²
14. $200\frac{1}{7}$ cm² **15.** $12\frac{4}{7}$ m²
16. 153.86 ft² **17.** 5 faces,
8 edges, 5 vertices; rectangular
pyramid **18.** 6 faces, 12 edges,
8 vertices; rectangular prism
19. 384 cm³ **20.** 6,300 in³
21. 353 m³ **22.** 2,308 ft³
23. 125 m² **24.** 102 cm²

Chapter 11

11-1 Exercises

1. +5
3.

```
 ‹─┼─┼─●─┼─┼─┼─●─┼─┼─›
  −4  −2   0   2   4
```

5.

```
 ‹─┼─●─┼─┼─┼─┼─┼─┼─┼─┼─●─┼─›
 −7 −5 −3 −1   1   3   5   7
```

9. −20 **11.** −39
13.

```
 ‹─●─┼─┼─┼─┼─┼─┼─┼─●─┼─›
 −6 −4 −2  0   2   4   6
```

15.

```
 ‹─┼─●─┼─┼─┼─┼─┼─●─┼─›
  −4   −2   0   2   4
```

19. spending $83 **21.** earning $15
23. +92 **25.** +25 **27.** 0 **29.** −3;
+5 **31.** +2.7 **33.** −6.2 **35.** +45
37. +2; −2 **39.** C **43.** D **45.** 1.7
47. 6.215

11-2 Exercises

1. > **3.** < **5.** −5, −4, 3, 7
7a. 3:30 A.M. **b.** 1°F **9.** > **11.** <
13. −8, 7, 15 **15.** −16, −9, −1, 13
17. −19, −3, 0, 8, 22 **19.** < **21.** >
23. < **25.** < **27.** −39, 14, 21
29. −26, −12, 0, 43
31. −73, −67, −10, 20, 82 **33.** C
35. San Augustin Cave, Dead Sea,
Mr. Rainier, Kilimanjaro, Mt.
Everest **39.** C **41.** acute
43. cannot form a triangle
45.

```
 ‹─●─┼─┼─┼─┼─┼─┼─┼─┼─┼─┼─┼─┼─●─┼─›
 −10 −8 −6 −4 −2  0   2   4   6   8  10
```

47.

```
 ‹─┼─┼─┼─┼─┼─┼─┼─●─┼─┼─●─┼─┼─┼─┼─›
 −10 −8 −6 −4 −2  0   2   4   6   8  10
```

49.

```
 ‹─┼─┼─┼─●─┼─┼─┼─┼─┼─┼─●─┼─┼─┼─›
 −10 −8 −6 −4 −2  0   2   4   6   8  10
```

11-3 Exercises

1. III **3.** I **5.** (1, 2)
7–9.

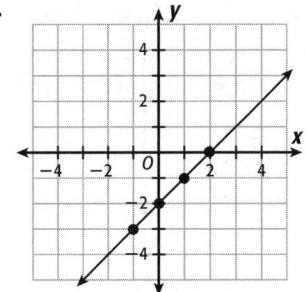

11. II **13.** I **15.** IV **17.** (−2, 4)
19. (4, 4) **21.** (−3, 0)

23.

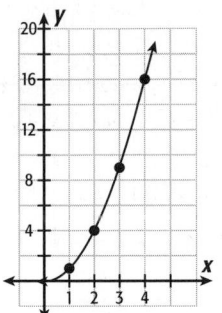

25.

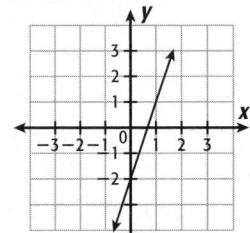

27.

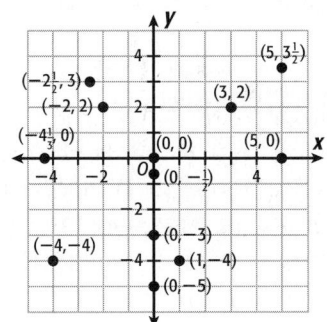

29. I **31.** III **33.** IV **35.** III
37–47.

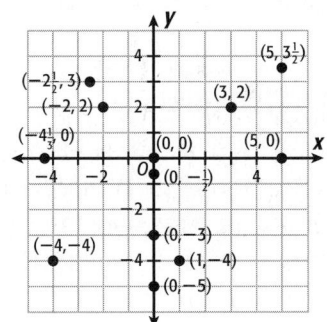

49. Gabon **55.** B **57.** 4.4 **59.** 5.75
61. 0.2 **63.** < **65.** <

11-4 Exercises

1. $3 + 2 = 5$ **3.** −5 **5.** 7 **7.** 4 **9.** 0
11. −17 **13.** −22 **15.** $6 + (−2) = 4$
17. 11 **19.** 0 **21.** −6 **23.** −7
25. −16 **27.** −8 **29.** −2 **31.** 2
33. 29 feet

35.

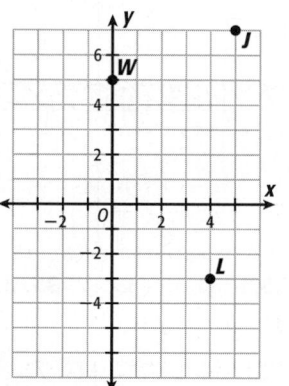

37.

39.

41.

43. 7 **45.** −11 **47.** −9 **49.** 17
51. 4 **53.** −1 **55.** −17 **57.** −6°F
63. B **65.** 5, 3, −1 **67.** 4 **69.** 1,728
71–75.

11-5 Exercises

1. $6 − 5 = 1$ **3.** −3 **5.** −8 **7.** 8
9. 13 **11.** −4 **13.** 11 **15.** 2
17. −5 **19.** 7 **21.** −12 **23.** −6
25. −1 **27.** 21 **29.** 30 **31.** 12
33. 4 **35.** −38 **37.** −19 m
39. 9°F **43.** D **45.** 2% **47.** 26%
49. 310% **51.** II **53.** III

11-6 Exercises

1. 24 **3.** −21 **5.** 9 **7.** 16 **9.** 9
11. 33 **13.** −24 **15.** 18 **17.** 45
19. −32 **21.** 39 **23.** −72 **25.** −24
27. −12 **29.** 40 **31.** 60 **33.** 14
35. 54 **37.** −90 **39.** 4 ft to −4 ft
45. positive; negative **47.** 9
49. −13 **51.** −3

11-7 Exercises

1. 8 **3.** 3 **5.** −2 **7.** −15 **9.** 5
11. −8 **13.** 6 **15.** 2 **17.** 1 **19.** 3
21. 16 **23.** 14 **25.** −6 **27.** 1
29. 10 **31.** −7 **33.** 3 **35.** 8
37. −3 **39.** 6 **41.** −11 **43a.** −300
43b. a decrease of 300 seals from
1976 to 1980 **45.** −20 **47.** 500
48. A **49.** G **50.** 6 cm **51.** 7 m
52. −1 **53.** 11 **54.** −9 **55.** 0
56. 20

11-8 Exercises

1. $m = 12$ **3.** $z = 9$ **5.** $p = −9$
7. $g = 8$ **9.** $b = −8$ **11.** $c = −7$
13. $f = −6$ **15.** $r = −900$
17. $g = 4$ **19.** $t = −14$
21. $x = −14$ **23.** $w = −10$
25. $j = 8$ **27.** $a = −52$
29. $m = −48$ **31.** $u = −60$
33. $x = 17$ **35.** $k = −4$
37. $m = −15$ **39.** $n = −3$
41. $g = −3$ **43.** $f = −8$ **45.** $d = 33$
47. $h = −84$ **49.** $b = 32$ **51.** $a = 8$
53. $t = −55$ **55.** $c = −13$
57. $n = −4$ **59.** $j = −3$
61. 70 dives **63.** −4
65. $x = −18,500$; sponge
67. −24 ft **71.** A **73.** always
75. −35 **77.** 12 **79.** 32

11-9 Exercises

1. 15 **3.** $j = b − 6$ **7.** $c = 12s − 2$
9. $p = 150m$ **11.** −54 **13.** −3; 1
15. Let c be the total cost and h be
the number of hours. $c = \$125 +$
$\$55h$ **17.** 9 hours **23.** G
25. $x = 3.9$ **27.** $p = 5.2$
29. 706.5 ft^3

11-10 Exercises

1. (1, 8); (2, 14); (3, 20); (4, 26)
3. no **5.** 2 **7.** 0

9.

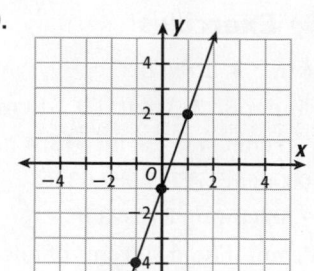

11. (1, −3); (2, −7); (3, −11);
(4, −15) **13.** yes **15.** 1 **17.** 0
19. 2

21.

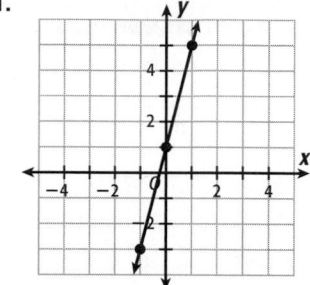

23.

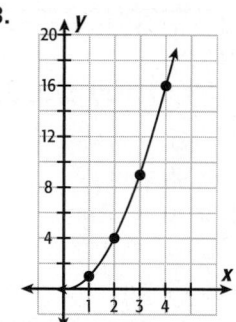

25.

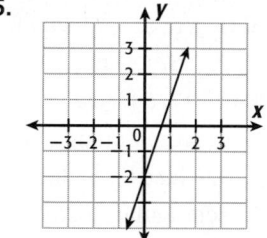

27. −3; −2; −1; 0 **29.** (1, 14)
31.

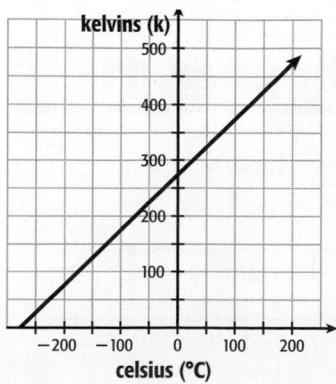

33. 219 kelvins **39.** H **41.** 6
43. $y = -120$ **45.** $j = -12$

Chapter 11 Extension

1. $1, \frac{1}{3}, \frac{1}{9}$ **3.** $1, \frac{1}{6}, \frac{1}{36}$ **5.** 7^{-1} **7.** 8^{-2}
9. 3^{-1} **11.** 7^{-2} **13.** 4^{-2} **15.** 3^{-4}
17. $\frac{1}{27}$ **19.** $\frac{1}{729}$ **21.** 256 **23.** $\frac{1}{64}$
25. $\frac{1}{125}$ **27.** 1 **29.** Any number
raised to the zero power is 1.

Chapter 11 Study Guide: Review

1. output, input **2.** coordinate
plane, quadrants **3.** $+10$ **4.** -50

5.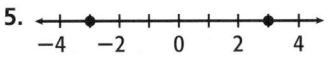

6.

7.

8.

9. $<$ **10.** $<$ **11.** $<$ **12.** $-1, 2, 4$
13. $-3, 0, 4$ **14.** $-8, -6, 0$
15. $(-2, -3)$ **16.** $(1, 0)$ **17.** III
18. II **19.** -2 **20.** 0 **21.** 1 **22.** -5
23. -17 **24.** 8 **25.** -8 **26.** 9
27. 13 **28.** -6 **29.** -10 **30.** 6
31. 6 **32.** -8 **33.** -18 **34.** 45
35. -3 **36.** 3 **37.** 2 **38.** -2
39. $w = 4$ **40.** $a = -12$ **41.** $q = -7$
42. $x = -5$ **43.** $y = 2x + 2; y = 18$

44. $\ell = 4w, \ell = $ length, $w = $ width
45. $(1, -3), (2, -1), (3, 1), (4, 3)$
46. $(1, 8), (2, 9), (3, 10), (4, 11)$
47. yes **48.** no

Chapter 12

12-1 Exercises

1. certain **3.** $0.4, \frac{2}{5}$ **5.** likely
7. unlikely **9.** $0.3, 30\%$
11. cashew **13.** unlikely
15. unlikely **17.** unlikely **19.** AB
negative **23.** C **25.** $2^2 \cdot 19$
27. 2^4 **29.** 2^7 **31.** 31.4 cm

12-2 Exercises

1. 6 **3.** no hits; 1 hit **5.** HTH
7. $\frac{13}{25}$ **9.** yellow **11.** $\frac{1}{31}$; unlikely
15. D **17.** 12 **19.** 21 **21.** 3

12-3 Exercises

1. turkey and fruit; turkey and
salad; tacos and fruit; tacos and
salad; pasta and fruit; pasta and
salad **3.** 9 **5.** 123, 132, 213, 231,
312, 321 **7a.** 18 **b.** 56 **9.** 9
13. C **15.** $1\frac{1}{12}$ **17.** $\frac{5}{8}$

12-4 Exercises

1. $\frac{1}{2}$ **3.** 74% **5.** $\frac{1}{6}$ **7.** $\frac{4}{9}$ **9.** 0.96
11. $\frac{5}{6}$ **13.** 1 **15.** $\frac{1}{6}$ **17.** 0 **19.** 50%

21. 53% **23.** $\frac{5}{12}$ **25.** 0.77 **26.** 0%
27. $\frac{1}{9}$ **29.** $<$ **31.** $<$ **33.** $>$ **37.** C
39. 21 **41.** 3 **43.** 12

12-5 Exercises

1. $\frac{1}{4}$ **3.** $\frac{1}{9}$ **5.** $\frac{1}{3}$ **7.** $\frac{1}{2}$ **9.** $\frac{1}{3}$ **11.** 0
13. 1 **15.** $=$ **17.** $<$ **19.** $\frac{1}{32}; \frac{1}{32}$
25. J **27.** 2.007, 2.02, 2.45, 2.678
29. 85%

12-6 Exercises

1. 600 **3.** 200 tickets **5.** 32 **7.** 129
donors **11.** about 90 **15.** B
17. $x = -12$ **19.** $x = -5$ **21.** $\frac{1}{6}$
23. $\frac{1}{3}$

Chapter 12 Extension

1. dependent **3.** $\frac{1}{24}$ **5.** $\frac{1}{3}$ **7.** $\frac{2}{15}$
9. $\frac{1}{45}$

Chapter 12 Study Guide: Review

1. equally likely **2.** experiment;
outcome **3.** probability
4. theoretical probability
5. sample space **6.** certain
7. $0.75, \frac{3}{4}$ **8.** white **9.** $\frac{20}{75} = \frac{4}{15}$
10. 18 combinations **11.** $\frac{1}{4}$ **12.** $\frac{1}{2}$
13. 75% **14.** $\frac{1}{6}$ **15.** $\frac{1}{8}$ **16.** 100
items **17.** 25 times **18.** 1,575
teenagers **19.** 100 students

Glossary/Glosario

A

ENGLISH	SPANISH	EXAMPLES
absolute value The distance of a number from zero on a number line; shown by │ │. (p. 762)	**valor absoluto** Distancia a la que está un número de 0 en una recta numérica. El símbolo del valor absoluto es │ │.	$\lvert -5 \rvert = 5$
acute angle An angle that measures less than 90°. (p. 421)	**ángulo agudo** Ángulo que mide menos de 90°.	
acute triangle A triangle with all angles measuring less than 90°. (p. 437)	**triángulo acutángulo** Triángulo en el que todos los ángulos miden menos de 90°.	
addend A number added to one or more other numbers to form a sum.	**sumando** Número que se suma a uno o más números para formar una suma.	In the expression 4 + 6 + 7, the numbers 4, 6, and 7 are addends.
Addition Property of Opposites The property that states that the sum of a number and its opposite equals zero.	**Propiedad de la suma de los opuestos** Propiedad que establece que la suma de un número y su opuesto es cero.	$12 + (-12) = 0$
adjacent angles Angles in the same plane that have a common vertex and a common side. (p. 424)	**ángulos adyacentes** Ángulos en el mismo plano que comparten un vértice y un lado.	∠1 and ∠2 are adjacent angles.
algebraic expression An expression that contains at least one variable. (p. 54)	**expresión algebraica** Expresión que contiene al menos una variable.	$x + 8$ $4(m - b)$
algebraic inequality An inequality that contains at least one variable.	**desigualdad algebraica** Desigualdad que contiene al menos una variable.	$x + 3 > 10$ $5a > b + 3$
alternate exterior angles A pair of angles formed by two lines intersected by a third line. (p. 433)	**ángulos alternos externos** Par de ángulos formados por dos líneas intersecadas por una tercera.	∠4 and ∠5 are alternate exterior angles.

ENGLISH	SPANISH	EXAMPLES
alternate interior angles A pair of angles formed by two lines intersected by a third line. (p. 433)	**ángulos alternos internos** Par de ángulos formados por dos líneas intersecadas por una tercera.	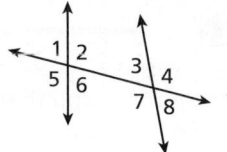 ∠3 and ∠6 are alternate interior angles.
angle A figure formed by two rays with a common endpoint called the vertex. (p. 420)	**ángulo** Figura formada por dos rayos con un extremo común llamado vértice.	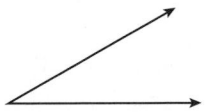
area The number of square units needed to cover a given surface. (p. 542)	**área** El número de unidades cuadradas que se necesitan para cubrir una superficie dada.	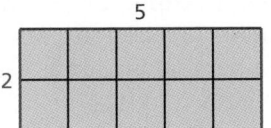 The area is 10 square units.
arithmetic sequence A sequence in which the terms change by the same amount each time. (p. 33)	**sucesión aritmética** Una sucesión en la que los términos cambian la misma cantidad cada vez.	The sequence 2, 5, 8, 11, 14. . . is an arthmetic sequence.
Associative Property of Addition The property that states that for three or more numbers, their sum is always the same, regardless of their grouping. (p. 26)	**Propiedad asociativa de la suma** Propiedad que establece que agrupar tres o más números en cualquier orden siempre da como resultado la misma suma.	$2 + 3 + 8 = (2 + 3) + 8 = 2 + (3 + 8)$
Associative Property of Multiplication The property that states that for three or more numbers, their product is always the same, regardless of their grouping. (p. 26)	**Propiedad asociativa de la multiplicación** Propiedad que establece que agrupar tres o más números en cualquier orden siempre da como resultado el mismo producto.	$2 \cdot 3 \cdot 8 = (2 \cdot 3) \cdot 8 = 2 \cdot (3 \cdot 8)$
asymmetrical Not identical on either side of a central line; not symmetrical.	**asimétrico** Que no es idéntico a ambos lados de una línea central; no simétrico.	
average The sum of the items in a set of data divided by the number of items in the set; also called *mean*.	**promedio** La suma de los elementos de un conjunto de datos dividida entre el número de elementos del conjunto. También se le llama *media*.	Data set: 4, 6, 7, 8, 10 Average: $\frac{4 + 6 + 7 + 8 + 10}{5} = \frac{35}{5} = 7$
axes The two perpendicular lines of a coordinate plane that intersect at the origin. (p. 610)	**ejes** Las dos rectas numéricas perpendiculares del plano cartesiano que se intersecan en el origen.	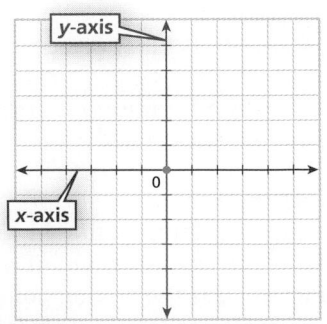

B

bar graph A graph that uses vertical or horizontal bars to display data. (p. 308)

gráfica de barras Gráfica en la que se usan barras verticales u horizontales para presentar datos.

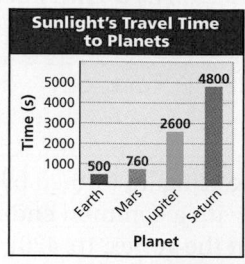

base (in numeration) When a number is raised to a power, the number that is used as a factor is the base. (p. 14)

base (en numeración) Cuando un número es elevado a una potencia, el número que se usa como factor es la base.

$3^5 = 3 \cdot 3 \cdot 3 \cdot 3 \cdot 3$; 3 is the base.

base (of a polygon or three-dimensional figure) A side of a polygon; a face of a three-dimensional figure by which the figure is measured or classified. (p. 566)

base (de un polígono o figura tridimensional) Lado de un polígono; la cara de una figura tridimensional, a partir de la cual se mide o se clasifica la figura.

 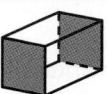

Bases of a cylinder   Bases of a prism

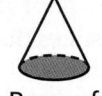 

Base of a cone   Base of a pyramid

bisect To divide into two congruent parts.

trazar una bisectriz Dividir en dos partes congruentes.

box-and-whisker plot A graph that displays the highest and lowest quarters of data as whiskers, the middle two quarters of the data as a box, and the median.

gráfica de mediana y rango Gráfica que muestra los valores máximo y mínimo, los cuartiles superior e inferior, así como la mediana de los datos.

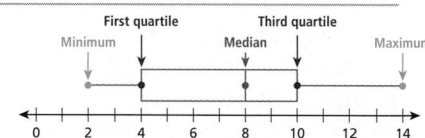

break (graph) A zigzag on a horizontal or vertical scale of a graph that indicates that some of the numbers on the scale have been omitted. (p. 309)

discontinuidad (gráfica) Zig-zag en la escala horizontal o vertical de una gráfica que indica la omisión de algunos de los números de la escala.

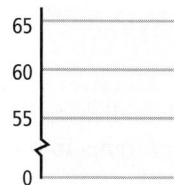

C

capacity The amount a container can hold when filled.

capacidad Cantidad que cabe en un recipiente cuando se llena.

Celsius A metric scale for measuring temperature in which 0°C is the freezing point of water and 100°C is the boiling point of water; also called *centigrade*.

Celsius Escala métrica para medir la temperatura, en la que 0° C es el punto de congelación del agua y 100° C es el punto de ebullición. También se llama *centígrado*.

ENGLISH	SPANISH	EXAMPLES
center (of a circle) The point inside a circle that is the same distance from all the points on the circle. (p. 520)	**centro (de un círculo)** Punto interior de un círculo que se encuentra a la misma distancia de todos los puntos de la circunferencia.	
center (of rotation) The point about which a figure is rotated.	**centro (de una rotación)** Punto alrededor del cual se hace girar una figura.	
certain (probability) Sure to happen; having a probability of 1. (p. 668)	**seguro (probabilidad)** Que con seguridad sucederá. Representa una probabilidad de 1.	
circle The set of all points in a plane that are the same distance from a given point called the center. (p. 520)	**círculo** Conjunto de todos los puntos en un plano que se encuentran a la misma distancia de un punto dado llamado centro.	
circle graph A graph that uses sections of a circle to compare parts to the whole and parts to other parts. (p. 524)	**gráfica circular** Gráfica que usa secciones de un círculo para comparar partes con el todo y con otras partes.	
circumference The distance around a circle. (p. 520)	**circunferencia** Distancia alrededor de un círculo.	
clockwise A circular movement in the direction shown.	**en el sentido de las manecillas del reloj** Movimiento circular en la dirección que se indica.	
clustering A method used to estimate a sum when all addends are close to the same value. (p. 112)	**aproximación** Método que se usa para estimar una suma cuando todos los sumandos se aproximan al mismo valor.	27, 29, 24, and 23 all cluster around 25.
combination An arrangement of items or events in which order does not matter.	**combinación** Agrupación de objetos o sucesos en la cual el orden no es importante.	For objects *A*, *B*, *C*, and *D*, there are 6 different combinations of 2 objects: *AB, AC, AD, BC, BD, CD.*
common denominator A denominator that is the same in two or more fractions. (p. 199)	**común denominador** Denominador que es común a dos o más fracciones.	The common denominator of $\frac{5}{8}$ and $\frac{2}{8}$ is 8.
common factor A number that is a factor of two or more numbers.	**factor común** Número que es factor de dos o más números.	8 is a common factor of 16 and 40.

ENGLISH	SPANISH	EXAMPLES
common multiple A number that is a multiple of each of two or more numbers.	**común múltiplo** Un número que es múltiplo de dos o más números.	15 is a common multiple of 3 and 5.
Commutative Property of Addition The property that states that two or more numbers can be added in any order without changing the sum. (p. 26)	**Propiedad conmutativa de la suma** Propiedad que establece que sumar dos o más números en cualquier orden no altera la suma.	8 + 20 = 20 + 8
Commutative Property of Multiplication The property that states that two or more numbers can be multiplied in any order without changing the product. (p. 26)	**Propiedad conmutativa de la multiplicación** Propiedad que establece que multiplicar dos o más números en cualquier orden no altera el producto.	6 · 12 = 12 · 6
compatible numbers Numbers that are close to the given numbers that make estimation or mental calculation easier. (p. 10)	**números compatibles** Números que están cerca de los números dados y hacen más fácil la estimación o el cálculo mental.	To estimate 7,957 + 5,009, use the compatible numbers 8,000 and 5,000: 8,000 + 5,000 = 13,000
compensation When a number in a problem is close to another number that is easier to calculate with, the easier number is used to find the answer. Then the answer is adjusted by adding to it or subtracting from it. (p. 30)	**compensación** Cuando un número de un problema está cerca de otro con el que es más fácil hacer cálculos, se usa el número más fácil para hallar la respuesta. Luego, se ajusta la respuesta sumando o restando.	
complement All the ways that an event can not happen. (p. 683)	**complemento** Todas las maneras en que no puede ocurrir un suceso.	When rolling a number cube, the complement of rolling a 3 is rolling a 1, 2, 4, 5, or 6.
complementary angles Two angles whose measures add to 90°. (p. 425)	**ángulos complementarios** Dos ángulos cuyas medidas suman 90°.	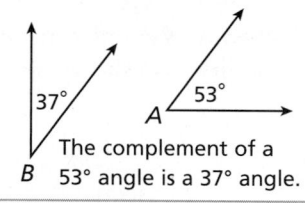 The complement of a 53° angle is a 37° angle.
composite number A number greater than 1 that has more than two whole-number factors. (p. 165)	**número compuesto** Número mayor que 1 que tiene más de dos factores que son números cabales.	4, 6, 8, and 9 are composite numbers.
compound event An event made up of two or more simple events. (p. 688)	**suceso compuesto** Suceso que consta de dos o más sucesos simples.	When tossing a coin and rolling a number cube, the event of the coin landing heads up and the number cube landing on 3 is a compound event.
cone A three-dimensional figure with one vertex and one circular base. (p. 567)	**cono** Figura tridimensional con un vértice y una base circular.	

ENGLISH	SPANISH	EXAMPLES
congruent Having the same size and shape. (p. 424)	**congruentes** Que tienen la misma forma y el mismo tamaño.	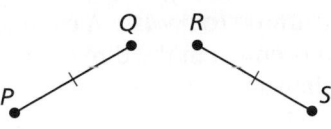
congruent angles Angles that have the same measure. (p. 424)	**ángulos congruentes** Ángulos que tienen la misma medida.	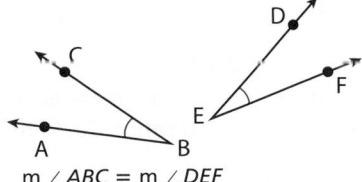 m ∠ABC = m ∠DEF
constant A value that does not change. (p. 54)	**constante** Valor que no cambia.	3, 0, π
coordinates The numbers of an ordered pair that locate a point on a coordinate graph. (p. 610)	**coordenadas** Los números de un par ordenado que ubican un punto en una gráfica de coordenadas.	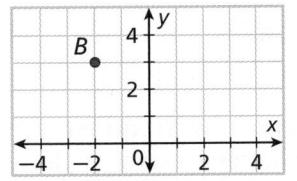 The coordinates of B are (−2, 3).
coordinate grid See *coordinate plane.*	**cuadrícula de coordenadas** Ver *plano cartesiano.*	
coordinate plane A plane formed by the intersection of a horizontal number line called the *x*-axis and a vertical number line called the *y*-axis. (p. 610)	**plano cartesiano** Plano formado por la intersección de una recta numérica horizontal llamada eje *x* y otra vertical llamada eje *y*.	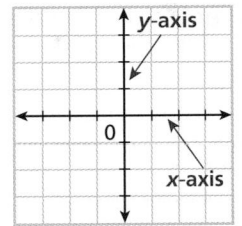
correspondence The relationship between two or more objects that are matched.	**correspondencia** La relación entre dos o más objetos que coinciden.	
corresponding angles (for lines) A pair of angles formed by two lines intersected by a third line.	**ángulos correspondientes (en líneas)** Par de ángulos formados por dos líneas intersecadas por una tercera.	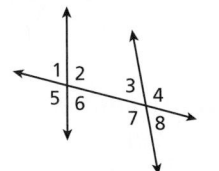 ∠1 and ∠3 are corresponding angles.
corresponding angles (in polygons) Matching angles of two or more polygons. (p. 366)	**ángulos correspondientes (en polígonos)** Ángulos que se ubican en la misma posición relativa en dos o más polígonos.	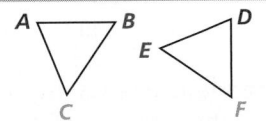 ∠A and ∠D are corresponding angles.
corresponding sides Matching sides of two or more polygons. (p. 366)	**lados correspondientes** Lados que se ubican en la misma posición relativa en dos o más polígonos.	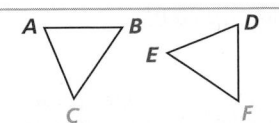 $\overline{AB}$ and $\overline{DE}$ are corresponding sides.

ENGLISH	SPANISH	EXAMPLES
counterclockwise A circular movement in the direction shown.	**en sentido contrario a las manecillas del reloj** Movimiento circular en la dirección que se indica.	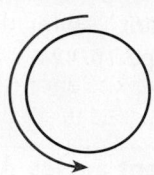
cross product The product of numbers on the diagonal when comparing two ratios. (p. 363)	**producto cruzado** El producto de los números multiplicados en diagonal cuando se comparan dos razones.	For the proportion $\frac{2}{3} = \frac{4}{6}$, the cross products are $2 \cdot 6 = 12$ and $3 \cdot 4 = 12$.
cube (geometric figure) A rectangular prism with six congruent square faces.	**cubo (figura geométrica)** Prisma rectangular con seis caras cuadradas congruentes.	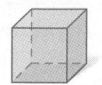
cube (in numeration) A number raised to the third power.	**cubo (en numeración)** Número elevado a la tercera potencia.	$5^3 = 5 \cdot 5 \cdot 5 = 125$
cumulative frequency The sum of successive data items. (p. 765)	**frecuencia acumulativa** La suma de datos sucesivos.	
customary system The measurement system often used in the United States. (p. 488)	**sistema usual de medidas** El sistema de medidas que se usa comúnmente en Estados Unidos.	inches, feet, miles, ounces, pounds, tons, cups, quarts, gallons
cylinder A three-dimensional figure with two parallel, congruent circular bases connected by a curved lateral surface. (p. 566)	**cilindro** Figura tridimensional con dos bases circulares paralelas y congruentes, unidas por una superficie lateral curva.	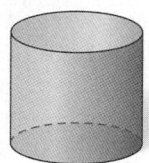

decagon A polygon with ten sides.	**decágono** Polígono de diez lados.	
degree The unit of measure for angles or temperature.	**grado** Unidad de medida para ángulos y temperaturas.	
denominator The bottom number of a fraction that tells how many equal parts are in the whole.	**denominador** Número de abajo en una fracción que indica en cuántas partes iguales se divide el entero.	$\frac{3}{4}$ ← denominator
dependent events Events for which the outcome of one event affects the probability of the other. (p. 700)	**sucesos dependientes** Dos sucesos son dependientes si el resultado de uno afecta la probabilidad del otro.	A bag contains 3 red marbles and 2 blue marbles. Drawing a red marble and then drawing a blue marble without replacing the first marble is an example of dependent events.
diagonal A line segment that connects two non-adjacent vertices of a polygon.	**diagonal** Segmento de recta que une dos vértices no adyacentes de un polígono.	

ENGLISH	SPANISH	EXAMPLES
diameter A line segment that passes through the center of a circle and has endpoints on the circle, or the length of that segment. (p. 520)	**diámetro** Segmento de recta que pasa por el centro de un círculo y tiene sus extremos en la circunferencia, o bien la longitud de ese segmento.	
difference The result when one number is subtracted from another.	**diferencia** El resultado de restar un número de otro.	
dimension The length, width, or height of a figure.	**dimensión** Longitud, ancho o altura de una figura.	
discount The amount by which the original price is reduced. (p. 394)	**descuento** Cantidad que se resta del precio original de un artículo.	
Distributive Property The property that states if you multiply a sum by a number, you will get the same result if you multiply each addend by that number and then add the products. (p. 27)	**Propiedad distributiva** Propiedad que establece que, si multiplicas una suma por un número, obtendrás el mismo resultado que si multiplicas cada sumando por ese número y luego sumas los productos.	$5(20 + 1) = 5 \cdot 20 + 5 \cdot 1$
dividend The number to be divided in a division problem.	**dividendo** Número que se divide en un problema de división.	In $8 \div 4 = 2$, 8 is the dividend.
divisible Can be divided by a number without leaving a remainder. (p. 164)	**divisible** Que se puede dividir entre un número sin dejar residuo.	18 is divisible by 3.
divisor The number you are dividing by in a division problem.	**divisor** El número entre el que se divide en un problema de división.	In $8 \div 4 = 2$, 4 is the divisor.
dodecagon A polygon with 12 sides.	**dodecágono** Polígono de 12 lados.	
double-bar graph A bar graph that compares two related sets of data. (p. 309)	**gráfica de doble barra** Gráfica de barras que compara dos conjuntos de datos relacionados.	
double-line graph A graph that shows how two related sets of data change over time. (p. 323)	**gráfica de doble línea** Gráfica lineal que muestra cómo cambian con el tiempo dos conjuntos de datos relacionados.	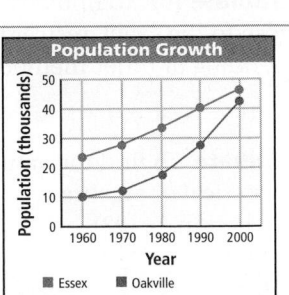

E

edge The line segment along which two faces of a polyhedron intersect. (p. 566)

arista Segmento de recta donde se intersecan dos caras de un poliedro.

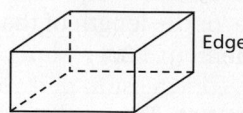
Edge

---

elements The words, numbers, or objects in a set. (p. 212)

elementos Palabras, números u objetos que forman un conjunto.

Elements of A: 1, 2, 3, 4

---

empty set A set that has no elements. (p. 212)

conjunto vacío Un conjunto que no tiene elementos.

---

endpoint A point at the end of a line segment or ray.

extremo Un punto ubicado al final de un segmento de recta o rayo.

---

equally likely Outcomes that have the same probability. (p. 682)

igualmente probables Resultados que tienen la misma probabilidad de ocurrir.

When you toss a coin, the outcomes "heads" and "tails" are equally likely.

---

equation A mathematical sentence that shows that two expressions are equivalent. (p. 70)

ecuación Enunciado matemático que indica que dos expresiones son equivalentes.

$x + 4 = 7$
$6 + 1 = 10 - 3$

---

equilateral triangle A triangle with three congruent sides. (p. 438)

triángulo equilátero Triángulo con tres lados congruentes.

---

equivalent Having the same value.

equivalentes Que tienen el mismo valor.

---

equivalent fractions Fractions that name the same amount or part. (p. 186)

fracciones equivalentes Fracciones que representan la misma cantidad o parte.

$\frac{1}{2}$ and $\frac{2}{4}$ are equivalent fractions.

---

equivalent ratios Ratios that name the same comparison. (p. 352)

razones equivalentes Razones que representan la misma comparación.

$\frac{1}{2}$ and $\frac{2}{4}$ are equivalent ratios.

---

estimate (n) An answer that is close to the exact answer and is found by rounding or other methods.

estimación (s) Una solución aproximada a la respuesta exacta que se halla mediante el redondeo u otros métodos.

---

estimate (v) To find an answer close to the exact answer by rounding or other methods.

estimar (v) Hallar una solución aproximada a la respuesta exacta mediante el redondeo u otros métodos.

---

evaluate To find the value of a numerical or algebraic expression. (p. 22)

evaluar Hallar el valor de una expresión numérica o algebraica.

Evaluate $2x + 7$ for $x = 3$.
$2x + 7$
$2(3) + 7$
$6 + 7$
13

---

even number A whole number that is divisible by two.

número par Un número cabal que es divisible entre dos.

ENGLISH	SPANISH	EXAMPLES
event An outcome or set of outcomes of an experiment or situation.	**suceso** Un resultado o una serie de resultados de un experimento o una situación.	
expanded form A number written as the sum of the values of its digits.	**forma desarrollada** Número escrito como suma de los valores de sus dígitos.	236,536 written in expanded form is 200,000 + 30,000 + 6,000 + 500 + 30 + 6.
experiment In probability, any activity based on chance. (p. 672)	**experimento** En probabilidad, cualquier actividad basada en la posibilidad.	Tossing a coin 10 times and noting the number of "heads."
experimental probability The ratio of the number of times an event occurs to the total number of trials, or times that the activity is performed. (p. 672)	**probabilidad experimental** Razón del número de veces que ocurre un suceso al número total de pruebas o al número de veces que se realiza el experimento.	Kendra attempted 27 free throws and made 16 of them. Her experimental probability of making a free throw is $\frac{\text{number made}}{\text{number attempted}} = \frac{16}{27} \approx 0.59$.
exponent The number that indicates how many times the base is used as a factor. (p. 14)	**exponente** Número que indica cuántas veces se usa la base como factor.	$2^3 = 2 \cdot 2 \cdot 2 = 8$; 3 is the exponent.
exponential form A number is in exponential form when it is written with a base and an exponent. (p. 14)	**forma exponencial** Cuando se escribe un número con una base y un exponente, está en forma exponencial.	4^2 is the exponential form for $4 \cdot 4$.
expression A mathematical phrase that contains operations, numbers, and/or variables.	**expresión** Enunciado matemático que contiene operaciones, números y/o variables.	$6x + 1$

F

face A flat surface of a polyhedron. (p. 566)	**cara** Lado plano de un poliedro.	
factor A number that is multiplied by another number to get a product. (p. 169)	**factor** Número que se multiplica por otro para hallar un producto.	7 is a factor of 21 since $7 \cdot 3 = 21$.
factor tree A diagram showing how a whole number breaks down into its prime factors. (p. 170)	**árbol de factores** Diagrama que muestra cómo se descompone un número cabal en sus factores primos.	12 / \\ 3 · 4 / \\ 2 · 2 $12 = 3 \cdot 2 \cdot 2$
Fahrenheit A temperature scale in which 32°F is the freezing point of water and 212°F is the boiling point of water.	**Fahrenheit** Escala de temperatura en la que 32° F es el punto de congelación del agua y 212° F es el punto de ebullición.	

fair When all outcomes of an experiment are equally likely, the experiment is said to be fair. (p. 682)

justo Se dice de un experimento donde todos los resultados posibles son igualmente probables.

When tossing a fair coin, heads and tails are equally likely. Each has a probability of $\frac{1}{2}$.

formula A rule showing relationships among quantities.

fórmula Regla que muestra relaciones entre cantidades.

$A = \ell w$ is the formula for the area of a rectangle.

fraction A number in the form $\frac{a}{b}$, where $b \neq 0$.

fracción Número escrito en la forma $\frac{a}{b}$, donde $b \neq 0$.

frequency table A table that lists items together according to the number of times, or frequency, that the items occur. (p. 314)

tabla de frecuencia Una tabla en la que se organizan los datos de acuerdo con el número de veces que aparece cada valor (o la frecuencia).

Data set: 1, 1, 2, 2, 3, 4, 5, 5, 5, 6, 6

Frequency table:

Data	Frequency
1	2
2	2
3	1
4	1
5	3
6	2

front-end estimation An estimating technique in which the front digits of the addends are added. (p. 113)

estimación por partes Técnica en la que se suman sólo los números enteros de los sumandos.

Estimate 25.05 + 14.671 with the sum 25 + 14 = 39. The actual value is 39 or greater.

function An input-output relationship that has exactly one output for each input. (p. 640)

función Relación de entrada-salida en la que a cada valor de entrada corresponde exactamente un valor de salida.

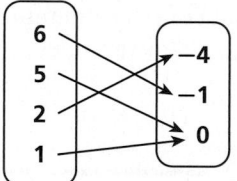

function table A table of ordered pairs that represent solutions of a function. (p. 640)

tabla de función Tabla de pares ordenados que representan soluciones de una función.

x	3	4	5	6
y	7	9	11	13

graph of an equation A graph of the set of ordered pairs that are solutions of the equation.

gráfica de una ecuación Gráfica del conjunto de pares ordenados que son soluciones de la ecuación.

greatest common factor (GCF) The largest common factor of two or more given numbers. (p. 173)

máximo común divisor (MCD) El mayor de los factores comunes compartidos por dos o más números dados.

The GCF of 27 and 45 is 9.

ENGLISH	SPANISH	EXAMPLES

height In a triangle or quadrilateral, the perpendicular distance from the base to the opposite vertex or side. (p. 543) In a prism or cylinder, the perpendicular distance between the bases. (pp. 572, 583)

altura En un triángulo o cuadrilátero, la distancia perpendicular desde la base de la figura al vértice o lado opuesto. En un prisma o cilindro, la distancia perpendicular entre las bases.

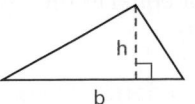

heptagon A seven-sided polygon.

heptágono Polígono de siete lados.

hexagon A six-sided polygon.

hexágono Polígono de seis lados.

histogram A bar graph that shows the frequency of data within equal intervals. (p. 315)

histograma Gráfica de barras que muestra la frecuencia de los datos en intervalos iguales.

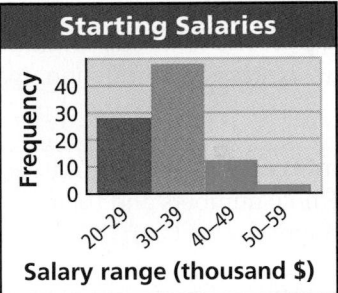

hypotenuse In a right triangle, the side opposite the right angle. (p. 761)

hipotenusa En un triángulo rectángulo, el lado opuesto al ángulo recto.

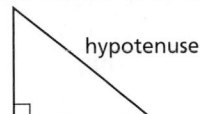

Identity Property of One The property that states that the product of 1 and any number is that number.

Propiedad de identidad del uno Propiedad que establece que el producto de 1 y cualquier número es ese número.

$5 \times 1 = 5$
$-8 \times 1 = -8$

Identity Property of Zero The property that states the sum of zero and any number is that number.

Propiedad de identidad del cero Propiedad que establece que la suma de cero y cualquier número es ese número.

$7 + 0 = 7$
$-9 + 0 = -9$

image A figure resulting from a transformation.

imagen Figura que resulta de una transformación.

impossible (probability) Can never happen; having a probability of 0. (p. 668)

imposible (en probabilidad) Que no puede ocurrir. Suceso cuya probabilidad de ocurrir es 0.

ENGLISH	SPANISH	EXAMPLES
improper fraction A fraction in which the numerator is greater than or equal to the denominator. (p. 192)	**fracción impropia** Fracción cuyo numerador es mayor que o igual al denominador.	$\frac{5}{5}$ $\frac{7}{3}$
independent events Events for which the outcome of one event does not affect the probability of the other. (p. 700)	**sucesos independientes** Dos sucesos son independientes si el resultado de uno no afecta la probabilidad del otro.	A bag contains 3 red marbles and 2 blue marbles. Drawing a red marble, replacing it, and then drawing a blue marble is an example of independent events.
indirect measurement The technique of using similar figures and proportions to find a measure. (p. 370)	**medición indirecta** La técnica de usar figuras semejantes y proporciones para hallar una medida.	
inequality A mathematical sentence that shows the relationship between quantities that are not equal. (p. 90)	**desigualdad** Enunciado matemático que muestra una relación entre cantidades que no son iguales.	$5 < 8$ $5x + 2 \geq 12$
input The value substituted into an expression or function. (p. 640)	**valor de entrada** Valor que se usa para sustituir una variable en una expresión o función.	For the rule $y = 6x$, the input 4 produces an output of 24.
integer A member of the set of whole numbers and their opposites. (p. 602)	**entero** Un miembro del conjunto de los números cabales y sus opuestos.	$\ldots -3, -2, -1, 0, 1, 2, 3, \ldots$
interest The amount of money charged for borrowing or using money, or the amount of money earned by saving money. (p. 400)	**interés** Cantidad de dinero que se cobra por el préstamo o uso del dinero, o la cantidad que se gana al ahorrar dinero.	
interior angles Angles on the inner sides of two lines intersected by a third line. In the diagram, $\angle c$, $\angle d$, $\angle e$, and $\angle f$ are interior angles. (p. 433)	**ángulos internos** Ángulos en los lados internos de dos líneas intersecadas por una tercera. En el diagrama, $\angle c$, $\angle d$, $\angle e$ y $\angle f$ son ángulos internos.	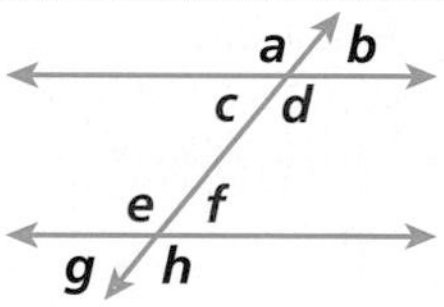
intersecting lines Lines that cross at exactly one point. (p. 428)	**líneas secantes** Líneas que se cruzan en un solo punto.	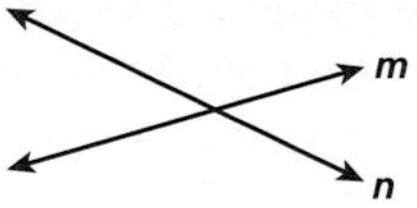
intersection (sets) The set of elements common to two or more sets. (p. 212)	**intersección (de conjuntos)** Conjunto de elementos comunes a dos o más conjuntos.	
interval The space between marked values on a number line or the scale of a graph.	**intervalo** El espacio entre los valores marcados en una recta numérica o en la escala de una gráfica.	
inverse operations Operations that undo each other: addition and subtraction, or multiplication and division.	**operaciones inversas** Operaciones que se cancelan mutuamente: suma y resta, o multiplicación y división.	

ENGLISH	SPANISH	EXAMPLES

isosceles triangle A triangle with at least two congruent sides. (p. 438)

triángulo isósceles Triángulo que tiene al menos dos lados congruentes.

lateral surface In a cylinder, the curved surface connecting the circular bases; in a cone, the curved surface that is not a base.

superficie lateral En un cilindro, superficie curva que une las bases circulares; en un cono, la superficie curva que no es la base.

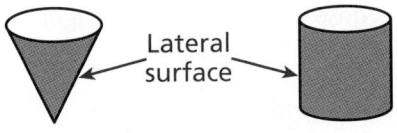

Lateral surface

---

least common denominator (LCD) The least common multiple of two or more denominators. (p. 234)

mínimo común denominador (mcd) El mínimo común múltiplo de dos o más denominadores.

The LCD of $\frac{3}{4}$ and $\frac{5}{6}$ is 12.

---

least common multiple (LCM) The smallest number, other than zero, that is a multiple of two or more given numbers. (p. 228)

mínimo común múltiplo (mcm) El menor de los múltiplos (distinto de cero) de dos o más números.

The LCM of 10 and 18 is 90.

---

like fractions Fractions that have the same denominator. (p. 198)

fracciones semejantes Fracciones que tienen el mismo denominador.

$\frac{5}{12}$ and $\frac{3}{12}$ are like fractions.

---

line A straight path that extends without end in opposite directions. (p. 416)

línea Trayectoria recta que se extiende de manera indefinida en direcciones opuestas.

---

line graph A graph that uses line segments to show how data changes. (p. 322)

gráfica lineal Gráfica que muestra cómo cambian los datos mediante segmentos de recta.

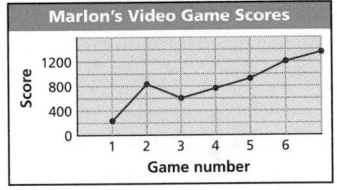

---

line plot A number line with marks or dots that show frequency. (p. 314)

diagrama de acumulación Recta numérica con marcas o puntos que indican la frecuencia.

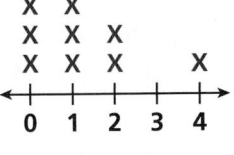

Number of pets

---

line of reflection A line that a figure is flipped across to create a mirror image of the original figure. (p. 459)

línea de reflexión Línea sobre la cual se invierte una figura para crear una imagen reflejada de la figura original.

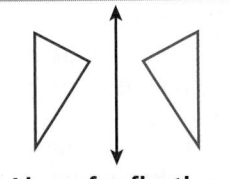

Line of reflection

---

line of symmetry The imaginary "mirror" in line symmetry. (p. 464)

eje de simetría El "espejo" imaginario en la simetría axial.

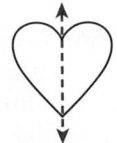

ENGLISH	SPANISH	EXAMPLES
line segment A part of a line between two endpoints. (p. 417)	**segmento de recta** Parte de una línea con dos extremos.	A •——————————• B
line symmetry A figure has line symmetry if one half is a mirror-image of the other half. (p. 464)	**simetría axial** Una figura tiene simetría axial si una de sus mitades es la imagen reflejada de la otra.	
linear equation An equation whose solutions form a straight line on a coordinate plane. (p. 647)	**ecuación lineal** Ecuación en la que las soluciones forman una línea recta en un plano cartesiano.	$y = 2x + 1$
lower extreme The least number in a set of data.	**extremo inferior** El número menor en un conjunto de datos.	Data set: 18, 23, 28, 29, 6, 42 Lower extreme: 6

M

ENGLISH	SPANISH	EXAMPLES
mean The sum of the items in a set of data divided by the number of items in the set; also called *average*. (p. 298)	**media** La suma de todos los elementos de un conjunto de datos dividida entre el número de elementos del conjunto. También se llama promedio.	Data set: 4, 6, 7, 8, 10 Mean: $\frac{4 + 6 + 7 + 8 + 10}{5} = \frac{35}{5} = 7$
median The middle number or the mean (average) of the two middle numbers in an ordered set of data. (p. 299)	**mediana** El número intermedio o la media (el promedio) de los dos números intermedios en un conjunto ordenado de datos.	Data set: 4, 6, 7, 8, 10 Median: 7
metric system A decimal system of weights and measures that is used universally in science and commonly throughout the world. (p. 492)	**sistema métrico** Sistema decimal de pesos y medidas empleado universalmente en las ciencias y por lo general en todo el mundo.	centimeters, meters, kilometers, grams, kilograms, milliliters, liters
midpoint The point that divides a line segment into two congruent line segments.	**punto medio** El punto que divide un segmento de recta en dos segmentos de recta congruentes.	A •——|——— B ———|——• C *B* is the midpoint of $\overline{AC}$
mixed number A number made up of a whole number that is not zero and a fraction. (p. 181)	**número mixto** Número compuesto por un número cabal distinto de cero y una fracción.	$5\frac{1}{8}$
mode The number or numbers that occur most frequently in a set of data; when all numbers occur with the same frequency, we say there is no mode. (p. 299)	**moda** Número o números más frecuentes en un conjunto de datos; si todos los números aparecen con la misma frecuencia, no hay moda.	Data set: 3, 5, 8, 8, 10 Mode: 8
multiple A multiple of a number is the product of the number and any nonzero whole number.	**múltiplo** El producto de un número y cualquier número cabal distinto de cero es un múltiplo de ese número.	
Multiplication Property of Zero The property that states that the product of any number and 0 is 0.	**Propiedad de multiplicación del cero** Propiedad que establece que el producto de cualquier número y 0 es 0.	$6 \times 0 = 0$ $-5 \times 0 = 0$

negative number A number less than zero. (p. 602)

número negativo Número menor que cero.

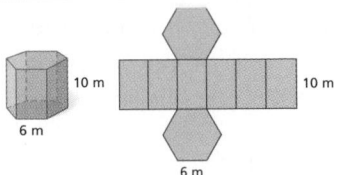
−2 is a negative number.

---

net An arrangement of two-dimensional figures that can be folded to form a polyhedron. (p. 582)

plantilla Arreglo de figuras bidimensionales que se doblan para formar un poliedro.

10 m   10 m
6 m
6 m

---

numerator The top number of a fraction that tells how many parts of a whole are being considered.

numerador El número de arriba de una fracción; indica cuántas partes de un entero se consideran.

$\frac{3}{4}$ ← numerator

---

numerical expression An expression that contains only numbers and operations. (p. 22)

expresión numérica Expresión que incluye sólo números y operaciones.

$(2 \cdot 3) + 1$

---

obtuse angle An angle whose measure is greater than 90° but less than 180°. (p. 421)

ángulo obtuso Ángulo que mide más de 90° y menos de 180°.

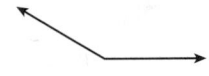

---

obtuse triangle A triangle containing one obtuse angle. (p. 437)

triángulo obtusángulo Triángulo que tiene un ángulo obtuso.

---

octagon An eight-sided polygon.

octágono Polígono de ocho lados.

---

odd number A whole number that is not divisible by two.

número impar Un número cabal que no es divisible entre dos.

---

opposites Two numbers that are an equal distance from zero on a number line. (p. 602)

opuestos Dos números que están a la misma distancia de cero en una recta numérica.

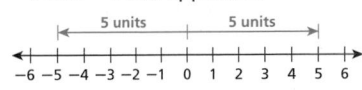
5 and −5 are opposites.

---

order of operations A rule for evaluating expressions: first perform the operations in parentheses, then compute powers and roots, then perform all multiplication and division from left to right, and then perform all addition and subtraction from left to right. (p. 22)

orden de las operaciones Regla para evaluar expresiones: primero se resuelven las operaciones entre paréntesis, luego se hallan las potencias y raíces, después todas las multiplicaciones y divisiones de izquierda a derecha y, por último, todas las sumas y restas de izquierda a derecha.

$3^2 - 12 \div 4$	
$9 - 12 \div 4$	Evaluate the power.
$9 - 3$	Divide.
6	Subtract.

ENGLISH	SPANISH	EXAMPLES
ordered pair A pair of numbers that can be used to locate a point on a coordinate plane. (p. 319)	**par ordenado** Par de números que sirven para ubicar un punto en un plano cartesiano.	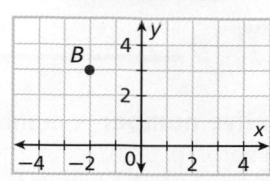 The coordinates of B are (−2, 3)
origin The point where the *x*-axis and *y*-axis intersect on the coordinate plane; (0, 0). (p. 610)	**origen** Punto de intersección entre el eje *x* y el eje *y* en un plano cartesiano: (0, 0).	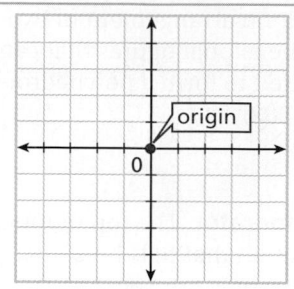
outcome A possible result of a probability experiment. (p. 672)	**resultado** Posible resultado de un experimento de probabilidad.	When rolling a number cube, the possible outcomes are 1, 2, 3, 4, 5, and 6.
outlier A value much greater or much less than the others in a data set. (p. 302)	**valor extremo** Un valor mucho mayor o menor que los demás valores de un conjunto de datos.	
output The value that results from the substitution of a given input into an expression or function. (p. 640)	**valor de salida** Valor que resulta después de sustituir un valor de entrada determinado en una expresión o función.	For the rule $y = 6x$, the input 4 produces an output of 24.
overestimate An estimate that is greater than the exact answer. (p. 10)	**estimación alta** Estimación mayor que la respuesta exacta.	100 is an overestimate for the sum 23 + 24 + 21 + 22.

parallel lines Lines in a plane that do not intersect. (p. 428)	**líneas paralelas** Líneas que se encuentran en el mismo plano pero que nunca se intersecan.	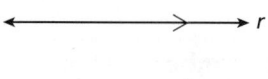
parallelogram A quadrilateral with two pairs of parallel sides. (p. 442)	**paralelogramo** Cuadrilátero con dos pares de lados paralelos.	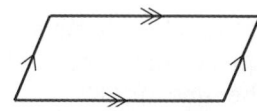
pentagon A five-sided polygon.	**pentágono** Polígono de cinco lados.	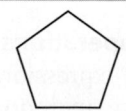
percent A ratio comparing a number to 100. (p. 381)	**porcentaje** Razón que compara un número con el número 100.	$45\% = \frac{45}{100}$
perfect square A square of a whole number.	**cuadrado perfecto** El cuadrado de un número cabal.	$5^2 = 25$, so 25 is a perfect square.

ENGLISH	SPANISH	EXAMPLES
perimeter The distance around a polygon. (p. 514)	**perímetro** Distancia alrededor de un polígono.	18 ft 6 ft perimeter = 48 ft
permutation An arrangement of items or events in which order is important.	**permutación** Arreglo de objetos o sucesos en el que el orden es importante.	For objects A, B, and C, there are 6 different permutations: ABC, ACB, BAC, BCA, CAB, CBA.
perpendicular bisector A line that intersects a segment at its midpoint and is perpendicular to the segment.	**mediatriz** Línea que cruza un segmento en su punto medio y es perpendicular al segmento.	ℓ is the perpendicular bisector of $\overline{AB}$.
perpendicular lines Lines that intersect to form right angles. (p. 428)	**líneas perpendiculares** Líneas que al intersecarse forman ángulos rectos.	
pi (π) The ratio of the circumference of a circle to the length of its diameter; $\pi \approx 3.14$ or $\frac{22}{7}$. (p. 520)	**pi (π)** Razón de la circunferencia de un círculo a la longitud de su diámetro; $\pi \approx 3.14$ ó $\frac{22}{7}$	
plane A flat surface that extends forever. (p. 416)	**plano** Superficie plana que se extiende de manera indefinida en todas direcciones.	plane R or plane ABC
point An exact location in space. (p. 416)	**punto** Ubicación exacta en el espacio.	P • point P
polygon A closed plane figure formed by three or more line segments that intersect only at their endpoints. (p. 446)	**polígono** Figura plana cerrada, formada por tres o más segmentos de recta que se intersecan sólo en sus extremos.	
polyhedron A three-dimensional figure in which all the surfaces or faces are polygons. (p. 566)	**poliedro** Figura tridimensional cuyas superficies o caras tienen forma de polígonos.	
population The whole group being surveyed. (p. 694)	**población** El grupo completo que es objeto de estudio.	In a survey about eating habits of middle school students, the population is all middle school students.
positive number A number greater than zero. (p. 602)	**número positivo** Número mayor que cero.	2 is a positive number. −4 −3 −2 −1 0 1 2 3 4
power A number produced by raising a base to an exponent.	**potencia** Número que resulta al elevar una base a un exponente.	$2^3 = 8$, so 2 to the 3rd power is 8.
prediction A guess about something that will happen in the future. (p. 694)	**predicción** Pronóstico sobre algo que puede ocurrir en el futuro.	

prime factorization A number written as the product of its prime factors. (p. 169)

factorización prima Un número escrito como el producto de sus factores primos.

$10 = 2 \cdot 5$
$24 = 2^3 \cdot 3$

---

prime number A whole number greater than 1 that has exactly two factors, itself and 1. (p. 165)

número primo Número cabal mayor que 1 que sólo es divisible entre 1 y él mismo.

5 is prime because its only factors are 5 and 1.

---

principal The initial amount of money borrowed or saved. (p. 400)

capital Cantidad inicial de dinero depositada o recibida en préstamo.

---

prism A polyhedron that has two congruent, polygon-shaped bases and other faces that are all rectangles. (p. 566)

prisma Poliedro con dos bases congruentes con forma de polígono y caras con forma de rectángulos.

---

probability A number from 0 to 1 (or 0% to 100%) that describes how likely an event is to occur. (p. 668)

probabilidad Un número entre 0 y 1 (ó 0% y 100%) que describe qué tan probable es un suceso.

A bag contains 3 red marbles and 4 blue marbles. The probability of randomly choosing a red marble is $\frac{3}{7}$.

---

product The result when two or more numbers are multiplied.

producto Resultado de multiplicar dos o más números.

The product of 4 and 8 is 32.

---

proper fraction A fraction in which the numerator is less than the denominator. (p. 192)

fracción propia Fracción en la que el numerador es menor que el denominador.

$\frac{3}{4}, \frac{1}{13}, \frac{7}{8}$

---

proportion An equation that states that two ratios are equivalent. (p. 362)

proporción Ecuación que establece que dos razones son equivalentes.

$\frac{2}{3} = \frac{4}{6}$

---

protractor A tool for measuring angles.

transportador Instrumento para medir ángulos.

---

pyramid A polyhedron with a polygon base and triangular sides that all meet at a common vertex. (p. 567)

pirámide Poliedro cuya base es un polígono; tiene caras triangulares que se juntan en un vértice común.

Q

quadrant The x- and y-axes divide the coordinate plane into four regions. Each region is called a quadrant. (p. 610)

cuadrante El eje x y el eje y dividen el plano cartesiano en cuatro regiones. Cada región recibe el nombre de cuadrante.

Quadrant II | Quadrant I
Quadrant III | Quadrant IV

---

quadrilateral A four-sided polygon. (p. 442)

cuadrilátero Polígono de cuatro lados.

ENGLISH	SPANISH	EXAMPLES
quotient The result when one number is divided by another.	**cociente** Resultado de dividir un número entre otro.	In $8 \div 4 = 2$, 2 is the quotient.

radius A line segment with one endpoint at the center of a circle and the other endpoint on the circle, or the length of that segment. (p. 520)	**radio** Segmento de recta con un extremo en el centro de un círculo y el otro en la circunferencia, o bien la longitud de ese segmento.	
range (in statistics) The difference between the greatest and least values in a data set. (p. 299)	**rango (en estadística)** Diferencia entre los valores máximo y mínimo de un conjunto de datos.	Data set: 3, 5, 7, 7, 12 Range: $12 - 3 = 9$
rate A ratio that compares two quantities measured in different units. (p. 353)	**tasa** Una razón que compara dos cantidades medidas en diferentes unidades.	The speed limit is 55 miles per hour or 55 mi/h.
rate of interest The percent charged or earned on an amount of money; see *simple interest*. (p. 400)	**tasa de interés** Porcentaje que se cobra por una cantidad de dinero prestada o que se gana por una cantidad de dinero ahorrada; ver *interés simple*.	
ratio A comparison of two quantities by division. (p. 352)	**razón** Comparación de dos cantidades mediante una división.	12 to 25, 12:25, $\frac{12}{25}$
ray A part of a line that starts at one endpoint and extends forever. (p. 417)	**rayo** Parte de una línea que comienza en un extremo y se extiende de manera indefinida.	
reciprocal One of two numbers whose product is 1. (p. 270)	**recíproco** Uno de dos números cuyo producto es igual a 1.	The reciprocal of $\frac{2}{3}$ is $\frac{3}{2}$.
rectangle A parallelogram with four right angles. (p. 442)	**rectángulo** Paralelogramo con cuatro ángulos rectos.	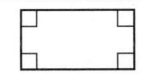
rectangular prism A polyhedron whose bases are rectangles and whose other faces are rectangles.	**prisma rectangular** Poliedro cuyas bases son rectángulos y cuyas caras tienen forma de rectángulos.	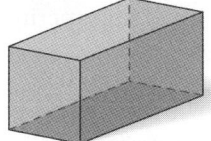
reflection A transformation of a figure that flips the figure across a line. (p. 459)	**reflexión** Transformación que ocurre cuando se invierte una figura sobre una línea.	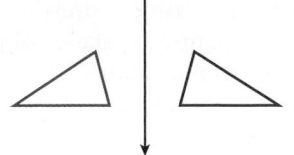
regular polygon A polygon with congruent sides and angles. (p. 446)	**polígono regular** Polígono con lados y ángulos congruentes.	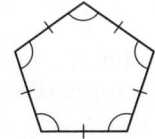

ENGLISH	SPANISH	EXAMPLES
repeating decimal A decimal in which one or more digits repeat infinitely. (p. 182)	**decimal periódico** Decimal en el que uno o más dígitos se repiten infinitamente.	$0.75757575\ldots = 0.\overline{75}$
rhombus A parallelogram with all sides congruent. (p. 442)	**rombo** Paralelogramo en el que todos los lados son congruentes.	
right angle An angle that measures 90°. (p. 421)	**ángulo recto** Ángulo que mide exactamente 90°.	
right triangle A triangle containing a right angle. (p. 437)	**triángulo rectángulo** Triángulo que tiene un ángulo recto.	
rotation A transformation in which a figure is turned around a point. (p. 459)	**rotación** Transformación que ocurre cuando una figura gira alrededor de un punto.	
rounding Replacing a number with an estimate of that number to a given place value.	**redondear** Sustituir un número por una estimación de ese número hasta cierto valor posicional.	2,354 rounded to the nearest thousand is 2,000; 2,354 rounded to the nearest 100 is 2,400.

S

ENGLISH	SPANISH	EXAMPLES
sales tax A percent of the cost of an item, which is charged by governments to raise money. (p. 394)	**impuesto sobre la venta** Porcentaje del costo de un artículo que los gobiernos cobran para recaudar fondos.	
sample A part of a group being surveyed. (p. 694)	**muestra** Parte de un grupo que es objeto de estudio.	In a survey about eating habits of middle school math students, a sample is a survey of 100 randomly-chosen students.
sample space All possible outcomes of an experiment. (p. 678)	**espacio muestral** Conjunto de todos los resultados posibles de un experimento.	When rolling a number cube, the sample space is 1, 2, 3, 4, 5, 6.
scale The ratio between two sets of measurements. (p. 374)	**escala** La razón entre dos conjuntos de medidas.	1 cm: 5 mi
scale drawing A drawing that uses a scale to make an object proportionally smaller than or larger than the real object. (p. 374)	**dibujo a escala** Dibujo en el que se usa una escala para que un objeto se vea proporcionalmente mayor o menor que el objeto real al que representa.	A blueprint is an example of a scale drawing.
scale model A proportional model of a three-dimensional object.	**modelo a escala** Modelo proporcional de un objeto tridimensional.	

ENGLISH	SPANISH	EXAMPLES
scalene triangle A triangle with no congruent sides. (p. 438)	**triángulo escaleno** Triángulo que no tiene lados congruentes.	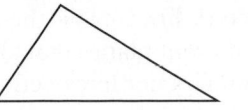
scientific notation A method of writing very large or very small numbers by using powers of 10. (p. 124)	**notación científica** Método que se usa para escribir números muy grandes o muy pequeños mediante potencias de 10.	$12{,}560{,}000{,}000{,}000 = 1.256 \times 10^{13}$
segment A part of a line between two endpoints.	**segmento** Parte de una línea entre dos extremos.	A———•———B *A* *B*
sequence An ordered list of numbers. (p. 33)	**sucesión** Lista ordenada de números.	2, 4, 6, 8, 10, . . .
set A group of items. (p. 212)	**conjunto** Un grupo de elementos.	
side A line bounding a geometric figure; one of the faces forming the outside of an object.	**lado** Línea que delimita las figuras geométricas; una de las caras que forman la parte exterior de un objeto.	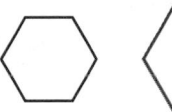
significant figures The figures used to express the precision of a measurement.	**dígitos significativos** Dígitos usados para expresar la precisión de una medida.	
similar Figures with the same shape but not necessarily the same size are similar. (p. 366)	**semejantes** Figuras que tienen la misma forma, pero no necesariamente el mismo tamaño.	
simple interest A fixed percent of the principal. It is found using the formula $I = Prt$, where P represents the principal, r the rate of interest, and t the time. (p. 400)	**interés simple** Un porcentaje fijo del capital. Se calcula con la fórmula $I = Cit$, donde C representa el capital, i, la tasa de interés y t, el tiempo.	
simplest form (of a fraction) A fraction is in simplest form when the numerator and denominator have no common factors other than 1. (p. 187)	**mínima expresión (de una fracción)** Una fracción está en su mínima expresión cuando el numerador y el denominador no tienen más factor común que 1.	Fraction: $\frac{8}{12}$ Simplest form: $\frac{2}{3}$
simplify To write a fraction or expression in simplest form.	**simplificar** Escribir una fracción o expresión numérica en su mínima expresión.	
simulation A model of an experiment, often one that would be too difficult or too time-consuming to actually perform. (p. 676)	**simulación** Representación de un experimento, por lo regular de uno cuya realización sería demasiado difícil o llevaría mucho tiempo.	

ENGLISH	SPANISH	EXAMPLES
skew lines Lines that lie in different planes that are neither parallel nor intersecting. (p. 428)	**líneas oblicuas** Líneas que se encuentran en planos distintos, por eso no se intersecan ni son paralelas.	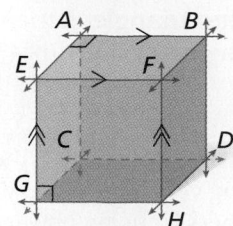 $\overrightarrow{AE}$ and $\overrightarrow{CD}$ are skew lines.
solid figure A three-dimensional figure.	**cuerpo geométrico** Figura tridimensional.	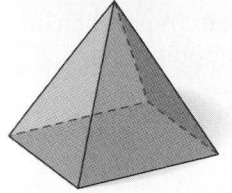
solution of an equation A value or values that make an equation true. (p. 70)	**solución de una ecuación** Valor o valores que hacen verdadera una ecuación.	Equation: $x + 2 = 6$ Solution: $x = 4$
solution of an inequality A value or values that make an inequality true. (p. 90)	**solución de una desigualdad** Valor o valores que hacen verdadera una desigualdad.	Inequality: $x + 3 \geq 10$ Solution: $x \geq 7$
solve To find an answer or a solution.	**resolver** Hallar una respuesta o solución.	
square (geometry) A rectangle with four congruent sides. (p. 442)	**cuadrado (en geometría)** Rectángulo con cuatro lados congruentes.	
square (numeration) A number raised to the second power. (p. 14)	**cuadrado (en numeración)** Número elevado a la segunda potencia.	In 5^2, the number 5 is squared.
square number A number that is the product of a whole number and itself.	**cuadrado de un número** El producto de un número cabal multiplicado por sí mismo.	25 is a square number since $5^2 = 25$.
square root One of the two equal factors of a number. (p. 645)	**raíz cuadrada** Uno de los dos factores iguales de un número.	$16 = 4 \cdot 4$ and $16 = -4 \cdot -4$, so 4 and -4 are square roots of 16.
standard form (in numeration) A number written using digits.	**forma estándar** Una forma de escribir números por medio de dígitos.	Five thousand, two hundred ten in standard form is 5,210.
stem-and-leaf plot A graph used to organize and display data so that the frequencies can be compared. (p. 330)	**diagrama de tallo y hojas** Gráfica que muestra y ordena los datos, y que sirve para comparar las frecuencias.	Stem | Leaves 3 | 2 3 4 4 7 9 4 | 0 1 5 7 7 7 8 5 | 1 2 2 3 *Key: 3|2 means 3.2*
straight angle An angle that measures 180°. (p. 421)	**ángulo llano** Ángulo que mide exactamente 180°.	

subset A set contained within another set. (p. 213)

subconjunto Conjunto que pertenece a otro conjunto.

substitute To replace a variable with a number or another expression in an algebraic expression.

sustituir Reemplazar una variable por un número u otra expresión en una expresión algebraica.

sum The result when two or more numbers are added.

suma Resultado de sumar dos o más números.

supplementary angles Two angles whose measures have a sum of 180°. (p. 425)

ángulos suplementarios Dos ángulos cuyas medidas suman 180°.

30° 150°

surface area The sum of the areas of the faces, or surfaces, of a three-dimensional figure. (p. 582)

área total Suma de las áreas de las caras, o superficies, de una figura tridimensional.

12 cm
6 cm
8 cm
Surface area = 2(8)(12) + 2(8)(6) + 2(12)(6) = 432 cm²

T

term (in a sequence) An element or number in a sequence. (p. 33)

término (en una sucesión) Elemento o número de una sucesión.

5 is the third term in the sequence 1, 3, 5, 7, 9, . . .

terminating decimal A decimal number that ends or terminates. (p. 182)

decimal finito Decimal con un número determinado de posiciones decimales.

6.75

tessellation A repeating pattern of plane figures that completely cover a plane with no gaps or overlaps. (p. 468)

teselado Patrón repetido de figuras planas que cubren totalmente un plano sin superponerse ni dejar huecos.

theoretical probability The ratio of the number of equally likely outcomes in an event to the total number of possible outcomes. (p. 682)

probabilidad teórica Razón del número de resultados igualmente probables en un suceso al número total de resultados posibles.

When rolling a number cube, the theoretical probability of rolling a 4 is $\frac{1}{6}$.

tip The amount of money added to a bill for service; usually a percent of the bill. (p. 394)

propina Cantidad que se agrega al total de una factura por servicios. Por lo general, es un porcentaje del total de la factura.

transformation A change in the size or position of a figure. (p. 459)

transformación Cambio en el tamaño o la posición de una figura.

ENGLISH	SPANISH	EXAMPLES
translation A movement (slide) of a figure along a straight line. (p. 459)	**traslación** Desplazamiento de una figura a lo largo de una línea recta.	
trapezoid A quadrilateral with exactly one pair of parallel sides. (p. 442)	**trapecio** Cuadrilátero con un par de lados paralelos.	
tree diagram A branching diagram that shows all possible combinations or outcomes of an event. (p. 678)	**diagrama de árbol** Diagrama ramificado que muestra todas las posibles combinaciones o resultados de un suceso.	
triangle A three-sided polygon.	**triángulo** Polígono de tres lados.	
Triangle Sum Theorem The theorem that states that the measures of the angles in a triangle add to 180°.	**Teorema de la suma del triángulo** Teorema que establece que las medidas de los ángulos de un triángulo suman 180°.	
triangular prism A polyhedron whose bases are triangles and whose other faces are rectangles.	**prisma triangular** Poliedro cuyas bases son triángulos y cuyas demás caras tienen forma de rectángulos.	

U

ENGLISH	SPANISH	EXAMPLES
underestimate An estimate that is less than the exact answer. (p. 10)	**estimación baja** Estimación menor que la respuesta exacta.	100 is an underestimate for the sum 26 + 29 + 31 + 27.
union The set of all elements that belong to two or more sets. (p. 212)	**unión** El conjunto de todos los elementos que pertenecen a dos o más conjuntos.	
unit conversion The process of changing one unit of measure to another.	**conversión de unidades** Proceso que consiste en cambiar una unidad de medida por otra.	
unit rate A rate in which the second quantity in the comparison is one unit. (p. 353)	**tasa unitaria** Una tasa en la que la segunda cantidad de la comparación es una unidad.	10 cm per minute
unlike fractions Fractions with different denominators. (p. 198)	**fracciones distintas** Fracciones con distinto denominador.	$\frac{3}{4}$ and $\frac{1}{2}$ are unlike fractions.

ENGLISH | **SPANISH** | **EXAMPLES**

V

variable A symbol used to represent a quantity that can change. (p. 54)

variable Símbolo que representa una cantidad que puede cambiar.

In the expression $2x + 3$, x is the variable.

Venn diagram A diagram that is used to show relationships between sets. (p. 212)

diagrama de Venn Diagrama que muestra las relaciones entre conjuntos.

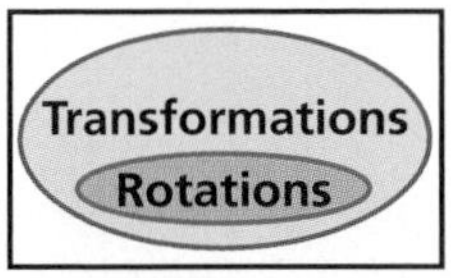

vertex On an angle or polygon, the point where two sides intersect. (p. 566)

vértice En un ángulo o polígono, el punto de intersección de dos lados

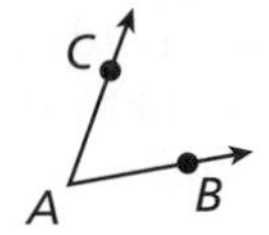

A is the vertex of $\angle CAB$.

vertical angles A pair of opposite congruent angles formed by intersecting lines. (p. 424)

ángulos opuestos por el vértice Par de ángulos opuestos congruentes formados por líneas secantes.

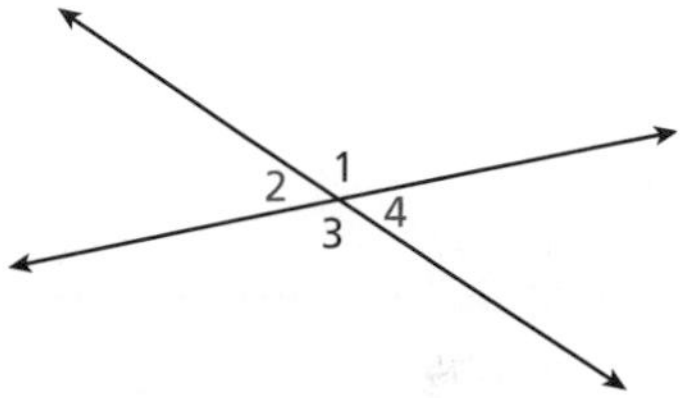

$\angle 1$ and $\angle 3$ are vertical angles.
$\angle 2$ and $\angle 4$ are vertical angles.

volume The number of cubic units needed to fill a given space. (p. 572)

volumen Número de unidades cúbicas que se necesitan para llenar un espacio.

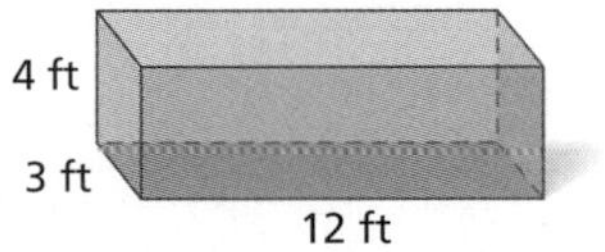

Volume $= 3 \cdot 4 \cdot 12 = 144 \text{ ft}^3$

X

***x*-axis** The horizontal axis on a coordinate plane. (p. 610)

eje *x* El eje horizontal del plano cartesiano.

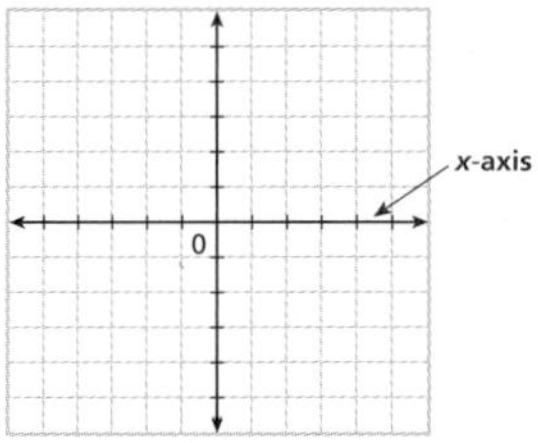

***x*-coordinate** The first number in an ordered pair; it tells the distance to move right or left from the origin, (0, 0). (p. 610)

coordenada *x* El primer número en un par ordenado; indica la distancia que debes avanzar hacia la izquierda o hacia la derecha desde el origen, (0, 0).

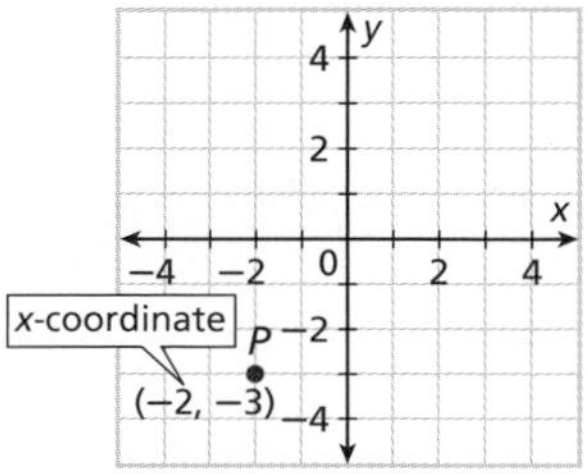

y-axis The vertical axis on a coordinate plane. (p. 610)

eje y El eje vertical del plano cartesiano.

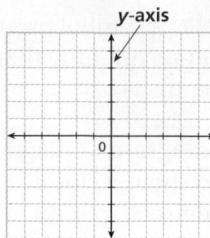

y-coordinate The second number in an ordered pair; it tells the distance to move up or down from the origin, (0, 0). (p. 610)

coordenada y El segundo número en un par ordenado; indica la distancia que debes avanzar hacia arriba o hacia abajo desde el origen, (0, 0).

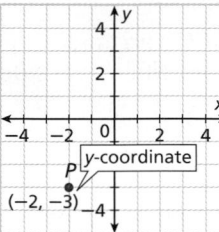

Z

zero pair A number and its opposite, which add to 0.

par nulo Un número y su opuesto, que sumados dan 0.

18 and −18

Index

A

Aaron, Hank, 36
Abacus, 9
Absolute value, 762
Accuracy, 767
Act It Out, 747
Acute angles, 421
Acute triangles, 437
Addition
of decimals, 118–119
exploring, 116–117
of fractions
with like denominators, 202–203
modeling, 232–233
with unlike denominators, 234–235
of integers, 617–618
modeling, 616
of mixed numbers, 238–239
in order of operations, 22
properties, 757
for solving fraction equations, 248–249
of whole numbers, 752
Addition equations, 74–75
Additional data, 302–303
Adjacent angles, 424
Africa, 2
Agriculture, 201
Algebra
The development of algebra skills and concepts is a central focus of this course and is found throughout this book.
absolute value, 762
equations, 70
addition, 74–75
checking solutions of, 70–71
decimal, solving, 144–145
division, 85–86
linear, 647
multiplication, 81–82
solutions of, 70–71
subtraction, 78–79
two-step, 762
exponential functions, 772
expressions, 54, 59
translating between tables and, 62–63
variables and, 54–55
functions,
exponential, 772
graphing, 646–647
integers and, 598–663
tables and, 640–641
inequalities, 90–91
proportions
and indirect measurement, 370–371
modeling, 362
in scale drawings and maps, 374–375

in similar figures, 366–367
solving, 363
tiles, 634–635
variables and expressions, 54
Algebra tiles, 634–635
Algebraic expressions, 54, 59
writing, 62–63
Alternate exterior angles, 433
Alternate interior angles, 433
Alvin submersible, 605
Angle measures in polygons, finding, 510–511
Angle relationships, 424–425
Angles, 420
acute, 421
adjacent, 424
alternate exterior, 433
alternate interior, 433
classifying, 420–421
complementary, 425
congruent, 424
corresponding, 366, 433
exterior, 433
interior, 433
measuring, with a protractor, 420–421
obtuse, 421
radians, 767
right, 421
straight, 421
supplementary, 425
in triangles, 441
vertical, 424
Anglo-Saxon, 491
Answer choices, eliminating, 46–47
Applications
Agriculture, 201
Archaeology, 25
Architecture, 421, 498, 513, 521, 547, 560, 569, 585
Art, 125, 451, 499, 552
Astronomy, 30–31, 110, 167, 192–193, 194, 375, 604
Biology, 358, 498
Career, 121
Chemistry, 393
Construction, 624
Consumer application, 23, 228, 457
Consumer Math, 132, 135, 136, 139, 353, 354, 390
Cooking, 199, 560
Crafts, 250
Earth Science, 28, 65, 87, 109, 127, 140, 286, 355, 382, 561, 605, 609, 618, 620, 624, 627
Economics, 246
Education, 300
Entertainment, 126, 276, 357, 388
Games, 685
Geography, 8, 9, 80, 91, 126, 500, 609
Geometry, 56, 146, 171, 392
Graphic Art, 369
Graphic Design, 643
Health, 112, 115
History, 9, 77, 140, 491, 523, 559

Hobbies, 376, 462
Language Arts, 387, 462
Life Science, 29, 71, 127, 184, 195, 202, 205, 209, 239, 240, 241, 263, 273, 277, 325, 376, 382, 639, 691, 696
Measurement, 56, 72, 141, 145, 194, 240, 245, 246, 250, 363, 371, 458, 523, 555, 579
Money, 57, 72, 115
Music, 251, 577
Patterns, 364, 506
Photography, 141
Physical Science, 77, 86
Physics, 495
Recreation, 543
School, 240, 256, 276
Science, 130, 579
Social Studies, 36, 58, 60, 72, 75, 80, 127, 142, 176, 195, 234, 236, 249, 255, 302, 307, 335, 383, 397, 440, 465, 549, 553, 639, 681, 684
Sports, 31, 118, 120, 121, 171, 184, 207, 250, 302, 437, 445, 498, 500, 511, 517, 561, 605, 620, 638
Technology, 126, 391, 393
Weather, 294, 675
Appropriate data displays, choosing, 333–334
Appropriate measuring tools, selecting and using, 486–487
Aquarium fish, 279
Archaeology, 25
Architecture, 421, 498, 513, 521, 547, 560, 569, 585
Are You Ready?, 3, 51, 103, 161, 225, 291, 349, 413, 483, 539, 599, 665
Area, 66, 542
of circles, 557–559
comparing perimeter and, 554–555
of composite figures, 551–552
estimating, 542–543
finding, 542–543
fractional part of a region, 758
of rectangles, 66–67, 542
surface, 582–583
of trapezoids, 546–547
of triangles, 546–547
Area formulas, 550
Arguments, writing convincing, 601
Arithmetic sequences, 33–34
Arizona, 346–347
Arizona-Sonora Desert Museum, 347
scenic roads, 346
Armadillos, 81
Armstrong, Lance, 500
Art, 125, 451, 499, 552
Assessment
Chapter Test, 45, 97, 155, 219, 285, 343, 407, 477, 533, 593, 659, 707
Cumulative Assessment, 48–49, 98–99, 158–159, 220–221, 288–289, 344–345, 410–411, 478–479, 536–537, 594–595, 662–663, 708–709

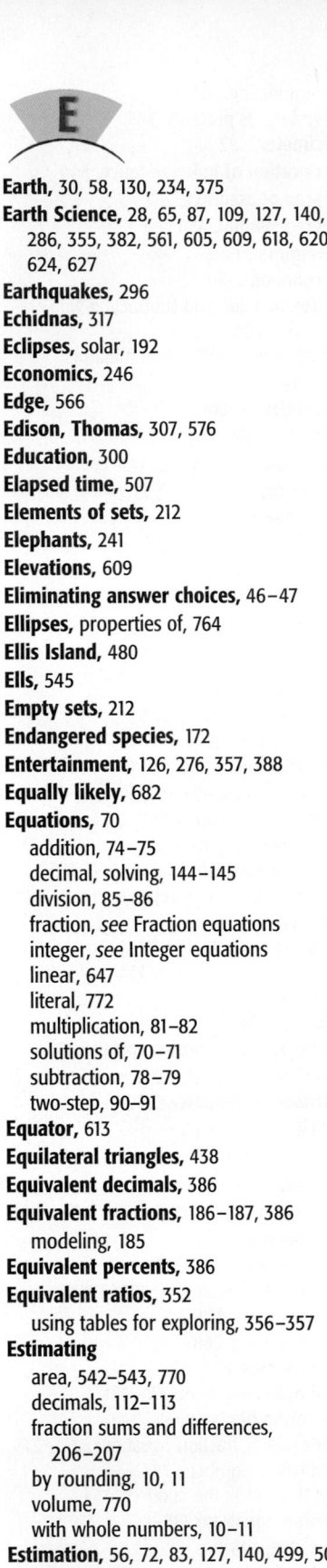
Index

modeling, 362
in scale drawings and maps, 374–375
in similar figures, 366–367
solving, 363
Protractor, 420, 512–513, 513
Proxima Centauri, 111
Pyramid, 567

Quadrants, 610
Quadrilaterals, 442–443, 446
Quart, 491
Quarter-inch ruler, 190
Quotients, interpreting, 141–142

Radians, 767
Radio station formats, 384
Radius, 520, 557
Range, 299
Rasmussen, Michael, 503
Rates, 353
interest, 398
unit, 353
using tables for exploring, 356–357
Rational numbers, 763
Ratios, 352–353
equivalent, *see* Equivalent ratios
surface area to volume, 771
Raven Cliff Falls, 596
Rays, 417
Reading
graphics, 293
lessons for understanding, 163
problems for understanding, 415
scales, 760
Reading and Writing Math, 5, 53, 105,
163, 227, 293, 351, 415, 485, 541, 601,
667
Reading Math, 70, 428
Reading Strategies, *see also* Reading and
Writing Math
Learn Math Vocabulary, 541
Read a Lesson for Understanding, 163
Read and Interpret Graphics, 293
Read Problems for Understanding, 415
Use Your Book for Success, 5
Ready to Go On?, 18, 38, 68, 88, 122,
148, 178, 196, 210, 252, 278, 306, 336,
378, 400, 434, 454, 470, 508, 526, 562,
586, 614, 632, 650, 686, 698, *see also*
Assessment
Real-world situations, integers in,
602–603
Reciprocals, 270–271
Recreation, 543
Rectangles, 442
area of, 542
exploring area and perimeter of, 66–67

golden, 402
perimeter of, 514
Rectangular prism, 566
Red Cube, 566
Reflection, 459
lines of, 459
Regrouping
to subtract fractions, 242–243
to subtract mixed numbers,
244–245
Regular polygons, 446
Relationships
angle, 424–425
geometric, 412–481
linear and nonlinear, exploring,
644–645
parallel line, 432–433
proportional, 348–411
Relative frequency, graph, 766
Remember!, 7, 10, 22, 113, 119, 131, 134,
135, 141, 144, 145, 181, 199, 202, 228,
229, 234, 255, 264, 274, 367, 382, 394,
438, 446, 450, 505, 577, 602, 606, 625,
626, 628, 629, 652, 682
Repeating decimals, 182
Representations, multiple, using, 485
Representing decimals, 108–109
Rhombuses, 442
Right angles, 421
Right triangle trigonometry, 761
Right triangles, 437
Rock, Paper, Scissors, 681
Rodinova, Yana, 523
Roman numerals, 9, 751
Rotations, 459
Rounding
decimals, 112, 750
estimating by, 10, 11
whole numbers, 750
Ruler, 186, 190–191
centimeter, 440
half-inch, 190
inch, 209
measure length using a, 760
quarter-inch, 190

Sales tax, 381, 394
Sample, 694
Sample space, 678
counting methods and, 678–679
San Diego image, 319
Satellite image, 294
Satellite map, 305
Saturn, 133
Scale, 374
reading a, 760
Scale drawings, 374–375
sketching, 373
Scale factor, 373

Scalene triangles, 438
School, 240, 256, 276
Science, 130, 579
Scientific notation, 124–125
Second, 506
Sector of a circle, 764
Selected Answers, 776–789
Selecting appropriate measuring tools,
486–487
Sequences
arithmetic, 33–34
finding patterns in, 37
patterns and, 33–34
Sets
empty, 212
intersection and union, 212
of numbers, 212–213
Seurat, Georges, 124
Shawnee State Forest, 222
Shea, Jim, 302
Shea Stadium, 445
Shipwreck diving, 710
Short Response, 13, 32, 80, 115, 156–157,
167, 205, 237, 296, 317, 325, 329, 355,
359, 393, 445, 453, 462, 467, 495, 513,
523, 534, 535, 549, 579, 609, 620, 639
Sides, corresponding, 366
Similar, 366
Similar figures, 366–367
Simple interest, 400
Simplest form, fractions in, 187
Simulations, 676–677
Sketching scale drawings, 373
Skew lines, 428
Skills Bank, 749–774
preview skills, 758–766
review skills, 749–757
science skills, 767–774
Sleeping, 260
Smileys, 435
Smoke alarm, 121
Snake lengths, 273
Snowman, 370
Social Studies, 36, 58, 60, 72, 75, 80, 127,
142, 176, 195, 234, 236, 249, 255, 302,
307, 335, 383, 397, 440, 465, 549, 553,
639, 681, 684
Software, geometry, 441, 550
Solar eclipses, 192
Solar system, 30
Solutions of equations, 70–71
Solve a Simpler Problem, 745
Solving
decimal equations, 144–145
fraction equations, 248–249, 274–275
integer equations, 636–637
2-step equations, 90–91
South Australia, 553
South Carolina, 596–597
Space exploration, 61
Spheres, properties of, 764

Credits

■ Staff Credits

Bruce Albrecht, Lorraine Cooper, Marc Cooper, Jennifer Craycraft, Martize Cross, Nina Degollado, Lydia Doty, Sam Dudgeon, Kelli R. Flanagan, Ronald Fowler, Mary Fraser, Stephanie Friedman, Jeff Galvez, José Garza, Diannia Green, Jennifer Gribble, Liz Huckestein, Jevara Jackson, Kadonna Knape, Cathy Kuhles, Jill M. Lawson, Peter Leighton, Christine MacInnis, Rosalyn K. Mack, Jessika Maier, Jonathan Martindill, Virginia Messler, Susan Mussey, Kim Nguyen, Matthew Osment, Manda Reid, Patrick Ricci, Michael Rinella, Michelle Rumpf-Dike, Beth Sample, Annette Saunders, John Saxe, Katie Seawell, Kay Selke, Robyn Setzen, Patricia Sinnott, Victoria Smith, Jeannie Taylor, Ken Whiteside, Sherri Whitmarsh, Aimee F. Wiley

■ Photo

Abbreviations used: (t) top, (c) center, (b) bottom, (l) left, (r) right, (bkgd) background

Cover (all), Pronk & Associates.

Title page (all), Pronk & Associates, cover and ii, Arcaid/Alamy

Master icons—teens (All): Sam Dudgeon/HRW.

Author photos by Sam Dudgeon/HRW; Jan Scheer photo by Ron Shipper

Front Matter: C2 AP Photo/NASA; vi ©Gary Randall/Getty Images/FPG International; vii ©Christian Michaels/Getty Images/FPG International; ix Peter Van Steen/HRW; x Peter Van Steen/HRW; xi Charles W. Campbell; xii Ralph A. Clevenger/CORBIS; xiii Art by Jane Dixon/HRW; xiv Sam Dudgeon/HRW; xv Florian Monheim/age fotostock; xvi Ernest Manewal/SuperStock; xvii SuperStock; xviii CORBIS/Brandon D. Cole; xix (t), Anna Clopet/CORBIS; xix (tr), ©corbisimages.com; xix (bl), Frank Siteman/Getty Images/Stone; xix (cl), Sam Dudgeon/HRW; xix (cr), Sam Dudgeon/HRW; xix (br), Carl and Ann Purcell/Index Stock Imagery, Inc.; xxii (tr), Bryan Berg; xxii (bl), Sam Dudgeon/HRW

Chapter One: 02 (br), Jeff Greenberg/MR/Photo Researchers, Inc.; 06; 06 (tc), Steve Ewert Photography; 06 (tr), Steve Ewert Photography; 06 (tr), Steve Ewert Photography; 06 (tr), Steve Ewert Photography; 06 (tr), Steve Ewert Photography; 09 (tl), ©Image Source/elektraVision/PictureQuest; 10 (t),; 11 (cr), Iowa State Fair; 13 (tr), James L. Amos/National Geographic Image Collection; 14 (tr), CORBIS/Bettmann; 17 (tr), CORBIS/Lester V. Bergman; 19 (br), Michael Dunning/Getty Images/FPG International; 23 (b), Sam Dudgeon/HRW; 23 Sam Dudgeon/HRW; 23 Sam Dudgeon/HRW; 23 Sam Dudgeon/HRW; 23 Sam Dudgeon/HRW; 25 (tr), Kenneth Garrett/National Geographic Image Collection; 25 (tc), Kenneth Garrett/National Geographic Image Collection; 26 DINODIA/Art Directors & TRIP Photo Library; 29 (c), Sam Dudgeon/HRW; 29 (r), PhotoDisc-Digital Image copyright © 2004 PhotoDisc; 29 (tl), C.K. Lorenz/Photo Researchers; 30 (tr), NASA; 33 Victoria Smith/HRW; 39 (t), AP Photo/Amy Sancetta; 39 (b), Getty Images; 40 (br), Jenny Thomas/HRW; 41 (b), HRW.   **Chapter 2:** 50 (br), Peter Yang/HRW Photo; 50–51 (bkgd), Christian Michaels/Getty Images/FPG International; 57 (tl), Sam Dudgeon/HRW; 61 (tr), AP Photo/NASA; 61 (all patches), NASA; 65 Adam Woolfitt/CORBIS; 69 (bl), David A. Northcott/CORBIS; 71 (r), CORBIS/Brandon D. Cole; 74 (tr), Franklin Jay Viola/Viola's Photo Visions; 77 (tl), Peter Yang/HRW; 78 (tl), Library of Congress; 78 (tr), AP Photo; 78 (bkgd), Corbis Images; 81 (tr), Bianca Lavies/National Geographic Image Collection; 84 (tr), Darwin Dale/Photo Researchers, Inc.; 85 (c), Eric Kamp/Index Stock Imagery/PictureQuest; 85 (tr), Takeshi Takahara/Photo Researchers, Inc.; 89 (tl), ©NorthWind/NorthWind Picture Archives; 93 HRW.   **Chapter 3:** 102 (br), Peter Yang/HRW Photo; 102 (bkgd), AP/Wide World Photos; 109 (cr), Jerry Schad/Photo Researchers, Inc.; 112 (tr), Cheryl Maeder/Getty Images/Stone; 115 Mark Tomalty/Masterfile; 118 AP Photo/John Russell; 121 (tl), Frank Siteman/Getty Images/Stone; 123 (bc), Peter Van Steen/HRW; 123 (bl), Peter Van Steen/HRW; 127 (tl), George Hall/Check Six; 130 (tr), NASA/Photo Researchers, Inc.; 133 (tr), CORBIS; 133 (br), Bettmann/CORBIS; 134 HRW; 136 (br), Victoria Smith/HRW; 137 (tr), Mark Gibson/Gibson Stock Photography; 140 (tl), Larry Stevens/Nawrocki Stock Photo;

141 (tr), Peter Yang/HRW; 144 (tr), CORBIS/Richard Hamilton Smith; 147 (tr), SuperStock; 149 (br), Stockbyte Platinum/Alamy; 150 (cr), Jenny Thomas/HRW; 151 HRW.   **Chapter 4:** 160 (bkgd), Peter Van Steen/HRW; 160 (br), Digital Image copyright © 2004 PhotoDisc; 164 (tr), Darren Carroll/HRW; 167 (tl), Mike Norton/Animals Animals/Earth Scenes; 172 (tr), Frans Lanting/Minden Pictures; 172 (t), Frans Lanting/Minden Pictures; 174 (tr), PhotoEdit; 176 (tl), Frans Lanting/Minden Pictures; 179 (b), Digital Image copyright © 2004 PhotoDisc; 181 (tr), Getty Images; 184 (cr), Pat Lanza/FIELD/Bruce Coleman, Inc.; 189 (tr), Bob Krist/CORBIS; 189 (br), Wendell Metzen/Bruce Coleman, Inc.; 190 (t), Peter Van Steen/HRW; 191 (egg), PhotoDisc-Digital Image copyright © 2004 PhotoDisc; 191 (shamrock), PhotoDisc-Digital Image copyright © 2004 PhotoDisc; 191 (acorn), PhotoDisc-Digital Image copyright © 2004 PhotoDisc; 191 (shell), PhotoDisc-Digital Image copyright © 2004 PhotoDisc; 191 (rock), PhotoDisc-Digital Image copyright © 2004 PhotoDisc; 191 (key), EyeWire-Digital Image copyright © 2005 EyeWire; 191 (penny), EyeWire-Digital Image copyright © 2005 EyeWire; 191 (cicada), Artville-Digital Image copyright © 2005 Artville; 192 (tr), Sam Dudgeon/HRW; 195 (tl), Science Photo Library/Photo Researchers, Inc.; 195 (cr), Sam Dudgeon/HRW Photo; 196 (tr), Peter French/Bruce Coleman, Inc.; 197 (bl), Tom Brakefield/CORBIS; 201 (tl), Peter Van Steen/HRW; 202 (tr), Mike Norton/Animals Animals/Earth Scenes; 202 (tc), Peter Van Steen/HRW; 205 (tl), Gary Meszaros/Bruce Coleman, Inc.; 206 Daryl Benson; 206 (tr), Carl Yarbrough; 206 (c), Beverly Barrett/HRW; 206 (b), Beverly Barrett/HRW; 207 (cr), SuperStock; 209 (tl), SuperStock; 209 (tr), Raymond A. Mendez/Animals Animals/Earth Scenes; 209 (tc), Mark Moffett/Minden Pictures; 214 Randall Hyman/HRW; 215 HRW; 222 (b) Mike Williams/Ohio Department of Natural Resources; 222 (cr), Richard Baumer; 222 (bc) Mike Williams/Ohio Department of Natural Resources; 223 (tr), Stimac/The Image Finders; 223 AP Photo/The Plain Dealer, Chris Stephens); 223 (br), Adam Jones/Visuals Unlimited.   **Chapter 5:** 224 (bkgd), Peter Van Steen/HRW; 224 (br), Digital Image copyright © 2004 PhotoDisc; 228 (tr), Carl Yarbrough; 228 (c), Beverly Barrett/HRW; 228 (b), Beverly Barrett/HRW; 237 (tr), SuperStock; 237 (br), Gerry Ellis/Minden Pictures; 237 (cr), Paul Chesley/National Geographic Image Collection; 237 (bl), Eric Hosking/CORBIS; 238 (tr), Frans Lanting/Minden Pictures; 239 (c), Frans Lanting/Minden Pictures; 241 (tl), Gerry Ellis/Minden Pictures; 248 (tr), Private Collection/Edmond Von Hoorick/SuperStock; 249 (cr), Alan Pitcairn/Grant Heilman Photography; 253 (br), Maximilian Stock Ltd./FoodPix; 257 (tr), Jeff Foott/Discovery Communications, Inc.; 263 (tl), Merlin D. Tuttle/Bat Conservation International; 264 (tr), Ken Karp/HRW; 265 (bkgd), Beverly Barrett/HRW; 270 Victoria Smith/HRW; 273 (tr), Allen Blake Sheldon/Animals Animals/Earth Scenes; 274 Lori Grinker/Contact Press Images/PictureQuest; 275 (cl), Beverly Barrett/HRW; 275 (tr), Beverly Barrett/HRW; 277 (tl), Frans Lanting/Minden Pictures; 279 Jell Kelly; 280 (br), Ken Karp/HRW; 281 HRW.   **Chapter 6:** 290 (br), CORBIS; 290–91 (bkgd), Charles W. Campbell; 294 (tr), Reuters NewMedia Inc./CORBIS; 294 (bl), Carl and Ann Purcell/Index Stock Imagery, Inc.; 298 (tr), Jenny Thomas Photography/HRW; 301 Stockdisc Classic/Alamy; 302 (tr), Trent Nelson/The Salt Lake Tribune; 302 (cl), AFP PHOTO/George FREY/Getty Images; 305 (tr), NASA/Science Photo Library/Photo Researchers, Inc.; 307 (bc), Victoria & Albert Museum/Art Resource, NY; 307 (br), U.S. Department of the Interior, National Park Service, Edison National Historic Site; 307 (bl), Index Stock/Alamy Photos; 307 (l), Pintail Pictures/Alamy Photos; 308 Tim Davis/Photo Researchers, Inc.; 308 Dr. Eckart Pott/Bruce Coleman, Inc.; 308 SuperStock; 308 Sharon Smith/Bruce Coleman, Inc.; 314 (l), Leonard Lessin/Peter Arnold; 314 (c), Federal Bureau of Investigation; 314 (r), Archive Photos; 317 (l), Roland Seitre/Peter Arnold, Inc.; 322 Bettmann/CORBIS; 325 GK Hart/Vikki Hart/Getty Images; 326 (cr), Shane Young/AP/Wide World Photos; 326 BrandX Pictures; 326 David Madison/Bruce Coleman, Inc.; 329 (tr), John Bavosi/Science Photo Library/Photo Researchers, Inc.; 329 (c), John Bavosi/Science Photo Library/Photo Researchers, Inc.; 329 (r), John Bavosi/Science Photo Library/Photo Researchers, Inc.; 330 (tr), Bryan Berg; 337 (bl), Travel Line/Alamy; 338 (br), Randall Hyman/HRW; 339 HRW; 346 (cr), Digital Vision; 346 (bl), Swerve/Alamy; 347 (br), Steve Lewis/The Image Bank/Getty Images; 347 (l), Jim Merli/Visuals Unlimited.   **Chapter 7:** 348 (br), Beth Davidow; 348 (bkgd), Ralph A. Clevenger/CORBIS; 352 (tr), Reuters NewMedia Inc./CORBIS; 356 AP Photo/Big Lots, Rene Macura; 359 Bettmann/CORBIS; 365 (tr), Ronald Zak/AP/Wide World Photos; 365 (tl), Imapress/Jean Claude N'Diaye/The Image Works; 365 (cr), AFP/CORBIS; 365 (cl), Jon Bower/Alamy Photos; 367 (tr), Mary

Cassatt, The Boating Party, Chester Dale Collection, Photograph © 2002 Board of Trustees, National Gallery of Art, Washington. 1893/1894, oil on canvas; 368 Jenny Thomas/HRW; 370 (tr), Sharon McNeill/Bethel Area Chamber of Commerce; 371 (tl), Thinkstock/Getty Images; 374 (l), Ngs Cartographic Division/National Geographic Image Collection; 374 (tr), Kerrick James/Getty Images/Stone; 374 (cr), W. Perry Conway/CORBIS; 376 (b), E. R. Degginger/Bruce Coleman, Inc.; 381 Jenny Thomas/HRW Photo; 384 (tr), Michelle Bridwell/PhotoEdit; 388 Bettman/CORBIS; 390 Sam Dudgeon/HRW; 393 (tl), Lucy Schaly/Beaver County Times/AP/Wide World Photos; 394 (t), Peter Van Steen/HRW; 394 (tl), J. & P. Wegner/Animals Animals/ Earth Scenes; 397 (cl), Sam Dudgeon/HRW; 399 (tl), foodfolio/Alamy; 401 (tl), foodfolio/ Alamy; 402 (br), Ken Karp/HRW; 402 (c), Mimmo Jodice/CORBIS; 402 (cl), Massimo Listri/CORBIS; 402 (cr), Gianni Dagli Orti/CORBIS; 403 (b), HRW. **Chapter 8:** 412 (br), ©Zhi Xiong China Tourism Press/Getty Images/The Image Bank; 412–13 (bkgd), Art by Jane Dixon/HRW; 420 Courtesy of Icon Health Fitness; 424 (cl), Michael Kelley/Getty Images/Stone; 424 (b), TempSport/CORBIS; 426 (tl), Peter Van Steen/HRW; 426 (tr), Peter Van Steen/HRW; 426 (cl), Werner Forman Archive/Piers Morris Collection/Art Resource, NY; 426 (cr), P. W. Grace/Photo Researchers, Inc.; 426 (tc), Peter Van Steen/HRW; 428 (t), Walter Bibikow/Index Stock Imagery/PictureQuest; 429 (tl), Emmanuel Faure/SuperStock; 429 (tr), Peter Van Steen/HRW; 429 (cl), ImageState/Alamy Photos; 429 (cr), Peter Van Steen/HRW; 437 (br), Bob Krist/CORBIS; 437 Peter Van Steen/HRW; 437 Peter Van Steen/HRW; 440 (tl), Peter Newark's Western Americana; 442 Digital Image (c) The Museum of Modern Art/Licensed by SCALA/Art Resource, NY; 445 (tl), David Forbert/SuperStock; 446 (cl), PhotoDisc-Digital Image copyright © 2004 PhotoDisc; 446 (bl), PhotoDisc-Digital Image copyright © 2004 PhotoDisc; 446 (t), Index Stock/Alamy; 447 PhotoDisc-Digital Image copyright © 2004 PhotoDisc; 448 (tl), Beverly Barrett/ HRW; 448 (tc), Peter Van Steen/HRW; 448 (tr), Peter Van Steen/HRW; 448 (bl), Eric Grave/Science Source/Photo Researchers, Inc.; 448 (bc), M. Abbey/Photo Researchers, Inc.; 448 (br), Kim Taylor/Bruce Coleman; 450 Lowe Art Museum, The University of Miami/SuperStock; 451 (cr), Peter Van Steen/HRW; 451 (bl), Peter Van Steen/HRW; 452 (c), Peter Van Steen/HRW; 453 (tr), Steve Vidler/SuperStock; 455 Michael Boys/CORBIS; 456 Ken Karp/HRW Photo; 458 (l), Original Artwork © "Sunflowers" by Mary Backer/Sam Dudgeon/HRW Photo; 458 (cl), "Sunflowers" by Mary Backer/Sam Dudgeon/HRW Photo; 458 (cr), "Sunflowers" by Mary Backer/ Sam Dudgeon/HRW Photo; 458 (r), "Sunflowers" by Mary Backer/Sam Dudgeon/ HRW Photo; 462 (l), Sam Dudgeon/HRW; 462 (cl), Sam Dudgeon/HRW; 464 John Greim/Index Stock Imagery/PictureQuest; 467 (cr), corbisimages.com; 467 (t), Anna Clopet/CORBIS; 471 (tl), Victoria Smith/HRW; 471 (b), Digital Vision/Getty Images; 473 (b), HRW; 473 (bc), HRW; 480 (cl), Catherine Karnow/CORBIS; 480 (tr), Catherine Karnow/CORBIS; 480 (bl), Westend61/Alamy; 480 (br), Westend61/Alamy; 481 (t), The Image Bank/Getty Images; 481 (b), Christie's Images/CORBIS. **Chapter 9:** 482 (bkgd), Sam Dudgeon/HRW; 482 V. C. L./Getty Images/FPG International; 489 HRW; 490 (t), HRW; 490 (b), HRW; 491 (l), Winchester Cathedral, Hampshire, UK, / Bridgeman Art Library; 493 HRW; 494 (t), Photonica/Getty Images; 494 (b), Siede Preis/Getty Images; 495 Stephanie Friedman/HRW Photo; 496 Michael Steele/Getty Images; 499 Pierre Gleizes/Still Pictures; 500 AP Photo/ Alessandro Trovati; 503 (tr), Robert Harding Picture Library Ltd/Alamy; 503 (tl), Taxi/ Getty Images; 504 Alan Copson City Pictures/Alamy; 507 (cr), Alan Schein Photography/CORBIS; 507 (tr), Michael S. Yamashita/CORBIS; 507 (br), Lonely Planet Images/Getty Images; 507 (t), Travel-Shots/Alamy; 509 Nic Hamilton/Alamy; 510 Royalty-Free/Corbis; 513 AP Photo/Fabio Muzzi; 514 (tr), Courtesy of Sigma Tau Pharmaceuticals, Inc.; 514 (b), Victoria Smith/HRW; 516 (tr), Barry L. Runk/Grant Heilman Photography; 516 (br), PhotoDisc-Digital Image copyright © 2004 PhotoDisc; 520 (c), Masterfile; 520 (tr), Masterfile; 523 Mark Mckeown/The Paris News/AP/WideWorld Photos; 527 (tl), Stone/Getty Images; 527 (b), Jean Carter/AGE FotoStock; 528 (br), Tim Davis/HRW Photo; 529 HRW **Chapter 10:** 538 Sam Dudgeon/HRW Photo; 538–9 Florian Monheim/age fotostock; 541 HRW; 542 (tr), Larry Lefever/Grant Heilman Photography; 545 (tr), William Hamilton/SuperStock;

545 (c), NASA/Science Source/Photo Researchers, Inc.; 546 Raymond Patrick/ Taxi/Getty Images; 549 Shirley Richards/SuperStock; 554 (tr), Kwame Zikomo/ SuperStock; 555 Steve Satushek/Getty Images/The Image Bank; 555 (tr), Steve Satushek/Getty Images/The Image Bank; 558 (tr), Getty Images; 561 (r), William Sallez/Duomo/CORBIS; 561 (l), David Parker/Photo Researchers, Inc.; 563 (bl), Omni Photo Communications Inc./Index Stock Imagery/PictureQuest; 566 (t), © 2006 The Isamu Noguchi Foundation and Garden Museum, New York/Artists Rights Society (ARS), New York/Corbis; 567 (c), Sam Dudgeon/HRW; 567 (b), Peter Van Steen/HRW; 568 (cl), Barry L. Runk/Grant Heilman Photography; 568 (c), Charles D. Winters/Photo Researchers, Inc.; 568 (cr), Charles D. Winters/Photo Researchers, Inc.; 569 (l), Richard Cummins/CORBIS; 569 (c), Joseph Sohm; ChromoSohm Inc./CORBIS; 569 (r), Hisham Ibrahim/CORBIS; 572 HRW; 572 HRW; 573 (cl), Sam Dudgeon/HRW; 573 (bl), Sam Dudgeon/HRW; 573 (cr), Sam Dudgeon/HRW; 573 (br), Sam Dudgeon/HRW; 573 (t), Sam Dudgeon/HRW; 575 (tr), TEK Image/ Science Photo Library/Photo Researchers, Inc.; 575 (c), Runk/Schoenberger/Grant Heilman Photography; 575 (br), Charles D. Winters/Photo Researchers, Inc.; 576 (r), U.S. Department of the Interior, National Park Service, Edison National Historic Site; 576 (tr), LOC/Science Source/Photo Researchers, Inc.; 585 (r), Peter Van Steen/HRW; 585 (l), Mark C. Burnett/Phot Researcher Inc.; 587 (l), NASA; 587 (r), CORBIS 588 (c), Tim Davis/HRW Photo; 589 (b), HRW; 596 (cr), Eyecon Images/Alamy; 596 (b), Andre Jenny/Alamy; 597 (t), Photri/ W. Kulik; 597 (cr), Photri/ W. Kulik.   **Chapter 11:** 598 (br), Peter Yang/HRW; 598–9 (bkgd), Ernest Manewal/SuperStock; 602 (tl), CORBIS/Bill Ross; 602 (tr), Patrick J. Endres/ AlaskaPhotographics.com; 605 (l), Emory Kristof/National Geographic Image Collection; 606 (tr), Getty Images/AFP; 607 Chris Trotman/Duomo Photography; 615 (br), AFP/Getty Images; 617 CORBIS/Douglas Peebles; 620 Robert Emmett Bright/Photo Researchers; 625 Dennis Degnan/CORBIS; 628 (t), AP Photo/News Ltd.; 631 (cr), Francisco Marquez; 631 (tr), Jacana/Photo Researchers, Inc; 633 Garry Black/Masterfile; 639 (l), Robert Frerck/Odyssey/Chicago; 640 (tr),; 646 (tr), Ken Karp/HRW; 649 (tr), Simon Fraser/MRC Unit, Newcastle General Hospital/Science Photo Library/Photo Researchers, Inc.; 651 (tl), Dorling Kindersley; 651 (b), The Image Bank/Getty Images; 654 (br), Jenny Thomas/HRW; 655 (b), HRW **Chapter 12:** 664 (br), Bill Varie/CORBIS; 664–5 (bkgd), SuperStock; 671 (tr), TEK Image/Science Photo Library/Photo Researchers, Inc.; 672 (cl), EyeWire-Digital Image copyright © 2004 EyeWire; 672 (cr), EyeWire-Digital Image copyright © 2004 EyeWire; 674 (cl), EyeWire-Digital Image copyright © 2004 EyeWire; 674 (c), EyeWire-Digital Image copyright © 2004 EyeWire; 674 (cr), Sam Dudgeon/HRW; 674 (l), Sam Dudgeon/HRW; 683 Peter Van Steen/HRW; 685 CORBIS; 687 Jason Hawkes/Getty Images/Stone; 688 Dynamic Graphics Group/i2i/Alamy; 689 (tl), Digital Image copyright © 2004 EyeWire; 691 Pat Doyle/CORBIS; 694 The Old Farmer's Almanac* and Design Mark* are used with permission of Yankee Publishing Inc., Dublin, New Hampshire; 697 (tr), Jeff Curtes/CORBIS; 697 (tl), Yvette Cardozo/Index Stock Imagery/PictureQuest; 697 (t), Richard T. Nowitz/CORBIS; 697 (tr), Reuters NewMedia Inc./CORBIS; 699 (t), Stockdisc/Superstock; 699 (b), Gail Mooney/Masterfile; 702 (b), Ken Karp/HRW; 703 (b), HRW; 706 (tl), Digital Image copyright © 2004 EyeWire; 706 (tr), Digital Image copyright © 2004 EyeWire; 706 (cr), Digital Image copyright © 2004 EyeWire; 707 Stockbyte-four food images; frame-Victoria Smith/HRW; 710 (c), Herb Segars-gotosnapshot.com; 710 (b), Steve Shott/Dorling Kindersley; 711 (r), Index Stock Imagery; 711 (t), Photo courtesy of Historic Cold Spring Village, an Early American Living History Museum, Cape May, New Jersey.

Back Matter: 712 Sam Dudgeon/HRW; 712 John Langford/HRW; 713 John Langford/HRW; 713 Sam Dudgeon/HRW; 739 ©Pictor/Alamy Photos; 740 (c), Victoria Smith/HRW; 740 (br), Sam Dudgeon/HRW; 740 (bl), Sam Dudgeon/HRW; 741 (tr), ©Charles Gupton/CORBIS; 742 (tr), Victoria Smith/HRW; 743 (tr), Victoria Smith/HRW; 743 (tr), Victoria Smith/HRW; 743 (tr), Victoria Smith/HRW; 745 Cleo Freelance Photography/Painet Inc.; 746 (tr), Sam Dudgeon/HRW; 746 (cl), Victoria Smith/HRW; 746 (bl), Victoria Smith/HRW

Table of Measures

METRIC

Length

1 kilometer (km) = 1,000 meters (m)

1 meter = 10 decimeters (dm)

1 meter = 100 centimeters (cm)

1 meter = 1,000 millimeters (mm)

1 centimeter = 10 millimeters

Capacity

1 liter (L) = 1,000 milliliters (mL)

Mass and Weight

1 kilogram (kg) = 1,000 grams (g)

1 gram = 1,000 milligrams (mg)

CUSTOMARY

Length

1 mile (mi) = 1,760 yards (yd)

1 mile = 5,280 feet (ft)

1 yard = 3 feet

1 yard = 36 inches (in.)

1 foot = 12 inches

Capacity

1 gallon (gal) = 4 quarts (qt)

1 gallon = 16 cups (c)

1 gallon = 128 fluid ounces (fl oz)

1 quart = 2 pints (pt)

1 quart = 4 cups

1 pint = 2 cups

1 cup = 8 fluid ounces

Mass and Weight

1 ton (T) = 2,000 pounds (lb)

1 pound = 16 ounces (oz)

TIME

1 year (yr) = 365 days

1 year = 12 months (mo)

1 year = 52 weeks (wk)

1 leap year = 366 days

1 week = 7 days

1 day = 24 hours (hr)

1 hour = 60 minutes (min)

1 minute = 60 seconds (s)

Centimeters